MAYFLOWER FAMILIES
THROUGH FIVE GENERATIONS

DESCENDANTS OF THE PILGRIMS WHO LANDED
AT PLYMOUTH, MASS., DECEMBER 1620

VOLUME TWENTY
PART 3

FAMILY OF HENRY SAMSON

Fifth -Generation Descendants of Henry's
sons Stephen and Caleb

Compiled by

Jane Fletcher Fiske, FASG

Robert Moody Sherman, FASG

Ruth Wilder Sherman, FASG

Published by
General Society of Mayflower Descendants
2006

Library of Congress Cataloging-in-Publication Data (revised for volume 20)
Mayflower Families Through Five Generations

Edited by L.M. Kellogg and others. Includes bibliographical references and indexes.

Contents:

1. Pilgrims (New Plymouth Colony): Genealogy.
  2. Massachusetts--Genealogy.
    I. Kellogg, Lucy Mary.
    II. General Society of Mayflower Descendants.

63.M39   929'.2'0973   75-30145
ISBN   0-930270-30-4

This book is dedicated to

Edith Bates Thomas

with gratitude for her unfailing support and encouragement.

The Society Expresses Thanks

The Mayflower Society wishes to thank Neil D. Thompson, FASG, Ann T. Reeves, and H. Clark Deane for their contributions to this family. The Society also thanks all those who sent information to Robert M. Sherman, and more recently to Jane Fiske.

FIVE GENERATIONS PROJECT CO-DIRECTORS
Edith Bates Thomas
Judith H. Swan

EDITED, INDEXED, AND PREPARED FOR PUBLICATION BY
Jane Fletcher Fiske, FASG

PREVIEWED BY
Ann S. Lainhart
John Bradley Arthaud, M.D.

PUBLICATION
Robert Allen Greene

History of the Five-Generations Project

The Five-Generations Project was authorized by the Board of the General Society of Mayflower Descendants in September 1959 with the goal of providing documentation from primary sources, whenever possible, for all statements, and of publishing the findings for the use of the Historian General, the State Historians, the membership, and the general public. Thus was formalized a project first conceived many years earlier, around the turn of the 19th and 20th centuries, by Herbert Folger in San Francisco and George E. Bowman in Boston.

Lewis Edwin Neff was the first chairman of the Five Generation Project. He was the driving force for this venture and recruited the first compilers. Dr. Lee D. van Antwerp was an early committee chairman in the formative years of the Project, serving from 1967 to 1975. Lucy Mary Kellogg, FASG, became chairman and gave professional advice and encouragement for a short time.

Robert Moody Sherman, FASG, served as chairman from 1976 to 1979. During his tenure the first two volumes entitled *Mayflower Families Through Five Generations* were published in "silver" hard cover: *Francis Eaton, Samuel Fuller, and William White*, in Volume 1 (1975); and *James Chilton, Richard More, and Thomas Rogers*, in Volume 2 (1978).

In 1980, Volume 3, the *Descendants of George Soule*, was published by the Society and the Soule Kindred in America, Inc.

Cathryn P. Lanham became the chairman of the "5Gs," as the project was familiarly called, before serving as Governor General, and she has continued preparing manuscripts for publication until recently. Under her supervision, beginning in 1986, a "pink" paperback was published under the title *Mayflower Families in Progress*. The publication of *MFIP*s has been continued under the present chairmanship and there are now many pink volumes in print.

Edith Bates Thomas, appointed director of the project in 1987, continues her remarkable accomplishments that began with the publication of Volume 4, Edward Fuller, in 1990, and now extend through Volume 23, John Howland, in 2005.

OFFICERS OF THE GENERAL SOCIETY

2005 – 2008

GOVERNOR GENERAL	Edward D. Sullivan
ASSISTANT GOVERNOR GENERAL	Terry J. McKane
SECRETARY GENERAL	Faith E. Edwards
TREASURER GENERAL	Judith H. Swan
HISTORIAN GENERAL	Ann S. Lainhart
ELDER GENERAL	The Reverend Jeanne Linderman
CAPTAIN GENERAL	Stuart T. Hall
SURGEON GENERAL	George P. Garmany, Jr., M.D.
COUNSELLOR GENERAL	J. Michael Phelps, Esq.

EXECUTIVE COMMITTEE MEMBERS AT LARGE

Lea S. Filson   Carroll R. Goslee

Benjamin G. Proctor Jr.

FIVE GENERATIONS PROJECT COMMITTEE

2006

Co-Directors, Edith Bates Thomas and Judith Haddock Swan
Assistant Director, Barbara Hensley Carpenter
Col. Robert Allen Greene
Caroline Lewis Kardell
Ann Smith Lainhart
Cathryn P. Lanham

The Authors

ROBERT MOODY SHERMAN and RUTH WILDER SHERMAN

Robert Moody Sherman was a descendant of Pilgrims John Alden, William Brewster and Richard Warren. A graduate of M.I.T. (1936), he was Chairman of the Division of Science at Bristol Community College in Fall River, Mass. Ruth Wilder Sherman, although not herself a descendant of any *Mayflower* passenger, believed in "shedding light where it's needed," and worked with her husband on his many projects. He served as Governor of the Rhode Island Society and was Chairman of the Five Generations Project. They co-authored the William White family, and together they transcribed the Marshfield and Yarmouth Vital Records and published articles on Pilgrim families. They were both elected Fellows of the American Society of Genealogists in 1975. In 1983 they became co-editors of *The American Genealogist*, and after Bob's death Ruth Ann carried on until she died, in 1991.

Mr. and Mrs. Sherman were co-authors of MF 20, Part 1: *Henry Samson of the Mayflower and His Descendants for Four Generations* (published posthumously in 2000 with Robert Wakefield as editor), and they left behind a considerable amount of material that they had collected towards the Fifth Generation.

JANE FLETCHER FISKE

Jane Fiske, a graduate of Swarthmore College, was elected a Fellow of the American Society of Genealogists in 1983. She has had a life-long interest in genealogy. She is the author of the award-winning *Thomas Cooke of Rhode Island* (1987) and numerous journal articles, as well as two volumes of Rhode Island court records, *Gleanings from Newport Court Files* and *Rhode Island General Court of Trials 1671-1704*, both published in 1998. After a term as president of the Rhode Island Genealogical Society in the 1980s, she was for eleven years editor of its journal, *Rhode Island Roots*. In 1987 she was appointed editor of the *New England Historical and Genealogical Register* and held that position until 2001, serving in addition as Director of Publications for NEHGS from 1995 to 2001. In a thirteen-year effort with the help of her husband John Wyman Fiske (who wrote the necessary software), she produced the *Cumulative Index* to the *Register*, published in 1994 in four volumes, which later provided the basis for searching the CD and on line versions of the *Register*.

She began working on the Henry Samson family in the summer of 2001, completing *Volume 20 Part 2* in 2005.

SPELLING AND ABBREVIATIONS

Spelling was far from consistent, even after the Revolutionary War. To a great extent names in this book have been spelled as found in each record. This practice often provides different spellings of an individual's name at his birth, upon marriage, and in a deed or will. For example, Hayford is found as Hafford and Heffords for the same person. Marcy and Mercy are often interchangeable, and nicknames were common. With variant spellings so commonplace, use of "[sic]" is restricted to exceptional examples. In the Index, most variant spellings of a surname are lumped together and cross-referenced, rather than separately alphabetized, and most given names have been standardized.

The following abbreviations are used throughout the book:

ae	age	int.	intentions of marriage
b.	born	LR	Land Records; Deeds
bp.	baptized	m.	married
bur.	buried	PR	Probate Records
ca	*circa* [about]	*q.v*	"which see" [look up]
calc.	calculated [from other evidence]	rec.	recorded
		[*sic*]	thus in original
CR	church records	*sub*	under [a different name]
d.	died	TR	Town Records
d.n.	docket number [court case]	VR	Vital Records

Some nicknames common in 17th – 19th centuries

Abigail = Nabby, Abbie, Abby	Martha = Patty
Anne = Nancy	Mary = Molly, Polly
Catherine = Kate, Katy	Sarah = Sally
Elizabeth = Betty, Betsey, Eliza	Temperance = Tempy
Experience = Peddy	

All places are assumed to be in Massachusetts unless otherwise stated.

SOME NOTES TO THE READER

Readers familiar with the format of most of the other *Mayflower Families Through Five Generations* books may notice that this volume does not strictly conform, particularly in its method of referencing. The following explanations are intended to provide clarification.

Numbering

The numbers for fifth-generation people in this book and in Volume 20 Part 2 (the first part of the Fifth Generation) are not the same as those used in MF20: Part 1 (Generations One through Four), published in 2000. This has caused some confusion.

Several new fifth-generation descendants were identified in the course of research for Parts 2 and 3. The options were to give each of these a letter following the number of the previous person in the text, or to re-number. We chose to re-number, not realizing that this would confuse some people. We apologize, but still believe we chose the wiser way. (One person has been added to Part 2 since its publication in 2005, and she has had to become 396A; see Additions and Corrections at the end of this volume, p. 561.)

Suggestion: At the beginning of Part 3, add 16 to the numbers given in Part 1 — Micah Sampson #498 there is #514 here. However, Bethiah Robinson, the last fifth-generation descendant, represents an increase of 23 over her number in Part 1 — #811 there, #834 here. Thus, the person sought may be anywhere from 16 to 23 numbers higher in this volume, but no more. This does not affect the index.

Spelling: *Sampson* or *Samson*?

Readers are certain to be confused by the spelling of the name. When we "inherited" the material on this family in 2001, it became apparent that someone in the distant past had made a decision to use the spelling "Samson" for descendants of Henry (who arrived on the *Mayflower*) and "Sampson" for descendants of Abraham (who did not). In fact, no such distinction existed, and any difference in the spelling of the surname usually has to do with the person keeping the record rather than the people he was recording. Thus in the census of one year everybody might be Samson, and in another year, Sampson. Only in the case of a Bible record can we be sure we have the true spelling a family used, or in a will if the testator signed it. As spelling of names became more standardized, "Sampson" seems to have been used by more descendants than the version without the "p".

In many kinds of records that are now searchable on line, such as the *Plymouth County Court Records* volumes, one must search under both spellings to be sure of picking up all the references to any single individual. The same is true of census indexes.

We have used Sampson in cases where we found it spelled that way in records, but we have not altered all the earlier references, and to change the name in the title of the book would not be a good idea. Suffice it to say that, if your name is Sampson *or* Samson, you may be descended from Henry or Abraham — in some cases both. Descent from Henry makes you eligible for the Society of Mayflower Descendants; descent from Abraham does not.

Method of Referencing

We've used a multi-level system to try to make the work suitable for anyone who may use it; these include casual readers, researchers who need more detail, and Mayflower Society staff looking to check application papers. While this way of presenting references may seem convoluted at first, we think that it will prove quicker and easier to use in the long run.

Short, specific citations are given at the relevant points in the text, hopefully not intrusive enough to distract the reader but sufficient to allow quick checks of the information.

Then, at the end of each family account, in smaller print, there is a list of "sources cited," consisting of the titles of whatever books or sets of records are referred to in that one sketch. Except in cases where the source is a very well-known title, the date of publication is included to help the reader evaluate the information. (It is well to keep in mind that recent works used here are likely to be more comprehensive and better documented, but older genealogies often include information obtained from 19th-century individuals who had personal knowledge of people or events concerned.)

The Bibliography beginning on page 565 includes full citations with publication information that should enable the reader to locate any of the sources easily. In a few cases, explanations or evaluations of manuscript sources are included. *Please note* that the alphabetical arrangement of works in the Bibliography is by family name, location, or subject rather than strictly by title or author. Journal articles cited only once or twice in the text may not be included in the bibliography, but the name of the journal will be, and the specific issue and date will be in the "Sources cited" where applicable.

Repetition of Surnames

Surnames are included in each list of children; although it is admittedly repetitive, this is a concession to the fact that we live in an electronic age. The text is computerized and may someday be used in an electronic publication. In such case, searching for names is easier if the given name and surname appear together. Moreover, looking at some 19th-century families who gave their children multiple names and other family names as middle names, it's often useful to have the surname there to prevent mistaking, say, a John Hamilton Jones for a John Hamilton.

Sixth and Seventh Generations

In researching the fifth-generation people, it was often necessary to figure out what became of some of their children in order to get a clear picture of the family's whereabouts. The time period concerned was one of much migration and scattering across the country, and sometimes a child's name on a census provided the best clue to the parents' last years. Often when we found an obscure source such as a Bible record that gave otherwise unavailable information on sixth and even seventh generations, it seemed useful to include that in this book so that the interested reader would not have to hunt it down all over again. The growing availability of census and other records on line made it tempting to try to trace as many families as possible as they moved around. While the picture given of each family is far from complete, we have tried to provide as much data as possible, after a reasonable search, to give the reader clues that will lead to more.

Whenever "human interest" information could be found, we have included such details in the fifth-generation sketches. Although the language used in many such accounts is fast fading or totally absent from literature produced today, it helps to flesh out the bare bones of our ancestors' lives if we can see them through the eyes of their contemporaries.

Our hope is that this volume will be of interest not only to readers who want to prove a line to the *Mayflower*, but to anyone who enjoys histories of our forebears. Although almost everyone in the book has the common thread of descent from Henry Samson (or married someone who did), their individual lives portray vast differences in culture and experience. In addition to numerous ministers, shoemakers, and farmers, as well as early governors of Maine and Iowa, the fifth, sixth, and seventh generations of the Samson family include the founder of a manufactory for mathematical instruments, a surgeon in the Royal Navy who was given 200 acres of land in Tasmania in recognition of long service, the compiler and publisher of the first Congressional Directory, and a Maine sea captain executed in Malta for piracy. This was a generation on the move in every sense.

Proving Eligibility for the Society of *Mayflower* Descendants

It must be realized that no five-generation genealogy is ever complete. Loose ends begging for further research must at last give way to printing deadlines. Proof depends on the presentation of solid evidence. The authors have assembled the family as correctly and as completely as circumstances have permitted. The work is based largely on carefully-researched articles in genealogical journals and family histories, verified wherever possible by research in probate and land records, town and church vital records, and other primary sources. Family tradition, in the absence of confirmatory evidence, has not been accepted as *proof* of a line, although it may be mentioned in order to provide possible clues for future research. Regretfully, a few lines that were accepted by the Society in its early years have been found to be based on insufficient or erroneous evidence and have thus had to be eliminated, but on the other hand, many potential new lines have been uncovered.

Occasionally the author offers tentative identifications using the word "probable," indicating that the evidence is *nearly* conclusive but positive proof has not been found. The word "possible" indicates that more research is needed (as does a question mark) to prove a connection for which the evidence is merely suggestive. While some might argue that these unproven links should not be mentioned at all, we feel that they may provide valuable clues to direct further research toward the discovery of more compelling evidence.

Please note that fifth-generation descendants of Henry Samson's daughters and of his son James [#171 through #413] are treated in Part 2, published in 2005. Relevant additions and corrections to Part 2 appear at the end of this volume.

A reader who finds either an error regarding any family or individual in this volume, or additional information (down to the birth of sixth-generation children) is urgently requested to send such materials, with documention, to:

FIVE GENERATIONS PROJECT, P.O. BOX 3297,

PLYMOUTH MA 02361

TABLE OF CONTENTS

514. MICAH⁵ SAMPSON (*Micah/Michael⁴, Benjamin³, Stephen², Henry¹*), son of Micah Sampson [110] and his wife Deborah Gardner, was born at Kingston 20 December 1740 (*VR* 130). He died at Falmouth (now Portland), Maine, 21 September 1821 aged 81 years, and is buried in the Eastern Cemetery, Portland (*Eastern Cem.*, 120). His death was noted in the *Eastport Sentinel* of 6 October 1821. He was a descendant also of *Mayflower* passengers Francis Cooke and Stephen Hopkins.

He married at Falmouth, Maine, 23 December 1762, Rev. Mr. Thomas Smith officiating (*Cumberland Co. Marriages*, 5), **ABIGAIL GOOKIN**, daughter of Simon and Prudence (Illsley) Gookin who married at Falmouth in 1742 (*NEHGR* 16:317), and a descendant of Massachusetts Governor Simon Bradstreet (*ibid.*, 8:322).

On 1 October 1744 Benjamin Samson, gentleman, of Kingston was appointed guardian of Micha Sampson (Plymouth PR 13:431). On 7 March 1755 Benjamin Sampson presented an accounting of his guardianship of his grandson Micah Sampson, for keeping "said Micha from four years old till he was seven, saving about half the time when he was with his mother" (*ibid.*, 13:507). On 1 April 1755 Micha Sampson, minor above the age of 14, chose "father in law" [stepfather] Jacob Gould, yeoman, of Weymouth as his guardian (*NEHGR* 143:47).

Benjamin Sampson, merchant of Kingston, in his will dated 20 February 1750/1, named his minor grandson Micah Sampson and directed that if Micah "should dwell or settle in Kingston my two sons Cornelius and Benjamin ... shall be obliged to keep him ... along with their own for the space of twelve years upon free cost" (Plymouth PR #17457, 14:523-26). Cornelius Sampson of Kingston gave bond 14 March 1759 as administrator of his father's estate, to pay Micah Sampson, grandson of the deceased, the sum of £133 6s 8d when he reached the age of 21 (*ibid.*, 15:233). Micah Sampson gave a receipt to his uncle Cornelius for his share on 24 February 1762; witnesses were Wrestling Brewster and Seth Tupper (*ibid.*, 16:324). Micah married Abigail later that year.

On 31 October 1765 Simon Gookin, gentleman, of Falmouth, Maine, conveyed land in Falmouth to his son-in-law Micah Samson of Falmouth, tinplate worker (Cumberland LR 3:263). The tax list taken 17 November 1766 in Falmouth lists Micah Sampson as one poll, taxed 8s 6d, with real estate taxable at 3s (*Falmouth First Church*, 96). In 1767 Simon Gookin sold other land bounded by land he lately sold to Micah Sampson; Simon's wife Prudence Gookin released her dower (*ibid.*, 5:115).

The will of Rebecca (Cooke) Sampson of Kingston, dated 6 January 1769, names among others grandson Micah Sampson (Plymouth PR #17631, 20:226). Micah gave a receipt for his share of the estate on 24 May 1770 (*ibid.,* 20:481).

Micah Sampson served extensively in Maine in the Revolutionary War (*MSSR* 13:762, 773). He was first a sergeant in Capt. Joseph Noyes's company, from 17 July to 31 December 1775, and from 1 March to 31 August 1776 and again from that date to 23 November 1776 a corporal in Capt. William Crocker's company, both companies stationed at Falmouth for defense of the seacoast; in 1777 he served as a matross and then as an end gunner in Capt. Abner Lowell's company. In the summer of 1779 he was in Capt. Peter Warren's company, Col. Jonathan Mitchell's regiment, on a Penobscot expedition.

In 1777 both Micah Sampson and Simon Gooking were taxpayers in Falmouth (*Me.G&B*, 1:116-17). Micah was "the first tinsmith who ever worked in [Portland], and when Mowatt bombarded and burned the city in the War of the Revolution, Mr. Sampson took his tinners' tools in a boat and rowed across Black Cove while the British shot were falling around him, thus saving his property from destruction" (*Harrison History,* 599). In 1790 Michael Samson at Falmouth, Maine, was head of a household consisting of two men over 16, two boys under 16, and seven females (*Heads of Fam. 1790,* 15).

Micah Sampson of Portland, plumber, sold land there to Samuel Motley on 9 May 1799; Micah's wife Abigail relinquished her dower (Cumberland LR 30:119). The 1800 census lists Micah Sampson in Portland with a household consisting of one man and one woman 45 or over, one young man and one young woman 16-26, and one boy 10-16 (p.260).

Micah Sampson founded a business in Portland dealing in ship's chandlery and supplies, later (1891) known as Sargent, Lord & Skillin and located at Nos. 8 and 12 Commercial Wharf (*Representative Business Men, Portland,* 69).

Children of Micah and Abigail (Gookin) Sampson, first eight bp. Portland, Me. (*Falmouth First Church,* 48):

i   [DAUGHTER][6] SAMPSON, bp. 22 June 1766.

ii JAMES GARDINER SAMPSON, bp. 17 July 1768; d. bet. 1830 and 1840 Falmouth, Me.; m. (1) Falmouth, 13 July 1794, HANNAH MOODY (*Cumberland Co. Marriages,* 108); m. (2) MARY (POTE) BUCKNAM, d. Fairhaven, widow of Jeremiah Bucknam (*Rep. Men Southeastern Mass.,* 1283). James was a ship carpenter at Falmouth, Me., and was killed by falling from a staging at the shipyards (*ibid.*). In 1830 his household at Falmouth consisted of himself ae 60-70, wife ae 5-60, one boy and two girls 15-20, and one boy 5-10 (p.207).

Children, first four with Hannah, rest with Mary (*Rep. Men Southeastern Mass.*, 1283): 1. *Joshua[7] Sampson*. 2. *Ann Sampson*. 3. *Thankful Sampson*. 4. *Benjamin Sampson*. 5. *George Sampson*, d. infancy. 6. *George I. Sampson*. 7. *Abigail Sampson*, b. 24 Aug. 1810; m. John Bucknam. 8. *James William Sampson*, b. 21 June 1812. 9. *Clarissa Sampson*, b. 23 April 1814; m. Stillman Leavitt. 10. *John Sampson*, b. 28 Nov. 1817; m. Elizabeth Eldridge Taber. 11. *Hannah M. Sampson*, b. 31 Jan. 1819; m. James R. Lawrence. 12. *Benjamin B. Sampson*, b. 11 June 1825.

iii   DEBORAH SAMPSON, bp. 14 April 1771; m. at Portland, 7 July 1793 (*VR* 21), ANDREW TWOMLEY.

iv   LUCY SAMPSON, bp. 17 Oct. 1773; m. at Portland, 16 April 1795 (*VR* 22), JOSEPH WILSON.

v   ABIGAIL SAMPSON, bp. 28 July 1776; m. int. Portland (as Nabby), 4 Oct. 1801 (*VR* 47), EPHRAIM TWOMBLEY of Falmouth.

vi   BETTY SAMPSON, bp. 3 Jan. 1779.

vii   JOSHUA SAMPSON, bp. 12 Aug. 1781; d. Roxbury 12 May 1857 ae 74y 10m, widower, tin plate worker, b. Portland [parents not listed] (Mass. VR 112:242); "of Bath [Me.]" when he m. at Milton, 21 June 1809 (*VR* 166), NANCY BABCOCK of Milton, d. Roxbury 12 May 1828 (*VR* 630); he m. (2) Roxbury, 23 Aug. 1829 (*VR* 352), NANCY (NEWMAN) DAVENPORT, widow of Enoch Davenport (m. Roxbury 1813, *VR* 105), d. Roxbury 1 Oct. 1852 ae 71y 9m, "wife of Joshua Sampson" (Mass. VR 67:221). Three children of Enoch Davenport d. Roxbury 1818, and Enoch d. there 8 Oct. 1823 ae 37y (*VR* 503). In 1830 Joshua Sampson was head of a household in Roxbury that included two boys and two girls under 10 and one boy 10-16 (p.76). In 1850 Joshua ae 68, b. Me., tin plate worker, and Nancy ae 70 were in Roxbury with Anne Davenport ae [? 24] (p.178). No Sampson children identified.

viii   DOROTHY SAMPSON, b 22 Aug. 1784.

ix   JOHN SAMPSON, b. 1788 (*Harrison History*, 599); d. 28 Aug. 1832 ae 44 yrs; bur. Eastern Cem., Portland, next to father (*Eastern Cem. Recs.*, 120); m. Otisfield, Me., 22 Oct. 1810 (*VR* 252), ABIGAIL ROBY, b. ca 1792 in Me., d. 3 April 1858 ae 66y, "wife of Col. John Sampson" (*Eastern Cem. Recs.*, 120). She was b. Otisfield, Me., 28 April 1790, dau. of Thomas Roby and his first wife, Lucretia Sturgiss (VR 125). John kept a grocery and provision store on Congress St., Portland, opposite Green St. In 1850 Abigail ae 58, was living in Ward 5, Portland, with dau. Lucretia ae 25 (p.160).

Children (*Harrison History*, 599): 1. *Thomas R. Sampson*[7], b. 11 Aug. 1811. 2. *Micah Sampson*, b. 1816; m. (1) Jane ___, (2) Susan H. ___; res. Portland 1870, dealer in ship stores. 3. *Lucretia S. Sampson*, b. 1821; res. 1870 in household of brother Micah, unm. (p.175).

Sources cited: *Kingston VR. Milton VR. Roxbury VR. Portland, Maine VR* (2005). Mass. Vital Records 1841-1910. Cumberland County Deeds at Portland, Me. Plymouth County Probate Records. "Marriages In Falmouth," ms. Maine Historical Society. "Records of Falmouth (now Portland), Me.," *NEHGR* 16 (1862) & 17 (1863). "Descendants of Gov. Bradstreet," *NEHGR* 8 (1854). *Baptisms & Admissions First Church Falmouth Maine* (1898). *Burial Records of Eastern Cemetery, Portland, Maine* (1987). Kelley, *Marriage Returns of Cumberland County, Maine prior to 1892* (1998). *Maine Genealogist & Biographer*, 1 (1875/76). *Vital Records from the* Eastport Sentinel *1818-1900* (1996). *Representative Families of Southeastern Massachusetts* (1912). *Centennial History of Harrison* [Maine] (1909). Bacon, *Portland: Its Representative Business Men and its Points of Interest* (1891). CENSUS: *Heads of Families 1790 – Maine;* Cumberland Co., Me.,[Portland 1800 (M32-6), 1850 (M432-252), & 1870 (M593-541), Falmouth 1830 (M19-46); 1850 Roxbury, Norfolk Co. (M432-330). See also: *Giles Memorial* (1864), 380.

515.   JOHN VEAZIE[5] (*Deborah*[4] *Samson, Benjamin*[3]*, Stephen*[2]*, Henry*[1]), son of Rev. Samuel Veazie and his wife Deborah Samson [111], was born 7 August 1746 at Duxbury (*VR* 179) and baptized at Hull 10 August 1746 (*VR* 36), a descendant also of *Mayflower* passengers Francis Cooke and Stephen Hopkins. He died 6 August 1806 aged 60 or 61 years, at Portland, Maine, his death noted in the *Columbian Centinel* of 13 August 1806 (*Me. Newsp. VR*, 620).

He married, probably at Hull, 16 October 1768, **RACHEL JONES**, who was born 5 November 1747 (*Bangor Hist. Mag.*, 2:72), and died at Portland, Maine, 10 November 1797, "wife of John ae 50 yrs" (*Me. Newsp. VR*, 620). She was probably the granddaughter Rachel Vezie named by Solomon Jones of Hull in his will dated 7 March 1780, proved 13 August 1792 (*NEHGR* 113:131). If this is correct, she was a niece of John Veazie's stepmother Sarah (Jones) Veazie. Rachel's mother was probably Solomon Jones' daughter Rachel Jones, who married in February 1745/6 Isaac Jones of Weymouth and is not mentioned in her father's will at all.

John and Rachel Veazie owned the covenant at the First Church in Falmouth, Maine (now Portland), 8 October 1769 (*Falmouth First Ch.*, 25). He was a town officer 26 March 1771 and purchased land there 17 April 1773, the deed witnessed by his father.

In 1790 John Veazie's family in Portland included one man over 16, four boys under 16, and four females (*Heads of Fam.*, 23). John Veazie of Portland acknowledged a deed 13 May 1798 with Robert Jordan and wife Deborah, of land that formerly belonged to Rev. Samuel Veazie of Harpswell (Cumberland LR 28:201).

The 1800 census (p.264) listed him in Portland, with a household consisting of one man over 45 [himself], one woman 26-45 [daughter Sarah?], two young men and one young woman 16-26 [sons John & Stephen; woman unidentified], two boys 10-16 [sons Samuel & Isaac], and one little girl under 10 [possibly grand-daughter Helen Hilton].

Children of John and Rachel (Jones) Veazie, bp. Falmouth (now Portland), Maine (*Falmouth First Church*, 105; *Bangor Hist. Mag.*, 2:72-73), as "Veasie":

i STEPHEN VEAZIE[6], bp. 12 Nov. 1769; d. before 1779.

ii RACHEL VEAZIE, b. 1 April, bp. 7 April 1771; d. Portland 10 Nov. 1797 of smallpox; m. in Maine, 13 Nov. 1791, Rev. Samuel Deane officiating, THOMAS HILTON (*Cumberland Co. Marriages*, 83).
     Hilton child: 1. *Helen L. Hilton*[7], m. at Bangor Joseph Smith, rem. to Washington.

iii SARAH VEAZIE, b. 6 Feb. 1773, bp. 20 Feb. 1774; d. Portland 17 Oct. 1867; m. 15 Oct. 1806, JOHN WARD.

iv SAMUEL VEAZIE, bp. 25 July 1775; d. 27 July 1775.

v JOHN VEAZIE, b. 25 April, bp. 4 May 1777; d. at Demerara 28 Sept. 1800 (*Me. Newsp. VR*, 620).

vi STEPHEN VEAZIE, b. 6 Nov., bp. 14 Nov. 1779; lost at sea in the privateer *Dart* in Sept. 1812; lived Portland; m. there 20 Oct. 1805 (*VR* 123), SALLY BEEMAN, who d. at the home of her daughter in Bangor, "late wife and widow of Stephen Veazie, dec'd." She m. (2) George D. Plaisted of Portsmouth, N.H.
     Children rec. Portland (*VR* 186): 1. *George Veazie*[7], b. 30 July 1806; d. 31 July 1806. 2. *Stephen Veazie* (twin), b. 19 Aug. 1807. 3. *Sally Veazie* (twin), b. 19 Aug. 1807; d. 22 Aug. 1807. 4. *John Veazie*, b. 12 Nov. 1808; bp. 31 May 1810 (*Falmouth First Ch.*, 105); m. Caroline Low. *Bangor Hist. Mag.* adds 4. *Adrianna Veazie*, m. George W. Merrill of Bangor; res. Eastport 1834.

vii SAMUEL VEAZIE, bp. 24 March 1782; d. 27 March 1783.

viii POLLY VEAZIE, b. 14 April, bp. 1 May 1785; d. 11 Oct. 1786.

ix SAMUEL VEAZIE, b. 22 April, bp. 6 May 1787; of Portland when he m. (1) 3 or 8 July 1809 SUSAN WALKER of Topsham (int. mid-Feb. 1809) (*Me. Newsp. VR*, 621), who d. 27 June 1852; m. (2) 17 May 1859 Mrs. MARY C. BLANCHARD. He served in War of 1812 and later became a general in the militia and a prominent citizen of Bangor.

Children: 1. *Jones P. Veazie[7]*, b. 2 June 1811; m. (1) Topsham (int. 13 Dec. 1834) Mary Jane Winslow, (2) Susan Townsend. 2. *John Walker Veazie*, b. 30 Oct. 1812; m. Ruth Maria Bartlett. 3. *Frances A. H. Veazie*, b. 18 July 1818; m. (1) Nathaniel Lord; m. (2) Rev. William W. or M. Willian [*sic*], Episcopal minister.

xi   ISAAC JONES VEAZIE, bp. 15 March 1789; d. St. Bartholomews 6 Jan. 1809 (*Me. Newsp. VR*, 620).

Sources cited: *Duxbury VR. Bangor Historical Magazine*, 2 (1886-87). Sprague, "Braintree Families." Cumberland County Deeds at Portland. Kelley, *Marriage Returns of Cumberland County, Maine prior to 1892* (1998). *Vital Records from Maine Newspapers, 1785 - 1820* (1993). CENSUS: 1800 Portland, Cumberland Co., Me. (M32-6); 1850 Bowdoin, Lincoln Co., Me. (M432-261).

516.   SAMUEL VEAZIE[5] (*Deborah[4] Samson, Benjamin[3], Stephen[2], Henry[1]*), son of Rev. Samuel Veazie and his wife Deborah Samson [111], was born at Duxbury 8 January 1751 (*VR* 179), and died in 1828 at Islesboro, Maine (*Bangor Hist. Mag.,* 2:74). He was a descendant also of *Mayflower* passengers Francis Cooke and Stephen Hopkins.

He married, about 1775, **PHEBE HOLBROOK** "of Harpswell, Me.," who died in 1832 (*ibid.*). She was born probably at Wellfleet 4 December 1750 and died at Islesboro in 1832 (*ibid.*).

During the Revolution, Samuel Veazey served as a sergeant in Capt. Nathaniel Larrabee's company, engaged 9 July 1775 for 6 months, 7 days, on the seacoast in Cumberland County (*MSSR* 16:304). In March 1777 Samuel Veasey of Casco Bay was a private in Capt. Samuel Johnson's company, Col. Wigglesworth's regiment, his name on a pay abstract for travel allowance from Albany home, 300 miles' travel allowed (*ibid.*). As Samuel Veasie of Harpswell, he was a sergeant in Capt. Benjamin Parker's company, Col. Nathan[iel] Wade's regiment; engaged 25 June 1778; stationed at Rhode Island for 6 months (*ibid.*).

About 1780 Samuel settled on the east side of Long Island, Islesboro, near Coombs' Cove. He was a mariner and town officer (*Islesboro History*, 290).

In 1790 Samuel Vezie was listed in the census at Islesboro with one man over 16, four boys under 16, and four females (*Heads of Fam.,* 29). The 1800 census of many Waldo County towns includes the name of the place from which each head of household had come, and Samuel Veazey of Islesboro was from Nantasket [Hull], head of a household consisting of one man 26-45 and a woman 16-26, one boy 10-15, and one boy and one girl under 10 (p.31). In 1810 both Samuel and Samuel Jr. were in Islesboro (p.510), but in 1820 only Samuel Jr. was listed there.

Children of Samuel and Phebe (Holbrook) Veazie (*Islesboro History*, 290-93; *Bangor Hist. Mag.*, 2:73-74):

i   STEPHEN VEAZIE[6], b. Nov. 1778; d. Caton, Steuben Co., N.Y., 13 Dec. 1855 (Veazie online); m. ca 1806 MARTHA HARDING, d. 7 March 1839 Corinna, Me (*ibid.*).

Children (Veazie on line):   1. *Isaac Veazie*[7], b. 5 Nov. 1806; m. Lydia Knowles.   2. *John Veazie*, b. 13 Nov. 1808.   3. *Paulina Veazie*, b. 4 April 1810.   4. *Laban Veazie*, b. 19 May 1812; m. Lucy ___.   5. *Stephen Veazie*, b. 1815; m. Sarah Chandler Folsom.   6. *Martha Hurstan* [*sic* – Harding?] *Veazie*, b. 1816; m. Dominicus Sewell.   7. *Mary Jane Veazie*, b. 17 Oct. 1820.   8. *Alden Veazie*, b. 3 Dec. 1823.   8. *Sewall Veazie*, b. 13 Nov. 1830.

ii SAMUEL VEAZIE, b. ca 1779; d. 4 Dec. 1841; m. BRIDGET COOMBS, b. 10 May 1788, d. 28 April 1858 (*VR* 1), dau. Field Coombs; res. Islesboro.

Children, rec. as "Veze" (*VR* 1; *Islesboro History*, 291): 1. *Johnson Veazie*[7], b. 6 Aug. 1804; d. on way to Bucksport on the stage[coach], m. (1) Sarah A. Hatch, (2) Ann C. Hatch.   2. *Jordan Veazie*, b. 15 Oct. 1806; m. Philena Parker.   3. *Samuel Veazie*, b. 7 April 1808; m. Deborah M. Hatch; res. Brewer.   4. *Wales Veazie*, b. 10 Jan. 1810; d. 1864 Hingham, unm.   5. *Azubah Veazie*, b. 27 Nov. 1812; m. Andrew P. Gilkey.   6. *Charles Veazie*, b. 3 July 1815; d. 1835, unm.   7. *Sally Veazie*, b. 3 May 1817; m. George Warren of Islesboro.   8. *Caroline Veazie*, b. 15 April 1819; m. William Avery Parker.   9. *Otis Coombs Veazie*, b. 14 June 1821; m. Deborah Coombs, who m. (2) John Veazie of Islesboro.   10. *William Veazie*, b. 12 April 1824; m. Deborah Parker.   11. *Albion P. Veazie*, b. 14 May 1826.   12. *Angela Veazie*, b. 24 Feb. 1828; m. Otis F. Coombs.

iii MARTHA VEAZIE, m. ca 1801 FIELD COOMBS [Jr.]. He m. (2) 26 Dec. 1814 (VR 23), BETSEY AMES[7] (Henry Samson desc. #215-i-4), with whom he had six *Coombs* children: Lucy Coombs[8], Louisiana Coombs, Samson Coombs, Thatcher Coombs, Hosea Coombs, and Jairus Coombs.

iv RACHEL VEAZIE, b. ca 1775; d. 17 April 1856 ae 81 (g.s.); m. LEMUEL DRINKWATER, b. prob. Northport, Me., 29 Jan. 1773, d. 27 Dec. 1848 ae 75 (g.s.), son of Micajah and Elizabeth (Bradford) Drinkwater, a descendant of William Bradford, James Chilton, and George Soule (*MF22*: 498-99). Capt. Lemuel and Rachel are bur. in Beech Hill Cemetery, Northport, Me.

Probable *Drinkwater* children: 1. *Siby Drinkwater*[7], b. ca 1800.   2. *Allen Drinkwater*, b. ca 1807.   3. *Olive Drinkwater*, b. ca 1811.   4. *Lemuel Drinkwater*, b. ca 1817.   5. *Martha Drinkwater*, b. ca 1819.   6. *Rachel Drinkwater*, b. ca 1821.

v   JOHN VEAZIE, b. 1786; d. 15 Sept. 1841; m. at Islesboro 18 June 1814 (*VR* 23), NAOMI COOMBS, b. ca 1790, d. 9 March 1872 ae 82y 1m 9d, dau. of Field Coombs of Islesboro, of whose estate John Veazie Jr. was administrator 2 May 1842 (*Bangor Hist. Mag.*, 2:74).

Children, b. Islesboro (*Islesboro History*, 292-93): 1. *Phebe Veazie⁷*, b. 20 Nov. 1814; m. Capt. John Seely of Islesboro. 2. *Rachel Veazie*, b. 21 April 1815 [*sic – prob. 1816*]; m. 1839, Isaac Roaks of Appleton. 3. *John Veazie*, b. 3 Feb. 1818; m. (1) 1841, Maria R. Sprague; m. (2) 28 Dec. 1859,. Deborah (Coombs) Veazie, widow of his cousin Otis. 4. *Rufus Veazie*, b. 24 June 1821; m. Lucinda E. Trim. 5. *Jane Veazie*, b. 27 May 1824; m. Michael Felker of Searsport. 6. *Clarinda Veazie*, b. 15 April 1825; m. Nathan F. Fuller of Searsport. 7. *James Harrison Veazie*, b. 18 May 1829; m. Adeliza Dix. 8. *Lorana Veazie*, b. 19 April 1832; m. Noah Roberts.

vi   LUCY VEAZIE, m. TIMOTHY HARDING.

vii   ABIEZER VEAZIE, b. ca 1789; d. Camden ca 1840, ae 51y 9m 21d; m. GRACE AMES⁷, dau. of Jabez and Jane (Gilkey) Ames of Islesboro (Henry Samson desc. #215-i-2). In 1810 and 1820 he was in Islesboro near Samuel Veazie and Samuel Veazie Jr. In 1850 Grace Veazee ae 62 was living in the household of Nathaniel Hosmer and wife Eliza, at Camden, Me. (p.181). *Islesborough History* says their descendants res. in Camden and Rockland.

Sources cited: *Duxbury VR. Mass. Soldiers & Sailors. History of Islesborough, Maine* (1883). *Bangor Historical Magazine*, 2 (1886-87). Northport, Me., cemetery inscriptions online at *www.mainweb.com*. Veazie online: *www.veazie.org* (well-documented website). CENSUS: Islesboro, Hancock Co., Me., 1800 (M32-7), 1810 (M252-11) & 1820 (M33-34); Camden, Waldo Co., Me., 1850 (M432-270).

517.   DEBORAH VEAZIE⁵ (*Deborah⁴ Samson, Benjamin³, Stephen², Henry¹*), daughter of Rev. Samuel Veazie and his wife Deborah Samson [111], was born at Hull 8 July 1753 (*VR* 36), a descendant also of *Mayflower* passengers Francis Cooke and Stephen Hopkins. Her mother died in 1755, and record of Deborah's birth was entered several years after the fact, as "daughter of Rev. Samuel and *Rebecca*." She was living 13 May 1798, when she acknowledged a deed, noted below.

She married at Harpswell, Maine, 26 July 1773, **ROBERT JORDAN** of Brunswick, Maine, Samuel Eaton V.D.M., officiating (*Cumberland Co. Marriages*, 14). Robert died at Brunswick, between 8 September 1806 when he acknowledged a deed, and 7 December 1807, when another deed referred to him as deceased.

In 1790 Robert Jordan was in Brunswick, head of a household consisting of two males over 16, two boys under 16, and four females (p.12). In 1800 Robert Jordan was listed in Brunswick, himself and wife 45 or older, with two young men and two young women 16-26, and one girl 10-16 (p.75).

Both Robert Jordan and his wife Deborah acknowledged a deed 13 May 1798, conveying land formerly belonging to Rev. Samuel Veazie of Harpswell, whereof Deborah was heir to thirds (Cumberland LR 28:201). On 24 July 1800, acknowledged 8 September 1806, Robert Jordan of Brunswick sold land there to Samuel Jordan and Robert Jordan Jr., both of Brunswick (*ibid.*, 49:629). On 7 December 1807, Samuel and Robert Jordan of Brunswick sold an undivided half part of the farm lately belonging to Robert Jordan of Brunswick deceased (*ibid.*, 55:2).

Children of Robert and Deborah (Veazie) Jordan, rec. Brunswick, Me. (*VR* 50):

i   SAMUEL JORDAN[6], b. 17 March 1776; m. Brunswick, 2 June 1803 (*VR* 100), JANE MARTIN (Marston in *Jordan Memorial*).
   Children (*Jordan Mem.*, 95): 1. *Thomas Marsten Jordan*[7], b. 28 April 1804; m. Lavina A. Weeks. 2. *Roseanna Jordan*, b. 1806.

ii   REBECCA JORDAN, b. 15 Oct. 1778; m. JOSHUA CUSHMAN of Woolwich; no children.

iii ROBERT JORDAN, b. 15 Oct. 1780; d. 20 March 1870; m. at Harpswell, MARY SNOW, b. there 29 Aug. 1787, d. 14 Oct. 1846 (*Bangor Hist. Mag.*, 2:71); res. Brunswick. In 1850 Robert Jordan ae 70, farmer, was living in Brunswick with Rebecca, Mary, and John (p.204).
   Children (*Jordan Memorial*, 96): 1. *Deborah Jordan*[7], b. 17 Sept. 1804; m. Joseph B. Ferren. 2. *Rebecca Jordan*, b. 17 Oct. 1806; d. 1870 unm. 3. *Mary Jordan*, b. 18 Aug. 1808; unm. 1875. 4. *Robert Jordan*, b. 10 June 1810; m. Hannah White. 5. *Jonathan Jordan*, b. 6 May 1812; unm. 6. *Shubael Jordan*, b. 12 Nov. 1814; d. 1838 unm. 7. *Samuel Jordan*, b. 25 Feb. 1818; m. Elizabeth Jordan. 8. *Henry Jordan*, b. 29 March 1820; m. Mary O. Sinnett. 9. *Isaiah Jordan*, b. 12 Aug. 1822; m. (1) Mary Reed, (2) Hannah S. Chapman. 10. *Delia Jordan*, b. 7 Sept. 1824; m. Robert Woodard. 11. *Bethia Jordan*, b. 25 Feb. 1826; m. Floyd Tolbert. 12. *Betsey Jordan*, b. 12 Aug. 1828; d. 1833. 13. *William Jordan*, b. 29 March 1833; m. Eliza Berry.

iv   SARAH JORDAN, b. 5 July 1782, m. _____ PURRINTON.

v   DEBORAH JORDAN, b. 18 Feb. 1785; m. Brunswick, 25 March 1803 (*VR* 100), JONATHAN SNOW; said to be living 1875, no ch.

Sources cited: *Hull VR*. Kelley, *Marriage Returns of Cumberland County, Maine prior to 1892*. Cumberland County Deeds. *Jordan Memorial* (1882). CENSUS: Brunswick, Cumberland Co., Me., 1790 (M637-2), 1800 (M32-6) & 1850 (M432-251). See also: *Bangor Historical Magazine*, 2 [1886-7].

518.   REBECCA VEAZIE[5] (*Deborah*[4] *Samson, Benjamin*[3], *Stephen*[2], *Henry*[1]), daughter of Rev. Samuel Veazie and his wife Deborah Samson [111], was baptized at Hull 24 August 1755 (*VR* 36), two days after the death of her mother (*VR* 74), and was living at Harpswell, Maine, 28 November 1835 when she acknowledged a deed. She was a descendant also of *Mayflower* passengers Francis Cooke and Stephen Hopkins.

She married at Harpswell, 21 May 1772, **JONATHAN HOLBROOK** (*Cumberland Co. Marriages*, 13), probably born at Wellfleet 21 July 1745. He died at Harpswell, before 27 February 1819 when Rebecca sold land, and certainly before 6 June 1835, when she was called widow in a deed, noted below.

Jonathan Holbrook settled at Harpswell before 1770, and is said to have been the ancestor of all of the Holbrook name in that vicinity (*Harpswell History*, 839, 873). On 17 April 1786 Samuel Veazie sold to [his daughter] Rebecca Holbrook part of lot no. 29 in Harpswell for £50 (*Bangor Hist. Mag.*, 2:71).

In 1790 Jonathan Holbrook was enumerated in Harpswell with two men over 16, two boys under 16, and five females (*Heads of Fam.*, 20). In 1800 Jonathan Holbrook in Cumberland County (p.46) was head of a household consisting of himself and wife 45 or older, two young men and one young woman 16-26, one girl 10-16, and one little girl under 10. In 1810 Jonathan Holebrooks was listed in Harpswell (p.39).

In deeds dated 1807 and 1810 Jonathan Holbrook, gentleman, and wife Rebecca of Harpswell sold land there; witnesses included Jonathan Holbrook Jr., Rebecah Holbrook, and Mary Holbrook (Cumberland LR 53:387, 59:64, 67:448). On 27 February 1819 Rebecah Holbrook of Harpswell sold land there for Jonathan Holbrook of Harpswell [probably her son, indicating that her husband was already deceased] (*ibid.*, 84:49). Rebecca Holbrook of Harpswell, "widowoman," sold land in Harpswell 6 June 1835 to [her son] Jonathan Holbrook of Harpswell, acknowledging the deed 28 November 1835 (*ibid.*, 152:131).

Children of Jonathan and Rebecca (Veazie) Holbrook, b. prob. Harpswell, Me. (*Harpswell History*, 839).

  i   ISRAEL HOLBROOK[6], b. 16 Jan. 1773; d. before 1850; m. HANNAH WILLIAMS (*Sinnett Gen.*, 93-94). Israel served as a private in Capt. Snow's Co. in 1814 (*Harpswell History*, 895). In 1850 Hannah ae 70 was living in the household of son Benjamin at Harpswell; the families of Abiezer and Johnathan [*sic*] ae 38 were listed next door (p.268).
        Children included (*Sinnett Gen.*, census): 1. *Abiezer Holbrook[7]*, b. ca 1810; m. Hannah ___. 2. *Jonathan T. Holbrook*, b. 2 Nov. 1812; m. Mary Orr. 3. *Benjamin Holbrook*, b. ca 1819; m. Susan ___.
 ii   DEBORAH HOLBROOK, b. 25 Feb. 1775; d.y.
iii   DEBORAH HOLBROOK, b. 14 March 1778; d.y.
 iv   ABIEZER HOLBROOK, b. 16 July 1779; d.y. [*sic*]
  v   ABIEZER HOLBROOK, b. 16 July 1780.

vi JONATHAN HOLBROOK, b. 26 Jan. 1783. He was a sgt. in Capt. Snow's
    Co. in 1814 (*Harpswell History*, 895).

vii REBECCA HOLBROOK, b. 10 April 1785.

viii DEBORAH HOLBROOK, b. 19 Feb. 1788.

ix HANNAH HOLBROOK, b. 10 July 1790.

x POLLY HOLBROOK, b. 10 Jan. 1792.

xi PRISCILLA HOLBROOK, b. 13 Sept. 1795.

Sources cited: *Hull VR*. Wheeler, *History of Brunswick, Topsham and Harpswell, Maine* (1878). *Bangor Historical Magazine*, Vol. 2 (1886-87). Rev. Charles Nelson Sinnett, *Michael Sinnett of Harpswell, Maine* ... (Concord, N.H.: The Rumford Press, 1910). CENSUS, Harpswell, Cumberland Co., Me.: 1800 (M32-6), 1810 (M252-11), 1850 (M432-251).

519. **CROCKER⁵ SAMPSON** (*Cornelius⁴, Benjamin³, Stephen², Henry¹*), son of Cornelius Samson [112] and his wife Desire Crocker, was born at Kingston 25 April 1749 and died there 7 July 1823 ae 74 (*VR* 127, 376). He was a descendant also of *Mayflower* passengers Francis Cooke, Stephen Hopkins, and John Howland.

He was "of Kingston" 4 May 1794 when he married at Barnstable (*VR* 3:293) **REBECCA HAWLEY**. She was born 21 November 1762 at Barnstable, daughter of Rev. Gideon and Lucy (Fessenden) Hawley (*MD* 25:130). She died 27 June 1844 at Kingston (*VR* 378), aged 81y 6m, "widow of Crocker Samson." In his will dated 5 April 1806, with codicil 10 August 1807, proved 10 November 1807, Rev. Gideon Hawley of Barnstable alias Mashpee, clerk, named two daughters, Lucy and Rebecca wife of Crocker Sampson, and appointed son Gideon executor (Barnstable PR 32:189; 33:33).

Crocker Sampson graduated from Harvard College in 1771 (Sibley, *Harvard Grads*, 12:410).

He served in the Revolutionary War. In his application for a pension he stated he entered the service as a quartermaster 1 January 1777 and remained to the end of the war; that he was a lieutenant [in 7th Mass. Regt. Continental Line] from 13 April 1780. On 17 July 1820 he stated that he was a husbandman, aged 71, living in Kingston with five others in his family: wife Rebecca, aged 57; an only son Benjamin, who was a cripple and of weak intellect from birth, aged about 25 and unable to contribute to his own support; eldest daughter Harriet, 23, and youngest daughter Lucy, 19, both of slender health and barely able to respond to necessary labor of the family; and colored boy Alexander Williams, 13 (White, 3004; pension file).

Crocker Sampson was granted license to sell liquor as a retailer in Kingston for the years 1791 and 1792 (*PCCR* 4:38). He was chosen a grand juror from Kingston in April 1798 (*ibid.*, 4:148), and in November 1798, called "Crocker Samson of Kingston, Gentleman," he was sued by Thomas Foster of Middleboro, blacksmith, for non-payment of two notes dated 31 January 1781, one for 70 dollars in "new emission currency," the other for 20 dollars in "old emission currency," the whole equal to £6 1*s* 6*d* in silver money; verdict was for the plaintiff, amount sued for plus costs (*ibid.*, 10:287).

In his will dated 28 January 1806, presented 21 July 1823, Crocker Sampson of Kingston, gentleman, named his wife Rebecca, son Benjamin under 21, and three daughters, Harriot, Rebecca, and Lucy (Plymouth PR 57:205; 59:78). In a division 20 September 1824, the widow's dower was excepted, and five equal shares were allotted: two to Benjamin Sampson, and one each to Harriet Fish, Rebecca Crocker, and Lucy H. Sampson.

Crocker Sampson and other members of his family are buried in the Ancient Burial Ground, Kingston (*MD* 7:170-71).

Children of Crocker and Rebecca (Hawley) Sampson, rec. Kingston (*VR* 126-29):

i   BENJAMIN[6] SAMPSON, b. 19 Aug. 1795; d. Kingston 22 Oct. 1832, ae 37 (*VR* 376); *non compos mentis*, unm.

ii   HARRIET SAMPSON, b. 9 Aug. 1797; m. at Kingston, 17 Sept. 1821 (*VR* 220, 273), CHARLES FISH, b. 22 Oct. 1799 Sandwich, son of Jonathan and Mary (Davis) Fish (*VR* 1:346, 540), d. June 1825, ae 27 yrs, lost in wreck of schooner *Herald* on passage from Charleston, S.C., to Falmouth (g.s. Spring Hill Cem., *Sandwich VR* 2:1569). Harriet m. (2) at Kingston, 5 Nov. 1843 (*VR* 221), as his second wife, CHARLES ADAMS, widower of her cousin Mary Sampson, dau. Josiah and Mary (Crocker) Sampson [#521-i].

   Fish child: 1. *Elizabeth Hawley Fish*[7], b. 28 June 1822 Kingston; m. there, 20 Sept. 1847 [her stepbrother] Capt. Henry Lincoln Adams, son of Charles and Mary (Sampson) Adams, b. 7 July 1810 Kingston (*VR* 74, 220, 11, 13).

iii   REBECCA SAMPSON, b. 4 Nov. 1799; m. Kingston, 6 Nov. 1817 (*VR* 274), ZENAS CROCKER of Barnstable. He d. 6 May 1877, ae 81y 2m, and she d. 25 Jan. 1887, ae 57y 2m 23d (*Barnst. Cem. Inscript.*, 119, 123). In 1850 (p.341) they were living next to her brother Josiah in Barnstable.

   Crocker children at home 1850: 1. *Gideon Crocker*[7], b. ca 1825, a seaman 1850. 2. *Mary B. Crocker*, b. ca 1827. 3. *Hannah B. Crocker*, b. ca 1829. 4. *Zenas Crocker*, b. ca 1831, a sailor 1850. 5. *Rebecca Crocker*, b. ca 1833. 6. *Malth—[dau.] Crocker*, b. ca 1835.

iv   LUCY SAMPSON, b. 18 Aug. 1801; living 1863 in California (*Giles Mem.*, 410), m. prob. after 1830 when named in will of her aunt Anne Sampson, _____ HOBSON (*ibid.*).

Sources cited: Barnstable VR. *Kingston VR. Sandwich VR.* Barnstable County and Plymouth County Probate Records. "Death Records from the Ancient Burial Ground at Kingston, Mass.," *Mayflower Descendant* 7 [1905], 25 [1923]. White, *Abstracts of Rev. War Pension Files*, 3004, citing #S33623. Konig, *Plymouth County Court Records.* Sibley's *Harvard Graduates.*

520.   JOSEPH⁵ SAMPSON (*Cornelius⁴, Benjamin³, Stephen², Henry¹*), son of Cornelius Sampson [112] and his wife Desire Crocker, was born at Kingston 10 February 1751 (*VR* 127), a descendant also of *Mayflower* passengers Francis Cooke, Stephen Hopkins, and John Howland. Col. Joseph Sampson died at Kingston 10 August 1804 aged 53 (*VR* 377) and is buried in the Ancient Burial Ground there (*MD* 7:171).

Capt. Joseph Sampson married at Kingston, 11 January 1787 (*VR* 212, 273), **JUDITH DREW**, who was born there 3 September 1768 and died there 24 May 1836 aged 67, "Judith (Drew) Samson Thomas," daughter of James and Deborah (Nye) Drew (*VR* 64, 211, 385). She married, second, 22 December 1805 at Kingston (*VR* 289), (Hon.) JOHN THOMAS, who died 21 February 1853 aged 87, with whom she is buried (*MD* 7:221). Judith had with her second husband a daughter, Hannah, born 1809, died Kingston 1891 (Mass. VR 419: 531), who married Theodore B. Cunningham and was named as an heir to the estate of her half-brother Joseph Sampson in 1845, noted below.

Among receipts from the heirs of James Drew is one for $52 received from Stephen Drew, administrator, in 1807, for "my wife's share of her father's estate," signed by J. Thomas (Plymouth PR 44:368).

Joseph Sampson served as an Ensign in the Revolutionary War in the company of "Eight months' men," commanded by Capt. (afterwards General) Peleg Wadsworth, in Col. Theophilus Cotton's regiment, from May to the end of December 1775 (*MSSR* 13:760).

At the Plymouth Court of Common Pleas in April 1788 (docket #8), Joseph Samson was sued by David Beal of Kingston, trader, over a right of passage to his barn that led through Beal's potato fields. Beal claimed that Joseph Samson, Gentleman, of Kingston, on 21 April 1788 "broke and entered the said David's close, being in Kingston ... [and] did break down one pane of the said Plaintiff's fence" valued at 5*s*, and "the Potatoes of the said David in said Close then planted to the value of [10*s*] with his cattle, to wit, oxen and Horses the said Joseph did eat and tread down and destroy," and that he had repeated the offence on other later occasions. Joseph, through his attorney, pleaded not guilty and claimed that he had a right of way of passage over the land, in "the Right of Cornilias Samson, by whose Command said Joseph entered." Croad Samson was admitted as a plaintiff with David Beal, and the verdict was for Beal. The defendant appealed, but there is nothing more in the records.

In his will dated 9 August 1804, proved 23 August 1804, Joseph Sampson of Kingston Esq., named Mr. John Faunce of Kingston executor and appointed wife Judith guardian of the children. Son Joseph was to have two-thirds of the real estate at age 21, and daughter Betsey Sampson to have the rest when Joseph reached 21 (Plymouth PR 40:109). The inventory, taken 1 October 1804, included the 27-acre homestead with buildings and part in the landing place, 8 acres near the meeting house, a 7-acre fresh meadow purchased of Anne Sampson on Jones River, the 25-acre furnace woodlot, 9 acres in Great Woods Pasture, 35 acres in the Sheep Pasture purchased of the town of Plymouth, a 15-acre woodlot, a 70-acre tract in Duxbury, 20 acres of salt marsh, a pew in the meeting house, and almost $1,000 worth of public securities of the United States (Plymouth PR 40:110-111).

Children of Joseph and Judith (Drew) Sampson, rec. Kingston (*VR* 126-29):

i   BETSEY[6] SAMPSON, b. 8 June 1790 (*VR* 126); m. Kingston, 5 April 1812 (*VR* 175, 272), Hon. THOMAS PRINCE BEAL, b. Kingston 12 Feb. 1786, d. 16 July 1852 (*Giles Memorial*, 483). Betsey Beal wife of T. P. Beal was named as niece in the will of Anne Samson of Kingston, dated 16 June 1830 (Plymouth PR 78:512), and she was one of only two heirs to the estate of her brother Joseph in 1845.

   Beal children, rec. Kingston (*VR* 22; see *Giles Memorial*, 483-84 for more detail): 1. *Thomas Beal*[7], b. 31 Jan. 1813; d. Kingston 14 April 1821 (*VR* 317). 2. *Joseph Sampson Beal*, b. 7 Aug. 1814; m. Pamela Holmes. 3. *Alexander Beal*, b. 26 Aug. 1819; m. Julia Ann Buckman. 4. *Judith Drew Beal*, b. 20 Nov. 1820. 5. *Lydia Prince Beal*, b. 12 Aug. 1822. 6. *Elizabeth Beal*, b. 7 Sept. 1827; m. Henry H. Warren. 7. *Helen Beal*, b. 2 Aug. 1828; m. George Rogers Hall.

ii   ELIZA SAMPSON, b. 13 April 1796; d. 13 July 1799, ae 3y 3m (*VR* 127, 377); bur. Kingston (*MD* 7:171).

iii JOSEPH SAMPSON, b. 25 Feb. 1799; d. 5 or 6 Dec. 1844 ae 45y 9m 10d; unm., "counsellor at law" (*VR* 128, 377); bur. Kingston (*MD* 7:171). Brown Univ., 1821; "a man of extensive reading and a thorough scholar; given to antiquarian research" (*Giles Mem.*, 410). He d. intestate, and his estate, which included "the homestead place at the Landing in Duxbury and Kingston," several other pieces of real estate, and a pew in Mr. Pope's meeting house, was divided between the only two heirs-at-law, his sister Betsey Beals and half-sister Hannah Cunningham (Plymouth PR #17573, 87:32, 251).

Sources cited: *Kingston VR.* Plymouth County Probate Records. "Death Records from the Ancient Burial Ground at Kingston, Mass.," *MD* 7 [1905]. *Mass. Soldiers & Sailors. Giles Memorial* (1864). Konig, *Plymouth County Court Records.*

521. JOSIAH[5] **SAMPSON** (*Cornelius*[4], *Benjamin*[3], *Stephen*[2], *Henry*[1]), son of Cornelius Sampson [112] and his wife Desire Crocker, was born at Kingston 9 May 1754 (*VR* 128), and died at Barnstable 14 July 1829 in his 76th year, "son of Cornelius and Desire" (VR 3:160). He was a descendant also of *Mayflower* passengers Francis Cooke, Stephen Hopkins, and John Howland. Josiah and both his wives are buried in the old cemetery on Route 169 at Marstons Mills (*Barnstable Inscript., 371*). He lived at various times in Kingston, Nantucket, and Barnstable (*Spooner Gen.*, 106-110).

He married first, at Falmouth 17 September 1777 after intentions 13 July 1777, "he of Barnstable, she of Falmouth" (*VR* 148), **MARY CROCKER** (called Polly in Barnstable int. 9 July, VR 3:160), who was born 9 September 1759, daughter of Timothy and Susanna (Robinson) Crocker, and baptized 29 March 1765 at Falmouth together with three siblings (*VR* 24, 205; CR 1:56). She died at Barnstable 16 March 1795 in her 36th year (*Barnstable Cem.*, 369). The will of Timothy Crocker of Falmouth, dated 24 January 1798, names wife Susanna and heirs of daughter Polly Sampson dec'd: Polly, Rebecca, Josiah, Joseph, William, Susanna and Lucy (Barnstable PR 28:499, 32:3).

Josiah married, second, at New Bedford 1 September 1798 (*VR* 462, 511), "he of Barnstable, she of New Bedford," **SARAH SPOONER**, who was born 22 June 1755 at Dartmouth (*VR* 2:262), daughter of Walter and Alathea (Sprague) Spooner. She died at Barnstable 12 February 1844, aged 88y 7m 10d, "widow of Josiah Samson and dau. of Walter Spooner" (VR 6:340).

Josiah was a merchant, farmer, and justice of the peace. He moved to Nantucket in 1777 and to Barnstable between 1790 and 1794. Two of his children were born in Falmouth, where their mother's family lived. In 1790 his household on Nantucket was enumerated as three men, three boys under 16 and four females (*Heads of Fam.*, 161). The earmark of Josiah Sampson, recorded at Barnstable in December 1794, was "a crop of the left ear and half crop under the same [later] recorded to Joseph and Benjamin Crocker" (Barnstable TR 3:280). In 1805 and 1806 Josiah Sampson, Esq., performed several marriages which were recorded by the Barnstable town clerk (VR 3:332).

On 11 August 1829 bond was posted by Josiah Sampson as administrator of the estate of [his father] Josiah Sampson late of Barnstable (Barnstable PR #1284). The inventory, taken 27 October 1829, included numerous pieces of real estate (*ibid.*, 47:524). Among these were 40 acres of cleared land and woodland called Gimquist, 80 acres of salt meadow at Rushy Marsh, 20 acres called "the old field," a 10-acre pond lot, 86 acres north of the mill road, and one-fourth of a pew in Great Marsh Meeting House; also an undivided half of further property, including 150 acres north of Rushy Marsh Road, two small islands, and a Grist Mill "with whatever belongs to it." Personal property included some silver spoons, a tankard, knives and forks, a watch, a desk, and a bookcase with stand. Nevertheless, the estate was declared insolvent 11 November 1829 and Josiah as administrator was given permission to sell some land to pay debts (*ibid.*, 49:326). The probate file includes several long, detailed accountings, listing many names.

On 14 December 1830, after some had been sold, a division of the land that remained in the estate of Josiah Sampson was made. Most of it was set off undivided, to Josiah Sampson and William Sampson, and some to widow Sarah Sampson as her dower (*ibid.*, 52:333). The surviving daughters and son Joseph do not appear to have shared in the division, and later records confirm that Josiah and William continued to "improve" their father's property together.

Sarah Sampson, aged widow of Barnstable, in her will dated 5 June 1835, proved 21 May 1844, left $400 to be divided between Sarah and Jane Spooner daughters of "my brother Alden Spooner." She named Josiah Sampson Esq., executor, and left to him a feather bed "in the bedroom chamber in which his workmen usually sleep"; all other beds and household furniture, along with the residue of the estate, were left to "Susan Sampson daughter of my late husband," and to "Lucy Crocker daughter of my late husband, now wife of Alvan Crocker" (Barnstable PR #1899, 60:348).

Children of Josiah and Mary (Crocker) Sampson (information not otherwise cited is from Sampson and Crocker Bibles):

i   MARY/POLLY[6] SAMPSON, b. Barnstable 21 Aug. 1778; d. Kingston 8 Nov. 1842, ae 64y 2m 12d, "delirious" (*VR* 312); m. Kingston, 27 June 1805 (*VR* 165), CHARLES ADAMS, b. 1 Oct. 1779, son of Ebenezer and Lydia (Cook) Adams. He m. (2) 5 Nov. 1843 her cousin Harriet (Samson) Fish [#519-ii]. Mary is named in the will of her Aunt Anne Samson (Plymouth PR 78:512) as Mary Adams, wife of Charles of Kingston.

  Adams children, rec. Kingston, of Charles & Mary (*VR* 11-14, 16): 1. *William Samson Adams[7]*, b. 12 March 1808; m. Lucy Eveline Holmes. 2. *Henry Lincoln Adams*, b. 7 July 1810; m. his stepsister Elizabeth Hawley Fish. 3. *Nathaniel Adams*, b. 24 Jan. 1812. 4. *Albert Adams*, b. 19 Jan. 1815. 5. *Charles Cook Adams*, b. 12 June 1817; d. Kingston 29 June 1837 of typhus fever (*VR* 311). 6. *Edwin Adams*, b. 24 May 1819.

ii   REBECCA SAMPSON, b. Barnstable 5 July 1780; d. 11 Feb. 1807 ae 27.

iii JOSIAH SAMPSON, b. Nantucket 6 Sept. 1782; d. Barnstable 7 Aug. 1861 ae
     78y 11m; m. (1) Barnstable 29 April 1837 (VR 6:172) or 1 June 1837 (Bible),
     HANNAH H. CROCKER, b. 31 Dec. 1820, d. 19 Jan. 1839; m. (2)
     Brewster 13 Nov. 1845 (*VR* 206) after int. Barnstable 8 Oct. (VR 1:199),
     DEBORAH R. (COBB) SAMPSON, widow of his brother Dr. Joseph
     Sampson, b. Brewster 28 Jan. 1794, d. 24 Feb. 1855 (Bible).
         In his lengthy will, dated 11 Dec. 1860, proved 5 Sept. 1861, Josiah Sampson
     called himself yeoman, in feeble health. He gave to his sisters Susan S. Bates,
     widow of William Bates late of New Bedford, deceased, and Lucy F. Crocker,
     wife of Alvan Crocker of Barnstable, the right to reside in his dwelling house if
     they wished, with detailed instructions about the parts of the house and land they
     might occupy. To Hannah B. Sampson, widow of his brother William, he left the
     improvement of his own half of the dwelling house and land set off to him in
     the division of his father's property, which he had shared with her. To
     grandnieces Mary S. Crocker and Hannah E. Crocker, children of Hiram and
     Rebecca S. Crocker, and to Lucy F. Sampson and Elizabeth C. Sampson,
     children of Benjamin T. and Joanna Sampson late of Barnstable, $500 each, and
     to Lucy and Elizabeth also land in Barnstable. To Charles F. Sampson and
     William F. Sampson, sons of nephew William Sampson, deceased, and their
     mother Augusta Sampson, land. To grandnephew Josiah W. Sampson, son of
     James T. Sampson and Mary N. Sampson, deceased, and to Benjamin S.
     Crocker, son of Hiram and Rebecca Crocker, a 100-acre woodlot in Sampson's
     Neck, and land also to niece Rebecca S. Crocker and her husband Hiram
     Crocker, mentioning Rebecca's mother Hannah B. Sampson. David and Hiram
     Crocker to be executors. In a codicil added 10 Oct. 1861 Josiah noted that
     Rebecca S. Crocker was "now very sick and liable to be removed by death before
     me," and if that happened, her share was to go to her children, Mary S., Hannah
     E., and Benjamin S. Crocker.
         The petition dated 5 Sept. 1861 named as heirs-at-law Susan S. Bates and
     Lucy T. Crocker, sisters, both of Barnstable. Approval of a final accounting
     dated 1 Sept. 1862 was signed by Lucy H. Sampson, Lizzie C. Sampson, David
     Crocker as guardian of Mary S. and Hannah E. Crocker, and Hiram Crocker as
     guardian of Rebecca S. and Hiram Crocker (Barnstable PR #4349; will *ibid.*,
     96:79, in file but too fragile to open).

iv   JOSEPH SAMPSON, b. Nantucket 17 April 1784; d. Brewster 4 Nov. 1844,
     ae 60y 7m, a physician, of disease of bladder (VR 222; Bible says Dec. 1844);
     m. after int. Brewster 11 March 1815 (*VR* 109-10), DEBBY REYNOLDS
     COBB, b. Brewster 28 Jan. 1794 (*VR* 1:173), d. 24 Feb. 1855 (Bible),
     daughter of Elijah and Mary (___) Cobb; she m. (2) in 1845 his brother
     Josiah Sampson.

In his will dated 10 Feb. 1844, proved 10 Dec. 1844, Joseph Sampson of Brewster, physician, left his whole estate to dearly beloved wife Deborah R. Sampson, except for certain bequests, and named her executrix. To "only brother" Josiah Sampson Esq. of Barnstable, he left his wearing apparel. To Frederic Augustus Freeman and Mary Ann Deborah Freeman, children of Frederic and Ann P. Freeman, "now in Trinidad de Cuba," he left $100 each in trust in Barnstable Savings Bank until they reached 21; to Doct. Benjamin F. Seabury of Orleans, several specific medical books; to Doctors George Atwood of Orleans, Samuel H. Gould of Brewster, and Alexander Poole of Dennis, the rest of his medical books and instruments. To Lucy, wife of Prince Matthew of Yarmouth, $100 and "my center table with my shells on … and all my other shells." To George Copeland of Brewster "my Gig"; to Elijah Winslow Cobb son of Elijah Cobb of Boston, "my two guns, pistol, and ammunition apparatus"; to Emily Cunningham Cobb, dau. of said Elijah, Mary Ann Copeland dau. of George, and Alice T. Williams dau. of Rev. Samuel Williams of Brewser, $10 each, "the income to be expended for Moral Books." (Barnstable PR #4349)

v   WILLIAM SAMPSON, b. Falmouth 13 Aug. 1786; d. Cotuit 27 Sept. 1834 ae 50y 4m (*New Bedford Mercury* of 2 Oct. 1834; *Nantucket VR* 526); m. Barnstable 16 April 1814 (VR 4:306, prob. int.) or 26 May 1814 (Bible), HANNAH B. THACHER (called Hannah Sampson in Bible), who d. Barnstable 1 Sept. 1874 ae 82y 9m (VR 6:73). He d. intestate and administration was given to Josiah Sampson 28 Oct. 1834 (Barnstable PR #804). The inventory taken 25 Nov. 1834 included undivided half parts of several pieces of property held in common with his brother Josiah, who in his own will provided for William's widow Hannah. The estate was declared insolvent 9 Dec. 1834, and the widow was allowed $225.

Children, rec. Barnstable (VR 6:73; Bible has minor differences); several named in will of their uncle Josiah: 1. *Mary Crocker⁷ Sampson*, b. 3 June 1815; d. 18 Nov. 1845 ae 30. 2. *James Thacher Sampson*, b. 2 March 1817; d. March 1856; m. Mary L. Hinckley. 3. *Nancy Sampson*, b. 13 Aug. 1819; d. 5 Oct. 1848. 4. *Rebeckah Sampson*, b. Barnstable 30 Aug. 1821; m. Hiram Crocker. 5. *William Sampson*, b. 27 July 1823; d. California 30 May 1854; m. Augusta Crocker. 6. *Freeman Hinckley Sampson*, b. 3 April 1825; d. Calif., 5 June 1850. 7. *Benjamin F. Sampson*, b. 12 March 1827; d. 5 Aug. 1855; m. Joanna Childs. 8. *Lucy F. Sampson*, b. 20 Jan. 1829; d. 1851.

vi   SUSAN SAMPSON, b. Falmouth 17 Sept. 1788; living Barnstable 1862 (brother's probate); m. after 1835 (stepmother's will), WILLIAM BATES of New Bedford, who d. before 11 Dec. 1860 (brother Josiah's will). An accounting dated 9 Nov. 1830 in her father's probate file includes "cash [$3] handed to Susan Sampson to go to Nantucket" (*ibid.*, 47:524). Sarah Bates ae

72 was living 1860 in the household of Henry A. and Mercy A. Lovell at Cotuit (p.381); record of her death not found.

vii LUCY SAMPSON, b. Barnstable 18 March 1793; d. there 17 Oct. 1872 ae 79y 7m; m. Barnstable, 31 Dec. 1832 (VR 6:280), ALVAN CROCKER, d. there 22 Nov. 1862 in 86th yr (*Barnstable Inscript.*, 106, 116).

viii NANCY SAMPSON, b. Barnstable 10 Feb. 1795; d. 23 Aug. 1795, ae 6m.

Sources cited: Barnstable VR, original pages cited on NEHGS CD. *Brewster VR. Falmouth VR. Kingston VR. Nantucket VR.* Barnstable County Probate Records. Sampson and Crocker Bibles, NEHGS Ms. Gen 1 S 391. Gravestones in Marston's Mills copied by Robert M. Sherman (see also *Barnstable Cemetery Inscriptions*). *New Bedford Mercury* Deaths, typescript, New Bedford Free Library. *Spooner Genealogy* (1883). CENSUS: Cotuit, Barnstable Co., 1860 (M653-486).

522. LUCY⁵ SAMPSON (*Cornelius⁴, Benjamin³, Stephen², Henry¹*), daughter of Cornelius Samson [112] and his wife Desire Crocker, was born at Kingston 29 October 1763 (*VR* 128) and died 10 November 1802, aged 39, "wife of Thomas [Jackson]," at Plymouth (CR 627; *Burial Hill*, 96). She was a descendant also of *Mayflower* passengers Francis Cooke, Stephen Hopkins, and John Howland.

She married at Kingston 8 January 1783, "he of Plymouth, she of Kingston" (*VR* 244, 275), **THOMAS JACKSON JR.**, who was born in 1754, baptized 25 October 1767 at Plymouth (*CR* 1:456), and died there 10 November 1840 (*CR* 683; *Burial Hill* 201), aged 86 or 87, son of Samuel and Experience (Atwood) Jackson. Thomas married, second, at Plymouth 25 April 1805 (*CR* 1:646), SARAH LEBARON, and with her had daughter Mary Anne baptized at Plymouth 2 April 1809 (*CR* 608) and possibly a second daughter Priscilla Alden. The will of Samuel Jackson of Plymouth, dated 26 March 1803, proved 24 April 1805, names wife Experience and son Thomas as an executor (Plymouth PR 40:192).

Thomas Jackson Jr. served in the Revolution as a private, under Capt. Abraham Hammett (*MSSR* 8:690).

In 1790 Thomas Jackson Jr. was head of a household in Plymouth consisting of one male 16 or over, two males under 16, and two females (*Heads of Fam.*, 176).

On 1 July 1807 Zacheus Bartlet conveyed land in Plymouth to the following children of Thomas Jackson of Plymouth and deceased wife Lucy Jackson: Cornelius Sampson Jackson, Frederick Jackson, Caroline Jackson, George Jackson Jr., Thomas Jackson III, and Lucy Jackson (Plymouth LR 113:213).

The will of Anne Samson of Kingston dated 16 June 1830 names her nephews George and Thomas Jackson and nieces Caroline and Lucy Jackson, daughters of Thomas Jackson of Plymouth (Plymouth PR 78:512).

No probate records were found for this Thomas or for Lucy Jackson.

Children of Thomas and Lucy (Samson) Jackson, b. Plymouth; births of only those who survived infancy recorded (*VR* 452), evidently from baptismal records; other birth dates calculated from ages at death. Caroline, George, Thomas, and Lucy were bapt. 2 April 1809 at Plymouth with their younger half-sister Mary Anne (CR 608):

i   EZRA THAYER JACKSON[6], b. ca 29 Oct. 1783; d. 23 Nov. 1783 ae 25d (*Burial Hill*, 56).

ii   CORNELIUS SAMSON JACKSON, b. 8 Dec. 1785; d. at Guadaloupe 31 Aug. 1815 ae 33y; m. NANCY B. CRANDON, d. 2 Nov. 1819 ae 27y 6m, dau. Benjamin Crandon (*Burial Hill*, 134).

      Child: 1. *Lucy Ann Jackson*[7], b. 1814; m. Asa Law of Medford.

iii FREDERICK JACKSON, b. March 1787; d. 15 March 1788 ae 1y 5d (*Burial Hill*, 60).

iv   DESIRE JACKSON, b. June 1788; d. 22 Aug. 1788 ae 2m 13d (*ibid.*, 61).

v   FREDERICK JACKSON, b. 19 May 1791; d. Plymouth 27 June 1857 ae 66y 1m 14d of inflammation, parents not named (Mass. VR 112:315); named in 1830 will of aunt Anne Samson (Plymouth PR 78:512). In 1850 he was a farmer at Plymouth with Phebe Cole ae 51 and Andrew Gardner ae 16 in his household (p.132).

vi   CAROLINE JACKSON, b. 17 March 1793; d. Plymouth 5 June 1841 ae 48, unm. (*Burial Hill*, 203); named in 1830 will of her aunt Anne Samson (Plymouth PR 78:512). In her will dated 16 April 1838, proved last Tuesday of Aug. 1841, Caroline Jackson of Plymouth left all her real estate to her brother Frederick Jackson, all her personal estate to Caroline Jackson, daughter of brother Thomas Jackson Jr., excepting certain articles of furniture to go to Lucy Ann Jackson, daughter of brother Cornelius S. Jackson dec'd; Nathaniel Russell Jr. to be executor (Plymouth PR #11177, 83:382). The inventory included one undivided sixth part of pasture and meadow land in the north part of Plymouth, formerly of Thomas Jackson dec'd, and "sundry articles of furniture in the house on the farm" (*ibid.*, 83:559).

vii LUCY JACKSON, b. ca June 1795; d. 10 Sept. 1796 ae 1y 3m 9d (*Burial Hill*, 76).

viii GEORGE JACKSON, b. 20 Feb. 1797; living June 1830 when he was named in the will of his aunt Anne Samson. No further record found.

ix   THOMAS JACKSON, b. 4 March 1799, d. Plymouth 25 Feb. 1879 (Mass. VR 311:295); m. (1) SOPHRONIA N. BISHOP, b. ca 1804, d. Plymouth 7 Aug. 1872 ae 67y 7m 29d of dysentery, dau. of Joseph and Joanna (___) Bishop of Rochester (Mass. VR 248:411); m. (2) Plymouth, 31 Aug. 1873 (Mass. VR 254:435), MARY ANN (PERKINS) SHAW, ae 66, b. Plymouth, dau. of Luke and Hannah (___) Perkins and widow of Silas Shaw. In 1850 Thomas was a farmer in Fairhaven, with Sophronia ae 46, Caroline, Lucy S., George F., Cornelius, and Betsey A. (p.195).

Children, with first wife Sophronia: 1. *Caroline Jackson*[7], b. ca 1834. 2. *Lucia S. Jackson*, b. 1838; m. George H. Griffin. 3. *George F. Jackson*, b. 1840; m. Hannah T. Mayo. 4. *Cornelius S. Jackson*, b. ca 1843; m. Emma L. Wright of Cambridge. 5. *Betsey A. Jackson*, b. 1845; m. Edward E. Green.

x   LUCY JACKSON, b. 3 May 1801; living, unm., in June 1830 when she was named in the will of her aunt Anne Samson (Plymouth PR 78:512).

Sources cited: *Kingston VR. Plymouth VR.* Mass. Vital Records 1841-1910. *Plymouth Church Records.* Plymouth County Deeds and Probate Records. *Epitaphs from Burial Hill, Plymouth. Mass. Soldiers & Sailors.* CENSUS: *Heads of Families 1790 – Mass.*; 1850 Fairhaven, Bristol Co. (M432-308), Plymouth, Plymouth Co. (M432-333).

523.   BENJAMIN[5] **SAMPSON** (*Benjamin*[4-3], *Stephen*[2], *Henry*[1]), son of Benjamin Samson [113] and his first wife Deborah Cushing, was born at Kingston 16 December 1759 (*VR* 130), and died there 9 February 1793, aged 33, or 9 February 1794 in his 35th yr. (*VR* 376; g.s. and CR differ). He was a descendant also of *Mayflower* passengers Francis Cooke and Stephen Hopkins. He was named in the will of his father, dated 4 November 1778, proved 1 March 1779, and on 3 May 1779, Benjamin Samson (over 14) chose Jos. Samson of Kingston as his guardian (Plymouth PR 35:542). He shared in the division of his father's estate on 16 April 1781 (*ibid.*, 28:155).

He married at Plymouth, 29 August 1786 (*VR* 366; *CR* 503), "he of Kingston, she of Plymouth," **PRISCILLA CHURCHILL.** Their intentions were published 15 April 1786 at Kingston (*VR* 272) and 18 April 1786 at Plymouth (*VR* 273). Priscilla was born 2 or 3 January 1766 and died at Kingston 4 or 6 April 1838, aged 72, "widow of Benjamin Jr." (*VR* 378). She was probably the daughter of Ansel and Bethia (Holmes) Churchill who married at Plymouth in 1765 (*VR* 356), but no probate records for them have been found. Benjamin and Priscilla are buried in the Ancient Burial Ground, Kingston (*MD* 7:170-71).

Benjamin Samson of Kingston is listed as a private in Capt. Joseph Stetson's company, Col. Dyke's regiment, in November 1776, paid a travel allowance for 76 miles to Dorchester Heights and back (*MSSR* 13:766). He served in December 1776 for 17 days on a march to Bristol, R.I. (*ibid.*, 13:757). He may be the Benjamin Sampson who was a seaman on the brigantine *Tyrannicide* from 20 May to 23 June 1779 (*ibid.*). He is said to have served also in 1778 for forty days, in Col. John Jacobs's regiment (*Giles Mem.*, 410).

He died intestate. At the request of the widow Priscilla Sampson on 8 April 1794 John Faunce of Kingston was appointed administrator of the estate of Benjamin Sampson late of Kingston, dec'd (Plymouth PR #17458; 27:476). The inventory was taken 13 April 1794 by Joseph Sampson, Nicholas Davis Jr., and Samuel Stetson (*ibid.*, 35:134), and dower was set off to the widow Priscilla Sampson on 3 April 1797 (*ibid.*, 36:92). John Faunce, yeoman of Kingston, was appointed guardian of Priscilla Sampson, a minor above 14 years,* on 10 August 1796, and of James Sampson, Isaac Sampson, George Sampson, and Deborah Sampson, all minors under 14, on 16 November 1796 (*ibid.*, 32:49, 60). On 23 May 1815 Isaac Sampson, trader of Plymouth, was appointed administrator *de bonis non* of Benjamin's estate, John Faunce having died; sureties included George Sampson 3rd, trader (*ibid.*, 46:437).

In her will dated 6 March 1838, proved 2nd Monday of August 1838, Priscilla Sampson of Kingston, widow, named her grandchildren George and Elizabeth Sampson, children of her son Isaac, and appointed her daughter Deborah Sampson executrix (Plymouth PR 80:260).

Children of Benjamin and Priscilla (Churchill) Sampson, last three rec. Kingston as "of Priscilla, widow" (*VR* 127):

 i JAMES⁶ SAMPSON, b. ca 1787; said to have gone "to sea at age 21, d. not long after" (*Giles Mem.*, 411).

 ii ISAAC SAMPSON, b. 16 Dec. 1789; d. Plymouth 7 May 1833 ae 42 (*CR* 678); m. Plymouth, 1 Jan. 1822 after int. 18 Nov. 1821 (*VR* 320, 446; *CR* 654), ELIZABETH SHERMAN, b. 19 June 1795, dau. William and Elizabeth (Drew) Sherman (*Giles Mem.*, 438).
  Children (*ibid.*; two eldest named in grandmother's will): 1. *Elizabeth⁷ Samson*, b. 15 Jan. 1824; m. John Kneeland of Dorchester; no ch. 2. *George Samson*, b. 28 May 1825; m. Rebecca Hovey; no ch. 3. *Isaac Samson*, b. 4 April 1830; d. 11 Dec. 1833.

 iii GEORGE SAMPSON, b. 5 May 1792; d. Providence, R.I., 8 May 1825 ae 33, of "liver complaint" (*Kingston VR* 377); unm.; bur. with parents (*MD* 7:171).

---

* Although it is possible to interpret this guardianship to mean that Priscilla was a daughter of Benjamin Jr. [#523], b. before 1782, there is no evidence to support this. The probable explanation is that when Cornelius Sampson [#112], uncle and guardian of his brother Benjamin's youngest surviving children (Micah and Priscilla) since 1784, died in March 1796, Micah was of age and Priscilla nearly so. John Faunce was already administrator of the estate of Benjamin Jr., and thus a logical choice to assume Priscilla's guardianship.

iv DEBORAH SAMPSON, b. 2 April 1793; living, apparently unm., in 1838 when she was executrix of her mother's will. In 1850, possibly the Deborah Sampson ae 56 in the household of Nathaniel Harlow ae 35, cooper, in Plymouth (p.112).

Sources cited: *Kingston VR. Plymouth VR.* "Death Records from the Ancient Burial Ground at Kingston, Mass.," *MD* 7 [1905]. *Plymouth Church Records.* Plymouth County Probate Records. *Mass. Soldiers & Sailors. Giles Memorial* (1864). CENSUS: 1850 Plymouth, Plymouth Co. (M432-333).

524. CROADE[5] SAMPSON *(Benjamin[1-3], Stephen[2], Henry[1])*, son of Benjamin Sampson [113] and his first wife Deborah Cushing, was born at Kingston 12 December 1763 (*VR* 130) and died there 4 October 1836, aged 72 or 73 (*VR* 376). He was a descendant also of *Mayflower* passengers Francis Cooke and Stephen Hopkins. He was named in the will of his father, dated 4 November 1778, proved 1 March 1779, and on 20 October 1780, Croade Samson, son of Benjamin, chose Nicholas Davis Jr. of Kingston as his guardian (Plymouth PR #17460). He shared in the division of his father's estate on 16 April 1781 (*ibid.*, 25:196-97).

He married at Kingston (*VR* 207, 272), 9 March 1794, **BETHANY DAW[E]S**, who was born 17 October 1773 and died at Kingston 2 March 1823, "wife of Croad," in her 50th year, of consumption (*VR* 376), daughter of Gideon and Sarah (Phillips) Dawes. Croade and Bethany are buried in the Ancient Burial Ground, Kingston, along with several of their children who died young (*MD* 7:170).

Croade served in the Revolution from September to December 1781 as a private in a regiment of militia raised to join Washington's army (*MSSR* 13:767). No evidence was found that he applied for a pension.

At the April 1788 Plymouth Court of Common Pleas, Croad Samson was admitted as a plaintiff with David Beal, who had sued Joseph Sampson [see family #520] for damaging his potato fields while exercising a right of passage to his barn (PCCR, April 1988, d.n.8). In November 1809 Seth Bradford of Duxbury, yeoman, sued William Rand of Kingston, Labourer, and "his trustee Croad Sampson." The defendant defaulted, but Sampson "appeared and after being examined upon Oath, was considered not to be a Trustee from which Judgement the Pltf. appealed" (*ibid.*, Nov. 1809, d.n.102).

The 1842 death record of his son Ezra says "Father shoemaker." No Plymouth probate records were found for Croade or Bethany Sampson, or for Gideon or Sarah Dawes.

Children of Croade and Bethany (Dawes) Sampson, rec. Kingston (*VR* 127-129; *Giles Mem.*, 411):

i   LUCY[6] SAMPSON, b. 2 June 1795; d. 26 March 1833 (*Giles Mem.*, 411); m. Kingston 27 Sept. 1827 (*VR* 273), FRANCIS DREW. He is prob. the Francis Drew ae 61, shipwright, res. Kingston 1850 (p.101), with wife Betsey ae 51 and dau. Elizabeth F. Drew, ae 15, who if age is correct cannot be Lucy's child.

ii BENJAMIN SAMPSON, b. 24 April 1797; d. prob. 1880 (Mass. VR 320:291); m. Kingston, 1823, SALLY BRADFORD, b. Kingston 8 July 1805, d. there 8 April 1870 of pneumonia, dau. of Lewis and Priscilla (Tupper) Bradford (Mass. VR 230:318). In 1850 Benjamin Sampson, yeoman, ae 53, res. Kingston with Sally B. ae 45, sons Charles L. and Martin H., both housewrights, George, a mason, Walter S., Columbus, William W., and Wendall A. Sampson (p.101). Huldah Sampson ae 31 [*sic*], surely his sister, was also in the household.

Children, rec. Kingston (*VR* 126-29): 1. *Catharine Bradford[7] Sampson*, b. 30 Sept. 1824. 2. *Charles Lewis Sampson*, b. 4 May 1826. 3. *Martin Henry Sampson*, b. 28 Oct. 1827. 4. *George Sampson*, b. 25 July 1829. 5. *William Wallace Sampson*, b. 4 Jan. 1831; d. 2 April 1838 (*VR* 378). 6. *Walter Scott Sampson*, b. 21 Feb. 1833. 7. *Lucy Sampson*, b. 3 Jan. 1835; d. 10 April 1838 of scarlet fever(*VR* 377). 8. *Columbus Sampson*, b. 11 Aug. 1836. 9. *William Wallace Sampson*, b. 26 April 1838. 10. *Wendell Sampson*, b. 5 Sept. 1846. 11. *Sarah Bradford Sampson*, b. 6 Sept. 1848; d. 24 July 1849 (*VR* 378).

iii STEPHEN SAMPSON, b. 11 Nov. 1798; d. 1 April 1802 ae 4 days [*sic* – 4y?], of "mortification" (*VR* 378).

iv CHANDLER SAMPSON, b. ca 1800; d. in April 1800 ae 6 weeks (*VR* 376); bur. with parents.

v   GIDEON SAMPSON, b. 1801; d. in April 1801 ae 1 week (*VR* 377); bur. with parents.

vi MARTIN SAMPSON, b. 24 Aug. 1804; m. at Boston, 18 April 1830 (*NEHGR* 90:48) LUCIA ANN BRADFORD, b. 27 April 1809, sister of his brother Benjamin's wife Sally. In 1850 he was a hatter in Boston, with Lucia A., ae 41, and three daughters .

Children at home 1850: 1. *S. M. Sampson[7]*, b. ca 1830. 2. *L. Ann Sampson*, b. ca 1832. 3. *M[aria] A. Sampson*, b. ca 1835; m. James C. Tucker.

vii CHARLES SAMPSON, b. 9 April 1807; d. Kingston 18 Aug. 1839 ae 32y 4m 9d, of consumption (*VR* 376); bur. with parents.

viii HULDAH SAMPSON, b. 9 July 1810; d. Kingston 10 Aug. 1884 of consumption, unm. (Mass. VR 356:311). In 1850 she was living in household of brother Benjamin.

ix EZRA SAMPSON, b. 3 Sept. 1815; d. Kingston 14 June 1842 ae 26y 10m 12d of consumption; under "occupation" is written "Father shoemaker dec" (Mass. VR 3:80).

Sources cited: *Duxbury VR. Kingston VR.* "Death Records from the Ancient Burial Ground at Kingston, Mass.," *MD* 7 [1905]. Mass. Vital Records 1841-1910. *Mass. Soldiers & Sailors.* Konig, *Plymouth Court Records. Giles Memorial* (1864). CENSUS: 1850 Boston, Suffolk Co. (M432-336), Kingston, Plymouth Co. (M432-333).

525. MICAH⁵ SAMPSON (*Benjamin⁴⁻³, Stephen², Henry¹*), son of Benjamin Samson [113] and his second wife Esther Weston, was born at Kingston 25 [*blank*] 1773 and baptized there 9 May 1773 (*VR* 130), a descendant also of *Mayflower* passengers John Alden, Francis Cooke, and Stephen Hopkins. He died at Falmouth 17 May 1839 aged 66 (*VR* 256). Micah is named in the wills of both his parents, and he shared in the division of his father's estate in 1781 (Plymouth PR 25:196-97). His mother in her will dated 10 May 1782, proved 7 October 1782, named [their grandfather] Cornelius Samson guardian of Micah and his sister Priscilla (*ibid.,* 28:481).

He married at Falmouth 10 January 1802, "both of Falmouth," **MARY CROSWELL** (*VR* 150, 205, incorrectly as "Crowell"), who was baptized 19 January 1783 at First Church, Plymouth (*VR* 1:466) and died 20 April 1869 aged 86 years and 3 months, or 26 May 1869 aged 84, as "widow of Micah," at Falmouth (*VR* 256). She was the daughter of Andrew and Sarah (Palmer) Croswell who married at Plymouth 30 September 1775 (*VR* 264). Division of the estate of widow Sarah Croswell, late of Falmouth, dated 8 August 1820, names daughter Mary, wife of Micah Samson (Barnstable PR #Z265, 43:350).

In his will dated 8 August 1832, proved 13 November 1839, Micah Sampson, mariner of Falmouth, left the improvement of his real estate to beloved wife Mary during her widowhood. His three daughters, Mary Ann, Abigail, and Sarah, were to have a home in his house as long as they remained single, and son Joseph was to "continue with them[,] be supported and have as good an education as his mother feels able to give him untill he can take care of himself." No division of the property was to be made as long as any of his daughters remained single. Personal estate was to be divided equally among his seven children: Andrew, Benjamin, Mary Ann, Abigail, Thomas, Joseph, and Sarah, "as many of them as shall then be home," with provision for any daughter who might then be married. He named his wife and son Andrew C. executors. (Barnstable PR 60:146-48, file 1285)

In 1850 Mary Sampson was living in Falmouth with her son Andrew C. Sampson, 47, a mariner, and daughter Abigail C. Sampson, 38 (p.413).

Capt. Micah, his wife Mary, and at least four of their children are buried in the Old Burying Ground on Mill Street, Falmouth.

Children of Micah and Mary (Croswell) Sampson, rec. Falmouth (*VR* 113):

i   ANDREW CROSWELL[6] SAMPSON, b. 14 April 1803; d. Falmouth 30 Aug. 1863, single, mariner, of disease of heart (Mass. VR 165:11). In 1860 he and his sister Abigail were living with their mother in Falmouth (p.163).

ii   BENJAMIN SAMPSON, b. 1 Aug. 1805. He may be the Capt. Benjamin Sampson who d. Farmington, Me., 13 Dec. 1862 ae 56, bur. Blake Memorial Cem. (Maine Cem. Recs.). In 1850 he was ae 44, a farmer b. Mass., with wife LOUISA ___, ae 41, b. Me., res. Farmington (p.173); in 1860 he was a farmer and their household included Elen D. Stinchfield ae 17, domestic, and Clarence Stinchfield ae 12, with a Thomas Crosswell family living nearby (p.34).

iii MARY ANN SAMPSON, b. 7 Sept. 1807; d. 29 March 1834 ae 26, Falmouth (*VR* 256).

iv   ABIGAIL C. SAMPSON, b. 2 Oct. 1811; d. Falmouth 7 May 1872 ae 60y 7m 5d, unmarried, of "pleuritis (chronic)" (Mass. VR 247:9).

v   THOMAS C. SAMPSON, b. 15 Oct. 1812; d. Mattapoisett 23 Oct. 1900 (Mass. VR 506:217); m. SETINA LEBARON PURRINGTON, b. ca 1814 Rochester, d. Mattapoisett 1904 (Mass. VR 1904, 64:500). In 1850 (p.289) and 1860 (p.404) he was a ship carpenter at Rochester; the 1850 census says he was b. Falmouth, she Rochester.

Children all b. Rochester (census): 1. *Andrew C.*[7] *Sampson*, b. ca 1841, a mariner 1860. 2. *Joseph T. Sampson*, b. ca 1843, a mariner 1860. 3. *Benjamin F. Sampson*, b. ca 1846. 4. *Mary/Mercy C. Sampson*, b. ca 1848. 5. *Elisha Sampson*, b. ca 1850. 6. *Sarah P. Sampson*, b. ca 1854.

vi   JOSEPH SAMPSON, b. 19 March 1814; d. 1 April 1814 ae 2 weeks, Falmouth (*VR* 256).

vii ESTHER WESTON SAMPSON, b. 26 July 1815; d. 25 Sept. 1816 ae 11m, Falmouth (*VR* 256).

viii JOSEPH WESTON SAMPSON, b. 15 Oct. 1818; drowned at Falmouth 18 July 1835 ae 16 yrs (*VR* 256).

ix   SARAH P. SAMPSON, b. 3 Dec. 1820; d. Falmouth 7 Sept. 1871 ae 50y 9m 4d, unm. (Mass. VR 238:11); not with mother and unm. siblings 1850.

Sources cited: *Falmouth VR* (deaths referenced p. 256 are from gravestones before 1850). *Kingston VR. Plymouth VR.* Mass. Vital Records 1841-1910. Barnstable County and Plymouth County Probate Records CENSUS: Falmouth, Barnstable Co., 1850 (M432-304) & 1860 (M653-486); Rochester, Plymouth Co., 1850 (M432-333) & 1860 (M653-519).

526. PRISCILLA⁵ SAMPSON (*Benjamin⁴⁻³, Stephen², Henry¹*), daughter of Benjamin Samson [113] and his second wife, Esther Weston, was born at Kingston 19 December 1776 (*VR* 130), and died at Falmouth 18 October 1860, "aged 72" (Mass. VR 138:10). She was a descendant also of *Mayflower* passengers John Alden, Francis Cooke, and Stephen Hopkins.

Priscilla was named in her father's will, dated 4 November 1778 and proved 1 March 1779, and in that of her mother, dated 10 May 1782, in which her uncle Cornelius Sampson was appointed guardian for her and her brother Micah. She was named also in the will of her sister Deborah dated 7 November 1788, presented 5 January 1789, when she would have been about twelve years old. (Plymouth PR 30:497). Her uncle Cornelius died in March 1796 and in August of that year John Faunce, yeoman of Kingston, who was administrator of the estate of her brother Benjamin Sampson, was appointed Priscilla's guardian; in November he also became guardian of Benjamin's orphaned children.

The statement in *Giles Memorial* (p 391) that Priscilla married _____ Nye, has sometimes been questioned. However, Priscilla's brother Micah and his family lived in Falmouth, and it was there that the marriage intentions of Priscilla Sampson with **NATHANIEL NYE** were recorded 20 June 1819 (*VR* 205). Priscilla, wife of Nathaniel Nye, died at Falmouth 18 October 1860 of paralysis, "aged 72; maiden name Sampson, birthplace and parents' names not known" (Mass. VR 138:10). Nathaniel was born at Falmouth 19 October 1787, son of Samuel and Elizabeth (___) Nye (*VR* 95) and died there 12 October 1862, aged 82, a widower.

Priscilla was 42 at marriage and 43 at the birth of her daughter, and the age on her gravestone is off by about 10 years. It should be noted, however, that her husband's age is incorrectly stated on his gravestone, too. Ages for both appear closer to the mark in the 1850 census of Falmouth (p.405b), which lists Nathaniel ae 62, Percilla ae 70, with Elizabeth E. Cook ae 29, and James F. Cook ae 4.

Child of Nathaniel and Priscilla (Samson) Nye, rec. Falmouth (*VR* 92):

 i ELIZABETH W./E. NYE⁶, b. 20 Sept. 1820, "dau. Nathaniel and Priscilla"; d. Mattapoisett 1898 (Mass. VR 482:675); m. (1) THOMAS COOK, b. Maine; m. (2) Falmouth 31 Aug. 1881, as his second wife,

SETH HILLER of Mattapoisett, ae 65, b. Nantucket, son of Seth and Mary (___) Hiller (Mass. VR 325:10). In 1850 Elizabeth and her son James F. Cook were living with her parents (p.405), and in 1860 Elizabeth, James, and Henry ae 9 were still there (p.147). In 1870 Elizabeth Cook's household in Woods Hole included James ae 25 and Henry ae 22 [*sic*], both laborers (p.175). In 1880 James Cook was a railroad section man at Woods Hole, with wife Martha A., dau. Roena, and mother Elisabeth Cook ae 59 (p.26, e.d.4).

    Cook children: 1. *James Franklin Cook[7]*, b. Falmouth (*VR* 23) 17 May [1846] (1746 in published *VR* surely wrong), "son of Thomas and Elizabeth E."; m. Falmouth, 15 Sept. 1878, Martha Hodson of Portland, Me. (Mass. VR 298:9) 2. *Henry Cook*, b. ca 1850, living 1870 (census).

Sources cited: *Kingston VR. Falmouth VR.* Mass. Vital Records 1841-1910. Plymouth County Probate Records. *Giles Memorial* (1864). CENSUS: Falmouth, Barnstable Co. 1850 (M432-304), P.O. Woods Hole, Falmouth, Barnstable Co., 1860 (M653-486), 1870 (M593-600), & 1880 (T9-519).

527. CEPHAS WADSWORTH[5] (*Lusanna[4] Samson, John[3], Stephen[2], Henry[1]*), son of Peleg Wadsworth and his wife Lusanna Samson [114], was born at Duxbury 12 August 1743 (*VR* 180) and died 12 September 1819 aged 76 or 77, at Kingston (*VR* 387). He was a descendant also of *Mayflower* passenger John Alden. He is buried in the Ancient Burial Ground, Kingston (*MD* 7:222).

    He was "of Duxbury" when he married at Kingston (*VR* 293), 5 November 1767, **MOLLY COOKE**, who was born 29 October 1743 at Kingston (*VR* 49) and died there 15 May 1827 ae 87, "widow" (*VR* 387). She was the daughter of John and Phebe (Crossman) Cooke and a descendant of *Mayflower* passengers Francis Cooke and Stephen Hopkins (*MF 12*:435-6). The property of John Cook, late of Kingston, yeoman, deceased, was divided 26 March 1753, with two-sixths going to his only son Silvanus Cook, and one-sixth each to Sarah Kent, wife of Samuel Kent Jr., Lydia Cook, Margaret Cook, and Molly Cook (Plymouth PR 13:107). Molly's share was "about twelve acres ... begining at the westerly side of and near Dea. Washburns House and thence bounded on the northwesterly side of a Cartway about ninty two rods to a Horn pine tree Standing on the Southerly Side of Second brook and from thence north four degrees westerly fifty six rods to a stake standing by Jones River and from thence bounded by the River down stream about seventy rods to the Widdows thirds...." On 18 December 1805 part of the dower of John Cooke's widow Phebe Kent was set off to Molly wife of Cephas Wadsworth (*ibid.*, 40:362).

Cephas was a private in the Revolution, serving in 1775 in the company commanded by his brother Capt. Peleg Wadsworth (*MSSR* 16:380).

In April 1774 (d.n.118) Cephas Wadsworth of Kingston, housewright, sued Ebenezer Robbins of Plymouth, wheelwright, for money due on a note dated 2 April 1771. In April 1786 (d.n.188) he sued Joseph Wadsworth, gentleman, of Duxbury, and Consider Drew of Duxbury, shipwright, for about £14 due on a note dated in 1782. He represented Kingston as a juror in October 1786.

In 1790 Cephas was head of a household in Kingston that included three boys under 16 and five females (*Heads of Fam.*, 170).

The will of Peleg Wadsworth, dated 1 June 1799 (Plymouth PR # 21,757; 37:76), includes a bequest of $68 to eldest son Cephas, with one third of the indoor moveables and "Bed & Bedding on which I commonly sleep."

Cephas Wadsworth as administrator of the estate of Jabez Washburn, late of Kingston, was given permission by the court to sell real estate in November 1802, and in November 1807 he was administrator of the estate of [his son-in-law] Daniel Perkins, late of Kingston (*PCCR*).

Cephas is called a housewright in the birth record of his son Alfred and also in the letters of administration on his estate issued to his son Cephas Wadsworth, mariner, of Kingston 20 September 1819 (Plymouth PR 46:362). On the same date the inventory, totaling $1450.25 and taken 18 September by Jer[h] Thomas, Nath[l] Thomas, and John Cook, was presented, and an allowance made to Molly Wadsworth, widow of the deceased (*ibid.*, 50:323).

Cephas Wadsworth of Kingston was appointed administrator 11 August 1828 of the estate of [his mother] Molly Wadsworth, late of Kingston, widow (*ibid.*, 61:220). Her estate was reported insolvent; James N. Sever and Timothy French were appointed 17 November 1828 to receive and examine the claims of her creditors. The distribution to the claimants (Gamaliel D. Adams, Elisha Washburn, Josiah Everson, Sally Mitchell, Constant Sampson, and the Administrator's Private Account) was recorded 15 June 1829 (*ibid.*, 67:244).

Children of Cephas and Molly (Cooke) Wadsworth, rec. Kingston (*VR* 147):

i   PELEG WADSWORTH[6], b. 19 Aug. 1768, bp. 5 July 1772; "fell from aloft" and drowned at sea 24 Feb. 1791 ae 21y 6m 5d, rec. Kingston (*VR* 387).

ii   WILLIAM WADSWORTH, b. 2 Aug. 1770, bp. 5 July 1772; d. 6 May 1790 ae 19y 9m 4d, of consumption, Kingston (*VR* 387); bur. with father.

iii LUCY WADSWORTH, b. 6 Nov. 1772; m. FREDERICK LEWIS (*Wadsworth Fam.*, 158).

iv   ALFRED WADSWORTH, b. 12 Sept. 1774; d. 1846 (*Wadsworth Fam.*); of Bristol when he m. Boothbay, Me., after int. 7 Jan. 1799, LYDIA KNIGHT, b. 1780, d. 8 Sept. 1873, dau. of Daniel and Mary (Winslow) Knight (*Boothbay History,* 270, 556). The 1810 census lists him at Boothbay ae 26-45 with a household consisting of one woman 45+, 1 woman 26-45, 1 young man 16-26, 1 boy and 1 girl 10-16, and 1 girl under 10 (p.206).

v   MOLLY / POLLY WADSWORTH, b. 28 Jan. 1777; m. Kingston, as Polly, 20 Nov. 1794 (*VR* 297), WASHBURN, b. Kingston 2 July 1771, son of Jabez Jr. and Mary (___) Washburn (*VR* 151), d. there 24 Dec. 1798 "in 28ᵗʰ yr of putrid fever" (*VR* 389).

      Washburn children rec. Kingston of Jabez and Polly (*VR* 153-54): 1. *Lucy Washburn⁷*, b. 7 Sept. 1795. 2. *Polly Washburn,* b. 23 Nov. 1797; m. Henry Cobb.

vi   WELTHEA WADSWORTH, b. 27 Jan. 1779; living 1850; m. (1) Kingston, 28 June 1798 (*VR* 294), DANIEL PERKINS, d. by Nov. 1807; m. (2) at Kingston, 6 Dec. 1807 (*VR* 260), CONSTANT SAMPSON, b. Bridgewater 16 Aug. 1770, d. Kingston 12 Nov. 1855 of cancer, son of Miles and Deborah (Bonney) Sampson (Mass. VR 94:195), and widower of Rebecca Partridge who d. of childbed fever Kingston 19 Jan. 1807 (*VR* 379). In 1850 he was a shipwright ae 80 in Kingston, with Wealthea ae 71 (p.92).

      Perkins child rec. Kingston: 1. *Lucy Wadsworth Perkins⁷,* b. 21 April 1799 (*VR* 114).

      Sampson children rec. Kingston (*VR* 130): 1. *Maria Sampson⁷,* b. 30 Sept. 1808. 2. *Philander Sampson,* b. 14 July 1811. 3. *Wealthea Sampson,* b. 7 Jan. 1814; m. her cousin Perez Woodward (*Kingston VR* 387). 4. *Julia Ann Sampson,* b. 24 April 1818 ["of Sampson & Wealthea"]. 5. *Hiram Sampson,* b. 2 Dec. 1820 ; m. Wealthea Bradford Drew (*VR* 273).

vii   CEPHAS WADSWORTH, b. 21 March 1781; m. Kingston (*VR* 293) 28 Jan. 1804 LUCY SYLVESTER.

      Children, b. Kingston to Cephas and Lucy (*VR* 147): 1. *Lewis Sylvester Wadsworth⁷* (twin), b. 17 Nov. 1805. 2. *William Wadsworth* (twin), b. 17 Nov. 1805; d. 19 Nov. 1822 ae 17y 2d. 3. *Lucy Sampson Wadsworth,* b. 10 May 1810. 4. *Eveline Wadsworth,* b. 6 June 1812. 5. *Hannah White Wadsworth,* b. 27 June 1817. 6. *Cephas Wadsworth,* b. 23 May 1820. 7. *William Alexander Wadsworth,* b. 30 June 1824, bp. 27 May 1827.

viii   LAVINA WADSWORTH, b. 4 or 14 Jan. 1783; d. Bristol, Me., 26 Feb. 1868; m. at Bristol, 4 Oct. 1807, JAMES WOODWARD, b. Scituate 20 Jan. 1783, d. Bristol, Me., 11 Dec. 1843 (*Wadsworth Fam.* 158). In 1850 Lavina Woodward's household in Damariscotta included Maria ae 37 and Cephas W. ae 26, a seaman (p.437).

Woodward children, b. Me. (prob. incomplete): 1. prob. *Perez Woodward[7]*, b. 22 March 1810 Bristol, Me.; m. Damariscotta 7 Oct. 1834, his cousin Wealtha Sampson. 2. *Maria Woodward*, b. ca 1813; at home 1850. 3. prob. *James Woodward*, b. ca 1815; m. Caroline ___; res. Damariscotta 1850, ship carpenter. 4. ? *Uriah Woodward*, b. ca 1818; a joiner in Damariscotta 1850. 5. ? *Samuel Woodward*, b. ca 1820; a ship carpenter in Damariscotta 1850. 6. *Cephas W. Woodward*, b. ca 1824, at home, a seaman 1850.

ix   ZILPHA WADSWORTH, b. 19 Aug. 1785; d. 30 Oct. 1787, ae 2y, Kingston (*VR* 387); bur. with father.

x   JOHN WADSWORTH, b. 3 Feb. 1788; d. 1861; m. at Strong, Me., SALLY WOODWARD (*Wadsworth Fam.*, 205).
      Children (*ibid.*): 1. *Maria C. Wadsworth[7]*, b. 1824; m. ___ Williams. 2. *Lucy W. Wadsworth*, b. 1828; m. [prob. Lorenzo] Tuck; res. N. Bridgewater 1850 (p.297). 3. *John Wadsworth*, b. 1831; m. Elizabeth Leonard.

Sources cited: *Duxbury VR. Kingston VR.* Plymouth County Probate Records. *Mass. Soldiers & Sailors.* *MF 12: Francis Cooke* (1996). "Death Records from the Ancient Burial Ground at Kingston, Mass.," *MD* 7 [1905]. *Wadsworth Family in America* (1883). CENSUS: *Heads of Families 1790 – Massachusetts.* 1810 Boothbay, Lincoln Co. (M252-12); 1850 North Bridgewater, Plymouth Co. (M432-333).

528.   ZILPAH WADSWORTH[5] (*Lusanna[4] Samson, John[3], Stephen[2], Henry[1]*), daughter of Peleg Wadsworth and his wife Lusanna Samson [114], was born 8 April 1746 at Duxbury (*VR* 184) and died there 3 January 1778 as "Zilpah Drew" (*VR* 375). She was a descendant also of *Mayflower* passenger John Alden.

She married 6 February 1772 at Duxbury (*VR* 249, 326), **PEREZ DREW**, who was born there 8 August 1740 (*VR* 71) and died in West Virginia in 1797 (*Va. Gen.* 24:222-23). He was the son of Perez and Abigail (Soule) Drew and a descendant of *Mayflower* passenger George Soule. Perez married, second, MARY _____. He appears to have had no surviving children with either wife.

Perez removed to Hampshire County, Virginia (now West Virginia), where he witnessed a deed in 1785. His will, dated 8 August 1797, proved 18 September 1797, names wife Mary and brother Sylvanus, who was left land in Plymouth, Mass., but does not mention children (*The Genealogist*, 1:242). The will of Zilpah's father, dated 1 June 1799 (Plymouth PR # 21,757; 37:76), does not mention her in any way.

Sources cited: *Duxbury VR. Virginia Genealogist*, 24 [1980] (book review citing Clara McCormick Sage and Laura Sage Jones, *Early Records, Hampshire County, Virginia* [1939; repr. 1969]). *The Genealogist*, 1 (1980).

529. PELEG WADSWORTH[5] (*Lusanna*[4] *Samson, John*[3], *Stephen*[2], *Henry*[1]), son of Peleg Wadsworth and his wife Lusanna Samson [114], was born 25 April 1748 at Duxbury (*VR* 183), and died 12 November 1829 aged 80, at Hiram, Maine, where he is buried in Wadsworth Hall Burying Ground (*Maine Families 1790*, 8:531). His death was reported in the *Columbian Centinel* of 2 December 1829. He was a descendant also of *Mayflower* passenger John Alden.

He married at Plymouth (*VR* 360; *CR* 497), recorded also at Duxbury (*VR* 326), 18 June 1772, "he of Duxbury she of Plymouth," **ELIZABETH BARTLETT JR.**, who was born at Plymouth 9 August 1753, "Thursday morning about 2 o'clock in the morning" (*VR* 81), baptized there 19 August 1753 (*CR* 448), and died at Hiram 20 July 1825 aged 72 (*Maine Fam. 1790*, 8:532), daughter of Samuel and Elizabeth (Lothrop) (Witherell) Bartlett. She was a descendant of *Mayflower* passenger Richard Warren.

Peleg Wadsworth was one of the sureties when Thomas Wetherell was appointed administrator 10 July 1793 of the estate of [Peleg's mother-in-law] Elizabeth Bartlett late of Plymouth (Plymouth PR 27:437, 35:291). Thomas Wetherell was ordered 10 July 1793 to prepare an inventory of the estate of Samuel Bartlett who died intestate, administration having been first granted to Elizabeth Bartlett who was now also deceased, and Peleg Wadsworth was again one of the sureties. Accounts of both estates 8 July 1795 indicate "apparell divided between Mr. Wadsworth and Mr. Doane ... sundry moveables to Peleg Wadsworth" (*ibid.*, 20:204, 27:535).

Peleg graduated from Harvard College in 1769. The story of his life and his service in the Revolutionary War (during which he was wounded, captured, and imprisoned), has been told many times, and most recently detailed by Clayton Adams in *Maine Families in 1790* (8:531-35).

The family lived in Portland from 1784 to 1806. In 1789 Peleg Wadsworth and wife Elizabeth were admitted to the first church in Falmouth, Maine (CRs 29, 105) from the church in Duxbury. In 1790 Peleg purchased a tract of 7,800 acres for 12½ cents per acre; the Wadsworth Grant extended from the Saco River to the Ossipee; it became the town of Hiram. Gen. Wadsworth reserved 1,400 acres for himself and his eldest son, and the remaining acres were sold to settlers "on easy terms" (*Hiram History*, 16-17).

In 1790 he was in Portland with a household consisting of two males 16 or older, five boys under 16, six females, and one other free person (p.23).

He was a member of Congress from 1793 to 1807, and during that time lived in his Portland home while his son Charles occupied the new house in Hiram (*Hiram History*, 18). The will of his father, Peleg Wadsworth, dated 1 June 1799

(Plymouth PR #21,757; 37:76), includes a bequest of $4 to son Peleg, "together with what he formerly received from me to defray the expences of his education."

In his will dated 11 November 1829, received and filed 4 January 1830, Peleg Wadsworth of Hiram, Maine, left his Portland house and lot to Zilpah Longfellow and Lucia Wadsworth. (In 2005 the Longfellow-Wadsworth House is headquarters of the Maine Historical Society.) He named Alexander Scammel Wadsworth; son Peleg Wadsworth, Jr.; son Charles Lee Wadsworth; grandson Frank Wadsworth, son of Charles; and son John; and mentioned but did not name the children of son Samuel Bartlett Wadsworth (Oxford PR # 104).

Children of Peleg and Elizabeth (Bartlett) Wadsworth (*Maine Families 1790*, 8:533-35, *q.v.* for further sources, unless otherwise cited):

 i ALEXANDER SCAMMEL WADSWORTH[6], b. Kingston 9 May 1774; d. 28 Aug. 1775.

 ii CHARLES LEE WADSWORTH, b. Plymouth 26 June 1776; bp. Duxbury with sister Zilpah 26 April 1778 (*VR* 180); d. Hiram, Me., 29 Sept. 1848 ae 72y 8m; m. (1) in 1795, RUTH CLEMENTS, b. ca May 1771, d. 1 Jan. 1839 ae 67y 8m; m. (2) Parsonsfield, Me., 2 Sept. 1841, JANE INGALLS, b. Fryeburg 2 June 1781, d. 28 March 1847; all bur. Hiram, Me. He built the first bridge across the Saco River at Hiram Village in 1805. Charles had a son *Frank* living Nov. 1829, named in the will of his grandfather.

 iii ZILPHA WADSWORTH, b. Duxbury 6 Jan. 1778, bp. there with brother Charles 26 April 1778 (*VR* 180); d. Portland, Me., 12 March 1851 ae 73y; m. Portland, 1 Jan. 1804 (*VR* 123), STEPHEN LONGFELLOW, b. Gorham 23 March 1776, d. Portland 3 Aug. 1849, son of Stephen and Patience (Young) Longfellow.

  Longfellow children rec. Portland (*VR* 176, 187, 200): 1. *Stephen Longfellow[7]*, b. 14 Aug. 1805. 2. *Henry Wadsworth Longfellow* [the poet], b. 27 Feb. 1807. 3. *Elizabeth Wadsworth Longfellow*, b. 24 Aug. 1808. 4. *Ann Longfellow*, b. 3 March 1810.

 iv ELIZABETH WADSWORTH, b. Boston 21 Sept. 1779, bp. Boston West Church 26 Sept. 1779; d. Portland 11 Aug. 1802 ae 22.

 v JOHN WADSWORTH, b. 1 Sept., bp. Plymouth 2 Sept. 1781 (*CR* 464); d. Hiram, Me., 22 Jan. 1860 ae 78y; m. ELLEN RUTH GEORGE, b. ca 1808, N.H., d. Dec. 1876. In 1850 they were in Hiram, Me., apparently living by themselves (p.87).

 vi LUCIA WADSWORTH, b. 12 June, bp. Plymouth 15 June 1783 (*CR* 466); d. unm. Portland 18 Oct. 1864; bur. there in Longfellow tomb in Western Cemetery.

vii HENRY WADSWORTH, b. Portland 21 June 1785; d. Tripoli 3 or 4 Sept. 1804, "while aiding in running a torpedo ship into the enemy's fleet."

viii GEORGE WADSWORTH, b. Portland 6 Jan., bp. 13 Jan. 1788 (*Falmouth CRs* 53); d. 8 April 1816 Philadelphia of a sore throat.

ix ALEXANDER SCAMMEL WADSWORTH, b. 7 May, bp. Portland 16 May 1790 (*Falmouth CR* 53); d. 5 April 1851 Washington, D.C; m. 19 Nov. 1824 LOUISA DENISON. See *Maine Families 1790*, 8:534 for details of his naval career, which included service on the *U.S.S. Constitution*.

   Children (*Wadsworth Fam.*, 151): 1. *Alexander S. Wadsworth[7]*, b. 1828; m. Helen McMorine. 2. *Louisa D. Wadsworth*, b. 1833; m. Charles G. Baylor. 3. *Annie D. Wadsworth*, b. 1841; m. Rev. John D. Wells.

x SAMUEL BARTLETT WADSWORTH ("7th son"), b. Portland 1 Sept. 1791, prob. the James bp. there 4 Sept. (*Falmouth CR* 53); d. 2 Oct. 1874 Eastport, Me; m. (1) N. Yarmouth, Me., 27 Feb. 1817, LUCY FIELD, b. there 23 Jan. 1794, d. Eastport, Me., 23 June 1818 ae 23y; m. (2) Eastport, Sept. 1823, ELIZA C. HARRINGTON of Dorchester, N.S. He had children mentioned but not named in father's will of Nov. 1829.

   Children (*Wadsworth Fam.*, 231): 1. *Elizabeth Harrington Wadsworth[7]*, b. 1824; m. (1) Augustus Norton, (2) G. E. Richie, (3) William D. Harrington. 2. *Anne H. Wadsworth*, b. 1827. 3. *Mary N. Wadsworth*, b. 1829; m. Charles C. Norton. 4. *Samuel L. Wadsworth*, b. 1830. 5. *Edward Henry Wadsworth*, b. 1835. 6. *Lucia Wadsworth*, b. 1839; m. E. E. Shead.

xi PELEG WADSWORTH, b. Portland 10 Oct. 1793, bp. 3 Nov. 1793 (*CR* 53); d. 17 Jan. 1875 Hiram; m. Hiram, 10 Sept. 1815, his cousin LU-SANNA WADSWORTH, b. Duxbury 11 Dec. 1797, d. 8 Jan. 1879, dau. Dura and Lydia (Bradford) Wadsworth [#534]. In 1850 he was a farmer at Hiram, ae 56, with Susanna ae 52 b. Mass., and children Frances, Louisa D., Peleg Jr., Alden B., and Cephas at home (p.90).

   Children (*Wadsworth Fam.*, 225): 1. *George Wadsworth[7]*, b. 1817. 2. *Joseph M. Wadsworth*, b. 1818. 3. *William Wadsworth*, b. 1820. 4. *Elizabeth Wadsworth*, b. 1824. 5. *George Wadsworth*, b. 1826. 6. *Frances Wadsworth*, b. 1828; m. Joseph Rounds. 7. *Lusannah Wadsworth*, b. 1830; m. (1) J. E. Osgood, (2) John P. Hubbard. 8. *Louisa Wadsworth*, b. 1832; m. John Rounds. 9. *Peleg Wadsworth*, b. 1834. 10. *Alden Bradford Wadsworth*, b. 1837. 11. *Cephas Wadsworth*, b. 1841.

Sources cited: *Duxbury VR. Plymouth VR. Portland, Maine VR* [2005]. *Plymouth Church Records.* Marquis F. King, *Baptism and Admission from the Records of the First Church in Falmouth. Now Portland, Maine* (1898). Plymouth County Probate Records. Oxford County, Me., Probate Records. Clayton R. Adams, "Peleg Wadsworth," *Maine Families in 1790*, 8 (2003), provides further detail and sources. Teg, *History of Hiram, Maine, Sesquicentennial Edition* (1964). *Wadsworth Family in America* (Lawrence, 1883). CENSUS: 1790 Portland, Cumberland Co., Me. (M637-2); 1850 Hiram, Oxford Co., Me. (M432-262 **See also:** Mary Jane Fry, *The Wadsworth Family in America, 1632–1985* (1985). Russell Clare Farnham, *A Longfellow Genealogy ...* (2002).

530.   URIAH WADSWORTH[5] (*Lusanna*[4] *Samson, John*[3], *Stephen*[2], *Henry*[1]), son of Peleg Wadsworth and his wife Lusanna Samson [114], was born 13 March 1750/1 at Duxbury (*VR* 183), and died there 20 March 1823 aged 72 (*VR* 433). He was a descendant also of *Mayflower* passenger John Alden.

He married at Duxbury, 8 January 1789 (*VR* 326), **EUNICE BRADFORD**, who was born there 8 May 1756 (*VR* 32) and died there 17 August 1795 in her 40th year, "wife of Uriah" (*VR* 433). She was the daughter of Eliphalet and Hannah (Prince) Bradford, and a descendant of *Mayflower* passengers William Bradford and Richard Warren (*Duxbury History*, 233-34).

In 1790 Uriah was in Duxbury, head of a household consisting of himself and two females (p.169). The will of his father, Peleg Wadsworth, dated 1 June 1799, includes a bequest of $150 to son Uriah (Plymouth PR # 21,757; 37:76).

In his will dated 18 March, proved 14 April 1823, Uriah Wadsworth of Duxbury, yeoman, made the following bequests:

> ... to beloved brother Ira Wadsworth, all that part of my pond woodlot lying northeast of a road that is made use of for to sled wood out of my lot down to Island Creek Pond, and over the pond when frozen hard, [and] $1,000 with one feather bed and half of my bedding and wearing apparel; ... to John Wadsworth son of my brother Dura Wadsworth, the remainder of my pond lot ... not to exceed three acres; ... to my nephew John Alden Jr., my pew in the Rev[d] Dr Allyn's meeting house; ... to my beloved sister Wealthy Alden wife of Judah Alden, Esq., $2,500; ... to my beloved brother Dura Wadsworth, the one half of what he oweth me on notes of hand, with the remaining half of my wearing apparel; ... unto my nephew Uriah Wadsworth son of Dura Wadsworth, the remaining half of what brother Dura oweth me; ... unto nephew Sylvanus Smith, all the monies he oweth me on notes of hand; ... unto niece Lucy S. Smith wife of Sylvanus Smith, $100; ... to my niece Sarah Wadsworth daughter of Ira Wadsworth, my feather bed with one half of my bedding.

Uriah named Judah Alden, Esq., executor and gave him full power to sell at public vendue a piece of woodland that he had purchased of Nathaniel Delano, or to dispose of any personal estate found that may have been omitted from the will (Plymouth PR 56:501).

Child of Uriah and Eunice (Bradford) Wadsworth, rec. Duxbury (*VR* 181, 431):

i   GAMALIEL WADSWORTH[6], b. 28 May 1793; d. Duxbury 23 Aug. 1795
     ae 2y 2m 23d.

Sources cited: *Duxbury VR.* Plymouth County Probate Records. Winsor, *History of Duxbury* (1849). CENSUS: *Heads of Families 1790 – Mass.*

531.   LUCIA WADSWORTH[5] (*Lusanna[4] Samson, John[3], Stephen[2], Henry[1]*), daughter of Peleg Wadsworth and his wife Lusanna Samson [114], was born 25 January 1753 at Duxbury (*VR* 182) and died 18 March 1780 aged 27y 1m 22d, at Pembroke (*VR* 445), "wife of Capt. Joseph."   She was a descendant also of *Mayflower* passenger John Alden.

She married at Duxbury, 20 August 1771 (*VR* 325), **JOSEPH SMITH**, who was born 22 November 1740 at Yarmouth (*VR* 73),   and died 11 August 1811, aged 70, at Pembroke (*VR* 445), son of Rev. Thomas and Judith (Miller) Smith. Joseph married, second, at Pembroke 1 January 1782 (*VR* 347), BATHSHEBA TORREY, with whom he had nine children recorded there: Bathsheba Smith, Catherine Smith, Christopher Smith, Joseph Smith, Joshua Smith, Judith Miller Smith, Lucia Smith, Thankful Smith, and Thomas Smith (*VR* 185-86).

Joseph served as a second lieutenant in the Revolutionary War in 1776 on the sloop *Republic,* commanded by Capt. John Foster Williams (*MSSR* 14:478).

In 1790 he was living in Pembroke, head of a household consisting of one male 16 or over, two boys under 16, and five females (*Heads of Fam.*, 176).

The will of Lucia's father, Peleg Wadsworth, dated 1 June 1799, includes a bequest of $4 to Sylvanus Smith, son of deceased daughter Lucia. On 4 September 1811 Silvanus Smith of Duxbury, mariner, was appointed administrator of the estate of Joseph Smith Esq. late of Pembroke deceased ((Plymouth PR #21,757; 37:76; 39:316; 44:12).

Children of Joseph and Lucia (Wadsworth) Smith, rec. Pembroke (*VR* 186):

i   JOSHUA SMITH[6], b. 28 Dec. 1776; d. y.
ii   SYLVANUS SMITH, b. 9 Aug. 1779; d. Duxbury 23 April 1865, widower,
     of valvular heart disease, ae 85y 8m, b. Hanson [*sic*] (Mass. VR 184:277);
     m. Duxbury, 30 Sept. 1804 (VR 212), his cousin LUCY SMITH ALDEN
     [#533-i], d. Duxbury 2 Feb. 1858 ae 77 of palsy and influenza (Mass. VR
     121-238). Their mutual uncle Uriah Wadsworth in his 1823 will left to
     nephew Sylvanus Smith "all the monies he oweth me," and to niece Lucy
     S. Smith, $100 (Plymouth PR 56:501). In 1850 he was a mariner in

Duxbury with Lucia S. Smith ae 69 and [her sister] Mary A. Alden ae 49 (p.75).

Sources cited: *Duxbury VR. Pembroke VR. Yarmouth VR.* Mass. Vital Records 1841-1910. Plymouth County Probate Records. *Mass. Soldiers & Sailors.* CENSUS: *Heads of Families 1790* – *Mass.*; 1850 Duxbury, Plymouth Co. (M432-333) **See also:** Susan A. Smith, *A Memorial of Rev. Thomas Smith (2nd Minister of Pembroke) & His Descendants* (1895), 97.

532. IRA WADSWORTH[5] (*Lusanna*[4] *Samson, John*[3], *Stephen*[2], *Henry*[1]), son of Peleg Wadsworth and his wife Lusanna Samson [114], was born 18 May 1757 at Duxbury (*VR* 181) and died there 28 December 1826, aged 70, "husband of Sarah" (*VR* 432). He was a descendant also of *Mayflower* passenger John Alden.

He married at Duxbury, 14 September 1783 (*VR* 325), **SARAH FREEMAN**, who was baptized there 28 March 1762 (*VR* 80) and died there 18 January 1836 aged 74, "widow of Ira Sr." (*VR* 433). She was the daughter of Joseph Jr. and Caroline (Chandler) Freeman.

Ira served 17 days in the Revolution as a private in Capt. Ebenezer Washburn's company, Col. Thomas Lathrop's regiment, marching to Bristol, R.I., on an alarm in December 1776 (*MSSR* 16:381).

In 1790 he was living in Duxbury with one boy under 16, and two females (*Heads of Fam.*, 169). In 1799 he and his brother Dura inherited the family property in Duxbury. Peleg Wadsworth in his will dated 1 June 1799, proved 5 August 1799, named his sons Ira and Dura executors, and left to them the homestead farm with two houses, barns, wharf, and other lands, his pew in the meeting house, a sloop named *Gabriel*, and all his livestock and farming tools (Plymouth PR #21,757; 37:76).

In 1800 Ira Wadsworth's household consisted of one man and one woman 26-45, one boy and one girl 10-16, one boy under 10 (p.99). In 1810 his household included a man and a woman over 45, a young man 16-26, and a woman 26-45 (p.126). Ira Wadsworth, shoemaker, and Dura Wadsworth, yeoman, both of Duxbury, agreed on 5 March 1818 to divide the land inherited from their father, and on 16 March 1818 Dura sold to Ira his half of the salt marsh "at high pines" (Plymouth LR 115:141; 140:56).

Ira's brother Uriah Wadsworth [#530], in his will dated 1823, left to beloved brother Ira half of his pond woodlot, $1,000, and a feather bed. To his niece Sarah Wadsworth, daughter of Ira, he left a feather bed and bedding (Plymouth PR 56:501). No Plymouth County probate records have been found for Ira or Sarah Wadsworth, or for Sarah's parents.

Children of Ira and Sarah (Freeman) Wadsworth, rec. Duxbury (*VR* 181-183):

i   SARAH WADSWORTH[6], b. 29 June 1784; unm. 1850 when res. Duxbury with brother Joseph, with real estate worth $216 (his was $6,000).

ii   IRA WADSWORTH, b. 26 Oct. 1789; d. 1857 (Mass. VR 112-69); of Cambridge when he m. at Concord, 28 Oct. 1822 (*VR* 390), NABBY JONES BROOKS, b. there 1 January 1803, dau. of Asa and Mary (___) Brooks (*VR* 277). In 1850 they were living in Cambridge (p.69); Ira was a grocer, and the household included George Wadsworth ae 24, a clerk; Frances Wadsworth ae 16; Matthew Brooks ae 26, clerk, b. Me.; Frank Conant ae 20; and Sarah A. Coldwell ae 40.
         Children at home 1850: 1. *George Wadsworth*,[7] b. ca 1826.   2. *Frances Wadsworth*, b. ca 1834.

iii JOSEPH F. WADSWORTH, b. 12 Nov. 1792; m. ANN ____; res. Duxbury 1850, no occupation, with Ann ae 52, [sister] Sarah ae 65, Susan Mears ae 16 and Alonzo T. Lewis ae 15 (p.60).

Sources cited: *Duxbury VR. Mass. Soldiers & Sailors.* Plymouth County Probate Records. CENSUS: Duxbury, Plymouth Co., 1800 (M32-16), 1810 (M252–21), & 1850 (M432-333); 1850 Cambridge, Middlesex Co. (M432–325).

533. WELTHEA WADSWORTH[5] (*Lusanna[4] Samson, John[3], Stephen[2], Henry[1]*), daughter of Peleg Wadsworth and his wife Lusanna Samson [114], was born 21 September 1759 at Duxbury (*VR* 184) and died there 2 or 3 March 1841 aged 81y 7m, of paralysis "wife of Maj. Judah" (*VR* 347). She was a descendant also of *Mayflower* passenger John Alden.

She married at Duxbury (*VR* 326), 17 February 1780, **JUDAH ALDEN,** who was born there on Wednesday 31 October 1750 (*VR* 17), and died there 1 or 12 March 1845 aged 94y 3m 10d, "merchant, widower, an officer of the Revolution" (*VR* 345). He was the son of Briggs and Mercy (Wadsworth) Alden, and a descendant of *Mayflower* passenger John Alden.

During the Revolution, Judah served as a captain in the 2nd regiment, Massachusetts Line (*MSSR* 1:109). He applied 3 July 1828 and received both a pension and a bounty land warrant for his service (White, 1:24).

In 1790 he was living in Duxbury, head of a household that included three boys under 16, and four females (*Heads of Fam.*, 169).

The will of Welthea's father, Peleg Wadsworth, dated 1 June 1799, includes a bequest of $4 to daughter Welthea, wife of Judah Alden (Plymouth PR #21,757, 37:76). The will of Uriah Wadsworth of Duxbury, dated 18 March, proved 14

April 1823, names among others his sister Wealthy Alden wife of Judah, and nephew John Alden Jr., and appoints Judah Alden executor (Plymouth PR 56:501).

In his will dated 6 December 1843 with codicil dated 21 December 1844, proved 2nd Monday of April 1845, Judah Alden of Duxbury, Esq., named daughter Lucia S. Smith and her husband Sylvanus, daughter Mary Ann, son John, daughter Welthea wife of William James, granddaughter Mercy A. wife of Robert W. Welsh [dau. Henry R. and Mercy (Alden) Packard], and son Samuel; he mentioned but did not name eldest son Briggs' children, and appointed as executor Sylvanus Smith (Plymouth PR #143).

Children of Judah and Welthea (Wadsworth) Alden, rec. Duxbury (VR 16-18):

i LUCIA SMITH ALDEN[6], b. 5 Dec. 1780; d. Duxbury 2 Feb. 1858 ae 77 of palsy and influenza (Mass. VR 121:238). m. Duxbury, 30 Sept. 1804 (VR 212), her cousin SYLVANUS SMITH [#531-ii], *q.v.*

ii JOHN ALDEN, b. 22 Nov. 1784; d. before 1844.

iii BRIGGS ALDEN, b. 6 Oct. 1786; Capt. Briggs Alden d. Duxbury 4 Jan. 1840 of abdominal adhesions ae 53 (VR 345); bur. Large Cemetery, Duxbury; m. ca 1819, HANNAH D. _____, b. Scituate ca Dec. 1786, d. Duxbury 15 April 1850, "wife of Briggs Alden," of cancer (Mass. VR 49:151). In 1850 several of the children were listed in Duxbury as noted below (pp. 66, 75).

Children rec. Duxbury, of Briggs and Hannah (VR 15-18): 1. *Judah Alden[7]*, b. 22 July 1820; d. Duxbury 18 or 23 Aug. 1823 (VR 346). 2. *William James Alden*, b. 22 April 1822; a shoemaker 1850; m. Lydia J. ___. 3. *Lydia P. Alden*, b. 17 or 20 April 1824; m. Caleb R. Moore; res. Duxbury 1850. 4. *Judah Alden*, b. 19 or 24 Aug. 1825; m. Julia W. [?Whitney]; a mariner Duxbury 1850. 5. *Samuel Alden*, b. 28 April 1827; res. Duxbury 1850. 6. *[Son] Alden*, b. 15 May 1830. 7. *Amherst Alden*, b. 15 May 1832; res. 1850 in household of sister Lydia.

iv MERCY / MARCIA ALDEN, b. 24 Sept. 1788; d. Duxbury 10 March 1841 (VR 397); m. Duxbury, 14 June 1812 (VR 212), HENRY R. PACKARD "of Bath"; Capt. Henry d. at sea of typhus fever, 12 Aug. 1834, rec. Duxbury (VR 397).

Packard children, rec. Duxbury "of Henry R. and Marcia" (VR 114): 1. *Marcia A. Packard[7]*, b. 4 June 1813; m. Robert W. Welsh. 2. *Hannah J. Packard*, b. 15 April 1815; d. 10 Aug. 1831 of typhus fever; bur. Duxbury (VR 397).

v JUDAH ALDEN, b. 11 Aug. 1790; d. 15 Dec. 1792 ae 2y 4m 2d (VR 346).

vi WELTHEA ALDEN, b. 13 Aug. 1792; m. Duxbury, 7 March 1816 (VR 212), WILLIAM JAMES. No children rec. Duxbury.

vii HANNAH ALDEN, b. 4 Jan. 1795; d. 25 April 1804 ae 9y 3m (VR 346).

viii JUDAH ALDEN, b. 9 June 1797; d. 20 April 1804 ae 6y 10m 11d (VR 346).

ix   MARY ANN ALDEN, b. 12 March 1801; living, unm. 1850 with sister Lucia
      Smith and her husband, Duxbury (p.75); d. prob. 1881 (Mass. VR 329:505;
      PR adm. #151).

x   SAMUEL ALDEN, b. 24 Jan. 1803 (rec. also Bridgewater); m. at Bridgewater,
      29 Jan. 1829 (*VR* 2:21), MARY ANGIER HYDE, b. prob. Bridgewater 12
      Jan. 1806, dau. of Ezra and Martha (Ames) Hyde (*VR* 174). Samuel was a
      physician at Bridgewater in 1850 with Mary A. and children Ezra H., William
      Alden, Lucia S., Alice W., and Mary A.; Jane Smith ae 24 was with them
      (p.33).

      Children, rec. Bridgewater (*VR* 1:17-21), of "Dr. Samuel and Mary": 1. *Ezra
      H. Alden*[7], b. ca 1831. 2. *Samuel Alden*, b. 9 March 1833, bp. 28 Sept. 1834; d.
      Bridgewater 9 May 1835 (*VR* 2:425). 3. *William Alden*, b. 11 Oct. 1836. 4. *Lucia
      S. Alden*, b. 3 May 1839. 5. *Francis/Frank Alden*, b. 23 June 1841; d. 22 Oct. 1847
      (*VR* 2:424). 6. *Alice W. Alden*, b. 5 Sept. 1843. 7. *Mary A. Alden*, b. 20 Oct.
      1845. 8. *Martha Williams Alden*, b. 11 or 21 Oct. 1847; d. Bridgewater 4 May
      1849 (*VR* 2:424).

Sources cited: *Bridgewater VR. Duxbury VR. Mass. Soldiers & Sailors.* White, *Abstracts of Rev. War
Pension Files*, citing S46364 and BLW 1716-300. Plymouth County Probate Records. *MF16: John
Alden Part 1* (2001). CENSUS: *Heads of Families 1790 – Mass.*; 1850 Bridgewater and Duxbury,
Plymouth Co. (M432-333). **See also:** *MF16: John Alden Part 3* (2004), 321-24.

534. DURA WADSWORTH[5] (*Lusanna*[4] *Samson, John*[3], *Stephen*[2], *Henry*[1]), son of
Peleg Wadsworth and his wife Lusanna Samson [114], was baptized at Duxbury 24
April 1763 (*VR* 180). He died probably at Hiram, Maine, 18 March 1846; his death
was recorded in the Gamaliel Wadsworth Bible as "my father, aged 82," no place
specified (*Duxbury VR* 430). He was a descendant also of *Mayflower* passenger John
Alden.

He married at Duxbury (*VR* 324), 17 January 1788, **LYDIA BRADFORD**,
who was born there 6 August 1765 (*MF* 22:391) and baptized there 15 September
1765 (*VR* 30), daughter of Seth and Lydia (Southworth) Bradford. She died,
probably at Hiram, Maine, 6 July 1836 (*Duxbury VR* 431), recorded in the family
Bible as "my mother." She was a descendant of *Mayflower* passengers William
Bradford, John Alden, Thomas Rogers, and Richard Warren.

In 1790 Dura Wadsworth was living in Duxbury, head of a household
consisting of one man, one boy under 16, and one female. In 1799 he and his
brother Ira inherited the family property in Duxbury. Peleg Wadsworth, in his will
dated 1 June 1799 (Plymouth PR. # 21,757, 37:76), named his sons Ira and Dura
executors, and left to them the homestead farm with two houses, barns, wharf, and

other lands, his pew in the meeting house, a sloop named *Gabriel*, and all his livestock and farming tools.

In 1800 Dura's household consisted of one man and one woman 26-45, two boys 10-16, two boys and three girls under 10 (p.99).

Ira Wadsworth, shoemaker, and Dura Wadsworth, yeoman, both of Duxbury, agreed on 5 March 1818 to divide their land, and on 16 March Dura sold to Ira his half of the salt marsh at high pines, his wife Lydia relinquishing her dower rights (Plymouth LR 115:141; 140:56).

The will of Uriah Wadsworth [#530] included bequests to his nephews John and Uriah Wadsworth, sons of his brother Dura; John received land and Uriah "the remaining half of what brother Dura oweth me" (Plymouth PR 56:501).

According to *History of Duxbury*, Dura's family removed to Maine. Their deaths as found in the *Duxbury Vital Records* are taken from the Bible of Gamaliel Wadsworth, recorded evidently by Gamaliel's father, Dura Wadsworth [Jr.].

Children of Dura and Lydia (Bradford) Wadsworth rec. Duxbury (*VR* 180-84):

i   DURA WADSWORTH[6], b. 4 Dec. 1788; m. (1) Duxbury, 17 March 1811 (*VR* 324), MERCY TAYLOR, b. Duxbury 11 Dec. 1793 (*VR* 173), d. there 29 July 1814 ae 21y 7m 18d, dau. of John and Marcy (___) Taylor (*VR* 432); m. (2) Duxbury, 3 Nov. 1816 (*VR* 324), NABBY CUSHMAN, b. ca 1794 Mass. In 1850 Dura was a housewright in Duxbury with Nabby ae 56 and children Abigail, Gamaliel, Dura, Elizabeth, Briggs C., Zilpha S., and William (p.62). His death was not found in Mass. VR on line.

Children rec. Duxbury (*VR* 179-82, 184): [with first wife Mercy:] 1. *Mercy T. Wadsworth*[7], b. 6 Sept. 1812. [with second wife Nabby:] 2. *Lucy Wadsworth*, b. 25 Sept. 1817. 3. *Abigail Wadsworth*, b. 4 April 1819. 4. *Henry Wadsworth*, b. 1 Jan. 1821; m. Abby O. Winsor. 5. *Gamaliel Wadsworth*, b. 2 Jan. 1823. 6. *Dura Wadsworth Jr.*, b. 25 Feb. 1825, a housewright 1850. 7. *Elizabeth Wadsworth*, b. 31 March 1827. 8. *Briggs C. Wadsworth*, b. 3 Dec. 1829, a mariner 1850. 9. *Zilpha S. Wadsworth*, b. 28 July 1832. 10. *William Wadsworth*, b. 8 Jan. 1839.

ii   PELEG WADSWORTH, b. 12 March 1791; d. after 1850; m. ELIZA ANN ___, b. ca 1810 Maine. In 1850 Peleg Wadsworth 2nd was a shoemaker in Hiram, Me., ae 59, with Eliza An [*sic*] ae 40 (p.90).

Children at home 1850: 1. *Eliza J. Wadsworth*[7], b. ca 1846. 2. *Joseph Wadsworth*, b. ca 1848. 3. *James Wadsworth*, b. ca 1849.

iii SETH WADSWORTH, b. 13 Nov. 1793; d. 1840-1850, prob. Baldwin, Me.; m. JANE ___, b. ca 1801 Maine. In 1840 Seth was head of the household at Baldwin, with one man 40-50, one woman 30-40, one young woman

15-20, one boy and two girls 10-15, and one girl 5-10 (p.227). In 1850 Jane Wadsworth was at Baldwin, Me., with all children except Jane (p.187).

Children rec. Duxbury (*VR* 181-183), first two b. Hiram, Me., four youngest with mother 1850: 1. *Jane Wadsworth*[7], b. 20 Dec. 1822. 2. *Anne Wadsworth*, b. 17 Sept. 1825. 3. *Mary Wadsworth*, b. 31 Aug. 1827. 4. *Seth Wadsworth*, b. 18 Aug. 1829, a farmer in Baldwin, Me., 1850. 5. *Ruth Wadsworth*, b. 9 Oct. 1831.

iv JOHN WADSWORTH, b. 16 Nov. 1794; m. Duxbury, 22 May 1815 (*VR* 325), LYDIA PERRY, b. ca 1789 Nova Scotia. In 1850 he was ae 55, in Duxbury, no occupation, with Lydia ae 61 and children Belinda and Peleg; the family of John Jr. shared the dwelling (p.62).

Children rec. Duxbury (*VR* 180, 182, 183): 1. *[Son] Wadsworth*[7], d. 1 Aug. 1815 [*sic*] (*VR* 433). 2. Lydia *Wadsworth*[7], b. 25 Aug. 1816. 3. *Catherine Wadsworth*, b. 16 Feb. 1819. 4. *John Wadsworth Jr.*, b. 9 Nov. 1820, a shoemaker 1850; m. Catherine T. _____. 5. *Belinda Wadsworth*, b. 14 Dec. 1822. 6. *Sarah B. Wadsworth*, b. 5 Oct. 1824. 7. *Peleg Wadsworth*, b. 28 Aug. 1828, a mariner 1850.

v   HANNAH WADSWORTH, b. 26 May 1796; m. at Duxbury, 26 Feb. 1815 (*VR* 223), STEPHEN BRADFORD, b. Duxbury 23 June 1791 (*VR* 32).

Bradford children rec. Duxbury (*VR* 28-32): 1. *Stephen Bradford*[7], b. 9 Oct. 1815. 2. *Otis Bradford*, b. 2 Dec. 1817; d. 5 Oct. 1818 (*VR* 353). 3. *Otis Bradford*, b. 13 Sept. 1819. 4. *Hannah Bradford*, b. 22 Feb. 1821. 5. *Lucy B. Bradford*, b. 2 April 1824. 6. *Erastus F. Bradford*, b. 16 Nov. 1827. 7. *Alexander Wadsworth Bradford*, b. 31 July 1830; d. 22 July 1834 ae 4y (*VR* 352). 8. *Julius Bradford*, b. 9 Dec. 1832. 9. *Alexander Wadsworth Bradford*, b. 9 March 1838.

vi LUSANNA WADSWORTH, b. 11 Dec. 1797; m. Hiram, Me., her cousin PELEG WADSWORTH, son of Peleg and Elizabeth (Bartlett) Wadsworth [#529-xi], *q.v.* for family (p.35).

vii ZILPAH WADSWORTH, b. 23 May 1800.

viii LYDIA WADSWORTH, b. 15 Nov. 1802.

ix URIAH WADSWORTH, b. 26 April 1808 Mass.; m. MARTHA ___, b. ca 1796 Maine. In 1850 Uriah ae 42 was a shingle maker at Limington, York Co., Me., with Martha ae 54 and ?Lemay [*male; name unclear*] Wadsworth, ae 10 (p.285).

Sources cited: *Duxbury VR.* Plymouth County Deeds and Probate Records. Winsor, *History of Duxbury* (1849). CENSUS: *Heads of Families 1790 – Mass.*; Duxbury, Plymouth Co., 1800 (M32-16) & 1850 (M432-333); Baldwin, Cumberland Co., 1840 (M704-138) & 1850 (M432-251), Hiram, Oxford Co., Me. (M432-262), & Limington, York Co., Me. (M432-276).

535. DANIEL BREWSTER[5] (*Priscilla*[4] *Samson, John*[3], *Stephen*[2], *Henry*[1]), son of William Brewster and his wife Priscilla Samson [115], was born 12 September 1747 at Duxbury (*VR* 33), and died at Williamstown 9 February 1784 (*VR* 140 citing g.s.) in his 36th year. He was a descendant also of *Mayflower* passenger William Brewster.

He married at Norwich, Conn., 22 November 1770 (*VR* 273), "both of Norwich," **MARY TRACY**, who was born there 1 April 1750 (*VR* 473), daughter of John and Margaret (Huntington) Tracy, and was living in September 1790. She married, second, 15 December 1784 at Williamstown (*VR* 107), DAVID JOHNSON. David's first wife, Phebe, with whom he had children Abigail, David Jr., Ethan, Nathaniel, Asael, and Hannah recorded at Williamstown 1766 through 1780, died there 27 December 1783 aged 36y 8m 27d (*VR* 153).

The marriage record states that Mary was David's second wife, but at that point confusion sets in: *Sarah*, wife of David Johnson, died at Williamstown 28 November 1811 in her 57th year (*VR* 153), and David, husband of Sarah, died there 7 December 1836 aged 89 (*ibid.*). David and *Mary* Johnson had a son Daniel born at Williamstown 28 July 1785 (*VR* 50), and Mary Johnson is named in September 1790 in the settlement of Daniel Brewster's estate. To complicate matters further, the death of a Lt. David Johnson at Granville, Washington County, N.Y., on 27 July 1812 is recorded at Williamstown (*VR* 153); he cannot be the David Jr. born to David and Phebe in 1768, because that child died in 1783 in his 15th year (*ibid.*). Two possible explanations come to mind: that "Sarah" may be an error for "Mary" (if so, her age at death is off by five years), or that Mary died and David married a third time. In 1800 there were two David Johnsons in Williamstown.

Daniel Bruster [*sic*] served as a private in the Revolutionary War in Samuel Clark's company, Col. John Brown's (Berkshire County) regiment, in the summer of 1777 (*MSSR* 2:720). The company took part in the battle of Wallumsick near Bennington on 16 August 1777, and later convoyed provisions to Pittsfield.

Mary Brewster was appointed administratrix of the estate of Daniel Brewster late of Williamstown, deceased on 1 June 1784; she signed the bond with sureties Elias Newbre and John George Krieger [?] both of Williamstown (Berkshire PR. #1212). The inventory taken 26 August 1784 included real estate valued at £193. On 16 September 1790 an allowance was made to Mary Johnson, late widow and relict of Daniel Brewster. An administrator's account filed the same day by David Johnson and Mary his wife on the estate of Daniel Brewster, included expenses for clothing, feeding, and schooling three children, viz. Lydia, Stephen, and Lucy, for 5 years and 9 months. Also claimed were expenses for trips "with horse" to

Stockbridge and Adams, and building materials to repair the house and barn; numerous individuals were named.

On 14 September 1790 Polly Brewster personally appeared before Wm. Towner, J.P., and chose Asa Standish of Williamstown as her guardian. Two days later, 16 September 1790, bond was given by Asa Standish and Daniel Burbank both of Williamstown, for Standish to be guardian for Polly Brewster, Lydia Brewster, Stephen Brewster, and Lucy Brewster, minor children of Daniel Brewster late of Williamstown, deceased (Berkshire PR #1486). On 22 January 1795 Samuel Mills, gentleman, and David Johnson, yeoman, both of Williamstown, gave bond for Mills to be guardian of Stephen Brewster, "about the age of fourteen ..." (*ibid.*).

The 1790 census listed David Johnson at Williamstown, with one man, four boys under 16, and four females (*Heads of Fam.*, 39). In 1800 two David Johnsons were listed there, and in 1810 David Johnson, over 45, was living with an apparent wife the same age and one man and one woman 16-26 (p.157).

On [*blank*] November 1795 Joel Dodge of New Ashford, yeoman, and Sarah his wife sold to John Sweet of Williamstown, yeoman, for £12 in lawful money of Massachusetts, a tract of land in Williamstown "containing six acres, one rood, and thirty-eight rods of Ground," it "being part of the real estate of Daniel Bruster late of said Williamstown deceased, already set off to said Sarah as her share ... situated on the west side of the land set of[f] to sister Polly and joining the east line of Lot No 20 ..." (Northern Berkshire LR 6:243).

Children of Daniel and Mary (Tracy) Brewster, no birth records found (*Brewster Gen.* 1:84-85); marriages at Williamstown (*VR* 107):

    i   SARAH BREWSTER[6], b. say 1771; m. 14 Aug. 1791, JOEL DODGE of New Ashford. In 1795 they sold land she had inherited, as noted above.

            A possible **Dodge** child, *Asariah*, b. Oct. 1792, is buried in South Williamstown Cem. with the family of Sarah's sister Lucy.

    ii   POLLY BREWSTER, b. prob. ca 1774; m. 28 April 1791, LEVI RICH, b. 3 Feb. 1767 Williamstown (*VR* 70), son of Moses and Lydia (___) Rich. No ch. or d. rec. Williamstown. Land set off to "sister Polly" is mentioned in the deed whereby Joel and Sarah Dodge sold Sarah's share in 1795.

    iii LYDIA BREWSTER, b. say 1777; living 1790 (guardianship).

    iv STEPHEN BREWSTER, b. ca 1781; d. at Sackett's Harbor, N.Y., in War of 1812.

    v   LUCY BREWSTER, b. ca 1783; d. Williamstown 26 Dec. 1823 ae 40 (*VR* 173); m. there after int. Sept. 1801 (*VR* 107) MOSES YOUNG JR., b. there 2 March 1779 (*VR* 96), living there 1850, son of Moses and

Susannah (___) Young; bur. South Williamstown Cem. He m. (2) Sally
_____, b. ca Feb. 1775 Williamstown, d. there 22 July 1856 ae 81y 5m,
parents unknown (Mass. VR 102:55).

   Young children rec. Williamstown (*VR* 96-97): 1. *Edward C. Young*[7], b. 19
June 1805. 2. *Maria Young*, b. 2 May 1807. 3. *Horace H. Young*, b. 2 Dec. 1809.
4. *Betsy Ann Young*, b. 1 Dec. 1812. 5. *Eliza Ann Young*, b. 6 Feb. 1817.

Sources cited: *Williamstown VR. Norwich [Conn.] VR.*   Berkshire County Probate Records at
Pittsfield. Northern Berkshire County Deeds at Adams. *Mass. Soldiers & Sailors.* CENSUS: *Heads of
Families 1790 – Mass. Brewster Genealogy* (1906). "Inscriptions in Cemeteries and Burying Grounds
in Williamstown, Mass.," ms. NEHGS (South Williamstown Cemetery).

536.   NATHANIEL BREWSTER[5] (*Priscilla*[4] *Samson, John*[3], *Stephen*[2], *Henry*[1]),
son of William Brewster and his wife Priscilla Samson [115], was born at Duxbury
23 November 1748 and baptized there 11 November 1750 (*VR* 35). He died about
1793 (Rev. pension #W7769). He was a descendant also of *Mayflower* passenger
William Brewster. This Nathaniel is readily confused with his cousin Nathaniel, the
son of Joseph and Jedidah (White) Brewster, who was also in the Norwich area
and later in Vemont.

   Nathaniel Brewster married at Williamstown, 8 December 1777, **ANNA
BURCHARD**, who was born 21 January 1759 and died at Warren, N.Y., 13
September 1850. The marriage is not recorded, but in her application for a
Revolutionary War pension, Anna gave the date and stated that it was performed
by "Elder Dewey a presbyterian minister in the town of Williamstown"; she further
stated that Mr. Isaac Ovett and wife, Mr. Colton and wife, and Benjamin Miller and
wife were present. Anna married, second, at Williamstown 7 December 1798, as
his second wife, ISAAC HOLMES, who was born about 1751 and died at Warren,
Herkimer County, N.Y., 17 December 1843 (pension file). Her second marriage
was performed by Ebenezer Fitch, President of Williamstown College [*sic* -
Williamstown Academy was renamed Williams College that year], and was not
recorded either. Isaac and Anna had three children: a daughter born about
November 1798, and sons Seth Holmes and John Wesley Holmes. Anna's sister,
wife of Benjamin Miller of Williamstown and later Laurens, N.Y., made
depositions supporting her statements.

   Most of what we know about Nathaniel Brewster is from Anna's application
for a pension. She had married and been widowed a second time, and in her
application did not specify for which husband's Revolutionary War service she was
claiming. She gave details about both marriages, but died without having made the
decision that would have allowed her to receive a pension.

Nathaniel Brewster served in the Revolutionary War from Norwich, Conn., as a corporal in the 2nd Co., 6th regiment, from 18 May 1775 to 10 December 1775 (*Conn. Men in Rev.*, 73), first as a lieutenant colonel until July, and then as captain (letter in pension file from Comptroller of Conn.). Anna declared in her deposition that he went into the service at Norwich soon *after* their marriage, as a sergeant and afterwards lieutenant in a company of horse, for three years or more, and she had seen him dressed in military uniform and it was generally understood in the neighborhood that he had been in service of the Revolution.

On 12 May 1777 Nathaniel Brewster of Norwich sold to John Ellis Jr. of Norwich one-half of the farm of his father William Brewster, deceased, excepting his mother's thirds (Norwich LR 22:211).

On 27 January 1779 Nathaniel Brewster shared in the distribution of the estate of his brother Stephen Brewster, late of Norwich, deceased (Norwich District PR #1574). On 24 March 1779 Nathaniel Brewster of Norwich sold to Amos Andrus of Norwich one-quarter of the farm of his father William Brewster, deceased, excepting the dower rights of Mrs. Priscilla Andrus, widow of William Brewster (*ibid.*, 23:262). Amos was probably the brother of John Andrus, second husband of Nathaniel's mother Priscilla (*NEHGR* 80:113), and a cousin of Temperance Andrus who married Nathaniel's brother Timothy.

No land records for this Nathaniel Brewster have been found in Berkshire County. He may be the Nathaniel Brewster listed at Pawlet, Vt., in 1790 with two boys under 16 and three females, on the same page with his brother Timothy and brother-in-law [True]love Brewster (p.41), but this was more likely his cousin of the same name. No listing has been found for Anna Brewster.

The *Vermont Gazette* of 11 December 1795 noted that Anna Brewster of Stamford, Vt., had petitioned the Bennington County Supreme Court for a bill of divorce "as her husband Nathaniel Brewster, has for seven years last, forsaken her without just provocation and he has gone to parts unknown" (*Vermont Newspaper Abstracts*, 150). Bennington court records have been lost to fire, and no divorce is mentioned in the pension papers, which say Nathaniel died about 1793. The most likely explanation is that relatives learned in 1795 of his death two years earlier, making a divorce unnecessary.

The 1800 census listed Isaac Holmes in Williamstown with a household consisting of one man 45+, two women 26-45, two young men and one young woman 16-26, three girls 10-16, and two little boys and two little girls under 10 (p.130). (In 1790 his household consisted of one man, one boy, and six females.) There are land records for Isaac Holmes in Williamstown, but none mentions wife Anna.

In 1850, the year she died, Anna Holmes, aged 91, was listed in the household of her son Seth Holmes, 48, and his wife Mary Ann in Warren, Herkimer County, N.Y. (p.33). In 1857 Seth took steps to claim her pension, stating that he was the only surviving child and administrator of the estate of Isaac Holmes. In Anna's pension file it is several times mentioned that she had a son Ezra Brewster who was living in Cattaraugus County, N.Y. There may have been other children not yet identified.

Child of Nathaniel and Anna (Burchard) Brewster (pension file):

i EZRA BREWSTER⁶, b. ca 1784; d. prob. between 1850 and 1855. He is surely the Ezra Birchard Brewster who m. at Westminster, Worcester Co., 26 March 1817, JOANN STEARNS REED (*VR* 120). Anna's pension records state that her son was living in Cattaraugus Co., N.Y., in 1848. In 1820 Ezra B. Brewster was in Plainfield, N.Y., with a household consisting of one man 26-45, one woman 16-26, and one boy and one girl under 10 (p.177). In 1850 Ezra P. [*sic*] Brewster was a farmer at Otto, Cattaraugus Co., N.Y., ae 66, b. Mass., with three children but no wife (p.310). However, a Joann J. Brewster is listed in the N.Y.S. 1855 census at East Otto (14/14/80), and there is no listing for Ezra after 1850.

Children, last three at home 1850; prob. others: 1. [*Son*] *Brewster*,⁷ b. ca 1818, perhaps *Martin S. Brewster*, b. ca 1819; a harness maker at Ellicottville, N.Y. (near Otto) 1850 (p.233). 2. [*Daughter*] *Brewster*, b. say 1820. 3. *Mary J. Brewster*, b. ca 1832. 4. *Myron Brewster*, b. ca 1835; d. 1870-1880; m. Mary J. Armstrong; he was a teacher Evanston, Ill., 1870 (p.125); she m. (2) Wm. H. Lunt. 5. *Marshall Brewster*, b. ca 1838.

Sources cited: *Duxbury VR. Westminster VR. Williamstown VR.* Norwich, Conn., Deeds. White, *Abstracts of Rev. War Pension Files. Connecticut Men in the Revolution.* Rising, *Vermont Newspaper Abstracts* (2001). *Brewster Genealogy* (1906). CENSUS: *Heads of Families 1790 – Connecticut; Heads of Families 1790 – Vermont;* 1820 Plainfield, Otsego Co., N.Y. (M33-74); 1850 Otto & Ellicottville, Cattaraugus Co., N.Y. (M432-479); Warren, Herkimer Co., N.Y. (M432-513); 1855 New York State, Cattaraugus Co. index online; 1870 Evanston, Cook Co., Ill. (M593-212); 1880 Pontiac, Livingston Co., Ill. (T9-226).

537. LYDIA BREWSTER⁵ (*Priscilla⁴ Samson, John³, Stephen², Henry¹*), daughter of William Brewster and his wife Priscilla Samson [115], was born at Norwich, Conn., 3 January 1757, a descendant also of *Mayflower* passenger William Brewster. She died probably in Rutland County, Vt., in 1840 (*Brewster Gen.* 140).

She married in Connecticut **TRUELOVE BREWSTER**, who was baptized at Duxbury 13 January 1760 (*VR* 35), son of Joseph Jr. and Jedidah (White)

Brewster. He was a descendant of *Mayflower* passengers William Brewster and William White. He disappeared about 1798 (*Brewster Gen.* 140).

Truelove Brewster served in the Revolution as a private in Capt. William Weston's company, June to November 1776, stationed at the Gurnet in defence of Plymouth Harbor; in June 1778 he enlisted again and served eight months guarding the passes of North River (*MSSR* 2:472).

According to *Brewster Genealogy* (p.140), Truelove moved from Duxbury to Connecticut, then to Albany, N.Y., where he was a merchant. About 1798 "he went to New York City to purchase stock, a shipment of which was received at Albany, but as he was never heard from again it is supposed that he met with an unnatural death."

On 27 January 1779 Lydia shared in the distribution of the estate of her brother Stephen Brewster, late of Norwich (Norwich District PR #1574).

Freelove [*sic*] Brewster and Lydia Brewster, both of Norwich, sold land there 17 February 1784, described as bounded by land set off to Timothy Brewster from the estate of his father, William, and by land set off to Daniel Brewster of Williamstown in the same division, it being the whole part set off to Lydia in the same division (Norwich LR 24:452).

He was probably the "Love" Brewster listed in Pawlet, Vt. in 1791 with three boys under 16 and two females (p.41). In 1800 Lydia Brewster was in Pawlet, 26-45 with one girl under 10 and one young woman 16-26 (p.146), listed next to [her brother] Timothy Brewster.

Children of Truelove and Lydia (Brewster) Brewster (*Brewster Gen.*, 140-41; b. rec. not found):

    i   JAMES OBERMAN BREWSTER[6], d. Pawlet, Vt., ae ca 13.

    ii   REBECCA BREWSTER, b. ca 1784, d. 12 Nov. 1871 Battle Creek, Mich.; m. ____ JOHNSON of Pawlet, Vt.; settled at Cape Vincent, N.Y. (*Brewster Gen.*, 140).

        Johnson children (*ibid.*, 140-41): 1. *Augustus Johnson*[7]. 2. *Marcus Johnson*. 3. *Juline Johnson*, d. ca 1888 Detroit, Mich., unm. 4. *Sarah Johnson*, m. (1) ____ Blaine, (2) Judge D. V. Belle; res. Watertown, N.Y.

    iii ETHAN ALLEN BREWSTER, b. ca 1787; m. (1) ____ ____, (2) MARTHA ____, b. ca 1800 in Vt. In 1850 Ethan A. Brewster ae 63, b. Mass. [*sic*], was a farmer in Castleton, Rutland Co., Vt., with Martha ae 50 and three children (p.187). In 1836 he claimed that he had two sons and was supporting his ancient mother (*Brewster Gen.*, 140).

        Children at home 1850: 1. *Samuel F. Brewster*[7], b. ca 1835. 2. *Oliver E. Brewster*, b. ca 1838. 3. *Martha Jane Brewster*, b. ca 1845.

iv AUGUSTUS ELLIOTT BREWSTER, b. 10 Jan. 1790; possibly the
Augustus Brewster ae 55, physician b. Vt., in Royal Oak, Oakland Co.,
Mich., in 1850, with wife Lydia ae 50 b. Vt. and ch. *Lafayette* ae 26 and *Jane*
ae 18, both b. N.Y. (p.238)

v DOLLY BREWSTER, prob. the girl under 10 with mother 1800.

vi LYDIA BREWSTER, d. Albany, N.Y., ae ca 2 years.

Sources cited: *Duxbury VR. Mass. Soldiers & Sailors.* Norwich, Conn., Deeds. *Brewster Genealogy*
(1906). CENSUS: Pawlet, Rutland Co., Vt., 1790 (M637:12), 1800 (M32-52); 1850 Castleton,
Rutland Co., Vt. (M432-927), Royal Oak, Oakland Co., Mich. (M432-359).

538. TIMOTHY BREWSTER⁵ (*Priscilla⁴ Samson, John³, Stephen², Henry¹*), son
of William Brewster and his wife Priscilla Samson [115], was born at Norwich,
Conn., 12 September 1759, a descendant also of *Mayflower* passenger William
Brewster. He died at Ellisburg, N.Y., 28 June 1848 (*Brewster Gen.* 135).

He married probably at Pawlet, Vt., 5 July 1781, **TEMPERANCE
ANDRUS**, who was born in Connecticut, probably at Norwich, 21 October 1759
(b. not rec.) and died at Ellisburg, N.Y., 17 December 1831, daughter of Daniel
and Temperance (Holmes) Andrus (*NEHGR* 70:113-14). She would have been a
cousin of John Andrus, second husband of Timothy Brewster's mother Priscilla
(*ibid.*, 113).

Timothy served as a private in the Revolution. When he applied for a pension
on 15 November 1834, Timothy Brewster of Ellisburg, Jefferson County, N.Y.,
aged 75, deposed that he was born in 1759 at Norwich, Conn. (according to his
father's Bible); he entered the service at Williamstown where he lived in August
1776 and later went to Norwich and enlisted there, and he lived in Pawlet for
about 30 years before moving to Ellisburgh, N.Y. (White, 1:378; file #R1190).

On 27 January 1779 Timothy Brewster shared in the distribution of the estate
of his brother Stephen Brewster, late of Norwich, deceased (Norwich District PR
#1574).

He lived on the Ezra Andrews homestead in Pawlet in 1784 (*Pawlet 100 Years*,
170). Timothy Bruster [*sic*] was among a group of men who signed a petition dated
6 September 1785 "to incorporate a religious society of the Congregational Order
in Pawlet" (*Vt. Religious Cert.*, 111). In 1790 his household at Pawlet consisted of
himself plus two boys under 16 and six females (p.41). In 1800 he was 26-45 and
his household included one woman over 45, one woman 26-45, one young man
and one young woman 16-26, one boy and two girls 10-16, and one boy and two
girls under 10 (p.146).

He was licensed to preach in the Baptist Church in 1791. After he removed in 1813 to Ellisburg, New York, he was pastor of the Baptist Church there.

Children of Timothy and Temperance (Andrews) Brewster, last seven b. Pawlet, Vt. (*Brewster Gen.*, 136):

i EPHRAIM BREWSTER[6], b. Norwich Landing, Vt., 9 April 1782; d. Ellisburg, N.Y., 16 April 1880 (*Brewster Gen.*, 254); m. (1) Pawlet, Vt., 6 Dec. 1804, ADA HARMON (VT VR), b. Dummerston, Vt., 3 Oct. 1791, d. Ellisburg 15 Oct. 1823, dau. of Joel and Chloe (Sheldon) Harmon (*Brewster Gen.*, 254); m. (2) Ellisburg, 13 Nov. 1823, ABIGAIL SMITH, b. Pawlet 11 June 1785, dau. of John Smith (*ibid.*). In 1850 he was a farmer at Ellisburg, N.Y., with son William Roderick at home (p.325).

   Children, first nine with Ada, last two with Abigail (*Brewster Gen.*, 254): 1. *Sheldon Brewster*[7], b. 6 Oct. 1806. 2. *Timothy Brewster*, b. 24 June 1808. 3. *Joel Harmon Brewster*, b. 2 May 1810. 4. *Selina Brewster*, b. 17 Feb. 1812. 5. *Sally Maria Brewster*, b. 5 July 1814. 6. *Adah Almira Brewster*, b. 11 June 1816. 7. *William Roderick Brewster*, b. 19 July 1819 (twin); living 1908 in Montana; m. Elcee Wild. 8. *Anna Antoinette Brewster* (twin), b. 19 July 1819; m. Theron Patterson Salisbury. 9. *Lydia Lavina Brewster*, b. 14 July 1821. 10. *Adoniram Judson Brewster*, b. 21 Oct. 1824. 11. *Angeline Brewster*, b. 25 Sept. 1826; d. 1849 unm.

ii ASENATH BREWSTER, b. 14 Dec. 1783; d. Sandy Creek, N.Y., 21 Nov. 1853 (*Brewster Gen.*, 255); m. Pawlet, 6 Jan. 1803 (VT VR), SALMON SMITH, b. Pawlet 17 May 1781, d. Sandy Creek, N.Y., 30 Oct. 1846, son of Nathaniel and Abigail (Stevens) Smith (*Brewster Gen.*, 255).

   Smith children (*ibid.*): 1. *Ahira B. Smith*[7], b. 27 Oct. 1805. 2. *Nathaniel Smith*, b. 25 Aug. 1810. 3. *Ferris Smith*, b. 28 Sept. 1813; d. unm. in Civil War. 4. *Temperance Ann Smith*, b. 28 Nov. 1819.

iii CLARISSA BREWSTER, b. 21 Nov. 1785; d. 1858/1859, unm. In 1850 she was living at Ellisburg, N.Y., near the families of her brothers Ephraim and Timothy, in a household evidently headed by Barnet Smith ae 40, a farmer, and wife Sarepta ae 31; also there were Lavina Brewster ae 56 and Olive Brewster ae 29.

iv HANNAH BREWSTER, b. 28 Jan. 1788; d. Auburn, Ohio, 1 May 1873; m. Pawlet, Vt., 12 Nov. 1807 (VT VR), HOSEA BARNES, b. Mass. 5 April 1781, d. Auburn, Ohio, 4 March 1854. In 1850 he was a farmer at Auburn with Hannah ae 62, Harriet, and George; sons A.E. and J.H. were nearby (p.264).

   Barnes children, some b. Danby, rest Pawlet, Vt. (*Brewster Gen.*, 255-56): 1. *Alanson Ellis Barnes*[7], b. 12 Dec. 1808; m. Cornitha Finlay. 2. *Fayette Bradford Barnes*, b. 20 June 1811. 3. *Sarah Ann Barnes*, b. 27 June 1813. 4. *Tempa Lorette*

Barnes, b. 8 Sept. 1815; m. Charles Dutton. 5. *Juliette Barnes*, b. 20 April 1818. 6. *John Hosea Barnes*, b. 24 June 1820; m. L. S. ___. 7. *Harriet C. Barnes*, b. 18 March 1822. 8. *Dr. Timothy B. Barnes*, b. 16 April 1827; unm. 9. *George W. Barnes*, b. 6 Oct. 1831; m. Mary Canfield.

v   ELISHA BREWSTER, b. 5 April 1790; d. Ellisburg, N.Y., 12 Dec. 1846; m. (1) Ellisburg, Sept. 1816, EUNICE BREWSTER, b. Rome, N.Y., 20 Jan. 1799, d. Mannsville, N.Y., 4 Aug. 1829, dau. Seth Brewster; m. (2) at Rome, N.Y., Jan. 1830, LAVINA BREWSTER, b. Rome 23 Oct. 1792, d. Eau Claire, Wisc., 6 Dec. 1876, dau. William Brewster (*Brewster Gen.*, 256).

   Children, first four with Eunice, last with Lavina (*ibid.*): 1. *Sarepta Brewster[7]*, b. 27 Feb. 1819. 2. *Olive Morgan Brewster*, b. 30 May 1821; d. 1886 unm. 3. *Alta Selestine Brewster*, b. 29 April 1823; m. William B. Parkhurst. 4. *Eunice Eliza Brewster*, b. 26 July 1829. 5. *Mary Lavina Brewster*, b. 6 Aug. 1833.

vi WILLIAM BREWSTER, b. 12 April 1794; m. at Paris, N.Y., 24 May 1824, SARAH TODD MALTBY, b. ca 1797 in N.Y., d. Auburn Ohio, dau. of Maurice and ___ (Todd) Maltby (*Brewster Gen.*, 257). In 1850 Sarah was head of the household at Ellisburgh, N.Y., but William was listed, ae 56, a farmer b. Vt.; sons William Jackson, Isaac D., Nathaniel, and M. M. were at home, all farmers (p.325). *Brewster Gen.* says William was a farmer and teacher, with a reputation for successfully handling tough children, and that he d. en route to California in 1848 and was buried at sea; perhaps news had not reached the family in 1850.

   Children (*Brewster Gen.*, 257-58; census): 1. *Charles Brewster[7]*, m. Amelia Barker. 2. *Charlotte Frances Fidelia Ann Brewster*, m. (1) John C. Bowler, (2) David Chamberlain. 3. *John Curren Brewster*, b. 5 June 1829; m. Isabella P. Leaton. 4. *William Jackson Brewster*, b. ca 1833. 2. *Isaac Degrasse Brewster*, b. 17 Aug. 1835; m. Elizabeth F. Boggs. 3. *Nathaniel Brewster*, b. ca 1837. 4. *M. M. Brewster* [son], b. ca 1839.

vii ANNA BREWSTER, b. 22 June 1796; d. Bangor, Mich.; m. at Ellisburg, N.Y., 15 March 1826, HIRAM DOOLITTLE, b. 26 Sept. 1794, d. Utica, N.Y., son of Joel and Huldah (Lucas) Doolittle (*Brewster Gen.*, 136).

   Doolittle children (*ibid.*): 1. *Hiram Lucas Doolittle[7]*, b. and d. 26 May 1828. 2. *Catharine Anna Doolittle*, b. 10 Aug. 1829; m. Elias Brewster Ferguson. 3. *Joel Doolittle*, b. 4 March 1831; d. 12 July 1832. 4. *Mary Ellen Doolittle*, b. 7 March 1833; m. James Edwin Ferguson. 5. *Hannah Doolittle*, b. 26 July 1835; d. 10 May 1840.

viii ROBA BREWSTER, b. 13 Jan. 1799; m. LYMAN BREWSTER.

ix TIMOTHY BREWSTER, b. 31 Oct. 1801. *Brewster Gen.* (p.136) says he d. a young man, unm., but he seems to be in the 1850 census at Ellisburg,

N.Y., a farmer, ae 49, b. Vt., with wife AMANDA C. ____, b. ca 1817, and six children (p.324).

    Children at home 1850: 1. *Gardiner Brewster*[7], b. ca 1835. 2. *Addison Brewster,* b. ca 1839. 3. *Elizabeth Brewster,* b. ca 1840. 4. *Ephraim Brewster,* b. ca 1843. 5. *Br—nard Brewster,* b. ca 1844. 6. *Thurstin Brewster,* b. ca 1848.

  x   LYDIA BREWSTER, b. 22 Feb. 1804; d. 16 April 1824, unm.

Sources cited: Vermont Vital Records to 1870. Mrs. Harriet Andross Goodell, "John[2] Andrews of Ipswich, Mass., and Norwich, Conn., and some of his Descendants," *NEHGR* 70 (1916). White, *Abstracts of Rev. War Pension Records,* and File #R1190. *Vermont Religious Certificates* (2003). *Pawlet Vt. for 100 Years* (1876). *Brewster Genealogy* (1906). CENSUS: *1790 Heads of Fam. – Vt.;* 1800 Pawlet, Rutland Co., Vt. (M32-52); 1850 Ellisburg, Jefferson Co., N.Y. (M432-516), Charlotte, Chittenden Co., Vt. (M432-823), Auburn, Geauga Co., Ohio (M432-682).

539. BARTLETT ALDEN[5] (*Elizabeth*[4] *Samson, John*[3], *Stephen*[2], *Henry*[1]), son of Wrestling Alden and his wife Elizabeth Samson [116], was born at Duxbury 22 March 1749/50 (*VR* 15), and died after 1817, when he was received into the Marshfield Church (see *MF16: John Alden,* Part 1:616). He was a descendant also of *Mayflower* passengers John Alden, William Brewster, and Richard Warren. No other record of him has been found.

Sources cited: *Duxbury VR. MF16: John Alden,* Part 1 (1999).

540.   SARAH ALDEN[5] (*Elizabeth*[4] *Samson, John*[3], *Stephen*[2], *Henry*[1]), daughter of Wrestling Alden and his wife Elizabeth Samson [116], was born at Duxbury 21 March 1758 (*VR* 18) and died at Marshfield 17 November 1790 in her 33d year (*VR* 378), a descendant also of *Mayflower* passengers John Alden, William Brewster, and Richard Warren. She is buried in Marshfield Hills Cemetery.

    She married after intentions at Scituate 15 January 1785 (*VR* 2:176), **LEMUEL LAPHAM,** who was born at Marshfield, 14 April 1761 (Rev. pension), son of Joshua and Mary (Wood) Lapham, and died at Pembroke 20 December 1843, aged 84 years, a farmer (*VR* 423).

    Lemuel was of Marshfield when he married second, at Pembroke 25 November 1792 (*VR* 301), LYDIA MAGOUN, who was born at Pembroke 2 October 1771 (*VR* 147), daughter of Aaron and Mary (Church) Magoun, and died at Dorchester 26 February 1858 (Mass. VR 121:190), aged 87y 4m 24d. Lemuel and Lydia had sons Melzar and Robert born at Pembroke (*VR* 135-136).

The 1790 census, taken just months before Sarah died, listed Lemuel at Marshfield with one female in his household (*Heads Fam.*, 171).

Lemuel and later his widow Lydia received a pension for his service in the Revolutionary War (White, 2:2014). In his will dated 9 December 1840, proved March 1844, Lemuel Lapham named his wife Lydia (executrix), and sons Melzar and Robert (Plymouth PR #12,321; 86:98).

Sarah (Alden) Lapham evidently had no surviving children.

Sources cited: *Marshfield VR. Pembroke VR. Scituate VR.* Mass. Vital Records 1841-1910. Plymouth County Probate Records. White, *Genealogical Abstracts of Rev. Pension* Files, citing files W15016, BLW 13873-160-55). *Heads of Fam. in 1790 - Mass.* **See also:** *MF16:* 1: 616.

541. HANNAH ALDEN[5] (*Elizabeth[4] Samson, John[3], Stephen[2], Henry[1]*), daughter of Wrestling Alden and his wife Elizabeth Samson [116], was baptized at Duxbury 20 August 1769 (*VR* 16), a descendant also of *Mayflower* passenger John Alden. She married at Duxbury, 28 November 1791, her cousin **JOHN SAMPSON** [#544], *q.v.* for more information.

542. SYLVANUS[5] **SAMSON** (*John[1-3], Stephen[2], Henry[1]*), son of John Samson [117] and his second wife, Abigail Stetson, was born at Duxbury 8 November 1761 (*Giles Mem.*, 392), and died there 2 March 1848, aged 86 (*VR* 412). He was a descendant also of *Mayflower* passenger William Brewster.

He married at Duxbury, 20 November 1787 (*VR* 302), **SYLVIA CHURCH WESTON**, who was born there 13 May 1768 (*VR* 195), and died there 23 February 1836 of measles, aged 66 or 67, "wife of Sylvanus" (*VR* 412). She was the daughter of Ezra and Sylvia (Church) Weston, and a descendant of *Mayflower* passengers George Soule and Richard Warren. A petition dated July 1823 by Sylvanus Sampson, administrator of the estate of Ezra Weston, names heirs as Ezra Weston, Jr., and the wife of the petitioner (Plymouth PR 57: 352).

The will of John Samson, dated 8 February 1804, proved 11 November 1805, includes a bequest of $2 to his son Sylvanus Samson (Plymouth PR 40:299).

In his will dated 25 July 1838, proved 2nd Monday in April 1848, Sylvanus Sampson of Duxbury named his sons Ezra W. and Sylvanus Jr., daughters Salumett W. Soule, Elizabeth Sampson, and Sylvia C. Owen wife of John; mentioned his deceased wife; and named as executor Samuel K. Williams of Boston (Plymouth PR 90:101).

Children of Sylvanus and Sylvia Church (Weston) Sampson, rec. Duxbury (*VR* 138, 139, 142, 143; *Giles Mem.*, 411):

i   SYLVIA CHURCH[6] SAMPSON, b. 3 Dec. 1788; d. Duxbury 5 Jan. 1798, ae 11m (*VR* 412).

ii   CHURCH SAMPSON, b. 17 Nov. 1790; d. 21 March 1793 (*VR* 409).

iii   SALUMITH WESTON SAMPSON, b. 25 Nov. 1793; m. Duxbury, 5 Feb. 1815 (*VR* 312*)*, OTIS SOULE, b. Duxbury 11 Feb. 1787 (*VR* 164), d. City Point, Va., Sept. 1821 (*MFIP Soule* #438-v), son of Ezekiel and Clynthia (Wadsworth) Soule [Samson #799-v]. In 1850 she was head of a household that included only her sister Elizabeth Sampson (p.60).

    Soule children (*Giles Mem.*, 439, 451): 1. *Salumith Weston Soule[7]*, b. 24 Oct. 1815; d. Duxbury 15 June 1821 ae 6 (*VR* 423). 2. *Mary Townsend Soule*, b. 22 Feb. 1819; m. Joseph A. Sampson (a desc. of Abraham Sampson).

iv   EZRA WESTON SAMPSON, b. 1 Dec. 1797; d. Dedham 15 Jan. 1867 of chronic pleurisy (Mass. VR 203:227); m. 8 Oct. 1820 (Sampson Bible), SELINA WADSWORTH, b. 25 May 1801 (*VR* 180), d. 25 July 1860 of cancer, dau. of Ahira and Deborah (Sprague) Wadsworth (Mass. VR 139:218). Ezra graduated from Harvard in 1816, was an attorney at Braintree and later Dedham; and was appointed clerk of the courts for Norfolk County in 1826 (Sprague 4144).

    Children, first b. Duxbury, next six at Braintree, last three at Dedham (Sampson Bible; *Giles Mem.*, 439): 1. *Augustus Wadsworth[7] Sampson*, b. 5 Aug. 1821. 2. *Frederick Alexander Sampson*, b. 22 March 1823; m. Annie T. Turner. 3. *Charles Edward Sampson*, b. 14 Feb. 1825; d. 1845 at sea. 4. *Elizabeth Church Sampson*, b. 1 Feb. 1827; m. Waldo Colburn. 5. *Ellen Constance Sampson*, b. 4 July 1829; m. Oscar H. Sampson. 6. *Albert De Wight Sampson*, b. 28 Aug. 1831; m. Flora E. Diem. 7. *Mary Otis Sampson*, b. 18 Jan. 1834; m. Henry Cormerais. 8. *Sylvanus Sampson*, b. 13 July 1837; m. Mary Harvey. 9. *Emily Frances Sampson*, b. 12 Sept. 1840; m. Benjamin H. Bailey. 10. *Selina Wadsworth Sampson*, b. 9 June 1842; m. Charles C. Loring.

v   ELIZABETH SAMPSON, b. 13 Oct. 1800; living Duxbury 1850 with sister Salumith W. Soule (p.60).

vi   [SON] SAMPSON, b. and d. 13 Jan. 1803.

vii   SYLVIA CHURCH SAMPSON, b. 21 Oct. 1804; d. 1891 (Mass. VR 419: 123, 531, rec. Cambridge and Kingston); m. Duxbury, 25 Jan. 1835 (*VR* 282), JOHN OWEN of Cambridge, b. ca 1805 Maine, d. 1882 (Mass. VR 338:58). In 1850 he was a "Book Seller" in Cambridge, and their household included Joanna Sullivan ae 20, Mary Halman ae 18, and Richard Evans ae 30, laborer, all b. Ireland (p.145-46).

Owen children at home 1850 (b. dates, *Giles Mem.*, 440): 1. *Elizabeth Sampson Owen[7]*, b. 17 Jan. 1836. 2. *Frances Owen*, b. 6 Sept. 1838. 3. *John Owen*, b. March 1842. 4. *Grace Owen*, b. 27 Sept. 1845.

viii SYLVANUS SAMPSON, b. 12 Oct. 1807; a farmer in Duxbury 1863; m. Duxbury, 20 March 1834 (*VR* 302), MARY CHAPMAN SOULE [#797-vii-2], b. 27 Oct. 1814, dau. of Capt. Richard and Prudence (Loring) Soule. In 1850 their household at Duxbury included Bridget Godfrey ae 21, b. Ireland (p.61).

Children at home 1850 (b. dates, *Giles Mem.*, 440): 1. *Mary Chapman Sampson[7]*, b. 10 Oct. 1835. 2. *Sylvia Church Sampson*, b. 19 March 1837; m. George M. Winslow. 3. *Elizabeth Seaver Sampson*, b. 28 April 1842. 4. *Helen Maria Sampson*, b. 3 Nov. 1844.

Sources cited: *Duxbury VR.* Plymouth County Probate Records. Sampson Bible, NEHGS Gen 1 S 244, follows family of Ezra Weston Sampson. *Giles Memorial* (1864). Sprague, "Braintree Families," ms. at NEHGS (numbers refer to cards). *MFIP George Soule*, pt. 2 (2002). CENSUS: 1850 Duxbury, Plymouth Co. (M432-333) & Cambridge, Middlesex Co. (M432-325

543. LUCY[5] SAMPSON (*John[4-3]*, *Stephen[2]*, *Henry[1]*), daughter of John Sampson [117] and his second wife, Abigail Stetson, was born at Duxbury 2 February 1764 (*Giles Mem.*, 392), and died there 14 February 1854, aged 90, of old age (Mass. VR 85:199). She was a descendant also of *Mayflower* passenger William Brewster. Her death record names her parents and calls her "wife of Wm. Bradford."

She married, 13 November 1788 (*Giles Mem.*, 392), **WILLIAM BRADFORD**, who was born at Duxbury 17 November 1761 (*VR* 32) and died probably after 1804 (father-in-law's will), son of Eliphalet and Hannah (Oldham) Bradford. He was a descendant of *Mayflower* passengers William Bradford and Richard Warren.

In 1790 William Bradford was living in Duxbury with two females in his household (*Heads Fam.*, 169). No Plymouth County probate has been found for him.

The will of John Sampson of Duxbury dated 8 February 1804, proved 11 November 1805, includes a bequest of $100 each to his "six daughters," one of whom was Lucy wife of William Bradford, and they were to share equally in the indoor moveables (Plymouth PR 40:299).

In 1850 Lucy Bradford, aged 86, was living in the household of her daughter at Duxbury (p.57).

Child of William and Lucy (Sampson) Bradford:

i   MARY BRADFORD[6], b. Duxbury 7 Sept. 1789 (*VR* 164, rec. as w. James
    Soule); m. at Duxbury, 9 Oct. 1820 (*VR* 223), JAMES SOULE, b. 20 Sept.
    1784 (*VR* 163), son of James and Abigail (Seaver) (Bosworth) Soule, a
    Henry Samson descendant [#797-vi]. In 1850 James was a shipwright at
    Duxbury, and their household included Mary's mother, Lucy Bradford ae
    86, and Dolly Sampson ae 75 (p.57).
        Soule children, rec. Duxbury (*VR* 161-165), four oldest at home 1850:
    1. *James O. Soule[7]*, b. 26 July 1821. 2. *Lucy B. Soule*, b. 11 July 1823. 3. *Justus Soule*,
    b. 21 Feb. 1825; a machinist 1850. 4. *Henry Martin Soule*, b. 23 Dec. 1826; a
    coppersmith 1850. 5. *Mary Soule*, b. 13 Sept. 1829; d. 10 May 1832 Duxbury (*VR*
    422), rec. as "[son]" so perhaps there were twins. 6. *[son] Soule*, b. 24 June 1832.
    7. *Benjamin True Soule*, bp. 19 Oct. 1837.

Sources cited: *Duxbury VR.* Mass. Vital Records 1841-1910. *MFIP George Soule* part 2 (2002).
Giles Memorial (1864) errs in giving mother of William Bradford as Hannah Prince. CENSUS: *Heads
of Families 1790 – Mass.;* 1850 Duxbury, Plymouth Co. (M432-333).

544.   JOHN[5] SAMPSON (*John[1-3], Stephen[2], Henry[1]*), son of John Samson [117]
and his second wife Abigail Stetson, was born at Duxbury 5 February 1766 (*Giles
Mem.*, 392; not in VR) and died probably about 1795. He was named in his father's
will, dated 8 February 1804, as deceased (Plymouth PR 40:299). He was a mariner,
and a descendant also of *Mayflower* passenger William Brewster.

He married at Duxbury, 28 November 1791 (*VR* 299), **HANNAH ALDEN**,
who was baptized at Duxbury 20 August 1769 (*VR* 16) and died there 10
December 1843, aged 75 (*VR* 409), daughter of Wrestling and Elizabeth (Samson)
Alden and a descendant of *Mayflower* passengers John Alden, William Brewster,
Henry Samson [#541], and Richard Warren.

The will of John Sampson, dated 8 February 1804, proved 11 November 1805,
includes a bequest of $5 to "Hannah Samson, widow, Relict of my deceased son
John" (Plymouth PR 40:299). John and Hannah's daughter was not mentioned.

On 22 November 1805 John Winslow of Duxbury, Esq., was appointed
guardian of Sarah Alden Sampson, a minor under the age of 14 years, daughter of
John Sampson Jr., late of Duxbury, mariner, deceased, and given authority to sue
for her right in the estate of her grandfather John Sampson, late of Duxbury,
yeoman, deceased (Plymouth PR 32:273). On 3 March 1806 the probate court
allowed a claim filed by John Winslow, guardian of Sarah Alden Sampson, only
child of John Sampson Jr. dec'd, for a one-tenth share of her grandfather's estate,
the same she would have had if he had died intestate (*ibid.*, 40:422). On

7 September 1818 a detailed accounting by John Winslow, "late guardian of Sarah A. Sampson of Duxbury ... singlewoman late a minor" was allowed (*ibid.*, 49:455), indicating that Winslow had been managing Sarah's land. In addition to itemized expenses, he claimed $2 per year for nine years of guardianship.

John Sampson probably died at sea. Mrs. Hannah Sampson is buried in the Large Cemetery, Duxbury, with her husband's family.

Children of John Jr. and Hannah (Alden) Sampson, rec. Duxbury:

i   SARAH ALDEN[6] SAMPSON, b. 12 Sept. 1792 (*VR* 142); d. unm. at Duxbury 2 Sept. 1864 of erysipelas (Mass. VR 175:306). There is no probate record for her in Plymouth Co.

ii   ANNE GREENE SAMPSON, b. 20 June 1795; d. Duxbury 1 Sept. 1795, ae 2m 12d (*VR* 137, 408).

Sources cited: *Duxbury VR. Giles Memorial* (1864). Plymouth County Probate Records. Mass. Vital Records 1841-1910.

545.   ANDREW[5] SAMSON (*John[4-3], Stephen[2], Henry[1]*), son of John Samson [117] and his second wife, Abigail Stetson, was born at Duxbury 3 May 1776 (*Giles Mem.*, 382), and died there 18 January 1846, aged 69y 8m, "son of John and Abigail" (*VR* 408).   He was a descendant also of *Mayflower* passenger William Brewster.

He married at Duxbury, 30 December 1804 (*VR* 297), **LYDIA SOULE**, who was born at Duxbury or Marshfield 18 May 1779 (calc.) and died at Marshfield 29 October 1871, aged 92y 5m 11d (Mass. VRs 239:327). She was the daughter of Nathaniel and Abigail (Tolman) Soule and a descendant of *Mayflower* passenger George Soule.

By the will of his father John Sampson, dated 8 February 1804, proved 11 November 1805, Andrew Samson inherited the southerly part of the homestead farm and other property, and was appointed sole executor (Plymouth PR 40:299). On 16 November 1811, following the death of Lydia's father, dower was set off to Abigail, widow of Nathaniel Soule of Duxbury, deceased, and an accounting by the administrator, Thomas W. Peterson, included children Andrew and Lydia Samson (Plymouth PR 44:35, 502).

On 13 April 1846, Samuel Stetson of Duxbury was appointed administrator of the estate of Andrew Samson late of Duxbury, deceased (Plymouth PR 11B:409). Dower was set off to Andrew's widow Lydia on 26 September 1846, and approval was given by his heirs: Wadsworth and Lydia S. Hunt, Charles C. and Arethusa Stevens, and Luther and Abigail T. Thomas (*ibid.*, 88:599; 90:108).

In 1850 Lydia Sampson, aged 69, and her older, unmarried sister-in-law Dolly Sampson were living in Duxbury with the family of her daughter Lydia Hunt (p.60).

Children of Andrew and Lydia (Soule) Sampson (*Duxbury VR* 137, 140):

i   LYDIA S.[6] SAMPSON, b. 29 March 1807; d. Duxbury 1878 (Mass. VR 302:270); m. at Duxbury, 10 Jan. 1830 (VR 268, 300), WADSWORTH HUNT, b. ca 1805, d. Duxbury 1889 (Mass. VR 401:362). Record of his son Cassius' birth calls Wadsworth Hunt a mariner.

> **Hunt** children rec. Duxbury (*VR* 94-96): 1. *Andrew W. Hunt[7]*, b. 4 July 1831. 2. *Henry A. Hunt*, b. 27 Feb. 1833. 3. *Mary S. Hunt*, b. 18 Sept. 1840; d. 1841 (*VR* 388). 4. *Edwin Hunt*, b. 13 Oct. 1842. 5. *Cassius Hunt*, b. 28 May 1844.

ii ARETHUSA SAMPSON, b. 5 Feb. 1813; m. (1) Marshfield, 1 Feb. 183[5] after int. 28 Dec. 1834 (*VR* 275, 286), CHARLES C. STEVENS, b. Marshfield ca 1807, d. there 25 Sept. 1863, consumption, ae 56y 10m 18d, married, shoemaker, son of Nathaniel and Lydia (___) Stevens (Mass. VR 166:299); res. Marshfield 1850 (p.154), no ch. in household or *VR*. Arethusa Stevens ae 56 m. (2) Marshfield, 24 Jan. 1870, JOHN CHURCH, ae 60, widowed, b. Pembroke, son of Cornelius and Huldah (___) Church (Mass. VR 227:387).

iii ABIGAIL T. SAMPSON, b. 23 May 1815; d. Marshfield 1888 (Mass. VR 392:365); m. Duxbury, 7 Jan. 1836 (VR 297, 320) after int. Marshfield 24 Jan. 1836 (*VR* 287), LUTHER THOMAS, b. Marshfield 30 Nov. 1811, d. there 1896 (Mass. VR 464:653), son of Luther and Abigail (___) Thomas (*VR* 103).

> **Thomas** children, first four rec. Marshfield *VR* (103, 318, 325), of Luther & Abigail, last from census; all at home 1860 (p.10): 1. *Anne Thomas[7]*, b. 19 June 1837. 2. *Henry Thomas*, b. 7 Feb. 1839, a mariner 1860. 3. *Alice Jane Thomas*, b. 24 Dec. 1844. 4. *Abby Frances Thomas*, b. May 1848. 5. *George H. Thomas*, b. ca 1852.

Sources cited: *Duxbury VR. Marshfield VR.* Mass. Vital Records 1841-1910. Plymouth Co. Probate Records. *Giles Memorial* (1864). CENSUS: 1850 Plymouth Co.: Duxbury (M432-333), Marshfield (M432-332); 1860 Marshfield, Plymouth Co. (M653-519).

546.   CLARISSA[5] SAMPSON (*John[4-3], Stephen[2], Henry[1]*), daughter of John Sampson [117] and his second wife, Abigail Stetson, was born at Duxbury 28 March 1779 (rec. Brewer, Me.), and died after 1850 when she was living at Scipio, Michigan, with the family of her son Lemuel. She was a descendant also of *Mayflower* passenger William Brewster.

She married at Duxbury, 12 April 1802 (*VR* 236), "he of Plymouth, she of Duxbury," **LEMUEL COBB**, who was born at Plymouth 16 April 1775, son of Lemuel and Hannah (Kempton) Cobb (*VR* 359). He died at Plymouth 4 January 1841 (*VR* 555) in his 66th year and is buried there (*Burial Hill,* #1540). By the terms of the will of John Sampson, dated 8 February 1804, daughter Clarissa Cobb wife of Lemuel Cobb, and her five sisters received $100 each and shared equally in the indoor moveables (Plymouth PR 40:299).

Lemuel Cobb Jr. was listed in the 1810 census at Plymouth with three little boys under 10 years (p.116). In the following decade the family removed to Brewer, Maine, where in 1818 Mrs. Clarissa, wife of Capt. Cobb, was admitted to the Congregational Church (*Bangor Hist. Mag.*, 3:153). The 1830 census listed the household of Lemuel Cobb at Brewer as consisting of a man and a woman 50-60 and one man 20-30 (p.331). He was back in Plymouth by 1840, when Lemuel Cobb of Plymouth, mariner, sued Samuel Thacher of Middleboro, dealer, for money due on a bond dated 19 April 1839 for £80; Thacher defaulted, the bond was chancered, and Cobb recovered £34 10d plus costs (*PCCR*).

William Cooper petitioned for administration on the estate of Lemuel Cobb of Plymouth, 18 January 1841 (Plymouth PR #4564; 10:412); an inventory was taken 2 April (*ibid.*, 83:156). Sylvanus Cobb requested administration 12 April 1841 and was appointed (*ibid.*,10:463); a more complete inventory, consisting of only personal items, was taken 2 August 1841; it included a fur cap and a pair of "silver-bowed spectacles," but most of the value was in "various gold coins of different kingdoms" and some silver (*ibid.*, 83:250). An account filed the same day by Sylvanus Cobb, administrator, included $5 to Lemuel Brown for a coffin, $57 to Hannah Robbins for board, $15 to John Kempton for gravestones, and $60 to himself for journies to and from Maine (83: 467). Distribution was made on 2 November 1841 to Clarissa Cobb the widow, $258.82, and to sons Lemuel Cobb, John K. Cobb, and Sylvanus Cobb, $172.54 $^1/_3$ each (*ibid.*).

In 1850 Clarissa Cobb, aged 70, born in Massachusetts, was listed in the household of her son Lemuel Cobb in Scipio, Hillsdale County, Michigan (p.442).

Children of Lemuel and Clarissa (Samson) Cobb (*Brewer, Me., History*, p. cxliv #23, "Capt. Lemuel Cobb's Family" from VR); not rec. Duxbury or Plymouth:

i   LEMUEL COBB[6], b. 30 Sept. 1805; m. _____ who d. evidently before 1850 when Lemuel was a farmer in Scipio, Mich., and his mother was keeping house for the family (p.442).
    Children at home 1850: 1. *Albion Cobb[7]*, b. Maine ca 1833. 2. *Albert Cobb*, b. Mich. ca 1844. 3. *Eugene Cobb*, b. Mich. ca 1846.

ii JOHN S./K. COBB, b. 17 May 1808; living 1841 (father's estate distrib.).

iii   SYLVANUS COBB, b. 27 Feb. 1810. In 1850 Sulvanus Cobb ae 40, was living in Brewer, Me., with CYNTHIA ____, b. ca 1826 Maine, and four children (p.177). (*Giles Mem.*, 392, confuses him with a Sylvanus Cobb, Universalist clergyman, who d. Boston 30 Oct. 1866 ae 68y 3m 14d, b. Norway, Me., son of Ebenezer and Elizabeth Cobb [Mass. VR 194:127]).

        Children at home 1850, all b. Me.: 1. *Clara Cobb*, b. ca 1844. 2. *William Cobb*, b. ca 1846. 3. *Josephine Cobb*, b. ca 1848. 4. *Maria Cobb*, b. 1850.

Sources cited: *Duxbury VR. Plymouth VR.* Mass. Vital Records 1841-1910. Plymouth County Probate Records. *Giles Memorial* (1864). *Brewer, Maine, History* , includes VR. *A History of the Cobb Family* (1907). CENSUS: 1820 Plymouth, Plymouth Co. (M33-21); Brewer, Penobscot Co., Me., 1830 (M19-51) & 1850 (M432-264); 1840 Scipio, Genesee Co., Mich. (M704-205); 1850 Scipio, Hillsdale Co., Mich. (M432-351).

547. LEWIS⁵ SAMPSON (*John⁴⁻³, Stephen², Henry¹*), son of John Samson [117] and his second wife, Abigail Stetson, was born at Duxbury 5 March 1783 (*Giles Mem.*, 392) and died at Constantia, Oswego County, N.Y., 2 June 1821 aged 38 (Weston Ts; *Giles Mem.*, 392) or 26 June 1822 (cem. rec.). He is buried in an unmarked grave in "Primitive Cemetery in the Town of Mexico, Oswego Co., N.Y." (*Early Settlers of N.Y.*, 2:572). He was a descendant also of *Mayflower* passenger William Brewster.

He married at Duxbury, 28 December 1801 (*VR* 300), **MARY / POLLY WESTON**, who was born there 16 January 1781, the daughter of Joseph and Rebecca (____) Weston (*VR* 193), and died at Mexico, N.Y., 15 July 1861, aged 82 (cem. rec.). She married, second, Jared Blount, with whom she is said to have had a daughter (Weston Ts, 102-03).

By the terms of the will of his father, John Samson, dated 8 February 1804, proved 11 November 1805, Lewis Samson was to receive the northerly part of the homestead farm in Duxbury, half of a woodlot, a salt meadow at the Gurnet, and a meadow at Duck Hill (Plymouth PR 40:299). However, birthplaces of the children as given in the 1850 census indicate that the family removed from Duxbury between 1804 and 1806, first to Vermont, and finally to Mexico, N.Y, by 1810 when Lucy was born.

The initial division of the real estate of Joseph Weston, late of Duxbury deceased, on 26 July 1815, includes Mary Sampson wife of Lewis Sampson; a subsequent division of remaining real estate on 15 November 1830 includes Polly Blount, wife of Jared (Plymouth PR 5:449; 46:27, 50; 50:254; 69:515).

In 1850 Jared Blount, aged 81, born in N.H., and Polly aged 80, born Mass., were living in Mexico, N.Y., in the household of William A. Davis, probably husband of Polly's daughter Lucy (p.93). The families of both John and Lewis Sampson were nearby.

Children of Lewis and Mary/Polly (Weston) Sampson (b. dates from GSH letter, cited below; other information from cem. rec.; Weston Ts, 102, says 14 ch.):

i   WESTON[6] SAMPSON, b. 18 Nov. 1802.

ii GEORGE SAMPSON, b. 18 Feb. 1804 in Mass.; d. 9 Nov. 1889; bur. Mexico, N.Y. (cem. rec.); m. (1) LUCY DAVIS, b. ca 1798, d. 1 May 1859, dau. Asa and Polly (Herring) Davis (cem. rec.); m. (2) MARIETTA ROBERTS, b. 1839, d. 1916 (*ibid.*). In 1850 (p.94), he was a farmer ae 58 [*sic*] with wife Lucy ae 54, b. Mass., and two sons. Sharing the household were [her parents] Asa Davis ae 78, Polly Davis ae 77, and two servants. George and both his wives are buried in the "Primitive Cemetery" at Mexico, N.Y., with his parents.
    Children with Lucy, at home 1850: 1. *Asa L.[7] Sampson*, b. ca 1829. 2. *William Augustus Sampson*, b. ca 1834; d. 28 Jan. 1859 ae 24y 4m 12d; bur. with parents; m. Sarah Brown, d. 16 Feb. 1858 ae 25y 11m (cem. rec.). Child with Marietta: 3. *George Sampson*, b. 1877; d. 1919; bur. Mexico, N.Y. (cem. rec.).

iii JOSEPH SAMPSON, b. 20 Oct. 1806.

iv LEWIS SAMPSON, b. 27 Aug. 1808 in Vt.; d. 12 March 1858 ae 50y 6m; bur. Mexico, N.Y. (cem. rec.). In 1850 he res. Mexico, N.Y. (p.93), a farmer ae 44 b. Vt. [*sic*], with wife RACHEL ____, ae 34, b. N.Y.
    Children at home 1850: 1. *Westren[7]* [*sic*] *Sampson*, b. ca 1836. 2. *Almira Sampson* (twin), b. ca 1837. 3. *Elvira Sampson* (twin), b. ca 1837.

v   LUCY SAMPSON, b. 22 April 1810; prob. m. WILLIAM A. DAVIS, b. ca 1807 N.Y., possibly a brother of the Lucy Davis who m. her brother George Sampson. In 1850 William was a farmer in Mexico, N.Y., with Lucy ae 40, b. N.Y., and their household included Lucy's mother and stepfather, Jared and Polly Blount (p.93). Lucy's brothers Lewis and John Sampson were listed on the same census page.
    Davis children at home 1850: 1. *Charles H. Davis[7]*, b. ca 1832. 2. *Althea R. Davis*, b. ca 1834. 3. *Ann Eliza Davis*, b. ca 1844. 4. *George W. Davis*, b. ca 1847.

vi REBECCA SAMPSON, b. 29 May 1812.

vii JOHN SAMPSON, b. 10 March 1814 in Vt.; d. 1895; bur. Mexico, N.Y. (cem. rec.); m. (1) EVALINA ANDERSON, d. 29 March 1857 ae 39y; m. (2) MARIA E. WIMPLE, b. 1833, d. 1913, dau. of Henry and Eliza (Dickenson) Wimple (*ibid.*). In 1850 John Sampson ae 36 was a farmer in Mexico, N.Y., with wife Evalina ae 33, and children Amelia G., Aurilla, James, and Ellen (p.93); his mother, sister Lucy, and brother Lewis were nearby.

Children with Evalina, at home 1850: 1. *Amelia G.⁷ Sampson*, b. ca 1841. 2. *Ellen Sampson*, b. ca 1842. 3. *Aurilla Sampson*, b. ca 1843. 4. *James Sampson*, b. ca 1845. Child with Maria, bur. with parents: 5. *Mary Sampson*, "dau. J. and M. E." d. 3 May 1866 ae 2m 5d.

viii   ELISHA SAMPSON, b. 12 March 1817.

ix   MARY SAMPSON, b. 4 June 1818.

x   MARTIN SAMPSON, b. 10 March 1819 [cem. rec. says 12 March 1817, but that is b. date of brother Elisha] in Mass.; d. 23 Oct. 1896 "ae 81y 7m" (cem. rec.); m. MARY V. EVARTS, d. 5 Oct. 1867 ae 47y, dau. of Philo and Venera (Carr) Evarts (cem. rec.). In 1850 Martin was a farmer ae 37 [*sic*] in Mexico, N.Y. (p.116), b. Mass., with Mary, ae 28, b. N.Y.

Children at home 1850: 1. *Frederick⁷ Sampson*, b. ca 1847. 2. *Algernon Sampson*, b. ca 1849.

Sources cited: *Duxbury VR.* Plymouth County Probate Records. "Tombstone Inscriptions, Primitive Cemetery in the Town of Mexico, Oswego Co., N.Y.," annotated by Edith Austin Moore, Brooklyn, N.Y., in *Early Settlers of New York*, 2:572 [orig. vol. 7 no. 12, June 1941]. Letter from Mrs. Gerald Rightmire enclosing children's births from Mrs. Gertrude Sampson Hotaling of Mexico, N.Y., to R. M. Sherman. Weston Typescript, Duxbury Library. *Giles Memorial* (1864). CENSUS: 1850 Mexico, Oswego Co., N.Y. (M432-577).

548.   PRISCILLA⁵ SAMPSON (*Elijah⁴, John³, Stephen², Henry¹*), daughter of Elijah Sampson [118] and his wife Ruth Bradford, was born at Duxbury 18 October 1762 (*VR* 141, year only from g.s.; *Giles Mem.*, 393) and died there 18 September 1844, aged 82y 11m [*sic*], "widow of William [Soule] and dau. of Elijah and Ruth Samson" (*VR* 423). She was a descendant also of *Mayflower* passengers John Alden, William Bradford, William Brewster, Thomas Rogers, and Richard Warren. *Giles Memorial* (p.393) cites the full birth dates of Priscilla and her siblings to a list provided by her daughter, but this seems inaccurate, as William and Priscilla had only one daughter, Lucy, and she died in 1814.

She married at Duxbury, 15 April 1784 (*VR* 313), **WILLIAM SOULE**, who was born at Duxbury 25 December 1759 and died there 14 January 1820 (*VR* 161,424), son of Joseph and Mercy (Fullerton) Soule [Samson #801]. He was a descendant also of *Mayflower* passengers George Soule and Myles Standish.

William served as a private in the Revolutionary War (*MSSR* 14:649). In 1790 he lived in Duxbury with two boys under 16 and two females (*Heads of Fam.*, 169).

He died intestate. On 22 September 1824 Samuel Soule of Scituate, and Stephen and Thomas Soule of Duxbury, all mariners, sold their rights in their father's estate to William and Elijah Soule of Duxbury, mariners (Plymouth LR 169:53). An account of Seth Sprague Jr., administrator of the estate of Elijah Soule, shows payments in March 1837 to Samuel Soule, Priscilla Soule, William Soule, and Stephen Soule (Plymouth PR. 79:123).

On 29 November 1845 eldest son [*sic*] Samuel Soule of Sumner, Maine, petitioned that Seth Sprague Jr. be appointed administrator of the estate of Priscilla Soule, widow, late of Duxbury, deceased (Plymouth PR #18858). An account of 12 April 1847 names Priscilla's heirs as William Soule, Stephen Soule, Thomas Soule, and Lucy Soule as attorney for Samuel Soule (*ibid.*, 89:149).

Children of William and Priscilla (Sampson) Soule, all b. probably Duxbury (Family Bible, *MF3*:201):

i LUCY SOULE⁶, b. 20 Sept. 1785 (*Duxbury VR* 163 has only year); d. at Duxbury 26 Jan. 1814, ae 19, unm. (*VR* 161, 422).

ii WILLIAM SOULE, b. 5 Dec. 1787 (*Duxbury VR* 165 has only year, from g.s.); d. 25 Oct. 1858 unm. (*MFIP Soule*, #440-ii). In 1850 he was a yeoman, living with the family of his brother Stephen in Duxbury (p.61).

iii SAMUEL SOULE, b. 15 Sept. 1789; d. Parma, Mich., 14 June 1870 (*MFIP Soule*, #440-iii); m. Duxbury, 24 Feb. 1815 (*ibid.; VR* 313), NANCY (DELANO) BATES, b. ca 1797 in Mass. He was of Sumner, Me., in 1845. The 1850 census lists the family in Rochester, N.Y., Ward 8 (p.379) with Lucy, Thomas H., Mary T., Abby A., and Elijah at home, and Mary Sampson ae 19, and Nancy ae 1, both b. Me. [prob. wife and child of Thomas H.].

Children (*MFIP Soule*, #440-ii), all but last b. Mass: 1. *Lucy S. Soule⁷*, b. 1815. 2. *Thomas Howard Soule*, b. ca 1827; a boatman 1850. 3. *Elizabeth Soule*. 4. *Hannah Soule*. 5. *Rebecca Soule*. 6. *Mary T. Soule*, b. ca 1835. 7. *Abby Soule*, b. ca 1839. 8. *Elijah William Soule*, b. ca 1841 Maine.

iv STEPHEN SOULE, b. 23 June 1792 (*Duxbury VR* 165 has only year, from g.s.); d. Duxbury 4 June 1868 (Duxb. TR [1868]:29); m. there, 16 Nov. 1816 (*VR* 313), LYDIA PIERCE, b. Duxbury 20 Jan. 1799, dau. of Luther and Lydia (Delano) Pierce (*VR* 126, 289). In 1850 he was a mariner, living in Duxbury with Lydia ae 51, the six younger children, and his brother William in his household (p.61).

Children rec. Duxbury (*VR* 161-65): 1. *Lydia Soule⁷*, b. 19 Jan. 1817. 2. *William Soule*, b. 24 Dec. 1819. 3. *Catherine Soule*, b. 8 Nov. 1822. 4. *Louisa Soule*, b. 18 Jan. 1825. 5. *Maria R./ Maria Lavinia Soule*, b. 22 June 1827. 6. *Lawrence Porter Soule*, b. 9 March 1831; a mason 1850. 7. *Fernando Soule*, b. 2 June 1833; a mariner 1850. 8. *Priscilla Bradford Soule*, b. 16 May 1836. 9. *Oscar H. Soule*, b. 14 July 1840.

v THOMAS SOULE, b. 27 May 1795; d. Duxbury 19 Dec. 1864 (Mass. VR 175:307); m. (1) Kingston, 13 Jan. 1828, JUDITH HOLMES (*VR* 281), b. ca

1809, d. Duxbury 12 May 183[2?] in 23rd yr (*VR* 422); m. (2) Duxbury, 25 Nov. 1832 (*VR* 313), DEBORAH DELANO SAMPSON, b. ca 1810, dau. of Stephen and Christiana (Lewis) Sampson [#551-i]. In 1850 he was a mariner ae 55 at Duxbury with Deborah D. ae 40, and children Aurelius, Thomas L., Joseph A., Christiana L., and Judith T. Soule (p.68) Rebecca Sampson ae 75 was next door.

Children rec. Duxbury (*VR* 161-63, 165; *MFIP Soule*, 2:#440-v), with 1st wife Judith: 1. *Judith Thomas Soule*[7], b. 12 Dec. 1830; d.y. Children with 2nd wife Deborah: 2. *Aurelius Soule*, b. 27 Oct. 1833; a shoemaker 1850. 3. *Elijah Soule*, b. 27 Dec. 1836. 4. *Thomas Lloyd Soule*, b. 17 July 1839. 5. *Joseph Alcide Soule*, b. 15 June 1842. 6. *Christiana Lewis Soule*, b. 5 Sept. 1844. 7. *Judith Thomas Soule*, b. 11 March 1847. 8. *Stephen Henry Soule*, b. 1851.

vi   ELIJAH SOULE, b. 3 Aug. 1798; d. Canton, China, 17 Sept. 1834, ae 36, of java fever, rec. Duxbury (*VR* 62,421); unm. (Plymouth PR #18,774).

Sources cited: *Duxbury VR*. Plymouth County Deeds and Probate Records. *Giles Memorial* (1864). *MFIP George Soule*, Part 2 (2002), William Soule [440], which includes spouses but not full birthdates for 7th generation and calls son Thomas's wife *Sarah* Delano Sampson. CENSUS: *Heads of Families 1790* – *Mass.*; 1850 Duxbury, Plymouth Co. (M432-333). **See also:** MD 29:179 (corrects "ae 5" in *Duxbury VR* d. rec. of William). *MF3*:201, cites for children a verified copy of a Family Bible in DAR Lineage #825888.

549.   ABIGAIL[5] **SAMPSON** (*Elijah*[4], *John*[3], *Stephen*[2], *Henry*[1]), daughter of Elijah Samson [118] and his wife Ruth Bradford, was born at Duxbury 16 January 1764 (*Giles Mem.*, 393), baptized there 27 April 1777 (*VR* 144), and died there 24 September 1837 in her 75th year [*sic*], "widow of Isaac" (*VR* 408). She was a descendant also of *Mayflower* passengers John Alden, William Bradford, William Brewster, Thomas Rogers, and Richard Warren.

She married at Duxbury, 20 April 1792 (*VR* 299), **ISAAC SAMPSON**, who was born there 21 March 1760 and died there 29 May 1827 in his 68th year, son of Abner and Deborah (Bisbee) Sampson (*VR* 145, 297, 410), a descendant of Abraham Sampson.

On 18 June 1827 Nathan C. Brewster of Duxbury was appointed administrator of the estate of Isaac Sampson, late of Duxbury, dec'd (Plymouth PR 61:113). On 16 June 1828 allowance was made to the widow, who was not named. (*ibid.*, 66:155)

Nathan C. Brewster was appointed administrator of the estate of the widow Abigail Sampson on 15 January 1828 (*ibid.*, 10A:148). An accounting dated 21 January 1839 lists payments to Weltha Sampson and Bradford Sampson. (*ibid.*, 81:28).

Children of Isaac and Abigail (Sampson) Sampson:

i   WELTHEA[6] SAMPSON, b. 14 Jan. 1793; evidently living, unm., in 1839, but not found in 1850 census.

ii BRADFORD SAMPSON, b. 25 Nov. 1797; d. 28 Dec. 1864, single, farmer, "found dead, probable hemerage ... from Duxbury" (Mass. VR 175:307); poss. the man of that name, ae 53, a farmer, listed in the 1850 census (p.99) in Worcester State Hospital.

iii ABIGAIL SAMPSON, b. 25 Sept. 1800; d. probably before 1839; prob. m. Duxbury, 23 Dec. 1821 (VR 226), NATHAN C[HANDLER] BREWSTER, b. there 30 April 1796, son of Joshua and Deborah (____) Brewster (VR 35). Nathan C. Brewster was administator of his mother-in-law's estate, as noted above.

   Brewster child, rec. Duxbury (VR 35): 1. *Nathan Brewster[7]*, b. 18 Oct. 1823.

Sources cited: *Duxbury VR.* Mass. Vital Records 1841-1910. *Giles Memorial* (1864) cites Abigail's birthdate to a list provided "from a daughter of William and Priscilla Soule [275]," who would have been her niece, but such a daughter has not been identified. Plymouth County Probate Records. CENSUS: 1850 Worcester, Worcester Co. (M432-342)

550.   RUTH[5] SAMPSON (*Elijah[4], John[3], Stephen[2], Henry[1]*), daughter of Elijah Sampson [118] and his wife Ruth Bradford, was born at Duxbury 24 April 1766 or 1767 (VR 142, citing several different recs.), and baptized there 27 April 1777 (VR 147). She died at Duxbury 10 May 1806, aged 40 years, 17 days [*sic*], "wife of Cyrus" (VR 356). She was a descendant also of *Mayflower passengers* John Alden, William Bradford, William Brewster, Thomas Rogers, and Richard Warren.

She married at Duxbury, 5 April 1798, "she dau. of Elijah, he son of Zadock" (VR 33, 224), **CYRUS BREWSTER**, who was born at Duxbury 7 December 1772 (VR 33) and died at Camden, Maine, 18 May 1854, son of Zadock and Lois (Brewster) Brewster. He was a descendant of Pilgrim William Brewster. He married, second, at Duxbury 22 November 1807 (VR 224), Ruth's younger sister, **DEBORAH SAMPSON** (Henry Samson #556), who was born at Duxbury 7 February 1780 and baptized there 16 April 1780 (VR 145). She died at Duxbury 19 March 1860 (Mass. VR 139:291).

In 1800 Cyrus Brewster was listed in the census at Duxbury, himself and his wife 26-45, with one boy under 10. In 1810 the household consisted of a man and a woman 26-45 [second wife, Deborah], one boy and two little girls under 10, and a woman 45 or older; the column that would list a man over 45 has been torn off the page. See also #556.

In 1850 Cyrus Brewster, aged 78, a mariner, was living at Duxbury with wife Deborah aged 70 (p.67). No probate records have been found for Cyrus in Plymouth County or in Maine.

On 21 May 1860 William Bradford was given administration on the estate of Deborah Brewster, late of Duxbury, deceased. The inventory, taken in August 1860 by Eden S. Sampson, Joseph Brewster, and Charles Latham, amounted to $162.50, and the administrator's account dated September 1860 balanced out so that there was no distribution (Plymouth PR #2736).

Children of Cyrus and Ruth (Samson) Brewster, recorded Duxbury (*VR* 33-36):

i ZADOCK BREWSTER[6], b. 21 Aug. 1799; d. St. Ubes, Portugal, 28 Aug. 1827 ae 28y 7d (*Duxb. VR* 356).

ii DORCAS BREWSTER, b. 9 Feb. 1801; d. Duxbury 1891 (Mass. VR 419:511); m. (1) Duxbury, 13 March 1827, GEORGE BARSTOW (*VR* 224), b. 28 Sept. 1798, d. Duxbury 11 Aug. 1835 (*VR* 23, 350). Dorcas m. (2) Duxbury, 1 or 10 Oct. 1839, as his second wife, WILLIAM BRADFORD (*VR* 216), widower of Sarah B. Cushman who d. 10 Dec. 1838 (*VR* 223, 354).

Barstow children, rec. Duxbury: 1. *Zadock B. Barstow*[7], b. ca July 1830; d. 21 Dec. 1830, ae 4m 24d (*VR* 350). 2. *George B. Barstow*, b. 1 Dec. 1832; m. Mary Ann Brown (*VR* 23).

Bradford child, rec. Duxbury: 1. *Hannah R[ogers] Bradford*, b. 4 Nov. 1841 (*VR* 29).

iii SALLY BREWSTER, b. 27 July 1803; d. Duxbury 1881 (Mass. VR 329: 305); m. Duxbury, 20 Nov. 1827, AUGUSTUS SAMPSON, b. Duxbury 24 Aug. 1806, son of Levi and Sophia (McGlauthlin) Sampson (*VR* 137, 226, 300), an Abraham Samson descendant.

Sampson children rec. Duxbury: 1. *Sarah Jane Sampson*[7], b. 14 July 1829 (*VR* 142). 2. *Ruth B. Sampson*, b. 17 Sept. 1831; m. Jonathan S. Ford (*VR* 142). 3. *Augustus C[abot] Sampson*, b. 16 June 1835 (*VR* 137). 4. *Frances E[lett] Sampson*, b. 29 May 1837; d. 14 Sept. 1839 of dysentery (*VR* 139, 409). 5. *Frances E[lliot] Sampson*, b. 5 May 1848 (*VR* 139).

Sources cited: *Duxbury VR*, where entries for this family cite P.R. 35, Elizabeth Bradford Bible, in possession [1911] of Miss Alice Holbrook of Duxbury. *Giles Memorial* (1864) cites Ruth's birthdate to a list provided "from a daughter of William and Priscilla Soule [275]," who would have been her niece. CENSUS: 1850 Duxbury, Plymouth Co. (M432-333). **See also:** *Brewster Genealogy*, 1:137.

551. STEPHEN[5] SAMPSON (*Elijah[4], John[3], Stephen[2], Henry[1]*), son of Elijah Samson [118] and his wife Ruth Bradford, was born at Duxbury 23 September 1768 (*VR* 142; *Giles Mem.*, 393), and baptized there with several of his siblings 27 April 1777. He died at Duxbury 1 April 1846, aged 78y 6m, a mariner, of heart complaint (*VR* 412). He was a descendant also of *Mayflower* passengers John Alden, William Bradford, William Brewster, Thomas Rogers, and Richard Warren.

Stephen married, first, at Duxbury in March 1797 (*sic*, *VR* 302 - prob. 1787), **DEBORAH DELANO**, who was born at Duxbury 25 July 1765 and died there 24 July 1790, aged 24y 10m 21d [*sic*], "wife of Stephen" (*VR* 409), daughter of Reuben and Deborah (____) Delano.

He married, second, at Duxbury 12 December 1802 (*VR* 302), **CHRISTIANA LEWIS**, who was born at Marshfield 11 April 1774 (*VR* 58), and died at Duxbury 20 February 1847, aged 73, "wife of Stephen," daughter of William and Christiana (White) Lewis (*VR* 409). She was a descendant of *Mayflower* passenger William White. Her brother William married Stephen's sister Welthea.

Stephen and both his wives are buried in the Large Cemetery, Duxbury. No probate records have been found for any of them. No daughters are named in the probate record of the estate of William Lewis in 1821 (Plymouth PR 12753).

Child of Stephen and Christiana (Lewis) Samson:

i DEBORAH DELANO[6] SAMPSON, b. 8 Nov. 1809 Duxbury (*VR* 138); d. 1880 (Mass. VR 320:278); m. there 25 Nov. 1832, her cousin THOMAS SOULE 2nd (*VR* 298), son of William and Priscilla (Sampson) Soule [Henry Samson # 548-v]. Her birth record says simply Deborah, but she is called Deborah Delano Sampson in her marriage record. See p. 64 for their children. She may be the "dau. of William and Priscilla Soule" who provided records for *Giles Memorial* ca 1863.

Sources cited: *Duxbury VR. Marshfield VR. Giles Memorial* (1864) cites Stephen's birthdate to a list provided "from a daughter of William and Priscilla Soule," who would have been Stephen's niece, but no such daughter has been identified — could Vinton have meant daughter-*in-law* Deborah Delano (Sampson) Soule?

552. WELTHEA[5] SAMPSON (*Elijah[4], John[3], Stephen[2], Henry[1]*), daughter of Elijah Sampson [118] and his wife Ruth Bradford, was born 22 April 1773 or 1774 (*Giles Mem.*, 393) and baptized with several of her siblings at Duxbury 27 April 1777 (*VR* 147). She died at Spencer 7 December 1845 aged 75y 7m 7d, "widow" (Mass. VR: 21:165). She was descended also from *Mayflower* passengers John Alden, William Bradford, William Brewster, Thomas Rogers, and Richard Warren.

She married at Duxbury, 4 November 1801 after intentions 11 October, he of Marshfield, she of Duxbury (*VR* 166, 273), **WILLIAM LEWIS**, who was born at Marshfield 27 February 1777 (*VR* 58) and died at Plymouth 14 or 15 July 1806 "aged 28" (*CR* 632), son of William and Christiana (White) Lewis. He was a descendant of *Mayflower* passenger William White. His sister Christiana Lewis married, as his second wife, Wealthea's brother Stephen Sampson. William was a shipwright. He built ships in Pembroke in 1796 and 1803, and later removed to Plymouth (*North River Shipbuilding*, 176). He is buried in Burial Hill, Plymouth, where the epitaph on his stone reads: "In Memory of Mᴿ WILLIAM LEWIS / who died July 15, 1806 / in the 30 year / of his age /*My flesh shall slumber in the ground / Till the last trumpets joyful sound / Then burst the chains with sweet surprise / And in my Saviors image rise*" (*Burial Hill* #904, p. 106).

On 6 August 1806 John Adams of Kingston was appointed to administer the estate of William Lewis Jr. late of Plymouth, shipwright, deceased. On 4 September 1807 an allowance was made to the widow (not named), and the estate was found to be insolvent (Plymouth PR 39:79; 44:318). On 21 June 1824 William Lewis of North Bridgewater, cordwainer, was appointed guardian of Welthea Lewis, Ruth B. Lewis, and Benjamin Lewis (minors over 14), children and heirs of William Lewis Jr., late of Plymouth, deceased (*ibid.* 51:249).

On 17 June 1833 William Lewis of North Bridgewater, and Welthea Lewis and Ruth B. Lewis of Duxbury, sold to Benjamin Lewis of Duxbury an undivided part of the estate of their grandfather William Lewis late of Marshfield, deceased; Mary wife of William released her dower rights (Plymouth LR 177:70).

No Worcester County probate records or deeds have been found for Welthea Lewis. As she died in Spencer, she probably was living with the family of her son Benjamin.

Children of William and Welthea (Samson) Lewis, first three rec. Duxbury (*VR* 34), last Marshfield (*VR* 58):

i   WILLIAM LEWIS[6], b. 10 Aug. 1802; d. Brockton 7 May 1875 of dropsy (Mass. VR 275:295); m. MARY PACKARD, b. ca 1803 in Mass; d. Brockton 1886 (Mass. VR 374:319). In 1850 they res. North Bridgewater; William was a shoemaker (p.327), but other records call him a painter.

   Children, all but Wealthy at home 1850, all b. Mass.: 1. *Mary E. Lewis*[7], b. ca 1832. 2. *William B. Lewis*, b. ca 1834; d. 1852 (Mass. VR 67:264). 3. *Horatio P. Lewis*, b. ca 1837. 4. *Benjamin F. Lewis*, b. ca 1839. 5. *Wealthy A. Lewis*, b. N. Bridgewater 7 Oct. 1844 (Mass. VR 11:144); evidently d. y. 5. *Sarah G. Lewis*, b. ca 1848.

ii   WELTHEA LEWIS, b. 9 Jan. 1803 [*sic*]; of Duxbury, unm., 1833.

iii RUTH BRADFORD LEWIS, b. 19 Feb. 1804; of Duxbury, unm., 1833.

iv BENJAMIN LEWIS, b. 25 Sept. 1806; m. 2 March 1834 (*NEHGR* 17:164), NANCY FROST, b. ca 1807 in Mass. In 1850 they res. Spencer, where Benjamin was a depot master (p.36); in 1863 res. S. Boston (*NEHGR* 17:164).

        Lewis children at home 1850, both b. Mass.: 1. *James Lewis*[7], b. ca 1835; a depot assistant 1850. 2. *Catherine Lewis*, b. ca 1839.

Sources cited: *Duxbury VR. Spencer VR. Marshfield VR. Plymouth Church Records.* Mass. Vital Records 1841-1910. *Epitaphs from Burial Hill, Plymouth* (1892). Briggs, *History of Shipbuilding on Old North River* (1899). John H. Sheppard, "Genealogy of the Lewis Family," *NEHGR* 17 (1863). *Giles Memorial* (1864) cites Welthea's birthdate to a list "from a daughter of William and Priscilla Soule," perhaps daughter-in-law Deborah Delano (Sampson) Soule (see p.67). CENSUS: 1850 North Bridgewater, Plymouth Co. (M432-332) & Spencer, Worcester Co. (M432-343).

553. BRADFORD[5] **SAMPSON** (*Elijah*[4], *John*[3], *Stephen*[2], *Henry*[1]), son of Elijah Samson [118] and his wife Ruth Bradford, was born at Duxbury 11 November 1772 (*Giles Mem.*, 393), and died there 24 September 1821 in his 49th year, "son of Elijah and Ruth, husb. of Rebecca Weston" (*VR* 408), a descendant also of *Mayflower* passengers John Alden, William Bradford, William Brewster, Thomas Rogers, and Richard Warren. He was a mariner.

He married at Duxbury, 23 November 1797 (*VR* 297), **REBECCA WESTON**, who was born at Duxbury 16 June 1774 and died there 14 July 1864, aged 90y 28d, a widow, daughter of Thomas and Martha (Chandler) Weston (Mass. VRs Deaths 175:306).

Rebecca Weston of Dartmouth, spinster, was one of several Westons who sold a meadow in Duxbury 5 May 1792 that had been set off to heirs of Thomas Weston late of Duxbury (Plymouth LR 84:115). In March 1801 Elijah Samson of Duxbury gave land there to his son Bradford Samson of Duxbury, mariner (*ibid.*, 89:243).

On 19 November 1821 Benjamin Alden Jr. was appointed administrator of the estate of Bradford Samson late of Duxbury, deceased, and an allowance was ordered to Rebecca, widow of Bradford Samson late of Duxbury, mariner, from his personal estate, on 19 September 1825 (Plymouth PR 52:86; 59:416). On 5 April 1833 Rebecca Samson petitioned that Benjamin Alden Jr. be appointed administrator in her stead of the estates of her two deceased children: Rebecca Sampson and Thomas W. Sampson, both late of Duxbury, deceased (*ibid.*, #17,634).

Rebecca may be the Rebecca Sampson, aged 75, who in 1850 was listed as head of her own household, sharing a dwelling with the family of Thomas and Deborah Delano (Sampson) Soule in Duxbury (see p. 64).

Bradford, Rebecca, and some of their children are buried in the Large Cemetery, Duxbury. No Plymouth County probate records have been found for Rebecca (Weston) Sampson.

Children of Bradford and Rebecca (Weston) Sampson, recorded Duxbury:

i BRADFORD[6] SAMPSON, b. 24 Sept. 1798 (*VR* 137) or 1799 (gs); d. Duxbury 30 Nov. 1832 (*VR* 408); m. Duxbury, 20 Aug. 1825, SOPHIA PETERSON (*VR* 297). "Capt. Bradford Samson fell from the ladder near the roof of his house and so far injured the spinal marrow that no sensation was ever felt below the wound" (*VR* 408 citing CR 1). Sophia W. Sampson, 45, was living in the alms house in Duxbury in 1850 because of "infirmity" (p.63).

Children rec. Duxbury: 1. *Julia' Sampson,* b. 9 Aug. 1830; d. Duxbury 7 or 10 June 1831 ae 10m (*VR* 149, 410). 2. *Sophia Sampson,* b. 1 June 1832, prob. Sophie Bradford Sampson, dau. —— and Sophia W., bp. 8 June 1838 (*VR* 142).

ii PELEG WESTON SAMPSON, b. 17 Oct. 1800; d. Calcutta, India, 28 Dec. 1819, ae 19y 2m 10d (*VR* 141, 411).

iii MARTHA C. SAMPSON, b. 22 Feb. 1804 (*VR* 141); d. 1878 (Mass. VR 302:270); m. Duxbury, 18 Nov. 1832 (*VR* 300), BENJAMIN ALDEN JR., b. Duxbury 22 March 1794, son of Isaiah and Mercy (Weston) Alden (*VR* 15, 211). In 1850 they res. Duxbury (p.85); he was 56, a yeoman, and his sisters Mercy Alden ae 57 and Ruth Alden ae 47, and brother Thomas Alden ae 22, a shoemaker, were in their household.

Alden child, rec. Duxbury (*VR* 17): 1. *Rebecca S. Alden',* b. 28 Oct. 1833; at home 1850.

iv REBECCA SAMPSON, b. 15 Jan. 1806; d. Duxbury 25 April 1831, ae 25, unm. (*VR* 411).

v THOMAS W. SAMPSON, b. 21 July 1815; d. Duxbury 8 Sept. 1824 ae 9y 1m (*VR* 143, 412).

Sources cited: *Duxbury VR.* Mass. Vital Records 1841-1910. Plymouth County Deeds and Probate Records. **See also:** *Giles Memorial* (1864) cites Bradford's birthdate to a list provided by "a daughter of William and Priscilla Soule," who would have been his niece (see note, p. 67). CENSUS: 1850 Duxbury, Plymouth Co. (M432-333).

554. ELIJAH⁵ SAMPSON (*Elijah⁴, John³, Stephen², Henry¹*), son of Elijah Sampson [118] and his wife Ruth Bradford, was baptized at Duxbury with his brothers Zophar and Bartlett on 27 April 1777 (*VR* 144). He was a descendant also of *Mayflower* passengers John Alden, William Bradford, William Brewster, Thomas Rogers, and Richard Warren. No further record of him has been found. *Giles Memorial*, 393, says that he was unmarried.

555. BARTLETT⁵ SAMPSON (*Elijah⁴, John³, Stephen², Henry¹*), son of Elijah Sampson [118] and his wife Ruth Bradford, was born at Duxbury about 1777, and baptized there with his brothers Elijah and Zophar on 27 April 1777 (*VR* 144). He died in the West Indies, a mariner, 6 August 1803 aged 25 "husb. of Welthea," recorded Duxbury (*VR* 408, has 1805, an error – see probate). He was a descendant also of *Mayflower* passengers John Alden, William Bradford, William Brewster, Thomas Rogers, and Richard Warren.

He married at Duxbury in February 1798 (*VR* 297), **WEALTHY WESTON**, who was born about 1776, daughter of Zabdiel and Hannah (Curtis) Weston (*NEHGR* 41:290-91). She died at Duxbury 28 April 1833, aged 57, "former widow [of] Bartlett [Samson]" (*VR* 412, citing g.s.) or 4 May 1833 as "Welthea Lee, wid." (*VR* 391), and is buried in the Large Cemetery, Duxbury. She married, second, after intentions at Duxbury 20 August 1809, ROGGERS LEE ("both of Duxbury") (*MF 20*: 1:99).

The 1800 census lists Bartlett Sampson in Duxbury, two families away from his brother-in-law Cyrus Brewster, and near Elijah Sampson Jr. and Studley Sampson (p.98). His household consisted of himself and wife, 26-45, and one little girl under 10.

On 16 September 1803 Studley Samson of Duxbury was appointed administrator of the estate of Bartlett Samson, late of Duxbury, deceased, mariner (Plymouth PR 17452). In December 1803 real estate was set off to the widow Wealthy Samson (*ibid.*).

The only census records found for a possible Rogers Lee about the right time are in 1820 at Wilmington, N.C., and in 1830 in another, unspecified, town in New Hanover County, N.C. The 1820 entry (p.219) lists him as 26-45 with wife 26-45, two girls 10-16, and one boy under 10. The 1830 census entry (p.145) is for a younger man with a younger family.

No probate record has been found in Plymouth County for Rogers Lee or Wealthy Lee.

In 1850 Welthea and Olive Sampson, aged 48 and listed as twins, were living at Duxbury in the household of Henry Lee, mariner aged 39, and his wife Sally H.

(Turner) (p.62; Lee m., 1840, *Duxbury VR* 273). Olive's death record identifies her as daughter of Bartlett and Wealthy, born Duxbury. Henry Lee's age makes him a possible child of Wealthy and her second husband Roggers Lee. In 1860 Sally H. Lee was a seamstress living in the household of David Turner at Duxbury, and there was no sign of her husband or of Wealthea Sampson.

Children of Bartlett and Wealthy (Weston) Sampson:

i [DAUGHTER][6] SAMSON, b. ca 1799; living 1800 when indicated by census.

ii WELTHEA SAMPSON (twin), b. ca 1802; d. unm. Duxbury 23 March 1884 ae 83, "dau. of Bartlett and Wealthy Sampson" (Mass. VR 356:300).

iii OLIVE W. SAMPSON (twin), b. ca 1802; d. unm. Duxbury 6 Aug. 1855 ae 53 of consumption, "dau. of Bartlett and Wealthy Sampson" (Mass. VR 94:186). In 1850 she and her twin were living in the household of Henry Lee aged 39, a mariner, at Duxbury, and his wife Sally H. (p.62).

prob. iv BARTLETT SAMSON, b. ca 1804 (posthumous ch.); drowned 29 Aug. 1829, ae 25, Duxbury (*VR* 408).

Sources cited: *Duxbury VR.* Mass. Vital Records 1841-1910. Plymouth County Probate Records. Thomas Weston, Jr., "The Descendants of Edmund Weston of Duxbury, Mass., for Five Generations," *NEHGR* 41 [1887]: 290-91, gives Wealthy Weston's parents but is incorrect in its account of earlier generations that claim a line to Myles Standish (*MF5*: 14:13). CENSUS: Duxbury, Plymouth Co., 1800 (M32-16) & 1850 (M432-333); New Hanover Co., N.C., 1820 (M33-84).

556. DEBORAH[5] SAMPSON (*Elijah[4], John[3], Stephen[2], Henry[1]*), daughter of Elijah Sampson [118] and his wife Ruth Bradford, was born at Duxbury 7 February 1780 and baptized there 16 April 1780. She died at Duxbury 19 March 1860 (Mass. VR 139:291). He was a descendant also of *Mayflower* passengers John Alden, William Bradford, William Brewster, Thomas Rogers, and Richard Warren.

She married, at Duxbury 22 November 1807 (VR 224), as his second wife, **CYRUS BREWSTER**, widower of her older sister Ruth Sampson [#550]. He was born at Duxbury 7 December 1772 (VR 33) and died at Camden, Maine, 18 May 1854, son of Zadock and Lois (Brewster) Brewster and a descendant of William Brewster.

For more information, see Family #550, page 65.

Sources cited: *Duxbury VR.* Mass. Vital Records 1841-1910.

557. **ELISHA[5] SAMPSON** (*Elijah[4], John[3], Stephen[2], Henry[1]*), daughter of Elijah Samson [118] and his wife Ruth Bradford, was born at Duxbury about June 1782 (calc.), and died there 6 October 1867, ae 85y 4m 2d, "widowed" (Mass. VR 203:290). He was a descendant also of *Mayflower* passengers John Alden, William Bradford, William Brewster, Thomas Rogers, and Richard Warren.

He married, first, at Duxbury, 22 January 1804 (*VR* 298), **LUCY WESTON**, daughter of Simeon and Honor (Hunt) Weston (Weston Ts, 103). She died at Duxbury 27 March 1828 (original VR, Births 91; "1831" in pub. *VR* 410 an error).

He married, second, at Duxbury, 28 June 1829 (*VR* 298), **REBECCA (WESTON) POLDEN**, widow of John Polden or Poulding who died in 1822 (*VR* 403). Rebecca was born at Duxbury 4 August 1793, daughter of Joseph and Rebecca (Thomas) Weston (*VR* 193) and died there 14 December 1864, aged 72y 4m (Mass. VR 175:306). With her first husband she had Joshua Thomas Polden and John Polden (*VR* 116).

A division of the estate of Joseph Weston, late of Duxbury, deceased (Plymouth PR #22405), on 26 July 1815 included Rebecca Polden. A later division of the remaining real estate on 15 November 1830 included Rebecca Sampson, wife of Elisha.

In 1860 Elisha Sampson, 77, master mariner, was living in Duxbury with Rebecca ae 66, son Bradford ae 26, and Briggs Weston ae 24; both young men were shoemakers (p.100). No probate records for him have been found.

Children of Elisha and Lucy (Weston) Sampson, recorded Duxbury:

i   LUCY[6] SAMPSON, b. 3 Sept. 1804 (*VR* 140) or 1805 (*VR* 92, g.s.); living 1860; m. Duxbury, 28 Jan. 1825 (VR 300), ELISHA HOLMES, b. Duxbury 10 Oct. 1805 (*VR* 92). In 1850 Elisha Holmes ae 44 was a shoemaker in Duxbury, with wife Lucy ae 44, and there were no children at home; in 1860 he was ae 53, a fisherman, with Lucy ae 53, and son William, mariner (p.90).
     Holmes children, rec. Duxbury (*VR* 92): 1. *Lydia Weston Holmes[7]*, b. 12 Dec. 1828. 2. *William E. Holmes*, b. 7 Dec. 1833; with parents 1860. 3. *George T. Holmes*, d. 2 March 1842; bur. Duxbury (*VR* 385).

ii   LYDIA W. SAMPSON, b. 8 Feb. 1807 (*VR* 141).

iii ELISHA SAMPSON Jr, b. 1 May 1809 (*VR* 138); d. Duxbury 24 April 1876, "shot by a gun" (Mass. VR 284:278); m. Duxbury, 4 Feb. 1838 (*VR* 298), ANN WESTON, b. 21 Aug. 1817 (*VR* 187), d. Winthrop 1 Feb. 1899 of influenza, dau. of Joseph and Anne (Cushman) Weston. In 1850 (p.77) and 1860 (p.100) Elisha Sampson, 51, master mariner, and wife Anna, 43, were living next to his father in Duxbury. In his will dated 7 April 1863, proved 13 Nov. 1876, Elisha Sampson Jr., master mariner, left "to each of my children, ten in number, $5 each," and named wife Ann sole executrix (Plymouth PR #17507, 142:37). Weston Ts says he was "shot and killed by an insane son."

Children (*ibid.*): 1. *Lydia A. Sampson*[7], b. ca 1840. 2. *Lucy W. Sampson*, b. ca 1842. 3. *Laura S. Sampson*, b. ca 1844. 4. *Julia F. Sampson*, b. ca 1846. 5. *Abbott Sampson*, b. ca 1848. 6. *Clara M. Sampson*, b. ca 1850. 7. *Simeon Sampson* (twin), b. ca 1852. 8. *Sylvia Sampson* (twin), b. ca 1852. 9. *Elisha Sampson*, b. ca 1857. 10. *[Child] Sampson*, living 1863.

iv SIMEON W. SAMPSON, b. 26 March 1812; d. Duxbury 9 Feb. 1830, ae 18y, typhus fever (*VR* 142, 412).

v JAMES L. SAMPSON, b. 17 Jan. 1815 (*VR* 139); d. prob. Duxbury 1879 (Mass. VR 311:272). In 1850 he was ae 36, a cooper, in the household of his brother Elisha.

vi SELINA SAMPSON, b. 11 May 1818 (*VR* 142; 194 *sub* Weston); d. 31 Aug. 1889; m. Duxbury, 13 Jan. 1837 (as Celina) (*VR* 298), JOSEPH WESTON JR., b. 3 Nov. 1814 (*VR* 191, citing Joseph Weston Family Bible, belonging to William Henry Weston of Duxbury in 1911), d. on Thanksgiving, 28 Nov. 1887, son of Joseph and Anna (Cushman) Weston (Weston Ts, 182). He was a ship carpenter and farmer.

Weston children, five rec. Duxbury (*VR* 190, 191, 193, 195; all in Weston Ts, 182): 1. *William H. Weston*[7], b. 15 May 1840. 2. *George Thomas Weston*, b. 4 Aug. 1842. 3. *Selina James Weston*, b. 4 Aug. 1844 in E. Sudbury; m Lewis Reed. 4. *Oscar Weston*, b. 14 July 1846; m. Sarah Bonney. 5. *Florean Weston*, b. 4 June 1848; m. E. Finney. 6. *Joseph A. Weston*, b. 5 July 1850; d. 1857, diptheria. 7. *Hannah S. Weston*, b. 27 May 1853; d. 1857, diptheria. 8. *Gershom Weston*, b. 23 Sept. 1855. 9. *Albert Weston*, b. 9 May 1858; d. 1864, diptheria.

vii PELEG W. SAMPSON, b. 4 July 1820 (*VR* 142); m. (1) _____; m. (2) Weymouth, 18 Sept. 1861, HANNAH (WHITE) TIRRELL, b. Weymouth, dau. of Silas and Hannah (___) White, 2nd m. for both (Mass. VR 145:228, 235). He served with distinction in the Civil War from Abington (Am. Civil War Soldiers database). In 1870 they were at Abington, where he was working in a boot factory (p.86). In 1880 he was still at Abington, married, but living alone in a boarding house (p.160).

Child at home 1870: 1. *Grace*[7] *Sampson*, b. ca 1867 in Wisconsin.

Children of Elisha and Rebecca (Weston) (Polden) Sampson, rec. Duxbury:

viii JASON SAMPSON, b. 3 Dec. 1830 or 1831 (VR 140); not with parents 1850, and prob. the Jason Sampson ae 20 who was a shoe cutter, living with several other single persons in the household of Abner Curtis, shoe mfr. in Abington (p.227).

ix   BRADFORD SAMPSON, b. 1 April 1834 (VR 137); ae 26, a shoemaker, with
     parents 1860; no death or marriage found in Mass. VR.

Sources cited: *Duxbury VR*, cites Joseph Weston Bible. Original Duxbury Births, p. 91, lists
births of the nine children and death of Lucy. Mass. Vital Records 1841-1910. Weston Typescript,
Duxbury Library. CENSUS: Duxbury, Plymouth Co., 1850 (M432-333) & 1860 (M653-519);
Abington, Plymouth Co., 1850 (M432-332), 1870 (M593-638), 1880 (T9-550, e.d. 557).

558.   SYLVIA[5] SAMPSON (*Elijah[4], John[3], Stephen[2], Henry[1]*), daughter of Elijah
Sampson [118] and his wife Ruth Bradford, was born at Duxbury 26 October 1784
(*Giles Mem.*, 393) and died there 26 January 1853, aged 67 [*sic*], "widow" (Mass. VR
76:197). She was a descendant also of *Mayflower* passengers John Alden, William
Bradford, William Brewster, Thomas Rogers, and Richard Warren.

She married, about 1803, **JAMES BURGESS** (*Giles Mem.*, 393), who was
born at Duxbury 12 January 1784, son of Jacob and Sarah (Glass) Burgess (*VR*
38). He drowned at Bordeaux, France, 23 July 1805 (*VR* 356, citing g.s.). His name
and dates are on a stone in Large Cemetery, Duxbury, where Sylvia is buried.

In 1850 Sylvia Burgess, aged 66, was living in the Duxbury alms house because
she was blind (p.63). No probate records have been found for this family.

Child of James and Sylvia (Sampson) Burgess, recorded Duxbury (*VR* 38):

i   JAMES BURGESS[6], b. 8 Aug. 1804; "[ae] 44, mariner, s. James and Sylvia,"
    when he m. at Duxbury, 6 Feb. 1848, ELLEN HEWES, 24, dau. John and
    Margaret (___) Hewes (*VR* 228). In 1860 they were living in Duxbury with
    the two children (p.93).
        Burgess children at home 1860: 1. *Sylvia J. Burgess[7]*, b. 25 Aug. 1849
    Duxbury (*VR* 38). 2. *William H. Burgess*, b. ca 1854.

Sources cited: *Duxbury VR.* Mass. Vital Records 1841-1910. *Giles Memorial* (1864) cites Sylvia's
birthdate to a list provided by "a daughter of William and Priscilla Soule," who was perhaps
Deborah Delano (Sampson) Soule and thus her niece. CENSUS, Duxbury, Plymouth Co., 1850
(M432-333) & 1860 (M653-519).

559.   DORCAS FISK[5] (*Dorcas Tyler[4], Hannah[3] Samson, Stephen[2], Henry[1]*), daughter
of Ebenezer Fisk and his wife Dorcas Tyler [119], was born 17 October 1740 at
Upton (*VR* 23). She died probably at Wilmington, Vt., after July 1785 when she
was named in her father's will.

She married at Hardwick, 26 February 1761 (*VR* 177), **WATSON
FREEMAN**, who was born at Rochester 25 October 1734 (*VR* 1:132), and died
at Wilmington, Vt., son of John and Joanna (Rickard) Freeman. The will of

Ebenezer Fisk of Shelburne, dated 18 July 1785, names daughter Darcus Freeman (Hampshire PR Box 56:53). He is called a weaver in *Deerfield History* (2:167).

Watson Freeman of Hardwick, husbandman, bought land in Rutland District from Elijah Perry of Sandwich on 19 May 1760 (Worcester LR 45:324). On 11 November 1761 Watson Freeman of Rutland, husbandman, sold land there (*ibid.*, 92:606), and, still of Rutland, bought 222 acres in Deerfield on 20 November 1761 (Hampden LR 18:376). He was of Deerfield on 1 November 1762 when he sold 122 acres there (*ibid.* 19:304). Watson Freeman of Shelburne, yeoman, on 15 April 1777 sold to Ebenezer Fisk Jr. of Shelburne 85 acres there; Dorcas also signed, and witnesses were Eben[r] and Levi Fisk (*ibid.* 28:39). On 20 October 1783 Watson Freeman of Hardwick, yeoman, sold land there to Stephen Johnson of Hardwick; Dorcas Freeman also signed and Susana Freeman was one of the witnesses; Watson acknowledged the deed 8 February 1785 (*ibid.* 98:301).

Watson Freeman and his family were dismissed from the church at Hardwick to Wilmington, Vt. in July 1785 (*Hardwick History*, 381). The 1790 census shows the family at Wilmington with Watson and four other men over 16 and three females (p.57). In 1800 Watson and his wife were over 45; also in the household were one man and one woman 26-45, and two boys and two girls under 10 (p.585).

Children of Watson and Dorcas (Fisk) Freeman, first four rec. Deerfield (*VR* 62), others at Hardwick (*VR* 45-46), all births as "of Watson and Dorcas"; bp. as "of Watson & — ":

    i   CHLOE FREEMAN[6], b. 31 Dec. 1761; d. Wilmington, Vt., 10 July 1841 in 80th yr; m. at Hardwick, 12 Oct. 1780 (*VR* 176), ANDREW HASKEL[L] "of Wilmington" [Vt.], b. by 1755, d. 11 March 1847, son of Thomas and Joanna (Hunt) Haskell; bur. Intervale Cem., Wilmington. In 1800 Andrew Haskell's household consisted of one man 45+, one woman 26-45, one boy 10-16, and four boys and one girl under 10 (p.234).

        Haskell children (VT VR): 1. *Alden Haskell*. 2. *Almira Haskell*, m. James P. Keyes. 3. *Mary Haskell*, m. Jehiel Swift. 4. *Chloe Haskell*, b. 14 Nov. 1781; d. 1787. 5. *Rhoda Haskell*, b. 13 Sept. 1783; m. ___ Boyd. 6. *Lucius Haskell*, b. 30 March 1786; d. 17 April 1786. 7. *Lucius Haskell*, b. 13 July 1788. 8. *Chloe Haskell*, b. 27 April 1791; m. Lawson Pratt. 9. *Thomas Haskell*, b. 28 Aug. 1793. 10. *Hori Haskell*, b. 30 Sept. 1795. 11. *Andrew Haskell*, b. Aug. 1797. 12. *Ephraim Haskell*, b. 1798. 13. *Hiram Haskell*, b. 16 Sept. 1800. 14. *Joanna Haskell*, b. 26 June 1802. 15. *Dorcas Haskell*, b. 9 July 1804; d. 1881 unm.

    ii   DORCAS FREEMAN, b. 22 Dec. 1762.

    iii PHEBE FREEMAN, b. 6 Nov. 1764.

iv   SUSANNA FREEMAN, b. 16 June 1766; living, unm., 1783 when she witnessed a deed at Hardwick.

v   ALPHEUS FREEMAN, b. 23 Nov. 1767.

vi   JOHN FREEMAN, b. 10 Aug. 1769; possibly the John Freeman in Wilmington 1800, 26-45 with wife the same age and 1 boy and 1 girl under 10 (p.585).

vii   ELIJAH FREEMAN, b. 7 Oct. 1770.

viii WATSON FREEMAN, b. 2 May 1772; d. Wilmington, Vt., 27 Jan. 1827 ae 56 (VT VR); m.Wilmington, 1 Oct. 1798 (VT VR; TR 1:108), SALLY PARMELEE, who d. Wilmington 8 July 1856 ae 88 (*ibid.*); both bur. Riverview Cem. In 1850 Sally and her son Watson were in the household of James Miller (p.233). On 5 March 1828 Jonathan Flagg was appointed administrator of the estate of Watson Freeman, late of Wilmington, deceased, including the homestead farm of 125 acres in Wilmington and his undivided one-eighth of land of John Flagg (the source of this land right is unknown). Sally, widow of Capt. Watson Freeman, petitioned for her thirds 11 Sept. 1828 (Marlboro Dist. PR, 12:223, 234, 339).

    Freeman children, b. Wilmington, Vt. (VT VR citing A:39): 1. *Watson Freeman[7]*, b. 24 Jan. 1805. 2. *Sally Freeman*, b. 30 Dec. 1806.

ix   MERCY FREEMAN, b. 14 March 1774.

x   ABIGAIL FREEMAN, b. 8 March 1777.

xi   EDMAND/EDWARD FREEMAN, bp. 11 July 1779.

xii   EUNICE FREEMAN, bp. 24 Feb. 1782.

Sources cited: *Deerfield VR. Hardwick VR.* Vermont Vital Records to 1870. Hampden County Deeds at Springfield. Hampshire County Probates at Northampton. Worcester County Deeds. *History of Deerfield* (1896). *History of Hardwick* (1882). CENSUS: Wilmington, Windham Co., Vt., 1790 (M637-12), 1800 (M432-929), 1850 (M432-929).

560.   ELIZABETH FISK[5] (*Dorcas Tyler[4], Hannah[3] Samson, Stephen[2], Henry[1]*), daughter of Ebenezer Fisk and his wife Dorcas Tyler [119], was born 28 January 1742/3 at Upton (*VR* 23) and died 22 October 1791 at Hardwick (VR 276).

She married at Hardwick, 12 November 1761 (*VR* 135), Ensign **DAVID ALLEN**, who was born at Hardwick 18 August 1738 to Joseph and Mercy (Livermore) Allen and died there 5 August 1799, aged 60y 11m 1d (*VR* 276; town rec. say 1800; g.s. & CRs 1799). He married, second, 22 January 1794 (*Hardwick History*, 326), LYDIA WOODS of New Braintree.

Elizabeth is named in the 1785 will of her father as Elizabeth *Alln*, and the family is listed in the 1790 census at Hardwick as *Allin*, with four males over 16, one boy under 16, and four females (*Heads of Fam.*, 221).

During the Colonial Wars, David served from 13 March to 1 December 1758 in Capt. Samuel Robinson's company, probably on an expedition to Canada (*Hardwick History*, 265-66). David Allen "was a very active citizen, selectman, and assessor ..." (*ibid.*, 326).

In his will dated 21 June 1799, proved 3 September 1799, David Allen of Hardwick named his wife Lydia; sons David and Moses; daughters Rhoda wife of David Barnard, Eunice wife of John Earl, and Elizabeth wife of Isaac Wing; daughter-in-law Keziah widow of son Daniel Allen dec'd; Daniel's children Betsey (under 18) and Justus (under 21); and daughters Mercy Allen, Lydia Allen (under 18); sons David and Moses Allen to be executors. (Worcester PR A1215).

Children of David and Elizabeth (Fisk) Allen, recorded Hardwick (*VR* 11-12):

    i   RHODA ALLEN[6], b. 27 Sept. 1763; d. Shelburne 30 Oct. 1813 ae 50y (*VR* 146); m. at Hardwick, 4 March 1783 (*VR* 136), DAVID BARNARD of Shelburne, b. ca 1757, d. Shelburne 6 June 1834 ae 77 (*VR* 145). He m. (2) at Shelburne, 12 May 1815 (*VR* 91), Keziah (Wing) Allen, widow of Rhoda's brother Daniel Allen.

        Barnard children rec. Shelburne (births *VR* 18-20, deaths *VR* 145): 1. *Betsey Barnard*, b. 30 Oct. 1783; d. 30 Nov. 1788. 2. *Ira Barnard*, b. 13 Oct. 1785. 3. *Dorinda Barnard*, b. 24 Sept. 1787. 4. *Allen Barnard*, b. 4 Jan. 1790. 5. *Anson Barnard*, b. 22 Feb. 1792. 6. *David Barnard Jr.*, b. 17 March 1794. 7. *Apollos Earl Barnard*, b. 6 Nov. 1795. 8. *Luther Barnard*, b. 24 March 1798. 9. *Calvin Barnard*, b. 21 Nov. 1801; d. 19 Aug. 1803. 10. *Calvin Barnard 2d*, b. 4 Aug. 1805. 11. *Betsey Barnard 2d*, b. 25 Jan. 1809; m. Worthington Nims.

    ii   EUNICE ALLEN, b. 22 Aug. 1765; d. 10 Sept. 1850; m. at Hardwick, 2 Oct. 1785 (*VR* 135), JOHN EARL, d. 17 Dec. 1832 ae 70 (*Hardwick History*, 366).

        Earl children (*ibid.*): 1. *Apollos Earl*, b. 1786; d. 1792. 2. *Lucius Earl*, b. 1788; d. 1794. 3. *Arathusa Earl*, b. 1790; d. 1792. 4. *Lewis Earl*, b. ca 1793. 5. *[Infant] Earl*, d. 10 Oct. 1795 ae 11d; 6. *Arathusa Earl*, b. 1799; m. Bradford Spooner. 7. *Luke Earl*, b. 1802. 8. *John F. Earl*, b. 1803; m. Chloe Keith.

    iii   DANIEL ALLEN, b. 20 Sept. 1767; d. Hardwick 1 Dec. 1796 ae 29y 2m 1w 3d (*VR* 276); m. at Hardwick, 20 Jan. 1791 (*VR* 135), KEZIA WING, b. Hardwick 19 Sept. 1765, dau. James and Ruth (____) Wing (*VR* 127). She m. (2) at Shelburne 12 May 1815 (*VR* 91), David Barnard, widower of her sister-in-law Rhoda Allen.

        Children rec. Hardwick (*VR* 11-12): 1. *Betsey Allen[7]*, b. 21 July 1792. 2. *Justis Allen*, b. 27 Aug. 1795.

iv ELIZABETH ALLEN, b. 27 Oct. 1768; m. at Hardwick, 24 Jan. 1793 (*Hardwick History*, 541), ISAAC WING, b. Hardwick 14 June 1770, son of James and Ruth (___) Wing (*VR* 127). Elizabeth wife of Isaac Wing was named in her father's will dated 21 June 1799.

v DAVID ALLEN, b. 12 May 1771; d. Hardwick 20 Jan. 1835 ae 63y (*VR* 276); m. at Hardwick, 27 April 1794 (*VR* 135), RUTH DEXTER, who d. 26 March 1847 ae 74y 7d (*VR* 277).

Children rec. Hardwick (births *VR* 11-12; deaths *VR* 277): 1. *Luthera Allen*[7], b. 12 April 1795. 2. *Clarissa Allen*, b. 7 Oct. 1796. 3. *Anna Allen*, d. Hardwick 14 Nov. 1803 ae 6y 10m 1w 4d [*sic* - must be error considering Clarissa's birth date]. 4. *Willard Allen*, b. 8 Feb. 1801. 5. *Mary Allen*, b. April 1803; d. 24 Nov. 1803 ae 7m 3w. 6. *Mary Allen*, b. 18 Nov. 1804; d. 3 Aug. 1818 ae 13y. 7. *Anna Allen*, b. 21 Nov. 1811.

vi MARY/MERCY ALLEN, b. 11 May 1773; d. Hardwick 6 Jan. 1857, unm. (Mass. VR 113:139). In 1850 Mercy Allen ae 77 res. Hardwick in the household of her nephew Anson F. Allen (p.334).

vii MOSES ALLEN, b. 9 March 1776; d. Hardwick 15 Sept. 1777 ae 18m 6d (*VR* 277).

viii MOSES ALLEN, b. 11 March 1779; d. Hardwick 22 April 1843 ae 64, of anaemia (*VR* 277); m. (1) at Hardwick, 20 or 26 June 1802 (*VR* 136), ANNA PAIGE, (2) after int. Hardwick in 1825, FANNY RICE.

Children rec. Hardwick, with Anna (*VR* 11): 1. *Almira Warner Allen*[7], b. 20 Feb. 1803. 2. *Anson Fish Allen*, b. 31 Jan. 1805. 3. *Daniel Freeman Allen*, b. 20 Sept. 1807. 4. *James Franklin Allen*, b. 26 Feb. 1809. 5. *Calvin Paige Allen*, b. 30 June 1811.

ix LYDIA ALLEN, b. 18 Oct. 1784; m. at Hardwick, 21 Jan. 1800 (*VR* 136), DANIEL MATTHEWS.

Sources cited: *Hardwick VR Shelburne VR.* Mass. Vital Records 1841-1910. Worcester County Probate Records. Paige, *History of Hardwick* (1883). CENSUS: 1850 Hardwick, Worcester Co. (M432-344).

561. JONATHAN FISK[5] (*Dorcas Tyler*[4], *Hannah*[3] *Samson, Stephen*[2], *Henry*[1]), son of Ebenezer Fisk and his wife Dorcas Tyler [119], was born at Upton 19 September 1746 (*VR* 24) and died probably after 1800 in Otsego County, N.Y.

He was of Shelburne when he married at Hardwick, 18 January 1770 (*VR* 229), **HANNAH RICE**, daughter of Solomon and Anna (Rice) Rice (*Hardwick History*, 461). She was born 25 March 1748 at Upton (*VR* 46), and died after 1775.

Jonathan Fisk of Shelburne, yeoman, bought 126 acres there on 3 March 1773 (Hampden LR 12:226). On 23 March 1774 Jonathan and Hannah both signed a deed selling the "west end of my land ... 52 acres"; Levi Fisk was a witness (*ibid.* 12:813). On 20 January 1775 when Jonathan and Hannah sold 53 acres in Shelburne, Watson Freeman was a witness; Jonathan acknowledged the deed 1 April 1778 (*ibid.* 16:227).

He is probably the Jonathan Fisk who was a private in Capt. Hugh McClallen's company of minute-men, Col. Samuel Williams' regiment, which marched 20 April 1775 in response to the alarm of 19 April 1775, from Colrain and Shelburne; serving 15½ days (*MSSR* 5:724). He may also be the Jonathan Fisk who was a private in Capt. William Tucker's company, Col. Jacob Gerrish's regiment, from 6 July 1778 to 1 December 1778, serving 4 months and 26 days (*ibid.*).

He may be the Jonathan Fisk in the 1790 census at German Flatts, Montgomery County, N.Y., with one man, three boys under 16, and one female (p.54). In 1791 Otsego County was established from Montgomery County, and in 1800 Jonathan Fisk was in the town of Otsego, Otsego County, N.Y. (p.12), himself and his wife over 45, with two young men 16-26, one boy and two girls 10-16, and two boys and two girls under 10. A younger Jonathan Fisk, a Solomon Fisk, and an "Abr^a" Fisk were listed nearby. However, the situation is confused by the fact that a different Jonathan Fisk applied for a Revolutionary War pension from Otsego County (White, 1202). The latter man stated that he was from Windham County, Conn., born about 1755, and his wife was Mehitable Smith. He also had sons Asa and Jonathan Jr., who, among several other children, were living in 1839 (*ibid.*).

Nothing helpful has been found in Otsego County Deeds or Probates.

Children of Jonathan and Hannah (Rice) Fisk, rec. Shelburne (*VR* 37, 38, 40):

i   ASA FISK[6], b. 13 July 1771.

ii   SOLOMON FISK, b. 2 May 1773; d. Taylor, N.Y., 1857; m. DIADAMA BILL (cem. rec. son Solomon). He was living in Otsego, N.Y. (p.590), in 1800, ae 26-45, with wife 16-26 and one boy and two girls under 10. In 1830 he was in Solon, Cortland Co., N.Y., himself and wife 50-60, one young man 15-20, and one woman 30-40 (p.10). In 1850 he was a laborer, ae 77, b. Mass., living at Taylor, Cortland Co., N.Y., in the household of Solomon Fisk Jr. ae 37, farmer b. N.Y. (p.185); his wife had evidently died.

Children included (1850 census): 1. *Diadama Fisk*[7], b. ca 1810; m. William Lieber. 2. *Solomon Fisk*, b. 18 Aug. 1813 Exeter, Otsego Co., N.Y.; m. Mercy Stone; bur. Taylor Cem., Otsego Co. ? 3. *Elijah Fisk*.

iii JONATHAN FISK, b. 27 Sept. 1775. A man of that name was living in Otsego, N.Y., in 1800, himself and wife aged 16-26, with one little boy under 10 (p.26).

Sources cited: *Hardwick VR. Shelburne VR. Upton VR.* Hampden County Deeds at Springfield. *Mass. Soldiers & Sailors.* White, *Abstracts of Rev. War Pension Files.* Information re d. and 2 ch. of son Solomon from *Ancestry of Louise Crankshaw,* online at ancestry.com, unverified. CENSUS: *Heads of Families 1790 –* N.Y.; 1800 Otsego, Otsego County, N.Y. (M32-25); 1830 Solon, Cortland Co., N.Y. (M19-88); 1850 Taylor, Cortland Co., N.Y. (M432-493). **See also:** F. C. Pierce, *History of the Fiske Family* (1896).

562. EBENEZER FISK⁵ (*Dorcas Tyler⁴, Hannah³ Samson, Stephen², Henry¹*), son of Ebenezer Fisk and his wife Dorcas Tyler [119], was born at Sutton 9 September 1749, his birth recorded at Upton (*VR* 23), and died 9 June 1841, aged 92, at Shelburne (*VR* 157). His birth, evidently adjusted for the calendar change, is recorded at Shelburne as 20 September 1749 (*VR* 37). His death record refers to him as the "father of missionary Pliny Fisk ... an original settler."

He married at Shelburne, 28 September 1779 (*VR* 103), **SARAH BARNARD**, whose birth on 24 July 1754 is recorded there (*VR* 40); she died there 15 April 1816 aged 62 years, as "wife of Ebenezer Jr." (*VR* 158). She was the daughter of John and Ruth (Catlin) Barnard, born at "Road Town" (now Shutesbury) 24 [or 5?] July 1754 (*Deerfield History,* 2:67), and thus sister of Samuel Barnard, the husband of Ebenezer's sister Abigail [#564]. John Barnard of Shutesbury in his will dated 27 April 1780, proved 13 February 1786, named among others his wife Ruth, son Samuel, and daughter Sarah Fisk (Hampshire PR 15:85; Box 9:48).

In 1790 Ebenezer Fisk Jr. was listed in Shelburne (p.122) with a household consisting of one man, five boys under 16, and three females, living next to his father.

In his will dated 4 May 1817, proved 24 August 1841, Ebenezer Fisk of Shelburne named his sons Ebenezer Fisk Jr., Levi Fisk, and Pliny Fisk; daughters Sarah Forbush, Lovina Taggart, and Ruth Fisk; and son Rufus, executor (Franklin PR # 1727). One of the witnesses was James Bishop.

Children of Ebenezer and Sarah (Barnard) Fisk, recorded Shelburne (*VR* 37-40):

i RUFUS FISK⁶, b. 22 March 1781; d. Shelburne in 1840 ae 59 yrs; m. at Shelburne (*VR* 104), 18 Nov. 1807, HANNAH WOODWARD. She is prob. the Hannah Fisk ae 70 in 1850 in the household of David O. Fisk ae 29 and Laura ae 30 (p.225).

Children rec. Shelburne (births, *VR* 37-40; deaths, *VR* 157): 1. *Anna Fisk[7]*, b. 22 April 1808; m. Daniel Fisk. 2. *Fidelia Fisk*, b. 24 Oct. 1810; d. 11 July 1814. 3. *Laura Fisk*, b. 30 Oct. 1813; d. 6 March 1815. 4. *Fidelia Fisk 2d*, b. 1 May 1816; teacher at Mt. Holyoke College and a missionary; d. unm. 5. *Laura Fisk 2d*, b. 20 May 1819; m. David O. Fisk. 6. *Hannah W. Fisk*, bp. June 1822; d. 17 Oct. 1840 ae 17. (See *Fiske Family*, 204-205 for further data.)

ii　SARAH FISK, b. 17 May 1783; d. 3 Feb. 1854 (*Fiske Family*, 132); m. 13 March 1814, ABIJAH FORBUSH, b. 11 May 1779 Upton (*VR* 26), d. Shelburne 27 June 1845 of inflammation of brain (*VR* 159), son of Samuel Jr. and Beaulah (Whitney) Forbush (*VR* 98). He was a farmer.

Forbush children, rec. Shelburne (*VR* 40, 104, 159): 1. *Catherine Forbush[7]*, b. 24 April 1815; d. 11 May 1843, unm. 2. *Sarah Forbush*, b. 20 Oct. 1816; d. 17 May 1858 (*Fiske Family*, 132). 3. *Lucy W. Forbush*, b. 2 May 1818; m. Shelburne, 8 Sept. 1840, Edmund Skinner of Charlemont. 4. *Rufus Forbush*, b. 1 Oct. 1820; d. Shelburne of consumption 27 Feb. 1846, a botanic physician; m. Shelburne, 28 Oct. 1841, Mabel Julia A. Dole. 5. *Alfred Forbush*, b. 19 Dec. 1822; d. 11 March 1825. 6. *Jane Forbush*, b. 12 Nov. 1828; d. of dropsy 2 April 1842, ae 15y 4m 14d.

iii　EBENEZER FISK 3d, Dea., b. 18 April 1785; d. Shelburne 25 Dec. 1846 (*VR* 157); of Shelburne when he m. at Abington, 22 Oct. 1809 (*VR* 2:74), HANNAH TERRILL, b. 2 March 1784 (calc.), d. 11 May 1866 ae 82y 2m 9d, dau. Isaac and Mary (___) Tyrrell (Mass. VR 202:256).

Children rec. Shelburne (*VR* 37-39): 1. *Clarissa Terrill Fisk[7]*, b. 18 Feb. 1811. 2. *Francis Alvares Fisk*, b. 8 July 1813. 3. *Ebenezer Fisk*, b. 28 Aug. 1815. 4. *Pliny Fisk*, b. 30 July 1817; m. Orilla Peck. 5. *Daniel Taggart Fisk*, b. 29 March 1819. 6. *Charlotte Fisk*, b. 6 April 1822. 7. *Isaac Terrill Fisk*, b. 27 July 1824. 8. *Henry Martyn Fisk*, b. 21 Aug. 1827. 9. *Levi Parsons Fisk*, b. 29 March 1829. (See *Fiske Family*, .204 for further data.)

iv　LOVINA FISK, b. 8 July 1787; m. at Shelburne 1815 (*VR* 103) after int. Nov. 1815 at Colrain (*VR* 79), DANIEL TAGGART of Colrain, prob. b. Colrain 25 April 1783, d. 22 Nov. 1818 in 36th yr, son of Rev. Samuel and Elizabeth (___) Taggart (*Colrain VR* 42, 185). *Fiske Family* (p. 132) reports a descendant, Mrs. Elizabeth Beals of Batavia, N.Y.

v　LEVI FISK, b. 21 Feb. 1790; d. Byron, N.Y., 16 Sept. 1878; of "Bergen" [Byron], Genesee Co., N.Y., when he m. at Buckland, 27 April 1819 (*VR* 83), CYNTHIA COLEMAN, b. 18 May 1779, d. 12 July 1852. He became a successful woolen manufacturer in Byron, N.Y., served in the New York State Legislature, and was a deacon in the Presbyterian Church.

Children: 1. *John Sheldon Fisk[7]*, b. 27 Feb. 1820. 2. *Clarissa Fisk*, b. 8 Sept. 1822. 3. *Cynthia C. Fisk*, b. 28 Jan. 1824. 4. *Abigail Fisk*, b. 25 Oct. 1825; m.

Loren Green, res. Calif. 5. *Eusebia N. Fisk*, b. 19 April 1829. 6. *Pliny Beyroot Fisk*, b. 8 Dec. 1830. (See *Fiske Family*, 205 for further data.)

vi   PLINY FISK, Rev., b. 24 June 1792; d. Beirut, Syria, 23 Oct. 1825 ae 33 yrs, rec. Shelburne (*VR* 157). A graduate of Middlebury College and Andover Theological Seminary, he became a missionary. (See *Fiske Family*, 132 for further data.)

vii   JOHN FISK, b. 2 May 1795; d. Shelburne (*VR* 157) 18 April 1819, ae 24.

viii RUTH FISK, b. 19 July 1797; m. at Shelburne (*VR* 104), in [Oct.] 1825, JAMES BISHOP. In 1850 he was a farmer in Shelburne ae 51, with Ruth ae 52, five children, and Sally Bishop ae 76 (p.225).

  Bishop children at home 1850: 1. *Pliny F. Bishop[7]*, b. ca 1834. 2. *Fanny F. Bishop*, b. ca 1836. 3. *Sarah B. Bishop*, b. ca 1838. 4. *Rufus Bishop*, b. ca 1841. 5. *Lucy F. Bishop*, b. ca 1844.

Sources cited: *Colrain VR. Shelburne VR* cites P.R. 14 (gen. notes of W. O. Taylor, in Arms Library, Shelburne Falls) for most of the records of this family, and includes Sarah's maiden name. *Upton VR.* Franklin County Probate Records at Greenfield. Hampshire County Probate Records at Northampton. *History of Deerfield* (1920). Jones, *History of Waitsfield, Vermont* (1909). Pierce, *Fiske Family* (1896) (p.195 lists births of children, but Sarah's is given as 1784), adds information on Rufus, Ebenezer, and Levi. CENSUS: *Heads of Families 1790 – Mass.*; 1850 Shelburne, Franklin Co. (M432-317).

563.   LEVI FISK[5] (*Dorcas Tyler[4], Hannah[3] Samson, Stephen[2], Henry[1]*), son of Ebenezer Fisk and his wife Dorcas Tyler [119], was born at Upton 16 December 1751 (*VR* 24) and died 6 May 1827, aged 75, at Shelburne (*VR* 157).

He married 7 October 1783 at Shelburne (*VR* 103), **HANNAH SEVER** of New London. She died 15 August 1841 at Shelburne (*VR* 157), aged 97, as "Hannah, wid. Levi, formerly of New London." Her name on her gravestone is inscribed "Johanna." No record of her birth has been found. They are buried in Old North Cemetery, also known as Hill Cemetery.

On 15 April 1775 Ebenezer Fisk Jr. of Shelburne sold to his brother Levi Fisk of Shelburne 29 acres there "purchased of my father Ebenezer" (Hampshire LR 19:305).

The 1790 census listed Levi Fisk in Shelburne with one man 16 and upwards and three females (p.122).

Levi Fisk of Shelburne sold land in Shelburne "that bounds on my father Ebenezer's land" on 29 September 1800, acknowledging the deed the same day (*ibid.*,103:320).

In his will dated 1 January 1821, presented 28 August 1827, Levi Fisk of Shelburne, yeoman, left "to beloved wife" one third of his estate, and the rest to Hannah Comstock and Lewis Farnsworth, "who has lived with me many years," who was to be executor (Franklin PR #1739). The day after making his will, 2 January 1821, Levi Fisk of Shelburne, yeoman, sold to Lewis Farnsworth of Shelburne one half of the "farm I now live on in Shelburne," about 50 acres, acknowledging the same day (Franklin LR 67:49).

No record has been found of children born to Levi and Hannah (Sever) Fisk, and Pierce (*Fiske Family*, 105) states that Levi died without issue.

Sources cited: *Upton VR. Shelburne VR.* Franklin County Deeds and Probate Records. Hampshire County Deeds. Pierce, *History of Fiske Family* (1896). **See also:** *Tyler Genealogy*, p. 100; Jones, *History of Waitsfield, Vermont* (1909), p. 310.

564.   ABIGAIL FISK[5] (*Dorcas Tyler[4], Hannah[3] Samson, Stephen[2], Henry[1]*), daughter of Ebenezer Fisk and his wife Dorcas Tyler [119], was born 7 October 1755 at Upton (*VR* 22) and died at Waitsfield, Vt., 7 March 1833 (*Waitsfield History*, 223).

She married at Shelburne, 26 November 1782 (*VR* 91, 102), **SAMUEL BARNARD**, who was born 12 October 1752 "at Road Town" (later Shutesbury), and died at Waitsfield, Vt., 3 November 1809 (*Waitsfield History*, 223), son of John and Ruth (Catlin) Barnard, and brother of Sarah Barnard who married Abigail's brother Ebenezer [#562]. The will of John Barnard of Shutesbury, yeoman, dated 27 April 1780, proved 13 February 1786, names among others his wife Ruth, son Samuel, and daughter Sarah Fisk (Hampshire PR 15:85; Box 9 #48).

Joseph Barnard of Deerfield on 1 June 1781 sold to Samuel Barnard of Shelburne, yeoman, 69 acres in Shelburne in lot #75 (Hampden LR 18:404). Samuel Barnard of Shelburne, yeoman, sold two parcels of land there on 18 June 1789 and 27 May 1790; Abigail also signed (Franklin LR 1:434-45). On 27 April 1792 Samuel and Abigail sold more land in Shelburne; both acknowledged 2 January 1793 (*ibid.*, 7:83). The family evidently removed to Waitsfield, Vt., in 1793.

Children of Samuel and Abigail (Fisk) Barnard, first four rec. Shelburne (*VR* 19-20), fifth prob. b. Shelburne, rest b. Waitsfield; all listed *Waitsfield History* (p.223):

    i   EBENEZER BARNARD[6], b. 30 Nov. 1783 Shelburne; d. Waitsfield, Vt., 21 Feb. 1872; m. 19 Jan. 1808, EXPERIENCE CHILDS, b. Deerfield 27 Jan. 1784, d. Waitsfield, Vt., 30 Sept. 1870, dau. of Samuel and Mary (Nims) Childs (*Waitsfield History*, 274; *Fiske*, 106, calls her Experience

Fiske). They lived on his parents' homestead farm in Waitsfield, and in 1850 were sharing it with the family of son William C. (p.12).

Children, b. Waitsfield, Vt.: 1. *Samuel Barnard*[7], b. 1808; d. 2 Nov. 1808. 2. *Joanna Barnard*, b. 10 Oct. 1810; m. Anson Fisk. 3. *Luana Barnard*, b. 12 March 1813; m. Seth Taylor. 4. *William Childs Barnard*, b. 11 Oct. 1815; m. Marilla ___. 5. *Caroline Samantha Barnard*, b. 29 April 1819; d. 30 Sept. 1819. 6. *Pliny Fisk Barnard*, b. 9 Nov. 1820; d. 28 May 1908; m. Julia Hobart.

ii   RUTH BARNARD, b. 28 June 1785; d. 13 April 1789 ae 3y, Shelburne (*VR* 146).

iii   JOANNA BARNARD, b. 24 April 1787; d. 29 Sept. 1803.

iv   PHILENA BARNARD, b. 4 Feb. 1789; m. at Waitsfield, Vt., 28 April 1811, RUFUS CHILDS, b. Deerfield 28 Feb. 1786, d. River Falls, Wisc., 26 Sept. 1861, son of Samuel and Mary (Nims) Childs (*Waitsfield History*, 274). In 1850 he was a farmer at Waitsfield living next to the Ebenezer Barnard family (p.12).

Childs children, b. Waitsfield, Vt. (*ibid.*): 1. *Samuel Barnard Childs*[7], b. 21 Jan. 1812; d. 1 April 1813. 2. *Sophronia Hortensia Childs*, b. 22 Aug. 1813; d. unm., Wisc. 3. *Philena Emeline Childs*, b. 13 Oct. 1816; d. unm. 4. *Sarah Childs*, b. 17 April 1819; d. 30 Aug. 1845, unm. 5. *Samuel Barnard Childs*, b. 9 June 1821; m. Laura ___. 6. *Marian Childs*, b. 11 July 1823; d. 13 Oct. 1896, Alexandria, Minn., unm. 7. *Edwin Ruthven Childs*, b. 25 Oct. 1827; d. unm. 8. *Jane Dorcas Childs*, b. 1830; d. 1863, unm. 9. *Israel Childs*, b. 1834; m. Delia Miles.

v   RUTH BARNARD, b. 25 April 1791; d. Genoa, Cayuga Co., N.Y., 9 Dec. 1868; m. at Waitsfield, Vt., 26 Oct. 1817, ITHAMAR SMITH, b. Shelburne 6 June 1787; d. Genoa, N.Y., 10 Feb. 1862, son of Salah and Mary (Taylor) Smith (*Waitsfield History*, 223). In 1850 Orsamus [*sic*] Smith ae 60 was a farmer at Waitsfield, with Ruth ae 60, Abigail ae 17, and Francis ae 15, near the families of her brother Ebenezer and sister Philena Childs (p.12).

Smith children, b. Waitsfield, Vt.: 1. *Chauncey Smith*[7], b. 11 Jan. 1819; m. Caroline E. Marshall. 2. *Salah Smith*, b. 13 Jan. 1821; d. 1823. 3. *Selah Smith*, b. 2 Aug. 1823; m. Elizabeth A. Bailey. 4. *Luther Leland Smith*, b. 23 June 1825; m. Elvira Matthews. 5. *Lucinda Wright Smith*, b. 31 Oct. 1828; m. John B. Taylor. 6. *Abigail Hortensia Smith*, b. 16 Jan. 1833; m. Charles Caverno. 7. *Francis Barnard Smith*, b. 1 Sept. 1835; m. Clara Carpenter.

vi   LINUS BARNARD, b. 13 Aug. 1793; d. Waitsfield, Vt., 8 March 1875; m. 22 May 1825, LUCY STICKNEY of Berlin, Vt., d. 27 March 1879 ae 86 (*Waitsfield History*, 224). In 1850 he was a farmer at Waitsfield ae 57 with Lucy ae 58 and Corless [*sic*] ae 21 (p.12).

Children (*Waitsfield History*, 224): 1. *John Barnard*[6], b. 11 June 1827; m. Frances M. Vandercook. 2. *Don Carlos Barnard*, b. 19 May 1829; m. Melissa A. Wheeler. 3. *Horace Barnard*, b. 6 Dec. 1836; d. 3 Jan. 1839.

vii   ABIGAIL BARNARD, b. 18 April 1796; m. ca 1832, JOHN HOBART of Middlesex, Vt. (*Waitsfield History*, 223). In 1850 he was a merchant ae 69 in Middlesex, b. N.H., with Abigail ae 54, Lucy ae 14, Ruth ae 11, and James ae 5; the household included Mariane Stearns ae 28 and Jane C. Stearns ae 20 (p.260).

   Hobart children, first three at home 1850, all in *Waitsfield History*: 1. *Lucy Irene Hobart*[7], b. ca 1836. 2. *Ruth Philena Hobart*, b. ca 1839. 3. *James Hobart*, b. ca 1844. 4. *Mary Hobart*.

Sources cited: *Shelburne VR. Upton VR.* Jones, *History of Waitsfield, Vermont* (1909). Pierce, *Fiske Genealogy* (1896). CENSUS: 1850 Washington Co., Vt., Middlesex (M432-928) & Waitsfield (M432-928). **See also:** *History of Deerfield*, 2: 67, 70; Waitsfield Town Vital Records and Cemetery Records, on microfilm.

---

565.   JOHN FISK[5] (*Dorcas Tyler*[4], *Hannah*[3] Samson, *Stephen*[2], *Henry*[1]), son of Ebenezer Fisk and his wife Dorcas Tyler [119], was born 27 September 1757 at Grafton (*VR* 50) and died 16 November 1811, aged 54 years, at Deerfield (*VR* 283). He is buried in the Old Cemetery, South Deerfield.

He was of Shelburne on 17 August 1786 when he published marriage intentions at Conway (*VR* 148) with **ANNA LELAND**. She was probably the daughter Anna born to James and Lucy (Warren) Leland 6 February 1760 at Grafton (*VR* 83, 242). She evidently died between 1799 (last rec. child) and 1804.

John Fisk of Ashfield married, second, after intentions there 3 March 1804 (*VR* 157), **DELIGHT BIGELOW** of Colchester, Conn. She was born at Colchester 24 December 1759, daughter of Jonathan and Elizabeth (Otis) Bigelow (*Greene Fam.*, 19n).

John Fisk of Conway bought land there 16 May 1789, and on the following 22 August sold 3½ acres there to James Leland of Conway (Franklin LR 3:223, 1:362). In the 1790 census he was listed at Conway (indexed as Fish), with a household consisting of two men over 16, one boy, and three females; James Leland was just before him on the list, and William Warren just before Leland (p.108). In 1792 John Fisk sold land in Conway to Nathaniel Goddard (*ibid.*, 4:445), and in 1795 to the Conway Southeastern School District (*ibid.*, 7:613).

The family has not been located on the 1800 census. In 1804 John married his second wife, and on 25 April 1809 John Fisk and Delight his wife, "late of Ashfield now of Deerfield" sold to Joseph Rice 2nd, for $500, one-fourth part of a piece of land in Conway, part of Lot No. 77, and one-fourth part of the Grist Mill standing on the premises; both signed (Franklin LR 27:42).

In 1810 John Fisk was in Deerfield, head of a household consisting of one man and one woman 45+, three young men 16-26, and one girl 10-16 (p.247).

Administration on the estate of John Fisk, who died leaving goods in Deerfield, was given to Delight Fisk on 21 July 1812 (Franklin PR #1735, 1:61). The inventory taken 10 August 1812 amounted to $221.79 and consisted of clothing and farming and household goods (*ibid.*, 1:63, 83). The account of Delight Fisk dated 22 June 1813 included "allowance to myself as widow," and a list of debts; the account was declared insolvent 16 February 1813 (*ibid.*).

Children of John and Anna (Leland) Fisk recorded Conway (*VR* 48-49):

  i   MARTHA FISK[6], b. prob. 1 Sept. 1788 (rec. says 1778, an obvious error).

  ii   HORACE FISK, b. 8 July 1790; d. unm. in Philadelphia (*Fiske Family* 131).

  iii [INFANT] FISK, d. 1793 Conway, "infant of Mr. Fisk," rec. bet. 5 Aug. and 23 Oct. (*VR* 232).

  iii ANNA FISK, b. 10 Sept. 1795.

  iv BETSEY FISK, b. 12 Feb. 1799.

Sources cited: *Ashfield VR. Conway VR. Deerfield VR. Grafton VR.* Franklin County Deeds and Probate Records at Greenfield. *Greene (Green) Family of Plymouth Colony* (1909). Pierce, *Fiske Family* (1896), has minimal account of this family. CENSUS: 1790 Conway, Hampshire Co. (M637-4); 1810 Deerfield, Franklin Co. (M252-19).

566. SARAH FISK[5] (*Dorcas Tyler[4], Hannah[3] Samson, Stephen[2], Henry[1]*), daughter of Ebenezer Fisk and his wife Dorcas Tyler [119], was born probably at Upton or Grafton about 1760, between the birthdates of her brothers John (1757) and Simeon (1762). The 1810 census indicates that she was 45 or over, thus born before 1765. Record of her birth has not been found, but her marriage record at Shelburne (*VR* 104) calls her "aunt of Pliny," who was the son of Ebenezer Fisk Jr. [562].* Sarah is not mentioned in her father's will dated 1785 (Hampshire PR Box 56 #53), but a comparison of the date of her marriage with the birthdate of her first child (if both are correct) offers a possible explanation for her exclusion

* Pliny was not born until nine years after Sarah's marriage, indicating that the information was added or the record was delayed. The entry in the VR is keyed to P.R. 14, "Genealogical notes of W.O. Taylor, at Arms Library, Shelburne Falls."

from that document. She died at Lockport, N.Y., 4 August 1843 (Rev. pension), aged 82, and is buried there with her husband in Cold Spring Cemetery.

She was called of Shelburne when she married there, 11 March 1783, **SILAS PARSONS** "of Goshen," born 26 September 1761, son of Benjamin and Rebecca (____) Parsons. His birthdate and parents' names are included in the marriage record at Shelburne (*VR* 104), and his Revolutionary War pension provides the information that he was born at Northampton and died at Lockport, N.Y., 6 December 1839, in his 79th year.

Silas Parsons served as a private in the Revolutionary War, in Capt. Enoch Chapin's company, Col. Jacob Gerrish's regiment, which was detached from the Hampshire County militia to guard stores at Springfield and Brookfield. He enlisted 6 July 1778 and was discharged 31 December 1778 after serving 5 months and 28 days (*MSSR* 11:978).

There is a detailed account of the Reverend Silas Parsons in the 2002 *Parsons Family* (pp.477-80). After their marriage Silas and Sarah lived in Shelburne for a few years, but were in Goshen by 1790. He was admitted to the Congregational Church there from Shelburne on 5 September 1790, and Sarah was admitted 2 July 1798; both were dismissed by letter to Charlemont in August 1802. Silas studied theology and was ordained pastor of the church in Sudbury, Vt., on 1 February 1807. About 1816 the family removed to New York, and in 1827 he became the first resident minister in what is now the town of Lockport.

The 1790 census lists the family in Goshen, with one male over 16, three boys under 16, and two females. In 1810 (p.136) they were at Sudbury, Vt., with a household consisting of a man and a woman 45 or older, one woman 26-45, four young men and one young woman 16-26, two girls 10-16, and one boy under 10.

When he applied for a pension on 14 September 1832, Silas Parsons was living in Lockport, N.Y. He stated that he had lived in Massachusetts until 1803 when he moved to Rutland, Vt.; in 1816 he moved to New York, where he lived at several places in that state before settling at Lockport. He made an affidavit in Niagara County on 21 August 1833 in support of the pension application of his brother Justin, who had enlisted at Pawlet, Vt., as a substitute for him.

On 11 June 1844, Silas Parsons Jr. gave the marriage record of his parents and their dates of death. He stated that they left children: Clarissa Hovey, Seth Parsons, William Parsons, Paulina Pratt, Theodosia Warner, Sarah Pratt, and Silas Parsons. (White, 2609, 2610).

Children of Silas and Sarah (Fisk) Parsons, first three born prob. at Shelburne, rest at Goshen where all were baptized (information not otherwise cited from *Parsons Fam.*, 480, *q.v.* for further sources):

i CLARISSA PARSONS[6], b. 10 March 1783 [*sic*]; bp. 10 March 1791; d. 17 May 1851, prob. Barre, Orleans Co., N.Y.; m. Sudbury, Vt., 23 May 1808 by her father, to Rev. JONATHAN HOVEY, b. 8 July 1782 Mansfield, Conn., son of Jonathan and Rebecca (Hall) Hovey, Middlebury College 1806.

    Hovey children (*Parsons 1912*, 163): 1. *Clarissa Hovey[7]*, b. 30 April 1809 Waybridge, Vt. 2. *Jonathan Parsons Hovey*, b. 11 Oct. 1810. 3. *Erastus S. Hovey*, b. 9 May 1812. 4. *John Hovey*, b. 17 Feb. 1814. 5. *John Storrs Hovey*, b. 19 Dec. 1816. 6. *Mary Paulina Hovey*, b. 6 Feb. 1822.

ii SETH PARSONS, b. 26 Feb. 1785; bp. 10 March 1791; d. Milwaukee, Wisc., 31 March 1851; m. at Sudbury, Vt., 16 June 1808, ACHSAH TENNEY, b. there 6 July 1787, dau. of Alvin Tenney.

    Parsons children (*Parsons 1912*, 164; correc. *Parsons 1920*): 1. *Melinda Fiske Parsons[7]*, b. 1809; m. ___ Fellows. 2. *William Leonard Parsons*, b. 25 June 1811; m. (1) Mary Ann Holt, (2) Lavinia Bradley, (3) Lucy Ann Seymour. 3. *Erastus Parsons*, b. 28 July 1813; m. (1) Alzina Grimes, (2) Angelina Grimes.

iii ERASTUS PARSONS, b. ca Dec. 1787; bp. 10 March 1791; d. Sudbury, Vt., 11 May 1813, ae 25y 5m, unm. He attended Middlebury College and taught school at Pittsford, Vt.

iv WILLIAM PARSONS, b. 18 Oct. 1790; bp. 10 March 1791; d. Lockport, N.Y., 4 April 1855 in 65th yr; m. at East Bloomfield, N.Y., 18 July 1817, AMANDA EGGLESTON, dau. of Nathaniel and Mary (Webster) Eggleston.

    Children (*Parsons 1912*, 165): 1. *Mary Louise Parsons[7]*, b. 8 Oct. 1818; m. (1) Oliver Perry Gooding, (2) Rollin Gooding Parks. 2. *William Fiske Parsons*, b. 12 Oct. 1820; m. Rebecca Hosmer. 3. *Levi Eggleston Parsons*, b. 8 Oct. 1822; m. Mary J. Baldwin. 4. *Nathaniel Spencer Parsons*, b. 4 May 1825; m. Julia M. Barber. 5. *Jonathan Child Parsons*, b. 12 Sept. 1835; m. (1) Martha Coryell, (2) Nettie Hoeger. 6. *Amanda Maria Parsons*, b. 4 Dec. 1837; m. Edwin Upson.

v PAULINA PARSONS, b. 10 Oct. 1792; bp. 30 Dec. 1792; living 1883 Lockport; m. 3 April 1825, GEORGE W. PRATT.

vi AUSTIN PARSONS, b. 6 Aug. 1794; bp. 20 Sept. 1794; said to have gone South and been lost to his family.

vii THEODOCIA PARSONS, b. 16 Sept. 1796; bp. as Dosia, 23 Oct. 1796; d. Lockport, N.Y., 3 Sept. 1883; m. Sudbury, Vt., 6 Oct. 1814, WARREN WARNER, b. 16 May 1794, son of Joseph and Asenath (Little) Warner.

    Warner children (*Parsons 1912*, 165): 1. *Joseph Warren Warner[7]*, b. 15 Jan. 1822. 2. *Julia Jackson Warner*, b. 10 June 1828; m. William Thayer Rogers.

viii SARAH PARSONS, b. 12 Aug. 1798; bp. 23 Oct. 1798; living 1883 Batavia, N.Y.; m. Sept. 1824 RICHARD PRATT.

ix   SILAS PARSONS, bp. 5 Nov. 1801; d. 9 Nov. 1803 Charlemont (*Parsons 1920*; d. date shown as a birth in *Charlemont VR* 61).

xi   SILAS PARSONS, b. 14 Nov. 1806; living 1883 at Buffalo, N.Y.; m. at Penfield, N.Y., 11 Aug. 1829 by his father, to LUCY VAN DAKE, b. 15 July 1807, d. Lockport 10 May 1871, dau. of Luke and Betsey (Baker) Van Dake.

    Children (*Parsons 1912,* 166): 1. *Silas Richmond Parsons*[7], b. 23 May 1834; d. 1854. 2. *William Wisner Parsons*, b. 10 Aug. 1838; m. Lucy Jane Havens.

Sources cited: *Shelburne VR. Mass. Soldiers & Sailors.* White, *Abstracts of Revolutionary War Pension Files,* 2609, citing W2661 (Justin Parsons) and 2610, citing W26841 (Silas Parsons). H. Barrus, *History of Goshen* (1881). Henry Parsons, *Parsons Family,* Vol. 1 (1912), Vol. 2 (1920). Gerald J. Parsons, *The Parsons Family, Volume One* (2002), includes further information and cites more primary sources.

567.   SIMEON FISK[5] (*Dorcas Tyler*[4], *Hannah*[3] *Samson, Stephen*[2], *Henry*[1]), son of Ebenezer Fisk and his wife Dorcas Tyler [119], was born 15 July 1762 at Hardwick (*Hardwick Hist.,* 376; *VR* 44) and died 8 September 1838 at Goshen, N.Y., aged 77 (*Goshen Church,* 97).

He married 10 January 1784 at Shelburne (*VR* 104), **DINAH WHITCOMB,** who was born in 1761 and died in Goshen in 1845 (*Fiske Family,* 131).

Simeon Fisk was named executor in the will of his father, Ebenezer Fisk of Shelburne, dated 18 July 1785 and proved 6 August following (Hampshire PR Box 56 #53). In 1790 Simeon Fisk was listed at Shelburne with a household consisting of one man, three boys under 16, and two females (*Heads of Fam.,* 122). In 1800, stilll in Shelburne (p.321), Simeon and his wife were 45+, and their household included a man and a woman 26-45, two young women 16-26, three boys 10-16, and two boys under 10.

On 21 November 1807 Simeon Fisk of Shelburne, yeoman, sold to Rufus Fisk and Ebenezer Fisk Jr., for $2,000, about 96 acres in the northwest part of Shelburne, Lot no. 64, bounded by land of David Barnard, Elijah Sever, Ebenezer Fisk, and Aaron White, and also a tract of land, eight acres, "on Bald Mountain so-called" beginning at the corner of Lot 76; Dinah Fisk also signed, (Franklin LR 28:89). On 1 December 1807 Simeon Fisk of Shelburne, yeoman, bought land in Gill, and the same day acknowledged the deed to Rufus and Ebenezer Jr. (*ibid.,* 27:384). He bought more land in Gill 4 November 1811 and 29 March 1813, and sold 20 acres there with wife Dinah 24 August 1814 to Aaron Leland *et al.* (*ibid.,* 29:580, 30:444, 32:635).

They moved to Orange County, N.Y., before 1830, when the 1830 census listed Simeon Fisk, 60-70, in Goshen with a woman 50-60, a woman 20-30, one boy 10-15, and a little girl under 5 years (p.280).

Children of Simeon and Dinah (Whitcomb) Fisk, rec. Shelburne (*VR* 38-40; some other information from *Fiske Family*, 131-32):

i   EZRA FISK[6], b. 10 Jan. 1785; d. 5 Dec. 1833 at Goshen, N.Y., "Dr. Ezra Fisk, Late Pastor, ae 48, inflammation of lungs with fever" (*Goshen Church*, 95). *Fiske Family*, 131-32, provides details of Dr. Fisk's distinguished career as a theologian, and says he m. _____ CUMMINS and had no surviving children.

ii PETER FISK, b. 15 Feb. 1787; d. unm.; a physician at Montague.

iii SIMEON FISK, b. 2 July 1788; d. at Montgomery, Ala., ae 33 yrs, "a native of Mass.", noted in the *Columbian Centinel* of 7 Nov. 1821; unm.; a merchant in western Georgia.

iv JONATHAN FISK, b. 18 Oct. 1790 (*Fiske Family*, 132); bp. Shelburne 28 Sept. 1794; d. 21 Aug. 1853, prob. at Terre Haute, Ind.; m. (1) at Leverett in May 1813, SUSANNA WILLIAMS, b. 25 May 1790, d. 17 July 1841 Coshocton, Ohio, dau. of Rev. Henry Williams; m. (2) in Ohio in 1843, MRS. MARIA ROBERTS, d. 1845; m. (3) at Terre Haute, Ind., in 1850 (evidently after the census), RELEAFY BLOOD, b. ca 1815 in N.Y., d. Sept. 1852. Jonathan removed with his first wife and oldest child to Wilkes Co., Ga., ca 1816, and ca 1824 returned North to Goshen, N.Y., then in 1834 to Coshocton, Ohio, and in 1849 to Terre Haute, Ind. He was a farmer and mechanic, a cooper by trade, a ruling elder in the Presbyterian Church, and a captain in the militia in Mass. at the outbreak of the War of 1812 but was never in battle (*Fiske Family*, 202). In 1850 the census listed Jonathan Fisk, ae 56 [*sic*], cooper b. Mass., with Israel Armstrong ae 28, a carpenter b. Ky., in Parke Co., Ind. (p.340). "Rafaly" Blood, ae 35, b. N.Y., was living in Vigo Co., Ind., in the household of George F. and Harriet Lyons (p.237).

Children, all with first wife (*Fiske Fam.*, 202-03): 1. *Esther Susanna Fisk*[7], b. 13 Feb. 1814; m. Jacob Welsh. 2. *Georgianna F. Fisk*, b. 14 Nov. 1818; m. Washington Burt. 3. *Ezra W. Fisk*, b. 29 May 1820; grad. from Princeton; m. Mary Van Dyke. 4. *Jonathan Fisk*, b. 15 Aug. 1825 Goshen, N.Y.; d. unm. 1879 in Kansas. 5. *Harriet Maria Fisk*, b. 25 Aug. 1823; m. Lewis D. Roderic. 6. *Henry Williams Fisk*, b. 6 Nov. 1833; m. Mary J. Stevenson. (See *Fiske Family*, 202-03 for further details.)

    v   DORCAS FISK, b. 1792; d. Shelburne 20 Aug. 1793 ae 1 yr.

    vi MOSES FISK, bp. 1800; d. Shelburne 14 Aug. 1802 ae 2y.

    vii HARRIET FISK, bp. 7 Oct. 1804; m. at Goshen, N.Y., 18 July 1829, JOHN M. GILLESPIE (*CR* 31). In 1850 Harriet Gallaspy ae 46, widow, b. Mass., was head of a household in Goshen, N.Y. (p.203).

          Gillespie children at home 1850: 1. *Mary C. Gillespie*, b. ca 1830. 2. *James S. Gillespie*, b. ca 1832; a painter 1850. 3. [*Son – name illegible*] *Gillespie*, b. ca 1834; a cabinet maker 1850. 4. *Matthew G. Gillespie*, b. ca 1836. 5. *Sarah Gillespie*, b. ca 1838.

Sources cited: *Hardwick VR. Shelburne VR.* Franklin County Deeds. Hampshire County Deeds and Probate Records. *History of Hardwick* (1882). *Early Records of the First Presbyterian Church at Goshen, N.Y.* (c1934). Pierce, *Fiske Genealogy* (1896). CENSUS: *Heads of Families 1790 – Mass.*; 1800 Shelburne, Hampshire Co. (M32-15); 1810 Deerfield, Franklin Co. (M252-19); 1830 Goshen, Orange Co., N.Y. (M19-113), 1850 Goshen, Orange Co., N.Y. (M432-574), Dist. 85, Parke Co., Ind. (M432-164), & Harrison, Vigo Co., Ind. (M432-177).

568.   MOSES FISK[5] (*Dorcas Tyler*[4], *Hannah*[3] *Samson, Stephen*[2], *Henry*[1]), son of Ebenezer Fisk and his wife Dorcas Tyler [119], was born at Deerfield 13 September 1764 (*VR* 61), and died 5 February 1847 at Waitsfield, Vt. (VR).

He married at Shelburne, 2 June 1789 (Waitsfield VR), **HANNAH BATCHELOR**, who was born at Upton 14 May 1770 and died at Waitsfield, Vt., 21 October 1853 (VR), daughter of Perrin and Martha (Fisk) Batchelor (*Waitsfield History*, 310).

Moses and Hannah settled in Waitsfield in 1794. They were among the original members of the Waitsfield Congregational Church, of which he was a deacon for 45 years (*ibid.*).

In 1850 Hannah Fisk, aged 80, was living with her daughter Emely, 32, next to the families of her sons Anson and Lyman, in Waitsfield; Abram Spofford, aged 80, a farmer born in Mass., shared the household (p.12).

Children of Moses and Hannah (Batchelor) Fisk, first three b. Shelburne, all rec. Waitsfield, Vt. (VR; *History*, 310; see *Fiske Family*, 133-34 for further information):

    i   JOEL FISK[6], b. 16 July 1790 "at Shelburne"; d. Waitsfield 18 July 1795.

    ii PERRIN BACHELLOR FISK, b. 6 July 1792 "at Shelburne"; d. 19 March 1846 Wardsboro, Vt.; m. at Montpelier, Vt., 1 May 1815, AZUBAH BLAISDELL, b. 14 Dec. 1794, d. Wardsboro 19 March 1846, dau. of Perrit and Ruth (___) Blaisdell (*Fiske Family*, 205). He was a saddler and later a Baptist minister (*Waitsfield History*, 310).

Children (*Fiske Family*, 205): 1. *Thomas Briggs Fisk*[7], b. 27 June 1823; m. Amaritt Bartlett. 2. *Moses Fisk*, b. 20 Oct. 1817; m. Orvilla Foster. 3. *William Wallace Fisk*, b. 5 March 1816; d. 16 July 1826. 4. *Ellen Hannah Fisk*, b. 4 Sept. 1832; m. Lewis Hart.

iii MOSES FISK, b. 25 July 1794 "at Shelburne"; d. Morrisville, Vt., 18 Feb. 1853; m. (1) MARY JOHNSON, (2) REBECCA (FERRIN) HENDEE. He was town clerk of Waterville, Vt., for 25 years, a J.P., State Representative and Senator, and a deacon of the Congregational Church (*Fiske Family*, 205).
Children (*ibid.*, 205-06): 1. [*Child*] *Fisk*[7], b. and d. 1826. 2. *Cornelia Ann Parmelee Fisk*, b. 19 Aug. 1828; m. Thomas Gleed. 3. *James Harvey Fisk*, b. 1830; d. 1855. 4. *Anna Mary Fisk*, b. 1832; m. J. Coleman Burnett. 5. *Josiah Moses Fisk*, b. 1834. 6. *Joel Batchelder Fisk*, b. 1837. 7. *Harris William Fisk*, b. 1840; d. 1841. 8. *Harris Myron Fisk*, b. 1842. 9. *Henry Clay Fisk*, 22 July 1852; m. Isabel M. Page.

iv JOEL FISK, b. 26 Oct. 1796; d. Plainfield, Vt., 16 Dec. 1856; m. 15 Oct. 1826, CLARINDA CHAPMAN, b. 21 June 1803, d. 15 Jan. 1878. He graduated from Middlebury College 1825 and became a minister and missionary (*Fiske Family*, 206).
Children (*ibid.*): 1. *Pliny Fisk*[7], b. 10 May 1828; m. (1) Helen Burlay, (2) Elizabeth C. Hall. 2. *Clarinda Chapman Fisk*, b. 27 Nov. 1829; m. L.W. Adgate. 3. *Harvey Fisk*, b. 26 April 1831; m. Louisa Green. 4. *Sarah J. Fisk*, b. 12 Dec. 1835; m. Henry Kinney. 5. *Mary I. Fisk*, b. 9 April 1838; m. L.W. Adgate, widower of her sister. 6. *Daniel C. Fisk*, b. Nov. 1840. 7. *Richard Henry Fisk*, b. 17 Nov. 1842.

v HARVEY FISK, b. 12 April 1799; d. 5 May 1831; m. 15 Feb. 1829, ANNA MARY PLUMB. Hamilton College 1826; Princeton Theological Seminary; State Missionary N.J. (*Fiske Family*, 206-07).
Child (*ibid.*): 1. *Harvey Jonathan Fisk*[7], b. 2 July 1830.

vi LYMAN FISK, b. 15 Oct. 1801; d. Waitsfield, Vt., 14 Dec. 1884; m. at Moretown, Vt., 14 Oct. 1828, MARY SPOFFORD, b. 14 Nov. 1801, d. 1 March 1879, dau. of Abram and Sarah (Spaulding) Spofford (*Fiske Fam.*, 207). In 1850 Lyman Fisk ae 48, a cooper, and Mary ae 48 were in Waitsfield with children Paul B. [*sic*], Mary, Betsey, and Harriet at home (p.12).
Children (*Waitsfield History*, 310): 1. *Narona Augusta Fisk*[7], b. 5 July 1830; m. Hiram Cross. 2. *Jonathan Albin Fisk*, b. 10 Jan. 1832; d. March 1842. 3. *Theron Ezra Fisk*, b. 5 May 1834; d. 9 Feb. 1839. 4. *Perrin Batchelor / Paul B. Fisk*, b. 3 July 1837; m. Harriet L. Bigelow. 5. *Mary Elmira Fisk*, b. ca 1840. 6. *Betsey Amanda Fisk*, b. 5 Feb. 1842. 7. *Harriet Clarinda Fisk*, b. 21 March 1845; m. Carl E. Gay.

vii   BETSEY FISK, b. 8 May 1804; d. 23 Feb. 1847; m. at Waitsfield, 20 Oct.
      1839, Rev. PHINEHAS BAILEY.
          Bailey children: 1. *Arabella Paulina Bailey*[7], b. 1842; d. 1852.   2. *Louisa
      Marietta Bailey,* b. 1844; m. Rev. Joel F. Whitney.   3. *Abbot Fisk Bailey,* b. 1847; d.
      1847.

viii ANSON FISK, b. 31 Oct. 1806; d. 2 Oct. 1880; m. 24 Nov. 1835, [his cousin]
      JOANNA BARNARD, b. 10 Oct. 1810, d. 21 Oct. 1891, dau of Ebenezer
      and Experience (Childs) Barnard (*Waitsfield History,* 311). In 1850 he was a
      farmer in Waitsfield with Joanna ae 40 and children Caroline, Edward,
      Phidelia, and Norman [*sic*] (p.12).
          Children (*Waitsfield History,* 311): 1. *Caroline Samantha Fisk*[7], b. 22 Nov. 1837;
      m. Orrin Hubbard Joslin.   2. *Edward Anson Fisk,* b. 1 Feb. 1842; m. Lillian
      Ramsey.   3. *Phidelia Joanna Fisk,* b. 14 Jan. 1845; d. 5 Oct. 1867.   4. *Pliny Barnard
      Fisk,* b. 6 May 1850; m. Caroline Clark.

ix   JONATHAN FISK, b. 6 May 1809; d. 5 Dec. 1872; m. at Allentown, N.J., 14
      Jan. 1834, MARY A. IMLAY, b. 23 March 1814; res. Trenton and
      Allentown, N.J. (*Fiske Family,* 207-08). In 1850 Jonathan Fiske was a "cashier
      in bank," living Trenton, N.J. (p.158); Pliny Fiske ae 22, b. Vt., was with
      them.
          Child: 1. *Harvey Fisk*[7], d.y.

x   ELVIRA / ALMINA ELIZA FISKE (twin), b. 20 Aug. 1811; d. 22 April
      1892; m. at Waitsfield, Vt., 3 March 1840, JOHN RUSSELL WHITNEY, b.
      18 April 1813, d. 23 July 1880; res. Wadham's Mills, N.Y. (*Fiske Fam.,* 133).
          Whitney children (*ibid.*): 1. *Elizabeth Hannah Whitney*[7], b. 11 Jan. 1841.
      2. *Marietta Thankful Whitney,* b. 2 Feb. 1842; m. Rev. A. T. Clarke; res. Ala. 3. *Joel
      Fisk Whitney,* b. 30 March 1843.   4. *Sarah L. Whitney,* b. 4 Sept. 1844; m. Edward
      D. Sturtevant.   5. *John R. Whitney,* b. 29 July 1847.   6. *Moses Fisk Whitney,* b. 18
      April 1849.   7. *Lemuel Whitney,* b. 12 Dec. 1850.   8. *Rosabelle Whitney,* b. 15 May
      1853; m. Rev. Wm. H. Wolcott.   9. *Elmina Eliza Whitney,* b. 7 Sept. 1855.

xi   HORACE ALONZO FISK (twin), b. 20 Aug. 1811; d. 29 Aug. 1851
      Waterville, Vt. (cem. rec.) ; m. 1841, CLARISSA FULLER, b. ca 1812 N.H.
      In 1850 he was a merchant in Waterville, and their household included
      Mercy Fuller ae 71, b. Mass. (p.76). No children.

xii   EMILY FISK, b. 12 Jan. 1817; d. 25 May 1891, unm.; in 1850 living with her
      mother near her brothers Anson and Lyman in Waitsfield (p.12).

Sources cited: Waitsfield, Vt., VR. Jones, *History of Waitsfield, Vt.* (1909). Pierce, *Fiske Genealogy*
(1896). CENSUS: 1850 Vermont: Waterville, Lamoille Co. (M432-925) & Waitsfield, Washington
Co. (M432-928).

569.   ROBERT FISK[5] (*Zilpha Tyler*[4], *Hannah*[3] *Samson, Stephen*[2], *Henry*[1]), son of Daniel Fisk and his wife Zilpha Tyler [120], was born at Upton 24 February 1746 and died there 25 September 1820, aged 74 (*VR* 25, 164).

He married at Upton (*VR* 96), 17 September 1768, **MARY HALL**, who died at Upton 7 February 1822, aged 78 (*VR* 163).

On 25 March 1793 Robert's younger half-brother and half-sister, Asher Aldrich and Faithful Aldrich, both of Upton, sold for £60 to Robert Fisk of Upton, yeoman, their half parts of rights to the thirds left by their "Mother Zilpher Aldrich by her late husband Isaac Aldrich deceased" (Worcester LR 118:450).

Robert Fisk of Upton, yeoman, on 21 April 1801 sold to William Fisk Jr. of Upton, yeoman, for $1,000, half of four undivided tracts of land in Upton and Milford; both Robert and his wife Mary signed, and Elisha and Daniel Fisk witnessed (Worcester LR 171:510). On 26 December 1812 Robert Fisk and wife Mary sold to William Fisk Jr. of Upton, yeoman, for $2,000, four pieces of land in Upton and Milford with half of the buildings, some of it land held in common with Benjamin Fisk; this deed was witnessed by Elisha Fisk and Elisha Bradish, and Mary signed but Robert made his mark (*ibid.*, 187:416). There are no probate records for Robert or Mary Fisk in Worcester County.

Children of Robert and Mary (Hall) Fisk recorded Upton (*VR* 22, 23, 25):

i   ELISHA FISK[6], b. 2 Sept. 1769 "in Holliston"; d. Wrentham 11 Jan. 1851, ae 81y 4m 9d of old age and exhaustion, a minister (Mass. VR 58:165); m. (1) LYDIA ROBINSON, b. Milford 30 Dec. 1773 (*VR* 150), d. Wrentham 11 July 1805 in 32nd yr (*VR* 2:446), dau. of John and Susanna (___) Robinson; m. (2) at Wrentham, 27 March 1811 (*VR* 2:298), MARGARET / PEGGY (SHEPHERD) BROWN, b. 1779, d. 30 April 1850, dau. of Benjamin and Hepzibah (Blake) Shepherd (*Fiske Family*, 227). Elisha graduated from Brown Univ. in 1795 and was minister at Wrentham for 52 years. (See *Fiske Family*, 227-28 for more.)

Children, b. or bp. rec. Wrentham (*VR* 1:89) for all but Charlotte (marriages, *VR* 2:298), all in *Fiske Family*: (With Lydia) 1. *Mary Hall Fisk*[7], b. 9 Nov. 1801; m. Rev. George Fisher. 2. *Charlotte Brown Fisk*, b. ca 1803; d. 31 Aug. 1838 ae 35; m. Rev. Amos A. Phelps; bur. Wrentham Center Cem. (*VR* 2:483). 3. *Charles Robinson Fisk*, b. 27 Oct. 1804. (With Margaret) 4. *Emily Frances Fisk*, b. 7 Nov. 1812; m. Wm. Sturtevant. 5. *William Jones Fisk*, bp. 1 Aug. 1813; d. 26 Jan. 1830. 6. *Frederick A. Fisk*, b. 15 April, bp. 2 June 1816. 7. *Harriett Josephine Fisk*, bp. 7 June 1818; m. Rev. Erasmus D. Moore.

ii   DANIEL FISK, b. 29 Oct. 1770 "in Holliston"; d. Upton in 1840 ae 69, Deacon Daniel, "son of Robert and Mary (Hall)" (*VR* 163); m. (1) at

Upton, 27 Sept. 1792 (*VR* 95), HANNAH PALMER, d. Upton 14 July 1815 in 39th yr (*VR* 163); m. (2) after int. Upton 23 Feb. 1816 (*VR* 95), RUTH CHAPIN of Mendon. *Fiske Family* (228-29), omits first marriage but has more about Daniel.

Children rec. Upton (*VR* 23-25), first two with Hannah, others with Ruth: 1. *Clarisa Fisk[7]*, b. 16 June 1796. 2. *Joanna Fisk*, b. 18 Dec. 1804. 3. *David Brainard Fisk*, b. 23 Jan. 1817. 4. *Hannah Palmer Fisk*, b. 29 Oct. 1818. 5. *Almira Chapin Fisk*, b. 22 April 1820. 6. *Daniel Edwards Fisk*, b. 4 March 1822. 7. *John Milton Fisk*, b. 17 Jan. 1824.

iii   WILLIAM FISK, b. 8 Nov. 1776; d. 15 Dec. 1862 (Mass. VR. 158:289); m. at Upton, 27 Feb. 1801 (*VR* 96), LUCY BRADISH, b. ca 21 July 1780, d. Upton, 26 Dec. 1860 ae 80y 5m 5d of typhoid fever, b. Upton, dau. of Elisha Bradish (Mass. VR 140:247).

Children rec. Upton (*VR* 22-24): 1. *Albert William Fisk[7]*, b. 16 Jan. 1802. 2. *Elisha Bradish Fisk*, b. 16 Feb. 1804. 3. *Judson H. Fisk*, b. 30 Aug. 1807; d. Upton 30 April 1816 ae 8y 8m (*VR* 163). 4. *Charles A. Fisk*, b. 4 April 1811. 5. *George R. Fisk*, b. 5 Jan. 1821.

iv   AMASA FISK, b. 17 Sept. 1780; d. Dover, Vt., 23 March 1847; m. _____ (*Fiske Family*, 230). Graduated from Brown; a lawyer.

Sources cited: *Milford VR. Upton VR. Wrentham VR.* Mass. Vital Records 1841-1910. Worcester County Deeds. Pierce, *Fiske Family* (1896).

570.   ZILPHA FISK[5] (*Zilpha Tyler[4], Hannah[3] Samson, Stephen[2], Henry[1]*), daughter of Daniel Fisk and his wife Zilpha Tyler [120], was born at Upton 16 April 1753 (*VR* 25) and died there 5 February 1833 aged 80, "wife of Peter [Forbush]" (*VR* 165; *Col. Cent.* of 2 March 1833).

She married at Upton, 26 January 1792 (*VR* 96), as his second wife, **PETER FORBUSH**. He was born at Upton 16 February 1754, son of Samuel and Margaret (Parker) Forbush, and died there 23 October 1839 (*VR* 165). Peter married first, at Upton, 6 May 1777 (*VR* 98), DEBORAH FLAGG, who died after 1783 (birth of last rec. child). Peter and Deborah had children recorded at Upton (*VR* 25-26): Elijah Forbush, b. 1778; Patty Forbush, d. 1780; Aaron Forbush, b. 1782; and Easter Forbush, b. 1783. Deborah's death is not recorded at Upton.

Peter served in the Revolutionary War as a private in Capt. Peter Penniman's company, Col. Job Cushing's regiment, from 17 August 1777 for 3 months, 24 days, with the Northern army (*MSSR* 6:206).

He is not listed in the 1790 Massachusetts census.

On 2 April 1808 Peter Forbush of Upton, yeoman, sold to Elijah Forbush of Upton, cooper, "one undivided half of my farm," half of all buildings, and half of all privileges; his wife Zilpah released her dower. Witnesses were Ephraim Forbush and Zilpah Nelson (Worcester LR 222:593).

In 1800 the household of Peter Forbush at Upton (p.387) consisted of one man and one woman 16-26 and one man and one woman 45+. The younger people were probably Peter's son and daughter by his first marriage.

There are no probate records for Peter or Zilpha Forbush in Worcester County, and no indication has been found that they had children.

Sources cited: *Upton VR.* Worcester County Deeds. Index, *Columbian Centinel. Mass. Soldiers & Sailors.* CENSUS: 1800 Upton, Worcester Co. (M32-16).

571. HANNAH FISK[5] (*Zilpha Tyler*[4], *Hannah*[3] *Samson, Stephen*[2], *Henry*[1]), daughter of Daniel Fisk and his wife Zilpha Tyler [120], was born at Upton 28 March 1756 (*VR* 24) and died there 17 July 1837, ae 81, "widow of Isaac [Nelson]" (*VR* 172).

She married at Upton (*VR* 95), 27 January 1778, **ISAAC NELSON**, who was born at Upton 16 October 1755 (*VR* 40), son of Lt. Jonathan and Ann (Jones) Nelson, and died there 28 December 1812 in his 58th year (*VR* 172), killed by the fall of a tree (*Job Tyler Desc.,* 101).

The 1790 census listed Isaac Nelson at Upton with a family consisting of one man over 16, one boy under 16, and four females (*Heads of Fam.,* 240).

Children of Isaac and Hannah (Fisk) Nelson, recorded Upton (births *VR* 39; marriages 118, 119):

i   ANNA NELSON[6], b. 17 Nov. 1778; m. Upton, 10 or 20 Feb. 1800 (*VR* 118), ELIJAH FORBUSH [stepson of her Aunt Zilpha], who d. Upton 17 April 1821 ae 43 (*VR* 165).
      Forbush children rec. Upton (*VR* 25-27): 1. *Holland Forbush*[7], b. 18 Aug. 1800. 2. *Aaron Forbush,* b. 24 March 1803; d. Upton Oct. 1807 (*VR* 164). 3. *Elijah Forbush Jr.,* b. 28 May 1805. 4. *Hannah Forbush,* b. 21 May 1808. 5. *Halford Forbush,* b. 24 Dec. 1811. 6. *Brigham Forbush,* b. 1 June 1813. 7. *Anny Melinda Forbush,* b. 3 Jan. 1816. 8. *Newel Forbush,* b. 9 Feb. 1819.

ii SYNTHA NELSON, b. 6 March 1783; m. Upton, 21 Aug. 1803 (*VR* 119), SOLOMON DAVIS, d. Upton 7 June 1812 (*VR* 161). A "son of widow Syntha" d. Upton 21 July 1815 (*VR* 161), but no births rec. there.

iii ZILPHA NELSON, b. 21 April 1786; m. at Upton, 18 Aug. 1809 (*VR* 132),
     ELIJAH STODDARD, prob. b. Upton 28 Nov. 1785, son of Ezekiel and
     Lucy (___) Stoddard / Stodder (*VR* 52).
          Stoddard children rec. Upton (*VR* 51) [*Tyler*, 101, says 8 ch.]: 1. *Ann Maria
     Stoddard*, b. 21 May 1810. 2. *Isaac Nelson Stoddard*, b. 29 Oct. 1812; m. Martha
     LeBaron Thomas. 3. *Lucy Jane Stoddard*, b. 12 March 1815. 4. *Lois Nelson
     Stoddard*, b. 10 July 1817. 5. *Electa Hale Stoddard*, b. 6 Jan. 1820; d. Upton 16 Sept.
     1821 (*VR* 180). 6. *[Child] Stoddard*, d. Upton 30 March 1828 (*ibid.*). 7. *Jennette C.
     Stoddard*, b. 27 April 1830.

iv   JONATHAN NELSON, b. 3 Dec. 1788; m. at Upton, 3 Oct. 1816 (*VR*
     118), CHLOE WARREN, b. ca 1796 in Mass. In 1850 Jonathan Nelson
     2^d ae 61, flour merchant, was living in Upton with Chloe ae 54, and Julia
     Warren ae 38, near son James A. (p.110).
          Child rec. Upton (*VR* 40): 1. *James Addison Nelson[7]*, b. 7 Aug. 1817; m.
     Martha B. ___; res. Upton 1850.

v   LOIS NELSON, b. 17 Aug. 1791; m. ELIJAH NELSON [#587-i], *q.v.*

Sources cited: *Upton VR. Heads of Families 1790 – Mass. Job Tyler Genealogy* (1912). CENSUS:
1850 Upton, Worcester Co. (M432-344).

572.   SUBMIT FISK[5] (*Zilpha Tyler[4], Hannah[3] Samson, Stephen[2], Henry[1]*), daughter
of Daniel Fisk and his wife Zilpha Tyler [120], was born at Upton 27 October 1758
(VR 25) and died at Buckland 19 September 1818 ae 60, "wife of Lt. William
Putnam and dau. Daniel Fiske" (*VR* 146).

Submit's father died when she was a child and her mother remarried, to Isaac
Aldrich. On 23 March 1767 Nathan Tyler was appointed guardian of Submit and
her two sisters (Worcester PR #A20843).

She married at Upton, 25 June 1778, **WILLIAM PUTNAM** of Upton (VR
96). He was born at Sutton 7 January 1758 (rec. *Buckland VR* 38), son of Elisha and
Lydia (Chase) Putnam, and died at Buckland 22 July 1818, aged 63 (*VR* 146).
William and Submit are buried in Buckland Center Cemetery.

William Putnam of Upton served in the Revolutionary War, first as a private in
Capt. Robert Taft's company, Col. Silas Wheelock's regiment, on a march to the
alarm of 19 April 1775; in 1778 he was in a regiment that marched to Rhode Island
to serve for six weeks; and in the summer of 1780 he was a corporal in Capt.
Thomas Baker's company, Col. Nathan Tyler's regiment, again marching to Rhode
Island (*MSSR* 12:878).

History of the Putnam Family (p. 275) relates that the family moved from Upton
to Buckland, where William was a farmer. On 22 April 1784 Samuel Taylor and

Lemuel Taylor, both of Buckland, sold land there to William Putnam of Buckland, yeoman (Franklin LR 1:449). On 11 April 1818, shortly before his death, William Putnam, gentleman, of Buckland, sold to William Putnam Jr. of Buckland, gentleman, all his land there; witnesses were Edward Fobes and Submit Putnam (*ibid.* 40:441).

Children of William and Submit (Fisk) Putnam, first two rec. Upton (*VR* 45); all rec. Buckland (*VR* 38):

i   LYD[I]A PUTNAM⁶, b. 7 March 1779 Upton; d. Buckland 6 July 1822, ae 43 (*VR* 157); m. Buckland, 15 Jan. 1799 (*VR* 102), JACOB WHITING, who d. Buckland "suddenly," 28 Dec. 1835 ae 73y, a Revolutionary pensioner (*VR* 157).

   Whiting children rec. Buckland (*VR* 59): 1. *Welcome Whiting*, b. 16 Oct. 1799. 2. *Hannah Whiting*, b. 8 March 1801. 3. *Patty Whiting*, b. 28 Dec. 1802. 4. *Emory Whiting*, b. 18 May 1812.

ii   POLLY PUTNAM, b. 8 April 1780; d. Buckland 10 May 1780 (*VR* 146).

iii   HANNAH PUTNAM, b. 14 May 1781 (June in *Buckland VR*); d. Buckland 9 May 1800 ae 19 yrs (*VR* 146).

iv   ZILPHA PUTNAM, b. 15 April 1784; d. Stockton, Chautauqua Co., N.Y. 11 July 1867 at home of son David (*Sabin Desc.*, 119); m. Buckland, 19 Feb. 1807 (*VR* 103), NEHEMIAH SABIN, b. 31 Dec. 1781 (rec. Buckland *VR* 40) of Halifax, d. 22 July 1856, son of Ebenezer Sabin. In 1850 they were living by themselves in Whitingham, Vt. (p.88).

   Sabin children, first rec. Buckland (*VR* 40), others Whitingham, Vt., all with marriages in *Sabin Desc.* (pp.119, 206-07): 1. *Dencea/Dency Sabin⁷*, b. 18 Nov. 1807; m. Martin Mason Ballou. 2. *Zilpha Sabin*, b. 5 Sept. 1809; m. William Burnham. 3. *David Sabin*, b. 28 Nov. 1811; m. Loisy ___. 4. *Louisa Lovina Sabin*, b. 18 Feb. 1814; m. ___ Williams. 5. *Laura Sabin*, b. 15 Feb. 1816; m. Hiram Gore. 6. *William Putnam Sabin*, b. 14 April 1818; m. Harriet Laura Clark. 7. *Harriet Olive Sabin*, b. 19 July 1824; d. 1826.

v   ELISHA PUTNAM, b. 18 May 1786; d. Shelburne 24 Dec. 1859 of consumption, a carpenter (Mass. VR 129:214); m. ZILPHA WHITNEY, b. ca 1790 Marlboro, Vt., dau. Nathaniel Whitney, d. Shelburne 29 Aug. 1863 ae 73 of stomach cancer (Mass. VR 165:304). In 1850 Elisha was a farmer in Whitingham, Vt., with Triphena [*sic*] ae 61, b. Vt., and Henry S. Brown ae 16, b. Vt. (p.85). The will of Elisha Putnam of Shelburne dated 12 Feb. 1856, proved 2 Jan. 1860, names wife Zilpher Putnam, executrix, to receive all his estate; upon her decease it was to go to Susan Shattuck and Milo P. Shattuck, children of Ezra Shattuck late of Readsborough, Vt., dec'd; to Sidney Smith of Stockton, Chautauqua Co., N.Y., and his wife Emeline, and to Henry S. Brown lately of Brattleboro, Vt., now resident in Shelburne (Franklin PR #6526).

vi WILLIAM PUTNAM, b. 15 March 1788; d. Buckland 30 Sept. 1865 ae 77y 6m 15d of paralytic shock (Mass. VR 183:276); m. LURANY L. SHEPARD, b. ca 1789 in Mass. In his will dated 13 Aug. 1858 he named wife Lurany, dau. Lexany wife of William H. Stetson, nephew William Putnam son of Abner ("my silver watch"), and granddaughter Idella; to "William" he left his right in the burying ground in Buckland adjoining the Baptist Meeting. He left $50 to Mary Dole, wife of Enos, without mentioning a relationship. In a codicil dated 18 July 1863 he appointed Josiah Trew executor in place of Amasa Ward of Buckland (Franklin PR #6551, 49:260). In 1850 he was a farmer at Buckland with Lurany ae 61, Lixana ae 33, and several persons of different surnames (p.203).

Child: 1. *Lexana L. Putnam⁷*, b. ca 1817; m. Buckland 10 April 1851 (Mass. VR 54:234), William H. Stetson.

vii DANIEL PUTNAM, b. 28 Feb. 1790; d. Buckland 7 Dec. 1828 ae 38 (*VR* 146); m. at Buckland, 31 March 1818 (*VR* 102), LOVINA LYON, d. 18 Sept. 1832 ae 37y at Hartford, Conn., and bur. Buckland Center Cemetery (*VR* 146). They removed to Ashfield, where he was a Deacon in the Baptist Church. Joseph Griswold was given adm. on the estate of Daniel Putnam of Buckland and Ashfield, deceased, 6 Jan. 1829; the inventory included 85 acres in Buckland (Franklin PR #6529). An accounting included $3 to Ellis Pratt for Daniel's coffin. All personal estate was given to the widow Lovina, and a third of the real estate, but the rest had to be sold: 46 acres for $340 to William Putnam and 22 acres and barn for $152 to the widow Lovina. On 21 July 1829 a guardian was appointed for minors William J., Sarah T. [? Submit F.], Lydia, and Daniel Putnam (*ibid.*, 2:12, 3:12).

Children (guardianship rec.): 1. *William J. Putnam⁷*. 2. *Sarah T./Submit F. Putnam*. 3. *Lydia Putnam*. 4. *Daniel Putnam*.

viii SARAH PUTNAM, b. 6 Feb. 1792; m. after int. Buckland 5 Aug. 1816 (*VR* 109), NATHAN SMITH, poss. son of Ebenezer and Keziah (___) Smith who lived nearby in 1850 when Nathan was head of a household at Stockton, Chautauqua Co., N.Y., ae 61, with Sally ae 58, both b. Mass., and five children (p.246).

Smith children at home 1850, all b. N.Y.: 1. *Pliney Smith⁷*, b. ca 1823. 2. *Jason Smith*, b. ca 1827. 3. *Sidney Smith*, b. ca 1829. 4. *Lydia Smith*, b. ca 1831. 5. *Newell Smith*, b. ca 1839.

ix ABNER PUTNAM, b. 28 July 1794; m. VESTA ____, b. ca 1795 in Vt.; removed to N.Y. In 1850 Abner was a farmer at Stockton, Chautauqua

Co., N.Y., near his brother-in-law Nathan Smith, with Vesta ae 55, and five children (p.244); sons Edwin and Corydon were also farmers.

Children, first five at home 1850, all b. N.Y.: 1. *Edwin Putnam⁷*, b. ca 1828. 2. *Emely Putnam*, b. ca 1830. 3. *Corydon Putnam*, b. ca 1831. 4. *Sarah Putnam*, b. ca 1833. 5. *Lucina Putnam*, b. ca 1837. 6. *William Putnam*, named in 1858 will of uncle William Putnam.

x   SUBMIT PUTNAM, b. 11 July 1797 (21 July in *Buckland VR*); d. 4 March 1883 (*Putnam Gen.*, 304); m. at Buckland, 9 Nov. 1820, both of Buckland (*VR* 103), NEWEL TOWNSLEY, b. 1791 or 1796 (*VR* 52), son of Daniel and Rachel (Bullard) Townsley. She is said to have outlived all the family. In 1850 Newell Townsley was a farmer at Buckland with Submit ae 52 and three sons; son Dan C. and his family were next door (p.203).

Townsley children rec. Buckland (*VR* 52, 154): 1. [*Twin son*] *Townsley⁷*, b. and d. 1821. 2. [*Twin daughter*] *Townsley*, b. and d. 1821. 3. *Daniel C. Townsley*, b. 1824; m. Eliza Williams (*VR* 118); a shoemaker 1850. 4. *Eliza S. Townsley*, b. 1826; d. 4 May 1840. 5. *William P. Townsley*, b. 1828; at home 1850. 6. *George N. Townsley*, b. 1830; at home 1850. 7. *Eliza Townsley*, b. 1832. 8. *Henry D. Townsley*, b. 1836; at home 1850. 8. *Jane A. Townsley*, b. 1838; d. 3 Sept. 1839.

Sources cited: *Buckland VR* [citing for Putnams PR 37, family rec. in poss. of Harry W. Kellogg of Greenfield, and for Townsleys PR 22, family rec. in poss. of Mrs. Laura T. Merriam of Buckland]. *Upton VR*. Franklin County Deeds and Probate Records at Greenfield. E. Putnam, *A History of the Putnam Family* (Salem, 1891). Morris and Hibbard, *William Sabin and his Descendants*, Vol. 1 (2000). CENSUS: 1850 Buckland, Franklin Co. (M432-317), Stockton, Chautauqua Co., N.Y. (M432-485), & Whitingham, Windham Co., Vt. (M432-929). See also: *History of Buckland* (1937), 583; Pierce, *Fiske Family* (1896), 201.

573.   ASHER ALDRICH⁵ (*Zilpha Tyler⁴, Hannah³ Samson, Stephen², Henry¹*), son of Isaac Aldrich and his wife Zilpha Tyler [120], was born at Upton 20 August 1763 (*VR* 10), and was living in Upton in 1794 but had probably died by August 1805. By his father's will, dated 11 February 1788, proved 25 November 1788, Asher was to divide the moveable estate "not yet given away" with his sisters Faithfull and Levisy, and he received half of his father's real estate "lying on the north side of my farm running east and west"; the other half went to his sisters, and his mother had a right of thirds in the property during her widowhood (Worcester PR #A841, 21:405).

On 25 March 1793 Asher Aldrich and Faithful Aldrich, both of Upton, "the one a husbandman and the other spinster," for £60 sold to Robert Fisk of Upton, yeoman (probably their older half-brother), their half parts of rights to the thirds left by their "Mother Zilpher Aldrich by her late husband Isaac Aldrich deceased";

both signed, before witnesses Isaac Nelson and Daniel Fisk Jr. (Worcester LR 118:450). On 18 April 1794 Asher Aldrich of Upton, yeoman, sold to Josiah Pease of Upton, yeoman, a 27-acre piece of land in Upton, "all the land said Asher is now in possession of by the will of his father Isaac Aldrich late of said Upton deceased," together with "my rite of widow's thirds ... and also my rite in the house and barn ..." (*ibid.*, 123:38).

The household of his mother, Zilpha Aldrich, in 1790 included a man over 16 and one other female (*Heads of Fam.*, 240), probably Asher and one of his sisters.

By a deed dated 14 May 1794, William Winter of Northbridge, yeoman, and Levice Winter his wife, for £3, sold to Ashur Aldrich of Upton "one fourth part of the old part so-called of the house which Isaac Aldrich died seized and possessed of and one sixth part of the barn" (*ibid.*, 159:592). This deed was recorded 14 August 1805, and on 20 August William and Levice sold to Timothy Aldrich their rights in land set off to "our mother Zilpha Aldrich late of Upton deceased, out of Isaac Aldrich's estate for her thirds" (*ibid.*, 158:432). There are no further land records for Asher in Worcester County.

No record of Asher has been found after 1794.

Sources cited: *Upton VR.* Worcester County Deeds and Probate Records. *Heads of Families 1790 – Mass.*

574.   LEVICY ALDRICH[5] (*Zilpha Tyler*[4], *Hannah*[3] *Samson, Stephen*[2], *Henry*[1]), daughter of Isaac Aldrich and his wife Zilpha Tyler [120], was born at Upton 1 September 1766 (*VR* 10), and died 27 May 1843 at Northbridge as "Louvise" (*VR* 202). She is named in the will of her father as "Levisy," and her marriage record calls her "Levice."

She married 13 January 1791 at Upton (*VR* 74), as his second wife, **WILLIAM WINTER** "of Northbridge." He was born at Uxbridge 18 August 1757 to Christopher and Ruth (Aldrich) Winter (*VR* 187), and died after 10 December 1806 when he sold land in Northbridge. He married, first, at Northbridge, 19 April 1781 (*VR* 168), ANNA CHAMBERLAIN of Grafton, and had with her two children: Willard Winter and William Chamberlain Winter, born at Northbridge in 1782 and 1790 respectively (*VR* 93).

William Winter, yeoman, and his wife Levicy Winter of Northbridge on 6 April 1793 sold land in Upton to Timothy Aldrich Jr. (Worcester LR 127: 370). On 14 May 1794, both signing, they sold to Ashur [*sic*] Aldrich of Upton, for £3, "one fourth part of the old part so-called of the house which Isaac Aldrich died seized and possessed of and one sixth part of the barn" (*ibid.*, 159:592). This deed was recorded 14 August 1805, and a few days later, on 20 August 1805, William Winter and wife Lovice quitclaimed to Timothy Aldrich Jr. land in Upton and Northbridge set off to "our mother Zilpha Aldrich late of Upton deceased, out of Isaac Aldrich's estate for her thirds" (*ibid.*, 158:432).

On 5 September 1805 William Winter and wife Levisa of Northbridge and Faithful Aldrich of Upton, yeoman and spinsters, quitclaimed to Timothy Aldrich of Upton their rights in land of Isaac Aldrich, deceased (*ibid.*, 158:557). On 10 December 1806, William Winter of Northbridge sold land there to Willard Winter, husbandman, acknowledging the deed the same day (*ibid.* 165:251).

In 1800 the household of William Winter in Northbridge (p.474) consisted of two young men 16-26 (probably William's two sons with his first wife), one girl 10-16, a woman 26-45 (Lovicy), and a man 45+ [*sic*]. If the age of the girl is correct, she was born 1790 or earlier and thus could not be daughter of Lovicy.

Sources cited: *Northbridge VR. Upton VR. Uxbridge VR.* Worcester County Deeds. CENSUS: 1800 Northbridge, Worcester Co. (M32–16).

575. FAITHFUL ALDRICH[5] (*Zilpha Tyler*[4], *Hannah*[3] *Samson, Stephen*[2], *Henry*[1]), daughter of Isaac Aldrich and his wife Zilpha Tyler [120], was born at Upton (*VR* 10) 2 October 1768. She died 14 May 1843 at Lancaster aged 74 years, of "fever," as "Faith[ful], wife of Mr. Rufus Fletcher" (*VR* 181).

She married at Upton, 19 May 1811 (*VR* 74) as his second wife, **RUFUS FLETCHER** of Lancaster. He was born at Lancaster 14 October 1764, son of Joshua and Mary (___) Fletcher (*VR* 93), and died there 30 September 1850 "aged 87y 8m" (Mass. VR 59:141). He married, first, at Lancaster 29 June 1786 (*VR* 130), POLLY SAWYER, who died 29 or 30 August 1808, aged 42; her name on her gravestone in Middle Cemetery, Lancaster, is "Mrs. Mary Fletcher" (*VR* 180, 427). Rufus and Polly/Mary had children: Elisha, Sophia, Artemas, Cynthia, Christopher, Rufus, Mary, and Lewis Fletcher, recorded at Lancaster between 1786 and 1805 (*VR* 118, 180, 304, 316-318, 337, 339, 340, 342), and two infants who died soon after birth (*VR* 351, 354).

By the will of her father, dated 11 February 1788, proved 25 November 1788, Faithful was to divide the moveable estate "not yet given away" with her brother Asher and sister Levisy, and the two sisters were to share in the half of the farm not given to Asher. In addition Isaac left to Faithful "a pair of Loombs and tackling for them," the only specific bequest he made. Their mother Zilpha had a right of thirds in all the property during her widowhood (Worcester PR #A841, 21:405).

On 25 March 1793 Asher Aldrich and Faithfull Aldrich, both of Upton, "the one a husbandman and the other spinster," for £60 sold to Robert Fisk of Upton, yeoman (probably their older half-brother), their half parts of rights to the thirds left by their "Mother Zilpher Aldrich by her late husband Isaac Aldrich deceased" (Worcester LR 118:450).

Faithful Aldrich, "spinster" on 31 August 1805 joined her sister Levisa and Levisa's husband William Winter in quitclaiming to Timothy Aldrich Jr. their rights in land in Upton that their father Isaac had sold to him (Worcester LR 158:557).

Faithful was 42 years old when she married, and no evidence has been found that she had any children.

Sources cited: *Lancaster VR. Upton VR.* Worcester County Deeds and Probate Records

576.   ANNA TYLER[5] (*Elijah*[4], *Hannah*[3] *Samson, Stephen*[2], *Henry*[1]), daughter of Elijah Tyler [121] and his wife Ruth Owen, was born at Upton 24 September 1750, recorded as Anne (*VR* 56). She died probably by 1780. She was a descendant also of *Mayflower* passenger John Alden.

Elijah Tyler, wife Ruth, and children Nathaniel, Ann, Stephen, Catherine, and Eunice, from Upton, were warned out of Mendon in September 1759 (*Worcester Co. Warnings*, 42).

She married at Mendon, 16 August 1770 (*VR* 416), **AMARIAH TAFT**; both were "of Upton," where intentions were recorded 10 July 1770 (*VR* 133, 138). He appears to be the same Amariah Taft who married Mary Johnson in Townshend, Vt., 9 May 1780, just six days before four children of "Amariah Taft and Mary his present wife" were recorded there on 15 May 1780 (Townshend VR, 1: pt 2: 24, 19). Amariah was born at Upton 10 March 1747/8, son of Israel Jr. and Mathew [Martha] (Smith) Taft (*VR* 52), and died at Townshend, Vt., 17 March 1818, aged 70. (Some sources claim as Anna's husband the Amariah Taft born at Mendon 13 February 1749/50, but the death of that child two weeks after birth is recorded.)

Taft family researchers believe that Amariah deserted Anna, and it seems clear that the children born in Townshend (Israel b. 24 March 1773; Martha b. 30 June 1774; Amariah b. 1 June 1776; and Elisha b. 5 Oct. 1778) were Mary's, born before her marriage. Record of Anna's death has not been found.

Sources cited: *Mendon VR. Upton VR.* Blake, *Worcester County Warnings* (1899). Townshend, Vt., VR, microfilm of originals examined 2006 by Neil D. Thompson, FASG.

577. NATHAN WEBB TYLER[5] (*Elijah*[4], *Hannah*[3] *Samson, Stephen*[2], *Henry*[1]), son of Elijah Tyler [121] and his wife Ruth Owen, was born at Upton 14 October 1752 (*VR* 56) and died at Columbus, Chenango County, N.Y., 24 March 1830 (pension file) or 1831 ae 77y 5m (g.s.); 1830 is probably correct. He was a descendant also of *Mayflower* passenger John Alden. He is buried with his wife Olive in Siloam Cemetery, Smithfield, Madison County, N.Y. (*Rev. War Veterans [of] Chenango County, N.Y.*, 4:1090). His gravestone bears the epitaph: *My children dear / assemble here / A fathers grave to see / not long ago I dwelt with you / and soon you'll dwell with me.*

He married at Goshen, 28 March 1776, "she of Chesterfield" (pension file), **OLIVE PATCH,** who was born at Union, Conn., 19 May 1756, daughter of Ephraim and Penelope (Dana) Patch, and died 21 July 1837 (g.s., Siloam Cem.).

Elijah Tyler, wife Ruth, and children Nathaniel [*sic*], Ann, Stephen, Catherine, and Eunice, from Upton, were warned out of Mendon in September 1759 (*Worcester Co. Warnings*, 42).

Buckland records state that Nathan Tyler was a resident there in 1790, and his brother Moses is listed there as a grantee a few years later. The 1790 census listed Nathan with a household of three boys under 16 and five females (*Heads of Fam.*, 105). In 1800 he was in Stephentown, N.Y., over 45, with one woman 26-45, one young man 16-26, two boys 10-16, and three little girls under 10 (p.912). He has not been located in 1810, but the 1820 census showed him still at Stephentown, himself and his wife 45+, with one young man 18-26, one young woman 16-26, two boys and one girl 10-16, and three boys under 10 (p.41), figures that suggest a married child and grandchildren. This is puzzling, since he called himself of Norwich, Chenango County, N.Y., in 1818 when he applied for a Revolutionary War pension (# W18180). However, the Revolutionary pensioner and the Stephentown Nathan are linked by information in the pension file, although no places of residence for him between 1776 and 1818 are given (see below).

On 1 May 1818 in Norwich, Chenango County, N.Y., Nathan Tyler signed a shaky signature to his deposition, stating that:

> ... he is aged [65] years ... [he] enlisted in the company of Captain Charles Soal of Col. Whitcums regiment (the name of which he has forgotten) of the Massachusetts line. That he continued to serve in the said company or in the service of the United States against the Common Enemy untill the full end & serrvice of One year thence next ensuing when he was discharged from said service at Fort Ticonderoga in the State of New York. That [he] assisted in rebuilding Castle William near Boston whilst in such service & to repair the fortifications at Ticonderoga, that he was in active service but never in any Battle ... he is in reduced circumstances & stands in

kneed [*sic*] of his country for support And that he has no other evidence now in his power of the said service.

On 11 October 1820 he was of Columbus, N.Y., and in a new declaration he said that he was 67 years old, and had enlisted 1 January 1776 for the term of one year, in Capt. Charles Sole's company, Col. Asa Whitmore's regiment, and although he was in no regular battle he was on Dorchester Point at the time of the cannonade. At the time of his declaration, he had no real estate, and his personal goods consisted of "2 [---], 1 Cracker Pot, 1 Tea Kittle, 1 Spider, 1 Dish [---], 1 Table, 2 Wheeles, 6 Plats, 1 Set Teacup & Saucer," the whole valued at $10.25. "My occupation is that of a farmer. I have a wife aged [64] years [who] has been sick for eighteen months under the Doctors care. My health is not good. I have had the Rheumatism and am unable to support my self & wife without some assistance." Charles Bellows of Marlboro, Vt., and Joseph Jepson of Goshen [Mass.], made depositions in October 1820 that they had served with Nathan Tyler

In her application on for a widow's pension, 21 January 1837 in Madison County, N.Y., Olive stated that she was eighty years old on 19 May last past, and she gave the date of Nathan's death and their marriage date. She stated that at the time of their marriage she was living with her father in Chesterfield where there was no minister, and Nathan "came home on a furlough for the purpose of being married." Ruth Bullard, sister of said Nathan Tyler, testified at Buckland, 2 November 1836, that she had attended their marriage. Ambrose Stone, Jr., town clerk of Williamsburg, provided a copy of a record of the marriage of Mr. Nathan Tyler of Chesterfield Gore and Olive *Pratt* of Chesterfield on 28 March 1776, along with the information that Chesterfield Gore was "now a part of the town of Goshen," and requested a dollar for his time, trouble, and postage. Documents in the file indicate that the difference in Olive's surname was questioned and adjudged to be a clerical error.

Lewis Nash deposed on 21 January 1837 in Madison County that Olive Tyler, widow of Nathan, was living in his family (pension file). Olive was dead by 1850, but the census that year showed that Lewis' wife was Nancy, who with further research can be identified as Nancy Tyler, born in Stephentown, N.Y.

Children of Nathan Webb and Olive (Patch) Tyler, several others suggested by census:

 i LYDIA TYLER, b. ca 1776; m. after int. Buckland, 5 April 1794, JAMES STEBBINS, both of Buckland (*VR* 119), b. Ware Sept. 1773, son of Abraham and Lydia (Damon) Stebbins (*Thomas Damon Gen.*). In 1850

James Stebbins ae 76 was living in Nelson, Madison Co., N.Y., with Lydia ae 74, both b. Mass. (p.310).

Stebbins children (*Thomas Damon Gen.*): 1. *Asa Stebbins[7]*, b. ca 1798. 2. *Hannah Stebbins*, b. ca 1800. 3. *Joel Stebbins*, b. ca 1802. 4. *Willard Stebbins*, b. ca 1804. 5. *Sumner Stebbins*, b. ca 1806. 6. *John Stebbins*, b. ca 1808. 7. *Emily Stebbins*, b. ca 1810. 8. *Frances Stebbins*, b. 2 Feb. 1812. 9. *Harriet Stebbins*, b. ca 1814. 10. *Allen Stebbins*, b. ca 1817.

ii   ELIJAH TYLER[6], b. Westhampton, Mass., ca 1777; m. LOUISA HEWITT of Castleton, Vt.; res. Chesterfield.

Children (*Job Tyler Desc.*, 366): 1. *Alsina Tyler[7]*. 2. *Almira Tyler*, drowned at Northampton trying to save a friend. 3. *Harriet Tyler*. 4. *Louisa Tyler*. 5. *Nathan Tyler*, b. 1812. 6. *Lidia Tyler*, m (2) Asa Tubbs. 7. *Elijah Tyler*, b. 24 Feb. 1815; bur. Conway (*VR* 103); m. Lucina S. Tower. 8. *Nancy A. Tyler*. 9. *Henry P. Tyler*, b. 1820; m. Frances Edwards. 10. *Sarah Tyler*. 11. *Julia Tyler*. 12. *Almira Tyler*, m. John Alrien.

? iii   *poss.* DANIEL TYLER, b. ca 1783 Mass.; m. WELTHY ___, b. ca 1794 Mass.; res. 1850 Smithville, N.Y. with daughters Dorcas ae 26, Susan ae 16, and Betsey ae 13 (p.482).

iv   [SON] TYLER, b. 1784-1790 (1800 census).

v   *prob.* ROYAL TYLER, b. ca 1790; in 1850 ae 58 [*sic*], a laborer, living in household of Lewis Nash at Smithfield, N.Y. (p.259).

vi   [DAUGHTER] TYLER, b. 1790-1800 (1800 census).

vii   [DAUGHTER] TYLER, b. 1790-1800 (1800 census).

viii   NANCY TYLER, b. Stephentown, N.Y., 11 Feb. 1797; m. [25 March 1824] LEWIS NASH, b. ca 1802 in N.H. In 1850 he was a blacksmith at Smithfield, Madison Co., N.Y., with Nancy ae 50 b. N.Y., three apparent children, and Royal Tyler ae 58 (p.259). In 1837 the widow Olive Tyler was living in the Nash household (pension file).

Nash children at home 1850, all b. N.Y.: 1. *?Delano C. Nash[7]*, b. ca 1828. 2. *Nancy F. Nash*, b. ca 1832. 3. *Celinda Nash*, b. ca 1838.

? ix   *poss.* ASA TYLER, b. ca 1802 N.Y.; a farmer in Norwich, N.Y., 1850, with *Asa Tyler Jr.[7]*, b. ca 1839 N.Y. (p.207).

Sources cited: *Buckland VR. Upton VR. Chesterfield Families.* Blake, *Worcester Co. Warnings* (1899). Revolutionary War Pension #W18180. *Descendants of Job Tyler* (1912). Nelson B. Tiffany, *Revolutionary War Veterans [of] Chenango County – New York* (1998). Richard A. Damon, Jr., *Thomas Damon of Wayland* (1997). CENSUS: *Heads of Families 1790 – Mass.;* 1800 Stephentown, Rensselaer Co., N.Y. (M32-26); 1850 Chenango Co., Norwich (M432-487), Smithville (M432-488), Madison Co., N.Y., Nelson (M432-527), & Smithfield (M432-526).

578.   STEPHEN TYLER⁵ (*Elijah⁴, Hannah³ Samson, Stephen², Henry¹*), son of Elijah Tyler [121] and his wife Ruth Owen, was born 9 June 1754 at Upton (*VR* 57), and died at Wilmington, Vt., 27 April 1833. He was a descendant also of *Mayflower* passenger John Alden.

He married, first, 12 August 1788, **ANNA STEVENS**, who died 2 June 1799 (*Buckland History*, 669). She may be the daughter of Jacob and Martha (Sherman) Stevens born at Grafton 10 April 1765 (*VR* 122).

Stephen married, second, 21 January 1801, **SARAH ALVORD**, who was born at South Hadley 14 March 1767 to Gideon and Sarah (Montague) Alvord, and died at Wilmington, Vt., 13 March 1817 aged 49 (Wilm. Cem. Rec.).

Stephen was among the children who were warned out of Mendon with their parents in September 1759 (*Worcester Warnings*, 42).

He served in the Revolution, marching on the Lexington Alarm (*Buckland History*, 669). On 2 June 1778 he was among those who signed a petition to have Westhampton set off as a new town (*Mass. Acts & Resolves* 5:989).

In 1790 Stephen and Anna were living in Buckland with one boy under 16 (*Heads of Fam.*, 105). In 1800, the year after Anna's death, Stephen was in Wilmington with an older couple in his household and four children [three boys and a girl] under 10 (p.587).

Children of Stephen and Anna (Stevens) Tyler, first two rec. Buckland (*VR* 53), all rec. Westhampton (Corbin):

    i   BENJAMIN OWEN TYLER⁶, b. 24 Sept. 1789, bp. 27 May 1790 (*Buckland History*, 669); m. ANN MARIA ___ (her name, Washington obits). He was a professor of penmanship, noted for having been the first person to make a facsimile of the Declaration of Independence (1818); lived 13 years at Washington, D.C.; supp. res. 1840 Albany, N.Y.; d. not found.

        Children (first two, *Job Tyler Desc.*, 366; rest, Washington obits); order uncertain: 1. *Howard Tyler⁷*, "res. and d. N.Y.C." 2. *Henry C. Tyler*, "moved west." 3. *Cecilia Minerva Tyler*, b. 1816; d. 3 Sept. 1818 ae 1y 10m, "dau. Benjamin O. and Ann Marie Tyler." 4. *Elizabeth Ann Maria Tyler*, b. ca 1818; d. 30 Nov. 1825 ae 7y after a short illness. 5. *Minerva Tyler*, b. ca Dec. 1820; d. 12 April 1822 ae 1y 4m. 6. *Benjamin Owen Tyler*, b. 1824; d. 23 Aug. 1827 ae 1y 3m, "youngest child of Benjamin O. Esq. of this city [Washington]."

    ii EPHRAIM TYLER, b. 19 April 1791; d. 24 Aug. 1878 Guilford, Vt.; m. 1 Dec. 1819, MARY BISSELL, d. 1861, dau. of Asahel and Polly (___) Bissell; res. Wilmington, Vt., until 1840 when rem. to Guilford.

        Children (*Job Tyler Desc.*, 366-67): 1. *Benjamin O. Tyler⁷*, b. 7 Sept. 1820. 2. *Ansel L. Tyler*, b. 11 Oct. 1822. 3. *D Clinton Tyler*, b. 10 Oct. 1825. 4. *Minerva Tyler*, b. 20 March 1828; d.s.p.; m. Dr. D. W. Jones. 5. *Sarah M. Tyler*, b. 12 Feb.

1831; d. unm. 6. *James M. Tyler*, b. 27 April 1835; res. Brattleboro, Vt. (*Buckland History*, 670). 7. *William H. Tyler*, b. 27 Nov. 1839; m. Belle Newcomb.

iii   ELI TYLER, b. 20 May 1793; d. Newfane, Vt.; m. FREELOVE ___, b. ca 1794 Vt. In 1850 Eli Tyler ae 60 [*sic*] was a farmer in Newfane with Freelove ae 56, and Lewis ae 15; Lucy Smith ae 75 shared the household (p.32).

Children (*Job Tyler Desc.*, 367; census): 1. *Stephen Tyler⁷*. 2. *Lewis Tyler*, b. ca 1835, at home 1850. 3. *Charles Tyler*; res. Newport, Vt.

iv   BETSEY TYLER, b. 20 May 1795; d. Wilmington, Vt., 10 Dec. 1803.

v   CHESTER GRENNELL TYLER, b. 19 Nov. 1797 Westhampton; d. Richmond, N.H., 11 Oct. 1854; bur. West Boylston; m. ROXANNA HARRIS; res. Whitingham and Bennington, Vt. (*Job Tyler Desc.*, 367). The family has not been located in census, but two of the sons m. in West Boylston, "b. Bennington, Vt., parents Chester & Roxa."

Children all but first b. Bennington (*Job Tyler Desc.*, 367-68), birthdates of last three uncertain: 1. *Anna Maria Tyler⁷*, b. Whitingham 20 Aug. 1824. 2. *Oscar Stephen Tyler*, b. 20 Jan. 1828; m. West Boylston, 20 Nov. 1856, Louise Rollins (Mass. VR 101:254). 3. *Jane Caroline Tyler*, b. 20 Jan. 1830; m. (1) Amos Burleigh, (2) ___ Ward. 4. *Elizabeth Celia Tyler*, m. George Munyon. 5. *Henry Clay Tyler*, b. 1835; m. West Boylston in 1862, Marrion Peirce (Mass. VR 155:226). 6. *Chester Warren Tyler*, b. ca 1838; d. in Civil War. 7. *Susan Sophia Tyler*, b. 1844; d.s.p.; m. ___ Fairbanks. 8. *Roxanna Tyler*, d. 1860. 9. *Frances Tyler*, m. ___ Taylor.

Children of Stephen and Sarah (Alvord) Tyler, born Wilmington, Vt. (*Job Tyler Desc.*, 190):

vi   WILLIAM TYLER, b. 19 March, d. 20 March 1802.

vii   STEPHEN TYLER, b. 9 Oct. 1803; d. same day.

viii   EBENEZER TYLER, b. 6 Oct. 1804.

ix   ANSON LYMAN TYLER, b. 8 Nov. 1808; d. "near Rochester, N.Y."; m. MARY E. ____, b. ca 1811 N.Y. In 1850 he was a mechanic at Avon, N.Y., with Mary E. ae 39, b. N.Y., and children as listed (p.304).

Children at home 1850, all b. N.Y.: 1. *Chester W. Tyler⁷*, b. ca 1835. 2. *Mary E. Tyler Jr.*, b. ca 1836. 3. *Ann A. Tyler*, b. ca 1840. 4. *Sarah A. Tyler*, b. ca 1842. 5. *Amanda Tyler*, b. ca 1847. 6. *Franklin W. Tyler*, b. ca 1849.

Sources cited: *Buckland VR* [citing PR 38, W. O. Taylor Collection, Ames Library, Shelburne Falls]. *Grafton VR.* Westhampton VR, Corbin Collection. Mass. Vital Records 1841-1910. Wilmington, Vt., Cemetery Records. Blake, *Worcester Co. Warnings* (1899). *History of Buckland, Massachusetts* (1937). *Job Tyler Descendants* (1912). *Mass. Acts and Resolves.* Washington, D.C., obits on line. CENSUS: *Heads of Families 1790 – Mass.*; 1800 Wilmington, Windham Co., Vt. (M32-52); 1850 Avon, Livingston Co., N.Y. (M432-524), Newfane, Windham Co., Vt. (M432-929).

579.　CATHERINE TYLER[5] (*Elijah[4], Hannah[3] Samson, Stephen[2], Henry[1]*), daughter of Elijah Tyler [121] and his wife Ruth Owen, was born at Upton 10 September 1756 (*VR* 56). She was a descendant also of *Mayflower* passenger John Alden. Catherine was among the children who were warned out of Mendon with their parents in September 1759 (*Worcester Co. Warnings,* 42).

She married, first, [probably **HEZEKIAH] MERIAM**, who died at Westhampton 25 November 1783, aged "(under 30)" (*sic,* CR 114). An "infant of Hezekiah Meriam" died there 24 January 1781 (*ibid.*). For Hezekiah's service in the Revolutionary War from Westhampton, see *MSSR* 10:369.

She married, second, at Westhampton 13 October 1785, as "widow Katherine Meriam," **ISAAC BULLARD** (CRs 43/213). He was born 2 April 1749 at Weston, son of Jonathan and Anna (Herrington) Bullard, and died in Susquehanna County, Pa., in 1842 ae 97 (*Susquehanna History,* 315).

Isaac Bullard served in the Revolutionary War. In his pension application, he stated that he enlisted at Roxbury and served also several times from Oakham (White, 1:458). He was of Westhampton when he bought 105 acres of land there on 7 February 1782, and on 2 December 1802 he sold his farm there "where I live" (Hampshire LR 4:430; 19:398).

In 1800 Isaac Bullard was at Westhampton, with a household consisting of himself and wife, 45+, two boys under 10, and one girl and one boy 10-16 (p.17). In 1810 they were in Wilmington, Vt. (p.249), with three young men and one young woman 16-26 in the household. The unusual format of the census in that town includes the information that they had clothes [prob. "cloths," not wearing apparel] consisting of 16 lbs. of wool and 16 lbs. of linen, no cotton, and no loom.

Isaac and Catherine Bullard evidently accompanied her brothers Moses and Simeon Tyler to settle in Susquehanna County, Pa. An account written in 1873 (*Susquehanna History,* 315), states:

> Isaac Bullard, a Revolutionary soldier, settled in 1812, where James Bunnell lives [in 1873], ... after a time he removed to the late location of his son, Hezekiah, in the south neighborhood. He died in 1842 aged 97. Of his sons, Elijah, the eldest, is now living in Montrose, over 80 years of age; Hezekiah and Otis have died recently aged respectively 79 and 77.

Census records indicate that all the grandchildren were born in Pennsylvania. Isaac Bullard was living at Bridgewater, Pa., aged 84, when he applied for a pension on 10 September 1832 (file #S2048).

Children of Isaac and Catherine (Tyler) Bullard:

　i　SALLY BULLARD[6], b. 18 Dec. 1786; apparently living, unm., in 1810.

ii ELIJAH BULLARD, b. 26 Nov. 1790; living Montrose, Pa., 1873 (*Susq. Co. History*, 315); m. in 1816, PHEBE DEANS. In 1850 he was a farmer at Bridgewater, Pa., with Phebe ae 52, b. Conn. (p.295).

Children at home 1850, all b. Penn: 1. *Catherine O. Bullard*, b. ca 1820. 2. *Zebulon D. Bullard*, b. ca 1825. 3. *Helen A. Bullard*, b. ca 1835. (Blackman says six children in all.)

iii HEZEKIAH BULLARD, b. 14 July 1793; d. Bridgewater, Pa., ae 79 (*Susq. Co. History*, 315); m. in 1816, MATILDA DEANS. In 1850 he was a carpenter ae 57, living at Bridgewater with Matilda, 53, b. Conn. (p.297).

Children at home 1850, all b. Pa.: 1. *Fanny D. Bullard*, b. ca 1819. 2. *Lucy F. Bullard*, b. ca 1826. 3. *Abigail Bullard*, b. ca 1831. 4. *Orson F. Bullard*, b. ca 1833; a clerk in 1850. 5. *Clarissa Bullard*, b. ca 1835. 6. *Frederick O. Bullard*, b. ca 1839. 7. *Julius L Bullard*, b. ca 1840. (Blackman says 10 ch. in all.)

iv OTIS BULLARD, b. March 1795; d. Bridgewater, Pa., ae 77 (*Susq. Co. History*, 315); m. MARY ANN CROOKER, b. 1799 in Conn. In 1850 they were living at Bridgewater, Pa. (p.292); Otis was 55, a farmer, b. Mass., with Mary Ann ae 51, and five children. In his will dated 19 Oct. 1864, proved 2 March 1872, Otis Bullard of Bridgewater Township asked to be buried in the South Bridgewater Cemetery according to rites of the Universalist Church; and left $100 to daughter Naomy Mary [*sic*], and all other property to son W. W. Bullard (Susquehanna Co. Wills 3:473-74).

Children at home 1850, all b. Pa.: 1. *Sally Caroline Bullard*, b. ca 1826. 2. *Hannah Jane Bullard*, b. ca 1830. 3. *Naomi Ruth Bullard*, b. ca 1832. 4. *Betsey Salome Bullard*, b. ca 1834. 5. *William Wallace Bullard*, b. ca 1837. (Blackman says there were one son and six or seven daughters.)

Sources cited: Westhampton Church Records, Corbin Collection. Blake, *Worcester Co. Warnings* (1899). Blackman, *History of Susquehanna County, Pennsylvania* (1873). Hampshire County Deeds at Northampton. Susquehanna County, Pa., Probate Records. Revolutionary War Pension Files. CENSUS: 1800 Westhampton, Hampshire Co. (M32-15); 1810 Wilmington, Windham Co., Vt. (M252-65); 1850 Bridgewater, Susquehanna Co., Pa. (M432-829).

580. EUNICE TYLER[5] (*Elijah[4], Hannah[3] Samson, Stephen[2], Henry[1]*), daughter of Elijah Tyler [121] and his wife Ruth Owen, was born at Upton 10 December 1758 (*VR* 56) as "Unice Tyler." She was a descendant also of *Mayflower* passenger John Alden. She was living in September 1759, among the children named when the family was warned out of Mendon (*Worcester Co. Warnings*, 42). No further record of her has been found.

Sources cited: *Upton VR. Worcester County Warnings.*

581.   RUTH TYLER[5] (*Elijah*[4], *Hannah*[3] *Samson, Stephen*[2], *Henry*[1]), daughter of Elijah Tyler [121] and his wife Ruth Owen, was born 27 February 1761 at Upton (*VR* 56) and died 21 April 1842 at Buckland (*VR* 133), aged 81, "widow of John Bullard." She was a descendant also of *Mayflower* passenger John Alden.

She married at Westhampton, 16 November 1786, "both of Westhampton" (VR Corbin, 89/213), **JOHN BULLARD II**. He was born about 1750 and died 24 February 1820 at Buckland (*VR* 133; pension), aged 70. John and Ruth are buried in Buckland Center Cemetery.

John served in the Revolution in the Continental and Massachusetts Lines. He was a resident of Buckland, Franklin County, when he applied for a pension 16 April 1818. His widow Ruth was living in Charlemont 16 October 1838, "aged 77 last February," when she applied. She stated that she was Ruth Tyler and that she and John were both of Westhampton when they were married. John was called John Bullard II in Westhampton, there being another John Bullard in that town. The marriage record was from Records of the Court of General Sessions of Hampshire County, Book II, p. 232. (Rev. pension #W15620.) The pension file includes records of several Westhampton marriages, including that of Ruth's sister Catherine (Tyler) Meriam, but not her own.

In his will dated 27 January 1818, presented 23 May 1820, John Bullard, husbandman, "late of Buckland," named his wife Ruth sole executrix. Witnesses were Sally Forbes, Enos Pomeroy, and Edw. Fobes (Franklin PR #645).

Ruth Bullard, sister of Nathan Tyler [#577], testified at Buckland 2 November 1836, in support of his widow's pension application, that she had attended his marriage. In 1840 Ruth Bullard, aged 79, was listed as a Revolutionary pensioner, in Charlemont in the household of [her nephew] Calvin Walker (p.31).

There is no indication that John and Ruth (Tyler) Bullard had any children.

Sources cited: *Buckland VR* [citing P.R. 38, family records in Collection of W. O. Taylor, at Arms Library, Shelburne Falls]. *Upton VR*. Westhampton Church Records, Corbin Collection. Franklin County Probate Records at Greenfield. *Other Bullards*, Supplement to *Bullard and Allied Families*. White, *Abstracts of Revolutionary War Pension Files*, citing #W15620. CENSUS: 1840 Charlemont, Franklin Co. (M704-183).

582.   MOSES TYLER[5] (*Elijah*[4], *Hannah*[3] *Samson, Stephen*[2], *Henry*[1]), son of Elijah Tyler [121] and his wife Ruth Owen, was born 10 June 1766 at Upton (*VR* 56) and died 11 April 1854 at Montrose, Pennsylvania (pension). He was a descendant also of *Mayflower* passenger John Alden.

He married at Hadley, 15 November 1791 (pension), after intentions 30 July 1791 at Westhampton (VR, Corbin), **SARAH COOK**, who was born at Hadley 14

February 1774 to Coleman and Hannah (Smith) Cook (*Hadley Families*, 26), and died in 1856 (*Susquehanna History*, 305).

Moses served in the Revolution, enlisting at Westhampton in 1777 as a private in Capt. John Banister's company and serving from September to the last of November in Col. Job Cushing's 6th Worcester County regiment, and again in 1779 from August to the end of December in Capt. Thomas Hovey's company, Col. Nathan Tyler's 3rd Worcester County regiment, in Rhode Island (pension rec.; *MSSR* 16:237).

Buckland records state that Moses Tyler was a grantee there in 1795 and a grantor in 1797. The family settled in Wilmington, Vt., about 1800, when they were listed there in the census; Moses and Sarah were 26-45, with four little girls under 10 in the household (p.587).

Emily Blackman in her 1873 *History of Susquehanna County* relates (p.304),

> Moses Tyler, an older brother of Simeon, and a native of Massachusetts, came from Wilmington, Windham County, Vt., in the spring of 1808, not then anticipating to find a home in this section; but, stopping in the south neighborhood to spend the Sabbath, it became known that he was a Congregationalist, and one ready to take an active part in a prayer-meeting. The circle of Christian mothers that had met from one Sabbath to another without the presence of a man to lead their devotions, now importuned him to bring his family to the settlement and remain to aid in sustaining religious services. Deeming this an indication of Providence, Mr. Tyler relinquished his intention of going farther west, and returned to Vermont. In the fall of that year he came with his wife and nine children, all girls but one, Moses C., late associate judge; and was accompanied by Samuel Davis and his family, which was also large, and all his children, but one, were boys. The party came in *via* Great Bend. Mr. Edward Fuller happening there on business, met them and hastened home with the joyful news, "Moses and the children of Israel are coming through the wilderness."

> Mr. Tyler stayed with all his family at the house of Stephen Wilson until he finished a log-house on what is now the Jessup farm, not far from the old brick-yard. He bought of the Pennsylvania landholder, J. B. Wallace. Afterwards, when the county was set off, the lands donated to it covered part of his tract. He received some indemnity for his improvements, and removed to the farm in Dimock which is now owned by John Wright. He moved back some years later, near his old location, to a small house that occupied the site of Dr. J. Blackman's present residence. Later, he resided again on a farm, just south of Stephen Wilson's old place, until his last removal to the home of his son in Montrose. He was a deacon of the Presbyterian church many years. He died April, 1854, aged eighty-eight; Mrs. T. in 1856, over eighty. They had twelve children. While living by the brick-yard (then

only a swamp), Mrs. Tyler went to visit Mrs. Wheaton, when she met a bear, sitting on his haunches and staring her in the face. She screamed and struck the brushwood, when the bear turned and walked quietly away, and she proceeded on her errand ....

Moses was 54 on 15 April 1818 when he applied for a pension in Susquehanna County, Pa. In 1820 he stated that he had wife Sarah, ae 46, and children at home: Moses 18, twins Emma and Emily 14, Eunice 10, and Eliza 8. In 1840 he was 74, living at Bridgewater, Pa. (p.302).

In 1850 (p.180), Moses Tyler, aged 83, and Sarah, 76, both born in Massachusetts, were living in Montrose, Pa., next to the family of their son Moses C. Tyler. Sarah applied for a widow's pension on 14 April 1854, and for a bounty land warrant on 15 March 1855.

Children of Moses and Sarah (Cook) Tyler, last three b. probably at Montrose, Pa. (order of the children has been corrected from that given in *Job Tyler Desc.*, 190-91, to match ages in census):

   i   MELINDA TYLER⁶, b. prob. 1792 (57 in 1850); m. THOMAS CARRIER, b. ca 1779 Conn. In 1850 he was a farmer in Auburn, Susquehanna Co., Pa. (p.53), with Melinda ae 57, b. Vt., Mary ae 20, Eldad ae 17, and Melinda ae 15, and a 17-yr-old girl ["B. Stout"?] whose name is illegible.
         Carrier children (*Job Tyler Desc.*, 191, omits Mary and Melinda) included: 1. *Sarah Carrier⁷.*   2. *Prudence Carrier.*   3. *Lucinda Carrier.*   4. *Moses Carrier.* 5. *Benjamin Carrier.* 6. *Sylvester Carrier.* 7. *Mary Carrier*, b. ca 1830; at home 1850. 8. *Eldad Carrier*, b. ca 1833; at home 1850.   9. *Melinda Carrier*, b. ca 1835; at home 1850.

   ii SALLY TYLER, b. ca 1794 (56 in 1850); m. JOSEPH BEEBE. In 1850 Joseph Beebe ae 59, b. Conn., was a farmer in Bridgewater, Pa. (p.296), with wife Sally ae 56, b. Mass.; sons Ezra, James Edward, and Orrin A.; and Margaret Kane ae 15, b. Ireland.
         Beebe children (*Job Tyler Desc.*, 191, omits James E. and Orrin A. who are in 1850 census): 1. *Owen Beebe⁷.* 2. *Angeline Beebe.* 3. *Hiram A. Beebe.* 4. *William L. Beebe.* 5. *Ezra Beebe*, b. ca 1822. 6. *Joseph Beebe.* 7. *Hannah Beebe.* 8. *Elizabeth Beebe.* 9. *James Edward Beebe*, b. ca 1830. 10. *Orrin A. Beebe*, b. ca 1822 (perhaps same as Owen?).

   iii HANNAH TYLER, b. 24 Feb. 1795 Hadley (*Job Tyler Desc.*, 191); m. 9 Feb. 1815, ELDAD BREWSTER, d. Dec. 1831 leaving his widow with nine children, the youngest five months old (*Susquehanna History*, 292). In 1850 Hannah Brewster ae 54, b. Mass., was living in the household of her son Horace at Bridgewater, Pa. (p.309).

Brewster children (*Job Tyler Desc.*, 368): 1. *Tyler Brewster*[7], b. 24 March 1815. 2. *Lucania Brewster*, b. 20 Nov. 1816. 3. *Horace Brewster*, b. 10 Oct. 1818; m. Augusta ___. 4. *Daniel Brewster*, b. 22 Nov. 1820. 5. *Warren Brewster*, b. 11 Dec. 1822. 6. *Andrew Brewster* (twin), b. 23 March 1827. 7. *Sally Brewster* (twin), b. 23 March 1827; m. S. A. Hempstead 8. *Moses Coleman Brewster*, d. 1859. 9. *Ann Mariah Brewster*, b. 18 July 1831; m. Ansel Stearns.

iv CLARISSA TYLER, b. ca 1799 (51 in 1850); m. at Montrose, Pa., JASON POTTER, b. ca 1794 in Conn. In 1850 he was a farmer in Orwell, Bradford Co., N.Y. (p.139), with Clarissa ae 51, Alonzo ae 28, Elizer ae 23, David ae 19, and Helen ae 13, and Peter Colegrove ae 23, blacksmith b. N.Y.

    Potter children at home 1850, all b. Pa.: 1. *Alonzo Potter*[7], b. ca 1822; a farmer 1850. 2. *Elizer Potter*, b. ca 1827, a groceryman 1850. 3. *David Potter*, b. ca 1831, a farmer 1850. 4. *Denison Potter*, b. ca 1833. 5. *Helen Potter*, b. ca 1837. (*Job Tyler Desc.*, 191, says ch. were Alonzo, Isaiah, Emmerline, and Denison.)

v MOSES COLEMAN TYLER, b. 7 April 1802 Wilmington, Vt.; d. 26 Jan. 1885; m. (1) Dec. 1825, MARY FRENCH, b. 24 June 1806, d. 1 March 1840; m. (2) 18 Oct. 1841, CORNELIA G. READ, b. Montrose, Pa., 8 Sept. 1820, d. 4 May 1845; m. (3) 15 May 1847, HARRIET HARRIS, b. 18 May 1807 North Sea, L.I., N.Y., d. 1897 (*Job Tyler Desc.*, 368-69). In 1850 (p.180) he was a merchant in Montrose, Pa., with wife Harriet H. ae 41; son Henry C. ae 13; Jerome Crocker ae 21, clerk, b. Pa.; and Ellen Caromody ae 23, b. Ireland. *Job Tyler Desc.* claims this line is "extinct."

    Children, first four with Mary, next two with Cornelia, last with Harriet (*Job Tyler Desc.*, 369): 1. *Owen Benjamin Tyler*[7], b. 16 Aug. 1826; d. 1860 unm. 2. *Clark Kellogg Tyler*, b. 13 Sept. 1828; d. 1857 unm. 3. *Coleman Merriam Tyler*, b. 22 Aug. 1831; d. 1837. 4. *Henry Cass Tyler*, b. 18 June 1837; m. Frances E. Wilcox; no ch. 5. *George Kearl Tyler*, b. 7 Oct. 1842; d. 1843. 6. *Ella Cornelia Tyler*, b. 27 Jan. 1845; d. 1852. 7. *William Cooper Tyler*, b. 4 Aug. 1851; d. 1852.

vi PARMELIA TYLER, b. 31 Jan. 1804 Wilmington, Vt.; d. 10 Aug. 1888 (*Job Tyler Desc.*, 191); m. WILLIAM SLOAN.

    Sloan child (*ibid.*): 1. *Ann Sloan*[7], m. David Quick.

vii EMMA TYLER (twin), b. 1807, prob. Wilmington, Vt.; d. Willet, N.Y., 10 Aug. 1863; m. 1 Jan. 1826, SAMUEL E. NEWCOMB, b. Bridgewater, Pa., 1 Dec. 1806.

    Newcomb children (*Job Tyler Desc.*, 369): 1. *Therese E. Newcomb*[7], b. 11 Oct. 1829; m. Gilbert Greene. 2. *Elizabeth E. Newcomb*, b. 5 March 1831; m. J. Cook. 3. *Adaline Newcomb*, b. 15 Oct. 1832; m. Orlando Avery. 4. *Sarah O. Newcomb*, b. 23 Aug. 1834; m. Stephen J. Adams. 5. *Louise Newcomb*, b. 25 July 1836; m. Angelos M. Clark. 6. *Gilbert L. Newcomb*, b. 19 April 1840; m. Lizzie Sunderland.

7. *Franklin Newcomb*, b. 19 July 1842; m. Libbie Thurston. 8. *Curtis S. Newcomb*, b. 5 March 1843; m. Pluma Mathews. 9. *Willis Newcomb*, b. 3 Nov. 1845. 10. *Ella Newcomb*, b. 3 March 1847; m. ___ Delavan. 11. *Marion Newcomb*, b. Aug. 1849; d. 1860. 12. *Cornelia Newcomb*, b. 7 Nov. 1851; d. 1852.

viii EMILY TYLER (twin), b. 1807, prob. Wilmington, Vt.; m. 4 Oct. 1826 URI NEWCOMB, b. Montrose, Pa., 2 Aug. 1806 (*Job Tyler Desc.*, 370). In 1850 he was a farmer in Bridgewater (p.295), with Emily ae 44, and children Emma, U. Clark, Alburn, Martin V., Adelia, Amanda, Ugene, and Frederick P.

   Newcomb children (*Job Tyler Desc.*, 370-71): 1. *Marvin Alonzo Newcomb*[7], b. 14 Sept. 1827; first mayor of Tama City, Iowa. 2. *Emma Ann Newcomb*, b. 20 Dec. 1828; m. James W. Wright. 3. *Uri Clark Newcomb*, b. 12 Oct. 1830; m. Caroline Munson. 4. *Alburn R. Newcomb*, b. 1 Aug. 1832; m. Lura Morgan. 5. *Martin Van Buren Newcomb*, b. 10 Sept. 1834; m. Roseltha Taylor. 6. *Frances Adelia Newcomb*, b. 1 Feb. 1837; m. Ezra B. Gord. 7. *Sarah Amanda Newcomb*, b. 26 June 1839; m. Thomas Smith. 8. *Eugene S. Newcomb*, b. 21 Aug. 1844; m. Jennie Trinter. 9. *Frederick Peter Newcomb*, b. 22 June 1847; m. Julia Munson. 10. *Emily Eudora Newcomb*, b. 27 Sept. 1850; d. 6 Feb. 1864.

ix EUNICE TYLER, b. 1810; m. CHAUNCEY TUBBS, b. ca 1811 N.Y. In 1850 he was a grocer in Greene, Chenango Co., N.Y. (p.332). with Eunice ae 40, b. N.Y., and W. M. Tubbs ae 17.

   Probable **Tubbs** child, at home 1850: 1. *W. M. Tubbs*[7], b. ca 1833; a painter 1850.

x ELIZA TYLER, b. 1812.

xi BENJAMIN OWEN TYLER, b. 1819; d. young.

Sources cited: *Upton VR.* Wilmington, Vt., VR. Revolutionary War Pension Files W25509 and Bounty Land Warrant 524-160-55. Boltwood, *Genealogies of Hadley Families* (1862). *Census of Pensioners 1840. Job Tyler Descendants* (1912). CENSUS: 1800 Wilmington, Windham Co., Vt. (M32-52); Bridgewater, Susquehanna Co., Pa., 1840 (M704-476) & 1850 (M432-829); 1850 Greene, Chenango Co., N.Y. (M432-488) & Orwell, Bradford Co., Pa. (M432-757).

583.   SIMEON TYLER[5] (*Elijah*[4], *Hannah*[3] *Samson*, *Stephen*[2], *Henry*[1]), son of Elijah Tyler [121] and his wife Ruth Owen, was born 9 September 1770, probably at Upton (not in VR) just before the family moved to Chesterfield. He died at Montrose, Pa., in July 1850 (*Susquehanna Hist.*, 301), just after he was listed in the census there, aged 80. He was a descendant also of *Mayflower* passenger John Alden.

He married 24 November 1796 at Westhampton after intentions there 9 April (CR 93, 138), **BETSEY BREWSTER**, who was born 10 April 1773 at Killingly, Conn. (*VR* 1:296, as Elisabeth), daughter of Nathan and Elizabeth (___) Brewster, and died at Bridgewater, Pa., 29 March 1839 (Alden Kindred). She was a descendant of *Mayflower* passengers John Alden and William Brewster.

The family settled in Wilmington, Vt., after 1800, and then in 1807 removed to Montrose, Pa., along with the family of Elizabeth's brother, Nathan Brewster. Emily Blackman, writing in 1873 (*Susquehanna History*, 299-301), described their struggles to get started:

> [They] came in together from Connecticut, February, 1807, with their families, ten persons in all, and all halted for five weeks at the house of Joseph Raynsford, whose only daughter was the wife of Nathan Brewster. Simeon Tyler began preparations for building a log-house large enough to accommodate his own and Mr. Brewster's family. Mr. B. was laid aside from work, having cut his foot in getting out boards. But, at length, when all was ready, the great "snow-storm" delayed their removal until some time in April. ... The cabin of Mr. Tyler was three miles from Mr. Raynsford, being at the northern foot of the first hill, due north of Montrose, one of the very longest and steepest of our hills. The season did not allow them to put up a chimney, and, until the frost was out of the ground, a hole in the roof was made to serve the purpose for *two* fires. Cooking was done on each side of a central pile of logs, and blankets served as a partition between the two families. Mr. Tyler had five children, and Mr. Brewster only one. ... In the fall of 1807, Nathan Brewster built a comfortable log-house directly opposite that of Mr. Tyler ... Both houses were near the source of one of the minor tributaries of the Wyalusing. ... Mr. Tyler had brought a yoke of oxen, but ... one was killed by the fall of a tree ... [he] finally succeeded in bartering off the ox for another horse, and thus a team was secured which was used in common by [Tyler and Brewster].... [Tyler] had eleven children, of whom the eldest [*sic*], Harvey, has been our late representative at Harrisburg.

Children of Simeon and Elizabeth (Brewster) Tyler (*Job Tyler Desc.*, 191-92):

i SIMEON TYLER⁶, b. 6 Dec. 1797 Westhampton; d. Brooklyn, Pa., 20 Nov. 1857; m. Bridgewater, Pa., 30 Oct. 1822, WEALTHY WARNER, b. ca 1801, d. Montrose, Pa., 24 March 1837; m. (2) by 1850 MARY _____, b. ca 1807 in Pa. In 1850 (p.298) Simeon Tyler ae 51, farmer, b. N.Y. [written over something else], was living in Bridgewater, Pa., with Mary ae 43, b. Pa., Edwin Roberts ae 17, and Casper Tyler ae 13.

Children (*Job Tyler Desc.*, 371): 1. *Amanda R. Tyler⁷*, b. 10 Feb. 1823. 2. *Eliza Ophelia Tyler*, b. 9 July 1825 Dimmock, Pa.; m. Orlando Gurdon Hempstead (Alden Kindred). 3. *Casper William Tyler*, b. 6 March 1837.

ii BETSEY TYLER, b. 6 Dec. 1799 Westhampton; d. Bridgewater, Pa., 1868 (Alden Kindred); m. (1) Bridgewater, Pa., 10 Oct. 1822 HARRY CLARK,

(2) 15 Oct. 1839, GEORGE W. LEWIS, a hotel-keeper in Dimock, Pa.
(*Job Tyler Desc.*, 371).

    Clark children (*ibid.*): 1. *Ruby F. Clark[7]*, m. James Bullard of Brooklyn, Pa.
2. *Anna Clark,* d. unm. 1863.

iii   ANSEL TYLER, b. 14 Feb. 1803 Wilmington, Vt.; d. E. Bridgewater, Pa.,
10 March 1848; m. at Yardleyville, Pa., Jan. 1835, ISABELLA LOUISA
YOUNG, b. 1805, d. 24 March 1895 E. Bridgewater (*Job Tyler Desc.*, 371).

    Children, four oldest b. Dimmock, others Bridgewater, Pa. (*Job Tyler Desc.*,
371-72): 1. *Leander Ansel Tyler[7]*, b. 23 Feb. 1836. 2. *Duane Legrange Tyler,* b. 26
July 1837. 3. *Ellen Lucenia Tyler,* b. 8 Sept. 1839; m. Jason Frost Whitney.
4. *Andrew Osias Tyler,* b. 4 Dec. 1840. 5. *Clark Lewis Tyler,* b. 20 Feb. 1842.
6. *Martha Tyler,* b. 5 March 1844.

iv   HARVEY TYLER, b. 1 April 1804 Wilmington, Vt.; d. Montrose, Pa., ca
1889 (Alden Kindred); m. (1) 27 Sept. 1827, SARAH COYLE of
Philadelphia, b. ca 1806; m. (2) 26 June 1849, AMANDA BULLARD, b.
ca 1820 Pa. (*Job Tyler Desc.*, 372). He was a Pennsylvania State Representative. In 1850 (p.187) Harvey Tyler ae 46, carpenter, b. Mass. [*sic*], was in
Montrose, Pa., with Amanda ae 22, and dau. Sarah.

    Children, b. Montrose, Pa. (*Job Tyler Desc.*, 372), with Sarah: 1. *William Larned
Tyler[7]*, b. 8 May 1833. 2. *Charles B. Tyler,* b. 21 Sept. 1834. 3. *Logan Osceola Tyler,* b.
22 June 1836; killed in Civil War at Chancellorsville 1863. 4. *Sarah Adelaide Tyler,*
b. 24 Nov. 1840; m. Thomas Williams. Children with Amanda: 5. *George W.
Tyler,* b. 16 Nov. 1850. 6. *Harvey J. Tyler,* b. 15 March 1859; d. 1863.

v   ABIGAIL TYLER, b. 19 Aug. 1806 Wilmington, Vt.; d. Bridgewater, Pa.,
5 Jan. 1835; m. there 6 Dec. 1827 LEVI B. GUERNSEY. He was ae 43 in
1850 at Bridgewater, Pa. (p.304) with [second] wife Hannah ae 34, who
was prob. mother of the younger Guernsey children: Abigail ae 13, Sophia
ae 11, Almira ae 9, James ae 5, and Maria ae 3; Leander Tyler ae 15 was
also in the household.

    Guernsey children (*Job Tyler Desc.*, 372-73; 1850 census): 1. *George Mortimer
Guernsey[7]*, b. 4 Oct. 1828 Tioga, Pa.; m. Martha Roach. 2. *Sarah Ophelia Guernsey,*
b. 2 Nov. 1830; m. ___ Sweet. 3. *Peter C. Guernsey,* b. 30 May 1833. ?4. *Ophelia
Guernsey,* d. y. [or is she same as Sarah Ophelia?]

vi   RAWSON TYLER, b. 20 May 1808 Montrose, Pa.; d. young.

vii   LUCENIA TYLER, b. 19 Jan. 1810 Montrose, Pa.; d. Bridgewater, Pa., 12
June 1836 (*Job Tyler Desc.*, 192).

viii   OSIAS TYLER, b. 20 June 1813 Montrose, Pa.; d. Bethlehem, Pa., 7 Feb.
1848; m. Montrose, 21 Aug. 1838, AUGUSTA L. HAMILTON, b. ca
1817 (Alden Kindred). No children (*Job Tyler Desc.*, 192).

ix   BREWSTER TYLER, b. 5 July 1814; d. Coxtown, Pa., 17 April 1835, drowned in Susquehanna River while rafting logs (*ibid.*).

Sources cited: Westhampton CR, Corbin Collection. Killingly VR as cited in Barbour Index. Blackman, *History of Susquehanna County* (1873). *Job Tyler Descendants* (1912). Alden Kindred web site. CENSUS: 1850 Montrose & Bridgewater, Susquehanna Co., Pa. (M432-829). **See also:** *Brewster Genealogy*, 1:104.

584.   SARAH / SALLY TYLER[5] (*Elijah⁴, Hannah³ Samson, Stephen², Henry¹*), daughter of Elijah Tyler [121] and his wife Ruth Owen, was born probably about July 1772 at Upton or Chesterfield and baptized 27 September 1772 at Chesterfield (CR, Corbin). She died 5 May 1859 at Dover [originally South Wardsboro], Vt., aged 86y 9m (g.s.). She was a descendant also of *Mayflower* passenger John Alden.

She married at Westhampton, 31 December 1795, **JOB WALKER**; their intentions published there 5 December call them both of Westhampton (CR 134, 92/144). He was born about January 1771 and died 29 December 1839 at Dover, Vt., aged 68y 11m (g.s.). He may be the Job Walker, son of Job and Mary (Williams) Walker, born at Dorchester 9 January 1771 "some months after decease of father who had resided in Dorchester some time" (*VR* 1:177).

The few census entries for the family that have been found suggest that they moved back and forth between northern Massachusetts and Vermont. The 1810 census listed Job Walker at Marlboro, Vt., himself and apparent wife 26-45, with two boys and one girl 10-16 and two boys and one girl under 10; the family had 55 lbs of woolen cloth, 60 lbs of linen, and 20 lbs of cotton (p.304). On 11 March 1811, Job Walker, his wife Sally, and children Ruth, William, Lucius, Calvin, and Alfred, were warned out of Marlboro (*Vt. Warnings*, 2:225). The only likely listing in 1830 is in Buckland, for a Job Walker aged 50-60 with a wife the same age, and one young woman 15-20 (p.26).

In 1850 Sarah Walker, aged 77, and her son Calvin were living in the household of George Hillman ae 29, and wife Elessa ae 26, in Charlemont (p.252). No probate records have been found for Job or Sally.

Children of Job and Sally (Tyler) Walker, listed in 1811 warning; (*Job Tyler Desc.*, 191 omits Ruth, Lucius, and Alfred, and adds Elijah and Mary; no birth recs. found):

i   RUTH WALKER[7], b. prob. 1796; living 1811; n.f.r.

ii   WILLIAM WALKER, b. ca 1798 in Mass.; living Dover, Vt., 1850; m. (1) LYDIA _____, d. Dover 24 Sept. 1834 in 32nd yr; m. (2) LUCY MIRANDA _____, d. 2 April 1848 ae 28y 3m 3d; m. (3) LAURANA _____, b. Vt. ca 1814, living 1850. William's first two wives are buried near his parents. In 1850 he was ae 42, a farmer with real estate worth $2400; the household included Laurana, 36, *Henry W.*, ae 9, and Washington Sparks, 34, farmer, b. Vt. (p.221).

iii   LUCIUS WALKER, b. prob. ca 1800; living 1811; *possibly* the Lucius Walker ae 50, b. Vt., who was a mason in Ward 13, N.Y.C., 1850, with wife HENRIETTE ___, b. ca 1810 Vt., and three children (p.221).
  Children at home 1850: 1. *Aldus Walker⁷*, b. ca 1836 Conn. 2. *Edna Walker*, b. ca 1843 Conn. 3. *Lucius Walker*, b. ca 1848 N.Y.

iv   CALVIN WALKER, b. ca 1803 Wilmington, Vt.; m. at Charlemont, 11 Dec. 1850, MARY MILLEN, b. ca 1819 Wilmington, Vt., dau. of Humphrey and Sarah (___) Millen (b. & m. info., Mass. VR 45:201). In 1850 he was ae 46, a shoemaker, living with his mother in the household of George Hillman in Charlemont (p.924); in 1860 he was ae 57, a shoemaker at Readsboro, Vt., with wife and son (p.924).
  Child: 1. *William Tyler Walker⁷*, b. 6 June 1852 Charlemont (Mass. VR 63:254).

v   ALFRED WALKER, b. ca 1805; d. Charlemont 1 Dec. 1831 ae 26 (*VR* 164); m. there after int. 5 Jan. 1828 (*VR* 127), LAURA DARBY, b. there 3 Sept. 1807, dau. of Samuel and Jerutia (___) Darby (*VR* 26). Laura m. (2) Thomas Weaver and in 1850 was living in Hawley with him, son Alfred Weaver ae 1, Jerusha Darby ae 72, and Laura Walker ae 20 (p.270).
  Child rec. Charlemont (*VR* 83): 1. *Lauraette/Laura Walker⁷*, b. 1 Aug. 1830.

vi   ELIJAH WALKER (*Job Tyler Desc.*); not with family 1811; n.f.r.

vii   MARY WALKER (*ibid.*); not with family 1811, but 1810 census indicates a girl b. 1800-1810; n.f.r.

Sources cited: *Charlemont VR. Dorchester VR [BRC* 21]. Mass. Vital Records 1841-1910. Chesterfield Church Records and Westhampton Church Records, Corbin Collection. Arthur D. Fiske, *Cemetery Records of Dover, Vermont to 1865* (1963). *Vermont Warnings Out*, Vol. 2. *Job Tyler Descendants* (1912). CENSUS: 1810 Marlboro, Windham Co., Vt. (M252-65); 1830 Buckland & Charlemont, Franklin Co. (M19-62); 1850 Dover, Windham Co., Vt. (M432-929) & Charlemont, Franklin Co. (M432-317); 1860 Readsboro, Bennington Co., Vt. (M653-1316).

585.   STEPHEN NELSON⁵ (*Hannah Tyler⁴, Hannah³ Samson, Stephen², Henry¹*), son of Francis Nelson and his wife Hannah Tyler [122], was born 29 April 1756 at Upton (*VR* 40) and died 1 February 1829 aged 72y 9m at Buckland (*VR* 144).

He married, at Upton, 6 October 1791 (*VR* 119), **AZUBA TAFT**, who was born at Upton 27 November 1761, daughter of Matthew Jr. and Hannah (Cutler) Taft (*VR* 52), and died 7 February 1846 aged 84y 2m 11d at Buckland, as "widow of Stephen" (*VR* 144). Stephen and Azuba are buried in Buckland Center Cemetery.

Stephen Nelson Jr., of Upton, yeoman, bought 50 acres in Buckland on 28 May 1787 (Franklin LR 65:71). He was of Buckland on 14 April 1819 when he bought Lot 250 there (*ibid.*, 32:356).

The will of Stephen Nelson of Buckland, dated 29 December 1828 and proved 19 May 1829, names his wife Azuba, daughter Azuba who was single, and sons Moses, Asa, and Levi; son Moses to be executor (Franklin PR #3336).

Children of Stephen and Azuba (Taft) Nelson, all but Betsey bp. Buckland 22 Nov. 1807 (*VR* 33-34) as "of Stephen":

i   MOSES NELSON⁶, b. ca 1792 Buckland (*Buckland History*, 552); d. 7 Sept. 1881, ae 89, Buckland (Mass. VR 328:312). He m. 11 March 1881 (at age 88), SUSAN BRONSON, ae 86, housekeeper, daughter of Smisson [?Smithson] and Elizabeth (___) Bronson of Buckland; it was the first marriage for both (Mass. VR 325:351). She d. 12 July 1901 (*Buckland History*, 552). In 1850 Moses Nelson ae 58 was a farmer at Buckland, with Euseba [prob. his sister Azubah] Nelson ae 53, Susanna Bronson ae 53, and Jas Nelson ae 11 (p.205).

ii   HANNAH NELSON, b. ca 1794; d. 10 June 1819, ae 25, Buckland, unm.; bur. with parents (*VR* 144).

iii AZUBAH NELSON, b. ca 1795; d. Buckland 14 Feb. 1864 ae 68y 8m 10d (Mass. VR 174:286). In 1850 census she was listed as Euseba, living with her brother Moses and Susan[na] Bronson who later became his wife.

iv   ASA NELSON, b. prob. 1801; d. after 1880, prob. at Franklin, Delaware Co., N.Y., where he was an assessor and one of the first trustees of the Presbyterian Church (*Delaware Co. History*, 181, 189). He was named in his father's will in 1828. Census records list him as a cooper and/or caskmaker, and in 1880 he was disabled by paralysis. He m. (1) MARY SQUIRES, b. ca 1806 in N.Y., dau. of Abraham and Matilda (___) Squires; she d. between 1850 and 1857, and he m. (2) MARGARET ____, b. ca 1812 N.Y.

Children (census), with first wife, Mary: 1. *Samuel W. Nelson⁷*, b. ca 1835. 2. *Levi Nelson*, b. ca 1838; living with Squires grandparents 1850 and named in both their wills (Delaware Co. Wills C:5, 50); d. 1858; m. Emma ____ (*ibid.,*, F:134). 3. *Pliny F. Nelson*, b. ca 1842; d. 1864 in Civil War service (*ibid.*, G:16); named in will of grandfather Squires (*ibid.*, C:5). 4. *William R. Nelson*, b. ca 1844; at home 1850; named in wills of brothers. 5. *Charles Nelson*, at home 1850. Children with second wife, Margaret: 6. *Mary L. Nelson*, b. ca 1857. 7. *Eliza Nelson*, b. ca 1859. 8. *John Nelson*, b. ca 1864.

v   BETSEY NELSON, b. ca 1800; d. 9 April 1802, ae 2, Buckland; bur. with
    parents (*VR* 144).

vi LEVI NELSON, bp. 22 Nov. 1807 with siblings; living 1828 when named
    in father's will.

Sources cited: *Buckland VR. Upton VR.* Mass. Vital Records 1841-1910. Franklin County
Probate Records at Greenfield. Delaware County, N.Y., Surrogate's Records. *History of Buckland*
(1937). *History of Delaware County, N.Y* (1880). CENSUS: 1850 Buckland, Franklin Co. (M432-317).

586. ANNE NELSON[5] (*Hannah Tyler*[4], *Hannah*[3] *Samson, Stephen*[2], *Henry*[1]),
daughter of Francis Nelson and his wife Hannah Tyler [122], was born 30 June
1757 at Upton (*VR* 39), and died there 12 or 16 June 1828, aged 71 years, as
"Anna, wife of John Brown" (*VR* 158).

She married, first, 18 November 1773 at Mendon (*VR* 352), "both of Upton,"
after intentions 29 October 1773 at Upton (*VR* 118), **LEVI RAWSON**, who has
not been identified.* Mrs. Anne Rawson married, second, at Upton 28 May 1782
(*VR* 124), **JOHN BROWN**, who was born about 1760 and died 10 August 1828,
aged 68, at Upton (*VR* 158).

John Brown was listed in the 1790 census at Upton with a household
consisting of himself, one boy under 16, and five females (*Heads of Fam.*, 240).

No children have been identified, although Anne is said to have had two
daughters with John Brown (*Job Tyler Desc.*, 102).

Sources cited: *Upton VR. Mendon VR. Heads of Families 1790 – Mass. Job Tyler Descendants*
(1912).

---

* It has been assumed that this Levi Rawson cannot be the Levi b. Mendon 27 March 1748,
son of Edward and Deborah (Green) Rawson (*VR* 145, 368), because that Levi d. Mendon 17
April 1819, aged 71, after having m. (1) 26 Oct. 1775, Thankful Warren of Grafton with whom
he had five children rec. Mendon from 1777 to 1790 [Warren, Olive, Hannah, Edward, and
Daniel Rawson], and, m. (2) 9 Sept. 1807, Nancy Fairbanks, with whom he had Hannah and
Silas Rawson (*NEHGR* 3 [1859]:320). However, these dates are not inconsistent with a first
marriage to 16-year-old Anne Nelson that did not last and evidently produced no children.

587.   ELIJAH NELSON⁵ (*Hannah Tyler⁴, Hannah³ Samson, Stephen², Henry¹*), son of Francis Nelson and his wife Hannah Tyler [122], was born 4 January 1759 at Upton (*VR* 40). Record of his death has not been found.

He married at Upton, 23 December 1787 (*VR* 118), **RACHEL RAWSON**, who has not been identified.

Elijah Nelson served in the Revolutionary War. On a descriptive list taken at Springfield in 1780 he is listed as aged 21, stature, 5 ft. 8 in., of light complexion, from Upton; during his term of service he marched from Upton to West Point and was discharged 17 December 1780 (*MSSR* 11:315). There is no record of his having applied for a pension.

Job Tyler Descendants (1:102) says of him "he moved to Buckland and had a son." Elijah Nelson of Buckland, yeoman, bought 40 acres there on 10 October 1789 (Franklin LR 3:543). He is listed in the 1790 census at Buckland with two boys under 16 and one female in his household (*Heads of Fam.*, 105). On 23 November 1792 he sold to Samuel Dean of Upton "a part of the land I live on" in Buckland; Rachel also signed, and both acknowledged the deed on 26 December 1792 (Franklin LR 5:376). The family has not been located in later censuses. (An Elijah Nelson in Dutchess County, N.Y., in 1810 and Putnam County 1820 is from a different family.)

In 1820 an Elijah Nelson was listed in Chautauqua, N.Y. (p 42), but he was aged 26-45, with a woman 45+, a woman 26-45, and one boy under 10. This is surely the Elijah who married at Upton in 1817, whose death record identifies him as son of our Elijah. The presence of the older woman in the household suggests that Elijah [Sr.] died before 1820.

Child of Elijah and Rachel (Rawson) Nelson :

i   ELIJAH NELSON⁶, b. Buckland ca 8 Jan. 1789 (calc.); d. Upton 23 Aug. 1864 ae 75y 7m 15d, widower, a farmer (Mass. VR 176:304). He was "of Chautauqua" when he m. at Upton, 1 Aug. 1817 (*VR* 118), LOIS NELSON, b. 17 Aug. 1791, d. Upton 9 July 1862 ae 70y 10m 12d, of cancer (Mass. VR 158:288), dau. of Isaac and Hannah (Fisk) Nelson (see #571-v). They evidently returned between 1820 and 1828 to Upton, where Elijah was listed in 1850, ae 62, a stonecutter, with Louise [*sic*] ae 59, and two sons (p.110).

Children, list perhaps incomplete: 1. *Isaac Nelson⁷*, b. ca 1819 N.Y.; a bootmaker 1850. 2. *Sally Nelson*, b. 1822; d. Upton 12 Aug. 1846 ae 24y 7m 23d, wife of ___ Field (*VR* 162). 3. *Edwin Nelson*, b. ca 1828 Mass.; "at college" 1850.

.**Sources cited:** *Upton VR.* Franklin County Deeds at Greenfield. *Mass. Soldiers & Sailors. Descendants of Job Tyler* (1912). CENSUS: *Heads of Families 1790 – Mass.*; 1820 Chautauqua, Chautauqua Co., N.Y. (M33-66); 1850 Upton, Worcester Co. (M432-344).

588.   ASA NELSON⁵ (*Hannah Tyler⁴, Hannah³ Samson, Stephen², Henry¹*), son of Francis Nelson and his wife Hannah Tyler [122], was born 10 November 1760 at Upton (*VR* 39). There is no marriage or death record for him in Upton. No further record of Asa Nelson of Upton has been found. The only Asa Nelson who served in the Revolutionary War was from Rowley.

589.   JOSEPH NELSON⁵ (*Hannah Tyler⁴, Hannah³ Samson, Stephen², Henry¹*), son of Francis Nelson and his wife Hannah Tyler [122], was born 10 January 1763 at Upton (*VR* 40) and died there 27 April 1843, aged 80 (*VR* 172).

He married at Upton, 24 December 1789 (*VR* 118), **ABIGAIL DEANE**, born about 1764, who died at Upton 26 November 1824, aged 60 (*VR* 172).

Children of Joseph and Abigail (Deane) Nelson, rec. Upton (*VR* 39-41; deaths, 172-73):

   i   DANIEL NELSON⁶, b. 9 March 1792; d. 24 Feb. 1841 Upton; m. at Upton (*VR* 118), (1) 13 April 1815, BETSEY NELSON, who d. 4 July 1824 ae 21, (2) after int. 27 Aug. 1825, ANNA NELSON, who d. 28 March 1829 ae 39, (3) 2 May 1830, BETSEY WOOD.
       Children, with first wife Betsey Nelson, rec. Upton (*VR* 40-41, 173): 1. *Samuel Austin Nelson⁷*, b. 9 Oct. 1819. 2. *Sylvia Ann Nelson*, b. 24 Aug. 1821; d. 4 Jan. 1824, ae 3. 3. *William Johnson Nelson*, b. 31 Jan. 1824; d. 12 Aug. 1825 ae 18m 12d; bur. with mother.

   ii   ELIJAH NELSON, b. 10 Aug. 1795; m. 12 June 1825 Upton (*VR* 118), MARY SADLER. In 1850 Elijah Nelson Jr. was a farmer ae 54 at Upton with Mary S. ae 53, son Granville, and Sarah Green ae 70 (p.118).
       Children rec. Upton (*VR* 40): 1. *Granville D. Nelson⁷*, b. 23 May 1831. 2. *Mary Jane Nelson*, b. 2 Dec. 1838; d. 29 Aug. 1840 ae 1y 9m 27d, Upton.

   iii   SYLVA NELSON, b. 14 Sept. 1797; d. 19 Nov. 1810 Upton.

   iv   ABIGAIL NELSON, b. 12 Feb. 1801; d. 26 Jan. 1817 Upton.

   v   LEVI NELSON, b. 2 March 1805; m. 23 June 1828 Upton (*VR* 118), ADALINE WOOD. In 1850 he was a farmer at Upton with Adeline ae 43 and Liberty ae 16 (p.118).
       Children: 1. *Abigail Dean Nelson⁷*, b. Jan. 1831; d. 5 March 1833 ae 2y 1m 17d, Upton. 2. *Liberty Nelson*, b. ca 1834.

vi   JULIA NELSON, b. 5 May 1807; d. Upton 6 Nov. 1828, ae 21.

Sources cited: *Upton VR.* 1850 census, Upton, Worcester Co. (M432-344). **See also:** *History of Milford, Mass.* (1882), 3:915-16.

590. HANNAH NELSON[5] (*Hannah Tyler*[4], *Hannah*[3] *Samson, Stephen*[2], *Henry*[1]), daughter of Francis Nelson and his wife Hannah Tyler [122], was born 18 March 1770 at Upton (*VR* 40), and died before 1850, probably at Homer, N.Y.

She married at Upton, 28 February 1796 (*VR* 75), **DANIEL ALEXANDER** of Upton, son of William and Sarah (Leonard) Alexander. He was born about 1774 and died after 1850, when he was living, aged 76, in the household of his son Leonard at Homer, N.Y. The will of William Alexander of Upton, dated 1813 and proved 1818 (Worcester PR #1085) names son Daniel.

This family moved to Dover, Vt., in 1797, and later to East Homer, N.Y., where "parents and children arrived Nov. 28, 1816" (*Boston Transcript*).

Children of Daniel and Hannah (Nelson) Alexander (*ibid.*, birthdates and marriages):

i   AUGUSTA ALEXANDER[6], b. 23 Sept. 1796 Upton (*VR* 11, *Allexander*); d. 7 Nov. 1887 ae 91; m. PELEG ARNOLD, b. ca 1793 in R.I., d. 5 Jan. 1871 ae 78; both bur. Glenwood Cemetery, Homer, N.Y. In 1850 Peleg was a farmer at Homer (p.308), and their household included Oliver M[*illegible*] ae 14 and Augusta M. Pratt ae 18, b. N.Y., perhaps dau. of Augusta's sister Electa.

ii   HANNAH ALEXANDER, b. Sept. 1798 Dover, Vt.; d. prob. 1850-1860; m. JACOB SCHERMERHORN, b. ca 1795 in N.Y. In 1850 they were living at Homer, N.Y., near her father and brother Leonard. Jacob was a farmer. In 1860 Jacob ae 66 was living in the household of Henry Schermerhorn ae 51 at Truxton, N.Y., without Hannah (p.603).

iii ELECTA ALEXANDER, b. 14 Nov. 1800 Dover, Vt.; d. April 1866; m. DAVID PRATT, b. 1795 Conn., d. 24 Sept. 1864, son of Joshua Pratt; both bur. Glenwood Cemetery, Homer, N.Y. In 1850 he was a mason, in Cortlandville, N.Y., with Electa ae 49, Caroline Davenport ae 27, b. Cortland Co., and Homer A. Davenport ae 5, b. Illinois (p.339). Franklin Pratt ae 15 b. Cortland Co., was next door with T. Mason and Polly M. Loring; another possible Pratt child, Augusta M., was in the household of Electa's sister Augusta Arnold.   A grandchild, "M.P.G.S.", sought information with a query 11 May 1932 in the *Boston Transcript*.

    iv   LEONARD ALEXANDER, b. 17 Feb. 1803 Dover, Vt.; d. 1887; m. MELVINA A. MINOR, b. ca 1808 in N.Y., d. 1878, dau. of Asahel and Rhoda (Keep) Minor. In 1850 Leonard was a farmer at Homer, N.Y. (p.304-05).

        Children at home 1850: 1. *Louisa Alexander*, b. ca 1833. 2. *Lagrange Alexander*, b. ca 1835. 3. *Orrissa Alexander*, b. ca 1837. 4. *Melvin Alexander*, b. ca 1838. 5. *Ervin Alexander*, b. ca 1840. 6. *Melvina Alexander*, b. ca 1844. 7. *Francis Alexander*, b. ca 1849. 8. *John Alexander*, b. 1850.

    v   LOUISA N. ALEXANDER, b. 25 March 1812 Dover, Vt.

Sources cited: *Upton VR. Boston Transcript*, Query #3662, 11 May 1932 by "M.P.G.S.," Answer 16 June 1932 by "W.A.," citing Vermont VR, Worcester Co. Deeds and Probate Records, "genealogies of the Tyler and Keep families," and Cutter's *Families of Central New York* "which is liable to be unreliable sometimes." Homer, N.Y., Cemetery Records, on line. CENSUS: 1850 Cortland Co., N.Y., Cortlandville & Homer (M432-493).

591. ABIGAIL NELSON[5] *(Hannah Tyler*[4], *Hannah*[3] *Samson, Stephen*[2], *Henry*[1]*)*, daughter of Francis Nelson and his wife Hannah Tyler [122], was born 6 May 1774 at Upton (*VR* 39) and died in Ohio in 1857, aged 82 (g.s.).

    She married, probably about 1798, **JOHN TAFT**, who was born 6 February 1773 at Upton (*VR* 54), son of John and Love (Whitney) Taft, and died in 1857, aged 84 (g.s.). John and Abigail are both buried in the Lamoreaux Cemetery, Huron County, Ohio (Huron Co. Cem. Rec., 3:3).

    In 1800 the household of John Taft, in the First Parish of Mendon (p.383), consisted of a man over 45, one man and one woman 16-26, and one boy under 10, figures that suggest John Sr. with John Jr. and Abigail and their young son. The birthplaces of the children indicate that they moved to Vermont soon after that. The first record found of them in Ohio is in the 1850 census, when John Taft, aged 76, was a cooper in Ripley Township, Huron County, with Abigail, 76, and Cullen Taft, 51, a cooper, all three born in Mass. (p 444).

    Children of John and Abigail (Nelson) Taft (Cullen from census; Austin from cem. rec.; other information from Pat Allen, Taft Family researcher):

    i   CULLEN TAFT[7], b. ca 1799 Mass.; with parents in 1850.

    ii   PRELATE TAFT, b. 27 Sept. 1802 Dover, Vt.; m. at Ripley, Ohio, 10 July 1836, PHEBE HINCKLEY, dau. Joshua and Hannah (Chase) Hinckley (Pat Allen), d. prob. before 1850 when P. Taft ae 46 was a cooper at Middlebury, Ohio, with all the children except Ezra and Susan (p.11).

        Children (*ibid.*; Pat Allen), first two b. N.Y., rest Ohio: 1. *Jane Taft*[7], b. ca 1824; at home 1850. 2. *Francis Taft*, b. ca 1832; a blacksmith 1850 3. *Lafayette*

Taft, b. ca 1834; m. Isabelle ___. 4. *Ezra Taft*, b. ca 1836 Ohio; not with father 1850. 5. *Eliza Ann Taft*, b. 3 June 1837 Ripley, Ohio; m. Ferdinand F. C. Schaefermeyer. 6. *Abigail Asenath Taft*, b. 11 June 1839 Ripley, Ohio; m. Frederick B. Spees. 7. *William Schenck Taft*, b. ca 1841; m. Mary McGill. 8. *Susan Matilda Taft*, b. 4 May 1844; d. 18 Aug. 1844 Ripley, Ohio.

iii ARABELLA TAFT, b. 180[–] in Vermont; d. 1839; m. HENRY T. DUBOIS.

iv AUSTIN TAFT, b. 26 May 1806 Worcester Co.; d. Bowling Green, Ohio, 12 Jan. 1888; m. 9 Feb. 1831, SUSAN BENEDICT, prob. the "SALLY," d. in 1850, ae 43, bur. with his parents and son Andrew; m. (2) after 1850, CATHERINE RIGEDON STRATTON, dau. of Daniel and Rachel (Logan) Stratton (Pat Allen). The cemetery rec. for his son calls him "Rev." In 1850 he was a farmer in Ripley, Ohio, with "Doresky," Andrew, Curtis, Austin, and Rothilla (p.223).

Children (*ibid.*; Pat Allen), with first wife, first two b. N.Y., rest Ohio: 1. *Helen Dorliska Taft*, b. 15 Jan. 1832; m. John Logan. 2. *Andrew Taft*, "son of Rev. A. and Sally," b. ca 1834; d. 1861 ae 27 (cem. rec.). 3. *Curtis Taft*, b. ca 1837; living 1850. 4. *Austin Taft*, b. 1839; living 1850. 5. *Rothilda Rithilla Rosetha Taft*, b. 1848; m. ___ Parks. Children with second wife: 6. *Emma Taft*, b. 1852; d.y. 7. *Melville Taft*, b. 1855; d.y.

v ARAMINTA ABIGAIL TAFT, b. ca 1818; m. P. O. GALLAGHER.

Sources cited: *Upton VR.* "Cemetery Records of Huron County, Ohio," typescript at Western Reserve Historical Society Library, Cleveland. Pat Allen, *Descendants of Matthew Taft* (web site). *Job Tyler Descendants* (1912). CENSUS: Mendon, Worcester Co., 1810 (M32-16); 1850 Ohio: Middlebury, Knox Co. (M432-700), Ripley, Huron Co. (M432-697).

592. ABIGAIL PARTRIDGE[5] (*Abigail Thayer*[4], *Mary*[3] *Samson, Stephen*[2], *Henry*[1]), daughter of John Partridge and his wife Abigail Thayer [123], was born 23 January 1754 at Wrentham (*VR* 157). She died 12 May 1802 as "— wife of John Allen," at Bellingham (*VR* 166), recorded as Abigail in the West Medway church records (*VR* 288).

Abigail was her parents' eighth child, born seven years after the early deaths of all but one of her siblings. Her brother John, 16 years older, lived to marry, but he too died in 1764, leaving Abigail the only survivor of eight children.

She married at Wrentham, 11 July 1771 (*VR* 243), **JOHN ALLEN**, who was born about 1739 and was "of Franklin" when he died at Bellingham (*VR* 166) 24 July 1815, aged 76 [*sic*], recorded also at Franklin (*VR* 150) and Medway (*VR* 288, from CR). Despite the stated age, he may have been the son of John and Huldah (Hill) Allen born at Medway 11 March 1747 (*VR* 19).

John Allen was administrator of the estate of Abigail's father, John Partridge, in 1792 (Suffolk PR #19934).

On 26 July 1815 a petition to grant administration on the estate of John Allen, late of Franklin, to Stephen Metcalf of Bellingham was signed by "lawful heirs of estate of John Allen": John Partridge Allen, Asa Allen, Simeon Allen, Ellery Allen, Samuel Allen, Stephen Allen, and Lucinda Allen (Norfolk PR #406). No widow was mentioned.

Several deeds, recorded together, document land transactions among the children (Norfolk LR 48:239-242). On 29 September 1815, Simeon Allen of Thompson, Conn., deeded to Ellery Allen of Franklin all his title in the estate of his late father John Allen of Franklin, deceased, held in common with Ellery, Samuel, Stephen, and Lucinda; Simeon's wife Elizabeth also signed. The same day, John P. Allen of Charlton deeded to Samuel Allen of Sturbridge his title in the estate of his father, held in common with Ellery, Samuel, Stephen, and Lucinda; John P.'s wife Betsy also signed. The same day, Asa Allen of Charlton, deeded his title to estate of his late father, held in common with Ellery, Samuel, Stephen, and Lucinda; Asa's wife Hannah also signed. On 13 September 1816, Samuel and Stephen Allen of Franklin deeded to Ellery Allen of Franklin land and buildings; Samuel's wife Polly also signed. The same day, Ellery and Stephen Allen of Franklin deeded land to Samuel Allen of Franklin; Ellery's wife Experience also signed. On 15 January 1817, Lucinda Allen of Franklin, single woman, deeded to Samuel Allen of Franklin one-third of the real estate of her father, referring to a quitclaim deed from Ellery and Stephen to Samuel on 13 September 1816; she also sold land to Ellery Allen and Stephen Allen.

On 8 December 1831, Stephen Allen and wife Betsey of Franklin deeded land in Franklin and Bellingham to Asa Allen of Charlton (Norfolk LR 95:148).

Children of John and Abigail (Partridge) Allen, first four rec. Franklin (*VR* 11), all bp. at Second Congreg. Church, Medway, first five together 30 April 1786 (*VR* 18-20):

  i JOHN PARTRIDGE ALLEN[6], b. 9 Nov. 1774; d. 15 Nov. 1843 Sturbridge, ae 68, yeoman, apoplexy, married; bur. New Cemetery there (*VR* 299); m. (1) Franklin, 13 March 1800, both of Franklin (*VR* 94), MEHETABLE WAKEFIELD; m. (2) BETSY ____.
      Children with Mehetable, rec. Franklin (*VR* 22): 1. *Hiram Allen*[7] (twin), b. 28 April 1803. 2. *Almira Allen* (twin), b. 28 April 1803.

  ii ASA ALLEN, b. 13 Dec. 1776; m. HANNAH ____; of Charlton 1831. A Hannah Allen, widow, d. Franklin 29 June 1845, ae 64, b. pl. unknown, "in care of family," consumption (*VR* 162).

Children rec. Bellingham (*VR* 11) and Charlton (*VR* 11): 1. *Melissa Allen[7]*, b. 19 Jan. 1806. 2. *Augustus Allen* (Bellingham) / *Augustus Thayer Allen* (Charlton), b. 25 Sept. 1808; m. int. Charlton 1839 with Aurelia Wakefield (*VR* 119).

iii SIMEON ALLEN, b. 11 March 1779; d. Thompson, Conn., 19 Sept. 1849; m. (1) HANNAH ___, d. 12 Nov. 1808 Thompson (VR 1:80); m. (2) at Thompson, 29 Oct. 1809 (*ibid.*), ELIZABETH LEAVENS. In 1830 figures for Simeon's household in Thompson match the children recorded there (p.115). In 1850 Elizabeth Allen ae 75 was living at Thompson with the family of Lucius Wheaton (p.128).

Children rec. Thompson, Conn. (VR 1:80): With Hannah: 1. *Hollis Allen[7]*, b. 2 May 1805. With Elizabeth: 2. *Jude Allen*, b. 22 Oct. 1810. 3. *Emily Allen*, b. 10 Feb. 1812. 4. *Ira Allen*, b. 27 April 1814. 5. *James Allen*, b. 26 Dec. 1815.

iv ELLERY ALLEN, b. 10 March 1783; m. (1) after int. 15 Oct. 1806 at Bellingham (*VR* 82), EXPERIENCE PARTRIDGE, b. Bellingham 14 Sept. 1786, d. there 8 Oct. 1841 ae 55, dau. of Job and Deborah (?Fairbank) Partridge (*VR* 50, 166); m. (2) Milford, 5 June 1842 (Mass. VR 3:218), LUCRETIA POND. In 1850 Elery Allen was a boot maker in Franklin with Lucretia ae 54 and Asa Pond ae 27, bootmaker (p.308).

Children, with first wife, rec. Franklin (*VR* 27, 29, 30, 33-35), first five bp. Medway 4 May 1817: 1. *Laura Allen[7]*, b. 13 Oct. 1807. 2. *Abigail Partridge Allen*, b. 29 April 1810. 3. *Fidelia Allen*, b. 7 March 1812. 4. *Calista Allen*, b. 22 March 1814; d. 18 Feb. 1825 (*VR* 153). 5. *Martha Allen*, b. 10 Dec. 1816. 6. *Mary Allen*, b. 30 Aug. 1819; m. Joseph Fisk. 7. *Lucinda Allen*, b. 22 Oct. 1821. 8. *Asa Allen*, b. 23 Dec. 1825. 9. *John Allen*, b. 30 Oct. 1827.

v SAMUEL ALLEN, b. ca 1786; m. POLLY ____, b. ca 1789 Conn. In 1850 he was a farmer ae 64 in Holliston, with Polly ae 61, Milton, Nancy, and Angeline, and Samuel Pond ae 45 (p.392).

Allen children, 1st rec. Franklin (*VR* 29), 2nd – 8th rec. Bellingham (*VR* 11-12): 1. *Dorcas Allen[7]*, b. 1 April 1816. 2. *Lucinda Allen*, b. 17 Oct. 1817. 3. *Bethesda Allen*, b. 18 March 1819. 4. *Asa Allen*, b. and d. 23 Oct. 1820 (*VR* 166). 5. *Milton Allen*, b. 16 Sept. 1821. 6. *Nancy Allen*, b. 5 May 1823. 7. *Reuel Allen* (twin), b. 27 Nov. 1824; d. 28 Nov. 1824. 8. *Rufus Allen* (twin), b. 27 Nov. 1824; d. 28 Nov. 1824 (*VR* 166). 9. *Angeline Allen*, b. ca 1833, at home 1850.

vi STEPHEN ALLEN, b. 21 Dec. 1788; bp. Medway 24 Feb. 1788; m. Brookfield, 17 Nov. 1816, he of Franklin (*VR* 254), BETSEY DANIELS, b. 3 June 1796 (g.s.). In 1850 he was a brick maker at Brookfield, with Betsey ae 54, Emily ae 30, Jane A. ae 22, James ae 18, William A. ae 16, shoemaker, and George ae 13 (p.54).

Children, all but last rec. Franklin (*VR* 34, 38): 1. *Adaline Allen*[7], b. 21 April 1818. 2. *Emily Allen*, b. 29 Dec. 1819. 3. *Edwin Francis Allen*, b. 23 Dec. 1821. 4. *Charlotte Jane Allen*, b. 9 Oct. 1823; d. Franklin 25 Feb. 1824 (*VR* 153). 5. *Hiram George Allen*, b. 22 May 1825; d. 3 Feb. 1826 (*ibid.*). 6. *Hiram Hazard Allen*, b. 31 Jan. 1827. 7. *Jane Amanda Allen*, b. 17 July 1828. 8. *Frederick Allen*, b. 16 June 1830. 9. *James Allen*, b. 7 April 1832. 10. *Willard Augustus Allen*, b. 13 Oct. 1835, William A. in census. 11. *George Allen*, b. ca 1837; at home 1850.

vii   LUCINDA ALLEN, b. Dec. 1795 (calc.), bp. Medway 21 Feb. 1796; d. Medway 17 Jan. 1881 ae 85y 1m, widowed, of congestion of lungs (Mass. VR 329:258); m. at Medway, 1 Nov. 1820 (*VR* 146), LEONARD HASELTON. In 1830 their household consisted of one man and one woman 30-40, two men 20-30, one young woman 15-20, one boy 5-10, and one boy under 5 (p.76). In 1850 Lucinda A. Haselton ae 55 was head of a household of several adults in Medway, apparently not related (p.339). In 1880 she was listed as mother in the household of Leonard Haselton ae 53, grocer, in Medway (e.d.521).

The only **Haselton** child identified is: 1. *Leonard Haselton*[7], b. ca 1827; m. Olive M. ____.

Sources cited: *Bellingham VR. Brookfield VR. Charlton VR. Franklin VR. Medway VR. Sturbridge VR. Wrentham VR.* Thompson, Conn., VR as cited in Barbour Index. Norfolk County Deeds and Probate Records. CENSUS: Medway, Norfolk Co., 1830 (M19-60), 1850 (M432-331), 1880 (T9-548); 1850 Holliston, Middlesex Co. (M432-326), Franklin, Norfolk Co. (M432-331), Brookfield, Worcester Co. (M432-343); Thompson, Windham Co., Conn. 1830 (M19-11), 1850 (M432-51).

593.   AMOS THAYER[5] (*Samuel Thayer*[4], *Mary*[3] *Samson*, *Stephen*[2], *Henry*[1]), son of Samuel Thayer [124] and his first wife, Sarah Farnum, was born 19 August 1757 at Uxbridge (*VR* 163) and died there 11 July 1838 in his 82nd year (*VR* 410).

Amos married at Uxbridge, 15 September 1785 (*VR* 323), **LOIS (EMERSON) WHITE**, widow of Samuel White. She was born evidently about 1748 and died 10 April 1822, aged 74 years, at Uxbridge (*VR* 420) as "—Thayer wife of Amos." Lois was of Glocester, R.I., 8 May 1766 when she married Samuel White at Uxbridge (*VR* 243), but her daughter Henrietta's death record says she was born at Uxbridge (not recorded there). Amos and his wife "Louis" are buried in Prospect Hill Cemetery, Uxbridge.

Lois had four children with her first husband, Samuel White, recorded at Uxbridge: Louies White b. 6 September 1769, Lucinda White b. 1 November 1771, Olive White b. 4 March 1778, and Samuel White b. 5 February 1781 (*VR* 180-81).

The 1790 census lists Amos Thayer's family in Uxbridge, consisting of one man, one boy under 16, and seven females (*Heads of Fam.*, 241).

The estate of Amos's father was insolvent, but in April 1793 land in the hands of his stepmother, Judith (Walker) Thayer, was set off to Amos Thayer of Uxbridge, "by judgement of last August" (Worcester LR 120:82).

Amos served in the Revolutionary War. When he applied for a pension on 15 April 1818, he was aged 60, "very infirm" (file #S33198). In 1820 he stated that he was a husbandman, very infirm for many years; his family consisted of five persons, himself and his wife, 70 years old, two maiden daughters: Sally, 34, and Sinderella, 32, and a fatherless grandson aged 2 years. He was disqualified for pension after testimony was given that he was partly deranged, a pauper, etc. On 19 June 1823 he applied again, saying he was aged 66, had no real estate, had two daughters, maidens aged 35 and 37, and an infant grandchild about 6 years old "with whom I live … My wife in whose right I was then seized during her life of a small low old house and 27 acres has deceased and I am deprived of the interest I then had in said house and land."

The probate record of his daughter Cinderella Thayer of Sutton includes a statement dated 15 September 1838: "My late father Amos Thayer 2d of Sutton, a Revolutionary pensioner of the U.S., died July 11, 1838 leaving three daughters now living: Sally Thayer, Henrietta Scott wife of Manley Scott, and myself — being his only children and heirs" (Worcester PR #A58612).

Either Sally or Cinderella evidently had an illegitimate son born ca 1817 who was living in 1823 when a "fatherless grandson" was mentioned by Amos. Sprague identifies the child as probably Augustus Thayer, but the 1850 census, when Augustus was living in Sutton (p.147), indicates that he was born about 1810 (which may be an error). The child mentioned in the pension file could have been son of a deceased son or daughter of Amos, but if so he must have died before 1838.

Children of Amos and Lois (Emerson) (White) Thayer, b. prob. Uxbridge but not rec. there:

i SALLY THAYER[6], b. 1 July 1786 (calc.); d. 5 Jan. 1858, ae 71y 6m 4d (g.s., Uxbridge). In 1850 Sarah Thayer ae 67 was living in Sutton with her sister Cinderilla Thayer ae 65, and their half-sister Olive White ae 72 (p.141).

ii LUCINDA RILLA / CINDERELLA THAYER, b. ca 1788; d. 15 Jan. 1855 of typhoid fever, unm., as Lucinda Rilla, dau of Amos and *Olive* Thayer (Mass. VR 95:159). In 1850 Cinderilla Thayer ae 65 was living in Sutton with her sister Sarah Thayer and half-sister Olive White (p.141).

iii HENRIETTA THAYER, b. 22 June 1790 (*VR* 131, from gs); d. at Uxbridge 21 Sept. 1882 ae 92, widow, of paralysis, she and both parents b.
Uxbridge (Mass. VR 339:445); m. after int. Mendon 10 March 1810 (*VR*
404) and Uxbridge __ March 1810 (*VR* 324), MANLEY SCOTT of
Mendon, b. Uxbridge 9 Oct. 1775 (*VR* 132). In 1850 Manly Scott, ae 71
[*sic*], carpenter, was living in Uxbridge with Henrietta ae 57, children John
V.B., Lois A., and Marion A. Scott, and Charles Fairbanks ae 34,
"finisher" (p.387).

 Scott children rec. Uxbridge (*VR* 131-32): 1. *Charles Amos Scott*, b. 17 May
1811. 2. *Anne Gray Scott*, b. 14 Sept. 1812; d.y. 3. *Sir George St. Clair Prevost Scott*,
b. 27 Feb. 1814. 4. *Maria Catharine Scott*, b. 18 May 1816. 5. *Anne Gray Scott*, b.
16 April 1818. 6. *Samuel White Scott*, b. 16 Oct. 1819; m. Susan ___. 7. *Abigail
Boyd Scott*, b. 15 Sept. 1821. 8. *Crysa Aurora Scott* (twin), b. 5 May 1823. 9. *Crysus
Tallamacus* (twin dau.), b. 5 May 1823; m. Eddy G. Smith. 10. *George Nahum Scott*
(twin), b. 2 March 1825. 11. *Charlotte Louisa Scott* (twin), b. 2 March 1825.
12. *Lois Amanda Scott*, b. 14 Feb. 1827; at home 1850. 13. *John Van Rensselaer
Scott*, b. 16 Oct. 1829; at home 1850. 14. *Marion Adalaide Scott*, b. 19 March 1831;
at home 1850.

Sources cited: *Uxbridge VR.* Mass. Vital Records 1841-1910. Worcester County Deeds and
Probate Records. W. C. Sprague, "Descendants of Thomas Thayer," Vol. 2. Revolutionary War
Pension File S33794, not included in White, *Genealogical Abstracts of Revolutionary War Pension Files.*
White's abstract of File #S33198 (p.3456) includes only Amos's age and residence. CENSUS:
Sutton and Uxbridge, Worcester Co., 1850 (M432-345).

594. ASA THAYER[5] (*Samuel Thayer*[4], *Mary*[3] *Samson, Stephen*[2], *Henry*[1]), son of
Samuel Thayer [124] and his first wife, Sarah Farnum, was born at Uxbridge
4 October 1761 (*VR* 163) and died there 9 April 1828, aged 67 years, "a
Revolutionary soldier" (*VR* 410). He is buried in Prospect Hill Cemetery,
Uxbridge.

He married 21 April 1782 (pension file) after intentions 19 April 1782 at
Uxbridge (*VR* 323), **MARY MURDOCK**, who was born 15 June 1764 at
Uxbridge (*VR* 113), daughter of John and Bethiah (Fuller) Murdock, and died
there 26 July 1844, aged 80 years (*VR* 410). John Murdock of Uxbridge in his will
dated 24 March 1804, proved 2 September 1806, named his daughter Mary Thayer,
wife of Asa (Worcester PR # A42517).

Asa served several enlistments in the Revolutionary War from Uxbridge,
described in *MSSR* (15:520). In 1778 he was at Fishkill, and signed a petition there
8 April 1779 with others, asking that they be paid for their mileage, etc., home
from Pennsylvania where they were to be discharged. In 1778 he was 16 years old,

5 ft. 7 in. tall, dark hair and complexion, with blue eyes; in July 1779 he was described as 17 years old, 5 ft. 9 in., complexion dark.

Asa Thayer of Uxbridge, yeoman, infirm in body, in his will dated 26 March 1828, proved 27 May 1828, left to his wife Mary a $20 annuity, a chaise, and furniture; to his sons Royal and Clinton Thayer $5 each, they having had their shares in full; to son Collins Thayer $300 "in addition to what he has"; to Sullivan Thayer and Turner Thayer $1000 each; to daughter Nancy wife of Arnold Taft or to their two daughters Harriet and Mary Taft $100; to daughter Olive, wife of Dea. Nicholas Baylies (who was "well off") $1; to daughter Louis [sic] wife of George Minot, or to her son Charles $200; to daughters Mary Thayer and Lovisa Thayer $300 each; to grandson Charles Minot $300; and to son Asa Thayer Jr. $1000; the residue to sons Asa Thayer Jr. and Amory Thayer who were to be executors (Worcester PR #A58621). Royal Thayer petitioned 21 May 1828 for a copy of the will for his brother (not named) who lived in the State of Maine.

Asa's widow Mary applied for a pension 23 October 1838 at Uxbridge, giving her maiden name, their marriage date, and his death date; her sons Asa and Sullivan Thayer of Uxbridge made affidavits, and birth dates for the children were given (White, 3456).

Mary Thayer of Milford, widow, in her will dated 12 September 1843, proved 24 August 1844, left her wearing apparel to her three daughters, Olive T. Balies, Nancy Taft, and Mary M. Sumner, equally, and the rest of her property to "all my surviving children equally, to wit: Olive, Nancy, Royal, Collins, Sullivan, Amory, Asa, Turner, and Mary M. Sumner (wife of Clark)," Sullivan to be executor. On 1 January 1846 Sullivan Thayer declined and asked that his brother Turner Thayer act as executor (Worcester PR # A58745).

Children of Asa and Mary (Murdock) Thayer, births rec. Uxbridge (VR 163-165) and also listed in pension rec.:

   i   OLIVE THAYER[6], b. 10 Aug. 1782 [18 Aug. pension]; m. (1) at Uxbridge, 29 Nov. 1804 (VR 325), EZEKIEL TAFT; m. (2) at Uxbridge, 3 July 1823, she of Sutton (VR 319), NICHOLAS BAYLIES.

  ii   CLINTON THAYER, b. 27 April 1784; d. Portland, Me., 11 March 1835; m. (1) at Watertown, 14 Feb. 1808, BETSEY CARTER (Col. Cent. of 18 March), bp. 28 April 1811 "at her house being very sick" (Sprague Ms), d. 13 May 1811 ae 25, bur. Watertown (ibid.); m. (2) in 1817, LUCY JONES GEORGE, d. Watertown Aug. 1821 ae 25; m. (3) Boston, 20 May 1824, MARGARET TYLER. Clinton was a merchant in Portland. On 1 June 1841 Catherine N. Andrews, widow, Lorenzo S. Cragin and wife Susannah, and Margaret Thayer, widow, children of William Tyler late of

Boston, sold land in Boston (Suffolk LR 468:292). A deed identifies Clinton's children living 11 Sept. 1856: George C. Thayer, by attorney, formerly of Portland, now of Chicago, Ill., Margaret A. Dow wife of John R. of Waterville, Me., Eliza L. Thayer of Brooklyn, N.Y., and Sarah M. Kingsland wife of Richard of Union Twp., Bergen Co., N.J., on that date sold land in Portland that had been of their father Clinton Thayer (Cumberland LR 272:416).

Children (Sprague Ms), with first wife: 1. *George Clinton Thayer*[7], b. 1809; bp. 28 April 1811; d. Baltimore 4 May 1834 (*Col. Cent.* 10 May). 2. *Charles Thayer*, bp. 28 April 1811; d.y. With second wife: 3. *Eliza L. Thayer*, b. 1818; unm. 1856. 4. *Charles Thayer*, b. ca 1821; d. 7 Feb. 1840 (*Col. Cent.* 8 Feb.). With third wife: 5. *Sarah M. Thayer*, b. ca 1825; m. Richard Kingsland. 6. *Margaret Ann Thayer*, b. ca 1826; m. John R. Dow. 7. *George Clinton Thayer*, b. after 1834.

iii   NANCY THAYER, b. 15 April 1786; m. at Uxbridge, 4 Sept. 1814 (*VR* 325), ARNOLD TAFT, prob. b. Uxbridge 8 March 1784, son of Thaddeus and Silence (___) Taft (*VR* 149). In 1850 Arnold Taft ae 56 [*sic*] was a "blocker" in North Providence with Nancy T. Taft ae 54 [*sic*] in the household of William and Ann Kane, both b. Ireland (p.339).

Taft children, named in grandmother's will: 1. *Harriet Taft*[7]. 2. *Mary Taft*.

iv   ROYAL THAYER, b. 19 March 1788; d. 30 March 1863, bur. Uxbridge (Sprague Ms); m. at Uxbridge, 21 June 1812 (*VR* 326), HANNAH SEA-GRAVES, b. 28 Aug. 1791, d. 5 March 1881, dau. of Bezaleel and Mary (Aldrich) Seagraves (Sprague Ms). In 1850 he was a farmer at Uxbridge (p.395), with Hannah ae 59, and five of the children.

Children, rec. Uxbridge (*VR* 163-65): 1. *Catharine Thayer*[7], b. 21 Jan. 1813; d. Uxbridge 13 Aug. 1844 ae 28y (*VR* 410). 2. *Sarah Ann Thayer*, b. 7 Oct. 1814; m. Henry Ridell. 3. *Charlotte Augusta Thayer*, b. 1817; at home 1850; m. Robert Rogerson. 4. *William Bainbridge Thayer*, d. 1 Nov. 1820 ae 1y 3m (g.s.). 5. *Hannah Adaline Thayer*, b. 28 March 1822; m. Edwin Armsby. 6. *Sylvia Wheaton Thayer*, b. 8 March 1824; at home 1850. 7. *William Walter Thayer*, b. 1 May 1827; at home, a clerk, 1850. 8. *Royal Thayer Jr.*, d. Uxbridge 21 March 1829 ae 2m (*VR* 410). 9. *Mary Aldrich Thayer*, b. 14 March 1830; at home 1850; m. Nathan Edward Goldthwaite. 10. *Royal Thayer Jr.*, b. 18 Dec. 1832; at home 1850; m. Cornelia K. Waters.

v   COLLINS THAYER, b. 7 April 1790; d. Norfolk, Va., 19 Sept. 1855 in an epidemic and bur. Elmwood Cemetery there (gs inscription, *NEHGR* 48:336); m. at Douglas, 6 Sept. 1819 (*VR* 150), ALMIRA TAFT, b. ca 1800 in Mass. In 1850 Collins Thayer ae 60 was a grocer in Norfolk, Va., with Almira and six children; Almarine Gwaltney ae 24, cabinetmaker, and Mary Gwaltney ae 22 shared the household (p.60).

Children [said to be nine in all], all but Susan at home 1850, all b. Virginia:
1. *Susan A. Thayer[7]*, m. Norfolk, 19 Feb. 1846, Charles H. Guild of Providence, R.I. (Sprague). ? prob. 2. *Mary Thayer*, b. ca 1828; m. Almarine Gwaltney. 3. *Almira Thayer*, b. ca 1831. 4. *Charlotte Thayer*, b. ca 1833. 5 *James Thayer*, b. ca 1835; a clerk 1850. 6. *Georgianna Thayer*, b. ca 1837. 7. *Olive Thayer*, b. ca 1840. 8. *Emily Thayer*, b. ca 1846.

vi SULLIVAN THAYER, b. 3 April 1792; d. Milford 7 Nov. 1865; bur. Pine Grove Cem. (Sprague); m. (1) at Uxbridge 6 Sept. 1814 (*VR* 326), CHARLOTTE MOWRY, b. 13 Feb. 1794, d. Uxbridge 30 Dec. 1815 ae 21y (*VR* 410), bur. old Mowry Cem., W. Uxbridge, dau. of Weston and Mary (___) Mowry (Sprague); m. (2) ca Feb. 1818, RUTH MOWRY, b. 1798, d. Milford 4 April 1879, sister of first wife. In 1850 Sullivan Thayer ae 58, coal dealer, was in Milford with Ruth ae 51, Henry B., and Harriet, and "Warriton Moorey" ae 83, b. R.I., was in their household (p.29).

In his will Sullivan Thayer of Milford, Esq., named wife Ruth, sons Edwin S. Thayer of Hopkinton and Henry B. Thayer, dau. Harriet L. Thayer, and granddaughter Ella F. Wiggins, only dau. of Samuel Wiggins (Worcester PR #58812).

Child with first wife Charlotte: 1. *Alonzo Thayer[7]*, b. Sept. 1815; d. Uxbridge 27 Feb. 1816 ae 5m 15d (*VR* 410). Children with second wife Ruth, b. Marlboro (*VR* 182-83), last two Uxbridge (*VR* 164, 410; Sprague Ms): 2. *Austin Thayer*, b. 1819; d. 16 Oct. 1819 ae 7m 7d. 3. *Sullivan Taft Thayer*, b. 17 April 1820; d. 1860 Calif. 4. *Charlotte Mowry Thayer*, b. 23 Nov. 1821; m. Samuel W. Wiggin. 5. *Mary Adeline Thayer*, b. 1824; d. 7 Jan. 1826 ae 2 yrs. 6. *Edwin Stephen Thayer*, b. 5 June 1826; m. Nancy P. Barstow. 7. *Asa Thayer*, b. 2 June 1828; d. Oct. 1849. 8. *Henry Bucklin Thayer*, b. 13 March 1832; with parents 1850. 9. *George Flagg Thayer*, b. 9 March 1834; d. 20 Feb. 1835 ae 11m 11d. 10. *Mary J. Thayer*, b. Jan. 1835; d. 2 June 1835 ae 5m 9d. 11. *Mary Thayer*, b. 1836; d. 1 June 1837 ae 9m 9d. 12. *Harriet Lydia Thayer*, b. 3 May 1839; at home 1850; d. unm. 1916. 13. *Herbert Morton Thayer*, b. 18 Feb. 1843; d. 10 Jan. 1844.

vii EMORY THAYER, b. 19 Feb. 1794; d. 12 Aug. 1862; m. Douglas, 8 Sept. 1816 [as Amory] (*VR* 150), SUSANNA TAFT, b. ca 1798 Mass., d. 4 May 1875 ae 77y; both bur. E. Douglas Cem. (Sprague). In 1850 Amory Thayer was a farmer in Douglas (p.349), with "Mrs. Thayer," ae 52, and daughters Angenette and Georgiana; son Ezekiel was next door with his own family.

Children b. Douglas, not rec. (Sprague, citing *Thayer Memorial*): 1. *Malonra Lavina Thayer[7]*, b. 2 Sept. 1819; m. Caleb Cummings. 2. *Matilda Ann Thayer*, b. 24 Sept. 1820; m. Douglas 1845, Allen Potter Jr. (*VR* 151). 3. *Ezekiel Taft Thayer*, b. 21 Nov. 1823; m. Douglas 1848 (*VR* 150), Mary D. Cook. 4. *Susan A. Thayer*, b. 1 Oct. 1826; m. Douglas 1843, James Sutton. 5. *Anjeline L. Thayer*, b. 10 Aug.

1830; m. Douglas 1849 (*VR* 150), Edwin C. Aldrich. 6. *Angenette Thayer*, b. 17 Aug. 1832; at home 1850. 7. *Georgiana Augusta Thayer*, b. 23 May 1835 (*VR* 61); d. 5 May 1836 (*VR* 187). 6. *Georgiana Thayer*, b. 6 July 1837; at home 1850.

viii   LOIS THAYER, b. 3 Oct. 1796; d. Uxbridge 29 March 1832 ae 35y (*VR* 388); m. 7 Jan. 1818 GEORGE MINOT (*Douglas History*, 175).

       Minot child, named in grandmother's will: 1. *Charles Minot⁷*, probably the *Charles Thayer Minot* bp. Uxbridge 26 May 1831 (*VR* 109).

ix   ASA THAYER Jr, b. 2 Sept. 1799; d. 7 March 1889; m. at Uxbridge 24 Sept. 1827 (*VR* 323), CHLOE T. CHAPIN, b. Uxbridge 8 April 1802, d. 5 Oct. 1881, dau. of Phineas and Eunice (___) Chapin; both bur. East Douglas Cem. Sprague says that Asa lived on his father's homestead on Hartford Turnpike in West Uxbridge, and then kept a public house in the village of East Douglas. In 1850 Asa was listed as a "boarding master" at Northbridge with Chloe ae 48 and seven of the children, head of a household that included many boarders (p.167).

       Children, first three rec. Uxbridge (*VR* 163-64), rest from Sprague Ms: 1. *Andrew Jackson Thayer⁷*, b. 19 Jan. 1829; Jackson A. Thayer, ae 21, clerk in 1850; m. Mary Ann Knapp. 2. *Charles Augustus Thayer*, b. 29 July 1830; d. 2 May 1856 Calif.; not with parents 1850. 3. *Francis Henry Thayer*, b. 8 June 1832; d. 26 Jan. 1852; at home, a clerk, in 1850. 4. *Anna F. or Eunice F. Thayer (Morgina F.* 1850), b. 3 Feb. 1835; m. William L. Shadlow. 5. *Elvira/Ella G. Thayer* (twin), b. 8 Jan. 1837; m. Isaac J. Wyman. 6. *Margaretta/Etta E. Thayer* (twin), b. 8 Jan. 1837; m. Amasa Alger. 7. *Lucius M. Thayer*, b. 18 Feb. 1840; m. Antoinette ___. 8. *Walter G. Thayer*, b. 23 Sept. 1842; d. 3 Jan. 1859 ae 16y 3m.

x   TURNER THAYER, b. 2 Feb. 1802; d. Douglas 18 Dec. 1853 of consumption (Sprague Ms); m. at Douglas, 25 Jan. 1824 (*VR* 152), LYDIA BATCHELER, b. Nov. 1805, d. 2 Jan. 1881; both bur. East Douglas. Turner Thayer was a storekeeper in Douglas 1850 (p.341), with "Mrs. Thayer," ae 44, and sons George, Henry, and Edward.

       Children, marr. and deaths (*VR* 187) rec. Douglas, birthdates from Sprague Ms: 1. *Lucy J. Thayer⁷*, b. 18 Oct. 1824; m. John C. Hammond. 2. *Lovisa H. Thayer*, b. 5 Nov. 1827; m. Douglas, 5 Oct. 1847, Philo Parker (*VR* 151). 3. *George Clyde Thayer*, b. 30 July 1830, a shoemaker 1850; m. Sarah A. Greeley. 4. *Mary B. Thayer*, b. 17 May 1835; m. (1) David J. Emery, (2) Amos Steere. 5. *Henry Thayer*, b. ca 1835; at home 1850. 6. *Olive Ellen Thayer*, b. June 1837; d. 7 Oct. 1838 ae 16m. 7. *Edward T. Thayer*, b. 18 Aug. 1839; d. 5 March 1841. 8. *Edward L. Thayer*, b. 4 March 1848; at home 1850.

xi   MARY M. THAYER, b. 4 Sept. 1803; m. Uxbridge, 3 Sept. 1833 (*VR* 325), as his second wife, Maj. CLARK SUMNER, b. ca 1794 Mass., widower of

Sally Clark who d. Milford 11 March 1832 ae 38 (*VR* 369). In 1850 he
was ae 56, a merchant in Milford (p.23).

Sumner children, rec. Milford: 1. [*Infant*] *Sumner,* d. Milford 9 April 1834
(*VR* 369). 2. *Sullivan Clark Sumner⁷,* b. Milford 9 Feb. 1836 (*VR* 163).

xii LOVISA THAYER, b. 4 April 1806; d. Uxbridge 30 Nov. 1828 (*VR* 410) in
her 23rd year.

Sources cited: *Douglas VR. Uxbridge VR.* Worcester County Probate Records. Edward W.
James, Esq., "Inscriptions at Norfolk, Va.," *NEHGR* 48 (1894). W. C. Sprague, Thayer Ms.
W. A. Emerson, *History of Douglas* (1879). CENSUS: 1850 Worcester Co.: Douglas (M432-341),
Milford (M432-344), Northbridge & Uxbridge (M432-345), North Providence, Providence Co.,
R.I. (M432-843), and Norfolk, Va. (M432-964).

595.   LOIS THAYER⁵ (*Samuel Thayer⁴, Mary³ Samson, Stephen², Henry¹*), daughter
of Samuel Thayer [124] and his first wife, Sarah Farnum, was born 15 February
1764 at Uxbridge (*VR* 164). She died probably between 1800 and 1810, since the
1820 census figures for her husband's household do not include a woman of her
age, and she would have been too old to be mother of the five children under 10
who were in the family.

She was of Uxbridge when she married at Milford, 1 July 1790 (VR 277),
ELIAS PHILIPS. He was born 27 February 1766 at Bellingham (VR 53), and
baptized at Milford 3 May 1772 (VR 140), son of Joshua and Mary (Heaton)
Philips "of Bellingham." He died after 1830 when he was listed in the census at
Leicester, N.Y. Census figures suggest that he married a second time, a woman
born between 1780 and 1790.

On 26 February 1790, Elias Phillips of Bellingham, cordwainer, bought land
with a dwelling and grist mill in Milford (Worcester LR 126:249). On 30 May 1793
Elias Phillips of Milford, yeoman, bought land in Milford from the estate of John
Tyler of Mendon (*ibid.,* 127:427). On 1 November 1794 Elias Phillips of Milford,
cordwainer, sold the property with the grist mill purchased in 1790; both he and
Loes [*sic*] acknowledged the deed on 12 February 1795 (*ibid.,* 124:632).

History of Milford (p.965), asks "whence they came, where dwelt, whither they
went?" It appears that they migrated to central New York State, probably by way
of Stafford, Conn. Elias Philips is listed in the 1790 census at Milford, with a
household consisting of just himself and one woman (p.229). In 1800 the family
appears at Stafford, Conn., with figures that match the known Milford family (a
man and a woman 26-45, three boys and one girl under 10) plus one boy 10-16
whose identity is not known (p.637). They have not been found in 1810, but Elias
is listed in 1820 at Leicester, Genesee County, N.Y. (p.162), over 45, with one boy

and four girls under 10, a girl 10-16, a young man 18-26, and a woman 26-45 (who was probably a second wife and mother of the younger children). Two members of the family were engaged in agriculture. In 1820 sons Nahum and Caleb were living in the adjacent town of Perry (p.230), which was set off from Leicester in 1814, and Caleb was still there in 1850, his age and birth place matching that of Elias and Lois's son of that name. Elias is listed at Leicester also in 1830, aged 60-70 with one woman 40-50, one woman 20-30, two young women 15-20, one boy and one girl 10-15, two girls 5-10, and one boy under 5 (p.162).

No probate records for Elias Philips have been found.

Children of Elias and Lois (Thayer) Philips, recorded Milford (*VR* 140):

   i   CALEB PHILIPS[6] (twin), b. 25 March 1791; m. ANNA _____, b. ca 1789 Mass. (census). In 1820 they were living at Perry, Genesee Co., N.Y., next to his brother Nahum, with one boy and one girl under 10 (p.230). In 1850 they were at Perry [by then in Wyoming Co.], N.Y., he ae 59, a farmer, b. Mass. (p.291).

         Children, last three at home 1850; prob. others: 1. [*Son*] *Philips*[7], b. 1810-1820. 2. *Carlista Philips*, b. ca 1818. 3. *Artemetia Philips*, b. ca 1822. 4. *Caleb Philips*, b. ca 1835.

   ii   JOSHUA PHILIPS (twin), b. 25 March 1791.

  iii   NAHUM PHILIPS, b. 7 April 1793. In his will dated 5 Dec. 1865, proved 4 Oct. 1867, Nahum Philips of Perry, N.Y., left his real estate to son Lyman M. Philips, and to daughter Mary M. Bolton "one melodion now owned by me" and $2000 in cash (Wyoming Co., N.Y., Wills 7:61-64).

         Children named in will: 1. *Lyman M. Philips*[7]. 2. *Mary M. Philips*, m. _____ Bolton.

   iv   MERINDA PHILIPS, b. 24 Nov. 1794.

Sources cited: *Milford VR. Uxbridge VR.* Worcester County Deeds. Wyoming Co., N.Y., Surrogate's Records. CENSUS: 1790 Milford, Worcester Co. (M637-4); 1800 Stafford, Tolland Co., Conn. (M32-2); 1820 Leicester, Genesee Co., N.Y. (M33-70); 1830 Leicester, Livingston Co., N.Y. (M19-93); 1850 Perry, Wyoming Co., N.Y. (M432-617).

596. MARY/ POLLY THAYER[5] (*Samuel Thayer*[4], *Mary*[3] *Samson, Stephen*[2], *Henry*[1]), daughter of Samuel Thayer [124] and his first wife, Sarah Farnum, was born 18 February 1766 at Uxbridge (*VR* 165), recorded as Polly, and died there 2 or 3 April 1818, aged 52 (*VR* 364) as "Mary, widow of Ebenezer Coffin." She is buried in Prospect Hill Cemetery, Uxbridge.

She married at Uxbridge, 28 May 1786 (*VR* 229), **EBENEZER COFFIN**, who was called "of Boston" in their intentions. His identity presents a puzzle. The ideal candidate, chronologically, is an Ebenezer born to William and Mary (Aston) Coffin of Boston 6 May 1763 (*VR* 305), but he is said in the *Coffin Family* to have married Mary Matthews and moved to South Carolina, and this is supported by a death notice in the *Columbian Centinel* of 24 May 1817 for Capt. Ebenezer Coffin on 9 May 1817 in Charleston, S.C., aged 54, and an earlier notice for the death on 26 June 1813 of Mrs. Mary, wife of Ebenezer Coffin, formerly of Boston, in Charleston. The Coffins of Boston were a merchant family, some of whom were Loyalists during the Revolution. Another Ebenezer, son of William and Ann (Holmes) Coffin was born 21 May 1736 in Boston.

Except for the birth of their daughter Elizabeth (five months after the marriage), there are no other Coffins in the Uxbridge records. The 1790 census lists Ebenezer Coffin in Uxbridge with one man and three females (*Heads of Fam.*, 241). No listing was found for the family in 1800. In 1810 Mary Coffin was head of the household, with two young women 16-26, one woman 26-45, and one woman 45+ (p.71). No land or probate records for Ebenezer or Polly have been found in Worcester County.

Child of Ebenezer and Mary [*sic*] (Thayer) Coffin, recorded Uxbridge (*VR* 48):

   i   ELIZABETH COFFIN[6], b. 26 Oct. 1786; n.f.r.

Sources cited: *Boston VR* [BRC 24]. *Uxbridge VR*. *Index to the Columbian Centinel.* CENSUS: *Heads of Families 1790 – Mass.*; 1810 Uxbridge, Worcester Co. (M252-22).

597. **STEPHEN THAYER**[5] (*Samuel Thayer*[4], *Mary*[3] *Samson, Stephen*[2], *Henry*[1]), son of Samuel Thayer [124] and his second wife Judith Walker, was born 10 February 1783 at Uxbridge (*VR* 165) and died 24 May 1852 at Waterville, Maine (*Maine Physicians*, 165).

He married, first, 13 May 1808 at Vassalboro, Maine (*VR* 2:106), **SOPHIA CARLETON**, daughter of Jonathan and Eunice (Lufkin) Carleton. She was born at Newbury 1 December 1790 (d. rec.; g.s.) and died 9 or 10 February 1831 at Fairfield, Maine (*VRs*; d. rec.).

He married, second, 10 February 1832, **MARY CARLETON**, a sister of his first wife; Mary died 23 March 1879 (*Stephen Thayer Desc.*). In 1860 she was aged 70, living in the home of her nephew and stepson Charles H. Thayer.

Stephen Thayer studied medicine with surgeon Dr. Reuben Dimond Mussey of Ipswich. After his training he moved to Maine and practiced in Vassalboro,

China, and Fairfield, settling finally in Waterville. He was commissioned as a surgeon in the War of 1812. It is written of him that he "was a man of brilliant speech, and he went through life sparking with witty stories, and exhibiting a most unkempt, shaggy head of hair" (*Maine Physicians*).

The family home in Waterville was the first brick dwelling house in that town, sold by Dr. Daniel Cook to Dr. Stephen Thayer about 1834. It is no longer standing. Stephen, Sophia, and Mary are buried in Pine Grove Cemetery, Waterville.

Stephen's mother, Judith (Walker) Thayer, evidently spent her last years with his family. The births of the children of Dr. Stephen Thayer and Sophia his wife, deaths of two of their children, and Sophia's own death are recorded all together in Fairfield. The death of Judith Thayer on 6 March 1816, "Mother of Stephen Thayer, Entered March 6 1824 ..." is listed in its chronological place among the births of the children, between George H. and Martha.

In 1850 the household of Stephen Thayer, M.D., at Waterville included his wife Mary, aged 57, children George, Eugene, Harriet, Emeline, and Elvirah, and George's wife Ellen (p.94).

In his will, dated 13 May 1852, less than two weeks before he died, Stephen Thayer of Waterville, in the County of Kennebec, Physician, mentioned his wife and appointed his son Charles H. Thayer executor, directing him to retain $500 out of the proceeds of his personal property "to be paid over by him to any one or more of my children whose situation and necessity may in his opinion most require it." To son Charles he left $100; to son Stephen his pew in the Baptist meeting house in Waterville, his chaise, horse cart and harness, and $200; to daughter Sophia Tuttle notes now in her possession made in part payment of purchase money for the house and lot in Canaan where she formerly lived, and $300; to son George $200; to daughter Almira Hale 15 shares of the stock of the Androscoggin & Kennebec Rail Road, provided she survive her husband Sherman Hale and not otherwise; and to daughter Martha Whitney & her heirs the lot of land and store and other buildings in the town of Plymouth "that I bought of her husband Chas. T. Whitney Apr. 1, 1851...." He named also Charles Atwood, son of daughter Sophia, and left the disposition of the household furniture to wife and daughters Emeline and Elvira. The residue was to go to son Eugene and daughters Emeline and Elvira to be equally divided, on condition they provide for his wife and pay to daughter Harriet an annuity of $60. The real estate was not to be divided for seven years. (Kennebec PR 23:177)

Children of Stephen and Sophia (Carleton) Thayer, rec. Fairfield, Me., *VR*, spouses and death dates from *Stephen Thayer Desc.*):

i   ALBERT C. THAYER[6], b. 3 March 1809; d. 28 Dec. 1834; m. ANN E. PUTNAM. No mention is made of heirs of Albert in his father's will.

ii CHARLES H. THAYER, b. 14 Oct. 1810; d. 11 Jan. 1864; m. SUSAN E. TOBEY. In 1860 he was a farmer at Waterville, with Susan E. ae 49, one son, and his aunt/stepmother, Mary C. Thayer ae 70 (p.824).
    Child (1860 census): 1. *Frederick C. Thayer*[7], b. ca 1845.

iii SOPHIA ANN THAYER, b. 11 March 1812; m. (1) REUBEN ATWOOD, M.D., d. ca 1845; m. (2) ca 1846, HIRAM TUTTLE, d. by 1850. In 1860 Sophia Tuttle was head of a household in Waterville with three children (p.785).
    Atwood children (census): 1. *Charles R. Atwood*[7], b. ca 1842. 2. *Abby F. Atwood*, b. ca 1844.
    Tuttle child (census): 1. *Lawrence O. Tuttle*[7], b. ca 1847.

iv MARY Y. THAYER, b. 26 May 1813; d. Fairfield, 30 Nov. 1833, unm.

v   STEPHEN S. THAYER, b. 5 May 1814; d. 13 June 1875; m. HANNAH BLACKWELL. In 1860 he was a farmer at Waterville, ae 46, with Hannah ae 46 and four children (p.725).
    Children: 1. *Albert Thayer*[7], b. ca 1848. 2. *Charles H. Thayer*, b. ca 1852. 3. *Mary L. Thayer*, b. ca 1853. 4. *William J. Thayer*, b. ca 1856.

vi HARRIET N. THAYER, b. 8 March 1816; living Waterville in 1906, unm.

vii GEORGE THAYER, b. 28 May 1817; d. Fairfield 8 Sept. 1818.

viii EMELINE F. THAYER, b. 22 Jan. 1819; d. 25 June 1906; m. WILLIAM L. HOWE, b. in Me. ca 1811, d. after 1860 when he was a farmer in Northfield, Minn., with Emeline ae 39 and Ida ae 4 (p.17).
    Howe child (census): 1. *Ida Howe*[7], b. ca 1856 in Tenn.

ix ALMIRA THAYER (twin), b. 6 March 1821; d. 23 Sept. 1891; m. SHERMAN HALE. He was a defendant in a debt case in Kennebec Co. in 1851, and has not been located after that.

x   ELVIRA THAYER (twin), b. 6 March 1821; d. 11 Oct. 1901; m. WILLIAM JORDAN, b. Me. ca 1813, d. after 1860 when he was a boot manufacturer in Waterville, ae 47, with Elvira T. ae 39, and two children (p.763).
    Jordan children (census): 1. *Mary E. Jordan*[7], b. ca 1856. 2. *William T. Jordan*, b. ca 1858.

xi GEORGE H. THAYER, b. 28 Dec. 1822; d. 16 June 1906; m. ELLEN A. BUTMAN. He is prob. the George Thayer ae 37 who in 1860 was a merchant in Plymouth, Me., with Ellen ae 31, and one son (p.24).
    Child (census): 1. *Samuel Thayer*[7], b. ca 1849.

xii   MARTHA THAYER, b. 6 May 1825; d. 2 Oct. 1891; m. CHARLES T.
      WHITNEY; said to have rem. to St. Paul, Minn., ca 1856. In 1850 Charles
      was a merchant in Plymouth, Me., ae 32, with Martha ae 26; no children
      were with them (p.10). They have not been found in 1860.

xiii LORENZO E. [EUGENE] THAYER, b. 3 Feb. 1828; d. 3 Oct. 1894; m.
      (1) 3 Jan. 1854, SARAH ABBY CHASE, b. Saco, Me., 6 Sept. 1833, d. 15
      April 1887, dau. Samuel Frye and Elizabeth (Pierson) Chase; m. (2)
      NELLIE (CHASE) EASTMAN, d. 10 Feb. 1902. In 1860 Lorenzo E.
      Thayer was a "dealer in ready made clothing" at Waterville, ae 32, with
      Sarah E. ae 26, and sons Francis C. and Edward (p.804).
            Children, with first wife: 1. *Francis C. Thayer⁷*, b. 15 Feb. 1855. 2. *Edward E
      Thayer*, b. 3 May 1857. 3. *Samuel C. Thayer*, b. 15 Jan. 1861.

Sources cited: *Uxbridge VR.* Vassalboro, Me., VR. Fairfield, Me., VR, original book not
paginated. Kennebec County, Me., Probate Records at Augusta. Spalding, *Maine Physicians of 1820
... (1928).* Dr. F.C. Thayer, comp., *Some Data relative to the Descendants of Stephen Thayer, M.D. of
Waterville, Maine* (1906), extends the genealogy to 1906. CENSUS: Waterville, Kennebec Co., Me.
1850 (M432-258) & 1860 (M653-440); 1860 Plymouth, Penobscot Co., Me. (M653-445) &
Northfield, Rice Co. Minn. (M653-573). **See also:** Alma Pierce Robbins, *History of Vassalborough.*
(1931), 243.

598.   SAMUEL THAYER⁵ (*Samuel Thayer⁴, Mary³ Samson, Stephen², Henry¹*), son
of Samuel Thayer [124] and his second wife, Judith Walker, was born 30 April 1784
at Uxbridge (*VR* 165). He died 14 April 1853 at Rutland, Vt., aged 69 years, and is
buried in Evergreen Cemetery there (Rutland Cem.).

He married, 1 April 1809, **ANNE BARNES** of Chester, Vt. She was born
about 8 August 1781 (calc.) at Bedford, N.H., daughter of Asa and Esther (___)
Barnes, and died at Rutland 17 September 1868 aged 87y 1m 9d (g.s.,VT VR).

They settled in Shrewsbury, Vt., where the 1810 census lists them with a
household consisting of a man and a woman 26-45, one boy 10-16, and one boy
under 10 (p.198). In 1850 Samuel Thayer aged 66, a farmer born Conn. [*sic*] and
Anna aged 68, born New Hampshire, were living in the household of their
daughter Esther Russell at Rutland, Vt. (p.43).

The only probate document recorded for Samuel Thayer is an administrator's
bond (Rutland Co., Rutland Dist. PR 29:94).

Children of Samuel and Anne (Barnes) Thayer, rec. Shrewsbury, Vt. (VT VR):

i   ALVA[H] BARNES THAYER⁶, b. 1 Oct. 1810; m. Shrewsbury, (1) 16 Feb.
      1835, MARIA ADAMS, (2) 8 Feb. 1843, LYDIA KENDALL, (3) 15 Feb.
      1847, FANNY KNIGHT (Sprague Ms), b. 10 June 1815, dau. of Thomas

and Phebe (Burnham) Knight. Alvah and his second wife, Lydia, appear to have separated, and in 1860 Lydia Thyer [sic] was in the household of William Russell ae 30 at Shrewsbury, Vt., with Louisa Thyer [sic] ae 15 (p.400). In 1860 Alvah B. Thayer ae 49, farmer, res. Rutland, Vt., with Fanny ae 44, children Julia ae 16, Louel [?] ae 12 [son], Edward ae 9, Clara ae 6, and Charles Pelky ae 23, b. N.Y. (p.308)

    Children (supp. six in all): 1. *Lydia Jane Thayer[7]*, b. 29 April 1844 (Sprague Ms). [Same as *Julia*, b. ca 1844, at home 1860, or twin?] 2. *Ann Louisa Thayer*, b. 26 July 1845 Shrewsbury, Vt. (Sprague Ms); res. Shrewsbury 1860 as Louisa, with her mother. 3. *Lowel* [?] *Thayer* [son], b. ca 1848. 4. *Edward Thayer*, b. ca 1851. 5. *Clara Thayer*, b. ca 1854.

ii   STEPHEN GALUSHA THAYER, b. 17 Aug. 1812; m. in 1840, RACHEL DODGE, b. ca 1822 Vt. In 1850 Stephen G. Thayer was a farmer in Rutland, Vt. (p.49).

    Children at home 1850: 1. *Savery Thayer[7]* [dau.], b. ca 1843. 2. *Alvin Thayer*, b. ca 1844.

iii JOSIAH RICHARDSON THAYER, b. 22 Aug. 1813; d. 26 Dec. 1816 ae 3y 5d (g.s. Brookside Cem., Chester, Vt.).

iv [MARY] ESTHER THAYER, b. 27 Oct. 1814; m. in 1838 A.E./EATON A. RUSSEL, b. ca 1808 Vt. In 1850 A. E. Russel was a farmer ae 42 in Rutland, Vt., and Esther's parents lived with them (p.43). In 1860 he was listed as Eaton A. Russel, and Esther's mother, Anna Thayer ae 78, was with them (p.343).

    Russell children at home 1850, 1860: 1. *Mary A. Russell[7]*, b. ca 1840, a teacher 1860. 2. *George Russell*, b. ca 1843, farm laborer 1860. 3. *Josephine Russell*, b. ca 1845. 4. *Josiah Russell*, b. ca 1849. 5. *Ellen Russell*, b. ca 1851. 6. *Alvin Russell*, b. ca 1857.

v   [son] THAYER, b. 5 Aug. 1819; d. in infancy.

Sources cited: *Uxbridge VR.* Vermont Vital Records to 1870. Rutland Cemetery Records. Rutland Co., Vt., probate records. W. C. Sprague, "Thomas Thayer" Ms., NEHGS. CENSUS: Rutland Co., Vt.: 1810 Shrewsbury (M252-65), 1850 Rutland (M432-927), 1860 Rutland & Shrewsbury (M653-1327). **See also:** *Memorial of Richard and Thomas Thayer*, pp. 291-92.

599. MARY THAYER[5] (*Samuel Thayer[4], Mary[3] Samson, Stephen[2], Henry[1]*), daughter of Samuel Thayer [124] and his second wife Judith Walker, was born at Uxbridge in 1786 (*MF20*: 1:104). Her birth is not recorded at Uxbridge. In 1790 her mother's household (in Douglas) consisted of two boys under 16 and two females (p.218), suggesting that Mary was alive at that date. No further record found.

Sources cited: *MF 20 – Henry Samson Pt. 1* (2000).   CENSUS: 1790 Douglas, Worcester Co. (M637-4).

600.   MICAH HOLBROOK[5] (*Zilpha Thayer[4], Mary[3] Samson, Stephen[2], Henry[1]*), son of John Holbrook and his wife Zilpha Thayer [125], was born 11 March 1744 at Uxbridge (*VR* 89) and died at Hamburg, N.Y., in 1810 (*Thomson Desc.*, 20). He is called in some records Mikel Holbrook.

He married 27 November 1766 at Uxbridge (*VR* 260), she of Douglas, **RHODA THAYER**, who was born about 1744 and died 20 September 1776 in her 32nd year at Mendon (*VR* 474), daughter of Joseph and Sarah (Balcome) Thayer. She is buried in Chestnut Hill Cemetery, Mendon.

Micah married, second, intentions 30 May 1779 at Uxbridge (*VR* 260), **MARY THOMSON** of Smithfield, R.I., born 9 August 1746, daughter of Benjamin and Martha (Darling) Thomson (*Thomson Desc.*, 19-20).

Micah Holbrook of Smithfield, R.I., yeoman, sold land in Uxbridge with a dwelling on 1 April 1793; his wife Mary released her dower (Worcester LR 126:161). Micah was still of Smithfield when he and Mary sold land in Uxbridge on 25 January 1803 (*ibid.*). On 1 September 1803 Micah Holbrook of Smithfield as guardian to Elizabeth Darling (who was insane), joined Peletiah Goldthwaite, Joseph Kelly Jr. and wife Hannah, all of Smithfield, and John Thompson and wife Lydia of Cheshire, N.H., in selling land in Mendon (*ibid.*, 154:560).

Micah was of Swanzey, N.H., by 10 June 1807 when he sold to Stephen Buffam of Smithfield, R.I., land in Uxbridge; Mary released her dower and he acknowledged the deed the same day in Smithfield (*ibid.*, 167:176).

Children of Micah and Rhoda (Thayer) Holbrook, rec. Uxbridge (*VR* 88-89):

   i   DAVID HOLBROOK[6], b. 4 Sept. 1767; d. Swanzey, N.H., 17 Jan. 1852; m. at Glocester, R.I. (not in *VRRI*), 4 March 1786, SARAH ARNOLD, b. 1 Sept. 1770, d. 22 Dec. 1850, dau. of Noah Arnold of Glocester (*Swanzey History*, 379). They settled in Richmond, N.H., then Swanzey. In 1850 David Holbrook ae 85 and Sarah ae 81, both b. R.I., were living in Swanzey in the household of Virgil Holbrook ae 41 and wife Rowena ae 34 (p.219).
       Children, first two b. Uxbridge, third at Richmond, N.H., rest at Swanzey, N.H. (*Swanzey History*, 379): 1. *Ann A. Holbrook[7]*, b. 19 May 1791; m. Ira Aldrich. 2. *Rhoda Holbrook*, b. 4 March 1793; m. Benjamin Kelton. 3. *Sarah B. Holbrook*, b. 13 May 1795; m. James Harris. 4. *Mary Holbrook*, b. 14 July 1797; m. Joseph Randall. 5. *David A. Holbrook*. 6. *Olive W. Holbrook*, b. 16 April 1804; m. David Aldrich. 7. *Betsey R. Holbrook*, b. 6 Jan. 1807; m. Charles C. Pratt. 8. *Virgil A.*

Holbrook, b. 19 Oct. 1809; m. Rowena T. Thompson. 9. *Lorenzo R. Holbrook,* b. 9 Oct. 1813; m. Electa E. Rogers. 10. *Aurilla T. Holbrook,* b. 9 Sept. 1817; m. Horace T. Slade.

ii SARAH HOLBROOK, b. 7 April 1769; d. 23 Oct. 1850; m. at Smithfield, R.I., 11 Oct. 1789, STEPHEN BUFFUM (*VRRI* 3: pt 6: 22), b. 16 Jan. 1762, son of Benjamin and Elizabeth (Sweet) Buffum (Smithfield Friends Recs., *VRRI* 7:184 [b.], 164 [par. m.]), d. Smithfield 21 March 1837 (*NEHGR* 138:120); both bur. Buxton Cem., North Smithfield, RI. (RI HCTP).

   Buffum children rec. Smithfield "of Stephen and Sarah" (*VRRI,* 3: pt 6: 93): 1. *Stephen Buffum⁷,* b. 15 April 1791; m. Ruth ___. 2. *Benjamin Buffum,* b. 17 March 1793. 3. *Allen Buffum,* b. 29 Jan. 1795.

iii ENOS HOLBROOK, b. 16 [or 7?] Dec. 1772; d. LaMoille, Ill., 18 Oct. 1853; m. Richmond, N.H., 14 Dec. 1797 ELIZABETH THOMPSON; rem. to Richmond, N.H., and later, by 1835, to Illinois. In 1850 Enos Holbrook ae 79, blacksmith b. Mass., was living in LaMoille, Ill. (p.199), with Rachall ae 45, b. N.H., and presumed sons Enos and Jonathan T. were nearby.

   Probable children, b. N.H. (1850 census): 1. *Enos Holbrook⁷,* b. ca 1793; m. Jerusha ____. 2. *? Jonathan T. Holbrook,* b. ca 1802; m. Lucy ____; a merchant in LaMoille, Ill., 1850. 3. *Rachel Holbrook,* b. ca 1805; with father 1850.

Children of Micah and Mary (Thomson) Holbrook, first two rec. Uxbridge (*VR* 89):

iv RHODA HOLBROOK, b. 6 Sept. 1781; m. TIMOTHY PEARSE.

v MARTHA HOLBROOK, b. 30 Jan. 1784.

vi BENJAMIN HOLBROOK, b. 8 Aug. 1786 Smithfield, R.I. (*VRRI* 3: pt 6:101); prob. Benjamin T. Holbrook at Harmony, Chautauqua Co., N.Y., 1850 (p.249), ae 63, farmer b. R.I., with wife BETSEY ____ ae 63, b. Mass., son Henry, and Betsey Wilkins ae 20, b. N.Y. In his will dated 5 June 1854, proved 2 May 1873, Benjamin T. Holbrook named wife Betsey and son Henry W. Holbrook and mentioned land in Harmony purchased of Alonzo Pearse (Chautauqua Co. Wills 5:367).

   Children, list prob. incomplete (1850 census): ?1. *Benjamin Holbrook⁷,* b. ca 1813 N.Y.; res. Harmony 1850. 2. *Henry W. Holbrook,* b. ca 1826 N.Y.; with father 1850.

Sources cited: *Douglas VR. Mendon VR. Uxbridge VR.* Arnold, *Vital Record of Rhode Island,* Vol. 3 [Smithfield], and Vol. 7 [Smithfield Friends Records]. Rhode Island Historical Cemeteries Transcription Project Data Base. "Deaths in Rhode Island and Massachusetts," *NEHGR* 138 (1984). Chautauqua Co., N.Y., Surrogate's Records. *History of Swanzey, N.H.* (1892). H. J. Amy,

Desc. of David & Amyes (Colle) Thomson ... (1962). CENSUS: 1850 LaMoille, Bureau Co., Ill. (M432-99), Swanzey, Cheshire Co., N.H. (M432-428), Harmony, Chautauqua Co., N.Y. (M432-484).

601. AMARIAH HOLBROOK⁵ (*Zilpha Thayer⁴, Mary³ Samson, Stephen², Henry¹*), son of John Holbrook and his wife Zilpha Thayer [125], was born 2 March 1747 at Uxbridge and died there 20 January 1817 (*VR* 88, 380).

He married at Douglas, 20 November 1777 (*VR* 114), **KEZIAH NYE**, who was born 20 April 1749 at Rochester (*VR* 1:225), daughter of David and Elizabeth (Briggs) Nye who moved from Rochester to Douglas (*Nye Fam.*, 79). She was living in November 1799 when she signed a deed with her husband.

On 5 December 1777 Amariah Holbrook of Uxbridge, husbandman, sold to John Holbrook of Uxbridge "part of the land left me by my father John Holbrook deceased by his will ..." (Worcester LR 83:523). On 14 November 1799 he sold to Daniel Aldrich of Glocester, R.I., "the farm whereon I now live in Uxbridge," Keziah releasing her dower (*ibid.*, 143:102). Amariah Holbrook of Mendon, laborer, sold land in Uxbridge 6 April 1805 (*ibid.*, 171:200).

In 1790 Amariah Holbrook of Uxbridge was head of a household consisting of one man, one boy under 16, and three females (p.241). In 1800 he was listed in Uxbridge with one man and one woman 45+ and one young man and one young woman 16-26 (p.465). In 1810 he was in Uxbridge, his household had one man and one woman 45+, one woman 26-45, one young man 16-26, and two girls under 10 (p.604).

No relevant Worcester County deeds or probate records were found.

Child of Amariah and Keziah (Nye) Holbrook, rec. Mendon; census figures suggest also a possible daughter b. between 1777 and 1783:

   i   OTIS HOLBROOK⁶, b. 24 Nov. 1783 at Mendon (*VR* 101); d. 15 July 1838 Uxbridge (*VR* 381); m. after int. 20 May 1810 Mendon (*VR* 322) and Uxbridge (*VR* 260), LEAR [LEAH] WILLSON of Mendon. He is listed in Uxbridge in 1820 (p.31) and 1830 (p.226), with figures that suggest several probable children, but their names have not been found.

Sources cited: *Douglas VR. Mendon VR. Rochester VR. Uxbridge VR. Genealogy of the Nye Family* (1907). CENSUS: Uxbridge, Worcester Co., 1800 (M32-16), 1810 (M252-22), 1820 (M33-54), 1830 (M19-68).

602. JOHN HOLBROOK⁵ (*Zilpha Thayer⁴, Mary³ Samson, Stephen², Henry¹*), son of John Holbrook and his wife Zilpha Thayer [125], was born in June 1748 at

Uxbridge (*VR* 89). He died 27 July 1817 at Swanzey, N.H., aged 69 years (*Swanzey History*, 375).

He was of Uxbridge when he married 6 December 1770 at Mendon (*VR* 322), **RHODA THAYER**, who was born there 11 November 1746 (*VR* 188), daughter of Moses and Hannah (____) Thayer. Rhoda Thayer, "daughter of Moses Thayer dec'd and now wife of John Holbrook," acknowledged a deed 8 November 1773 (Worcester LR 71:225). She died sometime between 1784, when son Thayer was born, and early 1797.

John married, second, after intentions 13 April 1797 at Uxbridge (*VR* 260, 291), **HANNAH (RICKARD) PRIME** "of Swanzey," widow of Josiah Prime (*Swanzey History*, 375). Hannah was born at Sutton 21 March 1763 (*VR* 146), daughter of Issachar and Mary (Carrill) Rickard/Record, and died at Swanzey, N.H., 31 May 1857 aged 94 (Swanzey Cem., 45). She married, first, as his second wife, JOSIAH PRIME, with whom she had Phebe, Josiah, and Rachel Prime, born at Swanzey (*Swanzey History*, 423). Hannah's father, Issachar Record, died in December 1776 "in York" while serving in the Revolution (*Sutton VR* 455).

On 29 May 1800 John Holbrook of Swanzey, N.H., yeoman, sold to Royal Farnum of Uxbridge land in Uxbridge bounded by land of Stephen and Henry Holbrook; John's wife Hannah also signed (Worcester LR 149:200). On 16 April 1806 John sold to Simeon Batcheller of Northbridge some land in Douglas; Hannah released her dower, and the deed was acknowledged by John 18 April 1806 in Cheshire County, N.H. (*ibid.*, 168:143).

In 1850 Hannah Holbrook, aged 87, was living at Swanzey with her unmarried children Aaron, Joshua, and Rhoda (p.220).

Children of John and Rhoda (Thayer) Holbrook, births rec. Uxbridge (*VR* 88-89); marriages from *Swanzey History* (p. 375):

i MOSES HOLBROOK[6], b. 21 June 1771; m. at Uxbridge, 20 March 1794 (VR 260), ANNA CRAGGIN, d. Uxbridge 18 Feb. 1848 ae 78 of liver complaint (*VR* 380).

   Children, first rec. Douglas (*VR* 36), rest Uxbridge (*VR* 88-89); all bp. Douglas 14 May 1809 (*VR* 36): 1. *Samuel Holbrook[7]*, b. 2 June 1795. 2. *Chloe Holbrook*, b. 18 Nov. 1799. 3. *Merit / Merrick Holbrook*, b. 22 March 1803.

ii EBER HOLBROOK, b. 12 Feb. 1773; d. prob. before 1800.

iii JOHN HOLBROOK, b. 16 Dec. 1774; d. y.

iv EZRA HOLBROOK, b. 17 Aug. 1776; m. (1) in 1803 at Richmond, N.H., SALLY PRIME, dau. of Joshua Prime, d. 1827 Roxbury; m. (2) in 1830 at Winchester, N.H., SUBMIT FIELD.

v   JOHN HOLBROOK 2d, b. 12 Sept. 1778 (g.s. says 11 Aug. 1778); d. 7 May
    1838 (*Swanzey History*, 375); m. after int. Mendon 15 Aug. 1801 (*VR* 319),
    "Massa Hill," prob. MERCY HILL b. Mendon 6 July 1780, dau. of Daniel
    and Mercy (Hayward) Hill (*VR* 99, 319).
        Children, b. Swanzey, N.H. (*Swanzey History*, 375): 1. *Rhoda Holbrook*[7], b. 26
    April 1804. 2. *Daniel Hill Holbrook*, b. 8 Jan. 1806. 3. *Abida Holbrook*, b. 11 Oct.
    1809. 4. *Sophia Holbrook*, b. 3 June 1811. 5. *Susan Ann Holbrook*, b. 11 Jan. 1814.
    6. *Chloe Holbrook*, b. 20 March 1816. 7. *John Holbrook*, b. 21 July 1818. 8. *Mercy
    Holbrook*, b. 3 Sept. 1821.

vi CATA HOLBROOK, b. 3 July 1781; m. GEORGE BROWN of Richmond
    (*Swanzey History*, 375).

vii THAYER HOLBROOK, b. 20 Feb. 1784; m. in 1811 at Swanzey, SALLY
    LAWRENCE of Winchester, N.H. (*Swanzey History*, 375). In 1850 he was
    a farmer at Girard, Pa., in the household of William S. Chapman ae 27, b.
    N.Y., and Nancy ae 28, b. N.H. (p.404).
        Possible child: 1. *Nancy Holbrook*[7], b. ca 1822 in N.H.

Children of John and Hannah (Rickard) (Prime) Holbrook, last four born Swanzey,
N.H. (*Swanzey History*, 375):

viii RHODAY HOLBROOK, b. Uxbridge 6 June 1798 (*VR* 89); d. 27 July
     1873 ae 75y 1m 21d (Swanzey Cem.), unm.

ix EBER HOLBROOK, b. 8 April 1800; m. MARIA ____, b. ca 1803 in Vt.
    In 1850 he was a farmer at Girard, Pa., with Maria and three children
    (p.416).
        Children at home 1850, all b. Pa.: 1. *Maria A. Holbrook*[7], b. ca 1836.
    2. *Josephine Holbrook*, b. ca 1838. 3. *George Holbrook*, b. ca 1840.

x   AARON HOLBROOK, b. 8 March 1802; d. 18 Oct. 1889 ae 87y 7m 10d
    (Swanzey Cem.); unm.

xi JOSHUA HOLBROOK, b. 12 March 1804; d. 2 Dec. 1878 ae 74y 8m 20d
    (Swanzey Cem.); unm.

xii PETER R. HOLBROOK, b. July 1806; m. SABRINA ___, b. ca 1814 in
    Pennsylvania. In 1850 he was a farmer at Girard, Pa., next to his brother
    Eber's family, with Sabrina, Caroline ae 5, and Helen and Emily Smith ae
    11 and 9, b. N.Y. (p.416).
        Child, b. Pa., at home 1850: 1. *Caroline Holbrook*[7], b. ca 1845.

Sources cited: *Douglas VR. Mendon VR. Sutton VR. Uxbridge VR.* Worcester County Deeds.
Read, *History of Swanzey, N.H.* (1892). W. F. Oakman, "Swanzey Cemetery Records," typescript
(1941), New Hampshire Historical Society. CENSUS: 1850 Swanzey, Cheshire Co., N.H. (M432-
428), Girard, Erie Co., Pa. (M432-778).

603. RHODA HOLBROOK[5] (*Zilpha Thayer*[4], *Mary*[3] *Samson, Stephen*[2], *Henry*[1]), daughter of John Holbrook and his wife Zilpha Thayer [125], was born in June 1750 at Uxbridge (*VR* 89), and was living in October 1774.

She married, after intentions at Uxbridge 22 July 1771 (*VR* 261, 346), **NATHAN WOOD**. Her father in his will dated 23 November 1773, left to "daughter Rhoda" £1 4s to be paid by her brother John Holbrook, and she signed a receipt to John at Uxbridge 9 October 1774 by mark as Rhoda Wood (Worcester PR # A30005; record book copy omits "Wood").

Nothing helpful has yet been discovered in records of Uxbridge and surrounding towns or of Worcester County, or in the *Wood Index*. A Nathan Wood born about 1744 served in the Revolutionary War from Douglas in 1775 and 1780, but no evidence has been found to identify him as Rhoda's husband. This man was described in July 1780 as aged 36, 5 ft. 3 in. tall, complexion dark, engaged for the town of Douglas (*MSSR* 17:760). Several Nathan Woods who served from Massachusetts or Connecticut applied for pensions, but all were either too young to have married in 1771 or can be otherwise accounted for.

The 1790 census is not helpful because it does not give break-downs of ages for adult men or females. In the 1800 census there are 19 Nathan Woods listed, but those who were 45 or older with wives in the same age range (and cannot be otherwise accounted for) were in Schoharie County, N.Y., and Townshend and Woodstock, Vt.

Sources cited: *Uxbridge VR.* Worcester County Probate Records. *Mass. Soldiers & Sailors.* John Sumner Wood, *The Wood Index* (1966). CENSUS: 1800 Bristol, Schoharie Co., N.Y. (M32-1215), Townshend, Windham Co., & Woodstock, Windsor Co., Vt. (M32-52)

604. SYLVANUS HOLBROOK[5] (*Thankful Thayer*[4], *Mary*[3] *Samson, Stephen*[2], *Henry*[1]), son of Sylvanus Holbrook and his wife Thankful Thayer [126], was born 21 April 1750 at Uxbridge (*VR* 89). He died before 1 September 1828 at Douglas, when administration was granted on his estate.

He married, intentions 20 January 1772 at Uxbridge (*VR* 261), **MOLLY THAYER**, who was born 17 June 1749 at Douglas (*VR* 61), daughter of Joseph and Sarah (___) Thair [*sic*]. On 23 November 1787, Sylvanus Holbrook of Uxbridge, yeoman, and Mary Holbrook his wife and daughter to Joseph Thayer, late of Douglas; Aaron Aldrich and wife Tirzah; and Martha Thayer sold to Thadeus Thayer of Douglas all their rights in the estate of their father Joseph Thayer. Sylvanus and Mary acknowledged 6 December 1787 (Worcester LR 144:588).

On 21 March 1826 Silvanus Holbrook of Douglas, for love and affection, deeded to his grandson Joseph Logee of Douglas, one-third of the "farm where I live," and on 7 November 1826 he deeded to him the other two thirds of the farm and lands (Worcester LR 252: 142, 622).

Sylvanus Holbrook of Douglas died intestate. The widow Mary Holbrook declined administration on 1 September 1828, saying she had no son living, but had a grandson Ezekiel Holbrook of Douglas, and on 16 September 1828 Nathaniel Carpenter was appointed administrator (Worcester PR #30118).

Children of Sylvanus and Molly (Thayer) Holbrook, first three rec. Uxbridge (*VR* 88-89):

i   PHEBE HOLBROOK[6], b. 16 Feb. 1773; m. int. 18 June 1790 Uxbridge (*VR* 317) and 17 Feb. 1791 Douglas (*VR* 114), with KEITH TAFT, b. 5 May 1761 Uxbridge (*VR* 155), son of Noah and Margaret (____) Taft.

ii   EZEKIEL HOLBROOK, b. 18 April 1777; d. 26 Jan. 1799 Douglas (*VR* 177); m. after int. 9 June 1798 Douglas (*VR* 114), SARAH COOK of Glocester, R.I., dau. of Israel and Sarah (Aldrich) Cook. Widow Sary Holbrook of Glocester m. (2) after int. Douglas 14 Feb. 1804 (*VR* 114), George Thayer, son of Thaddeus and Margaret (Holbrook) Thayer (see Family #607-i).

Child: 1. *Ezekiel Holbrook[7]*, b. prob. 1799; prob. m. Matilda Caswell.

iii JOSEPH HOLBROOK, b. 6 Nov. 1781; d. Douglas 2 Dec. 1802 (*VR* 177).

iv   MARY HOLBROOK, b. 16 Oct. 1784 Douglas (*VR* 36); d. 15 Aug. 1844 ae 60 of "disease in head" at Douglas (*VR* 180); m. after int. 22 Jan. 1804 at Douglas (*VR* 125), DANIEL LOGEE of Glocester [R.I.] They are buried in South Douglas Cemetery.

Logee children rec. Douglas (*VR* 44): 1. *Joseph Holbrook Logee[7]*, b. 17 Oct. 1804; m. Prudence Payne. 2. *Ira Sales Logee*, b. 9 Sept. 1808; d. 9 Feb. 1809 ae 5m (*VR* 180).

Sources cited: *Douglas VR. Uxbridge VR.* Worcester County Deeds and Probate Records.

605.   RUTH HOLBROOK[5] (*Thankful Thayer[4], Mary[3] Samson, Stephen[2], Henry[1]*), daughter of Sylvanus Holbrook and his wife Thankful Thayer [126], was born 10 August 1751 at Uxbridge (*VR* 89). She died 16 May 1781 at Mendon (*VR* 450) in her 30th year, and is buried in Chestnut Hill Cemetery, Mendon.

She was of Uxbridge when she married, 6 December 1770 at Mendon (*VR* 323), **BENONI BENSON JR.** He was born 11 June 1747 at Mendon (*VR* 31), son of Benoni Benson and probably his first wife Abigail (White). He died between 25 September 1798, when he was named in his father's will, and 19 September 1803, when his father added a codicil noting that son Benoni was deceased (*Benson Fam.* is incorrect on death date).

Benoni Benson Jr. of Mendon married, second, 3 January 1782 at Sutton (*VR* 211), RUTH SIBLEY of Sutton, perhaps the Ruth, daughter of Nathaniel and Ruth (Braddish) Sibley, born there 9 April 1745 (*Benson Fam.*, 301).

Benoni's brother John married Ruth's sister Molly Holbrook [#609]. In a distribution of the estate of Sylvanus Holbrook on 27 May 1783, one of the heirs was daughter Ruth Benson, deceased, wife of Benoni Benson. Benoni Benson Jr. of Mendon, husbandman, sold land in Uxbridge to Joseph Blake on 20 July 1779; his wife Ruth signed her consent (Worcester LR 95:362). On 12 December 1782 Benoni and John Benson of Mendon sold land there that belonged equally to them and to Seth Taft, deceased (*ibid.*, 89:29).

Benoni's three children, as "heirs of Ruth Benson deceased," shared in the distribution of the estate of their grandfather Sylvanus Holbrook of Uxbridge on 27 May 1783; Ruth's sister Molly Benson signed a receipt for them (Worcester PR #A30117). On the same date Benoni Benson Jr. was appointed guardian of Amasa, Chloe, and Benoni Benson, all under 14 (*ibid.*, 118:24, 217:241).

On 16 November 1794 Benoni Benson Jr. of Mendon, husbandman, sold the "whole of my farm," with (second) wife Ruth consenting; he acknowledged the deed at Worcester 21 January 1795 (*ibid.*, 97:117).

Benoni Jr. predeceased his father. In his will dated 25 September 1798, proved 17 May 1806, Benoni Benson of Mendon, greatly advanced in age, named his wife Abigail and son Benoni; in a codicil dated 19 September 1803 he noted that son Benoni was now dead and his children (not named) were to inherit, except that one-quarter of the estate left to Benoni was to revert to his brother John (Worcester PR #5145).

Children of Benoni and Ruth (Holbrook) Benson, first two rec. Mendon (*VR* 31):

i AMASA BENSON[6], b. 15 Jan. 1771; d. Mendon 7 March 1837 in 65th yr (*VR* 450); m. at Mendon, 28 Oct. 1798 (*VR* 248), LAVINA TURTILOT, b. there 20 Feb. 1777, dau. of Jesse and Lydia (___) Turtellot (*VR* 196).

Children rec. Mendon (*VR* 31-32): 1. *Henry Holbrook Benson*[7] (twin), b. 22 March 1801. 2. *Horis Benson* (twin), b. 23 March [*sic*] 1801. 3. *James Davis Benson*, b. 15 Nov. 1802. 4. *Chloe Benson*, b. 2 Oct. 1804. 5. *Meria Benson*, b. 17 Dec. 1806. 6. *Charles Benson*, b. 14 Sept. 1809. 7. *Angeline Benson*, b. 20 July 1811. 8. *Ann Eliza Benson*, b. 20 Feb. 1813. 9. *Elsa Benson*, b. 17 July 1815. 10. *Nathan Benson*, b. 30 Nov. 1817. 11. *William Hall Benson*, b. 24 Oct. 1819.

ii CHLOE BENSON, b. 28 Jan. 1774.

iii   BENONI BENSON, b. ca 1780 (guardianship); d. 1819 ae 39 at Sherburne, Vt. (*Benson Fam.*, 302n, citing VT VR).

Sources cited: *Mendon VR. Sutton VR. Uxbridge VR.* Worcester County Deeds and Probate Records. *The Benson Family of Colonial Massachusetts* (2003).

606.   RACHEL HOLBROOK⁵ (*Thankful Thayer⁴, Mary³ Samson, Stephen², Henry¹*), daughter of Sylvanus Holbrook and his wife Thankful Thayer [126], was born 6 November 1753 at Uxbridge (*VR* 89; VT VR says 9 Nov. 1752). She died at Danby 3 mo. 9, 1832 [9 March 1832], aged 79y 4m (g.s.; VT VR; Hemenway 3:649 says d. "about the year 1840").

She married, after intentions 12 December 1777 at Mendon (*VR* 323) and 29 December 1777 at Uxbridge (*VR* 310) **JONATHAN STAPLES**. He was born 29 March 1754 at Mendon (*VR* 163), son of Abraham Jr. and Marcy (Harvey) Staples, and died 11 mo. 28, 1832 [28 Nov. 1832] at Danby, Vt., aged 79 years (g.s.; VT VR). Jonathan and Rachel are buried in the Quaker Cemetery "near Dellingham farm" in Danby (VT VR citing Danby LR 13:153), described more recently as the Old Quaker Cemetery, on the southwest side of the road leading west from Danby Village (Jenks, 50-51).

Jonathan Staples of Mendon served in the Revolutionary War as a private in Capt. Joseph Daniels's company, marching to Roxbury on 19 April 1775; he was at Roxbury later, and in April and May 1777 served in Capt. Peter Penniman's company, Col. Wood's regiment, on a march for defense of Rhode Island; from August to October 1777 he served "at the Northward," including 180 miles travel home; in 1780 he was in Capt. Philip Ammidon's company, Col. Tyler's regiment, discharged 31 July 1780 after marching to Rhode Island on an alarm, 52 miles travel home (*MSSR* 14:847).

On 21 July 1781, Jonathan Staples, husbandman, and wife Rachel of Mendon, joined John Benson and wife Molly of Mendon, Thadeus Thayer and wife Margaret of Douglas, "heirs of our father Silvanus Holbrook late of Uxbridge, deceased," in deeding to Silvanus Holbrook of Uxbridge their rights in the estate; Rachel acknowledged 2 October 1781 and Jonathan on 27 November 1781 (Worcester LR 86:165). Heirs to whom payments made from the estate on 27 May 1783 included daughter Rachel Staples (Worcester PR #A30117).

The family removed to Wardsboro, Vt., by 1790 when they are listed in the census there with two boys under 16 and three females (p.56). In 1800, in addition to Jonathan and Rachel, over 45, the household consisted of two boys under ten, one boy 10-16 and one young man 16-26, and one girl 10-16 (p.83).

Children of Jonathan and Rachel (Holbrook) Staples, first two rec. Mendon (*VR* 164); all listed by Hemenway (3:649):

i SALLY STAPLES[6], b. 3 Oct. 1779; m. at Danby, Vt., 17 Feb. 1799, by Amos Brown, J.P., ISAAC ALLEN (VT VR), son of John and Sally (Brown) Allen; rem. to Collins, N.Y. (*Danby History*, 102).

ii SILVIA STAPLES, b. 5 Jan. 1781; m. Danby, 17 Feb. 1799, by Amos Brown, J.P., ELIJAH ALEXANDER (VT VR). In 1850 he was at Charlotte, Vt., ae 74, b. Mass., owner of $9,000 worth of real estate, with Sylva ae 70, three apparent daughters; farm laborers Isaiah Jones ae 38 b. N.Y. and Oscar Hazard ae 23 b. Vt.; and Arthur Barton ae 14 and Elijah H. Converse ae 4, both b. Vt. (p.93).

   Alexander children at home 1850, all b. Vt.: 1. *Sylvia Alexander*[7], b. ca 1805. 2. *Rachel Alexander*, b. ca 1814. 3. *Lydia Alexander*, b. ca 1826.

iii ELLERY STAPLES, b. 1784 in Mass. (1850 census); d. Danby, Vt., in 1861, ae 77; m. ALVIRA SKEELES, who d. 1870 ae 81 (Hemenway, 3:649). In 1850 Elory Staples ae 66, farmer b. Mass., and Almira ae 60, b. N.Y., were living in Danby in the household of Henry B. Kelley ae 26 and wife Rachael ae 21 (p.305).

   Children (*Danby History*, 267-68): 1. *Lydia Staples*[7], b. 1811; m. Graville Farrar. 2. *Sarah Staples*, b. 1812; m. Jonathan Crocker. 3. *Eunice Staples*, b. 1814; m. Linus Jennings. 4. *Amanda Staples*, b. 1816; m. Gilman Walker. 5. *Olive Staples*, b. 1818; d.y. 6. *William Staples*, b. 1819; d.y. 7. *Almira Staples*, b. 1820. 8. *Eliza Ann Staples*, b. 1822; d. 1846. 9. *Sylvia Staples*, b. 1824; m. William Robbison. 10. *Rhoda Staples*, b. 1826; m. Alvira Eldredge. 11. *Rachel Staples*, b. 1828; m. prob. Henry B. Kelley. 12. *William Ellery Staples*, b. 1829; d. 1832.

iv WILLARD STAPLES, b. prob. 1785; d. Granville, N.Y., on his birthday in 1858, ae 73 (*Danby History*, 268); m. Danby, 10 Sept. 1812, by Zoeth Allen, J.P. (VT VR), ELIZABETH ROGERS, d. 1861 ae 72, dau. of Stephen and Elizabeth (Lapham) Rogers (*Danby History*, 236, 268). Lived 28 years in Danby, "a man of standing and influence ... kind-hearted and highly respected" (*ibid.*, 268).

   Children (*ibid.*): 1. *Dorcas Staples*[7], b. ca 1815; m. Merrit Cook. 2. *David Staples*, b. ca 1817; m. Fanny Sherman. 3. *Stephen Staples*, m. Ann Slocum. 4. *Lydia Staples*. 5. *Edwin Staples*, res. Danby; m. (1) Louisa Vail, (2) Margaret V. Lapham.

v RACHAEL STAPLES, b. prob. ca 1788; m. Danby, [? 5] Dec. 1807, DEXTER BARTLETT (VT VR). Dexter was the son of Abner and Drusilla (Smith) Bartlett; he inherited his father's homestead, but in 1840 removed to the Holland Purchase, N.Y., where he d. 1866 (*Danby History*,

107, 267). In 1850 Dexter Bartlett ae 69, b. R.I., and Rachel ae 62, b. Vt., were living by themselves at Otto, Cattaraugus Co., N.Y. (p.318).

vi ABRAHAM STAPLES, b. prob. ca 1794; d. Stapleton Twp., Chickasaw Co., Iowa, by 1860 (census); m. at Danby, 23 March 1815, by Henry Herrick, J.P., CATHERINE / KATIE GRIFFITH (VT VR), d. 1868 ae 75, dau. of Thomas Griffith Sr. (*Danby History*, 150-51); rem. to Dorset, Vt., then west (*ibid.*, 268). In 1850 Abram Staples ae 55, Catherine Staples ae 54, and Phebe A. Webster ae 23, all b. Vt., were living with the family of Thomas G. Staples in Palatine, Ill. (p.97). In 1860 Catherine Staples ae 65 was in Thomas G.'s household at Stapleton, Ia. (p.102).

Children, b. Vt. (*Danby History*, 268; census): 1. *Abraham Staples*[7]. 2. *Thomas G. Staples*, b. ca 1825; m. Harriet ___. 3. *Lucinda Staples*. 4. *Phebe A. Staples*, b. Vt. ca 1827; prob. m. bef. 1850, ___ Webster.

vii JONATHAN STAPLES, b. prob. ca 1796; d. Granville, N.Y., 1868 ae 71 (*Danby History*, 268); m. Danby, 17 Dec. 1818, by Zoeth Allen, J.P. (VT VR), SYLVIA ROGERS, dau. of Stephen and Elizabeth (Lapham) Rogers (*Danby History*, 236). In 1850 he was ae 54, a farmer in Pawlet, Vt., with Sylvia ae 58, Ruth ae 22, and John ae 17, in the household as well as Stedman E. Carpenter ae 23, and Mary Welsh ae 26 (p.289).

Children (*Danby History*, 268): 1. *Anson Staples*[7]; m. Lydia Haviland. 2. *John Staples*, m. Lydia Cook. 3. *Phebe Staples*, m. Lucius M. Carpenter. 4. *Ruth Staples*, b. ca 1828; m. Pawlet, 31 Oct. 1850, Allen Whedon (VT VR). 5. *Eliza Staples*, m. Joseph Haviland.

Sources cited: *Mendon VR. Uxbridge VR.* Vermont Vital Records to 1870. Worcester County Deeds and Probate Records. Williams, *The History and Map of Danby, Vermont* (1869), *q.v.* for further information. Hemenway, *Vermont Historical Gazetteer.* Jenks, *Danby and Mount Tabor Cemetery Inscriptions* (1988, rev. 1993). CENSUS: 1790 Wardsborough, Windham Co., Vt. (M637-12); 1800 Danby, Rutland Co., Vt. (M32-52); 1850: Danby & Pawlet, Rutland Co., Vt. (M432-927), Charlotte, Chittenden Co., Vt. (M432-923), Palatine, Cook Co., Ill. (M432-103), & Otto, Cattaraugus Co., N.Y. (M432-479); 1860 Stapleton, Chickasaw Co., Ia. (M653-313).

607. MARGARET HOLBROOK[5] (*Thankful Thayer*[4], *Mary*[3] *Samson, Stephen*[2], *Henry*[1]), daughter of Sylvanus Holbrook and his wife Thankful Thayer [126], was born 14 August 1757 at Uxbridge (*VR* 89). She died 15 April 1806, aged 48, "wife of Thadeus," and is buried in Douglas in a cemetery described as "on east side of Douglas, ¼ mile west of S.E. Main St. on Perry St. Extension," with her son Thadeus and daughter Barbara.

Her marriage intentions with **THADDEUS THAYER** of Douglas were published 24 May 1778 at Uxbridge (*VR* 260) and 25 May 1778 at Douglas (*VR* 152). Thaddeus was born at Douglas 1 February 1755, son of Joseph and Sarah (___) Thayer (*VR* 62) and died 24 December 1826 (Sprague Ms). He married, second, after intentions 1 December 1807 at Douglas (*VR* 152), MILLA CUTLER, daughter of Zachariah Cutler of Thompson, Conn. (Sprague Ms). Thaddeus and Milla had children Alzada Thayer, Chapin Thayer, Almira Thayer, Albert Thayer, Milly Thayer, Zilpha Thayer, and Joseph Thayer (for full birthdates, see Sprague Ms). Milla died at Burrillville, R.I., 28 December 1855 aged 78 years (*ibid.*).

On 27 May 1781, Thaddeus Thayer of Douglas and wife Margaret joined John Benson and wife Molley, and Jonathan Staples and wife Rachel in selling their rights in the estate of their honored father Silvanus Holbrook, late of Uxbridge, to Silvanus Holbrook [Jr.] of Uxbridge (Worcester LR 86:165). In an accounting of the estate of Sylvanus Holbrook dated 27 May 1783, Margaret Thayer signed a receipt as one of the heirs (Worcester PR #A30117).

The 1790 census lists the family in Douglas with five boys under 16 and two females besides Margaret (*Heads of Fam.*, 218).

The will of Thaddeus Thayer of Douglas, yeoman, weak in body, dated 6 November 1826, proved 6 March 1827, left his 300-acre homestead (in the southeast part of Douglas on both sides of the turnpike from Providence to Douglas Meeting House) equally to sons Sylvanus, Chapin, Albert, Joseph, and daughters Elzada, Almira, Milley, and Zilpha Thayer [all except Sylvanus were children of second wife Milla]. He mentioned but did not name his wife, leaving her a bed, a cow, and five sheep. To sons George, Otis, and Ellis and daughter Diana Humes he left $20 each; to daughter Margery Aldrich $30, and to daughter Morandy Humes $40; to five grandchildren, heirs of daughter Ruth: Ellery, Warren, Lydia, Smith or Zoeth, and Healy Baker, $1 each; to grandchildren, heirs of daughter Margaret: Marble, Besulel, Margaret, Sarah, Madeline, and David Phetteplace, $1 each and to Thaddeus Phetteplace $5; to four grandchildren, heirs of son Thaddeus: Warren, Lilis, Lela-ann, and Margaret Thayer, $1 each. Mark Wood of Uxbridge was to be executor. (Worcester PR #A58820)

On 21 April 1827, Simon White of Uxbridge and Enoch Thayer of Burrillville, R.I., were appointed guardians with John Thayer and Paul White of Douglas to Alzada, Chapin, Almira, and Albert, over 14, and Milly, Zilpha, and Joseph Thayer, under 14, children of Thaddeus Thayer of Douglas, deceased. Dower was set off to Miley Thayer, widow of Thaddeus, on 23 August 1827 (Worcester PR #A58605).

On 23 April 1830 partition was made to the eight legatees of the homestead: Sylvanus Thayer, Chapin Thayer, Albert Thayer, Joseph Thayer, Jonathan Benson who purchased the share of Alzada wife of Ebenezer Benson, Almira Thayer, Milley Thayer, and Zilpha Thayer (Sprague Ms).

Children of Thaddeus and Margaret (Holbrook) Thayer (Sprague Ms):

i   GEORGE THAYER[6], b. 20 Jan. 1779; d. 27 May 1836 in 58th yr (Sprague); m. after int. 14 Feb. 1804 at Douglas (*VR* 150), SARAH (COOK) HOL-BROOK of Glocester, R.I., b. 8 June 1777, d. 2 April 1867 ae 89y 10m 24d, dau. of Israel and Sarah (Aldrich) Cook and widow of Ezekiel Holbrook (see Family #604-ii); they are bur. in a cemetery near the Uxbridge-Burrillville, R.I., line (Sprague). The will of George Thayer of Burrillville, laborer, dated 6 April 1836, names wife Sarah, sons Isaac and Ellis, daughters Sarah Ann Baker, Phebe Comstock, and Mary Thayer (Burrillville PR 2:327).

Children (Sprague, citing Preserved Thayer Ms.): 1. *George Thayer*[7], b. 19 Nov. 1804; d. 1809 ae 4y 9m 14d (g.s. Burrillville, R.I.). 2. *Sarah Ann Thayer*, b. 10 Feb. 1806; m. Simon Baker. 3. *Isaac W. Thayer*, b. 22 March 1810 (g.s.); m. Amy Mathewson. 4. *Phebe Thayer*, b. 6 Feb. 1813 (diary of son William Comstock); m. Simon Comstock. 5. *Mary Thayer*, b. 1815; d. 5 April 1838 ae 23 (g.s., Burrillville). 6. *Ellis Thayer*, b. ca 1816; d. 31 Dec. 1842 ae 26.

ii OTIS THAYER, b. 21 April 1780; d. Douglas 13 April 1841 (g.s., Baker Cem.); m. (1) Douglas, 20 Sept. 1801 (*VR* 151) SALLY BAKER, b. 1779, d. 30 Sept. 1831 ae 52 (g.s.), dau. of John Baker; m. (2) PHILA (MOWRY) ALDRICH, widow of Peter Aldrich, dau. of Eleazer and Eunice (Aldrich) Mowry (Sprague Ms).

Children, no b. rec. found (Sprague Ms): 1. *Lucy Thayer*[7], b. 1 April 1802; m. Douglas W. Logee. 2. *Chloe Thayer*, m. int. Douglas 19 Sept. 1825, Willard Steere. 3. *Archa Thayer*, b. ca Sept. 1806; m. Elizabeth Aldrich. 4. *Otis Thayer Jr.*, b. ca July 1809; m. Mercy Ann Wellman. 5. *Sylvanus Thayer*, b. 1810 (g.s., Douglas); d. Cumberland, R.I., 14 June 1832 ae 22 (*Thayer Family* calls him Lyman, says he drowned in Woonsocket River). 6. *Sally Thayer*. 7. *John Thayer*.

iii ARKEY [*sic*] (ARCHA/ARCHER) THAYER, b. 6 Dec. 1781; d. 20 Jan. 1783.

iv ELLIS THAYER, b. 9 March 1783 (rec. *Charlton VR* 96); d. 2 July 1863 ae 80 (g.s.); m. (1) after int. 5 Aug. 1806 at Douglas (*VR* 150), MARY COOK of Glocester, R.I., sister of his brother George's wife, b. 16 Aug. 1787 (rec. *Charlton VR* 96), d. Charlton 14 Sept. 1836 ae 49 (g.s.); m. (2) Killingly, Conn., 18 June 1837, PEGGY (DE ESTREES) McINTIRE, d. Charlton 11 Nov. 1859 as Margaret (g.s.), dau. of Jean B. A. P. [*sic – Jean Baptiste?*] and Olive (Carpenter) De Estrees and widow of Rufus McIntire (Sprague Ms).

Children, with first wife Mary; first two b. Burrillville, R.I., all rec. Charlton (*VR* 95-96): 1. *Remington Southwick Thayer*[7], b. 15 May 1809; d. Charlton 18 Sept. 1829 ae 20 (Sprague Ms). 2. *Elisha Cook Thayer*, b. 9 Nov. 1811; m. Mary W.

McIntire. 3. *Ellis Holbrook Thayer*, b. 21 Oct. 1818; m. Hannah E. Carpenter. 4. *Mary M. Thayer*, b. 3 March 1829; d. Charlton 5 Aug. 1853 ae 24.

v RUTH THAYER, b. 8 Nov. 1784; d. by March 1823; m. at Douglas, 26 Dec. 1806 (*VR* 151), BRAD F. BAKER; he m. (2) int. Charlton 28 March 1823, Hannah Gore (*VR* 122).

> **Baker** children, rec. Charlton (*VR* 14-15), first four b. Douglas: 1. *Elery Baker⁷*, b. 4 Feb. 1809. 2. *Ruth Baker*, b. 2 May 1810; d. 19 Nov. 1812 (*VR* 240). 3. *Warren Baker*, b. 3 Jan. 1812. 4. *Lydia Baker*, b. 10 Sept. 1813. 5. *Smith Baker*, b. 26 March 1815. 6. *Margaret Baker*, d. 12 Dec. 1815 (*VR* 240) 7. *Healy Baker*, b. 10 Sept. 1817. 8. *Ruth Baker*, b. 17 Feb. 1821.

vi SYLVANUS THAYER, b. 24 March 1786 (Sprague citing Preserved Thayer Ms); d. Franklin 7 March 1859 of consumption; m. after int. at Douglas 30 April 1819 (*VR* 151), OLIVE WHITING, d. 12 March 1865 ae 67y 2m 19d, dau. of David and Olive (___) Whiting (Sprague Ms). In 1850 he was a farmer in Bellingham, ae 60, with Olive, ae 40 [*sic*], and children Leprelate, Alexander, Merrick, Smith, and Francis at home (p.203). Wm. Bolkcom, farmer, and wife Sophia, both ae 53, were also in the household.

> Children, b. Douglas, not rec. (Sprague Ms): 1. *Leprelette M. Thayer⁷*, b. ca 1824; m. Alice Hood. 2. *Emeline E. Thayer*, b. ca 1825; m. Bellingham 1849, William Hart. 3. *Alexander Thayer*, b. ca 1827; m. Mary E. Hallett. 4. *Merrick P. Thayer*, b. 31 Aug. 1829; m. (1) Martha Darling, (2) Harriet H. Warfield. 5. *Stephen Thayer*, not at home 1850. 6. *Smith W. Thayer*, b. 1832 (g.s.); m. Lucinda Richards. 5. *Francis/Frank J. Thayer*, b. ca 1834; m. Manchester, N.H., 1866, Helen Whipple.

vii MARGARET THAYER, b. 11 Nov. 1787; m. at Douglas, 14 Oct. 1809 (*VR* 151), BEZALEEL PHETTEPLACE.

> **Phetteplace** children, named in grandfather's will: 1. *Marble Phetteplace⁷*. 2. *Bezaleel Phetteplace*. 3. *Margaret Phetteplace*. 4. *Sarah Phetteplace*. 5. *Madeline Phetteplace*. 6. *David Phetteplace*.

viii THADDEUS THAYER, b. 31 Nov. [*sic*] 1789; d. Douglas 4 March 1824 ae 35y; bur. with mother (g.s.); m. at Douglas, 29 Nov. 1810 (*VR* 152), MARGARET COOK.

> Children, first four named in grandfather's will, all in Sprague Ms: 1. *Warren B. Thayer⁷*, b. 3 May 1813; m. Ann Maria Sutton. 2. *Lilis Thayer*, b. 30 July 1815; m. Allen Crocker. 3. *Celia Ann Thayer*, b. 27 Nov. 1818; m. Albert S. Walls of Oakham. 4. *Margaret C. Thayer*, b. 21 Oct. 1820; m. William Metcalf. 5. *Thaddeus Thayer*, b. 3 Sept. 1822; d. ae 5m 2d, "son of Thaddeus and Margaret"; bur. Douglas with father.

ix MARGERY THAYER, b. 2 March 1792; m. int. 1 May 1811 at Douglas (*VR* 151) with JOHN ALDRICH.

x   MIRANDA THAYER, b. 3 Jan. 1794; m. at Douglas, 23 Aug. 1811 (*VR* 151), MOSES HUMES JR. Prob. the Moses Humes in 1840 census at Riga, Monroe Co., N.Y., ae 50-60 (p.126).

xi   BARBARA THAYER, b. 24 June 1797; d. 2 Feb. 1822, unm. (Sprague Ms); bur. Douglas with her mother

xii   DIANA THAYER, b. 6 Jan. 1800; m. int. 14 Dec. 1825 at Douglas (*VR* 150) with NAHUM HUMES. Nahum Humes, carpenter, and "Mrs. Humes," both ae 50, were living by themselves in Douglas in 1850 (p.350).

Sources cited: *Charlton VR. Douglas VR. Mendon VR. Uxbridge VR.* Worcester County Deeds and Probate Records. W. C. Sprague, "Thomas Thayer," Ms., NEHGS (1952), Vol. 2, not paginated; sometimes cites Preserved Thayer Ms. Thayer Cemetery Records [from Douglas] on line at www.thayer.com. Census: 1840 Riga, Monroe Co., N.Y. (M704-297); 1850 Douglas, Worcester Co. (M432-350).

608.   THANKFUL HOLBROOK (*Thankful Thayer[4], Mary[3] Samson, Stephen[2], Henry[1]*), daughter of Sylvanus Holbrook and his wife Thankful Thayer [126], was born 23 February 1760 at Uxbridge (*VR* 89), and died at Mendon 25 May 1831 (*VR* 480).

Thankful Holbrook of Mendon married at Uxbridge, 4 April 1802 (*VR* 261), probably as his fourth wife, **DAVID LEGG**, who was born at Mendon 11 May 1756, son of Aaron and Experience (Fish) Legg (*VR* 114, 337) and died at Uxbridge 25 April 1844 aged 87y 11m 14d (*VR* 387). He married at Mendon, first HANNAH DEWING, second MARGERY HOLBROOK, and third COMFORT WHITE (*VR* 338). Comfort died at Uxbridge 31 July 1800 aged 42 years (*VR* 387). David and Thankful are buried in Prospect Hill Cemetery, Uxbridge.

David Legg served extensively in the Revolutionary War from Mendon, and was at Valley Forge in 1778. A descriptive list signed at Springfield by Gen. John Glover 12 July 1780 describes him as 24 years old, 5 ft. 10 in. tall, with dark complexion (*MSSR* 9:656). He received a pension (White, 2050, citing #S13722).

On 27 May 1783 Thankful Holbrook shared in the distribution of her father's estate (Worcester PR #A30117).

Child of David and Thankful (Holbrook) Legg:

i   THANKFUL LEGG[6], b. ca 1803; m. at Mendon, 23 May 1821 (*VR* 338), STEPHEN PARKHURST of Milford. In 1870 he was a machine mfr. in Montclair, N.J., ae 62, with Thankful L. ae 56 [both ages obviously understated], and *Emily R. Parkhurst[7]* ae 34, all b. Mass. (p.271).

Sources cited: *Milford VR. Uxbridge VR.* 1870 Census, Montclair, Essex Co., N.J. (M593-861).

609. MARY / MOLLY HOLBROOK[5] (*Thankful Thayer*[4], *Mary*[3] *Samson, Stephen*[2], *Henry*[1]), daughter of Sylvanus Holbrook and his wife Thankful Thayer [126], was born 1 February 1762 at Uxbridge (*VR* 89). She died at Mendon 17 December 1814, in her 62nd year [*sic*], as "Mary, wife of Dea. John Benson" (*VR* 450). Her death was noted in the *Columbian Centinel* of 11 January 1815, with her age correctly given as 51 years.

She married 9 November 1780 as Mary, "she of Uxbridge, he of Mendon," (*VR* 322), as his second wife, **JOHN BENSON**. He was born 1 August 1749 at Mendon (*VR* 32), son of Benoni and Abigail (White) Benson (*Benson Fam.*, 148, 153). Deacon John Benson died 18 May 1818 in his 68th year at Mendon (*VR* 450), and is buried with Mary in Chestnut Hill Cemetery there. His brother Benoni Benson Jr. was the husband of Molly's sister Ruth Holbrook [#605]. With his first wife, JOANNA TAFT, who died at Mendon 3 October 1777 in her 26th year (*VR* 450), John had Lovett Benson, Lois Benson, Prudence Benson, and Phila Benson; Lovett and Prudence died young (*VR* 249, 450).

John Benson served in the Revolution (*MSSR* 1:971). He was a private in Capt. Joseph Daniels' company which marched on the alarm of 19 April 1775 to Roxbury. From 8 December 1776 to 21 January 1777 he served as a corporal in Capt. Peter Penniman's company, Lt. Col. Nathan Tyler's regiment. In 1780 he was a first lieutenant in Capt. Benjamin Read's company, Capt. Nathan Tyler's 6th (Worcester Co.) regiment, and then acting captain of Capt. Read's company on an alarm to Rhode Island.

On 27 May 1781, John Benson and wife Molley, with Thaddeus Thayer of Douglas and wife Margaret, and Jonathan Staples and wife Rachel, quitclaimed their rights in the estate of their honored father Silvanus Holbrook, late of Uxbridge, to Silvanus Holbrook [Jr.] of Uxbridge (Worcester LR 86:165). In an accounting of the estate of Sylvanus Holbrook dated 27 May 1783, a payment was made to Molly Benson as one of the heirs, and Molly also signed a receipt for the heirs of Ruth Benson, wife of Benoni Benson (Worcester PR #A30117).

The 1790 census listed two John Benson families in Mendon (*Heads of Fam.*, 227). Our John Benson is probably the man whose household consisted of two men over 16, three boys under 16, and five females.

John died intestate. Heirs listed on 7 June 1823 were Manassah Baker, John Benson, Ephraim Lee, Bailey Legg, Jos. B. Cook, Prudence Benson, Phila Benson, and George W. Benson. An accounting was presented 2 September 1823 by Jared Benson, administrator, and a final settlement included Nabby, now Nabby Lee, and Mary Legg, daughters of the deceased, and also Thankful Cook, Prudence Benson, Lois Baker, and Phila Benson (Worcester PR #A5181).

Children of John and Mary/Molly (Holbrook) Benson, all except Mary and Judson recorded Mendon (*VR* 31):

i   JOHN BENSON Jr[6], b. 22 July 1781; d. Uxbridge 21 Jan. 1842 (*VR* 358); m. at Uxbridge, in Dec. 1805 (*VR* 213), CHLOE TAFT, b. Uxbridge 7 July 1785, d. there 25 April 1826, daughter of Easman and Hannah (Taft) Taft (*Benson Family*, 343).

    Children, rec. Uxbridge (*ibid.*, 344): 1. *Charlotte Benson*[7], b. 30 Sept. 1807 Mendon. 2. *Abby Ann Benson*. 3. *Ezra Taft Benson*, b. 22 Feb. 1811 Mendon; joined the Church of Jesus Christ of Latter-day Saints and had eight wives. 4. *Hannah Benson*. 5. *John M. Benson*, b. ca 1819. 6. *George Taft Benson*, b. 1825.

ii GEORGE WASHINGTON BENSON, b. 25 May 1783; m. after int. 11 Feb. 1804 at Mendon (*VR* 248), ALINDA WARFIELD.

    Child rec. Mendon (*VR* 32): 1. *Otis Benson*[7], b. 28 Feb. 1806.

iii JARED BENSON, b. 3 Feb. 1785; m. at Mendon, 24 May 1807 (*VR* 248), SALLY TAFT.

    Children, rec. Mendon of "Jared and Sally" (*VR* 31-32, 450): 1. *James Sullivan Benson*[7], b. 19 Sept. 1808; d. 3 Jan. 1813 ae 4y 3m 14d. 2. *Putnam Taft Benson*, b. 28 Oct. 1814; d. 24 April 1834. 3. *Jared Benson*, b. 8 Nov. 1821. 4. *Sylvanus Holbrook Benson*, b. 23 June 1828. 5. *Laurette V.H. Benson*, b. ca 1830.

iv ABIGAIL BENSON, b. 13 Feb. 1787; d. 17 Nov. 1824 ae 37y at Mendon (*VR* 480) as Nabby Taft Lee, second wife of Ephraim; m. prob. (1) _____ TAFT; as Abigail Taft, m. (2) 27 June 1813 at Mendon (*VR* 337) as his second wife, EPHRAIM LEE. He m. (1) Lydia _____, with whom he had children Royal Lee, Salem Lee, and Caroline Lee; he m. (3) 12 Nov. 1826 at Mendon (*VR* 337), Nancy Nichols of Uxbridge, with whom he had a dau. Abby Ann Lee.

    Lee children of Ephraim and Abigail, rec. Mendon (*VR* 114): 1. *Judson B. Lee*[7], b. 18 April 1814. 2. *Pardon Lee*, b. 21 Dec. 1815. 3. *Phidelia Lee*, b. 9 Feb. 1817. 4. *Abby Ann Lee*, b. 21 July 1820; d. prob. y. 5. *Susan Elizabeth Lee*, b. 17 July 1824.

v   MARY / POLLY BENSON, b. ca 1788; m. 5 March 1812 at Mendon (*VR* 337), BAILEY LEGG, b. 9 May 1783 Mendon (rec. *Uxbridge VR* 104, as Basley), son of David and Margery (Holbrook) Legg. In 1850 he was a farmer at Norway, Herkimer Co., N.Y., with a household consisting of himself ae 66, Polly ae 62, Sylvanus ae 33, Harriet ae 28, David B. ae 26, all b. Mass., Abigail ae 21, Judson ae 15, Catharine C. ae 27, Mary ae 6, and Jerrod B. ae 5 (p.268); the ages of Sylvanus and Harriet seem to be transposed.

Legg children, first three rec. Uxbridge (*VR* 104), rest from 1850 census; prob. incomplete: 1. *Sylvanus B. Legg*[7], b. 20 June 1813 in Mendon; prob. m. Abigail ___. 2. *Mary H. Legg*, b. 7 July 1815. 3. *Harriet H. Legg*, b. 14 June 1817. 4. *David B. Legg*, b. ca 1824 Mass.; prob. m. Catharine C. ____. 5. *Judson Legg*, b. ca 1835 N.Y.

vi   PRUDENCE BENSON, b. 7 July 1795; unm. 1823.

vii   SYLVANUS HOLBROOK BENSON, b. 12 Jan. 1797; d. 24 Aug. 1812 at Mendon (*VR* 450), ae 15, "son of Dea. John."

viii   THANKFUL BENSON, b. 26 Nov. 1799; m. Mendon, 22 March 1818 (*VR* 249), JOSEPH B. COOK.

Cook children rec. Mendon (*VR* 51-54): 1. *William Walker Cook*[7], b. in Uxbridge 21 March 1820. 2. *Amanda Malvina Cook*, b. 12 Oct. 1821. 3. *Mary Adeliza Cook*, b. 18 April 1824. 4. *Emily Caroline Cook*, b. 8 Feb. 1826. 5. *Elma Ann Cook*, b. 29 Jan. 1827. 6. *Phila Adelia Cook*, b. 7 June 1830. 7. *Fanny Melia Cook*, b. 7 May 1832. 8. *Joseph Sullivan Cook*, b. 5 Feb. 1834. 9. *Henry Augustus Cook*, b. 12 Dec. 1835. 10. *Abba Jane Cook*, b. 12 Feb. 1839. 11. *Ellen Ardell Cook*, b. 4 May 1843. 12. *[Daughter] Cook*, b. 30 March 1844.

ix   JUDSON BENSON, d. Mendon 15 Oct. 1813 (*VR* 450), "son of Dea. John."

Sources cited: *Mendon VR. Uxbridge VR.* Worcester County Probate Records. *Mass. Soldiers & Sailors.* Richard H. Benson, *The Benson Family of Colonial Massachusetts* (2003).

610.   STEPHEN HOLBROOK[5] (*Thankful Thayer*[4], *Mary*[3] *Samson, Stephen*[2], *Henry*[1]), son of Sylvanus Holbrook and his wife Thankful Thayer [126], was born at Uxbridge 19 June 1764 (*VR* 89). He died 16 August 1830, aged 66 years, at Uxbridge (*VR* 381).

He married, 11 September 1788 at Uxbridge (*VR* 261), **HOPESTILL ALBEE,** who was born 17 January 1768 at Uxbridge (*VR* 11), daughter of James and Prudence (White) Albee. She died 18 January 1840 at Mendon (*VR* 474) as "Hope, wife of Stephen." The will of James Albee of Uxbridge, dated 23 January 1787 with codicil dated 7 September 1795, proved 24 November 1795, names his daughter Hopestill, now Hopestill Holbrook; Stephen and Hopestill Holbrook signed the release by heirs of James Albee (Worcester PR #A636; 26:421, 430).

Stephen Holbrook of Uxbridge, yeoman, in his will dated 22 July 1830, proved 7 September 1830, named his wife Hopestill, two sons Wilder and Henry Holbrook; daughter Rachel Verry wife of Foster Verry; daughter Chloe Southwick wife of Jonathan Southwick; five sons Sylvanus, Wilder, Willard, Henry, and Ellery; Sylvanus and Willard to be executors (Worcester PR #A30112).

Children of Stephen and Hopestill (Albee) Holbrook, rec. Uxbridge (*VR* 88-90):

i   RACHEL HOLBROOK[6], b. 22 April 1789; m. after int. 4 April 1810 Uxbridge (*VR* 260), FOSTER VERREY. In 1850 Foster Verry ae 60, a farmer, and wife Rachel, 61, were living in Blackstone, with James C. Carr, 45, farmer, b. R.I., in their household (p.349).

   Verry children, rec. Mendon (*VR* 198): 1. *Albert Verry[7]*, b. 15 July 1812. 2. *James Verry*, b. 27 Feb. 1814. 3. *Chloe Holbrook Verry*, b. 20 March 1816. 4. *Foster Verry*, b. 3 Oct. 1821.

ii SILVANUS HOLBROOK, b. 28 July 1792; m. (1) ELIZABETH FARNUM, who d. 1828; m. (2) HANNAH WHITNEY, who d. 1831; m. (3) int. 29 March 1840 at Northbridge (*VR* 133), MARTHA WATERS of Millbury.

iii WILLARD HOLBROOK (twin), b. 7 April 1795; d. Uxbridge 4 March 1862 ae 66, farmer, of "pleurisy and dropsy of chest" (Mass. VR 158:290); m. (1) after int. 7 July 1822 at Uxbridge (*VR* 261), ALICE COMSTOCK of Burrillville, R.I., b. ca 1800; m. (2) at Blackstone, 10 July 1860, PHILA DARLING ae 57, dau. of Peletiah and Phila (___) Darling (Mass. VR 137:159). In 1850 he was a farmer in Uxbridge with Alice ae 50, Daniel ae 20, and John Murry ae 58, laborer, b. Ireland (p.372). Three other Holbrook children listed (it appears accidentally) in the next household probably belonged to this family.

   Children, first three rec. Uxbridge (*VR* 88-89), last four from census: 1. *Adaline Holbrook[7]*, b. 8 Sept. 1823. 2. *Amanda C. Holbrook*, b. 6 May 1826. 3. *Daniel S. Holbrook*, b. 20 Feb. 1829. Probably also: 4. *Eliza Holbrook*, b. ca 1832. 5. *William Holbrook*, b. ca 1838. 6. *Chloe Holbrook*, b. ca 1840.

iv WILDER HOLBROOK (twin), b. 7 April 1795; m. after int. 12 April 1818 at Uxbridge (*VR* 261), TYLA BUFFUM of Smithfield, R.I. In 1850 he was a farmer in Smithfield, with Tyla ae 51, sharing a household with James and Eliza Southwick, both ae 25 (p.402).

v   CHLOE HOLBROOK, b. 13 Aug. 1801; m. 14 Nov. 1822 at Uxbridge (*VR* 259), JONATHAN F. SOUTHWICK.

vi HENRY HOLBROOK, b. 19 April 1804; d. Barre 10 July 1874 ae 70y 2m 21d of pneumonia, married (Mass. VR 267:303); m. after int. 11 March 1827 at Barre (*VR* 154), SALLY WADSWORTH, b. Barre 9 July 1802 (*VR* 89). In 1850 he was a farmer at Barre with Sally ae 48 and six children.

   Children at home 1850, three rec. Barre (*VR* 45): 1. *Franklin Holbrook[7]*, b. ca 1830. 2. *Stephen Holbrook*, b. Uxbridge 4 Nov. 1831 (*VR* 89). 3. *John Holbrook*, b. ca 1833. 4. *Joseph Wadsworth Holbrook*, b. Barre 6 July 1835. 5. *Mary Elizabeth*

Holbrook, b. Barre 18 Jan. 1841; m. Thomas Gordon Grassie (GSMD #68674).
6. *Henry C. Holbrook*, b. Barre 24 June 1842.

vii ELLERY HOLBROOK, b. 26 June 1810; d. at Uxbridge 10 July 1847 ae 37y 14d of consumption (*VR* 380); m. after int. at Uxbridge 7 April 1831 (*VR* 259), HANNAH C. HALE of Northbridge, b. 21 Oct. 1806 (*Uxb.* *VR* 89).

Children rec. Uxbridge (*VR* 88-89): 1. *Eliza Holbrook⁷*, b. 27 Feb. 1832; d. unm. 2. *William E. Holbrook*, b. 29 Feb. 1836; d. 7 Sept. 1836 (*VR* 381). 3. *Chloe Malvina Holbrook*, b. 17 Dec. 1839.

Sources cited: *Barre VR. Douglas VR. Mendon VR. Northbridge VR. Uxbridge VR.* Mass. Vital Records 1841-1910. CENSUS: 1850 Worcester Co.: Blackstone & Uxbridge (M432-345); Smithfield, Providence Co., R.I. (M432-843).

611. HENRY HOLBROOK⁵ (*Thankful Thayer⁴, Mary³ Samson, Stephen², Henry¹*), son of Sylvanus Holbrook and his wife Thankful Thayer [126], was born 11 February 1768 at Uxbridge (*VR* 89). He died 18 December 1828 at Mendon (*VR* 474), in his 60th year, and is buried there in Chestnut Hill Cemetery.

He was of Uxbridge when he married 22 September 1791, at Mendon (*VR* 322), **BARBARA THAYER**. She was born 27 February 1770 at Mendon (*VR* 180), daughter of John and Mary (Spencer) Thayer, and died there 14 July 1812 in her 43rd year (*VR* 474).

Henry married, second, 24 December 1812 at Mendon (*VR* 322), **NELLA ALBEE**. She was born 4 May 1788 at Uxbridge (*VR* 11), daughter of James and Ruth (White) Albee, and died at Blackstone 26 August 1867 of pneumonia (Mass. VR 204:201).

Nella Holbrook, widow, was given administration on the estate of Henry Holbrook late of Mendon, deceased, on 6 January 1829 (Worcester PR #29995). Elijah Thayer was appointed guardian of the three children of the deceased on 24 May 1831 (*ibid.*). On 3 Feb. 1838 Nelson Holbrook of Mendon sold to his mother Nella Holbrook of Mendon, widow, land purchased of Artemas Thayer and rights to the estate of his father Henry Holbrook late of Mendon deceased; his wife Mary also signed (Worcester LR 335:60). On 9 April 1842 all the children and heirs of Henry — Nelson, Limon, and Willard Holbrook — requested that dower be set off to "our mother Nellie" (Worcester PR #29995).

In 1850 Nella Holbrook, aged 63, and her son Lymon were sharing a dwelling with the family of son Willard.

Children of Henry and Nella (Albee) Holbrook:

i   NELSON HOLBROOK[6], b. 3 Aug. 1815 (calc.); d. Blackstone 22 Sept. 1854 ae 39y 1m 19d of "fits" (Mass. VR 86:112); m. at Mendon, 15 Dec. 1836 (*VR* 322), MARY KILBORN. In 1850 Nelson Holbrook ae 30 was a farmer in Blackstone with Mary ae 37, b. Vt., Henry ae 11, and Lucy Kilborn ae 76, b. Mass. (p.348).

Child at home 1850: 1. *Henry Holbrook[7]*, b. ca 1839.

ii LYMON HOLBROOK, b. ca 1818; d. Blackstone 23 July 1877 ae 59, of epileptic fits (Mass. VR 294:292); m. at Blackstone, 17 Jan. 1856 as her second husband, ANN MARIA MANN ae 34, b. Taunton, dau. of Joseph E. and Ruth Dean (Mass. VR 101:168). In 1850 he was a farmer ae 32 in Blackstone, living with his mother and sharing a dwelling with the family of his brother Willard.

iii WILLARD HOLBROOK, b. 11 April 1820 at Mendon (*VR* 101); m. (1) 24 Dec. 1840 at Mendon (*VR* 323), AMY M[ATILDA] LEGG, b. there 11 July 1820 (*VR* 115), dau. of Adna and Elsa (____) Legg, d. Blackstone 1898 (Mass. VR 483:637). Willard and Amy are buried in Chestnut Hill Cem., Mendon. In 1850 he was a farmer at Blackstone, with Amy M. ae 29, and three children; his mother Nella and brother Lyman shared the dwelling (p.349).

Children, all b. Blackstone; first three at home 1850: 1. *Oscar M. Holbrook[7]*, b. 9 Oct. 1844 "near Southwick Hill" (Mass. VR 11:168). 2. *Malvina Fitzlan Holbrook*, b. 31 Oct. 1845; m. 6 Dec. 1866, Davis Hill (Mass. VR 17:194, 191:185). 3. *Alice J. Holbrook*, b. 11 March 1848 (Mass. VR 29:195). 4. *Georgianna J. Holbrook*, b. 19 June 1850 (Mass. VR 44:136).

Sources cited: *Mendon VR. Uxbridge VR.* Mass. Vital Records 1841-1910. 1850 census, Blackstone, Worcester Co. (M432-345).

612. LUCY HOLBROOK[5] (*Thankful Thayer[4], Mary[3] Samson, Stephen[2], Henry[1]*), daughter of Sylvanus Holbrook and his wife Thankful Thayer [126], was born 13 September 1770 at Uxbridge (*VR* 89). She died 29 January 1843 at Northbridge (*VR* 174), aged 72, and is buried in the Old Cemetery at Northbridge Center.

She married 4 November 1795 at Uxbridge (*VR* 195), as his second wife, **ABNER ADAMS**. He was born 4 November 1757 at Uxbridge (*VR* 9), son of John and Mary (____) Adams, and died 18 January 1834 at Northbridge (*VR* 173), aged 76. He married, first, at Milford 16 January 1782, RUTH WOOD, who died in 1794 in her 32nd year at Northbridge (*VR* 174). Abner and Ruth had children recorded at Milford (*VR* 9): Becca Adams, Lois Adams, Parly Adams, and Warren Adams.

In his will dated 5 May 1832, proved 4 March 1834, Abner Adams of Northbridge, yeoman, named his wife Lucy, sons Sylvanus Adams, Washington Adams, Abner Adams, and Judson Adams; daughter Ruth wife of Amos Fairbanks; grandson Zebediah Adams; and daughters Rebecca Leland and Pearly Leland; son Sylvanus to be sole executor (Worcester PR # 86).

Administration on the estate of Lucy Adams, late of Douglas, was given to Sylvanus Adams, oldest son, 30 December 1843 (Worcester PR # 350).

Children of Abner and Lucy (Holbrook) Adams, rec. Northbridge, first three without dates (*VR* 9-12):

i   SYLVANUS ADAMS[6], b. 17 Oct. 1796 at Sutton; d. Milford 6 Feb. 1872 ae 75y 3m 19d of erysipelas (Mass. VR 249:328); m. at Milford, 13 May 1819 (*VR* 190), CHLOE HUNT ALBEE, bp. Milford 21 Aug. 1805, dau. of Abel and Annar (___) Albee (*VR* 12), d. there 7 Dec. 1871 ae 70y 2m 12d of "general debility" (Mass. VR 240:276).

    Children rec. Northbridge (*VR* 9-10, 12): 1. *Zebadiah Allbe Adams*[7], b. 31 March 1824. 2. *Harriet Thayer Adams*, b. 17 Nov. 1826. 3. *John Quincy Adams*, b. 20 Sept. 1829. 4. *Gilbert Franklin Adams*, b. 27 April 1832. 5. *Abner Adams*, b. 8 Dec. 1834. 6. *George Willard Adams*, b. 5 July 1837. 7. *Judson Laroy Adams*, b. 30 Sept. 1842. (one more – supp. 8 ch.)

ii OTIS ADAMS, b. Dec. 1797; d. Northbridge 21 Jan. 1798 (*VR* 174).

iii WASHINGTON ADAMS, b. 11 Dec. 1799 at Sutton.

iv RUTH ADAMS, b. 11 May 1802 (or 1803); m. after int. 1831 at Northbridge (*VR* 99), AMOS FAIRBANKS of Douglas, b. ca 1788. In 1850 Amos was ae 62, a farmer at Douglas, with "Mrs. Fairbanks" ae 48, and two *Adams* children, perhaps nephews: Franklin Adams ae 12, b. Ohio, and [Nelson?] Adams (a boy) ae 7, b. Mass. (p.337).

v   HARRIET THAYER ADAMS, b. 8 Oct. 1804; d. 29 Oct. 1825, ae 21, at Northbridge (*VR* 173).

vi ABNER ADAMS, b. 11 Feb. 1806; d. 1885 at Milford (Mass. VR 366: 425); m. after int. at Northbridge 21 Feb. 1830 (VR 97), ELIZABETH THAYER CLAFLIN. In 1850 he was a laborer in Milford with Elizabeth ae 38, and children Samuel W., James M., Mary L., Elizabeth, Warren, and Adeline (p.54).

    Children, some rec. Milford (VR 9-11, 318): 1. *Samuel W. Adams*[7], b. ca 1831 (census, ae 18). 2. *James Adams*, b. 10 Feb. 1833. 3. *Mary Adams*, b. 15 Dec. 1835 [prob. Dec. *1834*; 15 in 1850]. 4. *Elizabeth Adams*, b. 14 Feb. 1836 [14 in 1850]; m. Alanson Towne (g.s.). 5. *Warren Adams*, b. 17 July 1841 (ae 12 in 1850).

    6. *Adeline C. Adams*, b. ca 1840 (census, ae 10).   7. *Sullivan Adams*, b. 30 Dec. 1844; d. 22 Aug. 1847.

vii JUDSON ADAMS, b. 23 March 1808; m. at Grafton, 27 April 1834 (*VR* 158), EMILY E. GATES, b. ca 1814. In 1850 he was a farmer in Northbridge with Emily E. ae 36, Betsy Bridges ae 63, single, and Lucius T. Gates ae 4 (p.158). No record of any children for them.

viii ZEBEDIAH ADAMS, b. 3 Aug. 1814; d. 3 April 1815, ae 8m, Northbridge (*VR* 174).

Sources cited: *Milford VR.   Northbridge VR.   Uxbridge VR.* Worcester Co. Probate Records. CENSUS: 1850 Worcester Co., Douglas (M432-341) and Milford (M432-344). **See also:** *History of Milford,* 518-19.

614.   OLIVE FARNUM[5] (*Margaret Thayer*[4], *Mary*[3] *Samson, Stephen*[2], *Henry*[1]), daughter of Joshua Farnum and his wife Margaret Thayer [127], was born 2 December 1753 at Uxbridge (*VR* 70), mistakenly recorded as Oliver, "son." She died probably between 1800 and 1810 in New York State. She is named in the will of her grandfather, Samuel Thayer, dated 17 October 1761, proved 20 August 1764, as granddaughter Olive Farnum; she and her cousin Pern Thayer, also under 18, were to live with their uncle Stephen Thayer (Worcester PR #A58793).

    Olive Farnam [*sic*] published marriage intentions 16 April 1770 at Uxbridge (*VR* 244) with **JAMES CHASE.** He was born at Petersham 26 February 1750, son of Henry and Abigail (Stratton) Chase (*VR* 17), and died probably after 1810 in Oneida or Ontario County, N.Y.

    No Revolutionary War service record was found in Massachusetts for this James Chase.

    On 7 February 1789 James Chase of Warwick, yeoman, sold his homestead farm in Warwick, 50 acres, for £60 to Savel Metcalf of Orange; Olive Chase also signed the deed (Franklin LR 4:169). According to *Aquila Chase Descendants,* the family was in Pittstown, N.Y., in 1790, with two men over 16, two boys under 16, and five females. There are no land records for them in Albany or Rensselaer County, but they were of Steuben, Herkimer County, N.Y., on 3 September 1793 when James Chase and Nathaniel Allen of Steuben bought part of Lot 72 in Fonda's Patent for £257 from the executors of the estate of Jellis Fonda (Oneida LR 18:16). Nathaniel Allen sold 203¼ acres to James Chase, both of Steuben, Herkimer County, on 29 October 1794 for £200 (*ibid.*, 17:259), and the following day James Chase sold to Nathaniel Allen for £200, part of Lot 72 (*ibid.*, 18:144).

    They were in Floyd, Oneida County, N.Y., in 1800, listed in the census as an apparent couple over 45, with two young men and two young women 16-26, one boy and one girl 10-16, and one girl under 10 (p.78). On 11 February 1802 James Chase of Floyd, N.Y., yeoman, quitclaimed for $20 to James Lawton of Hardwick and spinster Deborah Chase of Petersham, all his interest in the land and personal property of his father Henry Chase, deceased (Worcester LR 162:97).

James Chase of Floyd sold part of Lot 72 to Stephen and Ellery Chase, also of Floyd, for $800 on 20 February 1809; no wife signed with him (Oneida LR 21:17). The 1810 census listed J. Chase in Floyd, aged 45+, with two men 16-25 and one young woman 16-25 (p.38), but no woman of Olive's age, suggesting that she had died by that date.

No probate records for James Chase were found in Oneida County. He may be the James Chase (over 45) listed in Henrietta, Ontario County, N.Y., in 1820, with a James Chase Jr. nearby (p.170), but no records of him were found there.

Children of James and Olive (Farnum) Chase, first three rec. Warwick (VR 1:13, 16, 20), all listed with birthdates in *Aquila Chase* (p.163):

i   MARGARET CHASE[6], b. 21 Nov. 1771; m. WILLARD MORSE.

ii SARAH / EUNICE CHASE, b. 21 Sept. 1773; unm. She is rec. as Sarah in the Warwick VR, and as Eunice in *Aquila Chase*.

iii OLIVE CHASE, b. 11 July 1775; unm.

iv DORCAS CHASE, b. 9 April 1777; living 1850; m. WILLIAM ALLEN, d. before 1850. Dorcas Allen ae 73, b. Mass., was living 1850 at Floyd, N.Y., in the household of Elias Allen ae 44; Jane Allen ae 19 was with them, and the family of Esek Allen ae 55, was next door (p.136).

   Probable *Allen* children, list incomplete, both b. N.Y., both farmers at Floyd, N.Y., 1850: 1. *Esek Allen[7]*, b. ca 1795. 2. *Elias Allen*, b. ca 1806.

v   OLIVIA CHASE, b. 12 March 1789 [*sic* – prob. 1779].

vi JAMES CHASE, b. 4 Oct. 1781; m. CLARISSA CORNWELL / CORNELL, b. Watertown, N.Y., 11 Aug. 1785. Ten children. (*Aquila Chase,* 355).

vii STEPHEN CHASE, b. 11 July 1783; unm.

viii ELLERY R. CHASE, b. 31 Jan. 1786 N.Y.; m. MARY POTTER, b. ca 1800 N.Y. In 1850 Elery R. Chase was a farmer at Floyd, N.Y., ae 63, with Mary ae 50, and four children (p.136).

   Children at home 1850: 1. *Cornelia Chase[7]*, b. ca 1826. 2. *Hamilton Chase*, b. ca 1832; a farmer 1850. 3. *Althera Chase*, b. ca 1835. 4. *Fanny Chase*, b. ca 1839.

ix SARAH CHASE, b. 6 Sept. 1789; m. ROBERT POTTER. In 1850 Robert Potter ae 65 and Sally ae 59 were living at Floyd with Julia ae 28, all b. N.Y. (p.132).

   Probable *Potter* child, at home 1850: 1. *Julia Potter[7]*, b. ca 1822.

x   FANNY CHASE, b. 26 Jan. 1792; m. DR. IRA CROSS.

Sources cited: *Petersham VR. Uxbridge VR.* Franklin County Deeds. Worcester County Probate Records. Oneida County, N.Y., Deeds. Chase and Chamberlain, *Seven Generations of the Descendants of Aquila and Thomas Chase* (1928). CENSUS: Floyd, Oneida Co., N.Y., 1800 (M32-23), 1810 (M252-82), 1850 (M432-565).

615.   PERN THAYER⁵ (*Susanna⁴, Mary³ Samson, Stephen², Henry¹*), daughter of Susanna Thayer [128], was born 11 December 1751 at Mendon (*VR* 187). She was named in the will of her grandfather, Samuel Thayer, dated 17 October 1761, proved 20 August 1764, as granddaughter Pern Thayer, under age 18. Pern and her cousin Olive Farnum, also under 18, were to live with their uncle Stephen Thayer (Worcester PR #A58793). No further record found.

Sources cited: *Uxbridge VR.* Worcester County Probate Records.

616.   PHILADELPHIA THAYER⁵ (*Stephen Thayer⁴, Mary³ Samson, Stephen², Henry¹*), daughter of Stephen Thayer [129] and his wife Rachel Davis, was born at Mendon 10 November 1763 (*VR* 187), and died at Brookfield 31 January 1837 (*VR* 498) or 1838 ae 73 (g.s.).

She married at Medway, 29 May 1788 (*VR* 205), as his second wife, **JOEL HAWES**, who was born at Medway 12 April 1757, son of Ichabod and Elizabeth (Fisher) Hawes (*VR* 73), and died at Brookfield 15 October 1839 aged 82 (*VR* 498). He married, first, at Medway 14 August 1777, JUDITH CLARK, who died there 24 May 1787 (*VR* 315). Joel and Judith had children recorded at Medway: Joel Hawes, b. 1777, d. 1779; Lewis Hawes, b. 1780; Polly Hawes, b. 1782; Betsey Hawes, b. 1784, d. 1802; and Judith Hawes, b. 8 Feb. 1787, who was adopted by Nathan and Rhoda Harding (*VR* 73, 315).

Children of Joel and Philadelphia (Thayer) Hawes, rec. Medway (*VR* 73-74):

i   JOEL HAWES⁶, b. 22 Dec. 1788. (A Joel Hawes ae 60, b. Mass., a Minister, was in Hartford, Conn., in 1850 (p.278) with wife Louisa ae 59, b. Mass., several students, and a teacher in their household; possibly the same, but no proof.)

ii   WINSLOW HAWES, b. 14 May 1790.

iii PRESTON HAWES, b. 14 Jan. 1792 ("Pressen" in b. rec.); d. Brookfield 4 March 1848 of "fever" (*VR* 498); m. at Brookfield, 13 Dec. 1812 (*VR* 337), FANNY OLDS, b. ca 24 March 1796 (calc.), d. 14 Oct. 1869 Brookfield, widowed, ae 73y 6m 20d, of "old age" (Mass. VR 222:234). In

1850 Fanny was living in Brookfield with dau. Clarinda A. ae 16, and son Preston W. ae 27, shoemaker (p.58).

Children rec. Brookfield (*VR* 121): 1. *Juliett Hawes⁷*, b. 29 Nov. 1813. 2. *Fanny Maria Hawes*, b. 1 Nov. 1816. 3. *Lydia Ann Hawes*, b. 10 Jan. 1818. 4. *Preston William Hawes*, b. 21 Feb. 1823; m. Ellen Nichols. 5. *Mary Jane Hawes*, b. 5 April 1825. 6. *Joel Hawes*, b. 10 April 1827. 7. *Betsey Smith Hawes*, b. 19 Jan. 1830. 8. *Clarinda Hawes*, b. 5 Feb. 1834. 9. *Kirkland Alanson Hawes*, b. 6 Jan. 1837.

iv   LYMAN HAWES, b. 18 Feb. 1794. In 1850 Lyman Haws was a farmer at Richmond, N.Y., ae 56, b. Mass., with RACHAEL ae 54, b. Vt.; three apparent children b. N.Y. (see below); James Clark ae 24 and Mary McGara ae 20, both b. Ireland; and Henry Hawes ae 3 and Sophia A. Hawes ae 23, both b. N.Y. (p.83).

Children, list prob. incomplete: 1. *prob. son Hawes⁷*, poss. d. before 1850 leaving wife Sophia A. and son *Henry Hawes* b. ca 1846. 2. *Joel Hawes*, b. ca 1829; "Dr's Student" in 1850. 3. *Ann E. Hawes*, b. ca 1832. 4. *Sanford Hawes*, b. ca 1837.

v   FANNY HAWES, b. 13 March 1796; d. Brookfield 29 Oct. 1812 (*VR* 498).

vi   RINDA HAWES, b. 1 Aug. 1798; m. 10 Nov. 1816 at Brookfield (*VR* 395), OLIVER RICE, b. ca 1788. In 1850 he was a farmer at Akron, Ohio, ae 62, with "Orinda" ae 58 [*sic*]; Preston Rice ae 28, b. Mass., and Almira Rice ae 19, b. N.Y.; William Darling ae 35, potter b. Mass., and apparent Darling children Fanny ae 8, Helen ae 3, and Orinda ae 7m, all b. Ohio; William Rice ae 19, miller, b. Mass., ended the list (p.411).

Rice children, first three rec. Brookfield (*VR* 185-87): 1. *Nancy Maria Rice⁷*, b. 7 Jan. 1817. 2. *Lyman Rice*, b. 20 Nov. 1818. 3. *Preston W. Rice*, b. 26 Oct. 1821; with parents, a grocer 1850. 4. [*prob. Daughter*] *Rice*, m. William Darling and d. ca 1850 leaving Fanny Darling b. ca 1842, Helen Darling b. ca 1847, and Orinda Darling b. 1849. 5. *Almira Rice*, b. ca 1831 N.Y.; at home 1850.

vii   MIRA HAWES, b. 18 March 1801.

Sources cited: *Brookfield VR. Medway VR. Mendon VR.* Mass. Vital Records 1841-1910. CENSUS: 1850 Brookfield, Worcester Co. (M432-343), Hartford, Hartford Co., Conn. (M432-41), Richmond, Ontario Co., N.Y. (M432-571), Akron, Summit Co., Ohio (M432-732).

617. STEPHEN THAYER⁵ (*Stephen Thayer⁴, Mary³ Samson, Stephen², Henry¹*), son of Stephen Thayer [129] and his wife Rachel Davis, was born 29 December 1765 at Mendon (*VR* 189), and died "last of August" 1821 at Rome, N.Y. (pension file). *Thayer Memorial* says he died there 3 March 1819.

He married 15 May 1787 at Milford (*VR* 298), **ANNA TWITCHELL**, who was born there 2 February 1770 (*VR* 172), daughter of Ephraim and Lydia (Parkhurst) Twitchell. She died 3 March 1851 (*Thayer Memorial,* 276), probably in Niagara County, N.Y. She married, second, in November 1842, JOSEPH OTIS, who died 22 March 1850 at Rome, N.Y. (Sprague Ms).

On 24 November 1802 Seth Nelson of Milford for $50 paid by Gershom Twitchell of Milford, Ephraim Twitchell of Stockbridge, Vt., Samuel Jones Esq. of Milford in behalf of Stephen Thayer of Shaftsborough, Vt., and wife Anna, Caleb Allen of Milford and wife Mercy, Polly Twitchell, single, Zuriel Hayword of Milford and wife Olivia, and David French of Westmoreland, N. H., as attorney for his children Sally, Lincoln, Zeba, Asapth, Lotty, Elijah, Raymond, Spencer, and David, quitclaimed to Gershom Twitchell their rights in property of Ephraim Twitchell late of Milford, deceased (Worcester LR 188:432). In a distribution of the estate of Ephraim Twitchell of Milford on 1 November 1803, son Gershom was directed to receive all the real estate and pay sums of money to the other heirs, who included Stephen Thayer (Worcester PR #A60282).

Stephen served in the Revolution. His widow applied for a pension on 11 September 1838 at Rome, Oneida County, N.Y. (Rev. pension #W21883). The pension file includes an original Bible record with birth dates for Stephen, Anna, and the first ten children. A copy of his discharge in the file says that he was a drummer in the 8th Mass. Regiment commanded by Michael Jackson, discharged with badge of merit for 3 years 5 months of service, dated Mendon 12 December 1804. A warrant for bounty lands issued in right of Stephen Thayer dated 27 January 1797 was sold to Josiah Nelson by Stephen Thayer [Jr.] and Anna Otis (BLW #5171-100-27).

The deed above places Stephen and Anna at Shaftsbury, Vt., in 1802. *Thayer Memorial* (p.276) says Stephen settled at Stratham, Vt., then Sunderland, Vt., about 1794, then lived at Fairfield, Vt., until 1810, when he moved to Oneida County, N.Y. In 1850 Ann Otis aged 77 [*sic*] was living with the family of her son Nathan in Pendleton, Niagara County, N.Y. (p.253).

Children of Stephen and Anna (Twitchell) Thayer (first ten from Bible in pension file, last three from *Thayer Memorial,* 276, which says first three b. Stratham, Vt., next at Sunderland, Vt., rest at Fairfield, Vt.; a few dates and spellings differ; last three not in Sprague Ms):

   i   LIMON ELANSON THAYER[6], b. 7 June 1790 (Lyman E. in *Thayer Mem.*); d. 12 Feb. 1864 Dayton, Wisc.; m. 8 Dec. 1810, FANNY BUTLER, b. 1 June 1788, d. 16 March 1862, dau. of Isaac Butler of Fairfield, Vt. They removed to Portage, Mich., 1836, and to Dayton, Wisc., 1850. In 1860

Lyman E. Thayer ae 70, occupation "hotel," and Fanny ae 71 lived in Dayton, Green Lake Co., Wisc., with two young servants, Caroline and Fred Calpelon, b. Germany (p.919).

Children, first six b. Middlesex, Ontario Co., N.Y., last four at Pendleton, Niagara Co., N.Y. (*Thayer Mem.*, 276-77). 1. *Sophrona H. Thayer⁷*, b. 5 April 1813; m. John Rouse. 2. *Stephen B. Thayer*, b. 11 Feb. 1815; m. Elizabeth Stoner. 3. *Huldah Adelaide Thayer*, b. 21 April 1817; m. William Sykes. 4. *Penelope A. Thayer*, b. 6 April 1819; m. John Eastland. 5. *Eleazur Isaac Thayer*, b. 8 April 1821; m. Eliza Mason. 6. *Napoleon B. Thayer*, b. 21 Oct. 1823. 7. *Julius Virgil Thayer*, b. 21 Nov. 1824. 8. *Charlotte Augusta Thayer*, b. 1 Jan. 1827. 9. *Lyman W. Thayer*, b. 21 April 1830. 10. *Ann Thayer*, b. 10 April 1832; d. 1 April 1834.

ii LUCINDIA THAYER, b. 25 Oct. 1792 (Lucinda, b. 15 Oct. 1791 in *Thayer Mem.*); m. 25 May 1814, STILLMAN CLARK.

    Clark children (*Thayer Mem.*, 278): 1. *Angeline Clark⁷*, b. 12 Jan. 1815. 2. *George W. Clark*, b. 3 June 1817. 3. *Stephen Clark*, b. 16 June 1820. 4. *Erastus F. Clark*, b. 8 Dec. 1822. 5. *Marietta Clark*, b. 2 July 1826. 6. *Jerome F. Clark*, b. 7 July 1829. 7. *Lyman H. Clark*, b. 9 Sept. 1831.

iii ANNA THAYER, b. Tuesday, 30 July 1793.

iv STEPHEN THAYER, JR., b. Thursday, 31 Oct. 1794; d. 6 Oct. 1839; m. in 1829 OLIVIA HAWLEY, b. 22 Jan. 1800, d. 4 Oct. 1853; res. Russell, Geauga Co., Ohio (*Thayer Mem.*, 278).

    Children (*ibid.*): 1. *George Thayer⁷*, b. 4 Sept. 1821; m. Charlotte Hunt. 2. *Murat Thayer*, b. 1823. 3. *Julia Thayer*, b. 1825. 4. *Jerald/Jared Thayer*, b. 12 Feb. 1828; m. Betsey E. Manly. 5. *Stephen Thayer*, b. 11 Feb. 1831; m. Mary Ann Brown. 6. *Virgil Thayer*, b. 15 Oct. 1834; m. Elizabeth I. Radcliff. 7. *Aaron Thayer*, b. 21 June 18__; m. Mabel Kelly.

v EL[L]ERY THAYER, b. Thursday, 1 June 1797 (1 April 1797 in *Thayer Mem.*); m. 7 July 1822, CLARISSA HAWLEY, b. 27 March 1803 (*Thayer Mem.*, 280). In 1850 Elery Thayre ae 52, farmer, and Clarissa ae 48, both b. Vt., were living in Floyd, Oneida Co., N.Y., with Crandle ae 18 and Jeraldine ae 17, both b. N.Y. (p.140).

    Children (*Thayer Mem.*, 280): 1. *Lyman Thayer⁷*, b. 29 Aug. 1823; m. Sarah Watson. 2. *Janette Thayer*, b. 30 March 1825; m. William Hamson. 3. *Freeman Thayer*, b. 20 April 1826; m. Emily Bartlett. 4. *Frances Thayer*, b. 10 Feb/ 1830; d. ae 5y. 5. *Crandall Thayer*, b. 12 Sept. 1832; m. Mary Ann Hawley. 6. *Jeraldine Thayer*, b. 28 Feb. 1834; m. John Morris. 7. *Everett Thayer*, b. 4 May 1836; d. ae 9y. 8. *Stephen Thayer*, b. 8 Aug. 1838; d. ae 12y. 9. *Darius Thayer*, b. 5 July 1840; d. ae 5y.

vi AARON THAYER, b. 25 Jan. 1799; d. 18 Sept. 1856; res. Rome, N.Y., 1838 (pension rec.); m. in 1819, CYNTHIA BRIGGS, d. 25 Nov. 1848

(*Thayer Mem.*, 279). In 1850 Aaron Thore ae 55, farmer, b. R.I.[*sic*] was living at Rome, N.Y., with Stephen Thore ae 14, b. N.Y., and William Nutt ae 42, b. N.Y. (p.53).

Children (*Thayer Mem.*): 1. *Delia Thayer⁷*, b. 19 Aug. 1820; m. Lewis West. 2. *Cordelia Thayer*, b. 30 May 1822; m. Henry C. Mallory. 3. *Charles Thayer*, b. 7 June 1824; m. Jane Lampson. 4. *George Thayer*. 5. *Jane Thayer*. 6. *Stephen Thayer*, b. ca 1836.

vii OLIVE THAYER, b. 22 Nov. 1800; d. 9 Aug. 1801, ae 8m 23d (b. 25 Nov. in *Thayer Mem.*).

viii NANCY THAYER, b. Tuesday, 11 May 1802; d. y.

ix NATHAN THAYER, b. Tuesday, 29 May 1804 (23 May in *Thayer Mem.*); d. 10 Sept. 1862; m. at Whitesboro, N.Y., 3 Feb. 1826, DORCAS BELKNAP, b. 18 Nov. 1805 (*Thayer Mem.*, 280). In 1850 Nathan was a farmer at Pendleton, Niagara Co., N.Y., with his mother in his household (p.253); birthplaces given for all the adults are wildly incorrect (England for Nathan, Ireland for Dorcas, N.Y. for Anna). Monroe, Vanburen, Alfred, Stephen, Sarah, and Freeman were at home.

Children (*Thayer Mem.*, 280): 1. *Martha Thayer⁷*, b. 27 July 1827; d. 13 March 1834. 2. *James Monroe Thayer*, b. 12 Nov. 1832; m. Mary Stebbins. 3. *Van Buren Thayer*, b. 2 Aug. 1835; m. Philena Bates. 4. *Alfred B. Thayer*, b. 22 April 1838. 5. *Stephen Thayer*, b. 13 Aug. 1840. 6. *Sarah Jane Thayer*, b. 18 Aug. 1842; d. 26 June 1850. 7. *Freeman Thayer*, b. 3 July 1846; d. 1 Sept. 1864.

x ELMIRIA THAYER, b. Monday, 2 June 1806 (Almira, b. 3 June in *Thayer Mem.*); m. BENJAMIN FULLER (*ibid.*).

xi SOPHRONA THAYER, b. 30 March 1808.

xii CHARLOTTE THAYER, b. 1810; m. NELSON ADSET (*Thayer Mem.*, 281).

xiii FANNY THAYER, b. 20 Jan. 1812; m. 24 Jan. 1831, ORSON WHEELER, b. 24 Nov. 1808; res. Rome, N.Y. (*Thayer Mem.*, 281).

Wheeler children (*ibid.*): 1. *Hepzibah Wheeler⁷*, b. 27 March 1832; d. 27 June 1856. 2. *Marion A. Wheeler*, b. 14 May 1835. 3. *Dimmist Earnest Wheeler*, b. 14 Sept. 1837. 4. *Philander Wheeler*, b. 16 March 1839; d. 18 Feb. 1841.

Sources cited: *Mendon VR. Milford VR.* Revolutionary War pension records. Worcester County Deeds and Probate Records. Bezaleel Thayer, *Thayer Memorial* (1874). W. C. Sprague Manuscript, NEHGS. CENSUS: 1850, Pendleton, Niagara Co., N.Y. (M432-560), Floyd and Rome, Oneida Co., N.Y. (M432-565); 1860 Dayton, Green Lake Co., Wisc. (M653-1410). **See also:** White, *Abstracts of Rev. War Pension Files*, 3:3459 (has first child as Simon Elanson).

618. **RACHEL THAYER**[5] (*Stephen Thayer*[4], *Mary*[3] *Samson, Stephen*[2], *Henry*[1]), daughter of Stephen Thayer [129] and his wife Rachel Davis, was born 14 March 1769 at Mendon (*VR* 187).

She married at Hopkinton, 26 March 1789 (*VR* 368), **MOSES RICE**. It seems likely that he was an unrecorded son of the Jason Rice of Hopkinton who married Susanna Haven at Framingham 14 February 1750/1, had children Abigail (1753) and Susanna (1755) recorded at Hopkinton (*VR* 351, 162-63), and died there 6 March 1801 aged 73 "of fever" (*VR* 446).

At the start of the Revolution, he was probably the Moses Rice on a roll of men from Framingham under the command of Capt. Micajah Gleason, who were at Concord and Cambridge 19 April 1775 (*Framingham History*, 278).

In the 1800 census of Hopkinton, Moses and his wife were 26-45, and they had with them one woman 16-26, one boy 10-16, and two boys and four girls under 10, indicating that all the children born before 1800 were living at that time. Just before Moses' household is listed that of Jason Rice, a man over 45, evidently living alone (p.885).

Where did this family go? Son Jason appears to have died in 1880 in Michigan, but no other trace of the family has been found. There are several listings for men named Moses Rice in the 1810 census, but none appears to fit. A Rachel Rice was head of a household in 1810 at New Ashford, Berkshire County, with only one girl 10-16 and one girl under 10 (p.178). No relevant probate or land records were found in Middlesex County.

Children of Moses and Rachel (Thayer) Rice, rec. Hopkinton (*VR* 162-63):

i ALANSON RICE, b. 23 Sept. 1789.

ii MOSES RICE, b. 10 April 1791.

iii NANCY RICE, b. 23 Dec. 1792. It has been suggested that she was the Nancy Rice who m. at Leominster, 21 Dec. 1826 (*VR* 249), John Burnham of Hopkinton, but if Nancy Burnham's age is correct on the 1850 census, she was b. ca 1808 (Ashland, Middlesex Co., p.439).

iv AARON RICE, b. 17 Aug. 1794.

v SUSANNA RICE, b. 3 Aug. 1796.

vi HITTE HARDING RICE, b. 26 May 1798; poss. the "child of Moses" d. Hopkinton 26 Oct. 1802 ae 3 (*VR* 446).

vii RACHEL RICE, b. 2 Feb. 1800.

viii JASON RICE, b. 26 Oct. 1801; d. prob. in Eggleston Twp., Muskegon Co., Mich., 7 Sept. 1880. Several as yet unverified internet sources provide further information.

ix   [INFANT] RICE, d. 18 Feb. 1804 (*VR* 446).

x   [CHILD] RICE, d. 25 Sept. 1805 ae 3w (*VR* 446).

Sources cited: *Hopkinton VR. Leominster VR. Mendon VR.* Temple, *History of Framingham* (1887). CENSUS: Hopkinton, Middlesex Co., 1800 (M32-17); 1850 Ashland, Middlesex Co. (M432-326).

619.   NANCY THAYER[5] (*Stephen Thayer*[4], *Mary*[3] *Samson, Stephen*[2], *Henry*[1]), daughter of Stephen Thayer [129] and his wife Rachel Davis, was born 24 May 1771 at Mendon (*VR* 186). She may have died 27 May 1822, probably at Mt. Holly, Vt. (IGI, unverified).

She married at Hubbardston, 28 July 1793 (*VR* 118; *Thayer Mem.*, 282), **JACOB AMES**. He was born perhaps at Mendon in November 1769 and died probably in Vermont or possibly New York, 22 December 1845 (IGI).

There is nothing further on this couple in Hubbardston records. An entry in the IGI, sourced only to a member [not named] of the LDS after 1991, appears to relate to this family, placing them at one point in Shaftsbury, Vt. It gives Jacob's birth date and death dates for both Jacob and Nancy.

The 1800 census lists Jacob Ames in Shaftsbury, aged 26-45 with wife 26-45, and four girls under 10 (p.169). A notice in *The Vermont Gazette* of 11 March 1805 says, "Jacob Ames of Shaftsbury is now confined to the Bennington jail, on execution of a judgement in favor of Oliver Wood, late of Townshend, Windham County [Vt.]. His attorney is to be served with notice as to why Ames should not take oath prescribed by law for the relief of prisoners" (*VT Newspaper Abstracts*, 287).

In 1810 Jacob Ames was in Dorset, Vt., about 20 northeast of Shaftsbury, himself and his wife 26-45, and with them were one woman 16-26, two girls 10-16, and three boys and two girls under 10 (p.294). Thankful Ames [his 20-year-old daughter] and Jacob Ames were among several people warned on 29 October 1817 in Mt. Holly, Vt., but he evidently satisfied the authorities and was listed there in the 1820 census, himself and his wife over 45, with one boy and one girl 10-16 (p.472).

Probable children of Jacob and Nancy (Thayer) Ames, birthdates from IGI, not found in Vermont VR, but supported by census figures:

i   CLARISSA AMES[6], b. 4 Feb. 1794 at Princeton (no rec. there).

ii   [Daughter] AMES, b. ca 1795.

ii   THANKFUL AMES, b. 24 May 1797 at Shaftsbury, Vt.; warned at Mt. Holly with father 1819.

iii   LUCY AMES, b. 4 Oct. 1800 at Shaftsbury, Vt.

iv   JONATHAN AMES, b. 13 Oct. 1802 Shaftsbury, Vt.

v   NAHUM AMES, b. 4 Aug. 1804; living 1870 at Rushford, N.Y.; m. EDITH
_____, b. ca 1798 in N.H. In 1850 Nathan [*sic*] was a farmer at Rushford, ae
46, b. Vt., with Edith ae 53, and four children (p.354). In 1870 Nahum and
Edith were at Rushford with Fletcher ae 42, farm laborer (p.726).

Children, from census: 1. *Nathan P. Ames*[7], b. ca 1828 Vt.; a farmer with
parents 1850; poss. the same as *Fletcher Ames*, b. ca 1828, with parents 1870.
2. *Rachael A. Ames*, b. ca 1830 Vt.; at home 1850. 3. *Clarissa M. Ames*, b. ca 1833
N.Y.; with parents, a milliner ae 36 in 1870. 4. *Alfred E. Ames*, b. ca 1839 N.Y.; at
home 1850.

vi   NANCY AMES, b. 4 Sept. 1806.

vii   ABEL AMES, b. 26 July 1808; m. SARAH [WATERBURY?], b. ca 1815 in
N.Y. In 1850 he was ae 42, b. Vt., a farmer in Rushford, N.Y., with Sally ae
29, and seven children, some too old to be Sally's if her age is right (p.349).
In 1860 he was a lumberman at W. Clarksville, N.Y., with Sarah ae 45 [*sic*],
and five children (p.282).

Children, from census: 1. *Nancy J. Ames*[7], b. ca 1832. 2. *Jacob S. Ames*, b. ca
1834. 3. *Silas I. Ames*, b. ca 1836. 4. *Jehiel Ames*, b. ca 1838. 5. *Lydia J. Ames*, b. ca
1840. 6. *Nathan E. Ames*, b. ca 1843. 7. *Alvin M./Milton Ames*, b. ca 1848.
8. *Alice Ames*, b. ca 1850. 9. *Helen Ames*, b. ca 1855. 10. *Abigail Ames*, b. 1859.

Sources cited: *Hubbardston VR. Mendon VR.* Mt. Holly, Vt., Town Records, Book 1. Rising,
Vermont Newspaper Abstracts (2001). Rollins, *Vermont Warnings Out,* Vol. 2 (1997). *Thayer Memorial*
(1874). *International Genealogical Index* of LDS. CENSUS: Bennington Co., Vt., Shaftsbury 1800
(M32-51) & Dorset 1810 (M252-64); 1820 Mt. Holly, Rutland Co., Vt. (M33-126); Allegany Co.,
N.Y., Rushford 1850 (M432-476) & 1870 (M593-905), 1860 W. Clarksville (M653-717).

620.   DOLINDA THAYER[5] (*Stephen Thayer*[4], *Mary*[3] *Samson, Stephen*[2], *Henry*[1]),
daughter of Stephen Thayer [129] and his wife Rachel Davis, was born 13 April
1774 at Mendon (*VR* 181).

Dolinda Thayer married at Milford, 25 January 1792 (*VR* 243) after intentions
17 December 1791 at Hopkinton (*VR* 368, call her "Dorathy"), **LEVI
HAYWARD** of Milford. He was born at Milford 22 July 1770 (*VR* 86), son of
Daniel Jr. and Ellen (Davis) Hayward of Mendon (*Milford History,* 794).

No further record of them has been found. A Levi Hayward in Townshend,
Vt., in 1800 and his wife were both too old to be this couple.

Sources cited: *Hopkinton VR. Mendon VR. Milford VR. History of Milford* (1882). *Thayer Memorial*
(1874), p. 282, says [incorrectly] that she m. 13 Jan. 1792 Samuel Goodell.

621. NAHUM THAYER⁵ (*Stephen Thayer⁴, Mary³ Samson, Stephen², Henry¹*), son of Stephen Thayer [129] and his wife Rachel Davis, was born 2 January 1776 at Mendon (*VR* 186) and died 1 May 1811, aged 36, at Wrentham (*VR* 501). He is buried in Norfolk (formerly North Wrentham) Cemetery.

He married, 21 December 1797 at Medway (*VR* 265), **MOLLY PIERCE**. She is called Mary in some of her children's birth records and Molly in others; her death record calls her Polly. She was born 15 December 1776 at Medway (*VR* 106), daughter of Jonathan and Rebecca (Carey) Pierce, and died 16 May 1848 at Wrentham (*VR* 501), aged 70, as "Polly, wife of Nahum Thayer."

Nahum Thayer of Medway, blacksmith, mortgaged land in the East Parish of Medway to Henry Ellis Jr. on 17 August 1805, and discharged it in 1809 (Norfolk LR 24:145). Nahum Thayer of Medway, blacksmith, sold land in Medway to the Medway Cotton Manufacturing Co. on 12 February 1811, the deed signed also by "Molley my wife" (Norfolk LR 39:24).

Calvin Sanger was appointed administrator of the estate of Nahum Thayer of Sherburne, blacksmith, 12 May 1812, with Samuel Perry Jr. of Natick and Asher Goodenow of Sudbury, gentleman, as bondsmen (Middlesex PR 206:45). On 12 January 1813 Simpson Jones of Medway, gentleman, was appointed guardian of Nancy Thayer of Sherborn, over 14, daughter of the late Nahum Thayer of Sherborn, blacksmith, and also of Roxana, Amory, Davis, and Lyman, under 14, children of Nahum Thayer and Polly who was now a widow (*ibid.*, 251:33).

Children of Nahum and Molly (Pierce) Thayer, recorded Medway (*VR* 122):

i NANCY THAYER⁶, b. 5 May 1798; d. prob. Sherborn 16 May 1852 ae 54y 11d of "dropsy on heart … dau. of Nahum and Polly Thayer" (Mass. VR 67:100); bur. Holliston; m. by 1817 CYRUS MARSH, b. Holliston 30 Oct. 1787, son of Esek and Sophia (___) Marsh (*VR* 103); d. there 23 March 1878 ae 90y 4m 23d of gangrene ("Cyprus," Mass. VR 302:83). In 1850 he was a shoemaker at Sherborn, with Nancy ae 52, Helen ae 15, and William W. Pond ae 12 (p.320).

   Marsh children rec. Sherborn (*VR* 64): 1. *Horatio Marsh⁷*, b. 29 May 1817. 2. *Cyrus Marsh*, b. 20 May 1821. 3. *Helen Maria Marsh⁷*, b. 20 Sept. 1834.

ii ROXANA THAYER, b. 18 Nov. 1801; d. Medway 12 June 1887 ae 85y 6m 27d of old age (Mass. VR 383:298); m. at Franklin, 13 Jan. 1823 (*VR* 101), NATHAN DANIELS JR., b. Franklin 14 Aug. 1791 (calc.), son of Nathan and Sarah (___) Daniels, d. Franklin 15 March 1872 ae 80y 7m 1d, of old age (Mass. VR 248:309). In 1850 Nathan Daniels ae 58, farmer, and Roxana ae 48, res. Franklin with three children (p.311).

Daniels children at home 1850: 1. *Thomas J. Daniels⁷*, b. ca 1827. 2. *Lucy G. Daniels*, b. ca 1829. 3. *Adaline Daniels*, b. ca 1835.

iii   STEPHEN THAYER, b. 8 Oct. 1803; d. 1812 (*Thayer Mem.*, 281).

iv   EMORY THAYER, b. 7 March 1806; m. 6 March 1838, ADELINE KELLY; settled Whitewater, Wisc. (*Thayer Mem.*, 281). In 1850 Emery Thayer was a tavern keeper in E. Troy, Walworth Co., Wisc., with Adeline ae 39, b. Vt., Caroline ae 9, b. N.Y., and Emery ae 7, b. Wisc. (p.174).
     Children (*Thayer Mem.*, 281; census): 1. *Catherine/Caroline Thayer⁷*, b. 9 Nov. 1840. 2. *Emery Thayer*, b. 7 Feb. 1843.

v   NAHUM DAVIS THAYER, b. 5 July 1808; d. Norfolk 7 Jan. 1895 ae 87y 7m of old age, b. Medway, parents unknown; m. HANNAH RIDER (*Thayer Mem.*, 281).

vi   LYMAN ALANSON THAYER, b. 1 Dec. 1810; m. 15 April 1832 at Medway (*VR* 265), HARRIET J. STORY, b. 22 Aug. 1812 (g.s., rec. Wrentham). In 1850 he was a farmer ae 39 at Wrentham with Harriet ae 37, six children, and Julia Story ae 57 (p.166).
     Children rec. Wrentham (*VR* 1:195): 1. *Mary Thayer⁷*, b. ca 1837. 2. *Lyman Le Barron Thayer*, b. 26 Dec. 1838. 3. *Stephen Erastus Thayer*, b. 18 Jan. 1841. 4. *Emery Davis Thayer*, b. 13 Jan. 1843. 5. *Maria Louisa Thayer*, b. 2 Oct. 1846. 6. *Harriet Jane Thayer*, b. 3 or 10 Dec. 1848.

Sources cited: *Franklin VR. Medway VR. Sherborn VR. Wrentham VR.* Mass. Vital Records 1841-1910. Middlesex County Probate Records. Norfolk County Deeds at Dedham. W. C. Sprague, Thayer Manuscript, NEHGS. *Thayer Memorial* (1874). CENSUS: 1850 Norfolk Co., Franklin & Wrentham (M432-331), Sherborn, Middlesex Co. (M432-322).

622.   WINDSOR THAYER⁵ (*Stephen Thayer⁴, Mary³ Samson, Stephen², Henry¹*), son of Stephen Thayer [129] and his wife Rachel Davis, was born 21 June 1778 at Mendon (*VR* 190), and died at Lockport, N.Y. (*Thayer Mem.*, 282).

He married, probably about 1799, **LYDIA _____**, who died at Lowville, Lewis County, N.Y. (*ibid.*).

The 1800 census lists Windson [*sic*] Thayer, himself and wife between 16 and 26, at Stockbridge, Vt., with one boy under 10 (p.341). He is probably the "Winslow" Thayer listed in 1810 at Barnard, Vt., himself and wife between 26 and 45, with three boys and two girls under 10 (p.477). In 1820 he was at Fort Ann, Washington County, N,Y, with a household consisting of an apparent wife 26-45, one young man and one young woman 16-26, a young man 16-18, a boy and a girl 10-16, and a boy under 10 (p.143).

Children of Windsor and Lydia (_____) Thayer (*Thayer Mem.*, 282), order unknown:

i   DANIEL THAYER[6], b. say 1799 (census).

ii LYDIA THAYER.

iii OVID THAYER, probably OEL / ORWELL THAYER, b. 4 Sept. 1806,
    Fairfield, Vt.; d. 4 Feb. 1876 or 1877, Lebanon, Boone Co., Ind.; m. at
    Pickinsville, S. C., Tuesday before 8 Sept. 1832 (Greenville, S. C. news-
    paper abstracts, *S. C. Mag. of Ancestral Research*, 8:45), HARRIETT
    CAROLINE OSBORNE, b. Pendleton, S. C., 5 May 1814, d. 21 Sept.
    1861. In 1850 Oel Thayer was a merchant in District 7, Boone Co., Ind.,
    b. Vt., ae 44, with Harriet C., 36, b. S.C., and the following children
    (p.173). It is said that three of his sons fought in the Civil War, two for the
    Union and one (Henry Osborne, briefly) for the Confederacy.
        Thayer children at home 1850: 1. *Byson Thayer[7]*, b. ca 1834 in S.C.; living
    1850, "idiotic." 2. *Albert Thayer*, b. ca 1836 in S.C. 3. *Amanda Thayer*, b. ca 1838
    in Miss. 4. *Henry Osborne Thayer*, b. 8 Jan. 1840 at Aberdeen, Miss.; m. Helen
    Elizabeth Boult. 5. *Adaline Thayer*, b. ca 1842 in Ind. 6. *James Thayer*, b. ca 1844
    in Ind. 7. *Daniel Thayer*, b. ca 1847 in Ind.

iv ALINDA THAYER.

v   IRA THAYER, b. ca 1810; m. PHILANDA ____, b. ca 1811 in Vt. In 1850
    he was a merchant in Indianapolis, Ind., ae 40, with Philanda ae 39, two
    children, and several other people (Howletts and Prescotts), in the
    household (p.229).
        Thayer children at home 1850: 1. *Francis W. Thayer[7]*, b. ca 1833 in S.C.
    2. *Evaline Thayer*, b. ca 1837 in Mass.

vi ALMIRA THAYER.

Sources cited: *Mendon VR. Thayer Memorial* (1874). *South Carolina Magazine of Ancestral Research*,
vol. 8 [1980]. CENSUS: 1800 Stockbridge, Windsor Co., Vt. (M32-52); 1810 Barnard, Windsor Co.,
Vt. (M252-65); 1820 Fort Ann, Washington Co., N.Y. (M33-76); 1850 Indiana, District 7, Boone
Co. (M432-136) & Indianapolis, Marion Co. (M432-229).

623. AARON CHANCE/CHENEY THAYER[5] (*Stephen Thayer[4], Mary[3]
Samson, Stephen[2], Henry[1]*), son of Stephen Thayer [129] and his wife Rachel Davis,
was born 29 June 1780 at Mendon (*VR* 179), and died 27 July 1856 in
Pennsylvania (*Thayer Mem.*, 282).

Aaron married 18 September 1803, at Medway (*VR* 264), **MARGARET
BULLARD**, whose name almost always appears in records as the nickname
PEGGY. She was born 27 July 1778 at Medway (*VR* 30), daughter of Adam and

Lois (Richardson) Bullard, and died 1 April 1851 (*Thayer Mem.*, 282), probably in Pennsylvania.

On 5 January 1795 Nehemiah Ward of Orange was appointed guardian of Aaron Cheney [*sic*] Thayer of Orange, son of Stephen Thayer late of Mendon, deceased (Hampshire PR #19096, Box 147 #10).

Aaron and Margaret lived for a short time at Fairfield, Vt., then in Lower Canada, returned to Medway, and finally removed about 1819 to Harford, Susquehanna County, Pennsylvania.

Aaron Thayer of Medway, yeoman, mortgaged 110 rods of land in Medway to Sylvanus Adams 13 January 1815; the mortgage was discharged 6 June 1817 (Norfolk LR 49:242). On 17 March 1815 Aaron Thayer of Medway, yeoman, sold to William Jackson 110 rods in Medway; wife Peggy released her dower (*ibid.*, 51:45).

In his will dated 31 August 1840, proved 4 April 1843, Adam Bullard of Medway, advanced in age, named his wife Nancy J. Bullard and directed that a suitable gravestone be erected for his deceased wife Lois Bullard. He left to his daughter Peggy Thayer, wife of Aaron Thayer, money to be held in trust by her son Ferdinand Davis Thayer, and mentioned four great-grandchildren under 21, sons of Cyrus Bullard Thayer, deceased. On 1 August 1844 Frederick [*sic*] Davis Thayer of Prompton, Wayne County, Pa., was appointed trustee, and Peggy Thayer signed a release on 12 July 1844 (Norfolk PR #2769).

The 1850 census lists Aaron Thayer, 70, farmer, with wife Peggy, 72, both born in Mass., living by themselves in Harford Twp., Pa., next to the family of daughter Alma Tiffany (p.332).

Children of Aaron Chance/Cheney and Peggy (Bullard) Thayer, i and v-viii rec. at Medway (*VR* 122); according to *Thayer Mem.*, both daughters Louisa lived to marry:

i   CYRUS BULLARD THAYER[6], b. 2 May 1804 at Medway "of Aaron and Pegga"; d. Havana, Cuba, 24 May 1840 (*Thayer Mem.*, 283); m. Somersworth, N.H., 23 March 1826 (Sprague Ms), ABIGAIL TILDEN, b. 17 June 1805, d. Lowell 15 Jan. 1857, dau. Josiah and Prudence (___) Tilden of Canton (*Thayer Mem.*, 282, says m. 3 March 1825). Four children named in will of great-grandfather Adam Bullard.
     Children (*Thayer Mem.*, 282): 1. *Helen Thayer*[7], b. 1 Aug. 1827; d. 19 Aug. 1827. 2. *Solon C. Thayer*, b. 9 Aug. 1828. 3. *Cyrus B. Thayer*, b. 18 Jan. 1830; m. Mary Stone. 4. *Clinton James Thayer*, b. 26 May 1832; d. Boston 28 Feb. 1833 ae 9m (*Col. Cent.*). 5. *Ambrose K. Thayer*, b. 16 Jan. 1834; m. Lizzie F. Clinton. 6. *Mary J. Thayer*, b. 14 July 1837; d. 25 Aug. 1838. 7. *William A. Thayer*, b. 25 Sept. 1839; d. 26 Aug. 1840.

ii   AMANDA M. THAYER, b. 6 Oct. 1805 Fairfield, Vt., "of Aaron and
      Pegga"; d. 1839, bur. near Independence, Warren Co., Ind.; m. 10 June
      1822, ASAHEL CARPENTER (*Thayer Mem.*, 283), b. Attleboro 1796, d.
      1842 Susquehanna, Pa., bur. Peck Cem. there, son of John and Polly
      (Tyler) Carpenter.
          Carpenter children, first five b. Pa., last Ind. (*Thayer Mem.*, 283, corrected):
      1. *Gideon Judd Carpenter*[7], b. April 1823; in 1850 a miner in Greenwood Valley,
      Calif. (p.455).   2. *Frederick D. Carpenter*, b. 1825; m. Marion Sickler.   3. *John
      Carpenter*, d.y.; bur. with mother.   4. *Cyrus Clay Carpenter*, b. 24 Nov. 1829; later
      Gov. of Iowa (*DAB*).   5. *Robert Emmet Carpenter*, m. Ella E. Vose.   6. *Amanda M.
      Carpenter*, b. 1837; d. 1842; bur. with father.

iii   LOUISA THAYER, b. 17 Dec. 1807 at Fairfield, Vt., "of Aaron and
      Pegga"; m. (1) 17 Oct. 1831, PRESTON RICHARDSON, d. Dec. 1836;
      m. (2) 10 Feb. 1844, EDWARD ALLEN; settled Carbondale, Pa. (*Thayer
      Mem.*, 283). Two Richardson children d. inf.
          Allen child (*ibid.*): 1. *George Hull Allen*[7], b. 28 Nov. 1849.

iv   ALMA THAYER (*Thayer Mem.*, 283, calls her Allen), b. 16 Jan. 1810 at
      Rome, Dist. Montreal, Lower Canada, "of Aaron and Pegga," bp. Medway
      5 May 1811 as "child of Aaron"; d. Harford, Pa., 29 Nov. 1861; m. 25
      Nov. 1830, EMILUS TIFFANY, b. Canterbury, Conn., 19 Feb. 1808, d.
      Harford, Pa., 5 May 1880 (Mortality List), son of Nathan Seneca and
      Anna (Pellett) Tiffany. In 1850 they were living next to her parents in
      Harford (p.332).
          Tiffany children, all at home 1850, all b. Pa. (full b. dates, *Thayer Mem.*, 283):
      1. *Lucinda Tiffany*[7], b. 13 Nov. 1832; m. Ziba Carey.   2. *Alonzo Tiffany*, b. 7 April
      1834.   3. *Judson Tiffany*, b. 2 May 1837.   4. *Malvina Tiffany*, b. 3 Feb. 1839.   5. *Cyrus
      Tiffany*, b. 14 July 1841.   6. *Edmund Tiffany*, b. 6 Nov. 1843.   7. *Emma Tiffany*, b.
      27 July 1848.

v   IRA THAYER, b. 24 Dec. 1811 at E. Medway; bp. 10 May 1812 Medway as
      "son of Aaron"; d. Medway 26 Sept. 1813, ae 1y 9m, "son of Aaron &
      Peggy" (*VR* 339).

vi   LOUISA THAYER, b. 13 July 1813 E. Medway; bp. Medway 12 Dec. 1813;
      d. 26 March 1837; m. 1835, GEORGE BLAKESLEE; settled Pa. (*Thayer
      Mem.*, 283).
          Blakeslee children (*ibid.*):   1. *Amanda Viola Blakeslee*[7], b. 1836.   2. *Louisa
      Blakeslee*, b. 3 March 1837.

vii   FERDINANDO DAVIS THAYER, b. 7 Oct. 1815 E. Medway; bp. Med-
      way 18 Aug. 1816; m. (1) SARAH or CATHERINE GRANT, b. 1 Aug.
      1822, d. 12 Sept. 1850; m. (2) 17 Dec. 1850, ELVIRA O. JENNINGS, b.
      5 Oct. 1812 (*Thayer Mem.*, 283-84) in Pa. In Davis Thayer [*sic*] ae 34, b.

Mass., was in Dyberry, Wayne Co., Pa., with Sarah ae 28, b. N.J., and three children; Emeline Fuller ae 22, b. Pa., was in the household (p.191). In 1860 F. D. Thayer, ae 44, was a farmer in Dyberry with Elvira ae 40, Levi [*sic*] ae 20, and Ann ae 18, a schoolteacher (p.230).

> Children (*Thayer Mem.*, 284), all b. Pa., with first wife: 1. *Levi Davis Thayer*[7], b. 14 Oct. 1839. 2. *Ann Elizabeth Thayer*, b. 13 March 1841. 3. *Aaron Everett Thayer*, b. 13 Jan. 1844; not at home 1860. Child with second wife: 4. *Alvira Caroline Thayer*, b. 26 April 1852; d. prob. before 1860.

viii MARGARET ANTOINETTE THAYER, b. 15 Dec. 1817 E. Medway; bp. Medway 13 May 1818; d. 2 July 1845; m. 3 Oct. 1842, HENRY TULLER; settled Johnstown, Licking Co., Ohio; no children (*Thayer Mem.*, 284). He m. (2) her sister Jemima.

ix JEMIMA B. THAYER, b. 8 June 1820 at Harford, Pa.; m. as his second wife, 7 Jan. 1846, HENRY TULLER, widower of her sister Margaret (*Thayer Mem.*, 284). In 1850 Henry Tullar [*sic*] was a merchant at Johnstown, Ohio, ae 33, b. N.Y., with Jemima B. ae 30, three Tullar children, and Ruhama Williams ae 10 (p.189).

> *Tuller* children (*ibid.*): 1. *Frank Tuller*[7], b. 17 Jan. 1847. 2. *Dick Tuller*, b. 6 Aug. 1848. 3. *Emma Tuller*, b. 9 Jan. 1850. 4. *Ella Tuller*, b. 26 Oct. 1852. 5. *Judd Tuller*, b. 7 March 1856. 6. *Fred Tuller*, b. 3 March 1858. 7. *Jemima Tuller*, b. 4 Sept., d. 21 Sept. 1859.

Sources cited: *Medway VR. Mendon VR.* Norfolk County Probate Records at Dedham. *Thayer Memorial* (1874). W. C. Sprague Ms. CENSUS: 1850 Johnstown, Licking Co., Ohio (M432-702), Harford, Susquehanna Co., Pa. (M432-829), Dyberry, Wayne Co., Pa., 1850 (M432-835) & 1860 (M653-1193). 1880 Mortality Schedule, Susquehanna Co., Pa.

624. LUCINDA THAYER[5] (*Stephen Thayer*[4], *Mary*[3] *Samson, Stephen*[2], *Henry*[1]), daughter of Stephen Thayer [129] and his wife Rachel Davis, was born 1 January 1782 at Mendon (*VR* 185). She is probably the widow Allard who died at Hopkinton 6 November 1828 aged "perhaps" 45 (*VR* 400, from CR).

She married at Hopkinton, as Lucy, 26 March 1801 (*VR* 368), **ANDREW AL[L]ARD**, who was born at Holden 23 February 1778 and died at Hopkinton 20 March 1824, aged "perhaps" 40 (*VR* 400, from CR), son of Andrew and Zerviah (Haven) Allard. He was evidently a posthumous child, as his mother's application for a widow's pension for his father's Revolutionary War service states that Andrew [Sr.] died at Blandford 23 August 1777 (White 31, citing #W14753). The military service record of Andrew Allard of Holden says that he was mustered in 3 June 1777 for a three-year term, and was reported deceased 1 September 1777

(*MSSR* 1:131). Zerviah (Haven) Allard married, second, at Framingham, 25 November 1784 (*VR* 229), Joseph Frail of Hopkinton.

The family of Andrew Allard [Jr.] and Lucinda has not been found in 1810, but their son Andrew's death record at Ashland (where he lived) gives his birthplace as Halifax, Vt., and parents as Andrew and Lucinda, while the record in Boston (where he died) lists his parents as Isaac and Mary. In 1810 the only Allard in Halifax, Vt., was Isaac Allard. Andrew Allard's grandfather was named Isaac Allard, and perhaps he had an uncle or brother of that name.

In 1820 Andrew Allard was listed in Hopkinton, himself and wife 26-45, with one boy and one girl 10-16 and two boys and three girls under 10 (p.433).

A record in the LDS Ancestral File (AFN:20WP-W2S) lists twelve children in this family with full birthdates. Much of the information seems correct, but there are a few errors and some details we have been unable to verify.

On 30 June 1824 Lucinda Allard signed a bond for $10,000, with sureties Fisher Metcalf and Matthew Metcalf, and was given administration on the estate of her husband, Andrew Allard, husbandman, "who last dwelt in Hopkinton" (Middlesex PR #296). The inventory, taken 28 June, included household goods consistent with a comfortable home, but no land and little livestock; one item was a cow "in the hands of Lyman Allard." The estate proved insolvent; Lucinda requested and was allowed her wearing apparel and "articles besides ... to the value of $100." There is no mention of the children.

Children of Andrew and Lucinda (Thayer) Allard, all listed in *History of Framingham* (p.457) without birthdates; dates and some other information from Ancestral File in IGI (verification not found):

   i   LYMAN ALLARD[6], b. 11 Dec. 1801; m. after int. 26 Dec. 1824 at Framingham (*VR* 228), NANCY MORSE.

   ii   HENRY ALLARD, b. 31 July 1803; d. 28 Jan. 1853 at Worth, Jefferson Co., N.Y.; m. at Shutesbury, 26 April 1826, CAROLINE WAILES. In 1850 Henry Allard was a farmer at DeRuyter, N.Y., ae 47, with Caroline ae 44, both b. Mass., and Caroline ae 1, b. N.Y. (p.297). This line is carried down in the Ancestral File.

   iii   ANDREW ALLARD, b. 13 March 1805 (IGI) or ca 21 Feb. 1805 (calc.); d. 30 Metropolitan Pl., Boston, 3 Dec. 1864 of heart disease, ae 59y 9m 10d, b. Halifax, Vt., a res. of Ashland, rec. both Boston [par. Isaac & Mary] (Mass. VR 176:185) and Ashland [par. Andrew & Lucinda] (Mass. VR 175:44); m. at Holliston, 23 Feb. 1832 (*VR* 168), CAMILLA EAMES, b. Holliston 18 Nov. 1807, dau. of Martin and Mary (Eames) Eames (*VR* 54). In 1850

Andrew was a farmer in Ashland, ae 45, b. Vt., with Camilla and the four youngest children (p.448).

Children, first rec. Holliston, others at home 1850: 1. *Henry Martin Allard*[7], b. Holliston 2 Jan. 1833 (*VR* 17). 2. *Abner Allard*, b. ca 1834. 2. *Albert A.* [*Allard*] *Whittemore*, b. Holliston 16 May 1837, "son of Andrew Allard and Camilla Allard, "an adopted son of Versal Whittemore" (*VR* 153). 3. *Charles Allard*, b. ca 1838. 4. *Ann M Allard*, b. ca 1840. 5. *Emely Allard*, b. ca 1843. 6. *Isaac W. Allard*, b. ca 1847.

iv ACHSAH ALLARD, b. 8 Aug. 1807; d. 1867 at Holliston (Mass. VR 205:125); m. at Hopkinton, 31 Aug. 1828 (*VR* 216), VERSAL WHITTEMORE of Brimfield. In 1850 he was a bootmaker at Holliston, ae 45, with Achsah ae 43, and [adopted] *Albert Whittemore*[7], ae 13, who was the son of Achsah's brother Andrew (see above).

v ORLIN ALLARD, b. 15 April 1809; d. Framingham 28 Feb. 1888 of paralysis, a farmer, b. Whitinsburg [*sic, prob. Whitingham, next to Halifax*], Vt., of Andrew & Lucinda, res. Southborough (Mass. VR 393:549); m. at Dudley 12 June 1831 after int. at Hopkinton 27 May 1831 (*VR* 216), SALLY WHITTEMORE of Dudley, b. Brookfield ca 1810. In 1840 they were in Jaffrey, N.H., both ae 30-40 with two boys under 5 and two girls ae 5-10 (p.33). In 1850 Alden [*sic*] Allard was a carpenter at Ashland, with Sarah and children Sarah A. ae 17, Mary F. ae 15, and Edmund B. ae 10 (p.435). In 1860 Orlin Allard was a book keeper in Ward 9, New York City, with Sarah and the same children, but ages are understated (10 yrs for both adults, 5 for Sarah); however, towns and states of birth were given (p.963), confirming the identity. In 1870 Orlin was a farmer in Oxford, ae 60, with Sarah ae 61 and son Edmund B.'s family (p.144). In 1880 they were in Southborough, with Sarah Pomeroy ae 47, widowed daughter (e.d.828).

Children (1860 census): 1. *Sarah Ann Allard*[7], b. 3 Oct. 1832, Hopkinton (*VR* 21, but 1860 census says b. Ashland); m. ___ Pomeroy. 2. *Mary F. Allard*, b. ca 1835 Ashland. 3. *Edmond Allard*, b. ca 1839 Jaffrey, N.H.; m. Susan ___, b. Pa.

vi SAMUEL R. ALLARD, b. 5 June 1811 Whitingham, Vt. (3rd m. rec.); d. after 1855; m. prob. (1) after int. at Greenfield, 14 April 1837 (*VR* 142), ELIZABETH SPEAR; m. (2) by 1842, MARY RUST, b. Chester 20 Aug. 1815, dau. of Joseph A. and Lovica (Bonner) Rust (*VR* 85, 177), d. Norwich 6 March 1853 of consumption (Mass. VR 76:18); m. (3) at Chicopee, 8 July 1853, LYDIA C. MAXWELL of Heath, ae 36, dau. of Benjamin and Mary (___) Maxwell (Mass. VR 69:369); poss. m. (4) ALICE ___. In 1850 he was at Norwich, ae 36, with wife Mary R., and children Mary L. ae 14, Sophia A. ae 7, William H. ae 5, Caroline ae 3, and Sarah ae 1m (p.52). He was called

Rev. at the birth of son William Henry at Chester, teacher at the birth of a son in 1846 and in 1850, and merchant at 3rd marriage. In 1860 Alice Allard ae 42 (female) was a farmer at Chester Village P.O., Huntington, head of a household that included Sophia ae 17 (teacher), William ae 15, Carrie ae 13, Harriet ae 1– [unclear], and Ada ae 5 (p.258). Hattie's m. rec. in 1870 (of Shelburne) says ae 28, b. Huntington, dau. of Samuel & Mary. No record found of deaths of Samuel, Lydia, Alice, or any of the children.

Children, first prob. with first wife; 2 - 7 with Mary; last with Lydia/Alice: 1. *Mary L. Allard²*, b. ca 1836; living 1850. 2. *Harriet Allard*, b. prob. ca 1841 (not at home 1850); m. at Huntington, 1870, J.A. Halligan (Mass. VR 227:81). 3. *Sophia A. Allard*, b. ca 1843; living 1860. 4. *William Henry Allard*, b. Chester 17 Sept. 1844 (*VR* 13); living 1860. 5. *[Son] Allard*, b. Chester 28 July 1846 (*VR* 13); d. prob. inf. 6. *Caroline Allard*, b. ca 1847; living 1860. 7. *Sarah Allard*, b. 1850; d. prob. before 1860. 8. *Ada Allard*, b. ca 1855; living 1860.

vii ESTHER G. ALLARD, b. 16 Oct. 1814; d. Ashland 27 Oct. 1877 ae 63y 0m 11d of congestion of lungs, b. Framingham of Andrew & Lucinda (Mass. VR 293:43); m. at Hopkinton, 18 Dec. 1832 (*Framingham VR* 229), HENRY J. DADMUN. In 1860 he was ae 53, a printer at Ashland with Esther ae 46; no children in the household (p.931).

viii LUCINDA ALLARD, b. 15 June 1815; m. 19 Oct. 1836 after int. 2 Oct. 1836 at Framingham (*VR* 228), EDWARD CLARK, b. 9 Jan. 1810, son of John and Mary (Dadmun) Clark; res. Framingham, Holliston, Ashland, Petersham, and finally Worcester in 1866 (*Hugh Clark Desc.*, 97, 164). In 1850 he was a market man in Ashland, with Lucinda and the six oldest children (p.448).

Clark children (all with b. dates in *Hugh Clark Desc.*, 164; first three rec. *Framingham VR*): 1. *Edward Franklin Clark⁷*, b. 7 Nov. 1837. 2. *Mary Jane Clark*, b. 5 Feb. 1839. 3. *David Brainard Clark*, b. 16 Nov. 1840; m. Mary Maria Haven. 4. *Alma Lucinda Clark*, b. 1 Nov. 1843; m. Royal C. Dickinson. 5. *Harriet Andrews Clark*, b. Holliston 20 April 1846 (*VR* 40); m. George R. Dickinson. 6. *John Eliot Clark*, b. 24 July 1848. 7. *Ellen Frances Clark*, b. 1 March 1851; d. 1 Sept. 1861. 8. *Alice Maria Clark*, b. 3 Aug. 1852. 9. *William Henry Clark*, b. 26 Aug. 1857.

ix NAHUM ALLARD, b. 15 June 1817.

x SARAH/SALLY ALLARD, b. 16 May 1818; m. CHARLES FINNEY.

xi MARY A[RADNEY] ALLARD, b. 15 June 1821; d. Northbridge 3 Aug. 1872, ae 51, b. Hopkinton, parents given only as "Allard" (Mass. VR 249:343); m. at Holliston, 12 October 1842 (*VR* 168), NELSON BATCHELLER, b. ca 1823. In 1860 he was a shoemaker at Northbridge with Mary ae 38 (p.743); in 1870 son George (a bootmaker) and his family shared the household and son Orrison was a "sole leather clerk" (p.44); in 1880 Nelson was a boarder in the home of his son George (e.d.858).

Batcheller children (census): 1. *George M. Batcheller⁷*, b. Northbridge 18 Feb. 1847 (Mass. VR 29:231); m. Imogene ___. 2. *Orrison J. Batcheller*, b. ca 1851. 3. *Marion V. Batcheller*, b. ca 1854. 4. *Willard F. Batcheller*, b. ca 1857.

xii ISAAC ALLARD, b. 30 March 1824 Hopkinton; d. Holliston 6 June 1845 ae 21y 2m 4d of consumption, a school teacher, "s. Andrew and Lucinda T." (*VR* 293).

Sources cited: *Chester VR. Framingham VR. Holliston VR. Hopkinton VR. Mendon VR.* Mass. Vital Records 1841-1910. Middlesex County Probate Records. Temple, *History of Framingham* (1887). John Clark, *Records of the descendants of Hugh Clark of Watertown, Mass., 1640 – 1866* (Boston: J. Clark, 1866). IGI, Ancestral File: *see* Bibliography. CENSUS: 1820 Hopkinton, Middlesex Co. (M33-51); 1840 Jaffrey, Cheshire Co., N.H. (M704-234); 1850 Norwich, Hampshire Co. (M432-320), Ashland, Holliston, & Hopkinton, Middlesex Co. (M432-326); 1860 Huntington, Hampshire Co. (M653-505), , & N.Y.C., Ward 9, Dist. 3 (M653-797); Northbridge, Worcester Co. 1860 (M653-531), 1870 (M593-655), & 1880 (T9-566).

625. JONAS THAYER⁵ (*Cornelius⁴, Elizabeth³ Samson, Stephen², Henry¹*), son of Cornelius Thayer [130] and his first wife Abigail Jones, was born 21 April 1750 at Bellingham (*VR* 64) and died probably in 1793 at Tyringham.

He married, but the name of his wife has not been learned.

Jonas Thair was a corporal in Capt. Andrew Lusk's company, Col. Brown's regiment, serving from 21 September to 13 October 1777, with the Northern army (*MSSR* 15:505).

On 16 May 1782 Jonas Thayer of Partridgefield, yeoman, sold land there to Phinehas Watkins; Oliver Watkins, one of the witnesses, attested it in January 1795 that it had been signed by "said Jonas who hath deceased" (Berkshire LR 35:37).

Jonas and his family settled in Pittsfield and joined the Shakers, living with them until his death (*Thayer Mem.*, 496). His brother Cornelius died at the Hancock Shaker community.

He is listed in the 1790 census in Tyringham as head of a household consisting of two men over 16, one boy, and two females (p.37). He was evidently alive on 24 April 1792 when he was named in the distribution of his father's estate (Worcester PR #A58648), but died before 1 October 1793 when William Clark of Tyringham was named guardian of Roswell Thayer, Abigail Thayer, Mary Thayer, and Anna Thayer, minor children of Jonas Thayer late of Tyringham, deceased, with Abel Allen fellow bondsman (Berkshire PR #1640).

On 2 August 1796 Jonathan Thayer of Partridgefield was appointed administrator of the estate of Jonas Thayer, late of Tyringham, giving bond with Nathaniel Tracy and Rufus Butts as sureties (Berkshire PR #1782). The inventory came to $77.14 and included no land; the estate was declared insolvent.

The only Thayers listed in any census in Tyringham are Jonas in 1790 and Mary in 1850 and 1860, noted below.

Children of Jonas Thayer, living 1 Oct. 1793 (Berkshire PR #1640):

i ROSWELL THAYER[6], b. ca 1772; "of Stanbridge, Canada" when he pub. m. int. 20 Dec. 1800 at Pittsfield with OLIVE PHINNEY (Sprague Ms), b. Mass. ca 1780 (census), d. 16 March 1859 (*Thayer Mem.*, 497). Roswell left the Shakers when he became of age, and settled at Pittsfield, then at Butternuts, N.Y. (*ibid.*). In 1850 Olive Thayer ae 70 was living in the household of Daniel and Charlotte Bacon at Paris, Oneida Co., N.Y. (p.190).

> Children (*Thayer Mem.*, 496-97): 1. *James Thayer[7]*, b. 6 Nov. 1800; m. Maria Thomas. 2. *Charlotte Thayer*, b. 1806; m. Daniel Bacon. 3. *Hiram Thayer*, b. 1810; m. Lydia Pratt. 4. *Cornelius Thayer*, b. 1812; m. Ruth Jacox. 5. *Simon Thayer*, b. 1814; d. 1817. 6. *Ann Maria Thayer*, b. 28 Nov. 1816; m. Jefferson Harrington. 7. *William Thayer*, b. 1818; m. Zerena Havens.

ii ABIGAIL THAYER.

iii MARY THAYER, b. ca 1778; d. after 1860 (not in Mass. VR). In 1850 (ae 71) and 1860 (ae 82) she was living at Tyringham in a Shaker community, in 1860 listed as "superannuated" (p.121; p.534).

iv ANNA THAYER.

Sources cited: *Bellingham VR.* Berkshire County Deeds and Probates. W. C. Sprague, Thayer Ms. *Thayer Memorial* (1874). CENSUS: Tyringham, Berkshire Co., 1790 (M637-4), 1850 (M432-306), 1860 (M653-488); 1850 Paris, Oneida Co., N.Y. (M432-562).

626. JONATHAN THAYER[5] (*Cornelius[4], Elizabeth[3] Samson, Stephen[2], Henry[1]*), son of Cornelius Thayer [130] and his first wife Abigail Jones, was born 7 April 1753 at Bellingham (*VR* 64). Capt. Jonathan Thayer, "Soldier of the Revolution," died 24 February 1827 at Lebanon, Madison County, N.Y., aged 74 years (g.s.).

He married, int. 30 --ember 1778 at Peru (*VR* 86), **MARTHA SMITH**, who died 12 February 1827 at Lebanon, N.Y., aged 68 years (g.s.). They are both buried in Lebanon Village Cemetery, with their son Jonathan. *Thayer Mem.* (p.498) says both died in January 1821.

In the Revolutionary War, Jonathan Thayer of Partridgefield [Peru] was a corporal in Capt. Nathan Watkins's company of Minute-men, which marched 22 April 1775 in response to the Lexington Alarm, and he served in the same company in Col. John Paterson's regiment several times later in 1775 (*MSSR* 15:541). In 1780 he was a sergeant (also given Lieutenant) in Capt. William Fletcher's company, Col. Simonds's regiment, marching to Pawlet [Vt.] in October of that year, and in October 1781 he served 10 days on a march to Stillwater [N.Y.] (*ibid.*, 542).

Jonathan Thayer of Partridgefield bought land there from Beriah Smith 29 October 1778; Rufus Butts and Cornelius Thayer Jr. were witnesses (Berkshire LR 21:396). Jonathan Thayer, gentleman, of Partridgefield, and wife Martha mortgaged land there 26 December 1781; the mortgage was discharged 25 August 1788 (*ibid.*, 21:405). On 16 September 1789, Cornelius Thayer and Jonathan Thayer of Partridgefield, gentlemen [evidently father and son], sold to Joseph Perry land in Partridgefield; their wives Abigail and Martha also signed (*ibid.*, 37:495).

The 1790 census listed him at Western (now Warren), with one man, three boys, and two females, near his father, Cornelius Thayer (p.242). His father died in October 1790 and Jonathan was appointed administrator of his estate (Worcester PR #A58648).

Jonathan Thayer and wife Martha of Western sold land there on 17 April 1792 to David Belcher of Thompson, Conn (Worcester LR 116:243. Jonathan was of Western, gentleman, when he bought 180 acres in Partridgefield on 12 May 1792 (*ibid.*, 38:469). He was of Partridgefield on 2 August 1796 when he was appointed administrator of the estate of his brother Jonas Thayer [#625]. On 23 September 1796 Jonathan Thayer of Partridgefield, gentleman, sold the north section of his farm there, bounded by land of Rufus Butts (*ibid.*, 40:385). On 6 January 1801, Jonathan Thair [*sic*], husbandman of Partridgefield, sold land there; Martha also signed, and witnesses were Rufus Butts and Patty Thayer; the deed was acknowledged 14 January 1801 (*ibid.*, 40:510).

Revolutionary Soldiers in Madison County, N.Y, says, "Capt. Jonathan Thayer came to Lebanon from Butternuts about 1800, settled on lot 61 and died there Feb. 24, 1827 aged 74. His wife Martha died there Feb. 12, 1827 aged 68 … had a son Jonathan Jr. and a grandson Sylvester, merchants of Lebanon …"

Children of Jonathan and Martha (Smith) Thayer, recorded Peru (*VR* 45-46):

i   JONATHAN THAYER Jr⁶, b. 9 Aug. 1782; d. Lebanon, N.Y., 20 May 1830 (g.s.); m. in 1807 CATHARINE BLAIR, b. Mass, d. Lebanon 23 Nov. 1853 ae 67, dau. of James Blair, Esq. (*Thayer Mem.*); both bur. Lebanon

Village Cem. He was "a Potash Maker, Post Master and Merchant ... sons Sylvester and Orin. Orin went west." (*Pioneer Settlers of Madison Co.,* 248).

Children (*Thayer Mem.,* 498): 1. *Sylvester Thayer*[7], b. 25 Feb. 1808; m. (1) Ruthena DeGrasse, d. 5 Aug. 1830, bur. Lebanon, N.Y. (g.s.); m. (2) Maria Emmons, (3) Electa/Eliza L. Redway. 2. *Caroline Thayer,* b. 26 June 1812; m. C.W. Sabin, in whose Lebanon household Catherine Thayer ae 64 was living 1850 (p.123). 3. *Orren Smith Thayer,* b. 16 April 1814. 4. *William Blair Thayer,* b. 19 Sept. 1820; m. Sophia Burchard.

ii PATTY THAYER, b. 5 Oct. 1784; witnessed father's deed in Jan. 1801.

iii ALANSON THAYER, b. 3 Aug. 1786; d. 21 Sept. 1848 ae 62; buried Earl-ville, N.Y. (*Pioneer Settlers of Madison Co.,* 248); m. 16 May 1816 JERUSHA BAKER, b. 25 May 1794, dau. of Solomon Baker (*Thayer Mem.,* 499).

Children (*ibid.,* 499-500): 1. *Harriet M. Thayer*[7], b. 27 Feb. 1818; m. Harlow Rogers. 2. *Orange W. Thayer,* b. 23 Feb. 1820; d. 2 March 1822. 3. *Charlotte A. Thayer,* b. 23 May 1823; m. Rufus A. Newton. 4. *Sylvester W. Thayer,* b. 4 Aug. 1825; m. Sarah M. Round. 5. *Giles G. Thayer,* b. 20 April 1828; m. Hannah Tillotson. 6. *Fairfax Thayer,* b. 16 Jan. 1834.

iv ISRAEL THAYER, b. 3 Dec. 1788; said to have d. Pulaski, Williams Co., Ohio, 28 June 1857; m. in Madison Co., N.Y., 1 Jan. 1812, SALLY LINSEY, b. ca 1792, d. 25 Oct. 1874 Le Sueur, Minn. Israel Thayer was a hatter at Lebanon, N.Y., 1815 (*Pioneer Settlers of Madison Co.,* 248). In 1850 he was a farmer in Montville, Ohio, near his brothers, listed as *Isaac* Thayer ae 61, with Sally ae 58, both b. Mass., Malvina ae 17 and William ae 14, both b. Ohio (p.304).

Children at home 1850: 1. *Malvina Thayer*[7], b. ca 1833. 2. *William Thayer,* b. 1836.

v ABIGAIL / NABBY THAYER, b. 22 Dec. 1790, "in Western" [Warren]; d. 11 April 1861.

vi BETSEY THAYER, b. 16 Feb. 1793; d. 15 Jan. 1839.

vii RUFUS THAYER, b. 24 Dec. 1794; m. 4 July 1813 SALLY NILES, b. ca 1799 N.Y. In 1850 he was a farmer ae 55 in Marathon, N.Y., with Sally ae 51, and children Mary ae 14, LeRoy ae 12, and Linus [?Lyman] ae 6 (p.226).

Children (*Thayer Mem.,* 500): 1. *Sally Thayer*[7], b. 10, d. 11 April 1814. 2. *William H. Thayer,* b. 6 Nov. 1815; m. Sarah Tarball. 3. *Electa Thayer,* b. 23 Aug. 1816; m. Giles Collins. 4. *Rufus Thayer,* b. 20 Feb. 1818; m. Joannah Tarball. 5. *Asahel Thayer,* b. 29 Nov., d. 6 Dec. 1819. 6. *Jonathan Thayer,* b. 4 Feb. 1821; d. 1 April 1825. 7. *Russell Thayer,* b. 8 Aug. 1822; m. Nancy Williams. 8. *Joel Langdon Thayer,* b. 8 Nov. 1823; m. Mary Ashcroft. 9. *Allen Thayer,* b. 16 Nov. 1825; d. 29 Jan. 1827. 10. *Sarah L. Thayer,* b. 17 Aug. 1827; m. George Isaacs. 11. *Clarissa Thayer,* b. 8 April 1829; d. 20 Sept. 1830. 12. *Wilford Alanson Thayer,* b. 3 May

1832; m. Jane Dutcher. 13. *Alberton Delos Thayer*, b. 22 March 1834. 14. *Mary Sophia Thayer*, b. 25 May 1836. 15. *Leroy Thayer*, b. 8 May 1838. 16. *Orlando Thayer*, b. 14 Sept. 1840; d. 1845. 17. *Lyman Niles Thayer*, b. 24 Sept. 1844.

viii RUSSEL THAYER, b. 2 Oct. 1796; d. 21 Nov. 1877 Medina, Ohio; m. 28 March 1821, BETSEY SMITH, b. 9 March 1801, dau. of Ithamar Smith (*Thayer Mem.*, 501). In 1850 he was a farmer in Montville, Medina Co., Ohio, with Betsey ae 50, Julia ae 21, Linas T. ae 18, and Harriet ae 12, listed on the same page with his brother Linas and brother-in-law John Hughs, and son Samuel M. Thayer (p.306).

Children (*Thayer Mem.*, 501): 1. *Samuel M. Thayer*[7], b. 21 Feb. 1823 N.Y.; m. Antoinette Clark. 2. *Julia Ann Thayer*, b. 9 Aug. 1824; d. 17 Feb. 1826. 3. *Julia M. Thayer*, b. 14 Aug. 1829; m. Linas L. Smith. 4. *Linas Smith Thayer*, b. 15 Sept. 1832; at home 1850; m. Charlotte J. Perkins. 5. *Mary C. Thayer*, b. 3 March 1835; d. 19 Sept. 1847. 6. *Harriet L. Thayer*, b. 17 July 1838; m. Thomas E. Rowe.

ix LINUS THAYER, b. 24 Feb. 1799; d. 23 April 1884; m. 10 Feb. 1825, MARY BILLINGS, b. 20 May 1800; no children (*Thayer Mem.*, 501-02). In 1850 he was a farmer in Montville, Ohio, with Mary ae 50, b. N.Y. (p.306).

x LUCY THAYER, b. 5 June 1802; d. 17 Nov. 1839; m. Jan. 1823, JOHN HEWES, b. 28 May 1798, d. 17 July 1872, son of Benjamin and Hannah (Gray) Hewes. He m. (2) Philura ___, b. ca 1802 Vt. In 1850 John Hughs [*sic*] was a farmer in Montville, Ohio, near his brothers-in-law Russel and Linas Thayer, with the seven youngest children (p.306).

Hughs/Hewes children (*Thayer Mem.*, 502), most at home 1850: 1. [*Daughter*] Hughs[7], d. inf. 2. *Elizabeth Hughs*, b. Jan. 1825; d. 1829. 3. *Hannah Hughs*, b. 3 Feb. 1827 N.Y. 4. *William Hughs*, b. Nov. 1829; d. 1851. 5. *Martha Hughs*, b. 29 Nov. 1831; d. 17 Jan. 1862. 6. *Lois Hughs*, b. 15 March 1833 Ohio; d. 30 May 1851. 7. *Jerusha Hughs*, b. 2 Jan. 1835; at home 1850. 8. *Alanson Hughs*, b. 7 May 1837; m. Mary Jane French. 9. *Lucy Ruthena Hughs*, b. 26 March 1839; at home 1850.

Sources cited: *Bellingham VR. Peru VR.* Berkshire County Deeds. Bracy, ed., *Pioneer Settlers of Madison County, N.Y.* (1984). *Rev. Soldiers of Madison County. Thayer Memorial* (1874). CENSUS: 1790 Western, Worcester Co. (M637-4); 1850 Quincy S. Ward, Adams Co., Ill. (M432-97), Marathon, Cortland Co., N.Y. (M432-493), Montville, Medina Co., Ohio (M432-709).

627. ABIGAIL THAYER[5] (*Cornelius*[4], *Elizabeth*[3] Samson, *Stephen*[2], *Henry*[1]), daughter of Cornelius Thayer [130] and his first wife Abigail Jones, was born 5 April 1755 at Bellingham (*VR* 62) and died 7 July 1814, aged 57, at Peru (*VR* 101), as "wife of Dea. Rufus Butts."

She married Capt. **RUFUS BUTTS**, who was born about 1755 at Canterbury, Conn. (DAR Lin. Bk 71:110), and died 13 February 1828 at Peru (*VR* 101), aged 73 (g.s.). She is named as Abigail Butts in the distribution of her father's estate dated 24 April 1792 (Worcester PR #A58648). Rufus married, second, intentions 25 October 1814 at Peru (*VR* 62), ABIGAIL (___) JACKSON of Hinsdale, who died 7 July 1832 at Hinsdale (*VR* 75), aged 66. She was perhaps the Mrs. Nabby Dickson whose marriage intentions with Joshua Jackson were published 8 December 1806 at Hinsdale (*VR* 52).

Rufus Butts served in the Revolution in 1777. His name is on a pay roll dated at Chesterfield 13 March 1777 as having marched to Ticonderoga with Capt. Benjamin Bonney's company, Col. Samuel Brewer's regiment to reinforce the Northern army. In July and August 1777 he served a total of 39 days in two Berkshire County companies, and in October 1781 he was a Sergeant in a detachment from Capt. Jonathan Thayer's co., Col. Barnes's regiment, which marched to Stillwater on an alarm (*MSSR* 2:974).

Rufus Butts of Coventry, Conn., bought land in Partridgefield 6 September 1775 and on 17 December 1796; and on 8 February 1797, as Rufus Butts of Partridgefield, gentleman, he bought more land there (Berkshire LR 19:451; 36:241; 59:192). Partridgefield was renamed Peru in 1807, and on 18 March 1809, Rufus Butts of Peru, gentleman, bought 15 acres there (*ibid.*, 49:229). On 13 January 1813 he sold land in Peru that had been deeded to him by Cornelius Thayer, now deceased, to Nathaniel Butts (*ibid.*, 54:688). He mortgaged land briefly in 1823, and on 8 March 1824 Rufus Butts of Peru, gentleman, and [second] wife Abigail sold land there to Lemuel Parsons (*ibid.*, 65:370; 67:121). He evidently moved to Canterbury, Conn., for on 26 March 1824 Rufus Butts of Canterbury, clothier, bought land in Hinsdale; on 21 October 1825 he was of Hinsdale, clothier, when he bought more land there (*ibid.*, 69:75, 77). On 8 February 1826 Rufus Butts of Hinsdale sold land there, including half the water from a dam to be built on his property (*ibid.*, 74:521).

There are no probate records for Rufus or Abigail in Berkshire County.

Children of Rufus and Abigail (Thayer) Butts, rec. Partridgefield/Peru (*VR* 17-18):

i   ABIGAIL BUTTS[6], b. 23 Dec. 1778; d. 14 Jan. 1779 (*VR* 101).

ii   ABIGAIL BUTTS, b. 15 May 1780; m., int. 18 April 1798 at Peru (*VR* 62) with STEVEN PAINE JR. No births of children rec. Peru, but *Lyman*, son of Stephen, d. there 29 May 1814 (*VR* 107).

iii RUFUS BUTTS, b. 2 Oct. 1781; d. 22 April 1808 at Peru (*VR* 101).

iv   POLLEY BUTTS, b. 22 Oct. 1783.

v NATHANIEL BUTTS, b. 9 Nov. 1785; d. Hinsdale 9 Jan. 1849 ae 63 of consumption (*VR* 75); m. POLLY PHILLIPS, b. Peru 26 Dec. 1791, d. Hinsdale 19 Oct. 1881 ae 89y 10m 3d, dau. of Smith and Lydia (____) Phillips (Mass. VR 328:37).

> Children, rec. Peru (*VR* 17-18, 101): 1. *Dilly Saphrona Butts*[7], b. 10 Nov. 1812; d. 8 Nov. 1830. 2. *Diantha Butts*, b. 20 July 1819. 3. *Mary Butts*, b. 18 March 1824; m. Phillip H. Sears. 4. *Lydia Leland Butts*, b. 31 March 1826; d. 22 Aug. 1842, ae 16.

vi DELIVERANCE BUTTS, b. 25 Sept. 1787; d. 4 Sept. 1807 Peru (*VR* 101).

vii JONATHAN BUTTS, b. 5 Feb. 1790; m. after int. 11 April 1813 at Peru (*VR* 62), LAURA MINOR, b. Peru 26 Dec. 1793 (*VR* 34, as *Lawry*), d. there 6 March 1865 ae 71y 3m, widowed, occ. "farmer's wife," dau. of Nathan and Dolly (Foot) Minor (Mass. VR 183:53).

> Children rec. Peru (*VR* 17-18, 101): 1. *Jonathan Averill Butts*[7], b. 6 Nov. 1814. 2. *Abigail Alzoa Butts*, b. 5 May 1817. 3. *Nathan Ozro Butts*, b. 5 Oct. 1819. 4. *Sarah Marie Butts*, b. 16 July 1822; d. 20 March 1841, ae 18. 5. *Rufus Marcellus Butts*, b. 11 Oct. 1825; d. 1 Jan. 1838, ae 12y 3m. 6. *Laura Butts*, b. 19 June 1828. 7. *Nelson Butts*, b. 4 Dec. 1831.

viii SARAH/SALLY BUTTS, b. 30 Jan. 1792; m. 13 May 1813 at Peru (*VR* 62), EBENEZER PHILLIPS.

> ***Phillips*** children rec. Peru (*VR* 38, 108): 1. *[Son] Phillips*[7] [twin?]. 2. *Smith Phillips*, "2d son" [twin?], b. 12 June 1813. 3. *Mary Ann Phillips*, b. 29 Dec. 1814. 4. *Mary Ann Phillips*, b. 25 March 1817. 5. *Lydia Isabel Phillips*, b. 31 July 1819; d. 29 Jan. 1839. 6. *Marilla Phillips*, b. 16 Nov. 1824; d. 2 Jan. 1839. 7. *Euphemia Phillips*, b. 17 March 1827. 8. *Ellen Louisa Phillips*, b. 18 May 1829.

ix DEBORAH BUTTS, b. 14 April 1794; m. 28 March 1813 at Peru (*VR* 62), WILLIAM MINOR, b. Peru 2 April 1792 (*VR* 34), son of Nathan and Dolly (Foot) Minor.

x LYDIA BUTTS, b. 25 July 1796.

Sources cited: *Bellingham VR. Hinsdale VR. Peru VR.* Berkshire County Deeds. Worcester County Probate Records. Gravestones from "Tombstone Inscriptions of Peru," Mss, Berkshire Athenaeum, Pittsfield. *Mass. Soldiers & Sailors.* CENSUS: 1850 Hinsdale, Berkshire Co. (M432-305).

628. CORNELIUS THAYER[5] (*Cornelius*[4], *Elizabeth*[3] *Samson, Stephen*[2], *Henry*[1]), son of Cornelius Thayer [130] and his first wife Abigail Jones, was born 27 May 1757 at Bellingham (*VR* 63). He died at the Shaker Community in Hancock 21 May 1813 aged 56 yrs (Shaker deaths, Cook Coll.).

He was "of Watertown, Conn.," when he married (Sprague Ms), **ASENATH BRADLEY**, who was born at New Haven, Conn., 15 September 1755 and baptized there 19 October 1755, daughter of Phinehas and Martha (Sherman) Bradley (*Fam. of Anc. New Haven*, 2:267). "Corn[s] Thare" served with his brothers Amos and Jonathan, marching on the expedition to Bennington, Vt., in August 1777 (*MSSR* 15:506). In 1779 Cornelius Thayer had a loss in the British raid on New Haven (Sprague Ms, citing *Conn. in Rev.*).

Asenath is named in the will of her father, dated 2 August 1777, proved 5 March 1781, as daughter Asenath, but she is called Asenath Thare in a distribution on 3 April 1782 (Conn. PR, New Haven Dist. #1749). On 8 April 1782, Phineas Bradley, John Hubbard and wife Martha, Elisha Gilbert and wife Sarah, all of New Haven, Zina Bradley of Watertown, and Cornelius Thayer and wife Asenath of Watertown, for £45 quitclaimed to "our brother Erastus Bradley" of New Haven, their rights in the house and barn in New Haven that had belonged to "our Hon'rd father Mr Phin[eas] Bradley Dec'd where he dwelt"; the Thayers were not among the grantors who acknowledged the deed (New Haven LR 39:484). On 17 March 1783, Lot Osborn of Watertown sold to Asenath, wife of Cornelius Thayer, of the same place, for £8, half an acre there (Watertown LR 2:75). On 20 November 1783, Zina Bradley of Litchfield and Cornelius and Asenath Thayer of Watertown signed a quitclaim to Erastus Bradley, evidently completing their part of the transaction above (New Haven LR 39:484-85). Then, on 13 July 1784, acknowledged the same day, Cornelius Thayer and wife Asenath sold to Aner Bradley, all of Watertown, for £100 [*sic*], the half-acre purchased a year earlier (Watertown LR 2:347).

Cornelius Thayer was listed in 1790 in Woodbury, Conn., one man with two boys under 16 and three females (*Heads of Fam.*, 79). He is named in a distribution of his father's estate dated 24 April 1792. The family has not been located in 1800; no further record of them has been found until 1813, when Cornelius died.

Census figures suggest two sons and two daughters born between 1780 and 1790, but none have been identified.

Sources cited: *Bellingham VR. Mass. Soldiers & Sailors.* New Haven, Conn., District Probate Records. New Haven and Watertown, Conn., Deeds. Sprague, Thayer Manuscript. D. L. Jacobus, *Families of Ancient New Haven*, Vol. 2 (Rome, N.Y., 1924). CENSUS: *Heads of Families 1790 – Conn*

629.   AMOS THAYER[5] (*Cornelius*[4], *Elizabeth*[3] *Samson, Stephen*[2], *Henry*[1]), son of Cornelius Thayer [130] and his first wife Abigail Jones, was born 16 March 1760 at Bellingham (*VR* 63), and died in 1833 at Albany, N.Y., where he was a jeweler (*Thayer Mem.*, 502).

He married in Massachusetts in 1783 **LUCY BACON PIERCE** (*ibid.*; rec. not found). She was born about 1763 and died 25 October 1817 in her 54th year, as "Lucy Thayer, wife of Amos Sr.," and was buried in the First Presbyterian Church Cemetery, Albany, N.Y. (Albany Cem. Recs.). That burial ground was among several removed to Albany Rural and other cemeteries in 1866, and the stones were recorded at that time.

During the Revolutionary War, Amos Thair entered service 17 July 1777 and served 13 days in Capt. William Clark's company, Col. Benjamin Simonds' regiment, marching from Gageborough to Manchester by order of Gen. Schuyler on an alarm. As Amos Thare he served with his brother Cornelius in Capt. William Fletcher's company, Col. Benjamin Simonds' regiment on a seven-day expedition to Bennington, Vt., in August 1777 (*MSSR* 15:506), and from 21 September to 13 October 1777 in Capt. Andrew Lusk's company, Col. John Brown's regiment, 23 days with the Northern Army (*ibid.*, 504). He was probably the Amos Thare, private in Capt. Daniel Brown's company, commanded by Lieut. William White, Col. Miles Powell's (Berkshire Co.) regiment, from 23 July 1779 to 1 September 1779, discharged at New Haven, Conn. (*ibid.*, 506).

In 1790 Amos was living at Partridgefield [later Peru], with three boys under 16 and two females (p.486). He shared in a distribution of his father's estate dated 24 April 1792. On 24 March 1795, Jason Watkins and John Fisk Jr., both of Partridgefield, each mortgaged 60 acres there to Amos Thayer of Partridgefield, yeoman (Berkshire LR 35:175, 36:232).

In 1800 Amos Thayer was listed in Ward 1, Albany, N.Y., aged 26-45, with a household consisting of a woman the same age, two boys 10-16, and two boys under 10 (p.131). In 1810 an Amos Thayer was again listed in Albany, but the figures (one woman over 45, two men and one woman 16-26, one boy 10-16, and one boy under 10) suggest that this was the household of Amos Jr., with his mother, but not his father, living there (p.40).

Lucy Thayer, wife of Amos, was admitted a member of the First Presbyterian Church of Albany on 17 July 1812 (*Church History*, on line).

The 1820 census lists Amos Thayer in Albany, over 45, with a household consisting of a woman the same age, one boy and three girls under 10, and one boy and one girl 10-16 (p.105). The younger children could not have been Lucy's if her age at death is correct. There are no land records for Amos Thayer in Albany County, N.Y.

Children of Amos and Lucy Bacon (Pierce) Thayer (*Thayer Mem.*, 502):

i   AMOS THAYER[6], b. July 1784; d. 1842; m. (1) 1807, MARY CHAMBERS, d. 1817; m. (2) 26 Dec. 1819, HARRIET SCHERMERHORN. He was a "jeweler, steam pump builder, and inventor of the city waters works of Philadelphia" (*Thayer Mem.*, 502). In 1850 Harriet Thayer ae 53, b. N.Y., was head of a household in Schenectady, N.Y., with Mary ae 30, Benjamin ae 17, and Charles ae 13 (p.166).

Children (*Thayer Mem.*, 502), with first wife: 1. *John Chambers Thayer*[7], b. 23 March 1809; m. Sarah Schermerhorn. 2. *Emeline Thayer*, b. 1811. 3. *Mary Ann Thayer*, b. 1813; unm. 1850. 4. *Joseph Thayer*, b. 1815. Children with second wife: 5. *William Henry Thayer*, b. 1 Jan. 1821; m. Susan Lord. 6. *George Washington Thayer*, b. 22 July 1829. 7. *Benjamin Franklin Thayer*, b. 21 April 1831. 8. *Charles Webster Thayer*, b. 17 Feb. 1833.

ii   JAMES THAYER, b. 29 April 1787; d. 25 Aug. 1861; m. 16 July 1810, FANNY MAINE of Plainfield, Otsego Co., N.Y., b. 3 Jan. 1792 Conn., d. 23 March 1856 (*Thayer Mem.*, 503). In 1850 he was a farmer at Ellisburg, N.Y., with wife Fanny, sharing the household of son Lewis ae 34 (p.342).

Children (*Thayer Mem.*, 503-04): 1. *Joseph McCheney Thayer*[7], b. 21 Dec. 1813; m. Mary Ann Smith. 2. *Lewis Maine Thayer*, b. 7 Sept. 1815; m. Rhoda Penny. 3. *Maryette Thayer*, b. 8 Oct. 1817; m. Lovius Fillmore. 4. *Lucy Bacon Thayer*, b. 27 Dec. 1819; m. Terry Fillmore. 5. *Zurial Campbell Thayer*, b. 18 Sept. 1822; m. Lucy Baker. 6. *Benjamin Franklin Thayer*, b. 1 Feb. 1824; m. Lovina Baker. 7. *James LaFrance Thayer*, b. 23 Jan. 1831; d. 5 Dec. 1856. 8. [adopted] *Maryline W. Thayer*[7], b. ca 1816.

iii JOSEPH THAYER (twin), b. 1788; d. young.

iv   [DAUGHTER] THAYER (twin), b. 1788; d. young.

v   BENJAMIN THAYER (twin), b. 1791; d. 1829; m. First Presby. Ch., Albany, 24 Jan. 1812, ISABELLA DOUGLASS (*Early Settlers of NY*, 2:35), prob. dau. of Thomas and Hannah (___) Douglas. Hannah Douglass, 70, relict of the late Thomas, d. in Albany 30 Jan. 1831 and her funeral was held from the home of Mrs. Isabella Thayer, 62 Ferry St. (Bowman, *Eastern N.Y. VRs*, #2625). Benjamin Thayer bought Lots 7 and 8, Ferry St., "near the lower ferry," in Albany 21 July 1827 from Daniel Bradt, attorney for Benjamin Bradt and his wife Margaret (Albany Co. LR 32:74). Isabella Thayer, widow, was given administration on the estate of Benjamin Thayer late of the city of Albany, deceased, on 29 Sept. 1829 (Albany Co. L/Adm., 5:193).

Possible child: 1. *Cornelius Thayer*[7], b. ca 1814, a farmer ae 36 in Morris, Otsego Co., N.Y., 1850 (p.260) with wife Ruth and children Andrew, Eliza J., and Isabella.

vi   [DAUGHTER] THAYER (twin), b. 1791; d. young.

vii EZRA JONES THAYER, b. 1793; d. 1826; m. ca 1820, RACHEL SPRINGSTEAD, d. Sept. 1840; res. Albany (*Thayer Mem.*, 504).

Children (*ibid.*): 1. *Mary Isabel Thayer[7]*, b. 1821; m. Orrister Burbanks. 2. *Amos Leonard Thayer* [M.D.], b. 27 Jan. 1824; m. Emeline Thurber.

viii BACON THAYER, b. 1796; d. ca 1803, ae 7y.

Sources cited: *Bellingham VR.* Albany County Deeds and Probate Records. *History of the First Presbyterian Church of Albany* (1877). Albany cemetery records on line. *Mass. Soldiers & Sailors.* Foley, *Early Settlers of New York. Thayer Memorial* (1874). CENSUS: *Heads of Families 1790 – Mass.*; Albany, Albany Co., N.Y., Ward 1, 1800 (M32-22), 1810 (M252-26), & 1820 (M33-63); 1850 N.Y.: Ellisburg, Jefferson Co. (M432-516), Morris, Otsego Co. (M432-580), Schenectady, Schenectady Co. (M432-594).

630. HANNAH THAYER[5] (*Cornelius[4], Elizabeth[3] Samson, Stephen[2], Henry[1]*), daughter of Cornelius Thayer [130] and his first wife Abigail Jones, was born 10 January 1763 at Sandisfield (*VR* 71). She was living in April 1792 when she shared in a distribution of her father's estate, named as Hannah Lincoln (Worcester PR #A58648). She married by 1792, _____ **LINCOLN**, who has not been identified.

Sources cited: *Sandisfield VR.* Worcester County Probate Records.

631. ELIZABETH THAYER[5] (*Cornelius[4], Elizabeth[3] Samson, Stephen[2], Henry[1]*), daughter of Cornelius Thayer [130] and his first wife Abigail Jones, was born at Sandisfield 13 February 1765 (*VR* 71). She was living in April 1792 when she shared in a distribution of her father's estate, named as Elizabeth Thompson (Worcester PR #A58648). She married by 1792, _____ **THOMPSON**, who has not been identified.

Sources cited: *Sandisfield VR.* Worcester County Probate Records.

632. ELEANOR THAYER[5] (*Cornelius[4], Elizabeth[3] Samson, Stephen[2], Henry[1]*), daughter of Cornelius Thayer [130] and probably his second wife Abigail Belcher, was born probably at Sandisfield or Partridgefield [Peru], before 1774. As Eleanor Thayer she shared in a distribution of her father's estate dated 24 April 1792 (Worcester PR #58648).

Eleanor Thayer published marriage intentions at Peru 26 January 1795 (*VR* 63) with **ZURIEL CAMPBELL** of Burlington, N.Y. Various census records indicate that he was born between 1755 and 1774 in Connecticut, and Eleanor was perhaps his second wife. He died probably at Plainfield, N.Y., in 1826, between 11 March when he made his will, and 14 April when it was proved (Otsego Co., N.Y., Wills G-43). He *may* be the Zuriel Campbell born at Mansfield, Conn., 6 December 1767, son of Zuriel and Lydia (Barrows) Campbell.

In 1800 Zurial Campbell was listed in Plainfield, N.Y., with a household consisting of a man and a woman 26-45, one young man 16-26, one boy 10-16, and one little boy and two little girls under 10 (p.673). Given the marriage date for Zuriel and Eleanor, only the children under 10 could be hers and some of those might be with his earlier wife. In 1810 the household of Z. Campbell in Plainfield consisted of one man and one woman 26-45, one young man 16-26, one boy and one girl 10-16, and two boys and two girls under 10 (p.119).

On 5 January 1818 Zerual Campbell of Plainfield purchased from Levi Carpenter, Jr., Henry Clark, Jr., and Oliver Brown, for $640, part of lot no. 31 in the "pattent of land granted to Leo Lespenard and others ... beginning at the east line of said lot in the center of the turnpike road ... Round an acre of land owned by said Campbell ... 40 acres more or less" (Otsego Co. LR Z-9). In 1820 Zuriel (indexed as *Luriel*) Campbell and his wife were 45 or older, and had with them one man 26-45, one young man 16-18, two young women 16-26, one boy and two girls 10-16, and two little boys under 10 (p.174).

In his will dated 11 March 1826, Zeriel Campbell of Plainfield left to his beloved wife Eleanor one-third of the estate during her widowhood, and "to my daughter Electy as she has been of great service to my family ... one-third more than any other of my sons and daughters providing she shall not call on the estate for her services but if she calls then she is to have only [$5] more ... Richard Campbell my son and James Thayer and John Hoxie of Brookfield" to be executors.

On 1 February 1834 John Hoxie and James Thayer, "surviving executors of Zuriel Campbell late of the Town of Plainfield in the County of Otsego deceased," applied to the Otsego County Surrogate for "aid in the final settlement of their accounts ... and did then and there produce receipts in full from all the heirs and Leatees of said Zuriel Campbell deceased ..." Receipts were proved by the oath of George W. Campbell, one of the heirs, who also stated that "each of the heirs and legatees was over the age of twenty one years at the time of the execution of said receipt ... producing a paper signed by Enoch T. Campbell, Geo. W. Campbell, Electa Campbell, Charles Church and Emeline his wife the heirs of said deceased" (Otsego Co. Surrogate's File and 2:360).

On 2 June 1843 Electa Campbell of the town of Plainfield, and Enoch T. Campbell and George W. Campbell of the town of Belvidere, county of Winnebago [later Boone], Illinois, by Electa Campbell of Plainfield their attorney, sold to Noyes Stillman of Plainfield for $285, part of lot no. 33 in the Leonard Lespenard patent, adjoining William Bassett, it being 14 acres, 2 roods, and 35 rods of land with all hereditaments and appurtenances (Otsego Co. LR 73:344).

Children of Zuriel and Eleanor (Thayer) Campbell; prob. incomplete; prob. all b. Plainfield, Otsego Co., N.Y.:

i RICHARD CAMPBELL[6], b. prob. ca 1795; d. between 1826 when named executor of father's will, and 1834.

ii ELECTA CAMPBELL, b. 1800; d. 1871. (g.s.). After selling the land in Plainfield, she lived with her brother George in Belvidere, Ill., where she was listed in 1870 as a seamstress.

iii EMELINE CAMPBELL, b. ca 1807; m. CHARLES CHURCH, b. ca 1803 N.Y. In 1850 he was a physician in Guilford, Winnebago Co., Ill., with Emeline ae 43, and four children (p.369).
   Church children at home 1850, all b. N.Y.: 1. *Richard Church[7]*, b. ca 1828. 2. *Charles Church*, b. ca 1835. 3. *Alanson Church*, b. ca 1837. 4. *Emma Church*, b. ca 1841.

iv ENOCH THAYER CAMPBELL, b. 1811; d. 31 March 1843 ae 32 (g.s.); m. JANE DERTHICK, b. 11 Feb. 1811 Richfield Springs, N.Y., d. 14 Feb. 1892 Belvedere, Ill. (*Belvidere Cem.* 106, 178). She m. (2) William Reed. Enoch T. Campbell is called "Dr." in death recs.
   Children: 1. *Elizabeth Stuart Campbell[7]*, b. 4 Oct. 1837. 2. *Jane Campbell*, b. 14 Nov. 1839. 3. *Zuriel T. Campbell*, b. 2 Dec. 1842; d. 9 July 1843 (*ibid.*, 26).

v GEORGE W. CAMPBELL, b. ca 1813; d. after 1880; m. (1) 7 Sept. 1843 in N.Y., CORNELIA MARSH, b. 2 Aug. 1816 (calc.), d. 22 April 1866, dau. of Alpheus and Sophia (___) Marsh, bur. Davis Cem., Belvidere, Ill. (all her data, *Belv. Cem.*, 35); m. (2) after 1866, CHARITY (___) ____, b. ca 1837 Michigan. Cornelia's obit. says she was from Plainfield, N.Y., gives date of m., and says she left her husband, one daughter, an aged father and four sisters (*ibid.*). In 1850 George was ae 37, head of a household at Belvidere, Ill., with Cornelia ae 33, Helen S. ae 5, b. Ill., [his sister] Electa ae 46, and Albert Kitchel ae 14, b. Ohio (p.16). In 1870 Geo. Campbell ae 57, was a farmer in Belvedere with wife Charity ae 37, b. Mich.; sister Electa ae 68, a seamstress; and dau. Mary ae 9m (p.315). In 1880 the household included a son and two daus. who were prob. Charity's by an earlier marriage, although listed as Campbells: Nettie ae 25, a nurse, William ae 23, and Lydia ae 20; three new children for George and Charity had been added (p.21).
   Child with first wife: 1. *Helen Campbell[7]*, b. ca 1845; at home 1850. Children with second wife, all living 1880: 2. *Mary Campbell*, b. 1869. 3. *George Campbell* (twin), b. ca 1872. 4. *Georgette Campbell* (twin), b. ca 1872. 5. *Frank Campbell*, b. ca 1875.

Sources cited: *Peru VR.* Otsego County, N.Y., Surrogate's Records at Cooperstown, N.Y. W. C. Sprague, Thayer Ms. *Thayer Memorial* (1874). *Belvidere Cemeteries 1836-1900* (1988). *Derthicks and*

Related Derricks (1986). CENSUS: *Heads of Families 1790*; Plainfield, Otsego Co., N.Y., 1800 (M32-25), 1810 (M252-34), 1820 (M33-74); Belvidere, Boone Co., Ill., 1850 (M432-189), 1870 (M593-189), 1880 (T9-176, e.d. 1); 1850 Guilford, Winnebago Co., Ill. (M432-134).

633.   EZRA THAYER[5] (*Cornelius*[4], *Elizabeth*[3] *Samson, Stephen*[2], *Henry*[1]), son of Cornelius Thayer [130] and probably his second wife Abigail Belcher, was born probably at Sandisfield or Partridgefield (later Peru) about 1775.

He married at the Reformed Dutch Church of Albany, N.Y., 25 January 1802, **JANE DOUGLAS** (*First Ref. Church Rec.*, 8:12), perhaps the daughter of Thomas and Hannah (_____) Douglas. Hannah Douglass, 70, relict of the late Thomas, died in Albany 30 January 1831 and her funeral was held from the home of Mrs. Isabella Thayer, 62 Ferry Street (Bowman, *Eastern N.Y. VRs*, #2625). (Isabella Douglass and Benjamin Thayer were married 24 January 1812, First Presbyterian Church, Albany [*Early Settlers of NY*, 2:35]; Benjamin may be Ezra's nephew of that name, and Jane and Isabella were perhaps sisters.)

On 26 April 1791 Jonathan Thayer was appointed guardian of Ezra Thayer, aged 16, son of Cornelius Thayer of Western, deceased; John Patrick and Samuel Blair were fellow bondsmen (Worcester PR #58673).

Ezra was named in a distribution of his father's estate dated 24 April 1792 (*ibid.*, #58648). In 1810 Ezra Thayer was head of a household in Albany consisting of one man over 45, one man and one woman 26-45, one woman 16-26, one boy 10-16, and two boys under 10 (p.64). In 1820 he was over 45, with wife the same age, one young man 16-18, two boys 10-16, and one boy and three girls under 10 (p.204).

He is probably the Ezra Thayer who on 5 January 1828 bought Lot 77, on the south side of the Albany-Schenectady Turnpike, from Thomas Herring and wife Lucy (Albany Co. LR 28:509). On 9 February 1829 this land, along with a lot on the corner of South Pearl and Hamilton Streets in Albany, was sold by sheriff's order to Eli Perry (*ibid.*, 31:132-33, 37:361). The time of that sale coincides with the death of Ezra's son Thomas, noted below, but the circumstances are not known.

Children of Ezra and Jane (Douglas) Thayer (*Thayer Mem.*, 505):

i   CORNELIUS THAYER[6].

ii   SARAH MARIA / SALLY THAYER, m. at Albany, N.Y., 15 Sept. 1831, by Rev. Meyer, GILBERT VANDENBURGH; all of Albany (Bowman, #9026, from *Albany Argus*); settled Albany or Troy, N.Y. (*Thayer Mem.*,

505). The only Gilbert Vandenburgh found in 1850 census was a carter in Albany, ae 42, with wife *Esther* ae 33 (p.166).

iii THOMAS DOUGLAS THAYER, d. Troy, N.Y., possibly the Thomas Thayer, son of Ezra, "d. recently … funeral held from his parents' home on the Schenectady Turnpike," noted in *Albany Argus* of 6 Feb. 1829 (Bowman, #8610). *Thayer Mem.* (p.505), however, says he m., was a harness maker, res. Troy, and d. ca 1867; not found in census.

iv ABIGAIL THAYER.

v DANIEL JONES THAYER, b. 11 Nov. 1815; m. 17 Sept. 1837, ANN SMITH of Troy; res. Amsterdam, then Rochester, N.Y., a butcher and dealer in cattle (*Thayer Mem.*, 505). In 1850 he was a butcher in Rochester with Ann ae 30, and children Ellen, Mary, Cornelius, and Lucianna (p.445).

   Children (*ibid.*): 1. *Ellen Jones Thayer*, b. 2 Oct. 1839. 2. *Mary Douglass Thayer*, b. 2 July 1843. 3. *Cornelius Thayer*, b. 13 Oct. 1844. 4. *Louisiana [Lucianna] Thayer*, b. 24 Aug. 1847. 5. *Susan Thayer*, b. 9 Feb. 1853; d. 27 Jan. 1855.

vi ELIZABETH THAYER, d. young (*ibid.*).

Sources cited: Worcester County Probate Records. *Records of the Reformed Dutch Church of Albany, New York* (1978). Albany County Deeds. Bowman, *10,000 Vital Records of Eastern New York 1777-1834* (1987). Foley, ed., *Early Settlers of New York State. Thayer Memorial* (1874). CENSUS: *Heads of Families 1790 – Mass.*; 1850 N.Y., Paris, Oneida Co. (M432-562), Ward 9 Rochester, Monroe Co. (M432-531), Ward 4 Schenectady, Schenectady Co. (M432-594).

634. NATHANIEL WIGHT[5] (*Sarah Thayer*[4], *Elizabeth*[3] *Samson, Stephen*[2], *Henry*[1]), son of Benoni Wight and his wife Sarah Thayer [131], was born 20 August 1753 at Wrentham (*VR* 223) and died 11 October 1832 at Barnard, Vt. (*Barnard History*, 2:427).

He married 9 March 1775 at Wrentham (*VR* 398), **MEHETABEL FULLER** of Wrentham, who died in February 1822 at Barnard, Vt. (*Barnard History*, 2:427).

Nathaniel served in the Revolution, enlisting for eight months before the Battle of Bunker Hill. In May 1775 he was replaced by his brother Jabez (*Wight Gen.*, 75).

As the oldest son, Nathaniel received his father's estate in 1778, and was directed to pay sums of money to his brothers and sisters (Suffolk PR # 15839). On 28 April 1796 he was named in the will of Sarah Wight of Wrentham, spinster, as cousin Nathaniel Wight (Norfolk PR # 20295).

This family moved to Barnard, Vt., in 1788. On 14 March 1833, Benoni Wight was appointed administrator of the estate of his father Nathaniel Wight, late of Barnard. The estate was insolvent and real estate was sold to pay the claimants, who included Rhoda Wight and Benoni Wight (Windsor Co., Hartford Dist. PR 11:33, 119).

Children of Nathaniel and Mehitable (Fuller) Wight, first three rec. Wrentham (*VR* 222-23), last two born Barnard, Vt. (*Barnard History*, 2:429):

    i   BENONI WIGHT[6], b. 20 Jan. 1776; d. 27 Feb. 1847 at Barnard, ae 71; m. at Barnard, 25 Sept. 1803, BRIDGET (NORRIS) BROCKAWAY, b. Cornish, Conn. ca May 1775, d. Barnard 3 Jan. 1867, ae 91y 7m, dau. of John and Mary (Ela) Norris (*Barnard History*, 2:429). Benoni lived on his parents' homestead (*ibid.*). In 1850 Bridget Wight, ae 74, was living in the household of Heman and Charlotte Gifford at Barnard (p.415).

        Children (*Barnard History*, 2:429): 1. *Lucy Wight[7]*, b. 17 Oct. 1804; m. Willard D. Crowell. 2. *Willard Wight*, b. 17 Oct. 1806; m. Mandana Gifford. 3. *Don Carlos Wight*, b. 12 Aug. 1810; m. Huldah Sessions. 4. *Mary Elizabeth Wight*, b. 6 May 1812; d. Barnard 6 Feb. 1814. 5. *Billings Wight*, b. 3 May 1814; d.y. 6. *Collins Wight*, b. 3 May 1815; m. Martha Jane Connover. 7. *Charlotte Wight*, b. 20 June 1816; m. Heman Gifford.

    ii   LUCY WIGHT, b. 30 Nov. 1777; d. 4 Aug. 1778 Wrentham (*VR* 515).

    iii JERUSHA WIGHT, b. 17 Oct. 1779; d. prob. by 1832.

    iv RHODA WIGHT, b. 20 April 1785 Barnard, Vt.; d. there 24 June 1857, unm. In 1850 she was ae 63, in the poor house, Barnard, the reason "ill health" (p.415).

    v   BETSEY WIGHT, b. 1 Sept. 1787 Barnard, Vt.; m. in 1812 ROBERT RAY "of Georgetown, Vt." (*Wight Gen.*, 141), a place not found. A Robert Ray was in Milton, Vt., 1820 with five children under 10 and three 10-16 (p.546), figures not consistent with marriage date.

Sources cited: *Wrentham VR.* Norfolk County Probate Records. Windsor County, Vt. Probate Records, Hartford District. *History of Barnard, Vermont* (1928). D. P. Wright, *The Wight Family Memoir of Thomas Wight of Dedham, Mass....* (1848). CENSUS: 1820 Milton, Chittenden Co., Vt. (M33-127; 1850 Barnard, Windsor Co., Vt. (M432-931).

635.   DAVID WIGHT[5] (*Sarah Thayer[4], Elizabeth[3] Samson, Stephen[2], Henry[1]*), son of Benoni Wight and his wife Sarah Thayer [131], was born 25 March 1761 at Wrentham (*VR* 222). He died 6 February 1829 at Barnard, Vt., aged 67 (*Barnard History* 2:428-29).

He married, first, 12 June 1792 at Barnard, Vt. (*ibid.;* VR say David *White*), **PATTY CHEEDLE**, daughter of John and Patience (_____) Cheedle.

He married, second, at Barnard, **POLLY D____** [perhaps DAY], who was born ca 1767 at Sutton, N.H., and died 26 July 1850 at Lawrence, Mass., aged 84 years (Mass. VR 48:116).

On 28 April 1796 David was named in the will of Sarah Wight of Wrentham, spinster, as "cousin David Wight" (Norfolk PR # 20295).

On 25 April 1829 a citation was issued to Daniel D. Wight, minor heir, over 14, of David Wight late of Barnard, deceased, and on 6 May 1829 Daniel chose [his older brother] David Wight of Barnard as his guardian (Windsor Co., Hartford Dist. PR 10:101).

Children of David and Patty (Cheedle) Wight, born Barnard, Vt. (*Barnard History* 2:428-29):

i   ANNA WIGHT⁶, b. 22 Sept. 1792.

ii RUTH WIGHT, b. 31 Dec. 1793; d.y.

iii DAVID WIGHT, b. 18 March 1796; d.y.

iv ASA WIGHT, b. 20 July 1797.

v   WELLS WIGHT, b. 29 April 1799.

vi POLLY WIGHT, b. 10 Jan. 1804; d. Barnard 6 Sept. 1884, unmarried.

vii DAVID WIGHT, b. 8 Jan. 1807; d. Barnard 14 Oct. 1889; m. at Barnard 8 Feb. 1846, MARTHA HUNTOON, b. ca 1848, d. 29 March 1888. In 1850 he was a farmer ae 43 at Barnard, with Martha ae 39, and a 4-month-old dau. (p.412).

    Children, first two b. and d. Barnard, 3ʳᵈ from census: 1. *Martha Jane Wight⁷*, b. ca 1848; d. 28 April 1849. 2. *David C. Wight* [twin?], b. ca 1850; d. 4 April 1850. 3. *Harriet E. Wight* [twin?], b. 1850.

viii RUTH WIGHT, b. 12 Aug. 1811; m. SAMUEL DAY.

ix DANIEL DAVIS WIGHT, b. 30 Oct. 1814; living 1829 (guardianship).

Sources cited: *Wrentham VR.* Barnard VR. *History of Barnard* (1928). Norfolk County Probate Records at Dedham. Vermont Probates, Hartford District, at Woodstock, Vt. CENSUS: 1850 Barnard, Windsor Co., Vt. (M432-931). **See also:** D. P. Wright, *The Wight Family Memoir of Thomas Wight of Dedham, Mass.* ...(1848).

636.   RUTH WIGHT[5] (*Sarah Thayer⁴, Elizabeth³ Samson, Stephen², Henry¹*), daughter of Benoni Wight and his wife Sarah Thayer [131], was born 17 October 1765 at Wrentham (*VR* 223), and died 17 March 1858 at Barnard, Vt., aged 92y 5m (*Barnard History* 2:171).

She married, 12 March 1805 at Barnard, Vt., as his second wife, "both of Barnard," **SETH DEAN**, who was born 3 October 1755 at Hardwick (*VR* 35; *Hardwick History*, 360), son of Paul and Mary (Whitcomb) Dean, and died 22 November 1851 at Barnard, Vt., aged 96y 1m 19d (*Barnard History*, 2:171). He married, first, 3 June 1782, MOLLY BICKNELL, who died at Barnard 9 September 1802, aged 39. Seth and Molly had Paul, Amos, Seth, and Asa Dean, who are not Henry Samson descendants.

Seth Dean served in the Revolution and was pensioned (File #W5262). In 1850 Seth, aged 94, farmer, and Ruth aged 84, were living in the household of his son Paul Dean at Barnard (p.403).

There is no evidence that Seth and Ruth had children.

Sources cited: *Wrentham VR. History of Barnard* (1928). *History of Hardwick* (1882). Census: 1850 Barnard, Vt. (M432-931).

637.   JONATHAN DAMON[5] (*Hopestill Thayer⁴, Elizabeth³ Samson, Stephen², Henry¹*), son of Joseph Damon and his wife Hopestill Thayer [132], was born 11 April 1751 at Bellingham (*VR* 29) and baptized 23 June 1751 at Milford (*VR* 54). He died 8 May 1823, aged 72, at Holden (*VR* 205) and is buried in Old Village Cemetery, Dedham (*VR* 369).

He married **MARY / POLLY MARSH**. She was called Polley Marsh in their intentions, published 8 May 1777 at Braintree (*VR* 880). She was born 5 November 1756 at Braintree, daughter of Moses and Sarah (Crosby) Marsh (*Marsh Gen.*, 23), and died 2 April 1806 at Dedham (*VR* 369), aged 49 years, as "Mary, wife of Jonathan Damon," of lung fever. Jonathan Damon and wife Mary were admitted to the Dedham church 1 February 1778 from Braintree (*Dedham VR* 611).

On 10 June 1809 Jonathan Damon of Dedham sold his homestead in Dedham with dwelling, etc., and other land in different towns to his two sons Ebenezer and Samuel Damon (Norfolk LR 33:212). Two days later, on 12 June 1809, Ebenezer Damon, yeoman, and Samuel Damon, cabinetmaker, both of Dedham, in consideration of money and considerations paid by Jonathan Damon of Dedham, agreed to care for Jonathan for his life and to support his sister Sarah Damon, giving bond of $10,000 (*ibid.*, 37:95). Jonathan signed a receipt for full satisfaction 29 January 1811. On 20 June 1811 Samuel Damon 2nd of Holden, cabinetmaker, for $10, quitclaimed to James Richardson of Dedham, Esq., all right in the estate lately the property of his father Jonathan Damon in Dedham which had been set off in executions (*ibid.*, 42:78).

Children of Jonathan and Mary (Marsh) Damon, recorded at Dedham (*VR* 43-44):

i JOSEPH DAMON[6], b. 3 Jan., bp. 10 Jan. 1779.

ii MARY/POLLY DAMON, b. 15 Aug., bp. (as Polly) 20 Aug. 1780.

iii REBECCA DAMON, b. 1 June 1782; m. 7 Jan. 1834 at Dedham (*VR* 291), prob. as his third wife, ELISHA MACINTOSH, widower of her younger sister Betsey, with whom he had eight children (see below), and previously of Elizabeth Crehore. On 17 March 1811 Rebecca Damon was accepted into full communion with the Church at Dedham (*VR* 611), and on 29 Oct. 1818 she and her sister Louisa were founders of the Orthodox (now Allin Congregational) Church there.

iv EBENEZER DAMON, b. 29 Jan. 1784; m. 25 March 1810 at Dedham (*VR* 246), MARY HOLMES of Stoughton.

v SAMUEL DAMON, b. 15 Jan. 1786; m. (1) int. 11 May 1811 at Holden (*VR* 118), KEZIA RUGGLES CALDWELL of Barre, who d. 21 Jan. 1844 ae 53 at Holden (*VR* 205); m. (2) 8 March 1847 at Holden (*VR* 118, 135), HANNAH W. GODDARD, b. ca 1806, daughter of Benjamin and Patty (___) Goddard.
Children, rec. Holden, with Keziah (*VR* 29, 205): 1. *Mary Damon*[7], b. ca Jan. 1813; d. 26 Aug. 1813 ae 7m. 2. *William Caldwell Damon*, b. 2 Oct. 1814. 3. *Mary Damon*, b. 23 July 1817. 4. *? Lucy Damon*, b. ca 1818; d. 29 March 1833, ae 15. 5. *Jane Damon*, b. ca 1822; d. 25 March 1823, ae 1. 6. *David D. Damon*, b. ca July 1826; d. 11 Sept. 1827 ae 14m.

vi BETSEY DAMON, b. 15 Jan. 1788; d. 14 May 1833 ae 45 at Dedham (*VR* 429); m. 1 Dec. 1808 at Dedham (*VR* 291), probably as his second wife, ELISHA MACINTOSH, both of Dedham. He m. (3) her older sister Rebecca. He probably m. (1) 15 Feb. 1807 at Dorchester (*Dedham VR* 291) Elizabeth Crehore of Milton, who d. in 1807 ae 29 and is bur. at Dedham (*VR* 429).
MacIntosh children, rec. Dedham (*VR* 140), first three as "of Elisha," rest "of Elisha & Betsey": 1. *Elisha MacIntosh*[7], bp. 24 April 1814. 2. *George MacIntosh*, bp. 24 April 1814; d. 16 July 1823 at Dedham (*VR* 429). 3. *Mary Elizabeth MacIntosh*, bp. 24 April 1814. 3. *Susanna MacIntosh*, bp. 11 Aug. 1816. 4. *William MacIntosh*, bp. 26 July 1818. 5. *Frances Maria MacIntosh*, b. 23 Nov. 1820, bp. 27 April 1821. 6. *George MacIntosh*, b. 8 Nov., bp. 31 Dec. 1824. 7. *Lauretta*

MacIntosh, b. 8 May, bp. 24 Aug. 1827. 8. *Edward Payson MacIntosh*, b. 6 May, bp. 3 Aug. 1832.

vii NANCY DAMON (twin), b. 26 Oct., bp. 2 Nov 1789; unmarried 25 April 1825 when she was admitted to the Orthodox Church, Dedham (*VR* 611).

viii [DAUGHTER] DAMON (twin), b. 26 Oct., d. 31 Oct. 1789 at Dedham (*VR* 369).

ix LUCY DAMON, b. 21 June 1791; m. 25 March 1810 at Dedham (*VR* 236), PITTS BUTTERFIELD, "both of Dedham" (*VR* 236). He was bur. 22 Aug. 1822 at Dedham (*VR* 357), ae. 34. Lucy Butterfield was admitted to the Episcopal Church in Dedham (*VR* 604) 27 Feb. 1824 and her four oldest surviving children were bp. there 2 March 1823 as "of Lucy."

   Butterfield children, bp. Dedham (*VR* 26): 1. *William Pitt Butterfield⁷*, b. 16 July 1810. 2. *Samuel Butterfield*, b. ca 1813; drowned 27 June 1815 at Dedham (*VR* 357). 3. *Lucy Ann Butterfield*, b. 25 Feb. 1815. 4. *Rebecca Damon Butterfield*, b. 8 May 1817. 5. *Georgianna Butterfield*, b. 30 Oct. 1819.

x [CHILD] DAMON, b. ca Nov. 1793; d. 23 July 1795 ae 20 months of putrid fever, at Dedham (*VR* 369).

xi LOUISA DAMON, 2 Aug. 1795; accepted into the Dedham Church 8 Feb. 1818 and withdrew 29 Oct. 1818 when she and her sister Rebecca were founders of the Orthodox (now Allin Congregational) Church at Dedham (*VR* 611).

xii LUCRETIA DAMON, b. 2 July, bp. 16 Aug. 1797; m. 9 March 1815 at Dedham (*VR* 244), JOHN COX. Lucretia Cox was admitted to the Orthodox Church (now the Allin Congregational Church) in Dedham (*VR* 609) 13 May 1832, and their five children were baptized there 14 Sept. 1832.

   Cox children, b. and bp. at Dedham (*VR* 41): 1. *Mary Thayer Cox⁷*, b. 18 Dec. 1818. 2. *Sarah Elizabeth Cox*, b. 6 Oct. 1821. 3. *John Edward Cox*, b. 6 March 1825. 4. *Caroline Frances Cox*, b. 29 May 1828. 5. *Samuel Henry Cox*, b. 7 Sept. 1830.

Sources cited: *Bellingham VR. Dedham VR* (Hanson, 1997 ed.). *Holden VR.* Norfolk County Deeds at Dedham. D. W. Marsh, *Genealogy of the Marsh Family* (1886).

638. SAMUEL DAMON⁵ (*Hopestill Thayer⁴, Elizabeth³ Samson, Stephen², Henry¹*), son of Joseph Damon and his wife Hopestill Thayer [132], was born 13 August 1755 at Dedham (*VR* 44) and died 27 May 1813, aged 57 years, at Holden (*VR* 205).

He married, 27 May 1779 at Medway (*VR* 182, 242), **ABIGAIL PENNIMAN**, who was born 19 March 1754 at Medway (*VR* 104), daughter of James and Abigail (Clark) Penniman, and died 18 March 1842, aged 87y 11m 29d, at Holden (*VR* 204). The will of James Penniman of Medway, gentleman, advanced in age, dated 4 February 1804, names his wife Abigail, and among his eight daughters Abigail Deming [*sic*], wife of Samuel Deming; in the account Samuel is named as, and signed as Samuel Damon (Norfolk PR #14,254).

Samuel Damon of Holden, weak in body, in his will dated 12 January 1813, proved 3 June 1813, directed that his beloved wife Abigail be "handsomely supported Clothing excepted, by my Executor during her natural life"; she was to have the use of a horse and chaise, the west room in his dwelling house and the chamber over it, with the west part of the back kitchen (for her own personal use, not to be rented), privileges in kitchen, cellar, and garret and a supply of wood sufficiently prepared for the fire and brought into the house, with option to sit at the table of the Executor and be furnished with food or to have her own table, and to have utensils "to treat a friend in decent hospitable manner," and $1,000 per year plus interest. To son Penniman he left $34, he having been given land as his share. Daughter Abigail was to have $1,620 and the "use of my pasture in Princeton," which was to go to her oldest son Jason at her death. Son Samuel was to be executor, and to him was bequeathed all the real and personal estate in Holden, he to pay the legacies. To son Penniman's wife Susanna he gave the use of a pasture near David Smith's, to go to her oldest son Samuel after her death. To sister Sarah Damon he left $10 per year, and to the town of Holden $100 for the use of the schools. He requested that son Samuel obtain a place in the burying place in Holden for a tomb for the use of the family. (Worcester PR #15188; 43:25)

Children of Samuel and Abigail (Penniman) Damon, only the first recorded at Holden:

i   PENNIMAN DAMON[6], b. 31 Oct. 1779 Holden (*VR* 29); m. after int. 12 Oct. 1801 at Holden (*VR* 118), SUSANNA WHEELOCK of Warwick.
     Children, b. Warwick (*Damon Mem.*, 22-33): 1. *Samuel Penniman Damon[7]*, b. 15 Feb. 1809; d. 7 Aug. 1860 Jamaica, L.I., N.Y.; m. Amanda M. Weeks. 2. *Susan Damon*; m. Lancaster; no children. 3. *Lucy Damon*, d. unm. at Holden. 4. *George Weeks Damon*, m. Emma L. Crossman; res. Jamaica, L.I.

ii   ABIGAIL DAMON, b. 3 June 1783; d. Phillipston 22 May 1838 (*VR* 106); m. 31 May 1801 at Holden (*VR* 118), IGNATIUS GOULDING, b. there Aug. 1774 (*VR* 44), d. Phillipston 15 July 1841 (*VR* 106), son of Ignatius and Elisabeth (___) Goulding. He m. (2) Boylston, 3 June 1840 (*VR* 73), Harriet (___) Sawyer. (His will, Worcester PR 25095)

> *Goulding* children (five in all) included   1. *Jason Goulding'*, named in grandfather's will; m. (1) Cynthia Knowlton, (2) Harriet B. Knowlton (*Phillipston VR* 24, 67). 2. *James Ignatius Goulding*, b. Phillipston 16 Sept. 1817 (*VR* 24).

iii   SAMUEL DAMON, b. 11 June 1786; m. 4 July 1810 at Holden (*VR* 112), ALONY CHENERY, b. 27 Jan. 1788 at Holden (*VR* 24), dau. Dr. Isaac and Susanna (Pierce) Chenery.

> Children, rec. Holden (*VR* 29): 1. *Susan Abigail Damon⁷*, b. 17 Dec. 1810; d. 30 July 1831. 2. *Alony Ann Damon*, b. 12 Feb. 1813. 3. *Samuel Chenery Damon*, b. 15 Feb. 1815, author of *Damon Memorial* and *History of Holden* (1841).* 4. *Isaac Peirce Damon*, b. 26 Oct. 1817. 5. *Frances Caroline Damon*, b. 11 Aug. 1820; d. 21 March 1834. 6. *Harriet Amelia Damon*, b. 29 June 1823. 7. *Charles Frederick Damon*, b. 21 May 1826. 8. *Augustus Franklin Damon*, b. 17 June 1828. 9. *Susan Abigail Damon*, b. 7 May 1833.

Sources cited: *Boylston VR. Holden VR. Phillipston VR.* Worcester County Probate Records. *Samuel Chenery Damon, *Damon Memorial : or notices of Three Damon Families* (Philadelphia for A. F. Damon and the Author, 1882). **See also:** *History of Holden* (1894).

639.   ABIGAIL THAYER⁵ (*Ezra Thayer⁴, Elizabeth³ Samson, Stephen², Henry¹*), daughter of Ezra Thayer [133] and his wife Judith Williams, was born 23 June 1763 at Ware (*VR* 19) and died 30 October 1840 at Stockbridge, in her 70th year.

She married 25 July 1791 at Stockbridge (*VR* 7-8), **STEPHEN WILLARD**, who was born there 24 November 1767, son of Benjamin and Naomi (Hale) Willard, and died there 19 November 1839 in his 72nd year ("Earliest Town Recs.," 43).

In his will dated 18 November 1839, proved 3 December 1839, Stephen Willard of Stockbridge gave all his estate and belongings to his wife Abigail and named her executrix (Berkshire PR #6100). Heirs at law who signed on 3 December 1839 stating that they were satisfied with the will were Enoch Willard, Jerusha Churchill, Sylvia Willard, and Anna Seymour.

Abigail Willard of Stockbridge in her will dated 26 October 1840, proved 1 December 1840, requested that a monument be erected on her grave similar to those of her mother and husband, stating name, age, and date of death (Berkshire PR #6222). The residue of her husband's property was to be equally divided between his brother Enoch and his sister Sylvia Willard. Abigail made a bequest to Mrs. Cynthia Sergeant, and to societies. Stephen and Abigail (Thayer) Willard apparently had no children.

Sources cited: Stockbridge Town Records. Ware VR. Berkshire County Probate Records. **See also:** *Memorial of Richard and Thomas Thayer*, p. 505.

640.   HENRY NELSON⁵ (*Elizabeth Thayer⁴, Elizabeth³ Samson, Stephen², Henry¹*), son of Josiah Nelson and his wife Elizabeth Thayer [134], was born 20 June 1754 at Milford (*VR* 127). His death on 13 September 1805, "son of Josiah and Elizabeth," was recorded at Milford (*VR* 356) but probably occurred elsewhere. The will of Josiah Nelson of Milford, dated 15 April 1806, proved 4 August 1807, names his grandson Henry, son of deceased son Henry (Worcester PR #42827).

He married, in 1780, **SIBBLE SMITH** (*DAR Patriot Index*; rec. not found), who is said to have been a daughter of Gad and Irene (Waite) Smith, and to have died in 1795 at Newburgh, N.Y. If her date of death is correct, Henry married again and his second wife was mother of the younger children. Records of the marriages of two other children of Gad and Irene Smith appear at Whately, Franklin County.

Henry Nelson served in the Revolution in the Massachusetts Line (White, 2478) as a lieutenant (*NEHGR* 114:182). A bounty land warrant was issued to his son Henry, who signed a power of attorney 9 July 1834 in Orange County, N.Y., for himself, Elizabeth Doughtey, Mary Ann wife of John Gisner, Ester wife of Lewis Nason, and Marcus Nelson, surviving children of the deceased soldier who died in 1805 (*ibid.*, citing BLW 2057-200).

Henry Nelson was listed in the 1790 census in New Cornwall, Orange County, N.Y. (p.144) with a household of three men, a boy under 16, and four females.

Children of Henry Nelson, living 1834 when named in pension file; uncertain whether Sibble Smith was mother of all:

  i   HENRY NELSON⁶, b. ca 1787 in N.Y. (perhaps twin to Elizabeth); d. New-
      burgh, N.Y., 16 March 1859 (probate petition) m. (1) SARAH ____ (*Milford
      History*); m. (2) ABIGAIL ____, b. ca 1800 with whom he was living 1850 at
      Newburgh, N.Y. (p.39), a carriage maker, ae 63, and Sarah, 37; the house-
      hold included Abram Budd 45, blacksmith, Sands Robison 23, and Charles
      Bush 19, the last two carriage makers, all b. N.Y. Henry is named in the will
      of his grandfather Josiah Nelson dated 15 April 1806. In his will dated 24
      Feb. 1857, Henry Nelson of Newburgh bequeathed $400 to daughter Sarah
      J. White wife of Thomas White, to be divided between his son Henry
      Nelson and son-in-law Thomas White should Sarah not survive for one year
      after her father's decease; to wife Abigail $40 annually for life; to son William
      M. Nelson and his heirs the residue, he to be executor. In a codicil dated 18
      April 1858 Henry revoked the bequest to Abigail and instead gave her a

$500 bond against the Trustees of the Village of Newburgh, and $100; reduced Sarah Jane's legacy to $100; and gave to daughter Mary White $200. The petition for probate by William M. Nelson, dated 14 April 1859, listed as heirs-at-law himself, of Buckingham, Pa.; Mary White wife of James White, Sarah Jane White wife of Thomas White, Ester Farley wife of Thomas Farley, all of Orange Co., N.Y.; Henry Nelson Jr., of McDonough Co., Ill., "when last heard from but whose present place of residence is unknown"; Lucinda Howell widow of James G. Howell of Bloomington, Ill.; and the widow Abigail Nelson of Newburgh, N.Y. (Orange Co. Surrogate's File).

Children (first two from *Milford History*, 2:927; rest from father's probate): 1. *Samuel Nelson[7]*, b. 7 May 1811; n.f.r. 2. *Clarissa Nelson*, b. 4 Dec. 1812; n.f.r. 3. *Sarah Jane Nelson*, b. ca 1813 (census); m. Thomas White. 4. *William M. Nelson*. 5. *Mary Nelson;* m. James White. 6. *Esther Nelson*, m. Thomas Farley. 7. *Henry Nelson*. 8. *Lucinda Nelson*, m. James G. Howell.

ii   ELIZABETH NELSON, b. 19 Sept. 1786 New Windsor (?twin to Henry); m. there 1 March 1802, SAMUEL DOUGHTY (NW Presbyt. Marr.).

iii MARCUS NELSON, b. ca 1801; living 1850 Bloomington, Ill. (p.8), ae 49, a wagonmaker, b. N.Y.; his wife had died or was elsewhere when the census was taken. Jonathan McM[urray?], wagonmaker, no age given, was in the household.

Children, from 1850 census, all b. N.Y.; all except Marcus living at home: 1. *Jane Ann Nelson[7]*, b. ca 1828. 2. *Marcus Nelson*, b. ca 1830; a wagonmaker living 1850 in Oskaloosa twp., Mahaska Co., Iowa (p.8), unm. 3. *Harriett Nelson*, b. ca 1832. 4. *Alx [Alexander?] Nelson*, b. ca 1833. 5. *James H. Nelson*, b. ca 1835. 6. *Mary E. Nelson*, b. ca 1838. 7. *Elizabeth Nelson*, b. ca 1840. 8. *Jonathan Nelson*, b. ca 1843.

iv   MARY ANN NELSON, b. ca 1803; living in New York City in 1850; m. by 1830 JOHN GISNER, b. ca 1799 in N.Y. In 1850 they were living in Ward 9, New York City (p.4); he was a policeman. The children as given below, and Mary Harris, 21, b. Ireland, were in the household.

Gisner children at home 1850: 1. *Mary E. Gisner[7]*, b. ca 1830. 2. *Lewis E. Gisner*, b. ca 1832, a clerk. 3. *Sarah Gisner*, b. ca 1835. 4. *Nelson Gisner*, b. ca 1837. 5. *Priscilla Gisner*, b. ca 1839. 6. *Charles Gisner*, b. ca 1841. 7. *Josephine Gisner*, b. ca 1845.

v   ESTHER NELSON, m. LEWIS NASON. He is surely the man of that name listed in the 1830 census in Ward 9, New York City (p.346), the same ward where Esther's sister Mary Ann Gisner was later living, and in the 1829/30 City Directory.

Sources cited: *Milford VR.* White, *Abstracts of Rev. War Pension Files.* Glenn Marshall, Historian of the Town of New Windsor, "Marriages at New Windsor Presbyterian Church," online at Orange Co., N.Y., GenWeb Site. Orange Co., N.Y., Surrogate's Records. *History of Milford* (1882). *DAR Patriot Index.* "Some Revolutionary Soldiers and their Heirs," *NEHGR* 114 [1960], from "Bounty Land Scripts — Act of 1833" at National Archives. CENSUS: 1830 New York City, Ward 9, 1830 (M19-97) & 1850 (M432-543); 1850 Newburgh, Orange Co., N.Y. (M432-573), McLean Co., Bloomington, Ill. (M432-117); & Mahaska Co., Oskaloosa, Iowa (M432-117).

641. STEPHEN NELSON[5] (*Elizabeth Thayer*[4], *Elizabeth*[3] *Samson, Stephen*[2], *Henry*[1]), son of Josiah Nelson and his wife Elizabeth Thayer [134], was born 12 December 1755 at Milford (*VR* 128). His death on 22 October 1793 occurred at Orange but was recorded at Milford (*VR* 356).

He married 29 May 1776, at Mendon (*VR* 352), **ANNA ATWOOD**, who was born there 11 September 1754 (*VR* 24), daughter of Benjamin and Joanna (Cheney) Atwood.

The 1790 census lists the family at Upton (*Heads of Fam.*, 240), with three boys under 16 and two females. There are no entries for them in the Upton VRs.

The will of Josiah Nelson, dated 15 April 1806, names four children of his deceased son Stephen: Levi, Nathaniel, Hallowel, and Lucinda (Worcester PR #42827).

Capt. Stephen Nelson, gentleman, of Orange, died intestate, and administration on his estate was given to Ebenezer Atwood and the widow Anna Nelson on 12 November 1793 (Hampshire PR box 104 #57). Among claimants were Josiah Nelson Sr., Josiah Nelson Jr., Paul Nelson, and Seth Nelson. Anna Nelson, widow and relict, petitioned on 5 January 1795 for an allowance for a family of four children. The file contains an accounting of Ebenezer Atwood, administrator, including setting off the widow's dower. On 10 April 1795 Anna Nelson and Ebenezer Atwood, administrators of the estate of Stephen Nelson, sold land to Oliver Chapin (Franklin LR 11:141). On 16 May 1795 Anna Nelson of Orange, widow and relict of Stephen Nelson, sold to Oliver Chapin all her right in Stephen's estate set off as her dower (*ibid.*,11:140).

Ebenezer Atwood was appointed guardian of Holloway Nelson, son of Stephen, late of Orange, deceased, on 3 December 1805 (father's PR).

Children of Stephen and Anna (Atwood) Nelson, births rec. Orange (VR 1:18); all named in will of their grandfather 1806:

   i   NATHANIEL NELSON[6], b. 7 Oct. 1778 "at Milford."

ii LEVI NELSON, b. 2 Feb. 1781 Upton; d. Providence, R.I., 19 Feb. 1815 ae 34 (Arnold 14 [*Prov. Gazette Deaths*]:132); m. at Milford, 21 Sept. 1806 (*VR* 268), SARAH PARK, d. 27 Dec. 1834 (*Milford History* 2:927).

    Nelson children (*ibid.*): 1. *Stephen Atwood Nelson*[7], b. 22 March 1807. 2. *Holloway Taylor Nelson*, b. 9 Dec. 1808.

iii ROSALINDA NELSON, b. 22 Sept. 1783 at Upton, bp. 11 Oct. 1801 at Milford (*VR* 128); d. after 1850 when "Linda" Nelson ae 65 and her brother "Holly" ae 60 were listed as town paupers at Milford (p.22).

iv HALLOWELL/HOLLOWAY NELSON, b. 25 Aug. 1789 at Upton, bp. 11 Oct. 1801 at Milford (*VR* 127), "of widow Anna." See note above.

Sources cited: *Mendon VR. Milford VR. Orange VR.* Franklin County Deeds. Hampshire County Probate Records and Deeds. Worcester County Probate Records. *History of Milford* (1882). Arnold, *Vital Record of R.I.,* Vol. 14 (newspapers). *Heads of Families 1790 – Mass.* 1850 census, Milford, Worcester Co. (M432-344).

642. RUTH NELSON[5] (*Elizabeth Thayer*[4], *Elizabeth*[3] *Samson, Stephen*[2], *Henry*[1]), daughter of Josiah Nelson and his wife Elizabeth Thayer [134], was born 11 October 1757 at Milford (*VR* 128), and died 12 July 1817 at Lewiston, Maine (*VR* 2:357).

She married 25 December 1777, at Mendon (*VR* 352), **NATHAN CUTLER**. He was born 22 February 1755 at Mendon (*VR* 58), son of David and Mehitable (Whitney) Cutler, and died 8 December 1827 at Lewiston, "Nathan Cutler Senior, Aged nearly 73" (*VR* 2:358). He married, second, at Lewiston 1 January 1818 (*VR* 2:415), HANNAH (___) BLANCHARD, probably widow of Joseph Blanchard and thus mother-in-law of Nathan's son Henry.

Ruth is named in the will of her father as Ruth, wife of Nathan Cutler (Worcester PR #42827).

Nathan served in the Revolutionary War as a private (*MSSR* 4:324-25).

Their first child was born in Auburn, Mass., but the family settled in Maine soon after. In 1790 Nathan Cutler's household in Lewiston consisted of a man over 16, two boys under 16, and four females (p.40, indexed as *Cutter*). The recently published *Lewiston Town Records* indicate that he served in town offices and in 1795 was a constable there.

Children of Nathan and Ruth (Nelson) Cutler, all but first prob. b. in Maine, all listed together in *Lewiston VR* 2:248:

i NATHAN CUTLER[6], b. 14 Sept. 1779 at Auburn (*VR* 27); d. 1 Nov. 1859 at Industry, Me. (*Industry History*, 568); m. (1) at Lewiston after int. 15 March

1800 (*VR* 2:398), "Mrs. Polly Moore" [MARY MOOAR], d. in 1822 ae 41; m. (2) after int. 16 Jan. 1823, LYDIA BAKER of Wilton. He res. Lewiston, then Minot, then New Vineyard on the part of the Gore set off as Industry in 1815 (*ibid.*). In 1850 Nathan ae 70, b. Mass., with Lydia ae 55, b. Me., were at Industry with Charles ae 19, Lydia A. ae 16, Ira and his wife Deborah and their son "Bub" ae 11m (p.78).

Children, last nine b. Industry, Me. (*Industry History*, 568-69), with first wife:: 1. *Henry Cutler*[7], b. 9 June 1800 Lewiston; m. Esther Hall. 2. *Hopestill Cutler*, b. 8 Jan. 1802 Minot; m. James Hardy. 3. *Harvey Cutler*, b. 26 Sept. 1803 Minot; m. Lucy Matthews. 4. *Nelson Cutler*, b. 25 April 1805 Minot; m. Love Thompson. 5. *Levi Cutler*, b. 27 Feb. 1807 Minot; m. Margaret Moore Norton. 6. *Seth Cutler*, b. 4 Feb. 1809 Minot; m. Abigail Stoyell Norton. 7. *Betsey Cutler*, b. 29 Dec. 1810 New Vineyard; m. Barzilla D. Dyer. 8. *Esther Cutler*, b. ca 1812 New Vineyard; m. William Heald. 9. *Nathan Cutler*, b. 11 Feb. 1815; m. Lucinda Barker. 10. *Josiah Cutler*, b. 26 March 1817; m. (1) Nancy Stanley, (2) Mary Margaret Craig. 11. *Ruth Cutler*, b. ca 1819; m. James B. Wood. 12. *Hiram Cutler*, b. ca 1822. Children with second wife: 13. *Mary Mooar Cutler*, b. 17 Oct. 1825; m. Ephraim Hartwell. 14. *Sarah A. Cutler*, b. ca 1827; m. Joshua Williams. 15. *Ira Vaughan Cutler*, b. ca 1829; m. Deborah Norton. 16. *Charles Cutler*, b. ca 1831; d. unm. 17. *Lydia Ann Cutler*, b. 17 Sept. 1833; m. James Norton. 18. *Cordelia J. Cutler*, b. ca 1835; m. Zebadiah M. Barker.

ii   HENRY CUTLER, b. 26 Aug. 1781; d. 26 March 1815, Lewiston (*VR* 2:357, "N. Henery son of Nat[n] & Ruth"); m. after int. at Lewiston 14 March 1806 (*VR* 2:398), HANNAH BLANCHARD, b. Lewiston 8 March 1787, dau. of Joseph and Hannah (___) Blanchard (*VR* 2:247).

Children (*Cutler Mem.*, 404): 1. *Horatio Nelson Cutler*[7], b. 28 Jan. 1806. 2. *Ruth Cutler*, b. 29 Nov. 1808; d. 29 July 1815. 3. *Hannah Cutler*. 4. *Olive Cutler*.

iii RUTH CUTLER, b. 15 March 1783; d. 28 June 1798, Lewiston (*VR* 2:357).

iv   BETSEY CUTLER, b. 10 Aug. 1785; d. Jan. 1811, Lewiston (*VR* 2:357).

v   OLIVE CUTLER, b. 10 March 1788; d. ca 1833; m. TIMOTHY MOOAR of Wilton, Me. In 1850 Timothy Mooar, b. ca 1785 Mass., was a farmer in Wilton with wife *Charlotte* ae 57 (p.64). *Cutler Mem.* says eight children.

vi   JOSIAH CUTLER, b. 22 Feb. 1791; d. 1 Jan. 1881 ae 90 in Chicago, Ill.; m. at Lewiston, 19 Feb. 1821 (*VR* 2:312), SALLY B. HANSCOM of Readfield; lived Livermore, Me., then Chicago. He was a farmer, much interested in raising bees (*Cutler Mem.*, 404). In 1860 Josiah was in Chicago in the household of his son, J. N. Cutler, who was a manufacturer of lightning rods (p.646).

Children (*Cutler Mem.*, 404): 1. *Sarah Jane Cutler*[7], b. 19 Jan. 1821; m. E.H. Gammond. 2. *Josiah Nelson Cutler*, b. 22 June 1823; m. Love Taylor. 3. *Mary*

Cutler, b. 2 June 1825; m. Samuel Taylor. 4. *Rhoda Carson Cutler*, m. John W. Ball of Natick.

vii   DAVID CUTLER, b. 14 July 1793; m. at Lewiston, 26 April 1820 (*VR* 2:415), LUCY LANDERS. *Cutler Mem.* says he lived on an old farm in Lewiston and d. at Haverhill, Mass., at the home of a daughter; had one son and three daughters.

viii ESTHER CUTLER, b. 11 Aug. 1795; d. 17 July 1812, Lewiston (*VR* 2:357).

ix   STEPHEN CUTLER, b. 3 Jan. 1799; d. 1 Nov. 1837, Lewiston (*VR* 2:358); m. at Lewiston, 12 Feb. 1821 (*VR* 2:415), ROXCEYLANIA BERRY of Minot, b. 6 July 1803, d. 8 Sept. 1865. Stephen lived on the homestead farm. Mrs. Roxceylania Cutler pub. m. int. 4 May 1839 with Josiah Cutler [?her brother-in-law] and cert. was granted 20 May, but the clerk noted, "not m. yet" (*VR* 2:510), and she evidently changed her mind and m. instead, 25 Nov. 1840 after int. 8 Nov., John Whittum(*VR* 2:514).
        Children rec. Lewiston (*VR* 2:309; *Cutler Mem.*, 405): 1. *Otis Nelson Cutler[7]*, b. 19 Feb. 1824. 2. *Stephen Corydon Cutler*, b. 8 July 1826. 3. *Vesta Augusta Cutler*, b. 16 Oct. 1828; m. Lewis C. Peck. 4. *Olive Amanda Cutler*, b. 27 June 1835.

x   CYNTHIA CUTLER, b. 7 July 1801; m. JOSIAH GREEN of Wilton, Me., b. ca 1802. In 1850 he was a farmer ae 48 at Farmington, Me., with Cynthia ae 48, children Olive A. and Josiah W. Green, and Lovina Chandler ae 35 and Apphia Chandler ae 6 (p.179). *Cutler Mem.* evidently errs in saying Cynthia d. ca 1833.
        Green children at home 1850 (said to be five in all): 1. *Olive A. Green[7]*, b. ca 1836. 2. *Josiah W. Green*, b. ca 1838.

Sources cited: *Auburn VR. Mendon VR. Milford VR.* Hodgkin, *Records of Lewiston, Maine*, 2 vols. (2001). Worcester County Probate Records. *History of Industry, Me.* (1869). *Mass. Soldiers & Sailors. Cutler Memorial and Genealogical History* (1889), has omissions and errors. CENSUS: Lewiston, Lincoln Co., Me., 1790 (M637-2), 1830 (M19-49); Farmington & Industry, Franklin Co., Me., 1850 (M432-253); Chicago, Cook Co., Ill., 1860 (M653-166).

643.   JOSIAH NELSON[5] (*Elizabeth Thayer[4], Elizabeth[3] Samson, Stephen[2], Henry[1]*), son of Josiah Nelson and his wife Elizabeth Thayer [134], was born 23 August 1761 at Milford (*VR* 127) and died there 15 October 1802 (*VR* 356). He was an innholder in Milford (*Milford History*, 2:920).

He married, after intentions 10 February 1786 at Milford (*VR* 268), **ANNA WARREN**, who was born 22 January 1767 at Mendon (*VR* 201), daughter of Samuel and Eunice (Corbett) Warren. She married, second, 30 May 1811 at Milford (*VR* 267), ABNER ALBEE of Chesterfield, N.H. Anna Albee, widow, died 25 March 1837 at Milford, aged 70, of fever (*VR* 318).

On 15 March 1796, Samuel Warren of Milford sold land there to Josiah Nelson Jr. of Milford, including a house where Josiah was dwelling that he had sold to Warren; no relationship was stated (Worcester LR 127:345). On 23 March 1803 Samuel Warren of Hopkinton and wife Eunice, and Anna Nelson of Milford, sold to Levi Chapin all rights in land and buildings in Milford as described in a deed given to Chapin by Samuel Warren and Josiah Nelson Jr.; Anna acknowledged in June 1803 (*ibid.*, 150:565).

Josiah's father in his will dated 15 April 1806, named Henry, John, Lucinda, Betsey, Mercy, and Julian, children of deceased son Josiah Nelson (Worcester PR # 42827).

Children of Josiah and Anna (Warren) Nelson, births rec. Milford (*VR* 125, 127) "to Josiah Jr. and Anne":

i   Capt. HENRY NELSON[6], b. 2 Sept. 1786; d. Milford 22 July 1874; m. at Milford 17 Jan. 1810 (*VR* 268) CATHARINE PARKHURST, b. 19 Aug. 1789, dau. of Nathaniel and Sarah (Brown) Parkhurst. Henry was adopted as his heir by Samuel Jones, Esq. (*Milford History*, 2:927)

       Children rec. Milford (*VR* 125-28): 1. *Warren J. Nelson*[7], b. 25 Nov. 1810. 2. *Maria Nelson*, b. 21 Feb. 1813; m. Oliver B. Parkhurst. 3. *Catharine Nelson*, b. 17 Oct. 1815; d. 26 April 1818 (*VR* 355). 4. *Nancy Parkhurst Nelson*, b. 15 Feb. 1818; m. Samuel Frink Jr. 5. *Angelina Parkhurst Nelson*, b. 4 Dec. 1821; m. Daniel S. Chapin. 6. *Catharine Nelson*, b. 21 Aug. 1824. 7. *Charlotte Helen Nelson*, b. 15 Aug. 1827; m. (1) Rev. L. P. Rand, (2) Arba Nelson [Samson **#648-iii**].

ii   LUCINDA NELSON, b. 15 Jan. 1789; d. 27 March 1818, of lung fever, at Hopkinton (*VR* 429); m. 21 April 1813 at Milford (*VR* 268), PHINEHAS HUBBARD, b. 8 March 1789 at Milford (*VR* 113), prob. son of Thomas and Lois (White) Hubbard. He m. (2) 30 March 1819 at Hopkinton (*VR* 304), Elizabeth Jones.

       Hubbard children rec. Hopkinton (*VR* 113): 1. *Josiah Nelson Hubbard*[7], b. 25 Oct. 1815. 2. *Nelson O. Hubbard*, b. 25 Oct. 1815 [*sic - twins or same child?*]. 3. *George Hubbard* (twin), b. 4 March 1818. 4. *Henry Hubbard* (twin), b. 4 March 1818; d. 17 May 1820 ae 2 at Hopkinton (*VR* 429). Some of the *VR* entries are from a Phinehas Hubbard Bible in possession (1911) of Mrs. Henry J. Hubbard of South Framingham.

iii   Dr. JOHN NELSON, b. 8 Sept. 1790; m. at Milford 6 July 1812 (*VR* 268), LUCINDA PARKHURST, b. ca 1790. *Milford History* says, "removed to

Carlisle," but in 1850 they were in Woburn, both ae 60, with Mercy A. Parkhurst ae 54 and Mary [—] ae 15, b. Ireland (p.268).

Child rec. Milford (*VR* 125): 1. *Albert Hobart Nelson⁷*, b. 12 March 1812 [*sic*].

iv BETSEY MELLEN NELSON, b. 18 June 1792; m. at Mendon, 26 Aug. 1818 (*VR* 352), CALEB V. ALLEN.

v MERCY JONES NELSON, b. 21 April 1794; m. at Milford 12 April 1818 (*VR* 268), MOSES LITTLEFIELD, b. Milford 14 Sept. 1789, son of Isaac and Elisabeth (____) Littlefield (*VR* 111).

vi JULIA ANN / JULIAN[A] NELSON, b. 22 Feb. 1798; d. 1867; m. at Milford, 3 April 1818 (*VR* 268), IRA CHENEY, b. Milford 23 Sept. 1798, son of Caleb and Sarah (Hunting) Cheney (*VR* 39, 212).

Cheney children, rec. Milford (*VR* 38-39): 1. *Maryannah Nelson Cheney⁷*, b. 30 Jan. 1821. 2. *Armenia Cheney*, b. 27 Jan. 1823. 3. *Samuel Jones Cheney*, b. 19 Sept. 1824. 4. *Francis Marion Cheney*, b. 28 Oct. 1832.

Sources cited: *Hopkinton VR. Mendon VR. Milford VR.* Worcester Co. Deeds and Probate Records. *History of Milford* (1882). CENSUS: 1850 Woburn, Middlesex Co. (M432-325).

644. PAUL NELSON⁵ (*Elizabeth Thayer⁴, Elizabeth³ Samson, Stephen², Henry¹*), son of Josiah Nelson and his wife Elizabeth Thayer [134], was born 3 September 1763 at Milford (*VR* 128). He died 1 April 1827 aged 63, at Pawtucket (*Milford History*, 2:920). He is named in the will of his father, dated 15 April 1806 (Worcester PR #42827).

He married, 21 December 1786 at Upton (*VR* 118) after intentions at Milford 6 April 1786 (*VR* 268*)*, **GRACE WOOD**, who was born at Upton 19 May 1766 (*VR* 66), daughter of Capt. Ezra and Anna (Chapin) Wood, and died 13 March 1838 (g.s.). The will of Ezra Wood, Esq., of Upton, dated 27 August 1811, proved 27 September 1815, names his wife Anna and daughter Grace Nelson (Worcester PR #A66986).

Paul's household in the 1790 census at Milford consisted of himself and three females (*Heads of Fam.*, 229). He "spent most of his adult life an innholder, first in West Upton several years, then in No. Providence, R.I., then in Bristol, R.I., about 5 yrs, and finally in Pawtucket 6 yrs … a popular landlord, and universally respected in all the relationships of life" (*Milford History* 2:920).

Paul and Grace (Wood) Nelson are buried in Swan Point Cemetery, Providence, along with several of their children (RIHCTP).

Children of Paul and Grace (Wood) Nelson (*Milford History* 2:920-21), first five rec. Upton of "Capt. Paul and Grace" (*VR* 39-40):

i   DULCINA NELSON[6], b. 23 April 1788 "at Milford"; d. 14 Nov. 1880 ae 92y (g.s.); bur. Swan Point Cem., Providence; m. 29 Sept. 1807 at Bristol, R.I., by Rev. Henry Wight, CHARLES HENRY TILLINGHAST, son of Joseph and Ann (___) Tillinghast (*VR* 53), d. ca 1809 (*Milford History*, 921). In 1850 Dulcina Tillinghast ae 60 was head of a large household in Ward 5, Providence (p.291); with her were her [daughter] Anna R. Tompkins ae 44, [sister] Abby G. Spencer ae 40, [grandchildren] Charles H. Tompkins ae 16, clerk, John A. Tompkins ae 13, both b. N.Y., and Eliza N. Rodman ae 29, and [niece] Abby N. Spencer ae 20, b. R.I. In addition there were several boarders, from several U. S. states, Germany, and Ireland, including clerks, accountants, a trader, and a music teacher.
    Tillinghast child: 1. *Anna Tillinghast*[7], b. ca 1808; m. (1) John Tompkins of Newburgh, N.Y., (2) A. D. Lippett (*Milford History*, 2:921).

ii DIANA NELSON, b. 20 April 1790 Upton; d. 17 June 1816 (g.s.); m. 1809 at Bristol, R.I. (not in VR), Rev. MATTHIAS MUNRO, an Episcopal clergyman, prob. son of Nathaniel and Abigail (___) Munro, b. Bristol 24 April 1785 (*VR* 93); bur. in East Burial Ground, Bristol (RIHCTP).
    Munro children (*Milford History*, 2:921): 1. *Diana Munro*[7], m. Willis G. Easton of Lowell. 2. *Grace Wood Munro*, m. Gilbert Richmond. 3. *William M. Munro*, m. ___ Noyes of Poland, Me.

iii PAUL NELSON Jr, b. 13 July 1792 Upton; d. at sea, 15 Oct. 1813, ae 21 (VR 152), of yellow fever on voyage to Cuba.

iv RUTH NELSON, b. 15 Oct. 1794 Upton; d. there 13 Sept. 1797 in 3rd yr (*VR* 173).

v   RUTH NELSON, b. 1 June 1798 Upton; d. 23 June 1825; m. 15 April 1824, at Pawtucket, PETER BUCKLIN HUNT, b. ca 1794, d. 28 April 1831. They are buried in Swan Point Cemetery (RIHCTP). No children.

vi ANGELINA NELSON, b. 15 Feb. 1801; d. 26 Feb. 1823 (g.s., year prob. not correct); m. 8 Nov. 1822, at New Grace Church, North Providence, R.I. (*VR* 30), JOSEPH TOMPKINS, b. 1787, d. 5 Jan. 1854 (g.s., Mineral Springs Cem., Pawtucket).
    Tompkins children (*Milford History*, 2:921; but if her m. and d. date are correct, these cannot be Angelina's): 1. *Susan G. Tompkins*[7]. 2. *Angelina N. Tompkins*, m. Theodore Horton.

vii ELIZA A. NELSON, b. 8 April 1803; d. 17 Oct. 1826 Pawtucket, unm. (*RIVR* 19:25)

viii HORATIO NELSON, b. 25 Feb. 1805; d. 19 Sept. 1805.

ix [CHILD] NELSON, d. 27 Aug. 1806 at Bristol, R.I. (not in *VR*).

x ABIGAIL GREEN NELSON, b. 25 Nov. 1807; d. 25 Dec. 1868 (g.s.); m. JONATHAN NILES SPENCER of Pawtucket (*Milford History*, 2:921), b. 1799, d. 7 May 1827 (g.s., Swan Point Cem.). In 1850 Abby G. Spencer and her daughter were living in Providence with her sister Dulcina Tillinghast.

> *Spencer* child: 1. *Abigail N. Spencer⁷*, b. ca 1830; m. Jerome Kimball of Providence, R.I.

xi MATTHIAS M. NELSON, b. 24 July 1810; d. 12 May 1857 (g.s., Swan Point Cem.); unm. In 1850 he was a book keeper in a boarding house in Blackstone (p.316).

Sources cited: *Milford VR. Upton VR.* Arnold, *Vital Record of R.I.*, 6: Pt 1 [Bristol]. R.I. Historical Cemeteries Transcription Project Data Base. *History of Milford* (1882). Worcester County Probate Records. *Heads of Families 1790 – Mass.* CENSUS: 1850 Blackstone, Worcester Co. (M432-345); Ward 5, Providence, Providence Co., R.I. (M432-845).

645. DEBORAH NELSON⁵ (*Elizabeth Thayer⁴, Elizabeth³ Samson, Stephen², Henry¹*), daughter of Josiah Nelson and his wife Elizabeth Thayer [134], was born 14 April 1765 at Milford (*VR* 126). Her death on 15 September 1817, aged 52, at Orange, is recorded there with the births of her children (*VR* 1). Her gravestone in the Jones Cemetery, Orange, bears the inscription: "*Death is a sweet sonorous sound / To those who have salvation found / It wafts them to the courts of bliss / Where all is joy and happiness.*"

She married 28 May 1786, at Milford (*VR* 267), **JONATHAN JONES JR.** of Orange. He was born at Milford 3 January 1763, son of Jonathan and Mary (____) Jones (*VR* 267), and died 14 March 1843 at Orange (g.s.), aged 80 years. He married, second, POLLY _____, who died 7 December 1836 at Orange, aged 47 (g.s.), and had with her daughters Martha C., Jane Augusta, Jeanette Miranda, and Maryette Ellen Jones. Jonathan's gravestone is inscribed: "*My flesh shall slumber in the Ground / Till the last trumpet's joyful sound / Then burst the chains with sweet surprise / And in my Saviour's image rise.*" His death was noted in the *Columbian Centinel* of 4 January 1812, "Jonathan Jones, formerly of Milford, died in Orange ae 80…" Polly's stone says, "*She was a kind and loving wife / To me she has always been / She's good to all her neighbors round/ And everybody's friend.*"

The will of Josiah Nelson dated 15 April 1806 names among others his daughter Deborah, wife of Jonathan Jones (Worcester PR #42827).

History of Western Massachusetts (2:413), under "Orange," relates that Jonathan Jones and his son Jonathan from Milford settled at a place called Goshen between 1772 and 1783; in 1791 Ward 1 included Jonathan Jones and Jonathan Jones Jr.

Jonathan's father, Jonathan Jones of Milford, innholder, bought 227 acres in Orange (formerly Goshen) on 24 December 1783 (Franklin LR 11:558). On 9 July 1787 Jonathan Jones of Orange, yeoman, sold to his son Jonathan Jones Jr. of Orange, yeoman, part of his homestead farm and half of his dwelling house, and on 9 February 1793 he sold 20 acres in Orange, bounded by Daniel Davison's land, to Jonathan Jr. (*ibid.*, 3:294; 11:561). The death in Orange of Jonathan Jones [Sr.], formerly of Milford, was noted in the *Columbian Centinel* of 4 January 1812.

Administration on the estate of Jonathan Jones, late of Orange, was given to George W. Jones on 26 April 1843, with Oliver Ward and Jesse Warrick as fellow bondsmen (Franklin PR #6284). On 9 May 1843 Jesse Warrick was appointed guardian of Jane Augusta Jones and Janette Miranda Jones, minors over 14, and Maryett Ellen Jones under 14. A petition to settle the estate was signed on 13 April 1844 by Levi Jones and Luke Cheney with Charlotte his wife, all of Londonderry, Vt.; Jeremiah R. Allen with wife Emily N. of Warwick; and George W. Jones, Martha C. Jones, and Jesse Warrick (guardian of Jane A. Jones, Janette M. Jones, and Mariette E. Jones, all of Orange), each holding one-eighth of undivided real estate. There was a division and settlement on 24 March 1845 among heirs: George W. Jones, Levi Jones, Charlotte Cheney wife of Luke, Emily N. Allen wife of Jeremiah R., Maryette E. Jones, Jenette M. Jones, Jane A. Jones, and Martha C. Jones. Jesse Warrick as guardian of Jenette M. Jones and Maryette E. Jones, minor children of Jonathan Jones deceased, petitioned 2 December 1846 to sell real estate.

Members of this family are buried in the Jones Cemetery, Read Road, Orange, where their inscriptions were copied in 1928.

Children of Jonathan and Deborah (Nelson) Jones, births of all and deaths of three recorded at Orange (*VR* 1: 6, 74):

   i   PHILIP JONES[6], b. 6 May 1787; d. 25 April 1794 in 7th year (g.s.).

   ii   LEVI JONES, b. 26 April 1789; m. ANNA ____, b. ca 1891 Mass. In 1850 he was a farmer in Londonderry, Vt., with Anna ae 59 and dau. Sylvia, adjacent to the families of Levi Jr. and Jonathan (p.301).

          Jones children, b. Vt. (1850 census; prob. incomplete): 1. *Jonathan Jones[7]*, b. ca 1813; m. Audelia A. ____. 2. *Levi Jones Jr.*, b. ca 1814; m. Sarah ____. 3. *Sylvia A. Jones*, b. ca 1831.

iii   JONATHAN JONES 3d, b. 4 Sept. 1791; d. 27 March 1816 ae 24y (g.s.; *Col. Cent.* of 25 May 1816); bur. Jones Cem., with epitaph: *"Friends and Physicians could not save / This mortal body from the grave / Nor can the grave confine me here / When Christ shall call me to appear."*

iv   CHARLOTTE JONES, b. 14 July 1793; m. LUKE CHENEY, b. Orange 27 Dec. 1790, son of Ebenezer and Hannah (___) Cheney (VR 1); of Londonderry, Vt., 1844.

      Probable *Cheney* children, farmers, living together 1850 Londonderry, Vt. (p.299): 1. *Josiah N. Cheney*[7], b. ca 1828. 2. *John Cheney*, b. ca 1830.

v   JOSIAH N. JONES, b. 21 May 1798; d. 11 Jan. 1815 ae 19y (g.s.).

vi   GEORGE WASHINGTON JONES, b. 28 Sept. 1800; d. 2 Jan. 1884 at Orange, ae 83y (g.s.; Mass. VR 355:336); m. ESTHER WARD, b. ca 1801 Mass., d. 1890 (Mass. VR 409:440). In 1850 he was a farmer at Orange, with Esther ae 49, and three children (p.362).

      Children at home 1850: 1. *Emeline W. Jones*[7], b. ca 1830. 2. *Caroline J. Jones*, b. ca 1836. 3. *Jonathan Jones*, b. ca 1839; m. Eunice Flagg.

vii   EMILY N. JONES, b. 13 Feb. 1810; d. 30 May 1845 ae 35y (g.s.); bur. Jones Cem., Orange; m. JEREMIAH R. ALLEN, b. ca 1804 Mass. In 1850 he was a farmer in Warwick, with three children but no wife (p.323). Emily's epitaph: *"Her lips proclaimed the path of light / Her own example made it plain, / Though gone from us to dwell in Heaven / Her kind instruction still remains."*

      Allen children at home 1850: 1. *Martha J. Allen*[7], b. ca 1833. 2. *Calvin D. Allen*, b. ca 1838. 3. *George J. Allen*, b. ca 1842.

Sources cited: Orange VR, transcription, Search & Research CD. Cemetery inscriptions, Jones Cemetery, Orange, copied 4 Aug. 1928 by Mrs. Grace F. Weymouth, on line. Franklin County Deeds and Probate Records at Greenfield. J.G. Holland, *History of Western Massachusetts* (1855). *Index, Columbian Centinel.* CENSUS: 1850 Franklin Co., Orange (M432-323) & Warwick (M432-317), Londonderry, Windham Co., Vt. (M432-929).

646.   ELIZABETH NELSON[5] (*Elizabeth Thayer*[4], *Elizabeth*[3] *Samson, Stephen*[2], *Henry*[1]), daughter of Josiah Nelson and his wife Elizabeth Thayer [134], was born 10 October 1768 at Milford (*VR* 126), and died at Craftsbury, Vt., 12 February 1842 (VT VR).

She married at Milford, 11 January 1789 (*VR* 225), **DANIEL DAVISON,** who was born at Conway 13 September 1764 (*VR* 40), son of Daniel Davison and Abigail Sumner who married at Mendon in 1759 (*VR* 286). He died at Craftsbury, Vt., 8 November 1854 (VT VR). Elizabeth was named in her father's will of 1806 as daughter Betsey, wife of Daniel Davison (Worcester PR # 42827). Daniel was brought up at Milford by Rev. R. A. Frost, the minister who had married his parents (*Milford History* 2:918).

Daniel Davison served in the Revolutionary War. He enlisted at Milford 30 March 1781 for a term of three years, described as aged 16, 5 ft. 8 in. tall, light complexion, occupation farmer. His name was on muster rolls at West Point and other places in New York, to February 1782; he was reported sick and absent in October and November 1781 (*MSSR* 4:554). His father also served, from Conway (*ibid.*).

On 2 May 1786 Jonathan Jones of Orange sold to Daniel Davison of Milford, laborer, 50 acres in Orange (Franklin LR 3:268). Daniel Davison of Reedsborough, Bennington Co., Vt., yeoman, sold five acres in Conway on 23 March 1791, and 10 more acres the same day (*ibid.*, 1:576, 578). On 3 April 1793 he bought 20 acres in Orange (*ibid.*, 11:562). Called "of Orange, yeoman," 13 February 1796, he sold 71 acres in Orange; wife Elizabeth relinquished her dower (*ibid.*, 11:586).

The family removed to Craftsbury, Vt., about 1796. Daniel's father, "Old Mr. Daniel Davison," died there 6 June 1828 aged 90 years (VT VR) and was buried in North Craftsbury Cemetery.

Daniel Davison applied for a pension 7 October 1832 in Orleans County, Vt., a resident of Craftsbury (White, 915, citing #S18792). He is listed as age 75, living at Craftsbury, in the *Vermont Pensioners* index of 1841 (p.63).

In 1850 Daniel Davidson [*sic*], aged 86, born Nova Scotia [*sic*] was living at Craftsbury in the household of Abigail S. Mason (probably his granddaughter), aged 33, born Vt., and her daughters Nancy and Susan (p.37).

Children of Daniel and Elizabeth (Nelson) Davison, rec. at Orange on the same page as the children of Betsey's sister Deborah Jones (VR 1) and also at Craftsbury, Vt. (VT VR):

i   AMORY DAVISON[6], b. 23 Jan. 1790; d. Craftsbury, Vt., 7 June 1868; m. at Bath, N.H., 1 Jan. 1815, NANCY DIXON MILLS, b. 1794 in Vt., d. Craftsbury 19 July 1862. In 1850 Emery Davidson was a farmer at Craftsbury ae 60, with Nancy ae 55, and children Daniel, Katherine, Emery, Solomon, and Almira (p.25) as well as several young people of other surnames.

Children, b. Craftsbury, Vt. (VT VR), Daniel and four youngest at home 1850: 1. *Susan Elizabeth Davison*[7], b. 22 Feb. 1816. 2. *Abigail Sumner Davison*, b. 20 Feb. 1818; m. Harrison Mason. 3. *Daniel Davison*, b. 6 Oct. 1820. 4. *William Davison*, b. ca 1822; d. inf. 5. *Katherine Mills Davison*, b. 9 Jan. 1824. 6. [*Child*] *Davison*, d. 16 Jan. 1829. 7. *Amory Davison*, b. 29 June 1830; m. Augusta ___.

8. *Solomon Van Rensalear Davison,* b. 4 July 1832. 9. *Almeda Merrill Davison,* b. 31 Oct. 1839.

ii   DANIEL DAVISON, b. 7 Jan. 1792; d. 25 June 1864; m. _____. In 1850 Daniel Davidson Jr. was a farmer ae 56 in Johnson, Vt., living in the household of Asa Andrews, farmer and innkeeper (p.66).
Children rec. Craftsbury, of "Daniel Jr." (VT VR): 1. *Charlotte Davison*[7], b. 15 Nov. 1821. 2. *Daniel Sumner Davison,* b. 12 May 1823. 3. *Maria Dulcena Davison,* b. 6 Feb. 1825. 4. *Lydia Angelina Davison,* b. 16 Dec. 1826; m. at Johnson, Vt., 28 March 1844, Atwood Andrews.

iii   ABIGAIL DAVISON (Nabby in Craftsbury VR), b. 17 Oct. 1793; d. 4 May 1869.

iv   ELIZABETH THAYER DAVISON, b. 10 June 1795; d. 26 May 1871; m. (1) 17 March 1812, JULIUS COLLINS; m. (2) 14 Feb. 1847, as his fourth wife, WILLIAM ELIJAH GREEN, whose first wife was Elizabeth's aunt Abigail Nelson [#651], *q.v.* (*Milford History,* 2:778, 918). Her two youngest sons were in Wisconsin in 1850: W. W. Collins was a storekeeper with wife and children in Oconomowoc (p.368), and Solon Y. Collins was a clerk in Racine (p.23).
Collins children, b. Vt.: 1. *Amory Davison Collins*[7], b. 12 Nov. 1813. 2. *Julia Nelson Collins,* b. 31 July 1815. 3. *Elizabeth Collins,* b. 29 June 1817. 4. *Abbie Sumner Collins,* b. 24 May 1820. 5. *Washington Wallace Collins,* b. 28 Aug. 1822. 6. *Solon Young Collins,* b. 15 April 1829.

Sources cited: Orange VR. Vermont Vital Records to 1870: Craftsbury. Franklin County Deeds. Worcester County Deeds and Probate Records. *Mass. Soldiers & Sailors.* White, *Abstracts of Rev. War Pension Files. History of Milford* (1892). CENSUS: 1850 Craftsbury, Orleans Co., & Johnson, Lamoille Co., Vt. (M432-925); Wisc.: Racine, Racine Co. (M432-1004) & Oconomowoc, Waukesha Co. (M432-1009).

647.   ESTHER NELSON[5] (*Elizabeth Thayer*[4], *Elizabeth*[3] *Samson, Stephen*[2], *Henry*[1]), daughter of Josiah Nelson and his wife Elizabeth Thayer [134], was born 16 September 1770 at Milford (*VR* 126). She died 23 July 1843, aged 72, at Greensboro, Vt. (cem. rec.).

She married 25 January 1805 at Milford (*VR* 267, 290), as his second wife, **LEVI STEPHENS** of Greensboro, Vt. He was born 22 January 1770 at Newbury, Vt., son of Simeon and Sarah (Hadley) Stephens (*Newbury History,* 697), and died 16 August 1859 at Greensboro, aged 89y 6m 24d (VT VR). He married, first, at Newbury 29 November 1790 (VR) SUSAN SHEPARD of Greensboro, who died 26 September 1802. He married, third, before 1850, SARAH / SALLY ___, who was born about 1792 and died in the spring of 1885 (Orleans District PR #388). In the will of her father, dated 15 April 1806 (Worcester PR #42827) Esther is called daughter Esther, "wife of Stephen or rather Levi Stephens," and in *History of Milford* (2:918) her husband is called Stephen Stephens, "not traced."

The 1790 census lists Levi in Newbury, Vt., with two females in his household. In 1800 he was in Greensboro with a boy 10-16 and four girls under 10. Hemenway (*Vt. Hist. Gazetteer* 3:212) states that Col. Levi Stevens' [first] wife and three children died in 1802. The Greensboro town records did not survive a fire.

The 1810 census lists the family in Greensboro (p 455), Levi and Esther between 26 and 45, with two boys and three girls under 10, a girl 10-16, and two young women 16-26; of these children only two or maybe three of the youngest could be Esther's. In 1850 Levi Stevens, aged 80, was head of a household in Greensboro that included [third wife] Sally, 58 [?], and [daughter] Belinda, 54, both born in Vermont (p.96).

In his will dated 29 September 1856, proved 15 September 1859, Levi Stevens of Greensboro, "being in a very infirm state of health and sensible too of my liableness to sudden death – at the same time being in my own apprehension of sound mind – do judge it best to make and accordingly do hereby make this my last will and testament ..." He gave ... "to my beloved wife Sally Stevens my dwelling house – barn – & out buildings connected therewith [with land and garden] in Greensboro Village, and all my household furniture, clothing and provisions (except what is otherwise particularly devised) also one cow" ... and $600 current money to be put in trust for her, to revert to his heirs if she remarried. To oldest daughter Belinda he left several household items, then crossed them out, replacing them with $600 to be invested for her support and maintenance during her natural life. Other bequests followed:

> ... to my son Josiah N. Stevens $300 ... to my daughter Susan Ewin widow the late Richard Ewin deseat [deceased] $100 ... to my daughter Abigail G. Stimpson $5 ... to my grandson Arba N. Waterman son of Loring S. Waterman, $50. ... to my grandson Levi Stevens son of Josiah N. Stevens $25 ... to my grandson Henry H. Stevens son of Josiah N. Stevens $50. ... to my granddaughter Ester Stevens daughter of Josiah N. Stevens $20 ... to the widow of Franklin Flint Deceased son of Wm S. Flint for the benefit of the child of the said Franklin $50.

He left the residue to son Josiah N. Stevens, and appointed him executor (Orleans District PR, Docket 2, Estate #388).

The probate file includes correspondence dated 1885. L. H. Haines of Waterbury, Vt., wrote to the probate judge on 5 August 1885 (on a very interesting letterhead for his wholesale grocery) informing him that the widow had died "last spring," the executor was dead also, and his own wife was one of the heirs. He requested that J. O Cutler of Greensboro be appointed administrator in order to settle the estate. A letter from Mr. Cutler to Judge Austin on 12 September enclosed a request signed by Mary S. Haines of Waterbury and a consent signed by Abbie M. Babbitt of East Hardwick, Vt., that the property be sold. Cutler wrote,

> as far as I can learn [they are] the only ayers [*sic*] in this State. The buildings are very much destroyed Sills all gone & some of the out buildings may brake down before Spring & it is thought best to have them disposed of this fall. I learn that there is no claims against the estate except Mr Haines he has a claim for paying taxes for a number of years past.

Children of Levi and Esther (Nelson) Stephens (from father's will):

i   SUSAN STEVENS[6], b. prob. 1805; m. RICHARD EWEN, d. before 1850, when Susan Ewen ae 45, b. Vt., was head of a household in Plainfield, Ill., with children Esther, Albert, and Henry, all b. Vt. (p.37). Her father's will calls her "widow of the late Richard Ewin." In 1860 Susan Ewing was a "Lady" living in the household of Walter B. and Esther Caswell (ae 31, b. Vt.) in Joliet, Ill.; [nephew] Arba N. Waterman was there too, ae 25, merchant, b. Vt. (p.464).
       Ewen children at home 1850: 1. *Esther Ewen[7]*, b. ca 1829; prob. m. Walter B. Caswell. 2. *Albert Ewen*, b. ca 1833. 3. *Henry Ewen*, b. ca 1838.

ii   MARY STEVENS, b. say 1807; d. prob. before Sept. 1858; m. LORING WATERMAN. Her husband and son are named in Levi Stevens' will but Mary is not.
       Waterman child (poss. others): 1. *Arba Nelson Waterman[7]*, b. Greensboro, Vt., 5 Feb. 1836; m. Chicago, Ill., 16 Dec. 1862, Eloise Hall. He became a prominent lawyer and editor in Chicago, editor of *Historical Review of Chicago and Cook County* (1898), *q.v.*, pp. 531-32, for an account of him.

iii JOSIAH NELSON STEVENS, b. 8 Sept. 1808 Greensboro, Vt. (VR); d. 1883; m. ROXANA HUNTINGTON, b. ca 1810, d. 1874. In 1850 he was a farmer in Greensboro (indexed as Stearns); with Roxana ae 40, eight children, Unice Huntington ae 23 and Thomas Boardman ae 20 (p.88). In 1860 his household in Greensboro included, in addition to his own family, [his sister] Abigail Stimpson ae 50, Mary Stimpson ae 17, Lydia Stevens [prob. Belinda] ae 64, and Henry Huntington ae 10 (p.978).
       Children (first nine at home 1850, last seven 1860): 1. *Levi Nelson Stevens[7]*, b. ca 1834. 2. *Henry H. Stevens*, b. ca 1836. 3. *Dan Stevens*, b. ca 1839. 4. *Caroline H. Stevens*, b. ca 1841. 5. *Helen Esther Stevens*, b. ca 1843, named in grandfather's will as Esther H. Stevens 6. *Pamelia Stevens*, b. ca 1846. 7. *Abbie M. Stevens*, b. ca

1847; m. Henry A. Babbitt (*DAR LB* 64:283); of Hardwick, Vt., 1885 when she consented to sale of her grandfather's real estate.   8. *Josiah N. Stevens*, b. ca 1849.   9. *Susan Estelle Stevens*, b. 1854; m. Samuel Gibson Updegraff (*DAR LB* 163:105).

iv   ABIGAIL G. STEVENS, b. ca 1810; m. ____ STIMPSON; named in father's will as Abigail Stimpson. In 1860 she was ae 50, living with her daughter Mary in the household of her brother Josiah N. Stevens at Greensboro, Vt.

Stimpson child (poss. others): 1. *Mary Stimpson⁷*, b. ca 1843 Vt. ; m. Leander H. Haines; res. Waterbury, Vt., with children 1880. She and her cousin Abbie M. Stevens Babbitt were the only heirs of Levi Stevens living in Vermont in 1885.

Sources cited: *Milford VR.* Vermont Vital Records to 1870: Greensboro. Orleans District Probate Records at Newport, Vt. *History of Milford* (1892).   *History of Newbury, Vermont* (1902). Hemenway, *Vermont Historical Gazetteer.* DAR Lineage Books 64 and 163. CENSUS: Greensboro, Orleans Co., Vt. 1850 (M432–925), 1860 (M653-1322); Waterbury, Washington Co., Vt., 1880 (T9-548); Will Co., Ill., Plainfield 1850 (M432-133), Joliet 1860 (M653-238).

648.   ARBA NELSON⁵ (*Elizabeth Thayer⁴, Elizabeth³ Samson, Stephen², Henry¹*), son of Josiah Nelson and his wife Elizabeth Thayer [134], was born 14 April 1772 at Milford (*VR* 125) and baptized 28 June 1772 at Mendon Mill River, Hopkinton (*VR* 140) as "Arbel, ch. of Josiah." He died 15 January 1835 at Craftsbury, Vt. (VR; cem. rec.) The will of Josiah Nelson, dated 15 April 1806, names his son Arba (Worcester PR # 42827).

He married at Milford, 2 October 1791 (*VR* 267), **ABIGAIL PARKHURST**, who was born there 9 May 1774, daughter of Nathaniel and Sarah (Brown) Parkhurst (*VR* 133, 273). She died 5 October 1860 at Craftsbury, aged 92y 5m, "usual residence Walcott" (Walcott VR). Abigail, wife of Arba Nelson, is named among heirs in the distribution of the estate of Nathaniel Parkhurst of Milford on 28 April 1819 (Worcester PR #45337).

The 1800 census listed Arba at Craftsbury, Vt., with three boys and one girl under 10 in the household (p.648). In 1820 the household included a boy under 10, two girls 10-16, a boy 16-18, and a girl 16-26 (p.354); in 1830 Arba and his wife were 50-60, with a boy 15-20, a man 20-30, another man 30-40, and a woman 20-30 in the household; Arba Jr. was listed that year by himself in Craftsbury (p.191).

On 17 May 1837 Arba Nelson of Craftsbury requested administration be granted on the estate of his father, Arba Nelson late of Craftsbury, deceased, and at the request of the widow (not named), Edwin Nelson was appointed (Orleans District PR 4:3).

Children of Arba and Abigail (Parkhurst) Nelson, six with full birthdates rec. Craftsbury; others probable, consistent with census:

    i   AMORY NELSON[6], b. 9 March 1792; indicated by census figures but n.f.r.

poss. ii   HORACE NELSON, b. ca 1794 Mass.; m. ELIZABETH ___. In 1850 Horace was a farmer ae 56 in Craftsbury with Elizabeth ae 52 b. N.H. or N.C., and four children (p.25).

        Children at home 1850, all b. Vt.: 1. *Abbie Nelson[7]*, b. ca 1833. 2. *Emily Nelson,* b. ca 1835. 3. *George Nelson,* b. ca 1840. 4. *Ellen Nelson,* b. ca 1843.

prob. iii   HELENA NELSON, b. say 1795; d. prob. ca 1848; m. Craftsbury, Vt., 13 Jan. 1822, HARVEY SCOTT, b. Peacham, Vt., ca 1800, son of William and Sabra (Elkins) Scott (*Haskell, Hayner Gen.,* 109).

        Scott children (*ibid.*): 1. *Laura Ellen Scott[7]*; m. John E. Hayner, partner of Arba Nelson Jr. in Alton, Ill., hardware business. 2. *Almira Scott.* 3. *Harvey Elkins Scott.*

    iv   STEPHEN NELSON, b. 4 June 1798; d. 16 June 1816 ae 18 (cem. rec.).

    v   ARBA NELSON, b. 19 Dec. 1800; d. Alton, Madison Co., Ill., after 1860; m. (1) ELLEN H. ___, b. ca 1815 Mass.; m. (2) his cousin CHARLOTTE H. (NELSON) RAND[7], dau. of Henry and Catharine (Parkhurst) Nelson (#643-i-7). He established a hardware business in Alton, Ill., before 1840, and donated land there to the Church of the Redeemer shortly before his death (*Madison Co. History*, 383).

        Children (census): 1. *Lawrence Nelson[7]*, b. ca 1848; d. poss. by 1860. 2. *Laura Nelson,* b. ca 1859.

    vi   NATHANIEL PARKHURST NELSON, b. 24 Dec. 1803; res. Craftsbury 1850 ae 46, in household of James M. and Ann Robins (p.25).

    vii   ELIZABETH NELSON, b. 10 Oct. 1806; d. 13 or 30 Oct. 1835 ae 19 (VT VR; cem rec.).

    viii   SARAH NELSON, b. 30 Aug. 1810; m. Craftsbury, 1832, PORTER CRANE, b. Williamstown, Vt., 27 Feb. 1804, d. Wolcott 23 Oct. 1880, son of Joseph and Eleanor (Buck) Crane (*Crane Gen.,* 2:116). In 1850 he was ae 46, a manufacturer b. Vt., in Wolcott, Vt., with Sarah P. ae 39, and five children (p.124).

        Crane children, all but Porter at home 1850, all b. Vt.; full b. dates from *Crane Gen.* 2:116: 1. *Arba N. Crane[7]*, b. 11 Jan. 1834. 2. *Franklin Crane,* b. 27 Dec. 1835. 3. *Edward P. Crane,* b. 14 Dec. 1837. 4. *Porter Crane,* b. 9 Dec. 1839; res. 1850 in household of George L. Martin, Williamstown, Vt. (p.278). 5. *Sarah E. Crane,* b. 17 April 1842. 6. *Frederick Crane,* b. 12 Sept. 1846; d. 28 April 1877.

prob. ix EDWIN NELSON, b. ca 1815; m. MARY E. ___, b. ca 1823 Vt. At the request of the widow of Arba Nelson, Edwin was appointed adm. in 1837 of Arba's estate (noted above). In 1850 Edwin Nelson ae 35 was a farmer at Craftsbury with Mary E. ae 27 and three children (p.25).

Children at home 1850: 1. *Charles Nelson⁷*, b. ca 1841. 2. *Hellen E. Nelson*, b. ca 1842. 3. *Arba Nelson*, b. ca 1847.

Sources cited: *Milford VR.* Vermont Vital Records to 1870: Craftsbury, Walcott. Orleans District, Vt., Probate Records at Newport. *History of Madison County, Illinois* (1912). Ellery Bicknell Crane, *Genealogy of the Crane Family*, vol. 2 (1900). *Haskell, Haynor and Allied Families* (1926). CENSUS: Craftsbury, Orleans Co., Vt., 1800 (M32-51), 1820 (M33-127), 1830 (M19-183), & 1850 (M432-925); 1850 Wolcott, Lamoille Co., Vt. (M432-925), Williamstown, Orange Co., Vt. (M432-926); 1850 Alton, Madison Co., Ill. (M432-119).

649. HOPESTILL NELSON⁵ (*Elizabeth Thayer⁴, Elizabeth³ Samson, Stephen², Henry¹*), daughter of Josiah Nelson and his wife Elizabeth Thayer [134], was born 10 October 1774 at Milford (*VR* 127). She died there 12 January 1857, aged 82 (Mass. VR 113:157).

She married, after intentions at Milford 27 October 1796 (*VR* 271), **AMASA PARKHURST**. He was born 23 November 1771 at Mendon (*VR* 134), son of Nathaniel and Sarah (Brown) Parkhurst, and died 23 November 1826, aged 55, at Milford (*VR* 358).

In his will dated 15 November 1826, proved 5 December 1826 (Worcester PR #45269), Amasa Parkhurst of Milford named his wife Hopestill; granddaughter Mariah Kendall; daughters Elmira Corbett, Ruba Webb, Hopestill Parkhurst, and Elizabeth Parkhurst; and sons Oliver B., Nelson, and Amasa Parkhurst. He appointed as executors his wife Hopestill and son-in-law John Corbett Jr., but the widow requested that Lt. John Corbett execute alone. A petition dated 6 January 1827 was signed by Mariah Kendall, Elmira Corbett, Ruba Webb, Hopestill Parkhurst, Elizabeth Parkhurst, Oliver B. Nelson, and Amasa Nelson. An accounting after April 1829 was signed by heirs: Jos. Webb, Coollidge Perry, Oliver Parkhurst, Sullivan Sumner, guardian for two of the heirs and "was guardian of another at the time the instrument was made."

On 27 May 1828 Sullivan Sumner was named guardian of Nelson Parkhurst, a minor over 14, and Amasa and Elizabeth Parkhurst, under 14, children of Amasa Parkhurst (Worcester PR #45270, #45339).

Children of Amasa and Hopestill (Nelson) Parkhurst, rec. Milford (*VR* 133-36):

i   ANNE / ANNA NELSON PARKHURST[6], b. 18 July 1797; d. 1823 ae 26 yrs and bur. Milford (*VR* 358), as "Annie M. Kendall, dau. of Amasa and Hopestill"; m. at Milford, 7 Nov. 1819 (*VR* 271), DANIEL KENDALL.
> **Kendall** child rec. Milford (*VR* 105): 1. *Lucy Mariah Kendall[7]*, b. 26 Sept. 1820.

ii   PAUL NELSON PARKHURST, b. 15 Aug. 1799; d. 10 Aug. 1802 at Milford (*VR* 359).

iii   ALMIRA / ELMIRA PARKHURST, b. 24 Oct. 1801; m. at Milford, 1 May 1825 (*VR* 271), MAJOR JOHN CORBETT JR.
> **Corbett** children rec. Milford (*VR* 49-50): 1. *Sarah Helen Corbett[7]*, b. 18 March 1826. 2. *Oliver Corbett*, b. 2 July 1829 [calc.]; d. 4 Oct. 1832 ae 3y 3m 2d, bur. Purchase St. Cem., Milford (*VR* 332). 3. *Carleton Corbett*, b. 12 Aug. 1831. 4. *Cyrus Barton Corbett*, b. 24 March 1836. 5. *Augustus Oliver Corbett*, b. 9 March 1837.

iv   RUBY BROWN PARKHURST, b. 7 Nov. 1803; m. 2 April 1822 at Milford (*VR* 273), JOSEPH WEBB, b. ca 1794 Mass. Said to have moved to R.I. and later Wisc. In 1850 Joseph Webb ae 56 was a depot master in Sutton, with Ruby ae 47 and four children (p.153).
> **Webb** children at home 1850 (said to be 10 ch. in all), one rec. Sutton: 1. *Henry Webb[7]*, b. ca 1830. 2. *George Webb*, b. ca 1835. 3. *Julia Webb*, b. ca 1841. 4. *Levi Webb*, b. 11 April 1846, Sutton (*VR* 184).

v   OLIVER BROWN PARKHURST, b. 20 July 1806; m. at Milford, 12 May 1833 (*VR* 273), MARIA NELSON, b. 21 Feb. 1813, dau. Henry and Catharine (Parkhurst) Nelson, at Milford (*VR* 127, 268).
> Children rec. Milford (*VR* 134-36): 1. *Ellen Maria Parkhurst[7]*, b. 10 June 1834; d. 4 July 1837 ae 3 yrs, Milford (*VR* 359). 2. *Eliza Bianca Parkhurst*, b. 19 Oct. 1835. 3. *George Oliver Parkhurst*, b. 4 Aug. 1837. 4. *Warren Jones Parkhurst*, b. 6 Oct. 1840; drowned 1 June 1844 ae 3y 8m, Milford (*VR* 360). 5. *Herbert Parkhurst*, b. 2 Dec. 1842. 6. *Mary Annah Parkhurst*, b. 1 Aug. 1845. 7. *John O.*, b. 14 Dec. 1847.

vi   NELSON PARKHURST, b. 30 April 1809; m. HANNAH JAYNE of Boston. In 1850 Nelson ae 41 was "foreman in Bootmaking" in Milford with Harriet [*sic*] ae 36, and four children (p.6).
> Children at home 1850, all b. Mass: 1. *Ann M. Parkhurst[7]*, b. ca 1833. 2. *Laura Parkhurst*, b. ca 1835. 3. *Charlotte Parkhurst*, b. ca 1837. 4. *Aurania Parkhurst*, b. ca 1839.

vii   HOPESTILL PARKHURST, b. 18 Nov. 1811; m. at Milford (*VR* 275, 276), (1) 25 Feb. 1827, COOLIDGE PERRY, who d. 13 Oct. 1836 ae 31 yrs, Milford (*VR* 361); m. (2) after int. 14 March 1839, WILLIAM P. HAVEN, b. Milford 8 Aug. 1815 (*VR* 83).

Perry children rec. Milford (*VR* 139-40): 1. *Mary Jane Perry*[7], b. 18 Dec. 1827. 2. *Amanda Mariah Perry*, b. 16 Feb. 1830. 3. *Nelson Parkhurst Perry*, b. 11 July 1832 or 1833. 4. *George F. Perry.*, d. 27 Feb. 1835 ae 4 wks, bur. Vernon Grove Cem., Milford (*VR* 362). 5. *Caroline E Perry*, b. 13 June 1836.

Haven children rec. Milford (*VR* 83): 1. *Ellen Frances Haven*[7], b. 13 Jan. 1840. 2. *Hopestill P Haven*, b. 17 Nov. 1841. 3. *Louisa P. Haven*, b. 1 Jan. 1843.

viii AMASA PARKHURST, b. 13 April 1815; m. (1) after int. at Mendon 20 Sept. 1839, ELIZABETH FRENCH BROWN, b. 18 May 1819, d. Milford 26 July 1840 ae 21, of dysentery, dau. of Abel and Polly (Pond) Brown (*VR* 28, 205, 359); m. (2) at Milford, 6 April 1842 (*VR* 271), HANNAH P. BROWN, b. 1822, sister of his first wife.

Children with Elizabeth: 1. *[Infant son]* Parkhurst, d. 24 July 1840 ae 2 wks, Milford (*VR* 358). Children with Hannah, rec. Milford (*VR* 133): 1. *Elizabeth Brown Parkhurst*[7], b. 29 May 1843. 2. *Edwin Parkhurst*, b. 9 Feb. 1846. 3. *Alton Parkhurst*, b. 3 Jan. or 3 Feb. 1848.

ix ELIZABETH CAROLINE PARKHURST, b. 12 Sept. 1820; m. 17 March 1839 at Milford (*VR* 247, 272), LEANDER HOLBROOK, Esq.

Holbrook children rec. Milford (*VR* 89-91): 1. *Orlando S. Holbrook*[7], b. 3 March 1842; d. 7 April 1843, ae 2y 1m, of canker rash. 2. *Lucinda B. Holbrook*, b. 8 April 1844. 3. *Emma L Holbrook.*, b. 21 April 1846. 4. *Mary Ava Holbrook*, b. 10 Nov. 1847. 5. *[Son]* Holbrook, b. 31 Dec. 1849.

Sources cited: *Mendon VR. Milford VR.* Mass. Vital Records 1841-1910. Worcester County Probate Records. CENSUS: 1850 Milford, Worcester Co. (M432-344). **See also:** *History of Milford*, 2:944.

650. EZRA NELSON[5] (*Elizabeth Thayer*[4], *Elizabeth*[3] *Samson*, *Stephen*[2], *Henry*[1]), son of Josiah Nelson and his wife Elizabeth Thayer [134], was born 8 May 1777 at Milford (*VR* 126). He died there 19 October 1835, aged 58 (*VR* 355).

He married 22 May 1800 at Milford (*VR* 267), **POLLY PARKHURST**, who was born there 25 February 1776, daughter of Nathaniel and Sarah (Brown) Parkhurst, and died there 19 March 1827, called on her gravestone "Mary, wife of Cap. Ezra Nelson" (*VR* 136, 356).

Ezra was named executor in his father's will dated 15 April 1806, proved 4 August 1807 (Worcester PR #42827).

A distribution of the estate of Nathaniel Parkhurst of Milford among the heirs on 28 April 1819 directed that one son make a payment to his sisters Polly Nelson wife of Ezra and Catharine Nelson wife of Henry (Worcester PR #45337).

Capt. Ezra Nelson spent most of his life in the family homestead bought by his father from Ebenezer Torrey in 1784, located in Milford on the road to Upton. He was captain of the Milford Artillery Company "and universally respected as a worthy man" (*Milford History*, 922).

In his will, dated 14 October 1835, proved 3 November 1835, Ezra Nelson of Milford named his sons James M., George C., and Ezra T. Nelson; daughters Martha M. Nelson, Mary M. Nelson, and Dian P. Nelson; executor, son James (Worcester PR #42797). On 8 January 1836 Diana P. Nelson chose Sullivan Sumner as her guardian; the bond lists Dian [*sic*] over 14, and Ezra under 14 (Worcester PR #42788). Ezra's file includes a petition dated 15 January 1836 for an auction of property of the "estate left by Ezra Nelson in his will to his six children, the three girls and Ezra being minors," signed by James M. Nelson for himself and as guardian of Martha and Mary, and Sullivan Sumner as guardian for Diana and Ezra, and a letter of assent from George C. Nelson from Plymouth, Michigan Territory.

Children of Ezra and Mary/Polly (Parkhurst) Nelson, rec. Milford (*VR* 125-28; *Milford History* 2:921):

i   WILLIAM NELSON[6], b. 19 April 1802; d. 13 Oct. 1803 (*VR* 356).

ii   NATHANIEL PARKHURST NELSON, b. 25 Aug. 1804; d. 20 April 1809 (*VR* 356).

iii CAROLINE NELSON, b. 10 May 1807; d. 7 March 1833 (*VR* 355).

iv   JAMES MADISON NELSON, b. 24 Nov. 1809; m. in June 1839 at Trinity Church, Boston, ABBA GRAY BRIDGE, b. Boston in May 1810, dau. of John and Sarah (Stearns) Bridge (*Milford History*, 2:929). He was a manufacturer of furniture in Grand Rapids, Mich. In 1850 their household in Grand Rapids included the four children, Peter Hendricks ae 19, laborer b. Holland, and An[n]a Gammon ae 20 b. Ireland (p.179).

   Children, all b. Mich. (*Milford History*, 2:929): 1. *Sarah Stearns Nelson[7]*, b. 1840; m. Stephen H. Ballard. 2. *Abbie Rebecca Nelson*, b. 1843; m. Rev. M. P. Jones. 3. *Caroline Bridge/Mary C. Nelson*, b. 1846; m. Charles W. Wright. 4. *Charlotte Gray Nelson*, b. 13 Sept. 1849.

v   GEORGE CLINTON NELSON, b. 24 March 1812; m. MARY E. TAYLOR, b. Rochester, N.Y. 12 May 1818 (*Milford History*, 2:929). In 1850 he was a merchant in Grand Rapids, Mich., with Mary E. ae 31 and two children (p.168).

   Children (*Milford History*, 2:930): 1. *George Kent Nelson[7]*, b. 1 July 1842; m. Henrietta Porter Thompson. 2. *James Francis Nelson*, b. 13 Dec. 1847; m. Julia Adel Boardman.

vi   MARY MIRILLA NELSON (twin), b. 17 April 1815; m. Grand Rapids, Mich., 2 April 1839, A. HOSFORD SMITH (*Milford History*, 2:930).

   Smith children (*ibid.*): 1. *Walter D. Smith[7]*, b. 20 April 1842. 2. *Martha Nelson Smith*, b. 11 Aug. 1844; m. Robert Baylies. 3. *Mary Elizabeth Smith*, b. 24 April 1846; m. John B. White. 4. *Frederick Smith*, b. 24 Aug. 1848.

vii   MARTHA MURTILLA NELSON (twin), b. 17 April 1815; m. 17 April 1838 at Milford (*VR* 268), AMBROSE CHAMBERLAIN of Cambridge.

   Chamberlain children rec. Cambridge (VR 1:124-25): 1. *Anne Nelson Chamberlain[7]*, b. 28 Feb. 1839. 2. *Charles Valentine Chamberlain*, b. 12 May 1844. 3. *Mary Parkhurst Chamberlain*, b. 24 June 1840. 4. *William Heath Chamberlain*, b. 10 Jan. 1842.

viii POLLY DIANA NELSON, b. 28 Jan. 1818; m. Rev. WILLIAM R. G. MELLEN; res. Toronto, Canada. Three children.

ix   EZRA THAYER NELSON, b. 9 May 1823; m. 9 Oct. 1848, AUGUSTA M. VALENTINE of Hopkinton, b. 31 Oct. 1824. He was a manufacturer of fine furniture in Grand Rapids, Mich., with his brother J. M. and was living there in 1850 with Augusta M. ae 33, and one child (p.171).

   Children, b. Mich. (*Milford History*, 2:930): 1. *Anne Valentine Nelson[7]*, b. 3 Aug. 1849; m. Charles M. McLaren. 2. *Isabel Augusta Nelson*, b. 7 May 1854; m. Frederick R. Blount. 3. *Elizabeth Gooch Nelson*, b. 28 Feb. 1855; d. 2 Sept. 1855. 4. *Louise Maud Nelson*, b. 18 Jan. 1860.

Sources cited: *Cambridge VR. Milford VR. History of Milford* (1892). Worcester County Probate Records. CENSUS: 1850 Milford, Worcester Co. (M432-344); Grand Rapids, Kent Co., Mich. (M432-353).

651. ABIGAIL NELSON[5] (*Elizabeth Thayer[4], Elizabeth[3] Samson, Stephen[2], Henry[1]*), daughter of Josiah Nelson and his wife Elizabeth Thayer [134], was born 12 February 1780 at Milford (*VR* 125). She died there 7 May 1804, aged 34, of consumption (*VR* 342).

She married, 21 February 1803 at Milford (*VR* 239), **WILLIAM ELIJAH GREEN** of Grafton. He was born 31 January 1777 at Worcester (*VR* 119), son of John and Mary (Ruggles?) Green, and was first called William; his middle name was assumed at the death of his brother Elijah in 1795. He died at Worcester 27 July 1865, aged 88y 5m 27d, a lawyer (Mass. VRs 185:293).

William E. Green married, second, 7 October 1806, LUCY MERRIAM of Grafton, who was born 1786 and died 8 September 1811, aged 25 at Grafton (*VR* 339). He married, third, 13 May 1813, JULIA PLIMPTON, who died 12 February 1833 aged 47, at Worcester (*VR* 481), and, fourth, 14 February 1847, **ELIZABETH**

THAYER (DAVISON) COLLINS (*Milford History*, 2: 778, 918), daughter of Daniel and Elizabeth (Nelson) Davison [Samson **#646**] and thus niece of his first wife. He evidently had with his third wife, Julia, daughters Julia E. and Lydia P. Green.

In 1850 William E. Green aged 73 was living in Worcester with (fourth wife) Elizabeth T., aged 55, Elizabeth Green, 76, Julia E., 34, and Lydia P., 26 (p.144). The will of Josiah Nelson names his grandson William E. Green (Worcester PR #42827). There are no probate records for William E. Green in Worcester County.

Child of William E. and Abigail (Nelson) Green:

i WILLIAM NELSON GREEN[6], b. 22 Feb. 1804 at Milford (*Worcester VR* 79); m. 1839, SARAH M. (BALL) STAPLES, b. ca 1806 Mass. In 1850 William N. Green, Justice, was in Worcester with Sarah M. ae 44, and their two surviving sons (p.156).

Children, rec. Worcester (*VR* 118-19, d. 481): 1. *William-Nelson Green*[7], b. 10 Jan. 1843. 2. *Timothy-Ruggles Green*, b. 22 June 1844. 3. *John Green* (twin), b. 28 July 1845; d. 14 Sept. 1845 ae 1m. 4. *Thomas Green* (twin), b. 28 July 1845; d. 18 Aug. 1845 ae 21d. 5. *Lucy-Nelson Green*, b. 29 Oct. 1846; d. 16 Aug. 1847 ae 8m.

Sources cited: *Grafton VR. Milford VR. Worcester VR.* Mass. Vital Records 1841-1910. *History of Milford.* (1891). CENSUS: 1850 Worcester, Wards 2 & 3 (M432-342).

652. JEDEDIAH THAYER[5] (*Micah Thayer*[4], *Elizabeth*[3] *Samson, Stephen*[2], *Henry*[1]), son of Micah Thayer [135] and his wife Lois Thayer, was born 29 March 1764 at Mendon (*VR* 184), and baptized at Ware with his mother and siblings on 1 June 1777 (CR 50). He died 14 September 1855 (*Thayer Mem.*, 506) at Portland, Chautauqua County, N.Y.

He married, intentions 24 November 1784 at Ware (*VR* 58), both of Ware, **RACHAEL ADAMS**. She was born 1 March 1767 at Brookfield (not in *VR*) and died 10 March 1844 (*Thayer Mem.*, 506) at Portland, N.Y.

A division of the estate of Micah Thayer of Ware dated 5 April 1785 named his widow Lois, eldest son Jedidiah, and other children Rhoda, Jonathan, Philatheta, and Howard Thayer (Hampshire PR Box 147 #57, 14:265). As eldest son, Jedediah received a double share.

On 22 October 1788 Jedidiah Thayer of Ware, cordwainer, sold land in Ware "where I now live," including house and barn, "because I am son and heir to Micah Thayer deceased ... and also right to my mother's thirds" (Hampshire LR 2:588). On 28 June 1791 Thomas Marsh, Jedidiah Thayer, Howard Thayer, and Phylothety Thayer, spinster, all of Ware, sold 33 acres there; Rachel Thayer also signed (*ibid.*, 9:331). Jedidiah Thayer of Ware sold land there 14 April 1794 and his wife Rachel released her dower (*ibid.*, 7:26). Finally, on 27 October 1803, Jedidiah Thayer of Ware, yeoman, sold half an acre of land with buildings there bounded by the widow Thayer's dower land (*ibid.*, 21:349).

On 4 October 1804 William Lawrence Jr. of Hawley sold to Jedediah Thayer of Hawley, yeoman, the north half of lot 45 in Hawley; Jedediah mortgaged that land, first on 25 February 1805, and again on 14 May 1812 to Oakes Tirrell of Abington (Franklin LR 19:491, 21:54, 17:237). On 19 November 1816 the Deputy Sheriff of Hinsdale, by execution against Jedediah Thayer of Savoy, sold all of Thayer's equity in lot 180 in Savoy in Bullock's grant (Berkshire LR 19:525).

Jedediah Thayer was among original purchasers of land in Chautauqua County, N.Y., in February 1817 (*Chautauqua Co. History*, 498).

Children of Jedidiah and Rachael (Adams) Thayer, all except Jonathan rec. Ware (VR 1:71):

i   PEREZ THAYER[6], b. 25 March 1786; m. 25 March 1811, HANNAH HASKINS, b. 18 June 1786 Mass. In 1840 he was in Quincy, Adams Co., Ill. (p.48). In 1850 Eres [*sic*] Thayer ae 64, farmer b. Mass., was in Honey Creek Twp., Adams Co., Ill., with Hannah ae 62, Horace ae 20, and Charles ae 19, both farmers b. N.Y. (p.111).

Children (*Thayer Mem.*, 506), two youngest at home 1850: 1. *Emily Thayer*[7], b. 10 Nov. 1812; m. David Haskins. 2. *Franklin Thayer*, b. 21 Dec. 1813. 3. *Phoebe Elvira Thayer*, b. 12 April 1815 Mass.; m. Jesse Jackson Kirkpatrick. 4. *Harriet Thayer*, b. 24 Sept. 1817; m. Oliver Thayer. 5. *Nathan Franklin Thayer*, b. 24 Oct. 1819; m. Sarah Burrows. 6. *Catherine Thayer*, b. 1822; d. 1840. 7. *Laura Alvina Thayer*, b. 26 Nov. 1827; m. Lorenzo Peter Thayer. 8. *Horace Thayer*, b. 8 Oct. 1829 N.Y.; m. Hannah Richardson 9. *Charles Thayer*, b. 4 May 1831 N.Y.; m. Alice Jane Tomlinson.

ii PARMELIA THAYER, b. 27 Nov. 1787; d. after 1860; m. 6 Feb. 1812, REUBEN B. PATCH; b. Mass. ca 1781, d. bet. 1850 and 1860, prob. Chautauqua Co., N.Y., where family moved in 1814. In 1850 Rubin B. Patch was ae 69, a farmer in Portland, Chautauqua Co., N.Y., with Permelia ae 67, Permelia E. ae 35, Rubin B. Jr. ae 34, Henry ae 30, Rhoda ae 27, and Violetta A. ae 19 (p.177). In 1860 Henry Patch's household at Brockton P.O., Portland, included [his mother] Permelia ae 72, [brother] Reuben B. ae 41, and Meletta C. Allen ae 18 (p.245).

Patch children at home 1850, all b. N.Y.: 1. *Permelia E. Patch*[7], b. ca 1815. 2. *Reuben B. Patch Jr.*, b. ca 1816. 3. *Henry Patch*, b. ca 1820. 4. *Rhoda Patch*, b. ca 1823. 5. *Violetta A. Patch*, b. ca 1831.

iii   RHODA THAYER, b. 9 April 1789; m. 23 Jan. 1806, JAMES GOULD; rem. to Va. and Ohio (Sprague Ms, citing Gould Gen.).

iv   ROYAL O./UMSTED THAYER [ROYAL OLMSTED?], b. 7 Sept. 1791; m. 4 July 1812, MERCY MOFFETT, who d. evidently by 1850, when Royal O. Thayer, ae 60, a farmer, was at Portland, N.Y., in the household of Paul C. Delee ae 35, and wife Mary ae 29, b. N.Y. (p.169). Royal is said to have had 16 children.

   Children, order uncertain: 1. [Child] Thayer[7]. 2. [Child] Thayer. 3. Willard Thayer, b. 1816; m. Mary Eddy (see Eddy Fam., 371). 4. Rena E. Thayer, m. Adelbert A. Bowers. 5. Mary P. Thayer; m. Paul C. DeLee. 6. Francis H. Thayer, m. Mary Ellis. 7. Royal O. Thayer Jr.; m. Margaret Carrier. 8. Daniel B. Thayer, m. Sarah Bly. 9. Almira M. Thayer; m. Oliver H. Perry. 10. Lois J. Thayer, m. L.C. Petit. 11. Rhoda E. Thayer; m. E. A. Owen. 12. Elbridge M. Thayer, m. Mary G. Merryfield. 13. James P. Thayer, m. Mary Stewart. 14. Gardner B. Thayer, m. Emily J. French. 15. [Child] Thayer. 16. William D. Thayer; m. Emma Abbott.

v   BETSEY THAYER, b. 7 Feb. 1794.

vi   JEDIDIAH THAYER, b. 26 Jan. 1796; d. 21 Oct. 1801 at Ware (VR 1:71).

vii HIRAM THAYER, b. 24 Aug. 1798; m. in 1828 MARYETTE EAMES, b. ca 1810 Vt.; res. Carroll, N.Y., 1871. The 1860 census listed Hiram at Frewsburgh P.O., Carroll, Chautauqua Co., N.Y., ae 61, b. Mass., with Mary ae 50, b. Vt., and children Ezra, Cible, Ellen, Horace E., and Frank E.; the household included Eliza J. Marsh ae 17, b. N.Y., Mary Lawsen [?] ae 43, servant, b. Sweden, and Isaac Eames ae 86, b. Mass. (p.573).

   Children (1850 census), b. N.Y. (said to be 10 in all): 1. Elmer H. Thayer[7], b. ca 1828; m. Mary L. ___, b. ca 1841 Sweden; living next to parents 1860. 2. Ezra Thayer, b. ca 1840. 3. Cible Thayer, b. ca 1844. 4. Ellen Thayer, b. ca 1846. 5. Horace E. Thayer, b. ca 1849. 6. Frank E. Thayer, b. ca 1851.

viii LOIS THAYER, b. 18 Oct. 1800; m. in 1816 WILLIAM DESMOND (Sprague Ms). Said to have had children.

ix   JONATHAN THAYER, b. 13 May 1803; d. 21 April 1805 (Sprague Ms).

Sources cited: *Mendon VR.* Ware Vital Records, town clerk. Berkshire and Franklin County Deeds. Hampshire County Deeds and Probate Records at Springfield. W. C. Sprague, Thomas Thayer Manuscript. Young, *History of Chautauqua County, New York* (1895). *Thayer Memorial* (1874). Ruth Story Devereux Eddy, *The Eddy Family in America* (1930). CENSUS: 1840 Adams Co., Ill. (M704-54), 1850 Adams Co., Ill. (M432-97) and Portland, Chautauqua Co., N.Y. (M432-485); 1860 Carroll & Portland, Chautauqua Co., N.Y. (M653-732).

653. RHODA THAYER[5] (*Micah Thayer*[4], *Elizabeth*[3] *Samson, Stephen*[2], *Henry*[1]), daughter of Micah Thayer [135] and his wife Lois Thayer, was born 2 October 1767 at Ware (VR 15), and baptized there with her mother and siblings on 1 June 1777 (CR 50). She died, as "Mrs. Stephen Damon," 3 July 1839 at Hawley (VR, *Hawley History*, 334).

She married, in November 1785 at Ware (*VR* 59), **STEPHEN DAMON**, who was born at Ware 16 February 1757 (*Damon of Wayland*, 23-24), son of Dr. Edward and Elizabeth (Smith) Damon, and died 18 November 1842 at Hawley (*ibid.*, 8, 23-24). He was a captain in the Revolutionary War, enlisting from Ware (*Hawley History*, 194).

A division of the estate of Micah Thayer of Ware dated 5 April 1785 named his widow Lois, eldest son Jedidiah, and other children Rhoda, Jonathan, Philatheta, and Howard Thayer (Hampshire PR 14:265).

Stephen Damon of Ware bought land there from (his father) Edward Damon of Ware on 19 August 1786 (Northampton LR 9:282). On 8 July 1789, Stephen Damon of Plantation #7 sold land in Ware to Thomas Damon of Ware (Northampton LR 10:524), and on the same day he bought from Thomas Daman land in Plantation No. 7 (Franklin LR 5:405). On 29 May 1790, Stephen Deamon of Hawley, yeoman, sold land in Hawley to Azur Hawk, acknowledging the deed 1 July 1795 (*ibid.*, 38:289). In 1790 Stephen Demmon [*sic*] was listed in Hawley with three females in his household.

On 29 February 1796 Stephen Damon of Hawley, yeoman, sold land in Hawley to David Parker (*ibid.*, 14:308-09). On 24 June 1822, Stephen Damon of Hawley, yeoman, sold land in Hawley and in Buckland to Bardine Damon, yeoman, of Hawley; Rhoda Damon relinquished her dower right (*ibid.*, 100:201).

Stephen Damon was a resident of Hawley, Franklin County, 17 October 1832 when he applied for a Revolutionary War pension (White, 369).

Children of Stephen and Rhoda (Thayer) Damon, rec. Hawley (*Hawley History*, 334); other information from *Damon of Wayland*, 48, which adds a dau. Minerva:

i   MALINDA DAMON[6], b. 3 Sept. 1786; d. Wilbraham 23 Feb. 1875; m. at Ware, 28 April 1841, DANIEL HILL, b. Spencer 29 April 1841, d. 10 Sept. 1843. Child (with George Newton): 1. *Aurelia F. Damon*[7], b. 10 June 1810; m. Abiel Eddy.

ii MATILDA DAMON, b. Jan. 1789; d. Hawley 26 Feb. 1858, unm.

iii BARDINE DAMON, b. April 1791; d. Hawley 18 Dec. 1848; m. (1) REBECCA _____, d. Hawley 31 Oct. 1822; m. (2) Hawley, 13 May 1830 (*Hawley History*, 71), LUCY W. DOANE, b. Hockanum 14 Aug. 1800, d. Hawley 7 Dec. 1869, dau. of James and Lucy (Woodbridge) Doane.

Rebecca and a child were killed by a cart and oxen passing over them (*Hawley History*, 319).

Children with Rebecca, rec. Hawley (*ibid.*, 319): 1. *Electa Ann Damon*[7], b. 21 Dec. 1818; d. 1851 unm. 2. *Fidelia R./Phildia Damon*, b. 12 June 1821; m. Moses Smith Blood. 3. *[Child] Damon*, b. and d. 20 Feb. 1820. 4. *[Child] Damon*, d. in accident with mother 1822. Children with Lucy: 5. *[Child]*, b. and d. 4 Nov. 1831. 6. *[Son] Damon*, b. and d. 9 Dec. 1832. 7. *[Child] Damon*, b. and d. 29 Sept. 1833. 8. *Allen Doane Damon*, b. 14 Dec. 1835; m. (1) Isabel Bernard Whipple, (2) Hannah Porter Johnson. 9. *Aurelia E. Damon*, b. 8 Feb. 1838; m. Charles Bliss Sanderson. 10. *Mary Rhoda Damon*, b. 28 June 1842; m. Gardner Dorrance Blackmer.

iv   STEPHEN DAMON, b. July 1793; d. Battle Creek, Mich., 9 Nov. 1843; m. ca 1814, RUTH ___. On 25 Aug. 1815, Stephen Damon of Conway, yeoman, bought land in Buckland from Ebenezer Wade of Buckland, blacksmith, and the same day mortgaged it to Wade; Ruth Damon also signed (Franklin LR 34:385, 633).

Children: 1. *Stephen Lyman Damon*[7], b. Buckland 14 Nov. 1816; m. (1) Elizabeth Victoria Winslow, (2) Amanda M. Brown. 2. *Lewis C. Damon*, b. 21 Nov. 1819; m. Nancy B. ___. 3. *Charles Palmer Damon*, b. 22 April 1824; m. Melissa Cross. 4. *William Damon*, b. ca 1825.

v   RHODA DAMON, b. Aug. 1795; m. at Hawley, 25 Nov. 1813, JUSTUS RUDDOCK, son of Edward and Martha (Sanderson) Ruddock. In 1850 he was a farmer in Berlin, Marquette Co., Wisc., with Rhoda and four children, another son next door (p.133).

Ruddock children, all b. Mass. (census): 1. *A. D. Ruddock*[7], b. ca 1822; m. Julia ___. 2. *Sylvester Ruddock*, b. ca 1826. 3. *Malinda Ruddock*, b. Conway 18 Oct. 1828 (*VR* 90); not at home 1850. 4. *Dianna Ruddock*, b. ca 1830. 5. *Adeline Ruddock*, b. ca 1832. 6. *Albert Ruddock*, b. ca 1836.

vi   JONATHAN [THAYER] DAMON, b. 9 April 1798; d. Amherst 17 June 1884; m. (1) at Ware, 3 June 1827, MARTHA GRAY, b. Ware ca 1803, d. Hawley 20 May 1855, dau. of Moses and Mercy Gray (Mass. VR 93:198); m. (2) at Greenwich, 20 Sept. 1855 (Mass. VR 88:11), SARAH GRAY, b. Ware 4 June 1809, d. Amherst 21 Dec. 1876, sister of first wife; m. (3) at Amherst, 1 May 1878, ARMEDIA (BARTLETT) JENKS, d. Amherst 5 Aug. 1885. In 1850 Jonathan was a farmer at Hawley, with Martha and the seven younger children at home; Roxana Marsh ae 62 was with them (p.270).

Children, first eight rec. Hawley (*Hawley History*, 59): 1. *Moses Gray Damon*[7], b. 21 July 1828. 2. *Cyrus Damon*, b. 9 Jan. 1830. 3. *Jonathan Thayer Damon*, b. 30 March 1832. 4. *Stephen Whitney Damon*, b. 7 May 1834. 5. *Charles Palmer Damon*, b. 27 Sept. 1836. 6. *Henry Clay Damon*, b. 9 Nov. 1838. 7. *Martha Ann Damon*,

14 Dec. 1840. 8. *Homer Franklin Damon,* b. 17 May 1843. 9. *William Lumby Damon,* b. 10 Feb. 1846.

vii   DEXTER DAMON, b. April 1801; d. 12 Dec. 1880 Oakland, Calif. (*Damon Mem.,* 62-63); m. at Pownal, Vt., 12 Dec. 1824, NANCY PECK, b. Cheshire, Conn., 6 Oct. 1802, dau. of Charles and Nancy (Fanning) Peck (*ibid.*). In 1850 Dexter Damon was ae 51, a painter in Bennington, Vt., with Nancy, Chester J. ae 22, carpenter, James C. ae 19, clerk, and [twins?] Catherine E. and Frances L. ae 12 (p.203). In 1870 Dexter and Nancy were in San Francisco; his occupation "out of business," son James E. was a dealer in real estate, and the daughters were music teachers (p.127). A son living in Oakland provided information ca 1880 for *Damon Memorial.*

Children: 1. *Charles P. Damon*[7], b. ca 1829. 2. *James E. Damon,* b. March 1831 Vt.; m. Amelia Spencer 3. *Catherine Elizabeth Damon,* b. Oct. 1836 Vt.; at home 1870. 4. *Frances L. Damon,* b. ca 1838 Vt.; m. John R. Kittredge.

viii MICAH T. DAMON (transcribed as "Mon T." in VR), b. Aug. 1803; d. April 1805 at Hawley.

ix   ROXANA DAMON, b. 17 July 1806; d. Ware 3 March 1882; m. at Hawley, 1 June 1837, JOHN RUGGLES GREENLEAF, b. Newton 24 Aug. 1797, d. Ware 8 Nov. 1895.

Greenleaf children, b. Ware: 1. *Rhoda Elizabeth Greenleaf,* b. 30 June 1838. 2. *John Ruggles Greenleaf,* b. 31 July 1810; m. Jennie F. Doake. 3. *Sarah Melinda Greenleaf,* b. 27 Sept. 1842; d. 1926 unm. 4. [*Child*] Damon, b. 23 April 1848; d. inf.

x   DIANTHA DAMON, b. August 1808; m. at Stamford, Vt., 16 Aug. 1830, WALTER B. THAYER, b. Douglas 20 Sept. 1809, d. 4 Nov. 1850; res. Albany, N.Y.

Thayer children: 1. *Frances Rhoda Thayer*[7], b. 22 Dec. 1833; m. Henry McBride. 2. *Josephine Thayer,* b. 30 Aug. 1840; m. James Redfern. 3. *Walter B. Thayer,* b. 22 June 1845. 4. *Marian Louise Thayer.*

xi   CYRUS DAMON, b. 8 March 1811; d. Strongsville, Ohio, 1847; m. there, 1 May 1836, ELIZABETH RABBITTS, b. 9 Jan. 1818, bp. 8 Feb. 1818 Horningsham, Wiltshire (IGI), dau. George and Rhoda (Nuth) Rabbitts [m. Babington, Somerset 1817, *ibid.*].

Children: 1. *Frances Laura Damon*[7], b. 6 Feb. 1837 Ohio; m. Rev. Elliot E. Swift. 2. *Rhoda Elizabeth Damon,* b. 10 April 1842 Ohio. 3. *George Cyrus Damon,* b. 6 Dec. 1845 Wisc.; d. 1868.

Sources cited: *Buckland VR. Hawley VR.* Ware VR. Mass. Vital Records 1841-1910. White, *Abstracts of Revolutionary War Pension Files,* citing file S30370. Franklin and Hampshire County Deeds. *History of Hawley* (1953). *Damon Family of Wayland* (1997). *Damon Memorial* (1882). CENSUS: Hawley, Franklin Co., 1850 (M432-317), Bennington, Bennington Co., Vt. (M432-921), Marquette Co. Wisc. (M432-1002); 1870 San Francisco Ward 6, Calif. (M593-81).

654. VIOLATY/PHILATHETA THAYER[5] (*Micah[4], Elizabeth[3] Samson, Stephen[2], Henry[1]*), daughter of Micah Thayer [135] and his wife Lois Thayer, was born 12 June 1772 at Ware (*VR* 19), and baptized there with her mother and siblings on 1 June 1777 (CR 50). She died 15 February 1848, aged 75, at Strongsville, Ohio (cem. rec., 456).

She married at Ware, 26 December 1796, the Rev. Reuben Moss officiating, after intentions 5 December 1796 (VR 215, 254), **EBENEZER POMEROY** of Hawley. He was born 29 June 1772 at Southampton, son of Ebenezer and Experience (Clark) Pomeroy (*Pomeroy Gen.*, 264, 391), and died 13 August 1835, aged 63, probably at Strongsville, Ohio, where they are buried with their son Alanson and his wife (cem. rec.).

A division of the estate of Micah Thayer of Ware dated 5 April 1785 named his widow Lois, eldest son Jedidiah, and other children Rhoda, Jonathan, Philatheta, and Howard Thayer (Hampshire PR 14:265).

Children of Ebenezer and Violaty (Thayer) Pomeroy (*Pomeroy Gen.*, 391, 578-79):

i   WALTER POMEROY[6], b. ca 1797.

ii   LORENCY POMEROY, b. ca 1800; m. ELISHA COLTRIN.

iii VIOLATRA POMEROY, b. 7 July 1801; m. (1) 1822, JOSIAH GALLUP, d. before 1850; m. (2) JAMES R. CLARK. In 1850 Violetta Gallup ae 50 (b. Canada !) was head of a household in Strongsville, Ohio, with two children (p.174). She is said to have had seven Gallup children.
     Gallup children at home 1850, b. Ohio: 1. *Josiah Gallup[7]*, b. ca 1833, a clerk 1850. 2. *Mary A. Gallup*, b. ca 1836.

iv   EBENEZER POMEROY, b. 22 Feb. 1803; m. (1) 1827, AMANDA BRONSON, (2) MARIA BINKLEY. In 1850 he was a merchant in Kenosha, Wisc., with Mary A. ae 41, b. Ohio, and four children (p.259).
     Pomeroy children at home 1850, first three b. Ohio: 1. *George W. Pomeroy[7]*, b. ca 1834. 2. *Mary A. Pomeroy*, b. ca 1837. 3. *Samuel B. Pomeroy*, b. ca 1838. 4. *Lucy A. Pomeroy*, b. ca 1841 Wisc.

v   ALANSON POMEROY, b. 20 Feb. 1805; d. Ohio, 4 Jan. 1875 ae 72 [*sic*]; m. KEZIAH POPE, b. ca 1809 in Mass.; d. Ohio 25 March 1898 ae 83 [*sic* – ? poss. 88]; bur. with his parents. In 1850 he was a merchant in Strongville, Ohio, with Keziah ae 41 and 5 children; Jonathan B. Thair ae 46, b. N.H., was in their household (p.169).
     Children at home 1850, all b. Ohio (poor handwriting makes spelling of three questionable – said to be nine ch. in all): 1. [*Abner ?* or *Elon?*] *Pomeroy[7]*, b. ca 1836. 2. *Orlando Pomeroy*, b. ca 1838. 3. *Elisabeth Pomeroy*, b. ca 1840. 4. [*Verona ?*] *Pomeroy*, b. ca 1843. 5. [*Nancy ?*] *Pomeroy*, b. ca 1849.

vi   MORRIS POMEROY, bp. 22 Aug. 1807; m. (1) 1831, CYNTHIA
      GOODWIN, (2) 1860, LUCY A. GALLUP. In 1850 he was a farmer in
      Kenosha, Wisc., with Cynthia ae 46, b. Conn., three children, and
      Margaret Callahan ae 17, b. Ireland (p.248).
           Children at home 1850 (said to be six ch. in all): 1. *Josiah Pomeroy*, b. ca
      1833. 2. *Elon H. Pomeroy*, b. ca 1837. 3. *Celia C. Pomeroy*, b. ca 1840.

vii   Dr. CALVIN THAYER POMEROY, b. 15 Nov. 1809 at Otisco Hill, N.Y.;
      m. 1836, JULIA COX. Four children.

viii LUCY POMEROY, b. 1811 at Otisco, N.Y.; d. prob. ca 1837; m.
      PHILANDER POPE, b. ca 1808 in Mass. In 1850 he was a farmer in
      Strongsville, Ohio, with second wife Orpha ae 33, b. Pa., and three
      children (p.166). Lucy is said to have had two children, so the youngest
      (George ae 10) was prob. Orpha's.
           Probable *Pope* children of Philander and Nancy (1850 census): 1. *Paulina
      Pope*, b. ca 1834. 2. *Charles Pope*, b. ca 1837.

Sources cited: Ware VR. Hampshire County Probate Records. E. H. Sherman and G. E. Metler,
"Cuyahoga County Cemeteries, Strongsville Township" (1929), at Western Reserve Historical
Society Library, Cleveland. A. A. Pomeroy, *History and Genealogy of the Pomeroy Family* (1912) [wrong
on Violaty's birth date and place]. CENSUS: 1850 Strongsville, Cuyahoga Co., Ohio (M432-673),
Kenosha Ward 1, Kenosha Co., Wisc. (M432-1000).

655.   HOWARD THAYER (*Micah⁴, Elizabeth³ Samson, Stephen², Henry¹*), son of
Micah Thayer [135] and his wife Lois Thayer, was born 23 December 1774 at Ware
(*VR* 19), and baptized there with his mother and siblings on 1 June 1777 (CR 50).
He was living 16 March 1818 at Ware when he bought land in Pelham.

A division of the estate of Micah Thayer of Ware dated 5 April 1785 named
his widow Lois, eldest son Jedidiah, and other children Rhoda, Jonathan,
Philatheta, and Howard Thayer (Hampshire PR 14:265).

On 12 July 1811 Thomas Marsh of Greenwich and wife Lois sold to Howard
Thayer of Greenwich, yeoman, the northwest corner of "the farm where I now
live," 50 acres in Greenwich (Hampshire LR 32:449). Howard Thayer of
Greenwich, yeoman, on 6 April 1814 sold to Clark Powers the same land, "bought
of my [step]father Thomas Marsh, deceased" (*ibid.,* 36:298). On 16 March 1818
Howard Thayer of Ware, yeoman, bought 85 acres in Pelham from Silas Wilkins
(*ibid.,* 42:579). There is no record of Howard Thayer in *Pelham VR,* and nothing
further about him has been learned.

Sources cited: Ware VR. Ware Church Records, Corbin Collection. Hampshire County Deeds
and Probates.

656. SIMON BRUCE⁵ (*Joseph Bruce⁴, Abigail³ Samson, Stephen², Henry¹*), son of Joseph Bruce [136] and his wife Elizabeth Farnsworth, was born 7 February 1756 at Mendon (*VR* 38). Capt. Simon Bruce died 20 March 1796 at Grafton (*VR* 325), aged 41.

He married 14 January 1787, at Grafton (*VR* 177), **SARAH WHIPPLE 2d**, who was born there 3 September 1765 (*VR* 144), daughter of James and Elizabeth (Hall) Whipple, and died there 27 October 1817 (*VR* 325), aged 52, "widow of Capt. Simon Bruce."

Simon predeceased his father. Joseph Bruce of Grafton, gentleman, in his will dated 15 March 1799 named among others his granddaughters Eliza and Sarah Bruce and grandson Joseph Bruce, who was to have all his grandfather's real estate when he reached age 25; Sarah, widow of son Simon and mother of the grandchildren, was also named (Worcester PR #A8534).

Bond for the administration of the estate of Simon Bruce of Grafton was given by Sarah Bruce, widow, and Joseph Bruce on 5 April 1796, signed also by Luke Drury and James Whipple; witnesses were Moses Wheeler and Thos. W. Millet. The division, dated 6 April 1812, names the widow Sarah Bruce; only son Joseph Bruce; and daughters Eliza Bruce and Sarah Bruce who also received land from their grandfather Joseph Bruce, deceased (Worcester PR #A8567).

Bond for the administration of the estate of Sarah Bruce, widow, late of Grafton, was given 10 December 1817 by Joseph Bruce, yeoman, as administrator, signed by Samuel Wood and Ambrose Chase of Sutton. The inventory mentions the three children of the deceased, and was signed by William and Eliza Eager and by Samuel Wood as guardian for Sarah Elizabeth Wood (Worcester PR #A8559).

Children of Simon and Sarah (Whipple) Bruce, recorded Grafton (*VR* 29); named in will of grandfather Bruce:

    i   JOSEPH BRUCE⁶, b. 13 March 1790; m. at Southborough, 27 Dec. 1813 (*VR* 99), HARRIET FAY.
          Children rec. Grafton (*VR* 29): 1. *Sarah Whipple Bruce⁷*, b. 4 April 1815. 2. *William Simon Bruce*, b. 20 May 1817. 3. *Harriot Fay Bruce*, b. 3 Aug. 1819. 4. *Elizabeth Eager Bruce*, b. 6 July 1822. 5. *Joseph Edward Bruce*, b. 6 Oct. 1825. 6. *Delia Augusta Bruce*, b. 16 Nov. 1828.

    ii ELIZA BRUCE, b. 21 Aug. 1792; m. at Grafton, 7 Dec. 1813 (*VR* 177, 198), WELCOME EAGER of Boston, b. Shrewsbury 1 Nov. 1786 (*VR* 33), son of Lewis and Sarah (Stacey) Eager. Welcome Eager of Boston, merchant, changed his name to William Eager on 14 June 1814 (*Name Changes in Mass.*), and he signed his mother-in-law's inventory, above, as William Eager. In 1830 William Eager was head of a household in Ward 8,

Boston consisting of 1 man 40-50, 1 woman 30-40, 1 woman 20-30, and 1 young man and 1 young woman 15-20 (p.281).

iii   SARAH BRUCE, b. 1 Sept. 1794; d. 2 June 1817 at Grafton (*VR* 376), ae 22; m. at Grafton, 8 Jan. 1815 (*VR* 177), SAMUEL WOOD, b. there 16 Dec. 1793 (*VR* 152), son of Samuel and Elizabeth (Kimball) Wood. He m. (2) Grafton, 22 Nov. 1818 (*VR* 212), Hannah P. Adams.

Wood child, rec. Grafton (*VR* 152), named in grandmother's will: 1. *Sarah Elizabeth Wood*[2], b. 17 May 1817; m. Grafton, 20 Dec. 1838 (*VR* 212), Nicholas H. Brigham.

Sources cited: *Grafton VR. Mendon VR. Shrewsbury VR. Southborough VR.* Worcester County Probate Records. *List of Persons whose names have been changed in Massachusetts 1780 – 1883* (1885). CENSUS: 1830 Ward 8, Boston, Suffolk Co. (M19-65).

657.   PHINEAS BRUCE[5] (*George Bruce*[4], *Abigail*[3] *Samson, Stephen*[2]*, Henry*[1]), son of George Bruce [137] and his wife Hannah Lovett, was born 7 January 1762 at Mendon (*VR* 38), his birth recorded also at Leicester (*VR* 19).   Phineas Bruce, Esq., died 4 October 1809, in his 48th year, "formerly of Machias," at Uxbridge (*VR* 360), and was buried in the Old Burying Ground there but later reinterred in Prospect Hill Cemetery.

Phineas Bruce Esq[r] of Machias, Maine, married at the Brattle Street Church, Boston, 29 March 1795 (*CR* 263), **JANE SAVAGE** of Boston. "Jenny" Savage was born 17 February 1768 in Boston (*VR* 317), daughter of Habijah and Elizabeth (Tudor) Savage. She died at Cambridge in 1854, aged 86, before 16 May when administration was granted on her estate (*Maine Hist. Mag.* 8:74).

Phineas Bruce graduated from Yale in 1786, studied law and became the first lawyer in Washington County, Maine (then part of Massachusetts), practicing in Machias. He was a member of the Massachusetts House of Representatives from 1791 to 1798 and in 1800, and was elected to the Eighth Congress beginning in March 1803 but was prevented by illness ("a violent attack of hypochrondriasis from which he had formerly suffered") from taking his seat (*Upton Mem.*, 515; *Biog. Dict. Am. Congress*, 905). His condition worsened and he was mentally ill until his death.

James S. Bruce, accountant, of Newton, was appointed administrator of the estate of Jane Bruce, widow, late of Cambridge, on 16 May 1854. J. S. Ryan signed a receipt for Henry Bruce for $2832 on 17 July 1854, and James Savage, designated to receive for George W. Bruce of Ascension, Louisiana, on 30 May 1854, signed for his share. In an accounting presented 15 August 1854, one-third each was paid to George W. Bruce and J. S. Ryan, guardian of Henry Bruce, and one-third was reserved by the administrator for himself (Middlesex Prob. File 28324).

The 1800 census (p 614) lists Phineas Bruce in Machias, himself and wife 26-45, with a household consisting of three boys under 10, one girl 10-16, two young men 16-26, and two extra women, one 26-45 and the other over 45. (The two young men were probably law clerks, one of them Phineas' future brother-in-law Daniel P. Upton.)

In 1850 Jane S. Bruce was living with the family of her son James S. Bruce in Brookline.

The Upton Memorial states that there were five sons and one daughter in the family, but their mother's probate clearly indicates that only three sons were alive in 1854. Only James S. has been found in census records.

Children of Phineas and Jane (Savage) Bruce:

i   [DAUGHTER] BRUCE⁶, b. prob. ca 1797; d. before 1854 without issue.

ii JAMES SAVAGE BRUCE⁶, b. 25 Nov. 1802 in Machias (g.s.); d. 9 June 1874 at Worcester, a resident of Brookline, clerk, "b. Calais, Me.," of heart disease (Mass. VR 267:415); m. at Duxbury 2 Dec. 1838 (*VR* 227), LUCY NICKERSON, b. 9 Aug. 1803 Provincetown (g.s.), dau. Joseph and Sally, d. Brookline 10 March 1874, "widowed," of anaemia, ae 70y 6m 1d (Mass. VR 266:230). In 1850 James was a clerk in Cambridge with Lucy and the two children; Jane S. Bruce ae 83 and Susan D. Nickerson ae 30 shared the household which included Joanna Crowley ae 24 b. Ireland (p.54). In 1860 James, Lucy, and Emma S. were in Newton (p.802). James was admitted to the Worcester Insane Asylum in 1863 (Middlesex PR #28323).

Children at home 1850: 1. *James W. Bruce⁷*, b. 1839. 2. *Emma S. Bruce*, b. ca 1844; requested adm. on her father's estate.

iii HENRY BRUCE, living 1854 when J. S. Ryan was his guardian.

iv GEORGE W. BRUCE, living 1858 when his uncle Stephen Bruce died; in 1854 he was in Ascension, La.

v   WILLIAM A. BRUCE; heir of [uncle] George Bruce [#649] in 1826; evidently d. before 1854 without issue.

vi [SON] BRUCE, d. before 1854 without issue.

Sources cited: *Boston VR. Cambridge VR. Duxbury VR. Mendon VR.* Middlesex County Probate Records. *Biographical Directory of the American Congress, 1774-1971, The Continental Congress ... and the Congress of the United States ...* (1971). *Maine Historical Magazine* (formerly *Bangor Historical Magazine*). *Upton Memorial* (1874). CENSUS: 1800 Machias, Washington Co., Me. (M32-8); 1850 Cambridge, Middlesex Co. (M432-325); 1860 Newton, Middlesex Co. (M653-510).

658. HANNAH BRUCE[5] (*George Bruce*[4], *Abigail*[3] *Samson, Stephen*[2], *Henry*[1]), daughter of George Bruce [137] and his wife Hannah Lovett, was born 27 December 1766 at Mendon (*VR* 38), recorded also at Leicester (*VR* 19). She died in Boston 2 March 1856 aged 87y 2m 4d (Mass. VR 104:15).

She married, 11 November 1801 (*Upton Mem.*, 205), **DANIEL PUTNAM UPTON**. He was born 12 August 1775 at [North] Reading (*VR* 233), son of Benjamin and Rebecca (Putnam) Upton, and died 31 December 1805.

Daniel graduated from Harvard College in 1797 and studied law with his future brother-in-law, Phineas Bruce, in Machias, Maine. He was admitted to the bar in 1800 and settled at Eastport. *Upton Memorial* (p.207) says of him,

> At the early age of thirty, he fell a victim to the ravages of pulmonary disease. What else could have been expected among the fogs of the Bay of Fundy? He took a severe cold, occasioned by exposure, and died in his native town, at his father's house, Dec. 31, 1805, having come thither for better medical aid than he could find in his eastern home.

Hannah, a widow for more than fifty years, lived with her brother George Bruce in Billerica until his death in 1826. On 6 June 1827 William Bruce of Bangor, Maine, merchant, Charles Bruce, merchant, Hannah Upton, widow, Abigail Bruce, and Martha B. Wait, singlewomen, all of Billerica, sold 13 acres in Billerica and a pew in the church; all except Charles acknowledged on 8 October 1827. The same day, the same group sold eight acres in Billerica bought by George Bruce in 1812 and 1813, another eight acres in Billerica conveyed by Samuel Whiting, administrator, to George Bruce, deceased, in 1814, and other land bought by George Bruce in 1819 and 1823 (Middlesex LR 277:218, 364, 446).

Hannah's obituary in the *Boston Daily Advertiser* of 4 March 1856, quoted in *Upton Memorial*, says of her:

> She was a person of rare intellectual endowments, gifted with uncommon conversational powers, of a cheerful, happy temperament ... ever a welcome guest.... Of a well cultivated mind and a retentive memory, she had a distinct recollection of the events of the Revolutionary War.... She took a deep interest in political matters, and being a disciple of the Washington School, she ever entertained a deep regard for that party.... She was well informed on the current events of the day, having been an extensive reader, until within a few years, when the loss of her eye sight deprived her of that privilege. ... Her religious principles were of the liberal class: her life was unblemished and exemplary, and she was truly a good woman.

There is a lengthy account of Daniel P. Upton and his family in Willis' *History of the Law, the Courts, and the Lawyers of Maine*, 323-27.

Children of Daniel and Hannah (Bruce) Upton (*Upton Memorial,* 208, 336), both bp. Billerica 25 Oct. 1809 as "ch. of widow Hannah" (*VR* 194):

i   DANIEL PUTNAM UPTON[6], b. Eastport, Me., 1 May 1803; d. 2 May 1849, unm.; bur. Mt. Auburn Cemetery, Cambridge. He was a shipmaster, long in the service of Enoch Train of Boston and captain of the packet ship *Washington Irving* at his death (*Lawyers of Maine,* 327).

ii   GEORGE BRUCE UPTON, b. Eastport, Me., 11 Oct. 1804; d. Boston 1 July 1874 of stomach cancer, at 79 Beacon St. (Mass. VR 267:132); m. at Nantucket 2 May 1826 (*VR* 4:480), ANN COFFIN HUSSY, dau. of Peter and Mary (Mooers) Hussey. He graduated from Harvard and became a prosperous Boston merchant (see *Upton Memorial,* 341-42).

   Children, first seven b. Nantucket (*VR* 2:601), eighth in Manchester, N.H. (*Upton Mem.,* 342): 1. *George Bruce Upton[7]*, b. 15 July 1829; m. Geraldine I. Rivers. 2. *Ann Coffin Upton,* b. 28 June 1831; m. Dr. George Hayward. 3. *Daniel Putnam Upton,* b. 19 Aug. 1833; d. unm. 4. *William Coffin Upton,* b. 7 Oct. 1835; d. Shanghai, China, 4 June 1864. 5. *Hannah Frances Upton,* b. 31 March 1838; d. Manchester, N.H., 1846. 6. *Mary Upton,* b. 21 Dec. 1839; m. Alexander Young. 7. *Elizabeth Upton,* b. 3 June 1843. 8. *Ellen Upton,* b. 1 July 1846.

Sources cited: *Billerica VR. Nantucket VR. Reading VR.* Middlesex County Deeds and Probate Records. Willis, *A History of the Law, the Courts, and the Lawyers of Maine* (1863). Vinton, *Upton Memorial* (1874).

658A. GEORGE BRUCE[5] (*George Bruce[4], Abigail[3] Samson, Stephen[2], Henry[1]*), son of George Bruce [137] and his wife Hannah Lovett, was born at Mendon 21 November 1768 (*VR* 38), and died at Billerica 4 September 1826, unmarried.

The will of George Bruce of Billerica dated in August 1824, presented 4 October 1826, names two sisters Hannah Upton and Abigail Bruce; niece Martha B. Wait; and brothers Stephen, William, and Charles Bruce; property left to Stephen was to be held by executors William and Charles, but William declined to serve (Middlesex PR #3264). Receipts of heirs, dated, 24 August 1824, were signed by Hannah Upton, Martha B. Wait, Abigail Bruce, and William Bruce for himself and again "in the claim of Stephen Bruce" who was *non compos mentis.* Permit to sell real estate was issued to Charles Bruce of Boston, merchant. Also Henry Bruce, James S. Bruce, and William A. Bruce, all of Boston, were among those heirs of George Bruce to whom a citation was sent on 15 September 1826 (*ibid.*).

Sources cited: *Billerica VR. Mendon VR.* Middlesex County Probate Files.

659. PATTY/MARTHA BRUCE⁵ (*George Bruce⁴, Abigail³ Samson, Stephen²,
Henry¹*), daughter of George Bruce [137] and his wife Hannah Lovett, was born 10
May 1771 at Mendon (*VR* 38), recorded also at Leicester (*VR* 19). She died at
Leicester 31 July 1794 (*Upton Mem.*, 515).

She married 11 November 1792 at Leicester (*VR* 130), **NATHAN WAITE
JR.** He was born 4 January 1768 at Leicester (*VR* 96), son of Nathan and Joanna
(Tucker) Waite, and died 20 February 1846, aged 78, at Sterling, a retired innholder
(Mass. VR 21:166). He married, second, at Sterling 17 January 1805 (*VR* 103),
TABITHA KENDALL, daughter of Josiah and Esther (Sawyer) Kendall, with whom
he had Josiah K. Waite, Esther Waite, Catherine Waite, and Lucyanne Waite, the
last two recorded Sterling (*VR* 44-45).

In his will dated 2 May 1834, proved [–] April 1846, Nathan Waite of Sterling
named his wife Taby Wait and her father Josiah Kendall; his daughter Martha B.
Waite who was not married, and four children: Josiah N., Esther N., Catherine,
and Lucy Ann (Worcester PR # A61031).

Child of Nathan and Patty (Bruce) Waite:

i   MARTHA / PATTY BRUCE WAITE⁶, b. 19 July 1794 at Leicester (*VR*
     96); d. 20 Sept. 1873 at East Bridgewater (Mass. VR 257:359), unmarried.

Sources cited: *Mendon VR.   Leicester VR.   Sterling VR.*   Mass. Vital Records 1841-1910.
Worcester County Probate Records. *Upton Memorial* (1874).

660. STEPHEN BRUCE⁵ (*George Bruce⁴, Abigail³ Samson, Stephen², Henry¹*), son
of George Bruce [137] and his wife Hannah Lovett, was born 1 August 1775, his
birth "at Mendon" recorded at Leicester (*VR* 19). He died at Worcester State
Hospital 12 April 1858, "from Billerica ... of old age" (Mass. VR 122:182).

On 8 September 1826 Stephen's brothers and sisters, Charles Bruce, Hannah
Upton, and Abigail Bruce, signed a petition requesting a guardian for Stephen
Bruce of Billerica, a lunatic, George Bruce who had been his guardian having lately
deceased; his brother William Bruce, of Bangor, Maine, merchant, offered himself
as guardian and was appointed 3 October 1826 (Middlesex PR # 3274). Stephen
was of Billerica, *non compos mentis*, on 5 June 1827 when his share of real estate
inherited from his father was sold to Charles Bruce of Boston by court order
(Middlesex LR 275:414). On 12 October 1840 it was noted that William Bruce,
guardian of Stephen Bruce, had lately died, and request was made that George B.
Upton be appointed. On 3 September 1847 Stephen was confined at the
Worcester Asylum, when a guardian was needed due to the death of his brother
Charles.

On 21 and 24 April 1858 a petition for administration on the estate of Stephen Bruce late of Billerica, deceased, was signed by his heirs: Susan W. Bruce, Eliza W. Bruce, James S. Bruce, and George B. Upton of Boston, who asked to be appointed administrator. When this was done 27 April 1858 it was stated that Stephen Bruce left no widow and no children. All heirs signed the release and receipts: Martha B. Waite, Susan W. Bruce, Eliza W. Bruce, James S. Bruce, and George W. Bruce by attorney James S. Bruce (Middlesex PR #28330).

Sources cited: *Mendon VR.* Mass. Vital Records 1841-1910. Middlesex County Deeds and Probate Records.

661. WILLIAM BRUCE[5] (*George Bruce*[4], *Abigail*[3] *Samson, Stephen*[2], *Henry*[1]), son of George Bruce [137] and his wife Hannah Lovett, was born 14 February 1778 "at Rutland," recorded at Leicester (*VR* 19). He died 22 May 1841 at Bangor, Maine, where he was a merchant.

He married 11 January 1813, at Bangor, Maine (*Me. Hist. Mag.* 1:83; int. 3:194), **SUSAN WILDER,** who was born 8 or 20 November 1794 at Salisbury, N. H., daughter of Luke and Susan (Poor) Wilder, and died 8 April 1863 in Philadelphia (*Me. Historical Mag.*, 8:39).

On 18 June 1827 William Bruce of Bangor, yeoman, sold for one dollar to Charles Bruce of Billerica, merchant and executor of the will of George Bruce of Billerica, deceased, land in Billerica to which he was entitled as heir of said George; his wife Susan relinquished her dower (Middlesex LR 275:417).

In 1860 Susan Bruce, widow, aged 53 [*sic*], born in New Hampshire, was living in Bangor, Me., with her daughter Susan W. Bruce, aged 43 (p.142).

Children of William and Susan (Wilder) Bruce (*Me. Historical Mag.*, 8:39):

i   SUSAN WILDER BRUCE[6], b. 15 Jan. 1814; d. Philadelphia, Pa., in 1863 ae 49.

ii   WILLIAM CHARLES BRUCE, b. 14 July 1815.

iii   GEORGE HENRY BRUCE, b. 3 July 1817; d. 1 April 1827.

iv   ELIZABETH BRUCE, b. 21 July 1819.

v   CAROLINE MOORE BRUCE, b. 5 April 1823; d. 26 May 1826.

vi   ELIZA WILDER BRUCE, b. 6 Feb. 1825; m. in 1859, PETER J. HASSARD. In 1870 Peter L. Hazzard [*sic*] was living in Ward 7, Dist. 20, Philadelphia, a retired druggist, with Eliza ae 45, b. Me., three children, and Isabel McFadden ae 29, domestic servant b. Ireland (p.469).

Hazzard children, b. Pa., at home 1870: 1. *Robert Hazzard*, b. ca 1860. 2. *William Hazzard*, b. ca 1862. 3. *Bessie Hazzard*, b. ca 1866.

vii   GEORGE BRUCE, b. 16 Feb. 1829.

viii CHARLES BRUCE, b. 7 Aug. 1830; d. Jan. 1832.

Sources cited: *Leicester VR. Maine Historical Magazine*, Vol. 8 [1893]. CENSUS: 1860 Bangor, Me. (M653-447); 1870 Philadelphia, Philadelphia Co., Pa. (M593-1392 – 1st enum., 10 June). **See also:** For more on Susan's parents, *Maine Historical Magazine*, 8:151, *Wilder Book*, 447, and John J. Dearborn, *History of Salisbury, N.H.* (Manchester, 1890), 860.

662.   CHARLES BRUCE[5] (*George Bruce*[4], *Abigail* Samson, Stephen[2], Henry[1]), son of George Bruce [137] and his wife Hannah Lovett, was born "at Rutland" 29 September 1781, recorded at Leicester (*VR* 19). His death on 29 August 1847 aged 65y 11m, a merchant, occurred in McLean Hospital and was recorded at Billerica (*VR* 347; Mass. VR 33:4).

He married at Northboro, 28 September 1823 (*VR* 119), **JULIA LAMBERT WHITNEY**, who was born there 16 March 1802 (*VR* 68), daughter of Thomas L. and Mary (____) Whitney. She died at Cambridge 8 November 1852, "wife of Charles … [of] inflammation" (Mass. VR 67:68).

They were living in Cambridge on 14 September 1843 when Charles Bruce of Cambridge, cooper, mortgaged to Jacob Eaton land and a dwelling in Cambridgeport; Julia L. relinquished her dower (Middlesex LR 433:112). The 1850 census listed Julia L. Bruce, aged 50, in Cambridge in a household headed by Charles Bruce aged 55, lather, but this was probably an error for aged 25, which would be correct for her son Charles; her husband having died three years before (p.49). Also in the household was Mary E. Bruce, aged 20, probably Charles' wife but possibly Julia's daughter.

Children of Charles and Julia L. (Whitney) Bruce:

i   CHARLES OTIS BRUCE[6], b. 3 Jan. 1825 Northboro (*VR* 23); res. Cambridge 1850.

ii   [*child*] BRUCE, b. 1835; bur. 13 Sept. 1836, ae 1 yr, Cambridge (*VR* 2:489).

Sources cited: *Billerica VR. Cambridge VR. Northboro VR.* Mass. Vital Records 1841-1910. Middlesex County Deeds. CENSUS: 1850 Cambridge, Middlesex Co. (M432-325).

663.   HANNAH HAZELTINE[5] (*Abigail Bruce*[4], *Abigail*[3] *Samson, Stephen*[2], *Henry*[1]), daughter of John Hazeltine and his wife Abigail Bruce [138], was born probably at Mendon about 1758. She died possibly at Sutton or at Stratton, Vt., about 1790.

She married at Sutton, 7 December 1780 (*VR* 279), **CLARK STONE**, who was born there 31 May 1757 (*VR* 167), son of Levi and Mary (Lawrence) Stone. He married, second, probably about 1791, CHLOE ____ [Kelley?], with whom he had eight children, two born at Stratton,Vt., and the rest at Wendell (*Gregory Stone*, 245).

He served 8 months in 1777 and 14 days in the summer of 1780, marching to Rhode Island on an alarm on the second occasion (*MSSR* 15:86).

They lived at Sutton until the close of the Revolution. On 2 May 1785, Clark Stone of Sutton sold land in Westminster to Ezra Putnam for £18 (Worcester LR 96:518).

The 1790 census shows him in Stratton, Vt., with a household of two men, one boy under 16, and one female (p.54). In 1800 he was in Wendell, with one boy and two girls under 10 years (p.668). In 1811 he represented Wendell in the Massachusetts State Legislature.

Gregory Stone, p. 245, says that Clark and Hannah "had issue, prob. d.y."; the 1790 census seems to indicate a son. However, the fact that Hannah's father, John Hazeltine, in his will dated 20 May 1802 did not mention Hannah in any way suggests that if she did have children, they were dead by that date

Sources cited: *Sutton VR.   Mass. Soldiers & Sailors.   Gregory Stone Genealogy* (1918).   CENSUS: 1790 Stratton, Windham Co., Vt. (M637-12), 1800 Wendell, Hampshire Co. (M32-15).

664.   CHLOE HAZELTINE[5] (*Abigail Bruce*[4], *Abigail*[3] *Samson, Stephen*[2], *Henry*[1]), daughter of John Hazeltine and his wife Abigail Bruce [138], was born at Mendon 29 April 1761 (*VR* 97). She died, probably at Sutton, before August 1797 when her husband remarried.

She married 23 December 1777, at Sutton (*VR* 279), perhaps as his second wife, **JONATHAN STONE**, who was born 27 April 1750 at Sutton (*VR* 167), son of Levi and Mary (Lawrence) Stone, brother of the husband of Chloe's sister Hannah. Jonathan died probably at Somerset, Vt., before 24 February 1813, when his will was proved.

Jonathan Stone published marriage intentions at Sutton 18 February 1775 (*VR* 363) with JUDITH RICE, who was born at Worcester 27 July 1751, daughter of Thomas and Judith (____) Rice, but no evidence has been found to indicate that the marriage took place (however, his first child with Chloe was named Judith). After Chloe's death, he married, second or third, at Sutton 20 August 1797 (*VR* 363), SARAH BIXBY, who was born 9 July 1757 and died there 30 November 1824 in her 68th year, "widow of Jonathan," (g.s.), daughter of Samuel and Lydia (Bond) Bixby (*VR* 21, 466). As Sarah Stone she signed a receipt 28 January 1814 for her legacy from her father's will dated 30 September 1796, proved 2 May 1809 (Worcester PR 36:359, 2A:121). Jonathan and Sally (Bixby) Stone had one child, Sally P. Stone, born at Somerset, Vt., 6 April 1800, who married Cornelius Bancroft and settled at Romeo, Michigan.

Jonathan Stone of Sutton served in the Revolutionary War as a private in the militia on several occasions in 1775 and 1776 (*MSSR* 15:106). He was an original grantee of Somerset, Vt., and a constable there in 1801 (*Vt. Hist. Gazetteer.* 5 (II): 528).

The family moved to Vermont about 1799 (*Gregory Stone,* 244). Jonathan Stone "late of Sutton now of Somerset, Vt.," was named as the husband of deceased daughter Chloe Stone in the will of his father-in-law, John Hazeltine, in 1802, and their children were mentioned (Westminster Dist. Prob. 2:119-23, 371-74; 2:371).

In his will dated 31 December 1810, Jonathan Stone of Somerset, Vt., named his children Judith Jacobs, Rhoda Rice, Jonathan Stone Jr., and Sally P. Stone, and appointed wife Sarah executrix (Marlboro Dist. PR 5:437). The will was presented by the widow Sarah 24 February 1813 (*ibid.*).

Children of Jonathan and Chloe (Hazeltine) Stone, b. Sutton, rec. Somerset, Vt. (VT VR, Somerset *VR* 2:26):

i   JUDITH STONE[6], b. 6 Nov. 1778; m. at Ward [now Auburn] (*VR* 82), 17 Sept. 1803 [?perhaps as his second wife], JAMES JACOBS. The 1810 census listed James Jacobs at Ward [Auburn], himself and wife 26-45, with one woman 16-26, one boy 10-16, and one little boy and two little girls under 10 (p.482). Judith Jacobs ae 71, b. Mass., was living 1850 in the household of Carter Jacobs ae 50, blacksmith, in Bethel, Vt. (p.194), but if his age is correct he was not her son.

   Jacobs children of "James and Judea," rec. Ward/Auburn (*VR* 37): 1. *Sally Jacobs[7]*, b. 5 April 1804. 2. *Jonathan Jacobs,* b. 14 Jan. 1807. 3. *Hannah Jacobs,* b. 2 March 1809.

ii   RHODA STONE, b. 11 Dec. 1782 (Bible rec. says 1783); d. 13 Aug. 1846 ae 63 at Dover, Vt. (VR 1:208) and bur. Mountain View Cem. there; m. 9 April 1809 at Somerset, Vt., HAZELTON RICE, b. there 20 Feb. 1788, d. at West Dover 15 Aug. 1870, son of Daniel and Sally (Ball) Rice (Bible rec.).

Rice children (Bibles), b. Somerset [later W. Dover], Vt.: 1. *Hiram Watkins Rice⁷*, b. 24 Dec. 1810. 2. *Nancy Rice*, b. 17 April 1813. 3. *Melinthy Rice*, b. 24 Feb. 1817; m. ___ Pike. 4. *Sally/Sarah Rice*, b. 23 Jan. 1821; m. James Alger. 5. *Hazelton Rice*, b. 9 Dec. 1822. 6. *Lewis Henry Rice*, b. 29 June 1826.

iii   JONATHAN STONE, b. 31 Jan. 1789; d. Genoa, Mich., 1844 (*Gregory Stone*, 402); m. at Guilford, Vt. (VR A:1), 4 Feb. 1810, SUSANNAH FORREST, b. ca 1790 Vt. In 1850 she was living in the household of her son David in Genoa, Livingston Co., Mich. (p.386).

     Stone children (*Gregory Stone*, 402): 1. *Jonathan Stone⁷*, b. 24 Nov. 1810, Somerset, Vt.; m. Lucinda Newton. 2. *David F. Stone*, b. 9 Sept. 1812, Somerset. 3. *Lyman Stone*, b. 4 March 1825, Dover, Vt.

Sources cited: *Auburn VR. Mendon VR. Sutton VR. Mass. Soldiers & Sailors.* Vermont Vital Records for Dover, Guilford, and Somerset. Worcester County Probate Records. Vermont Probate Records, Marlboro and Westminster Districts. Family Bible of James and Sarah (Rice) Alger, NEHGS Mss C181, and Hazelton Rice Bible, NEHGS Gen. 1 R 110, both on Bible Records CD, *q.v.* for further information. *Vermont Historical Gazetteer. Gregory Stone Genealogy* (1918). **See also:** The Hazelton Rice Papers (VT Hist. Soc. MSA 69-71), include correspondence between Rhoda Rice & Jonathan Stone Jr.

665.   JOHN HAZELTINE⁵ (*Abigail Bruce⁴, Abigail³ Samson, Stephen², Henry¹*), son of John Hazeltine and his wife Abigail Bruce [138], was born about 1765. He died before 15 March 1798 at Townshend, Vt.

He married by 1797, **POLLY** _____, who was living in September 1824 when she claimed John's share in his uncle Col. Simeon Hazelton's estate.

Letters of administration were issued 15 March 1798 to Polly Hazeltine, widow of John Hazeltine Jr. (Westminster Dist. PR 1:242). The will of John's father, dated 20 May 1802, named grandson John Hazeltine, only child of son John late of Townshend, deceased (2: 371-74), and on 5 July 1802, the day that will was proved, Benjamin Murdock of Townshend was appointed guardian for young John Hazeltine (Westminster Dist. PR 2:119-23, 294; D:23).

Child of John and Polly (___) Hazeltine:

i   JOHN HAZELTINE⁶, b. Townshend, Vt., 8 May 1787 [?1797]* (VR A:38); d. prob. 1850-1860, possibly in Chicago, Ill.; m. LYDIA _____, b. ca 1800. As a young child John was under the guardianship of Benjamin Murdock

---

* The Town Record gives 1787 as year of birth, but if that is correct John Jr. would be 21 in 1808 and thus would not require a guardian. His choosing Willard Taft as guardian 3 June 1811 suggests he had turned 14 about that time.

of Townshend, but on 3 June 1811, when he was 14, he chose Willard Taft of Putney as his guardian. He was of Hartland, Vt., in May 1828 when he received a deed for 115 acres of Sandgate property from the estate of his uncle Col. Simeon Hazeltine (Bennington LR 8:363).; of Sunderland, Vt., 3 June 1830; of Manchester 16 March 1832 (LR 10:51, 70, 89-96); and of Sandgate 25 Aug. 1841 when he sold to Isaac Binniger of Salem, N.Y., 205 acres formerly owned by Col. Simeon Hazeltine, dec'd., and distributed in 1828 to: 1) heirs of John Hazelton, dec'd.; 2) John Rice [whose heirs sold to grantor 25 Aug. 1841]; and 3) Simeon Hazelton (Bennington LR 10:355-6).

The 1830 census listing, at Sunderland, includes one boy and one girl under 5, and one man 30-39. The 1850 census lists John at Sandgate. ae 58 [sic], merchant b. Vt., Lydia ae 50, Lindsey ae 6 (male) and Weltha M. ae 2 (p.111), implying a second family [?or grandchildren?]. No land records were found in Sunderland, and no probate in Bennington Co. In 1860 Lydia Hazeltine ae 58, b. Vt., was living in Chicago, Ill., in the household of George W. Perkins ae 26, "agent," b. N.Y., and his wife Jula, ae 28, with Welthy ae 11 [surname under Perkins with ditto mark crossed out], and John Hazeltine ae 32, carpenter, all b. Vt. (p.91). The 1850 census shows Julia Hazeltine ae 17, b. Vt., in the household of John Stanley ae 75 and Nancy ae 66, in Lyman, Grafton Co., N.H. (p.63).

Probable children, all b. Vt.: 1. *John Hazeltine*[7], b. ca 1828; living 1860. 2. *Julia Hazeltine*, b. ca 1832; m. after 1850 George W. Perkins. ? 3. *Lindsey Hazeltine* [son], b. ca 1844; not with Lydia 1860. ? 4. *Welthy M. Hazeltine*, b. ca 1848 (poss. Julia's child and thus grandchild of John and Lydia).

Sources cited: Vermont Vital Records to 1870. Townshend, Vt. VR. Windham Co., Vt., Westminster District Probate Records. Bennington and Manchester, Vt., Deeds. Bennington Co. Probate Records, Manchester District. CENSUS: CENSUS: 1830 Sunderland, Bennington Co., Vt. (M19-184); 1850 Sandgate, Bennington Co., Vt. (M432-921) & Lyman, Grafton Co., N.H. (M432-431); 1860 Ward 5, Chicago, Cook Co., Ill. (M653-166).

666. POLLY HAZELTINE[5] (*Abigail Bruce*[4], *Abigail*[3] *Samson, Stephen*[2], *Henry*[1]), daughter of John Hazeltine and his wife Abigail Bruce [138], was born probably about 1767, and died before May 1802 when her father named her in his will as deceased (Westminster Dist. PR 2:119-23, 371-4).

She married at Worcester, 4 September 1793 (*VR* 371), **URIAH JOHNSON**, who was born 13 September 1759 and died at Hartford, Ohio, in May 1840 (pension file), after 14 May when he made his will. A Uriah Johnson, son of Solomon Jr. and Levina (____) Johnson, was born at Worcester 28 June 1752

(*VR* 152), but this date does not agree with the date given in the pension file; there is room for his birth, however, in the list of other children entered for that couple.

The 1850 census record of daughter Sophia says she was born in Mass., and records of Stephen say he was born in Sutton, Mass., but they are not recorded there. Uriah was of Weathersfield, Vt., in 1800, and was there in 1802 when his father-in-law died.

He was of Weathersfield, Vt., when he married, second, at Putney, Vt., 26 August 1805 (TR 1:2 of insert), OLIVE LOPER. Olive evidently died soon, for Uriah married, third, at Unity, N. H., 4 March 1807, BETSY WEED, who was born 7 May 1779. Uriah and Betsey had children (pension file): George F. Johnson, Alexander H. Johnson, Sally H. Johnson, Albert N. Johnson, Warren W. Johnson, Joseph R. Johnson, Solomon Johnson, Mary A. Johnson, and Emily W. Johnson.

Uriah Johnson of Worcester served in the Revolutionary War, mustered 4 September 1777 for three years (*MSSR* 8:879). His service included 20 mos. 6 days as a drummer in Capt. Pierce's company, Col. Timothy Bigelow's regiment, and 9 mos. 21 days as a private.

The 1800 census for Weathersfield, Vt., lists one man and one woman 26-45, and one boy and two girls under 10 (p.351).

The will of John Hazeltine of Townshend, Vt., dated 20 May 1802, proved 5 July 1802, names among others "the children of late daughter Polly Johnson late wife of Uriah Johnson of Weathersfield, Vt." Uriah Johnson Jr., Sophia Johnson, Stephen Johnson, and Eliza Johnson shared in a division of the estate on 28 September 1805 (Westminster Dist. PR 2:119-23, 371-74, 400).

On 11 December 1819, claiming to be aged 59, Uriah Johnson applied for a pension from Windham County, Vt., naming third wife Betsy and seven children (White, 1859). At age 74 Betsey applied for a widow's pension 6 October 1853 from Grafton County, N. H., stating that her husband had died May 1840 at Hartford, Ohio. She applied for a bounty land warrant 18 April 1855. Names of children of their marriage are given.

On 1 September 1834, Stephen Johnson, Sophia Sweat wife of Benjamin, and Eliza Johnson sold to Safety Dozenbury the land inherited from their grandfather John Hazeltine (Manchester LR 12:416-7).

Uriah Johnson's will, written in Trenton Township, Delaware County, Ohio, on 14 May 1840, was proved 16 June 1840. He named as heirs "my son-in-law Benjamin Sweat ... Eliza Johnson ... son Albert N. Johnson. ... and all the rest of my lawful heirs," and appointed Benjamin Sweat and Thomas Blackburn executors; witnesses were Merrson D. Cole and David M. Nitt (Delaware Co. PR 2:105-07).

Children of Uriah and Polly (Hazeltine) Johnson, all b. before May 1802 when they were named in will of their maternal grandfather:

i URIAH JOHNSON[6], b. say 1794; living 28 Sept. 1805 but not mentioned when his mother's heirs sold her land legacy from Simeon Hazeltine 1 Sept. 1834. (A Uriah Johnson of Haverhill, N. H., m. Sarah Swift of Weathersfield 29 Dec. 1831 (VT VR Weathersfield TR 3:89).

ii SOPHIA JOHNSON, b. ca 1796; d. Claridon, Ohio, 1 Nov. 1871 (Geauga Co. Deaths, 2:24, #409), ae 71 (g.s.) or 74 (*Geauga Co. History*); m. at Westminster, Vt., 19 Aug. 1821 (VT VR, TR 2:135), BENJAMIN SWEAT, b. in N. H. ca 1794-95, d. Claridon 24 March 1869 ae 74 (g.s.). In 1817 he and Benjamin Mastick, both bachelors, moved from Vermont to Geauga Co., Ohio, and settled on Lot 1 of Section 13 comprising 216 acres. Mastick married there but Sweat returned to Vermont for his bride (*Pioneer and General History of Geauga Co.*, 391-92). In 1850 Benjamin Sweat was a farmer in Claridon, ae 55, b. N. H., with Sophia, ae 54, b. Mass., and four children b. Ohio (p.229). His will was proved April 1869 in Geauga Co., Ohio (Geauga Co. Wills A:395).

Sweat children at home 1850, all b. Ohio: 1. *Maria Sweat'*, b. ca 1827. 2. *Sarah E. Sweat*, b. ca 1832; d. 9 Jan. 1858 ae 25 (g.s.). 3. *Emily Sweat*, b. ca 1834; d. 12 Sept. 1861 ae 27 (g.s.). 4. *Henry Sweat*, b. ca 1838.

iii STEPHEN JOHNSON, b. prob. ca 1798; d. 17 June 1882 Stockton, Ill.; m. in Vt., 10 Oct. 1814, LUCY STONE, b. Hinsdale, N. H., ca 1795, d. Ill. ca 1838 (Ray W. Justus). He was of Underhill, Vt., 1 Sept. 1834 when he joined his siblings in selling land inherited from their grandfather.

Children, all except Eliza b. Townshend or Underhill, Vt. (Ray W. Justus): 1. *Sophia/Sally Johnson'*, b. 15 March 1815. 2. *Lucy Mariah Johnson*, b. 31 Jan. 1817. 3. *Mary Ann Johnson*, b. 17 March 1819. 4. *Samuel Henry Johnson*, b. 3 Dec. 1821. 5. *Marsha Aurilla Johnson*, b. 14 Dec. 1822. 6. *Harriet Lenora Johnson*, b. 28 Dec. 1826. 7. *Stephen Randall Johnson*, b. 14 March 1829. 8. *Charlotte L. Johnson*, b. 1 April 1832. 9. *Eliza Rachel Johnson*, b. ca 1834 Claridon, Ohio.

iv ELIZA JOHNSON, b. say 1800; of Claridon, Ohio, 1 Sept. 1834; living 14 May 1840.

Sources cited: Putney, Vt., Town Records. Geauga Co., Ohio, Deaths, Probate Court 1867-1899. Manchester, Vt., Deeds. Windham Co., Vt., Westminster District Probate Records. Delaware Co., Ohio, Probate Records Geauga Co., Ohio, Probate Records. White, *Abstracts of Revolutionary War Pension Files*, citing files W1194 and BLW 11151-160-55. Claridon Township Cemetery Files, Geauga Co. Genealogical Society. *Pioneer and General History of Geauga County, Ohio* (1880). Ray W. Justus, "Justus-Painter Families," on line. CENSUS: *Heads of Families 1790 – Vermont;* 1800 Weathersfield, Winsor Co., Vt. (M32-52); Claridon Twp. Geauga Co., Ohio, 1850 (M432-682) & 1860 (M653-967).

667. SIMEON HAZELTINE[5] (*Abigail Bruce*[4], *Abigail*[3] *Samson*, *Stephen*[2], *Henry*[1]), son of John Hazeltine and his wife Abigail Bruce [138], was born 5 June 1779 at Sutton (*VR* 86). He died after 1830 when he was listed in the census at Bakersfield, Vt. He is probably the [Rev.] Simeon Hazeltine who died 10 August 1841 "at Nelson, N.Y. [having] labored in Pennsylvania, Ohio, and Concord, N.H.," noted in the Baptist newspaper *Morning Star* of 6 July 1842 (*Death Notices from Freewill Baptist Pub.*, 163).

He was of Townshend, Vt., 20 September 1801, when he married, at Westminster (*VR* H:332), **LYDIA REED**, who was born about 1782 and died 14 April 1829 at Berkshire, Vt. (TR).

In the 1800 census Simeon was recorded at Townshend as a single man between 16 and 26 years (p.148). In a deed dated 20 May 1802, recorded 24 May 1803, Lt. John Hazeltine of Townshend deeded to "only [surviving] son" Simeon Hazeltine of Townshend about 187 acres in Townshend, which Simeon deeded back to his stepmother on 5 October 1803 (Townshend LR 3:495; 4:215). Simeon's cousin Silas Hazeltine, an important landowner at Bakersfield, Vt., undoubtedly induced Simeon to settle there. From his cousin, Simeon purchased four and a half acres in Bakersfield 10 October 1805 and remained in that town at least until 27 January 1817 when he sold the property to Silas B. Hazeltine, son of Silas who had died before 18 June 1816 (Bakersfield LR 2:22; 4:167). He moved to Berkshire, Vt., near the Canadian border, where he purchased a lot 24 March 1819 from George W. Kendall of Sheldon (Berkshire LR 4:259).

An account of his grandson Nelson H. Farr in the *Baptist Encyclopedia* calls Nelson's mother "Wealthy C., daughter of Rev. Simeon Hazelton," and while this is the only indication found to date that Simeon was a minister, it explains to some extent his wandering. He was recorded in the 1810 census of Bakersfield (p.322) but does not appear at either Bakersfield or Berkshire in the 1820 census. He sold his lot in Berkshire 14 December 1829 to John Clendening of Sheldon (Berkshire LR 6:112), eight months after his wife died, and returned to Bakersfield where he was enumerated in the 1830 census aged 50-60 with one male 10-15, one female 40-50, one 10-15 and one 15-20 (p.65); evidently his three oldest daughters were not with him by then.

Except for the death of his youngest child and only son, of Berkshire in December 1839, and the marriage of daughter Welthy C., no trace of Simeon's family has been found.

Children of Simeon and Lydia (Reed) Hazeltine, all b. in Vermont:

   i   LYDIA HAZELTINE[6], b. 9 July 1802 Townshend (TR A:39).

ii PAMELA ANDREWS HAZELTINE, b. 31 Jan. 1804 Townshend (TR A:39).

iii ROWENA H. HAZELTINE, b. 4 July 1808 Bakersfield (TR 1:20).

iv WELTHY C. HAZELTINE, b. 30 June 1813 Bakersfield (TR 1:20); m. evidently before 1832, SAMUEL FARR (sketch of son Nelson H. Farr in *Baptist Encyclopedia*, 190). In 1850 Welthy C. Farr ae 37, b. Vt., was head of a household in Scipio, Seneca Co., Ohio; her husband was not with the family (p.48).

> *Farr* children at home 1850: 1. *Lyman M. Farr[7]*, b. ca 1832 Vt. 2. *Nelson H. Farr*, b. 10 Jan. 1834 Enosburg, Vt. (*Baptist Ency.*); m. Matilda Patterson. 3. *Emeline Farr*, b. ca 1837 N.Y. 4. *Mary J. Farr*, b. ca 1840 N.Y. 5. *Areal [?] J. Farr*, b. ca 1845 Ohio.

v ANGELINA HAZELTINE, b. 10 Nov. 1815 Bakersfield (TR 1:20).

vi JOHN WESLEY HAZELTINE, b. 28 Jan. 1818 Berkshire (TR 2:279); d. there 2 Dec. 1839 aged 22; bur. Calvary Church (TR index).

Sources cited: *Sutton VR.* Vermont Vital Records: Town VRs of Bakersfield, Berkshire, Townsend, and Westminster. Bakersfield, Berkshire, and Townshend Deeds. Young and. Taylor, *Death Notices from Freewill Baptist Publications 1811-1851* (1985). CENSUS: Franklin Co., Vt., Bakersfield and Berkshire, 1800 (M32-52), 1810 (M252-64), 1830 (M19-183). **See also:** Franklin Probate District G:188, distribution of Silas Hazelton's land.

668. MARGARET RAWSON[5] (*Elizabeth Bruce[4], Abigail[3] Samson, Stephen[2], Henry[1]*), daughter of John Rawson and his wife Elizabeth Bruce [139], was born Monday 14 December 1761 at Mendon (*VR* 145). She died in 1850, aged 89, at Hartland, Vt. (*NEHGR* 121:217).

She married 20 April 1795, at Sudbury (*VR* 198), **ZELOTES GATES** of Rutland (*VR* 182). He was born 24 December 1755 at Rutland, son of Stephen and Demaris (Howe) Gates (*NEHGR* 121:217), and died 19 March 1823, aged 67, at Hartland, Vt. (*ibid.*). The will of Stephen Gates dated 8 September 1770 and proved 22 October 1773, named among others his wife Damaris and son Zelotes (*ibid.*).

Zelotes Gates of Rutland served in the Revolutionary War as a private, first in 1775 in response to the Lexington alarm, in August 1777 on a march to Bennington, in 1778 on a reinforcement of the Rutland barracks and on a march to escort troops from Saratoga to Enfield, Conn., and finally in 1779 at Claverack [N.Y.] (*MSSR* 6:326).

Zelotes Gates, in his will dated 1 November 1822 and proved 15 April 1823, named his wife Margaret, who received one-third of his real estate, two sons, Benjamin Franklin (to be executor) and Thomas Jefferson; son John Nelson Gates; son James Addison Gates; and "my sons' aunt Catherine Rawson" (Windsor, Vt. PR, Hartford District 7:565).

Children of Zelotes and Margaret (Rawson) Gates, rec. Hartland, Vt. (*VR*; Hartland Cem. Rec.):

  i   BENJAMIN FRANKLIN GATES[6], b. 4 Dec. 1797; d. 1870, ae 72; m. MARY CROSLEY (cem. rec.). In 1850 Benjamin F. Gates ae 52, farmer, was in Hartland with Mary ae 52, and 3 children; the household included James Peterson ae 20, farmer, and Eldad French ae 58, laborer, everyone b. Vt. (p.283).
        Children at home 1850: 1. *Emily Gates[7]*, b. ca 1832. 2. *Mary F. Gates*, b. ca 1841. 3. *Elbridge Gates*, b. ca 1843.

  ii JOHN NELSON GATES, b. 6 Dec. 1799; living Nov. 1822.

  iii ELIZABETH GATES, b. 20 April 1801; d. 12 Aug. 1822, ae 21 (g.s.).

  iv JAMES ADDISON GATES, b. 2 April 1803; m. LUCY ___. In 1850 he was a farmer in Hartland with Lucy ae 43, and two children (p.283b)
        Children at home 1850: 1. *Adalaide Gates[7]*, b. ca 1836. 2. *Adaline Gates*, b. ca 1842.

  v   THOMAS JEFFERSON GATES, b. 5 Dec. 1804; d. 26 Aug. 1844 ae 40 (g.s.); m. at Woodstock, 1 Dec. 1836 (VT VR), POLLY SANDERSON. The 1840 census listed them in Hartland, both 30-40, with one girl and one boy under 5 (p.442). Polly is not listed there in 1850.

Sources cited: *Mendon VR*. *Rutland VR*. Vermont Vital Records: Hartland and Woodstock.. Windsor, Vt., Probates, Hartford District. Clarence Almon Torrey, "Stephen Gates of Hingham, Lancaster and Cambridge, Mass., ...", *NEHGR* 121 [1967]. CENSUS: 1850 Hartland, Windsor Co., Vt. (M432-931). **See also:** Charles O. Gates, *Stephen Gates of Hingham and Lancaster* (New York, 1898), 36, 75.

669.   TURNER RAWSON[5] (*Elizabeth Bruce[4], Abigail[3] Samson, Stephen[2], Henry[1]*), son of John Rawson and his wife Elizabeth Bruce [139], was born Thursday 3 September 1767 at Mendon (*VR* 147). He died 17 January 1811, ae 43, at Grafton (*VR* 359).

He married at Sutton, 30 December 1805 (*VR* 338), **PATTY KING**, who was born there 30 May 1779, daughter of John and Elizabeth (Town) King (*VR* 102). She died at Holden 14 October 1864, ae 85y 4m 14d (Mass. VR 176:245). She married, second, in 1812 at Uxbridge, as his second wife, PHINEAS LELAND (*History of Sutton*, 679).

The will of Turner Rawson of Grafton, dated 10 January 1811 filed 4 February 1811, left all his estate to his wife Patty and named her executrix (Worcester PR #A48863). Phineas Leland of Grafton in his will dated 20 August 1818, proved 2 May 1820, named his wife Patty and his children, all by his first marriage (Worcester PR #A37000).

In 1850 Patty Leland, aged 72, was living at Grafton, listed as head of her own household, sharing a dwelling with Joshua W. Leland [age unclear] and Polly, 67 (p.419). Patty Leland of Holden in her will dated 4 April 1859, proved 8 November 1864, named her sister Polly King and mentioned without naming "my nieces" (Worcester PR #A36999).

Turner Rawson and his wife Patty had no children.

Sources cited: *Grafton VR. Mendon VR. Sutton VR.* Mass. Vital Records 1841-1910. Worcester County Probate Records. *History of Sutton* (1878).

670. ELIZABETH RAWSON[5] (*Elizabeth Bruce*[4], *Abigail*[3] *Samson, Stephen*[2], *Henry*[1]), daughter of John Rawson and his wife Elizabeth Bruce [139], was born 7 February 1778 at Mendon (*VR* 144), recorded as "Betsey." She died in August 1847 (*John Hill of Dover*, 12).

She married 13 April 1800, at Salem (*VR* 3:498), **SAMUEL HILL**, who was born 13 April 1777 at Kittery (later Eliot), Maine, son of Isaac and Elizabeth (Estes) Hill. He died in October 1865 at Eliot (*John Hill of Dover*, 12, 14). He inherited his father's estate in Eliot.

In 1850 Samuel Hill was a farmer in Eliot, Maine, aged 73, with Nancy Rosin [*sic*] aged 70, born in Massachusetts, surely his sister-in-law Nancy Rawson (n.f.r., *MF 20* 1:118).

Children of Samuel and Elizabeth (Rawson) Hill, iii-xii b. Eliot, Me. (*John Hill of Dover* unless otherwise cited):

i   JOSEPH HILL[6], b. 18 June 1800 at Salem (not rec.); m. (1) ELIZA AUGUSTA HAMMOND, (2) MARY FAIRFIELD.

ii ELIZA HILL, b. 19 Dec. 1801; d. 1 Jan. 1805.

iii JOHN HILL, b. 28 Nov. 1802 at Eliot; d. there in Oct. 1827.

iv STEPHEN HILL, b. 29 Oct. 1805; m. CHARLOTTE LAMB.

v   MARY HILL, b. 6 Dec. 1807; m. (1) JOHN GOODWIN, (2) EDWARD K. PAUL.

vi   SAMUEL HILL, b. 28 June 1809; d. Townsend 14 Jan. 1887 (Mass. VR 383:233); m. (1) OLIVE M. HOLMAN, (2) at Townsend 29 Dec. 1841 (*VR* 184), LYDIA PALMER, b. there 24 March 1812 (*VR* 291), dau. of Rev. David and Chloe (___) Palmer of Townsend. Samuel, Lydia, and several of their children are bur. in New Cemetery, Townsend (*VR* 363).

      Children with first wife: 1. *Samuel Edwin Hill*, b. 1833, d. 1804, "son of Samuel Hill and Olive Holman" (g.s.). Children with second wife: 2. *Charles William Hill*, b. 11 Oct. 1842; m. Katherine L. Struckman. 3. *Mary Caroline Hill*, b. 29 Dec. 1843; m. James A. Doane. 4. *Lucia Thompson Hill*, b. 26 March 1846; m. Rev. Henry Hyde. 5. *Annie Elizabeth Hill*, b. 11 July 1847; m. Albert L. Fessenden. 6. *John Kingsley Hill* (twin), b. 4 Oct. 1848; d. 4 Feb. 1853. 7. *Levi Palmer Hill* (twin), b. 4 Oct. 1848; m. N. S. Farmer. 8. *Henry Arthur Hill*, b. 2 Aug. 1850. 9. *John Frederick Hill*, b. 9 March 1853; m. Ida Frances Parker.

vii   ELIZABETH HILL, b. 27 May 1811; m. IVORY GOODWIN, b. Me. ca 1813. In 1850 he was a butcher at S. Berwick, Me., with Elizabeth ae 34 [*sic*], and three children (p.276).

      Goodwin children at home 1850: 1. *Charles C. Goodwin*[7], b. ca 1840. 2. *Elizabeth R. Goodwin*, b. ca 1842. 3. *Mary Goodwin*, b. ca 1848.

viii   ASA A. HILL, b. 26 Dec. 1812; d. in July 1838.

ix   IRA HILL, b. 20 Dec. 1814; m. HANNAH FAIRFIELD, b. ca 1817 Me. In 1850 he was a butcher in Brighton, with Hannah ae 33 and a daughter (p.70).

      Child at home 1850: 1. *Augusta Hill*, b. ca 1843 in Me.

x   MARTHA ESTES HILL, b. 5 Dec. 1816; m. 13 Oct. 1839, LEONARD SPINNEY.

xi   CHARLES ESTES HILL, b. 28 Aug. 1819; m. MARY MASON.

xii   WILLIAM HILL, b. 4 Feb. 1821; m. (1) 27 Nov. 1849, MIRIAM LEIGHTON, dau. of Andrew and Sarah C. (Odiorne) Leighton, d. 9 Nov. 1876; m. (2) JENNIE BROOKS.

      Children: 1. *Ella Bruce Hill*, b. 19 Sept. 1850; m. Homer H. Hobbs. 2. *John Fremont Hill*, b. 29 Oct. 1855; m. (1) Lizzie G. Vickery, (2) Laura (Colman) Leggett; he was Gov. of Maine 1901-05. 3. *Lizzie Rawson Hill*, b. 23 March 1857; m. William L. Hobbs. 4. *Howard Hill*, b. 5 Dec. 1861; d. 2 Jan. 1863.

Sources cited: *Salem VR*. Lapham, *John Hill of Dover in 1649* (1889), wrong date for marriage of Samuel and Elizabeth. CENSUS: 1850 Brighton, Middlesex Co. (M432-326), S. Berwick, York Co., Me. (M432-329). **See also:** *Old Eliot*, 5:71-76, account of Hill Family of Eliot and sketch of Gov. John F. Hill.

671.   LYDIA BOSWORTH[5] (*Lydia*[4] *Samson, David*[3], *Caleb*[2], *Henry*[1]), daughter of
Nathaniel Bosworth and his wife Lydia Samson [140], was baptized 17 June 1739
at Plymouth (*CR* 1:442). She was apparently living in September 1759 when her
son was baptized, but no further record of her has been found. She was a
descendant also of *Mayflower* passengers John Alden and Myles Standish.

She married, intentions 26 January 1756 at Chelsea (*Chelsea History* 2:392),
AMOS BROWN. He may be the Dea. Amos Brown who died at Boston
3 February 1812 aged 73 years (*NEHGR* 78:419).

It has been assumed that Amos was the man of that name born 26 October
1737 at Attleboro, son of Benjamin and Sarah (Freeman) Brown (*Brown Families,*
27). The will of Benjamin Brown of Attleboro, dated 23 August 1742, proved 19
October 1742, names his wife Sarah, sons Jeremiah (not yet of age), and Benjamin
(to provide for his mother), and mentions but does not name four youngest sons
and seven daughters, all under age (Bristol PR 10:193-95). There are, however,
problems with this identification. An "Order respecting the Militia," dated 25
October 1754, requests the names "of the Persons by Law obliged to appear upon
Alarms ...," and the list returned for Point Shirley (then part of Chelsea, now
Winthrop), includes Benjamin Bosworth, Nathaniel Bosworth [Lydia's father], and
Amos Brown (*NEHGR* 20:233-34). The Amos Brown born in Attleboro in 1737
would have been only 17 in 1754 (old enough to be obliged to turn out for training
with the militia), and not yet 19 at marriage. The statement in *History of Chelsea* that
Amos "was a resident of Point Shirley about 1750" was probably drawn from that
same list, but if he really was a resident at that date he must have been born earlier
than the Attleboro man. Possibly the Point Shirley man was an older Amos who
may have been father of Lydia's husband.

Child of Amos and Lydia (Bosworth) Brown, only one identified:

i   AMOS BROWN[6], bp. 9 Sept. 1759 at King's Chapel, Boston, "infant ... of
      Amos and Lydia"; sponsors were George Lish, Samuel Ward, and Mary
      Burrel (Boston Ch. CD). He is prob. the Capt. Amos Brown who d.
      Duxbury 9 April 1823 "ae 63y 6m" (*VR* 356); m. at Duxbury 1 Jan. 1784
      (*VR* 226), RHODA WINSOR, b. Duxbury 6 June 1764, dau. of Samuel and
      Rhoda (Delano) Winsor (*VR* 204, 338). This Amos Brown was "from
      Boston" (*Duxbury History*, 238). In 1790 he was listed at Duxbury with
      one man, one boy, and three females (p.169).
          Children, prob. b. Duxbury (*Duxbury History*, 238): 1. *John Brown*[7], b. 17 Feb.
      1784; m. Cornelia Little. 2. *Rhoda Brown*, b. 1787; m. as 2nd wife, Henry Gooding
      (*VR* 85). 3. *Elizabeth/Betsey Brown*, b. 1790; m. as 1st wife, Henry Gooding (*ibid.*).

4. *Nancy Brown*, m. Duxbury 14 Sept. 1820 (*VR* 291), Charles Prior.   5. *Charles Brown*.   6. *Adriana Brown*, b. Jan. 1805 (*VR* 36).

Sources cited: *Attleboro VR. Chelsea VR. Plymouth Church Records.* Records of King's Chapel, Boston (Boston Churches CD). Bristol County Probate Records. "Order Respecting the Militia" [25 Oct. 1754], *NEHGR* 20 (1866). "Deaths in Boston and Vicinity," *NEHGR* 78 (1924). *History of Chelsea* (1908). Winsor, *History of Duxbury* (1849). Boyer, *Brown Families of Bristol* (1981).

672.   NATHANIEL BOSWORTH[5] (*Lydia*[4] *Samson, David*[3], *Caleb*[2], *Henry*[1]), son of Nathaniel Bosworth and his wife Lydia Samson [140], was born probably at Plymouth about 1741. He died at Boston or at sea, between 11 August 1788 and 8 June 1789, when his widow was appointed administratrix of his estate (Suffolk PR #19291). He was a descendant also of *Mayflower* passengers John Alden and Myles Standish.

He married 13 June 1771, at Boston (*VR* 49), **ELIZABETH POPE**. She was born 20 February 1750 at Falmouth (now Portland), Maine, daughter of Robert and Phebe (Brown) Pope (*Bosworth Gen.*, 5:699). She was living in Duxbury in October 1790 when she sold land in Boston.

On 15 September 1778 Nathaniel Bosworth, mariner, bought a house and land on the north side of Hollis Street in Boston from Samuel Pope (Suffolk LR 129:55). On 20 April 1787, the dwelling houses of Nathaniel Bosworth, Robert Pope, and Joseph Pope, all on the west side of Orange Street, Boston, were destroyed in a fire that started in a malt house and burned about one hundred buildings, sixty of them dwellings (Dexter, 190).

Nathaniel was called "Capt." in the inventory of his estate. Elizabeth Bosworth, widow, was appointed administratrix 8 June 1789 of the estate of Nathaniel Bosworth, late of Boston, mariner deceased. On 16 June 1789 an allowance was made for her four children (not named) under seven years; and again on 11 May 1790 for her children under seven. On 29 October 1790 Elizabeth Bosworth of Duxbury, administratrix of the estate of Nathaniel Bosworth of Boston, mariner, deceased, deeded to Abraham Adams, leather-dresser, land on the north side of Hollis Street, Boston (Suffolk LR 168:221).

The 1790 census listed Eliza Bozworth in Duxbury with one male 16 or over, one under 16, and four females (*Heads of Fam.*, 169).

The most accurate account found of the children in this family is a photocopy captioned "An exact copy of the brothers and sisters of Lydia who married Jno Bernard Swanton," in *The Swanton Genealogy* (1976).

Children of Nathaniel and Elizabeth (Pope) Bosworth, all b. probably at Boston, from photocopy in *The Swanton Genealogy*, seven in *Bosworth Gen.* without full birthdates:

i   NATHANIEL BOSWORTH⁶, b. 19 Feb. 1772.

ii   ELIZABETH BOSWORTH, b. 30 Jan. 1773; m. ca 9 Jan. 1793 at Duxbury, Capt. CLARK DREW (*Col. Cent. Index* 1:389), b. ca 1765, d. before 29 June 1797 when an administrator was appointed for his estate (Plymouth PR #6682; 34:118). *Bosworth Gen.* incorrectly attributes this marriage to Elizabeth (Pope) Bosworth, Nathaniel's widow.

iii ROBERT BOSWORTH, b. 24 April 1775; d. before 1820, "drowned in the mouth of the Kennebec river with two other sea captains while fishing"; m. at Bath, 16 Jan. 1799 (Winter St. Cong. CR, 2), SALLY/SARAH PETERSON, b. 1780 Maine, d. 1851 ae 71, dau. of John and Sarah (Hewitt) Peterson and a descendant of *Mayflower* passenger George Soule. In 1850 Sarah was living at Bath, Me., with her youngest daughter, near the family of son Robert (p.154).

     Children, b. Bath, Me. (*Bosworth Gen.*, 5:956): 1. *Robert Bosworth⁷*, b. 17 March 1800; m. Mary Ann McDonald or McDaniel (Bath Marriages, DAR). 2. *Nathaniel Bosworth*, b. ca 1802; went to sea and never heard from again. 3. *John Bosworth*, b. 23 March 1806; d. 1866; m. Viola M. Derout. 4. *Sarah Bosworth*, d. infancy. 5. *Sarah Bosworth*, d. unm. 6. *Elizabeth Ann Bosworth*, b. 1820; d. 20 March 1892 unm.

iv   JOSEPH BOSWORTH, b. 25 April 1776.

v   JOHN BOSWORTH, b. 18 July 1778; poss. the John Bosworth who d. in Florida in 1828 ae 50y (*Bath History*, 145). He was employed 1818-1821 by Green and Emerson of Bath to take 100 men to Florida and Georgia and cut live-oak timber to fulfill a contract with the U.S. for naval use (*ibid.*).

vi   BENJAMIN BOSWORTH, b. 26 Dec. 1780; d. 21 Aug. 1783.

vii ABIGAIL BOSWORTH, b. 18 March 1782; d. 18 Nov. 1865 Dexter, Me., unmarried. *Bosworth Gen.* says she cared for her sister Mary's children after the deaths of their parents. In 1860 she was in the household of her nephew John B. Arnold ae 38 at Dexter, listed as "Domestic" (p.434).

viii LYDIA BOSWORTH, b. 21 March 1784; d. 25 Feb. 1865 at Dresden, Me.; m. at Bath, Me., 16 Sept. 1804, JOHN BERNARD SWANTON, b. Bath 29 May 1782, son of William and Elizabeth (Donnell) Swanton (*Swanton Gen.*, n.p.). He was Collector of Customs at Bath 1825-1829, appointed by Pres. John Quincy Adams; "a prominent man and member of the Swedenborgian Church, having previously belonged to the Calvinist Baptist" (*Bath History*, 185). In 1850 John B. Swanton ae 68 was a farmer at Bath with Lydia B. ae 65, Abigail S., Samuel B., and George W. Swanton, and Darius Cathorn ae 17. Buried Maple Grove Cem., Bath.

    Swanton children (*Swanton Gen.,* 160): 1. *John Bosworth Swanton Jr.*[7], b. 29 Nov. 1804; m. Catherine Reed. 2. *Henry Gilbert Hunt Swanton,* b. 21 Sept. 1806; m. Elizabeth Glazier. 3. *William Swanton,* b. 6 Feb., d. 23 Feb. 1808. 4. *Lydia Bosworth Swanton,* b. 10 Jan., d. 17 Jan. 1809. 5. *Joseph Bosworth Swanton,* b. 14 June 1810; m. Philena Pratt. 6. *William King Swanton,* b. 20 Feb. 1812; d. 1827. 7. *Andrew Jackson Swanton,* b. 26 May 1815; m. Martha Pierce. 8. *Abigail Sprague Swanton,* b. 19 March 1817; d. Hallowell. 9. *Edward Wheelock Swanton,* b. 3 July, d. 21 July 1819. 10.*Thomas Ripley Swanton,* b. 16 July 1920; m. Lucy Pierce. 11. *George Stearns Swanton,* b. 29 Oct. 1822; d. 1837. 12. *Lydia Elizabeth Swanton,* b. 19 Sept. 1824; m. Joseph Marson. 13. *Margaret Tingley Swanton,* b. 28 April, d. 26 May 1826. 14. *Samuel Benjamin Swanton,* b. 28 May 1829; d. 8 Aug. 1850.

ix   POLLY / MARY BOSWORTH, b. 27 March 1785; b. ca Jan. 1787; d. Monmouth, Me., 6 Sept. 1840 ae 53y 8m; m. at Bath, Me., ca 1811, JOHN ARNOLD JR., b. Lebanon, Conn., 6 March 1781, d. Monmouth 22 Feb. 1845 ae 64y, son of John and Hannah (Loomis) Arnold. John, Mary, and four of their daughters are bur. Center Cem., Monmouth, with his father.

    Arnold children: 1. ? *Mary Arnold*[7], b. ca 1812; living in household of brother John B. Arnold in 1860. 2. *Wealthy Arnold,* b. ca 1817; d. 28 April 1848 ae 31y. 3. *Julia Arnold,* b. ca 1819; d. 12 July 1849 ae 30y. 4. *John B. Arnold,* b. ca 1822; m. Drusilla ___. 5. *Nathaniel Arnold,* b. 23 Nov. 1823 Monmouth; m. Welthy Swanton. 6. *Fannie M. Arnold,* b. ca 1827; d. 1 Nov. 1847 ae 20y. 7. *Elizabeth Arnold,* b. ca 1830; d. 20 Oct. 1848 ae 18y. 8. *[Daughter] Arnold,* m. Davis Hatch of Bath (*Swanton Gen.,* 163b).

x   BENJAMIN BOSWORTH, b. 10 Aug. 1787.

Sources cited: *Duxbury VR. Boston VR* (BRC 30). "Marriages and Baptismal Records of Winter Street Congregational Church, Bath 1796–1838 (Me. DAR). Plymouth County Probate Records. Suffolk County Probate Records. *Index to Marriages in the Columbian Centinel.* Louise May Swanton, *The Swanton Genealogy* (1976). *Memoranda of John Haven Dexter. Bosworth Genealogy* (1926-40). Reed, *History of Bath* (1894). CENSUS: *Heads of Families 1790 – Mass.;* 1850 Lincoln Co., Me., Bath & Dresden (M432-261); 1860 Bath, Penobscot Co., Me. (M653-447).

673.   BENJAMIN BOSWORTH[5] (*Lydia*[4] *Samson, David*[3], *Caleb*[2], *Henry*[1]), son of Nathaniel Bosworth and his wife Lydia Samson [140], was born probably at Plymouth in January 1743. He died 15 November 1769 in Boston or at sea (*Bosworth Gen.,* 5:704).

He married at Boston 17 August 1766, by Rev. Mather Byles (*VR* 44), **ABIGAIL SEAVER**, who was born 4 January 1743/4 at Dorchester, daughter of Joshua and Abigail (Foster) Seaver (*VR* 1:99, 115), and died at Duxbury 26 August 1832, aged 88 years (*VR* 420). She married, second, 17 January 1773, at Duxbury (*VR* 221), **JAMES SOULE** [Henry Samson # 797], *q.v.*, with whom she had seven children. James was a descendant of George Soule as well as of Henry Samson.

Abigail joined the Hollis Street Church in Boston on 26 April 1767 (*Hollis St. CR*, 24). After Benjamin's death she returned to Duxbury.

On 12 January 1773 Abigail Bosworth of Duxbury, widow, was appointed administrator of the estate of Benjamin Bosworth late of Boston, mariner, intestate; Joseph Soule of Duxbury and John Fullerton of Boston were sureties on her bond (Suffolk PR #15291, 72:330). On the same date she was given guardianship of Benjamin and Abigail, both under 14, children of Benjamin deceased (*ibid.*, #15290, 15292). The inventory was dated 8 October 1773.

Children of Benjamin and Abigail (Sever) Bosworth, bp. Hollis St. Church, Boston, as "of Abigail" (*Hollis St. CR*, 25):

i BENJAMIN BOSWORTH[6], b. prob. Boston, 25 June 1767 (*Duxbury VR* 27); bp. Boston 28 June 1767; m. at Duxbury, 8 Sept. 1791 (*VR* 292), MERCY / MARCY PRIOR, b. there 22 Aug. 1767 (*VR* 130), d. Boston 6 April 1844 ae 83 [*sic*], dau. of Benjamin and Sarah (Soule) Prior, and also a Henry Samson desc. [#796-ii] (*Bosworth Gen.*, 5:957).

Children, rec. Duxbury (*VR* 26–27; m. from *Bosworth Gen.*): 1. *Abigail Bosworth*[7], b. 22 June 1792; d. unm. 2. *Benjamin Bosworth* (twin), b. 8 May 1793; m. Lucretia Tuckerman. 3. *Nathaniel Bosworth* (twin), b. 8 May 1793; d. ae 12d. 4. *Hiram Bosworth*, b. 23 Feb. 1795; m. Alethea S. Hall. 5. *Sally Bosworth*, b. 9 Jan. 1797; d. ae 2y 7m. 6. *Mercy Bosworth*, b. 27 April 1799; m. Capt. Eden Wadsworth [#802-iii]. 7. *Betsey Bosworth*, b. 29 July 1801; d. ae 23 unm. 8. *Nathaniel Bosworth*, b. 1 May 1803; d. 1811. 9. *Joshua S. Bosworth*, b. 23 Aug. 1804; m. Susan Hallet. 10. *Mary T. Bosworth*, b. 11 July 1807; d. 1868 unm. 11. *William Bosworth*, b. 3 Sept. 1811; m. Diana Day.

ii ABIGAIL BOSWORTH, bp. 12 March 1769; living Jan. 1773 (guardianship).

Sources cited: *Duxbury VR. Dorchester VR. Boston VR* [BRC 30]. *Hollis Street Church Boston ...* (1998). *Bosworth Genealogy*, Vol. 5. *MFIP Soule*, pt 2. **See also:** *Bosworth Genealogy*, 4:490; 5:704-05; 6:957.

674.   MARY BOSWORTH[5] (*Lydia[4] Samson, David[3], Caleb[2], Henry[1]*), daughter of Nathaniel Bosworth and his wife Lydia Samson [140], was born probably at Plymouth about 1745. She died 14 August 1778 at Duxbury, and her youngest child died three days later (*VR* 437). She was a descendant also of *Mayflower* passengers John Alden and Myles Standish.

She married 25 January 1767, at Duxbury (*VR* 221, 332), **WARREN WESTON**, who was born there 24 August 1738 (*VR* 195), son of Eliphaz and Priscilla (Peterson) Weston, a descendant of *Mayflower* passenger George Soule. He died at Duxbury in 1799, before 27 November when administration was granted on his estate. He married, second, in February 1780 at Duxbury (*VR* 332), MARTHA (CHANDLER) WESTON, widow of Thomas. She is probably the Martha Weston, widow, who died at Duxbury 16 February 1804 in her 72nd year (*VR* 437).

Warren Weston inherited his father's homestead at Powder Point, Duxbury. As a ship carpenter, he made trips to and from Broad Bay in Maine (Weston Ts, 86½). Records of the Plymouth County Court of General Sessions indicate that he was granted a license in July 1764 to sell strong liquor, and in 1777 he was serving as a constable whose duty it was to warn persons from Duxbury (*PCCR*).

On 20 May 1770 Warren and Mary Weston renewed their covenant with the Duxbury Church and had their first child baptized there (*Bosworth Gen.,* 5:605).

Warren Weston of Duxbury, shipwright, was sued by Ichabod Briggs of Scituate, shipwright, in April 1773 (*PCCR*, CCP, d.n.28), for money due by note dated 10 July 1772, the first of several such cases in which he invariably defaulted, allowing the judgment to go against him.

He served in the Revolutionary War as a sergeant at Lexington, and later was a seaman on a brig captured by the British ship *Rainbow*, taken prisoner and confined at Halifax, N. S. (*MSSR* 16:920).

Warren Weston, shipwright of Duxbury, was appointed administrator on the estate of [his mother] Priscilla Weston, late of Duxbury, on 7 December 1778 (Plymouth PR 23:216).

At the Plymouth Court of Common Pleas in April 1782 (d.n. 136), Eliphaz Weston of Weymouth, mariner, sued Warren Weston of Duxborough, shipwright, to recover money due on four notes: one dated 7 April 1776 "for value received ... for one Third part of the Real Estate of the Father of the said Warren Weston, deceased ... to pay [£11 4s 9d] at the death of the said Warren's Mother, to wit, on the first day of March A.D. 1781"; the other notes were dated in 1772, 1773, and 1779, one to Joshua Hall and endorsed to the plaintiff. The defendant defaulted and judgment was satisfied by seizing 6½ acres of his land in Duxbury, delivered 7 April 1783. On 17 December 1787 seven acres belonging to Warren Weston of

Duxbury, shipwright, were sold to satisfy a debt owed to Silvanus Delano of Duxbury, shipwright (*Bosworth Gen.* 5:705). The easterly end of his dwelling house at Powder Point, with a barn and three acres of land, adjoining land of Ezra Weston and the sea, were sold 3 January 1788 to satisfy a debt of £66 2s 3d due since the previous October (*ibid.,* 706).

In 1790 Warren Weston was head of a household in Duxbury consisting of himself and one other male over 16 and two females (*Heads of Fam.,* 169).

Joshua Brewster, mariner, and Ezra Weston, gentleman, both of Duxbury, on 27 November 1799 were appointed administrators of the estate of Warren Weston late of Duxbury, shipwright (Plymouth PR #22453; 34:212).

Children of Warren and Mary (Bosworth) Weston, rec. Duxbury:

i   LYDIA WESTON[6], b. 17 Sept. 1768 (not "1778" as shown in VR); bp. 20 May 1770 (*VR* 192); d. Duxbury 22 Oct. 1841, "w. Capt. Joshua, ae 73y 1m 5d" (*VR* 355); m. Duxbury, 5 June 1785 (*VR* 330), JOSHUA BREWSTER, b. Duxbury 14 July 1755, d. there 2 April 1851 (Mass. VR 58:170, gives mother's name as Jane), son of Job and Elizabeth (__) Brewster (*VR* 34, 225).

    Brewster children rec. Duxbury (*VR* 33-36): 1. *Daniel W. Brewster*[7], b. 25 Sept. 1788. 2. *Job E. Brewster,* b. 4 April 1791. 3. *Polly B. Brewster,* b. 16 July 1793. 4. *William M. Brewster,* b. 10 May 1796. 5. *Betsey E. Brewster,* b. 26 Feb. 1799. 6. *Sally C. Brewster,* b. 7 June 1801. 7. *Warren W. Brewster,* b. 10 Nov. 1803. 8. *Priscilla W. Brewster,* b. 12 Feb. 1806. 9. *Harriet G. Brewster,* b. 9 Oct. 1808.

ii DANIEL WESTON, b. 5 April 1772 (*VR* 188); apparently living 1790; n.f.r. found.

iii WARREN WESTON, b. in March 1777; bp. 16 Aug. 1778, "the child being dangerous sick" (*VR* 195); d. 17 Aug. 1778, ae 17m (*VR* 439), 4 days after the death of his mother.

Sources cited: *Duxbury VR. Mass. Soldiers & Sailors.* Plymouth County Probate Records. *Bosworth Genealogy.* Konig, *Plymouth County Court Records.* CENSUS: *Heads of Families 1790 – Mass.*

675.   HEZEKIAH BOSWORTH[5] (*Lydia[4] Samson, David[3], Caleb[2], Henry[1]*), son of Nathaniel Bosworth and his wife Lydia Samson [140], was born at Boston or Duxbury about 1750 and was lost at sea about 1798 (*Bosworth Gen.,* 5:706). He was a descendant also of *Mayflower* passengers John Alden and Myles Standish.

He was of Boston when he married 18 November 1782, at Scituate (*VR* 2:33) or Hanover (*VR* 114), **SARAH EELLS**. She was born 12 May 1758 at Hanover (*VR* 22), daughter of William Witherell and Sarah (Pillsbury) Eells, and died 17

January 1825 at North Yarmouth, Maine, where she is buried in Walnut Hill Cemetery (*Bosworth Gen.*, 5:706).

In 1790 Hezekiah was living at Hanover with one boy under 16 and three females (p.170). Sarah moved to Freeport, Maine, sometime before 17 November 1811, when she united with the Congregational Church there (*Bosworth Gen.*, 5:706). No probate records have been found in Plymouth or Suffolk Counties for Hezekiah.

Children of Hezekiah and Sarah (Eells) Bosworth, b. prob. Hanover but only Sally rec. there (*VR* 42):

i SOPHIA BOSWORTH[6], b. 22 March 1784; d. 17 Dec. 1870 Athens, Somerset Co., Me.; m. at Athens, in 1804, Rev. LEVI LORING, b. New Gloucester, Me., 29 Sept. 1783, d. Saco, Me., 16 Jan. 1860, son of Bezaleel and Elizabeth (Mason) Loring (*Bosworth Gen.*, 5:958, *q.v.* for more).
    Loring children (*ibid.*, 958-59): 1. *Albert Smith Loring*. 2. *Samuel Veazie Loring*, m. Eliza E. Low and/or Eliza E. Brackett. 3. *Isaac S. Loring*, m. Naomi S. Hill. 4. *Levi Loring*, b. 6 Nov. 1819; d. Pasadena, Calif. 5. *Elizabeth Loring*, m. (1) Tyrrell White, (2) Elder J. Follette. 6. *Mary R. Loring*, b. 1822; m. James F. Follette. 7. *Ann Sophia Loring*, m. Cyrus Roby. 8. *Henry P. C. Loring*, m. (1) Amy Taft, (2) Anna M. Wiatt. 9. *Frederick Cannon Loring*, b. 17 Feb. 1826; m. (1) Mary Abby Hill, (2) Virginia Rose Primm.

ii LYDIA BOSWORTH, b. ca 1786.

iii JOSEPH POPE BOSWORTH, b. 26 Oct. 1789; d. Duxbury 31 May 1877; m. at Duxbury, 18 Feb. 1816 (*VR* 221), REBECCA DELANO, b. 7 June 1793 (*VR* 65), d. 15 Aug. 1855 ae 62y 2m 6d of dysentery (Mass. VR 94:186, says dau *John* & Lydia Delano), dau. Ichabod and Lydia (Wakefield) Delano, a Henry Samson descendant [**#793-iv**]. In 1860 Joseph was living with the family of his son Daniel E. at Duxbury (p.63/111).
    Children, rec. Duxbury, first three as b. Vienna, Me. (*VR* 27, 351): 1. *Daniel Eaton Bosworth[7]*, b. 5 Dec. 1816; m. Mary Towle Follett. 2. *Sophronia Eaton Bosworth*, b. 5 July 1821; m. (1) Abner Alden, (2) Stillman Peterson. 3. *Sophia Loring Bosworth*, b. 9 April 1823; m. Hiram Peterson. 4. *Joseph Bosworth*, b. 21 June, d. 9 Sept. 1825. 5. *Joseph Pope Bosworth Jr.*, b. 4 July 1829; m. Susan J. Simmons. (See *Bosworth Gen.*, 5:960, for more information.)

iv DAVID H. BOSWORTH, b. ca 1794; d. 1876 unm., North Yarmouth, Me.; bur. Walnut Hill Cem. (*VR* 358). He served an apprenticeship at Duxbury as a cobbler, then settled in Maine (*Bosworth Gen.*, 5:707). In 1860 he was a cordwainer at North Yarmouth, ae 60 [*sic*], living next to the family of David H. Loring, a sea captain (p.13/541).

v   SARAH BOSWORTH, b. 5 Nov. 1797 (*Hanover VR* 42 as Sally, dau. of Hezekiah and *Abby*); m. STEPHEN HANSON (*Bosworth Gen.*, 5:707); said to m. (2) NATHANIEL LUFKINS and d. 3 Sept. 1869, Chelsea (*ibid.*), but d. rec. of Sarah Lufkin at Chelsea on that date does not match.

Sources cited: *Hanover VR. Scituate VR. Bosworth Genealogy.* CENSUS: 1860 Duxbury, Plymouth Co. (M653-519), North Yarmouth, Cumberland Co., Me. (M653-437).

676.   DEBORAH[5] SAMPSON (*Charles[4], David[3], Caleb[2], Henry[1]*), daughter of Charles Samson [141] and his wife Mary Church, was baptized 26 April 1741 at Marshfield (*MD* 32:17), and died 5 April 1824, aged 83, "widow." She was a descendant also of *Mayflower* passengers John Alden, Myles Standish, and Richard Warren.

She married at Marshfield, 24 December 1761 (*VR* 142), **ABIJAH THOMAS,** who was born at Marshfield 30 June 1734, son of Samuel and Rebecca (Howland) Thomas (*VR* 50, 349). He died 15 March 1801 in his 67th year and is buried in the Old Burying Ground at the Congregational Church, Marshfield (*VR* 410).

On 29 March 1769 Asa Thomas of Marshfield sold to Abijah Thomas of Marshfield, yeoman, the homestead farm of "our father, Samuel Thomas" (Plymouth LR 57:123).

In 1790 Abijah was living at Marshfield with a household consisting of one man over 16 and two females (*Heads of Fam.*, 171).

Deborah Thomas, widow, and Peleg Thomas, gentleman, were appointed 1 June 1801 as administrators of the estate of Abijah Thomas late of Marshfield, yeoman, deceased (Plymouth PR 34:281). In a partition of the estate 26 November 1803, Peleg Thomas and Charles Thomas were directed to pay their sister Bethiah, wife of Nathan Sherman; a further settlement was to be made upon the decease of the widow, not named (*ibid.*, 38:195).

Children of Abijah and Deborah (Sampson) Thomas, rec. Marshfield (*VR* 62):

i   PELEG THOMAS[6], b. 12 Oct. 1763; d. Marshfield 9 Nov. 1849 (*VR* 366), a ship master, ae 88y 28d of old age; bur. South Cemetery; m. 6 Oct. 1782 at Marshfield (*VR* 175), BETHIAH WALKER.
     Children rec. Marshfield (*VR* 62): 1. *Bethiah Thomas[7]*, b. 23 Jan. 1783. 2. *Peleg Thomas*, b. 26 June 1785.

ii BETHIAH THOMAS, b. 12 July 1766; m. at Marshfield, 16 Aug. 1785 (*VR* 176), NATHAN SHERMAN, prob. b. Marshfield 18 March 1760, son of Ignatious and Abigail (Chapman) Sherman (*VR* 67, 150).

iii   CHARLES THOMAS, b. 1 Oct. 1769; d. 28 June 1839 ae 69y 9m; bur.
      Marshfield (*VR* 410); m. after int. at Marshfield 15 Oct. 1793 (*VR* 120),
      POLLEY CUSHMUN [*sic*] of Duxbury, prob. the Mary, dau. of Joshua
      and Mercy (Wadsworth) Cushman, b. Duxbury 15 Aug. 1768 (*VR* 57).
          Children rec. Marshfield, of Charles & Mary (*VR* 76, 239): 1. *Charles
      Thomas⁷*, b. 9 Dec. 1795; d. at sea 30 Aug. [1816] ae 20y 8m (*VR* 207). 2. *John
      Wadsworth Thomas*, b. 19 Jan. 1796. 3. *Joshua Thomas*, b. 24 Dec. 1797. 4. *Deborah
      Thomas*, b. 2 Jan. 1802; d. Marshfield 25 Aug. 1805 ae 2y 7m (*VR* 207). 5. *Asa
      Thomas*, b. 22 July 1804; d. 17 Aug. 1806 ae 2y 1m (*VR* 207). 6. *Loriann Thomas*,
      b. 10 July 1808. 7. *Sarah W. Thomas*, b. 1 Jan. 1813.

iv   DEBORAH THOMAS, b. 30 Dec. 1780; d. 6 May 17[96] in 16th yr; bur.
      Marshfield (*VR* 410).

Sources cited: *Duxbury VR. Marshfield VR. Mayflower Descendant*, 32 [19??]. Plymouth County
Deeds and Probate Records.

677.   CHARLES⁵ SAMPSON (*Charles⁴, David³, Caleb², Henry¹*), son of Charles
Samson [141] and his wife Mary Church, was baptized 22 April 1744 at Marshfield
(*MD* 32:19). He died 28 February 1804 at Waldoboro, Maine, aged 63 (*Col. Cent.* of
17 March 1804). He was a descendant also of *Mayflower* passengers John Alden,
Myles Standish, and Richard Warren.

Charles Samson Jr. of Duxbury married, first, 12 January 1769 at Marshfield
(*VR* 163), **SARAH DINGLEY**. She was born 27 February 1747, daughter of
John Jr. and Kesiah (Thomas) Dingley, at Marshfield (*VR* 97, 139), and died
between 31 January 1780 (when she gave oath as sister of Thomas, Jabez, and
Keziah Dingley and of Lucy Bourn), and 12 July 1781, when Charles remarried.
The will of John Dingley of Marshfield, yeoman, dated 2 January 1770, proved
3 February 1779, names his wife Kesia and daughter Sarah Sampson (Plymouth
PR. 25:146). On 29 November 1792 Charles Samson of Waldoboro sold land in
Duxbury, partly a lot owned by John Dingley, deceased, and willed to "my first
wife, his daughter" (Plymouth LR 74:133).

Charles was of Waldoboro when he married, second, 12 July 1781 at
Marshfield (*VR* 175), **ELIZABETH SPRAGUE**. She was born 28 November
1751 at Marshfield (*VR* 93), daughter of James and Patience (Ford) Sprague, and
died 7 May 1833 at Thomaston, Maine. Elizabeth, wife of Charles Sampson of
Waldoboro, gentleman, on 1 May 1794 joined several other heirs to the estate of
Mr. James Sprague Jr. late of Marshfield, in selling their title to land in Marshfield,
reserving unto the widow Patience Sprague, relict of said James, her dower
(Plymouth LR 77:252).

Charles went to Waldoboro with his parents about 1770; father and son had engaged in coastal trade and worked in close collaboration. *History of Old Broadbay and Waldoboro* (pp. 414-15) calls Captain Charles [Sampson], Jr., "one of the early Waldoborough capitalists, or dealers in land," and details some of his dealings from the time he first bought land for a home. "He played a very active part in local affairs. His name appears on the first slate of town officers [of Broad Bay] in 1773. He was literally in everything — a member of the Committee of Correspondence and Inspection in 1777, first selectman in 1781, Town Treasurer in 1798, second postmaster of Waldoborough ... and a representative to the Legislature in 1825, not to mention an array of other offices, and with all this keeping a tavern."

Charles Sampson, mariner, and Abijah Waterman, both of Broad Bay, bought 90 acres there on 3 April 1770 from Jonathan Robbins, and a few days later Charles Sampson Jr. bought 100 acres there from the heirs of the late Brigadier General Samuel Waldo, dec'd (*ibid.*, 7:206; 8:66). He continued to add to the property in Waldoboro, and in 1779 he bought 3¼ aces in Warren, Maine, and in 1787 further land there (*ibid.*, 13:65; 21:21). On 13 July 1792 he bought 50 acres at Meduncook from Nathaniel Bartlett (*ibid.*, 29:8).

In the 1800 census his household consisted of one man and two women 45 or older, one woman 26-45, two women 16-26, and one boy 10-16 (p.575).

Appraisers were appointed 21 March 1804 for the estate of Capt. Charles Sampson, late of Waldoboro, gentleman deceased (Lincoln PR 10:306). The inventory, dated 3 May 1805, included one third of the schooner *Independence*, five-eights of the schooner *Sally*, one "coat of arms," a farm in Waldoboro, a farm in Meduncook, four acres of salt marsh in Thomaston, and promissory notes from several people; the total came to $8962.92 (*ibid.*, 11:165). Receipts to Elizabeth Sampson, administratrix, from "our father's estate," were signed by Church C. Trouant; William Henry Little, attorney for Lucy Trouant; Daniel Samson; Sally D. Samson; and Charles Samson (*ibid.*, 22:322).

Elizabeth Samson of Thomaston, widow, in her will dated 21 September 1831, proved 15 May 1834 (Lincoln PR 40:122-23), left to her son Daniel Samson of Waldoboro all her household furniture and utensils, and her stock of cows and sheep; the remainder of the estate to Oliver Fales, Esq. of Thomaston in trust for daughter Sarah Dingley Haskell "for her sole and separate use and benefit during her coverture." The inventory taken 6 November 1834 by Halsey Healey, Hezekiah Prince Jr., and William I. Farley totaled $724.00 and included land near Shepard Robbins, land and buildings near Loring's Store, and a pew in the Congregational Meeting House (*ibid.*, 40:326).

Children of Charles and Sarah (Dingley) Samson, b. probably Waldoboro, Me.:

i   CHARLES[6] SAMPSON, b. ca 1774; d. Waldoboro 21 May 1853; m. after int. Waldoboro 5 May 1798 (*VR* 8), SALLY THOMAS, dau. Waterman and Hannah (Dexter) Thomas. The children in *Waldoboro VR* (births, 8, 11) to Charles and *Dolly* Sampson are surely of Charles and *Sally*. The g.s. rec. of dau. Sarah Ann Balch in Sproul Cem., Waldoboro, calls him Capt. Charles Sampson. In 1810 his household consisted of one man and one woman 45+, one man and one woman 26-45, one young man 16-26, one boy and one girl 10-16, one boy and one girl under 10, and two other free persons (p.91). In 1850 Charles was 76, a farmer, with Sarah 72, one family away from his brother Daniel (p.210).

      Children rec. Waldoboro (*VR* 8-12, transcribed as of Charles & *Dolly*): 1. *Eliza Sampson[7]*, b. 30 Nov. 1799; m. Alfred Hovey (Weyman Ms). 2. *Sarah Sampson*, b. 30 July 1803; m. John Balch (*Waldoboro Cem.*, 119*)*. 3. *Dinah Collins Sampson*, b. March 1808. 4. *Charles Sampson*, b. 6 April 1810. 5. *George N. Sampson.*

ii   LUCIA / LUCY SAMPSON, b. ca 1779 Waldoboro; d. 7 Oct. 1867, ae 88, Marshfield (VR Reg. 2:17); m. CHURCH C. TROUANT, b. Marshfield 10 July 1771, son of Samuel and Rhoda (_____) Trouant (*VR* 104), d. 20 March 1855 ae 83 yrs; both bur. Marshfield (*VR* 412).

      Trouant children, rec. Marshfield (*VR* 225): 1. *Church Clift Trouant[7]*, b. 24 Dec. 1801. 2. *Charles Sampson Trouant*, b. 2 Sept. 1803. 3. *Lucy Sampson Trouant*, b. 29 May 1806. 4. *Samuel Trouant*, b. 27 March 1809. 5. *Sarah Dingley Trouant*, b. 13 May 1814; m. John Capron (Weyman Ms).

Children of Charles and Elizabeth (Sprague) Sampson, b. probably at Waldoboro:

iii   DANIEL SAMPSON, b. ca 1782; living 1862, Waldoboro, "at an advanced age" (*Giles Memorial*, 412); m. JANE _____. In 1810 his household at Waldoboro (p.91), next door to that of his brother Charles, consisted of one man 45+, one man and one woman 26-45, one young man 16-26, and two girls under 10. In 1850 (p.210) he was 67, a farmer, with wife Jane 69; the household included Elizabeth ae 43, William ae 23, a joiner; John Sampson ae 34, farmer with wife Aldrain and child Daniel Jr. ae 8.

      Children at home 1850: 1. *Elizabeth Sampson[7]*, b. ca 1807. 2. *John Sampson*, b. ca 1816. 3. *William Sampson*, b. ca 1827.

iv   SARAH DINGLEY SAMPSON, b. 6 July 1783 at Waldoboro; m. JOHN HASKELL.

      Haskell children (Weyman Ms): 1. *Sarah Elizabeth Haskell*, b. 11 Feb. 1810; m. (1) Eusebius Fales, (2) Charles Loring. 2. *John E. Haskell*, b. 1 Feb. 1811. 3. *Mary Sprague Haskell*, b. 16 Nov. 1813; m. Edmund Wilson. 4. *Martha Brookhouse Haskell*, b. 3 Nov. 1818; m. Shubael Waldo.

Sources cited: *Marshfield VR. Scituate VR. Waldoboro, Maine VR.* Plymouth County Deeds and Probate Records. Lincoln County, Me., Deeds and Probate Records. *History of Old Broad Bay and Waldoboro* (1956). *Giles Memorial* (1864), account incomplete. *Mayflower Descendant. Index to Obituaries in the Columbian Centinel.* Weyman Manuscript, box 408, bundle 11. CENSUS: Waldoboro, Lincoln Co., Me., 1800 (M32-6); 1810 (M252-12).

678. **MARY**[5] **SAMPSON** (*Charles*[4], *David*[3], *Caleb*[2], *Henry*[1]), daughter of Charles Samson [141] and his wife Mary Church, was baptized 17 November 1751 at Scituate with her brother Melzar (*VR* 1:315). She died 15 January 1828, aged 76y 8m 15d, "wife of Capt. William Kent," at Marshfield (*VR* 418). She was a descendant also of *Mayflower* passengers John Alden, Myles Standish, and Richard Warren.

She married, 1 April 1773 at Marshfield (*VR* 163), **WILLIAM KENT**, "he of Marshfield, she of Duxborough." He was born 31 October 1742 at Marshfield (*VR* 77), son of Elisha and Lusanna (Ford) Kent, and a descendant of *Mayflower* passengers Richard Warren and Edward Doty. He died after 30 December 1831, when he made a life-lease arrangement with his son Elisha, noted below.

William was a mariner, called "Capt." on his wife's tombstone. The 1790 census (p 171) listed him in Marshfield with a household consisting of two males under 16, one 16 or over, and four females. On 30 December 1831 William Kent of Marshfield sold to his son Elisha Kent of Marshfield, yeoman, his homestead farm and buildings in Marshfield that he had bought of his father Elisha Kent, reserving for himself the use of the property during his natural life; Elisha was to discharge all of his father's debts, and to support his sister Alice W. Kent as long as she remained unmarried (Plymouth LR 175:10).

No Plymouth County probate records have been found for William or Mary Kent.

Children of William and Mary (Samson) Kent, rec. Marshfield (*VR* 55-56):

i   WILLIAM KENT[6], b. 5 Sept. 1773; m. Marshfield, 26 Dec. 1799 (*VR* 169), SARAH JOYCE. In 1850 William Kent ae 79, mariner, and Sally ae 77, were living in the household of [son-in-law] Elisha T. Cushman at Kingston (p.91).
        Children rec. Marshfield to William Jr. and Sarah (*VR* 227): 1. *Sarah Kent*[7], b. 20 Nov. 1800. 2. *Christiana Kent*, b. 25 Nov. 1802. 3. *Eliza Smith Kent*, b. 12 Oct. 1804. 4. *William Kent*, b. 7 or 9 Sept. 1806; m. 1831 Harriet Keen. 5. *Mary Sampson Kent*, b. 2 Oct. 1808; m. 1829 Elisha T. Cushman. 6. *Lydia Kent*, b. 29 Dec. 1810. 7. *Caroline Kent*, b. 10 Dec. 1813.

ii POLLY KENT, b. 28 Dec. 1775; m. at Marshfield, 27 Dec. 1798 (*VR* 169), ASA SHERMAN, b. Marshfield 12 April 1773, d. 26 April 1870, son of Ignatius and Abigail (Chapman) Sherman (*VR* 67). In 1850 he was a farmer ae 77 at Marshfield, with Polly ae 75, Polly ae 50, Welthea ae 47, Allice W. ae 39, Sarah D. ae 6 [prob. dau. Asa Jr.], and Pelham W. Dingley ae 13 (p.160); the family of Asa Jr. was nearby.

Sherman children rec. Marshfield (*VR* 238): 1. *Polly Sherman[7]*, b. 15 Sept. 1799; unm. 1850. 2. *Asa Sherman*, b. 28 Feb. 1801; m. Anne Phillips Loring (Weyman Ms). 3. *Wealthy Sherman*, b. 22 Feb. 1803; unm. 1850. 4. *Abigail Sherman*, b. 15 Aug. 1806. 5. *Alice Warren Sherman*, b. 24 Feb. 1810; d. unm. 6. *William Sherman*, b. 25 May 1813.

iii LUSANNA KENT, b. 15 Nov. 1778; d. (as Lucy) 7 July 1868 ae 89y 7m (*VR* 415); m. at Marshfield, 21 Nov. 1805 (*VR* 264), ROBERT AMES, b. ca 1778, d. 18 or 19 July 1824 ae 44 or 46y 3m, bur. cemetery near Cong. Ch., Marshfield. (*VR* 415). In 1850 Louceana Ames ae 71 was head of a household at Marshfield, with dau. Mary ae 36 (p.155).

Ames children, first two rec. Marshfield as of Robert and Susannah (*VR* 210), prob. incomplete: 1. *Lucy Ames[7]*, b. 3 Oct. 1808. 2. *Mary Ames*, b. 3 Feb. 1812. 3. *Priscilla W. Ames*, b. 1822; d. Sharon 14 Sept. 1849 ae 27y 5m 13d, drowned; bur. with parents (*VR* 366, 415).

iv SMITH KENT, b. 28 Oct. 1783.

v SILVIA CHURCH KENT, b. 2 July 1786; m. after int. Marshfield 11 Dec. 1810 (*VR* 187), JACOB AMES. In 1850 he was ae 64, a seaman, in Marshfield, with Sylvia C. ae 64, Sylvia C. ae 34, George ae 21, fisherman, and Robert ae 17, shoemaker (p.162).

Ames children rec. Marshfield (*VR* 223, 225): 1. *Jacob Smith Ames[7]*, b. 8 April 1813. 2. *Sylvia C. Ames*, b. 12 Oct. 1815; unm. 1850. 3. *Nathaniel Ames*, b. 27 June 1819. 4. *Harriet Ames*, b. 6 Nov. 1826. 5. *George Ames*, b. 10 Aug. 1829. 6. *Robert Ames*, b. 23 March 1833.

vi ELISHA KENT, b. 17 Oct. 1789; m. at Marshfield, 2 April 1817 (*VR* 271), BETSEY SPRAGUE. In 1850 Elisha was a farmer at Marshfield with Elizabeth ae 59, dau. Sarah and the twins; his sister Elliss Kent was in the household (p.161).

Children, first three rec. Marshfield (*VR* 229): 1. *Betsey Ford Kent[7]*, b. 2 Dec. 1817; m. 1843 Nathan Tucker. 2. *Sarah Kent*, b. 24 Jan. 1820. 3. *Elisha W. Kent*, b. April 1822; m. Ann Williamson. 4. *Ann M. Kent* (twin), b. ca 1830. 5. *James W. Kent* (twin), b. ca 1830.

vii ELAS/ALICE WARREN KENT, b. 8 April 1793; d. 15 Sept. 1867 at Marshfield, unm. (Mass. VR 203:303).

Sources cited: *Marshfield VR. Scituate* VR. Mass. Vital Records 1841-1910. Plymouth County Deeds. Weyman Manuscript, NEHGS, box 408, bundle 11. CENSUS: *Heads of Families in 1790 - Mass.*; 1850 Marshfield, Plymouth Co. (M432-332), Kingston (M432-333). **See also:** *Giles Memorial*, 393; *Kent Genealogy*, 58, 80-81.

679. MELZAR⁵ SAMPSON (*Charles⁴, David³, Caleb², Henry¹*), son of Charles Samson [141] and his wife Mary Church, born at Duxbury "near the Marshfield line" (*Giles Memorial*, 412), and was baptized 17 November 1751 at Scituate with his sister Mary (*VR* 1:315). He died at Duxbury before 7 February 1787, when an administrator was appointed on his estate. He was a descendant also of *Mayflower* passengers John Alden, Myles Standish, and Richard Warren.

He married, 2 March 1779 at Marshfield, after intentions there 7 February 1779 (*VR* 175, 131), **SARAH KENT**, he of Duxbury, she of Marshfield. Sarah was born 19 February 1756 at Marshfield (*VR* 77), daughter of Elisha and Lusanna (Ford) Kent, and a descendant of *Mayflower* passengers Richard Warren and Edward Doty. Her brother William married Melzar Sampson's sister Mary. She is probably the Sarah Sampson who married at Marshfield, 26 March 1801 (*VR* 264), as his second wife, STEPHEN CARVER, who was born at Marshfield 2 April 1743 (*VR* 81) and died at Vinalhaven, Me., in 1823, son of Caleb and Abigail (Sherman) Carver and widower of Deborah Kent (*Robert Carver Gen.*, 74).

At the Plymouth Court of General Sessions in December 1783, three selectmen of Duxbury, Jonathan Peterson, Abel Chandler, and Elijah Baker, petitioned that "one Mary Sampson the widow of David Sampson late of Duxborough" had become a town charge, although her children and grandchildren ("viz, Ebenezer Sampson and Charles Sampson, Children, and Charles Sampson and Melzar Sampson, Grand Children") were able to support her, had been asked to do so, and had refused. All four were ordered to show cause at the next court term as to why they would not support her. In December the Duxbury selectmen requested that the court order the family of Mary Sampson to maintain her, "a poor indigent Person," who had been under care of the town since 1 January 1783, although her two sons Charles Sampson and Ebenezer Sampson, both of Duxborough, yeomen, and grandson Melzar Sampson of Duxborough, mariner, were capable of doing so. In July 1785 it was finally settled by arbitrators William Drew, Esq., Col. John Gray, and Capt. John Turner, who reported that "the said Charles Sampson [was to] pay one eighth part of the Charge of Supporting the said Mary Sampson, and that the said Melzar Sampson pay one other eighth part ... and the said Charles and Melzar pay in the like proportion of the Costs of Suit and Reference" (*PCCR* 4:28, 33).

On 7 February 1787, William Kent, mariner, and Sarah Sampson, widow, both of Marshfield, were appointed administrators of the estate of Melzar Sampson, late of Duxbury, deceased, mariner (Plymouth PR # 17593). They attested the inventory on 17 February 1787 (*ibid.*, 30:94).

Vinton in *Giles Memorial* (p.412), wrote, "It is believed that this family, after the after the death of the father, removed to the Fox Islands, in Maine." (Fox Island was incorporated 1789 as the town of Vinalhaven.) This is supported by census records. In 1790 Sarah Sampson was head of a houseold at Marshfield consisting of one boy under 16 and three females (p.171). In 1800 her household consisted of one boy 10-16, one young woman 16-26, and a woman 26-45 (p.93). No Sarah Sam[p]son is listed in Massachusetts in 1810.

Stephen Carver was living at Vinalhaven in 1790 with one female (p.32). The 1800 census of Vinalhaven stated that he was from Marshfield, 45 or over, alone except for a little girl under 10 (p.7). In 1810 his household consisted of one man and one woman over 45, and one man and one woman 16-26 (p.541).

Children of Melzar and Sarah (Kent) Sampson, rec. Duxbury (*VR* 140-42):

i   SARAH[6] SAMPSON, b. 31 Dec. 1780.

ii LUCY SAMPSON, b. 31 Oct. 1783; d. Vinalhaven, Me., 26 Aug. 1872; m. at Vinalhaven, 25 Nov. 1803 (*VR* 31), THOMAS WATERMAN, b. there 21 Oct. 1775, d. before 1850 when Lucy Waterman ae 67, b. Mass., was living at North Haven, Me., with Mary A. ae 31 and Adeline ae 24 (p.62).

    Waterman children, b. Vinalhaven, Me. (*VR* 31): 1. *Joseph Waterman*[7], b. 4 Dec. 1804. 2. *Melzar Waterman*, b. 10 July 1806; m. Sarah ___. 3. *John Waterman*, b. 22 March 1808; m. Eliza ___. 4. *Sally Waterman*, b. 29 April 1810. 5. *Deborah Waterman*, b. 12 Feb. 1812. 6. *Lucy Waterman*, b. 21 March 1814. 7. *Thomas Waterman*, b. 2 Sept. 1815. 8. *Winslow Waterman*, b. 2 Sept. 1816. 9. *Mary Ann Waterman*, b. 17 Oct. 1818; unm. 1850. 10. *Julia G. Waterman*, b. 11 Oct. 1820. 11. *Albion P. Waterman* (father's will). 12. *Adaline Waterman*, b. ca Feb. 1826; unm. 1850.

iii MELZAR SAMPSON, b. 14 March 1785; d. 1860 – 1870, North Haven, Me.; m. ANNA ___, b. ca 1790, d. after 1870. In 1850 and 1860 he was a farmer at North Haven (*VR* 102, 135); in 1870 Anna, ae 80, widow, was living with her son Warren (*VR*, 135).

    Child (*VR* 48, 68; census): 1. *Warren K. Sampson*[7], b. April 1824; m. Emily J. Whitmore.

Sources cited: *Duxbury VR. Marshfield VR. North Haven, Me., VR.* Plymouth County Probate Records. Konig, *Plymouth County Court Records. Giles Memorial* (1864). CENSUS: *Heads of Families in 1790 - Mass.*; 1800 Marshfield, Plymouth Co. (M32-16) & Vinalhaven, Knox Co., Me. (M32-7); 1810 Vinalhaven, Knox Co., Me. (M252-11); 1850 North Haven, Waldo Co., Me. (M432-271).

680.   ELIZABETH⁵ SAMPSON (*Ebenezer⁴, David³, Caleb², Henry¹*), daughter of Ebenezer Samson [142] and his wife Hannah Harlow, was born at Plymouth 24 July 1741 and was living 13 May 1809 when she acknowledged a deed (*TAG* 51:94). She was a descendant also of *Mayflower* passengers John Alden, Myles Standish, and Richard Warren.

She married, first, at Plymouth 13 August 1761 (*VR* 354), **SAMUEL KEMPTON JR.**, born at Plymouth 5 November 1738 "at 6 clock in the morn," son of Samuel Jr. and Mabell (Partridge) (Soule) Kempton (*VR* 129), a descendant of *Mayflower* passenger Richard Warren.

She married, second, at Plymouth 10 April 1774 (*VR* 360) as his second wife, **EPHRAIM BARTLETT**, who was born at Plymouth 8 September 1737 (*VR* 124) and died at Plymouth 26 October 1801 (CR 625), son of Robert and Rebecca (Wood) Bartlett. He was a descendant of Francis Cooke of the *Mayflower*. Ephraim married, first, at Plymouth 18 January 1759, MERCY CHURCHILL, with whom he had children at Plymouth: James C., Sylvanus, Susannah (*VR* 214), and Rebecca Bartlett (*MF12*:474), and probably also Lazarus, "Ephraim Bartlett's son," who drowned while fishing 19 July 1787 (*Plymouth CR* 415).

Samuel Kempton of Plymouth, mariner, was sued by Abner Ripley of Duxbury, cordwainer, in October 1770 for £2 2s 10d due on a note dated 27 April 1767 that had been given to Samuel Partridge who endorsed it to Ripley. Kempton defaulted and Ripley received a judgment for the amount sued for plus costs (*PCCR*, CCP Oct. 1770).

The 1790 census listed Ephraim Bartlett's household at Plymouth as consisting of three men over 16 and four females (p.177), figures that do not fit. In 1800 Ephraim and his wife were 45 or older, with one man 26-45 and two young men and two young women 16-26 (p.15).

By a deed dated in April 1799, Ephraim Bartlett, mariner, and wife Elizabeth joined several of her siblings and heirs of deceased siblings, in selling to Oliver Kempton all their rights in the part of a dwelling that had been set off to Mrs. Hannah Sampson, deceased wife of Ebenezer Sampson and daughter of William Harlow, from said William Harlow's estate (Plymouth LR 88:113). By a second deed dated 29 December 1803, Elizabeth Bartlett, widow, with her siblings or their heirs, sold to Rositer Cotton of Plymouth some land and swamp that had belonged to her mother, Hannah, from William Harlow's estate (*ibid.*, 98:184).

Elizabeth Bartlett, widow of Ephraim Bartlett and administratrix of "my mother Hannah Samson, formerly wife of Ebenezer Samson" acknowledged a deed on 13 May 1809 (Plymouth LR 113:211).

Children of Ephraim and Elizabeth (Sampson) Bartlett (*MF12*:474 unless otherwise cited):

i ELIZABETH BARTLETT[6], b. prob. May 1775; d. prob. 1856; m. at Plymouth, 17 Dec. 1795 (*VR* 371), EPHRAIM WHITING, son of Elisha and Betsey (Holmes) Whiting (Davis, 286). In 1850 Elizabeth Whiting ae 75, was living in Plymouth with Benjamin Whiting ae 51 and Mary Brown ae 61, near [her sister] Mercy Leach (p.140). Two d. recs. at Plymouth for a Betsey Whiting 27 Sept. 1855 ae 80y 5m (Mass. VR 94:209), and another 26 Aug. 1856 ae 81y 4m (Mass. VR 103:218), both of "old age," b. Plymouth, line for parents' names blank, suggest that this was the same woman recorded twice in error; the age in both cases is consistent with Elizabeth Bartlett.

    Whiting children (Davis, 286): 1. *Ephraim Whiting[7]*, b. prob. ca 1796; m. Plymouth 4 Nov. 1819 (*VR* 445) Patience Everson. 2. *Benjamin Whiting*, b. ca 1798; m. Plymouth June 1823 (*VR* 479), Phebe R. Flemmons.

? ii EPHRAIM BARTLETT, b. prob. ca 1777; "lost at sea on 9th Sept. [1800] with Ebenezer Sampson and — Bartlett" (*CR* 622); m. at Plymouth, 20 Jan. 1799 (*CR* 170), ABIGAIL HOLMES, dau. of Richard and Abigail (Damon) Holmes (Weyman Ms). His epitaph in Burial Hill (Kingman, #752; not in Robinson) reads: "... Mr Ephraim Bartlett who was drowned on the Grand-bank Sepbr 9th 1800 in the 34th year of his age" [*sic* – ? 24th yr]. Davis and Weyman place him in this family; *Harlow Gen.* accepts gravestone age, which if correct means he was son of Ephraim Sr.'s first wife.

iii MERCY BARTLETT, b. ca 19 Jan. 1779 (calc.); d. Plymouth 23 April 1865 ae 86y 3m 4d (Mass. VR 184:302); m. at Plymouth, 11 Feb. 1800 (*VR* 435), FINNEY LEACH, b. ca 1774, d. Plymouth (as Capt.) 5 Nov. 1839 (*VR* 516) in 65th yr (*Burial Hill* #1505), son of Lemuel and Sarah (Holmes) Leach (Weyman Ms). In 1850 Mercy Leach ae 70 was in Plymouth with Josiah Leach ae 30, seaman; Albert's family was nearby (p.140).

    Leach children rec. Plymouth (*VR* 460, 516; some info. from Weyman Ms): 1. *David Leach[7]*, b. 1 June 1803; d. 9 Aug. 1803 ae 2m 8d (*CR* 628). 2. *Marcia Leach*, b. 10 Feb. 1805; d. 6 Oct. 1806 (*Bur. Hill* #909). 3. *Phineas Leach*, b. 26 July 1807; m. Sally Barnes Dunham. 4. *Robert B. Leach*, b. 27 Aug. 1809; d. 12 Sept. 1821. 5. *Albert Gallatin Leach*, b. 16 Aug. 1811; m. Ellen/Eleanor Churchill. 5. *[Child] Leach*, b. 1815; d. 22 Dec. 1820 ae 5y (*CR* 669). 6. *Louisa Leach*, b. prob. 1816; d. Oct. 1818 ae 2y (*CR* 632). 7. *[Child] Leach*, d. 4 May 1818 ae 9w (*CR* 666). 8. *Josiah Leach*, b. 2 Nov. 1819; with mother 1850. 9. *George E. Leach*, d. 21 Dec. 1820.

iv ISAAC BARTLETT, b. ca Jan. 1781; d. Plymouth 3 May 1845 ae 64y 4m of consumption, mariner, b. Plymouth, son of Ephraim and Elizabeth (*VR* 630); m. (1) at Plymouth, 18 April 1801 (*VR* 290), FEAR COBB, dau. of

Lemuel and Hannah (Kempton) Cobb (Weyman Ms); m. (2) at Plymouth, as Capt. Isaac Bartlett, int. 19 Aug. 1812 (*VR* 308), REBECCA BARTLETT (*VR* 462), dau. of Caleb and Elizabeth (Holmes) Bartlett (Weyman Ms).

Children, first three with Fear, rest with Rebecca (*VR* 462): 1. *Isaac Bartlett*, b. 9 Dec. 1801. 2. *Eliza Ann Bartlett*, b. 26 July 1807; m. Stephen Palmer Brown (Weyman Ms). 3. *Ephraim Bartlett*, b. 7 Feb. 1809; d. 3 Dec. 1832 (*Burial Hill* #1343). 4. *Rebecca Bartlett*, b. 1813; d. 14 Nov. 1817 ae 4y 3m (*ibid.*, #1066). 5. *Robert Bartlett*, b. 8 Oct. 1817. 6. *Rebecca Bartlett*, b. — 1819. 7. *[Son] Bartlett*, b. 6 June, d. 9 June 1822 (*ibid.*, #1142). 8. *Caleb Bartlett*, b. 21 April 1824; d. 24 July 1826 (*ibid.*).

Sources cited: *Plymouth VR. Plymouth Church Records.* Kingman, *Epitaphs from Burial Hill, Plymouth* (1892); also Robinson, *Burial Hill in the 1990s* (1999). Robert M. Sherman, "Three New Heirs of Ebenezer Samson of Plymouth: Elizabeth Bartlett, Mary Covington, & Hannah Southwick," *TAG* 51 [1975]. Weyman Manuscript, box 408, bundle 11. *Harlow Family* (1997). *MF12* Francis Cooke. *MFIP George Soule*, 4th ed. (2002). CENSUS: 1790 Plymouth, Plymouth Co. 1790 (M637-4), 1800 (M32-16), 1850 (M432-333).

681.   HANNAH⁵ SAMPSON (*Ebenezer⁴, David³, Caleb², Henry¹*), daughter of Ebenezer Samson [142] and his wife Hannah Harlow, was born 2 October 1744 at Plymouth (*VR* 123; Bible rec. says 13 October) and died there 23 September 1826, aged 82, as "Hannah, widow of Richard Cooper" (*VR* 476; Bible rec.). She was a descendant also of *Mayflower* passengers John Alden, Myles Standish, and Richard Warren.

She married, 22 January 1761 at Plymouth after intentions there 3 January (*VR* 350, 250), **RICHARD COOPER**; both were of Plymouth. He was born 29 June 1740 (Bible rec.), the son of John and Hannah (Rider) Cooper and a descendant of *Mayflower* passenger James Chilton. Capt. Richard Cooper died 10 September 1819 at Plymouth, aged 80 (*Burial Hill*, #1091). Richard Cooper's brother John was the first husband of Hannah's sister Sarah Sampson [#684].

On 18 June 1763 Richard Cooper, mariner, was appointed administrator of the estate of his father John Cooper, deceased, of which the widow Hannah now deceased had been administratrix (Plymouth PR 16:393, 484). In a distribution of this estate, Richard was called eldest son of John (*ibid.*, 16:512).

In a deed dated in April 1799, Richard Cooper, gentleman, and wife Hannah joined several of her siblings and heirs of deceased siblings, in selling to Oliver Kempton all their rights in the part of a dwelling that had been set off to Mrs. Hannah Samson, deceased wife of Ebenezer Samson and daughter of William Harlow, from said William Harlow's estate (Plymouth LR 88:113). In a second deed dated 29 December 1803, the same group of heirs sold to Rositer Cotton of

Plymouth some land and swamp that had belonged to her mother, Hannah, from William Harlow's estate (*ibid.*, 98:184).

Hannah Cooper, widow of Richard Cooper of Plymouth, sued Daniel Jackson of Plymouth, merchant, in August 1820, for dower "as per writ." Details of the case are missing, but the court found the defendant's plea sufficient; Hannah appealed, but there is no further record (*PCCR* 13:243, #25).

No Plymouth County Probate was found for Richard or Hannah Cooper.

Children of Richard and Hannah (Sampson) Cooper, born at Plymouth, all listed in Bible record copied by Bowman in 1897; some information from Weyman Ms):

i   HANNAH COOPER[6], b. 1 July 1761 (*VR* 206); d. Plymouth 6 Sept. 1836 while visiting her son Schuyler (*Plympton VR* 511); m. at Plymouth, 8 Oct. 1780 after int. 24 June (*VR* 363, 268), GEORGE SAMPSON of Plympton, b. Plympton 3 Sept. 1755, d. there 25 Nov. 1826 of consumption, son of Zabdiel and Abiah (Whitmarsh) Sampson, a descendant of Abraham [not Henry] Sampson (*Giles Mem.*, 418). His sister Hannah m. his wife's brother Richard Cooper.
        Sampson children (*ibid.*, 419): 1. *Zabdiel Sampson*[7], b. 22 Aug. 1781; m. Ruth Lobdell. 2. *George Sampson*, b. 8 June 1783; m. Sally Bartlett. 3. *Marston Sampson*, b. 1 Oct. 1785; m. (1) Leonice Holmes, (2) Caroline Bartlett. 4. *John Sampson*, b. 6 April 1788; m. Priscilla Bramhall. 5. *Alvan Sampson*, b. 18 March 1791; m. Susan Crandon. 6. *Joseph Sampson*, b. 4 Oct. 1794; m. Harriet Rider. 7. *Schuyler Sampson*, b. 16 Jan. 1797; m. (1) Mary Ann Bartlett, (2) Sarah Taylor Bishop. 8. *Hannah Sampson*, b. 24 Dec. 1799; m. Roswell Ballard. 9. *Caroline Sampson*, b. 10 Dec. 1801; d. 5 Feb. 1824, unm.

ii   RICHARD COOPER, b. 30 Jan. 1763 (*VR* 206); d. Plympton 30 Jan. 1844 (Weyman Ms); m. ca 1780 HANNAH SAMPSON, b. Plympton 3 March 1762 (*VR* 180), d. 7 March 1813, dau. of Zabdiel and Abiah (Whitmarsh) Sampson (Weyman Ms). Hannah wife of Richard Cooper was rec. into the Plymouth Church 12 Aug. 1781 and Richard on 11 Nov. 1781 after having been dism. for fornication (*CR* 375). At their request, they were dismissed to the 3rd Church 28 June 1804 (*CR* 551).
        Children rec. Plympton (*VR* 76-77; spouses, Weyman Ms): 1. *Richard Cooper*[7], b. 1 Dec. 1784; m. (1) Mercy Wright, (2) Deborah Sampson. 2. *Hannah Cooper*, b. 13 Dec. 1786; m. John Fuller. 3. *Eleanor Cooper*, b. 3 April 1788; m. Ezra Rider. 4. *Polly Cooper*, b. 5 Oct. 1791. 5. *Betsey Cooper*, b. 6 Aug. 1793. 6. *Priscilla Virgin Cooper*, b. 11 April 1797; m. Barzillai Ellis Wright. 7. *Eliza Cooper*, b. 23 Sept. 1799. 8. *John Dexter Cooper*, b. 1 Dec. 1802; m. (1) Sarah Bullard Newton, (2) Sarah Adelaide Adams.

iii ELIZABETH COOPER, b. 25 July 1764 (*VR* 206); d. E. Bridgewater 18 June 1841 (*VR* 372); m. at Plymouth, 26 Oct. 1782 after int. 13 March (*VR* 364, 269), NYMPHAS MARSTON, b. 24 July 1760 at Marstons Mills, son of Prince and Sarah (Winslow) Marston (*Marston Gen.*, 475).

Marston children, b. Plymouth but not rec. there (*ibid.*, 477): 1. *George Marston⁷*, b. ca 1784; d. at sea. 2. *Elizabeth Marston*, b. ca 1787. 3. *Henry Marston*, b. ca 1793; m. Abigail (Cobb) Bradford. 4. *Elizabeth Marston*, b. 21 Nov. 1795. 5. [*Daughter*] *Marston*, b. ca 1799; d. Plymouth 3 Nov. 1806 ae 7y (*CR* 632).

iv PRISCILLA COOPER, b. 10 July 1767; d. 30 May 1853 ae 86y (*Burial Hill* #1737); m. (1) Plymouth, 22 Dec. 1791, Capt. JOHN VIRGIN (*VR* 368), b. ca 1767, d. 3 Oct. 1814 ae 47 (*Burial Hill* #1021); m. (2) Duxbury, 4 July 1817 (*VR* 330) as his third wife, Capt. EZRA WESTON, d. Duxbury 13 Oct. 1822 ae 79y 2m 17d, son of Eliphaz and Priscilla (Peterson) Weston and widower of (1) Sylvia Church and (2) Salumith Wadsworth (*VR* 436).

Virgin children (Davis 269; *Burial Hill* #696, 1149): 1. *John Virgin⁷* , b. ca 1792; d. at sea 23 Oct. 1822 on passage from St. Ubes, "in 32ⁿᵈ yr" (*Burial Hill* #1149; *VR* 530); m. Plymouth, 3 Dec. 1816 (*VR* 443), Abigail Davie. 2. *William Henry Virgin*, b. 4 Dec., d. 9 Dec. 1792. 3. *George William Virgin*, m. 1816 Mary Barnes. 4. *William Henry Virgin*, b. ca Jan. 1798; d. 13 Sept. 1798 ae 9m 4d.

v JOSEPH COOPER, b. 1 July 1769 (*VR* 454); d. 25 Nov. 1851 (*Burial Hill 1999*, #24); m. Plymouth, 29 July 1791 after int. 28 May (*VR* 368, 278), LUCY TAYLOR, b. 19 Nov. 1772, dau. Edward Taylor (*VR* 454), d. Plymouth 16 Oct. 1842, "wife of Joseph, ae 70, paralytic" (*VR* 531; *Burial Hill 1999*, #25). In 1850 Joseph Cooper was ae 81, a trader, at Plymouth, with [dau.] Lucy T. ae 44, Mary ae 28, and William B. ae 15, a student; [son] George Cooper's household was nearby (pp.128-29).

Children, rec. Plymouth (*VR* 454): 1. *Joseph Cooper⁷*, b. 14 Dec. 1791; m. Sylvia Paty. 2. *George Cooper*, b. 16 Oct. 1793; d.y. 3. *George Cooper*, b. 23 Aug. 1797; m. Mary Covington [his 2d cousin]. 4. *Edward Taylor Cooper*, b. 11 Feb. 1800; m. Caroline Paty. 5. *Lucy Taylor Cooper*, b. 28 March 1802; d. y. 6. *Lucy Taylor Cooper*, b. 12 Dec. 1805; d. unm. 7. *Wm. Brewster Cooper*, b. 27 Dec. 1807; m. (1) Emeline De Palace, (2) Ruth Flint Edwards. 8. *Mary Calvin Cooper*, b. 14 April 1810; d. unm. 9. *James Bartlett Cooper*, b. 4 Sept. 1812. (See Weyman Ms for continuation.)

vi POLLY COOPER, b. 13 Oct. 1770 (Bible rec.).

vii GEORGE COOPER, b. 11 July 1773; d. ca April 1775 (Bible rec.)

viii CALVIN COOPER, b. 14 May 1775; d. 18 Oct. 1776, as "Richard Cooper's child," ae 1y 5m (Bible rec.).

ix ESTHER COOPER, b. 29 Oct. 1777; d. Plympton ca 1824 (Plymouth PR #21669); m. at Plymouth, Sept. 1801, Capt. SAMUEL VIRGIN (*VR* 436),

b. 18 Sept. 1776 Williamston, N.C., d. Sept. 1824, lost in schooner *Martha Forbes* in a hurricane, son of Samuel Virgin (Weyman Ms; *Plympton VR* 77). **Virgin** children (Weyman Ms): 1. *Mary Henderson Virgin⁷*, b. 4 March 1802. 2. *Priscilla Cooper Virgin*, b. 3 May 1804; d. 1818. 3. *Adeline Virgin*, b. 25 Dec. 1805; m. Arioch Thompson. 4. *Samuel Virgin*, b. 4 July 1808; m. Melissa Cobb Hammond.

x   JOHN COOPER, b. 30 March 1780; m. at Plymouth, 25 Jan. 1801 (*VR* 375), JERUSHA COBB, dau. of Lemuel and Hannah (Kempton) Cobb.
Children (Weyman Ms): 1. *Esther* (*Ellen* in Weyman) *Cooper⁷*, b. 1801; d. 9 Sept. 1803 ae 2y 2m, dau. John and Jerusha (*Burial Hill 1990s*, 53). 2. *John Cooper*. 3. *Southworth Cooper*. 4. *William Henry Cooper*, m. Harriet Augusta Babbitt. 5. *Francis Cooper*, b. 20 Oct. 1814; m. Keziah Winsor.

xi   LUSHA/LUCIA SAMSON COOPER, b. 1 July, bp. 7 July 1782; d. ae 1yr, prob. "Richard Cooper's child" d. Plymouth 14 July 1783 (*CR* 412).

xii NANCY COOPER, b. 10 Jan., bp. 23 Jan. 1785; d. ae 2y.

xiii CALVIN COOPER, b. 20 Sept., bp. 5 Oct. 1788; d. 1818 Martinique, W.I.; m. after int. at Plymouth 15 Dec. 1810 (*VR* 306), SARAH MORTON, b. Plymouth 1790, d. Boston 11 June 1863, dau. of Eleazer and Jemima (Taylor) Morton (Weyman Ms). She m. (2) Joseph Atkins (*ibid.*).
Children (*ibid.*): 1. *Sarah Winslow Cooper⁷*, b. 1813; m. Thomas Hall. 2. *Elizabeth Taylor Cooper*, m. Hart Bailey.

Sources cited: *Duxbury VR. Plymouth VR. Plympton VR. Plymouth Church Records.* Bible Record "copied from old bible, printed 1791, said to have belonged to Capt. Richard Cooper of Plymouth, Mass. The entries are evidently made very soon after the book was printed," by George Ernest Bowman 25 Sept. 1897, at GSMD, Plymouth. Plymouth County Probate Records. Weyman Manuscript, box 408, bundle 11. *Plymouth County Court Records. Giles Memorial* (1864). *Epitaphs from Burial Hill, Plymouth* (1892). *Burial Hill in the 1990s* (1999). *Marston Genealogy* (1888). **See also:** *Harlow Family* (1997).

682.   JOHN⁵ SAMPSON (*Ebenezer⁴, David³, Caleb², Henry¹*), son of Ebenezer Sampson [142] and his wife Hannah Harlow, was born 21 October 1746 at Plymouth (*VR* 123). He died at Plymouth before 7 December 1786, when administration was granted on his estate. He was a descendant also of *Mayflower* passengers John Alden, Myles Standish, and Richard Warren.

He married, 11 February 1768 at Plymouth (*VR* 357), **HANNAH SHERMAN**, probably the daughter of Caleb and Rebecca (Rider) Sherman who was born 27 October 1751 at Plymouth (*VR* 27) and died after 9 January 1787.

Administration was granted 7 December 1786 to Hannah Samson of Plymouth on the estate of John Samson late of Plymouth, mariner of Plymouth

(Plymouth PR 27:222). Hannah attested the inventory 9 January 1787 and the estate was declared insolvent the same day (*ibid.*, 30:52-53).

Two deeds involving numerous heirs of Ebenezer Sampson identify Hannah (Samson) (Churchill) Southwick as daughter of John Sampson, and Elizabeth (Samson) Bartlett as daughter of either John or his brother George (see *TAG* 51 [1975] for a detailed discussion).

Children of John and Hannah (Sherman) Sampson, b. Plymouth (*TAG* 51:99):

i HANNAH⁶ SAMPSON, b. say 1769; m. (1) 2 Dec. 1787 at Plymouth (*VR* 2:272), REUBEN CHURCHILL, b. Plymouth 1 Aug. 1765, d. by 13 July 1797 (Plymouth PR 34:121), son of Jonathan and Hannah (Foster) Churchill (*Churchill Gen.*, 24-25); m. (2) 27 Nov. 1800 after int. 25 Oct. 1800 at Plymouth (*VR* 290, *TAG* 51:98), WILMARTH SOUTHWICK, "resident in Plymouth," b. prob. Newport, R.I., in 1775, d. Albany, N.Y., 19 Aug. 1843, son of Solomon and Ann (Gardiner) (Carpenter) Southwick (*Southwick Gen.*, 89). In 1800 Reuben Churchill's household in Plymouth consisted of one man and one woman (p.177). In 1810 William [*sic*] Southwick was head of a household in Plymouth, himself and wife 26-45, with a woman 16-26, one boy and one girl 10-16, and one boy under 10 (p.141); the older children may be Churchills, but no b. recs. found. In 1820 the family was in Albany, N.Y. (p.197). Wilmarth Southwick is listed in Albany City Directories as a "ropemaker, textiles (m)," at 37 Steuben St. in 1815, and in 1826 and 1827 at the "upper end of Maiden Lane."

    Southwick children (*Southwick Gen.*, 89): 1. *William Southwick⁷*, b. Plymouth 18 Aug. 1801; in 1850 a bookbinder ae 40 [*sic*] in Albany, N.Y. (p.197) 2. *Solomon Southwick*, b. 12 Jan. 1804; d. Albany 31 July 1835; m. Sarah Rice. 3. *Mary Ann Southwick*, b. 30 Aug. 1807; d.y. 4. *Mary Ann Southwick*, b. 30 June 1808; d. 1824. 5. *Sarah Sherman* Southwick, b. 12 April 1812; m. William Greene Fry.

ii [CHILD] SAMPSON, d. 11 Aug. 1776 Plymouth (*CR* 406).

iii [CHILD] SAMPSON, d. 22 Nov. 1776 Plymouth (*ibid.*).

prob. iv ELIZABETH SAMPSON, b. say 1774; m. 9 Nov. 1794 at Plymouth (*VR* 370) ZEPHANIAH BARTLETT, prob. son of Joseph and Lucy (___) Bartlett b. Plymouth 17 Feb. 1772, living April 1799. Deeds show that she was dau. of either John or his brother George Sampson [#683], and, given her marriage date, she seems to fit better in John's family.

Sources cited: *Plymouth VR.* Plymouth County Probate Records. Robert M. Sherman, "Three New Heirs of Ebenezer Samson of Plymouth: Elizabeth Bartlett, Mary Covington & Hannah Southwick," *The American Genealogist*, 51 [1975]:94-100, citing Plymouth County Deeds. *Southwick Genealogy* (1881). CENSUS: 1810 Plymouth, Plymouth Co. (M252-21); 1820, Albany, Albany Co., N.Y. (M33-63); 1850 Albany Ward 10 (M432-472). Albany City Directories.

683.   GEORGE⁵ SAMPSON (*Ebenezer⁴, David³, Caleb², Henry¹*), son of
Ebenezer Sampson [142] and his wife Hannah Harlow, was born 22 August 1748
at Plymouth (*VR* 123). He died before April 1799, when his children Deborah,
Mary, and George signed a deed for land that he had inherited, cited below. He
was a descendant also of *Mayflower* passengers John Alden, Myles Standish, and
Richard Warren.

He married, after intentions 20 November 1771 at Plymouth (*VR* 260), "both
of Plymouth," **MARY KEMPTON**, who was living on 30 April 1802 when she
was mentioned in a deed. She was probably the daughter of John and Elizabeth
(Randall) Kempton born 15 September 1749 at Plymouth (*VR* 128).

Two deeds in 1799 and 1803 involving numerous heirs of Ebenezer Samson
identify Mary Covington, Deborah Bradford, and George Sampson as children of
George Sampson, and Elizabeth (Sampson) Bartlett as daughter of either George
or his brother John (see *TAG* 51:94-100 for a detailed discussion).

In 1800 the household of Mary Sampson in Plymouth consisted of one boy
10-16, one young man and four young women 16-26, and a woman 45 or older
(p.23). On 30 April 1802, Joseph Cooper of Plymouth [George Sampson's
nephew, son of sister Hannah Cooper] and his wife Lucy sold to Mary Covington
of Plymouth, widow of Isaac Covington, deceased, part of a house, bounded south
by Deborah Kempton's land; the deed includes the stipulation, "I the abovenamed
Mary Covington for $50 paid by my mother Mary Sampson of Plymouth, agree
with her ... on use of half the premises during her life" (Plymouth LR 96:223).

No Plymouth County probate records were found for the correct John
Kempton, or for George or Mary Sampson.

Children of George and Mary (Kempton) Sampson, born probably at Plymouth
(*TAG* 51:99, citing Plymouth LR):

  i MARY⁶ SAMPSON, b. say 1772; d. between 2 March and 5 Dec. 1807 at
     Plymouth; m. 21 Sept. 1794 at Plymouth after int. there 10 May (*VR* 370,
     281), ISAAC COVINGTON, d. before 1802.
       Covington child: 1. *Mary Covington⁷*, m. Plymouth, 6 Feb. 1824 (*VR* 447),
     George Cooper, son of Joseph and Lucy (Taylor) Cooper (*TAG* 51:97).
  ii GEORGE SAMPSON, b. 10 Jan. 1775 (calc.); d. Plympton 9 Nov. 1826
     (*VR* 511), ae 51y 9m 28d; buried Old Cemetery, Plympton Centre; m.
     Plymouth 24 March 1796 (*VR* 371), PATIENCE RYDER, b. 16 Feb.
     1777, d. 18 Oct. 1835 in 58ᵗʰ yr (g.s., *Burial Hill*).
       Children rec. Plymouth (*VR* 398): 1. *Harriot⁷ Sampson*, b. 11 Feb. 1797; m.
     Daniel Gale. 2. *Patience Howland Sampson*, b. 27 Oct. 1799; m. Joseph White.

3. *George Sampson,* b. 9 Feb. 1802; d.y.   4. *Mary Sampson,* b. 7 Aug. 1805; m. Ichabod Shaw.

iii   DEBORAH SAMPSON, b. 29 May 1776; m. (1) Plymouth, 6 March 1796 (*VR* 371), BENJAMIN WRIGHT, who d. Oct. 1796 in the West Indies; m. (2) after int. Plymouth 1 Dec. 1798, NATHANIEL BRADFORD JR., son of Nathaniel and Rebecca (Holmes) Bradford, and removed to New York City. At least five *Bradford* children.

poss. iv   ELIZABETH SAMPSON; m. in 1794 ZEPHANIAH BARTLETT. Deeds show that she was dau. of George Sampson or his brother John [#682], and given her marriage date, she appears to fit more easily into John's family. See p. 279.

v   [CHILD] SAMPSON, d. 1 July 1779 at Plymouth (*CR* 409).

Sources cited: *Plymouth VR. Plympton VR.* Plymouth County Deeds. *Epitaphs from Burial Hill, Plymouth.* Robert M. Sherman, "Three New Heirs of Ebenezer Samson of Plymouth: Elizabeth Bartlett, Mary Covington & Hannah Southwick," *The American Genealogist,* 51 [1975]. *Churchill Family* (1904). CENSUS: Plymouth, Plymouth Co., 1800 (M32-16). **See also:** *Harlow Family* (1997).

684.   SARAH[5] SAMPSON (*Ebenezer[4], David[3], Caleb[2], Henry[1]*), daughter of Ebenezer Sampson [142] and his wife Hannah Harlow, was born 25 May 1751 at Plymouth (*VR* 123) and died there as "Sally Simmons" in October 1825 (*VR* 340). The death of "widow Simmonds," aged 73, was noted in the *Columbian Centinel* of 20 October 1825 (*Col. Cent. Obits,* 4079). She was a descendant also of *Mayflower* passengers John Alden, Myles Standish, and Richard Warren.

She married, first, 19 January 1769 at Plymouth after intentions 2 December 1768 (*VR* 358, 257), "both of Plymouth," **JOHN COOPER**. He was born in 1749, son of John and Hannah (Rider) Cooper and a descendant of *Mayflower* passenger James Chilton. John died before 16 July 1779 when administration was granted on his estate (Plymouth PR 27:23; 28:136-38).

Sarah's sister Hannah Sampson [#681] married John Cooper's brother Richard. A distribution in 1763 of the estate of John Cooper, mariner late of Plymouth, deceased, included eldest son Richard Cooper and son John Cooper (Plymouth PR 14:86; 16:512, 393).

Sarah married, second, 11 February 1784 at Plymouth (*VR* 270, 364), **BENNET SIMMONS**, who was born there 17 August 1757 (*VR* 190) and died there [25] November 1801 (*VR* 340), son of Nathan and Lydia (Holmes) Simmons and also a descendant of Henry Samson [#722-iii].

On 16 July 1779 administration on the estate of "your husband" John Cooper, late of Plymouth, yeoman, was granted to Sarah Cooper, widow, of Plymouth

(Plymouth PR 27:23). Dower was set off to her on 10 October 1782, consisting of half a house adjoining Capt. Richard Cooper, and the estate was declared insolvent; on 12 December 1782 Sarah's account included an item "for support of my children" (*ibid.*, 28:136-38).

Bennet Simmons served throughout the Revolutionary War, from 16 March 1777 until discharged 10 June 1783 by Gen. Washington, and was among men entitled to honorary badges for faithful service. He was described as a cordwainer, born in Plymouth, with black hair, dark complexion, and of stature varying in different lists as 5 ft 7in., 5 ft 8½ in., and 5 ft. 10 in. (*MSSR* 14:227).

On 23 June 1788, Bennet Simmons, fisherman, of Plymouth, sold his rights in a dwelling and garden in Plymouth that had been "set off to Sally Simmons my wife as her dower in the estate of John Cooper late of sd. Plymouth dec'd," for £16 (Plymouth LR 68:217).

In 1790 Bennet Simmons was living in Plymouth with four females (p.176). In 1800 his household consisted of one boy under 10, two girls 10-16, and one man and one woman over 45 (p.11). No record has been found of any children born to Bennet Simmons in Plymouth, nor any probate record there for Bennet or Sarah. Sarah Simmons is not listed in the census in 1810 or 1820.

Children of John and Sarah (Samson) Cooper, b. prob. at Plymouth, list evidently incomplete as more than one child was living in Dec. 1782; no birth records found:

i   BENJAMIN COOPER[6], b. ca 1773 (Davis, 70); d. Paris, Me., 8 Jan. 1847 (Weyman Ms); m. at Plymouth, 5 May 1794 (*VR* 370), SUSANNA KING, b. 1771, d. 2 June 1857 Paris, Me., dau. of William and Susanna (Harlow) King (Weyman Ms). They evidently moved to Maine ca 1802. The 1820 census listed the family at Paris, Oxford Co., Me., Benjamin and his wife 45+ with two young women 16-26, a man 18-26, two girls 10-16, and one boy and three girls under 10 (p.32).

   Children, first three b. Plymouth but not rec. there, rest b. Paris, Me. (all in Weyman Ms): 1. *Susan Cooper[7]*, b. ca 1797; m. John Briggs. 2. *Harriet Cooper*, b. 4 July 1799. 3. *John Cooper*, b. 1801; m. Rebecca Matthews. 4. *Sarah/Sally Cooper*, b. 16 June 1803; m. Daniel Finney (Davis, 70) or John Billings (Weyman Ms). 5. *Hannah Cooper*, b. 28 Feb. 1806; m. Elliot Smith. 6. *Miranda Cooper*, b. 16 July 1808; m. George W. Cole. 7. *Emily Cooper*, b. 20 Feb. 1810. 8. *William Cooper*, b. 23 March 1814; m. Charity ___.

ii [CHILD] COOPER, d. 27 Nov. 1771 at Plymouth (*CR* 400).

iii [CHILD] COOPER, d. 2 Feb. 1777 at Plymouth (*CR* 407).

Census figures in 1800 suggest that Bennett and Sarah (Samson) (Cooper) Bennett had two daughters b. 1784-1790 and one son b. 1790-1800.

Sources cited: *Plymouth VR. Plymouth Church Records. Index to Obituaries in the Columbian Centinel.* Plymouth County Probate Records. Davis, *Ancient Landmarks ...* (1899). Robert M. Sherman, "Three New Heirs of Ebenezer Samson of Plymouth: Elizabeth Bartlett, Mary Covington & Hannah Southwick," *The American Genealogist*, 51 [1975]. Weyman Manuscript, box 408, bundle 11. CENSUS, Plymouth, Plymouth Co., 1790 (M637-4), 1800 (M32-16); Paris, Oxford Co., Me., 1820 (M33-37). **See also:** *Harlow Family* (1997).

685.   LYDIA⁵ SAMPSON (*Ebenezer⁴, David³, Caleb², Henry¹*), daughter of Ebenezer Sampson [142] and his wife Hannah Harlow, was born 16 July 1753 at Plymouth (*VR* 123). She was probably "the widow Edwards" who died at Plymouth 7 October 1838 aged 86 (*CR* 682). She was a descendant also of *Mayflower* passengers John Alden, Myles Standish, and Richard Warren.

She married, 18 April 1771 at Plymouth after intentions 9 March (*VR* 359), "both of Plymouth," **JOHN EDWARDS**, who died 7 June 1795 at Plymouth (*CR* 423).

In 1790 John Edwards was listed in Plymouth with a household of three boys under 16 and four females (*Heads of Fam.*, 177).

Lydia Edwards, widow, joined other heirs of Hannah (Harlow) Sampson in selling land in 1799 and 1803 (*TAG* 51:95). No Lydia Edwards is listed in the 1800 Massachusetts census, and no Edwards families were living in Plymouth in the 1810 census. No Plymouth County probate records were found for either John or Lydia Edwards.

Children of John and Lydia (Samson) Edwards, b. prob. at Plymouth but not recorded there; list prob. incomplete:

i   JOHN EDWARDS⁶, b. prob. ca 1772; d. by 1797; m. at Plymouth, 2 April 1795 (*VR* 371), SARAH COVINGTON. She m. (2) Plymouth, 10 Feb. 1799 (*VR* 373), Daniel Doten. On 12 April 1797 guardianship of Mary Edwards, under 14, daughter of John Edwards late of Plymouth, mariner, deceased, was granted to Thomas Covington of Plymouth, mariner (Plymouth PR 32:83).

Child: 1. *Mary Edwards⁷*, b. ca Jan. 1796; d. Plymouth 22 June 1879 ae 83y 5m 27d, "dau. John & Sally (Covington) Edwards" (Mass. VR 432-333); m. William Morey.

    ii   LYDIA EDWARDS, b. 17 March 1777 (GSMD #7765); d. 1865 (Mass. VR 184:301); m. after int. Plymouth 22 April 1797 (*VR* 285), JOHN SYLVESTER, prob. son of Abner and Abigail (Washburn) Sylvester. In 1850 John Sylvester ae 71 was a seaman at Plymouth with Lydia ae 70 (p.153).

            Sylvester children (Davis, 257): 1. *Abigail Washburn Sylvester[7]*, b. 1801; d.y. 2. *Abigail Washburn Sylvester*, 1803; prob. d. 27 March 1803 (*CR* 628). 3. *Lydia Sylvester*, m. James Wadsworth. 4. *John Sylvester*, m. Sally Burbank. 5. *Abby Sylvester*.

    iii POLLY EDWARDS, b. 1786; d. 11 Sept. 1791 at Plymouth (*Burial Hill*, #612), ae 5y 3m, dau. "of Mr John and Mrs Lydia Edwards."

    iv [CHILD] EDWARDS, d. 15 Nov. 1789 at Plymouth (*CR* 417), "John Edward's child."

Sources cited: *Plymouth VR.* Mass. Vital Records 1841-1910. *Plymouth Church Records.* Plymouth County Probate Records and Deeds. *Epitaphs from Burial Hill, Plymouth* (1892). Robert M. Sherman, "Three New Heirs of Ebenezer Samson of Plymouth: Elizabeth Bartlett, Mary Covington & Hannah Southwick," *The American Genealogist*, 51 [1975]. Davis, *Ancient Landmarks* … (1899). CENSUS: *Heads of Families 1790 – Mass.*; 1850 Plymouth, Plymouth Co. (M432-333).

686. MARY[5] SAMPSON (*Ebenezer[4], David[3], Caleb[2], Henry[1]*), daughter of Ebenezer Sampson [142] and his wife Hannah Harlow, was born 4 June 1755 at Plymouth (*VR* 123). She died 21 December 1790 in her 36th year, "wife of Lemuel Bradford," at Plymouth (*Burial Hill*, #598). She was a descendant also of *Mayflower* passengers John Alden, Myles Standish, and Richard Warren.

    She married 23 March 1775 at Plymouth (*VR* 361), **LEMUEL BRADFORD**. He was born 20 February 1750/1 at Plymouth (*VR* 50), and died there 22 May 1828, aged 77, called "Capt." (*Burial Hill*, #1260), son of Nathaniel and Sarah (Spooner) Bradford and a descendant of Pilgrim William Bradford. He married, second, 28 August 1791 at Plymouth (*VR* 368), LYDIA HOLMES, daughter of Cornelius and Lydia (Drew) Holmes, and had with her six children born at Plymouth: Cornelius, Lydia, David, William Holmes, Lewis, and Lewis Bradford again (*VR* 390).

    During the Revolutionary War, Lemuel Bradford served seven days on the alarm of 18 April 1775, and as a seaman on the sloop *Sally* on the Penobscot Expedition in 1779 (*MSSR* 2:405).

In a deed dated 1792 he was called a housewright, and Plymouth Court Records indicate that he was paid for several construction projects in and around the jail and the court house.

In 1790 Lemuel Bradford was living in Plymouth with one man, three boys under 16, and four females (*Heads of Fam.*, 176). In 1810 his household consisted of one boy under 10, three boys and one girl 10-16, one man 26-45, plus himself and presumably his wife, both 45 or over (p.110).

Lemuel Bradford Sr., Lemuel Bradford Jr., Thomas Bradford, housewright, and Mary Bradford, spinster, all of Plymouth (as heirs of Mary Sampson Bradford), joined other heirs of Hannah (Harlow) Sampson in selling land in 1799 (*TAG*, 51:95-96). The 1803 deed involving the same rights was signed by Thomas Bradford and wife Polly, Polly Bradford Holmes and husband Ephraim, and Eleanor Bradford (*ibid.*).

On 24 May 1821 Lemuel Bradford of Plymouth, housewright, mortgaged to his son David Bradford of Plymouth, part of the dwelling house on Summer Street "I now live in," and Lemuel's wife Lydia released her dower rights (Plymouth LR 168:198). Stephen Lucas and David Holmes made a deposition in front of the Registrar of Deeds that on 10 February 1830 they "were present and within the dwelling house now occupied by David Bradford of said Plymouth, Gentleman, and formerly the residence of his late father Lemeul Bradford deceased, and that ... David Bradford was then and their present holding in his hands a deed of Mortgage of the premises upon which we were then standing from ... Lemuel Bradford deceased to the said David Bradford dated" 24 May 1821. All the persons duly notified who were "to us known as interested in the property" were listed as William H. Bradford, Lydia Bradford, John Tribbel and Mary Tribbel, Eleanor Faunce, and Andrew Mechie and Mehitable Mechie (Plymouth LR 167:98). (Of these, William H. and Lydia were children of Lemuel's second wife; Mary Tribbel and Eleanor Faunce were daughters of first wife Mary Sampson, and Mehitable Mechie was Mary's granddaughter by son Lemuel Bradford.)

Lemuel does not appear in the 1820 census, and he did not claim a federal pension. No Plymouth County probate records were found for him or for Mary.

Children of Lemuel and Mary (Sampson) Bradford, rec. Plymouth (*VR* 390):

i   LEMUEL BRADFORD[6], b. 6 Dec. 1775; killed in battle of Sackett's Harbor at Lake Champlain, N.Y., 17 Sept. 1814; m. after int. at Portland, Me., 16 Feb. 1800 (*VR* 39) MEHITABLE HINCKLEY of Barnstable, b. 1780, d. 9 Feb. 1809, dau. of Ebenezer and Esther (Shays?) Hinckley (Weyman Ms). On 29 Jan. 1799 Lemuel was censured by the Plymouth Church for "*playing at Cards*, in a public place, before several, who were not of the Ch[urch]h, (&

who express^d their surprize at such Conduct in Members of the Church).″ He acknowledged "the Fact charged against him — that he did not, at the time of it, reflect so much upon it or think it so great an Evil — that he was drawn into it — & was ignorant of the explicit Vote of this Ch[urc]h against playing Cards, (having lived out of town for some years) but, that had he known what he now does, he sho^d not have comply^d — he own'd he did it, thro the Temptation of Satan, & his own wicked heart, & is sorry." At a meeting 12 Feb. 1799, it was voted to "forgive & restore [him] to … christian Charity" (*CR* 535-37).

The 1800 census listed him in Cumberland Co., Me., ae 26-45 with one woman 16-26 (p.283).

Children (Weyman Ms): 1. *Abigail Chandler Bradford*[7], b. 10 Feb. 1801; m. Isaac Jackson Bicknell. 2. *Mehitable/Hetty Amelia Bradford*, b. Portland 11 April 1803; d. New Bedford 30 Aug. 1880 (Mass. VR 319:135); m. Dr. Andrew Mackie. 3. *George Frederick Bradford*, b. April 1805; d. 1832. 4. *Charles Augustus Bradford*, b. 24 May 1808; m. Abigail Clapp Beal.

ii   THOMAS BRADFORD, b. 25 Feb. 1778; d. 1837 (Weyman Ms); m. Plymouth, 27 April 1800 (*VR* 435), MARY HOLMES, b. Plymouth 18 May 1779 ("Polly"), dau. of Richard and Mercy (Barnes) Holmes (*VR* 186).

Children, eight rec. Plymouth (*VR* 449): 1. *Mary Samson Bradford*[7], b. 25 Aug. 1800; m. "___ Campbell of Shaw's Crossing?". 2. *Thomas Bradford*, b. 21 Feb. 1803; d. 7 Jan. 1804. 3. *Abigail Holmes Bradford*, b. 21 Sept. 1804. 4. *Thomas Lewis Bradford*, b. 21 Aug. 1806. 5. *Amos Sturtevant Bradford*, b. 22 June 1808. 6. *Sarah Spooner Bradford*, b. 15 Dec. 1810. 7. *David Bradford*, b. 19 Aug. 1813. 8. *Lewis Bradford*, b. 20 Jan. 1816. Weyman Ms has four more: ? 9. *James Russell Bradford*. ? 10. *Lydia Bradford*. ? 11. *Maria Bradford*. ? 12. *Thomas Bradford*.

iii MARY BRADFORD, b. 19 Dec. 1780; d. Plymouth 4 Sept. 1856, ae 75y 8m (Mass. VR 103:219); m. (1) at Plymouth 30 March 1800 as "Polley Bradford" (*VR* 375) EPHRAIM HOLMES, d. 14 Aug. 1811 at sea 3 days out of Havana, son of Ephraim and Lucy (Barnes) Holmes; m. (2) at Plymouth, 26 May 1816 (*VR* 443), as his second wife, JOHN TRIBBLE, b. 23 Nov. 1782 (*VR* 453), d. Plymouth 2 June 1862, a painter (Mass. VR 157:368), son of Joseph and Sarah (Dunham) Tribble and widower of Bathsheba Holmes, d. 24 July 1815, with whom he had five children rec. Plymouth (*VR* 453).

Holmes children (Weyman Ms): 1. *Ephraim Holmes*[7], b. 29 Oct. 1801; d. 1803. 2. *Joan Holmes*, b. 20 Jan. 1803; m. Jacob Jackson. 3. *Ephraim Holmes*, b. 29 Aug. 1805; m. Mary Ann Atwood. 4. *Mary Ann Holmes*, b. 6 Aug. 1808; m. (1) Sylvanus Davie, (2) Corban Barnes.

Tribble children, first rec. Plymouth (*VR* 453), all in Weyman Ms: 1. *Marcia Tribble²*, b. 9 Sept. 1817. 2. *Albert R. Tribble*, b. 8 April 1819; m. Lydia Harlow. 3. *Levantha Tribble*, b. 31 May 1821; d. 1824.

iv GEORGE BRADFORD, b. 19 Sept. 1783; d. 1849; m. 1808, HARRIET CHURCHILL, dau. of Amaziah and Betty (Bartlett) Churchill.
    Children (Weyman Ms): 1. *George Bradford²*, b. 24 Aug. 1808; m. Sarah Prince Browne. 2. *Edmund Bradford*, b. 7 June 1810; m. Mary E. Hall. 3. *Lemuel Bradford*, b. 10 March 1813; m. Lucy Ann Damon. 4. *Henry Churchill Bradford*, b. 21 May 1816. 5. *Harriet Bradford*, b. 9 Aug. 1819.

v   ELENER BRADFORD, b. 25 Aug. 1785; d. 13 Sept. 1868; m. at Plymouth, 13 Nov. 1806 as Ellen (*VR* 438), SOLOMON FAUNCE, b. 1784, d. 1815, son of Thaddeus and Elizabeth (Sylvester) Faunce (Weyman Ms).
    Faunce children (*ibid.*): 1. *Solomon Faunce²*, b. 27 Oct. 1809; m. Mary Olive Harlow. 2. *Lemuel B. Faunce*, b. 18 Aug. 1811; m. (1) Lydia Vaughan Wood; m. (2) Plymouth, 23 March 1845, Elizabeth A. Morton (*VR* 611). 3. *William Faunce*, b. July 1813.

Sources cited: *Plymouth VR. Plymouth Church Records.* Plymouth County Deeds. *Epitaphs from Burial Hill, Plymouth.* Weyman Manuscript, box 408, bundle 11. Konig, *Plymouth County Court Records.* Robert M. Sherman, "Three New Heirs of Ebenezer Samson of Plymouth: Elizabeth Bartlett, Mary Covington & Hannah Southwick," *The American Genealogist,* 51 [1975]. CENSUS: 1800 Cumberland Co., Me. (M32-6).

687. EBENEZER⁵ SAMPSON (*Ebenezer⁴, David³, Caleb², Henry¹*), son of Ebenezer Sampson [142] and his wife Hannah Harlow, was born 1 April 1764 at Plymouth (*VR* 202). He died 9 September 1800, lost at sea with his nephew Ephraim Bartlett (see # 680-ii) and ___ Bartlett (*Plymouth CR* 622). He was a descendant also of *Mayflower* passengers John Alden, Myles Standish, and Richard Warren.

He married at Plymouth, 5 October 1786 (*VR* 366), "both of Plymouth," **SUSANNA FINNEY,** daughter of Josiah and Alice (Barnes) Finney. She is on census records through 1830, and is probably the Susannah Sampson who died at Plymouth in October 1836 (*VR* 526).

Ebenezer served in the Revolutionary War as a private in Capt. Stephen Churchill's company, Col. Theophilus Cotton's regiment, in March 1781 for 24 days, at Newport, R. I.; the company was raised by order of His Excellency John Hancock to serve for 40 days unless sooner discharged (*MSSR* 13:767).

In 1790 Ebenezer Sampson Jr. was living in Plymouth with three females (*Heads of Fam.,* 177). On 30 September 1794, Ebenezer Sampson Jr., mariner, and wife Susanna, with others, all of Plymouth, sold land that had descended to them by heirship from "our mother" Ellice Finney, late of Plymouth, deceased, which had descended to her from her grandfather William Barnes (Plymouth LR 77:78).

The household of Ebenezer Sampson in Plymouth in 1800 consisted of one boy and two girls under 10, three girls 10-16, one man and two women 26-45, and one man over 45 (p.15); these figures suggest that the family of Ebenezer Jr. was sharing a household with his father, following the death of his mother in 1792.

In 1810 Susanna Sampson was living in Plymouth, head of a household consisting of two girls 10-16, one young woman 16-26, and one woman, presumably herself, 26-45 (p.140). In 1820 she was 45 or older and living with her were one woman 26-45, one boy 10-16, and one boy under 10 (p.369). Susan Sampson was head of a household in Plymouth in 1830, aged 60-70, with one woman 40-50, one man 20-30, and one boy 10-15 (p.77).

No Plymouth County probate records were found for Ebenezer or Susanna Samson, or for Josiah Finney, or guardianships for children of Ebenezer.

Children of Ebenezer and Susanna (Finney) Sampson, b. probably Plymouth (Davis, 229); several more daughters suggested by census:

    i   OLIVE W.[6] SAMPSON, b. ca Jan. 1788; d. Plymouth 21 May 1858 ae 70y 4m of dropsy, widow, b. Plymouth, no parents listed (Mass. VR 121:259); m. at Plymouth, 29 Nov. 1807 after int. 22 Aug. 1807 (*VR* 301, 381) PERREY GRIFFIN. In 1850 Olive Griffin was in Plymouth in the household of John A. Morse ae 40 and Nancy ae 39 (p.151) [Nancy was not a Griffin dau.; John Morse m. Nancy Doten 1834 Plymouth (*VR* 325).]

           Probable ***Griffin*** child: 1. *Ebenezer S. Griffin[7]*, b. ca 1816; m. Plymouth 14 April 1841 (*VR* 557), Rebecca Rogers; res. Plymouth 1850 (p.146).

    ii   EBENEZER SAMSON, b. bet. 1790 and 1800. He was not with his mother in 1810, but poss. apprenticed or gone to sea. [Is he the Ebenezer Sampson listed as father on records of Benjamin F. Sampson in New Bedford? – age fits but no evidence found.]

   ?iii HANNAH SAMSON.

Sources cited: *Plymouth VR.* Mass. Vital Records 1841-1910. Plymouth Church Records on CD. *Mass. Soldiers & Sailors.* Robert M. Sherman, "Three New Heirs of Ebenezer Samson of Plymouth: Elizabeth Bartlett, Mary Covington & Hannah Southwick," *The American Genealogist*, 51 [1975], citing Plymouth County Deeds. Davis, *Ancient Landmarks* ... (1899). CENSUS: Plymouth, Plymouth Co., 1800 (M32-16), 1810 (M252-21), 1820 (M33-50), 1830 (M19-64), 1850 (M432-333).

688. GAMALIEL LITTLE[5] (*Mary*[4] *Samson, David*[3], *Caleb*[2], *Henry*[1]), son of John Little and his wife Mary Samson [143], was born 18 January 1741/2 at Lebanon, Conn. (VR 1:180). Capt. Gamaliel Little died at Columbia, Conn., before 6 August 1800 when administration was granted on his estate. He was a descendant also of *Mayflower* passengers John Alden and Richard Warren.

He married, 16 August 1765 at Hebron, Conn. (VR 2:60), **SARAH PHELPS**, who was born at Hebron 30 March 1745 (not in *VR*), daughter of John and Ann (Horsford) Phelps, and died in 1831 at Columbia, Conn. The will of John Phelps of Hebron, dated 28 January 1769, proved 20 February 1769, names wife Ann and daughter Sarah; a distribution names daughter Sarah, but neither record includes her surname (Conn. PR, E. Haddam Dist.). However, Anna, widow of John Phelps, of Hebron, conveyed land to her son-in-law, Gamaliel Little, on 20 February 1773 (*Horsford Family*).

John Little of Lebanon in his will dated 13 June 1777, proved 8 January 1799, bequeathed to son Gamaliel £125 (Conn. PR, Windham Dist. #2,467).

During the Revolutionary War, Gamaliel Little was a cornet in the Second Regiment of Light Horse Militia (*Conn. Men in Rev.*, 443).

There are two listings for Gamaliel Little in Lebanon in 1790. One is for a household of one man, three boys under 16, and seven females (p.145), and the other of two men, two boys under 16, and seven females (p.146).

Bond was posted on 6 August 1800 by Sarah Little, widow of Gamaliel Little of Lebanon, deceased, as administratrix of his estate; there are no other papers in the file (Conn. PR, Lebanon Dist.). In 1800 Sarah Little was head of a household in Lebanon consisting of one boy 10-16, one girl under 10, two girls 10-16, four young women 16-26, one woman 26-45, and two women over 45 (p.718).

Children of Gamaliel and Sarah (Phelps) Little, first three rec. Lebanon (VR 1:190), probably all b. there; three bp. Columbia:

i   THEODOSIA LITTLE[6], b. 28 July 1766; poss. m. __ Gary (Weyman Ms).

ii DAVID LITTLE, b. 23 March 1768; d. 17 Nov. 1832, Springfield, N.Y.; m. 30 Sept. 1792, ALICE LOOMIS, b. 1 Sept. 1768 Colchester, Conn., d. 23 April 1846 Cherry Valley, N.Y., dau. of Daniel and Alice (Chamberlain) Loomis (Weyman Ms).

    Children, b. Springfield, N.Y. (*ibid*): 1. *Eliza Olivia Little*[7], b. 9 Nov. 1795; m. Dr. Delos White. 2. *Sarah Little*, b. 5 Aug. 1800; d. 15 Aug. 1802. 3. *George Little*, b. 10 July, d. 19 July 1802. 4. *David Hervey Little*, b. 3 Aug. 1807; m. Julia Elizabeth Seelye.

iii JOHN PHELPS LITTLE, b. 15 Feb. 1770.

   iv   [CHILD] LITTLE, d. 1775.

   v   CHARLES LITTLE, b. 12 Sept. 1776; poss. the child who d. 1777.

   vi   SALLY LITTLE, bp. 1779; m. DAVID YEOMANS (Weyman Ms).
          Yeomans child: 1. *William Austin Yeomans[7]*, b. 14 June 1805 Columbia, Conn.; m. [cousin] Harriet Rebecca Dewey.

   vii   ARETHUSA LITTLE (twin), bp. June 1781; d. 30 May 1863, ae 82 (g.s.); bur. near brother Norman in West St. Cem., Columbia (Hale 803-3:59).

   viii   AMANDA LITTLE (twin), bp. June 1781.

   ix   MINDWELL LITTLE, b. 1783; m. 15 Feb. 1807, SILAS HOLBROOK, b. 1 Feb. 1782 Columbia, Conn., d. there 19 Feb. 1861, son of John and Sarah (Pineo) Holbrook (Weyman Ms).
          Holbrook children (*ibid.*): 1. *Sally Emeline Holbrook[7]*, b. 8 March 1808; m. Henry W. Abel. 2. *Nancy Adelia Holbrook*, b. 10 April 1810; m. Jonathan Clarke Fuller. 3. *Amanda Melvina Holbrook*, b. 27 April 1812; m. Hiram Belcher Ware. 4. *Mary Elmina Holbrook*, b. 3 April 1814; m. Luke Palmer. 5. *Maria Holbrook*, b. 22 Sept. 1816; m. James B. Goodwin. 6. *Anson Holbrook*, b. 27 April 1819; m. Ann Elizabeth Abell. 7. *Silas Abel Holbrook*, b. 16 May 1821; m. Elizabeth J. Wright. 8. *Harriet Holbrook*, b. 9 Jan. 1824; m. John Webster Gilbert.

   x   NORMAN LITTLE, b. 10 Nov. 1785; d. 3 Dec. 1867 ae 82 (g.s.); m. ca 1812 POLLY LOOMIS, b. Lebanon, Conn., 9 Aug. 1789, d. 22 Jan. 1865 ae 76 (g.s.); bur. West St. Cem., Columbia (Hale 803-3:59), dau. of Benoni and Grace (Parsons) Loomis (Weyman Ms). In 1850 he was a farmer ae 64 in Columbia, with Polly ae 62 and Norman P. ae 16, David D. Little ae 28 was next door (p.359). These two sons and their wives were members of the Ecclesiastical Society, Columbia, in 1866-67.
          Children, b. Columbia, Conn. 1. *Agnes Prudence Little[7]*, b. ca 1813. 2. *Andrew Judson Little*, b. ca 1815. 3. *Henry Bliss Little*, b. ca 1818. 4. *Eleanor Little*, b. ca 1820. 5. *Edwin Little*, b. ca 1821. 6. *David Dickinson Little*, b. ca 1822; m. Elizabeth Amelia Scoville, (2) Maria Jane Loomis. 7. *Norman Prescott Little*, b. ca 1834; m. Mary Ann ____.

   xi   NANCY LITTLE; m. ____ TOWNSEND.

Sources cited: Hebron and Lebanon VRs as cited in the Barbour Index. Columbia Church Records, CSL. Connecticut Probate Records, East Haddam District and Lebanon District. Hale Collection of Conn. Cemetery Inscriptions. *Record of Service of Connecticut Men in the War of the Revolution. The 150th Anniversary of the Organization of the Congregational Church in Columbia, Conn. Ye Horseforde Booke: Horseford-Hosford families in the United States of America* (1936). Weyman Manuscript, box 408, bundle 11. CENSUS: *Heads of Families in 1790 – Connecticut*, 1800 Lebanon, Windham Co., Conn. (M32-2).

689.   OTIS LITTLE⁵ (*Mary⁴ Samson, David³, Caleb², Henry¹*), son of John Little and his wife Mary Samson [143], was born 1 April 1744 at Lebanon, Conn, (1:180). He died probably between 1796 and 1800 (see below). He was a descendant also of Mayflower passengers John Alden and Richard Warren.

He married, 17 September 1773 at Fair Haven Church, Columbia (*Early Conn. Marriages*, 7:74), **SARAH ___** [no surname listed], who died 15 September 1775 at Columbia, aged 21 (g.s.). The inscription on her gravestone in the Old Cemetery, Columbia, calls her "consort of Otis Little" (Hale 803-1:14).

Otis Little served in the French and Indian War under Capt. Azel Fitch (*Conn. Soldiers, French & Indian War, 1755–1762*, 340).

John Little of Lebanon in his will dated 13 June 1777, proved 8 January 1799, bequeathed to son Otis £30, stating, "I have already given him a Traid" (Windham Dist PR #2467). On 20 April 1790 Otis Little of Lebanon leased the farm "on which he lives" to his father, John Little, for 27 years of John's lifetime (Lebanon LR 15:91). Otis is named in an endorsement to his father's will dated 20 May 1796, but he did not share in a division on 5 May 1800.

Otis has not been found in any census. A man indexed as "Otis Little" was noted in Litchfield, Conn., in 1790, but an examination of a copy of the original census page (p.68) indicates that Otis was the surname; all entries are written with given name first, and this one is Little [or Settle] Otis. In 1800 there were two Otis Littles, both in Maine; one in Castine (p.39) came there from Marshfield and the other, in Bath (p.493), was too young to be the Connecticut man. Nothing relevant has been found in Columbia or Litchfield VRs.

Sources cited: Lebanon VR as cited in the Barbour Index. Connecticut Probate Records, Windham District. Columbia Church Records, CSL. Hale Collection of Conn. Cemetery Inscriptions. *Conn. Soldiers, French & Indian War, 1755–1762. Early Connecticut Marriages.* CENSUS: 1790 Litchfield, Litchfield Co., Conn. (M637-1); 1800 Bath, Lincoln Co., Me. (M32-6) & Castine, Hancock Co., Me. (M32-7). **See also:** *MF 16 [Alden]*, 2:112-13.

690.   CONSIDER LITTLE⁵ (*Mary⁴ Samson, David³, Caleb², Henry¹*), son of John Little and his wife Mary Samson [143], was born 24 March 1746 at Lebanon, Conn. (VR 1:180). He died 3 August 1831, aged 85, at Columbia, Conn. (g.s.). He was a descendant also of *Mayflower* passengers John Alden and Richard Warren.

He was "of Lebanon, Conn.," when he married, 1 February 1774 "in the Gore adjoining Chesterfield" (*VR*, Corbin), **REBECCA BUCKINGHAM**. She was born 13 May 1751 at Lebanon (VR 1:33), daughter of William and Rebecca (Clark) Buckingham, and died 25 October 1825 at Columbia, aged 75, "wife of Consider

Little" (g.s.). They are both buried in the Old Cemetery, Columbia (Hale 803-23). No probate records for her parents have been found.

John Little of Lebanon in his will dated 13 June 1777, proved 8 January 1799, bequeathed to son Consider £170 and other items (Windham Dist PR. #2467).

In 1790 Consider was living in Lebanon with one man 16 or over, three boys under 16, and nine females. In 1810 he was in Columbia, his household consisting of one man and one woman 26-45, and one man [himself] and one woman over 45 (p.615).

The will of Consider Little of Columbia, dated 28 February 1825, recorded 23 August 1831, names his wife Rebecca; son Samuel; daughter Mary; sons Levi and George; daughters Sarah and Rebecca; grandson Philo; and granddaughters Cynthia and Mary. Receipts dated 5 March 1832 were signed by Samuel Little, Mary Lathrop, Sally Scovill, Rebecca Dewey, Levi Little, and George Little (Lebanon Dist. PR #).

Children of Consider and Rebecca (Buckingham) Little, b. Columbia, Conn., births not recorded:

    i   SAMUEL LITTLE⁶, b. 18 Aug. 1774; d. 22 Sept. 1853 (g.s.); m. (1) ca 1801 LEVINA RICHARDSON, d. Columbia 16 June 1807 (VR 32) ae 29 (g.s.); m. (2) Columbia, 23 June 1808, JERUSHA BAILEY, b. Lebanon 21 April 1781 (g.s.), d. 3 Nov. 1857, dau. of Saxton and Lois (Hunt) Bailey (Weyman Ms); all bur. Old Cemetery, Columbia (Hale Coll., 803:2) In 1850 he was a farmer in Columbia with Jerusha; the family of son William was nearby (p.349). The Columbia Public Library is named for their son Saxton B. Little.

        Children with Levina: 1. *Levina Little⁷*, b. 11 May 1802; d. 24 May 1807 (VR 32). 2. *Samuel Little Jr.*, b. 6 March 1804; m. (1) 1829, Amey Pinneo, (2) 1840, Clarissa Pinneo (VR 30, 86). 3. *Anson Little*, b. 20 June 1806; m. Ann Eliza Welles (Alden Kindred). Children with Jerusha: 4. *Emily Little*, b. 27 April 1809 (VR 30); d. Columbia 14 June 1830 (VR 32). 5. *Saxton Bailey Little*, b. 19 April 1813 (VR 30); m. 1836, Sarah M. Tracy (VR 90). 6. *William Buckingham Little*, b. 6 June 1815 (VR 30); m. Harriet Newell Palmer. 7. *Charles Little*, b. 26 Sept. 1818; m. Amelia Newton.

   ii MARY LITTLE, b. 28 Feb. 1776; d. 12 Aug. 1853 ae 77 (g.s.); bur. Old Cem., Columbia, near parents (Hale 803-24), m., prob. as his second wife after 1814, DARIUS LATHROP (g.s.), b. Norwich 14 July 1760, d. 15 Sept. 1827, son of Jonathan and Theoda (Woodworth) Lathrop (*Lo-Lathrop Family*, 113). He m. (1) in 1786, Lydia McCall of Lebanon, who d. 22 March 1814, with whom he had Sophia, Mira, Elizabeth, and John Backus Lathrop (*ibid.*, 165). Distribution of his estate was to Mary Lathrop of Columbia, Daniel and Sophia Morse of Norwich, Chester and Mira Bell of Lebanon, Seymour and Elizabeth Morse, and John B. Lathrop (*ibid.*). Mary had no children of her own.

iii   SARAH/SALLY LITTLE, b. 29 Dec. 1777; d. 25 July 1853, Lebanon; m. at Columbia, 9 Oct. 1798 (VR 67), AMHERST SCOVILLE, b. Tolland Co., Conn., 20 Oct. 1774, d. 22 March 1854, son of Nathan and Elizabeth (Gates) Scovel (Weyman Ms).

   Scoville children, first five rec. Columbia, of "Amhurst & Sally" (VR 68), all in Weyman Ms: 1. *Amherst Scoville[7]*, b. 9 May 1800; d. 22 April 1803, drowned in Mill Pond. 2. *Charles Amhurst Scoville*, b. 23 March 1801. 3. *Elizabeth Scoville* (twin), b. 29 March 1802; m. Darius Kingsley. 4. *Sally Scoville* (twin), b. 29 March 1802; m. Clement Wakeley. 5. *Fanny Little Scoville*, b. 22 March 1806; m. 1827 Elisha H. Hayward of Buffalo, N.Y. (VR 59) 6. *Lydia Little Scoville*, m. 1838 Sanford Yeomans. 7. *Mary Ann Scoville*, m. 1831 Daniel P. Sprague (VR 89). 8. *Caroline Scoville*, b. 10 Dec. 1811. 9. *John Buckingham Scoville*, b. 16 June 1814. 10. *Dan Carpenter Scoville*, b. 16 Oct. 1816.

iv   REBECCA LITTLE, b. 17 June 1779; d. 5 June 1866 ae 87 (g.s.); m. 28 May 1807, as his second wife (*Dewey Fam.*, 431), ELEAZER DEWEY, b. Lebanon, Conn., 4 Dec. 1778, d. 10 May 1872 ae 93, son of Solomon and Elizabeth (Cady) Dewey (g.s.; *Dewey Fam.* and Weyman Ms say d. 1871); bur. Center Cem., Columbia (Hale 803-49). He m. (1) Lydia Wright, who d. 28 April 1805 ae 25 (*Dewey Fam.*), with whom he had a son, Lorenzo Dewey.

   Dewey children (*ibid.*, 431-32): 1. *Elmore Gervase Dewey[7]*, b. 6 Nov. 1808; m. Elizabeth Collins Lyman. 2. *Lydia Amelia Dewey*, b. 3 May 1811; m. Samuel Edson Lyman. 3. *Elizabeth Henrietta Dewey*, b. 9 Aug. 1813; d. 12 March 1851 unm. 4. *Harriet Rebecca Dewey*, b. 8 April 1817; m. William Austin Yeomans. 5. *Mary Little Dewey*, b. 23 Nov. 1819; m. Alanson Hills Fuller.

v   FANNY LITTLE, b. 3 March 1781; d. 13 Sept. 1794, ae 13 (g.s.); bur. with parents.

vi   LEVI LITTLE, b. 1 Dec. 1783; d. Columbia 20 June 1854 ae 70 [*sic*] (g.s.); m. (1) LAURA BARKER, d. 22 Feb. 1825 ae 34 (g.s.); m. (2) Columbia, 5 Feb. 1826 (VR 83), MATILDA WRIGHT, d. 29 July 1860 ae 58, dau. of Horatio and Hannah (Collins) Wright (Weyman Ms); Levi and Laura bur. Old Cemetery, Columbia (Hale 803:10), Matilda in Center Cem. (*ibid.*, 33). In 1850 he was a farmer in Columbia "ae 56" with wife Matilda and son Horatio W. ae 24 (p.358). Levi's age is prob. a clerical error, as the age for the person on the line directly above him is also 56.

   Children (Weyman Ms), with Laura: 1. *Philo Little[7]*, b. 22 Aug. 1819; m. Esther Burroughs Hill. 2. *Cynthia Little*, b. 17 June 1821; m. Edward Dyer.

3. *Mary Lathrop Little*, b. 9 Nov. 1823; m. John Merrick. Children with Matilda:
4. *Horatio Wright Little*, b. 26 April 1826; m. Esther E. Vinton. 5. *Anson Little*, b.
ca 1833; d. 8 April 1839 ae 5y 7m; bur. with father.

vii   GEORGE LITTLE, b. 25 March 1788 [g.s. says 1789]; d. 6 April 1864 (g.s.);
m. NANCY HUNT, b. 15 Oct. 1796, d. 28 April 1876, dau. of Eldred and
Huldah (Benton) Hunt; bur. Center Cem., Columbia (Hale 803). In 1850 he
was a hatter in Columbia, with Nancy ae 56, and children William and Sarah
(p.349).
Children (Weyman Ms): 1. *George Oren Little*[7], b. 22 Jan. 1817; m. (1) Emily
Holbrook, (2) Emma Woodruff Rowley; a hatter 1850. 2. *Nancy Amelia Little*, b.
7 Sept. 1819; m. Samuel Gray Byrne. 3. *Edwin Hunt Little*, b. 9 Feb. 1822; m.
Eliza Melvina West. 4. *Horace Benton Little*, b. 1 July 1824; m. Mary C. Hawley.
5. *Charlotte Huldah Little*, b. 15 Oct. 1826. 6. *Lydia Louise Little*, b. 3 Oct. 1830;
m. Justin Holbrook; she was unm., in household of brother George in 1850, next
to parents. 7. *William W. Little*, b. 23 May 1833; at home 1850; m. Sarah
Ingraham Joslyn. 8. *Mary Delia Little*, b. 1 Dec. 1835; d. unm. 9. *Sarah Kittredge
Little*, b. 19 April 1838; d. 8 May 1856; at home 1850.

viii   LYDIA LITTLE, b. 20 March 1791; d. 20 or 29 June 1807, ae 16.

Sources cited: Chesterfield VR. Columbia and Lebanon, Conn., VR as cited in Barbour Index.
CSL Church Records: Columbia. Gravestones: Louis M. Dewey, "Inscriptions from Old
Cemeteries in Connecticut," Columbia, *NEHGR* 60 (1906).   Hale Collection of Cemetery
Inscriptions: Columbia. Connecticut Probates, Lebanon District. Weyman Manuscript, NEHGS,
box 408, bundle 11 (continues several lines). *Dewey Family* (1898). Huntington, *Lo-Lathrop Family*
(1884). CENSUS: 1790 Lebanon, Windham Co., Conn. (M637-1); Columbia, Tolland Co., Conn.,
1810 (M32-252, 253), 1850 (M432-50). **See also:** *MF 16 [Alden]*, 2:112-13.

691.   JOHN LITTLE[5] (*Mary*[4] *Samson, David*[3], *Caleb*[2], *Henry*[1]), son of John Little
and his wife Mary Samson [143], was born 9 March 1750 at Lebanon, Conn. (VR
1:180). He died 1 July 1833, aged 83, at Columbia, Conn. (g.s.), and is buried with
all three of his wives in the Old Cemetery there (Hale 803-1:23). He was a
descendant also of *Mayflower* passengers John Alden and Richard Warren.

He married, first, at Lebanon, 16 June 1774 (not in VR), **REBECCA
WHITE**, who was born 27 April 1752 at Lebanon, daughter of Nathaniel and
Lois (Coomer) White (VR 1:345), and died 14 December 1787 at Columbia, aged
35, "wife of John Jr." (g.s.).

He married, second, at Lebanon, 2 August 1789, **ANNE HUTCHINSON**,
who was born 5 September 1760 at Lebanon (VR 1:152), and died 5 June 1815 at
Columbia, aged 54, "second wife of John" (g.s.), daughter of Eleazer and Ruth
(Long) Hutchinson.

He married, third, 10 September 1817 at Coventry, Conn. (*VR* 261), **SUBMIT LYMAN**, who was born there 14 September 1771, daughter of Jacob and Mehitable (Bushnell) Lyman (VR 80) and died 31 March 1842, aged 70, "relict," at Columbia (g.s.). The will of Jacob Lyman of Coventry, dated 29 March 1792, proved 27 January 1802, names his wife Mehitable and daughter Submit with the condition "so long as she remains unmarried." A distribution of his estate 4 May 1805 included Submit Lyman.

John Little of Lebanon in his will dated 13 June 1777, proved 8 January 1799, bequeathed to son John £30, "he having a Traid" (Windham Dist. PR #2467).

In 1790 John was living in Lebanon with a household of one man, four boys under 16, and three females (p.16). In 1800 both John and his wife were listed as 45 or older (although Ann was only 40), and their family appears to have included two young men and one young woman 16-26, one girl 10-16, and one boy and four girls under 10 (p.718); either one of the children was married and living in their household with spouse and daughters, or John and Ann had at least three more daughters born between 1790 and 1800 than have been identified.

In his will, dated 23 November 1826, recorded 10 July 1833, John Little of Columbia requested that he be buried in Columbia close to his late dear wife. He named his wife Submit and brother Gamaliel, and mentioned but did not name heirs of daughter Rebecca West, deceased; heir of son Nathaniel Little, deceased; and heir of daughter Louisa Hunt, deceased. He named his sons John Little Jr. and Alanson Little executors (Andover District PR #1467).

Children of John and Rebecca (White) Little, recorded Hebron (VR 2:205):

i REBECCA LITTLE⁶, b. 14 March 1775; d. 8 May 1821 ae 47y; m. SAMUEL WEST, who d. 16 Oct. 1863 ae 87y 10m (g.s.). His gravestone and those of his wives and children refer to him as Col. Samuel West, and his grave has a War of 1812 marker (Hale 803-42). He m. (2) Ruby Bliss, d. 8 July 1831 ae 49; m. (3) Lucy Manning, d. 29 Aug. 1861 ae 76; and m. (4) Amanda Woodward, d. 11 Aug. 1878 ae 74. All are bur. Center Cem., Columbia.

West children, g.s. say "of Col. Samuel & Rebecca" (Hale 803-43): 1. *Eliza D. West⁷*, b. 18 Sept. 1798; d. 9 Oct. 1818 ae 20. 2. *Cynthia M. West*, b. 18 July 1801; d. 15 Jan. 1816 ae 15. 3. *John O. West*, b. 5 Dec. 1803; d. 9 Nov. 1822 ae 19. 4. *Marianna West*, b. 4 Feb. 1806; d. 7 Nov. 1817 ae 12. 5. *Malvina West*, b. 12 April 1808; d. 21 Nov. 1817 ae 10. 6. *Malinda West*, b. 2 Sept. 1810; m. George W. Morgan. 7. *Samuel Ferdinand West*, b. 13 Dec. 1812; m. Catherine Porter. 8. *William W. West*, b. 17 July 1815; d. 3 Nov. 1817 ae 3. 9. *Hannah Lucretia West*, b. 23 Sept. 1817.

ii   NATHANIEL LITTLE, b. 10 Sept. 1777; d. before 1826 leaving an "heir."

iii   WILLIAM LITTLE, b. 24 Dec. 1779; not in father's will.

iv   OTIS LITTLE, b. 5 March 1782; not in father's will.

v   JOHN LITTLE, b. 22 April 1784; d. 1 July 1833 ae 77 (g.s.); m. (1) SALLY
      ___, d. 8 May 1845 ae 57 (g.s.); bur. Center Cem., Columbia (Hale 803-
      2:33); m. prob. (2) ABIGAIL ____, b. ca 1804 Mass., his wife in 1850
      when he was a farmer ae 65 at Columbia, Conn. (p.348).
          Probable child: 1. *Samuel Little*[7], b. ca 1804; m. Clarissa ___; a farmer in
      Columbia 1850 (p.348).

vi   MELINDA LITTLE, b. 14 May 1787 (*VR* 1:191), d. 9 Sept. 1811 ae 25;
      bur. with parents but stone says "dau. of John and Anne."

Children. of John and Anne (Hutchinson) Little:

vii   ALANSON LITTLE, b. 4 May 1790 Lebanon (VR 1:191); d. 19 Aug. 1861
      ae 71 (g.s.); m. (1) PERCY YEOMANS (Weyman Ms; g.s. read as Tericy),
      d. 15 May 1843 ae 48; m. (2) Columbia, 1 Jan. 1845, LAVINIA
      YEOMANS (VR 16), d. 24 March 1847 ae 45 (g.s.); m. (3) WEALTHY
      (STRONG) BROWN, d. 22 July 1869 ae 79, "formerly wife of Russell
      Brown and widow of Alanson Little" (g.s., West St. Cem., Columbia). All
      except Wealthy are bur. Old Cem., Columbia (Hale 803-1:20). In 1850
      Alanson ae 57 was a farmer in Columbia, with Giles, Adeline, Isabella, and
      Julia O. (p.353).
          Children, all with first wife; some bur. with parents (census and g.s.); prob.
      incomplete: 1. *Abby Ann Little*[7], b. ca 1815; d. 28 March 1843 ae 28 (g.s.).
      2. *Giles Little*, b. ca 1822; m. 1850 Amanda C. Little (VR 29). 3. *Julia Orintha
      Little*, b. ca 1826; d. 27 Oct. 1851 ae 25 (g.s.). 4. *Jane Little*, b. ca 1831; d. 7 Oct.
      1859 ae 28 (g.s.). 5. *Adeline Little*, b. ca 1833. 6. *Isabella Little*, b. ca 1836.

viii LEMIRA LITTLE (twin?), b. ca 1793; d. 16 July 1812 ae 20 (g.s.); bur. with
      parents.

ix   AMIE LITTLE (twin?), b. ca 1793; d. 2 Dec. 1811 ae 18 (g.s.); bur. with
      parents.

x   LOUISA LITTLE, b. 2 July 1796; d. 14 April 1824; m. Dr. ORRIN HUNT,
      b. Columbia 12 Jan. 1793, d. there 24 Aug. 1850, son of Eldred and
      Huldah (Benton) Hunt; he m. (2) Adeline Cone (Weyman Ms). John
      Little's will notes that dau. Louisa is deceased and mentions her "heir."
          Hunt children (Weyman Ms): 1. *Louisa A. Hunt*[7], b. 23 April 1820; d. 1823.
      2. *John O. Hunt*, b. 27 Sept. 1822; m. Mary J. Kirkland.

xi   ABILINE LITTLE, b. ca 1803; d. 28 Nov. 1818 ae 15 (g.s.); bur. with parents.

Sources cited: *Coventry* VR. Lebanon VR as cited in the Barbour Index. Columbia Congregational Church Records, CSL. Hale Collection of Cemetery Inscriptions. Weyman Manuscript, box 408, bundle 11 (continues several lines). CENSUS: Lebanon, Windham Co., Conn. 1790 (M637-1) & 1800 (M32-2); Columbia, Tolland Co., Conn., 1850 (M432-50).

692. ELIZABETH LITTLE[5] (*Mary⁴ Samson, David³, Caleb², Henry¹*), daughter of John Little and his wife Mary Samson [143], was born at Lebanon, Conn., 1 April 1752 (VR 1:180), and baptized there 1752 (CR). She was living on 1 June 1803. She was a descendant also of *Mayflower* passengers John Alden and Richard Warren.

Elizabeth was named in the will of her father, John Little, dated 13 June 1777, proved 8 January 1799, and she shared in the distribution, signing a receipt on 1 April 1801 as Elizabeth Little (Windham Dist. PR #2467). She was of Lebanon, unmarried, on 25 June 1803 when she sold to her brother Consider 2½ acres inherited from her father's estate (Lebanon LR 18:393). She is assumed to have had no children.

Sources cited: Lebanon VR as cited in the Barbour Index. Columbia Congregational Church Records, CSL. Lebanon, Conn., Deeds. Conn. Probates, Windham District.

693. PRISCILLA LITTLE[5] (*Mary⁴ Samson, David³, Caleb², Henry¹*), daughter of John Little and his wife Mary Samson [143], was born at Lebanon, Conn., 19 October 1754 (VR 1:180), and was baptized at Columbia Congregational Church in 1754. She died at Columbia, Conn., 5 October 1838 aged 81 (g.s.). She was a descendant also of *Mayflower* passengers John Alden and Richard Warren.

She married, about 1776, **ELIPHALET WOODWORTH**. He was born in 1751 at Lebanon, Conn., son of Eliphalet and Anna (Lyman) Woodworth, and died at Columbia 16 October 1826 aged 76, as Eliphalet Woodward (g.s.).

John Little of Lebanon in his will dated 13 June 1777, proved 8 January 1799, left £120 to be divided among his four daughters Elisebeth, Priscila, Faith, and Elinor; Priscilla Woodworth shared in the distribution on 5 May 1800 (Windham Dist. PR #2467). On 17 March 1803 Eliphalet Woodworth and his wife Priscilla of Lebanon sold to her brother Consider Little the 57 rods that had been set off to her from the estate (Lebanon LR 18:358).

In 1800 the household of Eliphalet Woodworth, at Coventry, Conn., included a man and a woman 45 or over, two young men and one young woman 16-26, a girl 10-16, and a boy under 10 (p 667).

In 1850 three of the children of Eliphalet and Priscilla (Eliphalet ae 53, Charles ae 72, and Persilla ae 70) were living together in West Springfield; Lucina Pinneo aged 70 was also in the household (p.160).

Children of Eliphalet and Priscilla (Little) Woodworth, b. Lebanon (Weyman Ms; no VR Lebanon or Columbia):

    i   CHARLES WOODWORTH[6], b. 1777; d. West Springfield 29 Aug. 1853 of consumption, "married" (Mass. VR 75:228). In 1850 he was a farmer in West Springfield. Charles Woodworth of Columbia, Conn., pub. m. int. West Springfield, 17 Oct. 1829, with LAURA PERKINS of West Springfield (*VR* 2:177); poss. m. (2) PRISCILLA MINER.

    ii   PRISCILLA WOODWORTH, b. 1780. A Persilla Woodworth ae 70 was living with Eliphalet and Charles in West Springfield in 1850, but she seems to be the Priscilla who d. Springfield 26 Aug. 1856 ae 76, b. Stonington, Conn., of Thomas and Lucretia (___) Miner (Mass. VR 102:233), so she may have been wife of one of the two brothers.

    iii JASPER WOODWORTH, b. 24 Aug. 1782; d. 6 Sept. 1811 at South Coventry, Conn.; m. 24 Nov. 1803, SARAH ELIZABETH REED, b. 23 Aug. 1783, d. 13 Sept. 1849.
        Children: 1. *Asahel Allen Woodworth*[7], b. 9 Sept. 1804; living Ohio 1837. 2. *Sarah Elizabeth Woodworth*, b. 1 May 1807. 3. *Charles B. Woodworth*, b. 4 Feb. 1808.

    iv ZERVIAH WOODWORTH, b. 1785; d. 18 Jan. 1810 (Weyman Ms).

    v   CHESTER WOODWORTH, b. Feb. 1789.

    vi SARAH WOODWORTH, b. 1793; d. 18 March 1796 (Weyman Ms).

    vii ELIPHALET WOODWORTH, b. 1797; d. 17 Dec. 1869, Chicopee, widowed (Mass. VR 221:9); his wife evidently d. before 1850 when he was a farmer at West Springfield. He, of Columbia, Conn., pub. m. int. 25 April 1824 with POLLY BAILEY of West Springfield (*VR* 2:177).
        Children included: 1. *Solomon B. Woodworth*[7], b. ca 1828 Conn.; a machinist, of Springfield when he m. West Springfield, 17 Sept. 1854, Ann Maynard of Norwich, Conn., ae 18 (Mass. VR 78:338).

Sources cited: *West Springfield VR. Coventry, Conn., VR.* Lebanon VR as cited in the Barbour Index. Columbia Congregational Church Records, CSL. "Inscriptions from Old Cemeteries in Connecticut, Columbia," *NEHGR* 60 [1906]. Weyman Manuscript, box 408, bundle 11. CENSUS: 1850 West Springfield, Hamden Co. (M432-318). **See also:** *MF 16 [Alden]*, 2:112-13.

694. FAITH LITTLE[5] (*Mary[4] Samson, David[3], Caleb[2], Henry[1]*), daughter of John Little and his wife Mary Samson [143], was born probably at Lebanon or Colchester, Conn., in November 1756 and baptized later that year at Columbia Congregational Church. She died at Columbia 12 October 1844, aged "87 and [11]/[12] years ... widow of Cap. Nathan" (g.s.). She was a descendant also of *Mayflower* passengers John Alden, Myles Standish, and Richard Warren.

She married, evidently as his second wife, probably about 1795, **NATHAN[IEL] HYDE**, probably the son of Nathaniel and Anna (Dunham) Hyde born at Lebanon 1 February 1744/5 (VR 1:149). He died at Lebanon in 1798. He married, first, SUBMIT ____, who died as "wife of Capt. Nathaniel Hyde," 8 January 1794 aged 48 years, and is buried in the Old Cemetery, Columbia, with several of their children (Hale 803-1:15).

John Little of Lebanon in his will dated 13 June 1777, proved 8 January 1799, left £120 to be divided among his four daughters: Elisebeth, Priscila, Faith, and Elinor; Faith Hyde signed a receipt for her share on 1 April 1801 (Windham Dist. PR #2467).

Nathaniel Hyde Jr. was living in Lebanon in 1790 with one boy under 16 and seven females (p.146). Nathaniel Hyde Sr. was nearby with two men over 16 and one female (*ibid.*).

Bond was posted 8 November 1798 by Joel Loomis of Lebanon as administrator of the estate of Capt. Nathaniel Hyde "the younger," deceased. On May 1800 Asahel Dewey was appointed guardian to Nathaniel Hyde, aged about 16 years. A distribution dated 6 May 1800 included widow Faith Hyde; youngest daughter Lydia Hyde; Submit; youngest and only son Nathaniel Hyde; Elizabeth, wife of John Adams; Sarah, wife of Benjamin Coleman; land set out to heirs of Capt. Nathaniel Hyde out of the estate of Mr. Nathaniel Hyde the elder, deceased. A second distribution on 3 April 1802 at Lebanon mentions articles of Capt. Nathaniel Hyde the younger, late of Lebanon, deceased: to wife of John Adams; to wife of Benjamin Coleman; to Submit Hyde; to Lydia Hyde; and to Nathaniel Hyde. Nothing further was found in Columbia or Lebanon VR.

The distribution of the estate of Mr. Nathaniel Hyde Sr., of Lebanon, 3 March 1800, included "heirs of Nathaniel Hyde Jr." (Lebanon Dist. PR).

The 1800 census listed Faith Hyde in Lebanon with a household consisting of herself, 45 or over, and one young man and two young women 16-26 (p.866). She was of Lebanon on 21 April 1803 when she sold to her brother Consider Little the one-half acre and 31 rods that had been set off to her from their father's estate (Lebanon LR 18:359).

In 1820 Widow Faith Hyde was living alone in Columbia, and [her stepson] Nathaniel Hyde was living next door (p.588). In 1830 she was still there, alone, aged 70-80, next to Nathaniel Jr.'s widow Asenath Hyde (p.283). She was 83 years old, living at Tolland, in 1840 when she made an affidavit in support of her sister Eleanor's application for a pension (White, 33). Probably all of Nathaniel's children were with his first wife. There is no indication that Faith had any children of her own.

Sources cited: Columbia Church Records. White, *Abstracts of Revolutionary War Pension Files,* citing W25346. Hale Collection of Conn. Cemetery Inscriptions. Conn. Probate Records, Lebanon and Windham Districts. CENSUS: Tolland Co., Conn., Lebanon 1790 (M637-1), 1810 Lebanon (M32-2) & Coventry (M32-3), Coventry 1820 (M33-3) & 1830 (M19:8). **See also:** *MF 16 [Alden],* 2:112-13.

695.   ELEANOR LITTLE⁵ (*Mary⁴ Samson, David³, Caleb², Henry¹*), daughter of John Little and his wife Mary Samson [143], was born 20 May 1762 (Rev. pension rec.), probably at Colchester, Conn. She was living in 1840 (*ibid.*). She was a descendant also of *Mayflower* passengers John Alden and Richard Warren.

She married, 2 November 1791 at Hebron, Conn. (VR 2:4), **ASAHEL ALLEN**, who was born at Lebanon, Conn., 4 March 1763, and died 12 April 1837 (pension rec.).

John Little of Lebanon in his will dated 13 June 1777, proved 8 January 1799, left £120 to be divided among his four daughters: Elisebeth, Priscila, Faith, and Elinor (Conn. PR, Windham Dist. #2467). It is not clear why Eleanor did not share in the distribution of her father's estate on 5 May 1800.

Asahel Allen served in the Revolutionary War in the Connecticut Line. He was living at Columbia when he applied for a pension 21 August 1832 in Tolland County. Eleanor applied for a widow's pension 11 February 1839 in New London County, Conn., and her sister Faith Hyde, aged 83, of Tolland made an affidavit (White, 33). The file contains pages from a Bible giving birth dates of Asahel and Eleanor, and his date of death, and their marriage record certified by the Hebron town clerk.

In 1810 the household of Asahel Allen at Columbia consisted of a man and a woman 45 or older and one little boy under 10 (p.617).

The will of Asahel Allen of Columbia, dated 31 March 1837, recorded 20 April 1837, names his wife Elleaner; nephew Joseph Collins, who was living with his family "in part of my dwelling house." Among others who are named, without relationship, is Ashel Allen Woodworth of Ohio [grandson of Eleanor's sister Priscilla].

There is no indication that Asahel and Eleanor had any surviving children.

Sources cited: Hebron VR as cited in Barbour Collection. White, *Abstracts of Revolutionary War Pension Files*, citing W25346. CENSUS: 1810 Lebanon, Tolland Co., Conn. (M252-3). **See also:** *MF16: Alden*, 2:112-13.

696. SARAH⁵ SAMPSON (*Jonathan⁴, David³, Caleb², Henry¹*),daughter of Jonathan Samson [144] and his first wife, Sarah Drew, was born probably at Plymouth, probably in August 1748. (Her parents married in September 1747, and her mother died in August 1748, most likely as a result of childbirth.)

Evidence that she was the daughter of Sarah (Drew) Sampson comes from land records. On 13 April 1748 Sarah, wife of Jonathan Sampson, received one-sixth part of real estate that had descended to [her mother] Hannah (Barnes) Drew from John Barnes and wife Mary (Plymouth PR 11:2-5). On 18 April 1798, Jonathan Sampson of Plymouth, labourer [a term that indicates he owned no land], and Sarah Sampson his daughter sold an undivided half part of a lot in South Meadows cedar swamp in Carver to Nathaniel Goodwin, Esq., of Plymouth, for $10 (*ibid.*, 85:81). Some of the record is illegible, but it states that the other half of the lot was purchased by Goodwin from Zacheus Barnes in 1775, so the property involved had evidently belonged to the Barnes family.

Sarah was unmarried on 24 April 1798 when she acknowledged the deed. She was at that time about 50 years old, so she cannot be the Sarah Sampson who married in 1803 Consider Clark and had children born in 1803, 1805, and 1808 (*VR* 414). If Sarah married at all it was in later life and she did not have children.

Sources cited: *Plymouth VR*. Plymouth County Deeds

697. PETER PINEO⁵ (*Elizabeth⁴ Samson, David³, Caleb², Henry¹*), son of Peter Pineo and his wife Elizabeth Samson [145], was born at Lebanon, Conn., 30 July 1745 (VR 1:243). He died 14 September 1790, of Granville, Nova Scotia (Marble, 2:63), in Providence Island, Bahamas, aged 45 (Pineo Ms). He was a descendant also of *Mayflower* passengers John Alden and Myles Standish.

He married, first, at Cornwallis, Nova Scotia, 14 May 1772, **EUNICE BENTLEY**, who was born at Lebanon 8 May 1750, daughter of David and Ann (Baldwin) Bentley (VR 1:32). She was living in 1815 when her son Austin named her in his will. Two of his brothers married two of her sisters. Peter is said to have married, second, Sarah, probably Cox (*Kings Co. History*, 778), but this cannot be correct as Eunice was named as the widow in his estate papers.

Peter's father was an early emigrant to Cornwallis in 1763, taking up land from which Acadians had been evicted several years earlier. On 4 June 1772, Peter Pineo of Cornwallis, yeoman, deeded land there to his son Peter (Kings Co. LR 2:307). Peter was, among other things, a merchant, and he had a store opposite his home on Queen St., Bridgetown, Nova Scotia (Pineo Ms). In 1790 he sailed to the West Indies with a cargo of lumber, but the ship was lost with all on board (*ibid.*). Peter Pineo Sr. is "said to have been a loyalist; his son Peter certainly was" (*ibid.*, 1:85)

Letters of administration on the estate of Peter Pineo late of Granville were given to Charles Coulbourn of Digby, a creditor, on 22 December 1790; the widow Eunice was named (*Annapolis Co. PR Abstracts*, 1:232 R).

Children of Peter and Eunice (Bentley) Pineo, first three rec. Cornwallis, N.S. (*Kings Co. History*), rest at Granville, Annapolis Co., N.S. (Pineo Ms.):

i   AUSTIN PINEO[6], b. 28 Jan. 1773; d. 1815. In his will dated 1815 [day and month blank], Austin Pineo of Annapolis in the county of Annapolis, weak in body, left to "my dearly beloved mother Eunice Pineo and to my sister Betsey Pineo the use and occupation of all my estate real and personal (that is to say, the interest arising from said estate)" equally during the life of his mother, and after her death, to sister Betsey and her heirs. "Immediately after my decease my Mother and Sister are to have a complete suit of mourning, as also my Brother George Pineo's two daughters to have a common mourning suit," and named "dearly beloved brother William Pineo of Cornwallis and Samuel Vetch Bayard of Wilmot, Annapolis County, executors and sister Betsey executrix" (Annapolis Co. Est. Folio P18 [1815]).

ii JOB PINEO, b. 10 Oct. 1774; d. Aylesford, N.S., 13 June 1846 (Marble 4:35); m. by 1798 MARGERY BURNS, dau. of Francis Burns of Wilmot Twp., Annapolis Co., N.S. Job was a blacksmith and farmer at Black Rock, N.S. (Pineo Ms, 15:5-8). Margery Pineo shared in the distribution of the estate of Francis Burns, yeoman, 30 Aug. 1798 (*Annapolis PR Abstracts*, #3327; Estate Folio B15 [1798]), and was named as the wife of Job Pineo in the administration of her brother William Burns of Digby in 1801 (*ibid.*, #3330; Estate Folio B19 [1801]).

Children, b. Black Rock, Colchester, N.S. (Pineo Ms 15:5-8): 1. *Charles Pineo[7]*, d. 20 June 1889, a policeman; no ch. 2. *Thomas Pineo*, m. Mary Dunham, "several children. Well off." 3. *Job Pineo*, lost at sea. 4. *William Pineo*, "d. in U.S." 5. *Bentley Pineo*, m. ___ Johnson; res. Ontario. 6. *George Pineo*, farmer at Grafton, N.S.; m. ___Fitch. 7. *Amelia Pineo*, m. Gurdon Fenner. 8. *Ann Pineo*, m. David White of Harborville, N.S. 9. *Nettie Pineo*, m. Hiram Balser or Baker. 10. *Lucy Pineo*, m. ___ Saunders of Boston.

iii BETTY PINEO, b. 29 Oct. 1776; d. Granville 24 May 1777 (Marble, 2:63).

iv GEORGE PINEO, b. 6 April 1778; d. 3 Aug. 1801, Annapolis Royal (Marble, 4:35); m. ELIZABETH ____, who was given letters of adm. on the estate of George Pineo, shoemaker, of the township of Annapolis, 3 Aug. 1801 (*Annapolis PR Abstracts*, #3896; Est. Folio P12 [1801]). The will of his brother Austin in 1815 says that George left two daughters.

v PETER BENTLEY PINEO, b. 3 Dec. 1779; m. 2 Sept. 1802, OLIVE COMSTOCK, b. 15 Dec. 1775, d. ca 1844, dau. of Ezekiel and Phebe (DeWolf) Comstock (*Cornwallis Twp Book*).

> Children (*Kings Co. Hist.*, 778; Pineo Ms 15:10; first three *Cornwallis Twp Book*): 1. *Perigreen /Austin Peregrine Pineo*[7], b. 9 July 1803; m. Jemima Porter. 2. *Edward Henry Pineo*, b. 22 Feb. 1805; d. in Ill.; m. ____ Pineo, dau. Stephen Pineo. 3. *Phebe Gore Pineo*, b. 17 May 1807; m. Benjamin Cleveland Morse. 4. *George Pineo*, b. ca 1810; d. unm. 5. *Jehial DeWolf Pineo*, b. 17 July 1815; m. Mercy M. Woodworth. 6. *Caroline Pineo*, b. 11 July 1817; m. Charles Bradford Darling (Weyman Ms).

vi CHARLES PINEO, b. 6 July 1781.

vii JOSEPH PINEO, b. 16 March 1783; d. Granville, N.S., 2 Nov. 1786 ae 3 (Marble, 2:63).

viii BETTY PINEO, b. 23 July 1786; prob. the Betsy Pineo, of Annapolis, named as executrix in will of her brother Austin in 1815.

ix JOSEPH PINEO, b. 1 April 1788.

x WILLIAM PINEO, prob. d. Cornwallis 15 Feb. 1832 (Marble, 4:35); named in will of brother Austin.

Sources cited: Lebanon, Conn., VR. *Cornwallis Township Book*. Marble, *Deaths, Burials, and Probate of Nova Scotians, 1749 – 1799, From Primary Sources* (1990). *Annapolis County Probate Abstracts*, citing Probate Will Book 1:232. Eaton, *History of Kings County* (1910). Pineo Manuscript (see Bibliography).

698. DAVID PINEO[5] (*Elizabeth*[4] *Samson, David*[3]*, Caleb*[2]*, Henry*[1]), son of Peter Pineo and his wife Elizabeth Samson [145], was born at Lebanon, Conn., 8 September 1747, a twin with his brother Jonathan (VR 1:243). He died 3 January 1843 at Machias, Me., and is buried there (Pineo Ms), or 3 February 1843 (Marble, 5:35). He was a descendant also of Pilgrims John Alden and Myles Standish.

He married at Cornwallis, Nova Scotia, 12 November 1767, **REBECCA WEST**, daughter of Capt. Stephen and Margery (____) West (*Twp Book*, 67). She was born about 1749, perhaps at Tisbury, Martha's Vineyard, died 23 May 1803, and is buried in Canard Burying Ground, Canard, N.S. (*Twp Book*, 76).

On 3 February 1769 Peter Pineo of Cornwallis, yeoman, deeded land there to his son David (Kings Co. LR 1:168).

The Pineo Manuscript (10:11) says of David,

> He was a very religious man ... scrupulously kept Saturday night and had the catechism taught in his family. In his last years a cancer developed in his hand. He set his house in order, bade goodbye to his children, saying he might never see them again, and went for treatment to Machias, at the house of his twin brother Jonathan. He died at Machias and was buried there ... A copy of his family record in his own hand was taken from the family Bible.

Children of David and Rebecca (West) Pineo, b. Cornwallis, N.S. (Bible rec.; *Twp Book*, 46); Bible record (spelling *Pinneo*) used when birth dates differ:

i   SARAH PINEO[6], "my first daughter," b. 3 Sept. 1768, on Saturday at two o'clock p.m.; d. Tappan, N.Y., 23 April 1842 (Weyman Ms); m. at Cornwallis, 4 May 1786 (*Twp Book*), HENRY GESNER, b. 10 Nov. 1756 Tappan, N.Y., d. Cornwallis 13 Oct. 1850, son of John Henry and Femetjie (Brouwer) Gesner. He was a Loyalist who fled to Nova Scotia.

    Gesner children, rec. Cornwallis, N.S. (*Twp Book.*, 35): 1. *Rebecca Gesner[7]*, b. 27 May 1787. 2. *John Henry Gesner*, b. 20 March 1789. 3. *Elizabeth Gesner*, b. 11 March 1791. 4. *David H. Gesner*, b. 7 March 1793. 5. *Famicha Gesner*, b. 27 March 1795. 6. *Abraham Pineo Gesner*, b. 2 May 1797; d. Halifax, N.S., 1864; a physician and geologist who patented the discovery of kerosene oil (*Appleton's Ency.*). 7. *Gibbs Henry Gesner*, b. 1 July 1799. 8. *Sarah Gesner*, b. 21 Feb. 1802. 9. *Henry Gesner*, b. 17 April 1804; m. Harriett S. Pineo. 10. *Ann Maria Gesner*, b. 28 Sept. 1806. 11. *Lavinia Caroline Gesner*, b. 22 May 1809. 12. *Charlotte Amelia Gesner*, b. 8 Sept. 1813.

ii   DAVID SAMSON PINEO, "my first son," b. 13 Oct. 1770, "Saturday two o'clock in the night"; prob. the David S. Pineo who d. Pugwash, N.S., 28 Jan. 1838 ae 66; m. Ann ___, d. 25 — 1847 ae 72; bur. Anglican Cem., Pugwash (Marble, 4:35).

    Possible son: 1. *Henry G. Pineo[7]*, whose dau. Amelia, d. 1 Jan. 1840 ae 18m, is bur. with David S. and Ann (Marble, 4:35).

iii   GIBBS PINEO, "my second son," b. 12 May 1773, "Tuesday 6 a m"; d. 12 May 1829 Wolfville, N.S., ae 56 (Marble, 5:35); m. at Cornwallis, 29 Jan. 1801, CHARLOTTE COMSTOCK, b. ca 1785, dau. of Ezekiel and Phebe (DeWolf) Comstock (*Twp Book*, 63).

    Children, first four rec. Cornwallis (*Twp Book* 47), rest Pineo Ms (10:198-99): 1. *Thomas Lewis Pineo[7]*, b. 24 April 1802; m. (1) Mary Randolph, (2) Mary Robertson. 2. *Charlotte Pineo*, b. 23 March 1804; m. (bond 6 Oct. 1825) Thomas Manning. 3. *Parlina Pineo*, b. 6 April 1806; d. unm., "a fine girl" (Pineo Ms.).

4. *Jonathan Pineo*, b. 5 Sept. 1808; m. (bond 7 June 1846) Phebe Ann Turner. 5. *David Gibbs Pineo*, m. Abigail Louise Forsythe. 6. *Lavinia Pineo*, prob. m. (bond 24 Dec. 1823) Oliver King. 7. *Sarah Pineo*, m. Thomas Manning (Pineo Ms). 8. *Ezekiel Pineo*, m. Catherine Harris; res. Chelsea or Revere.

iv   ESTHER PINEO, "second daughter," b. 12 April 1775, "Tuesday 8 p m at night"; m. 29 May 1795 LEMUEL BORDEN, b. 26 Sept. 1768, son of Perry and Mary (Ells) Borden (*Horton Twp. Book*, 85).

       Borden children rec. Horton (*ibid.*; marriages, Pineo Ms 10:248-49): 1. *Rebecca Borden[7]*, b. 26 Feb. 1796 Cornwallis; m. Joseph Lockhart, a sea captain. 2. *Peace Borden*, b. 24 Feb. 1800; d. 30 Oct. 1885; m. John Gould. 3. *Mary Ann Borden*, b. 13 Feb. 1802; m. Stephen Gould. 4. *Lemuel Perry Borden*, b. 30 Sept. 1804; m. Margaret Cummings. 5. *Ruby Borden*, b. 2 Aug. 1811; m. Gurdon Cox. 6. *David Henry Borden*, b. 23 Sept. 1815.

v   LEVINIAH PINEO, "third daughter," b. 2 June 1777, "9 p m"; m. as his second wife, BENJAMIN BORDEN, b. 28 April 1779 (Weyman Ms), son of Perry and Mary (Ells) Borden, brother of Lemuel who m. Lavinia's sister Esther, widower of Martha Wells; no ch. (Pineo Ms 10:290).

vi   ELIZABETH PINEO, "fourth daughter," b. 17 Oct. 1779, "Sunday 1 a m"; m. ROBERT HOLMES SMITH.

       Smith children (Pineo Ms 10:292): 1. *Rebecca Smith[7]*, m. (1) ___ Stewart, (2) ___ Creelman. 2. *David Smith*, m. ___ Brown. 3. *Isaiah Smith*, m. ___ Brown, dau. of Squire Brown. 4. *Lavinia Smith*, m. James Nelson. 5. *Eleanor Smith*, m. ___ Bradley. 6. *Stewart Smith*, Rev., a Presbyterian minister in U.S.

vii   JOHNATHAN PINEO, "third son," b. 4 May 1782, "Saturday, five [?] a m"; d. unm. Miramichi, N.S.

viii   RUBY PINEO, "fifth daughter," b. 19 July 1784, Monday 6 p m"; m. Cornwallis, N.S., 17 Feb. 1813 (*Twp Book* 64), DANIEL HUNTLEY, b. Horton, N.S., 28 Oct. 1839.

       Huntley children, b. Cornwallis, N.S. (Twp Bk 37): 1. *Daniel Huntley[7]*, b. 6 March 1814. 2. *Rebeckah Ann Huntley*, b. 15 May 1816; d. 1893. 3. *Sarah Jane Huntley*, b. 10 April 1819. 4. *Esther Huntley*, b. 15 Dec. 1821. 5. *David Rufus Huntley*, b. 11 July 1826.

ix   ELIJAH PINEO, "fourth son," b. 22 July 1786, "Tuesday 12 at night"; d. ("Alijah") 30 Aug. 1869 ae 82 (g.s.); bur. Old Cemetery, Union Church of Scots Bay; m. 7 April 1813, ELIZABETH NEWCOMB, b. 10 Oct. 1787 Perraux, N.S., d. 1869, dau. of Benjamin and Abigail (Sanford) Newcomb; res. Scots Bay, N.S. (*Kings Co. History*, 778; Pineo Ms 10:330). He was a farmer at Sheffields Mills, Cornwallis, "a kind, good man, and very industrious [but] drank so family was poor" (Pineo Ms 10:330).

Children (first three births rec. *Twp Book*, 47; all in Pineo Ms 10:331):
1. *Eleanor Pineo*[7], b. 28 Aug. 1814; m. George Edward Newcomb. 2. *Rebecca Pineo*,
b. 9 March 1817; d. 26 April 1839 unm., "as fine a girl as ever lived" (Pineo Ms).
3. *Elijah West Pineo*, b. 18 March 1819; m. Rachel Barteaux. 4. *Barnaby Newcomb*
Pineo, b. 19 July 1822; m. Almira Lydia Jenks. 5. *David Pineo*, b. 23 June 1824; d.y.
6. *Elizabeth Pineo*, b. 21 Feb. 1827; m. William Jess.

x   REBECCA PINEO, "sixth daughter," b. 1 June 1792; d. 17 Jan. 1856; m.
Cornwallis, 7 Feb. 1810, BARNABY NEWCOMB, b. 13 April 1786, d. 21
Nov. 1821 ae 36, son of Benjamin and Abigail (Sanford) Newcomb (*Twp*
Book 66); m. (2) 19 May 1826, Capt. JOHN NEWCOMB, b. 8 Sept. 1795,
brother of her first husband.

   Newcomb children with first husband, rec. Cornwallis (Twp Bk, 43; each
birth one year later in Pineo Ms 10:360-61 and Weyman Ms): 1. *Rebeckah*
Newcomb[7], b. 20 Nov. 1811; m. Gardiner Dodge. 2. *[William] Freeman Newcomb*, b.
22 Aug. 1814; m. Cinderella Aurelia Lyons. 3. *Lavinia Newcomb*, b. 12 Aug. 1817;
m. George F. Jackson. 4. *Elizabeth Newcomb*, b. 15 Sept. 1819; m. Stephen North.

   Newcomb children with second husband (Pineo Ms): 5. *David Barnaby*
Newcomb, b. 6 Sept. 1827; m. Lucilla Borden. 6. *Sarah Alice Newcomb*, b. 27 Jan.
1830; m. Henry Loomer. 7. *Hester Ann Newcomb*, b. 15 May 1833; m. Joseph A.
T. Jackson. 8. *John Henry Newcomb*, b. 2 Dec. 1837; d.y.

Sources cited: Lebanon, Conn., VR, as cited in the Barbour Index. *Cornwallis and Horton Township*
Books. Nova Scotia Marriage Bonds, on line. Pineo Manuscript, includes David Pineo's Family
Bible, transcribed by Mrs. George Jackson of Cornwallis. Eaton, *The History of Kings County* (1910).
Appleton's Encyclopedia of American Biography.

699.   JONATHAN PINEO[5] (*Elizabeth*[4] *Samson, David*[3], *Caleb*[2], *Henry*[1]), son of
Peter Pineo and his wife Elizabeth Samson [145], was born at Lebanon,
Connecticut, 8 September 1747, "third son," a twin with his brother David (VR
1:243). He died at Cooper, Maine, 10 June 1821, at the house of his son Otis
(Pineo Ms 14:1). He was a descendant also of *Mayflower* passengers John Alden and
Myles Standish.

   He married, first, about 1769, **ESTHER LIBBY**, who was born at Machias,
Maine, in May 1750, and died there 10 January 1796, daughter of Timothy and
Sarah (Stone) Libby (*Maine Hist. Mag.,* 8:70).

   He married, second, at Eastport, Maine, 3 October 1796, **BRIDGET**
(BYRON) DOTY, who was born in Dublin, Ireland, about 1764, and died at
Cherryfield, Maine, aged 99 years. She was the widow of [probably James] Doty,
supposedly of St. Andrews, New Brunswick. Her first husband may have been the
James Doty born at Plymouth 28 November 1757, son of Edward and Phebe

(Phinney) Doten, who is said to have gone to New Brunswick (*Doty Fam.*, 159). Bridget is said to have been a "very intelligent woman, a good historian, having a remarkable memory" (Pineo Ms 14:1).

Jonathan went to Machias about 1770, it is claimed either from New Haven, Conn., or from Nova Scotia. He joined the Congregational Church there and was among those who subscribed to the building of a meeting house in 1774; he was an active participant in town affairs, serving as assessor and surveyor from 1784 to 1795. In 1790 Jonathan "Pinco" was living in Machias with three men, four boys under 16, and three females (p.52).

Jonathan was a sergeant in the Revolutionary War; and called lieutenant in the muster roll of Machias in May 1794. He was last noted in Machias in 1798 (the last mention of any Pineo there was of David in 1801). The next Maine census to list Jonathan was that of 1820, when Jonathan Pineo Sr. was in Plantation No. 15, Washington County (p.271). In 1850 Bridget Pineo, aged 86, born in Maine [*sic*], was living in Cherryfield, Me., in the household of Joseph C. Lewis, a trader aged 33, and wife Mary (p.21).

Volume 14 of the Pineo Manuscript, which covers Jonathan's family, bears no date but begins with a notation, "this book belongs to Rev. Addison P. Foster, Beacon St., Room 85, Boston, Mass." A note recorded with the family of grand-daughter Louisa (Pineo) Hand says "grandmother [Bridget] was at the Harbor [Sag Harbor, N.Y.] in 1814 — Stephen H. Hand."

Children of Jonathan and Esther (Libby) Pineo, b. Machias, Me. (Pineo Ms Vol. 14, cites Machias records and a list of Jonathan's children in an "old document found in the trunk of George Pineo who was lost at sea"):

i JONATHAN PINEO[6], b. 1 April 1770; d. 1860, Cooper, Me. (Weyman Ms); m. (1) 23 Oct. 1794, BETSY BRACY, b. 1779, d. 1824 (Pineo Ms 14:10-16); m. (2) ___ (___) SPRAGUE. In 1850 he was living at Cooper, Me., in the household of Eli T. Sprague (p.229).

Children (spouses, Weyman Ms): 1. *Lydia Pineo[7]*, b. 1796; m. William Hitchings. 2. *Esther Pineo*, b. 1798; m. John Hodgdon; res. Cooper, Me., then Iowa. 3. *Mary Pineo*, b. 1800; m. Jonathan Munson. 4. *Otis Pineo*, b. 1802. 5. *Hiram Pineo*, b. 1804; m. Sarah Bryant. 6. *Bethiah Pineo*, b. 1806. 7. *Betsey Pineo*, b. 1808; m. Solomon Munson. 8. *Sally Pineo*, b. 1810; m. Otis Mitchell. 9. *Julia Pineo*, b. 1812; m. Lewis Foster. 10. *Caroline Pineo*, b. 1814; m. Samuel Sevey. 11. *Ellen Pineo*, b. 1816; m. Lyman Jones.

ii OTIS PINEO, b. 1 March 1772; d. April 1858 Harrington, Me., ae 86; m. (1) at Machias, 4 Nov. 1797, LOIS HANSCOM, dau. Aaron and Sally and Sally (Sevey) Hanscom; m. (2) ca 1802, his stepsister MARY ANN DOTY, b. Sept. 1783, d. 22 July 1866 ae 82 (Pineo Ms 14:14).

Children (*ibid.*), order uncertain: 1. *Louisa Pineo*[7], b. 22 April 1803; m. Capt. Robert F. Hand of Sag Harbor, N.Y. 2. *Priscilla Pineo*, d. soon after m. 21 Jan. 1818 to Jonathan Carey. 3. *Mary Ann Pineo*, m. Capt. Jesse Halsey of Sag Harbor, N.Y. 4. *William Pineo*, b. 5 March 1809 Columbia, Me.; m. Mary Putnam. 5. *Otis Pineo*, b. 12 Feb. 1811 Machias, Me.

iii DAVID PINEO, b. 17 Feb. 1774; d. 24 Jan. 1863 Calais, Me.; m. at Machias, Me., 13 Dec. 1796, PRISCILLA HILL, b. Machias 28 July 1780, d. St. Stephen's, Me., 13 Sept. 1850, dau. of Japhet and Hannah (Knight) Hill. He was a Universalist minister (Pineo Ms, 14:48-49).

Children (*ibid.*): 1. *Eliza C. Pineo*[7], b. 24 Jan. 1798; m. Joseph Wilson; rem. to N.Y. 2. *Mary Ann Pineo*, b. 2 Dec. 1800; m. James Boies. 3. *John Pineo*, b. 4 March 1802; d. 11 Oct. 1802. 4. *David Pineo*, b. 25 Sept. 1803; m. Amelia Sedgeley (see *MD* 46:260). 5. *Hannah Hill Pineo*, b. 7 Nov. 1806; m. Ferdinand Tinker. 6. *Amelia Pineo*, b. 19 March 1809; m. William P. Trott of Woolwich, Me. 7. *Stephen Hill Pineo*, b. 19 April 1811; m. Sarah Potter. 8. *Jane Smith Pineo*, b. 23 Dec. 1820; d. 21 Oct. 1841 ae 21, unm.; bur. St. Stephens, N.B.

iv GEORGE PINEO, b. 26 Feb. 1776; d. ae 39, lost at sea. He "sailed from Boston in the War of 1812 and was never heard from again ... he was a Frenchman in appearance, wore ruffled shirts ..." (Pineo Ms 14:5). His trunk survived and in it were found several documents in cipher, one listing the dates of his brothers' marriages, and a record of the births of the children in the family.

v ELIZABETH PINEO, b. 24 March 1778; d. 1808, ae 30, killed by a runaway horse (Pineo Ms 14:36); m. ISAAC HANSCOM, son of Aaron and Sally (Sevey) Hanscom; he m. (2) Betsey Drisco, (3) Eliza Corey (Weyman Ms).

Hanscom children (Pineo Ms 14:102): 1. *Otis Pineo Hanscom*[7]. 2. *George W. Hanscom*, m. Bethiah Andrews. 3. *Ellis Hanscom*, b. 14 April 1802; m. Sarah Bowker. 4. *John Hanscom*, m. ___ Getchell. 5. *Lovina Hanscom*, m. Benjamin Harmon. 6. *Eliza Hanscom*, m. Aaron Andrews.

vi TIMOTHY PINEO, b. 26 Sept. 1780; d. Jonesboro, Me., Oct. 1861; m. SUSANNAH (NOYES) WATTS, widow of Thomas Greenleaf Watts and dau. of Josiah and Eunice (Watts) Noyes of Yarmouth, Me., b. Rowley ca 1776, d. Jan. 1855 ae 78; res. Jonesboro (Pineo Ms 14:138).

Children (*ibid.*): 1. *William O. Pineo*[7]; m. Abiah W. Dunbar. 2. *Mary Pineo*, d. 1892 ae 85 at Deblois, Me.; m. Edmund Libby. 3. *Jacob Pineo*, b. 11 Nov. 1813 Jonesboro; d. unm. 4. *Abigail Pineo*, b. 6 Jan. 1817; d. 1892; m. Peter Farnsworth.

vii ESTHER PINEO, b. 27 Jan. 1783; d. Machias ca 1844, unm.

viii PETER PINEO, b. 8 April 1785; d. 30 Dec. 1860 ae 75; m. (1) 1 Nov.
      1814, HANNAH LAMB, who d. 1821, dau. of James Lamb; m. (2) at St.
      Stephen's, N.B., 5 Jan. 1822, JANE CHRISTIE, b. 13 Oct. 1805, dau. of
      James and Susannah (Hill) Christie and sister of Priscilla who m. Peter's
      brother David. He served in the War of 1812 and later was in the lumber
      business at St. Stephen's. In 1860 they were in Topsfield, Me., in
      household of son Hiram C. (p.88). Jane was living in 1888 at Topsfield,
      Me., ae 84 (Pineo Ms 14:40). See biographical note in brother Dan's
      account, below.
           Children, b. St. Stephen's, N.B., first two with Hannah, rest with Jane (Pineo
      Ms 14:158-60): 1. *George William Pineo*[7], b. 20 Dec. 1818; m. (1) Eliza Jane
      Courtland, (2) Lydia Maria Robbins 2. *William Pineo*, d. 15 May 1821 as inf.
      3. *Peter Pineo*, b. 8 Oct. 1825; d. 22 June 1842 ae 18. 4. *Hannah Pineo*, b. 24 March
      1829; d. 8 Nov. 1833 ae 4. 5. *Hiram Christie Pineo*, b. 18 Nov. 1830; m. Susan R.
      Knight.

ix   DAN PINEO, b. 10 Sept. 1787; d. 9 Aug. 1866 ae 79 on visit to St.
      Stephen's, N.B.; m. MARY CHRISTIE, b. 10 June 1801 St. Stephen's, d.
      there 26 Oct. 1888 ae 88, dau. of James and Susannah (Hill) Christie and
      sister of Jane who m. Dan's brother Peter. Pineo Ms (14:46-48), says,
      "Peter and Dan were never separated in boyhood days ... at the close of
      the War of 1812, they started from Machias through the woods and traced
      their way through the wilderness on an Indian trail [to] what is now called
      Sprague's Falls on the St. Croix river, the dividing line between Maine and
      New Brunswick, five miles above St. Stephen's. ... After 30 years they
      settled up their lumber business in St. Stephen's and moved to Topsfield
      and went to farming and lived there the rest of their days. Dan built a
      meeting house for the Congregationalists and gave it to them just before
      his death; he was not a church member. He kept a Public House in
      Topsfield and a large farm ... was a man of means." In 1860 he was a
      farmer in Topsfield, Me. (p.87); the Pineo Ms says no children, so the
      Mary Ann Pineo, b. ca 1826, in their household was probably a niece.

x   GAMALIEL PINEO, b. 3 Sept. 1790; d. 31 Aug. 1863 Columbia, Me.; bur.
      Great Hill Cem. there; m. in N.H., 3 July 1815, CHARLOTTE D.
      CHAMBERLAIN, b. Gilmanton, N.H., 26 Dec. 1794, d. 1 Oct. 1875
      Columbia, Me., dau. of Ephraim and Sarah (___) Chamberlain (*Early
      Pleasant River*, 459-60); res. first Annsburg, Me., later Columbia Falls,
      where in 1850 he was a farmer, with Charlotte ae 56 and the five youngest
      children; Jonathan and Ephraim had adjacent households (p.216).
           Children (*Early Pleasant River*, 460), 1st and 3rd b. N.H., others Columbia, Me.:
      1. *Ephraim Chamberlain Pineo*[7], b. 28 Dec. 1816, Gilmanton, N.H.; m. Lorana

Leighton. 2. *Mercy Drisko Pineo,* b. 5 Nov. 1818; m. William Joseph Tupper. 3. *Sarah Chamberlain Pineo,* b. 30 Sept. 1820; m. Daniel Merritt. 4. *Jonathan Pineo,* b. 24 Aug. 1822; m. Elizabeth Leighton. 5. *Priscilla Pineo,* b. 24 Sept. 1824; d. 1847 unm. 6. *George Chamberlain Pineo,* b. 17 April 1826; m. Delana Ann Look. 7. *John Franklin Pineo,* b. 26 April 1828; m. Amanda T. Longfellow. 8. *Elizabeth W. Pineo,* b. 3 Feb. 1830; m. Joseph W. Farnsworth. 9. *Benjamin Chamberlain Pineo,* b. 9 July 1832; m. Cordelia Wilson Ramsdell. 10. *Jane C. Pineo,* b. 29 Oct. 1834; m. George W. Kilton.

xi   MARY/POLLY PINEO, b. 14 March 1793; d. ae 69; m. at Machias, 13 June 1815 (Jackman, 43), JOSEPH FENNO of Columbia, Me., b. 7 March 1766 at Canton, d. 4 Dec. 1839 Machias, Me., son of Joseph and Jerusha (Robinson) Fenno (*NEHGR* 51:453). Pineo Ms (14:102) says, "Joseph is now living Machias, a shoemaker and harness maker ... at further end of the old toll bridge going to E. Machias." The 1850 census listed Mary F. Fennoe ae 57 at Machias, head of a household consisting of Mary A. ae 29, Elizabeth ae 25, Joseph ae 22 (merchant), and apparent boarders A. G. Peabody, physician ae 32, b. Mass., Edmund Pearson ae 25, merchant b. Me., and James Pearl ae 50, laborer b. Ireland (p.23).

    Fenno children, prob. all b. Machias (all in Pineo Ms): 1. *George Washington Fenno[7],* b. 16 Sept. 1816. 2. *Mary Ann Fenno,* b. 30 Jan. 1818; d. 20 Sept. 1819. 3. *Mary Ann Fenno,* b. 25 Sept. 1819. 4. *Elizabeth Fenno,* b. ca 1825; "Lizzie" ae 45 in 1870 in household of brother Joseph, unm. 4. *Joseph William Fenno,* b. ca 1830; m. Mary ___; in 1870 was a shoemaker in Machias with four children (p.360).

Children of Jonathan and Bridget (Byron) (Doty) Pineo, b. Machias (Pineo Ms 14:9):

xii   JAMES DOTY PINEO, b. 1797; d. 23 April 1838 ae 40; m. ROSANNA SMITH, dau. of James Smith. He was a tailor; res. Braddington, Me., and afterwards Waite, Me. (Pineo Ms 14:104).

    Children (*ibid.*): 1. *Eliza Pineo[7].* 2. *Mary Ann Pineo,* b. 9 Dec. 1825; m. Charles Wesley Butterfield. 3. *Delia Pineo,* b. 12 Feb. 1828; m. (1) Robert Thaxter, (2) Samuel Longfellow Getchell. 4. *Caroline A. Pineo,* b. 30 Sept. 1831; m. Dr. Charles Jordan. 5. *Ruby Pineo.* 6. *Dan Pineo,* b. 6 Nov. 1836; m. Cynthia A. Getchell; desc. in Minnesota.

xiii JOHN RICHARDS PINEO, b. 1800.

xiv   RUBY W. PINEO, b. 23 Aug. 1803; d. Columbia, Me., 1836; m. 11 Feb. 1821, EDWARD ELSMORE, b. 24 July 1799 E. Machias, d. 9 Dec. 1889, son of Moses and Lydia (___) Elsmore (Pineo Ms 14:154). In 1850 the family of Edward Elsimore [*sic*], a laborer ae 51, and Rheuby ae 47, was one of only four families in Twp 18, Washington Co., Me., three of whom were Elsimores; seven children were still at home (p.52). The family business was apparently lumbering.

Elsimore children, first from Pineo Ms, others from census: 1. *Bridget Elsmore*[7], m. D. A. Fenderson. 2. *Charles B. Elsimore*, b. ca 1832. 3. *George F. Elsimore*, b. ca 1835. 4. *Hiram Elsimore*, b. ca 1837. 5. *Leonice Elsimore*, b. ca 1840. 6. *Eliza J. Elsimore*, b. ca 1843. 7. *Edward O. Elsimore*, b. ca 1846. 8. *Gilbert Elsimore*, b. ca 1848.

xv CHARLES BYRON PINEO, b. 2 Sept. 1805; d. 1875; m. (1) SUSAN DENSMORE of Cherryfield, Me.; m. (2) after 1850 MARY MORRELL He was a shoemaker at W. Harrington, Me., and Pineo Ms says, "a cripple [because of a] stiff leg" (Pineo Ms 14:153). In 1850 he was a shoemaker at Milbridge, Me., ae 40 [*sic*] with Susan ae 34, and four children (p.134).

Children, first four with first wife, last two with Mary (Pineo Ms; census): 1 *John F. Pineo*[7], b. ca 1837. 2. *Mary A. Pineo*, b. ca 1842. 3. *Susanna Pineo*, b. ca 1844. 4. *Gifford/Gilford Pineo*, b. ca 1847. 5. *Salinda Pineo*. 6. *Charles B. Pineo*, b. Cutler, Me.; res. Bar Harbor.

xvi RUFUS PATTEN PINEO, b. 1806; prob. d. infancy.

Sources cited: Lebanon, Conn., VR as cited in the Barbour Index. Pineo Manuscript. Weyman Manuscript. "Notes about Machias with some account of its First Settlers," *Maine Historical Magazine*, 8 [1893] (calls second wife widow *Mary Ann* Doty). Tibbetts and Lamson, *Early Pleasant River Families of Washington County, Maine* (1997). Allen H. Bent, "Fenno Family," *NEHGR* 52 [1898]. CENSUS: Washington Co., Me., Machias 1790 (M637-2), Plantation No. 5, 1820 (M33-37); Cherryfield, Columbia, & Milbridge 1850 (M432-272); Machias 1850 (M432-273) & 1870 (M593-563), Topsfield 1860 (M653-455). **See also:** Account of Jonathan in *Genealogy and History of the State of Maine* (1909).

700. DAN PINEO[5] (*Elizabeth*[4] *Samson, David*[3], *Caleb*[2], *Henry*[1]), son of Peter Pineo and his wife Elizabeth Samson [145], was born at Lebanon, Conn., 25 February 1749/50 (VR 1:243) and died 3 February 1843, aged 94, at Habitant (a village in Cornwallis), N.S., where he was a farmer (Pineo Ms 10:1); Marble (*Nova Scotians*, 4:35) says *Daniel* Pineo died 6 February 1843, aged 93. He was a descendant also of Pilgrims John Alden and Myles Standish.

He married, first, at Cornwallis, N. S., 21 October 1773 by Rev. B. Phelps, **ANNA BENTLEY**, daughter of David and Anna (Baldwin) Bentley (*Township Book*, 1:63). She was born at Norwich, Conn., 13 October 1752 (*VR* 1:315) and died at Cornwallis 5 December 1778, aged 26, as "wife of Daniel" (Marble, 2:63).

He married, second, between December 1778 and 1784, **KEZIAH COX**, described in the Pineo Ms as a "high spirited woman ... her husband drank, and she finally left him and refused to live with him" (Pineo Ms, 10:1).

On 28 April 1774 Peter Pineo of Cornwallis, yeoman, deeded land to his son Dan (Kings Co. LR 2:527). The Pineo Ms (10:1) says he was "lame in his last days."

Children of Dan and Anne/Anna (Bentley) Pineo, b. Cornwallis (*Twp Book*, 46):

i   ERASTUS PINEO[6], b. 3 Sept. 1774; d. Cornwallis 8 May 1826 (Marble 5:35); m. there, 14 May 1795, PRUDENCE BECKWITH, b. 9 March 1779, d. 5 June 1847 (*ibid.*), dau. of John and Katharine (Chipman) Beckwith (*Twp Book*, 61).

Children included (*ibid.*), order uncertain: 1. *Eunice Pineo*[7], b. 11 Oct. 1798; m. Judah Eaton. 2. *Caroline Eliza Pineo*. 3. *Sarah Malvina Pineo*; m. Wells Borden. 4. *Catharine Pineo*, m. ___ Woodworth. 5. *Ann Pineo*, m. Samuel Cowdell (*Twp Book*, 63). 5. *Prudence Pineo*, m. John Parker. 6. *Ruth Olivia Pineo*. 7. *John O. Pineo*, b. 15 April 1807; res. Canard, N.S. 8. *George Chipman Pineo*. 9. *Daniel Pineo*.

ii   EUNICE PINEO, b. 20 Jan. 1776.

iii OBADIAH PINEO, b. 8 Sept. 1777; rep. d. 31 Dec. 1848; m. ca 1824, ANN CHARLOTTE ____, b. Purbrook, Hants, ca 1789, d. after 1851. According to their son, writing ca 1889, Obadiah was a physician, educated at King's College, Windsor, N.S., became a surgeon's assistant on board H. M. frigate *Boston*, then a surgeon in the Royal Navy, serving in the Baltic campaign and at the blockading of French ports 1805-1820. As surgeon superintendant of ships carrying criminals to Botany Bay, he was granted 200 acres in Australia, and adopted arms associated with John Quincy Adams (Pineo Ms 10:1-7, citing letter from C. W. Eustace Pineo to Clarence Pineo of N.Y. ca 1889).

O. Pineo, Surgeon, R.N., in his will dated 18 May 1846 at Launceston, V.D. Land [Van Diemen's Land, now Tasmania], wrote, "Should anything happen to me during my absence at Port Philip or elsewhere ..., I bequeath to my dear son C.W.E. Pineo a [---] piece of land in ... Cornwallis, N.S., a gift from my departed Father Dan Pineo and now in the use of my two sisters at a pepper corn rent / viz. one pint of beech nuts yearly, ... to my dear son George Douglas Pineo my land on the Weriby River Port Philip 200 acres (a Crown Grant for upwards of 40 years service in the Royal Navy). He is to provide for his three sisters. To my dear son Francis Thornhill Pineo I have no legacy to bequeath but confide him to the care of Capt. W.A. Hamilton R.N. who I am sure will provide for him either in the R. Marine Corps or in his own Office at the Admiralty. My dear wife C.A. Pineo will have my Pension as a Naval Surgeons Widow ... My Arab Pony I give with all my books household furniture etc. to my three daughters enjoining my Sons never to neglect their dear Mother & Sisters. I regret not having more property to bequeath them but a good education will more or less supply the want to this with the prudent and good counsel of an excellent Mother. Should Francis not be provided for under Government he is to have one half of the Port Philip property subject to the care & support of his Sisters with his brother George more particularly the youngest Anna who will from her unfortunate affliction require peculiar care." The will was proved 19 Jan. 1848 by Ann Charlotte Pineo, Widow, and administration given to her 30 Jan. 1848 (PCC, PROB11/2087).

The 1851 English census listed Ann C. Pineo, widow, at 170 Queen [?Green] St., Portsea, ae 62, annuitant b. Purbrook, Hants; with her were Mary Waller ae 42, sister (married, annuitant, b. Pipers Hill, Purbrook); Anne Pineo ae 28, dau. (b. Portsea); C.W.E. Pineo ae 27, son, civil engineer & architect (b. Portsea); Francis Pineo ae 19, lawyer's clerk (b. Deal, Kent); and Eliza Bray ae 39, servant (fol.298, p.28).

Children (will; letter in Pineo Ms; census): 1. [Daughter] Pineo[7]. 2. [Daughter] Pineo. 3. Charles W. Eustace Pineo, b. ca 1824; res. 1889, W. Kensington, London. 4. Anne Pineo, b. ca 1825 ("youngest dau."). 5. George Douglas Pineo, prob. res. Melbourne, Aus., 1889. 6. Francis Thornhill Pineo, b. ca 1832; retired from War Office 1887, res. Southsea, Hants, England; m. Eliza Jane ___ (1871 census).

Children of Dan and Keziah (Cox) Pineo, b. Cornwallis (Twp Book, 46):

iv GEORGE DAVENPORT PINEO, b. 29 May 1785; d. 31 May 1846 ae 61 (Marble 5:35); m. at Cornwallis, 26 June 1805 (TB 1:64), MARTHA NESBIT, b. 1779, d. 29 Oct. 1854 ae 75 (g.s.), dau. of John Nesbit. They lived at Canning, N.S., and George was known as "Pesky" because one of his favorite expressions was "pesky creatur" (Pineo Ms 10:86).

Children (Twp Book 47, 76; Marble, 4:35; Pineo Ms 10:86): 1. Rebecca Pineo[7], b. 13 March 1806. 2. Eliza Kezia Pineo, b. 23 Dec. 1807. 3. Martha Jane Pineo, b. 13 Dec. 1809. 4. Mary Pineo, b. 2 May, d. 15 July 1811. 5. Mary Ann Pineo, b. 21 July 1812. 6. Eunice Pineo, b. 12 Oct. 1814. 7. Prudence Mariah Pineo, b. 19 Oct. 1816. 8. George Nesbit Pineo, b. 1 July, d. 5 July 1818. 9. George Nesbit Pineo again, b. 30 May, d. 2 June 1819.

v ELIZABETH PINEO, b. 29 Oct. 1786; unm.; res. Cornwallis; had a son Charles Pineo[7], who m. ___ Baxter, res. Elmwood, Ill. (Pineo Ms 10:112).

Sources cited: Lebanon, Conn., VR as cited in the Barbour Index. Norwich, Conn., VR. Cornwallis Township Book [TB = film of originals]. Pineo Manuscript. Weyman Manuscript, NEHGS, box 408, bundle 12, continues some lines. Eaton, History of Kings County, N.S. 1851 Census of England, Portsea, Hampshire (H0107/1658). U. K. National Archives, PROB11/2087.

701. JOHN PINEO[5] [Rev.] (Elizabeth[4] Samson, David[3], Caleb[2], Henry[1]), son of Peter Pineo and his wife Elizabeth Samson [145], was born in Coos County, N.H., about 1753, and died at Cornwallis, N.S., 21 June 1835, aged 81 (g.s.) or 82 (Kings Co. History, 778), and is buried in Habitant Cemetery there.

He married at Cornwallis, 22 February 1778, HANNAH LOOMER, daughter of Stephen and Hannah (Chapman) Loomer (TB 1:8). She was born at

Norwich, Conn., 18 February 1754 (*VR* 1:278), and died at Cornwallis, N.S., 29 December 1835 in her 81st year (*Kings Co. History*, 778). The will of Stephen Loomer of Cornwallis, dated 13 July 1790, proved 3 November 1790, names among others his daughter Hannah Pineo (Marble, 2:13, 147).

The Pineo Manuscript (13:1-2) claims that Rev. John Pineo was "in full sympathy with the colonists in the rebellion and much against the will of his elder brother Peter ... he joined the Revolutionary army ... his brother tried to impress him into the King's troops but he escaped and perhaps he is the John Pineo on the rolls of Connecticut men who served in the Revolution ... After the [war] he returned to Cornwallis and spent his life there as a Congregational minister."

On 21 January 1780 and on 8 November 1784 Peter Pineo of Cornwallis, yeoman, deeded land there to his son John (Kings Co. LR 1:418; 2:508).

John was minister in the New Light Congregational Church of Cornwallis from 1807 until his death in 1835 (*Kings Co. History*, 779).

Children of John and Hannah (Loomer) Pineo, rec. Cornwallis, N.S., except Hannah (*Township Book*, 47), additional data from Pineo Ms:

   i   ANNE PINEO[6], b. 29 Jan. 1779; d. before 1861; m. ca 1797 WILLIAM BREWSTER, b. ca 1775, d. 12 Jan. 1819 at sea, son of John Pierce and Margaret (Morrison) Brewster; buried Harvey, N.B.

   ii   LUKE PINEO, b. 15 April 1782; m. at Cornwallis, 6 May 1806, ELIZABETH MILLER, dau. of John Miller (*Twp Book*, 67). A "substantial good old man ... without fingers on his left hand ... sea captain and school teacher ... lived at Lower Pereaux, Cornwallis" (Pineo Ms 13:40).
        Children (*ibid.*, 12:25, 13:41-42): 1. *James Pineo[7]*, d. at sea, unm. 2. *John Pineo*. 3. *Phoebe Ann Pineo*; m. ___ Pickles. 4. *Eliza Pineo*, m. Thomas Crouch. 5. *Harriet Pineo*, m. David Weaver. 6. *Vina Pineo*, m. ___ Lovelace. 7. *Hannah Pineo*, m. Jacob Lockhart. 8. *Cynthia Pineo*, m. Jonathan West; res. Wisconsin. 9. *Jane Pineo*, m. ___ Lockhart. 10. *Levinie Pineo*, d.y. (Weyman Ms differs, lists only: 1. Lavinia, 2. Ruth, 3. Hannah, and 4. John; says Lavinia had three out-of-wedlock children: William Jess, Paul Coffin, and Freeman Coffin, whose lines are continued.)

   iii   JOHN PINEO, b. 30 June 1785; m. at Cornwallis, 7 Dec. 1809 (TB 1:63), SARAH ELLS; the space for her parents' names is blank. He was a farmer at Upper Pereaux in Cornwallis (Pineo Ms 13:56-57).
        Pineo children (*ibid.*, 12:26, 13:57): 1. *Frank Pineo[7]*, a farmer in Lower Pereaux. 2. *Luke Pineo*, a farmer in Lower Pereaux. 3. *Sarah Pineo*, m. William Green [*sic*]. 4. *John Pineo*. 5. *Betsey Pineo*, m. William Green [*sic*]. 6. *Margaret Pineo*, b. 1807/8; m. William Huntley. 7. *Mark Pineo*, b. 17 Dec. 1812; m. Orenda Scofield. 8. *Stephen Pineo*.

iv PHOEBE PINEO, b. 3 Jan. 1788; m. ELISHA ELLS; res. Lower Pereaux, Cornwallis (Pineo Ms 12:27, 13:74).

Ells children (*ibid.*): 1. *John Ells[7]*. 2. *Watson Ells*, m. ___ Robinson. 3. *George Ells*, m. ___ Robinson. 4. *Sophia Ells*, m. ___ Ward. 5. *Phoebe Ells*.

v PETER PINEO, b. 1790; d. 2 May 1859 ae 68; m. ca 1810, SARAH STEADMAN, b. 5 April 1791, d. 17 Jan. 1870, dau. of Enoch and Elizabeth (Cogswell) Steadman; bur. Presbyterian churchyard, Cornwallis; "a liberal, deputy sheriff, etc.," res. Canard, N.S. (Pineo Ms 13:5).

Pineo children (*ibid.,* 13:7-8): 1. *Ellison Pineo[7]*, b. 6 Sept. 1811; m Richard Crowe. 2. *Enoch Pineo*, b. 16 Oct. 1813; d. 19 March 1814. 3. *Susan Pineo*, b. 1815; m. Samuel Denison. 4. *Nancy Pineo*, b. 23 March 1818; m. John Terry Newcomb. 5. *John Pineo*, b. 4 April 1821. 6. *Isaac Pineo*, m. Elizabeth (Adams) Taylor. 7. *Peter Pineo*, M.D., b. 6 March 1825; m. Elizabeth Crosby. 8. *Mason Pineo*, b. 30 Nov. 1827; m. Eliza C. Bagwell. 9. *Georgiana Pineo*, b. 23 Oct. 1830; m. William Muhlig. 10. [*Infant*] *Pineo*, b. and d. 11 June 1834. 11. *Sarah Pineo*, b. 18 Dec. 1832; m Stephen Harris.

vi HANNAH PINEO, m. JOSEPH MCLELLAN of Cumberland Co., N.S. (Pineo Ms 13:85).

McLellan children (*ibid.,* 87): 1. *John A. McLellan[7]*, res. Central Economy, N.S. 2. *Ann McLellan*. 3. [*Daughter*] *McLellan*, m. ___ Brewster.

vi STEPHEN PINEO, m. (1) MARGARET ____, (2) ____ HUNTLEY (Pineo Ms 13:95-97). He had a daughter and a son *Burton Pineo[7]* (*ibid.*).

Sources cited: Norwich, Conn., VR. *Cornwallis Township Book* [TB = film of original]. Eaton, *The History of Kings County* (1910). Marble, *Deaths, Burials, and Probate of Nova Scotians* (1990). Pineo Manuscript. Weyman Manuscript, box 408, bundle 12.

702. WILLIAM PINEO[5] (*Elizabeth[4] Samson, David[3], Caleb[2], Henry[1]*), son of Peter Pineo and his wife Elizabeth Samson [145], was born probably in New Hampshire about 1755. He was living in 1803. He was a descendant also of *Mayflower* passengers John Alden and Myles Standish.

He married at Cornwallis, Nova Scotia, 18 July 1776, **PHEBE BENTLEY**, daughter of David and Ann (Baldwin) Bentley (TB 1:63). She was born at Norwich, Conn., 27 February 1758 (*VR* 1:315), and was living January 1789 (last recorded child).

On 23 December 1773 Peter Pineo of Cornwallis, yeoman, deeded land there to his son William (Kings Co. LR 1:222).

William Pineo was a Lieutenant in the First Regiment, Kings County, in 1793. In 1803 he bought 2,000 acres of land, which became known as Pineoville, but was later changed to Waterville (Pineo Ms).

Children of William and Phebe (Bentley) Pineo, births rec. Cornwallis (*Twp Book* 47), other data from Pineo Ms (15:5-6):

i   JAMES PINEO[6], b. 22 Aug. 1777; d. Cornwallis 28 June 1841 (*Nova Scotians,* 4:35); m. GRACE CRANE.
    Children (Pineo Ms 15:8): 1. *Rachel Pineo[7],* b. Waterville. 2. *William Pineo,* b. ca 1810; d. Dec. 1849 ae 39 (*Nova Scotians,* 4:35); m. Margaret Randall. 3. *Locker Pineo,* d. ae 21. 4. *Robert Pineo,* m. Phoebe Randall. 5. *Maria Pineo,* m. Benjamin Lyons. 6. *Jonathan Pineo,* m. Elizabeth Lyons. 7. *Elizabeth Pineo,* m. John L. George. 8. *Elijah Pineo,* b. ca 1823; d. 29 Aug. 1849 ae 26 (*Nova Scotians,* 4:35). 9. *Matilda Ann Pineo,* m. Robert Lyons.

ii AUGUSTINE PINEO, b. 13 July 1779; m. MARTHA BECKWITH, dau. of Capt. Samuel Beckwith (Weyman Ms).
    Children (Pineo Ms 12:12, 15:50-52): 1. *Rebecca Pineo[7],* m. John Baldwin Bentley. 2. *David Pineo,* m. (1) Rebecca Forsythe, (2) Louisa Bridge. 3. *Samuel William Pineo,* m. Sophia Miller. 4. *Lydia Keziah Pineo,* m. David H. Rouse. 5. *Phoebe Pineo,* m. William or Tristram Best. 6. *Sarah Ann Pineo,* m. William Sandford. 7. *Mariah/Mary Pineo,* m. Peter Lawson. 8. *Augustine Allerson Pineo,* m. (1) Elizabeth Nichols, (2) Eunice Nichols.

iii ANNE PINEO, b. 4 Jan. 1781; m. NATHAN KNOWLES.
    Knowles children (Pineo Ms 12:27): 1. *Baldwin Knowles[7].* 2. *Rebecca Knowles.*

iv LYDIA PINEO, b. 23 Dec. 1783; m. JOHN SESSIONS or JESSIONS.

v   OLIVE PINEO, b. 23 Dec. 1785; m. by bond dated 24 June 1820 (as Olivia), ARUNAH RANDALL; William Pineo Jr. co-signed.

vi SALLY PINEO, b. 10 Jan. 1787; d. unm.

vii WILLIAM PINEO, b. 23 Jan. 1789; m. HARRIET SHAW.
    Children (Pineo Ms 12:27): 1. *Henry Pineo[7],* m. Hannah E. Rusman. 2. *Margaret Pineo.* 3. *George Davenport Pineo,* m. Ann Eliza Bligh. 4. *Isaiah Shaw Pineo,* m. Elizabeth Bowles.

viii DAVID PINEO, d.y.

Sources cited: *Norwich, Conn., VR. Cornwallis Town Books* [TB = film of originals]. Nova Scotia Marriage Bonds, on line. Marble, *Nova Scotia … From Primary Sources* (1990), Vol. 4 (1999). Eaton, *History of Kings County* (1910). Pineo Manuscript. Weyman Manuscript, box 408, bundle 12.

703.   ELIZABETH PINEO[5] (*Elizabeth[4] Samson, David[3], Caleb[2], Henry[1]*), daughter of Peter Pineo and his wife Elizabeth Samson [145], was born probably about 1757, either in New Hampshire where her parents lived for a few years after leaving Lebanon, Conn., or in Cornwallis, Nova Scotia, where they settled.   She is called daughter of Peter and Elizabeth in her marriage record. She was a descendant also of *Mayflower* passengers John Alden and Myles Standish.

She married at Cornwallis, N.S., 3 August 1775, **ELIJAH BEWEL**, son of Timothy and Margaret (_____) Bewel (*Township Book*, 61).

"Elizabeth Buel *et al.*" were listed as recipients of one of the land grants given in Horton, N.S., "subsequent to the large Grant of 1761" (*Kings Co. History*, 86).

Children of Elijah and Elizabeth (Pineo) Bewel, rec. Cornwallis (*Twp Book*, 23):

i   TIMOTHY HAMMON BEWEL[6], b. 11 April 1776.

ii CHAPIN BEWEL, b. 22 June 1777.

Sources cited: *Cornwallis Township Book.* Eaton, *History of Kings County* (1910).

704.   MARCY PINEO[5] (*Elizabeth[4] Samson, David[3], Caleb[2], Henry[1]*), daughter of Peter Pineo and his wife Elizabeth Samson [145], was born at Cornwallis, N.S., 18 January 1763 (*Township Book*, 47). She died at Horton, N.S., in March 1815. She was a descendant also of *Mayflower* passengers John Alden and Myles Standish.

She married at Cornwallis, 8 January 1778 (*Township Book*, 71), **WILLIAM WOODWORTH JR.**, son of William and Sarah (_____) Woodworth. He was born at Hebron, Conn., 3 August 1755, and died at Cornwallis 11 May 1839 (Marble, 4:345).

Children of William and Marcy (Pineo) Woodworth, births of all except Rebecca, William, and Marcy rec. Cornwallis, N.S. (*Township Book*, 60; Weyman Ms):

i   ELIZABETH WOODWORTH[6], b. 16 Dec. 1779; d. 16 March 1784 (*Twp Book*, 78).

ii SARAH WOODWORTH, b. 27 Jan. 1782; d. Eastport, Me., 7 June 1839; m. (1) HENRY DE FOREST, (2) BENJAMIN G. WEAVER (Weyman Ms).

   De Forest children (*ibid.*): 1. *Elizabeth De Forest[7]*; m. Caleb Hearsey. 2. *Sarah B. De Forest.* **Weaver** child: 3. *Jane E. Weaver,* b. 1826; d. 1882; m. John E. Kennedy.

iii PETER PINEO WOODWORTH, b. 23 Dec. 1783; d. Milwaukee, Wisc., 29 Oct. 1874; m. at Cornwallis, N.S., 30 Dec. 1810 (*Twp Book*, 71), MARY KINSMAN, b. 24 June 1790, d. 13 July 1817, dau. of Robert and Mehitable (Rand) Kinsman.

   Children (Weyman Ms): 1. *Ephraim Kinsman Woodworth[7]*, b. 5 Nov. 1811. 2. *James William Woodworth[7]*, b. Cornwallis, N.S., 9 Nov. 1813; m. (1) Mary Cerena Loomer, (2) Hannah (Loomer) Fisk. 3. *Mary Mehitable Woodworth*, b. 16 June 1815; m. (1) Jehial DeWolf Pineo, (2) Peter Bentley.

iv   JAMES WOODWORTH, b. 23 Dec. 1785; poss. m. CATHERINE PINEO, b. 29 Sept. 1800 (Weyman Ms).

v   MATTHEW WOODWORTH, b. 8 Jan. 1788; d. Cornwallis 13 Sept. 1843, a blacksmith (*Nova Scotians*, 4:345).

vi   ELIZABETH WOODWORTH, b. 5 June 1790; m. NATHAN PALMETER (Weyman Ms).
   Palmeter children (*ibid.*): 1. *James Palmeter*[7]. 2. *Oliver Palmeter*. 3. *William Palmeter*. 4. *Eunice Palmeter*. 5. *Waity Palmeter*. 6. *[Judith?] Palmeter*. 7. *Mercy Palmeter*.

vii REBECCA WOODWORTH, b. 26 Nov. 1793; d. 18 June 1879, Cornwallis; m. DENISON HAINES, son of Jonathan Haines; res. S. Norridgewock, Me. (Weyman Ms).
   Haines children (*ibid.*): 1. *Henry A. Haines*[7]. 2. *James H. Haines*. 3. *Mercy L. Haines*. 4. *Gideon C. Haines*, b. 1818; d. 9 Oct. 1819 ae 1y 19d, Pembroke, Me. 5. *Sarah R. Haines*. 6. *Denison J. Haines*. 7. *Leonard Haines*. 8. *Mary R. Haines*; m. ___ Blasedell. 9. *William J. Haines*.

viii WILLIAM WOODWORTH, b. 20 Dec. 1796; d. 8 July 1879 W. Pembroke, Me.; m. MARY HERSEY, b. 20 Sept. 1798 Pembroke, Me., d. W. Pembroke 10 April 1884, dau. of Zadoc and Abigail (Lewis) Hersey (Weyman Ms). William was a farmer and town clerk of Pembroke, Me., for 47 years.
   Children (*ibid.*): 1. *William Lewis Woodworth*[7], b. 6 April 1818. 2. *Mary Eliza Woodworth*. 3. *James Hearsey Woodworth*. 4. *Amelia Rebecca Woodworth*. 5. *Ephraim Woodworth*. 6. *Olive Perry Woodworth*. 7. *Sarah Ann Woodworth*.

ix   MARCY/MARY WOODWORTH, b. 3 May 1798; d. 15 Nov. 1883 (Weyman Ms); m. as Mary, dau. of William and Marcy, at Cornwallis 6 Nov. 1816, CHARLES MORTON, d. 9 Feb. 1868, son of Elemuel and Martha (___) Morton (*Twp Book*, 60).
   Morton children, all but 4th rec. Cornwallis (*ibid.*, 42), all in Weyman Ms: 1. *Mary Ann Morton*[7], b. 3 Nov. 1817; d. 23 Aug. 1820 (*ibid.*, 76). 2. *Mary Ann Morton*, b. 22 March 1821. 3. *Lemuel Guy Morton*, b. 28 March 1823. 4. *William Charles Morton*, b. 1826. 5. *Martha Alice Morton*, b. 12 June 1828. 6. *John Leander Morton*, b. 24 Feb. 1831. 7. *Rebecca Adlice Morton*, b. 2 Feb. 1834. 8. *Sarah Elizabeth Morton*, b. 3 April 1836.

x   RUBY WOODWORTH, b. 10 Jan. 1802; m. ODIORNE LOVEJOY, b. ca 1795, d. 1847 ae 52, son of Nathaniel Lovejoy; res. Calais, Me., and Milltown, N.B. (Weyman Ms).
   Lovejoy children (*ibid*): 1. *Mary Ann Lovejoy*[7]. 2. *Sarah Percy Lovejoy*. 3. *Lucretia Maria Lovejoy*. 4. *William Odiorne Lovejoy*. 5. *Charles Norman Lovejoy*. 6. *Leonard Hiram Lovejoy*. 7. *James Loren Lovejoy*. 8. *Amanda Elizabeth Lovejoy*. 9. *Ruby Melvina Lovejoy*. 10. *Harry Lovejoy*. 11-13. [*Three daughters*], d.y.

xi OLIVER WOODWORTH, b. 10 April 1804; d. 10 April [*sic*] 1884, Cornwallis; m. (1) ISABEL O'BRIAN, dau. of Robert O'Brian, (2) EUNICE LYONS, dau. of William Lyons (Weyman Ms).

   Children (*ibid.*): 1. *Samuel Woodworth*[7], b. 1827. 2. *William Woodworth*, b. 1829; d. 1854. 3. *James Woodworth*, b. 1830. 4. *Sarah Woodworth*, b. 1832. 5. *Isabella Adelia Woodworth*, b. 1834; m. John Burbridge Best. 6. *Robert Woodworth*, b. 1836. 7. *Lucy Maria Woodworth*, b. 26 Dec. 1839. 8. *Thomas O. Woodworth*, b. 4 Feb. 1841. 9. *Richard Watson Woodworth*, b. Oct. 1842. 10. *Mercy Woodworth*. 11. *Anna Rebecca Woodworth*, b. 1850.

xii AMY WOODWORTH, b. 2 May 1805; d. 2 March 1884 Pembroke, Me.; m. ADNA LEIGHTON, d. 26 June 1891 (Weyman Ms).

   Leighton children (*ibid.*): 1. *Amy Leighton*[7]. 2. *Leah Leighton*. 3. *Sarah Leighton*. 4. *Ellen Leighton*. 5. *Lorenzo Leighton*.

xiii LEONARD WOODWORTH, b. 19 Dec. 1808; m. LOVINA MACK, dau. of Dr. Jason Mack; res. Jay, Me. (Weyman Ms).

   Children (*ibid.*): 1. [*name illegible*] *Woodworth*[7]. 2. *Lucy Woodworth*. 3. *William Woodworth*. 4. *James Woodworth*. 5. *Rebecca Woodworth*. 6. *Lavinia Woodworth*.

Sources cited: *Cornwallis Township Book.* Marble, *Nova Scotians … 1800 – 1850* (1999). Weyman Manuscript, NEHGS, box 408, bundle 12 (continues some lines).

705. RUBY PINEO[5] (*Elizabeth*[4] *Samson, David*[3], *Caleb*[2], *Henry*[1]), daughter of Peter Pineo and his wife Elizabeth Samson [145], was born at Cornwallis, Nova Scotia, 17 September 1765 (*Township Book*, 47). She died evidently before 1819 when her husband remarried. She was a descendant also of *Mayflower* passengers John Alden and Myles Standish.

She married, at Cornwallis, 25 April 1782, **OLIVER WOODWORTH**, son of Thomas and Zerviah (Fox) Woodworth (TB 1:85). He was born at Norwich, Conn., 19 January 1756 (*VR* 1:347), and died at Cornwallis 11 August 1829, "husband of Alice" (*Nova Scotians*, 4:345). He married, second, at Cornwallis, 7 September 1819, ELLEN BENTLEY, daughter of Asahel and Lucy (___) Bentley (TB 1:70; Weyman Ms calls her Alice Bentley).

Child of Oliver and Ruby (Pineo) Woodworth:

   i NATHAN WOODWORTH[6], b. 16 June 1785; d. 22 July 1866 (Weyman Ms); m. (1) at Cornwallis, 24 Feb. 1807 (bond dated 31 Dec. 1806), SARAH BAXTER, dau. William and Ruth (Sheffield) Baxter (*Twp Book*, 71; *Kings Co. History*, 880); m. (2) JULIA BAXTER, sister of Sarah (Weyman Ms).

Children, all but Sarah Eliza rec. Cornwallis (*Twp Book*, 60), all in Weyman Ms: 1. *William Oliver Woodworth*[7], b. 18 July 1808. 2. *Prudence Ruth Woodworth*, b. 8 June 1810; d. 31 Aug. 1813 (*Twp Book*, 78). 3. *Benjamin Baxter Woodworth*, b. 15 May 1812. 4. *Ruth Woodworth*, b. 15 May 1814. 5. *Douglas Woodworth*, b. 5 Aug. 1817; d. 8 Jan. 1818 (*Twp Book*, 78). 6. *Ruby Woodworth*, b. 1 June 1819. 7. *Douglas Woodworth*, b. 19 Feb. 1821. 8. *Sarah Eliza Woodworth* (Weyman Ms).

Sources cited: *Norwich, Conn. VR. Cornwallis Township Books* [TB = film of original town book]. Nova Scotia Marriage Bonds, on line. Weyman Manuscript, NEHGS, box 408, bundle 12 (continues some lines). Eaton, *History of Kings County* (1910).

706. MARY PINEO[5] (*Elizabeth*[4] *Samson, David*[3], *Caleb*[2], *Henry*[1]), daughter of Peter Pineo and his wife Elizabeth Samson [145], was born at Cornwallis, Nova Scotia, 23 May 1768 (*Township Book*). She was a descendant also of *Mayflower* passengers John Alden and Myles Standish. (Weyman Ms calls her Elizabeth but has correct birth date.)

She married at Cornwallis, 14 September 1786, **MATTHEW FISHER**, son of Richard and Hannah (____) Fisher; the marriage record identifies both sets of parents (TB 1:7). Matthew was a purser on an English man-of-war, *S.S. Torbay*, from Somerset, and later a teacher in Cornwallis, described in Pineo Manuscript as "very severe ... Hon. Samuel Chipman of Cornwallis aged 99 in 1888 went to school to him."

On 30 December 1799 Peter Pineo of Cornwallis, yeoman, deeded land there to his son-in-law Matthew Fisher (Kings Co. LR 4:155).

A sampler made 17 May 1809 by Eliza Fisher in Cornwallis names all nine children.

Children of Matthew and Mary (Pineo) Fisher, rec. Cornwallis, N.S. (*Township Book*, 35):

i   MERCY/MARY FISHER[6], b. 26 April 1787.

ii   ELIZABETH FISHER, b. 26 Feb. 1789; d. Port Williams, N.S., 12 Aug. 1865 (Weyman Ms); m. at Cornwallis, 1 Jan. 1807, DAVID NEWCOMB, b. 3 April 1784, d. 21 Dec. 1854 (*ibid.*), son of Benjamin and Abigail (Sanford) Newcomb (*Township Book*, 66). She is probably the Eliza Fisher who made the sampler dated 17 May 1809 that names her siblings.

Newcomb children, rec. Cornwallis (*Twp Book*, 43); Weyman Ms lists 14 children, some differences: 1. *William Edward Newcomb*[7], b. 11 Dec. 1807. 2. *John Sanford Newcomb*, b. 14 Aug. 1809. 3. *David Benjamin Newcomb*, b. 14 April 1813. 4. *Mary Eliza Newcomb*, b. 28 Sept. 1816. 5. *Matthew Fisher Newcomb*, b. 29 Nov. 1820. 6. *Simon Barnaby Newcomb*, b. 1 July 1823. 7. *Samuel Harmon Newcomb*, b. 10 Nov. 1825. 8. *Rebekah Fisher Newcomb*, b. 28 March 1828. 9. *Asaph Wallie Newcomb*, b. 21 March 1830. 10. *Gideon Emmerson Newcomb*, b. 26 Nov. 1835.

iii MATTHEW FISHER, b. 2 June 1791; m. HARRIET CONDON (Weyman Ms).

Children (*ibid.*): 1. *George Watkins Fisher*[7], b. 4 Sept. 1820; m. Mary Seraphina Parker. 2. *Adaline Fisher*, m. Robert Collins. 3. *John Wesley Fisher*, b. 7 Aug. 1835; m. Elizabeth Rand Porter. 4. *Sampson Kerr Fisher*, d. 31 May 1865; m. Helena Augusta Bligh. 5. *Eunice Fisher*, m. Joseph Purdy. 6. *Matthew Fisher*, m. Jessie Saunders.

iv SARAH FISHER, b. 29 June 1793.

v JOHN FISHER, b. 6 June 1795; d. Cold Brook, 18 Oct. 1872 ae 77; m. (1) at Aylesford, N.S., 25 Sept. 1823, REBECCA CRANE (*Twp Book*, 35), d. 25 April 1857; m. (2) in 1857 ADELIA GILLMORE, b. ca 1822, d. 9 Feb. 1873 ae 51, widow of Lewis Gillmore and dau. of Perry Borden (*Township Book, Horton* 99). He was a blacksmith and merchant at Horton, N.S.; no children (Weyman Ms).

vi RICHARD FISHER, b. 22 June 1797.

vii RUTH FISHER, b. 18 June 1799.

viii NATHAN WOODWORTH FISHER, b. 5 Jan. 1802; m. Aylesford, 10 March 1825 (*Twp Book*, 43), ISABELLAH WEST. He was a carpenter and wheelwright (Weyman Ms).

Children, first two births rec. Aylesford (*Twp Book*, 43), all in Weyman Ms: 1. *Mary Jane Fisher*[7], b. 9 Jan. 1826. 2. *Isabella Fisher*, b. 11 April 1828; m. Samuel Harmon Newcomb. 3. *James Edwin Fisher*, b. 29 May 1830; m. Eunice Louisa Woodworth. 4. *Charlotte Fisher*, m. ___ Graves. 5. *Melissa Fisher*, unm. 6. *Prudence Fisher*, unm. 7. *Malvina Fisher*, unm. 8. *Harmon Fisher*, unm.

ix WILLIAM HENRY FISHER, b. 10 July 1810; d. 29 April 1890, Somerset, N.S. (Weyman Ms); m. (1) MARY BECKWITH, d. 1846, dau. of Asa Beckwith (*ibid.*); m. (2) as widower, of Cornwallis, 3 April 1848, CHARLOTTE BRENNAN (N.S. Marriage Bonds), b. 25 Jan. 1820, d. 9 April 1890, dau. of Thomas and ___ (Miller) Brennan (Weyman Ms). He was a carpenter and carriage builder (*ibid.*).

Children, b. Somerset, N.S. (*ibid.*), order uncertain, with first wife: 1. *Mary Eliza Fisher*[7]. 2. *Amer Beckwith Fisher*, b. 23 Oct. 1837; m. Maria Jane Elliot. 3. *Betsey Fisher*. 4. *Prudence Fisher*, b. 25 Jan. 1843; d. 1866 unm. 5. *Amos Patterson*

Fisher. With second wife: 6. *William Wallace Fisher,* b. 8 March 1850. 7. *Roxanna Sophia Fisher,* b. 8 Aug. 1852; unm. 8. *Edwin Ruthven Fisher,* b. 17 Feb. 1854; unm. 9. *Henry Sampson Fisher,* b. 7 Jan. 1856; m. Carrie Elizabeth Franklin. 10. *Thomas L---- Fisher,* b. 3 May 1861; d. 1922 unm.

Sources cited: *Township Books, Cornwallis and Horton* [TB = film of original town books]. Nova Scotia Marriage Bonds, 1763-1849, on linc. Weyman Manuscript, NEHGS, box 408, bundle 12.

707.   SARAH   HUTCHINSON[5] (*Mercy[4] Samson, David[3], Caleb[2], Henry[1]*), daughter of Timothy Hutchinson and his wife Mercy Samson [146], was born at Lebanon, Conn., 9 November 1750 (VR 1:148). She died 11 September 1843 (rec. of husband's estate) at Tunbridge, Vt., and is buried in the "old cemetery across the branch from the old meeting-house, and her grave is not known" (*Royalton History,* 736). She was a descendant also of *Mayflower* passengers John Alden, Francis Cooke, and Myles Standish.

She married, about 1775, **ELIAS CURTIS**, who was born at Lebanon, Conn., 1 June 1748 (VR 1:53), son of Simeon and Sarah (Hutchinson) Curtis. Elias Curtis, Esq., died at Tunbridge, Vt., 18 October 1827, aged 72, and was buried in the Buzzell Cemetery at North Tunbridge (VR B:187).

Sarah was a child in 1758 when her father died, and her mother soon remarried to William White. A distribution to the heirs of Dr. Timothy Hutchinson dated 12 April 1768 included Sarah Hutchinson (Conn. PR, Windham Dist. #2122).

Elias removed from Lebanon, Conn., to Norwich, Vt., with his father, Simeon, in 1773, and then to Tunbridge; he lived for a time in Royalton and served in the Revolutionary War from there (*Royalton History,* 736-37). After the war, he built a house in Tunbridge, octagon-shaped, "in the S.E. corner of the present mill yard at Tunbridge. The upper floor was a hall where meetings were held" (*ibid.,* 737).

In 1790 Elias was in Tunbridge with two men 16 or over, five boys under 16, and four females (p.92). In 1800, over 45, Elias was living in Tunbridge with a woman 26-45, three young men 16-26, one girl 10-16, and one girl under 10 (p.599). Elias Jr. was next listed as head of his own household.

A list of seven "subscribers calling for a meeting to form 'a society in ... Tunbridge by the name of the Presbyterian or Congregational Society,' April 17, 1807," includes the names of Elias Curtis and Hezekiah Hutchinson (*Vt. Religious Cert.,* 88).

The will of Elias Curtis of Tunbridge, dated – 1827, presented 27 October 1827, names Elias Curtis Jr. and Abijah Curtis executors, and mentions but does not name his widow (Orange Co., Randolph Dist. PR 10:246). The estate was insolvent. Reports mention land occupied by Stephen Baker in Tunbridge, 30 November 1832; monies until 1 May 1838 to support the widow; and finally the death 11 September 1843 of Sarah, widow of Elias Curtis (*ibid.*, 11:255, 257, 425).

Children of Elias and Sarah (Hutchinson) Curtis, first and third rec. at Norwich and Tunbridge; Simeon rec. at Royalton; last three rec. at Tunbridge (VT VR):

i ELIAS CURTIS[6], b. 14 July 1776 Norwich and rec. Tunbridge (VR A:101); m. (1) at Tunbridge, 8 April 1798 (VR A:135), ABIGAIL / NABBY CLEMENTS, b. 24 Oct. 1778, d. 4 Sept. 1816, dau. William and Mary (__) Clements (*Royalton History*, 737); m. (2) Tunbridge, 13 Nov. 1817 (VR B:132), ANNA BINGHAM, b. ca 1785 Vt. In 1800 Elias Jr. and his wife were 16-26, with 1 boy under 10 and 1 older man 26-45 in the household (p.599). In 1850 Elias was a farmer in Tunbridge, with Anna ae 65, Abby Curtis ae 28, both b. Vt., and Mary Curtis ae 12, b. N.H. (p.5).

  Children with first wife (*Royalton History*, 737): 1. *John Phelps Curtis[7]*, b. 9 Feb. 1799. 2. *Sarah Curtis* (twin), b. 25 March 1801 (VR A:142). 3. *Mary Curtis* (twin), b. 25 March 1801. 4. *Cyrus Curtis*, b. 14 Feb. 1803. 5. *Azro Benton Curtis*, b. 6 May 1805. 6. *Betsey Curtis*, b. 21 March 1807. Children with second wife: 7. *Cacy Curtis*, b. 30 Dec. 1818. 8. *Elizabeth Ann Curtis*, b. 1822; d. 1 Oct. 1841. 9. *Abby Curtis* (?twin), b. ca 1822; at home 1850.

ii SIMEON CURTIS, b. Royalton 15 Sept. 1778 (VR 60); n.f.r. There was an older Simeon in Tunbridge not to be confused with this one.

iii ABIJAH CURTIS, b. Norwich 11 March 1781 (VR 1), rec. also Tunbridge (VR A:101), d. prob. 1830-1840; m. at Tunbridge, 9 July 1817, RUHAMAH ALLEN, the marriage performed by Jacob Allen, minister (VR B:131). In 1830 he was head of a household in Tunbridge, Vt., consisting of one man 40-50, one woman 80-90 [? his mother], one woman 50-60, one woman 30-40, one young man 15-20, two boys 10-15, and one boy and two girls under 5 yrs (p.195). *Royalton History* (p.737) says "Abijah went west and died there. His wife returned and married a former lover."

  Children (*Royalton History*, 737; VT VR): 1. *Timothy Curtis[7]*, b. 8 Aug. 1818. 2. *Elias Curtis*. 3. *Mercy Curtis*. 4. *Sarah Curtis*. 5. *Fidelia Curtis*.

? iv [SON] CURTIS, b. poss. ca 1783; living 1800.

v SARAH CURTIS, b. 17 Aug. 1785 (VR A:101); d. Royalton 16 March 1826 (*Royalton History*, 737); m. at Tunbridge, 1 Jan. 1804, STEPHEN BAKER (VR A:374), b. 21 May 1778, d. 24 Dec. 1838 (*Royalton History*, 737).

Baker children, all prob. b. Tunbridge, Vt. (*ibid.*): 1. *Lucy Curtis Baker[7]*, b. 14 June 1805. 2. *Chester Baker*, b. 9 Aug. 1807; m. Abigail Colby. 3. *Louisa Maria Baker*, b. 6 April 1810; m. (1) Clark Brown, (2) Jonathan Emerson. 4. *Charles Baker*, b. 21 March 1812; d. 1824. 5. *Mary Baker*, b. 4 June 1815; d. 1817. 6. *Elias Curtis Baker*, b. 9 Aug. 1817; m. Mary ___; res. Tunbridge 1850. 7. *Calvin Porter Baker*, b. 11 Aug. 1819; m. Eliza Pierce. 8. *Mary Baker*, b. 6 March 1826; m. Joseph Whitney.

vi LUCY CURTIS, b. 24 Feb. 1788 (VR A:101); m. at Tunbridge, 31 Dec. 1809, PETER SANBORN JR., by Calvin Noble, minister (VR A:380). He was prob. the Peter b. 7 March 1784, son of Peter and Patty (Dow) Sanborn (see pension rec. Peter Sanborn [Sr.], White, 3008).

vii POLLY CURTIS, b. 25 Aug. 1792 (VR A:110); m. at Tunbridge, 6 Nov. 1820, DAVID HUTCHINSON, by Jacob Allen, minister (VR B:140).

Hutchinson children (*Royalton History*, 737): 1. *Sarah Hutchinson[7]*, m. Milo Douglass. 2. *Harriet Hutchinson*. 3. *Thomas Hutchinson*. 4. *Ellen Hutchinson*.

Sources cited: Lebanon, Conn., Vital Records as cited in Barbour Index. Conn. Probate Records, Windham District. Orange Co., Vt., Randolph District Probate Records. Vermont Vital Records to 1871: Norwich, Royalton, Tunbridge. *History of Royalton, Vermont* (1911). *Vermont Religious Certificates* (2003). CENSUS: Tunbridge, Orange Co., Vt., 1790 (M637-12), 1800 (M32-51), 1830 (M19-185), 1850 (M432-926).

708. HEZEKIAH HUTCHINSON[5] (*Mercy[4] Samson, David[3], Caleb[2], Henry[1]*), son of Timothy Hutchinson and his wife Mercy Samson [146], was born at Lebanon, Conn., 6 October 1752 (VR 1:148). He died at Tunbridge, Vt., 20 August 1851, aged 99. He was a descendant also of *Mayflower* passengers John Alden, Francis Cooke, and Myles Standish.

He married, first, at Salisbury, Conn., 4 January 1776, **PHEBE FARNUM**, "both of Salisbury." She was born at Killingworth, Conn. (VR 2:108), 19 October 1752, daughter of Bezaleel and Phebe (Kirtland) Farnum, and died at Tunbridge, Vt., 26 November 1819, aged 68, "wife of Deac. Hezekiah" (VT VR). A distribution of the estate of Bezaleel Farnam late of Salisbury, dec'd, on 28 August 1782, includes widow Phebe Farnam and Phebe Hutchinson (Conn. PR, Salisbury Dist.). Phebe's sister Meriam married Hezekiah's brother Abijah Hutchinson.

Hezekiah was "of Tunbridge" when he married, second, at Royalton, Vt., 12 July 1820, **SUSANNA (RIX) DURKEE**, who was born at Preston, Conn., 30 June 1765, daughter of Daniel and Rebecca (Johnson) Rix and widow of Col. Heman Durkee. She died at Royalton 9 September 1852, aged 87 (VT VR).

Hezekiah was five years old in 1758 when his father died, and his mother soon remarried to William White. A distribution to the heirs of Dr. Timothy Hutchinson dated 12 April 1768 included eldest son Hezekiah Hutchinson (Conn. PR, Windham Dist. #2122).

Hezekiah was employed by the government during the Revolutionary War. He moved from Salisbury, Conn., to Tunbridge, Vt., with his family about 1786. In 1790 he was living in Tunbridge with three boys under 16 and three females (p.35). A list of seven "subscribers calling for a meeting to form 'a society in … Tunbridge by the name of the Presbyterian or Congregational Society,' April 17, 1807," includes the names of Elias Curtis and Hezekiah Hutchinson (*Vt. Religious Cert.*, 88).

In 1850 Hezekiah and his second wife were living in the household of his son Amos in Tunbridge, next door to son Harvey (p.12).

Children of Hezekiah and Phebe (Farnum) Hutchinson, first five rec. Salisbury, Conn. (VR 2:78-79), rest at Tunbridge, Vt. (VT VR):

i TIMOTHY HUTCHINSON[6], b. 29 April 1777; m. (1) BETSY [? LASELL]. He may be the man of that name, ae 72, b. Conn., with wife Sophia, in Bennington, Wyoming Co., N.Y., in 1850, in the household of [his nephew] Lysander Cushman (p.111). He poss. m. (2) his nephew's mother-in-law, SOPHIA ____ SANBORN, b. ca 1784 N.H.

   Children, b. Tunbridge, Vt. (VT VR): 1. *Olive Hutchinson*[7], b. 25 Dec. 1804. 2. *Aroline Hutchinson*, b. 3 Nov. 1807; m. Levi Baker. 3. *John Lasell Hutchinson*, b. 30 Nov. 1809. 4. *Mary Ann Hutchinson*, b. 8 Aug. 1811. 5. *Elizabeth Hutchinson*, b. 13 May 1813. 6. *James Dana Hutchinson*, b. 25 Jan. 1816.

ii POLLY HUTCHINSON, b. 1 Nov. 1778; prob. m. at Tunbridge, 2 Nov. 1796, CALEB SWAN.

iii OLIVE HUTCHINSON, b. 28 May 1781.

iv AMOS HUTCHINSON, b. 24 Dec. 1782; d. 21 Dec. 1861 Tunbridge of dropsy of the heart; m. at Royalton, Vt., 28 May 1806, JERUSHA RIX, b. there 23 Aug. 1780, d. Tunbridge 10 April 1860, dau. of Daniel and Rebecca (Johnson) Rix; bur. Central Cemetery. In 1850 Amos was a farmer at Tunbridge, head of a household that included his father and stepmother, and daughter Emily ae 34 and her husband Jonathan Morse ae 37, machinist, and their son Charles (p.12).

   Children, b. Tunbridge (*Royalton History*, 832): 1. *Daniel Hutchinson*[7], b. 1807; d. inf. 2. *Louisa Maria Hutchinson*, b. 1 Oct. 1808; m. C. M. Lamb. 3. *Laura Farnham Hutchinson*, b. 6 Aug. 1811; m. Jeremiah Foster. 4. *Susan Hazen Hutchinson*, b. 29 April 1814; m. Joseph Rix Jones. 5. *Emily R. Hutchinson*, b. 23

March 1816; m. Jonathan Morse. 6. *Hezekiah Hutchinson,* b. 7 May 1818; d. 3 May 1819. 7. *William Amos Hutchinson,* b. 1821; d. 8 March 1822.

v PHEBE HUTCHINSON, b. 16 Nov. 1785; d. Tunbridge 29 Sept. 1843; m. 8 Dec. 1807 BENJAMIN HOLMES CUSHMAN, b. 26 Sept. 1778 Norwich, Vt., d. Tunbridge 25 Aug. 1870, son of Capt. Solomon and Sarah (Curtis) Cushman; he m. (2) Phebe Swan (Weyman Ms). In 1850 he was a farmer at Tunbridge, Vt., with [second] wife Phebe ae 52, Benjamin ae 39 and Harper ae 25 (p.11). In 1870 Benjamin ae 91 and Phebe ae 72 were in the household of son Earl at Tunbridge (p.464).

   Cushman children (Weyman Ms): 1. *Benjamin Cushman*[7], b. 1 June 1811; at home 1850. 2. *Lysander Cushman,* b. 28 April 1812; m. Elizabeth Freeman Sanborn. 3. *Maria Cushman,* b. 6 June 1813. 4. *George Provost Cushman,* b. 9 Jan. 1815; m. Lydia Emerson Dustin. 5. *Valmore Brock Cushman,* b. 14 Sept. 1816; m. Sarah L. Dustin. 6. *Earl Percy Cushman,* b. 29 Nov. 1818; m. Sarah Ann Mastin. 7. *Solomon Cushman,* b. 1 March 1821; m. Lucy B. Brigham. 8. *William Amos Cushman,* b. 24 Nov. 1822; m. Sarah Samantha Gibbs. 9. *Harper Gaffney Cushman,* b. 23 July 1824; m. Lydia Smith. 10. *Sarah Phebe Cushman,* b. 30 May 1830; m. Norman Dudley.

vi HARVEY HUTCHINSON, b. 26 March 1788; d. Tunbridge 9 May 1860 ae 72y 1m 13d of spasmodic asthma, bur. Hutchinson family cemetery (VT VR); m. (1) 12 Sept. 1811, ELIZABETH LADD, b. 16 Aug. 1788 (Weyman Ms), d. Tunbridge 11 Feb. 1813 ae 25y 6m, bur. Town Cemetery; m. (2) at Sharon, Vt., 19 Aug. 1813, SOPHIA BARNARD, b. ca 1790, d. 12 May 1844 ae 54y (VT VR). In 1850 Harvey was a farmer at Tunbridge with Hezekiah ae 29 and Mary Ellen ae 16, and Rachel M. Fuller ae 34 b. Canada with Ruth E. Fuller ae 2 (p.12).

   Children (VT VR; all in Weyman Ms), first with Elizabeth, rest with Sophia, b. and d. Tunbridge: 1. *Sophia Hutchinson*[7], b. 9 Jan., d. 25 Jan. 1813 ae 16d. 2. *Eliza Hutchinson,* b. 15 July 1814; d. 8 April 1848, unm. 2. *Sarah Sophia Hutchinson,* b. 20 Aug. 1816; d. 25 May 1844 ae 27y 9m. 3. *Phoebe Hutchinson,* b. 8 Sept. 1818; m. Alva Tracy. 4. *Hezekiah Hutchinson,* b. 29 Sept. 1820; m. Lucretia P. Butterfield. 5. *Emmeline Electa Hutchinson,* b. 24 Feb. 1823; m. William Pitt Brown. 6. *Ellen Jane Hutchinson,* b. 8 Jan. 183[1?]; d. 23 Sept. 1832 ae 1y 8m. 7. *Mary Ellen Hutchinson,* b. 15 Dec. 1833; m. Joseph Wardner Smith.

vii JOHN FARNAM HUTCHINSON, b. 27 July 1791; prob. m. at Tunbridge or Norwich, Vt., 10 March 1814, OLIVE WRIGHT.

Sources cited: Killingworth and Lebanon, Conn., Vital Records as cited in Barbour Index. Connecticut Probate Records, Salisbury District. Conn. Probate Records, Windham District. Vermont Vital Records to 1870: Royalton and Tunbridge. Lovejoy, *History of Royalton* (1911). *Vermont Religious Certificates* (2003). Weyman Manuscript. CENSUS: 1850 Bennington, Wyoming

Co., N.Y. (M432-616); Tunbridge, Orange Co., Vt., 1790 (M637-12), 1850 (M432-926) & 1870 (M593-1622).

709. JOHN HUTCHINSON⁵ (*Mercy⁴ Samson, David³, Caleb², Henry¹*), son of Timothy Hutchinson and his wife Mercy Samson [146], was born at Lebanon, Conn., in October 1754, according to an affidavit in his brother Abijah's pension application (White, 1788). He died at Royalton, Vt., 21 October 1847 in his 93rd year (*Royalton History*, 831). He was a descendant also of *Mayflower* passengers John Alden, Francis Cooke, and Myles Standish.

He married, 3 or 25 November 1779 at Royalton (*ibid.*), **HANNAH PARKHURST**, who was born at Plainfield, Conn., 14 March 1748 (VR 2:79), and died at Royalton 19 August 1831, aged 84, daughter of Joseph and Judith (Johnson) Parkhurst.

John was three or four years old in 1758 when his father died, and his mother soon remarried to William White. A distribution to the heirs of Dr. Timothy Hutchinson dated 12 April 1768 included John and Hezekiah Hutchinson (Conn. PR, Windham Dist. #2122).

In Lebanon, Conn., when the Revolution began, John enlisted at Colchester in November 1775 for 13 months and saw service at Roxbury. He went to Orange County, Vt., in 1777, and volunteered for service again there; he saw action at Saratoga, including the surrender of Burgoyne. He was living in Tunbridge, Vt., in 1780, where his was the first house in town. In October 1780 he was captured by Indians, who burned his house and took him to Canada for a year. Upon his return to Vermont he lived at Royalton, where he bought from Joshua Hutchins a farm on which he lived until his death (*Royalton History*, 831).

In 1790 the census listed him there with one man 16 or over and four females (p.63). In 1800 he was in Royalton, over 45, with one little boy under 10, one boy and one girl 10-16, a young woman 16-26, a woman 26-45, and a woman over 45 (p.462).

John applied for a pension 1 August 1832 at Royalton, aged 77 (White, 1789). In June 1839 he deeded 110 acres to [grandsons] Calvin, Charles, and John Bliss, in return for a bond promising lifetime support (*Royalton History*, 831). Charles W. Bliss of Royalton was appointed administrator 8 March 1848 of the estate of John Hutchinson of Royalton who died 21 October 1847 (Windsor Co. PR, Hartford Dist. 19:63). John and Hannah are buried in North Royalton Cemetery (*Royalton History*, 831).

Children of John and Hannah (Parkhurst) Hutchinson, rec. Tunbridge, Vt. (*Royalton History*, 831; all in Weyman Ms):

  i　REBECCA HUTCHINSON[6], b. 14 Aug. 1778; d. Royalton 16 June 1850; m. at Royalton, 11 Nov. 1802, JOHN BLISS, b. Rehoboth 17 Sept. 1773, d. Royalton 29 Aug. 1859, son of Nathan and Rebecca (___) Bliss (*Royalton History*, 688) or Nathan and Joanna (Bowen) Bliss (Weyman Ms).
    Bliss children, b. Royalton, Vt. (*ibid.*): 1. *Emily Bliss[7]*, b. 21 Oct. 1803; m. Othniel Dunham. 2. *Calvin Parkhurst Bliss*, b. 10 Dec. 1805; m. Maria Nichols. 3. *Nathan Bliss*, b. 16 Jan. 1808; d. 1824. 4. *Charles Bliss*, b. 26 July 1810; d. 1813. 5. *Sarah Anne Bliss*, b. 15 Sept. 1812; m. Isaac Brown. 6. *Charles William Bliss*, b. 16 Sept. 1814; m. Henrietta Whitney. 7. *Mary Lazette Bliss*, b. 6 Feb. 1816; m. Nathan Parker. 8. *John Hutchinson Bliss*, b. 24 July 1819; m. Harriet Cornelia Blodgett. 9. *Rebecca Jane Bliss*, b. 9 March 1822; m. Ira Holt.
  ii　JOHN HUTCHINSON, b. 4 Aug. 1782; d. 5 Aug. 1782.
  iii　ROXANNA HUTCHINSON, b. 1 Oct. 1784; d. 2 Jan. 1828; m. ___ PERRY.
  iv　PAMELA HUTCHINSON, b. in Feb. 1786; d. in Oct. 1786.
  v　SARAH HUTCHINSON, b. 3 March 1787; d. 29 Oct. 1847; m. at Royalton, 25 Oct. 1817, HENRY CHAMBERLAIN of Chelsea, Vt.
  vi　JOHN HUTCHINSON, b. 3 March 1790; d. 8 March 1790.

Sources cited: Plainfield Vital Records as cited in Barbour Index:. Vermont Vital Records to 1870: Royalton and Tunbridge. Conn. Probate Records, Windham District. Windsor Co., Vt., Probate Records, Hartford District. White, *Abstracts of Revolutionary War Pension Files*, citing S13491 [Abijah] and S22321 [John]. Weyman Manuscript. Lovejoy, *History of Royalton* (1911). CENSUS: Royalton, Windsor Co., Vt., 1790 (M637-12) & 1800 (M32-52).

710.　ABIJAH HUTCHINSON[5] (*Mercy[4] Samson, David[3], Caleb[2], Henry[1]*), son of Timothy Hutchinson and his wife Mercy Samson [146], was born at Lebanon, Conn., 4 July 1756 (White, 1788), and died at Geneseo, Livingston County, N.Y., 11 February 1843. He is buried in Temple Hill Cemetery there (*Abstracts of Graves of Rev. Patriots*, 2:#8163, vol. 4). He was a descendant also of *Mayflower* passengers John Alden, Francis Cooke, and Myles Standish.

He married 27 February 1783 at Salisbury, Conn., by Abial Camp, J.P. (VR 2:42), "he of Lebanon, she of Salisbury," **MERIAM FARNUM**. She was born at Killingworth, Conn., 31 January 1761 (VR 2:108), and died at Tunbridge, Vt., 4 May 1815, aged 54 (VT VR), daughter of Bezaleel and Phebe (Kirtland) Farnum. A distribution of the estate of Bezaleel Farnam late of Salisbury, dec'd, on 28

August 1782, names daughter Meriam Farnam (Conn. PR, Sharon Dist.). Meriam's sister Phebe was the first wife of Abijah's brother Hezekiah Hutchinson.

Abijah was just two years old in 1758 when his father died, and his mother soon remarried to William White. A distribution to the heirs of Dr. Timothy Hutchinson dated 12 April 1768 included son Abijah Hutchinson (Conn. PR, Windham Dist. #2122).

Abijah's pension records tell the story of his service in the Revolutionary War. He enlisted at Canada (now Hampton), Conn., for eight months in 1777 as a private. Afterwards he enlisted on the sloop *Oliver Cromwell* for two longer terms. On his discharge he returned to visit his brother Hezekiah at Salisbury, then went on from there in March 1780 to Tunbridge, Vt., where in October 1780 he was captured by Indians and taken to Montreal. When he was released in 1782 and sent to Boston, he went to Salisbury, Conn., where he married Meriam, and they left for Tunbridge in March 1783.

In 1790 Abijah was living in Tunbridge with one boy under 16 and one female (p.35). In 1800 the household consisted of himself, 45+, a woman 26-45, and a boy 10-16 (p.600).

Abijah was still in Tunbridge in November 1833, but in February 1835 he moved to Geneseo, N.Y., to live with his son James, his only living child, who was aged 58 in June 1843 (pension rec.). James published his father's story, *Memoir of Abijah Hutchinson.*

Children of Abijah and Meriam (Farnum) Hutchinson (VT VR):

i   SILVA HUTCHINSON[6], b. ca 1784; d. Tunbridge 14 June 1788, ae 4y.

ii JAMES HUTCHINSON, b. Tunbridge 14 April 1785; d. Libertyville, Ill., 18 Jan. 1863; m. at Tunbridge, 27 March 1809, BETSEY CLEMENTS, b. there 14 Nov. 1790, d. 7 Dec. 1854, both bur. Lakeside Cem., Libertyville. In 1840 James' household at Geneseo, N.Y., consisted of one man 80-90 [his father, listed as Rev. pensioner Abijah Hutchinson ae 83], one man 50-60, one woman 40-50, one man and two women 20-30, one young man 15-20, one boy and one girl 10-15, one boy 5-10, and one boy under 5 (p.249). They were in Geneseo in 1843, but moved to Libertyville, Lake Co., Ill., by 1850 when James Hutchinson ae 64, farmer b. Vt., had in his household Betsey ae 60, b. Vt., Harriet H. ae 22, Walter S. ae 20, both b. Vt., George W. ae 13 b. N.Y., and two Irish servants, Helen Finch ae 13 and James McCarton ae 20 (p.46)

Children, all but last b. Tunbridge, Vt.: 1. *Mary Clements Hutchinson[7]*, b. 20 March 1810. 2. *James O. Hutchinson*, b. 25 April 1813. ? 3. *Kirtland Hutchinson.* 4. *Miriam F. Hutchinson*, b. 18 Nov. 1820; d. 5 Sept. 1822. 5. *Henry C. Hutchinson*,

b. 5 April 1825. ? 6. *William O. Hutchinson*, b. ca 1827. 7. *Harriet H. Hutchinson*, b. ca 1828. 8. *Walter S. Hutchinson*, b. ca 1830. 9. *George W. Hutchinson*, b. 17 Jan. 1837.

Sources cited: Killingworth and Salisbury, Conn., VR as cited in the Barbour Index. Vermont Vital Records to 1870. Orange Co., Vt., Probate Records, Hartford District. White, *Abstracts of Revolutionary War Pension Files*, citing S13491. Connecticut Probate Records, Sharon District (included Salisbury to 1847). CENSUS: Tunbridge, Orange Co., Vt., 1790 (M637-12) & 1800 (M32-51); 1840 Geneseo, Livingston Co., N.Y. (M704-294); 1850 Libertyville, Lake Co., Ill. (M432-114). **See also:** K. M. Hutchinson, *Memoir of Abijah Hutchinson* (Rochester, N.Y.: W. Alling, 1843, available also on microfiche).

711.   JONATHAN FARNHAM[5] (*Eleanor*[4] *Samson, David*[3]*, Caleb*[2]*, Henry*[1]), son of Joseph Farnum and his wife Eleanor Samson [147], was born 7 December 1753, probably at Marshfield although not recorded there, and died 29 May 1823 at Boothbay, Maine (pension rec.). He was a descendant also of *Mayflower* passengers John Alden and Myles Standish.

He was of Marshfield when he married at Plymouth, 30 April 1782 after intentions 25 March 1780 (*VR* 267, 364), **DORCAS BARNES JR.** of Plymouth. She was born at Plymouth 18 February 1756, daughter of Lemuel and Sarah (LeBarron) Barnes (*VR* 49, 145), and died at Boothbay 12 December 1840 (pension rec.).

Jonathan served extensively in the Revolutionary War. He enlisted from Duxbury as a private in Capt. Samuel Bradford's company, Col. Theophilus Cotton's regiment, and is on a company return dated Roxbury Camp, 7 October 1775. He was also a Sergeant, in the Capt. Judah Alden's (7th) company, Col. John Bailey's regiment, on Continental Army pay accounts for service from 31 December 1776 to 31 December 1779, including a return dated Camp at Valley Forge, 24 January 1778 (*MSSR* 5:515).

The 1790 census listed Jonathan Farnham at Boothbay living next to his father Joseph and brothers Ansel and Chapen, with a household consisting of one man, one boy under 16, and three females (p.34). In 1800 he and his wife were both listed as 26-45 (a bit inaccurate in his case), and their family consisted of two boys and two girls 10-16 and two boys and two girls under 10 (p.369). Although he was listed next to his brothers Ebenezer and John, his name was spelled Farnham and theirs Farnom.

Jonathan Farnham was a resident of Boothbay when he applied for a pension 9 May 1818 in Lincoln County, Maine. In 1820 daughter Hannah, 27, was living at home, and in 1837 daughter Dorcas Holbrook, 51, made an affidavit, along with

Ezekiel Holbrook, 59. Dorcas applied for a widow's pension 30 December 1837, aged 81 (White, 1154, citing W24231).

Children of Jonathan and Dorcas (Barnes) Farnham, first two recorded Plymouth (*VR* 239), rest born Boothbay, Me. (*Boothbay History*, 525):

i   SARAH BARNES FARNHAM[6], b. 4 March 1785; m. after int at Boothbay, 21 April 1806, THOMAS SARGENT, b. there ca 1784, d. there 31 Jan. 1861, son of Benjamin Sargent.

   Sargent children, b. Boothbay, Me.: 1. *Isaac Sargent* [7], b. 8 Oct. 1806. 2. *Francis Sargent*, b. 19 April 1808. 3. *Sarah Sargent*, b. 24 June 1810. 4. *Hannah Sargent*, b. 10 Feb. 1813. 5. *Dorcas Farnum Sargent*, b. 18 June 1815; m. Joseph Farnham [#717-v]. 6. *Elizabeth Sargent*, b. 17 June 1818. 7. *Mary Sargent*, b. 26 Nov. 1820. 8. *Thomas Sargent*, b. 16 Jan. 1825.

ii   DORCAS FARNHAM, b. 18 Dec. 1786; d. Boothbay, 18 May 1884; m. there 9 Dec. 1806, EZEKIEL HOLBROOK, b. Wellfleet 1778, d. Boothbay 5 March 1863. In 1850 he was a farmer at Boothbay ae 72, with Dorcas ae 62, and the five youngest children; Mary E. Bennet ae 15 and Dorcas Farnum ae 31 were also in the household (p.51).

   Holbrook children, b. Boothbay: 1. *Lucy Holbrook*[7], b, 8 Oct. 1807. 2. *Daniel Holbrook*, b. 5 July 1809. 3. *Fanny Holbrook*, b. 6 Jan. 1812. 4. *Nancy F. Holbrook*, b. 16 April 1814. 5. *Sally F. Holbrook*, b. 7 July 1816. 6. *Dorcas Holbrook*, b. 30 Aug. 1818; m. her cousin Joseph Farnum, son of John and Abigail (Plummer) Farnum [#712-xii]. 7. *Ezekiel Holbrook*, b. 3 May 1822; a farmer 1850. 8. *Eliphalet Holbrook*, b. 17 Sept. 1824; a mariner 1850. 9. *William Holbrook*, b. 17 May 1827; a mariner 1850. 10. *Sarah Sophrona Holbrook*, b. 1 July 1830.

iii JOSEPH FARNHAM, b. 8 Oct. 1789; d. Boothbay, 1 May 1867; m. there, (1) after int. 11 Feb. 1820, his cousin NANCY FARNHAM [#712-ii], b. there 8 April 1795, d. before 1850, daughter of John and Abigail (Plummer) Farnham. In 1850 he was a master mariner at Boothbay with wife MARY ae 48, and all the surviving children except Nancy Jane; sons John, George, Andrew, and Israel H. were mariners (p.57).

   Children, b. Boothbay (*Boothbay History*, 526): 1. *Israel Farnum*[7], b. 16 Aug. 1822. 2. *John Farnum*, b. 24 Feb. 1824; m. Mary J. [prob. Farnum, #714-i-2]; next to parents 1850. 3. *George Farnum*, b. 19 Sept. 1826. 4. *Andrew Farnum*, b. 23 Dec. 1828. 5. *Israel Harvey Farnum*, b. 23 March 1831. 6. *Isaac Farnum*, b. 3 Aug. 1833. 7. *Nancy Jane Farnum*, b. 8 Feb. 1836; not at home 1850. 7. *Eliza A. Farnum*, b. 24 May 1838.

iv   HANNAH BARNES FARNHAM, b. 9 Sept. 1792; d. Boothbay, 25 Feb. 1856; m. int. there, 2 Dec. 1815, with JOHN PAGE, but *Boothbay History* says she d. unm.

    v   GEORGE FARNHAM, b. 12 March 1794; d. unm.

    vi   JONATHAN FARNHAM, b. 12 Nov. 1798.

Sources cited: *Plymouth VR. History of Boothbay* (1906). White, *Abstracts of Rev. War Pension Files.*
CENSUS: Boothbay, Lincoln Co., Me., 1790 (M637-2), 1800 (M32-6).

712.   JOHN FARNHAM[5] (*Eleanor[4] Samson, David[3], Caleb[2], Henry[1]*), son of
Joseph Farnum and his wife Eleanor Samson [147], was born about 1755, probably
at Marshfield, and died at Boothbay, Maine, 25 March 1849 (*Boothbay History*, 525).
He was a descendant also of *Mayflower* passengers John Alden and Myles Standish.

    He married, after intentions 8 June 1793, **ABIGAIL PLUMMER** of Bristol
(*Old Bristol VR*, 1:80), who was born about 1773 (1850 census) and died about
1858 (*Boothbay History*, 525). The marriage intentions erroneously call him "son of
Jonathan 1st."

    On 3 December 1791 Chapen Farnum, signing his name as Chafen Varnum,
of Boothbay, yeoman, quitclaimed to John Farnum of Boothbay, yeoman, for £24,
67 acres more or less, on the west side of the Damascotty [*sic*] River in Boothbay,
beginning at a spruce tree marked on four sides standing on the northern point of
Camp Cove, running thence northwest 250 rods to George Bace's easterly line,
thence south to the head of Ponch Island Cove, southerly by the shore of said
Pond [*sic*] to Benjamin Linneken's northwest corner, thence east southeast to the
Damariscotta River, with all buildings and appurtenances (Lincoln LR 52:154).
Chafen acknowledged the deed 5 December 1798 and it was recorded 3 September
1804 with a deed whereby Joseph Farnam of Boothbay, yeoman, quitclaimed 23
acres to John Farnum of Boothbay, yeoman, for $50 on 30 September 1796,
Ebenezer Farnam as a witness (*ibid.*).

    An incident in January 1798 involving John Farnham, in which his brother
Ansel was drowned, is described by Rice in *Shipping Days of Old Boothbay* (pp.19-20).
The two men, with James McFarland, had gone to help free a sloop that had struck
on a reef at Heron's Island, and coming back in their dugout canoe, John lay down
and fell asleep. After setting McFarland ashore, Hansel somehow fell overboard,
and when John woke up, he was (according to the *Kennebeck Intelligencer*),

> near two leagues outside the White Islands drifting to sea ... alone in the canoe without
> either paddle or oar. After being at sea four days and nights, without anything to subsist
> on excepting snow, the canoe drifted ashore on the Isles of Shoals, which being
> discovered by the inhabitants they repaired to the canoe and found him crawling on his
> hands and knees upon the rocks; they carried him to a house and gave him some

refreshments which he feebly partook of and then some people brought him to Portsmouth on the same day, but in a very weak situation.

There he met a captain from home, who, with another master, paid his expenses and obtained passage for him in a vessel bound direct to Boothbay, Farnham insisting that the canoe be taken on board. On arrival he was received as one from the dead, since the mystery of his disappearance and that of the canoe had been unexplainable. It had drifted at least seventy miles.

In his eighties Captain William Reed wrote: "Your story in regard to the Farnham canoe is very correct. This canoe was dug out of a big pine tree. It was over twenty feet long and from three to four feet wide and quite high sided. It was very able."

In 1800 the household of John Farnom [sic] at Boothbay consisted of one man and one woman 26-45 and two boys and two girls under 10 (p.369). The 1810 census listed John Farnham as head of a household of one woman over 45, one man and one woman 26-45, one boy and two girls 10-16, and one boy and two girls under 10 (p.198). In 1850 Abigail Farnum aged 77 was living in the household of her son John Farnum in Boothbay (p.51).

Children of John and Abigail (Plummer) Farnum, b. Boothbay, Maine (*Boothbay History*, 525):

i JOHN FARNHAM⁶, b. 24 Aug. 1793; d. ca 1885 unm. In 1850 he was a mariner at Boothbay ae 52, with a household that included his mother Abigail ae 77, his brother Michael [sic] ae 32 [sic], also a mariner, and prob. sister Sarah ae 40 [sic] (p.51).

ii NANCY FARNHAM, b. 8 April 1795; m. her cousin JOSEPH FARNHAM [#711-iii], *q.v.*, son of Jonathan and Dorcas (Barnes) Farnum.

iii SARAH FARNHAM, b. 18 Jan. 1797; prob. the Sarah ae 40 in her brother John's household 1850.

iv JAMES FARNHAM, b. 24 Aug. 1800; d. 1809.

v ELIZABETH/BETSY FARNHAM, b. 18 Nov. 1801; m. DAVID POOR.

vi DAVID FARNHAM, b. 11 Sept. 1803.

vii BEUFIELD FARNHAM, b. 10 March 1805; d. prob. y.

viii MARY FARNHAM, b. 18 Aug. 1808.

ix JAMES FARNHAM, b. 10 Jan. 1811; m. ABIGAIL TAYLOR.

x CHAPIN FARNHAM (twin), b. 21 Jan. 1813; d. unm.

xi MICAH FARNHAM (twin), b. 21 Jan. 1813; m. HANNAH SMALLEY. He is prob. the Michael ae 32, mariner, in his brother John's household 1850.

xii   JOSEPH FARNHAM, b. 22 June 1816; m. DORCAS HOLBROOK. It
       was prob. his wife or widow, Dorcas Farnum ae 31, who was in the
       household of [her parents] Ezekiel and Dorcas (Farnum) Holbrook in
       1850 (p.51).

xiii   MARY FARNHAM, b. 16 Feb. 1819; m. ISAAC W. SMALLEY, b. ca 1824
       Maine. In 1850 he was a sailor in Belfast, Me., with Mary ae 29, and three
       children (p.120). He was prob. son of Isaac and Martha (Farnum) Smalley
       [#717-ii].

           Smalley children at home 1850:   1. *Christiana Smalley*[7], b. ca 1845.
       2. *Alexander Smalley*, b. ca 1846. 3. *Martha Smalley*, b. ca 1849.

Sources cited: *VR of Old Bristol and Nobleboro. History of Boothbay* (1910). Rice, *Shipping Days of
Old Boothbay* (1938). CENSUS: Boothbay, Lincoln Co., Me. 1800 (M32:6), 1810 (M252-12), & 1850
(M432-260); Belfast, Waldo Co., 1850 (M432-270).

713.   CHAPIN/CHAFIN FARNHAM[5] (*Helena*[4] *or Eleanor Samson, David*[3],
Caleb[2], *Henry*[1]), son of Joseph Farnum and his wife Helena/Eleanor Samson [147],
was born about 1757, named for his mother's brother, Chapin Samson, and died
after 1798 when he acknowledged a deed. He was a descendant also of *Mayflower*
passengers John Alden and Myles Standish.

It appears that he married, but the name of his wife has not been found.

Chapin, spelled also Chapfin, Farnum served in the Revolution, as a private in
Capt. Woodbridge's Company, Col. Calvin Smith's (formerly Wigglesworth's)
Regiment, paid for service from January 1 to January 31, 1780; it was noted that he
had enlisted for a term of three years (*MSSR* 5:524).

On 20 March 1782 Samuel Montgomery of Boothbay, husbandman, for
diverse good causes and £48, deeded to Chaffen [*sic*] and Hanson [*sic*] Farnham,
both of Boothbay, 140 acres of land on the west side of the Damariscotta River,
running to the head of Island Cove (Lincoln LR 56:108).

The 1790 census listed Chapen Farnham [*sic*] in Boothbay next to his father,
Joseph, and brothers Ansel and Jonathan, with one man over 16, one boy under
16, and two females (p.34).

On 3 December 1791, Chafen Farnum of Boothbay, yeoman (signing as
Chafen Varnum), sold for £24 to John Farnum of Boothbay, yeoman, all his right
in a tract of 67 acres of land on the west side of the Damariscotta River in
Boothbay; one of the witnesses was Samuel Montgomery, from whom he had
bought the land with his brother Hansel; he acknowledged the deed 5 December
1798 (Lincoln LR 52:154-55).

No further record of him has been found.

Sources cited: *Mass. Soldiers & Sailors.* Lincoln County Deeds at Wiscasset, Me. CENSUS: Boothbay, Lincoln Co., Me., 1790 (M637-2).

714.   ANSEL/HANSEL/ANSELM FARNUM[5] (*Helena[4]* or *Eleanor Samson, David[3], Caleb[2], Henry[1]*), son of Joseph Farnum and his wife Helena / Eleanor Samson [147], was born about 1760, probably at Boothbay, Maine. He died in early January 1798 when he fell out of a canoe (*Shipping Days of Old Boothbay*, 19). He was a descendant also of *Mayflower* passengers John Alden and Myles Standish.

An Anselm Farnum published marriage intentions at Newburyport, 20 May 1784, with Amey Moore (*VR* 2:159), but no marriage is recorded.

On 20 March 1782 Samuel Montgomery of Boothbay, husbandman, for diverse good causes and £48, deeded to Chaffen [*sic*] and Hanson [*sic*] Farnham, both of Boothbay, 140 acres of land on the west side of the Damariscotta River, running to the head of Island Cove (Lincoln LR 56:108).

He was "of Boothbay" when he married at Bristol, Maine, 30 October 1789 after intentions 13 October (*Old Bristol VR*, 1:80), **ELIZABETH / BETSEY PLUMMER**, who was born there about 1768 and died after 1800 (census).

Hansel Farnom/Anselm Farnum served in the Revolutionary War. His name is on a list of men raised to serve in the Continental Army from Capt. Thomas Brackett's Company, 3rd Lincoln County Regiment; his residence was Bristol and he was engaged for that town and also for Woolwich, Maine. Pay accounts list his service from 11 March 1777 to 31 December 1779 as a private in Capt. John Burnam's company, Col. Michael Jackson's regiment, and also 82 days in the spring of 1777 in Capt. John Bayley's company, Col. Jackson's regiment (*MSSR* 5:517, 524).

On 20 March 1782 Samuel Montgomery of Boothbay, husbandman, for diverse good causes and £48, deeded to Chaffen [*sic*] and Hanson [*sic*] Farnham, both of Boothbay, 140 acres of land on the west side of the Damariscotta River, running to the head of Island Cove (Lincoln LR 56:108).

The 1790 census listed Ansel Farnham living at Boothbay next to his father, Joseph, and brothers Chapen and Jonathan, with a household consisting of one man over 16 and one female (p.34).

History of Boothbay states cryptically that "Records are unobtainable in this fam.," but the date and manner of Ansel's death are clarified elsewhere (Rice, *Shipping Days of Old Boothbay*, 19-20):

> An unusual incident occurred early in January 1798, when a Marblehead sloop, commanded by a Captain Brooks, struck on a reef at Heron's Island, and after futile attempts to get her off the master went ashore for aid. Two sons of Jonathan

Farnham, John and Hansel, together with James McFarland, agreed to assist him and paddled out to the stranded vessel in a dugout canoe. Thoroughly chilled in the wintry weather while freeing the sloop, they were invited on board, where all partook freely of liquor. They then departed in the canoe for home. The *Kennebeck Intelligencer* continues the tale:

> John Farnham soon said he would lie down on some straw and take a nap, as he was fatigued and sleepy, while his brother and Mr. McFarland paddled the canoe up the Damariscotta River. His brother accordingly set Mr. McFarland ashore on the eastern side of the river where he lived and then attempted to paddle to the western side of the river where he and his brother dwelt, but the wind blowing fresh and strong against him in the growing dark, it is supposed he felt cold and stood up in the canoe to thresh his arms and staggered or fell overboard. His brother, who was asleep, never wakened till he was near two leagues outside the White Islands drifting to sea when he found his brother and Mr. McFarland missing, and he alone in the canoe without either paddle or oar. ...

Elizabeth Farnom was listed at Boothbay in the 1800 census, aged 26-45 with two boys and three girls under 10 (p.369).

Children of Ansel and Elizabeth/Betsey (Plummer) Farnum, b. Boothbay, Me., spellings Farnam or Farnham also used:

     i   ANSEL FARNUM[6], b. ca 1794; d. Boothbay 28 June 1873 ae 79; bur. Holbrook Cem., E. Boothbay; m. at Bristol, 26 Dec. 1824 (*Old Bristol VR* 1:80), MINA/JEMIMA GAMAGE, b. ca 1800 Bristol, d. Boothbay 17 Sept. 1877. Hancil Farnum ae 48 [*sic*], mariner, was head of a household at Boothbay in 1850 with Mina ae 48 and all the children except Mary J.; all the boys from Simon up were mariners (p.51). Ansel Farnam, mariner of Boothbay, with wife Jemima sold land in Boothbay, nine acres to James Race in 1848 referring to the spruce tree marked on four sides (see his father's deed), and on 10 Dec. 1853, 3½ acres to Frederic F. Farnam of Boothbay, mariner, who sold it the same day to Nathaniel Foster (Lincoln LR 189:437).

         Children (*Boothbay History*, 526; 1850 census): 1. *Frederic F. Farnam[7]*, b. 5 June 1825. 2. *Mary J. Farnam*, b. 23 Aug. 1827; poss. m. her cousin John, son of Joseph and Nancy (Farnum) Farnum [#711-iii-2]. 3. *William G. Farnam*, b. 5 Oct. 1829. 4. *Ambrose C. Farnam*, b. 11 Feb. 1832. 5. *Simon H. Farnam*, b. 21 Sept. 1834. 6. *Albion Farnam*, b. 30 Oct. 1836. 7. *Ansel Farnam*, b. 9 May 1839. 8. *Lucinda Farnam*, b. 23 Sept. 1841. 9. *George M. Farnam*, b. 12 Aug. 1845.

     ii   CHAPIN FARNAM, b. ca 1796; m. ca 1816, MARIA MANN. He was called Chapen Varnum, mariner, of Bristol on 14 Feb. 1854 when he and wife Maria sold to Ansel Farnam of Boothbay their right in 45 acres of land in Boothbay bounded by land of Ebenezer and John Farnam (Lincoln LR 201:526).

iii MARY FARNAM, b. ca 1798.

iv [DAUGHTER] FARNAM, b. 1790 – 1800.

v [DAUGHTER] FARNAM, b. 1790 – 1800.

Sources cited: *VR of Old Bristol and Nobleboro. History of Boothbay* (1906). Rice, *Shipping Days of Old Boothbay* (1938). CENSUS: Boothbay, Lincoln Co., Me. 1790 (M637-2) & 1800 (M32-6).

715. MARTHA FARNHAM⁵ (*Helena⁴* or *Eleanor Samson, David³, Caleb², Henry¹*), daughter of Joseph Farnham and his wife Helena/Eleanor Samson [147], was born about 1762, probably at Boothbay, Maine, and died there 5 February 1825 aged 62 years (*Old Bristol VR*, 1:197). She was a descendant also of *Mayflower* passengers John Alden and Myles Standish.

She married after intentions at Bristol, Maine, 16 March 1794 (as Martha *Varnom*, **JAMES PLUMMER** of Bristol (*Old Bristol VR*, 2:290). He was born probably about 1759 in New Hampshire (1850 census) and died after 1850 when he was living at Bristol, Me. He evidently married, second, after 1825, ZABERINA ____, who was born in Maine about 1769 and was living in 1850.

In 1800 James Plummer's household in Bristol consisted of himself and presumably Martha, both 26-45, and two boys and one girl under 10 (p.390). In 1820 the family had increased: James and Martha were over 45, and with them were one man and one woman 26-45, two young men 16-26 of whom one was 16-18, two boys 10-16, and one boy and one girl under 10 (p.356). In 1850 James aged 91, and his second wife, Zaberina, aged 81, were living in the household of Ebenezer Pool Jr. aged 44 and wife Martha aged 37 in Bristol (p.32).

Probable children of James and Martha (Farnum) Plummer, b. Bristol, Me., list incomplete; census indicates several sons:

i LYDIA PLUMMER⁶, b. April 1797; d. Bristol, Me., 18 Aug. 1859; m. at Bristol, 21 Dec. 1822, JOSHUA HOUSE, b. there 30 Oct. 1797, d. there 30 May 1881, son of Joshua and Abigail (____) House. In 1860 Joshua was a farmer at Nobleboro, Me., with Mary A. ae 22, David ae 32, farmer, [David's wife] Lucinda ae 30, Adderson A. ae 26, "soldier in the armey," and Elbridge ae 24, mariner (p.60).

House children, b. Bristol, Me.: 1. *James House⁷*, b. 1823; m. Hellen Foster. 3. *Maria House*, b. 1825. 4. *Charlotte House*, b. April 1827. 5. *David Plummer House*, b. 28 Feb. 1829; m. (1) Lucinda Briggs, (2) Clara Lillian Dodge. 6. *Addison House*,

b. ca 1834. 7. *Elbridge N. House*, b. ca 1836; m. Delia S. Dole. 8. *Mary Ann House*, b. ca 1838.

? ii   DAVID PLUMMER, b. ca 1810; m. NANCY ____, b. ca 1809 Maine. In 1850 he was a farmer in Bristol with Nancy ae 41, and five sons (p.33).

Children at home 1850: 1. *Zenas F. Plummer*[7], b. ca 1831; a carpenter 1850. 2. *William H. Plummer*, b. ca 1834; a farmer 1850. 3. *Albert G. Plummer*, b. ca 1838. 4. *David E. Plummer*, b. ca 1840. 5. *Leander M. Plummer*, b. 1849.

iii   MARTHA PLUMMER, b. ca 1813; m. EBENEZER POOL JR., b. ca 1806. In 1850 he was a farmer in Bristol, Me., with Martha ae 37 and seven children; her father James and his second wife were living in their household (p.32).

Pool children at home 1850: 1. *Martha Pool*, b. ca 1837. 2. *Willard Pool*, b. ca 1839. 3. *Samuel Pool*, b. ca 1841. 4. *Nancy Pool*, b. ca 1843. 5. *James Pool*, b. ca 1845. 6. *Lydia Pool*, b. ca 1847. 7. *Ebenezer Pool*, b. 1850.

Sources cited: *Vital Records of Old Bristol and Nobleboro.* CENSUS: Bristol, Lincoln Co., Me., 1800 (M32-6), 1820 (M33-36), 1850 (M432-260); Nobleboro, Lincoln Co., Me., 1860 (M653-442).

716.   ELINOR FARNHAM[5] (*Helena*[4] *or Eleanor Samson, David*[3], *Caleb*[2], *Henry*[1]), daughter of Joseph Farnum and his wife Helena/Eleanor Samson [147], was born about 1764, probably at Marshfield, and died 5 April 1845 at St. George, Maine (*Maine Fam. 1790* 2:185). She was a descendant also of *Mayflower* passengers John Alden and Myles Standish.

She married at Boothbay, Maine, 24 April 1787 after intentions there 2 April, **DAVID LINNEKIN**, who was born there 22 April 1763 (*Boothbay History*, 564) and died at St. George 6 July 1838, son of Benjamin and Mary (____) Linnekin (*Maine Fam. 1790*, 2:185). They are buried in Wylie Corner Cemetery, St. George, Maine.

Children of David and Eleanor (Farnum) Linnekin, rec. St. George, Me. (*VR* 29) as "David Linnekin Family":

i   MARY LINNEKIN[6], b. 18 Jan. 1788; d. St. George in 1864; m. at St. George, 29 July 1805, JOHN CLARK, b. Beverly 1782, d. St. George 10 Aug. 1841, son of John and Mary (Wilson) Clark.

Clark children, b. St. George, Me.: 1. *Harriet Clark*[7], b. 1805. 2. *Josiah Clark*, b. 1806. 3. *Lavinia Clark*. 4. *Sarah Clark*. 5. *Eleanor Clark*. 6. *Eliza Jane Clark*, b. 1816. 4. *Catherine Clark*, b. 1818. 5. *Benjamin Clark*, b. 1819. 6. *Julia Clark*, b. 1825. 7. *Lucinda Clark*, b. 1826. 11. *James Clark*. 12. *Nancy Clark*. 13. *Levi Clark*, b. 1831. 14. *Andrew Jackson Clark*, b. 18 Nov. 1832.

ii JAMES LINNEKIN, b. 16 Dec. 1792; d. 1 May 1844 St. George (*VR* 22); m. at St. George, 1 May 1844, SARAH GILCHREST, b. 29 March 1798, d. 9 Dec. 1874, dau. of Samuel and Hannah (Robinson) Gilchrist (*Maine Fam. 1790*, 2:185).

Children rec. St. George (*VR* 22): 1. *Louisa Linekin[7]*, b. 26 Aug. 1818. 2. *George Linekin*, b. 9 Aug. 1820; d. Feb. 1847. 3. *David Linekin*, b. 19 April 1822. 4. *Barbary Linekin*, b. 31 July 1824; d. 27 March 1853. 5. *Ephia Linekin*, b. 18 Nov. 1827. 6. *Elvira Linnekin*, b. 7 March 1831. 7. *Alden G. Linekin*, b. 31 Aug. 1836. 8. *T. Whitney Linekin*, b. 1 Sept. 1838; d. 5 Jan. 1842.

iii NANCY LINNEKIN, b. 30 Dec. 1794; prob. d. 19 Jan. 1885 St. George (*VR* 50).

iv BENJAMIN LINNEKIN, b. 20 Dec. 1796; d. Rockland 24 Feb. 1879; m. Boothbay 18 Jan. 1821 [his cousin] HARRIET FARNHAM [#717-i], b. 24 Oct. 1797, d. Rockland 3 Feb. 1873, "wife of Capt. Benjamin Linneken of Belfast, ae 75" (*Belfast History*, 576), dau. of Ebenezer and Mary (Herrin) Farnham (*Maine Fam.* 2:185). In 1850 Benjamin (indexed as "Lemkin") was in Belfast, Me., a sailor, head of a household that included Harriett ae 53, seven apparent children, and Benjamin Smalley ae 23, a sailor, and his wife Acinith ae 19 [perhaps a Linnikin dau.?] (p.147). In 1870 Benjamin, a retired master mariner, and Harriet were in Belfast with only [?dau.] Mary E. Murray ae 47, no occupation, in their household.

Children at home 1850: 1. *Mary E. Linniken[7]*, b. ca 1822; poss. m. ____ Murray. 2. *Eben F. Linniken*, b. ca 1824; a sailor 1850. 3. *Ira Linniken*, b. ca 1826; a sailmaker 1850. 4. *Sarah Linniken*, b. ca 1829. 5. *Benjamin Linniken*, b. ca 1831; a sailor 1850. 6. *Hannah Linniken*, b. ca 1833. 7. *Reliance Linniken*, b. ca 1835.

v JOHN LINNEKIN, b. 16 Dec. 1799; d. St. George 1 April 1873; m. there, 22 Nov. 1827 (*VR* 199), ELIZA SMALLEY, b. there 9 Oct. 1809, d. 21 April 1843, dau. of Thomas and Elizabeth (Wyley) Smalley (*Maine Fam.* 2:185).

vi SARAH/SALLY LINNEKIN, b. 20 March 1801; m. St. George, Me., 21 Nov. 1822 by Benj[n] Eames (*VR* 36), SAMUEL WATTS, b. 14 Feb. 1799 (*ibid.*). In 1850 he was a farmer ae 51 at St. George, Me., with Sally ae 50, and daus. Catherine and Ephia (p.37). He was town clerk at St. George.

Watts children rec. St. George (*VR* 36): 1. *Harriet E. Watts[7]*, b. 1 Dec. 1823. 2. *Katharine Watts*, b. 13 April 1827. 3. *Ephia Watts*, b. 8 Aug. 1832.

vii MARTHA LINNEKIN, b. 13 July 1804.

viii LUCY LINNEKIN, b. 12 June 1806; d. 19 Jan. 1889 St. George (*VR* 2); m. 13 March 1829, LEVI SMALLEY, b. 18 Sept. 1804, d. 4 March 1872 (*VR* 2, from g.s.). He was the first keeper of Tenants Harbor lighthouse (*Maine*

Fam. 2:185). In 1850 he was a master mariner living at St. George with Lucy ae 44 and all six children (p.48).

> **Smalley** children rec. St. George (*VR* 2): 1. *Adam Smalley[7]*, b. 27 May 1831; a sailor 1850. 2. *Ellen Smalley*, b. 24 Dec. 1832; d. 7 April 1857. 3. *George G. Smalley*, b. 30 Nov. 1834. 4. *Levi Smalley*, b. 30 Sept. 1837; d. 2 May 1926. 5. *Farnsworth B. Smalley*, b. 3 Aug. 1839; d. 4 July 1859. 6. *Sarah Catharine Smalley*, b. 3 Dec. 1845; d. 24 Nov. 1922.

ix EPHIA LINNEKIN, b. 12 Dec. 1808; d. 25 Dec. 1832, St. George (*VR* 6); m. there (1) 25 Dec. 1832 (*VR* 201), THOMAS WHITNEY, b. 25 May 1806, d. 8 Oct. 1837, son of Artemas W. Whitney (*VR* 6); m. (2) 25 Aug. 1842 (*VR* 208), OBEDIAH GARDINER JR.

> **Whitney** child (*VR* 6): 1. *Mary Thomas Whitney[7]*, b. 23 Sept. 1837; d. 1 March 1838.

x ELIZA LINNEKIN, b. 23 Feb. 1812; m. at St. George, 2 May 1842 (*VR* 441), as his second wife, JAMES KELLER, b. ca 1806 Maine, widower of Louisa Keller (*VR* 202). In 1850 he was a master mariner in St. George, Me., ae 44, with Eliza ae 37, and six children, three of whom (Charles ae 16, Edwin ae 14, and Albert ae 11), could not be Eliza's, and three others whose ages indicate that they were hers (p.34).

> **Keller** children of James and Eliza at home 1850: 1. *Alvin Keller[7]*, b. ca 1843. 2. *William S. Keller*, b. ca 1845. 3. *Emily J. Keller*, b. ca 1849; m. Edward A. Watts.

Sources cited: *St. George, Me., VR. History of Boothbay* (1906). *History of Belfast, Me.* (----). Janet Ireland Delorey, "David Linniken," *Maine Families in 1790*, Vol. 2 (1990). CENSUS: 1850 St. George & Washington, Knox Co., Me. (M432-259).

717. EBENEZER FARNUM[5] (*Eleanor[4] Samson, David[3], Caleb[2], Henry[1]*), son of Joseph Farnum and his wife Eleanor Samson [147], was born about 1766, probably at Boothbay, Me., and died there 26 May 1823 (*Boothbay History*, 525). He was a descendant also of *Mayflower* passengers John Alden and Myles Standish.

He married, after intentions at Boothbay 27 October 1796 (*Boothbay Int.*), **MARY/POLLY HERRIN**, who died 10 December 1835.

Shortly before his marriage, on 5 October 1796, Joseph Farnum of Boothbay, yeoman, sold to Ebenezer Farnum of Boothbay, fisherman, 50 acres bordering land he had sold to John Farnum the previous week (Lincoln LR 52:154)

Children of Ebenezer and Mary (Herrin) Farnum, born Boothbay, Me. (*Boothbay History*, 525):

i HARRIET FARNUM[6], b. 24 Oct. 1797; m. [her cousin] BENJAMIN LINEKIN [# 716-v], *q.v.* for their family (p 339).

ii MARTHA FARNUM, b. 11 Aug. 1799; m. ISAAC SMALLEY, b. ca 1896 Me. In 1850 he was a sailor in Belfast, Me., with Martha ae 50 and six children (p.121).

Smalley children, list prob. incomplete; six youngest at home 1850: prob. 1. *Isaac W. Smalley[7]*, b. ca 1824; m. Mary Farnham 712-xiii. 2. *Jane H. Smalley*, b. ca 1835. 3. *Thomas Smalley*, b. ca 1836. 4. *Harvey Smalley*, b. ca 1838. 5. *James C. Smalley*, b. ca 1840. 6. *Harriett H. Smalley*, b. ca 1842. 7. *Aledia Smalley*, b. ca 1843.

iii EBENEZER FARNUM, b. 8 May 1802; d. 1809.

iv ALEXANDER FARNUM, b. 7 May 1804; m. at Boothbay, 18 Aug. 1828 (*Boothbay Int.*), EUNICE TAYLOR of Newcastle. In 1850 he was a master mariner at Newcastle ae 44, with Eunice ae 42, and six children (p.401).

Farnum children at home 1850: 1. *Mary Farnum[7]*, b. ca 1829. 2. *Alexander Farnum*, b. ca 1831, a mariner 1850. 3. *Sarah Farnum*, b. ca 1836. 4. *Eunice Farnum*, b. ca 1838. 5. *Laura Farnum* (?twin), b. ca 1843. 6. *Ephraim Farnum* (?twin), b. ca 1843.

v JOSEPH FARNUM, b. 7 April 1806; m. as Joseph Farnham 2d, after int. at Boothbay 13 Jan. 1838 (*Boothbay Int.*), DORCAS SARGENT, b. ca 1816, living 1860. He was listed in the 1850 census at Boothbay as *Ebenezer* Farnum ae 45, mariner (p.62), an error confirmed by the names and ages of the four oldest children for Joseph Farnham at North Boothbay in 1860 (p.58). In 1860 he was a rigger; son David was a fisherman.

Children, b. prob. Boothbay, spelling Farnham (census): 1. *Joseph C. Farnham[7]*, b. ca 1838. 2. *David Farnham*, b. ca 1840. 3. *Marriah/Marcia Farnham*, b. ca 1843. 4. *Ebenezer/Ebin Farnham*, b. ca 1848. 5. *Levi Farnham*, b. ca 1851. 6. *Lucy Farnham*, b. ca 1854. 7. *Charles Farnham*, b. ca 1856.

vi SARAH FARNUM, b. 4 July 1808; m. at St. George, 2 Aug. 1829 by Rev. Benjamin Eames (*VR* 200), THOMAS KELLOCH JR., both of St. George.

vii EBENEZER FARNUM, b. 1 Oct. 1810; d. 8 April 1870 St. George (*VR* 35); m. at St. George, 16 Jan. 1834 (*VR* 202), LYDIA WATTS, b. 26 Jan. 1809, d. 23 March 1870 St. George (*VR* 35). In 1850 he was a merchant at St. George with Lydia ae 42, and five children; Clarisa Rivers ae 19, John Watts Jr. ae 36, merchant, and Sarah M. Watts ae 19 shared the household (p.54).

Children, all but last two rec. St. George (*VR* 35), spelling Farnham: 1. *John Albert Farnham[7]*, b. 18 April 1835. 2. *Mary Augusta Farnham*, b. 10 Feb. 1837. 3. *Edward Watts Farnham*, b. 22 March 1840; d. 18 March 1883. 4. *Eben Francis Farnham*, b. 29 Aug. 1842; d. 11 March 1921. 5. *Lydia M. Farnham*, b. ca 1847. 6. *Alexander R. Farnham*, b. ca 1851, at home 1860.

viii	RACHEL FARNUM, b. 19 Jan. 1813; m. DAVID LANG, b. ca 1811 in Maine. In 1850 he was a master mariner at Boothbay with Rachael ae 37 and six children (p.56).

  Lang children at home 1850: 1. *Mary Lang*, b. ca 1836. 2. *John Lang*, b. ca 1839. 3. *Elenor Lang*, b. ca 1840. 4. *Sarah Lang*, b. ca 1842. 5. *Harriet Lang*, b. ca 1846. 6. *Charles Lang*, b. ca 1848.

Sources cited: *Boothbay Marriage Intentions* (2001). *History of Boothbay* (1906). CENSUS: Lincoln Co., Me.: Boothbay & Newcastle 1850 (M432-260), Boothbay 1860 (M653-442); St. George, Knox Co., Me., 1850 (M432-259) & 1860 (M653-440).

**718.	ELIZABETH⁵ SAMPSON** (*Chapin⁴ or Chaffin Samson, David³, Caleb², Henry¹*), daughter of Chapin/Chaffin Sampson [148] and his wife Betty Clift, was born at Duxbury 10 June 1762 (*VR* 145), and died at Brunswick, Maine, 20 August 1843, aged 82, "wife of Capt. W. Weston." She was a descendant also of *Mayflower* passengers John Alden, Myles Standish, and Richard Warren.

  She married, at Duxbury 8 March 1781 (*VR* 303), **WILLIAM WESTON**, son of Jacob and Deborah (Simmons) Weston. He was a descendant of *Mayflower* passengers Henry Samson [#748] and George Soule.

  On 30 November 1774 widow Betty Samson of Duxbury was appointed guardian of the minor children of Chafin Samson, late of Duxbury, mariner: Chapin Samson, Job Samson, Briggs Samson, Judith Clift Samson, and Elizabeth Samson (Plymouth PR 22:35).

  For an account of the family of William and Elizabeth (Samson) Weston, see William Weston [#748], p. 405.

Sources cited: *Duxbury VR.* Plymouth County Probate Records. Weston Typescript.

**719.	CHAPIN⁵ SAMPSON** (*Chapin⁴ or Chaffin Samson, David³, Caleb², Henry¹*), son of Chapin/Chaffin Sampson [148] and his wife Betty Clift, was born at Duxbury 14 August 1764 (*VR* 144), baptized in the First Church at Marshfield (*MQ* 47:34), and died at West Gardiner, Maine, 30 December 1850 (*NEHGR* 114:316) or 29 December 1853 (g.s., *Kennebec Co. History*, 678b). He was a descendant also of *Mayflower* passengers John Alden, Myles Standish, and Richard Warren.

  He married at New North Church, Boston, 13 July 1788 (*CR* 103), **SARAH SMITH**, who was born about 1768 and died at West Gardiner 10 June 1851 (g.s.), "widow of Chapin Sampson." Sarah Sampson owned the covenant at New North

Church 14 September 1788 and their daughter Sally was baptized there two weeks later (*CR* 103).

On 30 November 1774 widow Betty Samson of Duxbury was appointed guardian of the minor children of Chafin Samson, late of Duxbury, mariner: Chapin Samson, Job Samson, Briggs Samson, Judith Clift Samson, and Elizabeth Samson (Plymouth PR 22:35).

Chapin was master of the ship *Betsy*, owned by William Boardman of Boston and Nathan Long of Amesbury, which was captured by an Algerian corsair off Spain while on a voyage bound to Naples (*NEHGR* 114:316). *History of Kennebec County* (p. 671), dates the event as "about 1786," and continues,

> He and his crew were stripped of their clothing and driven through the streets of Algiers as a show, being the first Americans ever seen there. They were treated with all manner of indignities, thrown in loathsome dungeons, and at the end of ten days they were sent into the country to labor as slaves. Captain Chapin and his master soon discovered that they were brother Masons, and at the risk of his life the overseer proved his loyalty to the order by helping his slave to escape.

The family attended New North Church in Boston at least until 1794 when son William Smith was baptized there.

Chapin Sampson was a grantee of land from Charles Sampson Jr. in Waldoboro (Lincoln LR 37:54). By a deed recorded 21 January 1801, Chapin Sampson and wife Sally sold land to Charles Sampson Jr. of Waldoboro, (*ibid.*, 46:202).

He signed his name to a deposition 16 August 1802 in Lincoln County, calling himself "Chapin Sampson of lawful age," but giving no place of residence, stating that

> I commanded the ship *Astrea* of Wiscasset owned by Abiel Wood Senr Esq., ... I sailed in said ship from Wiscasset as Master about the fifth of March AD 1800 bound to Liverpool in the Kingdom of Great Britain with a cargo of oak & pine timber, spars, masts, lathwood & staves & was consigned to Mess[rs] John & William Finlayson Merchants in Liverpool ... I arrived in said Ship in Liverpool aforesaid in the month of May following, & on my arrival at Liverpool I heard it reported that said John & William Finlayson were about to fail in their business, which report I informed them of, they then informed me that their affairs had been under some embarrasments but that they were all all settled, in consequence of which I delivered the cargo of said Ship into their hands, & on my departure from Liverpool [they] handed me an account of sales of said cargo which amounted to two thousand nine hundred & fifty eight pounds eleven shillings & nine pence British sterling, & that there remained unaccounted for about thirty four thousand staves & a quantity of heading which was not included in the account of sales handed me, and which I understood by them we sold for eight guinea p[r] thousand.

I further testify & say that my orders from Mr Wood was to take a full load of salt on board said ship *Astra* at Liverpool, that after being detained by said John & William Finlayson six weeks waiting for salt was obliged to leave Liverpool in said ship with little more than half the quantity of salt ordered.

Chapin Sampson, mariner, was of Boston on 13 October 1805 when he purchased a farm of 100 acres in Hallowell, Maine, from William Morse and Nathan Bachelder, merchants (Kennebec LR 10:341). He settled later in Bath, Maine.

In 1850 the household of Chapin Sampson, 85, master mariner, included Sarah Sampson, 82, and Maria Sampson, 49, all born in Mass. (p.298). The households of William Stevens and Job Sampson were next door.

Maria Samson was appointed administratrix of the estate of Chapin Sampson, late of West Gardiner, on 28 April 1851, and posted $500 bond with John Stevens and John Bachelder as sureties (Kennebec Co. PR 67:464, 87:139). The inventory, taken 6 May 1851, totaled $318.87½ and included two notes of hand from John Stevens secured by a mortgage on real estate, two cows, a cooks stove, two beds, a clock, some other furniture, one portrait, two pictures, and a Bible "& several other books" (*ibid.*,82:307). The widow Sarah petitioned for her share of the personal estate and was directed to give notice thereof for three successive weeks in the *Hallowell Gazette*, but "deceased before return day" so the proceedings were discontinued (*ibid.,* 96:17). The final accounting presented by Maria Sampson as administratrix, 2nd Monday of December 1852, included expenses of the last sickness and funeral of the widow Sarah (*ibid.,* 107:19).

Capt. Chapin Sampson and his wife Sarah are buried in a family cemetery near their house, "on the road to Litchfield" in West Gardiner, Me. (*Kennebec History,* 678b; g.s.).

Children of Chapin and Sarah (Smith) Sampson (*NEHGR* 114:316-17); first three bp. New North Church, Boston (*CR* 103):

 i SARAH^6 SAMPSON, b. ca July 1788; bp. 28 Sept. 1788 as SALLY; d. 5 Oct. 1869, ae 81y 3m; m. WILLIAM STEVENS, d. 3 July 1855, ae 74y 10m. In 1850 he was ae 69, a farmer, in Gardiner, Me., with Sally ae 61; dau. Sarah was with them and son John's family shared the dwelling (p.298).

   Stevens children at home 1850: 1. *John Stevens^7*, b. ca 1809; m. Harriet L. French (MSMD #3979). 2. *Sarah Stevens,* b. ca 1815; unm. 1850.

 ii CHAPIN SAMPSON, bp. 6 Jan. 1793; d.y.

 iii WILLIAM SMITH SAMPSON, bp. 12 Oct. 1794; drowned in 1819 (*Col. Cent.*, 11 Aug. 1819).

iv THOMAS B. SAMPSON, b. Waldoboro, Me., 6 Feb. 1797; d. 31 Aug. 1873; bur. Sampson Cem., West Gardiner; m. at Gardiner, Me., 15 May 1826 (*VR* 453), HARRIET B. CURRIER, b. ca 1808, d. Auburn, Me., 19 Oct. 1897, dau. of Nathaniel and Sarah (Abbott) Currier. He was a sea captain. An account of him in *History of Kennebec County* (p.678b; portrait opp. p. 679) says: "[he] received the advantages of the common schools of those times, and at an early age began an apprenticeship to a spar maker in Boston, where he remained until the beginning of the war of 1812. Circumstances transpired in 1813 that fired the patriotism of the young mechanic, and he abandoned the tools of his craft and at once enlisted in the navy, where he served his country for two years." Later he was in the merchant service, and in 1824 became master of his own vessel, operating in the European trade for 34 years before retiring to his farm.

Children rec. Gardiner (VR 156, 641) all d. before 1892 (*Kennebec History*, 678b): 1. *Harriette E.[7] Sampson*, b. 9 Feb. 1827; m. Dr. Chadbourn W. Whitmore. 2. *Adelia B. Sampson*, b. 5 June 1829; d. 19 Sept. 1831. 3. *William C. Sampson*, b. 7 March 1831; d. 7 Jan. 1832. 4. *Thomas C. Sampson*, b. 12 March 1834; m. Charlotte M. Jackson.

v MARIA SAMPSON, b. ca 1801; living 1852 when adm. father's estate.

vi JOB SAMPSON, b. 2 June 1802; d. West Gardiner 19 July 1889 (g.s.), a blacksmith; m. after int. at Gardiner 29 Aug. 1829 (*VR* 453), HANNAH BRAN, b. 27 July 1811, d. Boston 2 Sept. 1891, daughter of John and Rachel (Edgecomb) Bran. Job and Hannah are bur. with his parents. In 1850 he was a blacksmith living in Gardiner with Hannah and nine children (p.298).

Children (*NEHGR* 114:317): 1. *Mary Ann[7] Sampson*, b. 22 Dec. 1829; d. 20 July 1844. 2. *Rufus Sampson*, b. 4 March 1832; d. 19 Sept. 1833. 3. *Oliver Roscoe Sampson* (twin), b. 22 Sept. 1834; m. Emily J. Stevens. 4. *Osgood Manceno Sampson* (twin), b. 22 Sept. 1834. 5. *Josephine Sampson*, b. 15 Oct. 1836; m. (1) William McCausland, (2) James Littlefield. 6. *Isaac Smith Sampson*, b. 5 Sept. 1838; m. Sarah Elizabeth Neal. 7. *Eugene Grant Sampson*, b. 1 Aug. 1840; m. Rachel Francena Stevens. 8. *Alonzo Sampson*, b. 2 Nov. 1842; d. 1866; m. Sarah E. Kezer. 9. *Mary Jane Sampson*, b. 7 Feb. 1845; d. 14 June 1864. 10. *Hannah Virginia Sampson*, b. 14 May 1847; m. Elisha P. Seavey. 11. *Georgia Ann Sampson*, b. 30 May 1849; m. Frank A. Leavitt. 12. *Sophia Larrabee Sampson*, b. 6 Sept. 1851; m. (1) John H. Collins, (2) Enoch Dill.

vii LUCY SAMPSON, b. say 1806; d. prob. ca 1835; m. at Gardiner, Me., 27 Sept. 1830 (*VR* 453), JULIUS NEAL, b. 19 March 1803, d. Hallowell 26 March 1842. He m. (2) int. Nov. 1836, Sarah Seavey.

viii RUFUS SAMPSON, b. 1808; d. New Orleans, La., 1831, ae 23 (*Col. Cent.* 13 July 1831).

ix MARY ANN SAMPSON, b. 11 Aug. 1810; d. 5 July 1887; m. (1) at
Gardiner, 25 April 1830 (*VR* 453), THOMAS BRANN, b. 16 July 1802,
d. 9 April 1849, son of Capt. John Bran and brother of her brother Job's
wife Hannah; m. (2) 16 Oct. 1859 (*VR* 325), DANIEL HILDRETH, b.
Gardiner 1 Sept. 1818. In 1850 Mary A. Bran and her children lived near
her parents in Gardiner (p.302).

Bran children at home 1850: 1. *Ellen M. Bran⁷*, b. ca 1833. 2. *William S.
Bran*, b. ca 1836. 3. *Sarah J. Bran*, b. ca 1838. 4. *Thomas A. Bran*, b. ca 1840.
5. *Emory M. Bran*, b. ca 1843. 6. *Adelaide Bran*, b. ca 1848.

Sources cited: *Duxbury VR. Boston VR* [BRC 30]. *Gardiner, Maine VR.* Marshfield Baptisms,
Mayflower Quarterly 47 (1981). *Records of New North Church, Boston.* Kennebec County, Me., Probate
Records. *Illustrated History of Kennebec County* (1892). West Gardiner, Me., gravestone inscriptions
on line. *Giles Memorial* (1864). James T. Seavey of Bethlehem, Pa., "Sampson Family Notes,"
NEHGR 114 [1960], *q.v.* for further detail. *Columbian Centinel Index.* CENSUS: 1850 Gardiner,
Kennebec Co., Me. (M432-257).

720. JOB⁵ SAMPSON (*Chapin⁴ or Chaffin Samson, David³, Caleb², Henry¹*), son of
Chapin / Chaffin Samson [148] and his wife Betty Clift, was born at Duxbury 19
September 1766 (*VR* 145), and died there 9 November 1822, aged 56 (*VR* 410).
He was a descendant also of *Mayflower* passengers John Alden, Myles Standish, and
Richard Warren.

He married at Duxbury, 15 June 1787 (*VR* 303), **BETSEY WINSOR**, who
was born there 3 February 1768, daughter of Samuel and Rhoda (Delano) Winsor,
and a descendant of *Mayflower* passenger John Alden. She died at Como, Illinois,
5 October 1854 (*Giles Mem.*, 413).

On 30 November 1774 widow Betty Samson of Duxbury was appointed
guardian of the minor children of Chafin Samson, late of Duxbury, mariner:
Chapin Samson, Job Samson, Briggs Samson, Judith Clift Samson, and Elizabeth
Samson (Plymouth PR 22:35).

Job was a shipmaster. He was commander of a vessel which in 1786 hoisted
the second American flag ever raised in the harbor of Leghorn [Livorno, Italy]
(*Giles Mem.*, 413). After his death, Betsey moved with her sons and their families to
Illinois, where in 1839 she was the oldest person living in Whiteside County
(*Whiteside Co. History*, 251-52).

The will of Job Sampson of Duxbury, dated 4 August 1819, proved 18
November 1822, names his wife Betsey; daughter Betsey wife of Thomas Power;
daughter Judith Sampson, and two sons: Henry B. Sampson and William Sampson
(Plymouth PR 56:248).

In 1850 Betsey S. Sampson, aged 82, was living in the household of her son Henry B. Sampson in District 37, Whiteside County, Illinois (p.383).

Children of Job and Betsey (Winsor) Sampson, b. probably at Duxbury (*Giles Mem.*, 413, 441):

i   [HENRY] BRIGGS[6] SAMPSON, b. 14 July 1787; res. Como, Ill., in 1862; m. NANCY TURNER, b. 8 May 1789, d. 8 Nov. 1862 Como, Ill., daughter of Col. William and Eunice (Clapp) Turner (Weyman Ms). In 1850 Henry B. Sampson was ae 62, a tavern keeper at District 37, Whiteside, Ill., with Nancy ae 60, Ann B. Sumwalt ae 33, Juliette Sampson ae 24, Florana H. Sampson ae 18, all b. Mass., and Albert Sampson ae 15, b. Me. (p.383).

    Children, b. Duxbury except the last (Weyman Ms): 1. *Frances Elizabeth[7] Sampson*, b. 8 Jan. 1814; m. Winfield Scott Wilkinson. 2. *Ann Briggs Sampson*, b. 22 March 1817; m. before 1850 Henry A. Sumwalt. 3. *Henry Rollins Sampson*, b. 6 Sept. 1819; m. Emma Dickerson. 4. *John Turner Sampson*, b. 7 Aug. 1822; d. 3 Oct. 1826. 5. *Julia Turner Sampson*, b. 16 June 1825; m. Charles Nash Russell. 6. *Georgiana Sampson*, b. 1 Feb. 1829; m. Charles P. Mallett. 7. *Florence Helen Sampson*, b. 2 April 1832; m. Edwin Clark Whitman. 8. *Albert Soule Sampson*, b. 1 Oct. 1834 Hallowell, Me.; m. Lucetta A. Cook.

ii   BETSEY SAMPSON, b. 27 Sept. 1789; m. 8 June 1813, THOMAS POWER, b. Boston 8 Oct. 1786, d. Framingham 9 Sept. 1868, son of Thomas and Hannah (Lincoln) Power (Weyman Ms). In 1850 Thomas Power ae 64 was a clerk of police court in Ward 10, Boston, with Betsy S. ae 40, and Charles J. ae 25, grocer; the household included Henry R. Sampson ae 30, [prob. Betsey's nephew], and [her sister] Judith Sampson ae 55 (p.475).

    Power children (Weyman Ms): 1. *Thomas Frederick Power[7]*, b. Duxbury 25 Aug. 1817; m. Susan Huntington (Odiorne) Shepherd. 2. *Charles Jackson Power*, b. Boston 11 April 1824; m. Catharine F. Coolidge. 3. *Elizabeth Julia Power*, b. 9 Dec. 1827; d. 12 June 1832.

iii   WILLIAM SAMPSON, b. 25 May 1792; d. 11 Aug. 1851, Chicago, Ill., of cholera; m. at Duxbury 4 Feb. 1816 (*VR* 314), CAROLINE SPRAGUE, b. there 6 Oct. 1795, dau. of Seth and Deborah (Sampson) Sprague (*VR* 168). In 1850 W. Sampson ae 58 was a broker in Ward 3, Chicago, with a household that included Mrs. C. Sampson ae 55, M. L. Merrit ae 25, W. Sampson ae 20, Josephine Sampson ae 18, F. A. Sampson ae 14, E.J.P. Sampson ae 12, Amos Merrit ae 26, clerk, b. Pa., and Chas. P. Merrit ae 1, b. Ill. (p.225).

    Children (Weyman Ms; first eight rec. Duxbury *VR* 138-43): 1. *Caroline Amelia[7] Sampson*, b. 6 Feb. 1817; m. Simeon Sampson. 2. *William Henry Sampson*, b. 19 June. 1819; m. Caroline Hopkins. 3. *George W. Sampson*, b. 7 Sept. 1821; d. 9 Sept. 1822. 4. *Edward Sampson*, b. 15 Feb. 1823. 5. *Maria Louisa Sampson*, b. 16 April 1825; m. Amos Coburn Merrill or Merrit. 6. *Virginia Sampson*, b. 15 July

1827; m. Henry Garnsey. 7. *Marilla Sampson*, b. 5 Nov. 1829; d. 1861, unm., "burned to death." 8. *Josephine Sampson*, b. 24 May 1832; m. Jeremiah Thompson. 9. *Frederick Sampson*, b. 1836; m. Eliza Farr. 10. *Elizabeth Julia Samson*, b. 6 Sept. 1838; unm. 1863.

iv   JUDITH SAMPSON, b. 6 Sept. 1797; d. Framingham 27 Oct. 1873 of bilious fever and typhoid fever, single, ae 76y 2m 12d, b. Duxbury (Mass. VR 257:162; parents' names incorrect), res. with her sister in Boston 1850 (p.475) and in Framingham 1863 (*Giles Mem.*).

Sources cited: *Duxbury VR. Plymouth VR. Weymouth VR. Giles Memorial* (1864), has more detail. Charles Bent, *History of Whiteside County, Illinois* (1877). CENSUS: 1850, Ward 10, Boston, Suffolk Co. (M432-337), Chicago, Cook Co., Ill. (M432-102), Dist. 37, Whiteside Co., Ill. (M432-132).

721. JUDITH CLIFT⁵ SAMPSON (*Chapin⁴ or Chaffin Samson, David³, Caleb², Henry¹*), daughter of Chapin/Chaffin Sampson [148] and his wife Betty Clift, was born at Duxbury 10 December 1768 (*VR* 146), and died after October 1806 (birth of last rec. child), but before 1827 when her husband remarried. She was a descendant also of *Mayflower* passengers John Alden, Myles Standish, and Richard Warren.

She married at Duxbury, 15 December 1791 (*VR* 300), he of Marshfield, she of Duxbury, **NATHANIEL CHANDLER WESTON**, who was born about 1770 and died about 1846 (Plymouth PR #22423), son of William and Ruby (Chandler) Weston and a descendant of *Mayflower* passenger George Soule. He married, second, about 1827, **ANNE ___**, born about 1795, with whom he had Sarah Chandler (b. 1828), William 2d (b. 1832), Betsey C. (1834-1838), and Nathaniel B. Weston (1837), all recorded at Duxbury (*VR* 188, 193-95) as "of Nathaniel C. and Anne (second wife)."

On 30 November 1774 the widow Betty Sampson of Duxbury was appointed guardian of Judith and her siblings, Chapin, Job, Briggs, and Elizabeth, minor children of Chafin Sampson, late of Duxbury, mariner: (Plymouth PR 22:35).

On 21 March 1797 Briggs Sampson of Duxbury, trader, sold to Nathaniel Chandler Weston of Duxbury, mariner, his rights in real estate of his father, Chapin Sampson, reserving his mother's dower and referring to his brother Job Sampson's deed of 7 March 1793 (Plymouth LR 82:81).

The will of Nathaniel's father, William Weston of Marshfield, dated 20 June 1804, presented 25 February 1805, names his [second] wife, Keziah, and, among his children, son Nathaniel C. Weston (Plymouth PR 40:171). On 28 March 1811 Nathaniel C. Weston filed an account as administrator of his father's estate (*ibid.*, 43:384).

Benjamin Alden, administrator of the estate of Nathaniel C. Weston, late of Duxbury, deceased, petitioned in November 1846 to sell part of the real estate, indicating that the personal estate had been allowed to the [unnamed] widow (Plymouth PR 3P:37).

In 1850 Ann Weston aged 55 was living at Duxbury with sons William D. ae 17 and Nathaniel B. ae 12 (p.80).

Children of Nathaniel C. and Judith C. (Samson) Weston, b. Duxbury (*VR* 188-94):

i   NATHANIEL WESTON[6], b. 22 Oct. 1793; prob. Capt. Nathaniel who d. 3 Aug. 1835 in West Indies (Weston Ts, 145; see also *Duxbury VR* 438); m. at Duxbury, 19 May 1831 (*VR* 331), ABIGAIL FRAZER, b. there 7 Aug. 1796 (*VR* 77), dau. of Samuel A. and Abigail (Drew) Frazer. In 1850 she was living in Duxbury with her sister Mercy C. Frazar and the children, her mother next door (p.73-74); Weston Ts says she d. in San Francisco.

   Children rec. Duxbury (*VR* 188, 193; Weston Ts 145): 1. *Arabella Weston*[7], b. 6 March 1832. 2. *Nathaniel Weston Jr.*, b. 6 June 1834.

ii JUDITH WESTON, b. 15 July 1796; d. Duxbury, unm., 24 April 1872 of consumption (Mass. VR 248:383).

iii CHURCH WESTON, b. 6 Aug. 1799; lost at sea in 1846; m. ELEANOR WINSOR (d. & m. *VR* 438), b. Duxbury 23 April 1804, dau. of James and Sarah (Gray) Winsor (*VR* 200), d. 1891, Paris, France, bur. Duxbury (Weston Ts 145). In 1850 Ellen W. Weston ae 46 was living at Duxbury with Ellen C. ae 13 (p.67).

   Child, rec. Duxbury (*VR* 189): 1. *Helen/Ellen Church Weston*[7], b. 14 March 1836; m. Capt. Dwight Boyden (Weston Ts; Weyman Ms).

iv RUBY WESTON, b. 29 July 1803; d. 1848 (Weston Ts; *VR* 438); bur. Large Cem., Duxbury; m. Capt. ALVIN BAKER, b. Duxbury 18 July 1803 (*VR* 21). No ch. rec. Duxbury. He m. (2) Martha James ___.

v   LUCY WESTON, b. 30 Oct. 1806; d. Duxbury 12 Oct. 1903 ae 96y 11m 12d, dau. of "Chandler Weston and Judith Sampson" (Mass. VR 1903, 18:64); m. at Duxbury, 8 Feb. 1832 (*VR* 336), EDEN WINSOR, b. Duxbury 4 Aug. 1806 (*VR* 200), d. there 6 Oct. 1882 of heart disease, a mariner, son of Charles and Beulah (Wadsworth) Winsor (Mass. VR 338:303).

Sources cited: *Duxbury VR*. Plymouth County Deeds and Probate Records. Weston Typescript. Weyman Ms has errors in account of this family. CENSUS: Duxbury, Plymouth Co., 1810 (M252-21) & 1850 (M432-333).

722.   NATHAN SIMMONS⁵ (*Zachariah Simmons⁴, Lora³ Samson, Caleb², Henry¹*), son of Zachariah Simmons [149] and his wife Deborah Bishop, was born at Duxbury 3 April 1732 (*VR* 190), and died at Plymouth 1 or 3 November 1758, aged 27y 6m [*sic*] (*VR* 190, 298). He was a descendant also of *Mayflower* passengers John Alden and Myles Standish.

He married at Plymouth, 24 October 1753 (*VR* 347), published as "he of Kingston, she of Plymouth," **LYDIA HOLMES**, who was born at Plymouth 17 November 1735 (*VR* 68), daughter of Cornelius and Lydia (prob. Bennet) Holmes, and died there 29 April 1821, aged 86, as "widow Lydia Mason" (*CR* 669).

She married, second, at Plymouth, 20 October 1767 (*VR* 351), STEVENS MASON, who died there 31 December 1789 (*CR* 417). Stevens and Lydia (Holmes) (Simmons) Mason had four children born at Plymouth (*VR* 224): Stevens Mason, Lydia Mason, Polly Mason, and Susanna Mason.

Nathan Simmons and his family, "who came from Plimouth the 6ᵗʰ day of Aprill last" were warned out of Duxbury 4 January 1757 (*PCCR* 3:78].

Nathan was a mariner. Bond on Lidia Simmons of Plymouth, widow, as administratrix of the estate of Nathan Simmons, mariner, late of Plymouth, deceased, was issued 10 September 1767, with Dr. William Thomas and John Nelson as sureties (Plymouth PR 19:527).

Stevens Mason was paid 40 shillings in September 1778 and again in December 1778, and £4 in April 1779 for "Sweeping and taking Care of the Court House" (PCCR 3:502, 504, 508).

In 1790 Bennett Simmons was listed in Plymouth with four females (p.176); there were no Masons and no Nathan Simmons. No listing was found for Lydia Mason in Plymouth in 1810. No Plymouth Probate records were found for Stevens or Lydia Mason, or for Lydia's parents, Cornelius and Lydia Holmes.

Children of Nathan and Lydia (Holmes) Simmons, rec. Plymouth (*VR* 190):

i   NATHAN SIMMONS⁶, b. 29 July 1754; "deceased 11 Aug. following."

ii NATHAN SIMMONS, b. 11 Aug. 1755 [*sic*]; d. prob. ca 1814. The only record of a Nathan Simmons serving in the Revolutionary War is a man in Capt. Isaac Wood's company, Col. Theophilus Cotton's regiment, who had an order for bounty coat or its equivalent in money dated Roxbury Camp, 17 Nov. 1775 (*MSSR* 14:233), and this might be a confusion with a Nathaniel Simmons of Duxbury. Despite his age, his children's names suggest that was the Nathan Simmons of Plymouth who m. there 26 June 1809 [after b. of first ch.] (*VR* 386), after int. 1 Oct. 1808 (*VR* 303), NANCY SIMMONS of Plymouth. She appears to have pub. int. Plymouth 20 April 1805 (*VR* 296) with Caleb Alexander Spooner "now res. Plymouth, he came from New Beadford" but no marriage is recorded. She prob. m. (2) at Plymouth, as Nance Simmons, 21 April 1816 after int. 1 Sept. 1815, Joseph Muxsom (*VR* 311, 379). He had pub. int. Plymouth 3 May 1812 with Cintha Hall (*VR* 307). In 1820 Joseph Maxham's household at Plymouth consisted of one man and one woman 26-45 and two boys under 10 (p.364).

Children rec. Plymouth (p.429): 1. *William Simmons⁷*, b. 4 June 1809. 2. *Nathan Bennit Simmons*, b. 9 Nov. 1811; d. 18 June 1812. 3. *Nathan Bennit Simmons* again, b. 20 Oct. 1813.

iii   BENNET SIMMONS, b. 17 Aug. 1757; d. Plymouth Nov. 1801 (*VR* 340); m. there, 11 Feb. 1784 (*VR* 364), SARAH⁵ (SAMPSON) COOPER, also a descendant of Henry Samson [#684], *q.v.* (p.281) for an account of this family.

Sources cited: *Kingston VR. Plymouth VR. Plymouth Church Records.* Plymouth County Probate Records. Konig, *Plymouth County Court Records.* CENSUS: Plymouth, Plymouth Co., 1790 (M637-4), 1820 (M33-50).

723. ELEAZER SIMMONS⁵ (*Zachariah Simmons⁴, Lora³ Samson, Caleb², Henry¹*), son of Zachariah Simmons [149] and his wife Deborah Bishop, was born at "Marshfield in New England, March 15ᵗʰ, 1739," as recorded at Liverpool, Nova Scotia, with his marriage and births of his children (VR 59). His birth was recorded at Duxbury as 14 March 1738/9 (*VR* 152), and he was baptized at Marshfield 18 March 1738/9 (*MD* 32:16). He was living at Liverpool, N. S., in 1780 (based on birth of last child), but evidently returned to Duxbury and died there, in the alms house, "burned," 23 November 1827 aged 88 (*VR* 416). He was a descendant also of *Mayflower* passengers John Alden and Myles Standish.

He was "resident in Chatham" when he married there, 2 April 1767 after intentions 14 March (*VR* 1:60, 65), **PRISCILLA MAYO**, who was born at Chatham 29 April 1748, daughter of Judah and Mary (Hamilton) Mayo. She died at Liverpool 26 November 1803 (Simeon Perkins Diary). She is said to have been homesick and to have run away to Chatham after her marriage (*ibid.*).

Eleazer Simmons was of Duxbury in April 1761 when he was administrator of his brother Zachariah's estate (Plymouth PR 17:32). He was of Chatham at the time of his marriage and the late-recorded birth record of his son Judah suggests that the family was still there in 1770, although the children are recorded at Liverpool, N.S.

The family of Eleazer Simmons is listed in the 1787 Queens County Census as consisting of three men, one woman, and six children (RGI, 443:45). He was taxed there in 1791 (sh.023) and 1792 (sh.052).

Children of Eleazer and Priscilla (Mayo) Simmons, first seven recorded in one grouping at Liverpool, N.S. (VR 59):

i   BENJAMIN SIMMONS[6], b. 25 March 1768. He was taxed in Queens County in 1791 (sh.023, Simmonds) and 1792 (sh.052, Simmons).

ii   JUDAH MAYO SIMMONS, b. 26 June 1770; d. after 1811; m. (1) at Liverpool, N.S., 7 Dec. 1792 (VR 136), ABIGAIL WOODS, b. there 17 Jan. 1771, d. there 26 Nov. 1803 (Perkins Diary), dau. of Joseph and Sarah (___) Woods; m. (2) at Chatham, 7 Feb. 1805 (VR 196), ABIGAIL ELDREDGE. Judah had his own birth recorded at Chatham (VR 129), "b. in America ... given me by sd Simmons 30 May & recorded ..." His name is on a plaque at Chatham Library as a founder of Herring Cove, N.S. (Sandra Johansen).

Judah was taxed in Queens County in 1792 (sh.052). He was impressed into the British Navy at Halifax, N.S., in 1801, returned to Liverpool when his mother died, came to Chatham, but returned to N.S. in 1811 and was jailed there for debt; his sister Priscilla cared for his chidren (Sandra Johansen).

Children, first two rec. Chatham (VR 127), all with first wife: 1. *Joseph Simmons[7]*, b. 26 Sept. 1793; d. 14 Nov. 1793. 2. *Robert Simmons*, b. 7 Nov. 1794; d. Chatham 9 Sept. 1829; m. Abigail Hopkins (VR 204, 207). 3. *Richard Simmons*, b. 1797 Liverpool. 4. *Abigail Simmons*, b. 1800. 5. *Judah Mayo Simmons*, b. 2 Feb. 1802 Chatham; m. Monisa Parker Post.

iii PRISCILLA SIMMONS, b. 20 Sept. 1772; d. 25 Feb. 1773 "from burns" (VR from Perkins, 10).

iv   PRISCILLA SIMMONS, "the second of that name," b. 9 Feb. 1774.

v   DEBORAH SIMMONS, b. 24 April 1776.

vi   PERTHINA SIMMONS, b. 3 April 1779; d. 20 April 1779 (VR from Perkins, 10).

vii PERTHINA SIMMONS, "the second of that name," b. 9 Aug. 1780.

viii ELEZER SIMMONS, b. 10 Oct. 1781; "resident Chatham" 30 May 1807 when pub. m. int. with SALLY SNOW (VR 179).

ix   LUCY SIMMONS, b. prob. ca 1783; m. at Liverpool, N.S., 31 Dec. 1801 (VR 226), ELDAD NICKERSON, son of James and Hannah (___) Nickerson. The marriage rec. includes Lucy's parents' names.

x   MARY SIMMONS.

Sources cited: *Chatham VR. Duxbury VR.* "Baptisms of First Church, Marshfield," *MD* 32 (1934). "Vital Records of Liverpool, N.S.," in *NEHGR* 126 [1972] and 127 [1973]. Muriel M. Davidson, "Early Records of Liverpool, N.S. from Extracts: The Diary of Simeon Perkins" (ms., Brampton, Ont., 1994). Nova Scotia Poll tax rolls, 1791-1793, RG1 vol. 444, NSARM microfilm no. 13580. *History of Chatham* (1909), 249, says Eleazer Simmons was "of Northfield" at time of marriage, prob. error for Marshfield. Sandra Johansen of Denver (Myrtle1893@att.net) has done extensive work on this family.

724. PEREZ SIMMONS⁵ (*Benjamin Simmons⁴, Lora Samson³, Caleb², Henry¹*), son of Benjamin Simmons [150] and his wife Fear Samson, was born probably about 1732 at Duxbury and baptized there with most of his siblings on 19 October 1740 (*VR* 157). He was said to be living at Salisbury, Conn., on 21 May 1801 when he joined many relatives in deeding land in Duxbury, but he did not sign that deed (see below). He may have died before 1800, when Mary Simmons was head of the only Simmons household in Salisbury. He was a descendant also of *Mayflower* passengers John Alden and Myles Standish.

He probably married **MARY** ____, who was born by 1755 (census), and was living at Salisbury, Conn., in 1800, aged 45 or older.

Isaac Partridge of Duxbury was appointed guardian on 1 August 1748, of Perez Simmons, minor son of Benjamin Simmons Jr. late of Duxbury (Plymouth PR #18307, 11:202).

In 1790 Perez Simmons (indexed as *Perer*) was listed at Litchfield, Conn., which that year included census results of several other towns, among them Salisbury. His household consisted of one man, three boys under 16, and four females (*Heads of Fam.*, 70); the three other Simmons households in Litchfield County were listed together several pages away (p.64), almost certainly in a different town. Mary Simmons' household in 1800 consisted of one woman 45 or over, three women 16-26, two boys 10-16, and one little boy and one little girl under 10 (p.776).

In a deed dated 21 May 1801, Perez Simmons of Salsbury [*sic*], yeoman, joined many other heirs of the estate of [his maternal grandfather] Nathaniel Samson of Duxbury, deceased, in selling to Joseph White of Duxbury, blockmaker, a salt meadow in Duxbury; although named as one of the grantors, Perez was among those who did not sign (Plymouth LR 89:262). This deed and its genealogical implications are discussed in an article by Robert M. Sherman in *TAG* (51:172-74).

It seems likely that Perez died between 1790 and 1800, probably close enough to the latter year that relatives in Duxbury were unaware of his death when writing up the deed. Mary has not been found in later census records, and she probably accompanied children on a move further west.

A Periz Simmons listed in the 1820 census at LeRoy, N.Y., aged 16-26 with wife but no children, may be a son or grandson. No land or probate records have been found for this family in Salisbury, Conn.

Census figures suggest several possible children for Perez and Mary (___) Simmons: three sons b. 1774-1790, three daughters b. 1774-1784, and one son and one daughter b. 1790-1800. However, if Perez' estimated birthdate is correct, some of these may be grandchildren.

Sources cited: *Duxbury VR.* Plymouth County Deeds and Probate Records. Robert M. Sherman, "Descendants of Nathaniel Samson of Duxbury," *The American Genealogist,* 51 [1975]. CENSUS: Litchfield Co., Conn., Litchfield 1790 [includes Salisbury] (M637-1) & Salisbury 1800 (M32-2).

725. MICAH SIMMONS[5] (*Benjamin Simmons*[4], *Lora*[3] *Samson, Caleb*[2], *Henry*[1]), son of Benjamin Simmons [150] and his wife Fear Samson, was born probably about 1736 at Duxbury and baptized there with most of his siblings on 19 October 1740 (*VR* 157). Mr. Micah Simmons aged 82 or 83, died at Lancaster 30 January 1817 of dropsy (*VR* 190, 359). He was a descendant also of *Mayflower* passengers John Alden and Myles Standish.

He married, first, at New North Church, Boston, 18 March 1762 (*VR* 58; *CR* 106), **SARAH (JEFFS) WHITTEMORE**, who was born at Boston 28 December 1733 (*NEHGR* 107:98) and died at Dorchester in January 1792, "the wife of Micah Symmonds" (*VR* 1:273), daughter of James and Anne (Payson) Jeffs. She married first, at Boston 14 October 1756 (*VR* 30:369), NATHAN WHITTEMORE, with whom she had a son Nathan.

On 22 March 1748 Moses Simmons of Duxbury was appointed guardian of Lucy Simmons, Micah Simmons, Benjamin Simmons, Elizabeth Simmons, and Keturah Simmons, minor children of Benjamin Simmons Jr., late of Duxbury, deceased (Plymouth PR 11: 202-06).

Micah Symmonds [*sic*] owned the covenant at New North Church, Boston, 12 December 1762 (*CR* 106).

Micah was of Dorchester when he married, second, at Weymouth 9 April 1794 (*VR* 2:173), **NABBY (BURRELL) WEBB**, who was born at Weymouth 21 April 1763 (*VR* 1:65), daughter of Andrew and Elizabeth (Porter) Burrell (*Weymouth History,* 3:136), and died at Lancaster 23 June 1817, "relict of Mr. Micah Simmons," of dropsy (*VR* 190, 359), less than five months after the death of her husband. She married, first, at Weymouth 18 March 1784, JOSEPH WEBB JR. (*VR* 2:42), with whom she had a son Joseph Webb Jr. born 31 January 1785, baptized at Weymouth in 1788 as "son of the widow Abigail Webb" (*VR* 1:333). The will of Andrew Burrell, dated 15 March and proved 14 May 1799, names among others daughter Nabby Simmons (Norfolk PR 5:195).

Micah Simmons was a matross in Capt. Daniel Vose's company, Col. Robinson's company of Train Militia who "Traveled to Roxbury and served as a Standing Company in the defence of Liberty before the Standing Army was completed after the battle of Concord" (*Milton History*, 433). Afterwards he served from Dorchester, several times in 1775 and again in 1778; on 26 June 1778 he signed a receipt for £10 received of Maj. Stephen Badlam, it being the balance due him from Patrick Clerk who had enlisted to serve in the Continental Army for the term of nine months from the time of arrival at Fishkill in place of said Simmons" (*MSSR* 14:232-33).

Micah Simmons, wheelwright of Dorchester, and wife Sarah on 28 April 1779 deeded to Sarah's son Nathan Whittemore of Roxbury, wheelwright, "for 5 shillings in money and the love and affection we bear unto [him]" a tenement on Lynde Street in Boston (Suffolk LR 133:95).

Warnings from the town of Dorchester include the notation that "Micah Symonds came into this Town to live in the year [*blank*] from Boston (*NEHGR* 61:44).

In 1790 the household of Mich¹ Simmonds in Dorchester included one man 16 or over and two females (p.199). Although he was called a carpenter, of Dorchester, in a deed dated 21 May 1801 in which he joined other heirs of his maternal grandfather, Nathaniel Samson, in selling a piece of salt marsh in Duxbury (Plymouth LR 89:262), the 1800 census listed him in Concord. He was head of a household consisting of one boy under 10, three boys and one girl 10-16, two young men 16-26, one man and one woman 26-45, and one man over 45 (p.9). Nabby's age seems to have been understated by two years, and some of the younger people may have been her children by her first marriage (the household of Joseph Webb at Weymouth in 1790 consisted of two men and five females [p.209]).

Micah has not been found in the 1810 census, and no records other than his death record and that of his wife have been found for him in Lancaster.

Children of Micah and Sarah (Jeffs) (Whittemore) Simmons, first three bp. New North Church, Boston, as Symmonds (*CR* 106); list perhaps incomplete:

i JAMES JEFFS SIMMONS⁶, bp. 9 Jan. 1763.

ii GEORGE SIMMONS, bp. 24 June 1764; prob. m. at Dorchester, 10 March 1789, both of Dorchester (*VR* 1:239), MARY WALES.

iii SARAH SIMMONS, bp. 29 Sept. 1765; poss. the Sarah who owned the covenant at New North Church 31 March 1782 (*CR* 106).

iv   BENJAMIN SIMMONS, b. Dorchester 14 June 1770 [not rec. there]; d.
     Dorchester 11 Sept. 1831 (VR 2:261); m. (1) HANNAH ____, d. Dor-
     chester 2 Aug. 1800 (VR 1:280); m. (2) at Dorchester, 23 March 1801, both
     of Dorchester (VR 1:333), DORCAS LEEDS, d. 20 Oct. 1812 (VR 2:361);
     m. (3) at Dedham, 31 May 1813 (VR 315), ELIZABETH GOULD.
          Children, all but first rec. Dorchester; with first wife, Hannah: 1. *Benjamin
     Simmons[7]*, b. ca Jan. 1799; d. Boston 25 Feb. 1873 ae 74y 1m 5d, widowed, a
     trader, b. Dorchester of Benjamin & Hannah (Mass. VR 258:44). 2. *Stephen
     Simmons*, b. Dorchester Aug. 1795 (VR 1:212); of Milton when m. 27 Jan. 1831,
     Martha P. Henry (*Dorchester VR* 2:188). child with second wife, Dorcas: 3. *Louisa
     Bourne Simmons*, b. Oct. 1806 (VR 1:290). Children with third wife, Elizabeth:
     4. *Elizabeth Simmons*, b. 16 June 1815 (VR 1: 304). 5. *Hannah Simmons*, b. 8 Aug.
     1817 (VR 1:305) m. Newton, 3 Dec. 1840 (*Dorchester VR* 2:188), Benjamin
     Whittemore. 6. *John Simmons*, b. 6 Sept. 1821 (VR 1:330). ? 7. *Abagail Frances
     Simmons*, of Newton when m. 29 July 1857 (*Dorchester VR* 2:188), Calvin Hager.

Sources cited: *Boston VR* [BRC 30]. *Dedham VR. Dorchester VR 1* [BRC 21] & *2* [BRC 36].
Lancaster VR. Weymouth VR.   Mass. Vital Records 1841-1910. *Records of New North Church.*
"Strangers in Dorchester," *NEHGR* 61 (1907). "Whittemore Family," *NEHGR* 107 (1953).
History of Milton (1887). *History of Weymouth* (1923). CENSUS: *Heads of Families 1790 – Mass.*; 1800
Concord, Middlesex Co. (M32-17), Dorchester & Roxbury, Norfolk Co. (M32-18).

726.   KETURAH SIMMONS[5] (*Benjamin Simmons[4], Lora[3] Samson, Caleb[2],
Henry[1]*), daughter of Benjamin Simmons [150] and his wife Fear Samson, was born
about 1738 (based on age at death), and baptized with most of her siblings at
Duxbury 19 October 1740 (VR 156). She died at Hanover 21 June 1790, aged 52,
"wife of Jabez" (VR 304). She was a descendant also of *Mayflower* passengers John
Alden and Myles Standish.

     She married at Marshfield (VR 163), 30 March 1769, **JABEZ STUDLEY** of
Hanover. He was born at Hanover in August 1738 and died there 14 February
1825, aged 86, son of Jabez and Elizabeth (____) Studley (VR 208).

     On 22 March 1748 Moses Simmons of Duxbury was appointed guardian of
Lucy, Micah, Benjamin, Elizabeth, and Keturah Simmons, minor children of
Benjamin Simmons Jr., late of Duxbury, deceased (Plymouth PR 11: 202-06).

     Jabez Studley served in the Revolutionary War from Hanover (*MSSR* 15:215).

     In 1790, the year Keturah died, Jabez was living in Hanover with one boy
under 16 and two females (p.263). In 1800 his household consisted of one young
man and one young woman 16-26, a man over 45, and a woman 26-45 (p.126). In
1810 Jabez was apparently sharing a household with the family of son Jabez; the
household consisted of three boys and two girls under 10, one man and two

women 26-45, and a man over 45 (p.9). In 1820 Jabez Studley of Hanover was head of a household consisting of one man [himself] and one woman over 45 [dau. Rebecca], and Jabez Jr. was listed separately (p.202).

"The heirs of Keturah Studley late of Hanover" were among many heirs of Nathaniel Samson of Duxbury who sold land to Joseph White 21 May 1801 (Plymouth LR 89:262).

Children of Jabez and Keturah (Simmons) Studley, b. at Hanover:

i   [SON] STUDLEY[6], d. 19 Jan. 1770 in infancy.

ii [DAUGHTER] STUDLEY, d. 22 Oct. 1773 in infancy.

iii REBECCA STUDLEY, bp. 2 Jan. 1774; d. 16 April 1829 ae 59y [g.s.]; m. at Hanover, 15 June 1823 (*VR* 264), as his second wife, LUTHER SPRAGUE, b. Marshfield 31 July 1767 (*VR* 61), d. there 26 April 1849 ae 82, son of James and Sally (___) Sprague; both bur. in cem. near Cong. Chapel, Marshfield (*VR* 419).

iv JABEZ STUDLEY, bp. 22 Sept. 1776; d. Hanover 31 May 1868 ae 91, widowed (Mass. VR 212:306); m. at Hanover, 23 Feb. 1800 (*VR* 124), CHLOE MANN CLARK. In 1850 Jabez ae 74 was a farmer in Hanover, with Chloe M. ae 72, sharing a dwelling with Robert, near George (p.103).

   Children (*Hanover History*, 398): 1. *Keturah Studley*[7], b. 20 March 1801; m. Robert S. Curtis. 2. *Elizabeth Studley*, b. 10 July 1803; m. Stephen Josselyn. 3. *John Studley*, b. 20 July 1805; m. Eliza A. Herrick. 4. *George Studley*, b. 25 Aug. 1807; m. Judith Curtis; a carpenter 1850. 5. *Horace Studley*, b. 6 Jan. 1810; m. Marcia Rose. 6. *Hiram Studley*, b. 28 April 1812; m. (1) Sarah A. Brett, (2) Esther Hollis. 7. *Robert C. Studley*, b. 31 Oct. 1815; d. 19 Jan. 1817. 8. *Robert H. Studley*, b. 8 Dec. 1818; m. Lucy J. Bonney; a shoemaker in 1850.

Sources cited: *Duxbury VR. Hanover VR. Marshfield VR.* Plymouth County Deeds. Robert M. Sherman, "Descendants of Nathaniel Samson of Duxbury," *The American Genealogist,* 51 [1975]. Barry, *History of Hanover* (1853). CENSUS: Hanover, Plymouth Co., 1790 (M637-4), 1800 (M32-16), 1810 (M252-21), 1820 (M33-50), & 1850 (M432-332).

727. LUCY SIMMONS[5] (*Benjamin Simmons*[4], *Lora*[3] *Samson, Caleb*[2], *Henry*[1]), daughter of Benjamin Simmons [150] and his wife Fear Samson, was baptized at Duxbury 10 May 1741 (*VR* 157), and died 8 April 1813 at Worthington, aged 71 or in her 71st year (*VR* 135). She was a descendant also of *Mayflower* passengers John Alden and Myles Standish.

She married at Scituate, 15 November 1786 (*VR* 2:259), perhaps as his second wife, **HOSEA DUNBAR**, who was born about 1752 and died at Worthington 18 or 19 April 1828, called "husband of Lucy," aged 78(*VR* 135). They are buried in Worthington Center Cemetery (*ibid.*).

On 22 March 1748 Moses Simmons of Duxbury was appointed guardian of Lucy Simmons, Micah Simmons, Benjamin Simmons, Elizabeth Simmons, and Keturah Simmons, minor children of Benjamin Simmons Jr., late of Duxbury, deceased (Plymouth PR 11: 202-206).

Hosea Dunbar served as a private from Scituate in the Revolutionary War, from 1775 to 1778; in 1777 he was aged 25 (*MSSR* 5:28). In 1790 Hosea was living in Worthington, head of a household consisting of himself plus one boy under 16 and four females (p.133). In 1800 census figures record Hosea and his wife living by themselves (p.299).

In a deed dated 21 May 1801, Hosea Dunbar of [*blank*] and wife Lucy joined many other heirs to the estate of Lucy's maternal grandfather Nathaniel Samson of Duxbury, deceased, in selling to Joseph White of Duxbury, blockmaker, a salt meadow in Duxbury; Hosea and Lucy were among those heirs named who did not sign (Plymouth LR 89:262). This deed and its genealogical implications are discussed more fully in an article by Robert M. Sherman in *TAG* (51:172-174).

Lucy was 45 years old when she married, and it is unlikely that she and Hosea had any children. No record has been found of any.

Sources cited: *Duxbury VR. Scituate VR. Worthington VR. Mass. Soldiers & Sailors.* Robert M. Sherman, "Descendants of Nathaniel Samson of Duxbury," *The American Genealogist*, 51 [1975]. CENSUS: Worthington, Hampshire Co., 1790 (M637-4), 1800 (M32-15).

728. BENJAMIN SIMMONS[5] (*Benjamin Simmons*[4], *Lora*[3] *Samson, Caleb*[2], *Henry*[1]), son of Benjamin Simmons [150] and his wife Fear Samson, was born about December 1743 (calculated), and died at Marshfield 15 March 1812, aged 68y 2m 16d (*VR* 419). He was a descendant also of *Mayflower* passengers John Alden and Myles Standish.

He was of Marshfield when he married at Scituate, 20 December 1770, **SARAH DAMON** of Scituate (*VR* 259). She was born 29 August 1747 (calculated), daughter of Israel and Sarah (Meritt) Damon, baptized at Scituate 17 September 1749 (*VR* 126), and died at Marshfield 25 February 1839, aged 91y 5m 26d, "widow of Benjamin" (*VR* 419). Benjamin and Sarah are buried in the cemetery near the Congregational Chapel, Marshfield, with their daughter Keturah (*ibid.*).

On 22 March 1748 Moses Simmons of Duxbury was appointed guardian of Lucy Simmons, Micah Simmons, Benjamin Simmons, Elizabeth Simmons, and

Keturah Simmons, minor children of Benjamin Simmons Jr., late of Duxbury, deceased (Plymouth PR 11: 202-206).

In her will dated 2 December 1837, proved first Tuesday of July 1839, Sarah Simmons of Marshfield, widow of Benjamin Simmons, refers to herself as aged and infirm, and includes bequests of one dollar each to her children: Abraham, Sylvanus, Joseph, Israel D., Sally, Hannah C., and Phillipi; and to her daughter Keturah Simmons the real estate in Marshfield that "descended to me as heir to my grandchild Lydia T. Hart deceased, late wife of Peter Hart of Boston"; John Ford Jr. was to be executor (Plymouth PR 81: 360). An account dated 28 October 1839 indicated one dollar each paid to: Abraham Simmons, Hannah C. Baker, Joseph Simmons, Silvanus Simmons, Israel D. Simmons, Phillipi Brewster, and Sarah Litchfield; with balance to Keturah Simmons (*ibid.*, 82:256).

Children of Benjamin and Sarah (Damon) Simmons, rec. Marshfield (*VR* 66):

i   ABRAHAM SIMMONS⁶, b. 12 Aug. 1771; m. at Marshfield (*VR* 264), 26 March 1801, PENELOPE CHANDLER, dau. Thomas and Rhoda (Blackmore) Chandler and a desc. of Henry Samson [#469-iv; *MF20* pt.2: 455].

ii BENJAMIN SIMMONS, b. Duxbury 13 Oct. 1772; d. Marshfield 21 Feb. 1832 ae 63 [*sic*] (VR 208); m. after int. Marshfield, 6 Jan. 1799 (*VR* 115), MRS. LYDIA VINAL JR., d. Marshfield 12 March 1836 (*VR* 208).
    Children rec. Marshfield (*VR* 214): 1. *Lydia Tilden Simmons⁷*, b. Marshfield 15 Aug. 1802; d. 25 Nov. 1837 (*VR* 376), wife of Peter Hart; named in her grandmother's will. 2. *Mercy Hewet Simmons*, b. 25 July 1806; d. 10 June 1831 Marshfield (*VR* 208).

iii SARAH SIMMONS, b. 6 July 1774; d. Carlisle 25 Nov. 1850 ae 76 of consumption (Mass. VR 49:43); m. at Marshfield, 6 Jan. 1803 (*VR* 264), DAVID LITCHFIELD, b. prob. 21 Sept. 1768, Scituate, son of Thomas and Lydia (___) Litchfield, d. Carlisle 1853 (Mass. VR 76:47). In 1850 he was a farmer at Carlisle, ae 82, with Sarah ae 76 and James ae 37 (p.483).
    Litchfield children, b. and bp. rec. Scituate (*VR* 1: 228, 235, 237, 238): 1. *Ruth Litchfield*, b. 21 April 1803. 2. *William Litchfield*, b. 1 Sept. 1805. 3. *Thomas Jefferson Litchfield*, b. 20 Sept. 1807. 4. *Israel Litchfield*, b. 30 May 1810. 5. *James Jenkins Litchfield*, b. 8 July 1814.

iv ISRAEL SIMMONS, b. 15 Oct. 1775; d. prob. young.

v   SYLVANUS SIMMONS, b. 17 Oct. 1777; d. at Scituate 7 Sept. 1859 ae 82y 11m of old age (Mass. VR 130:232); m. (1) at Scituate, 4 Dec. 1800 (*VR* 2:260) after int. Marshfield 13 Sept. 1800 (*VR* 113), ELIZABETH DAMAN, b. Scituate 24 Aug. 1780, dau. of John and Elizabeth (Collier) Daman (*VR* 1:123, 2:99), d. there as "— w. of Silvanus," 25 Feb. 1819 (*VR*

2:440). He m. (2), at Scituate, 15 March 1820 (*VR* 2:260), ELIZABETH WHEELWRIGHT, b. ca March 1787, d. Scituate 16 May 1860 ae 73y 2m of "mortification" (Mass. VR 139:328). In 1850 Sylvanus and Elizabeth were living by themselves in Scituate (p.62).

Children rec. Scituate, first seven with Elizabeth Daman, last three with Elizabeth Wheelwright (*VR* 1:322-23): 1. *John Damon Simmons*[7], b. 4 March 1803; lost at sea Dec. 1825 (*VR* 2:440). 2. *Benjamin Simmons*, b. 13 April 1804; poss. "ch. of Sylvanus" d. 1805. 3. *Joseph Simmons*, b. 18 May 1808. 4. *Elizabeth Simmons*, b. 17 April 1810. 5. *Gridley Simmons*, b. 15 March 1812; d. Scituate 9 April 1835 (*VR* 2:440). 6. *William Henry Simmons*, b. 19 March 1814. 7. *Sylvanus Simmons*, b. 21 Aug. 1816. 8. *Hiram Simmons*, b. 8 Dec. 1820. 9. *Sarah E. Simmons*, b. 20 Jan. 1823. 10. *Charles Simmons*, b. 8 Dec. 1825.

vi HANNAH COWEN SIMMONS, b. 17 May 1780; m. at Marshfield, 26 May 1822 (*VR* 271), THOMAS BAKER of Duxbury. In 1850 Hannah Baker ae 71 was living in Duxbury with her sister Philipe Brewster (p.85).

vii PHILIPPI SIMMONS, b. 2 Jan. 1783; d. 1869; m. at Marshfield, 20 July 1815 (*VR* 266), STEPHEN BREWSTER, d. Duxbury 4 March 1840 ae 57y 2m 4d, "h. Philippi" (*VR* 355), son of Joseph and Deborah (Hunt) Brewster (*Brewster Gen.*, 138). In 1850 Philipe Brewster ae 68 was living in Duxbury with her sister Hannah Baker (p.85).

   Brewster children, d. rec. Duxbury: 1. *[Infant son] Brewster*[7], d. 28 Oct. 1819 (*VR* 356). 2. *Philippi Brewster*, b. June 1824; d. 29 Sept. 1824 ae 3m 21d (*VR* 355).

viii JOSEPH SIMMONS, b. 19 Nov. 1784; d. Duxbury 5 Nov. 1863 ae 79y 11m 19d, of heart disease (Mass. VR 166:281); m. after int. Marshfield 5 Sept. 1808 (*VR* 186), ASENATH FREEMAN of Duxbury. In 1850 Joseph was a housewright in Duxbury with Asenath ae 68 (p.81).

   Children rec. Duxbury (*VR* 151-54, 416, 417): 1. *Gamaliel A. Simmons*[7], b. 21 Sept. 1811; d. 7 Nov. 1811. 2. *Joseph Simmons*, b. 21 Oct. 1816; d. 1 or 3 Dec. 1816. 3. *Asenith F. Simmons*, b. 22 April 1818. 4. *Rebecca A. Simmons*, b. 14 March 1822; d. Oct. 1844 ae 22y 6m 10d.

ix ISRAEL DAMON SIMMONS, b. 23 Oct. 1787; m. int. Marshfield, 3 Oct. 1814, with RUBY GULLIFER, both of Marshfield (*VR* 189). In 1820 he was ae 26-45, head of a household at Marshfield that included one boy under 10; the columns showing females is torn and illegible (p.252). Sarah Simmons ae 45+ (probably his mother), was next door with a household that included one boy and one girl under 10 as well as one woman 26-45 and possibly more; some columns are illegible.

x KETURAH SIMMONS, b. 15 Nov. 1791; d. 21 Nov. 1839, ae 47y 11m 7d; bur. with parents at Marshfield (*VR* 419). The will of Keturah Simmons of Marshfield, singlewoman, weak in body, dated 8 Oct. 1839, proved third

Monday in Jan. 1840, left all her estate to her daughter Lucy D. Simmons (Plymouth PR 82:13).

Child: 1. *Lucy D. Simmons*[7], m. Marshfield 26 Nov. 1840 (*VR* 303), Marston Samson.

Sources cited: *Marshfield VR. Scituate VR.* Mass. Vital Records 1841-1910. Plymouth County Probate Records. Robert M. Sherman, "Descendants of Nathaniel Samson of Duxbury," *The American Genealogist*, 51 [1975]. CENSUS: 1820 Marshfield, Plymouth Co. (M33-50), 1850 Duxbury & Scituate, Plymouth Co. (M432-332, 333); 1850 Carlisle, Middlesex Co. (M432-324).

729. MARY SIMMONS[5] (*Mercy Simmons*[4], *Rachel*[3] *Samson, Caleb*[2], *Henry*[1]), daughter of Nathaniel Simmons and his wife Mercy Simmons [151], was born at Duxbury 19 June 1742 (*VR* 157). She was living at Waldoboro, Maine, on 2 March 1820 when she released her dower in a land record. She was a descendant also of Mayflower passengers John Alden and Myles Standish.

She married at Duxbury, 24 April 1764 (*VR* 267), **JOHN HUNT JR.**, who was born there 6 October 1734, son of John and Esther (Wright) Hunt (*VR* 96), and a descendant of *Mayflower* passenger Francis Cooke (*MF 12*:481). John died, probably at Waldoboro, between 30 June 1803 and January 1804, as indicated by a Lincoln County deed cited below. His brother Judah Hunt married Betty Oldham, a Henry Samson descendant [#208].

Mary's parents were living in Waldoboro by 1773. In his will dated 22 January 1787, proved 22 January 1789, Nathanael Simmons left, among other bequests, to his four daughters, Mary wife of John Hunt, Dorothy wife of John Winslow, Sarah Simmons, and Rachel Simmons, "all that my Farme which I bought of Mrs Jane Cleveland ... one Hundred Acres and lyeth on the Southerly side of Jacob Wades farme ... within the Township of Waldoborough ... Except the Long Island Lot"; he also gave to Mary and Dorothy £4 apiece and to each a cow (*Lincoln Probate*, 180-82).

History of Old Broadbay and Waldoboro (pp. 410-11) relates that John Hunt of Pembroke, cordwainer, bought land in Waldoboro, Maine, on 28 August 1772 from Michael Ried, who was

> ... a second-generation German about to remove to some unoccupied land at the town back on Old County Road, [for £82 13s 4d] ... a parcel of land being one half of lot No. 21 on the west bank of the river, 12½ rods wide and containing about 50 acres, with all improvements, stock, dwelling house, one half of the barn and a right of way through to the river. ... John's wife, Mary ... brought with her to Waldoborough her church letter from the church in Pembroke and was one of the original members of the Congregational Society in the town. John was one of the

first two tax collectors, held many minor offices, and discharged many committee duties relating to the town's affairs. Later the family spread into the northeast recesses of the town ... descendants in present-day Waldoboro, though few who still bear the name.

A John Hunt was constable in Waldoboro in 1773, and served in the Revolution from Waldoboro in 1777. John Hunt signed as a witness to the will of Christian Cline of Waldoboro dated 20 March 1783, proved 1 October 1783 (*Lincoln Probate*, 123-24).

On 12 November 1790 Joseph Simmons, Zebedee Simmons, and Stephen Simmons, "all sons of Nathaniel Simmons late of the town of Waldoborough, husbandman, deceased, and John Winslow and Dorothy Winslow, son in law and daughter of the aforesaid Nathaniel Simmons, living in the town of Nobleborough," for £58 6s 8d quitclaimed to John Hunt of Waldoboro, cordwainer, their right in a lot of land in Waldoboro containing 100 acres, "the lot our father bought of Mrs. Jean Cleveland ... our share from our father's will" (Lincoln LR 52:112-13). On 18 November 1790 John Hunt of Waldoboro, cordwainer, sold land there, and his wife Mary relinquished her dower (*ibid.*).

The 1790 census listed the family in Waldoboro with one man, one boy under 16, and three females (p.42). In 1800 John Hunt was over 45, his wife the same, and the rest of the family consisted of one woman 26-45, two young men and two young women 16-26, and two girls under 10 (p.519).

On 30 June 1803 John Hunt of Waldoboro, yeoman, "in consideration of the Love & good [*sic*] which I bear toward my beloved son Asa Hunt, and for the tender care which he has always shown to be [*sic – me?*] both in sickness & in health & also for the further consideration that he supply myself & his honored mother Mary Hunt in a comfortable & decent manner during our natural lives," gave to him "a certain lot of land in Waldoborough, part of the Lot number twenty nine the same on which I now live," beginning at a stake on the shore of Broad Bay River at the southwest corner of Sarah Simmons' lot, containing 70 5/6 acres, 285 feet in width north and south; witnesses were Benj[a] Brown and Peleg Oldham (Lincoln LR 53:202). Peleg Oldham acknowledged the deed at January term 1804, stating that "the said John Hunt is dead," and the deed was recorded 22 February 1804.

Children of John and Mary (Simmons) Hunt, bp. Pembroke (*VR* 114):

i   BWYS [?] HUNT[6] [son], bp. 13 April 1766.
? ii   *poss.* JOHN HUNT, b. 1765-1774 [poss. the "Bwys" bp. 1766?]. He was a housewright of Waldoboro 8 Sept. 1803 when he bought from Barnabas

Simons of Union, yeoman (for $350), a tract of land on the east side of the Mescongus River in Waldoboro, adjoining land of Sarah Simons and running east to Goose River, the deed witnessed by Waterman Thomas and Samuel A. Thomas, rec. 12 Jan. 1804 (Lincoln LR 53:165-66). On 7 Jan. 1813 John Hunt of Waldoboro, yeoman, bought (for $111) 52 acres in the same area from Benjamin Joy of Boston, merchant, who had bought the land "at auction of the executrix of General Knox" (*ibid.*, 80:147). In 1810 John was listed next to Asa Hunt in Waldoboro, 26-45, with a wife 26-45, and one boy and one girl under 10 (p.88). In 1820, still in Waldoboro, he was over 45; his wife was 26-45, and the two children were both 10-16 (p.209).

iii   MERCY HUNT, b. 9 Nov. 1768 at Duxbury (*Old Bristol VR* 1:374); bp. Pembroke 17 Jan. 1768 (*VR* 114); d. Waldoboro, Me., Dec. 1848 ae 81; m. (1) at Waldoboro, 24 Jan. 1793 (VR 2:140), JOSEPH WINSLOW, b. Scituate 3 Sept. 1753 (*Old Bristol VR* 1:744), d. Waldoboro 28 Sept. 1796 ae 43y 28d, son of Oliver and Bethia (Prior) Winslow; m. (2) at Union, Me., 28 Oct. 1801, DAVID ROBBINS (VR 1:374), b. Walpole 21 March 1751/2, d. Union 12 Aug. 1831, son of Philip and Jemima (Smith) Robbins and widower of Elisabeth Chapman with whom he had 12 children (*Maine Fam. 1790*, 8:435-36). Adm. on estate of Joseph Winslow, late of Waldoborough, joiner, was given to Mercy Winslow, widow, 19 Sept. 1797, and on 10 Sept. 1799 she was named guardian of minor daus. Bethiah and Esther (*Lincoln Co. Probate*, 298).

   Winslow children, b. Waldoboro (*Old Bristol VR* 1:742-43): 1. *Bethiah Winslow*[7], b. 24 Sept. 1793; m. Nathaniel Glidden. 2. *Esther Winslow*, b. 7 May 1797; m. Spencer Mero (see *Maine Families 1790*, 8:339).

   Robbins children (*ibid.*): 1. *Eliza Robbins*[7], b. 14 Aug. 1802; d.y. 2. *Sally Simmons Robbins*, b. 25 Sept., d. 7 Oct. 1807. 3. *Sarah Simmons Robbins*, b. 2 Dec. 1808; m. (1) James Woodcock, (2) Nathaniel Hunt.

iv   ESTHER HUNT, bp. 1 July 1770.

v   ASA HUNT, b. after 1774; d. prob. 1829 at Waldoboro, intestate (Lincoln PR); m. _____. His father deeded land to him in 1803 in return for lifetime support for himself and his wife Mary. In 1810 he was living at Waldoboro, 26-45, with a wife 16-26, and one boy and two girls under 10 (p.88). In 1820 he and his wife, both 26-45, had one boy and two girls 10-16 and two girls under 10 in their household (p.209).

   Children, rec. Waldoboro (VR 9-12) as "of Asa"; mother not named: 1. *Jane Hunt*[7], b. 29 Sept. 1804. 2. *Sally Hunt*, b. 19 May 1807. 3. *Samuel Hunt*, b. 3 May 1809. 4. *Maria Hunt*, b. 11 Nov. 1812. 5. *Rebecca Hunt*, b. 13 March 1816.

Sources cited: *Duxbury VR. Pembroke VR. VR of Old Bristol and Nobleboro. Waldoboro, Maine VR.* Patterson, *Lincoln County Probate Records* (1895). Lincoln Co. Deeds at Wiscasset, Me. Margaret F.

Viens, "Amariah Mero" and "David Robbins," *Maine Families in 1790,* Vol. 8 (2003). Stahl, *History of Old Broad Bay and Waldoboro* (1956). CENSUS: 1790 Nobleboro, Lincoln Co., Me. (M637-2) Waldoboro, Lincoln Co., Me., 1800 (M32-6), 1810 (M252-12), 1820 (M33-36). **See also:** Frederick Johnson Simmons, "A Genealogy of a Few Lines of the Simmons Family of Maine and Massachusetts," *Sprague's Maine Journal,* 7 (1919) and 8 (1920).

730.   JOSEPH SIMMONS[5] (*Mercy Simmons[4], Rachel[3] Samson, Caleb[2], Henry[1]*), son of Nathaniel Simmons and his wife Mercy Simmons [151], was born at Duxbury 19 September 1744 (*VR* 156, as Simons). He died at Nobleboro, Maine, 24 May 1816, at the home of his son James (*Sprague's Me. Journal,* 8:100). He was a descendant also of Mayflower passengers John Alden and Myles Standish.

He married at Bridgewater, 4 December 1770 as Joseph Symmonds of Pembroke (*VR* 2:361), **ELIZABETH CHAMBERLAIN**, who was born there 13 September 1751, daughter of Job and Rachel (Bonney) Chamberlain, and died at Waldoboro, Maine. In an order of distribution of the estate of Job Chamberlain late of Bridgewater, deceased, dated 24 September 1794, one of the heirs named is Elizabeth, wife of Joseph Simmons (Plymouth PR 27:263; 35:150; 42:197).

Joseph moved to Waldoboro about 1772 or 1773, at about the same time as his parents.

His father, Nathanael Simmons, in his will dated 22 January 1787, proved 22 January 1789, named his two oldest sons, Joseph and Zebedee Simmons, executors, and left to them "the whole of that my Farme it Being the Homestead Farme on which I Dwell after their mothers Improvement ... further I give to s'd Joseph and Zebedee my four best oxen together with my Horse and two thirds of all my tools of all sorts; further I give [them] the two Gunes that they now Improve and my two Swoards" (*Lincoln Co. Probate,* 180-82).

On 12 November 1790 Joseph Simmons, Zebedee Simmons, and Stephen Simmons, "all sons of Nathaniel Simmons late of the town of Waldoborough, husbandman, deceased, and John Winslow and Dorothy Winslow, son in law and daughter of the aforesaid Nathaniel Simmons, living in the town of Nobleborough," for £58 6s 8d quitclaimed to John Hunt of Waldoboro, cordwainer, their right in a lot of land in Waldoboro containing 100 acres, "the lot our father bought of Mrs. Jean Cleveland ... our share from our father's will" (Lincoln LR 52:112-13).

In 1790 Joseph Simons was living at Waldoboro with two boys under 16 and two females (p.42). On 11 February 1795, Charles Samson, Joseph Simmons, and Nathan Sprague appraised the annual rent of real estate owned by Cornelius Bradford, late of Meduncook, mariner (*Lincoln Co. Probate,* 199). On 19 September

1797 he was one of the appraisors of the inventory of Sarah Soule, late of Waldoboro, widow (*ibid.*, 276). When his brother Zebedee died in 1794, Joseph Simmons was one of the executors (*ibid.*, 238-39).

His brother Stephen died in 1795, and Joseph Simmons was appointed guardian of Stephen's minor children Peabody, Stephen, and Urainy Sprague Simmons on 20 September 1796, filing an account on 11 January 1805 (*ibid.*, 248). In December 1795 he was an appraisor of the inventory of Church Nash, late of Waldeboro, and a surety for the widow, Eve Nash (*ibid.*, 261).

In 1800 his household consisted of one boy and one girl under 10, one boy 10-16, two young men 16-26, and one man and one woman over 45 (p.577).

The Simmons Genealogy in *Sprague's Journal of Maine History* states that Joseph "spent his last days with his son Col. James Simmons, Nobleboro," and mentions a Bible and various personal items that were passed down among his descendants.

No probate records were found for this family.

Children of Joseph and Elizabeth (Chamberlain) Simmons, all but first born probably at Waldoboro, Me. (*Sprague's Journal*, 8:102; order given there by F. J. Simmons changed to reconcile with other evidence):

i   NATHANIEL SIMMONS[6], bp. Pembroke 12 Jan. 1772 (*VR* 185); d. at Waldoboro 22 Oct. 1788, ae 17y 3d.

ii   SOPHIA/ZERVIAH SIMMONS, b. prob. ca 1775; m. after int. Waldoboro, 23 July 1794 (VR 7), JOSIAH OLDHAM [#755, *q.v.*]. F. J. Simmons called her "Sovia" and listed her without a birthdate, next to last among the children, with note that she "m — Oldham," but she must have been born earlier.

iii   JOB SIMMONS, b. possibly ca 1777; d. prob. y.

iv   JAMES SIMMONS, b. 10 Jan. 1781; d. Nobleboro, 2 Oct. 1872 (*Sprague's Journal*, 101); m. after int. at Waldoboro 5 June 1802 (*VR* 9), CRESSY KEEN [Christiana Keene]. In 1850 James Simmons ae 69, blacksmith, and Christiana ae 66 were living in Nobleboro with John N.[?] Simmons ae 19, blacksmith (p.449).

v   THOMAS SIMMONS, b. ca 1782; d. 4 Aug. 1868 ae 86y 4m (*Sprague's Journal*, 101); called Colonel due to service in War of 1812; a surveyor and carpenter; m. at Waldoboro after int. 30 Dec. 1804 (VR 10), CATHERINE FEYLER, b. ca 1785, d. 1872 ae 87 (*Old Broad Bay*, 416). Thomas built the house later known as the Jameson House (*ibid.*). In 1850 Thomas ae 67, "land surveyor," Catharine, and dau. Susan F. shared a dwelling with the family of son Thomas J., a farmer (p.210).

Children, rec. Waldoboro as "of Thomas" (VR 11-13): 1. *Catherine Louisa Simmons*[7], b. 8 April 1805. 2.*Thomas Jefferson Simmons*, b. 23 April 1808; m. Clarissa ___. 3. *John Simmons*, b. 29 July 1810. 4. *Susan Farley Simmons*, b. 27 Sept. 1813; unm. 1850. 5. *Joseph Warren Simmons*, b. 16 Nov. 1815. 6. *Elizabeth Simmons*, b. 16 Jan. 1818.

iv   MERCY SIMMONS, b. 14 Dec. 1790; d. Belfast, Me., 1884, ae 93y 5m (*Sprague's Journal*, 101).

v   JOSEPH SIMMONS, b. say 1792 (under 10 in 1800); "lived and d. in Palermo, Me." (*Sprague's Journal*, 101).

Sources cited: *Bridgewater VR. Duxbury VR. Waldoboro VR.* Patterson, *Lincoln County Probate Records* (1895). Frederick Johnson Simmons, "A Genealogy of a Few Lines of the Simmons Family of Maine and Massachusetts," *Sprague's Journal of Maine History*, 7 (1919), 8 (1920). Stahl, *History of Old Broad Bay & Waldoboro* (1956). CENSUS: Waldoboro, Lincoln Co., 1790 (M637-2), 1800 (M32-6).

731.   ZEBEDEE SIMMONS[5] (*Mercy Simmons*[4], *Rachel*[3] *Samson, Caleb*[2], *Henry*[1]), son of Nathaniel Simmons and his wife Mercy Simmons [151], was baptized at Duxbury 10 August 1746 as Zebedy Simons (*VR* 157). He died while trying to cross the Medomack River on the ice to Waldoboro, Maine, "hurrying to secure a doctor for his sick wife" (*Sprague's Journal*, 101-02), probably shortly before 25 April 1794, when administration was given on his estate. He was a descendant also of Mayflower passengers John Alden and Myles Standish.

Marriage intentions of Capt. Zebedee Simmons and **MARY (THOMAS) WATERMAN** were published at Waldoboro 21 April 1787 (*VR* 3). Mary was born at Marshfield 17 February 1749 (*VR* 101), and died at Waldoboro 18 March 1809, aged 60 years, daughter of William and Mary (Hill) Thomas. She married, first, at Marshfield, 26 April 1770 (*VR* 163), ABIJAH WATERMAN, He was born at Marshfield 25 December 1745, son of Thomas and Abigail (Thomas) Waterman, and a descendant of James Chilton and Richard Warren. Abijah and Mary had children Thomas Waterman, Deborah Waterman, and Mary Waterman.

Mary Waterman, widow, of Waldoboro, was given administration on the estate of her husband Abijah Waterman late of Waldoboro, 20 February 1782, with Charles Samson as one of the sureties (*Lincoln Co. Probate*, 110). Zebedee Simmons was appointed guardian unto Thomas, minor son, and Deborah and Mary, minor daughters, on 1 June 1785. Later, in 1794 after Zebedee died, Deborah and Thomas both chose Charles Samson of Waldoboro as their guardian (*ibid.*).

The will of William Thomas of Marshfield, dated 4 October 1796 and proved 21 August 1798, names among others his wife Abiah and daughter Mary Simmons

(Plymouth PR 36:406). Mary is buried in the Slaigo burial yard on family property in Waldoboro (*Sprague's Journal,* 102).

Nathanael Simmons in his will dated 22 January 1787, proved 22 January 1789, named his two oldest sons, Joseph and Zebedee Simmons, executors, and left to them "the whole of that my Farme it Being the Homestead Farme on which I Dwell after their mothers Improvement ... further I give to s'd Joseph and Zebedee my four best oxen together with my Horse and two thirds of all my tools of all sorts; further I give [them] the two Gunes that they now Improve and my two Swoards ... to my three children now Living at home viz Zebedee Sarah and Rachel after my wifes Improvement as above the three Cows and five Sheep together with all the House movables to be Equally divided among them further I give to Zebedee Six Sheep ..." (*Lincoln Co. Probate,* 180-82).

F. J. Simmons wrote (ca 1920), "Zebedee was the first of the Simmons brothers to come to Waldoboro, Me. One of his descendants informs me that he was interested in and owned sailing vessels and had something to do with salt and fish business and quarries near Friendship, Me., as well as farming in Waldoboro. The District of Maine census, 1798 shows that the heirs of Zebedee Simmons held 165 acres of land valued at $850, and a house valued at $90. [He] served the town ... as selectman in 1778, 1779, and as town treasurer in 1790" (*Sprague's Journal,* 102). On 28 January 1784 he was one of the appraisers of the inventory of Nathan Soule, late of Waldoboro (*Lincoln Co. Probate,* 129).

In 1790 Zebedee Simons was living at Waldoboro with two boys under 16, and two females (p.42).

On 12 November 1790 Joseph Simmons, Zebedee Simmons, and Stephen Simmons, "all sons of Nathaniel Simmons late of the town of Waldoborough, husbandman, deceased, and John Winslow and Dorothy Winslow, son in law and daughter of the aforesaid Nathaniel Simmons, living in the town of Nobleborough," for £58 6s 8d quitclaimed to John Hunt of Waldoboro, cordwainer, their right in a lot of land in Waldoboro containing 100 acres, "the lot our father bought of Mrs. Jean Cleveland ... our share from our father's will" (Lincoln LR 52:112-13).

The will of Zebedee Simmons, dated 16 October 1793, proved 25 April 1794, mentions but does not name wife and children (Lincoln PR 4:20).

> I give to my wife the income of the Sloop till she thinks best to Sell her and then to be Devided between her and the Children as the rest of my Estate likewise one Hundred Dollars in Cash. Likewise I give to Polly Haupt [his stepdaughter neé Mary Waterman] Fifty Dollars, and Thomas Waterman Fifty Dollars, and Deborah Waterman Fifty Dollars, and I likewise give to my Sister Sarah Simmons a Note of Hand against my

Brother Stephen for [£24]. ... the Income of my Place to my wife and Children one third to my wife and the other two thirds to my Children till they come of age and then to be Eaqualy Devided ... [also] the Debts due to me Except the Note of Hand and the Other Legacies that I have bequeathed above Likewise I would give Thomas Waterman my part of the Timber that I own in a Vessel frame but not as a gift but for him to have the Refusal of it towards what I owe him; Likewise I give my Mare to my wife to be Disposed of according to her Desire ... [all the rest to wife and children equally]; Likewise appoint my Brother Stephen Simmons Thomas Waterman and my Brother Joseph Simmons Executors to this my will ... my wife Guardian to my Children till Thomas Waterman comes of Age and then I appoint him their Guardian

Ezekiel G. Dodge and Robt. Farnsworth were witnesses; the inventory was taken by William Farnsworth, Peleg Oldham, and Nathaniel Pitcher, all of Waldoboro (*Lincoln Co. Probate*, 238-39). Mary Simmons of Waldoboro, widow, was appointed guardian on 26 April 1794 of Zebedee, minor son of Zebedee Simmons of Waldoboro, gentleman, deceased (*ibid.*). At her death Joseph Farley was appointed guardian of Zebedee (Lincoln PR 13:174, 17:265), and when Zebedee's estate was settled in 1815 it included Farley's accounting from 1809, noting that he had paid to Zebedee Simmons $288.38, and stating that a note of hand against Thomas Mace signed by James and Thomas Simmons "could not be collected and had to be given up." An item dated 11 May 1809 recorded 62½¢ "received of Mrs. Davis for wool she had of your mother," and another noted cash from John and Loren Sides for timber sent to Boston by Capt. Ewell (*ibid.*, 17:265).

Mary Simmons is not listed in the 1800 census in Maine.

Children of Zebedee and Mary (Thomas) (Waterman) Simmons, b. probably Waldoboro, Me.:

i   ZEBEDEE SIMMONS[6], b. ca 1790; d. prob. 1815; m. at Waldoboro, 22 July 1813 (VR 15), SALOME SPRAGUE, probably dau. of Capt. Michael and Deborah (___) Sprague with whom the Simmons sons are buried. Inventory of Zebedee's estate taken 15 July 1815 included a Bible and Psalm book, arithmetic and singing books, Hersey's *Meditations*, works by Sterne, Swift, and Milton, "school books," several other books, and joiner's tools (Lincoln PR 16:86). On 17 Jan. 1816 Salome Simmons, widow of Zebedee Simmons, late of Waldoboro, dec. intestate, presented an accounting and the remainder of the estate was distributed to Salome Simmons, widow, Zebedee Simmons, and Michael Simmons, $114.12 ⅓ to each (*ibid.*, 16:75).

On 5 July [1816?] Michael Sprague was appointed guardian of Zebedee Simmons and Michael Simmons, minor children of Zebedee Simmons deceased (*ibid.*, 16:169). Real estate was sold and Salome presented an account 22 Jan. 1817 (*ibid.*, 16:201).

Children, both bur. Old German Cem., Waldoboro (*Waldoboro Cem.*, 35):
1. *Zebedee Simmons*, b. ca 1815; d. 28 May 1827 ae 12 yr. 2. *Michael Simmons*, b. ca
Dec. 1813; d. 16 Aug. 1842 ae 27y 9m.

? ii [CHILD] SIMMONS, b. ca 1792; d.y. (Zebedee's will refers to children,
plural.)

Sources cited: *Duxbury VR. Marshfield VR. Waldoboro, Maine VR.* Patterson, *Lincoln County
Probate Records* (1895). Lincoln County Probate Records at Wiscasset, Me. *Waldoboro, Maine,
Cemetery Inscriptions.* Frederick Johnson Simmons, "A Genealogy of a Few Lines of the Simmons
Family of Maine and Massachusetts," *Sprague's Journal of Maine History,* 7 [1919] and 8 [1920].
CENSUS: Waldoboro, Lincoln Co., 1790 (M637-2).

732. STEPHEN SIMMONS[5] (*Mercy Simmons*[4], *Rachel*[3] *Samson, Caleb*[2], *Henry*[1]),
son of Nathaniel Simmons and his wife Mercy Simmons [151], was born probably
at Duxbury about 1748, his birth not recorded. He died at Waldoboro, Maine,
before 11 February 1795, when administration was given on his estate. He was a
descendant also of Mayflower passengers John Alden and Myles Standish.

He married, first, between 1778 and 1783, *possibly* **URANIA SPRAGUE**,
daughter of Nathan and Martha (Spooner) Sprague, born at Marshfield 9 June
1755 (*VR* 71). No marriage record has been found, but the reasons for this
identification are discussed below. She was the mother of his older children, and
died before September 1789, when he remarried.

He married, second, at Waldoboro, 21 September 1789, "both of Waldoboro"
(VR 4), **BETSEY VINAL**, who was living on 5 April 1799 when Stephen's estate
was divided. She may be the Betty, daughter of Ezekiel and Molley (Wade) Vinal
born at Scituate 27 August 1769 (VR 1:385); Ezekiel Vinal over 45 was living at
Waldoboro in 1820 (p.373). Betsey married, second, before 17 September 1798,
Ephraim Patch, and was probably the woman 26-45 in his household in Bath, Me.,
in 1800 (p.496).

Nathanael Simmons, in his will dated 22 January 1787, proved 22 January
1789, among other bequests, left to son Steven Simmons "the Long Island farme
which I bought of Benjamin Bradford Lying on Long Island near a Place Called
the midle narrows [and] Half of the farme on which he he the s'd Steven now Does
now Dwells on [*sic*] — further I give Steven the gun that he Improves ..." (*Lincoln
Co. Probate,* 180-82).

In 1790 Stephen was living at Waldoboro with two boys under 16 and four
females (p.42). He was a selectman there in 1793 and 1794 (*Sprague's Jounral,*
8:103).

On 12 November 1790 Joseph Simmons, Zebedee Simmons, and Stephen Simmons, "all sons of Nathaniel Simmons late of the town of Waldoborough, husbandman, deceased, and John Winslow and Dorothy Winslow, son in law and daughter of the aforesaid Nathaniel Simmons, living in the town of Noble-borough," for £58 6s 8d quitclaimed to John Hunt of Waldoboro, cordwainer, their right in a lot of land in Waldoboro containing 100 acres, "the lot our father bought of Mrs. Jean Cleveland ... our share from our father's will" (Lincoln LR 52:112-13).

Stephen and his brother Joseph were executors of the will of their brother Zebedee in 1794 (*Lincoln Co. Probate*, 238). On 11 February 1795, Betsey Simmons of Waldoboro, widow, was appointed administratrix of the estate of Stephen Simmons, late of Waldoboro; the inventory was taken 20 February by Jacob Ludwig, Peleg Oldham, and Nathaniel Pitcher, all of Waldoboro. On 20 September 1796 minor daughter Abigail chose Spooner Sprague of Waldoboro as guardian, and Joseph Simmons of Waldoboro was apointed guardian of Peabody, Stephen, and Urainy. An account dated 17 September 1798 indicates that the administratrix had married Ephraim Patch. A division was made 5 April 1799 among: the widow, Abigail, Peabody, Stephen, Urany Sprague, Nancy, Betsy, and Rachel.

The 1798 Tax List valued the house of Stephen Simmons' heirs (occupied by William Groton) at $200 (*Sprague's Journal*, 8:103).

Accounts were filed by guardian Joseph Simmons on 11 January 1805; and by Ezekiel Vinal, guardian of Nancy, and Nathan Sprague, guardian of Urania Simmons, on 21 June 1809 (*Lincoln Co. Probate*, 248). On 29 July 1805 Michael Sprague, Ezekiell Vinal, and Nathan Sprague, all of Waldoboro, yeomen and guardians to Stephen Simmons, Urana Simmons, Nancy Simmons, Elizabeth Simmons, and Rachel Simmons, minors and heirs to Stephen Simmons late of Waldoboro, yeoman, deceased, by order of the Superior Judicial Court on the 2nd Tuesday of June last past, sold to William Grotton of Waldoboro, for $1,000, land in Waldoboro; this deed was recorded 24 June 1809 along with a deed from Peabody Simmons to William Grotton (Lincoln LR 71:170-71).

No probate record for Ephraim or Elizabeth Patch was found in Lincoln County. The only Ephraim Patch listed in the 1800 census in Maine was in Bath, over 45 with wife 26-45, two boys under 10, and one girl 10-16 (p.496).

Betsey Vinal must have been Stephen's second wife, for daughter Abigail was at least 14 before she chose a guardian in 1796, thus born by 1782, and son Peabody deeded land in 1804. Stephen's father's will, quoted above, indicates that Stephen had his own household on the Long Island farm by January 1787, and this is reflected by the figures in the 1790 census.

It seems likely that Stephen's first wife was somehow connected to the family of Nathan and Margaret (Spooner) Sprague, married about 1746, who settled in Waldoboro. Among their children were daughters Abigail born at Marshfield 22 April 1749 (*VR* 70) and Urane born there 9 June 1755 (*VR* 71). Stephen's oldest daughter was named Abigail, and a younger daughter, with second wife Betsey, was given the full name Urania Sprague Simmons, possibly demonstrating a practice normal at that time, of honoring a deceased first spouse by naming a child after him or her. Nathan and Margaret also had a son Spooner Sprague, who was probably the guardian of that name chosen by Stephen's oldest child in 1796. Nathan Sprague was guardian of Urania Sprague Simmons in 1809. All in all, it seems more than possible that Stephen Simmons' first wife *was* the Urane Sprague born in 1755, but no proof has been found.

Children of Stephen Simmons, b. probably Waldoboro, Me.; probably first three with first wife [? Urania Sprague]; last four with second wife Betsey Vinal, all living 1799 at distribution and all but Abigail in 1805 at sale of land:

i   ABIGAIL SIMMONS[6], b. by 1782; living 1796 when she chose Spooner Sprague as guardian; d. possibly before 1805 when her siblings deeded land to William Groton. However, she may be named under a married name in another deed that has been missed.

ii   PEABODY SIMMONS, b. before 1783; m. MARY or MERCY REED. Polly Reed Simmons, dau. of Caty (Smouse) Reed, was named in her grandfather's will 1809 (*Broadbay History*, 564). Peabody was probably named after his father's grandmother, Mercy (Peabody) Simmons. Peabody Simmons of Waldoboro, blacksmith, on 8 Dec. 1804 sold to William Grotton of Waldoboro, yeoman, a lot "of which my father Stephen Simmons died possessed, being land on which William Grotton now lives" (Lincoln LR 71:170). His wife Mary or Mercy signed a deed with him in 1812 when he sold to Abner Keene of Waldoboro two parcels of land there, one 30 acres, the other 20 acres (*ibid.* 80:59). There are several other land transactions for Peabody recorded in Lincoln County. F. J. Simmons says that Peabody m. — Groton and lived and d. at Hope, Me. (*Sprague's Journal*, 8:104).
     Children (*ibid.*): 1. *Adeline Simmons[7]*, m. C. G. Bachelor in Camden. 2. *Stephen Simmons*, m. Sophia Sprague.   3. *Nathaniel Simmons,* m. Chloe Dunton (see *Sprague's Journal,* 8:104, for desc.). 4. *Peabody Simmons,* b. 1817 at Union, Me.; d. March 1894 at Somerville, Mass. (Mass. VR 446:354); m. Salome Sprague.

iii STEPHEN SIMMONS; living July 1805, under guardianship. Possibly m. S.___ and had dau. Hellen C. who d. 2 April 1819 ae 2y 9m, bur. with

Spooner Sprague and his wife in the Ancient part of the Old German Cem., Waldoboro, "dau. of Stephen and S. Simmons" (*Waldoboro Cem.*, 8).

iv   URANIA SPRAGUE SIMMONS, b. ca 1794; d. 4 July 1850 in New York City; m. WILLIAM SAVAGE.

v   NANCY SIMMONS; living July 1805, under guardianship.

vi   BETSEY SIMMONS; living July 1805, under guardianship.

vii RACHEL SIMMONS; living July 1805, under guardianship.

Sources cited: *Marshfield VR. Scituate VR. Waldoboro, Maine VR. Waldoboro Cemetery Inscriptions.* Patterson, *Lincoln County Probates* (1895). Lincoln County Deeds at Wiscasset, Me. Stahl, *History of Old Broad Bay* (1956). Frederick Johnson Simmons, "A Genealogy of a Few Lines of the Simmons Family of Maine and Massachusetts," *Sprague's Journal of Maine History*, 7 [1919] and 8 [1920]. CENSUS: Waldoboro, Lincoln Co., 1790 (M637-2).

733.   DOROTHY SIMMONS[5] (*Mercy Simmons*[4], *Rachel*[3] *Samson, Caleb*[2], *Henry*[1]), daughter of Nathaniel Simmons and his wife Mercy Simmons [151], was baptized at Duxbury 11 May 1753 as "Doritey Simons" (*VR* 156), and died at Nobleboro, Maine, 23 September 1814 (*VR* 2:742). She was a descendant also of Mayflower passengers John Alden and Myles Standish.

She married at Nobleboro, by 1777 (*Simmons Gen.*, 51), **JOHN WINSLOW**, who was born at Scituate 23 January 1743, baptized at Hanover 5 February 1743 (*Hanover First Church*, 126), and died at Nobleboro 8 or 17 January 1827, aged 85, son of Oliver and Agatha (Bryant) Winslow. He was a descendant of *Mayflower* passenger Richard Warren. John Winslow was a ship carpenter. His younger half-brother Joseph Winslow married Dorothy's niece, Mercy Hunt [#729-iii].

On 31 August 1773 John Winslow of Marshfield sold to Pelham Winslow of Plymouth and Isaac Winslow of Marshfield his right to land in Winslow [Maine] "which I have as proprietor in common with others" (Plymouth LR 10:192).

Dorothy's father, Nathanael Simmons, in his will dated 22 January 1787, proved 22 January 1789, among other bequests, left to his four daughters, Mary wife of John Hunt, Dorothy wife of John Winslow, Sarah Simmons, and Rachel Simmons, "all that my Farme which I bought of Mrs Jane Cleveland ... one Hundred Acres and lyeth on the Southerly side of Jacob Wades farme ... within the Township of Waldoborough ... Except the Long Island Lot"; he also gave to Mary and Dorothy £4 apiece and to each a cow (*Lincoln Co. Probate*, 180-82).

On 12 November 1790 Joseph Simmons, Zebedee Simmons, and Stephen Simmons, "all sons of Nathaniel Simmons late of the town of Waldoborough, husbandman, deceased, and John Winslow and Dorothy Winslow, son in law and daughter of the aforesaid Nathaniel Simmons, living in the town of Nobleborough," quitclaimed to John Hunt of Waldoboro, cordwainer, their right in a lot of land in Waldoboro containing 100 acres, "the lot our father bought of Mrs. Jean Cleveland … our share from our father's will" (Lincoln LR 52:112-13).

In 1790 John Winslow was in Nobleboro, Maine, with three boys under 16 and six females in his household (p.35). In April 1795 he was one of three men who set off the dower of Hannah Hussey, widow of Benjamin Hussey of Nobleboro (*Lincoln Co. Probate*, 227-28). In 1800 the census listed him in Nobleboro with a household consisting of two boys and one girl under 10, one boy and one girl 10-16, two young men 16-26, and one man and one woman 45 or older (p.458). In 1810 the household consisted of two boys 10-16, one young woman 16-26, and a man and a woman 45 or over (p.265).

See the account of John and his family in *Winslow Memorial*, 668.

Children of John and Dorothy (Simmons) Winslow, b. Nobleboro (*VR* 742-747); see *Winslow Memorial* for more detail:

i   RUTH WINSLOW[6], b. 4 Oct. 1777; d. 7 June 1838 (*VR* 747); m. at Nobleboro, 18 Dec. 1797 (*VR* 307), NATHANIEL MESERVEY "of Barretstown," b. Bremen, Me., ca 1769, d. 19 May 1849, son of Nathaniel (*Winslow Mem.*, 668-69).

        Meservey children, first two b. Nobleboro, 7th – 10th b. Jefferson, Me. (*ibid.*): 1. *Nathaniel Meservey*[7]. 2. *Samuel Meservey*, b. 8 Aug. 1799. 3. *Miles Meservey*. 4. *Elsie Meservey*. 5. *Sally Meservey*. 6. *Alden Meservey*. 7. *John Meservey*. 8. *William Meservey*, b. 31 July 1811. 9. *Caroline Meservey*, b. 10 Aug. 1813. 10. *Nancy Meservey*, b. 16 Oct. 1816. 11. *Jane Meservey*. 12. *Daughter*, d.y. 13. *Son*, d.y.

ii   DOROTHY WINSLOW, b. 18 May 1779; d. 28 June 1860 (*VR* 742); m. at Nobleboro, int. 20 Oct. 1795 (*VR* 305), ELIJAH HALL, b. 7 July 1773, d. 19 Jan. 1827 (*Winslow Mem.*, 671). In 1850 Dorothy was living at Nobleboro with Augustus L., Julia A., Harriet M., and Gardner (p.446).

        Hall children, all but poss. first b. Nobleboro (*Winslow Mem.*, 671): 1. *Zenas Hall*, b. 7 April 1796; m. Hannah Austin. 2. *Demaris Hall*, b. 24 July 1798; m. (1)Daniel Chapman, (2) Stacy Rollins. 3. *Seth Hall*, b. 25 Dec. 1800; m. (1) Jerusha Rollins, (2) Lydia Rollins. 4. *Winslow Hall*, b. 27 Dec. 1802. 5. *Horace Hall*, b. 14 May 1805; m. Silence Oliver. 6. *Almond G. Hall*, b. 6 Oct. 1807; m. Dorcas Rollins. 7. *Elbridge G. Hall*, b. 19 Dec. 1810; m. (1) Mary Vannah, (2) Charlotte Varney. 8. *Jane Oldham Hall*, b. 10 July 1818; m. William Siderlinger. 9. *Thomas Gardner Hall*, b. 19 July 1816; m. Lucinda Rollins. 10. *Julia Ann Hall*, b. 5 March 1819; unm. 1872. 11. *Harriet Newell Hall*, b. 25 June 1821; d. unm. 12. *Augustus Lyman Hall*, b. 12 Nov. 1823; m. Henrietta P. Rollins.

iii   JOHN WINSLOW, b. 30 Nov. 1780 (*VR* 744); m. at Nobleboro (1) 9 May 1802, NANCY HALL, (2) after int. 15 May 1808, JANE CLARK, (3) 15

Nov. 1810, CHARLOTTE CLARK (*VR* 306). In 1850 they were in Noble-boro with Jane, Bradford D., Albion K., Abby, and Joseph; Josiah 2d, a blacksmith, was next door (pp.459-60). (See *Winslow Mem.*, 677, for more.)

Children (*VR* 744), with Nancy: 1. *Isaac Winslow⁷*. 2. *Harvey Winslow*. With Jane: 3. *John Winslow*. With Charlotte: 4. *Nancy Winslow*. 5. *Josiah Winslow 2d*, b. ca 1811; m. Nancy Rowell. 6. *Jane Winslow*, b. ca 1817. 7. *William B. Winslow*. 8. *Percival Winslow*. 9. *Bradford D. Winslow*, b. ca 1821. 10. *Albion K. Winslow*, b. ca 1823. 11. *Abigail Winslow*, b. ca 1825. 12. *Harriet Winslow*. 13. *Joseph Winslow*, b. ca 1829. 14. *Jackson Winslow*.

iv NATHANIEL OLIVER WINSLOW, b. 14 May 1783; d. 2 June 1847; m. (1) at Nobleboro, 24 Feb. 1806, ABIGAIL HALL, b. 25 May 1778, d. 25 May 1783, dau. of James and Hannah (Keene) Hall; m. (2) at Nobleboro, 4 March 1841, RACHEL CHAPMAN, b. 5 Oct. 1798, dau. of Jonathan and Rachel (Knowlton) Chapman (see *Winslow Mem.*, 682-83 for more detail).

Children (*ibid.*), b. Nobleboro: 1. *Rachel Sampson Winslow⁷*, b. 18 Jan. 1808.. 2. *Elsie Winslow*, b. 29 Nov. 1810. 3. *Nathaniel Oliver Winslow*, b. 9 Nov. 1813; m. Sarah Dunbar. 4. *Martha Hopkins Winslow*, b. 25 Jan. 1815. 5. *James Hall Winslow*, b. 5 Oct. 1817. 6. *Cyrus Newcomb Winslow*, b. 17 April 1820. 7. *William Winslow*, b. 22 March 1822; d. 1841. 8. *Hartson Winslow*, b. 8 Aug. 1825; d. 1842.

v JOSEPH WINSLOW, b. 26 Jan. 1786; d. 2 Feb. 1869 (*VR* 744); m. at Nobleboro, 12 Oct. 1809 (*VR* 306), CHLOE HALL. In 1850 he was a farmer in Nobleboro with Chloe ae 58, John A. ae 27, and Vesta M. ae 16; Lyman's family shared the dwelling (p.448).

Children, all at home 1850: 1. *John A. Winslow⁷*, b. ca 1823. 2. *Lyman Winslow*, b. ca 1826; m. Lydia S. ___. 3. *Vesta M. Winslow*, b. ca 1834.

vi SARAH WINSLOW, b. 1 Oct. 1787; d. Nobleboro 3 Aug. 1868 (*VR* 747); m. there, 25 Dec. 1805 (*VR* 307), JESSE DUNBAR JR.

vii RACHEL WINSLOW, b. 26 May 1789; d. Nobleboro 19 Aug. 1879 (*VR* 746); in household of her brother Josiah at Nobleboro 1860.

viii JOSIAH WINSLOW, b. 29 Feb. 1792; d. Nobleboro 28 April 28 April 1880 (*VR* 744); m. at Nobleboro (1) 28 Dec. 1815, MARY AUSTIN, (2) 10 March 1850, SARAH (DUNBAR) WINSLOW, dau. of Joseph and Martha (Chapman) Dunbar and widow of Nathaniel O. Winslow (*VR* 306). In 1850 he was a farmer at Nobleboro with Sarah and three children; sister Racheal Winslow ae 54 [*sic*] was with them (p.448). (See *Winslow Mem.*, 684 for more).

Children, with first wife (*VR* 744; 1850, 1860 census): 1. *Josiah A. Winslow⁷*, b. ca 1827; m. Hannah ___; a farmer living next to father 1850. 2. *Oscar N./Nathaniel O. Winslow*, b. ca 1839. 3. *Abigail Winslow*, b. ca 1841, not at home 1860. 4. *Zerelda Winslow*, b. ca 1843.

ix SNOW WINSLOW, b. 4 Jan. 1796; d. Nobleboro 13 Oct. 1854 (*VR* 747); m.
after int. at Nobleboro 6 Dec. 1818 (*VR* 307), BETSEY HANNAH
HOCH, b. there 9 March 1799 (*Broadbay History*, 212). In 1850 he was a
farmer in Nobleboro with Elizabeth ae 54 and sons Joel and Roscoe (p.447).
        Children (*VR* 747), order uncertain: 1. *Joel Winslow⁷*, b. ca 1832; a joiner
1850. 2. *Elizabeth A. Winslow.* 3. *Roscoe G. Winslow*, b. ca 1836. 4. *Asa Winslow.*
5. *Newell Winslow.* 6. *Harriet R. Winslow.*

Sources cited: *Duxbury VR. Hanover First Church Records. Old Bristol and Nobleboro VR. Waldoboro,
Maine VR.* Plymouth County Deeds. Patterson, *Lincoln County Probate Records* (1895). Stahl, *History
of Old Broadbay and Waldoboro* (1956). *Winslow Memorial* (1888). CENSUS: Nobleboro, Lincoln Co.,
Me., 1790 (M637-2), 1800 (M32-6), 1810 (M252-12), 1850 (M432-260), 1860 (M653-442).

734. CONSIDER SIMMONS⁵ (*Ichabod Simmons⁴, Rachel³ Samson, Caleb²,
Henry¹*), son of Ichabod Simmons [152] and his first wife Lydia Soule, was born at
Duxbury 27 September 1744 and baptized there 1 May 1748 (*VR* 152). He died 23
February 1826, recorded at Pembroke (*VR* 445) as of Duxbury. He was a
descendant also of Pilgrims John Alden, George Soule, and Myles Standish.

He married at Duxbury, 25 February 1763 (*VR* 306), **NEPHELA SOULE**,
who was baptized at Duxbury as Aphela, 19 April 1741 (*VR* 159) and died there
1 December 1827 as Aphelia, wife of Consider Simmons (*VR* 418), daughter of
Micah and Mercy (Southworth) Soule. She was a descendant of Pilgrims John
Alden and George Soule. In his will, dated 20 October 1778, proved 7 December
1778, Micah Soule among other bequests left £10 to daughter Nephele, wife of
Consider Simmonds (Plymouth PR #18,842).

Consider Simmons of Duxbury served for three days in the Revolutionary
War, as a private in Capt. Benjamin Wadsworth's militia company, Col. Warren's
regiment, marching on the Lexington alarm 19 April 1775 (*MSSR* 14:228).

In 1790 the household of Consider Simmons at Duxbury consisted of two
men 16 or older, and three females (p.168). In 1810 Consider and his wife, both
over 45, had living with them one other woman 45+ and one woman 26-45,
figures that fit their two daughters (p.227).

Consider and Nephebe [*sic*] Simmons sold a part of their homestead to
Thomas W. Peterson on 3 January 1820 (Plymouth PR 149:133); there is no reference to any relationship.

Children of Consider and Nephele/Aphele (Soule) Simmons, rec. Duxbury (*VR*
159):

i   LYDIA SIMMONS⁶, b. ca Aug. 1763; d. Duxbury 1 July 1766 ae 2y 10m (*VR*
417); probably the Lydia bp. there 28 June 1766.

ii LUCY SIMMONS, bp. 26 July 1767; prob. the Lucy Simmons who d. 28 Aug. 1834, ae 69, in Duxbury almshouse of "debility and age" (*VR* 417).

iii LYDIA SOUL SIMMONS, bp. 24 July 1768; prob. the Lydia Simmons who d. 28 July 1835 in Duxbury almshouse of consumption, ae 70 (*VR* 417).

iv JONATHAN SOUL SIMMONS, bp. 6 June 1773; d. poss. 5 Nov. 1819 "of Marshfield" (*Pembroke VR* 445); m. at Marshfield, 29 Nov. 1804 (*VR* 260), MERCY JOYCE, dau. Jonathan and Abigail (Holmes) Joyce, b. 9 April 1779, a Henry Samson descendant [#325-viii, *MF20*, pt. 2:251-52]. By Jonathan Joyce's will, dated 10 Dec. 1806, proved 6 March 1809, dau. Mercy Simmons inherited all his real estate and remainder of personal estate not before disposed of, and son-in-law Jonathan Simmons was appointed sole executor (Plymouth PR 42:482-83). In 1850 Mercy Simmons ae 71 was living at Marshfield with her three youngest sons, next door to family of son-in-law Samuel Keen; Mary Joyce ae 78 was also there (p.164).

Children, first six rec. Marshfield (*VR* 231-32): 1. *Jonathan Joyce Simmons⁷*, b. 20 Nov. 1805. 2. *Hewit Simmons*, b. 22 July 1807. 3. *Biram Simmons*, b. 29 July 1809. 4. *James Hervey Simmons*, b. 1 May 1811. 5. *Elbridge Simmons*, b. 9 Oct. 1813. 6. *Winthrop Brigham Simmons*, b. 1 Feb. 1816. 7. *Mercy S. Simmons*, b. ca 1819; ae 28 when m. Duxbury, 24 Nov. 1847, Samuel Keen, parents' names given (*VR* 342-43).

Sources cited: *Duxbury VR. Marshfield VR. Pembroke VR. Mass. Soldiers & Sailors.* Plymouth County Deeds and Probate Records. CENSUS: Duxbury, Plymouth Co., 1790 (M637-4) & 1810 (M252-21); 1850 Marshfield, Plymouth Co. (M432-332

735. NOAH SIMMONS⁵ (*Ichabod Simmons⁴, Rachel³ Samson, Caleb², Henry¹*), son of Ichabod Simmons [152] and his first wife Lydia Soule, was born at Duxbury 2 September 1745 and baptized there 1 May 1748 (*VR* 154). He died at Duxbury 26 June 1832 aged 86 (*VR* 417). He was a descendant also of *Mayflower* passengers John Alden, George Soule, and Myles Standish.

He married at Duxbury, 2 July 1769 (*VR* 308, 314), **SYLVIA SOUTH-WORTH**, daughter of Benjamin Jr. and Mary (Hunt) Southworth (*MF 16*: 2:49). She was born at Duxbury 22 November 1747 (*VR* 168), and died there 1 September 1831 aged 83y 8m 29d (Simmons Fam. Rec., 7). She was a descendant of *Mayflower* passengers John Alden and George Soule.

On 20 October 1775 Noah Simmons, his wife Silvia, and their children Peleg Southworth and Charles "who came here sometime in October last past from Duxborough" were warned out of Marshfield (*PCCR*, 3:358).

In 1790 Noah was in Duxbury, with two boys under 16 and five females (p.169).

In April 1806 Noah Simmons of Duxbury, yeoman, won a judgment of $14.53 plus costs against Peres Chandler when the defendant defaulted (*PCCR* 11:365).

In 1810 Noah's household consisted of one man and one woman 45 or older, one man 26-45, and one woman 16-25 (*Heads of Fam.*, 169).

No Plymouth County probate record has been found for this Noah or Sylvia Simmons or for an appropriate Benjamin Southworth.

Children of Noah and Sylvia (Southworth) Simmons, all but last rec. Duxbury as noted, all in Simmons Family Record:

i WEALTHEA SIMMONS[6], b. 10 March 1770, bp. 28 April 1771 (*VR* 155); d. 3 May 1771 ae 1y 2m (*VR* 418).

ii PELEG SOUTHWORTH SIMMONS, b. 24 Feb., bp. 1 March 1772 (*VR* 154); d. at sea 1803 ae 31 yr, unm. (Simmons Fam. Rec., 6).

iii CHARLES SIMMONS, b. 23 Nov. 1774, bp. 27 Jan. 1777 (*VR* 152); d. 1 Sept. 1857 ae 82y 11m 8d; m. at Duxbury, 25 Jan. 1798, LYDIA WESTON (*VR* 306), dau. of Simeon and Honor (Hunt) Weston.
   Children rec. Duxbury (*VR* 151-55; Simmons Fam. Rec., 3): 1. *Joshua W. Simmons[7]*, b. 14 Sept. 1798 [compiler of the Fam. Rec.]. 2. *Alden Simmons*, b. 4 May 1801. 3. *James Simmons*, b. 4 Aug. 1803. 4. *Peleg Simmons*, b. 21 Aug. 1806. 5. *Caroline Simmons*, b. 10 March 1809. 6. *Henry Simmons*, b. 13 Aug. 1811. 7. *Sylvia S. Simmons*, b. 19 July 1814.

iv DANIEL SIMMONS, b. 17 Feb. 1777, bp. 16 Sept. 1778 (*VR* 152); d. 23 Sept. 1778 ae 1y 7m (*VR* 416).

v NATHAN SIMMONS, b. 18 April, bp. 25 April 1779 (*VR* 154); d. 26 Oct. 1779 ae 6m (*VR* 417).

vi DANIEL SIMMONS, bp. Aug. 1781 (*VR* 152); d. Hallowell, Me., 29 July 1825 ae 45 yrs (VR 6:39); m. (1) SARAH/SALLY _____, d. Duxbury 1806 or 1809 ae 23y 8m 183 (*VR* 418); m. (2) after int. Hallowell, Me., 1 Nov. 1810 (VR 5:61), SALLY MAYO.

vii WELTHEA SIMMONS, b. 22 April, bp. 3 May 1783 (*VR* 155); d. Duxbury 27 Sept. 1785 (*VR* 418).

viii SYLVIA SIMMONS (twin), b. 27 Sept., bp. 29 Sept. 1785 (*VR* 155); d. Duxbury 4 March 1796 (*VR* 418).

ix [CHILD] SIMMONS (twin), b. and d. 27 Sept. 1785 (*VR* 418*)*.

x VIOLATA SIMMONS, b. 5 April 1788 (Simmons Family Rec., 3); d. Duxbury 11 Nov. 1875, unm. (Mass. VR 275:301).

Sources cited: *Duxbury VR. Hallowell, Maine, VR.* "Family Record of Births, Marriages, and Deaths by Joshua W. Simmons, [b.] 1798 [son of Charles and Lydia (Weston) Simmons]," typescript GSMD Library. *Mass. Soldiers & Sailors. Heads of Families 1790 – Mass.* **See also:** *Philip Delano, Fifth and Sixth Generations,* Part 1 (2004), 81-82.

736.   LEMUEL SIMMONS⁵ (*Ichabod Simmons⁴, Rachel³ Samson, Caleb², Henry¹*), son of Ichabod Simmons [152] and his first wife Lydia Soule, was born at Duxbury 22 February 1749 (*VR* 153). He died at Plympton 11 December 1833 aged 84y 9m 6d, and was buried at Plymouth (*Burial Hill* #1366). He was a descendant also of *Mayflower* passengers John Alden, George Soule, and Myles Standish. His Plympton death record calls him Lt. Lemuel Simmons, "father of Avery Deane's wife, father of Pelham."

He married at Duxbury, 15 March 1769 or 1770 (*VR* 307), **ABIGAIL PIERCE,** who was born about 1752 and died at Plymouth 2 October 1817 in her 66th year. Their shared gravestone in Burial Hill, Plymouth, bears the epitaph:. "*Their happy spirits onward rise / To yon blest world above the skies. / Come children view this place of rest / Prepare and be forever blest.*"

Abigail has not been identified. It has been suggested that she was probably the daughter of Abraham and Abigail (Peterson) Pierce of Pembroke (*Philip Delano* 2004, 82), but there is no record of a daughter Abigail in that family, and Abigail (Peterson) Pierce died about 1750 (*MFIP Soule*, 148-49). Abraham Peirce in his will dated 30 March 1784, proved 20 May 1785 (Plymouth PR 29:335), included a bequest of £2 5s to granddaughter Abigail Simmons but did not name her parents; he also left 5s to daughter Hannah Simmons (bp. 1737; m. William Simmons #155). It has been assumed (MF20:1:131) that the Abigail named in the will was Hannah's daughter, although no such child is recorded (see #753, p. 415). The fact that *both* Hannah and Abigail received legacies suggests that Abigail may have been the daughter of a deceased child, inheriting in place of a parent. Such a chronology fits the Abigail who married Lemuel Simmons.

Lemuel Simmons served as a lieutenant in the Revolutionary War (*MSSR* 14:228). In July 1780 he was one of several innholders in Plymouth who were licensed to sell spiritous liquors (*PCCR*, General Sessions). At the August 1792 session of the court Lemuel Simmons of Plymouth, cordwainer, sued John Watson of Plymouth, gentleman, and received a judgement for £4 18s 6d plus costs (*PCCR*, CCP Aug. 1792, #41).

He applied for a pension 15 August 1832 at Plympton, stating that he was born at Duxbury in 1749 and had enlisted from there (White, 3137).

There are no probate records for him in Plymouth County.

Children of Lemuel and Abigail (Pierce) Simmons, ii - vi bp. Duxbury, vi-x births rec. together at Plymouth (*VR* 426); see *Philip Delano* (2004), 80-83 for more detail:

    i   MARY / POLLY SIMMONS, b, ca 1770; bp. Duxbury 28 March 1779 (*VR*
         154); d. Plymouth 30 March 1843 ae 73 (g.s.); m. at Plymouth, 27 July 1797
         (*VR* 372), GEORGE STRAFFIN, b. Plymouth 9 March 1771 (*VR* 243,

258), "kill'd with lightning in the Bay of Biscay Jan. 10, 1801" (g.s.), son of William and Susannah (Kember) Staffin. There is one stone in Burial Hill (#765) for parents and both sons.

> **Straffin** children b. Plymouth (*VR* 426); lost at sea: 1. *George Straffin[7]*, b. 30 Aug. 1798; d. 1824. 2. *Robert Straffin*, b. 4 Oct. 1800; d. 1821..

ii MOSES SIMMONS[6], b. ca 1772; d. Duxbury 30 Oct. 1777, ae 5 (*VR* 417).

iii BEULAH SIMMONS, bp. Duxbury 28 March 1779 (*VR* 152); m. at Plymouth, 3 April 1794 (*VR* 370), DANIEL GODDARD.

> **Goddard** children rec. Plymouth (*VR* 427): 1. *Mary Simmons Goddard[7]*, b. 2 Dec. 1795; d. 1798. 2. *Daniel Goddard*, b. 12 May 1797. 3. *William Goddard*, b. 20 May 1799; d. 1804. 4. *Mary Goddard*, b. 26 Aug. 1801; d. 1803. 5. *Beulah Goddard*, b. 30 Aug. 1802. 6. *Lemuel Simmons Goddard*, b. 20 Aug. 1804. 7. *Lucia Goddard*, b. 26 June 1806; d. 1807. 8. *Lucia William Goddard*, b. 1 Dec. 1808. 9. *Abigail Perce Goddard*, b. 7 May 1809. 10. *Mary Ann Goddard*, b. 30 Jan. 1811.

iv ANDERSON SIMMONS, b. ca 1776; bp. Duxbury 2 March 1779 (*VR* 151); d. there 7 Nov. 1779, ae 3 (*VR* 415), d. rec. also as Andrew.

v LYDIA ANDERSON SIMMONS, bp. Duxbury 26 March 1780 (*VR* 153); d. Plympton 17 Dec. 1844 ae 63y 9m of "inward cancer" (*VR* 473); m. (1) at Plymouth, 15 Jan. 1800 (*VR* 435), SIMON RICHMOND, d. 22 April 1809 at sea in 35th year, "Capt." (g.s.); m. (2) at Plymouth, 30 May 1817 (*VR* 443), AVERY DEANE of Plympton, b. there 1 Sept. 1789, son of Dr. Ebenezer and Hannah (Whitman) Deane (*VR* 91).

> **Richmond** children rec. Plymouth (*VR* 426): 1. *Anderson Simmons Richmond[7]*, b. 18 Jan. 1801; d. 1802. 2. *Anderson Simmons Richmond*, b. 19 May 1803. 3. *Susan William Richmond*, b. 4 May 1806. **Deane** children, rec. Plympton (*VR* 92): 1. *Rebecca Whitman Deane[7]*, b. 20 Sept. 1818. 2. *George Avery Richmond Deane*, b. 9 June 1825.

vi GEORGE SIMMONS, b. Plymouth 7 June 1782 (*VR* 426); bp. Duxbury 9 June 1782 (*VR* 152); m. at Plymouth, 12 April 1804 (*VR* 437), MARY BATES, called Mercy in birth records of their children.

> Children rec. Plymouth (*VR* 426): 1. *George Simmons[7]*, b. 3 Sept. 1805. 2. *Mercy Simmons*, b. 28 Nov. 1806. 3. *Moses Simmons*, b. 4 Oct. 1808. 4. *William Davis Simmons*, b. 8 April 1811. 5. *Augustus Frederick Simmons*, b. 16 March 1813. 6. *John Brooks Simmons*.

vii ABIGAIL SIMMONS, b. Plymouth 3 June 1784 (*VR* 426); bp. there 13 July 1794; m. at Plymouth, 30 Dec. 1805 (*VR* 438), ALPHEUS RICHMOND.

> **Richmond** children rec. Plymouth (*VR* 425): 1. *Alpheus Richmond[7]*, b. 22 Nov. 1806. 2. *Abigail Simmons Richmond*, b. 4 June 1809. 3. *William Richmond*, b. 3 June 1814. 4. *John Atwood Richmond*, b. 30 Jan. 1818.

viii   EUNICE TERRY SIMMONS, b. Plymouth 28 July 1787 (*VR* 426); bp. 13
       July 1794; m. at Plympton, 14 Aug. 1828 (*VR* 393), PELHAM
       CHURCHILL, b. there 14 March 1800 (*VR* 69), son of Josiah and Deborah
       (Phinney) Churchill. In 1850 he was a farmer at Plympton, ae 50, with
       Eunice T. ae 58 [*sic*] and their two sons (p.46).
           Churchill children rec. Plympton (*VR* 67, 69): 1. *Pelham Francis Russell
           Churchill*, b. Newport, R.I., 11 Dec. 1828.   2. *Lemuel Pierce Churchill*, b. 2 April
           1831.

ix   LEMUEL SIMMONS, b. Plymouth 12 Aug. 1790 (*VR* 426); bp. there 13 July
       1794; d. 6 Dec. 1863; m. at Plymouth, 17 May 1818 (*VR* 444), PRISCILLA
       SHERMAN, b. ca 1793, d. 1 March 1835 in 42d yr; both bur. Burial Hill,
       Plymouth (#1395, #1906).
           Children rec. Plymouth (*VR* 228): 1. *Priscilla C. Simmons*[7], b. 1 Nov. 1819.
           2. *Mary S. Simmons*, b. 23 April 1821.   3. *Lemuel Simmons*, b. 23 Jan. 1823; d. 26
           Jan. 1823.   4. *Eunice T. Simmons*, b. 30 March 1824.   5. *Lemuel Simmons*, b. 26 Feb.
           1826.

x   CYNTHIA DAVIS SIMMONS, b. Plymouth 19 May 1794 (*VR* 426); bp.
       there 13 July 1794; m. at Plymouth, 18 Sept. 1813 (CR 2:181), ELKANAH
       BARNES. They are bur. in Burial Hill, "on the southwest side of the hill,
       near the boundary line," no dates legible (*Burial Hill*, p.287, #2233).
           Barnes children rec. Plymouth (*VR* 429): 1. *Alexina Carlowitzs Barnes*[7], b. 26
           Dec. 1813.   2. *Lavonzo Barnes*, b. 23 July 1816.   3. *Catharine Harriet Barnes*, b. 14
           Dec. 1818.   4. *Churles* [*sic*] *Elkanah Barnes*, b. 15 Sept. 1820.

Sources cited: *Duxbury VR. Plymouth VR. Plympton VR. Plymouth Church Records. Epitaphs from
Burial Hill, Plymouth* (1892). Plymouth County Probate Records. Konig, *Plymouth County Court
Records. Mass. Soldiers & Sailors.* White, *Abstracts of Rev. War Pension Files*, citing File S30703.
CENSUS: *Heads of Families 1790 – Mass.;* 1850 Plympton, Plymouth Co. (M432-333). **See also:**
Philip Delano, Fifth and Sixth Generations, Part 1 (2004), 81-82.

737.   ABIGAIL SIMMONS[5] (*Ichabod Simmons*[4], *Rachel*[3] *Samson, Caleb*[2], *Henry*[1]),
daughter of Ichabod Simmons [152] and his first wife Lydia Soule, was born at
Duxbury 24 May 1753 (*VR* 151) and died there 6 November 1807 in her 55th year
(*VR* 350). Abigail was a descendant also of *Mayflower* passengers John Alden,
George Soule, and Myles Standish.
    She was of Plymouth when she married there, 24 August 1784, **JOHN
BARTON** (*Duxbury VR* 305), who was born in Great Britain about 1759 and died
at Duxbury 20 December 1835 or 9 January 1836, aged 79, of "debility and age"
(*VR* 350). He married, second, at Duxbury, 21 February 1809, AMY DELANO,

born Duxbury 29 January 1759, daughter of Lemuel and Lydia (Bartlett) Delano (*Philip Delano 2004*, 67).

John Barton served in the Revolutionary War, enlisting in 1777 in Capt. Joseph Wadsworth's company, Col. Gamaliel Bradford's regiment when he was 18. At age 22 he was described as 5 ft. 10 in. tall, with light hair and light complexion, born in Great Britain, residing in Duxbury. He was reported transferred to Gen. Washington's guard in 1781 (*MSSR* 1:740). When he applied for a pension 14 June 1818, he was aged 59, of Duxbury (White, 177, citing #S34002).

On 22 September 1832 John Barton of Duxbury gave all his property to [brother-in-law] John Bailey of Hanover in return for one dollar and a bond to provide him with support and nursing (Plymouth LR 176:42).

Children of John and Abigail (Simmons) Barton, rec. Duxbury as "Bartin" (*VR* 24):

i   GEORGE WASHINGTON BARTON[6], b. 23 July 1785; d. prob. Bath, Me., before 1850; m. at Bridgewater, 17 Sept. 1809 (*VR* 41), CHRISTIANA WHITMAN, b. there 18 Dec. 1785 (*VR* 1:341).

    Child: 1. *George W. Barton[7]*, b. ca 1814 in Maine (*MFIP Soule*, 2:145).

ii   JOHN DOUGLASS BARTON, b. 9 Feb. 1788; d. Waltham, Vt., after 1850; m. (1) at Duxbury, 1 Feb. 1807 (*VR* 216, as *Barlin*), his cousin ANN[A] (SIMMONS) DELANO [#738-iii]; m. (2) BETSEY ____. In 1850 John D. Barton ae 62 was a farmer in Waltham, Vt., with Betsey ae 55, and four children; Betsey Taylor ae 83 was in the household (p.222).

    Children at home 1850: 1. *Amos M. Barton[7]*, b. ca 1827. 2. *Fanny D. Barton*, b. ca 1829. 3. *Franklin D. Barton*, b. ca 1833. 4. *Julia E. Barton*, b. ca 1837.

iii JEDIDIAH S. BARTON, b. 31 Dec. 1789; d. Pembroke (*VR* 386) 21 Sept. 1847 [rec. without date *Duxbury VR* 350]; m. at Duxbury, 9 May 1811 (*VR* 216, as *Barlin*), SALLY WESTON.

    Children rec. Duxbury (*VR* 24, as *Bartin*): 1. *Abigail S. Barton*, b. 8 July 1812. 2. *Sally W. Barton*, b. 30 Nov. 1814. 3. *Cordianna Barton*, b. 19 June 1817. 4. *Mary A. Barton*, b. 4 Sept. 1821. 5. *James M. Barton*, b. 2 Dec. 1823. 6. *Caroline Barton*, b. 10 March 1826. 7. *Jerusha B. Barton*, b. 14 June 1828. 8. *Elisabeth C. Barton*, b. 8 April 1831; d. 21 Aug. 1834 (*VR* 350). 9. *Susan J. Barton*, b. 28 Jan. 1833; d. 20 Aug. 1835. 10. *Elisabeth C. Barton*, b. 24 April 1835.

iv   ANDERSON BARTON, b. 17 Feb. 1793; d. Duxbury 6 Oct. 1796 (*VR* 350).

v   MATHEW BARTON, b. 2 Sept. 1795; d. poss. Searsmont, Me., after 1850; m. at Georgetown, Me., ca 1825, LUCY ____ , b. Georgetown ca 1799. In 1850 Mathew Barton was a farmer in Searsmont, Me., ae 54, with Lucy ae 51 and six children all b. Searsmont (p.157).

Children at home 1850, b. Searsmont, Me.: 1. *Martha Barton[7]*, b. ca 1826. 2. *Lucy Ann Barton*, b. ca 1829. 3. *George Barton*, b. ca 1831. 4. *Catharine Barton*, b. ca 1836. 5. *Oleva A. Barton*, b. ca 1839. 6. *Caroline Barton*, b. ca 1842.

Sources cited: *Duxbury VR. Pembroke VR. Mass. Soldiers & Sailors.* CENSUS: 1850 Waltham, Addison Co., Vt. (M432-920), Searsmont, Waldo Co., Me. [includes birthplaces] (M432-271). *Philip Delano* (2004). **See also:** *Philip Delano of the Fortune ... Fifth and Sixth Gen.* (2004), 84-85. *MFIP Soule*, Part Two (2002) includes 7th-generation spouses.

738. NATHANIEL SIMMONS[5] (*Ichabod Simmons[4], Rachel[3] Samson, Caleb[2], Henry[1]*), son of Ichabod Simmons [152] and his first wife Lydia Soule, was born at Duxbury 3 April 1757 (*VR* 154). He died there 22 January 1835 in his 78th year, "husband of Lydia, son of Ichabod" (*VR* 417). Nathaniel was a descendant also of *Mayflower* passengers John Alden, George Soule, and Myles Standish.

He married at Duxbury, 7 December 1780 (*VR* 308), **LYDIA SPRAGUE**, who was born there 21 March 1761 (*VR* 153), daughter of Samuel Jr. and Sarah (Oldham) Sprague and a descendant of *Mayflower* passenger Henry Samson [#206-ix, MF20:.2:61]. She died at Duxbury 28 November 1829 in her 68th year, of consumption (*VR* 417). Nathaniel and Lydia and other members of this family are buried in the Large Cemetery, Duxbury. Lydia Sprague, "fifth daughter," is named in the division of the estate of Samuel Sprague of Duxbury dated 11 June 1770 (Plymouth PR 20:381-85).

Nathaniel served in the Revolutionary War as a private (*MSSR* 14:233). When he applied for a pension on 21 August 1832 he stated that he was born in 1757, had enlisted from Duxbury, and had always lived there (White, 3137 citing #S15981). In 1790 his household in Duxbury included one boy under 16 and five females (p.169).

Bond was filed 13 April 1835 on Nathaniel Simmons of Marshfield, yeoman, as administrator on the estate of Nathaniel Simmons late of Duxbury, yeoman; Lemuel Harlow and Jacob Smith were sureties (Plymouth PR 71:309). The inventory was taken 23 December 1835, and an account filed 5 December 1836 made no mention of children (*ibid.*, 78:148, 503).

Children of Nathaniel and Lydia (Sprague) Simmons, b. at Duxbury:

    i   PARTHENA SIMMONS[6], b. 5 Aug. 1781 (*VR* 151, as *Barthenia*); d. at Duxbury, as "Parthenia" 15 June 1840 in her 60th yr, unm. (*VR* 417).

    ii   SARAH SIMMONS, b. 9 March 1784 (*VR* 155); poss. m. at Duxbury, 13 Jan. 1825 (*VR* 308), PEREZ WHITING.

iii ANNA SIMMONS, b. 27 March 1786 (*VR* 151); d. prob. in Vermont ca 1820; m. (1) as Anne, at Duxbury, 16 June 1801 (*VR* 306), CORNELIUS DELANO, a Henry Samson descendant [#459-viii, *MF20:*.2:437]; m. (2) at Duxbury, 1 Feb. 1807 (*VR* 216), as his first wife, her cousin JOHN DOUGLASS BARTON [#737-ii].

iv NATHANIEL SIMMONS, b. 24 June 1788 (*VR* 154); m. (1) ca 1809, NANCY ____; m. (2) at Bristol, Me., 15 July 1817, SARAH HILTON.
   Children, from d. rec. at Duxbury, first two "of Nathaniel and Sarah" (*VR* 416, 418): 1. *Leander H. Simmons*, b. ca 10 Nov. 1818; d. Duxbury 12 Sept. 1838, ae 20y 10m 2d. 2. *George Simmons*, b. ca 15 Nov. 1822; d. Duxbury 23 Jan. 1842 ae 19y 2m 8d. 3. [*Son*] *Simmons*, d. 1 Feb. 1828. 4. [*Daughter*] *Simmons*, d. 15 June 1830.

v REBECCA SIMMONS, b. 4 Oct. 1791 (*VR* 154); m. at Duxbury, 4 Oct. 1815 (*VR* 308), JOHN SPRAGUE, b. Marshfield 7 Sept. 1790 (*VR* 69). In 1850 he was a whitesmith in Marshfield with Rebecca ae 58, Augustus ae 34, Nancy ae 32, and Marian M. ae 15 (p.168); in 1860 John was a machinist and Augustus was the only child at home (p.41).
   Sprague children, first rec. Duxbury (*VR* 168), rest Marshfield (*VR* 245): 1. *Augustus Frederick Sprague[7]*, b. 21 Sept. 1816. 2. *Nancy Sprague*, b. 26 July 1818. 3. *Huldah Sprague*, b. 30 July 1822. 4. *Marion Melville Sprague*, b. 17 Feb. 1835.

vi ALATHEA SIMMONS, b. 24 Sept. 1793 (*VR* 151); res. Marshfield 1850; m. there, 21 Dec. 1841 (*VR* 304), as his second wife, JOSEPH P. CUSHMAN, b. Marshfield 12 Oct. 1785, son of Robert and Persis (Phillips) Cushman and widower of Betsey Gray (*VR* 181, 192).

vii LYDIA SIMMONS, b. 1 May 1795 (*VR* 153); d. Marshfield 17 July 1844 of pulmonary consumption (*VR* 358); m. at Duxbury, 21 May 1826 (*VR* 307), WILLIAM WILLIAMSON, prob. b. Marshfield 3 Nov. 1797, son of Nathan and Hannah (Ewell) Williamson (*VR* 215). He m. (2) int. Marshfield 4 Oct. 1846, Mrs. Sarah A. Woodbury (*VR* 311), and in 1850 they res. Boston with several Woodbury children (p.270).
   Williamson child, b. rec. Duxbury (*VR* 197): 1. — [*dau.*] *Williamson* b. 24 April 1831; n.f.r.

viii LUCY SIMMONS (twin), b. 18 Dec. 1798 (*VR* 153); d. Marshfield, 30 Nov. 1864, ae 66y 6m, unm., of consumption (Mass. VR, 175:323).

ix NANCY SIMMONS (twin), b. 18 Dec. 1798; d. Duxbury 26 May 1801 (*VR* 417).

x ICHABOD SIMMONS, b. 17 Feb. 1801 (*VR* 153); d. at 78 Emerald St., Boston, 12 Sept. 1869 ae 68y 6m 25d of phthsis, "Captain" (Mass. VR 222:151), Plymouth TR [1869]:46); m. at Plymouth, 25 Dec. 1828 (*VR* 466), MARCIA BATES SIMMONS, b. Plymouth 28 Nov. 1806 (*VR* 426).

Children, first three rec. Duxbury (*VR* 153, 154, 156; all in *MFIP Soule*, 2:148): 1. *Marcia A*[*nn*] *B*[*ates*] *Simmons⁷*, b. 11 April 1830. 2. *Ichabod Simmons*, b. 24 Dec. 1831. 3. *Joanna Adelaide Simmons*, b. 24 Nov. 1834. 4. *Victorine Annette Simmons*, b. 1837. 5. *Eugene Simmons*, ca 1842; d. 1845. 6. [*Daughter*] *Simmons*, b. 1844. 7. *Walter Simmons*, b. 1846.

xi   MARY SIMMONS, b. —— 1804 (*VR* 154) or Feb. 1805 (calc.); d. Duxbury 22 March 1872 ae 67y 1m 19d; m. there 5 Dec. 1827 (*VR* 309), THOMAS KENT WESTON, b. 20 Feb. 1795 (rec. *Duxbury VR*, 195 as husb. Mary Simmons, from g.s.). In 1850 he was a mariner at Duxbury with Mary ae 46, Sarah ae 18, and Ann F. ae 16 (p.77).

        Weston children, rec. Duxbury (*VR* 188, 194): 1. *Sarah D. Weston⁷*, b. 22 June 1831. 2. *Anne F. Weston*, b. 14 June 1833.

xii   JOSHUA SPRAGUE SIMMONS, b. 28 April 1807 (*VR* 153); d. at Duxbury 4 Sept. 1838 ae 30y 4m 7d (*VR* 416: Capt. Joshua S., h. Jane W., from g.s.); m. after int. Duxbury 11 May 1833, JANE W. SOULE (*MD* 30:42). In 1850 Jane W. Simmons ae 39 was in the household of Lot and Elizabeth Soule at Duxbury (p.71). No record found of children.

Sources cited: *Duxbury VR. Plymouth VR.* "Records of Publishments [in Duxbury]," *Mayflower Descendant* 30 (1932). *Mass. Soldiers & Sailors.* White, *Abstracts of Revolutionary War Pension Files.* Plymouth County Probate Records. *MFIP Soule*, 2 (2002). CENSUS: Plymouth Co., Duxbury 1850 (M432-333); Marshfield 1850 (M432-332) & 1860 (M653-519). **See also:** *Philip Delano of the Fortune ... Fifth and Sixth Gen.* (2004), 85-87.

---

739. ICHABOD SIMMONS⁵ (*Ichabod Simmons⁴, Rachel³ Samson, Caleb², Henry¹*), son of Ichabod Simmons [152] and his first wife Lydia Soule, was born at Duxbury 25 May 1761 (Bible; *VR* 153), and died at Kingfield, Franklin County, Maine, 12 January 1833 (Bible), aged 71y 8m (g.s.). He was a descendant also of *Mayflower* passengers John Alden, George Soule, and Myles Standish.

He married at Duxbury, 16 January 1783 (*VR* 265), **URANIA HOLMES**, who was born there 29 August 1760 (Bible; not in VR) and died at Kingfield 3 September 1845, aged 85 (g.s.), probably the daughter of Jeremiah and Phebe (Crymble) Holmes (*Delano 2004*, 87). Ichabod and Urania are buried in Riverside Cemetery, Kingfield, Maine.

Ichabod served in the Revolutionary War. He was a resident of Readfield, Maine, aged 56, when he first applied for a pension in May 1818. He stated that he enlisted in July 1779 for two months on an expedition to Rhode Island and was discharged at Tiverton; he again enlisted in May or June 1780 for four months, in Capt. Clift's company, Col. Sproat's regiment, and went under the command of General Sullivan to Rhode Island. "In June of the year that Gen. Benedict Arnold went over to the enemy," he again enlisted and served six months in Capt. Haskell's company, Col. Gamaliel Bradford's regiment, receiving his discharge at West Point in December. "I have a small farm, am considerbly in debt, and depend principally upon my labor for support, am rendered infirm and decrepid by the rheumatism … am in need of the bounty of the government." He applied again in 1832 under the Act passed that June, and in his declaration said he "was one of the soldiers [at West Point] who guarded [Major John] Andre to the gallows when he was executed." He stated that he was born in Duxbury in 1761 and moved to Readfield, Maine, in 1782, then to Kingfield in Somerset County in 1824. Luther Sampson, aged 72 years, testified that he had served with Ichabod, and described the various campaigns, including the time in 1780 at West Point, "it being when Major Andre the British spy was hung."

Urania applied for a widow's pension 12 February 1839 (file #W24971). Her son Moses Simmons testified that he had cared for her since his father's death, and he provided two sheets of Bible records that give dates for his parents' marriage, Urania's birth, Ichabod's death, and births and some marriages and deaths of their children.

Children of Ichabod and Urania (Holmes) Simmons, b. Readfield, Maine (Bible):

i MOSES SIMMONS[6], b. 19 July 1784; d. 25 Sept. 1841 (g.s.); m. at Readfield, 10 Sept. 1809, BETSEY HAYWARD (Bible), d. 4 Oct. 1867 ae 77y 9m 6d (g.s.). They are buried in Riverside Cem., Kingfield, with his parents. In 1850 Betsey Simmons ae 51, b. Mass., was at Kingfield with her three youngest sons, and the family of Daniel next door (p.219).

Children (1850 census; prob. incomplete): 1. *Daniel Simmons[7]*, b. ca 1812; m. Beulah ___; ch. 1850 included Betsey W. and Moses. 2. *Joshua H. Simmons*, b. 1822; d. 28 Jan. 1876 ae 53y 9m; bur. with parents. 3 *Charles H. Simmons*, b. ca 1824. 4. *George Simmons*, b. ca 1828. 5. *Tristram N. Simmons*, b. ca 1832.

ii LYDIA SIMMONS, b. Tuesday 28 Aug. 1787; m. at Readfield, 2 Jan. 1812, SAMUEL WALTON (Bible), b. ca 1786 Mass., d. 11 March 1859, bur. Fellows Cem., Fayette, Me. In 1850 he was a farmer at Fayette, with Lydia ae 63, Ichabod ae 31, Caroline ae 25, and Amanda Butler ae 35; Samuel S. Walton ae 34 was nearby (p.418).

Walton children (1850 census; prob. incomplete): 1. *Samuel S. Walton[7]*, b. ca 1816. 2. *Ichabod Walton*, b. ca 1819. 3. *Caroline Walton*, b. ca 1825.

iii ZERUJAH SIMMONS, b. Thursday 22 April 1790; d. 16 Jan. 1834 at Mt. Vernon, Me., as "Zerujah *Newton* aged 44 years" (Bible); m. at Augusta, Me., 5 April 1814, JOSIAH NORTON (Augusta VR).

iv SAMUEL SIMMONS, b. Thursday 20 Sept. 1792; d. 23 Feb. 1814 at St. Andrews in "the Province of [*blank – prob. New Brunswick*]."

v DANIEL SIMMONS, b. Friday 20 April 1795; d. Readfield 17 Sept. 1803.

vi PATTY SIMMONS, b. Friday 15 Sept. 1797; d. Readfield 28 March 1843, ae 46 yrs (g.s.); m. after int. at Readfield 19 Dec. 1818, JONATHAN WHITTIER, b. ca 1786, d. 21 Dec. 1869 ae 83 (g.s.). Both bur. East Readfield Cem.

Whittier child (*ibid.*): 1. *Almeda S. Whittier*[7], b. ca 1822; d. 1852.

Sources cited: *Duxbury VR.* White, *Abstracts of Revolutionary War Pension Files,* and Bible records in File W24971. Readfield Cemetery Inscriptions on line. *Philip Delano of the Fortune ... Fifth and Sixth Generations* (2004). *MFIP Soule,* Part Two (2002). CENSUS: 1850 Fayette, Kennebec Co., Me. (M432-257), Kingfield, Franklin Co., Me. (M432-253).

740. ALPHEUS DELANO[5] (*Lydia Simmons*[4], *Rachel*[3] *Samson, Caleb*[2]*, Henry*[1]), son of Judah Delano and his wife Lydia Simmons [153], was born at Duxbury 2 October 1744 (*VR* 67), and died at Friendship, Maine, 9 March 1826 (pension file). He was a descendant also of *Mayflower* passengers John Alden and Myles Standish.

He married at Duxbury, 26 April 1770 (*VR* 241), **MARGARET / PEGGEY SIDES,** who was born about 1752 and died at Warren, Maine, 12 June 1845 (pension, final payment). She was probably the daughter of Laurentz Sides/Seitz of Waldoboro who was killed by Indians on his farm there in 1757.

A well-documented sketch of this family in *Maine Families in 1790* (5:77-79) relates details of Alpheus' life. He was shipwrecked on Plum Island in December 1761 while returning from Halifax during military service, and his father petitioned the Governor for expense relief to bring him home to Duxbury (*Mass. House of Rep.,* 1762, 37:326).

> The petition of Judah Delano humbly showeth that in behave of my son Alpheus Delano inListed a private soldier in Col. Haress Company on Cor'll Thwing's Regiment on ye 12 Day of may 1761 perseded to Hallafax & there did Duty Untill December & then went on Board a ship in Bound to Boston but was unfortunately Cast away att Ipswich and was so frozen that he was not abel to travill Which Caused me a journey to Ipswich to Bring him home which was acomplished ye 1 day of January 1762 & after a grate Deal of troubel for Nigh two months he gote so as to walk out though not with out ye Loss of a joint or two.

Judah requested "something alowed for" his trouble and expense, and a note on the bottom of the petition, signed by Jerathmeel Bowers, indicates that the

Committee allowed £1-16-0. A notice in the *Boston Evening Post* of 28 December 1761 describes the incident. Evidently Alpheus was in one of three transport vessels filled with Provincial Troops who had been in His Majesty's service in Nova Scotia. One of the transports was "cast ashore at Plumb Island in the storm weather we had last Tuesday (22 Dec. 1761), but no lives were lost, tho some of the men had their hands and feet much frozen."

Alpheus Delano recovered to serve in the Revolutionary War, after settling in Maine about the same time as his father, 1770. After the war he lived at Meduncook [now Friendship], Me., where he held office as town clerk, surveyor of roads, assessor, and collector.

He was of Meduncook on 24 September 1784 when he sold land there; his wife Margaret Delano also signed (Lincoln LR 29:66). In 1790 they were in Meduncook with one man over 16, two boys, and five females (p.40c). Alpheus Delano, yeoman, of Meduncook sold land there 13 March 1797, Margaret also signing, and on 13 March 1801 Alpheus sold land to Nathan Delano, mariner (Lincoln LR 39:50; 61:208). Called "Alpheus Dellano" of Friendship, he sold land there 26 December 1811 to Juda Delleno of Friendship, mariner (Lincoln LR 85:181).

Alpheus' application for a pension on 8 August 1820 in Lincoln County, Maine, indicates only his wife, aged 69, living with him. Peggy was aged 84, of Warren in 1836 when she applied for a widow's pension; the file includes information on their marriage and his death, and states that he was a private in the Revolution. The "final payment" record of 1 September 1845 gives her death [erroneously calling him "Alfred"], and names as the only [surviving] children: Judah Delano, Margaret Copeland, Lydia Vose, Eliza Copeland, and Mary Cobb.

Children of Alpheus and Margaret (Sides) Delano, first seven rec. Meduncook/Friendship, Me. (p.26) (see also *Maine Fam. 1790*, 5:78-79):

i NATHAN DELANO[6], b. 18 Jan. 1771; bp. Duxbury 2 June 1771 (*VR* 65); d. at sea 9 April 1826 between Boston and Monhegan; m. at Friendship, Me., ca 1798, POLLY LAWRY, d. Friendship 19 May 1842. In 1850 sons Christopher and Judah res. Friendship (p.160).
   Children (1850 census): 1. *Annice Delano*[7]. 2. *Margaret Delano*, b. 8 Oct. 1799. 3. *Christopher Delano*, b. 18 Nov. 1801; m. Polly Benner. 4. *Judah Delano 2nd*, b. 10 Jan. 1804; m. Jane ___.

ii LYDIA DELANO, b. 20 June 1773; d. 22 July 1851; m. ca 1800 SETH VOSE of Warren, Me., b. 1772, d. 18 Oct. 1846.
   Vose children (*Vose Desc.*, 224): 1. *Alpheus Vose*[7], b. ca 1795. 2. *Seth Vose*, b. ca 1797. 3. *Nancy Vose*, b. ca 1799. 4. *Eliza Vose*, b. ca 1801. 5. *Harriet Vose*, b. ca 1803. 6. *Abigail Vose*, b. ca 1805.

iii   MARGARET DELANO, b. 27 Oct. 1775; d. Warren 10 Dec. 1847; m. at
      Bristol, Me., 24 July 1794, MOSES COPELAND, b. Warren, Me., 3 Sept.
      1773, son of Moses and Patience (Sweet) Copeland, d. Aug. 1853. In 1850
      he was a farmer in Warren, Me., sharing a household with Josiah Morse ae
      48 whose apparent wife was Lydia D. ae 52 (p.171).
          Copeland children (*Copeland Family*, 245; 1850 census): 1. *Lydia D. Copeland*,
      b. ca 1798; m. Josiah Morse. 2. *Amasa Delano Copeland*, b. ca 1803. 3. *Charles
      Copeland*, b. 19 Nov. 1805. 4. *Eliza D. Copeland*, b. 17 Feb. 1807. 5. *Seth Copeland*,
      b. ca 1809. 6. *Patience Copeland* (twin), b. 1 March 1814. 7. *Margaret Copeland*
      (twin), b. 1 March 1814.

iv   CHRISTOPHER DELANO, b. 21 Jan. 1778; d. Malta 4 Feb. 1820, executed
      for piracy. He m. in St. Nicholas Church, Liverpool, England, as Charles
      Christopher Delano, 21 July 1805 (St. Nicholas PRs), ELLEN ABBOTT,
      about whom nothing has been learned. (His brother Philip married in the
      same parish in 1815.)
          His crime was reported in *The London Times* of 5 Nov. 1819, under "Piracy in
      the Mediterranean." Christopher Delano, master of the English brig *William*
      from Liverpool, and his crew had plundered the ship *Helen* that was carrying a
      cargo of manufactures from Dartmouth to Genoa. They had nailed down the
      hatches, trapping the crew below, in the expectation that the *Helen* would sink;
      however, the crew managed to escape in a longboat and were rescued by a
      Dutch vessel, and the ship itself came ashore on the coast of Spain. The *William*
      reached Malta, where the men sold some of the stolen goods before sailing on to
      Smyrna. Word of the crime reached Malta, and the Royal Navy sent Lieut.
      Hobson, of H. M. *Spey*, and a complement of men to Smyrna to deal with the
      situation. They seized the *William* and put the crew into Quarantine-prison. [The
      other members of the crew are named.] The trial was set for 26 Oct. [1819], and
      the *Times* commented that "Little doubt was entertained at Malta of the con-
      viction of the pirates." *The London Times* of 20 Nov. 1819 also reported on the
      matter, quoting a letter dated 2 Oct. at Smyrna, stating that Delano, "said to be
      born in North America, had been sailing between Liverpool and this port
      [Smyrna] for some years, and though reputed to be a clever man, his character
      was not liked." *Malta Family History* reported that Delano and his men were tried,
      found guilty, and all but two (one pardoned for his young age, the other for
      previous good character) were hanged.

v   SALOME DELANO, b. 29 March 1781; d. Waldoboro, Me., 23 July 1840; m.
      ca 1799, JOHN LAWRY, b. ca 1774 Friendship, d. there Sept. 1824, son of
      Samuel and Mercy (Cromwell) Lawry (*Lawry Fam.*,189, 192; *Delano 2004*, 17).
          Lawry child: 1. *Annis Lawry*, b. Nov. 1800.

vi   JUDAH DELANO, b. 18 April 1784; d. Friendship, Me., 19 Dec. 1865; m. (1)
      Thomaston, Me., 21 Feb. 1810, JUDITH WEED, b. South Thomaston

5 Dec. 1791, dau. James and Annah (Williams) Weed, d. Friendship 4 Nov. 1844; m. (2) at Waldoboro, 1845, CATHARINE WINCHENBACH, b. there ca 1799. In 1850 Judah Delano ae 66, farmer, was living in Friendship with Catharine ae 51, Sanford ae 22, a trader, and Edward ae 14 (p.160).

   Children, b. Friendship, Me.: 1. *Malachi Delano[7]*, b. 21 Nov. 1813. 2. *Hannah Delano*, b. 10 April 1816. 3. *Mary Ann Delano*, b. 13 Aug. 1818. 4. *Elizabeth Delano*, b. 4 June 1820. 5. *James Weed Delano*, b. 8 Aug. 1822; d. 27 Jan. 1824. 6. *James Weed Delano*, b. 31 Oct. 1823. 7. *Antoinette Delano*, b. 22 Aug. 1826. 8. *Sanford Delano*, b. ca 1828. 9. *Emeline Delano*, b. 30 May 1830. 10. *Louisa Delano*, b. 9 Dec. 1831. 11. *Nancy Delano*, b. 15 Feb. 1834. 12. *Edward Prescott Delano*, b. 27 Nov. 1835.

vii   PHILIP DELANO, b. 12 Sept. 1786; said to have d. at sea, unm. However, there is a marriage record for him in Liverpool, England, 13 June 1815, to ELIZABETH LLOYD, in St. Nicholas Church, the same parish in which his brother Christopher married in 1805.

viii   ELIZABETH DELANO, b. 1788; d. Friendship 26 Oct. 1860; m. there 15 March 1811, JAMES COPELAND, b. Warren, Me., ca 1786, son of Nathaniel and Barbara (Blackington) Copeland, d. 26 Nov. 1860 [?or 1868]. In 1850 he was a farmer in Warren, Me., ae 59 [*sic*], with Elisabeth ae 53 [*sic*], and Oliver ae 33 and his family (p.171).

   Copeland children (*Delano Gen.*, 132): 1. *Elona Delano Copeland[7]*, m. Richard Elliott. 2. *Caroline J. Copeland*, m. 1832, Ezekiel Demith. 3. *Oliver Copeland*, b. 11 Oct. 1817; m. Lydia Sweetser.

ix   MARY L. DELANO, b. 29 April 1793; d. 12 Aug. 1876; m. at Friendship, 20 Sept. 1813, NATHANIEL COBB, b. 6 Dec. 1788, d. Warren, Me., 9 Sept. 1869, son of Roland and Jerusha (Bartlett) Cobb. In 1850 he was a farmer in Warren, ae 62, b. Mass., with Mary L. ae 57, Elethea, Elisebeth C., Aldin M., and Rebecca F. Cobb, and Nancy E. Copeland ae 6 (p.170).

   Cobb children (*Delano Gen.*, 132; 1850 census): 1. *Rebecca Francis Cobb[7]*. 2. *Elethea Cobb*, b. ca 1823; d. 1865. 3. *Elisebeth C. Cobb*, b. ca 1825; d. 1853 Calif. 4. *Alden M. Cobb*, b. ca 1829. 5. *Lewis Cobb*, b. ca 1833; m. Eliza Dickey. 6. *Nathaniel Cobb*, d. 7 Sept. 1820. 7. *Mary Cobb;* m. Alexander Copeland. 8. *Margaret Cobb*, b. 1829; d. 3 Oct. 1833.

Sources cited: *Duxbury VR.* Lincoln County, Maine, Deeds at Wiscasset. *Journals of the House of Representatives of Mass.* White, *Abstracts of Revolutionary War Pension Files.* File #W22932 & Final Payment, National Archives. Sanford R. Delano, "Alpheus Delano," *Maine Families in 1790,* Vol. 5 (1996). *Philip Delano of the Fortune … Fifth and Sixth Generations* (2004). *Delano Genealogy* (1899). *Copeland Genealogy* (1937). *Lawry Family* (1992). *Vose Descendants* (1932). *The London Times,* on line. Parish Registers of St. Nicholas, Liverpool, Lancashire (FHL microfilm #009339, #0093840). *Malta Family History,* on line. CENSUS: Friendship, Lincoln Co., Me., 1850 (M432-259).

741. SALOME DELANO[5] (*Lydia Simmons*[4], *Rachel*[3] *Samson, Caleb*[2], *Henry*[1]), daughter of Judah Delano and his wife Lydia Simmons [153], was born at Duxbury 16 July 1746 (*VR* 69), and died there 23 September 1781, aged 35y 2m (*VR* 441). Her gravestone in the Old Cemetery, Chestnut Street, South Duxbury, records her age as 35y 1m 26d, evidently adjusted for the calendar change that occurred in 1752. She was a descendant also of *Mayflower* passengers John Alden and Myles Standish.

She married at Duxbury, 21 December 1780, as his second wife (*VR* 246), **JOSHUA WINSLOW,** who was born at Harwich 22 November 1740, son of Kenelm and Zerviah (Rider) Winslow (*VR* 36). He had first married, 3 December 1772, HANNAH DELANO, who died 16 September 1778, aged 29 "wanting 21 days" (*VR* 441), evidently the daughter of Lemuel and Lydia (Bartlett) Delano born at Duxbury 26 September 1749 (*VR* 67). Joshua and Hannah had three children who died young at Duxbury (*VR* 440-41), births not recorded: Gilbert, Charles, and Sophia Winslow. Joshua married, third, at Pembroke 9 December 1784 (*VR* 376), RUTH (OLDHAM) WALKER of Pembroke, daughter of Isaac and Mary (Stetson) Oldham and widow of Gideon Walker (*Delano 2004*, 135).

Child of Joshua and Salome (Delano) Winslow:

　i　[CHILD] WINSLOW[6], b. not rec.; d. Duxbury 20 April 1781, "infant of Joshua" (*VR* 441).

Sources cited: *Duxbury VR. Harwich VR. Philip Delano of the Fortune ... Fifth and Sixth Generations* (2004).

742. MALACHI DELANO[5] (*Lydia Simmons*[4], *Rachel*[3] *Samson, Caleb*[2], *Henry*[1]), son of Judah Delano and his wife Lydia Simmons [153], was born at Duxbury 16 October 1748 (*VR* 68), and died there 9 October 1832 (pension file). He was a descendant also of *Mayflower* passengers John Alden and Myles Standish.

He married, first, at Duxbury 19 September 1770 (*VR* 244), **PATIENCE BURGESS,** who was born at Duxbury 26 December 1752, daughter of Nathaniel and Ruth (Chandler) Burgess (*Delano 2004*,17), and died there in 1776, "wife of Malichi" (*VR* 371).

He married, second, at Duxbury 1 November 1778 (*VR* 244), **SYBIL DELANO**, who has not been identified.

He married, third, at Bridgewater 22 July 1807, **ABIGAIL / NABBY KINGMAN,** who was born at Bridgewater 6 August 1758, recorded as "Nabba" (*VR* 1:198), daughter of David and Abigail (Hall) Kingman. The will of David Kingman of Bridgewater, dated 22 April 1805 and proved 3 June 1805, directs that his daughter Nabby Kingman was to have the use of his homestead and buildings until she married (Plymouth PR #12137).

He married, fourth, at Middleborough 13 November 1813 (*VR* 2:197), **LYDIA COX**, who was living at Duxbury on 2 July 1833, when final payment was made on his pension. She may be the Lydia Delano who died at Duxbury 2 November 1838, aged 76, of cancer (*VR* 370).

Malachi was a private in the Revolutionary War, first serving with his brother Judah in Capt. Benjamin Wadsworth's (2d Duxbury) company of minute-men, Col. James Warren's (Plymouth Co.) regiment, which marched on the alarm of 19 April 1775, for three days. He also served for 15 days in the 2d Duxbury company commanded by Lieut. Nathan Samson, Col. Thomas Lothrop's regiment, marching to Bristol, R. I., 10 December 1776 on an alarm, and also in Capt. Andrew Samson's company, among men stationed at the Fort at the Gurnet, on a muster roll dated 20 May 1777 (*MSSR* 4:647).

In October 1788 and August 1799 he served as a juror in the Plymouth Court of Common Pleas (*PCCR*).

In 1790 he was living in Duxbury [as "Malaca"] with three boys under 16 and two females (*Heads of Fam.*, 169). On 1 March 1790, his father, Judah Delano of Duxbury, wife Lydia also signing, sold land there to their son Malachi; the deed was witnessed by Malachi's brothers Judah and Jephtha (Plymouth LR 70:229).

On 1 April 1798 Malachi Deleno of Duxbury, yeoman, sold land in Duxbury and Marshfield to his son Asa Deleno of Duxbury (Plymouth LR 89:237).

In his pension application he claimed to be 83 on 21 August 1832 and born in Duxbury in 1749, but said his birth was not on the record [*sic – it is*], and that he had always lived in Duxbury. The final payment on 2 July 1833 provided his death date and indicated that his wife Lydia was still living (Rev. Pension #S5342 & Final Payment).

No Plymouth County probate records were found for Malachi or for any of his wives.

Children of Malachi and Patience (Burgess) Delano; rec. at Duxbury:

i   JABEZ DELANO[6], b. 1771; bp. 24 Feb. 1773 (*VR* 68). *Delano Gen.*, p. 132, says he was unmarried. No further record of him found.

ii ASA DELANO, b. 12 April 1772; bp. 13 June 1773 (*VR* 60, 67); d. Duxbury 10 March 1851 of erysipelis (Mass. VR 58:170); m. at Duxbury, 13 Dec. 1795 (*VR* 242), LYDIA SOULE CUSHMAN, b. Middleborough 19 Nov. 1772, d. 31 Jan. 1865 of old age (Mass. VR 184:277), daughter of Joseph and Elizabeth (Sampson) Cushman.

Children rec. Duxbury (*VR* 61, 63-65, 370, 371, citing Bible): 1. *Joseph Soule Delano⁷*, b. 27 Sept. 1796. 2. *Patience Burgess Delano*, b. 11 Sept. 1798; m. Simeon Soule. 3. *Elisabeth Sampson Delano*, b. 28 Oct. 1800. 4. *Otis Briggs Delano*, b. 28 Jan. 1803; lost at sea, 23 Feb. 1833 in shipwreck off N.C. 5. *Mary Soule Delano*, b. 28 Oct. 1805; d. 11 Sept. 1836. 6. *Edith Alden Delano*, b. 5 Jan. 1808. 7. *Lydia Soule Delano*, b. 23 June 1810; m. Joseph Waterman Simmons [#751-ii]. 8. *Asa Sampson Delano*, b. 30 Oct. 1812; m. Eunice Thomas. 9. *Deborah Cushman Delano*, b. 17 Sept. 1815; m. Melzar Hunt. 10. *Joshua Cushman Delano*, b. 12 Dec. 1818; d. 3 Dec. 1834. 11. *John Porter Delano*, b. 15 Nov. 1822; d. 4 Sept. 1825.

iii   NATHANIEL DELANO, b. 12 July 1773; bp. 25 Sept. 1774 (*VR* 68); d. Duxbury 24 Aug. 1855 (Mass. VR 94:186); m. at Duxbury, Nov. 1796 (*VR* 245), ABIGAIL PIERCE, b. Pembroke 17 March 1773 (*VR* 160), d. Duxbury 20 Jan. 1849 ae 75y 9m 27d (*VR* 368), dau. of Joseph and Olive (Fish) Pierce. In 1850 Nathaniel was in the household of his son Nathaniel C. at Duxbury (p.70).

Children rec. Duxbury (*VR* 59-66; some dates differ in *Delano Gen.*, 134-35, *q.v.* for more): 1. *Abigail Delano⁷*, b. 13 Oct. 1797; m. Ichabod Alden. 2. *Judith Delano*, b. 22 July 1799; m. Jotham Horton. 3. *Salome Delano*, b. 27 Feb. 1803; m. Melzar Weston (*VR* 246). 4. *Sophronia Delano*, b. 22 July 1805; m. Eben Taylor. 5. *Almira Delano*, b. 29 April 1808; m. (1) Whitcome S. Cox, (2) Nathaniel Ford. 6. *Augusta N. Delano*, b. 1 May 1810; m. Arad T. Harlow (*VR* 242). 7. *Nathaniel C. Delano*, b. 22 Aug. 1811; m. Abigail Taylor (*VR* 245). 8. *Olive C. Delano*, b. 30 May 1814; m. Ivory Harlow.

Children of Malachi and Sybil (Delano) Delano:

iv   NATHAN DELANO, b. 8 Sept. 1780 Duxbury (*VR* 64); d. Plympton 15 Oct. 1851; m. at Kingston, 1 July 1802, MERCY HOLMES, b. Kingston 10 Sept. 1781 (rec. *Duxbury VR* 65), dau. of Levi and Lydia (Bradford) Holmes. They moved to Plympton in 1837 and the children are recorded there also with minor differences. (See also *Delano Gen.*, 136-37.)

Children, b. and d. rec. Duxbury (*VR* 60-61, 65-66; 372-373): 1. *Marcia Delano⁷*, b. 7 July 1804; d. 11 Sept. 1804. 2. *Sarah Holmes Delano*, b. 12 July 1805; d. 14 Feb. 1826 ae 20y 7m 2d. 3. *Briggs B. Delano*, b. 30 Oct. 1807. 4. *Sophia Delano*, b. 2 Jan. 1810; d. 11 Oct. 1826 ae 16y 9m 9d, of consumption. 5. *Nathan Delano*, b. 4 April 1814. 6. *Catherine Delano*, b. 16 June 1822; m. Shadrach Standish. 7. *Sarah Pruden Delano*, b. 25 April 1827; m. Ansel Churchill.

v   [INFANT] DELANO, d. 15 June 1783 (*VR* 373).

Sources cited: *Duxbury VR*, including many references to P.R. 24, Bible Record of Joseph W. Simmons, husband of Asa's daughter Lydia Soule Delano. *Pembroke VR. Plympton VR.* Mass. Vital Records 1841-1910. Revolutionary War Pension File S5342 & Final Payment, at National Archives. *Delano Genealogy* (1899). *Philip Delano of the Fortune ... Fifth and Sixth Generations* (2004).

743. JUDAH DELANO[5] (*Lydia Simmons*[4], *Rachel*[3] *Samson, Caleb*[2], *Henry*[1]), son of Judah Delano and his wife Lydia Simmons [153], was born at Duxbury 1 May 1751 (*VR* 68), and died in Boston 9 September 1801 (*Delano Gen.*, 137). He was a descendant also of *Mayflower* passengers John Alden and Myles Standish.

Judah Delano "of Duxboro" and **PENELOPE SAMSON** "of Plimouth" published their intentions at Plymouth 20 January 1781 and were married there 15 March 1781 (*VR* 268, 363; *CR* 2:500). She was born at Plymouth 16 June 1761 (*VR* 56), the daughter of Stephen and Abigail (Morton) Samson and a descendant [#478] of Henry Samson. She died at Topsham, Maine, in April 1814 at the home of her brother James Samson.

Judah was a private in the Revolutionary War, in Capt. Benjamin Wadsworth's (2d Duxbury) company of minute-men, Col. James Warren's (Plymouth Co.) regiment, which marched on the alarm of 19 April 1775; service, three days (*MSSR* 4:647).

In 1790 Judah Dellino [*sic*] was living in Plymouth with one man, one boy under 16, and two females (*Heads of Fam.*, 176). Judah was called a mariner on 26 or 20 March 1793, when his father deeded to him all his real estate, including his homestead (Plymouth LR 74:107).

Penelope was admitted to the Plymouth Church 7 September 1794 and three of the children, Elizabeth, Judah, and Priscilla, were baptized there on 19 October 1794 (*CR* 477, 482). Judah was received into the church on 4 January 1795 (*ibid.*).

The obituary of his daughter Priscilla, written in 1897, relates,

> ... when she was a small child her father moved to Portland, Maine. He owned and was captain of a passenger packet plying between Portland and Boston. Capt. Delano often took one of his children with him on these trips. During one of them Priscilla took a deep interest in some object in the water and while gazing intently upon it she fell overboard. There was excitement on the boat and it was supposed that Priscilla's life was lost. While looking for his child the father saw her long hair floating on the water. He caught the hair with his hands and pulled the nigh-drowned child from the water. It was some time before she fully recovered from her startling experience.

The family is listed in Cumberland County, Maine, in 1800; Judah was 45 or older and his wife was 26-45, with one boy and two girls under 10 and a boy and a girl 10-16 (p.262), figures that check except for the extra boy 10-16.

Judah was just 50 years old when he died, and his death may have been sudden on one of his trips to Boston. Cumberland County [Maine] probates were destroyed by fire, and no probate records for him have been found in Plymouth or Suffolk counties. The obituary of daughter Priscilla, who was just seven years old when her father died, relates that she then went to live with her uncle James Sampson, of Topsham, Maine. Probably the whole family moved in with James, as that was where Judah's widow Penelope died in 1814. Later Priscilla "returned to school to Portland. "

Judah Delano of Philadelphia, printer, John Sanford in the right of his wife Priscilla and she in her own right, and William Titcomb in the right of his wife Salome, all of New Portland, Somerset County, on 1 May 1819 sold three undivided fourth parts of 30 acres in Duxbury, part of the homestead of Judah Delano, late of Duxbury, deceased; the sale was acknowledged by attorney at Cumberland County on 24 May 1819 (Plymouth LR 137:173).

Children of Judah and Penelope (Samson) Delano, first seven rec. Plymouth (*VR* 243) as of "Judah Dellano & Penelope his wife," first three without dates:

i   SALOME DELANO[6], b. 29 April 1782; d. 6 Sept. 1783 ae 1y 5m (*Burial Hill*, #522).

ii   PENELOPE DELANO, b. 7 April 1784; d. 9 April 1784, ae 2d (*ibid.*).

iii [DAUGHTER] DELANO, b. 3 Feb. 1785; d. 4 Feb. 1785, ae 1d (*ibid.*, #597).

iv   ELIZABETH DELANO, b. 4 April 1786 "Tuesday half past 8 o'clock AM.";
     bp. Plymouth with siblings Judah and Priscilla 19 Oct. 1794 (*CR* 2:482); m.
     (1) after int. N. Yarmouth, Me., 19 June 1811 (*VR* 131), as "Betsey Delano
     of Portland," ELISHA CUTLER, Esq., b. 18 Oct. 1780 Amherst (*Maine
     Lawyers*, 476); d. N. Yarmouth 29 Aug. 1813 (*VR* 314) of a "pulmonary
     complaint," son of Robert and Esther (Pomeroy) Cutler (*Maine Lawyers*, 476-
     77). He grad. from Williams College 1798 and practiced law at Hardwick
     before moving to N. Yarmouth. Elizabeth Cutler m. (2) at N. Yarmouth, 22
     Jan. 1815 (*VR* 260), prob. as his second wife, JOSIAH W. MITCHELL
     Esq., of Freeport, Me., where he is listed on census 1820 through 1840. He
     m. (1) Sarah Angier (*Bridgewater History*, 106). In 1860 Elizabeth Mitchell ae
     74 was living in the household of E. W. Mitchell ae 42, attorney, and wife
     Abby, whose young children included Josiah W. and Elizabeth D. Mitchell
     (p.8). In 1820 Josiah W. Mitchell's household included four boys under 10,
     but how many of these were Elizabeth's is not clear (p.442).
         Cutler children rec. N. Yarmouth (*VR* 21): 1. *William Henry Cutler*[7] (twin), b.
     23 May 1812; d.y. 2. *Elisha Pomeroy Cutler* (twin), b. 23 May 1812.
         Mitchell children (*Lawyers of Maine*, 478, says there was "a large family of
     children"): 1. *E. W. Mitchell*, b. ca 1818; m. Abby ___; he was an attorney in
     Freeport 1860.

v   HENRY DELANO, b. 6 July 1788 "Sunday 53 minutes past 9 o'clock AM";
     d. 14 Nov. 1790; bur. with his unnamed sister (*Burial Hill*, #597).

vi   JUDAH DELANO, b. 26 Feb. 1792; bp. Plymouth with sisters Elizabeth and
     Priscilla 19 Oct. 1794 (*CR* 482); d. Edenton, N.C., 19 Aug. 1839 (*Delano
     2004,* 19); m. MARY ANN MOORE, b. Dover, Del., 6 April 1799, d. 6 Oct.
     1864 St. Louis, Mo. (*ibid.*). He was of Philadelphia in 1819, a printer. His
     sister Priscilla's obituary in 1897 says Judah Jr. "was for a number of years
     publisher of the *Sentinel,* at Albemarle, N.C. Previous to that he was for 15
     years a proof reader on the *National Intelligencer* at Washington, D.C." In 1822
     the first directory of Washington, *The Washington Directory, showing the name,
     occupation, and residence, of each head of a family and person in business; the names of the
     members of Congress, and where they board; together with other useful information,* by
     Judah Delano, was published (*Delano Gen.,* 138-39, has more on this family.)
          Children: 1. *William Judah Delano[7],* b. Philadelphia 27 June 1819; m. (1) Sarah
     Ann Given, (2) Eleanor Odlin. 2. *Mary Elizabeth Delano,* b. 13 Jan. 1822.
     3. *Penelope Delano,* b. 25 Dec. 1825; m. John T. Coleman. 4. *Rufus Bacon Delano,* b.
     15 Oct. 1827; d. 30 Sept. 1831. 5. *Salome Delano,* b. 3 Oct. 1830; d. 31 Jan. 1833.
     6. *Catherine Delano,* b. 1 May 1834. 7. *Salome Titcomb Delano,* b. 19 Nov. 1837; d.
     4 Sept. 1839.

vii PRISCILLA DELANO, b. 11 Dec. 1793; bp. Plymouth with siblings Judah
     and Elizabeth 19 Oct. 1794 (*CR* 2:482); d. Kent, Ohio, 9 July 1897 ae 103;
     m. (1) at Topsham, Me., in 1811, JOHN SANFORD, b. there 22 Feb. 1780,
     d. New Portland Oct. 1840, brother of Hezekiah Sanford; John was an
     inventor of, among other things, the old tide-mill at Bowdoinham, Me.
     (Priscilla's obit.); m. (2) at New Portland in 1847, as his second wife, Dr.
     WARD SPOONER, b. 10 July 1777, son of Ward and Abigail (Pease)
     Spooner, a "popular and skilled physician" (*ibid.*). In 1870 Ward Spooner
     was living at New Portland but Priscilla Spooner was in the household of her
     daughter Lucia Sawyer in Mars Hill, Aroostook Co., Me.; towns as well as
     states of birth were given (p.277). She went with the Sawyers to Ohio in
     1872 (obit.). (*Delano Gen.,* 140-43, includes the entire obituary and more
     information; see also *Delano 2004.*)
          Sanford children: 1. *Judah Delano Sanford[7],* b. 14 Aug. 1812; d. unm.
     2. *Thomas Sanford,* d. ae 2 yrs. 3. [*Daughter*] *Sanford,* d.y. 4. *William Titcomb Sanford,*
     b. 21 Feb. 1818. 5. *Mary Elizabeth Sanford,* b. 28 May 1820. 6. *Susan Salome
     Sanford,* b. 8 Feb. 1823; unm. 7. *Harriet Penelope Sanford,* b. 19 July 1825; m.
     William Paul Gettys. 8. *John Q. A. Sanford,* b. 4 March 1829; d. unm. 9. *Henry
     Cutler Sanford,* b. 11 Sept. 1831. 10. *Lucia Maria Sanford,* b. 8 May 1834; m.
     Edward T. Sawyer.

viii SALOME DELANO, b. 27 May 1796; d. Boston 23 Sept. 1869, ae 73, a res.
     of 47 Sharon St., of gastric disease (Mass. VR 222:159, says b. Portland, m.n.
     Delano, parents Judah & *Cornelia*); m. at Brunswick, Me., 18 July 1817 (*VR*

173), WILLIAM TITCOMB, b. Portland, Me., 8 May 1791, d. Norridge-wock, Me., 17 March 1850. In 1860 Salome res. Ward 7, Boston, with dau. Sophia, sharing a dwelling with son-in-law M. Allen Mayhew, bookseller and pub., and his wife Marian (p.52).

    Titcomb children (*Delano Gen.*, 144): 1. *William Henry Titcomb[7]*, b. 28 March 1819; m. Mary Crockett. 2. *Mary Ann Elizabeth Titcomb*, b. 9 April 1821; d. 1 June 1824. 3. *Benjamin Titcomb*, b. 13 Jan. 1823; m. Ann Williams. 4. *Marion Ann Titcomb*, b. 10 July 1827; m. Boston 30 Nov. 1854 Matthew A. Mayhew (Mass. VR 80:172). 5. *Josiah Whitman Delano*, b. 6 Sept. 1829; d. 1849. 6. *Helen Maria Delano*, b. 15 Aug. 1832; m. Aaron D. Blant. 7. *Sophia Ann Titcomb*, b. 23 March 1835; unm. 8. *Lucretia Hamlin Delano*, b. 6 Feb. 1838; m. George F. French.

Sources cited: *Duxbury VR. Plymouth VR. Plymouth Church Records. Epitaphs from Burial Hill, Plymouth.* Plymouth County Deeds. *Delano Genealogy* (1899) has much more for this family. Obituary of "Grandma Spooner" [Priscilla Delano Sanford Spooner], from *Kent, Ohio Courier*, 10 July 1897, on line at Ancestry.com. Willis, *A History of the Law, the Courts, and the Lawyers of Maine* (1863). CENSUS: *Heads of Families 1790 – Mass.*; Freeport, Cumberland Co., Me., 1820 (M33-34), 1840 (M704-138), 1860 (M653-437); New Portland, Somerset Co., Me., 1850 (M432-269) & 1870 (M593-559); Boston, Suffolk Co., 1860 (M653-522); Mars Hill, Aroostook Co., Me., 1870 (M593-538). **See also:** *Philip Delano of the Fortune ... Fifth and Sixth Generations* (2004), 18-20.

744.   PRISCILLA DELANO[5] (*Lydia Simmons[4], Rachel[3] Samson, Caleb[2], Henry[1]*), daughter of Judah Delano and his wife Lydia Simmons [153], was born at Duxbury 22 or 24 November 1755 (*VR* 68) and died there 17 February 1836 of "debility and age" (*VR* 444). She was a descendant also of *Mayflower* passengers John Alden and Myles Standish.

    She married at Duxbury, in March 1795 (*VR* 338), as his second wife, **WILLIAM WINSOR**, who was born there 27 January 1753, son of Samuel and Rhoda (Delano) Winsor (*VR* 205), and died there 7 January 1836, aged 83 of "infirmities of age" (*VR* 444). He was a descendant of *Mayflower* passenger John Alden. William married, first, at Duxbury 23 July 1775 (*VR* 335, *sub* Winslow), ANNE HUNT, with whom he had: Melzar, Sally, Waity, Clark, William, Nancy, Mary, and Rhoda Winsor (*Duxbury History*, 342).

    In 1790 William was listed in Duxbury with three boys under 16 and four females (*Heads of Fam.*, 169). The 1800 census enumerated him and his wife as 26-45, with two girls under 10, one boy and one girl 10-16, and one young man and one young woman 16-26 (p.96). In 1810 his household in Duxbury consisted of one boy under 10, one man 45 or older, one girl between 10 and 16, two young women 16-26, and one woman 45 or older (p.234). In 1830, William and his wife, both aged 70-80, were living by themselves, next to Otis Weston on one side and Mary Ann Winsor on the other (p.135).

In his application for a pension for his Revolutionary War service, William Winsor of Duxbury, aged 79 on 21 August 1832, claimed that he was born at Duxbury in 1753 and had always lived there.

Priscilla was nearly 40 when she married William. Chronologically, she could have been mother of the one of the two girls listed as under 10 in 1800 who was 10-16 in 1810 (thus b. 1794-1800), but no children are recorded for either of William Winsor's marriages. In 1810 the household included a boy under 10, but no evidence has been found to identify him either.

No Plymouth County probate records were found for either William or Priscilla.

Sources cited: *Duxbury VR.* Revolutionary War Pension File S30,217. Winsor, *History of Duxbury* (1849). CENSUS: *Heads of Families 1790 – Mass.;* Duxbury, Plymouth Co. 1800 (M32-16), 1830 (M19-64) **See also:** *Delano Genealogy,* (1899) 127, 144; *Philip Delano of the Fortune ... Fifth and Sixth Generations* (2004), 20.

745.   JEPTHAH DELANO⁵ (*Lydia Simmons⁴, Rachel³ Samson, Caleb², Henry¹*), son of Judah Delano and his wife Lydia Simmons [153], was born at Duxbury 29 October 1758 (*VR* 63), and died there 23 December 1843, aged 85y 1m 24d, as "husband of Rebecca, son of Judah" (*VR* 369). He was a descendant also of *Mayflower* passengers John Alden and Myles Standish.

He married, first, at Duxbury 22 December 1784 (*VR* 244), **REBECCA CHANDLER,** who was born at Duxbury 25 October 1764, baptized there 10 November 1771 (*VR* 46), and died there 10 or 14 February 1816 in her 53rd year (*VR* 373), daughter of Asa and Martha (Delano) Chandler and a descendant of *Mayflower* passengers John Alden, James Chilton, and Edward Doty.

He married, second, at Plympton 17 November 1816 (*VR* 306), **SARAH (SOULE) CHURCHILL,** who was born at Plympton 21 July 1768, daughter of Ebenezer and Silence (Hudson) Soule (*VR* 196). She married, first, at Plympton 16 February 1794, JAMES CHURCHILL Jr. with whom she had Sarah Hudson Churchill (*MF3*:169). Jepthah and Sarah had no children.

Jepthah Delano of Duxbury served extensively in the Revolutionary War, and was at the Battle of Valley Forge (*MSSR* 4:645-46, *q.v.* for details).

In 1790 he was living at Duxbury with five females in his household (*Heads of Fam.,* 169).

In his application for a pension, dated 13 April 1818, Jepthah Delano of Duxbury, now in his 60th year, claimed that he served over six years in the

Revolution; that he was a cordwainer, unable to work; that his family consisted of himself, wife Sally aged 51, feeble and almost blind, a daughter aged 23 in good health, and son Jeptha aged 13 in health, but unable to support himself (file #W7008).

On 23 August 1853, Sarah Delano of Reading, Windsor County, Vt., aged 85, widow of Jeptha Delano deceased, applied for pension benefits. On 5 November 1855 she was 87 and of Weathersfield, Vt., in a claim for bounty land, when she stated that she was the widow of Jeptha Delano, a deceased soldier of the Revolution, and former pensioner in Massachusetts; that she was presently a pensioner in Vermont; indicated the above marriage date and place, and the death date and place of her husband; and that she was Sarah Churchil before the marriage (*ibid.*).

The will of Jephtha Delano of Duxbury, dated 17 August 1841, proved third Monday in February 1844, named his wife Sarah; daughter Joanna wife of Martin Chandler; son Henry S.; daughters Rebecca Field, Martha wife of Nathaniel Weston, Salome wife of Nathaniel Snow, Abigail widow of Isaac Chandler; and sons Asa C. and Jephtha Jr. (Plymouth PR 86:56).

Children of Jepthah and Rebecca (Chandler) Delano, rec. Duxbury:

i   SALOME / SALOMITH DELANO[6], b. 6 April 1785 (*VR 66*); d. 23 May 1855 (*Delano Gen.*, 145); m. at Duxbury (1), 6 Dec. 1802 (*VR 246*), PELEG GULLIFER, d. Duxbury 26 or 27 Sept. 1806 (*VR 381*), son of Peleg and Ruby (Sampson) Gullifer (*VR 260*); m. (2) in May 1809 (*VR 260*), NATHANIEL S. SNOW (*VR 260*), b. Randolph ca 1784, d. Duxbury 12 Jan. 1856 of consumption, ae 71 (Mass. VR 103:197).

    Gullifer children rec. Duxbury, "of Peleg and Sally" (*VR 86*): 1. *Sally Gullifer[7]*, b. 27 June 1803. 2. *Caroline Gullifer*, b. 15 July 1805. 3. *Peleg Gullifer Jr.*, b. 21 Jan. 1807.

    Snow children rec. Duxbury, "of Nathaniel S. and Sally" (*VR 159*): 1. *Mary Ann Snow[7]*, b. 6 Dec. 1809. 2. *Susan Snow*, b. 6 Nov. 1814. 3. *Nathaniel Snow*, b. 11 Aug. 1816. 4. *Rebecca Snow*, b. 20 Feb. 1822; m. George P. Freeman. 5. *Hannah Snow*, b. ca 1824; d. Duxbury 28 May 1846 ae 19y 9m, of consumption (*VR 420*).

ii   MARTHA DELANO, b. 25 May 1786 (*VR 64*); d. 2 Nov. 1873 (Mass. VR 257:357); m. at Duxbury, 2 May 1803 (*VR 245*), NATHANIEL WESTON, b. there 2 Sept. 1779, son of Samuel and Abigail (Bisbe) Weston (*VR 193*). In 1850 he was ae 71, a shipwright at Duxbury, with Martha ae 63, Nelson Stetson and wife Rebecca C. ae 34, Georgiana W. Clap ae 17, and Elizabeth G. Watson ae 12 (p.72).

Weston children rec. Duxbury (*VR* 188-94): 1. *Maria Weston⁷*, b. 12 June 1804; m. Claudius Bradford. 2. *George Weston*, b. 24 Aug. 1807; d. 28 June 1833 (*VR* 436). 3. *Betsey F. Weston*, b. 30 Sept. 1809. 4. *Martha D. Weston*, b. 29 March 1812; m. Albert Clapp. 5. *Rebecca C. Weston*, b. 20 June 1816; m. Nelson Stetson. 6. *Sarah S. Weston*, b. 10 Aug. 1819. 7. *Samuel N. Weston*, b. 17 July 1821. 8. *Nathaniel Weston* (twin), b. 12 Aug. 1825. 9. *Susan Weston* (twin), b. 12 Aug. 1825.

iii ABIGAIL DELANO, b. 29 Aug. 1787 (*VR* 59); m. at Duxbury, 20 Dec. 1804 (*VR* 241), ISAAC CHANDLER, b. Kingston 3 Sept. 1782 (*VR* 39), d. Duxbury 13 Nov. 1837 (*VR* 359). In 1850 Abigail was living at Duxbury in the home of her son Alden (p.72).

 Chandler children rec. Duxbury (*VR* 43-44): 1. *Jephthah D. Chandler⁷*, b. 11 Dec. 1805; d. 26 Sept. 1806 ae 9m 15d (*VR* 360). 2. *Isaac W. Chandler*, b. 8 July 1807. 3. *Alden Chandler*, b. 14 Nov. 1809; m. Lydia James Prior. 4. *Abigail D. Chandler*, b. 28 June 1813. 5. *Joan Maria Chandler*, b. 13 March 1822. 6. *Henry D. Chandler*, b. 13 July 1825. 7. *Luther Chandler*, b. 28 Feb. 1828. 8. *[Daughter] Chandler*, b. 26 Jan. 1833.

iv JOANNA S. DELANO, b. 19 Nov. 1789 (*VR* 63); d. Duxbury 31 Oct. 1792 (*VR* 369).

v ASA C. DELANO, b. 27 Dec. 1791 (*VR* 60); d. Duxbury 16 Oct. 1792 (*VR* 368).

vi JOANNA SAMPSON DELANO, b. 3 Sept. 1796 (*VR* 63); m. at Duxbury, 11 Oct. 1840, as his second wife (*VR* 244), MARTIN S. CHANDLER, b. rec. Duxbury 25 Sept. 1796 (*VR* 44), son of Asa and widower of Nancy Delano [#793-viii].

vii ASA CHANDLER DELANO, b. 17 Aug. 1799 (*VR* 60, 368); d. Boston 21 July 1868, a cabinet maker, of "old age" (Mass. VR 213:115; *Duxbury VR* gives his b. date also as his d. date). He m. at Kingston, 25 Feb. 1823 (*VR* 207), CHRISTIANA D. COVEL, b. Kingston 4 May 1803 (*VR* 207), d. Boston 2 Nov. 1894 (Mass. VR 447:442), dau. of Ebenezer and Mary D. (___) Covel. In 1840 Asa was in Duxbury;, but in 1850 A. C. Delano was a cabinetmaker in Boston, Wd. 12, with Christianna and Mary, and the family of Moses Libby ae 20, clerk b. N.H., and Adelaide (p.314).

 Children rec. Duxbury (*VR* 60-64; spouses from *Delano Gen.*, 146): 1. *George H. Delano⁷*, b. 20 Oct. 1823; m. Caroline W. Frederick. 2. *Christiana C. Delano*, b. 14 April 1825; m. Amos Hale Brainard. 3. *Adelaide M. Delano*, b. 16 Feb. 1828; m. Moses Libby. 4. *Mary Romer Delano*, b. 22 April 1833; m. Thomas Church Byrnes.

viii REBECCA MALCOLM DELANO, b. 31 March 1801 (*VR* 66); d. Taunton 17 Dec. 1879 of heart disease (Mass. VR 310:144); m. at Duxbury, 17 Oct.

1819 (*VR* 246), ABNER FIELD, b. Taunton 13 Feb. 1795, son of Zebulon and Hannah (Hall) Field (*VR* 1:158, 2:182). In 1850 they res. Taunton with Eliza ae 30 and Susan ae 15; Abner's occupation was "none" (p.161).

Field children, b. Taunton (*Delano Gen.*, 147): 1. *Eliza Everett Field[7]*, b. 15 June 1820. 2. *Chester Isham Field*, b. 7 Aug. 1825. 3. *Susan Amelia Field*, b. 12 Nov. 1834. 4. *Ezra Alden Field*, b. 4 March 1837.

ix HENRY SAMSON DELANO, b. 29 Dec. 1803 (*VR* 62); m. at Easton, 7 April 1830 (VR 300), KEZIAH KINSLEY AMES, b. Easton 29 Aug. 1808, dau. of Parmenas and Mehetable (Ames) Ames. In 1850 he was ae 46, a cabinet maker, in Easton, with Keziah ae 42, and children Harrison, Charles, and Lydia (p.2). In 1870 he was a farmer, and his household included "Kessie" and children Henry ("works on farm"), Charles M. ("makes boots"), Lydia M. ("sews straw"), and Emma J., plus [grandchild] Thomas Delano ae 6, and Martin and Henry Ripley (p.187).

Children (one rec. Easton; *Delano Gen.*, 147): 1. *Mehitable Ames Delano[7]*, b. 13 July 1832; d. 1833. 2. *Elwood Murray Delano*, b. 6 July 1837; d. 1842. 3. *Henry Harrison Delano*, b. 21 Sept. 1840; m. Emma Weaver. 4. *Charles Morris/Maurice Delano*, b. Easton 27 Oct. 1842 (VR 339); m. (1) Helen Maria Pratt, (2) Caroline E. White. 5. *Lydia Maria Delano*, b. 11 Nov. 1846; m. Charles Knowles Dailey. 6. *Emma Jane Delano*, b. 28 Dec. 1852; m. William Frederick Shaw.

x   JEPHTHA DELANO, b. 13 Sept. or Nov. 1806 (*VR* 63); d. Cambridgeport 9 Dec. 1874 ae 65y 2m 2d [*sic*] of pneumonia (Mass. VR 266:85); m. at Boston, 7 June 1829 (*Delano Gen.*, 147), SARAH PITCHER, b. Saco, Me., 8 Aug. 1812. In 1850 he was ae 45, a cabinet maker, in Charlestown, with Sarah ae 39, and six children; the household included Eunice Pitcher ae 72 b. Mass., Benjamin C. Brownell ae 23, cabinet maker, and Lydia Brownell ae 20, both b. N.H. (p.45).

Children, two rec. Charlestown (*VR*; census; *Delano Gen.*, 148): 1. *William Q. Delano[7]*, b. 12 Aug. 1831 Duxbury (*VR* 66); a jeweler 1850; m. Anna Clemtina Pollo. 2. *John Willard Delano*, b. 16 Oct. 1833; d. 1837. 3. *Charles H. Delano*, b. 9 Feb. 1836; m. Helen Maria Williams. 4. *Joanna Sampson Delano*, b. 27 Feb. 1838; d. 1839. 5. *Sarah Elizabeth Delano*, b. 18 March 1840; m. David Hall Barnes. 6. *Mary Davis Delano*, b. 26 Dec. 1842; m. Frederick Riley. 7. *Jeptha Delano 3d*, b. 8 Aug. 1845, Green St. (*Charlestown VR* 1:566); m. Anna Mary Sutter. 8. *Helen Taylor Delano*, b. 19 March. 1848, Bow St. (*ibid.*, 1:628). 9. *Anna Bowdoin Delano*, b. and d. 24 Aug. 1853.

Sources cited: *Charlestown VR. Duxbury VR. Easton VR. Kingston VR. Plympton VR. Taunton VR.* Mass. Vital Records 1841-1910. Plymouth County Probate Records. Revolutionary War Pension File W7008. *Delano Genealogy* (1899), has much more on this family. CENSUS: *Heads of Families 1790 – Mass.*; Duxbury, Plymouth Co. , 1840 (M704-195) & 1850 (M432-333); 1850

Easton and Taunton, Bristol Co. (M432-307), Boston, Suffolk Co. (M432-339), & Charlestown, Middlesex Co. (M432-322); 1870 Easton, Bristol Co. (M593-603). **See also:** *Philip Delano* ... (2004), 20-22.

746.   PHILIP DELANO⁵ (*Lydia Simmons⁴, Rachel³ Samson, Caleb², Henry¹*), son of Judah Delano and his wife Lydia Simmons [153], was born at Duxbury 24 May 1761 and baptized there 25 July 1761 (*VR* 65). He died there 29 April 1836, aged 74, of "influenza and infirmity" (*VR* 371). He was a descendant also of *Mayflower* passengers John Alden and Myles Standish.

He married at Duxbury, 14 October 1783 (*VR* 245), **MARY FULLER,** who was born at Kingston 31 May 1763 as "Molly" (*VR* 83) and died at Duxbury 1 September 1835 (*Delano Gen.*, 148, not in *VR*), aged 72, daughter of Ezra and Elizabeth (Weston) Fuller, and a descendant of *Mayflower* passengers Samuel Fuller, Francis Eaton, John Billington, and Stephen Hopkins. The will of Ezra Fuller of Kingston, dated 20 March 1771, proved 5 August 1771, names his wife Elizabeth, sons Samuel, Consider, and James, and daughters Susannah and Molly, all minors; Ebenezer Washburne was to be guardian of the three youngest children, including Molly (Plymouth PR 21:20).

In his application for a pension for service in the Revolutionary War, Philip stated that he enlisted as a private, but was later appointed a non-commissioned officer, and had served over six years, which is supported by records. He was a fifer in Capt. Elijah Crooker's company, Brig. Gen. John Thomas's regiment, in 1775. Various muster rolls and pay accounts follow him from May 1777 to April 1782 when he was reported deserted. He evidently was at Valley Forge in January 1778, and in 1781 at Peekskill, N.Y. (for more detail, see *MSSR* 4:648).

In 1790 he was living at Duxbury with one boy under 16 and two females (*Heads of Fam.*, 169). The 1800 census listed him in Duxbury, himself and wife 26-45, with one boy and two girls under 10, a girl 10-15, and a young man 16-25 (p.96). The household in 1810 consisted of a man and a woman 45 or older, two boys under 10, two girls 10-15, and two young men 16-25 (p.118).

When he applied for a pension on 21 November 1820 he was aged 59, of Duxbury, and his family consisted of four people: himself, his wife aged 58, daughter Hannah who was aged 22 and weakly, and a boy James, aged 13, who was not well (file #S34,321).

Children of Philip and Mary (Fuller) Delano, b. Duxbury (*Delano Gen.*, 148; births not rec. *VR*):

i   EZRA FULLER DELANO⁶, b. 20 March 1783 [*sic – prob. 1784*]; lost at sea.

ii   TIRZA DELANO, b. 14 Nov. 1786; d. Pembroke 14 May 1839, "Tirzy, w.
     Ichabod" (*VR* 422); m. at Duxbury, in Dec. 1805 (not in VR), ICHABOD
     KEENE, b. 1785 (*Pembroke VR* 133 from g.s.); d. Pembroke 16 Aug. 1852
     ae 68, shipwright, parents not listed (Mass. VR 67:265); bur. High St. Cem.,
     Pembroke. He m. (2) at Pembroke, 1840 (*VR* 303), Ruth Ward of Marsh-
     field, with whom he had dau. Tirza Keene. In 1850 Ichabod Keen ae 66 was
     in Pembroke with Ruth ae 48 and Tirzah ae 9 (p.139).

     Keene children, b. Duxbury or Pembroke (*Delano Gen.,* 149), not in VR:
     1. *Mercy Shepherd Keene[7]*, b. 20 Dec. 18—; m. John P. Sampson.   2. *Ezra Fuller
     Keene*, b. 20 Feb. 18—; unm.   3. *Judah Belknap Keene* (twin) b. 27 May 1809, m.
     Hannah Bennett.   4. *William Whitridge Keene* (twin), b. 27 May 1809; m. (1) Eliza
     Ramsdell, (2) Mehitable Bosworth.   5. *Zoeth Keene*, b. 20 March 1812; m. Mary J.
     Small.   6. *Eliza Magoun Keene*, b. 1 Feb. 1814; m. James M. Richards.   7. *Mary
     Fuller Keene*, b. 20 Sept. 1817; d. unm.   8. *Seneca Loring Keene*, b. 20 April 1820.
     9. *Caleb Turner Keene*, b. 1823; m. Emeline Fuller.   10. *Aaron Magoun Keene*, b.
     1824; m. Abbie Robinson.   11. *Briggs Otis Keene*, b. 1825; m. Maria Chandler.
     12. *Andrew Jackson Keene*, b. 28 Sept. 1826; m. Julia Messer.

iii ABIGAIL DELANO, b. 30 March 1791; m. at Duxbury, 21 June 1812 (*VR*
     241, he as *Robbins*), after int. Bridgewater 21 March (*VR* 2:108), WILLIAM
     ROBINSON, b. Bridgewater 12 July 1784 (*VR* 1:283), son of William and
     Hannah (Egerton) Robinson (*Delano 2004*, 22).

iv   JOHN DELANO, b. 20 July 1793; lost at sea.

v   HANNAH DELANO, b. 16 May 1796; m. LEWIS CREHORE; no children.

vi   RUFUS DELANO, b. 11 July 1799; d. Swampscott 16 Dec. 1864 of
     consumption (Mass. VR 174:280); m. at Duxbury, 6 Jan. 1822 (*VR* 246),
     DEBORAH D. PIERCE, b. Duxbury 16 Nov. 1800, dau. of Luther and
     Lydia (Delano) Pierce. In 1850 they were in Lynn; Rufus and son Israel
     [Ezra F.?] were fishermen; children "Israel," Mary F., Augusta R., and
     Elizabeth F. were at home, and Risley P. Rich ae 19, fisherman, lived with
     them (p.225).

     Children, first five rec. Duxbury (*VR* 61), last from 1850 census (all in *Delano
     Gen.* with slightly different birthdates): 1. *Rufus Delano[7]*, b. 15 Oct. 1822; m.
     Lynn, 1844, Tabitha Newhall (Mass. VR 12:88); m. (2) Elizabeth Keyes; m. (3)
     Ellen Herbert.   2. *Deborah P. Delano*, b. 1 Aug. 1825; m. Lynn, 1844, Paul Newhall
     Jr. (*ibid.*)   3. *Mary F. Delano*, b. 2 April 1830; m. Samuel A. Lewis.   4. *Ezra F.
     Delano*, b. 22 March 1832; prob. same as "Israel" ae 18 in 1850; d. Andersonville
     Prison, Ga., in Civil War.   5. *Augusta R. Delano*, prob. the "dau. of Rufus" b.
     Duxbury 17 July 1834; ae 16 in 1850.   6. *Elizabeth F. Delano*, b. 13 May 1839,
     Swampscott.

vii JUDAH BELKNAP DELANO, b. 10 Sept. 1804; d. Duxbury 19 May 1884 (Mass. VR 356:300); m. at Duxbury, 2 Jan. 1842 (*VR* 244), REBECCA (CHANDLER) AMES, b. Duxbury 20 April 1811 (*VR* 46), d. there 17 Nov. 1891 (Mass. VR 419:511), dau. of Samuel and Nancy (Winsor) Chandler and widow of Jonathan E. Ames. In 1850 Judah was a mariner in. Duxbury with Rebecca ae 39, next to brother James F., no children in household (p.79).

viii JAMES FULLER DELANO, b. 10 Oct. 1807; d. Duxbury 5 May 1891 of angina pectoris, a shoemaker (Mass. VR 419:511); m. at Middleborough, 19 Nov. 1837 (*VR* 2:288), PRISCILLA MORTON, b. there 24 June 1819 (*VR* 1:369), dau. of Samuel and Esther (Churchill) Morton. In 1850 he was a shoemaker in Duxbury with Priscilla ae 30, next to brother Judah; no children at home (p.79).

Children (*VR* 62-63, 369; *Delano Gen.*, 150): 1. *Edgar Francis Delano[7]*, b. 23 Sept. 1843; d. 13 Sept. 1846. 2. *John Delano*, b. 7 March 1845 in E. Duxbury; d. 7 Oct. 1846 ae 1y 7m, scarlet fever. 3. *Ella F. Delano*, b. 25 Dec. 1847; d. 25 Aug. 1848 ae 8m, scarlet fever (*VR* 62, 369). 4. *Myron Lawrence Delano*, b. 19 March 1852; m. Addie Churchill.

Sources cited: *Duxbury VR. Kingston VR.* Mass. Vital Records 1841-1910. Plymouth County Probate Records. *Mass. Soldiers & Sailors.* White, *Abstracts of Revolutionary War Pension Files. Delano Genealogy* (1899), has further information; many birthdates vary from VR. CENSUS: Duxbury, Plymouth Co., 1800 (M32-16), 1810 (M252-21), 1850 (M432-333); 1850 Lynn, Essex Co. (M432-311). **See also:** *Philip Delano …* (2004), 22-23.

747. ANNIS DELANO[5] (*Lydia Simmons[4], Rachel[3] Samson, Caleb[2], Henry[1]*), daughter of Judah Delano and his wife Lydia Simmons [153], was born at Duxbury 17 December 1767 and baptized there 27 March 1768 (*VR* 60). She died at West Bridgewater 24 August 1859, aged 89y 11m 6d, "widow" (Mass. VR 130:235). Various records call her Anise, Annas, and even Eunice. She was a descendant also of *Mayflower* passengers John Alden and Myles Standish.

She married at Duxbury, 5 August 1792 (*VR* 284), **CALVIN PERKINS**, who was born at Plympton 25 December 1763, son of Josiah and Deborah (Soule) Perkins (*VR* 147). Capt. Calvin Perkins, "husband of Annis," a master mariner, died at sea in 1815 (g.s. Jerusalem Cem., West *Bridgewater* (*VR* 212). He was a descendant of *Mayflower* passengers John Alden, George Soule, and Myles Standish.

On 1 August 1815 Annas Perkins of Duxbury, widow, was appointed administratrix of the estate of Calvin Perkins late of Duxbury, mariner (Plymouth PR #15542, 46:114). An inventory taken by Judah Alden, Esq., Samuel A. Frazer, shipwright, and Malachi Delano, yeoman, all of Duxbury, was presented 26

December 1815 (*ibid.*, 48:152). No Plymouth County probate record was found for Annis Perkins, nor guardianships for Nathan, Daniel, and Deborah.

In 1850 Annis Perkins, aged 80, was living with the family of her son Daniel Perkins in West Bridgewater.

Children of Calvin and Annis (Delano) Perkins (*Philip Delano 2004*, 24), only the first rec. Duxbury:

    i   JOSIAH PERKINS[6], b. 30 May 1795 at Duxbury (*VR* 116); lost at sea.

    ii   ELIZABETH PERKINS, b. 24 June 1797; d. Duxbury 24 July 1890 ae 92y 1m (Mass. VR 410:416, says father Daniel Perkins, mother unknown); m. at Duxbury, Nov. 1818 (VR 284), ALDEN WINSOR, b. Duxbury 2 Feb. 1793 (*VR* 199), d. there 28 June 1880, son of Samuel and Asenith (Hunt) Winsor, a shoemaker (Mass. VR 320:278). In 1850 he was a mariner at Duxbury with Eliza and children Harvey D., Susan B., Samuel A., and James E. (p.65).

        Winsor children rec. Duxbury (*VR* 199-205; in *Delano Gen.*, 150, some dates differ): 1. *Catharine Winsor*[7], b. 21 Aug. 1821. 2. *Maria Winsor*, b. 31 Oct. 1822. 3. *Harvey D. Winsor*, b. 3 July 1824. 4. *Eliza Ann Winsor*, b. 15 March 1828. 5. *Susan B. Winsor*, b. 22 Feb. 1831. 6. *Samuel A. Winsor*, b. 22 March 1836. 7. *James E. Winsor*, b. 3 Sept. 1840.

    iii NATHAN PERKINS, b. 1799 [*sic*], more likely 1800 or after (1810 census); lost at sea.

    iv DANIEL PERKINS, b. 25 Sept. 1804; d. West Bridgewater 1897 (Mass. VR 473:701); m at Duxbury, 27 Sept. 1828 (*VR* 284), MARIA GLASS, b. 7 April 1805 (rec. *West Bridgewater VR* 88 *sub* Perkins), d. West Bridgewater 24 Aug. 1861 (Mass. VR 473:355), dau. of Ezekiel and Mary (Thomas) Glass (*Delano Gen.*, 151). Daniel was oldest res. of West Bridgewater in 1895 and recalled years at sea from age 14, then 50+ years as employee of Dwelley Iron Foundry (*Delano Gen.*, 151). In 1850 he was a "founder" at West Bridge-water, with Maria ae 44, Annie J., and Nathan, and [his mother] Annis Perkins ae 80; Henry Howland ae 24, blacksmith, and Mary ae 20 shared the household (p.273).

        Children: 1. *Mary Perkins*[7], b. 2 May 1830 Duxbury (*VR* 116); m. Henry Howland. 2. *Annis J. Perkins*, b. 24 Jan. 1832 West Bridgewater (*VR* 87). 3. *Nathan Perkins*, b. West Bridgewater 16 May 1838 (*VR* 89).

    v   DEBORAH PERKINS, b. 1 Jan. 1809; m. at Duxbury, 7 Nov. 1830 (*VR* 284), JOSEPH TILDEN of Hanover. In 1850 he was a farmer ae 41 in Tecumseh, Lenawee Co., Mich., with Deborah ae 40, Joseph ae 19, b. Mass., and Julia ae 9, b. Mich. (p.85).

        Tilden children at home 1850: 1. *Joseph Tilden*[7], b. ca 1831. 2. *Julia Tilden*, b. ca 1841.

Sources cited: *Duxbury VR. Plympton VR. West Bridgewater VR.* Mass. Vital Records 1841-1910. Plymouth County Probate Records. *Delano Genealogy* (1899), has further information but some birthdates differ from VR. CENSUS: Duxbury, Plymouth Co., 1850 (M432-333); West Bridgewater 1850 (M432-332); Tecumseh, Lenawee Co., Mich., 1850 (M432-355). **See also:** *Philip Delano of the Fortune* ...(2004), 24.

748. WILLIAM WESTON[5] (*Deborah Simmons*[4] *Rachel*[3] *Samson, Caleb*[2], *Henry*[1]), son of Jacob Weston and his wife Deborah Simmons [154], was born at Duxbury 24 August 1758 (Weston Ts; not in VR) and died at Brunswick, Maine, 25 May 1838, aged 82 or 83 (pension rec.). He was a descendant also of *Mayflower* passengers John Alden, George Soule, and Myles Standish.

He married, at Duxbury, 8 March 1781 (*VR* 303), **ELIZABETH SAMPSON**, a descendant of Henry Samson [#718] and Richard Warren. She was born at Duxbury 10 June 1762 (*VR* 145), daughter of Chapin/Chaffin and Betty (Clift) Samson, and died at Brunswick, Maine, 21 August 1843, aged 82, "wife of Capt. W. Weston" (Weston Ts, 106).

William Weston served in the Revolutionary War in both the Massachusetts and the Continental Lines, and also in the Navy Service (see *MSSR* 16:920-21 for details). He removed to New Meadows, in the township of Brunswick, Maine, with his father about 1785 (Weston Ts). Figures for the household of Jacob Weston in Brunswick in 1790 (2 men, 4 boys under 16, 2 females) indicate that the two families were living together (p.12).

Jacob Weston of Brunswick, housewright, on 16 April 1802 sold to William Weston of Brunswick, mariner, all the real estate in Brunswick that he had bought from Samuel Dunken and Nehemiah Peterson, along with all his personal estate in Brunswick "immediately after my decease" (Cumberland LR 56:43).

William applied for a pension 25 April 1818 at Brunswick. In 1820 he was 66, with wife Elizabeth aged 60, and children at home were daughters Abigail, 22, and Lucy, 18; his parents Jacob and Deborah, both aged 90, were also living with him (White, 3760). Elizabeth applied for a widow's pension on 31 August 1838, aged 76. At her death in 1843 she left two daughters: Lucy W. Larrabee, wife of Nehemiah Larrabee, and Abigail Weston, both of Brunswick; Lucy made an affidavit stating that she and her sister were the only surviving children (*ibid.*).

Children of William and Elizabeth (Sampson) Weston, first two b. Duxbury (not rec.), others probably b. Brunswick, Me. (Weston Ts, 106):

i   WILLIAM WESTON[6], b. 22 Jan. 1781 [*sic*]; d. St. Croix, W.I., 4 May 1837; m. at Brunswick, 2 June 1804 (*VR* 100), MARY THOMAS of Brunswick.
     Child: 1. *Mary Weston*[7], res. Freeport, Me., 1844.

ii   CHAPIN WESTON, b. prob. Duxbury, 2 Nov. 1783; lost at sea 17 Dec. 1809
     with his brother Charles on the brig *Eagle* out of Bath, Me., bound to
     Dublin, Ire. (Weston Ts, 106).

iii JACOB WESTON, b. 21 Nov. 1785; d. before 1843; m. after int. Brunwsick
     12 Nov. 1814 (*VR* 169), HANNAH PETERSON, living April 1843.
          Children: 1. *Chapin Weston*[7], b. 5 Dec. 1817; m. Christiana Coombs; res.
     Brunswick (*VR* 527). 2. *[Daughter] Weston.*

iv   CHARLES WESTON, b. 29 March 1789; lost at sea with his brother Chapin
     17 Dec. 1809.

v   JOB WESTON, b. 18 July 1792; lost at sea in 1816; unm.

vi   ABIGAIL WESTON, b. 27 June 1798; d. 3 Sept. 1881, unm.; living with
     family of sister Lucy 1850.

vii LUCY WESTON, b. 26 Jan. 1802; m. at Brunswick, 21 April 1822 (*VR* 162),
     NEHEMIAH LARRABEE, b. ca 1800. In 1850 he was a mariner ae 50 at
     Brunswick, with Lucy W., Charles W., and the three daughters; Mary Eaton
     ae 56 and Lucy's sister Abigail Weston shared the household (pp.251-52).
          Larrabee children at home 1850: 1. *Charles W[eston] Larrabee*[7], b. ca 1821;
     Bowdoin College ca 1845 (*Giles Mem.*, 412), a lawyer 1850. 2. *Sophia S. Larrabee*,
     b. ca 1829. 3. *Mary W. Larrabee*, b. ca 1831. 4. *Abby F. Larrabee*, b. ca 1832.

Sources cited: *Brunswick VR. Duxbury VR.* White, *Abstracts of Revolutionary War Pension Files,*
citing file #W22555. Samuel N. Weston, "Genealogy of the Weston Families of Duxbury,"
typescript at Duxbury Public Library. *Giles Memorial* (1864). CENSUS: 1850 Brunswick, Cumberland
Co., Me. (M432-251).

749.   JACOB WESTON[5] (*Deborah Simmons*[4] *Rachel*[3] *Samson, Caleb*[2], *Henry*[1]), son
of Jacob Weston and his wife Deborah Simmons [154], was born probably at
Duxbury 19 July 1760 (pension rec., not in VR). Capt. Jacob Weston died at
Duxbury 17 January 1832, aged 70 years, "burnt" (*VR* 436). He was a descendant
also of *Mayflower* passengers John Alden, George Soule, and Myles Standish.

He married at Duxbury in November 1784 (*VR* 330), **ALICE SOUTH-
WORTH**, who was baptized there 13 May 1764 (*VR* 166) and died there 9 June
1827, aged 65 of consumption (*VR* 439), daughter of William and Betty (Fullerton)
Southworth. Jacob and Alice are buried in the Large Cemetery, Duxbury.

Jacob Weston Jr. of Duxbury served as a private in Capt. Benjamin Wadsworth's (2d Duxbury) company of militia, Col. James Warren's (Plymouth Co.)
regiment, which marched on the alarm of 19 April 1775 (*MSSR* 16:912).

In 1790 he was living in Duxbury with two boys under 16 and two females
(*Heads of Fam.*, 168). In 1800 he and Alice were listed as 26-44 and there was one

older woman in the household; the apparent children were two boys and a girl 10-15 and one boy and one girl under 10 (p.93).

Jacob Weston was appointed administrator of the estate of Seth Simmons, mariner, of Duxbury, deceased, on 15 March 1805 (Plymouth PR 34:395, 40:450). Jacob and Seth were first cousins (see Family #752).

At court in November 1808, continued from the previous August, Isaac Winslow of Marshfield sued Jacob Weston of Duxbury, yeoman, for trespass, for breaking and entering his close in Marshfield with force and arms. Weston pleaded not guilty and the court ruled that he was to recover his costs (*PCCR* 12:75). In 1810 his household in Duxbury consisted of himself and two women 45 or over, two young men and two young women 16-26, and a girl 10-16 (p.125).

Court records for October 1816 show John Winsor of Duxbury, master mariner, suing Jacob Weston of Duxbury, merchant, for $81 due for wages for 24 days as master of Weston's schooner *Ardent* "laden for a voyage from Boston to Alexandria and back" (*PCCR* 13:14-15). Judgement was for the defendant, but Winsor appealed and referees awarded to him $61 and costs.

In November 1819 the petition of Jacob Weston and others for a new road in Duxbury, continued from August, was dismissed by the court (*PCCR*, General Sessions, Nov. 1819).

At the court of common pleas in November 1820 Jacob Weston of Duxbury was a traverse juror. In the census that year his family consisted of one man and one woman 45 or over, one man 26-45, a young man 18-26, and a young woman 16-26 (p.428). Around this time Jacob's financial situation appears to have deteriorated so that he could not meet his bills. That November he was sued by John Watson Jr., for "work and labour done and performed"; both men were shipwrights of Duxbury (*PCCR* 13:249). In April 1821 he was sued by William Barstow, Sr., for money due by note (*ibid.*, 13:259); by the Duxbury Manufacturing Co. for $200 for goods, wares, and merchandise sold and delivered (*ibid*); by Peleg Weston of Duxbury for "work and labour done [and] divers goods and wares sold and delivered" (*ibid.*); by Benjamin Ford of Marshfield, yeoman (who included Peleg Weston of Duxbury, yeoman, in his suit) for $391.51 due (*ibid*); by Solomon Washburn of Duxbury, blockmaker (*ibid.*,13:260); by Benjamin Cushman of Duxbury, cordwainer, for money due on note (*ibid.*, 13:261); by Otis Weston of Duxbury, housewright (*ibid.*); and finally by Judah Alden Esq. of Duxbury, for four notes (*ibid.*). In all of these actions Jacob defaulted and there were judgements against him.

Jacob Weston applied for a pension for his Revolutionary War service on 20 November 1820. He gave his age as 60; and said his family consisted of himself and his wife [not named] aged 59; "I have no children under me"; and stated his birth date and war service (file #33,883).

On 8 May 1821, after Peleg Weston won a judgment against him that he was unable to pay, 10 acres of Jacob's land in Duxbury were seized to satisfy the debt of $91.54 damages and $25.35 costs of suit (Plymouth LR 145:96).

On 4 June 1821 Jacob Weston of Duxborough, merchant, sold to [son-in-law] William Barstow of Duxburough, shipwright, "all my right in equity of redemption in and to certain real Estate situated in Duxborough and Marshfield, [the] same premises which I mortgaged to Hiram Simmons by deed dated July 26th 1820 (Plymouth LR 143:112).

Jacob died in a house fire. Samuel N. Weston in his "Genealogy of the Weston Families of Duxbury" (p.125) tells the story:

> He lived and died in the house of which he was the owner, in the part of town known as Duck Hill. He was a ship carpenter [and] built several vessels of 300 tons on the shallow creek near his home. On Tuesday night 7 January 1832 his house burned and three aged persons perished in flames. It was not very late in the night, but soon after all had retired, except Mr. Weston, and were sleeping soundly. Mr. Barstow's dog set up howling and barking, and woke him and his wife Mary (Weston's daughter), with whom all boarded, in time to save himself, his wife, and child [*correction over* children] of 1½ [*correction over* 2½] years. Her father, old Mrs. Southworth and Mr George Cushing Senior died in the flames. Mr. Weston had been in a chair in his own room reading newspapers, and it is supposed he fell asleep and the paper fell on the flame of the lamp — all was consumed.

Administration on the estate of Jacob Weston of Duxbury was given to Ezra Weston Jr. of Boston, attorney-at-law, on 17 February 1834, and G. B. Weston and Ezra Weston were appointed to appraise the estate, which consisted mainly of six certificates of money due under the Neapolitan Treaty, cash value unknown (Plymouth PR #22399, 71:221). An accounting was presented 2 June 1835 and allowed, with sums paid to various persons, but there is no reference to heirs (*ibid.*, 77:299-300).

Jacob and Alice had two children who died young at Duxbury, their deaths but not their names or ages recorded. Samuel N. Weston's typescript provides names and some details for three children who lived to adulthood that have been confirmed in other records. Census figures 1800 through 1820 suggest that there may have been other children, but all must have been financially independent by November 1820 when Jacob applied for his pension.

Children of Jacob and Alice (Southworth) Weston:

i   DANIEL WESTON[6], b. say 1785; d. Duxbury 8 April 1841, of "intem-
    perance" (*VR* 436); m. at Marshfield, 17 Jan. 1811 (*VR* 265), PERSIS
    PHILLIPS CUSHMAN, b. Marshfield 14 Oct. 1788 (*VR* 181), d. Westford
    1 Aug. 1866 ae 76y 9m 16d, rec. Weymouth (Mass. VR 193:289), dau. of
    Robert and Persis (Phillips) Cushman of Marshfield. The Weston Genealogy
    (p.157) says, "[Daniel] was not a good husband ... did not provide for his
    family as well as men are expected to ... was suffocated by smoke 8 April
    1841 while asleep in a shanty at Duck Hill, near where his father built vessels
    of the schooner class. Her father provided for the family [after his death] ...
    they removed to Weymouth and finally Westford [corrected from *Westport*]."
    In 1860 Persis and her unmarried daughter Persis were living in the
    household of her son-in-law Jacob Smith, who was a farmer at Westford
    (p.564).
        Children (Weston Ts.; not in VR): 1. *Robert Cushman Weston*[7], m. 1836 Nancy
    Richards Shaw (line carried forward in Weston Ts, 185). 2. *Fannie Weston.*
    3. *Mary Ann / Ann Weston*, b. ca 1813; m. Jacob Smith. 4. *[Child] Weston*, d.
    1 May 1818. 5. *Persis Weston*, b. 1818; unm. 1860.

ii HIRAM WESTON, b. say 1788; m. at Duxbury, 27 Sept. 1818 (*VR* 330),
    OLIVE LITTLE, d. Boston 19 May 1849 ae 58y 4m, dau. of Isaac Little of
    Pembroke. Hiram, a Unitarian minister, moved his family South to preach
    there but d. after a few years at Beaufort, N.C. (Weston Ts, 157); his
    daughter Mary Ann's m. rec. calls him a merchant. Olive returned to
    Duxbury.
        Children: 1. *Mary Ann F. Weston*[7], b. 27 Feb. 1820 Duxbury (*VR* 193); m.
    Charles Frederick Winsor (*VR* 331). 2. *Elizabeth Weston*, who was deaf from
    birth (Weston Ts).

iii [CHILD] WESTON, b. by 1790 census; d. Duxbury 9 Oct. 1791, "child of
    Jacob and Alice" (*VR* 439).

iv [CHILD] WESTON, d. Duxbury in Aug. 1796, "child of Jacob" (*VR* 439).

v   MARY S. WESTON, b. 8 May 1799; d. 17 Jan. 1877 of erysipelas, ae 77y 5m
    10d; m. at Duxbury, 20 Sept. 1829 (*VR* 217), WILLIAM BARSTOW, b. ca
    30 June 1796, d. 22 Feb. 1871 ae 74y 7m 22d. He was a shipwright and
    leader of the choir at the Unitarian Church, Duxbury. In 1850 all four
    children were at home (p.77).
        Barstow children rec. Duxbury (*VR* 23-24): 1. *Hiram W. Barstow*[7], b. 5 July
    1830 (ae 1½ on 17 Jan. 1832 when escaped house fire); a shoemaker 1850.
    2. *Mary Jane Barstow*, b. 14 Feb. 1833, bp. 7 Dec. 1834. 3. *William R. Barstow*, b.
    1 Jan. 1836. 4. *Daniel Weston Barstow*, b. 11 July 1839.

Sources cited: *Duxbury VR.* Mass. Vital Records 1841-1910. Plymouth County Deeds. *Mass. Soldiers & Sailors.* Samuel N. Weston, "Genealogy of the Weston Families of Duxbury," typescript at Duxbury Public Library. Konig, *Plymouth County Court Records.* Rev. Pension File #33,883. CENSUS: *Heads of Families 1790 – Mass.;* Duxbury, Plymouth Co. 1800 (M32-16), 1810 (M252-21), 1820 (M33-50); 1860 Westford, Middlesex Co. (M653-506).

750.   ABIGAIL WESTON[5] (*Deborah Simmons*[4] *Rachel*[3] *Samson, Caleb*[2]*, Henry*[1]), daughter of Jacob Weston and his wife Deborah Simmons [154], was born probably at Duxbury 3 June 1765 (calculated) and died there 13 September 1855, aged 90y 3m 10d (Mass. VR 94:186). She was a descendant also of *Mayflower* passengers John Alden, George Soule, and Myles Standish.

She married at Brunswick, Maine, 6 October 1784 (*VR* 95), **NATHANIEL KENT**, who died at Duxbury 8 or 11 April 1838, aged 78, of lung disease (*VR* 390, 8 April; pension, 11 April). Their marriage intentions, published at Marshfield 31 May 1784, called them "Nathie[l] Kent of this town & Abigail Weston of Duxborough" (*VR* 126). He was born about 1760, probably an unrecorded son of Joseph and Lydia (Thomas) Kent with whom two of his children are buried in the Winslow Cemetery at Marshfield (*VR* 388). His first son was named Thomas, and daughter Hannah had the middle initial T. Another Nathaniel Kent born that year is otherwise accounted for (*Philip Delano 2004*, 111).

Nathaniel Kent of Marshfield served in the Revolutionary War as a private in Capt. Elijah Crooker's company, Gen. John Thomas's regiment in 1775, and in 1777 in Capt. Andrew Samson's company, stationed at the fort at the Gurnet (*MSSR* 9:134). The gravestone of one of his young sons calls him "Capt. Nathaniel."

In 1790 Nathaniel was in Marshfield with one boy under 16 and three females (*Heads of Fam.,*172). In 1800 his household included one man and one woman 45 or older, one man and two women 26-45, one girl 10-16, and three little girls under 10 (p.94). In 1810 the household had expanded to include one man and two women 45 or older, one young man and one young woman 16-26, two girls 10-16, and two girls under 10 (p.20).

When he applied for a pension on 22 November 1821, he was aged 62, a mariner, living with his wife, aged 58, and three minor daughters (file #W14986). Abigail in her application in March 1855 for pension and bounty land stated that they had been married outside of Brunswick, Maine, 6 October 1784, and that Nathaniel died 11 April 1838 at Duxbury; her signature was witnessed by Abigail Kent and Maria Kent (*ibid.*).

In 1850 Abigail Kent, aged 84, was living at Duxbury with her daughters Abigail Kent Jr., 55, Mariah Kent, 51, Deborah Soule, 49, and grandson Daniel L. Soule, 25 (p.77).

Since birth records for this family are lacking, an analysis of census figures may prove useful to further research. The names and ages of two sons, both of whom died young, are known, and it appears that the rest of the children were all daughters. If all the girls enumerated with the family were all children of Nathaniel and Abigail, there were six daughters: one born 1784 – 1790, one 1790 – 1794, two more 1794 – 1800 [Abigail and Maria], and another two 1800 – 1810 [Deborah and Hannah]. The oldest daughter [Sarah] was married by 1810. In 1800 an extra man and woman over 45 and a woman 26-45, perhaps grandparents and an aunt, were present, and by 1810 that man was gone and only one extra woman, then over 45, was still there.

Children of Nathaniel and Abigail (Weston) Kent:

i   SARAH SMITH KENT[6], b. Marshfield 13 Sept. 1786, date rec. Duxbury (*VR* 97); d. Duxbury 12 April 1870 of fever (Mass. VR 230:307); m. at Duxbury, 15 Dec. 1807, SAMUEL HUNT JR., b. there 26 Jan. 1784, d. there 24 June 1861, son of Thomas and Susanna (Fuller) Hunt (*VR* 97, 388).

   Hunt children, rec. Duxbury (*VR* 94-97): 1. *Samuel Hunt 3d'*, b. 6 June 1809. 2. *Sarah Hunt*, b. 29 April 1811. 3. *Elizabeth B. Hunt*, b. 8 May 1813. 4. *Nathaniel K Hunt*, b. 15 Aug. 1815. 5. *Abigail W. Hunt*, b. 15 Jan. 1818. 6. *Ellis W. Hunt*, b. 2 Nov. 1820. 7. *Susan T. Hunt*, b. 30 Aug. 1822. 8. *Marcia Hunt* (twin), b. 6 July 1825. 9. *Martha Hunt* (twin), b. 6 July 1825. 10. *Zilpha S. Hunt.*, b. 7 Feb. 1828.

ii   THOMAS KENT, b. ca 1788; d. Marshfield 2 Dec. 1792, ae 4y 4m 26d; bur. Winslow Cem., Marshfield, with grandparents (*VR* 388).

? iii   [DAUGHTER] KENT, b. 1790-1794; living 1810.

iv   ABIGAIL KENT, b. ca 1793; d. Duxbury 2 Aug. 1880 ae 87, of "old age" (Mass. VR 320:278).

v   MARIA KENT, b. ca 1799; d. Duxbury 1887 (Mass. VR 383:345), unm.

vi   DEBORAH W. KENT, b. ca 11 Feb. 1801 (calc.); d. Duxbury 24 Sept. 1862 of typhoid fever, widow, ae 61y 7m 13d (Mass. VR 157:337); m. at Duxbury, 8 Dec. 1822 (*VR* 271), DANIEL SOULE, son of Nathaniel and Lydia (Freeman) Soule (see Soule *MFIP*, 2:121-22, #406). He was lost at sea ca 1825, and in 1850 Deborah and her son were living in her mother's household.

   Soule child: 1. *Daniel Lucius Soule[7]*, b. Duxbury 23 Nov. 1824 (*VR* 161).

vii HANNAH T. KENT, b. ca 1803 (calc.); d. 2 April 1897 ae 93y 5m 23d (Mass.
VR 473:661); m. at Duxbury, 27 Jan. 1833 (*VR* 271), THOMAS D.
HATCH of Marshfield, prob. Thomas Durfee Hatch, son of Jabez and
Keturah (Gullifer) Hatch, b. Marshfield 10 Dec. 1807 (*VR* 217, 113), d.
there 1890 (Mass. VR 410:431). In 1850 he was a laborer in Marshfield ae
49, with Hannah ae 45, Eliza E. ae 15, and [mother] Keturah ae 69 (p.158).
    Hatch child: 1. *Eliza Ellis Hatch⁷*, b. Marshfield 21 Oct. 1835 (*VR* 300).

viii NATHANIEL KENT, b. ca 1806; d. Marshfield 13 Dec. 1806, ae 15d, son of
Capt. Nathaniel and Abigail; bur. Winslow Cem. (*VR* 388).

Sources cited: *Marshfield VR. Duxbury VR.* Mass. Vital Records 1841-1910. *Mass. Soldiers &
Sailors.* Rev. pension file #W14986. *MFIP George Soule,* part 2 (2002). CENSUS: *Heads of Families
1790 – Mass.*; Duxbury, Plymouth Co. 1800 (M32-16), 1810 (M252-21), & 1850 (M432-333).

751.   WILLIAM SIMMONS⁵ (*William Simmons⁴, Rachel³ Samson, Caleb², Henry¹*),
son of William Simmons [155] and his wife Hannah Peirce, was born probably
about 1764 at Duxbury. He died between October 1837, when he sold land in
Duxbury, and 1850. He was a descendant also of *Mayflower* passengers John Alden,
George Soule, and Myles Standish.

He married at Marshfield, 15 January 1794 (*VR* 169) after intentions there 14
December 1793 (*VR* 120), **SARAH HEWITT**, who was born at Marshfield 30
September 1768 (*VR* 156, 134) and died at Duxbury 9 October 1852, a widow,
aged 82, daughter of Joseph and Ann (Waterman) Hewitt (Mass. VR 67:244). The
published record of the marriage gives her name incorrectly as Sarah Kent. Her
own death record and that of her son William give it as Hewitt, as does the
marriage intention, and this identification is confirmed by land records.

William Simmons Jr. was a mariner, of Duxbury, on 23 March 1798 when his
father sold to him and his brother Seth, his homestead and all his real estate in
Duxbury (Plymouth LR 84:191). On 21 April 1806, Jacob Weston, administrator of
the estate of Seth Simmons late of Duxbury, sold Seth's half of the property to
William Simmons Jr. (*ibid.*, 104:60).

On 20 March 1810 Joseph Hewet and Luther Thomas and Abigail his wife,
both of Marshfield, yeomen, Lucy Hewet of Marshfield, singlewoman, and William
Simmons Junʳ of Duxbury, mariner, and Sarah his wife, shared in a division of "the
90ᵗʰ lot of woodland in the second division of commons of Duxbury and Pembroke ... sold by Eliphalet Bradford to Joseph Hewet and at his decease left to his
children equally. Ann sold her share to Joseph C. Waterman, Asa and John sold
theirs to Abigail, Lucy, and William Simmons Junʳ, therefore we have divided said

lot into four parts." All signed and acknowledged the same day (Plymouth LR 115:43).

In 1810 William Simmons was aged 45 or older, with a presumed wife the same age, one man 26-45, a girl 16-26, and one boy under 10 (p.229). In 1820 his household consisted of two men and two women 45+, one man 18-26, and one boy under 10 (p.424). In 1830 the listing included one man 90-100 [his father d. 1831], one man 50-60, one young man 15-20, and two women 50-60 (p.130); that year William H. Simmons had his own household (p.134).

William Simmons and wife Sarah of Duxbury on 21 October 1837 sold to [their son] J. W. Simmons two pieces of land in Duxbury, one five acres, the other seven acres, for $191 (Plymouth LR 192:236). J. W. Simmons and wife Lydia S. Simmons sold land the same day to Judah Chandler of Duxbury (*ibid.*, 192:235).

In 1850 Sarah Simmons aged 79 was living with her son Joseph at Duxbury.

Children of William and Sarah (Hewitt) Simmons:

i WILLIAM H. SIMMONS[6], b. Duxbury 28 Aug. 1802 (*VR* 155); d. there 4 July 1875 ae 77 of paralysis, a teacher, b. Duxbury, son of William Simmons and Sarah Hewitt (Mass. VR 275:301); m. BEULAH [prob. GODDARD, b. Duxbury 10 Oct. 1802, dau. of Daniel and Beulah (Simmons) Goddard and granddau. of Lemuel Simmons #736]. In 1850 William H. Simmons ae 48, a teacher, was in the Duxbury alms house, insane (p.63); Bulah Simmons ae 48 and the families of her daughters were sharing a household in Plymouth (p.112).

Children rec. Duxbury (*VR* 152, 153, 155): 1. *Sarah H. Simmons[7]*, b. 13 May 1824; m. Lysander Dunham. 2. *Beulah G. Simmons*, b. 12 Feb. 1826; m. Nathaniel C. Sampson Jr. 3. *John W. Simmons*, b. 30 Aug. 1828; d. 21 May 1832 (*VR* 416).

ii JOSEPH WATERMAN SIMMONS, b. Duxbury 10 April 1811, "son of William and Sarah" (*VR* 153); d. there 17 Jan. 1887 ae 75y 9m of phthisis, a farmer, "parents William and Mary" (Mass. VR 374:324); m. at Duxbury, 10 Jan. 1833 (*VR* 307), LYDIA S. DELANO, b. there 23 June 1810, dau. of Asa and Lydia Soule (Cushman) Delano, a Henry Samson descendant [granddau. of Malachi Delano #742]. In 1850 he was a yeoman in Duxbury with his mother, Sarah Simmons ae 79, in his household (p.77).

Children rec. Duxbury (*VR* 152, 154, 155), all at home 1850: 1. *Mary O. Simmons[7]*, b. 8 Dec. 1838. 2. *George Simmons*, b. 5 Oct. 1841. 3. *Sally T. Simmons*, b. 12 Sept. 1843.

Sources cited: *Duxbury VR. Marshfield VR.* Mass. Vital Records 1841-1910. Plymouth County Deeds. CENSUS: Duxbury, Plymouth Co., 1800 (M32-16), 1810 (M252-21), 1850 (M432-333). **See also:** *MF16* [Alden], 2:86.

752.   SETH SIMMONS[5] (*William Simmons[4], Rachel[3] Samson, Caleb[2], Henry[1]*), son of William Simmons [155] and his wife Hannah Peirce, was born at Duxbury 15 November 1769 (*VR* 155), and died there before 15 March 1805 when an administrator was appointed on his estate. He was a descendant also of *Mayflower* passengers John Alden, George Soule, and Myles Standish.

His marriage intentions with **NABY BAKER**, he of Duxbury, she of Marshfield, were published 3 April 1794 at Marshfield (*VR* 118). Her birth on 1 August 1773 was recorded at Duxbury (*VR* 154) as "Nabby —, wife of Seth [Simmons]"; no other record for her has been found. Her son Seth's death record says she was born at Marshfield. Nabby married, second, intentions at Marshfield 10 September 1810 (*VR* 187), as his second wife, JOSHUA TILDEN FORD of Duxbury. He was born at Marshfield 24 June 1766, son of Elisha and Elizabeth (Tilden) Ford (*VR* 180; rec. *Duxbury VR*, 76, as 29 June 1760]. He married, first, 31 March 1789, Deborah Hatch, who died at Marshfield 5 April 1809 (*VR* 153, 416), with whom he had children Joshua Tilden and Deborah Hatch Ford at Marshfield (*VR* 181), and Oakman, Benjamin, Celia, and Elisabeth at Duxbury (*VR* 75-77).

Seth Simmons was a mariner of Duxbury on 23 March 1798 when his father sold to him and his brother William, his homestead and all his real estate in Duxbury (Plymouth LR 84:191).

On 15 March 1805 Jacob Weston of Duxbury was appointed administrator of the estate of Seth Simmons late of Duxbury, mariner, deceased (Plymouth PR 34:395, 40:450), and on 21 April 1806, Jacob Weston as administrator sold Seth's half of the property to his brother William Simmons, Jr. (Plymouth LR 104:60). On 1 May 1806 Jacob Weston was appointed guardian of Seth, Abigail, and Hiram Simmons, minors under 14, children and heirs of Seth Simmons late of Duxbury, mariner, deceased (Plymouth PR 32:293, 44:136). An accounting dated 4 March 1812 indicates that the widow had been paid one-third of the personal estate, and the guardian of Seth Simmons, Nabby Baker Simmons, and Hiram Simmons had also been paid (*ibid.*, 44:135).

Joshua and Nabby (Baker) (Simmons) Ford had children Ruth, Elisha, and George Ford recorded at Duxbury, 1812–1817 (*VR* 76-77). After 1817, no further record of Nabby or of Joshua T. Ford has been found.

Children of Seth and Abigail/Nabby (Baker) Simmons, rec. Duxbury:

    i   SETH SIMMONS[6], b. 27 July 1795 (*VR* 155); d. Boston 26 March 1875, congestion of lungs, res. 1276 Washington St. (Mass. VR 276:77); of Boston when he m. at Marshfield, 3 April 1823, ELIZABETH TILDEN FORD, "she belonging to the first Christian Church and Society in Marshfield" (*VR* 272). The 1850 census recorded the family in Boston, Ward 10: Seth was ae

55, a carpenter, Betsey G. ae 45, b. Maine, Ellen ae 20, Adeline ae 10, Edward ae 9, Ellen Crowley ae 31, b. Ireland, Ruth Ford ae 45, b. Mass., and Elizabeth Ballard ae 65, b. Mass. (p.318).

    Children at home 1850: 1. *Ellen Simmons[7]*, b. ca 1830. 2. *Adeline Simmons*, b. ca 1840. 3. *Edward Simmons*, b. ca 1841.

ii   ABIGAIL BAKER SIMMONS, b. 2 Aug. 1797, rec. as Nabby B. (*VR* 154); m. after int. Marshfield, 8 March 1819, she of Duxbury, BENJAMIN FORD of Marshfield (*VR* 191), probably her stepbrother, son of Joshua T. and Deborah (Hatch) Ford, b. 19 Feb. 1797 at Duxbury (*VR* 75).

    Ford children rec. Marshfield (*VR* 224): 1. *Nabby Williams Ford*, b. 30 June 1820. 2. *Ann Maria Ford*, b. 23 July 1822. 3. *Benjamin Franklin Ford*, b. 22 Feb. 1824. 4. *Augustus Hiram Ford*, b. 4 Nov. 1825. 5. *Marcia Elizabeth Ford*, b. July 1827; d. Duxbury 6 Aug. 1828 ae 1y 1w, rec. Marshfield (*VR* 417) where she is buried.

iii HIRAM SIMMONS, b. 5 April 1801 (*VR* 153); d. Boston 22 [?] April 1881 at 134 St. James St., ae 80, of stomach cancer (Mass. VR 330:105); m. SUSAN _____, b. ca 1801 Mass. In 1850 (p.338) and 1860 he was a carpenter in Boston, Ward 6 (p.752); in 1850 the household included Walter Phillips ae 24, apothecary, and H. Sullivan ae 20 and C. McDonald ae 15, both b. Ireland; in 1860 included Julia Kenney ae 21 b. Ireland, servant.

    Children (census; list prob. incomplete): 1. *Augusta Simmons[7]*, b. ca 1834. 2. *Susan Simmons*, b. ca 1843. 3. *Harriet L. Simmons*, b. ca 1846. 4. *Walter C./Channing Simmons*, b. ca 1848. 5. *Hiram Simmons*, b. ca 1856.

Sources cited: *Duxbury VR. Marshfield VR.* Mass. Vital Records 1841-1910. Plymouth County Deeds and Probate Records. CENSUS: Boston, Suffolk Co., 1850 Wards 6 and 10 (M432-336, 337), 1860 Ward 6 (M653-521).

753.   **ABIGAIL SIMMONS[5]** (*William Simmons[4], Rachel[3] Samson, Caleb[2], Henry[1]*), *possible* daughter of William Simmons [155] and his wife Hannah Peirce, was born probably at Duxbury, and was living on 30 March 1784, unmarried, when she was given a legacy of £2 5s in the will of her grandfather Abraham Pierce (Plymouth PR #15,388, 27:508; 29:335). She was a descendant also of *Mayflower* passengers John Alden, George Soule, and Myles Standish.

    No birth, marriage, or death record for this Abigail has been found. It is possible that this is the wrong identification for the granddaughter of Abraham Pierce, and that she was instead the Abigail Pierce who was the wife of Lemuel Simmons (see Family #736).

Sources cited: Plymouth County Probate Records.

754. MERCY OLDHAM[5] (*Anne Simmons*[4], *Rachel*[3] *Samson, Caleb*[2], *Henry*[1]), daughter of Anne Simmons[4] [#156] and her husband Peleg Oldham[5] [#210], was baptized at Duxbury 21 August 1768 (*VR* 113). She was a descendant also of *Mayflower* passengers John Alden and Myles Standish. Her family moved to Waldoboro, Maine, by January 1787. No marriage or death record for Mercy has been found.

755. JOSIAH OLDHAM[5] (*Anne Simmons*[4], *Rachel*[3] *Samson, Caleb*[2], *Henry*[1]), son of Anne Simmons[4] [156] and her husband Peleg Oldham[5] [210], was baptized at Duxbury 10 September 1769 (*VR* 113) and was living at Waldoboro, Maine, in 1798 when he was listed on a tax list there (*Gen. Adv.*, 4:45). He probably died between 1800 and 1810 (see discussion below). He was a descendant also of *Mayflower* passengers John Alden and Myles Standish.

His marriage intentions with **ZERVIAH SIMMONS**, "both of Waldoboro," were published 23 July 1794, but there was no marriage return (Waldoboro VR 7). She was probably born at Waldoboro about 1775, the daughter of Joseph and Elizabeth (Chamberlain) Simmons, the same called "Sovia [who] married — Oldham" by F. J. Simmons (*Sprague's Me. Journal*, 8:102), but born earlier in her parents' marriage than he indicated. Her parents moved from Duxbury to Maine about 1772 (*ibid.*, 101). She was also a Henry Samson descendant [#730-ii].

In 1798 Josiah Oldham was living in Waldoboro and had 17 acres valued at $68, with a house worth $99 (*Gen. Adv.*, 4:34). He has not been found in Maine census records, but figures for his father in 1800 suggest that Josiah and Zerviah were living with Peleg and Anna in Waldoboro, and probably had a daughter under 10 (p.575).

Josiah has not been found in later records, but an analysis of census figures for his father's household offers a possible scenario for further research. In 1810 Peleg and Anna, both over 45, had with them another woman 45 or over, and a girl 10-16; these could be Josiah's wife and daughter, suggesting that he died between 1800 and 1810. In 1820 the household of Peleg Olden [*sic*] consisted of himself, a woman 45 or older (who could be either Anna, for whom we have no death date, or Zerviah), and one woman 26-45, the right age to be the apparent granddaughter.

The only other possibility found is a Josiah Olden who was living in Whitingham, Vt., in 1820, where his name is last on the page, and the first on the next is a Caleb Olden (p.203-204); however, the 1810 census gives this Josiah's age as 45 or older (p.398), slightly too old for Peleg's son.

Further research may find evidence, but from what is now known it appears that Josiah Oldham probably died between 1800 and 1810.

Possible child of Josiah and Zerviah (Simmons) Oldham:

? i   [DAUGHTER] OLDHAM, b. 1794-1800; living in grandparents' home 1820.

Sources cited: *Duxbury VR.* Waldoboro VR. *Genealogical Advertiser. Sprague's Journal of Maine History,* 8 (April-Dec. 1920). CENSUS: Whitingham, Windham Co., Vt., 1810 (M252-65) & 1820 (M33-128).

756.   ANNA OLDHAM[5] *(Anne Simmons*[4]*, Rachel*[3]* Samson, Caleb*[2]*, Henry*[1]*),* daughter of Anne Simmons[4] [156] and her husband Peleg Oldham[5] [210], was baptized at Duxbury 13 June 1773 (*VR* 112). She was a descendant also of *Mayflower* passengers John Alden and Myles Standish.

Her family moved to Waldoboro, Maine, by January 1787. No marriage or death record for Anna has been found.

757.   SYLVIA[5] **SAMSON** *(Paul*[4]*, Caleb*[3-2]*, Henry*[1]*),* daughter of Paul Samson [157] and his wife Esther Chandler, was born at Duxbury 10 February 1755 (*VR* 147), and died at Pembroke 24 March 1817, "Mrs. Sylva [Turner], wife of Jabe" (*VR* 459). She was a descendant also of *Mayflower* passengers John Alden and Myles Standish.

She was of Marshfield 1 January 1794 (*VR* 169), when she married there, as his second wife, **JOB TURNER**. He was born at Pembroke 2 April 1751, son of John and Mary (Randall) Turner (*VR* 212), and died there 17 February 1823, aged 72 (*VR* 458). He married, first, at Pembroke 5 May 1776 (*VR* 367), SARAH JAMES, with whom he had: Abel, Betsey, Deborah, Enoch, Job, Lydia, Nabby, and Sarah Turner. He married, third, at Pembroke, 6 October 1818, NABBY CLIFT (*VR* 367) of Bridgewater, identified as ABIGAIL (BYROM) CLIFT in the Weyman Manuscript. Job is buried in Centre Cemetery, Pembroke (*Graves of Rev. Patriots,* 4:11507).

Job Turner served in the Revolutionary War as a private in Capt. Freedom Chamberlain's company, Col. Bailey's regiment, which marched on the alarm of 19 April 1775 (*MSSR* 16:172). He was a private in Capt. William Weston's company from 1 October 1776 to 19 November 1776, stationed at the Gurnet for defence of Plymouth Harbor. He was discharged after his father, John Turner, petitioned the General Court on 28 October 1776, stating that two of his sons, one of them Job, were in the Continental service, and inasmuch as he had no son or servant to assist him in his business or in taking care of his family, requested that Job might be discharged and permitted to return home (*ibid.*).

In 1810 Job Turner's household in Pembroke consisted of a man and a woman both 45+, a young man 16-26, and one boy and one girl 10-16 (p.61).

On 4 March 1823 Seth Whitman of Pembroke was appointed administrator of the estate of Job Turner, late of Pembroke, yeoman, deceased. An account dated 20 February 1824 included cash paid to Job Turner for money paid to purchase Nabby's right of dower (Plymouth PR 52:202; 57:535, 551; 58:232).

Children of Job and Sylvia (Sampson) Turner, rec. Pembroke (*VR* 213-14):

   i   PAUL SAMPSON TURNER[6], b. 22 June 1795; d. Boston 14 Aug. 1841, rec. Pembroke (*VR* 459); m. 24 Dec. 1831(Weyman Ms), CHARLOTTE E. TIRRELL, b. Boston ca 1814, dau. of Artemas Tirrell; she m. (2) ca 1843, Rufus L. Tay with whom she had Rufus T., Lucy Hobart, and Joseph N. Tay. In 1840 Paul Turner was in Boston, Ward 3 (p.401). In 1850 Rufus L. Tay ae 35 was a coal dealer in Charlestown, and his household included, in addition to his wife and children, parents-in-law Artemas and Eliza Tirrell, and stepdau. Charlotte E. Turner ae 18 (p.115).

          Children: 1. *Charlotte Elizabeth Turner*[7], b. 8 Aug. 1832 Charlestown; m. Gordon Burleigh (followed in Weyman Ms). 2. *Armenelda Malvina Turner*, b. 9 June 1834; d. 27 June 1836 (Weyman Ms).

   ii SYLVIA SAMPSON TURNER, b. 15 March 1797; d. Medford 8 April 1881 (Mass. VR 329:144); m. at Pembroke, 14 May 1820 (*VR* 368), JOHN SPARRELL, b. Scituate 26 Sept. 1793, son of James and Betsey (___) Sparrell, d. Medford 29 March 1876 ae 82y 6m 3d, a surveyor, of pneumonia (Mass. VR 284:133; Middlesex PR #10287). In 1850 John's household in Medford included Sylvia ae 53, John H., Emeline, and Elbridge K. Sparrell, Roena Williams ae 9, and Mary McGowen ae 35 (p.412).

        Sparrell children, some rec. Medford (*VR* 129), all in Weyman Ms: 1. *Sylvia Turner Sparrell*, b. 8 Sept. 1821. 2. *Sarah Elizabeth Sparrell*, b. 18 Dec. 1822; m. Lorenzo Clisby. 3. *Anjelina Sparrell*, b. 7 June 1825. 4. *John Sparrell Jr.*, b. 20 March 1827. 5. *John Henry Sparrell*, b. 26 Sept. 1828, a cabinetmaker 1850; m. Caroline A. ___. 6. *Emeline Sparrell*, b. 7 Feb. 1830. 7. *Elbridge Kirkwood Sparrell*, b. 4 Oct. 1832, a 17-yr-old shipwright 1850. 8. *Herbert Everett Sparrell*, b. 11 Oct. 1833; d. 4 Aug. 1834. 9. *Maria Josephine Sparrell*, b. 14 June 1835; d. 10 Sept. 1836. 10. *Angelina Maria Sparrell*, b. 5 April 1839; d. 2 Oct. 1839.

Sources cited: *Charlestown VR. Marshfield VR. Medford VR. Pembroke VR.* Mass. Vital Records 1841-1910. Middlesex County Probate Records. Plymouth County Probate Records. *Abstracts of Graves of Rev. Patriots. Mass. Soldiers & Sailors.* Weyman Manuscript. CENSUS: Pembroke, Plymouth Co., 1810 (M252-21); 1840 Boston, Suffolk Co. (M704-198); 1850 Charlestown, Middlesex Co. (M432-322); Medford, Middlesex Co., 1850 (M432-323). **See also:** *Giles Memorial* (1864), 394, 478.

758. **OLIVE[5] SAMSON** (*Paul[4], Caleb[3-2], Henry[1]*), daughter of Paul Samson [157] and his wife Esther Chandler, was born at Duxbury 8 April 1756 (*VR* 146), and died 16 October 1825, aged 69, at Marshfield, where she is buried in the Old Burial Ground with her husband (*VR* 401). She was a descendant also of *Mayflower* passengers John Alden and Myles Standish.

She married at Marshfield, 4 October 1781 (*VR* 175), **PELEG FORD**, who was born there 1 March 1746/7, son of Thomas and Jane (Thomas) Ford (*VR* 92, 171), and died there 23 November 1798 (*VR* 401).

In 1790 Peleg was living in Marshfield with three boys under 16, one man 16 or over, and three females (p.172).

Olive Ford, widow of Marshfield, on 4 March 1799 was appointed administratrix of the estate of Peleg Ford late of Marshfield, yeoman (Plymouth PR 34:176). The real estate was settled on Consider Ford, Francis Gray Ford, Peleg Thomas Ford, and Chandler Ford, who agreed to pay the other heirs and children: Ruth Ford and Rebecca Ford (*ibid.*, 42:335).

Children of Peleg and Olive (Samson) Ford, rec. Marshfield (*VR* 98-100; *Giles Mem.*, 478):

i CONSIDER FORD[6], b. 19 July 1782; d. 17 Sept. 1840 Marshfield (*VR* 203, 401); m. at Marshfield, 20 Feb. 1826 (*VR* 272), MARY SAMPSON HARLOW of Plympton, b. ca 1800. She m. (2) Marshfield, 9 Nov. 1842 (*VR* 304), Josiah Hatch, "both of Pembroke." In 1850 Mary S. Hatch ae 50 was in the household of David Wight Jr., orthodox clergyman, and his young dau., at Scituate (p.66), and in 1860 she was in the household of her son Thomas P. Ford at Marshfield (p.8).
   Children rec. Marshfield (*VR* 252): 1. *Mary Norton Stanley Ford[7]*, b. 26 April 1827; d. 19 April 1848; bur. with father. 2. *Thomas Peleg Ford*, b. 20 April 1832; m. Sally S. ___.

ii FRANCIS GRAY FORD, b. 6 April 1784; d. Hingham 1 Jan. 1843, a merchant, of consumption, ae 58y 9m (Mass. VR 3:77); m. at Marshfield, 17 March 1811 ("Capt." in int.) (*VR* 187, 265), RUTH BARKER THOMAS, b. there 9 Nov. 1790, dau. of John and Lucy (Baker) Thomas (*VR* 244, 176).
   Children rec. Marshfield (*VR* 229): 1. *Francis Anglin Ford[7]*, b. 20 July 1814. 2. *Peleg Ford*, b. 1 June 1817; d. 26 Nov. 1820 (*VR* 203). 3. *Lucy Thomas Ford*, b. 24 July 1821; prob. m. George M. Soule.

iii PELEG THOMAS FORD, b. 13 June 1786; d. Hingham 20 May 1873, merchant, of old age (Mass. VR 257:366); m. at Marshfield, 9 March 1815 (*VR* 266), LUCY BAKER THOMAS, b. there 22 April 1792, dau. of John and Lucy (Baker) Thomas (*VR* 244, 176), d. Hingham 1883 (Mass. VR

347:319). The 1850 census listed Peleg T. Ford ae 60 [*sic*], dealer in coal, and wife Lucy T. ae 57, at Marshfield in the household of George M. Soule ae 36, wife Lucy T. ae 29 [perhaps Peleg's niece] (p.98).

iv   RUTH FORD, b. 29 Aug. 1789; d. before 1863; m. at Marshfield, 18 Dec. 1823 (*VR* 272), her cousin JOHN BOURNE JR., son of John and Martha (Samson) Bourne. For his data and their children, see Family #761-i.

v   REBECCA FORD, b. 15 July 1792; res. Marshfield 1863. In 1850 she was living in the household of her sister Ruth, unm.

vi   CHANDLER FORD, b. 18 June 1794; d. 19 Aug. 1850, ae 56y; bur. Marshfield (*VR* 401); m. at Marshfield, 19 Sept. 1844 (*VR* 334-35), BETHIA S. WALKER, 24, dau. of Seth Walker of Worcester. The 1850 census listed Chandler Ford ae 55, farmer, in Marshfield with Bethia ae 31, and John Angelo ae 12 (p.61). Chandler and Bethia evidently had no surviving children.

Sources cited: *Marshfield VR.* Mass. Vital Records 1841-1910. Plymouth County Probate Records. *Giles Memorial* (1864). CENSUS: Marshfield, Plymouth Co., 1790 (M637-4), 1850 (M432-332).

759.   LUTHER⁵ SAMSON (*Paul⁴, Caleb³⁻², Henry¹*), son of Paul Samson [157] and his wife Esther Chandler, was born at Duxbury 25 March 1760 (*VR* 146), and died at Readfield, Maine, 31 August 1847, aged 87 (pension file). He is buried in Kent's Hill Cemetery, Readfield (g.s.). He was a descendant also of *Mayflower* passengers John Alden and Myles Standish.

He was of Marshfield when he married, first, at Pembroke, 18 September 1783 (*VR* 342), **ABIGAIL FORD** of Pembroke. She was born at Pembroke 8 July 1760 (*VR* 86), daughter of John Jr. and Mary (Baker) Ford. She died 14 December 1798 at Pembroke (*VR* 442) or Marshfield, aged 38y 5m 6d and is buried in the Cemetery near the Congregational Chapel, Marshfield (*VR* 418) with her husband's parents and her daughter Harriet. Her name and dates appear also on her husband's stone in Kent's Hill Cemetery, Readfield.

Giles Memorial (p.479) states that in the latter years of her life Abigail was "greatly disordered in mind." The will of her brother John Ford Jr. of Pembroke, dated 20 April 1793, proved 3 June 1793, mentions sisters Lydia Ford and Abigail Sampson, and father John Ford. No Plymouth County probate records were located for their father, John Ford, who died in 1813, or mother, Mary (Baker) Ford, who died in 1827, both at Pembroke.

Luther married, second, at Readfield, Maine, in September 1799, **LYDIA FORD** (pension file), born at Pembroke 18 July 1768 (*VR* 89), daughter of John

Jr. and Mary (Baker) Ford and sister of his first wife. She died at Readfield 17 December 1859 aged 91 and is buried with her husband (g.s.).

Luther served extensively in the Revolution, from January 1776 when he was in Capt. Thomas Turner's company of militia at Boston for about six months, to December 1781 when he was discharged at West Point in Capt. William White's company which had been sent to reinforce the Continental Army for three months. In 1777 he took part in two expeditions to Rhode Island, and in 1778 he was at Cambridge, and again on a march to Rhode Island. A descriptive list of men raised to reinforce the Continental Army for six months, dated 10 July 1780, found Luther at Springfield, described as 20 years old, 5 ft. 8 in. tall, of light complexion, from Marshfield (*MSSR* 13: 761, 772). *Giles Memorial* (p.479) states that Luther was in the army on Long Island at the time of its evacuation by the Americans in 1776, at Trenton and Princeton the winter following, and at West Point at the time of Benedict Arnold's treason.

Following the death of his first wife and daughter Harriet in the winter of 1798-1799, Luther removed to Readfield, Maine. He married his first wife's sister, and in 1800 his household at Readfield consisted of one man and one woman 26-45, two young men 16-26, two girls 10-16, and one little girl under 10 (p.387).

In his application for a pension at Readfield, 23 July 1832, he stated that he was born in 1760 at Duxbury and at age six moved with his father to Marshfield, where he lived during the Revolution; in 1799 he moved to Readfield in Kennebec County and there he married Lydia Foord of Pembroke in September 1799. His widow applied for pension 6 November 1848, aged 80, and for bounty land on 28 March 1855, at age 87; D. Richmond Sampson and Amos A. Sampson [her grandsons] were witnesses for her (#W1939).

Luther's gravestone is inscribed "Founder of the Maine Wesleyan Seminary" [Methodist Seminary at Kent's Hill] and "Revolutionary Soldier."

In his will, dated 12 October 1839, presented 18 November 1847, Luther Sampson of Readfield, bequeathed:

… unto my beloved wife Lydia Sampson [$50] at my decease and [$30] annually … and one half of all my household goods, which shall include two beds and beding but not the desk bookcase nor clock. And she shall have and injoy in addition another sum of [$30] annually … paid quarterly, and the right of occupying and improving that part of my dwelling house I now improve, and a right in the seller out houses & well as she needs and as much hard drey wood fited for the fier & in the house as she needs for her comfort and as much Wheat Rey & Corn meal Meat sauce & apels all of each kind to be such as she choses in reason as she needs for her self, and assisstance and the milk of a good cow well kept and the use of a slay and shay with a gentel horse tackeled into either of them when she choused for her own use. And the use and improvement of the other half of my house hold goods and to dispose of them to my children and granchildren by Will or otherwise, as she chouses ... I have given heretofore to my Daughter Charlotte Thomas as my heir by her & her Husband['s] Resate [receipt] in full as my heir to their satisfaction ... unto my son David F. Sampson all the rest, resedue, and Remander [he to be executor and manage the widow's legacy for her benefit].

A vague codicil added 30 December 1840, concerning notes of hand due, along with other considerations, resulted in a delay of probate and generated a large file that has not been further examined (Kennebec PR file).

In 1850 Lydia Sampson, aged 81, was living at Readfield with the family of D. F. Sampson, who was both her stepson and her nephew.

All of Luther and Abigail's children are listed on a family stone in Kent's Hill Cemetery, Readville, with dates of birth and death (*Kennebec Inscriptions*, 2373-74), but probably not all are buried there.

Children of Luther and Abigail (Ford) Sampson:

   i   DAVID FORD[6] SAMPSON, b. at Pembroke or Duxbury 26 Jan. 1784 (*VR* 138); d. 24 May 1870; m. in 1812 MARY RICHMOND, b. 5 March 1792, d. 25 March 1864 (*Kennebec Inscriptions*, 2374). In 1850 D. F. Sampson was a farmer in Readfield, ae 66, with Mary ae 58, Susan ae 29, D.R. ae 28, a trader, and Amos ae 20, farmer, sharing a dwelling with his stepmother/aunt Lydia Sampson (p.416).

         Children (*Kennebec Inscriptions*, 2373): 1. *Abigail[7] Sampson*, b. 3 Feb. 1813; d. 26 March 1835. 2. *Luther Sampson*, b. 28 Sept. 1814; d. 10 Nov. 1842. 3. *Mary Pierce Sampson*, b. 20 Nov. 1816; d. 30 July 1840. 4. *Susanna Sampson*, b. 27 July 1820; d. 28 Sept. 1865. 5. *David Richmond Sampson*, b. 9 March 1822; d. 7 Feb. 1887. 6. *Lydia Sampson*, b. 30 May 1825; d. 7 Jan. 1842. 7. *Amos Atwell Sampson*, b. 1 April 1830; d. 3 Sept. 1905; m. Nancy J. Stevens (g.s.).

  ii HARRIET SAMPSON, b. 19 Oct. 1785; d. 3 Jan. 1799, ae 13y 2m 15d at Marshfield (*VR* 419), two weeks after her mother's death; bur. Marshfield. Her name is also on the family stone in Readfield, Me., with dates 19 June 1785 – 3 July 1799.

 iii CHARLOTTE SAMPSON, b. 12 June 1787 at Duxbury (*VR* 138); d. 11 Oct. 1876 (*Kennebec Inscriptions*, 2374); m. MARKWELL THOMAS (*Giles Mem.*, 414).

 iv SYLVIA SAMPSON, b. 19 March 1790 Duxbury (*VR* 147); d. 5 Oct. 1824, unm. (g.s.)

v ROZELLA SAMPSON, b. 9 June 1792 Duxbury (*VR* 141); d. 23 May 1803 (g.s.).

?vi [DAUGHTER] SAMPSON, d. 4 June 1794 "ae 19" [days?], Duxbury (*VR* 413).

Sources cited: *Duxbury VR. Marshfield VR. Kennebec Co., Maine Cemetery Inscriptions. Mass. Soldiers & Sailors.* White, *Abstracts of Rev. War Pension Files. Giles Memorial* (1864). CENSUS: Readfield, Kennebec Co., Me., 1800 (M32-7) & 1850 (M432-257), New Gloucester, Cumberland Co., Me., 1850 (M432-250

760. CALEB⁵ SAMSON (*Paul⁴, Caleb³⁻², Henry¹*), son of Paul Samson [157] and his wife Esther Chandler, was born at Duxbury 24 June 1762 (*VR* 144) and died in 1823 (*Giles Mem.*, 478) at New Hartford, N.Y. (Weyman Ms). He was a descendant also of *Mayflower* passengers John Alden and Myles Standish.

He married at New Hartford, New York (*ibid.*), **JANE PLANT**.

Caleb served in the Revolution, about six months before his marriage according to *Giles Mem.* (see also *MSSR* 13:767). He removed to Whitestown, N.Y., where he was a physician (*Giles Mem.*).

In 1800 Caleb Samson of Paris, Oneida County, N.Y., was head of a household consisting of himself, 26-45, one young man and one young woman 16-26, and one boy and one girl under 10 (p.126). In 1820 he was in Whitestown, N.Y., over 45, with a woman 26-45, two young men and one young woman 16-26, and two boys and one girl under 10 (p.299).

No federal pension was found for Caleb, nor is there a will for him or anyone else in his family in Oneida County.

Children of Caleb and Jane (Plant) Samson (*Giles Mem.*, 479; Weyman Ms):

i PROCTOR C.⁶ SAMSON, b. ca 1793; d. prob. 1860-1870; m. ALMIRA _____, b. ca 1803. He was a physician; res. New York 1863; lived for a time in Georgia (*Giles Mem.*). In 1840 he was in Hancock Co., Ga., himself and wife ae 30-40, with one boy and one girl under 5 and one boy and one girl 10-15 (p.210). Dr. Proctor C. Samson was received as a member for the First Presbyterian Church of Syracuse on 25 March 1844 by examination (*Early Records*, on line). In 1860 Proctor C. Samson ae 57, physician, was in the 7ᵗʰ Ward, Syracuse, with Almira ae 57, Mary ae 30, and Ellen ae 21 (p. 925). He is mentioned in an 1899 history of the Syracuse church (p.116) as "Dr. Proctor C. Samson, long clerk of the session." In 1870 Ellen E. Samson ae 29, b. N.Y., was the only Samson living in Syracuse (p.408).

Children at home 1860; two possible sons also suggested by census: 1. *Mary⁷ Samson*, b. ca 1830. 2. *Ellen Samson*, b. ca 1839.

ii   ELIZA SAMSON, b. Paris, Oneida Co., N.Y., 23 Nov. 1794; d. April 1875
      Buffalo, N.Y. (Weyman Ms); m. at Paris, N.Y., 3 Sept. 1815, JOSEPH
      HOOKER, b. Farmington, Conn., 26 Oct. 1786; d. Oswego, N.Y., 2 Oct.
      1820, son of Joseph and Mary (Ingersoll) Hooker (*ibid.*). In 1860 Eliza
      "Hecker" was living in the household of her son-in-law, B. F. Sherman, a
      lawyer in Buffalo (p.397).
          Hooker children (followed in Weyman Ms): 1. *Jane Eliza Hooker⁷*, b. Oswego
      5 July 1816; d. 12 July 1876; m. 1838 Benjamin Franklin Sherman. 2. *Charles
      Joseph Hooker,* b. 1818.

iii   CHARLES P. SAMSON, b. 1790-1800; d. unm. before 1863.

iv   CALVIN P. SAMSON; res. New York City 1863.

Sources cited: *Duxbury VR. Giles Memorial* (1864). Weyman Manuscript. *Seventy-fifth anniversary
of the First Presbyterian Church in the village of Syracuse* … (1899). *Early Records of the First Presbyterian
Church of Syracuse, N.Y., 1826 – 1850* (1902), on line. CENSUS: 1800 Oneida Co., N.Y., Paris (M32-
23), 1820 Whitestown (M33-73); 1840 District 102, Hancock Co., Ga. (M704-43); 1860 Ward 7,
Buffalo, Erie Co., N.Y. (M653-747); Ward 7, Syracuse, Onondaga Co., N.Y., 1860 (M653-830) &
1870 (M593-1063).

761.   MARTHA⁵ SAMSON (*Paul⁴, Caleb³⁻², Henry¹*), daughter of Paul Samson
[157] and his wife Esther Chandler, was born at Duxbury 23 June 1764 (*VR* 146)
and died at Marshfield 23 October 1830, aged 66, "wife of John [Bourne]" (*VR*
416). She was a descendant also of *Mayflower* passengers John Alden and Myles
Standish.

She married at Marshfield, 16 March 1789 (*VR* 135), **JOHN BOURNE JR.**,
who was born at Marshfield 10 April 1759 and died there 7 October 1859, aged
100y 5m 26d, son of John and Lucy (Dingley) Bourne (*VR* 142).

John Bourn served in the Revolutionary War. He enlisted as a private 26 June
1776 in Capt. William Weston's company, stationed at the Gurnet for defense of
Plymouth Harbor, serving until 7 January 1777; on 7 November 1777 he was on a
return of men enlisted into the Continental Army from the 2nd Plymouth County
regiment, for Marshfield, for three years (*MSSR* 2:308-09). His obituary, quoted
below, states that he was a prisoner of war when peace was declared.

In 1850 John Bourne, aged 91, a farmer, was living in Marshfield; with him
were his daughters Hannah [Harriet?], 47, and Elizabeth Bourne, 41 (p.156). John
Bourne Jr., aged 60, was living next door. On 5 December 1859 the only son
petitioned that John H. Bourne [grandson of the deceased] be appointed
administrator of the estate of John Bourne, late of Marshfield, there being no
widow. John H. was duly appointed and gave an account of the estate (Plymouth
PR #2386).

An obituary for John Bourne appeared in the *New England Historical and Genealogical Register* in 1860 (14:82). Following an account of his ancestry, the author, "M. A. T." continues:

The venerable centenarian whose departure is recorded at the head of this article, married Martha, dau. of Paul and Esther (Chandler) Sampson, in 1788. She died, deeply lamented, Oct. 23, 1830, a. 66. They were the parents of six children, half of whom are living. Two unmarried daughters resided with their father at the ancient homestead.

He entered the Revolutionary service at the commencement of the struggle, and was a prisoner of war when peace was declared.

He was buried the Sabbath afternoon succeeding his decease from the house of the First Congregational Society, of which church he had been a worthy member seventy years. His remains rested near the spot where his parents offered him in baptism one hundred years before; and within the shadow of this temple stood the humble headstones that marked the spots where the ashes of those parents, with their parents, and other kindred, were deposited.

Children of John and Martha (Sampson) Bourne, rec. Marshfield (VR 51, 52):

i   JOHN BOURNE[7], b. 7 Feb. 1790; m. at Marshfield, 18 Dec. 1823 (*VR* 272), his cousin RUTH FORD, daughter of Peleg Ford and Olive Samson [#758]. The 1850 census listed John Bourne Jr., ae 60, farmer, at Marshfield, with Ruth ae 60, Olive L. ae 25, and John H. ae 21, a carpenter; Ruth's sister Rebecca Ford ae 58, Seneca White ae 52, a clergyman, and Elizabeth White ae 66, were also in the household (p.157).
      Children: 1. *Olive Sampson Bourne*[7], b. 5 Oct. 1824; unm. 1850. 2. *John Henry Bourne*, b. 9 March 1829 Marshfield (*VR* 250).

ii   PROCTOR BOURNE, b. 4 Aug. 1791 (*VR* 51); m. at Marshfield, 15 May 1821 (*VR* 268), TEMPERANCE THOMAS of Marshfield.
      Children rec. Marshfield (*VR* 252): 1. *Proctor Bourne*[7] (twin), b. 30 Aug. 1824; d. 6 Oct. 1831; bur. Marshfield (*VR* 399, 416). 2. *Temperance Bourne* (twin), b. 30 Aug. 1824; m. Alden Harlow (*VR* 340-41).

iii OLIVE BOURNE, b. 1 Feb. 1794; d. 13 June 1835 Marshfield, ae 41 yrs (*VR* 416).

iv   JAMES BOURNE, b. 11 Sept. 1799; d. 1849; bur. Marshfield (*VR* 399); m. MARY RITTER, "dau. of Thomas and Anne Ritter of Lunenburg," b. 1805, d. 1885 (*ibid*).
      Children bur. with parents: 1. *James S Bourne*[7], b. 1832; d. 1833. 2. *Martha A. Bourne*, b. 1834; d. 1864; living 1850 with grandmother Anna Ritter ae 67, Boston (p.362). 3. *Harriet P. Bourne*, b. and d. 1839. 4. *George R Bourne*, b. 1841; d. 1842.

v   HARRIET BOURNE, b. 8 March 1803; living at home, unm., in 1859.

vi   ELIZABETH BOURNE, b. 28 Feb. 1809; living at home, unm., in 1859.

Sources cited: *Marshfield VR.* "Marriages and Deaths," *NEHGR* 14 [1860]. *Mass. Soldiers & Sailors.* CENSUS: 1850 Ward 10, Boston, Suffolk Co. (M432-337) & Marshfield, Plymouth Co. (M432-332).

762. ESTHER⁵ SAMSON (*Paul⁴, Caleb³⁻², Henry¹*), daughter of Paul Samson [157] and his wife Esther Chandler, was born at Duxbury 30 August 1766 (*VR* 145), and died at Pembroke 1 March 1837, aged 70 (*VR* 429). She was a descendant also of Pilgrims John Alden and Myles Standish.

She married at Marshfield, 27 June 1799 after intentions 3 March (*VR* 116, 169), **ELIAS MAGOUN** of Pembroke. He was born at Pembroke 5 March 1770, son of John and Huldah (Shurtleff) Magoun (*VR* 146, 315), and died there 23 September 1823, aged 53 (*VR* 429).

In his will dated 6 September 1823, proved 7 October 1823 (Plymouth PR 57:331), Elias Magoun of Pembroke, Gentleman, left all his personal estate to beloved wife Esther to be at her disposal during her widowhood, and at the end of that, all his estate both real and personal was to be divided equally among his sons Elias, Calvin, John, and Luther Magoun. To son William Magoun he left "the money expended for his education at Brown University." *Giles Memorial* (p.479) states that Elias and Esther "had five sons, of whom four are now [ca 1863] living, one a resident of Turin, Italy."

Children of Elias and Esther (Sampson) Magoun, rec. Pembroke (*VR* 145-48):

   i   ELIAS MAGOUN⁶, b. 10 March 1801; d. Warren, R.I., 9 Jan. 1847; bur. Two-Mile Cem., Pembroke (*VR* 429); m. at Providence, R.I., 22 Sept. 1834, SUSAN HAILE, b. there 16 Aug. 1806, d. Warren 12 Oct. 1852 (Weyman Ms; date of marriage given in *Pembroke VR* is obviously wrong.) Elias was a teacher and bank cashier (Weyman Ms). In 1850 Susan and her son Elias, ae 13, were living in Warren in the household of John G. and Susan Waterman (p.83).

           Children (Weyman Ms): 1. *Annie Magoun⁷*, b. 29 July 1835; d. 7 Aug. 1836 Warren, R.I., bur. Pembroke (*VR* 429). 2. *Elias Magoun*, b. 28 Sept. 1837; d. unm., Havana, Cuba, 22 Feb. 1858. 3. *William Magoun*, b. 18 March 1844; d. 10 March 1845 Warren, R.I., bur. Pembroke (*VR* 429).

  ii WILLIAM MAGOUN, b. 15 Sept. 1802; d. unm. at Turin, Italy, 26 Sept. 1871 (Weyman Ms); educated Brown University, a teacher and scholar.

 iii CALVIN SAMPSON MAGOUN, b. 30 May 1804; d. Marshfield 16 Oct. 1866 (Mass. VR 193:315); of Boston, a housewright, when he m. at Marshfield, 21 May 1843 [his cousin] MARTHA SAMPSON, b. Marshfield 9 Sept. 1807, d. there 1 Feb. 1883 (Weyman Ms), dau. of Chandler Sampson [#763]

(*VR* 330-31). In 1850 Calvin ae 46 and Martha ae 42 were living in her father's household in Marshfield. Weyman Ms says one child, d. at birth.

iv JOHN MAGOUN, b. 14 June 1806; d. 20 Jan. 1878 unm.; a banker, res. Bloomington, Ill. (Weyman Ms).

v LUTHER MAGOUN, b. 16 Sept. 1808; d. 8 Aug. 1887 (Mass. VR 383:361); m. at Marshfield 15 May 1836, by John Adams "a transient preacher" (*VR* 266), ELIZA SAMPSON of Marshfield, b. 19 March 1809, d. Marshfield 12 April 1894 (Mass. VR 446:611), sister of his brother Calvin's wife.

Children rec. Pembroke (*VR* 146-48): 1. *Luther S. Magoun*[7], b. 30 Aug. 1837; d. 29 July 1839 (*VR* 430). 2. *Calvin Sampson Magoun*, b. 14 Nov. 1839; d. 19 June 1862 unm. 3. *John Magoun*, b. 20 July 1841. 4. *Esther S. Magoun*, b. 9 Oct. 1843. 5. *Nancy Thomas Magoun*, b. 28 Jan. 1846. 6. *Susan Haile Magoun*, b. 14 May 1850; d. 1 Sept. 1852 (Weyman Ms).

Sources cited: *Duxbury VR. Marshfield VR. Pembroke VR.* Mass. Vital Records 1841-1910. Plymouth County Probate Records. *Giles Memorial* (1864). Weyman Manuscript. CENSUS: 1850 Marshfield, Plymouth Co. (M432-332).

763. CHANDLER[5] **SAMSON** (*Paul*[4], *Caleb*[3-2], *Henry*[1]), son of Paul Samson [157] and his wife Esther Chandler, was born at Marshfield 10 July 1768 (*VR* 61), and died there 28 [VR] or 29 [g.s.] August 1850, aged 82y 1m 18d, a widower, "son of Paul and Esther" (Mass. VR 49:160). He is buried with his two wives in the Burial Ground at the Old Congregational Church, Marshfield (*VR* 407). He was a descendant also of *Mayflower* passengers John Alden and Myles Standish.

He married, first, at Marshfield, 5 March 1795 (*VR* 169), **NANCY THOMAS**. She was born at Marshfield 20 March 1769, daughter of Nathan and Sarah (Bourn) Thomas (*VR* 111, 140), and died there 15 July 1821, aged 52 (*VR* 207, 407). The will of Nathan Thomas of Marshfield, dated 19 March 1802, proved 5 September 1803, names his wife Sarah and daughter Nancy Sampson, wife of Chandler (Plymouth PR 38:364).

Chandler married, second, at Marshfield, 25 November 1822 (*VR* 272), **LYDIA (TURNER) FORD**. She was born at Scituate 28 October 1767, daughter of James and Deborah (Lincoln) Turner (*VR* 1:378), and died at Marshfield 26 April 1834 aged 66 (*VR* 407). She married, first, at Scituate 4 January 1787 (*VR* 2:304), ELISHA FORD Jr., with whom she had children, recorded at Marshfield (*VR* 180-81): Lydia Turner, Abigail, Elisha, Elizabeth, James Turner, Nathaniel, Priscilla, Deborah Lincoln, Rozella, Peleg, and [*torn*]ane [a dau.] Ford. Chandler and Lydia had no children.

In 1850 Chandler Sampson, aged 82, was head of a household in Marshfield that included his daughters Esther Sampson, aged 54, Martha Magoun and her husband Calvin, and granddaughters Joanna A. and Sarah J. Bessey (p.163).

The will of Chandler Sampson of Marshfield, yeoman, dated 14 September 1849, presented the last Monday in September 1850, names his six children: Esther C., Sarah B., Nancy T., Martha, Eliza, and Calvin C. Sampson, who was of Charlestown (Plymouth PR 92:380). Receipts from heirs include Martha S. Magoun, Sarah B. Thomas, Nancy Waterman, Esther C. Sampson, Eliza S. Magoun, and Calvin C. Sampson (*ibid.*, 95:30).

Children of Chandler and Nancy (Thomas) Sampson, rec. Marshfield (*VR* 238-39):

  i   ESTHER CHANDLER[6] SAMPSON, b. 1 Feb. 1796; d. 6 Aug. 1884; bur. with parents (*VR* 407); unm.

 ii   SARAH BOURNE SAMPSON, b. 24 May 1798; d. 10 Aug. 1884 (g.s.); m. (1) at Marshfield, 9 Sept. 1821 (*VR* 271), CAPT. MARSHALL BESSEY, b. 24 Sept. 1791, d. 23 Oct. 1842 (g.s.), son of Adam Bessey (Weyman Ms); both bur. Old Burial Ground at Cong. Church, Marshfield (*VR* 399). Sarah B. m. (2) at Marshfield, after int. 20 March 1849 (*VR* 313), WATERMAN THOMAS, widower of Sarah Deering Thomas who d. Marshfield 13 Dec. 1847 (*VR* 411). In 1850 Waterman Thomas, 66, a farmer, and wife Sarah B., 52, were in Marshfield, next door to Sarah's sister Nancy and her husband Asa Waterman (p.156).

   Bessey children, only the first rec. Marshfield (all in Weyman Ms): 1. *Nancy Chandler Bessey[7]*, b. 2 Aug. 1822 (*VR* 241); m. William Page, Jr. (*VR* 241, 330-31). 2. *Marshall Bessey*, b. 22 Sept. 1824; m. Lucy Bush. 3. *Joanna Adams Bessey*, b. 3 May 1827; m. Moses Clement. 4. *Sarah Jane Bessey*, b. 8 Jan. 1830; m. Ezra Smith. 5. *Permelia A. Bessey*, b. 8 Jan. 1837; m. (1) William Holmes, (2) Henry Stanton. 6. *Lucius Bessey*, b. 10 Feb. 1838; drowned Marshfield 28 July 1846 ae 8y 5m 18d (*VR* 361, 399). 7. *Martha Sampson Bessey*, b. 30 Nov. 1840; m. William Francis Harlow.

iii   [SON] SAMPSON, b. 15 Sept. 1800; d. 25 Oct. 1800, Marshfield (*VR* 407).

 iv   [SON] SAMPSON, b. 12 Jan. 1802; d. 13 Jan. 1802, Marshfield (*VR* 407).

  v   NANCY SAMPSON, b. 29 Aug. 1805; m. there, 2 Nov. 1828 (*VR* 273), CAPT. ASA WATERMAN, b. there 4 Feb. 1800 (*VR* 65), d. there 19 May 1863 of kidney disease (Mass. VR 166:299), son of Asa and Ruth (Little) Waterman. In 1850 they were living in Marshfield next to her sister Sarah B. (Sampson) (Bessey) Waterman, with [niece] Permelia A. Bessey ae 13, and Obed Catlett ae 29, laborer (p.156).

   Waterman child: 1. *Asa Granville Waterman[7]*, d. 26 Sept. 1839, ae 3m (*VR* 412).

vi   MARTHA SAMPSON, b. 9 Sept. 1807; m. CALVIN S. MAGOUN [#762-iii], *q.v.* for more information.

vii   ELIZA SAMPSON, b. 19 March 1809; m. LUTHER MAGOUN [#762-v], *q.v.* for more information.

viii CALVIN CHANDLER SAMPSON, b. 5 Nov. 1812 (year rec. also *Cambridge VR* 1:619); d. Marshfield 9 Aug. 1868 of typhoid fever, a merchant, res. Charlestown (Mass. VR 212:316); m. at Marshfield, 4 Oct. 1840 (*VR* 303), HANNAH HARLOW, b. Duxbury 8 Feb. 1818 (*Cambridge VR* 1:619), d. Manchester 20 Sept. 1908 (Mass. VR, Deaths 1908, 64:162), dau. of Gideon and Olive (Thomas) Harlow. In 1850 the household of Calvin C. Sampson, occupation "furniture," in Charlestown included Harriet H. ae 32 and children Charlotte, Francis G., Oliver H., and Junius, and also Catherine Nelson ae 27, Gideon T. Harlow ae 24, chair painter, and Olive Harlow ae 16 (p.138). In 1860 the family consisted of Calvin C., Hannah, Chandler, Francis G., Olive, Junius, Calvin P., and Thomas H. (p.240).

  Children (Weyman Ms): 1. *Chandler⁷ Sampson*, b. 14 March 1842; m. Alice Marie Russell; he was a senior at Amherst in 1863. 2. *Francis Gray Sampson*, b. 1 April 1844; m. Nancy Jane Russell. 3. *Olive Harlow Sampson*, b. 27 April 1846; m. Charles Richard Shaw. 4. *Junius Sampson*, b. Charlestown 4 July 1849, rec. name blank (*VR* 1:674); m. Ella Rose. 5. *Calvin Proctor Sampson*, b. 17 March 1853; m. Annie Marston Sawyer. 6. *Thomas Harlow Sampson*, b. 8 Nov. 1854; m. Susan A. ___ .

Sources cited: *Cambridge VR. Charlestown VR. Marshfield VR.* Mass. Vital Records 1841-1910. Plymouth County Probate Records. *Giles Memorial* (1864). CENSUS: 1850 Marshfield, Plymouth Co. (M432-332); Charlestown, Middlesex Co., 1850 (M432-322) & 1860 (M653-512).

764. PROCTOR⁵ SAMSON (*Paul⁴, Caleb³⁻², Henry¹*), son of Paul Samson [157] and his wife Esther Chandler, was born at Marshfield 23 December 1772 (*VR* 61), and died at the Shaker community at New Lebanon, N.Y., 30 April 1855, aged 82y 4m 2d (*NEHGR* 115:37). He was a descendant also of *Mayflower* passengers John Alden and Myles Standish.

He married, first, at Scituate, 10 December 1801 (*VR* 2:254), intentions at Marshfield 16 November 1801 (*VR* 166), **RACHEL STETSON**, who died 3 3rd m [3 March] 1803 (Pembroke FR).

He married, second, at Marshfield, 7 July 1805 (*VR* 258), **KEZIA HALL,** who was born at Marshfield 30 December 1764, daughter of Adam Jr. and Kezia (Ford) Hall (*VR* 102, 162), and died there 31 5m [May] 1811 (Pembroke FR). Adam Hall of Marshfield in his will, dated 9 June 1806 and proved 15 March 1808, named his wife Kezia and daughter Kezia Sampson (Plymouth PR 42:256). The will of Keziah Hall of Marshfield, dated 1 July 1809, proved 4 September 1809, also names daughter Kezia Sampson (*ibid.*, 43:29).

Proctor Sampson was living in Marshfield in 1810, his household consisting of one boy and one girl under 10, and one man and two women 26-45 (p.18).

Proctor was among six sons named in the will of Paul Samson of Marshfield, dated 25 February 1806, was proved 3 June 1811 (Plymouth PR 43:463). On – 11ᵗʰ month [Nov.] 1813 Proctor Sampson of Marshfield sold land lately owned by his father Paul Sampson (Plymouth LR 120:264). In August 1816 Proctor Sampson of New Lebanon, N.Y., yeoman, successfully sued Joseph Estes of Pembroke, housewright, to recover $44 due by note dated 9 September 1815 (*PCCR* 13:29).

After his second wife died he joined a group of Shakers and was probably included in a household headed by someone else in 1820 and 1830. In 1840 Proctor Sampson was in Canaan, Columbia County, N.Y., with a household consisting of 38 people of both genders and all ages (p.49). In 1850 he was at the Shaker community in New Lebanon, N.Y., aged 77, a gardener, and [his daughter] Rachel Sampson, 47, born in Massachusetts, was there too (p.26).

Child of Proctor and Rachel (Stetson) Sampson:

i   RACHEL⁶ SAMPSON, b. prob. at Marshfield, 20 1m [Jan.] 1803 (Pembroke FR 325:19); d. at New Lebanon, N.Y., 22 April 1886 ae 83y 3m 2d, with the Shakers (*NEHGR* 115:39).

Child of Proctor and Kezia (Hall) Sampson:

ii   ADAM HALL / JOSEPH SAMPSON, b. prob. at Marshfield, 20 10m [Oct.] 1805 (Pembroke FR 325:19); d. (as Joseph Sampson) at New Lebanon, N.Y., 14 Dec. 1825, ae 20y 1m 24d, with the Shakers (*NEHGR* 115:35).

Sources cited: *Marshfield VR. Scituate VR.* Pembroke Friends Records, microfilm. Rachel (Wilkins) (Baker) Cottrell, "Shaker Death Records," *NEHGR* Vol. 115 [1961]. Plymouth County Deeds and Probate Records. Konig, *Plymouth County Court Records.* CENSUS: 1810 Marshfield, Plymouth Co. (M252-21): 1840 Canaan, Columbia Co., N.Y. (M704-272), 1850 New Lebanon, Columbia Co., N.Y. (M432-492).

765.   JOSEPH⁵ SAMPSON (*Michael⁴, Caleb³⁻², Henry¹*), son of Michael Samson [158] and his first wife, Hannah Pool, was born at Abington 6 April 1757 (*VR* 1:199), and died at Greene, Maine, 9 January 1830, a minister in the Society of Friends (Leeds FR 39). He was a descendant also of *Mayflower* passengers John Alden and Myles Standish.

He married, first, at Bridgewater (*VR* 2:330), 28 December 1780, **HANNAH GURNEY**. She was born at Abington 12 March 1761, daughter of Perkins and Jane (Derby) Gurney (*VR* 1:93), and died at Greene 13 or 27 March 1822, "an elder" (Leeds FR 39). The will of Perkins Gurney of Bridgewater, dated 5 January 1790, proved 13 March 1792, names his wife Patience and daughter Hannah Sampson (Plymouth PR 31:499).

Joseph married, second, at Greene, Maine, 22 May 1823, **MARY (COHOON) WING** of Leeds, Maine, daughter of James and Thankful (___) Cohoon of Wellfleet (*Leeds History*, 323). She died at Monmouth, Maine, 22 September 1840 and was buried at Leeds 24 September (Leeds FR, 39).

Joseph was in Greene, Maine, by 1788, and the 1790 census indicated two boys under 16 and four females in his household (p.38). In 1800 the family consisted of one boy and four girls under 10, one boy and one girl 10-16, two young men and two young women 16-26, and a man and a woman 26-45 (p.109).

On 10 September 1804 Joseph Sampson of Greene joined his brothers Michael, Martin, and Stephen Sampson, and sisters Huldah and Bethiah Sampson, Hannah Gardner and her husband John, and Ruth Stowel and her husband Caleb, in transferring to Michael Sampson of Bridgewater land left by "our mother Hannah Sampson" late of Abington; Joseph was one of three named in the deed who did not sign it (Plymouth LR 87:161). No census listing was found for him in 1810, but in 1820 he was still at Greene, with a household consisting of one boy 10-16, two young men 18-26, two young women 16-26, and a man and a woman 45 or older (p.631). He was a voter and property holder in Greene in 1818 (*Greene History*, 38).

History of Kennebec County (p.287) says that Joseph Sampson was probably the first member of the Leeds Friends Meeting, "he having been a soldier in the revolutionary war, but was brought over to the society of peace loving Friends through the efforts of David Sands." He was one of three men appointed to attend the opening of the meeting of the Winthrop Friends (*ibid.*, 291).

No probate record for Joseph or Hannah Sampson was found.

Children of Joseph and Hannah (Gurney) Samson (Leeds FR, 39-40, except Hannah and Lydia):

i   CYRUS[6] SAMPSON, b. 17 May 1781 East Bridgewater; d. Manchester, Me., 23 Oct. 1865 ae 84y 5m 6d (b. & d. Leeds FR, 40); m. at Greene, 4 Dec. 1803, NABBY WING of Leeds (*Greene Hist.*, 139), b. Sandwich 29 Aug. 1781; d. Winthrop, Me., 22 March 1852 (Leeds FR 40). They were members of the Harlem and later Leeds Monthly Meeting; bur. Manchester Friends Cemetery.

Children (Leeds FR 40): 1. *Fanny Sampson⁷*, b. Greene 9 Jan. 1805; m. Elias Pinkham. 2. *Daniel Sampson*, b. Leeds 3 April 1806. 3. *Alden Sampson*, b. Greene 29 Dec. 1807; m. Sarah T. Pope. 4. *Mary Wing Sampson*, b. China 30 Sept. 1809; m. Moses S. Varney. 5. *Eunice Sampson*, b. China 8 Aug. 1812; m. ___ Robinson. 6. *Almira Wing Sampson*, b. 28 March 181[-]; m. ___ Rice. 7. *Henry Sampson*, b. Leeds 1 Sept. 1817; d. at Friends School, Providence, R.I., 19 Nov. 1837, scarlet fever. 8. *George Sampson*, b. Leeds 14 May 1819; d. Friends School, Providence, R.I., 17 Nov. 1837, scarlet fever. 9. *William Almy Sampson*, b. Leeds 5 May 1822; m. Elizabeth G. Wingate. 10. *Anna Almy Sampson*, b. Leeds 26 May 1825; d. there 13 May 1826.

ii HANNAH SAMPSON, b. ca 1783; prob. m. 31 Dec. 1812, JAMES JONES (*NEHGR* 70:274), b. Durham, Me., son of Caleb and Peace (Goddard) Jones (Durham FR). Hannah Jones rem. to Vassalboro Monthly Meeting from Leeds 19 June 1813 (Leeds FR). "James Jones was known among Friends throughout the United States as a minister of the gospel ... had the power of prophecy ... brothers James and Elisha and cousin Stephen Jones came into Fairfax ... [and China] from Durham ..." (*Kennebec History*, 283). In 1850 James Jones ae 60, no occupation listed, res. China, Me., with Hannah Jones ae 67, Josiah Philbrook ae 28, Hannah S. Philbrook ae 27, and two Philbrook children; also James J. Jones ae 25; and Gustavus Austin ae 11 (p.203).

   Jones children, from census: 1. *Hannah S. Jones⁷*, b. ca 1823; m. Josiah Philbrook. 2. *James J. Jones*, b. ca 1825.

iii MARY SAMPSON, b. say 1784; possibly the Mary Sampson who m. at Greene, Me., in April 1812, AMOS MURRAY (*Greene History*, 142).

iv SARAH SAMPSON, b. say 1786; m. MOSES HAWKES (Leeds FR 39).

v   JOSEPH SAMPSON, b. say 1788; disowned by Friends 21 July 1815 (*ibid.*).

vi JANE SAMPSON, b. say 1790; m. at Greene, in Dec. 1816, as his first wife, MARCUS GILBERT of Leeds (*Greene History*, 144; *Leeds History*, 328). Jane was disowned by Leeds Friends 22 May 1813, evidently for marrying out of meeting (Leeds FR 39). Marcus, "a maker of carpenter's bench tools," m. (2) Marian Coburn (*Leeds History*, 78).

   Gilbert children of Marcus and Jane (*ibid.*): 1. *Aranda Gilbert⁷*, b. ca 1818; m. Diana T. Wing. 2. *Jane Gilbert*; m. William Cushing.

vii LYDIA SAMPSON, b. say 1792.

viii ANNE SAMPSON, b. 18 Oct. 1794; m. (as Anna) at Greene, in March 1815, WILLIAM T. GILBERT of Leeds (*Greene Hist.*, 143), prob. son of Capt. William and Betsey (___) Gilbert (*ibid.*, 262). Anna was disowned by the Leeds Friends 19 May 1815 (Leeds FR, 39). They lived at S. Leeds, then Hallowell, Me. (*Leeds History*, 78).

Gilbert children (*ibid.*): 1. *Proctor Gilbert[7]*, res. Norfolk, Va. 2. *Earl Gilbert.* 3. *Jane Gilbert.*

ix   JACOB SAMPSON, b. 27 July 1796; d. 18 May 1874 ae 77y 9m 22d; bur. Friends Cem., Manchester, Me. (g.s.); m. (1) Oct. 1826, RUTH COLLINS of Litchfield (*Leeds History,* 332); m. (2) at Manchester, 7 Dec. 1845 (VR), ELIZA GODDARD, b. 1817, d. 11m 18 [18 Nov.] 1897 ae 80y 7m 16d (g.s.). He was disowned by Leeds Friends (p.39) 20 Oct. 1826, was received back by request 16 Aug. 1839, disowned again 16 Jan. 1846, and reinstated 16 May 1862 (p.40). In 1860 he was a farmer ae 63 in Manchester, Me., with Eliza ae 43 and daughters Mary, Julia, Irena, and Rhoda (p.81/459). Ruth's g.s. is evidently illegible, as the transcription of it makes no sense [8 mo 1830 ae 79].

    Children, first three with Ruth, last two with Eliza (Leeds FR 41, 42): 1. *Mary [A. H.?][7] Sampson[7]*, b. ca 1833. 2. *Julia E. Sampson,* b. 31 May 1840. 3. *Irena J. Sampson,* b. Nov. 1843; m. J. Adams. 4. *Elvira Sampson,* b. Hallowell 7 Oct. 1850; d. 11 Jan. 1851. 5. *Rhoda Elvira. Sampson,* b. 4 Oct. 1853.

x   RUTH SAMPSON, b. 29 Aug. 1798 (Leeds FR 39); m. ELIJAH FARR. In 1850 Ruth Farr ae 51 was head of a household at Hallowell, Me., that included two Farr children and Jane Gilbert ae 27 (p.212).

    Farr children at home 1850: 1. *Lorin Farr[7]*, b. ca 1835. 2. *Maria Farr,* b. ca 1837.

xi   DAVID SAMPSON, b. 1801; d. 13 Feb. 1821; bur. Leeds 15 Feb. 1821 (Leeds FR 39).

xii   PHILENA SAMPSON, b. 11 June 1803 (Leeds FR); m. at Manchester, 20 June 1830 (VR), WILLIAM MORGRIDGE; b. there 12 Dec. 1789 (VR). She was disowned by Leeds Friends 22 April 1831 for marrying out of meeting (p.39). In 1850 William Morgridge ae 60 was a farmer in Chesterville, Me., with Philena ae 46, and four children (p.94).

    Morgridge children at home 1850: 1. *Sarah E./Ellen Morgridge[7]*, b. Manchester 18 July 1831 (VR). 2. *Harriet S. Morgridge,* b. ca 1835. 3. *William J. Morgridge,* b. ca 1844. 4. *Adelia P. Morgridge,* b. ca 1847.

xiii   PROCTOR SAMPSON, b. Leeds 21 May 1806; d. 18 May 1893 ae 87 (g.s.); m. 23 Oct. 1834, LYDIA FARR (Leeds FR 40), b. 9 Jan. 1811 (*ibid.,* 41), d. 4 Sept. 1854 ae 43y 9m (g.s.); m. (2) Manchester, 1 June 1859 (VR), HANNAH MORILL, d. 28 Oct. 1863 ae 37 (g.s.); m. (3) Manchester, 31 May 1865 (VR), HANNAH HAMLIN, d. 20 Feb. 1876 ae 53 (g.s.); all bur. Friends Cem., Manchester, Me. Proctor Sampson cleared a farm in the part of Hallowell that in 1850 became Manchester, "and brought his young bride to the shore of the lake and made the second Friends family [there]" (*Kennebec History,* 293, 875). He served six terms as selectman in Manchester (*ibid.*, 881). In 1850 he was a farmer in Hallowell, with Lydia F., ae 39, and four children, next to the family of his brother Jacob (p.211).

Children with Lydia, at home 1850, b. Hallowell (Leeds FR 42): 1. *William F.*[7] *Sampson,* b. 18 Aug. 1835; m. Marcia Paine. 2. *Sarah A. Sampson,* b. 4 Nov. 1837; m. I. W. Hawkes. 3. *Abby E. Sampson,* b. 8 March 1840; d. 5 Jan. 1858 ae 17y 10m; bur. with parents. 4. *Joseph G. Sampson,* b. 24 May 1843; m. Henrietta L. Freeman.

Sources cited: *Abington VR. Bridgewater VR.* Manchester, Me., VR (FHL microfilm #0011545). Plymouth County Deeds and Probate Records. Pembroke Friends Records, "Births, Deaths, Marriages" (FHL film #0,001,335). Mabel R. Whiting, "Part of Book I, Leeds Monthly Meeting of Friends ..." *Illustrated History of Kennebec County* (1892). Cemetery records, Friends Cemetery, Manchester, Me., on line. *History of Greene, Maine* (1938). Stinchfield, *History of Leeds* (1901). CENSUS: Greene, Kennebec Co., Me. 1790 (M637-2), 1800 (M32-7), 1820 (M33-35); 1850 Chesterville, Franklin Co., Me. (M432-253) & Hallowell, Kennebec Co., Me. (M432-256); 1860 Manchester, Kennebec Co., Me. (M653-439).

766.   HANNAH[5] **SAMPSON** (*Michael*[4], *Caleb*[3-2], *Henry*[1]), daughter of Michael Sampson [158] and his first wife, Hannah Pool, was born at Abington 9 November 1760 (*VR* 1:199) and died there 8 May 1833, aged 74, of lung fever (*VR* 2:283). She was a descendant also of *Mayflower* passengers John Alden and Myles Standish.

She married at Abington, 18 August 1785 (*VR* 2:186), **JOHN GARDNER**. He was born about 1765 and died at Abington 27 June 1829, aged 65, of consumption, son of Amos and Betsey (_____) Gardner (*VR* 2:284).

No John Gardner is indexed in Plymouth County in the 1790 census. John and Hannah Gardner of Abington joined her siblings on 10 September 1804 in transferring to Michael Sampson of Bridgewater, land left "by our mother Hannah Samson" late of Abington (Plymouth LR 87:161).

John's household in Abington in 1810 consisted of one boy 10-16, a man 26-45, and a woman 45 or over (p.96). No Plymouth County probate records were found for John, Hannah, or Amos Gardner. John's birth is not recorded in the vital records of Abington, any of the Bridgewaters, Duxbury, Pembroke, or Scituate.

Children of John and Hannah (Samson) Gardner, rec. Abington (*VR* 1:85-86):

i   DAVID GARDNER[6], b. 25 Jan. 1786; prob. m. (1) at Abington, 2 Feb. 1808 (*VR* 2:82) or Weymouth (*VR* 2:76), POLLY PAIN, bp. Weymouth 7 June 1778, "ch. of the Widow Pain" (*VR* 1:204), d. Weymouth 12 July 1811 (*VR* 2:273). In 1810 and his household, near his father, included a boy under 10.

Children: 1. [*Son*] *Gardner*[7], b. ca 1809. 2. [*child*] Gardner, d. Weymouth 10 May 1811 (*VR* 2:273). [Possibly same child, b. & d.]

ii OLIVE GARDNER, b. 1 April 1787; d. Abington 9 or 10 Dec. 1806 ae 20, "dau. John Esq. and Hannah" (*VR* 2:284).

Sources cited: *Abington VR. Weymouth VR.* CENSUS: Plymouth Co., Abington 1810 (M252-21), Plymouth 1850 (M432-332).

767. BETHIAH⁵ SAMPSON (*Michael⁴, Caleb³⁻², Henry¹*), daughter of Michael Sampson [158] and his first wife, Hannah Pool, was born at Abington 22 January 1765 (*VR* 1:198). If the marriage identification for her is correct, she was living at Sharon on 10 February 1809 when she and her husband signed a deed. She was a descendant also of *Mayflower* passengers John Alden and Myles Standish.

She is probably the Bethiah Samson of Bridgewater who married there, 20 August 1808 (*VR* 2:330) after intentions 3 May at Sharon, as his second wife, **SIMEON WHITE**. (In *Brockton VR*, taken from church records, her name appears as Bethiah *Jamison*). Simeon was born at Sharon 26 June 1766, son of David and Lois (Morse) White (*VR* 65), and was living there on 10 February 1809. He married, first, at Foxboro, in 1797, ELIZABETH (WHITE) WADE, widow of Ira Wade, with whom he had four children: Anna White, Betsy White, Eli White, and Rufus White, recorded at Sharon (*VR* 64).

Bethiah was a singlewoman, of Bridgewater, on 10 September 1804 when she and her sister Huldah joined their siblings in transferring to Michael Sampson of Abington land that had belonged to their mother, Hannah Sampson (Plymouth LR 87:161). Simeon White of Sharon, laborer, sold land there on 10 February 1809 to Jared White of Sharon; Simeon and Bethiah White signed the deed (Norfolk LR 33:108). There are several Simeon Whites listed on the 1810 census, and none has been identified.

If this identification is correct, Bethiah was 43 years old at the time of her marriage, and it seems unlikely that she had any children.

Sources cited: *Bridgewater VR. Foxboro VR. Sharon VR.* Norfolk County Deeds. Plymouth County Deeds.

768. MICHAEL⁵ SAMPSON (*Micah⁴, Caleb³⁻², Henry¹*), son of Micah or Michael Sampson [158] and his first wife, Hannah Pool, was born at Abington 26 January 1767 (*VR* 1:199), and died at Leeds, Maine, 22 February 1845, aged 78 (*VR*). He was a descendant also of *Mayflower* passengers John Alden and Myles Standish.

He married at Turner, Maine, 11 June 1791, **BETSEY HOUSE** (*Turner History*, 161). She was born about 1772 and died at Leeds 30 August 1854, aged 82, "Elizabeth wife of Michael" (*VR*).

Michael Sampson was living in Leeds in 1800, when his household consisted of one boy and four girls under 10, and a man between 26 and 45; no older woman was enumerated (p.259), so perhaps Betsey had gone elsewhere to have the next baby, Ira, who was born in May of that year. On 10 September 1804 Michael Sampson of Greene, Me., joined his siblings in quitclaiming to Michael Sampson of Bridgewater [their father], their rights in land of land left "by our mother Hannah Samson" (Plymouth LR 87:161). In 1810 Micah Sampson was in Leeds with a household consisting of two boys and two girls under 10, one boy and one girl 10-16, two young women 16-26, and one man and one woman 45 or older (p.927).

On 31 May 1817 in a supplement, *The American Advertiser* published a list of landowners in Leeds who had not paid taxes since an assessment in 1815; if not paid by 26 June 1817 with 20 per cent added, the property was to be sold at public sale in Hallowell. The list included Michael Sampson, with 50 acres, house and barn, bounded east by Jabez Daggett, tax $1.98.

In 1820 Micah Samson was still at Leeds with a household consisting of a man and a woman 45 or older, one woman 26-45, one young woman 16-26, two young men 18-26, and two girls 10-16 p.620). No probate records for Michael / Micah Sampson were found in Kennebec County.

In 1850 Betsey Sampson, aged 77, born in Massachusetts, and Sylva Sampson, aged 39, born in Maine, were living in the household of Marcus Gilbert, aged 39, at Leeds, Maine (p.316).

Children of Michael and Betsey (House) Sampson, rec. Leeds, Me. (*VR* 114):

   i   BETSY[6] SAMPSON, b. 15 Nov. 1791. She may be the Betsey Sampson who m. as his 2nd wife BARNUM JONES, son of Sylvester Jones who went from Taunton to Turner, Me., 1797, and widower of Deborah or Mary Lincoln (*Turner History*, 56).

   ii   LYDIA SAMPSON, b. 19 July 1793; m. July 1812 (*Leeds History*, 326), SYLVESTER JONES of Turner, b. ca 1791. In 1850 he was a farmer at Livermore, Me., with Lydia ae 57, Clarissa M. Jones ae 15, and Laura Sampson ae 22 (p.272).

      Jones children, from census: 1. prob. *Charles Jones[7]*, b. ca 1826. 2. *Clarissa Jones*, b. ca 1835.

   iii   DEBORAH SAMPSON, b. 7 Aug. 1795; m. at Turner, Me., 29 May 1816, SALMON TOWNSEND (*Leeds History*, 328), b. Taunton 19 Jan. 1793 (*Boston Transcript*, 16 July 1919).

Townsend children (*ibid.*): 1. *Jane Townsend⁷*, b. 12 July 1816. 2. *Salmon Townsend,* b. 14 May 1818. 3. *Elisha Townsend,* b. 5 July 1821. 4. *Elizabeth Townsend,* b. 3 Feb. 1828.

iv ELISHA SAMPSON, b. 12 July 1797; prob. Elisha H. Sampson who m. at Leeds or Winthrop, Me., Sept. 1826 (*Leeds History,* 332), SYLVIA GURNEY.

v IRA SAMPSON, b. 8 May 1800; m. (1) SUSAN GILBERT, dau. of Cornelius Gilbert (*Leeds History,* 76), d. prob. ca 1833. "They settled on the bank of the Androscoggin river—near the recent ferry ... in a delicate state of health, in rescuing a child from drowning, she took cold and died therefrom" (*ibid.,* 76-77). He m. (2) at Leeds, Feb. 1834, PATIENCE FISH (*ibid.,* 336).

Children (*ibid.*): 1. *Laura Sampson⁷,* b. ca 1828; in household of aunt Lydia Jones 1850. 2. *Julia Sampson.* 3. *William Sampson.* 4. *Ira Sampson.*

vi SYLVIA SAMPSON, b. 29 Aug. 1802; probably the "Sylva Sampson" ae 39 [*sic*], b. Me., living with her mother in household of Marcus Gilbert in Leeds, 1850, evidently unm.

vii JUDETH SAMPSON, b. 22 July 1805. In 1880 Judith A. Sampson ae 75, milliner, was living by herself in Turner, Me. (p.463B).

viii POLLY SAMPSON, b. 13 Aug. 1808.

Sources cited: *Abington VR.* Leeds (Maine) VR. *History of Leeds* (1901). *Boston Transcript,* 16 July 1919. CENSUS: Leeds, Kennebec Co., Me., 1800 (M32-7), 1820 (M33-35), & 1850 (M432-258); 1880 Turner, Androscoggin Co., Me. (T9-475).

769. MARTIN⁵ SAMPSON (*Michael⁴, Caleb³⁻², Henry¹*), son of Michael Sampson [158] and his first wife, Hannah Pool, was born at Abington 6 March 1769 (*VR* 1:199), and died there 16 March 1842, aged 73, "son of Michael" (*VR* 2:349). He was a descendant also of *Mayflower* passengers John Alden and Myles Standish.

He was of Bridgewater when he married at Pembroke, 8 September 1808 (*VR* 343), his first cousin, **HEPZIBAH⁵ SAMPSON** of Pembroke, a Henry Samson descendant [#779]. She was baptized at Duxbury 2 April 1775 (*VR* 145), daughter of Gideon and Keziah (Carver) Samson, and died at Abington 3 December 1826, aged 52, as "— wife of Martin Sr." (*VR* 2:349).

Martin was of Greene, Maine, in 1804 when he and his siblings signed a deed quitclaiming to their father their rights in land left by their mother (Plymouth LR 87:161). He did not settle in Maine, however, for in 1810 his household in Abington consisted of one boy under 10, one woman 26-45, and one man and one woman 45 or older (p.99). No probate records were found for Martin or Hepzibah Sampson in Plymouth County.

Children of Martin and Hepzibah (Sampson) Sampson, rec. Abington (*VR* 1:198-99):

i   MARTIN[6] SAMPSON, b. 20 March 1809; d. 15 Dec. 1825, ae 16 (*VR* 2:349).

ii   NANCY SAMPSON, b. 4 Feb. 1811; m. at Hanson, 26 March 1843 (*VR* 70), as his second wife, ALBERT HOUSE, b. ca 1805 Mass. In 1850 he was a shoemaker in Hanson, ae 45, enumerated next to Turner Sampson, with Nancy ae 39, Sarah J. ae 20, Albert Jr. ae 18, and Nancy T. ae 5; Deborah House ae 83 lived with them (p.134). Sarah and Albert Jr. were ch. of Albert's first wife, Jane Barnes Everson.
     House child of Albert and Nancy: 1. *Nancy T. House[7]*, b. ca 1830.

iii ABIGAIL CARVER SAMPSON, b. 21 Oct. 1812.

iv   TURNER SAMPSON, b. 16 April 1815; d. Hanson in 1893 (Mass. VR 437:623); m. at Abington, 7 May 1835 (*VR* 2:186), EUNICE BRIGGS TOLMAN, b. Pembroke 28 July 1815, dau. of John and Averick (Everson) Tolman (*VR* 206, 363). In 1850 Turner Sampson was a shoemaker at Hanson, ae 35, with Eunice B. ae 35, and two children (p.134).
     Children: 1. *Turner[7] Sampson*, b. ca 1837; d. Abington 21 Feb. 1839 (*VR* 2:349). 2. *Elizabeth T. Sampson*, b. 14 June 1842 Pembroke (*VR* 180); at home 1850; res. Whitman 1910, unm. 3. *Frances W. Sampson*, b. ca 1848; at home 1850.

v   RUTH SAMPSON, b. 20 Oct. 1817; d. 23 Nov. 1831, ae 14 (*VR* 2:349).

Sources cited: *Abington VR. Bridgewater VR. Duxbury VR. Hanson VR. Pembroke VR.* Plymouth County Deeds. CENSUS: 1810 Abington, Plymouth Co. (M252-21); 1850 Hanson, Plymouth Co. (M432-332).

770.   RUTH[5] SAMPSON (*Michael[4], Caleb[3-2], Henry[1]*), daughter of Michael Sampson [158] and his first wife, Hannah Pool, was born at Abington 4 September 1771 (*VR* 1:199), and died at Hamilton, N.Y., probably after 1830. She was a descendant also of *Mayflower* passengers John Alden and Myles Standish.

She married at Plainfield (VR), 26 July 1803 after intentions at Ashfield 9 June 1803 (*VR* 207), "both of Ashfield," as his second wife, **CALEB STOWELL**. He was baptized at Abington 18 November 1764, son of Samuel and Hannah (Lambert) Stowell, died 27 May 1839, aged 74, and is buried at Lebanon, N.Y. (*Pioneers of Madison Co.*, 242).

Caleb was of Plainfield when he married, first, at Cummington 4 November 1788 (*VR* 158), MOLLY TORREY. Caleb and Molly had: Barney, Polly, Betsey,

Davis, Rachael, and Susan Stowell, born at Easthampton. He married, third, at Lebanon, N.Y., ROXANNA (___) TORREY, who died in 1849.

In 1800 Caleb Stowell was at Ashfield with a household consisting of one boy and two girls under 10, one boy and two girls 10-16, and a man and a woman 26-45 (p.345). On 10 September 1804 Caleb Stowell and wife Ruth, of Plainfield, Hampshire County, joined her siblings in transferring to Michael Sampson of Bridgewater land left by their mother Hannah Sampson, late of Abington; Caleb Stowell was one of three grantors named who did not sign the deed (Plymouth LR 87:161).

In 1810 Caleb Stowel was in Sherburne, Chenango County, N.Y., where his household consisted of one man and one woman 26-45, one young man 16-26, and three little boys under 10 (p.350). No Caleb is indexed for 1820 in New York, and *Pioneers of Madison County* (p.242) states that in 1820 Cabel [*sic*] Stowell was on the jail limits for debt. In 1830 Caleb Stowel of Lebanon, Madison County, N.Y., had a household consisting of one man 30-40, and one man and one woman 60-70 (p.345).

On 25 April 1850, John Pettet of Lebanon requested letters of administration on the estate of Roxanna Stowell of Lebanon. He stated that she died in Lebanon "sometime last Fall," that he was the husband of a granddaughter of the deceased, and that her only heirs were his wife and Theodore Torrey, a son, who "resides in one of the western states" (Madison Co. Surrogate's Rec.).

Children of Caleb and Ruth (Samson) Stowell (the Torrey and Stowell genealogies confuse Caleb's first and second marriages, calling Ruth his first wife and attributing to her Caleb's children with Molly Torrey, and Ruth's children to Molly):

   i   CHANDLER STOWELL[6], b. 26 Nov. 1804; d.y.

   ii CALEB STOWELL, b. 29 March 1807; m. at Hamilton, N.Y., RHODA TEFFT, b. 18 April 1802 in R.I., d. 16 May 1881 Chautauqua, N.Y., dau. of John and Elizabeth (Dye) Tefft (*Torrey Gen.*, 34). In 1860 Caleb ae 53 was a farmer in the town of Chautauqua with Rhoda ae 58, and John ae 21, all b. N.Y. [*sic*] (p.55).

        Children (*Torrey Gen.*): 1. *Rhoda Elnora Stowell*, b. 12 Sept. 1835. 2. *Eliza Ann Stowell*, b. 25 March 1837. 3. *John Caleb Stowell*, b. 17 April 1839.

   iii RANSFORD STOWELL, b. 6 May 1809. He is prob. the Ransford Stowell who in 1850 was listed as ae 38, a farmer in Jay, Wabash Co., Ind., b. Mass., with wife Catharine ae 28, b. Vt., and four children (p.316).

        Children at home 1850, first three b. Ohio: 1. *William Stowell*, b. ca 1841. 2. *George Stowell*, b. ca 1843. 3. *Edwin Stowell*, b. ca 1844. 4. *Vanderwoof Stowell*, b. ca 1849 Indiana.

iv   WILLIAM STOWELL, b. 15 June 1810 in N.Y.; m. (1) ORILLA ___, b. N.Y. ca 1815, d. prob. between 1850 and 1857; m. (2) LOUISA [?OLNEY], b. N.Y. ca 1824. In 1850 he was at Ellington, Chautauqua Co., N.Y., a millwright, with Orilla ae 35 and three children (p.164). In 1860 he was at Fredonia P.O., Pomfret, Chautauqua, N.Y., ae 50, a head sawyer, b. N.Y., with Louisa ae 26, five children, and John Delin ae 19, b. Sweden (p.563).

Children at home 1850 and/or 1860, first three with Orilla, rest with Louisa: 1. *Electa Stowell*, b. ca 1834; not at home 1860.   2. *Jane E. Stowell,* b. ca 1828. 3. *Warren Stowell,* b. ca 1831, a sawyer 1860.   4. *Ransford Stowell,* b. ca 1857. 5. *Albert Stowell,* b. ca 1858.

v   DIANA STOWELL, b. 4 May 1812; d. 18 Jan. 1888, Palmyra, Mich.; m. at Hamilton, N.Y., 23 Jan. 1831, HORATIO G. POPE (*Stowell Gen.*, 136).

Sources cited: *Abington VR. Ashfield VR. Cummington VR.* Plainfield VR. Elmer I. Shepard, "Cummington & Plainfield Marriages," NEHGS Mss C 2487. Plymouth County Deeds. Madison Co., N.Y., Surrogate's Records. Tuttle, *Names and Sketches of the Pioneer Settlers of Madison County, New York,* Isabel Bracy, ed. (1984). D. Torrey, *A contribution toward a genealogy of all Torreys in America* (1895). *Stowell Genealogy* (1922). CENSUS: 1800 Ashfield, Franklin Co. (M32-15); 1810 Sherburne, Chenango Co., N.Y. (M252-26); 1830 Lebanon, Madison Co., N.Y. (M19-93); 1850 Jay, Wabash Co., Ind. (M432-153); Chautauqua Co., N.Y., 1850 Ellington (M432-484), 1860 Chautauqua (M653-732) & Pomfret (M653-731).

771.   STEPHEN⁵ SAMPSON (*Michael⁴, Caleb³⁻², Henry¹*), son of Michael Samson [158] and his first wife, Hannah Pool, was born at Abington 2 September 1775 (*VR* 1:199), and died there 26 May 1812, aged 37 (*VR* 2:349). He was a descendant also of *Mayflower* passengers John Alden and Myles Standish.

He published marriage intentions at Bridgewater, 19 March 1796 (*VR* 2:330), with **LUCY HARRIS** of Easton.

In 1800 Stephen Sampson was in Bridgewater, his household consisting of one boy and one girl under 10, one man 16-26, and one woman 26-45 (p.56); his brother Micah Sampson was living nearby. Stephen was still there in September 1804 when he joined several of his siblings in quitclaiming to their father land that had belonged to their mother (Plymouth LR 87:161).

He is not listed in Bridgewater in 1810, and the other Stephen Sampsons listed that year in Massachusetts were all in the same places in 1800. There are no probate records for Stephen or Lucy in Plymouth County. No further record of Lucy was found.

Census records indicate probable children of Stephen and Lucy (Harris) Sampson: a son and a daughter, both born between 1796 and 1800.

Sources cited: *Abington VR. Bridgewater VR.* CENSUS: 1800 Bridgewater, Plymouth Co. (M32-16).

772. WILLIAM SAMPSON⁵ (*Michael⁴, Caleb³⁻², Henry¹*), son of Michael Sampson [158] and his second wife, Deborah Richmond, was born at Abington 4 October 1782 (*VR* 1:199). He was a descendant also of *Mayflower* passengers John Alden, Thomas Rogers, and Myles Standish.

He may be the William Samson [*sic*] listed in the 1820 census at Leeds, Maine, near his brother Abel Sampson [*sic*]. William and presumably his wife were both aged 26-45, and they had in their household two girls 10-16 and two boys and two girls under 10 (p.425). Nothing further has been learned.

Sources cited: *Abington VR.* CENSUS: Temple, Kennebec Co., Me., 1820 (M33-35).

773. ABEL⁵ SAMPSON (*Michael⁴, Caleb³⁻², Henry¹*), son of Michael Sampson [158] and his second wife, Deborah Richmond, was born at Abington 1 August 1784 (*VR* 1:198), and died at Temple, Maine, 6 September 1861, aged 89y 1m 5d, called "Deacon" (VR 1:49, date blank; Franklin Co. Cem.). He was a descendant also of *Mayflower* passengers John Alden, Thomas Rogers, and Myles Standish.

He married at Norton, 27 November 1806, **MARTHA / PATTY KEITH WHITE,** who was born at Raynham 2 December 1786, daughter of John and Martha (Keith) White (*Nicholas White*, 94), and died at Temple, Maine, 24 June 1861, aged 74y 8m (g.s.; VR 1:49, date blank ; Franklin Co. Cem.). A note with the family record of Abel and Martha Sampson at Temple, Maine, says, "Old Mrs White Died July 8th 1847 lived with Abe[l] Sampson" (VR 1:49). Dea. Abel Sampson and his wife Martha K. are buried in the Scales Cemetery, Temple.

In 1820 Abel Sampson was living in Temple, Me., his household consisting of two boys and two girls under 10, one boy and two girls 10-16, and one man and one woman 26-45 (p.425). In 1850 Abel Sampson was still in Temple, aged 67, a blacksmith, with Martha, 66, Martha, 38, Mehitable, 36, and Abby Sampson, 23 (the last three b. Maine), and Ella A. Farmer, 4; Abel Sampson, Jr., 31, born in Maine, lived next door with his family (p.211).

Children of Abel and Martha Keith (White) Sampson, first three b. Greene, Me., rest Temple, Me., all births and some deaths rec. together Temple (VR 1:49); marriages performed by Simeon Hacket, "Minister of the Gospel in Temple":

   i   ALMIRA⁶ SAMPSON, b. 31 Aug. 1807; d. 10 Aug. 1861; m. at Temple, Me., 21 Jan. 1833 (VR 2:n.p.), DAVID TUCK, b. ca 1779 Me. In 1850 David

Tuck was at Temple, ae 71, with Almira ae 42; their household included Walter Morton ae 3, perhaps related to Rev. Alpha Morton who lived next door (p.212).

ii   HARRIET SAMPSON, b. 29 June 1809; d. 1 May 1836.

iii   CROCKER WILLIAM SAMPSON, b. 12 July 1810; d. 11 March 1901; bur. Scales Cem., Temple, Me.; m. (1) after int. Temple, Me., 25 April 1840 (VR 2:1), JANE LAWRENCE, who d. Temple, Me., 16 Feb. 1847 (VR 79); m. (2) at Farmington, Me., 7 March 1849, SARAH PRATT TUCK, b. there 8 Aug. 1823, d. 25 July 1905; bur. Bragg Cem., Farmington. They divorced 7 Oct. 1868 and Sarah m. (2) William T. Brackley. C. W. Sampson was town clerk of Temple in 1842 when he recorded marriages of his brother Abel Sampson Jr. and cousin Ammi Colcord.

    Children (Temple VR): With Jane: 1. *Almira Jane⁷ Sampson*, b. 11 April 1841. With Sarah: 2. *Wallace* [name changed in infancy to] *Frank Darius Sampson*, b. 23 May 1850 (VR 1:79), d. 1873; m. Margaret Worthley.

iv   PATTY K. / MARTHA KEITH SAMPSON, b. 7 March (Temple VR) or Dec. 1812; d. 16 March 1881; m. at Temple, Me., 16 Nov. 1851 (VR 2: n.p.), as his second wife, JOSEPH FAIRBANKS, d. 8 Jan. 1871, son of Joseph Fairbanks; no children (*Farmington History*, 469).

v   MEHITABLE [COLCORD] SAMPSON, b. 17 Feb. 1814; unm. 1850.

vi   FRANCIS SAMPSON, b. 7 Feb. 1816; m. at Temple, Me., 27 Feb. 1840 (VR 2:1), MARY CONANT, b. ca 1818. In 1850 he was a mechanic at Temple, with Mary and four children (p.211).

    Children at home 1850: 1. *Harriet M.⁷ Sampson*, b. ca 1841. 2. *Le Roi Sampson*, b. ca 1843. 3. *Elliot Sampson*, b. ca 1844. 4. *John A. Sampson*, b. ca 1847.

vii   ABEL SAMPSON, b. 2 June 1818; d. 12 April 1878; m. at Temple, Me., 28 April 1842 (VR 2:10), ZERIAH FLETCHER STEWART of Farmington, b. 23 Nov. 1815, dau. of Capt. Henry and Sophia (Church) Stewart (*Farmington History*, 578), d. 12 April 1878.

    Children rec. Temple (VR 1:84): 1. *Henry Le F.⁷ Sampson*, b. 13 June 1843. 2. *Rolla S. Sampson*, b. 19 Jan. 1845. 3. *Augustus S. Sampson*, b. 23 July 1850. 4. *Hellen Marion Sampson*, b. 1860.

viii DANIEL C[OLCORD] SAMPSON, b. 24 Dec. 1820; m. at Temple, Me., 31 Dec. 1844 (VR 2:16), PHEBE STAPLES, b. ca 1823. He was a shoemaker at Temple 1850 (p.211).

    Children rec. Temple (VR 1:85): 1. *Samuel W.⁷ Sampson*, b. 22 Feb. 1847. 2. *William Sampson*, b. 19 Oct. 1848; d. 2 or 29 April 1865. 3. *Vester Jane Sampson*, b. 19 March 1852; d.y. 4. *Abby L. Sampson*, b. 14 Jan. 1856; d. 26 March 1858. 5. *Addie Sampson*. 6. *Millie May Sampson*.

ix ALZADA SAMPSON, b. 1 Aug. 1823; d. 5 Jan. 1848 (VR 1:49); m. at Temple, Me., 7 Nov. 1844 (VR 2:17), MOSES FARMER 3rd.

x ROSANNA SAMPSON, b. 1 March 1825; m. at Temple, Me., 15 April 1846 (VR 2:19), ANDREW KENNISON, b. ca 1825. In 1850 he was a farmer in Norridgewock, Me., with Rosanna and two children; William B. Kennison ae 33, "tinker," was in the household (p.155).

    Kennison children at home 1850: 1. *Alpha M. Kennison*[7] [male], b. ca 1847. 2. *Harriet A. Kennison*, b. ca 1849.

xi ABIGAIL / ABBIE DEWEY SAMPSON, b. 18 Aug. 1827; unm. 1850.

Sources cited: *Abington VR. Norton VR.* Temple, Me., Town Records (FHL film #012,263) and "old record book that appears to be a local census," from town clerk Jeanette T. Stevens to Priscilla K. Simms (GSMD #60919). Dorothy Wirth, "36 Cemeteries of Franklin County, Maine" (typescript, 1960), now on line. Butler, *A History of Farmington, Maine* (1885). Lothrop, *Nicholas White Family* (1902). CENSUS: Temple, [in] Kennebec Co., Me., 1820 (M33-35), [in] Franklin Co., Me., 1850 (M432-253); Norridgewock, Somerset Co., Me., 1850 (M432-268).

774. MEHITABLE SAMSON[5] (*Michael*[4], *Caleb*[3-2], *Henry*[1]), daughter of Michael Samson [158] and his second wife, Deborah Richmond, was born at Abington 10 March 1786 (*VR* 1:199), and died at North Yarmouth, Maine, 12 February 1830 (*VR*, orig. 2:113). She was a descendant also of *Mayflower* passengers John Alden, Thomas Rogers, and Myles Standish.

She married at Exeter, N.H., 16 June 1810, **DANIEL COLCORD**, who was born at Exeter 30 June 1786, son of Samuel and Anna (Walden) (Gilman) Colcord, and a twin with his brother Thomas (*TAG* 18:41). He died at North Yarmouth 28 December 1825 (VR, orig. 2:112).

The 1810 census listed them in Exeter, their household consistent with that of a newly-married couple between 16 and 26 (p.248). In 1820 Daniel Colcut [*sic*] was head of a household in North Yarmouth, Me., that consisted of one man and one woman 26-45 and three boys under 10 (p.460). The last three children are not recorded in either Yarmouth or North Yarmouth, Maine.

Daniel's death record calls him a potter. Gravestone records for Daniel and Mehitable are at Yarmouth Historical Society, but their stones in a cemetery next to a church were lost or removed after a large tree uprooted the area (P. K. Simms).

Children of Daniel and Mehitable (Samson) Colcord (*Colcord Gen.*, 35, 52-53):

i SAMUEL COLCORD[6], b. Exeter, N.H., 27 July 1811; d. Greenville, Ill., 12 Nov. 1893 (*Rogers Gen.*, 249); m. 1 May 1836, ELIZABETH PERHAM (*Colcord Gen.*, 53), b. Wilton, Me., 1 May 1813. In 1860 he was "A.G.

Implement Maker" at Greenville, Bond Co., Ill. , with Elisabeth ae 47 and five children (p.319). In 1880 his household included his sister Jane Clark and nephew George Colcord [son of Ammi Mitchell Colcord] (p.232B).

Children at home 1860, b. Ill.: 1. *Josiah Colcord*[7], b. ca 1843. 2. *Jennie Colcord*, b. ca 1845. 3. *Samuel Colcord*, b. ca 1847. 4. *Mary Colcord*, b. ca 1850. 5. *Ida Colcord*, b. ca 1855.

ii   WILLIAM SAMPSON COLCORD, b. Exeter 17 Oct. 1815; d. 1892 (*Colcord Gen.*, 53); m. (1) MARY E. BECKETT, (2) FRANCES W. PLANT, b. ca 1834 Ill. In 1850 he was an accountant in Bond Co., Ill., in the household of Charles Hoiles or Horles, not far from brother Otis (p.384). In 1860 he was a clerk in Greenville, Ill., with Frances and two children (p.321). *Colcord Gen.* says he was a storekeeper and postmaster in Greenville.

Children at home 1860, b. Ill.: 1. *Willy F. Colcord*[7], b. ca 1853. 2. *S.E. Colcord* [dau.], b. ca 1856.

iii OTIS BRIGGS COLCORD, b. Yarmouth, Me., 16 March 1818; d. 1898 (*Colcord Gen.*, 53); m. prob. (1) _____ who d. ca 1846; m. (2) in Bond Co., Ill., 28 May 1853, HARRIET E. EBLIN, b. ca 1820 Ill.; m. (3) in Bond Co., 1 Jan. 1859, HARRIET J. WHITE. In 1850 Otis B. Colcord ae 33, b. N.H., no occupation given, and Tapley Colcord ae 4 [m], b. Ill., were in Bond Co., among several people in the household of Jacob B. Drake ae 62, physician and surgeon (p.385). In 1860 Otis was in Greenville, Ill., a trader, with Harriet ae 30 and son Otis T. ae 15 (p.321). *Colcord Gen.* says Otis was a dealer in live stock and owned a farm near Greenville.

Child: 1. *Tapley/ Otis T. Colcord*[7], b. ca 1845-46; m. Jennie Laughlen.

iv   AMMI MITCHELL COLCORD, b. Yarmouth 15 Oct. 1820; d. after 1910 census; m. after int. Temple, Me., 12 March 1842, both of Temple (VR 2:9), SARAH CONANT. The int. was entered by [Ammi's cousin] C. W. Sampson, town clerk. In 1850 Ammi M. Colcord ae 29, was a farmer in Temple, with Sarah C. ae 27, and two children (p.211); they were still there in 1860, when son Edward was called George Ammi (p.29). In 1910 Ammi M. Colcord, ae 89, widowed, and his two youngest daughters (unmarried) were living at Bunker Hill, Ill. (p.7B).

Children, b. Temple, Me. (VR): 1. *Jane Colcord*[7], b. 6 June 1848; m. Henry Sampson. 2. *Edward / George Ammi Colcord*, b. 16 April 1850; m. Julia Longley Maynard. 3. *Ida Colcord*, b. 25 Oct. 1858. 4. *Eula Colcord*, b. 2 Oct. 1863.

v   JANE COLCORD, b. Yarmouth 11 June 1824; living 1880; m. in Bond Co., Ill., 3 Jan. 1843, JACOB CLARK (Ill. Marriages; *Colcord Gen.*, 53). He was ae 47, b. Mass., a school teacher in 1860 in Macoupin Co., Ill., with Jane but no children (p.253). In 1880 she was living in the household of her brother Samuel (p.232B).

Sources cited: *Abington VR.* North Yarmouth (Me.) VR. Temple, Me., VR. Meredith B. Colket, Jr., "The Descendants of Edward Colcord of New Hampshire," *TAG* 18 [1941-42]. *Descendants of Edward Colcord of New Hampshire* (1908). *Thomas Rogers, Pilgrim ...* (1980). Illinois Marriages, online data base. CENSUS: 1810 Exeter, Rockingham Co., N.H. (M252-25); 1820 North Yarmouth, Cumberland Co., Me. (M33-34); Bond Co., Ill., 1850 (M432-98) & 1860 (M653-156); 1910 Bunker Hill Twp., Macoupin Co., Ill. (T624-308).

775. SILENCE FORD⁵ (*Bethiah⁴ Samson, Caleb³⁻², Henry¹*), daughter of Abner Ford and his wife Bethiah Samson [159], was baptized at Marshfield 30 April 1758 (Weyman Ms), and died at Montville, Maine, 11 November 1811 (TR I:196 She was a descendant also of *Mayflower* passengers John Alden and Myles Standish.

She married, about 1784, **JOSEPH MACCARES CARR**, who was born at Salisbury 25 December 1757 (*VR* 42) and baptized at Newbury 1 January 1758, son of Maccares (or Macries) and Elizabeth (Wait) Carr (*VR* 297). He died after 1820, when he was listed in the census at Montville, Maine. The Joseph Carr listed in the 1830 census of Montville was evidently his son.

Silence Ford's family settled in Ballstown (now Jefferson), Maine, when she was a child.

A letter in the files of the Mayflower Society Historian General indicates that Joseph moved about 1780 from Ballstown (now Jefferson, Me.) to Montville, where he was among the first settlers. In 1790 Joseph Carr was living at Harpswell, Maine, with one boy under 16, one man over 16, and one female (p.271). In 1800 Joseph Carr resided in Davis Town, Hancock Co., Maine (organized as Montville in 1806), head of a household consisting of a man and a woman 26-45, two boys and two girls 10-16, and one boy and one girl under 10 (p.360).

The mark for Joseph Carr's sheep, "left ear loped with a swallows tail in the right," was recorded at Montville in August 1807, just after that of his son-in-law Nicholas Twitchel (TR 1:265). In 1810 Joseph Carr of Montville had a household consisting of a man and a woman 45 or older, two young men and two young women 16-26, a boy 10-16, and one little girl under 10 (p.302).

In 1820, after Silence's death, Joseph was living at Montville, over 45, with one young woman between 16 and 26 and a little boy under 10 (p.298).

Children of Joseph and Silence (Ford) Carr, b. at Montville, Me. (TR 1:196):

i SARAH CARR⁶, b. 30 July 1785; m. (as *Sally* Carr) after int. Montville 25 May 1806 (TR 1:3), NICHOLAS TWITCHEL. His mark for sheep ("a crop off right ear and half crop the uper side the left ear") was recorded Montville 25 July 1807 (TR 1:265).

ii   HANNAH CARR, b. 6 March 1787; m. (1) at Montville, 21 Dec. 1810, both
      of Montville (TR 1:226), NATHANIEL BATCHELOR; m. (2) Montville,
      30 March 1848 at "the residence of said Tasker" (TR 2:138), evidently as his
      second wife, JOHN TASKER. In 1850 he was a farmer at Montville, ae 60,
      b. N.H., with Hannah [ae 46 !] and two Tasker sons who must have been
      with an earlier wife (p.265).

iii   ESTHER CARR, b. 6 Oct. 1788; m. after int. Montville 15 Sept. 1811 (TR
      1:252), BENJAMIN STEVENS.

iv   MECRES CARR, b. 25 March 1790; m. MARY ____, b. ca 1796 Maine. In
      1850 Micris Carr was a farmer in Liberty, Me., ae 60, with Mary ae 54, and
      two children (p.41).
          Children at home 1850 (prob. incomplete): 1. *Julia G. Carr⁷*, b. ca 1832.
      2. *John C. Carr*, b. ca 1835.

v   JOSEPH CARR, b. 24 Jan. 1792; m. at Montville, 1 July 1818 (TR 2:549),
      MARY McALLISTER, "both of this town." In 1830 his household con-
      sisted of a man 30-40, a woman 20-30, two boys and one girl 5-10, and one
      little girl under 5 (p.458). He is prob. the Joseph Carr in Burnham, Me.,
      1850, a farmer ae 58 with wife Mary ae 54, and six children (p.238).
          Children at home 1850: 1. *Richard Carr⁷*, b. ca 1820; m. Lucinda ____.
      2. *Willard Carr*, b. ca 1822. 3. *David Carr*, b. ca 1831. 4. *Rosana Carr*, b. ca 1832.
      5. *Thomas Carr*, b. ca 1835. 6. *Esther Carr*, b. ca 1838.

vi   MEHITABLE CARR, b. 4 Dec. 1793; m. at Montville, 8 July 1815 (TR 2:548),
      JOHN GERRY of Freedom, Me. In 1850 John Garey ae 58 was a farmer at
      Dover, Me., with Mahitable ae 55, and seven children; another apparent son
      and his family shared the dwelling (p.283), next to the family of Mehitable's
      sister Abigail Ayer.
          Garey children at home 1850: 1. *Ebenezer Garey⁷*, b. ca 1818. 2. *James McC.
      Garey*, b. ca 1825. 3. *E. M. Garey* (?twin), b. ca 1825; m. Mary R. ____. 4. *Esther A.
      Garey*, b. ca 1828. 5. *Susan C. Garey*, b. ca 1830. 6. *Peleg A. Garey*, b. ca 1832.
      7. *J. W. Garey* [m], b. ca 1836. 8. *Susan Garey*, b. ca 1838.

vii   MARTIN CARR (twin?), b. 24 Nov. 1795; m. after int. Montville 19 March
      1828 (TR 2:541), BETSEY PHILLIPS, b. ca 1806 Maine; res. 1850 Mont-
      ville (p.276). Montville records show that he was town clerk there 1846-47
      (3:35-36).
          Child at home 1850: 1. *Joseph I. or S. Carr⁷*, b. ca 1829.

viii SUSANNA CARR, either a twin or d. y., as her name is interlined after
      Martin's, with birthdate blank.

ix   ABIGAIL CARR, b. 27 June 1801; m. at Montville, 28 April 1827 (TR 2:378),
      PARLY AYER. In 1850 P. M. Ayer ae 49, b. N.H., was a farmer in Dover,

Me., with Abagael ae 49, and six children, the oldest two listed as farmers (p.283), next to the family of Abigail's sister Mehitable Garey.

    Ayer children at home 1850: 1. *B.S. Ayer*[son], b. ca 1828. 2. *A.M. Ayer* [son], b. ca 1830. 3. *Emma Ayer*, b. ca 1831. 4. *Mary Ayer*, b. ca 1832. 5. *Hazen Ayer*, b. ca 1836. 6. *D--- Ayer* [son], b. ca 1838.

Sources cited: *Newbury VR. Salisbury VR.* Montville, Maine, Town Records. Letter and affidavit with *Mayflower* Membership #13632, Historian General. CENSUS: 1790 Harpswell, Cumberland Co., Me. (M637-2); 1800 Davis Town, Lincoln Co., Me. (M32-7); Montville, Waldo Co., Me., 1810 (M252-12), 1820 (M33-36), 1830 (M19-50), & 1850 (M432-271); 1850 Dover, Piscataquis Co., Me. (M432-267), Burnham, Waldo Co., Me (M432-270), and Liberty, Waldo Co., Me. (M432-271).

776.   ABNER FORD[5] (*Bethiah*[4] *Samson, Caleb*[3-2], *Henry*[1]), son of Abner Ford and his wife Bethiah Samson [159], was baptized at Marshfield 8 September 1765 (*MQ* 46:133), and was living at Jefferson, Maine, 21 May 1811 when he acknowledged a deed. He is probably the Abner Ford who died at Mayfield, Maine, 22 May 1850, aged 93 [*sic*] (*Maine Farmer*, 4 July 1850). He was a descendant also of *Mayflower* passengers John Alden and Myles Standish.

He married, first, _____ **TRASK,** who died before March 1794.

He married, second, at Ballstown, "both of this plantation," 10 March 1794, **SUSANNA FOWLES** (*NEHGR* 46:12). She was probably living in 1830 when census figures for [her stepson] William Ford include a woman aged 60 to 70.

Abner Ford Jr. of Ballstown bought land there 7 July 1786 (Lincoln LR 44:105). In 1790 he was living there with three boys under 16 and one female (p.33). His father was also listed, with three females. In 1800 the household of Abner Ford Jr. of Ballstown consisted of a man and a woman 26-45, one boy 10-16, and two boys and three girls under 10 (p.345).

On 4 September 1804 Abner Ford of Ballstown sold to Abner Ford Jr. of Ballstown 200 acres of land there (Lincoln LR 55:250).

Ballstown was organized as Jefferson in 1807. In 1810 Abner Ford of Jefferson had a household consisting of one woman 45 or older, one man 26-45, three young men and one young woman 16-26, one boy and three girls 10-16, and two little boys and two little girls under 10 (p.285). Census figures suggest more children than have been identified.

On 20 May 1811, acknowledged next day, Abner Ford of Jefferson sold 200 acres there to William Ford of Jefferson (Lincoln LR 77:28).

Abner was probably the man aged 70-80 in the household of his son Abner in 1840, in Piscataquis County, Maine (p.47).

Children of Abner and _____ (Trask) Ford, b. prob. Ballstown (Jefferson), Me. (affidavit):

i   DAVID FORD[6]

ii   BETHIAH FORD

iii   WILLIAM FORD, b. ca 1789; living 1850; m. NANCY ___, b. ca 1798 in Maine. In 1811 his father sold 200 acres in Jefferson to him, noted above. In 1850 William ae 61 and Nancy ae 52 were living in Jefferson in a household headed by William H. Ford ae 27, that included two other probable children and 13 other people, mostly elderly, of varying surnames (p.342).
        Children at home 1850 (earlier census indicates more): 1. *William H. Ford*, b. ca 1823. 2. *Lucinda J. Ford*, b. ca 1829. 3. *Guy M. Ford*, b. ca 1839.

iv   NATHAN FORD, b. ca 1791; living 1850; m. MARGARET _____, b. ca 1791 Me. In 1850 he was ae 59, a tavern keeper at Jefferson, Me., with Margaret ae 59, four Ford children, and George W. Trask ae 24 (p.342).
        Children at home 1850 (earlier census indicates more): 1. *Joshua Ford*, b. ca 1827; a ship carpenter. 2. *Joseph Ford*, b. ca 1829; a farmer. 3. *Margaret Ford*, b. ca 1831. 4. *Amasa Ford*, b. ca 1836.

Children of Abner and Susanna (Fowles) Ford, b. prob. Ballstown (Jefferson), Me. (affidavit):

v   ABNER FORD, b. ca 17 June 1795; d. 10 Nov. 1858 Sebec, Me, ae 63y 4m 23d (Sebec Village Cem. Rec., 4).; m. MEHITABLE HATCH (Cutter, *New England Fam.*, 1:197), b. 1789, d. 1883. He was a machinist and millwright and manufactured tubs in Sebec. In 1840 his household, at an unnamed place in Piscataquis Co., Me., included a man 70-80, probably Abner's father (p.47). In 1850 he was a millwright at Sebec, ae 50, with Mahitable ae 44, and children Llewellyn, Eliza J., Melvina, Asenath, and Frank (p.342).
        Children, births rec. Sebec, burials in Sebec Village Cemetery; spouses from Cutter, 197): 1. *Caleb Jewett Ford*, b. 31 Dec. 1820; m. Helen P. Snow. 2. *Caroline D. Ford*, b. 11 May 1822; m. Theodore Wyman. 3. *Lucy Ann Ford*, b. 24 July 1825; d. 9 May 1838, scarlet fever. 4. *Llewellyn Ford*, b. 18 May 1828; d. 1 July 1862, typhoid fever. 5. *Eliza Jane Ford*, b. 23 July 1831; m. John Morrison. 6. *David S. Ford*, d. 8 June 1838 ae 3y 7m 15d. 7. *Melvina C. Ford*, b. 1 Dec. 1837; m. Judson Parker. 8. *Annette/Asenath Ford*, b. 24 April 1841; m. Henry M. Richardson. 9. *Frank M. Ford*, b. 23 Aug. 1843; d. unm.

vi   SILENCE FORD

vii   ENOCH FORD, b. prob. ca 1801; m. JANE _____, b. ca 1802 Maine. In 1850 he was a farmer ae 48 in Mayfield, Somerset Co., Me. (where Abner Ford Sr. d. that year), with Jane ae 48 and five children (p.236). In 1860 Enoch and Jane, both ae 60, were in Twp. 1, Range 13, Piscataquis Co., and he was a hotel keeper; daughter Susanna Flanders and her two sons were with them (p.985).

Children (1850 census): 1. *Susanna Ford*[7], b. ca 1825; m. before 1850 Barnet Flanders. 2. *Benjamin F. Ford*, b. ca 1827. 3. *Jane Ford*, b. ca 1835. 4. *Olinda Ford*, b. ca 1837. 5. *Ruth Ford*, b. ca 1839. 6. *Jno. F. Ford*, b. ca 1842.

viii SUSAN FORD

ix ELIZA FORD, b. 8 Jan. 1804 (Maine VR); m. at Sebec, Me., after int. 6 Dec. 1834, JOHN SPRINGER (TR 2:25), b. ca 1813 Maine. In 1850 he was a millwright at Lincoln, Penobscot Co., with Eliza ae 46, and six children (p.346).

Springer children at home 1850: 1. *Hannah Springer*[7], b. ca 1836. 2. *Elizabeth A. Springer*, b. ca 1838. 3. *David F. Springer*, b. ca 1839. 4. *Lewis T. Springer*, b. ca 1841. 5. *Roumelia J. Springer*, b. ca 1843. 6. *Mary E. Springer*, b. ca 1847.

x ASEANETH FORD

xi ELIJAH FORD, b. ca 1806; living 1860; prob. m. HARRIET ___, b. ca 1803 in Maine; res. 1840 at Weston, Aroostook Co., Me (p.89). In 1860 he was a house carpenter in Old Town, Penobscot Co., with wife Harriet ae 47, and six children (p.336). No other Elijah Ford appears in any Maine census.

Children at home 1860: 1. *Warren W. Ford*[7], b. ca 1830. 2. *Anga Ford*, b. ca 1832. 3. *Julia Ford*, b. ca 1834. 4. *Hannah H. Ford*, b. ca 1836. 5. *Alverta W. Ford*, b. ca 1838. 6. *George W. Ford*, b. ca 1841.

Sources cited: Marshfield Baptisms, *Mayflower Descendant*, 46 (1980). "Lincoln County Marriages," *NEHGR* 46 (1892). Sebec, Me., Town Records. Sebec Village Cemetery Records, courtesy of Betty Ellis. Lincoln County, Maine, Deeds. Cutter, *New England Families Genealogical and Memorial: Third Series* (1915). *Deaths from the Maine Farmer* (1997). Affidavit with GSMD #13632. CENSUS: Maine: 1790 Ballstown, Lincoln Co. (M637-2) & 1800 (M32-6); 1810 Jefferson, Lincoln Co. (M252-12); 1840 Weston, Aroostook Co. (M704-136); 1860 Penobscot Co., Old Town (M653-445); 1840 Piscataquis Co., unnamed place (M704-150), 1850 Lincoln, Penobscot Co. (M432-266), Sebec (M432-267) & Mayfield, Somerset Co. (M432-269); 1860 Twp. 1, Range 13, (M653-433); **See also:** *Biographical Review Volume 23: Sketches of Leading Citizens of Penobscot, Piscataquis, Hancock, Washington, and Aroostook Counties, Maine* (Boston, 1898), for family of Abner Ford Jr. (but confused about earlier generations).

777. GIDEON FORD[5] (*Bethiah*[4] *Samson, Caleb*[3-2], *Henry*[1]), son of Abner Ford and his wife Bethiah Samson [159], was baptized at Boothbay, Maine, 8 October 1770 ("Rev. John Murray's Recs."), and died probably just before 18 October 1808 when his widow sold land. Their last child was born, evidently posthumously, in late July 1809. A history of Jefferson says "Gideon, Sr., died in October 1805 at Mayhew's Corner and was buried near the First Baptist Church, his grave being one of the three that were formerly seen there" (*Centennial Jefferson*, 34), but the date on the stone was perhaps misread. He was a descendant also of *Mayflower* passengers John Alden and Myles Standish.

He married at Newcastle, Maine, 13 May 1793 (VR; *Maine Fam. 1790*, 2:204), **MARY LINDSEY MURPHY**, who was born at Phippsburg, Maine, 11 October 1770, baptized at Georgetown 29 December 1770 (*ibid.,* citing VR), and died at Jefferson, Maine, 21 February 1863, aged 93, "wife of Gideon Ford" (g.s.). She is buried in Boynton Hill or Highland Cemetery, Jefferson. She was the eldest of nine children of James and Sarah (Linsey) Murphy, born at Pleasant Pond (*Centennial Jefferson,* 34).

Gideon Ford of Sheepscut Great Pond, Maine, bought land there 20 October 1798 from Jeremiah Crommet, and he sold land there 3 September 1801, the deed signed by Gideon and Mary Ford (Lincoln LR 48:7-8). Mary Ford of Jefferson, widow, on 18 October 1808 sold land in Jefferson bounding her dwelling house, and she sold additional land 1 September 1846 (*ibid.,* 64:198; 225:282).

The 1800 census listed Gideon and his wife both 26-45 in Jefferson with one boy and two girls under 10 (p.355). In 1810 Mary Ford was living in Jefferson, her household consisting of one woman 45 or over, one woman 26-45, and one boy and one girl 10-16 (p.285). In 1820 "Wid°" Mary Ford, over 45, was living in Jefferson with one boy 10-16 and one young man 18-26 (p.71). In 1850 Mary Ford, aged 80, was living at Jefferson with her 50-year-old son Gideon (p.334). It is said that she "outlived all her family" (*Centennial Jefferson,* 34), but her son Gideon appears to have been living in Jefferson in 1870.

No Lincoln County probate records were found for Gideon or Mary.

Children of Gideon and Mary Lin[d]sey (Murphy) Ford, rec. Jefferson as "the late Gideon Ford family" (VR 1:8):

i   SARAH FORD[6], b. 3 Feb. 1794; not at home 1810.

ii   GIDEON FORD, b. 21 Oct. 1795; prob. d. unm. He can be followed in the census in Jefferson: in 1850 he was living with his mother; in 1860 he was a mariner, and in 1870 a farmer, ae 74, living alone.

iii MARY FORD, b. 14 Oct. 1797 "at Somerville, Me." (affidavit); evidently m. _____ CLARK, who d. by 1850 when she was head of household at Newcastle, Me., with four children (p.395).
     Clark children at home 1850: 1. *John S. Clark[7]*, b. ca 1826. 2. *? Soresta M. Clark* [female], b. ca 1831. 3. *Frank Clark,* b. ca 1835. 4. *Ephraim Clark,* b. ca 1837.

iv   SUMNER M. [MURPHY] FORD, b. 25 July 1809 [*sic*], perhaps an error for 1805; not with mother 1810 (census).

Sources cited: "Rev. John Murray's Book of Records ..." (1947 Me. DAR). Mary Kelton Dummer Clap, "Jefferson Maine Cemeteries," Manuscript, NEHGS. Jefferson, Me., VR, *NEHGR* 73 (1919) and Maine State Archives. Lincoln County, Me., Deeds. Marjorie Barnes Thompson, "James Murphy," in *Maine Families in 1790*, Vol. 2 (1990). *Centennial Celebration of the Town of Jefferson* (1908). Affidavit of Susie (Clark) Haggett dated June 15, 1938, in GSMD File #13632, Historian General. CENSUS: Lincoln Co., Me., Jefferson 1800 (M33-36), 1810 (M252-12), 1820 (M33-36), with Newcastle 1850 (M432-260).

778. ABIGAIL FORD[5] (*Bethiah*[4] *Samson, Caleb*[3-2], *Henry*[1]), daughter of Abner Ford and his wife Bethiah Samson [159], was born about September 1774, at Boothbay, or at Jefferson, Maine (son Converse's d. rec.). She died at Farmingdale, Maine, 21 March 1853, aged 78y 8m, "wife of James," recorded at Gardiner (*VR* 610). She was a descendant also of *Mayflower* passengers John Alden and Myles Standish.

She married at Hallowell, Maine, [date blank in record but probably ca 1792], **JAMES McCURDY** (*VR* 4:61). He was born at Bristol, Maine, 30 March 1765 (*Hallowell VR* 1:189), son of John and Anna (Hilton) McCurdy, and died at Farmingdale 1 or 22 July 1843, aged 77, recorded at Gardiner (*VR* 611).

In 1800 James McCurdy was living in Hallowell, Maine, himself and his wife aged 26-45, with three boys and two girls under 10 (p.113). No probate records were found for James or Abigail.

Children of James and Abigail (Ford) McCurdy, rec. Hallowell, Maine (*VR* 1:189):

i   NANCY McCURDY[6], b. 14 Nov. 1793; m. at Gardiner, Me. (*VR* 383), after int. 1 April 1815 Hallowell (*VR* 4:61), SAMUEL CLAY. In 1850 Nancy Clay was head of a household at Hallowell that consisted of two sons, her brother Abner, and their mother Abigail ae 76 (p.299).
    Clay children at home 1850: 1. *Frederick Clay*[7], b. ca 1834. 2. *Melvin Clay*, b. ca 1838.

ii ROBERT McCURDY, b. 24 Feb. 1795; d. 30 March 1817 ae 21.

iii JAMES McCURDY, b. 26 Aug. 1796; d. Gardiner 25 or 26 Oct. 1867 ae 70 (*VR* 611); m. at Gardiner, 11 July 1824 (*VR* 383), JOANNA BROWN, b. there Dec. 1803 (*VR*), d. there 17 Feb. 1882 (*VR* 611); res. Gardiner, Me., 1850, a carpenter (p.331-2).
    Children, b. Gardiner (*ibid.*, and *VR*): 1. *Caroline McCurdy*[7], b. ca 1826. 2. *James S. McCurdy*, b. 12 May 1828 (VR). 3. *Delia F. McCurdy*, b. ca 1832.

iv BETHIAH McCURDY, b. 14 Jan. 1798; m. after int. Hallowell 16 June 1825 (*VR* 4:60), ISAAC GOLDSMITH of Gardiner.

v   ABIGAIL McCURDY, b. 20 Sept. 1799; prob. the Abby who m. at Gardiner, 9 Feb. 1823 (*VR* 383), EPHRAIM C. KEITH, b. ca 1797 Mass. In 1850 he was a shoemaker in Bridgewater with Abby G., and six children (p.19).
    Keith children at home 1850, all b. Mass.: 1. *Anna J. Keith[7]*, b. ca 1824. 2. *Abby A. F. Keith*, b. ca 1829. 3. *Ephraim C. Keith Jr.*, b. ca 1831. 4. *George F. Keith*, b. ca 1836. 5. *Esther M. Keith*, b. ca 1839. 6. *Seth D. Keith*, b. ca 1843.

vi   PROCTOR McCURDY, b. 28 Jan. 1800 [*sic*]; d. 2 March 1827 ae 27.

vii   ABNER McCURDY, b. 17 Sept. 1801; a laborer ae 45 [*sic*], living in household of sister Nancy Clay in 1850 (p.299).

viii   GEORGE McCURDY, b. 4 March 1802 [*sic*]; d. Gardiner, 30 Jan. 1864 ae 61y 11m (*VR* 610); m. after int. Gardiner 23 May 1828 (*VR* 383), ELIZABETH SMITH, d. Gardiner 20 Dec. 1874 ae 67 (*VR* 610); res. Gardiner 1850, a carpenter (p.322).
    Children at home 1850 (*ibid.*): 1. *Ellen A. McCurdy[7]*, b. ca 1834. 2. *Rufus S. McCurdy*, b. ca 1836. 3. *Mary A. McCurdy*, b. ca 1837. 4. *Henry M. McCurdy*, b. ca 1840. 5. *Harriet M. McCurdy*, b. ca 1842; d. Gardiner 31 Aug. 1859 ae 18 (*VR* 610). 6. *Frances A.M. McCurdy*, b. ca 1844; d. Gardiner as *Frances Ellis McCurdy* 22 Jan. 1851 ae 6y (*VR* 610). (The George McCurdy ae 20 in household of Emerald McCurdy may also belong in this family.)

ix   ESTHER McCURDY, b. 9 Jan. 1804; d. Jan. 1823 ae 19.

x   LORANIA McCURDY, b. 13 Oct. 1807; m. at Gardiner, 2 Sept. 1827 (*VR* 383), JOHN D. JONES.

xi   CONVERSE L. McCURDY, b. 17 May 1809; d. Wakefield 22 Nov. 1876 of consumption, clergyman, widowed, b. Hallowell, Me. of James b. Bristol and Abigail b. Jefferson (Mass. VR 284:185); m. EVELINE BRADFORD, b. Plympton, d. Lawrence 12 April 1876 of consumption, ae 66y 1m 12d, dau. of [Daniel] and Bathsheba [Carver] Bradford (Mass. VR 283:205; *Plympton VR*). Her mother was a "doctress and midwife" at Plympton. In 1850 Converse S. McCurdy ae 41, b. Me., was a Methodist minister in Palmer, with Eveline ae 40, and three children (p.273).
    Children at home 1850, all b. N. H.: 1. *Charles W. McCurdy[7]*, b. ca 1833. 2. *Hannah M. McCurdy*, b. ca 1838. 3. *Mary A. McCurdy*, b. ca 1845.

xii   SUMNER McCURDY, b. 19 May 1811.

xiii   ARIEL McCURDY, b. 10 June 1813; d. Dec. 1814 ae 1y 6m.

xiv   CYNTHIA McCURDY, b. 2 May 1815.

xv   ZILPHA S. or L. McCURDY, b. 11 Sept. 1816; d. Boston 26 Aug. 1856 ae 46 [*sic*] of a tumor, b. Sullivan, N.H. [*sic*], parents' names not given (Mass. VR 104:61); m. at Gardiner, Me., 2 April 1843 (*VR* 383), JOHN T. BROWN, b. ca 1816 Maine. In 1850 he was a machinist in Newton, with Zilphia ae 36 [*sic*], b. Me., and two children; Zilpha's sister Octavia McCurdy ae 28 was in the household (p.54).

> **Brown** children at home 1850, both b. Mass.: 1. *Charles Brown⁷*, b. ca 1836. 2. *Maria Brown*, b. ca 1849.

xvi EMERALD McCURDY [son], b. 9 Nov. 1818; d. Gardiner 17 or 18 Nov. 1867 (*VR* 610); m. MARY A. _____. In 1850 he was a tinplate worker in Gardiner, with wife Mary A. ae 32, and Edwin Yeaton ae 18, Rufus Hastings ae 16, and George A. McCurdy ae 20, all tinplate workers (p.269).

xvii OCTAVIA L. McCURDY, b. 1 Aug. 1822; d. Cambridge 1 Nov. 1880 ae 58y 3m of tubercular phthisis, single (Mass. VR 320:68). In 1850 she was living in the household of her sister Zilpha Brown in Newton.

Sources cited: *Plympton VR.* Farmingdale, Me., VR. *Gardiner [Me.] VR. Hallowell [Me.] VR.* Mass. Vital Records 1841-1910. *Old Bristol and Nobleboro VR.* Affidavit GSMD #13632.. Hall, "Cemetery Inscriptions of Central Maine" (NEHGS typescript ME 60 40, 1939). CENSUS: 1830 Hallowell, Kennebec Co., Me. (M32-6); 1850 Newton, Middlesex Co. (M432-326), Palmer, Hampden Co. (M432-319), & Gardiner, Kennebec Co., Me. (M432-257).

779.   HEPHZIBAH⁵ SAMSON (*Gideon⁴, Caleb³⁻², Henry¹*), daughter of Gideon Samson [160] and his first wife Keziah Carver, was baptized at Duxbury 2 April 1775 (*VR* 145). She was a descendant also of *Mayflower* passengers John Alden and Myles Standish. She married at Pembroke 8 September 1808 (*VR* 343) her cousin **MARTIN SAMSON**. See **Family # 769** for their information.

780.   PETER⁵ SAMSON (*Gideon⁴, Caleb³⁻², Henry¹*), son of Gideon Samson [160] and his second wife, Millicent Bates, was born about March 1789 (calculated from d.), probably at Pembroke, and died at Alvordton, Williams County, Ohio, 17 February 1863 aged 73y 11m 11d (g.s.). He was a descendant also of *Mayflower* passengers John Alden and Myles Standish.

He married, first, at Pembroke 15 March 1812 (*VR* 343), **MARGARET MUNRO**, who was born there 31 January 1787, daughter of Henry Jr. and Margaret (___) Munro (*VR* 154). No Plymouth County probate records were found for her parents. Margaret was dead by about 1824.

Peter married, second, in New York State, **ESTHER HAKES**. She was born in New York about December 1795, daughter of George Hakes (LR noted below), and died 17 February 1876 at Alvordton, Ohio, aged 80y 2m 11d (cem. rec.). Peter and Esther are buried in Primrose Cemetery, near Alvordton.

Peter Samson of Pembroke was appointed administrator of the estate of his father, Gideon Samson, on 5 September 1814, with David Oldham Jr. and Elisha

R. Josselyn as sureties (Plymouth PR 46:59). The estate was insolvent, and in April 1815 he was given permission to sell real estate (*ibid.,* 47:139, 268).

By 1820 Peter was in New York State, enumerated that year in Brutus, Cayuga County with two boys under 10; other figures in the listing are unclear (p.27). Margaret died probably after 1820, and Peter married Esther about 1824. A deed dated 19 April 1828 whereby heirs of George Hakes sold land in Cayuga County includes Peter Sampson and wife Esther (Cayuga Co. LR, MM:21). In 1830 Peter was in Mentz, Cayuga County, 40-50, with a household consisting of one woman 30-40, one boy and one girl 15-20, one boy 10-15, two girls 5-10, and two little girls under 5; a woman 60-70 was also living in their home (p.395).

He was in Ohio by about 1833; on 6 August 1835 he and his wife Esther acknowledged a deed in Seneca County, Ohio (Seneca Co. LR 8:130). In 1840 Peter was living in Thompson Township, Seneca County, 50-60, with Esther 40-50; their household included one girl 15-0, two girls 10-15, and one girl and one boy 5-10 (p.221).

In 1850 Peter Sampson ae 60, born in Mass., farmer, was in Sherman Township, Huron County, Ohio, with Hester ae 55, Lucetta ae 23, Ester ae 21, John ae 16, and Rebecca ae 25, all born in New York (p.108). In 1860 Peter aged 70 and Esther aged 66 were of Mill Creek, P.O. Primrose, Williams County, Ohio (p.129). In 1870 Esther Sampson aged 74, born in N.Y., was living with the family of her daughter Esther Wheeler (p.129).

No estate or deeds were found in Williams County for Peter or Esther Sampson.

Children of Peter and Margaret (Munro) Samson [*sic*], b. Pembroke (*VR* 182; *Giles Mem.,* 478):

    i   PETER[6] SAMSON, b. 28 Dec. 1812.

    ii MILLISENT BATES SAMSON, b. 14 June 1815.

Children of Peter and Esther (Hakes) Samson, b. New York State (1850 census), list perhaps incomplete; prob. used spelling *Sampson:*

    iii REBECCA SAMPSON, b. ca 1825; unm. 1850.

    iv LUCETTA SAMPSON, b. ca 1827; unm. 1850.

    v   ESTHER SAMPSON, b. ca 1829; m. ca 1851 CHARLES WHEELER, b. ca 1821 Baden, Germany. In 1860 (p.129) and 1870 (p.129) [*sic*] he was a cooper in Mill Creek Twp., P.O. Primrose, Williams Co., Ohio; in 1870 Esther's widowed mother was living with them.

        Wheeler children (1860 & 1870 census): 1. *Juliette Wheeler*[7], b. ca 1852. 2. *Franklin Wheeler,* b. ca 1853. 3. *Elizabeth Wheeler,* b. ca 1856. 4. *John Wheeler,* b.

ca 1858. 5. *Rebecca Wheeler*, b. ca 1861. 6. *George Wheeler*, b. ca 1863. 7. *Mary Wheeler*, b. ca 1866. 8. *Sarah Wheeler*, b. ca 1868.

vi   JOHN C. SAMPSON, b. ca 1834; m. ca 1860, MARGARET ____, b. ca 1842 Ohio. In 1870 he was a cooper in Mill Creek Twp., P.O. Primrose, Williams Co., Ohio, next to brother-in-law Charles Wheeler.

Children at home 1870: 1. *William Sampson⁷*, b. ca 1861. 2. *Clarence Sampson*, b. ca 1864. 3. *Mary Sampson*, b. ca 1866. 4. *Enos Sampson*, b. ca 1868.

Sources cited: *Pembroke VR. Giles Memorial* (1864). Cayuga County, N.Y., Deeds. Seneca County, Ohio, Deeds. Certified copies of gravestone records of Peter and Esther Sampson from Primrose Cemetery, near Alvordton, Ohio, GSMD, Historian General. CENSUS: 1820 Brutus, Cayuga Co., N.Y. (M33-68); 1830 Mentz, Cayuga Co., N.Y. (M19-88), 1840 Thompson, Seneca Co., N.Y. (M704-426), 1850 Sherman, Huron Co., Ohio (M432-697), Mill Creek, Williams Co., Ohio, 1860 (M653-1052), and 1870 (M593-1282).

781.   LYDIA⁵ SAMSON (*Amos⁴, Joshua³, Caleb², Henry¹*), daughter of Amos Samson [161] and his wife Deborah Samson, was born at Duxbury 6 April 1747 (*Giles Mem.*, 395) and baptized there with her siblings 16 September 1759 (*VR* 146). She died 1 or 3 September 1811 in her 65th year, and is buried with her husband in Large Cemetery, Duxbury (*VR* 426). She was a descendant also of *Mayflower* passengers John Alden and Myles Standish.

She married at Duxbury, 23 November 1769 (*VR* 316), **URIAH SPRAGUE,** born at Duxbury 11 January probably 1747/8 (pension rec.; not in *VR*), son of Samuel and Sarah (Oldham) Sprague; his mother was a Henry Samson descendant [#206]. His sister Lydia Sprague married Nathaniel Simmons [#738], and his sister Hannah Sprague married Lydia's brother Elijah Samson [#785]. Uriah died at Duxbury 1 February 1842 (*sic, VR* 427). His birth year has been given as 1742/3 (*MF 20*, 2:60), but in 1840 he was listed as 92, and at his death, "in 94th year"; his pension record says he was born 1747 in Duxbury (White, 3279). He is called "oldest son" in his father's will, but this is consistent with a birth year of 1747/8, which also fits into the chronology of the other children. He would have been the third child, younger than sisters Sarah and Lucia, but older than brother Joshua.

At the December 1785 term of the Court of General Sessions, Uriah Sprague was paid for 31 days' work during a large project to build a new well for the county gaol (*PCCR* 4:27). In 1790 his household at Duxbury consisted of one man, one boy under 16, and five females (p.172).

Uriah served in the Revolutionary War. He applied for a pension 21 August 1832, stating that he was born in Duxbury in 1747 and had always lived there

(White, 3:3279 citing #S30125). In 1840 Uriah Sprague was listed as a pensioner, aged 92 and head of a family.

In his will, dated 24 September 1831, proved in April 1842, Uriah Sprague of Duxbury named his son Eden, daughters Alathea Sprague, Lurana Freeman wife of Weston Freeman, and Lydia Sprague, and mentioned children [not named] of late daughter Betsey Smith wife of Jacob Smith (Plymouth PR 84:203; file #19125). He appointed no executor, and administration was given to his daughter Lydia Sprague (*ibid.*, 10A:519).

Children of Uriah and Lydia (Samson) Sprague, births not recorded, named in father's will (dates from Winsor, 320; *Giles Mem.*, 395):

i   EDEN SPRAGUE[6], b. 12 April 1770; living 1842 when named in father's will; prob. m. at Boston, 6 Nov. 1792 by Rev. Samuel Stillman (*VR* 106), SARAH FOSTER. Winsor in *Duxbury History* (p.320) says he m. Sarah Hinckley, but record not found. *Sprague Family* (p.131) says no children. An Eden Sprague arrived in Philadelphia 29 April 1801 in the brig *George* from St. Bartholomew's (Nat. Arch. 425-2, list 28). Nothing further found.

ii   ALETHEA SPRAGUE, b. 10 April 1772; living unm., in 1850 in the household of her sister Laurana Freeman at Duxbury.

iii LYDIA SPRAGUE, b. 17 April 1776; d. 12 Oct. 1843, unm., of typhoid fever; bur. Duxbury with parents (*VR* 426). She was administratrix of her father's will in 1842. In her own will, dated 13 Sept. 1843, proved 4 Dec. 1843, Lydia Sprague of Duxbury left to her sister Laurana wife of Weston Freeman, the dwelling house and homestead farm "on which I now live, it being the same bequeathed to me by my late father Uriah Sprague, deceased," after Laurana's death to go to her three sons, Weston Jr., Enoch, and Joshua S. Freeman; to sister Alathea Sprague a featherbed and bedstead belonging to their father, after her death to go to Enoch Freeman; to sister Laurana the looking glass in the southeast parlor, after her death to go to niece Betsey S. Foster, wife of Bradford Foster of Kingston; other household furniture and personal things to nephew Weston Freeman Jr. and nieces Abigail Farrington wife of David, Ruth T. Freeman, Lydia Ring wife of Samuel, and Martha Stetson wife of Samuel; nephew Joshua S. Freeman was to have her silver watch (Plymouth PR #19078, 85:543).

iv   LAURANA SPRAGUE, b. 18 May 1780; m. at Duxbury 26 Jan. 1803 (*VR* 315), WESTON FREEMAN, b. Duxbury 6 Feb. 1777, son of Enoch and Abigail (Weston) Freeman (*VR* 81, 255). In 1850 he was a housewright at Duxbury with Lurany ae 70 and her sister Alethea Sprague ae 78 (p.62). No d. recs. for them found in Mass. VR.

Freeman children rec. Duxbury (VR 78-81): 1. *Lydia Freeman*[7], b. 31 March 1805; m. Samuel Ring. 2. *Ellis Freeman*, b. 13 Aug. 1806. 3. *Weston Freeman Jr.*, b. 7 June 1808. 4. *Mary Cooper Freeman*, b. 20 Jan. 1810. 5. *Abigail Freeman*, b. 9 Nov. 1811; m. David Farrington. 6. *Betsey Sprague Freeman*, b. 7 March 1814; m. Bradford Foster. 7. *[Child] Freeman*, d. 26 Nov. 1816. 8. *Enoch Freeman*, b. 9 Oct. 1818. 9. *Joshua Soule Freeman*, b. 11 Jan. 1821; m. Hannah Gray Hunt [#790-ii-6]. 10. *Ruth F. or T. Freeman*, b. 25 Feb. 1823.

v JOSHUA SPRAGUE, b. 17 May 1783; d. 9 Feb. 1807 at sea, ae 25; on cem. stone with parents (VR 426).

vi BETSEY SPRAGUE, b. 28 Aug. 1788; d. 11 May 1814 ae 25 (VR 419); m. 26 May 1805, JACOB SMITH, b. at Duxbury 11 March 1780, son of Benjamin and Sarah (____) Smith, d. 3 July 1844, ae 64, at Marshfield, a mariner (VR 158, 419). He m. (2) 14 or 16 Dec. 1816, Deborah Cushman.

Smith children, rec. Duxbury (VR 157, 158): 1. *[child] Smith*[7], b. Dec. 1806; d. 11 Jan. 1807 ae 1m (VR 419). 2. *Caroline Smith*, b. 2 Sept. 1808. 3. *Martha Smith*, b. 9 Aug. 1810; m. Samuel Stetson. 4. *Jacob Smith Jr.*, b. 11 Sept. 1812.

Sources cited: *Boston Marriages* [BRC 30]. *Duxbury VR.* Plymouth County Deeds and Probate Records. White, *Abstracts of Rev. War Pension Files.* Passenger and Immigration Lists, National Archives, index on line. *Giles Memorial* (1864). Winsor, *History of Duxbury* (1849). CENSUS: Duxbury, Plymouth Co., 1790 (M637-4), 1850 (M432-333). **See also:** *Sprague Genealogy* (1849).

782.   JOSHUA[5] **SAMSON** (*Amos*[4], *Joshua*[3], *Caleb*[2], *Henry*[1]), son of Amos Samson [161] and his wife Deborah Samson, was born about 1750 and baptized with his siblings at Duxbury 16 September 1759 (VR 146). He lived at Braintree and died at Weymouth at the home of his son Isaac (*Giles Mem.*, 415), 9 April 1834 aged 85 (Sprague #4138, citing CR). He was a descendant also of *Mayflower* passengers John Alden and Myles Standish.

He was of Duxbury when he married, first, at Braintree 2 April 1773 (VR 877), **RACHEL FRENCH**, who was born at Braintree 19 April 1753, daughter of Gideon and Elizabeth (Thayer) French, and died 23 June 1787 aged 34 (VR 804; Sprague). The will of Gideon French [Jr.], dated 19 May 1832, filed 7 December 1841, names among others his deceased sister Rachel Sampson (Norfolk PR #7396; 74:181). Another sister, Joanna French, married Joshua's brother Amos Samson [#784].

Joshua married, second, in Boston 26 May 1790 (VR 30:105) after intentions at Braintree 29 April (VR 862), **SUSANNA PARKHURST** (*Parkis* in record) of Boston, who was born at Waltham 14 May 1770, daughter of Isaac and Sarah (Corey) Parkhurst (VR 69), and died at Braintree 3 November 1821 (Sprague).

Joshua served in the Revolutionary War from Braintree as one of the "Eight months' men" (*Giles Mem.*, 415). He enlisted first as a private in Capt. Silas Wild's company, 36th regiment, from 28 April to 1 June 1775, then as a corporal in Maj. Thomas Pierce's company, Col. Richard Gridley's (artillery) regiment, and his name is on various muster rolls and returns through the end of 1775 (*MSSR* 13:760, 772).

John Adams Vinton in *The Giles Memorial* (p.415) wrote of Joshua,

> ... [he] removed, early in life, from Duxbury to Braintree, where he exercised the trade of a shipwright, in company with Lieut. Daniel Loring ... they built vessels at the Iron-Works Landing in East Braintree, at the head of tide-water on Monatiquot River, at the place where the South Shore Railroad now [1863] crosses that river. The compiler remembers him as living in that vicinity, more than fifty years ago.

Joshua Samson was chosen one of three surveyors of lumber for the town of Braintree at town meetings in March 1780, 1781, 1785, 1787, and 1788; in 1789 and 1790 as one of three "cullers of staves" (*Braintree TRs*, 506, 519, 554, 571, 579, 585, 592). In April 1790 at the town meeting it was voted "to choose a Committee of six who shall have power to limit the time for catching the herrens [herrings] and cause passage ways to be opened for them," and Mr. Joshua Samson was the first of the six chosen for that committee (*ibid.*, 595). In 1792 he was both a surveyor of lumber and a surveyor of highways (*ibid.*, 613, 614).

Joseph (surely an error for Joshua) Sampson was living at Braintree in 1790 with two boys under 16 and two females (*Heads of Fam.,*195). In 1793 he "bought a place on Commercial St. E. side of Josiah Vinton, opposite his house at top of hill ... torn down before 1856" (Sprague). Joshua Sampson of Braintree, gentleman, sold one-half a house there on 14 November 1793, and Susanna also signed the deed; they signed another deed together on 8 March 1799 (Norfolk LR 1:47; 8:203). Joshua Sampson of Braintree, shipwright, sold land on 30 July 1801 (*ibid.*, 15:228).

In his application for a pension on 3 April 1818 Joshua Sampson was of Braintree, aged 69. On 19 July 1820, still of Braintree, he was 70, a shipwright, and stated that he had a wife to maintain. Joshua appointed Zephanaiah Sampson attorney to receive his pay, attesting 11 March 1834 that he was of Weymouth, where he had been for the past two years. On 14 April 1834 Zephaniah made oath that no sale, transfer or mortgage of the pension had occurred, but no death date was given for Joshua (Rev. pension file #S33632).

No Middlesex County probate records or deeds were found for Isaac or Sarah Parkhurst, nor any deeds for Joshua or Susanna Samson, Gideon or Elizabeth French, or Isaac or Sarah Parkhurst. No Norfolk County probate records were found for Joshua or Susanna Sampson.

Children of Joshua and Rachel (French) Sampson, b. Braintree (*VR* as noted; also Sprague 4139):

i RACHEL[6] SAMPSON, b. 3 Sept. 1774 (*VR* 839); d. 6 Nov. 1856, unm.; bur. Elm St. Cem. (Sprague). *Giles Memorial* includes a vivid description of her, noting her "uncommonly retentive memory ... [she] possessed extensive information of persons, families and facts ... In genealogy, and dates, she was without a rival, at least in the old town of Braintree. ... A tailoress by trade, she was employed in that capacity by many of the first families of Braintree and Quincy ..."

ii JOSHUA SAMPSON, b. 1 March 1776 (*VR* 839); d. South Boston 29 Dec. 1834; bur. Elm St. Cem. (Sprague, #4140), a ship-carpenter (*Giles Mem.* 443); m. 11 Sept. 1797 LUCY HOLBROOK, b. 20 May 1778, d. 2 June 1865, dau. James and Rhoda (Vinton) Holbrook (Mass. VR 184:223); living 1850 with family of dau. Mary Lincoln in Quincy (p.241).

   Children, b. Braintree (first three, *VR* 859-60; all Sprague, #4140): 1. *Rachel Sampson*, b. 31 March 1798; m. (1) William Mead, (2) Benjamin V. Mead. 2. *Zephaniah Sampson*, b. 17 Dec. 1799; went to sea at ae 21. 3. *Joshua Sampson*, b. 14 Nov. 1801; m. Susan Lloyd (*Cambridge VR* 619-20). 4. *Ruth Holbrook Sampson*, b. 25 Nov. 1803; m. Phineas Spear Jr. 5. *Lucy Sampson*, b. 9 April 1806; m. (1) Martin Winch, (2) ___ Clay. 6. *Hannah Pearson Hayward Sampson*, b. 17 Feb. 1809; m. ___ Perkins. 7. *Mary Sampson*, b. 9 Sept. 1810; m. (1) Samuel Packard, (2) William Lincoln. 8. *Susan Sampson*, b. 15 March 1814; m. Oliver Harris. 9. *Elias Holbrook Sampson*, b. 18 Feb. 1816. 10. *Albert Sampson*, b. 24 Jan. 1819; m. Leora Barker. 11. *William Henry Sampson*, b. 17 Sept. 1823; m. Anna Blanchard. (See *Giles Mem.* for further information.)

iii ZEPHANIAH SAMPSON, b. 20 Nov. 1777 (*VR* 840); d. Oct. 1858; res. Charter St., Boston, a mason and held city office; m. at Trinity Church, Boston, 4 Dec. 1803 (*CR* 755), ELIZABETH CROSBY, dau. Daniel Crosby; m. (2) Charlestown, 30 June 1833 (*VR* 1:330), his cousin RACHEL FRENCH SAMPSON [#784-v], dau. of Amos Sampson of Charlestown (*Giles Mem.*, 443-44).

   Children with first wife: 1. *Daniel Crosby[7] Sampson*, b. 23 May, bp. Trinity Church 28 Dec. 1804 (*CR* 676). 2. *Elizabeth Godfrey Sampson*, b. 31 March 1806. 3. *Nancy Crosby Sampson*, b. Jan. 1807; d.y. 4. *Henry Sampson*, b. 19 June 1809. 5. *George Robinson Sampson*, b. 3 May 1811. 6. *Ann Rachel Sampson*, b. 7 June 1813. (See *Giles Mem.* for further information.)

iv ELIZABETH THAYER SAMSON, b. 9 Nov. 1780; d. Braintree 9 Aug. 1787 (*VR* 841).

v GIDEON SAMSON, bp. 1783 (Sprague); died young.

Children of Joshua and Susanna (Parkhurst) Samson, b. Braintree (*VR* 856-57):

vi ELIZABETH SAMPSON, b. 15 Dec. 1791; d. Weymouth, 18 Aug. 1816, as Betsey (*VR* 2:335).

vii ISAAC PARKS SAMPSON, b. 12 Dec. 1794; d. Weymouth 1 Aug. 1854 (Mass. VR 85:189); of Braintree when he m. (1) at Weymouth 1 May 1816 (*VR* 2:168), LUCY B. TIRRELL, dau. of Noah Tirrell of Weymouth (*Giles Mem.*, 415); m. (2) after int. Marshfield 13 Aug. 1843 (*VR* 308), HANNAH WILLIAMSON, b. Marshfield 28 July 1807, dau. of Nathan and Hannah (Ewell) Williamson (*VR* 182, 121), d. Weymouth 15 May 1866, lung fever (Mass. VR 193:289). In 1850 he was a shoemaker at Marshfield ae 55, with Hannah ae 36, their daus. Hannah L. and Bertha, and Franklin Williamson ae 16 (p.154).

    Children with first wife, Lucy, rec. Weymouth (*VR* 1:265): 1. & 2. [*Twins*][7] *Sampson*, b. and d. Jan. 1817. 3. *Harrison F. Sampson*, b. 8 Aug. 1818; drowned 14 June 1824 ae 6y (*VR* 2:335). 4. *Lucy B. Sampson*, b. 5 March 1822; m. William Holbrook. 5. *Elizabeth/Eliza G. Sampson*, b. 16 Nov. 1824; m. James Edmundson. 6. *Harrison Sampson*, b. 18 Oct. 1826. Children with second wife, Hannah: 7. *Hannah Lucilla Sampson*, b. 23 Nov. 1846, Weymouth (*VR* 1:265). 8. *Bertha Sampson*, b. Marshfield 13 Aug. 1849 (*VR* 328).

viii GIDEON FRENCH SAMPSON, b. 15 Oct. 1797 (*VR* 857); res. Weymouth 1862; m. (1) Weymouth, 31 Aug. 1820 (*VR* 2:167), ELIZABETH (TORREY) FENNO, d. Weymouth 4 Jan. 1849 ae 58 of carditis (*VR* 2:335), dau. of Joshua and Sarah (___) Torrey and widow of Oliver Fenno; m. (2) after int. 20 May 1849 Weymouth (*VR* 2:167), ELIZA (HUSSEY) STARBUCK of Quincy. In 1850 Gideon F. Sampson ae 52 was a farmer in Weymouth, with Eliza ae 45, sons Edwin, George, and Albert (all shoemakers), and George Starbuck ae 13, prob. Eliza's son.

    Children with first wife, two rec. Weymouth from g.s. (*VR* 1:265); at home 1850: 1. *Edwin[7] Sampson*, b. Nov. 1822. 2. *George Sampson*, b. ca 1824. 3. *Albert Sampson*, b. July 1828.

ix SUSANNA SAMSON, b. 11 Dec. 1801 (*VR* 857); res. Abington in 1862; m. (1) at Weymouth, 20 May 1822 (*VR* 2:168), she of Braintree, JOSEPH F. PRATT; m. (2) ___ RIPLEY.

Sources cited: *Charlestown VR. Duxbury VR. Marshfield VR. Waltham VR. Weymouth VR. The Records of Trinity Church, Boston 1728–1830*, Vol. 2, Colonial Society of Mass., 56 (1982). *Giles Memorial* (1864). Sprague, "Braintree Families," ms NEHGS (numbers refer to cards). Rev. Pension file #S33632. CENSUS: *Heads of Families 1790 – Mass.*; 1850 Marshfield, Plymouth Co. (M432-332).

783. **LAURANA⁵ SAMSON** (*Amos⁴, Joshua³, Caleb², Henry¹*), daughter of Amos Samson [161] and his wife Deborah Samson, was born probably about 1752 and baptized at Duxbury with her siblings 16 September 1759 as "Lurany, child of Amos" (*VR* 146). She was a descendant also of *Mayflower* passengers John Alden and Myles Standish (*Philip Delano*, 83).

She married at Duxbury, 20 January 1774 (*VR* 299, as "Irene"), **LUTHER DELANO**, son of Ebenezer and Lydia (Delano) (Wormall) Delano and also a Henry Samson descendant. See **Family #408** (*MF 20* [*Henry Samson*]: pt. 2:369) for information about this family.

784. **AMOS⁵ SAMSON** (*Amos⁴, Joshua³, Caleb², Henry¹*), son of Amos Samson [161] and his wife Deborah Samson, was born 24 September 1756 (*Charlestown VR* 1:150) and baptized with his siblings at Duxbury 16 September 1759 (*VR* 144). He died at Charlestown 3 August 1843 aged 87, a Revolutionary pensioner, of "old age" (Mass. VR 9:16). He was a descendant also of *Mayflower* passengers John Alden and Myles Standish.

He married at Braintree, 11 May 1783 (*VR* 868), **JOANNA FRENCH**, who was born there 11 August 1758, daughter of Gideon and Elizabeth (Thayer) French, and died at Charlestown 10 or 13 January 1847 aged 88 years, widowed, of "decline" (*VR* 2:872; Mass. VR 27:20). The will of Gideon French [Jr.] of Quincy, dated 19 May 1832, filed 7 December 1841, names his sister Joanna Sampson of Charlestown (Norfolk PR #7396; 74:181). Another sister, Rachel, married Amos's brother Joshua Samson [#782]. The birth dates of Amos and Joanna are recorded at Charlestown with those of their children (*VR* 1:150).

Amos Samson of Duxbury served in the Revolutionary War as a private in Capt. Samuel Bradford's company, Col. Theophilus Cotton's regiment, from 8 May 1775 until the end of October 1775. He was among men raised to serve in the Continental Army from 1st Duxbury company, Col. Cotton's regiment, joining Capt. Joseph Wadsworth's company, Col. Gamaliel Bradford's regiment, 9 September 1777 for 8 months; and was in the same regiment at Valley Forge, 28 January 1778 (*MSSR* 13:765).

Amos Sampson owned the covenant at the Brattle Street Church in Boston 5 June 1785 and his daughter Joanna was baptized the same day (*CR* 192). In 1790 he was living in Charlestown with one boy under 16 and three females (p.137). He was the first sexton of Harvard Church there, 1816 to 1820.

Amos's pension records give his age as 70 on 22 August 1832. On 15 August 1843 Mrs. Joanna Sampson of Charlestown, aged 85, attested that she was widow of Amos, a native of Duxbury, private in the Revolution; that she married him in

Braintree 13 May 1783 (although the town clerk cited a record of marriage 11 May); and that he died on 3 August 1843. Middlesex Probate records (#26247 under date 12 June 1847) show that Joanna Sampson, widow of Amos, was a pensioner; she died in Charlestown 10 January 1847 leaving six children living: Joanna Frothingham, Amos Sampson, Betsy Putnam, Rachel Sampson, Gideon Sampson, and Ebenezer Sampson.

Appraisers were appointed 27 April 1847 on the estate of Amos Sampson, late of Charlestown, and Isaac Frothingham was appointed administrator the same day, with the approval of the heirs: Amos Sampson, Betsy Putnam, Joanna Frothingham, Rachel F. Sampson, Gideon Sampson, Ebenr. Sampson, and Joseph L. Bates, guardian of three children of the late George A. Sampson.

Children of Amos and Joanna (French) Sampson, rec. in group in Charlestown (*VR* 1:150); information not otherwise cited from *Giles Memorial*:

i   AMOS⁶ SAMPSON, b. 24 Feb. 1784; d. 6 April 1784 (*Charlestown VR* 1:301).

ii   JOANNA SAMPSON, b. 13 May 1785; bp. Brattle St. Church 5 June 1785 (*CR* 192); res. Charlestown 1863; m. at Charlestown, 4 June 1806, after int. there 11 May 1806 (*VR* 1:348, 523), ISAAC CALL FROTHINGHAM, b. Charlestown 31 Dec. 1787, son of Richard and Mary (Kettell) Frothingham (*VR* 1:65), d. 20 Sept. 1853 (*Giles Mem.*, 444).

     Frothingham children (first four rec. *Charlestown VR* 1:67): 1. *Mary Ann Frothingham*, b. 17 Sept. 1806. 2. *George Odin Frothingham*, b. 6 Aug. 1808. 3. *Elizabeth Thayer Frothingham*, b. 7 Aug. 1810. 4. *Nathaniel Francis Frothingham*, b. 4 Nov. 1813. 5. *Sarah Kettell Frothingham*, b. 9 Feb. 1817. 6. *Rachel Sampson Frothingham*, b. 31 March 1821. 7. *Maria Sargent Frothingham*, b. 28 Oct. 1826. (See *Giles Memorial*, 444, for further information.)

iii AMOS SAMPSON, b. 19 May 1787; d. Charlestown 29 Sept. 1867 of consumption (Mass. VR 203:112); m. 6 Dec. 1812, ANN MATILDA SMITH, dau. of Isaac and Rebecca (___) Smith of Taunton, d. 1 Jan. 1855 ae 66 (*Giles Mem.*, 444-45). He apprenticed at the *Columbian Centinel* and later worked for the publishers of the *Boston Gazette*. In 1850 he was a printer in Boston living with Ann ae 60 and the two youngest children (p.262).

     Children: 1. *Joanna⁷ Sampson*, b. 30 Oct. 1814. 2. *William Henry Allen Sampson*, b. 6 Aug. 1816. 3. *Charles Augustus Ludlow Sampson*, b. 12 June 1824; at home, a "carver" in 1850. 4. *Mary Elizabeth Sampson*, b. 10 Oct. 1826 [?1822 - ae 28 in 1850]. (See *Giles Memorial*, 444-45, for further information.)

iv   BETSY THAYER SAMPSON, b. 15 Oct. 1789; res. Charlestown 1863; m. in Danvers, after int. Charlestown 1 Dec. 1811 (*VR* 1:537), GILBERT PUTNAM, who d. 5 Oct. 1820 ae 35.

Putnam children, last three b. Malden: 1. *Betsey Putnam[7]*, b. Danvers, 13 June 1813. 2. *Rachel Sampson Putnam*, b. 24 Oct. 1815. 3. *Joanna Sampson Putnam*, b. 28 May 1817. 4. *George Sampson Putnam*, b. 20 April 1819. (See *Giles Memorial*, 445, for further information.)

v RACHEL FRENCH SAMPSON, b. 29 Aug. 1791; m. as his second wife, her cousin ZEPHANIAH SAMPSON [#783-iii], *q.v.*

vi GIDEON SAMPSON, b. 5 Jan. 1794; living 1847.

vii DEBORAH SAMPSON, b. 27 Jan. 1796; d. 18 July 1833, unm.

viii EBENEZER SAMPSON, b. 21 Jan. 1798; m. (1) in Boston, 7 July 1822, HARRIET HOWE, d. Charlestown 25 May 1841, "Ebenezer Samson's wife, ae 35½ yrs, of fever" (*VR* 1:279; Mass. VR 1:50); m. (2) in Boston, 9 Oct. 1842 after int. 10 Sept. 1842 Charlestown (*VR* 1:677), SARAH HOWE, sister of his first wife. He res. Charlestown in 1863, a wheelwright and later messenger of the Eagle Bank.

Children with first wife; first five b. in Boston, last two in Charlestown: 1. *Harriet Maria[7] Samson*, b. 24 Sept. 1823. 2. *Sarah Howe Samson*, b. 15 Sept. 1825. 3. *Eben Rhoades Samson*, b. 18 June 1828. 4. *Hannah Howe Samson*, b. 3 Aug. 1830. 5. *Mary Elizabeth Samson*, b. 19 July 1833. 6. *Ellen Samson*, b. 1 April 1837 (*Charlestown VR* 1:164). 7. *William Harrison Samson*, b. 22 May 1841. (See *Giles Memorial*, 445-46, for further information.)

ix GEORGE ADAMS SAMPSON, b. 20 July 1800; d. at Portland, Me., 23 July 1834, ae 34, while traveling to Bangor; m. 10 Oct. 1825 after int. Charlestown 3 Sept. 1825 (*VR* 1:579), MARY LEACH BATES, b. 2 Nov. 1802, dau. of Elihu and Mary (Leach) Bates of Boston, res. Boston 1863.

Children, b. Boston: 1. *George Amos[7] Sampson*, b. 20 Sept. 1826. 2. *Hilman Barnes Sampson*, b. 30 March 1828. 3. *Albert Patterson Sampson*, b. 18 Sept. 1830. (See *Giles Memorial*, 446, for further information.)

Sources cited: *Charlestown VR. Duxbury VR. Records of the Church in Brattle Square, Boston 1699–1872* (1902). Middlesex County Probate Records. Norfolk County Probate Records at Dedham. *Giles Memorial* (1864). CENSUS: 1790 Charlestown, Middlesex Co. (M637-4); 1850 Ward 3, Boston, Suffolk Co. (M432-334) & Weymouth, Norfolk Co. (M432-329).

785. ELIJAH[5] SAMSON (*Amos[4], Joshua[3], Caleb[2], Henry[1]*), son of Amos Samson [161] and his wife Deborah Samson, was born at Duxbury 25 October 1757 (*Giles Mem.*, 416) and baptized with his siblings at Duxbury 16 September 1759 (*VR* 145). He died at Duxbury 21 August 1834 (pension rec., final payment). He was a descendant also of *Mayflower* passengers John Alden and Myles Standish.

He married, first, at Duxbury 12 December 1782 (*VR* 298), **HANNAH SPRAGUE**, who was born 19 May 1764 and died at Duxbury 11 or 23 September

1817 (*VR* 413; *Giles Mem.*, 416), daughter of Samuel Sprague Jr. and his wife Sarah Oldham, a Henry Samson descendant [#206].

He married, second, at Scituate 29 October 1818, **HANNAH (FORD) WRIGHT**, who was born at Marshfield 23 April 1756, daughter of Elijah and Eleanor (Thomas) Ford (*VR* 72, 162), and was living at Duxbury 18 September 1834 when her husband made his will. She married, first, at Marshfield 8 November 1781 (*VR* 175), JESSE WRIGHT. The will of Elijah Ford of Marshfield, dated 14 October 1792, presented 17 December 1792, names wife Eleanor and daughter Hannah, wife of Jesse Wright (Plymouth PR 33:234).

Elijah served in the Revolutionary War. He was a private in Capt. Samuel Bradford's (1st Duxbury) company of militia, Col. Warren's (Plymouth Co.) regiment, which marched on the alarm of 19 April 1775; in the same company in Col. Theophilus Cotton's regiment during several months later in 1775; and in Capt. Bildad Arnold's company, Col. Thomas Lothrop's (Plymouth Co.) regiment, which marched to Rhode Island on the alarm of 10 December 1776 (*MSSR* 13:768). Vinton (*Giles Memorial*, 416) says that Elijah was in a company of 100 men, under Capt. Andrew Sampson, stationed in the fort at the Gurnet for the defence of Plymouth Harbor from 19 June 1776 until the end of the summer of 1777, and also mentions the march to Rhode Island in December 1776.

In 1790 Elijah Samson Jr. was living in Duxbury with two boys under 16 and two females (*Heads of Fam.*, 169). His household in Duxbury in 1810 consisted of one boy 10-16, and one man and one woman 45 or older (p.231). In his application for a pension Elijah gave his age on 21 August 1832 as 77, and said that he was born at Duxbury and had always lived there. The final payment indicated that he died 21 August 1834.

In his will dated 1 January 1825, presented 25 November 1834, Elijah Sampson of Duxbury left to wife Hannah $200 and the furniture she had brought with her; he named his sons Martin, Thomas, and Eden; mentioned four children left by his daughter Hannah Ventress; and named son Martin executor (Plymouth PR #17506). Elijah is called a cordwainer in estate papers; *Giles Memorial* (p.416) calls him a shoemaker.

Children of Elijah and Hannah (Sprague) Sampson, b. Duxbury:

   i   MARTIN[6] SAMPSON, b. 10 Oct. 1783 (*VR* 141); m. (1) Duxbury, 12 Nov. 1807 (*VR* 300), SARAH FREEMAN, dau. Enoch and Sarah (___) Freeman, d. Duxbury July 1813 (*VR* 411); m. (2) SARAH SMITH.
        Children, first three with first wife, rec. Duxbury (*VR* 139, 141, 142): 1. *Hannah[7] Sampson*, b. 17 June 1808. 2. *Martin Sampson Jr.*, b. 4 Sept. 1810; d. 21

May 1834 "on passage to Amsterdam" (*VR* 411). 3. *Sarah F. Sampson*, b. 1 March 1813. 4. *William S. Sampson*, b. 29 March 1818.

ii THOMAS SAMPSON, b. 27 Feb. 1786 (*VR* 143); d. Duxbury 7 July 1840 of consumption (*VR* 412); m. at Duxbury, 2 Oct. 1808 (*VR* 302), POLLY THOMAS, b. Braintree 17 April 1791, rec. Duxbury (*VR* 141).

Children rec. Duxbury (*VR* 138-43*)*: 1. *Thomas⁷ Sampson Jr.*, b. 30 Jan. 1808 [*sic*]. 2. *Mary Sampson*, b. 25 April 1811; m. George Loudon. 3. *Catherine Sampson*, b. 24 March 1814. 4. *Martha Sampson*, b. 10 Sept. 1817. 5. *George A. Sampson*, b. 26 or 28 April 1820. 6. *Elijah Sampson*, b. 29 or 30 April 1823. 7. *James P. Sampson*, b. 2 July 1826. 8. *Elizabeth Sampson*, b. 18 Nov. 1832.

iii HANNAH SAMPSON, b. 23 July 1788 (not in*VR*); d. by 1821; m. at Duxbury, 25 Sept. 1808 (*VR* 323), MOSES VENTRESS. He m. (2) Pembroke, 15 July 1821 (*VR* 369), Deborah Keith.

Ventress children rec. Duxbury (*VR* 179): 1. [*Child*] *Ventress⁷*, d. Duxbury 6 May 1810. 2. *Magnus Ventress⁷*, b. 7 Oct. 1811. 3. *Betsey Smith Ventress*, b. 29 June 1813. 4. *Hannah Sprague Ventress*, b. 20 Nov. 1815. 5. [*Child*] *Ventress*, mentioned in grandfather's will 1825.

iv EDEN SPRAGUE SAMPSON, b. 11 Dec. 1797 (*VR* 138); d. Duxbury 5 March 1882, a mechanic, of nephritis (Mass. VR 338:303); m. at Duxbury, 3 Dec. 1818 (*VR* 298), POLLY SAMPSON, b. 8 Nov. 1799 rec. Duxbury as w. Eden S. (*VR*, 141), d. Duxbury 3 Nov. 1878 ae 79, dau. of Nathaniel and Hannah (Ames) Sampson (Mass. VR 302:270).

Children rec. Duxbury (*VR* 138, 140, 142-43): 1. *Eden⁷ Sampson*, b. 24 Aug. 1819; d. 2 Oct. 1819 (*VR* 409). 2. *Eden Sampson*, b. 30 June 1820. 3. *Eden Sampson 2d*, b. 5 July 1822. 4. *Caroline Sampson*, b. 13 Aug. 1823. 5. *Jane T. Sampson*, evidently a twin, b. 14 Aug. 1824 [*sic*]. 6. *Seneca Sampson*, evidently a twin, b. 16 Aug. 1824 [*sic*]. 7. *Jane Frost Sampson*, b. 7 Sept. 1826; m. John Glover. 8. [*Twin Daughter*] *Sampson*, b. 2 Nov. 1828; d. — Nov. 1828 (*VR* 413). 9. [*Twin Daughter*] *Sampson*, stillborn 2 Nov. 1828 (*VR* 413). 10. *Ellen Maria Sampson*, b. 22 May 1833.

Sources cited: Duxbury VR. Marshfield VR. Plymouth County Probate Records. *Giles Memorial* (1864) overstates Elijah's age at death (ae. 86y 9m 26d) by ten years. *Heads of Families 1790 – Mass.* CENSUS: 1810 Duxbury, Plymouth Co. (M252-21). Revolutionary War Pension File #S30078 & Final Payment (Elijah Sampson). **See also:** Weyman Manuscript, NEHGS.

786. STUDLEY⁵ SAMPSON (*Amos⁴, Joshua³, Caleb², Henry¹*), son of Amos Samson [161] and his wife Deborah Samson, was born at Duxbury 27 April 1759 (*VR* 142), and died there 9 March 1835, "A soldier of the Revolution" (*VR* 412). He was a descendant also of *Mayflower* passengers John Alden and Myles Standish.

He married, first, at Duxbury, 16 November 1780 (*VR* 302), **ABIGAIL PRIOR**, who was born there 20 July 1753, daughter of Jabez and Abigail (Samson) Prior (*VR* 128) and died there 3 or 23 February 1824 in her 71st year (*VR* 408). Studley Sampson and his first wife are buried in the Large Cemetery, Duxbury, with some of their children.

He married, second, at Duxbury, 7 May 1825 (*Duxbury Hist.*, 304; *VR* 302), **HANNAH (HOSEA) CHURCHILL**. She was born at Plymouth in March 1772 (calc.), daughter of Daniel and Hannah (Bartlett) Hosea, and baptized there 13 August 1780 with her brother William as "grandchildren of Dea. Bartlett and wife" (*CR* 463). She died at Brookline 26 November 1848 aged 76y 8m 14d, "widow of Studley Sampson and mother of William Churchill" (Mass. VR 41:9). She married, first, after intentions at Plymouth 14 May 1791 (*VR* 278), Peleg Churchill, who died at Duxbury 15 November 1810 in his 42nd year (VR 363); they had children: Peleg, Otis, Ezra, Harriet, Eliza, and William Churchill.

Studley Sam[p]son served in the Revolutionary War, in the "Eight Months' service" in 1775 and also in Capt. Calvin Partridge's company of Duxbury men, which marched to Rhode Island in August 1777; he was also a sailor on board the brigantine *Dolphin*, described 25 May 1780 as of Duxbury, aged 22, 5 ft. 5 in. tall, of dark complexion (*MSSR* 13:775, 763; *Giles Mem.*, 416). In 1790 he was living at Duxbury with two boys under 16 and three females (*Heads of Fam.*, 169).

On 13 October 1799, Abigail Prior, tailoress, of Duxbury gave, for love and affection, a dwelling house in Duxbury to son-in-law Studley Samson and his wife Abigail (Plymouth LR 89:240).

Studley Sampson's application for a pension includes the information that in July 1820 he was a mariner, and his family consisted of himself, aged 61, and four others: wife Abigail aged 67, daughter Deborah Churchill, widow, aged 26, with her daughter Elizabeth aged 14 months, and his granddaughter Abigail Prior Simmons aged 13, whom he had adopted into the family. On 21 August 1832 Studley Sampson was 73, of Duxbury, born there and had always lived there, and had been an inspector in the Plymouth District custom house (pension rec.).

Hannah Sampson, widow, of Duxbury on 13 April 1835 was appointed administratrix of the estate of Studley Sampson late of Duxbury; inventory was presented 18 May 1835 (Plymouth PR 71:310; 77:185).

Children of Studley and Abigail (Prior) Samson, rec. at Duxbury:

i   JABEZ PRIOR[6] SAMPSON, b. 29 July 1781; d. 15 Jan. 1782 (*VR* 139, 410).
ii   DEBORAH SAMPSON, b. 21 Feb. 1783; d. 21 March 1783 (*VR* 138, 413).
iii STUDLEY SAMPSON, b. 10 May 1784; d. 10 Oct. 1809, lost at sea, drowned
     on a passage from Lisbon to Boston, ae 25y 5m (*VR* 142, 412).

iv   GAIUS SAMPSON, b. 26 June 1785 (*VR* 139); d. Boston 9 July 1842; bur.
     Duxbury (*VR* 409); m. at Kingston, 7 Jan. 1808 (*VR* 274), MARY SAMP-
     SON, dau. of Oliver Samson [#787], d. 26 Aug. 1839, ae 51 (*VR* 411).
        Children rec. Duxbury (*VR* 139-41): 1. *George⁷ Sampson*, b. 13 Oct. 1808; m.
     Isabella Soule. 2. *Gaius Sampson*, b. 18 April 1811; d. 5 Oct. 1811. 3. *Marcia
     Sampson*, b. 10 Dec. 1812; d. 7 Jan. 1815, "languished after measles" (*Kingston VR*
     378). 4. *Mary Otis Sampson*, b. 2 June 1815; m. George O. Frothingham. 5. *Gaius
     Sampson*, b. 15 Dec. 1818; m. Sarah Harvey Lowden. 6. *Benjamin Sampson*, b. and
     d. 6 May 1822. 7. *Louisa Williams Sampson*, b. 11 April 1830; m. Charles H.
     Herbert.

v   ABIGAIL SAMPSON, b. 24 Sept. 1787 (*VR* 141); bp. 19 July 1798 (*VR* 137);
     d. Charlestown 17 Jan. 1866 of consumption (Mass. VR 193:303); m. at
     Duxbury, 24 Nov. 1804 (*VR* 300), NOAH SIMMONS, who d. Duxbury in
     August 1821, "h. Nabby," no age given (*VR* 417).
        Simmons children rec. Duxbury of Noah Jr. and Nabby (*VR* 151-52, 155):
     1. *Abigail Prior Simmons⁷*, b. 21 Aug. 1806. 2. *Elvira Simmons*, b. 13 Sept. 1808; m.
     Daniel Titus; res. Charlestown 1863. 3. *Deborah Simmons*, b. 8 Dec. 1810.
     4. *Gershom Simmons*, b. 21 March 1813. 5. *Edwin Simmons*, b. 27 Nov. 1815; d.
     [bef. 1850]. 6. *Augusta Simmons*, b. 18 Sept. 1817. 7. *Sarah Studley Simmons*, b.
     6 Dec. 1819.

vi   ALFRED SAMPSON, b. 12 Feb. 1790 (*VR* 137); m. at Duxbury, 5 May 1816
     (*VR* 296), WEALTHEA JOYCE, b. Duxbury 5 Sept. 1795, dau. of Stephen
     and Lucy (Peterson) Joyce (*VR* 100), d. Duxbury 18 Aug. 1889 ae 93y 11m
     13d (Mass. VR 401:362), Henry Samson descendant #812-i. In 1850 he was
     a mariner in Duxbury with Weltha P. Sampson and all the children (p.64).
        Children rec. Duxbury (*VR* 137-39, 141; *Giles Mem.*, 448): 1. *Alfred Sampson⁷*,
     b. 26 Feb. 1818; unm. 2. *George Frederic Sampson*, b. 6 Aug. 1820; m. Maria
     Richards. 3. *Studley Sampson*; m. Nellie Buckley. 4. *Catharine P[atten] Sampson*, b.
     3 Aug. 1822; m. ___ Lincoln of Bath, Me. 5. *Olive W./Robinson Sampson*, b. 17
     Aug. 1824; unm. 1864. 6. *Maria F[rothingham] Sampson*, b. 18 Feb. 1827; m.
     David Cook. 7. *Mary F[rances] Sampson*, b. 2 Sept. 1831; unm. 1864.

vii DEBORAH SAMPSON, b. 6 Sept. 1793 (*VR* 138); d. Duxbury 24 March
     1854 ae 60y 6m (Mass. VR 85:199); m. at Duxbury, 3 Dec. 1817 (*VR* 235,
     298), STEPHEN CHURCHILL, b. ca 1791, d. 21 May 1820 in his 29th yr,
     son of Stephen and Elizabeth (Gray) Churchill (*VR* 363). In 1820 Deborah
     and her daughter were living with her father (pension rec.). She m. (2) at
     Duxbury, 26 May 1822 (*VR* 268), as his second wife, SAMUEL HUNT
     [#790-ii], *q.v.*, p. 474.
        Churchill child: 1. *Elizabeth Churchill⁷*, b. ca May 1819. ***Hunt*** child:
     2. *Hannah Gray Hunt⁷*, b. 15 March 1823; m. Joshua Soule Freeman.

viii   JOANNA SAMPSON, b. 5 Oct. 1795 (*VR* 140); d. 30 June 1798 (*VR* 410)

.**Sources cited:** *Duxbury VR. Plymouth VR.* Mass. Vital Records 1841-1910. Plymouth County Probate Records. *Mass. Soldiers & Sailors.* Revolutionary War Pension File #S30,082. *Giles Memorial* (1864), varies from the *VR* in some dates. Winsor, *History of Duxbury* (1849). *Philip Delano 2004* confuses Deborah's marriages. CENSUS: *Heads of Families 1790 – Mass.*

787.   OLIVER⁵ SAMSON (*Anthony⁴, Joshua³, Caleb², Henry¹*), son of Anthony Samson [162] and his first wife, Anna Samson, was born 9 September [1754?] (*Kingston VR*, 128, says [1751], from P.R. 23, but 1754 seems a more likely fit with his siblings; see *MF20* Pt. 1:137). He was baptized at Duxbury 7 August 1757 (*VR* 147), and died at Kingston 26 September 1812, aged 59 or 61 (*VR* 378). He was a descendant also of *Mayflower* passengers John Alden and Myles Standish.

He married at Kingston, 21 November 1782 (*VR* 275), **SARAH McLAUGHLIN**, who was born 19 November [1764] (rec. *VR* 128, as "___ (__), w. Oliver, mason and yeoman"), and died at Kingston 1 June 1836, aged 71y 6m, "fell in fire ... widow of Joshua Brewster and formerly widow of Oliver Samson," daughter of John and Jedidah (Samson) McLaughlin (*VR* 324). She married, second, intentions at Kingston in July 1818, JOSHUA BREWSTER. On 6 January 1777 Jedidah McLaughlin of Kingston was appointed guardian of Sarah age 12, and John age 5, minor children of John McLaughlin, deceased (Plymouth PR #13837).

Oliver Samson of Duxbury served as a private in the Revolutionary War in Capt. Samuel Bradford's company, Col. Warren's regiment which marched on the alarm of 19 April 1775, and also two enlistments in 1776 and 1777 in companies stationed at the fort at the Gurnet for defense of Plymouth (*MSSR* 13:773). His brother Thomas evidently served at least one enlistment in place of his brother Oliver (pension rec.; see p. 471).

Oliver is called "mason and yeoman" in birth records of his wife and children. In 1790 he was living at Kingston with one man 16 or over and four females (*Heads of Fam.,* 171).

John McLaughlen of Kingston on 4 January 1813 was appointed administrator of the estate of Oliver Sampson of Kingston, bricklayer, deceased (Plymouth PR 39:386). The widow's portion was set off to Sarah Sampson 15 May 1817, and division was made 27 May 1817 among widow Lucy Peirce, Mary wife of Gaius Sampson, Oliver Sampson, and Sally Sampson (*ibid.,* 49:6, 202).

The "heirs of Oliver Sampson, deceased," received 23 acres plus ¾ acre of woodland in Duxbury in the division of the real estate of their grandfather Anthony Sampson on 12 April 1816 (Plymouth LR 48:33).

Children of Oliver and Sarah (McLaughlin) Sampson, rec. Kingston (*VR* 127-29):

i   LUCY[6] SAMPSON, b. 17 Sept. 1784; d. 5 June 1842, ae 57y 7m 19d; m. (1) CALVIN PEARCE (*Giles Mem.*, 435), who d. before May 1817, and (2) 3 Jan. 1820, SPENCER HOLMES, b. Kingston 13 Jan. 1781, d. 16 June 1846, son of Jedidiah and Sarah (Adams) Holmes (*ibid.*, 219).

        Holmes children: 1. *Lucy Sampson Holmes[7]*, b. 6 June 1821. 2. *Mary A. Holmes*, b. 15 Aug. 1823. 3. *Alphonso Holmes*. (See also *Giles Memorial*, 219.)

ii   MARY / POLLY SAMPSON, b. 27 Oct. 1788; m. GAIUS SAMPSON [#786-iv], *q.v.*, p. 467, for their children and more information.

iii OTIS SAMPSON, b. 4 April 1793; lost at sea in 1811, ae 17 (*VR* 378).

iv GEORGE SAMPSON, b. 18 April 1795; d. 6 July 1798, ae 3y 2m 18d.

v   SALLY SAMPSON, b. 9 June 1799; d. Marshfield 2 May 1900 ae 100y 10m 23d (Mass. VR 506:216); m. at Kingston 18 April 1818 (*VR* 274) OTIS BAKER, b. Duxbury 4 Aug. 1794, son of Edward D. and Olive (___) Baker (*VR* 22), d. Marshfield 18 June 1868 (Mass. VR 212:316). In 1850 he was a farmer in Marshfield with Sally ae 50, son Otis Jr. and his family, and ch. Henry A., Ann M., and Sally (p.156).

        Baker children rec. Duxbury (*VR* 21-22, 349): 1. *Otis Baker Jr.[7]*, b. 11 Jan. 1819; a shipmaster 1850; m. Mary A. ___. 2. *Sally Baker*, b. 28 Oct. 1820; prob. m. 1839 Hiram Winsor. 3. *Edward L. Baker*, b. 27 Feb. 1823; m. Lucy A. Simmons (*VR* 329). 4. *Olive W. Baker*, b. 5 April 1825; d. 12 Sept. 1826. 5. *Horace E. Baker*, b. 27 Oct. 1830. 6. *Henry A. Baker*, b. 27 May 1833; d. 15 Nov. 1833. 7. *Henry A. Baker*, b. 23 Dec. 1835; at home 1850. 8. *Ann M. Baker*, b. 12 March 1837; at home 1850. 9. *Olive W. Baker*, b. 13 June 1839; d. 7 Oct. 1839. 10. *Sally Baker*, b. ca 1843; at home 1850.

vi OLIVER SAMPSON, b. ca 1802 ("rec. after ch. b. June 1799"); m. EMELINE WASHBURN, b. Duxbury 1 Feb. 1806, dau. of Soloman and Hannah (___) Washburn (*VR* 185). In 1850 he was a yeoman at Kingston ae 48 with Emeline ae 44 and Benjamin ae 6 (p.107).

        Child at home 1850: 1. *Benjamin[7] Sampson*, b. ca 1844.

vii ALDEN SAMPSON (*Giles Mem.*, 435), b. ca 1807; prob. the unnamed "son of Oliver" d. Kingston 18 May 1811 ae 4 of quinsy (*VR* 378).

Sources cited: *Duxbury VR. Kingston VR.* Mass. Vital Records 1841-1910. Plymouth County Probate Records. *Mass. Soldiers & Sailors. Giles Memorial* (1864). CENSUS: *Heads of Families 1790 – Mass.;* 1850 Plymouth Co., Marshfield (M432-332) & Kingston (M432-333).

788. **KETURAH[5] SAMSON** (*Anthony[4], Joshua[3], Caleb[2], Henry[1]*), daughter of Anthony Samson [162] and his first wife, Anna Samson, was baptized at Duxbury 16 July 1758 (*VR* 146). She is probably the "Widow of John Stevens" who died at

Marshfield "sometime in July 1831" (*CR, MQ* 50:104). She was a descendant also of *Mayflower* passengers John Alden and Myles Standish.

She married at Duxbury, 16 February 1790 (*VR* 303), **JOHN STEVENS** of Marshfield. He was born at Marshfield 14 February 1756, son of John and Eleanor (Jarmin) Stevens (*VR* 109, 141), and died evidently between 1810 and 1820 (census).

In 1790 John Stevens [father or son?] was living in Marshfield with three females (*Heads of Fam.*, 171). In 1800 John Stevens of Marshfield had a household consisting of two boys and two girls under 10, and a man and a woman 26-45 (p.95). Figures for the household of John Stephens in 1810 indicate one man and one woman 45 or older, one young man and one young woman 16-26, and two girls and two boys 10-16 (p.19). In 1820 Katura Stevens was head of the household, over 45 with one man and two women 26-45 and one young woman 16-26 (p.248).

In a distribution of the real estate of Anthony Sampson of Duxbury, deceased, on 12 April 1816, Keturah Stephens received land bordering that of Anna Sampson and of Thomas Phillips (Plymouth LR 48:34-35).

There are no appropriate Plymouth County probate records for Lucy, Keturah, Oliver, or John Stevens.

Children of John and Keturah (Samson) Stevens, rec. Marshfield; census figures suggest several more:

    i   JOHN STEVENS[6], b. at Marshfield 28 Oct. 1790 (*VR* 213).

    ii   OLIVER STEVENS, b. prob. Marshfield 14 Feb. 1795 (*VR* 291); Capt. Oliver Stevens d. 17 Feb. 1844 ae 49, drowned in No. River, Marshfield a mariner (*VR* 357); m. at Marshfield, 9 Jan. 1823 (*VR* 263), DEBORAH JONES, b. 13 Nov. 1801 (*VR* 291), d. Marshfield 1892; bur. Marshfield Hills Cem. (*VR* 383).

        Children rec. Marshfield (*VR* 291): 1. *Hannah T. Stevens[7]*, b. 27 Oct. 1823. 2. *Thomas Stevens*, b. 22 Nov. 1825. 3. *Peleg Stevens*, b. 29 Sept. 1828. 4. *Harriet A. Stevens*, b. 18 Oct. 1831; d. 1862. 5. *John O. Stevens*, b. 29 Oct. 1834; d. 1836. 6. *Ellen P. Stevens*, b. 15 Sept. 1838. 7. *Charles Stevens*, b. 23 July 1841. 8. *Andrew O. Stevens*, b. 28 Sept. 1843.

? iii   *poss.* LUCY STEVENS, b. ca 1808; d. Marshfield 9 June 1831, ae 23y, "dau. of John Stevens" (*VR* 208; CR, *MQ* 50:104). The age doesn't dovetail with census, but note that this is just a month before Keturah died.

Sources cited: *Duxbury VR. Marshfield VR.* "The Second Church of Christ at Marshfield, Mass., The Rev. Elijah Leonard's Record of Deaths, 1789–1834," *Mayflower Quarterly,* 50 [May 1994].

789.   THOMAS⁵ SAMSON (*Anthony⁴, Joshua³, Caleb², Henry¹*), son of Anthony Samson [162] and his first wife, Anna Samson, was born at Duxbury in 1764 and baptized there 10 June 1764 (*VR* 147). He died at Duxbury 7 or 17 February 1834, aged 69 (*VR* 412; pension rec.). He was a descendant also of *Mayflower* passengers John Alden and Myles Standish.

He was of Duxbury when he married at Marshfield, 28 December 1786 (*VR* 176), **LUCY THOMAS JR.** of Marshfield, born there about 1760, daughter of Samuel and Mary (Cushing) Thomas (*Thomas Gen.*, 171). She died at Duxbury 2 January 1840 (*VR* 413), as " — [Sampson], wife of Thomas, mother of Samuel Bradford." The will of Abigail Thomas of Marshfield dated 1802 names granddaughter Sarah Sampson (Plymouth PR 38:147).

Thomas was a private in the Revolutionary War. In his pension application he stated that he served in a company commanded by Andrew Sampson (White, 3006).

In 1790 he was living at Duxbury with one other man 16 or over and four females (*Heads of Fam.*, 169). In 1810 his household in Duxbury consisted of a man and a woman 45 or older, two young women 16-26, and two boys 10-16 (p.231).

Thomas Sampson was administrator of the estate of his father, Anthony Samson of Duxbury, mariner. In a division of Anthony's real estate, made 12 April 1816, Thomas Sampson received a share of the home farm and salt marsh in Common Island (Plymouth PR 48:33-34).

On 7 October 1834 William Freeman of Duxbury was appointed administrator of the estate of Thomas Sampson late of Duxbury, mariner; the whole of the personal estate went to Lucy Sampson, widow of the deceased, on 1 December 1834 (Plymouth PR 71:261; 76:546).

Lucy applied for a pension to commence 4 March 1836 (Rev. pension file #W15301). Information in the file indicates that Thomas died 17 February 1834 in Plymouth County; he was 68 on 21 August 1832; he was of Duxbury when he entered the service, taking the place of his brother Oliver Sampson; he was born at Duxbury in 1764 and had always resided there; and on 28 December 1786 he married Lucy Thomas of Marshfield, who was aged 78 on 16 August 1838. She died 2 January 1840, with final payment in June, leaving three children all living and of age: Clark in Scituate and Anna and Sally in Duxbury.

Children of Thomas and Lucy (Thomas) Sampson, b. prob. South Scituate (not recorded):

i   ANNA/ANNE⁶ SAMPSON, b. 4 Sept. 1789 (*VR* 28, *sub* Bradford); m. at Duxbury (as Anna), 17 March 1815 (*VR* 297), SAMUEL BRADFORD, b. Duxbury 6 March 1786 (*VR* 31).

> ***Bradford*** children rec. Duxbury (*VR* 28, 30-31): 1. *Anne Bradford*[7], b. ca
> 1816, "rec. bef. ch. b. 30 Nov. 1817." 2. *Lucy T Bradford.*, b. 30 Nov. 1817.
> 3. *Lydia A Bradford.*, b. 18 March 1822. 4. *Samuel Bradford Jr.*, b. 1 Feb. 1825.

ii   SALLY SAMPSON, b. ca 1793; m. at Duxbury, 1 Dec. 1812 (*VR* 301),
     THOMAS PETERSON, b. ca 1786, prob. son of Reuben and Abigail
     (Soule) Peterson (*Duxbury History*, 290). In 1850 he was a sailmaker at
     Duxbury, ae 64, with Sally ae 57, dau. Sally, and the family of dau. Sylvia
     Weston (p.71).

> ***Peterson*** children rec. Duxbury (*VR* 118-23): 1. *Henry Peterson*[7], b. 15 July
> 1816; d. 22 June 1841 Liverpool, Eng., in fall from mast of *Oneco* (*VR* 399).
> 2. *William Peterson*, b. 19 Oct. 1820. 3. *Lewis Peterson*, b. 24 Oct. 1822; d. 29 Feb.
> 1823 (*VR* 401). 4. *Sylvia Peterson*, b. 6 Nov. 1824; m. John Weston. 5. *Sally Peter-
> son*, b. 6 Nov. 1826; unm. 1850. 6. *Mary Peterson*, b. 25 Jan. 1829. 7. *Clark Peterson*,
> b. 19 Feb. 1831. 8. *Lewis Peterson*, b. 15 Feb. 1833; d. 13 Aug. 1848 (*VR* 400).

iii THOMAS SAMPSON, b. Oct. 1797; d. Duxbury 29 Oct. or 1 Nov. 1810 ae
     13y 1m 6d (*VR* 413).

iv   CLARK SAMPSON, b. 2 Aug. 1799 (calc.); d. S. Scituate 4 Feb. 1882 ae 82y
     6m 2d (Mass. VR 338:338); m. at Scituate, 23 March 1834 (*VR* 254), LOIS
     STETSON, b. rec. at Scituate as "— 1797" (*VR* 315 *sub* Sampson, from g.s.,
     Church Hill Cem., Norwell), d. S. Scituate 8 Jan. 1864 ae 64, dau. of Abner
     Stetson (Mass. VR 175:344). In 1850 Clark Sampson, a shoemaker ae 51 was
     living in South Scituate with Lois ae 51 and two children (p.82).

> Children at home 1850: 1. *Thomas C.*[7] *Sampson*, b. ca 1835. 2. *Sarah L.*
> *Sampson*, b. ca 1837.

Sources cited: *Duxbury VR. Scituate VR.* Mass. Vital Records 1841-1910. Plymouth County
Probate Records. White, *Abstracts of Rev. Pension Files*, and Pension #W15301. Winsor, *History of
Duxbury* (1849). *Thomas Genealogy* (1980). CENSUS: *Heads of Families 1790 – Mass.*; 1810 Duxbury
(M252-21); 1850 Scituate, Plymouth Co. (M432-332). **See also:** R. M. Sherman, "Descendants of
Nathaniel Sherman of Duxbury," *TAG* 51 (1975), at p. 176.

790.   MARY / MOLLY)[5] SAMPSON (*Sarah*[4], *Joshua*[3], *Caleb*[2], *Henry*[1]), daughter
of Abner Samson and his first wife, Sarah Samson [163], was born at Duxbury 22
March 1750 (*VR* 146), and died there 22 or 28 August 1813 (*VR* 388), aged 63.
She was a descendant also of *Mayflower* passengers John Alden and Myles Standish.

She married at Duxbury, 4 March 1773 (*VR* 267), **LOT HUNT**, born about
1750, who was baptized at Duxbury 9 May 1756 (*VR* 96) and died there 17
October 1822 (*VR* 388), aged 72, "Capt. ... husband of Mary", son of John and
Deborah (Soule) Hunt and a descendant of *Mayflower* passenger George Soule. He
married, second, at Duxbury 22 March 1814 (*VR* 268), ABIGAIL (SAMSON)

HANKS, widow of John Hanks and daughter of Ebenezer and Zerviah (Soule) Samson (*Delano 2004,*150). Lot and Abigail had no children.

Mary is named in the will of her father, dated 11 February 1780, as daughter Mary Hunt (Plymouth PR 25:483).

Lot Hunt of Duxbury served as a private in the Revolutionary War in Capt. Nehemiah Allen's company, Col. Theophilus Cotton's regiment, for 33 days on a secret expedition to Rhode Island in September and October 1777 (*MSSR* 8:529).

In 1790 Lot was living at Duxbury with four boys under 16 and three females (*Heads of Fam.,* 169). In his pension application 10 July 1820 he stated that he was aged 69, a resident of Duxbury, living with wife Abigail, aged 68, grandson Ziba Hunt aged 16, and girl Lucy Joice aged 22 (White, 1771; pension #S32868).

In his will dated 26 May 1815, allowed 21 October 1822, Lot Hunt of Duxbury left to his wife Abigail Hunt the furniture "she brought with her when I married her"; he named his "only son" Samuel Hunt; daughters Sarah Brewster and Jane Prior; and three grandchildren by son Ziba Hunt deceased: Ziba, Henry, and Mary Hunt under 21; son Samuel to be executor (Plymouth PR 56:158). In an account and order of distribution on 19 May 1823, mention is made of Jane Joyce's note against the estate; William Joyce's note; payment to be made to Sarah Brewster, to Jane Joyce late Jane Prior, and heirs of Ziba Hunt (*ibid.,* 57:168).

Duxbury VR record the birth of "Beulah Hunt, grand d. Lot and Mary," on 11 March 1793 (p.95), possibly the same Beulah who died 30 July 1813 "ae 22" (*VR* 387).

Children of Lot and Mary (Samson) Hunt, rec. Duxbury (*VR* 95-97):

i SARAH HUNT[6], b. 28 Nov. 1773; d. Duxbury 10 Feb. 1856 (Mass. VR 103:197); m. at Duxbury 28 Dec. 1802 (*VR* 225), JOSEPH BREWSTER JR., b. 5 Nov. 1777, son of. Zadock and Lois (Brewster) Brewster of New London, Conn. (Weyman Ms), d. Duxbury 12 or 20 Nov. 1846 ae 69y 7d, "h. Sarah" (*VR* 355). In 1850 Sarah Brewster ae 75 was head of a household in Duxbury that included Nathaniel Ellis ae 34, shoemaker, and wife Eunice ae 32 (p.67).

  Brewster children rec. Duxbury (b. *VR* 32-35; d. 355-56); spouses from Weyman Ms: 1. *Eunice Brewster[7],* b. ca March 1804; d. 15 Dec. 1805 ae 1y 9m. 2. *Joseph Brewster,* b. 28 June 1805; m. Almira Baker. 3. [*Samuel*] *Brewster,* b. ca Oct. 1806; d. Jan. 1808 ae 1y 3m. 4. *Nancy Brewster* (twin), b. 21 July 1810; m. James Churchill Ellis. 5. *Sarah Brewster* (twin), b. 21 July 1810; m. Nathaniel Delano 3d. 6. [*Child*] *Brewster,* b. ca April 1812; d. 28 Oct. 1813 ae 1y 6m. 7. *Asaph Brewster,* b. 18 Dec. 1815; m. Lydia Bradford Drew. 8. *Eunice Brewster,* b. 27 Dec. 1818; m. Nathaniel Ellis.

ii SAMUEL HUNT, b. 22 Sept. 1775; bp. 6 Oct. 1776; d. at sea by drowning 26 Dec. 1823 rec. Duxbury (*VR* 388); m. (1) at Duxbury, 31 March 1801 (*VR* 268), HANNAH GRAY, bp. 23 Aug. 1778, dau. of Samuel and Eunice (Delano) Gray (*Philip Delano 2004*, 137), d. Duxbury 27 or 29 Sept. 1818 ae 40 (*VR* 387); m. (2) at Duxbury 26 May 1822 (*VR* 268), DEBORAH (SAMPSON) CHURCHILL, b. 6 Sept. 1793, d. Duxbury 24 March 1854 ae 60y 6m (Mass. VR 85:199), dau. of Studley and Abigail (Prior) Sampson [Samson #786-vii] and widow of Stephen Churchill who d. May 1820. In 1850 Deborah was living in the household of son-in-law Joshua S. Freeman at Duxbury (p.67).

   Children rec. Duxbury; births of two who d. y. rec. without parents, but deaths say of Samuel & Hannah; b. of Hiram and Allan Mellville rec. as of Samuel & *Deborah,* although mother must have been Hannah (*VR* 94-96, marr. 267): 1. *Hannah Hunt*[7], b. 11 Dec. 1802; d. 7 or 9 Sept. 1804 ae 1y 8m 26d (*VR* 388). 2. *Samuel Hunt,* b. 1 Nov. 1804; d. 17 June 1806 ae 1y 7m 17d (*ibid.*). 3. *Hiram Hunt,* b. 13 Oct. 1806; m. Hannah Cushing Sampson. 4. *Allan Mellville Hunt,* b. 24 Nov. 1808; m. Caroline Wadsworth. 5. *Edward Gray Hunt,* b. 15 or 18 March 1818; m. (1) Lucia W. Prior, (2) Emma Prior. Child with Deborah: 6. *Hannah Gray Hunt,* b. 15 March 1823; m. Joshua Soule Freeman [#781-iv-9].

iii ASA HUNT, b. 21 March 1778; d. Duxbury 10 Dec. 1806 ae 28y 8m 17d (*VR* 387); m. at Duxbury, 8 Dec. 1801 (*VR* 267), ABIGAIL SOULE, dau. of James and Abigail (Sever) Soule [see #797-v].

iv ZIBA HUNT, b. 26 July 1780; d. at Duxbury 26 Aug. 1809 ae 29y 1m; m. at Duxbury, 10 Oct. 1802 (*VR* 268), SYLVIA WADSWORTH [#824-iii], dau. of Wait and Jerusha Bartlett (Robinson) Wadsworth.

   Children rec. Duxbury (*VR* 95-97, 387); spouses from Weyman Ms: 1. *Ziba Hunt*[7], b. 25 Nov. 1802; m. Diana Chandler. 2. *Henry Hunt,* b. 2 Dec. 1805; m. Deborah Freeman. 3. *Asa Hunt,* b. 30 Oct. 1806; d. 1 Jan. 1808 ae 14m 2d. 4. *Mary Lewis Hunt,* b. 15 Oct. 1809; m. Weston Freeman.

v JANE HUNT, b. 6 March 1784; d. Duxbury 25 Aug. 1864 of typhoid fever (Mass. VR 184:277); m. there (1) 19 Nov. 1800 (*VR* 267), EZRA PRIOR, b. 16 Nov. 1773, lost at sea 9 Oct. 1809 (*VR* 404), son of Joseph and Bethiah (Peterson) Prior (Weyman Ms); m. (2) 15 Nov. 1818 (*VR* 291), WILLIAM JOYCE JR. [Samson #811-I], son of Asa and Lucy Ann (Southworth) Joyce. See p. 510 for her children with William Joyce.

   Prior children rec. Duxbury (*VR* 128-29, 404-05); marriages from Weyman Ms: 1. *Ezra Prior*[7], b. 11 July 1801; lost at sea 13 May 1821. 2. *Otis Prior,* b. 23 July 1803; d. July 1822. 3. *Erastus Prior,* b. 9 March 1805; d. 18 March 1806. 4. *Jane Prior,* b. 29 Sept. 1807; m. Elbridge G. Ramsdell. 5. *Deborah Prior,* b. 26 June 1809; m. Daniel Studley Crocker.

vi LOT HUNT, b. 15 April 1789; d. at sea 26 Oct. 1811 "with Capt. Herrick" rec. Duxbury (*VR* 388).

Sources cited: *Duxbury VR* (many entries keyed to PR 85, "private record, from the Samuel Hunt Bible, now [1911] in the possession of Frank Holmes of Duxbury"). Mass. Vital Records 1841-1910. Plymouth County Probate Records. *Mass. Soldiers & Sailors.* White, *Abstracts of Rev. War Pension Files. Philip Delano of the Fortune …Fifth and Sixth Gen.* (2004). CENSUS: 1850 Duxbury, Plymouth Co. (M432-333). *MFIP George Soule* (2000). **See also:** R. M. Sherman, "Descendants of Nathaniel Sherman of Duxbury," *TAG* 51 (1975), at p. 177.

791. ABNER⁵ SAMSON (*Sarah⁴, Joshua³, Caleb², Henry¹*), son of Abner Samson and his first wife, Sarah Samson [163], was born at Duxbury 1 or 10 April 1752 (*VR* 144) and died there 15 April 1843 aged 91y 3m 2d, "husband of Ruth" (*VR* 408). He was a descendant also of *Mayflower* passengers John Alden and Myles Standish. The will of Abner Samson dated 11 February 1780, proved 3 April 1780, names among others his eldest son Abner (Plymouth PR 25:483).

He was of Duxbury when he married there, 2 April 1781 (*VR* 297), **RUTH BURGESS** of Plymouth, who was born in 1758, daughter of Nathaniel and Ruth (Chandler) Burgess, and died at Duxbury 5 January 1847, aged 88y 10m, "of old age" (*VR* 411).

Abner Samson of Duxbury served as a private in the Revolutionary War (*MSSR* 13:765). In 1790 he was living at Duxbury with two females in his household (*Heads of Fam.,* 169). In 1800 his household consisted of one man and one woman 26-45 (p.98).

He was listed as a pensioner in Duxbury, aged 88, in 1840 (p.29). In his pension application on 21 August 1832, he gave his age as 80 and claimed he was born and had always lived at Duxbury. His widow, Ruth, age 85 on 11 September 1843, gave the dates of their marriage and of Abner's death.

In his will dated 28 October 1837, proved first Tuesday in June 1843, Abner Samson of Duxbury named his wife Ruth, and several grandnieces and grand-nephews (Plymouth PR 85:273). Ruth Samson of Duxbury in her will dated 28 June 1844, proved the third Monday in February 1847, named only her two Burgess brothers and three married sisters (Plymouth PR 89:63).

Abner and Ruth evidently had no surviving children.

Sources cited: *Duxbury VR. Mass. Soldiers & Sailors.* White, *Abstracts of Rev. War Pension Files.* Pension File W15306. Plymouth County Probate Records. CENSUS: *Heads of Families 1790 – Mass.;* 1800 (M32-16). **See also:** R. M. Sherman, "Descendants of Nathaniel Sherman of Duxbury," *TAG* 51 (1975), at p. 177.

792. HULDAH DELANO[5] (*Huldah*[4], *Joshua*[3], *Caleb*[2], *Henry*[1]), daughter of Ichabod Delano and his first wife, Huldah Samson [164], was born probably in July 1762 at Duxbury, her birth not recorded. She was a descendant also of *Mayflower* passengers John Alden and Myles Standish.

She is probably the Huldah Delano who married at Duxbury, 6 August 1780 (*VR* 240), **GAMALIEL DAMON**, who was born at Pembroke (*VR* 74) 14 October 1756, son of Thomas and Alice (Pierce?) Damon (Damon typs., 1:22; see Corrections to Part 2, p. 559, for discussion of Alice's identity), a descendant of Henry Samson [#190-ii]. "—— wife of Gamaliel Damon" died 18 December 1781 at Duxbury, aged 19y 5m (VR 367).

Huldah's father, Ichabod Delano of Duxbury, in his will dated 15 February 1786, provided for his other children but did not mention daughter Huldah, nor is she mentioned in any of the probate documents (Plymouth PR # 6261; 30:82, 288; 42:126; 70:173). It is presumed that she died without surviving children.

Gamaliel Damon married, second, in 1783, HELENA GARDNER, and settled in Washington County, Maine, where they "raised a large family of children" (pension rec., White, 1:946 citing W24030). For further information, see Family #190-ii, *MF20: Henry Samson*, part 2:30-31.

Sources cited: *Duxbury VR.* Plymouth County Probate Records. D. Bradford Damon, "John Damon of Scituate," typescript NEHGS. White, *Abstracts of Revolutionary War Pension Files.*

793. ICHABOD DELANO[5] (*Huldah*[4], *Joshua*[3], *Caleb*[2], *Henry*[1]), son of Ichabod Delano and his first wife, Huldah Samson [164], was born probably at Duxbury 17 August 1764, and died there 4 July 1831 (*Delano*, 509; not in *VR*). He was a descendant also of *Mayflower* passengers John Alden and Myles Standish.

He married, about 1787, **LYDIA WAKEFIELD**, who was born at Medford 8 May 1767 (*VR* 159) and died at Duxbury 25 February 1858, aged 90y 9m 19d, daughter of Samuel and Elizabeth (_____) Wakefield (Mass. VR 121:238).

Ichabod's father in his will dated 15 February 1786, proved 11 September 1786, named Ichabod [Jr.] and Charles as his two eldest sons, leaving to them "all the salt meadow that I die seized of that was their mother's, to be equally divided between them," and "the moveable estate of my first wife"; and also the improvement of two-thirds of the remainder of his real estate, to keep it in repair until his three younger sons were of age to act for themselves; son Ichabod was to be executor (Plymouth PR #6261; 30:82-83). In 1806 an equal division was made between Ichabod, the heirs of his brother Charles, and his half-brother Elijah, of land bounded on the widow's thirds (Plymouth LR 55:222). In April 1831, not long before his own death, Ichabod shared with Elijah and the heirs of Charles in a division of the real estate that had belonged to their father's widow (*ibid.,* 71:174).

On 8 August 1831 Wadsworth Chandler of Duxbury was appointed administrator on the estate of Ichabod Delano late of Duxbury (Plymouth PR 71:469, 515; file #6262). On 5 December 1831 an allowance was made from the estate to Lydia Delano, widow of Ichabod. An account of 3 July 1832 mentions sale of "reversion in the widdow third to Samuel Delano," and part of the barn and land to Samuel Delano. On 9 April 1832, there was set off to the widow of Ichabod Delano late of Duxbury, deceased, all of the dwelling he owned at his death and part of the barn. The numerous creditors of the estate were paid at the rate of 29 and 316/1000ths on the dollar. Among claims of the administrator allowed 3 July 1832 were sums for "making devisions in the widdow Howland's third April 9 1831," and "going to Isaiah Alden's to take oath" (*ibid.,* 72:299-300).

In 1850 Lydia was living in the household of her son Samuel Delano 2^d at Duxbury.

Children of Ichabod and Lydia (Wakefield) Delano, rec. Duxbury (*VR* 60, 63-66):

i   HULDAH DELANO[6], b. 17 Sept. 1788; d. Duxbury 30 May 1835 (*VR* 435); m. at Duxbury, 1 Jan. 1809 (*VR* 243), WILLIAM WATSON.

        Watson children rec. Duxbury (*VR* 186): 1. *George Watson[7]* [twin], b. 31 July 1813. 2. *William Watson* [twin], d.y. (*Delano,* 510). 3. *Almeda Watson,* b. 1 July 1816

ii   BETSEY DELANO, b. 23 March 1790; d. Duxbury 12 April 1840 (*VR* 368, no date, "child of Ichabod and Lydia"; d.d. *Delano,* 509).

iii   LYDIA W. DELANO, b. 3 Nov. 1791; m. at Duxbury 9 April 1812 (VR 244), SAMUEL G. WINSOR, b. Duxbury 30 Oct. 1790, son of James and Sarah (Gray) Winsor (*VR* 204), d. Bridgewater 1874 (Plymouth PR #23259). In 1850 he was a farmer in Bridgewater ae 59 with Lydia ae 58 and Francis [a grandson?] ae 13 (p.28).

        Winsor children rec. Duxbury (*VR* 199-203): 1. *Elizabeth Winsor[7],* b. 10 Dec. 1812. 2. *Daniel H. Winsor,* b. 14 Oct. 1814. 3. *Maria Winsor,* b. 13 June 1817. 4. *Samuel Winsor,* b. 28 Jan. 1822. 5. *Elbridge Winsor,* b. 18 Feb. 1824. 6. *Harrison Gray Winsor,* b. 28 Dec. 1825; d. 1834.

iv   REBECCA DELANO, b. 7 or 9 June 1793; d. Duxbury 15 Aug. 1855 of dysentery (Mass. VR 94:186); m. at Duxbury, 18 Feb. 1816 (*VR* 246), JOSEPH P. BOSWORTH [Samson #675-iii]. In 1850 he was a housewright at Duxbury, with Rebecca ae 53 [*sic*] and Joseph P. Jr. ae 20 (p.85); in 1860 he was living with the family of his son Daniel E. at Duxbury (p.63/111). See p. 264 for their children.

v   OLIVE DELANO, b. 2 July 1795; d. Duxbury 8 Sept. or 18 Oct. 1848 (*VR* 360); m. at Duxbury, 26 Nov. 1815 (*VR* 245), BISBE CHANDLER, b.

Duxbury 2 July 1789, son of Bisbe and Abigail (Bradford) Chandler (*VR* 40, 230), "lost on Grand Bank" 18 Sept. 1844 (*VR* 358).

vi   SOPHIA DELANO, b. 7 Aug. 1797; d. Duxbury 24 Jan. 1839 unm. (*VR* 372, no date; *Delano*, 510).

vii   SAMUEL DELANO, b. 22 Oct. 1798; d. Duxbury 8 Aug. 1861, disease of stomach (Mass. VR 148:310); m. LUCY WARREN (*Delano*, 510). In 1850 Samuel Delano 2[d], ae 50, was a yeoman at Duxbury with Lucy W. ae 49, ch. Henry ae 22, and Almira ae 14, and his mother Lydia Delano ae 83 (p.84).
     Children rec. Duxbury (*VR* 60, 62-63): 1. *Henry Delano[7]*, b. 14 Dec. 1827; a shoemaker 1850. 2. *Almira Delano*, b. 9 June 1833. 3. *Nancy Delano*, b. 24 Nov. 1839; d. 28 Oct. 1849 (*VR* 371).

viii   NANCY DELANO, b. 16 May 1800; d. Duxbury 8 March 1840 (*VR* 360) ae 39y 9m 22d; m. there 12 May 1819 (*VR* 232, 245), MARTIN S. CHANDLER, b. Duxbury 25 Sept. 1796, son of Asa and Diana (Simmons) Chandler (*VR* 44, 229). He m. (2) at Duxbury, 11 Oct. 1840 (*VR* 232), Joanna S. Delano [#745-vi], dau. of Jephtha and Rebecca (Chandler) Delano (see p. 399). In 1850 he was a brickmaker at Duxbury with Joanna and the two youngest children (p.84).
     Chandler children rec. Duxbury (*VR* 40, 44, 46): 1. *Celina Chandler[7]*, b. 6 Feb. 1820. 2. *Rebecca B. Chandler*, b. 25 Sept. 1821. 3. *Martin Chandler*, b. 20 Jan. 1824. 4. *Bailey Chandler*, b. 31 Dec. 1825. 5. *Ichabod D. Chandler*, b. 5 March 1828. 6. *Maria V. Chandler*, b. 2 June 1832. 7. *Calvin Chandler*, b. 29 Oct. 1834.

ix   MARY DELANO, b. 3 June 1807; d. Duxbury 2 Aug. 1893; m. (1) PELEG CHANDLER, (2) NATHANIEL WATERMAN, (3) WILLIAM CURTIS GARDNER; no children (*Delano*, 510).

Sources cited: *Duxbury VR. Medford VR.* Mass. Vital Records 1841-1910. Plymouth County Deeds and Probate Records. *The American Genealogist* 49:37-38, 107. *Delano Genealogy* (1899). CENSUS: 1850 Bridgewater and Duxbury, Plymouth Co. (M432-333); 1860 Duxbury (M653-519). **See also:** *Philip Delano of the Fortune ... Fifth and Sixth Gen.* (2004).

794.   CHARLES DELANO[5] (*Huldah[4], Joshua[3], Caleb[2], Henry[1]*), son of Ichabod Delano and his first wife, Huldah Samson [164], was born probably at Duxbury about 1767, and died there in April 1806 (*VR* 368). He was a descendant also of *Mayflower* passengers John Alden and Myles Standish.

He married at Duxbury, 17 November 1791 (*VR* 242), **HANNAH PIERCE**. She was born at Pembroke 6 June 1771 (*VR* 160), daughter of Joseph and Olive (Cushing) (Fish) Pierce, and died at Duxbury 18 December 1812, "--- widow of Charles Delano," ae 4[0] (*VR* 373), a descendant of *Mayflower* passenger George Soule. Her sister Abigail married Nathaniel Delano [Samson #742-iii].

(*Delano 2004*, p. 176, confuses Hannah's husband with a different Charles, born in 1779 and thus only 12 at date of marriage).

Charles's father in his will dated 15 February 1786 named Ichabod [Jr.] and Charles as his two eldest sons, leaving to them "all the salt meadow that I die seized of that was their mother's, to be equally divided between them," and "the moveable estate of my first wife," along with the improvement of two-thirds of the remainder of his real estate which they were to keep in repair until his three younger sons were of age to act for themselves (Plymouth PR #6261; 30:82-83). The estate was divided 16 August 1806 among surviving sons Ichabod and Elijah, and the heirs of son Charles, deceased (Plymouth LR 55:222). In April 1831 the heirs of Charles (not named) shared with Ichabod and Elijah in a division of the real estate that had belonged to their father's widow (Plymouth LR 71:174).

Hannah Delano, widow of Charles late of Duxbury, deceased, declined administration of his estate, and at her request Isaiah Alden of Duxbury was appointed on 7 July 1806. The inventory dated 13 October 1806 included a dwelling house, one-third of a barn, and land (Plymouth PR #6236; 39:71, 40:516). Isaiah Alden, administrator of the estate of Charles Delano late of Duxbury, by court order sold real estate at public vendue on 16 January 1807 in order to satisfy debts. The resulting deeds were executed on 6 April 1807: to Ichabod Delano one and a half acres with part of the barn for $33; to Judah Peterson of Duxbury, four acres of woodland for $44; and to Gideon Harlow for $150 half an acre with the dwelling house, except for the part set off to the widow Hannah Delano (Plymouth LR 175:30, 123:120). No Plymouth probate records were found for Hannah's parents, or any relevant appointment of a guardian 1806 – 1815.

In 1800 Charles Delano and his wife, both 26-45, had a household that included three little girls under 10 (p.104). In 1810 the household of Hannah Delano of Duxbury consisted of herself (26-45), and one little boy under 10 (p.219), the only child indicated by census who has been positively identified.

Child of Charles and Hannah (Pierce) Delano (three daughters b. 1790-1800 also indicated by census):

    i   CHARLES DELANO (called Charles Delano 2d in marriage records and 1850 census, Charles 3rd in children's births and 1860 census), b. 1 June 1806; supp. d. East Boston 5 April 1893 but rec. not found; m. (1) Duxbury, 24 Nov. 1833 (*VR* 242), ABIGAIL BATES, b. 17 Aug. 1809 Pembroke, d. Duxbury 30 May 1864 ae 54y 9m 13d of an ovarian tumor, dau. of Edward and Margaret (Howland) Bates (Mass. VR 175:306); m. (2) in Boston, as Charles Delano ae 55, mariner, b. Duxbury, son of Charles and Hannah, 25 Dec. 1864, MATILDA (STILLMAN?) PETERS, ae 39, b. Prince Edward

Island, dau. of William and Mariet Stillman, second m. for both (Mass. VR
173:151). In 1850 Charles Delano 2^d was a cordwainer at Duxbury, with
Abigail ae 41, and four children (p.70). In 1860, at Duxbury, he and son
Daniel were both in "market fishing" (p.84), and in 1870, in Boston with his
second wife, he was working for a shoemaker (p.8).

Children rec. Duxbury of Charles 3rd and Abigail (*VR* 61, 65, 66); all at home
1850, two youngest in 1860: 1. *Rebecca G. Delano*[7], b. 31 Oct. 1834; m. 1852 John
Cushman (Mass. VR 61:228); had ch. 2. *Charles E. Delano*, b. 18 Sept. 1838; d.
Duxbury 20 Oct. 1859, consumption (Mass. VR 130:203). 3. *Daniel W. Delano*, b.
24 Jan. 1841; d. "Charity Hosp., N.C.," 22 March 1863, soldier, fisherman,
congestion of lungs (Mass. VR 166:282). 4. *Rosetta A. Delano*, b. 17 Dec. 1842; d.
Duxbury 17 Sept. 1863, pthisis (Mass. VR 166:281).

Sources cited: *Duxbury VR. Pembroke VR.* Mass. Vital Records 1841-1910. Plymouth County
Deeds and Probate Records. CENSUS: Duxbury, Plymouth Co., 1800 (M32-16), 1810 (M252-21),
1850 (M432-333) & 1860 (M653-519); 1870 Ward 1, Boston [E. Boston], Suffolk Co. (M593-640).

795.   JOSHUA SOULE[5] (*Mercy Fullerton*[4], *Joshua*[3], *Caleb*[2], *Henry*[1]), son of Joseph
Soule Jr. and his wife Mercy Fullerton [165], was born at Duxbury 14 November
1742 (*VR* 160), and died at Avon, Maine, 8 May 1808 (Ridlon, 1:402). He was a
coaster, called Captain. He was a descendant also of *Mayflower* passengers John
Alden, George Soule, and Myles Standish.

He married at Duxbury, 14 February 1765 (*VR* 310), **MARY CUSHMAN**,
who was born at Plympton 23 December 1744, daughter of Allerton and Alathea
(Soule) Cushman (*VR* 86), and died at Phillips, Maine, 27 March 1819 (*VR* 86).
She was a descendant of *Mayflower* passengers Isaac Allerton and George Soule
(*MFIP Soule* 2:172, #434). Capt. Joshua Soule and his wife Mary are buried at
Livermore, Maine (*MD* 36:156; Ridlon 1:402).

After the deaths of the two older children in May 1771, Joshua and Mary with
their son Joseph moved from Duxbury to Bristol, Maine, and later to what is now
Avon, Maine, on Sandy River (Ridlon 1:402). In 1790 the family was enumerated at
Sandy River, Upper Town [Avon], Maine, with two boys under 16, two men 16 or
older, and four females. Joshua provided civil service in the Revolution (*DAR
Patriot Index* 3:2741).

In his will dated 13 August 1806, proved 2 August 1808, Joshua Soule mentioned his "widow," and named his sons Nathan and Joshua, unmarried daughter
Polly who was under 21, son William, daughter Ruba, and grandsons Joshua and
Thomas Soule, and noted that his son Joseph had left "three heirs"; he directed
that one feather bed be reserved for the use of Methodist preachers and other
visitors (Kennebec PR 4:416-17).

Children of Joshua and Mary (Cushman) Soule (Ridlon 1:401-02, 425-30, unless otherwise cited; see *MFIP Soule*, 2:172-74 for further information):

   i   LUTHER SOULE[6], b. Duxbury Dec. 1765; d. there 21 May 1771 ae 5y 5m (*VR* 422); bur. Old Cemetery, Chestnut Street, South Duxbury.

   ii   ALATHEA SOULE, b. Duxbury 28 Aug. 1769, bp. there 8 Oct. 1769; d. there 20 May 1771 (*VR* 420, from g.s.); bur. with brother Luther.

   iii JOSEPH SOULE, b. Duxbury 8 Sept. 1771, bp. there 27 Oct. 1771; d. Avon, Me., 3 March 1805; m. at Duxbury, June 1796 (*VR* 322), MARY DARLING.

        Children (Ridlon, 1:425-6): 1. *Joshua Soule[7]*, b. 22 July 1797; m. Hannah Collier. 2. *Mary/Polly Soule*, b. 11 Aug. 1802; m. Stephen Folsom. 3. *Joseph Soule*, b. 1 Aug. 1804; m. Judith Soule.

   iv WILLIAM SOULE, b. Bristol, Me., 29 May or 22 Nov. 1774; d. Avon, Me., 21 May 1841; m. (1) Farmington, Me., 18 Oct. 1796, MARY THOMPSON; m. (2) 1832, CLARISSA GOODWIN. (See Ridlon 1:429)

        Children with Mary: 1. *Isaac Thompson Soule[7]*, b. 1794 [?1796]. 2. *David Thompson Soule*, b. 1797. 3. *Luther Soule*, b. 1798; m. Abigail Kersey. 4. *William Soule*, b. 1802; m. Rebecca Hardy. 5. *George Soule*, b. ca 1813; m. Sarah Doyen. Children with Clarissa: 6. *John Wesley Soule*, b. 7 Feb. 1834; m. Clemena Whitney. 7. *Nathan Soule*, b. 1836; d.y.

   v   RUBY SOULE, b. Bristol, Me., 1 Oct. 1776; d. prob. Ohio, Feb. 1844; m. (1) Bristol, Me., ca 1798, PETER DUDLEY, (2) in Ohio, PETER FULSOM.

        Dudley children: 1. *Joshua Dudley[7]*. 2. *Cyrus Dudley*. 3. *Elias Dudley*. 4. *Daniel Dudley*. 5. *Rhoda Dudley*. 6. *James Dudley*. 7. *George Dudley*. 8. *Mary Dudley*. 9. *Peter Dudley*. 10. *Joseph S. Dudley*.

   vi JAMES SOULE, b. Bristol 1 Oct. 1779; d. Livermore, Me., 30 March 1806; m. (1) ca 1800, MARGARET COOK, (2) Mainsville, Ohio, ca 1805, _____.

        Children: 1. *Thomas House Soule[7]*, b. 11 Nov. 1801; m. (1) Mary Shields, (2) Barbara Hildebrand. 2. *Judith Soule*, b. 9 Feb. 1804; m. her cousin Joseph Soule Jr.

   vii JOSHUA SOULE, b. Bristol 1 Aug. 1781; d. near Nashville, Tenn., 6 March 1867; m. at Providence, R.I., 18 Sept. 1803, SARAH ALLEN. He was founder of the Methodist Episcopal Church South; see Ridlon for much more information. In 1850 he was listed alone in District 8, Williamson, Tenn. (p.185).

        Children (Ridlon 1:411-14): 1. *Mariah Soule[7]*, b. 10 July 1804, Nantucket; m. Rev. Henry Van Dyke. 2. *Joshua Soule*, b. 6 Dec. 1805, Nantucket; m. (1) Julia Lawton, (2) Eliza M. Lawson. 3. *Amelia Soule*, b. Aug. 1807, Winthrop, Me.; m. Rev. William Miller. 4. *Jane Augusta Soule*, b. 28 Sept. 1809, Lebanon, Ohio. 5. *Ernestine Cordelia Soule*, b. 1812. 6. *James Soule*. 7. *Joseph Allen Soule*, b. 1815.

8. *Sarah Soule*, b. 1817. 9. *William McKindree Soule*, b. 1821. 10. *Martha Soule*, b. 1822. 11.*George Soule*, b. 1824.

viii   NATHAN SOULE, b. Avon, Me., 2 July 1784; d. Harmony, Me., 17 Jan. 1849; m. at Avon, 29 June 1806, NANCY HOWLAND, b. Avon 23 May 1788 (Ridlon 1:416). He was 6 ft. 3 in. tall, 225 lbs (see Ridlon 1:401).

   Children, first four b. Avon, rest Livermore (*ibid.*): 1. *Asa Whiting Soule*[7], b. 8 Jan. 1808. 2. *Pliny Britt Soule*, b. 25 July 1810; m. Anna Carroll. 3. *Fanny Cushman Soule*, b. 4 Sept. 1812. 4. *Sophronia Soule*, b. 30 Aug. 1814. 5. *Francis Asbury Soule*, b. 27 April 1817. 6. *Nancy Howland Soule*, b. 30 Oct. 1819. 7. *Nathan Augustus Soule*, b. 6 Feb. 1822; m. Almira Timberlake. 8. *James Harvey Soule*, b. 11 May 1824; m. Julia A. Rolf. 9. *Mary Jane Soule*, b. 20 Dec. 1826; m. (1) Calvin Dore, (2) John R. Kenney. 10. *Elijah Hedding Soule* (twin), b. 26 Aug. 1828. 11. *Joshua Emery Soule*, b. 26 Aug. 1828. 12. [*child*] *Soule*, stillborn 1830.

ix   POLLY SOULE, b. Avon, Me., 1 Oct. 1786; d. Phillips, Me., 1 Jan. 1868; m. April 1811, THEODORE MARSTON, b. 1792 Me. In 1850 he was a merchant ae 58 at Phillips, Me., with Polly ae 63, and Jeremiah ae 35; the household included Olive W. Soule ae 21 and Geo. R. Osbeton ae 28, farmer (p.148).

   Marston children (Ridlon 1:402): 1. *Daniel Marston*[7], b. 22 June 1813; m. Rosanna Dow. 2. *Jeremiah Marston*, b. 6 Feb. 1815. 3. *Mary Ann Marston*, b. 22 May 1818; m. William H. Josselyn.

Sources cited: *Duxbury VR. Phillips* [Me.] *VR.* Kennebec Co., Me., Probate Records. Ridlon, *Soule Family* (1926). *MFIP Soule*, Pt. 2 (2002). CENSUS: 1850 Phillips, Franklin Co., Me. (M432-253); Williamson Co., Tenn. (M432-900).

796.   SARAH SOULE[5] (*Mercy Fullerton*[4], *Joshua*[3], *Caleb*[2], *Henry*[1]), daughter of Joseph Soule Jr. and his wife Mercy Fullerton [165], was born at Duxbury 20 February 1746 (*VR* 160) and died there 12 or 14 March 1830, aged 84, a widow (*VR* 405). She was a descendant also of *Mayflower* passengers John Alden, George Soule, and Myles Standish.

   She married at Duxbury, 8 January 1765 (*VR* 313), **BENJAMIN PRIOR JR.**, who died there in December 1820 or 1 January 1821 (*VR* 404), probably the son of Benjamin and Deborah (Weston) Prior born at Duxbury 23 October 1740 (*VR* 128). He was a descendant of *Mayflower* passenger John Alden.

   By the will of his father, dated 3 February 1763, Benjamin Prior received a share in a salt meadow and a share of the residue of the estate (Plymouth PR #16,253). He served as a private in the Revolution in Capt. Bildad Arnold's company, Col. Thomas Lothrop's regiment, for twelve days on a march to Rhode Island on the alarm of 10 December 1776 (*MSSR* 12:796).

In 1790 the family was living in Duxbury with a household consisting of three men, one boy under 16, and five females (p.169). On 21 August 1801 Sarah Pryor shared in a division of the estate of her father, Joseph Soule, and an executor's accounting on 9 January 1808 included a payment to Benjamin Prior for his wife Sarah (Plymouth PR #18820, 37:254-55, 270-71, 486, 42:243; *MD* 30:145-49).

On 25 May 1804 Benjamin Prior, cordwainer, and his wife Sarah, of Duxbury, sold one half of their homestead to their son Benjamin Prior Jr., shipwright (Plymouth LR 107:110).

Children of Benjamin and Sarah (Soule) Prior, rec. Duxbury (*VR* 128-30):

i   JABEZ PRIOR[6], b. 23 Dec. 1765; drowned 23 May 1768 ae 2y 5m (*VR* 404).

ii   MERCY PRIOR, b. 22 April 1767 and bp. 28 April 1771; d. Boston 6 April 1844 ae 83; m. at Duxbury, 8 Sept. 1791 (*VR* 292), BENJAMIN BOS-WORTH, b. Duxbury 25 June 1767 (*VR* 27), a desc. of Henry Samson. See Family #673-i for more information and names of their 11 children.

iii JOANNA PRIOR, b. 22 March 1769; d. Duxbury 15 Sept. 1843 ae 74y 5m 7d (*VR* 365); m. there, 11 Sept. 1791 (*VR* 291), JOSHUA CUSHING, b. there 20 Nov. 1767 or 29 Nov. 1761 (*VR* 54).
     Cushing children, rec. Duxbury (*VR* 54-55): 1. *Mary Cushing[7]*, b. 14 March 1792. 2. *Joan Cushing*, b. 28 Dec. 1795. 3. *Nancy Cushing*, b. 17 Feb. 1798. 4. *Joshua S. Cushing 3d*, b. 11 June 1801. 5. *Sally Cushing*, b. 14 June 1803. 6. *Jane Cushing*, b. 19 Nov. 1807.

iv   ANNE/ANNA PRIOR, b. 21 Oct. 1770; d. Duxbury 18 or 21 March 1810 in 40th yr (*VR* 385); m. there, in Dec. 1796 (*VR* 291), NATHANIEL HOLMES, b. ca 1773, d. Duxbury 20 Sept. 1821 in 48th yr (*VR* 385); bur. Large Cem., Duxbury.
     Holmes children rec. Duxbury (*VR* 91-93): 1. *John Holmes[7]*, b. 24 Feb. 1798. 2. *Nathaniel Holmes*, b. 30 July 1800. 3. *Lewis Holmes*, b. 14 March 1802. 4. *Mason Holmes*, b. 18 Sept. 1804; d. 1821. 5. *Anna Prior Holmes*, b. 27 Oct. 1806.

v   JABEZ PRIOR, b. 26 April 1772; d. at sea; m. SARAH HOLMES, b. Plymouth (d. rec. son William). In 1800 Jabez Prior was listed in Duxbury next to Benjamin and Matthew Prior, 26-45 with one woman 26-45, and one boy and one girl under 10 (p.100). In 1810 his household consisted of one man and one woman 26-45, and four boys under 10 (p.226).
     Children: 1. *Henry Prior[7]*, b. 16 June 1799; d. 19 Oct. 1803 ae 4y 4m 3d (*VR* 405). 2. *William Prior*, b. 1804; d. Boston 1 March 1881, a fisherman, in an accident; b. Duxbury of Jabez and Sarah (Holmes) Prior (Mass. VR 329:305). Prob. a dau. b. before 1800, d.y. [Probably three more sons b. 1800-1810.]

vi   MATTHEW PRIOR, b. 2 April 1774; d. at sea in 1816 (*Duxbury VR 405*); m. at Duxbury, 19 Nov. 1797 or 1798 (*VR* 292), ESTHER BRYANT. In 1800 they were in Duxbury, he 26-45, she 16-26, with one boy under 10 (p.100). In 1810 they were in Bath, Me., both 26-45, with one woman 16-26, one boy 10-16, and one boy and two girls under 10 (p.336). Esther Prior in 1820 was head of a household at Bath, Me., with one girl under 10 (p.136).

vii   BENJAMIN PRIOR, b. 30 Oct. 1776; m. (1) Duxbury, 12 Sept. 1801 (*VR* 291), POLLY MCGLAUTHLIN, b. 14 Feb. 1781 (rec. *Duxbury VR* 130 *sub* Prior), d. Duxbury 22 Nov. 1832 (*VR* 405); m. (2) Duxbury, 24 Aug. 1834 (*VR* 291), SALLY FREEMAN, b. 13 Feb. 1784 (rec. *Duxbury VR* 130 *sub* Prior). His household in Duxbury in 1810 consisted of one man and one woman 26-45 and one girl under 10 (p.226).

      Child: 1. *Holmes Prior⁷*, b. ca 1809; d. Duxbury 3 Dec. 1814 ae 5 (*VR* 404).

viii   SARAH PRIOR, b. 17 May 1779; bp. 23 May 1779; d. Duxbury 9 Oct. 1848 or 1849 ae 69y 5m, as "Sally" (*VR* 401); m. there, 5 April 1801 (*VR* 292), GEORGE PETERSON, b. Duxbury 5 July 1778, son of Jonathan and Lucy (Hunt) Peterson (*VR* 119, 286), d. 3 Nov. 1818 in Havana, rec. Duxbury as "Capt. George" (*VR* 399).

      Peterson children, rec. Duxbury (117, 119, 121; differing dates cite P.R. 100, Edwin Peterson Bible): 1. *George Peterson ⁷*, b. 7 July 1801; d. Duxbury 7 Oct. 1828 (*VR* 399). 2. *Augusta Peterson*, b. 15 June 1807. 3. *Otis Peterson*, b. 11 Aug. 1809. 4. *Sally Peterson*, b. 5 Aug. 1812. 5. *Edwin Peterson*, b. 6 Feb. 1814 or 4 Feb. 1815. 6. *Lucy Peterson*, b. 19 Jan. 1819 or 19 June 1817.

Sources cited: *Duxbury VR*, many entries keyed to P.R. 93, the "Benjamin Prior Bible, now [1911] in possession of Mrs. Philander Wadsworth of Duxbury." Plymouth Co. Deeds and Probate Records. CENSUS: Duxbury, Plymouth Co., 1790 (M637-169), 1800 (M32-16), 1810 (M252-21); Bath, Lincoln Co., Me. 1810 (M252-12) & 1820 (M33-36).

797. JAMES SOULE⁵ (*Mercy Fullerton⁴, Joshua³, Caleb², Henry¹*), son of Joseph Soule Jr. and his wife Mercy Fullerton [165], was born at Duxbury 12 April 1747 (*VR* 160), and died there 29 or 30 August 1794 aged 48 (*VR* 421). A newspaper account in the *Independent Chronicle* of 4 September 1794 referred to the death of Capt. James Soule on the previous Saturday. He is buried in the Large [Mayflower] Cemetery, Duxbury, with his wife. He was a descendant also of *Mayflower* passengers John Alden and Myles Standish.

He married at Duxbury, 17 January 1773 (*VR* 310), **ABIGAIL (SEAVER) BOSWORTH**, who was born at Dorchester 4 January 1743/4 (*VR* 1:99) and died at Duxbury 26 August 1832, aged 88 (*VR* 420), daughter of Joshua and Abigail (Foster) Seaver and widow of BENJAMIN BOSWORTH [Samson # 673], with whom she had Benjamin and Abigail (see Family #673, pp. 260-61). Her son Benjamin Bosworth married her husband's niece Mercy Prior [#796-ii].

Joseph Soule in his will dated 14 July 1794, left to son James a meadow right in Hammer Island and an equal share with his brothers in land in North Yarmouth [Maine], but James died before his father, so in a codicil dated 12 June 1798, Joseph directed that the property go to his other sons, who were to pay James' heirs. In the settlement 21 August 1801, the heirs of James received $24.30 (Plymouth PR #18820; *MD* 30:146-49).

On 30 October 1794 Joseph Soule and Ezekiel Soule, yeomen of Duxbury, were appointed administrators of the estate of James Soule late of Duxbury, mariner (Plymouth PR 34:20). The inventory included a farm, the schooner *Belinda* and the sloop *Phoenix*. An account dated 9 January 1808 indicates that payments had been made to widow Abigail, and to Joshua, Joseph, and Abigail, three heirs of the deceased, and to James and Richard Soule (*ibid.*, 42:245; see *MD* 30:150).

In 1810 Abigail Soule was head of a household in Duxbury that consisted of one man 26-45, and two women 45 or older (p.230).

Children of James and Abigail (Seaver) (Bosworth) Soule, bp. rec. Duxbury (*VR* 160-64;, birthdates from *Duxbury History*, 313):

i SALLY SOULE[6], b. 7 July 1774; bp. 2 Oct. 1774 (*VR* 160); d. 12 Sept. 1775 (Winsor, 312).

ii JOSEPH SOULE, b. 27 Dec. 1775; bp. 11 Aug. 1776; d. 27 Aug. 1778 ae 2 yrs (*VR* 163, 422).

iii JOSHUA SOULE, b. 19 Dec. 1777; bp. 26 April 1778; d. 17 Sept. 1803.

iv JOSEPH SOULE, b. 2 Jan. 1780; d. 5 Jan. 1806.

v ABIGAIL SOULE, bp. 16 June 1782; d. Duxbury 10 or 13 Feb. 1804 in 22nd yr (*VR* 387); m. at Duxbury, 8 Dec. 1801 (*VR* 310), ASA HUNT [#790-iii], b. there 21 March 1778, son of Lot and Mary (Sampson) Hunt (*VR* 95), d. there 8 or 10 Dec. 1806 ae 28y 8m 17d (*VR* 387).

vi JAMES SOULE, b. 20 Sept. 1784; m. at Duxbury, 9 Oct. 1820 (*VR* 311), MARY BRADFORD, b. Duxbury 7 Sept. 1789, dau. of William and Lucy (Sampson) Bradford. (See Family #543-i, p.56 for their children.)

vii RICHARD SOULE, b. 7 Nov. 1786; bp. 17 Aug. 1788; d. 17 Crescent Pl., Boston, 25 July 1866, merchant (Mass. VR 194:77); m. at Duxbury (1) 24 June 1810 (*VR* 312), PRUDENCE LORING, b. there 11 Aug. 1789 (*VR* 164), d. there 15 Dec. 1823 (*VR* 423); m. (2) 4 Nov. 1824, LUCY LORING (*VR* 312), b. Duxbury 8 Sept. 1790 (*VR* 163), sister of his first wife.

Children, rec. Duxbury: 1. *Richard Soule*[7], b. 8 June 1812 (*VR* 164). 2. *Mary Chapman Soule*, b. 27 Oct. 1814; m. Sylvanus Sampson [#542-viii, p.55].

3. *Elizabeth Seaver Soule*, b. 6 April 1818 (*VR* 162); m. Isaac Sweetzer. 4. *Prudence Loring Soule*, b. 10 March 1823 (*VR* 164); m. Charles Soule Jr. 5. *[Son] Soule*, b. and d. Aug. 1825 (*VR* 165, 424). 6. *Horace Homer Soule*, b. 13 Sept. 1827 (*VR* 162). 7. *Helen Maria Soule*, b. 20 Oct. 1829; d. 20 Jan. 1834 (*VR* 162, 421). 8. *Charles Carroll Soule*, b. 26 June 1832 (*VR* 161).

Sources cited: *Duxbury VR.* Mass. Vital Records 1841-1910. Plymouth County Probate Records. Winsor, *History of Duxbury* (1849), errs in several birth dates; has some omissions. CENSUS: *Heads of Families 1790 – Mass.*; Duxbury, Plymouth Co., 1810 (M252-21). **See also:** Ridlon, 1:399; *Soule MFIP* 2 (2002): 177-78 (further information on 7th gen.).

798. OLIVE SOULE[5] (*Mercy Fullerton*[4], *Joshua*[3], *Caleb*[2], *Henry*[1]), daughter of Joseph Soule Jr. and his wife Mercy Fullerton [165], was born at Duxbury 29 March 1749 (*VR* 164), and died there 28 October 1833, aged 85 (*VR* 443). She was a descendant also of *Mayflower* passengers John Alden and Myles Standish.

She married at Duxbury, 19 January 1768 (*VR* 337), **NATHANIEL WINSOR**, who was born at Duxbury 15 June 1747 (*VR* 203), son of Samuel and Rhoda (Delano) Winsor, and died there 17 October 1839, "father of Nathaniel Jr., husband of Olive" (*VR* 443, says 1840, clearly an error), aged 93, of "age and cold." They are buried in the Large Cemetery, Duxbury.

Nathaniel served as a private in the American Revolution (*MSSR* 17:645). In 1790 he was living in Duxbury in 1790, head of a household that included three boys under 16 and six females (p.169).

In his will dated 8 April 1831, Nathaniel Winsor of Duxbury, merchant, mentioned but did not name his wife; he made bequests to granddaughter Maria, daughter of son Samuel deceased; son Nathaniel Winsor and his son Henry; son Martin (after his decease to Albert Winsor); daughter Welthea Little; daughter Sylvia Waterman; daughter Mahala and her son Daniel Wadsworth; daughter Betsey Turner wife of David, and her son William Turner; daughter Nancy wife of John Howland (after her death to Lucian Howland); and daughter Sally (Plymouth PR #23250). A codicil 31 January 1839 revoked daughter Nancy Howland's bequest, giving it instead to Cordelia Howland of Duxbury as trustee. Order to appraise the estate was given 5 November 1839 and bond on the administrators taken 2 December 1839 (*ibid.*).

Children of Nathaniel and Olive (Soule) Winsor, rec. Duxbury (*VR* 203-205):

    i   WELTHEA WINSOR[6], b. 17 Oct. 1769; bp. 3 Oct. 1778; m. at Duxbury or Pembroke (*VR* 311), 15 Jan. 1788, ISAAC LITTLE, b. Pembroke 22 June 1761, son of Isaac and Lydia (Hatch) Little (*VR* 311).

Little children, first six rec. Pembroke (*VR* 139-40), rest and all spouses from *Duxbury History* (p.341): 1. *Wealthy Little⁷*, b. 31 Oct. 1790; m. Seth Sprague Jr. 2. *Olive Little*, b. 27 Feb. 1792; m. Rev. Hiram Weston. 3. *Sally Little*, b. 29 Sept. 1794; m. Isaac Barker. 4. *Isaac Little*, b. 18 Nov. 1796. 5. *Lydia Hatch Little*, b. 4 Oct. 1798. 6. *Nancy/Ann Little*, b. 4 Oct. 1804; m. George Frazar. 7. *Betsy Little*, m. Benjamin Standish. 8. *Otis Little*, m. Betsy Hoskins. 9. *Samuel Little*, m. Elizabeth Simmons.

ii   SYLVINA WINSOR, b. 19 June 1771, bp. 22 July 1780; d. Duxbury 5 Feb. 1835 (*VR* 434); m. there, 25 Nov. 1790 (*VR* 338), ELIPHALET WATERMAN (*Duxbury History*, 333), d. Duxbury 25 May 1836 (*VR* 434).

    Waterman children rec. Duxbury (*VR* 185): 1. *Martin Waterman⁷*, b. 1 Oct. 1793. 2. *Betsey Waterman*, b. 12 July 1796. 3. *[child] Waterman*, d. 23 Jan. 1805 (*VR* 434). ?4. *Thomas W. Herrick Waterman*, b. 9 Oct. 1806; d. Duxbury 1853 (Mass. VR 76:197); m. Emily Winsor (*Duxbury History*, 333). He m. and d. with surname Herrick, but d. rec. says he was b. Brighton, parents Eliphalet and Sylvia Winsor.

iii NATHANIEL WINSOR (twin), b. 8 Sept. 1775, bp. 3 Oct. 1778; m. at Duxbury, 7 or 12 Dec. 1800 (both dates, *VR* 337), HANNAH LORING, b. 16 May 1780, dau. of Samuel and Prudence (Chapman) Loring (*Duxbury History*, 278).

    Children rec. Duxbury (*VR* 199-201, 203; see *Duxbury History*, 342-43 for more details): 1. *Gershom Winsor⁷*, b. 23 Nov. 1801. 2. *Daniel L. Winsor*, b. 7 July 1804. 3. *Nathaniel Winsor*, b. 30 June 1806; m. Ann T. Howland; parents of Justin Winsor, historian and author of *History of Duxbury*. 4. *Elizabeth Winsor*, b. 25 July 1808. 5. *Mary Winsor*, b. 18 Aug. 1810. 6. *Edward Winsor*, b. 28 April 1813. 7. *Gustavus Winsor*, b. 5 Dec. 1814. 8. *Samuel Loring Winsor*, b. 19 Dec. 1816. 9. *Charles Frederick Winsor*, b. 7 May 1819. 10. *Henry Winsor*, b. 22 April 1826.

iv   OLIVE WINSOR (twin), b. 8 Sept. 1775; d. 3 July 1776 Duxbury (*VR* 443).

v   SALLY WINSOR, b. ca Feb. 1777, bp. 3 Oct. 1778 (*VR* 204); d. Duxbury 7 Oct. 1778 ae 1y 7½ m (*VR* 444).

vi   MAHALA WINSOR, bp. 3 Oct. 1778 (*VR* 203); m. ("Matilda" in VR) at Duxbury, Dec. 1795 (*VR* 326), ZENITH WADSWORTH, b. Duxbury 5 Oct. 1766, son of Wait and Abigail (Bradford) Wadsworth (*Duxbury History*, 329, 331), d. there 10 July 1832 (*VR* 433).

    Wadsworth children, rec. Duxbury (*VR* 179-83): 1. *Olive Wadsworth⁷*, b. 22 May 1797. 2. *Rufus Wadsworth*, b. 26 May 1799. 3. *John Wadsworth*, b. 16 June 1801; d. 10 or 11 July 1822 ae 19 (*VR* 432). 4. *Daniel Wadsworth*, b. 27 July 1803. 5. *Alden Wadsworth*, b. 27 March 1805. 6. *Mahalah Wadsworth*, b. 6 Feb. 1807. 7. *Harvey Wadsworth*, b. 6 June 1811. 8. *Lawrence Wadsworth*, b. 3 July 1813.

vii SAMUEL WINSOR, b. ca March 1779 and bp. 23 May 1779 (*VR* 204); d. 24 March 1805 ae 26y 20d, "on board the ship *Arcturus* in the port of Kingston

Jamaika" (*VR* 444 from g.s.); m. at Duxbury, 22 Oct. 1801 [*sic*], OLIVE CHANDLER (*VR* 338), b. Duxbury 3 July 1782, dau. Samuel and Mary (Johnson) Chandler (*VR* 45, 233).

Children rec. Duxbury (*VR* 200, 203, 204): 1. *Maria Winsor*[7], b. 9 Nov. 1800 [*sic*]; m. Samuel A. Frazer Jr. 2. *Eliza Winsor*, b. 21 Oct. 1802; m. John Holmes (*Duxbury History*, 343). 3. *Samuel Winsor*, b. 1 Aug. 1804.

viii   SALLY WINSOR, bp. 1 July 1781 (*VR* 204); d. at Columbus [Ohio?] after 1849 (not found in 1850 census); m. (1) at Duxbury in Sept. 1805 (*VR* 338, 263), THOMAS HERRICK of Boston, b. Gloucester, d. Richmond, Va., 1814, ae 40, son of Wm. Haskell Herrick (*Duxbury History*, 341); m. (2) at Duxbury, 9 July 1827 as Sarah Herrick, widow (*VR* 263), Rev. THOMAS ASBURY; res. Columbus, Ohio. 1849.

ix   MARTIN WINSOR (Capt.), b. 4 Nov. 1784 (*VR* 203); d. at 1305 Washington St., Boston, 28 Jan. 1877, mariner (Mass. VR 293:306; 294:19); m. at Pembroke, 8 Sept. 1805 (*VR* 375, as *Windsor*), HANNAH ROGERS of Hanover. In 1850 Martin was a mariner at Duxbury, ae 65, with Hannah ae 66, and [dau.?] Hannah A. Baker ae 35; his sister Nancy Howland and her dau. Cordelia shared the same dwelling (p.65).

Children, rec. Duxbury (*VR* 199, 201, 203, 205; marriages from *Duxbury History*, 343): 1. *Albert Martin Winsor*[7], b. 13 Oct. 1807; m. Augusta Merry. 2. *Susan Winsor*, b. 10 July 1809; m. Capt. Thomas Winsor. 3. *Caroline Winsor*, b. 28 Aug. 1811; m. Capt. George Prior. 4. *Hannah Augusta Winsor*, b. 2 Dec. 1815; m. Elijah Baker. 5. *Olive Soule Winsor*, b. 17 Nov. 1824; d. 14 June 1835.

x   BETSEY WINSOR, b. 4 March 1787 (*VR* 177, *sub* Turner); d. Duxbury 26 Jan. 1880 ae 92y 10m 22d (Mass. VR 320:278); m. at Pembroke, 12 June 1803 (*VR* 375 as *Windsor*), DAVID TURNER, b. Pembroke 24 Nov. 1780 (*VR* 177).

Turner children rec. Duxbury (*VR* 177-78): 1. *Betsey Anne Turner*[7], b. 18 April 1804 or 1806. 2. *David Turner Jr.*, b. 14 Aug. 1808; d. 1828 on voyage Boston to New Orleans (*Duxbury VR* 430). 3. *William Turner*, b. 30 Oct. 1809. 4. *Sally H. Turner*, b. 2 Nov. 1812.

xi   NANCY WINSOR, b. 27 Dec. 1788 (*MFIP Soule*, #437-xi), bp. 24 May 1789 (*VR* 203); m. at Duxbury [ca. 1808], as "Ann" (*VR* 266) JOHN HOWLAND, b. 23 Nov. 1780, son of Daniel and Thankful (Morse) Howland (*Duxbury History*, 269-70). In 1850 Nancy and her dau. Cordelia M. had their own household but shared a dwelling with her brother Martin Winsor at Duxbury, and the family included Lucian H. Howland ae 3 (p.65).

Howland children rec. Duxbury (*VR* 94, 386): 1. *Ann Thomas Howland*[7], b. 12 Feb. 1809. 2. *John Howland Jr.*, b. 30 March 1812; d. 20 Sept. 1832, "killed by lightning at sea." 3. *Cordelia Maria Howland*, b. 16 Dec. 1813; unm. 1850.

4. *Lucian Lorenzo Howland*, b. 25 July 1819. 5. *Jerome Howland*, b. 18 July 1822; d. 16 April 1823. 6. *Jerome F. Howland*, b. 23 Feb. 1827.

Sources cited: *Duxbury VR.* Plymouth County Probate Records. Winsor, *History of Duxbury* (1849). CENSUS: Duxbury, Plymouth Co., 1850 (M432-333). **See also:** *MFIP George Soule*, Part Two (2002).

799.   EZEKIEL SOULE[5] (*Mercy Fullerton*[4], *Joshua*[3], *Caleb*[2], *Henry*[1]), son of Joseph Soule Jr. and his wife Mercy Fullerton [165], was born at Duxbury 16 February 1752 (*VR* 160) and died there 3 November 1843 aged 94 (*VR* 421). He was a descendant also of *Mayflower* passengers John Alden and Myles Standish.

He married at Duxbury, 7 January or February 1777 (*VR* 311), **CLINTHEA WADSWORTH**, who was born at Duxbury 25 March 1756 (*VR* 180), recorded as "Cleanthos," daughter of Wait and Abigail (Bradford) Wadsworth. Clynthia, wife of Ezekiel Soule, died at Duxbury 28 August 1827 aged 71, of "internal cancer" (*VR* 421). She was a descendant of *Mayflower* passengers John Alden, William Bradford, William Brewster, Thomas Rogers, and Richard Warren. Ezekiel and Clynthia are buried in the Large Cemetery, Duxbury. His sister Ruby Soule married Clynthia's brother Eden Wadsworth [Family #802].

Ezekiel Soule served in the Revolutionary War (*MSSR* 14:647). In 1790 he was living in Duxbury with five boys under 16, and one female (p.169). Joseph Soule of Duxbury in his will dated 14 July 1794, proved 16 June 1800, left to son Ezekiel two-thirds of the farm "Where I now Live," and named him executor (Plymouth PR 37:254; see *MD* 30:146-49).

In 1810 the family consisted of one man and two women 45 or older, one man 26-45, and one young man and one young woman 16-26 (p.228).

In his will dated 19 June 1837, presented third Monday in February 1844, Ezekiel Soule of Duxbury named sons Charles and Marshall executors; children of "my late sons George Soule and Otis Soule": George M., Laura A., James, Nickolas B., and Mary T.; and daughter Clynthia Soule, "unwell" (Plymouth PR 86:58).

Children of Ezekiel and Clynthea (Wadsworth) Soule, rec. Duxbury (*VR* 161-64):

  i   MARSHALL SOULE[6], b. 24 April 1778; d. Duxbury 27 Feb. 1861 ae 82y 10m, farmer, single, of congestion of lungs (Mass. VR 148:310). In 1850 he was living alone at Duxbury, "yeoman," ae 72, next to family of brother Charles (p.61).

 ii GEORGE SOULE, b. 4 Dec. 1779; d. at St. Thomas, W.I., 11 Feb. 1820 (*VR* 421); m. at Duxbury, 9 Nov. 1806 (*VR* 311), RUTH SPRAGUE, b. Duxbury 4 Dec. 1785, dau. Seth and Deborah (Sampson) Sprague (*VR* 165, 169, 316), d. there 25 March 1836 (*VR* 423).

    Children rec. Duxbury (*VR* 162-64, 421-22): 1. *George Soule*[7], b. 31 Aug. 1807; d. 28 or 30 Oct. 1812. 2. *Laura Soule*, b. 14 Jan. 1811; d. 28 Sept. 1813. 3. *George Marshall Soule*, b. 2 Dec. 1813. 4. *Laura Ann Soule*, b. 14 March 1816. 5. *James Soule*, b. 13 March 1818. 6. *Nicholas Brown Soule*, b. 6 June 1820.

iii   CHARLES SOULE, b. 22 April 1782; d. Duxbury 19 Oct. 1868 ae 86y 6m (Mass. VR 212:302); m. (1) at Duxbury, 25 June 1809 (*VR* 311), MERCY SPRAGUE, b. Duxbury 25 Dec. 1789 (*VR* 169), dau. Seth and Deborah (Sampson) Sprague, d. 16 Dec. 1846 ae 57y 11m 21d, of "canker" (*VR* 422); m. (2) at Duxbury, 19 Dec. 1847 (*VR* 311), MARY B. (SAVERY) ALEXANDER, 34, widow, b. Plymouth, dau. Thomas and Joanna (Burbank) Savery. In 1850 Charles was a mariner at Duxbury, ae 67 with Mary B. ae 36, sons Marcellus (mariner), Otis and Edwin A. (both house-wrights), and prob. stepdau. Mary A. Alexander ae 9 (p.61).

    Children rec. Duxbury (*VR* 161-65): 1. *Isabella Soule*[7], b. 23 March 1810. 2. *Caroline Sprague Soule*, b. 8 Aug. 1811. 3. *Harvey Soule*, b. 16 Nov. 1812. 4. *Elizabeth Soule*, b. 24 Oct. 1814. 5. *Susan Soule*, b. 1815. 6. *Charles Soule*, b. 13 April 1819; d. 22 July 1820 ae 15m (*VR* 421). 7. *Charles Soule*, b. 3 Jan. 1821. 8. *Otis Soule*, b. 2 or 3 Aug. 1823. 9. *Edwin Augustus Soule*, b. 3 Aug. 1825 (twin). 10. *Susan Augusta Soule*, b. 3 Aug. 1825 (twin). 11. *William Marcellus Soule*, b. 27 May 1827. 12. *Peleg Sprague Soule*, b. 9 Nov. 1831. 13. *Mercy Sprague Soule*, b. 15 May 1835.

iv   HARVEY SOULE, b. 29 May 1785 (*VR* 162); d. (*VR* 421, no date), before 1837 (father's will).

v   OTIS SOULE, b. 11 Feb. 1787, bp. 17 Aug. 1788 (*VR* 164); d. City Point, Va., Sept. 1821 (*MFIP Soule* #438-v); m. at Duxbury, 5 Feb. 1815 (*VR* 312), SALUMITH WESTON SAMPSON, dau. Sylvanus and Sylvia Church (Weston) Sampson [#542-iii]. In 1850 she was living Duxbury with her sister Elizabeth Sampson ae 49 (p.60). (See Family #542, p. 55, for their children.)

vi   CLYNTHIA SOULE, b. 20 April 1791 (*VR* 161); d. 4 Aug. 1846 unm. (*Duxbury Hist.*, 312). Charles Soule petitioned as her brother, second Tuesday in April 1857, to administer the estate of Clenthea Soule late of Duxbury (Plymouth PR 13D:397).

Sources cited: *Duxbury VR*. Mass. Vital Records 1841-1910. Plymouth County Probate Records. *Mass. Soldiers & Sailors*. Winsor, *History of Duxbury* (1849). Ridlon, *Soule Family* (1926). *MFIP George Soule*, Part Two (2002), Ezekiel Soule [#438]. CENSUS: *Heads of Families 1790 – Mass.*; Duxbury, Plymouth Co., 1810 (M252-21), 1850 (M432-333). **See also:** *Philip Delano of the Fortune … Fifth and Sixth Generations* (2004).

800. JOANNA SOULE[5] (*Mercy Fullerton*[4], *Joshua*[3], *Caleb*[2], *Henry*[1]), daughter of Joseph Soule Jr. and his wife Mercy Fullerton [165], was born at Duxbury 19 January 1756 (*VR* 160), and died 16 May 1840 aged 84, "widow of Lot [Stetson]," at Pembroke. She is buried in Mt. Pleasant Cemetery, Bryantville (*VR* 448). She was a descendant also of *Mayflower* passengers John Alden and Myles Standish.

She married at Duxbury, 8 May 1777 (*VR* 311), **LOT STETSON**, who was born at Pembroke 21 September 1751 (*VR* 193), son of Nathaniel and Elizabeth (Stetson) Stetson. He died at Pembroke 17 December 1811, aged 60, and is buried in Pembroke Centre Cemetery (*VR* 449).

Lot was a fisherman in summer and a coaster in winter (*Delano* 2004, 104). He served as a corporal in the Revolutionary War (*MSSR* 14:945). In 1790 he was living in Pembroke with two boys under 16 and three females (*Heads of Fam.*, 174).

On 9 January 1808 it was recorded that Lot Stetson had signed a receipt "for Joa his wife," for $24.30, her share of the estate of her father, Joseph Soule (Plymouth PR 42:243).

On 15 April 1812 Harvey Stetson of Fairhaven, shipwright, was appointed administrator of the estate of Lot Stetson late of Pembroke deceased (Plymouth PR 39:351). Dower was set off to the widow Joanna Stetson on 17 December 1813. In an account dated 17 March 1814, Harvey mentions a "note I hold against my father," and money paid to Joanna, widow of Lot Stetson (*ibid.*, 45:299).

Joanna applied for a widow's pension 6 September 1838, giving the place and date of her marriage and date of her husband's death (White, 3319). Following her death, on 9 August 1841 there was a division of her dower in Lot's estate; eldest son Harvey purchased rights of his brothers Lot and Joseph and shared with his sisters Joanna Caswell, Nancy wife of Seth L. Stratton, Caroline Caswell wife of Daniel, and Mercy S. White wife of Charles B. (Plymouth PR 84:186).

Children of Lot and Joanna (Soule) Stetson, b. at Pembroke, births not rec.:

i   HARVEY STETSON[6], b. 3 April 1778; bp. Pembroke 16 Aug. 1778 (*VR* 192); d. there 6 March 1851 of cancer (Mass. VR 58:184); m. at Scituate, 25 Nov. 1802 (*VR* 2:268), POLLY / MARY LANMAN (Landman, m. rec.), b. Plymouth ca May 1776, dau. of Edward Lanman (d. rec.), d. Pembroke 29 April 1860 (Mass. VR 139:318); res. Pembroke 1850 (p.139).
   Children: 1. *Harvey Stetson*[7], b. 1806; ship carpenter 1850; m. Pembroke 1832, Abigail D. Walker (*VR* 353). 2. *Mary A. Stetson*, b. 1808; at home 1850. 3. *Edward Stetson*, b. 1813; at home, a shoemaker 1850.

ii   CAROLINE STETSON, b. ca 1780; d. Foxboro 1 Aug. 1857, ae 77 (Mass. VR 112:221); m. ca 1800 DANIEL CASWELL (father's dist.), b. ca 1781, d.

Foxboro 23 July 1847, ae 66, a shipwright, of consumption, b. Middleboro, parents' names unknown (Mass. VR 33:116).

    Caswell child: 1. *Harvey Caswell*[7], b. ca 1800; d. 1805 (*MFIP Soule*, #439).

iii LOT STETSON JR., b. 15 Sept. 1785; d. Plymouth 20 April 1853, ae 71, carpenter, of consumption (Mass. VR 103:217); m. at Plymouth 14 April 1808 (*VR* 381), HANNAH RIDER, d. Plymouth 11 April 1848 ae 58, consumption, "wife of Lot Stetson" (*VR* 641).

    Children, b. Pembroke (*MFIP George Soule*, 2:184 unless otherwise cited): 1. *Hannah Ryder Stetson*[7], b. 1809; m. Isaac S. Kempton. 2. *Nancy Stetson* (twin?), b. 1816; d.y. 3. *Samuel Stetson* (twin?), b. 1816; d.y. 4. *Mary D. Stetson*, b. 1817. 5. *Asenath Stetson*, b. 1820; d. Plymouth 6 July 1823 (*VR* 526). 6. *Lucy Stetson*, b. 1822; m. Plymouth 1843, Benjamin Dillard (*VR* 603). 7. *Asenath Stetson 2d*, d. Plymouth 3 Nov. 1825 (*VR* 526). 8. *Nathaniel R. Stetson*, b. 1827.

iv JOANNA STETSON, b. ca 1788; m. at Pembroke 28 Sept. 1808 (*VR* 251), ALANSON CASWELL of Plymouth. In 1850 Johannah Caswell ae 61, b. Mass., was living in Bridgeport, Conn., with Mary Caswell ae 31 and Mary E., 11m, both b. Conn., and Catherine Luna ae 19, b. Ireland (p.265), near her sister Nancy Stratton.

v JOSEPH S. STETSON, b. ca Feb. 1791; d. Pembroke 1 Dec. 1814 ae 22y 9m; unm. (*VR* 449).

vi MERCY / MARY S. STETSON, b. ca 1795; d. Pembroke 24 Nov. 1842 ae 47y (*VR* 462); m. at Duxbury, 5 Feb. 1836 (*VR* 317), CHARLES B. WHITE of Boston. In 1840 he was head of a household in Pembroke consisting of himself ae 50-60, and one woman 40-50 (p.107), so there were prob. no children.

vii NANCY SOULE STETSON, b. ca 1802, bp. 12 June 1803 (*VR* 194); m. at Seventh Presbyterian Church, N. Y. City, 9 Dec. 1827, SETH LEGRAND STRATTON (*MFIP Soule*, #439-vii). In 1850 he was ae 43, a carpenter in Bridgeport, Conn., with Nancy ae 47 and five children b. N.Y. (p.266), near her sister Johanna Caswell.

    Stratton children at home 1850 (prob. others, older): 1. *Adeline F. Stratton*[7], b. ca 1833. 2. *Augusta G. Stratton*, b. ca 1836. 3. *George S. Stratton*, b. ca 1837. 4. *Seth LeGrand Stratton*, b. ca 1841. 5. *John H. Stratton*, b. ca 1843.

Sources cited: *Duxbury VR. Pembroke VR. Plymouth VR. Scituate VR.* Mass. Vital Records 1841-1910. Plymouth County Probate Records. *Mass. Soldiers & Sailors.* White, *Abstracts of Rev. War Pension Files*, citing #W15394. *MFIP George Soule*, Part Two (2002). CENSUS: Duxbury, Plymouth Co., 1810 (M252-21); 1850 Ward 4, Bridgeport, Fairfield Co., Conn. (M432-37). **See also:** *Philip Delano of the Fortune ... Fifth and Sixth Generations* (2004).

801. WILLIAM SOULE[5] (*Mercy Fullerton*[4], *Joshua*[3], *Caleb*[2], *Henry*[1]), son of Joseph Soule Jr. and his wife Mercy Fullerton [165], was born at Duxbury 25 December 1759 (*VR* 161), and died there 14 January 1820 (*VR* 424). He was a descendant also of *Mayflower* passengers John Alden and Myles Standish.

He married at Duxbury, 15 April 1784 (*VR* 313), **PRISCILLA SAMSON** [#548], who was born there 18 October 1762 (*VR* 141) and died there 18 September 1844, aged 82y 11m [*sic*, g.s. says d. 1843], "widow of William and dau. of Elijah and Ruth Samson" (*VR* 423). She was also a descendant of Pilgrim Henry Samson. See **Family #548** (p. 64) for an account of this family.

802. RUBY SOULE[5] (*Mercy Fullerton*[4], *Joshua*[3], *Caleb*[2], *Henry*[1]), daughter of Joseph Soule Jr. and his wife Mercy Fullerton [165], was born at Duxbury 23 April 1762 (*VR* 160), and died there 3 or 6 April 1816, aged 54, "— wife of Capt. Eden Wadsworth" (*VR* 433). She was a descendant also of *Mayflower* passengers John Alden and Myles Standish.

She married, about 1786 (b. of first child), **EDEN WADSWORTH**, who was born at Duxbury 12 May 1759 (*VR* 180) and died there 26 or 30 April 1818, aged 59, "drowned," son of Wait and Abigail (Bradford) Wadsworth (*VR* 431). Eden and Ruby are buried in the Large Cemetery, Duxbury. He was a descendant of *Mayflower* passengers John Alden, William Bradford, William Brewster, Thomas Rogers, and Richard Warren. His sister Clynthia married Ruby's brother Ezekiel Soule [Family #799].

Eden Wadsworth served in the American Revolution (*MSSR* 16:380).

At the court of General Sessions in November 1803, the court allowed Eden Wadsworth $6 "for the use of his House etc. at a Court held there by Joshua Thomas Esq." (*PCCR* 4:215). In November 1805 he was licensed as an innholder and retailer in Duxbury (*ibid.*,4:233). In August 1806 he was called a mariner of Duxbury when he and Arthur Howland were sued by Luke Wadsworth of Marshfield for money due by notes dated February 1801; the defendants defaulted (*ibid.*, 11:383).

In 1810 his household in Duxbury consisted of a man and a woman 45 or older, a woman 26-45, and a young man and a young woman 16-26 (p.233).

On 19 December 1817 Eden Wadsworth of Duxbury, mariner, deeded for love all his property to his son Eden Wadsworth Jr. (Plymouth LR 132:187).

Children of Eden and Ruby (Soule) Wadsworth, rec. Duxbury (*VR* 180-84):

  i   BEULAH WADSWORTH[6], b. 25 May 1787 (*VR* 180); d. Duxbury 22 Feb. 1863 ae 75 yrs (Mass. VR 166:281); m. at Duxbury, 25 Jan. 1805 (*VR* 324),

CHARLES WINSOR, b. there 17 Sept. 1781, son of Samuel and Acenith (Hunt) Winsor (*VR* 199).

Winsor children rec. Duxbury (*VR* 199-205); spouses from *Duxbury History* (p.344): 1. *Eden Winsor*, b. 4 Aug. 1806; m. Lucy Weston. 2. *Emily M. Winsor*, b. 15 July 1808; m. Thomas Waterman Herrick. 3. *Nancy Winsor*, b. 2 July 1810. 4. *Asenith Winsor*, b. 14 Aug. 1813; d. 5 Sept. 1835. 5. *Hiram Winsor*, b. 10 Nov. 1815; m. (1) Sally Baker, (2) Lydia Delano. 6. *Whitman S. Winsor* (twin), b. 31 July 1818. 7. *[infant daughter] Winsor* (twin), b. 31 July, d. 24 Aug. 1818. 8. *Ruby S. Winsor*, b. 17 Feb. 1821; d. 13 March 1837. 9. *Abby Otis Winsor*, b. 11 April 1823; m. Henry Wadsworth. 10. *Laura Ann Winsor*, b. 28 Oct. 1825. 11. *Helen Mar Winsor*, b. 10 Oct. 1827; m. ___ Burbeck. 12. *Clara Winsor*, b. 31 Aug. 1829; m. Rufus Holmes.

ii   NANCY WADSWORTH, b. 13 May 1789; d. Duxbury 4 March 1859 of consumption (Mass. VR 130:203); m. ca 1811 JOSEPH BARSTOW, b. Duxbury 14 Aug. 1787, son of Joseph and Lydia (Soule) Barstow, d. there 22 April 1813 (*VR* 23, 350). In 1850 she was living at Duxbury with dau. Beulah ae 37, and son-in-law Francis H. Barstow ae 27, apparently sharing a dwelling with the family of her brother Eden (p.60).

Barstow child rec. Duxbury: 1. *Beulah W. Barstow*, b. 16 Aug. 1812 (*VR* 23); m. Francis H. Barstow (*VR* 216).

iii EDEN WADSWORTH (twin), b. 15 May 1793; d. Duxbury 29 June 1878 (Mass. VR 302:270); m. ca 1822 MERCY BOSWORTH [Samson #673-i-6], b. Duxbury 22 April 1799, dau. Benjamin and Mercy (Prior) Bosworth (*VR* 27, 221). In 1850 he was a mariner at Duxbury, with Mercy ae 51, Eden Jr., Walter H., Fernando, and Claudius and his family; the three older sons were machinists (pp.59-60). Eden's sister Nancy Barstow and her daughter Beulah were part of a household headed by Beulah's husband Francis H. Barstow in the same dwelling.

Children rec. Duxbury (*VR* 180-81, 184): 1. *Claudius Wadsworth*, b. 23 July 1823. 2. *Eden Wadsworth Jr.*, b 9 July 1825. 3. *Walter Hamlet Wadsworth*, b. 26 July 1827. 4. *Fernando Wadsworth*, b. 16 Oct. 1832; d.y. 5. *Fernando Wadsworth*, b. 10 July 1839; m. before 1850 Ellen C. ___.

iv   ZENITH WADSWORTH (twin), b. 15 May 1793; d. 17 Jan. 1810, lost at sea, ae 16y 8m 3d (*Duxbury VR* 433).

Sources cited: *Duxbury VR.* Mass. Vital Records 1841-1910. Winsor, *History of Duxbury* (1849). *MFIP George Soule*, Part Two (2002). CENSUS: *Heads of Families 1790 – Mass.*; Duxbury, Plymouth Co., 1810 (M252-21), 1850 (M432-333).

803.   JOHN FULLERTON[5] (*John Fullerton*[4], *Ruth*[3] *Samson*, *Caleb*[2], *Henry*[1]), son of John Fullerton [166] and his wife Molly Noyes, was born at Abington 19 March 1756 (*VR* 1:84), and died evidently after 1780 (son's birth). He was a descendant also of *Mayflower* passengers John Alden and Myles Standish.

John's father served in the Revolutionary War from Abington, but no record has been found of an appropriate John Jr. from Plymouth County, unless he was the John who was a private in Capt. Edward Cobb's company, Col. Edward Mitchell's regiment, which marched 4 March 1776 to the Farms at Braintree, for five days (*MSSR* 6:195); that service, however, may belong to his father.

No separate census listing for this John Fullerton has been found. The listing for a John Fullerton in Abington in 1810 is that of his son John.

No marriage, death, or probate record for him has been found in Plymouth County. The only record of him so far discovered is on the death record of his son in 1856. The younger John lived in Abington in proximity to his uncle Asa Fullerton and Asa's sons, but neither Asa's family nor that of his grandfather John Fullerton include a boy under 16 in 1790.

Although indications are that John Fullerton died relatively young, it is possible that he left the area, and that his son returned to settle there in 1808.

Child of John Fullerton and _____:

i   JOHN FULLERTON[6], b. 6 July 1780 (calc.); d. 19 Aug. 1856 at High St., Abington, ae 76y 1m 13d of "affection of kidneys," father John Fullerton, mother's name not given (Mass. VR 103:189); m. at Abington, 5 June 1808 (*VR* 2:80), SARAH NOYES, b. ca 1784, d. Abington 6 Jan. 1868 of lung fever, ae 84, parents unknown (Mass. VR 212:292). He is probably the John Fullerton of Abington, yeoman, who sued John Noyes *et al* in Nov. 1809 concerning partition of a certain piece of land in Abington that was undivided between them; he discontinued the suit in April (*PCCR* 12:186). John is listed in census records at Abington from 1810 through 1850, when he was a farmer ae 70 with wife Sarah ae 66 (p.190). In 1810 he was next to his uncle Asa with no children listed (p.96); in 1820 his household included one boy 10-16 and a woman over 45 in addition to Sarah (p.455); in 1830 John and Sarah were 40-50 with one boy and one girl 10-15 (p.388). No record of children's births has been found.

Sources cited: *Abington VR.* Mass. Vital Records 1841-1910. *Mass. Soldiers & Sailors.* Konig, *Plymouth County Court Records.* CENSUS: Abington, Plymouth Co., 1810 (M252-21), 1820 (M33-50), 1830 (M19-388), 1850 (M432-332).

804.   ASA FULLERTON[5] (*John Fullerton*[4], *Ruth*[3] *Samson, Caleb*[2], *Henry*[1]), son of John Fullerton [166] and his wife Molly Noyes, was born at Abington 29 January 1764 (*VR* 1:83), and died there 6 June 1847 aged 83 (*VR* 2:281). He was a descendant also of *Mayflower* passengers John Alden and Myles Standish.

He married at Abington, 29 January 1782 (*VR* 2:80), **MARY HUNT**, who was born at Weymouth and died at Abington 10 January 1851, aged 86, "widow of Asa Fullerton, of old age," parents' names not given (Mass. VR 58:166).

Asa and presumably his wife were living in Abington in 1790 with three boys under 16 (p.164). In 1810 the household consisted of two men and one woman 45 or older, and one young man and two young women 16-26 (p.96). In 1840 Asa and his wife, aged 70 to 80, were living in Abington next to the families of their sons Noah and Jairus (p.163).

No probate records were found in Plymouth, Norfolk, or Suffolk County for Jonathan Hunt, or for Asa Fullerton in Plymouth County.

Children of Asa and Mary/Molly (Hunt) Fullerton, rec. Abington (*VR* 2:83-84):

i   JACOB FULLERTON[6], b. 4 March 1782; d. Abington 20 Feb. 1858 of dropsy (Mass. VR 121:226); m. at Abington, 19 Sept. 1806 (*VR* 2:80), HANNAH REED, b. Abington ca 1786, d. there 19 April 1853 ae 67 of "congestion of brain," dau. of James W. and Abby (___) (Mass. VR 76:191). The 1840 census listed them in Abington, ae 50-60, with two men 20-30, and one girl 10-15 (p.154).

   Children, rec. Abington (*VR* 1: 82-84), some as Fullarton: 1. *Hannah Reed Fullerton*[7], b. 27 Nov. 1808. 2. *Betsey Jane Fullerton*, b. 5 Dec. 1813; d. 1815. 3. *James Reed Fullerton*, b. 16 Feb. 1817; m. Arabella Brewster. 4. *Jacob Fullerton*, b. 1 Nov. 1819; m. Mary Torrey. 5. *Timothy Reed Fullerton*, b. 22 June 1824; d. 26 Oct. 1824 (*VR* 2:282).

ii   NOAH FULLERTON, b. 2 April 1785; d. Abington 11 Sept. 1859 ae 74y 5m, of "disease of brain" (Mass. VR 130:195); m. at Abington, 27 April 1806 (*VR* 2:80), SILENCE DAYLEY, b. ca 1786 Easton, d. Abington 3 Oct. 1859 of "softening of brain," dau. of Daniel and Silence (___) Dayley (Mass. VR 130:195). In 1850 he was a farmer in Abington with his wife Silence, Silence D., Myra, and Henry W., and his mother Mary ae 85 (p.190).

   Children rec. Abington (*VR* 1:82-84), some as *Fullarton*: 1. *Oliver Fullerton*, b. 13 Aug. 1806; m. Rachel Ford. 2. *Silence Dailey Fullerton*, b. 12 Jan. 1809. 3. *Daniel Morton Fullerton*, b. 16 July 1812. 4. *Noah Fullerton*, b. 1 June 1815; m. Martha T. Packard. 5. *Mary Fullerton* (twin), b. 9 March 1818. 6. *Myra Fullerton* (twin), b. 9 March 1818. 7. *Nahum Fullerton*, b. 17 Feb. 1821. 8. *Lucretia Persons Fullerton*, b. 23 March 1824; m. Richard Vining Jr. 9. *Henry Williams Fullerton*, b. 21 Sept. 1827.

iii JAIRUS FULLERTON, b. 19 Dec. 1788; d. Abington 1859 (Plymouth PR #8312); m. at Abington, 27 Feb. 1815 (*VR* 2:79), ABIGAIL KEENE, b. Pembroke 17 Oct. 1797, dau. Galen and Diana (Garnet) Keene (*VR* 127, 303), d. Abington 8 Feb. 1871 ae 75y 3m 22d (Mass. VR 239:319). In 1850 Jairus was a shoemaker ae 60 at Abington with Abigail ae 54, and the five youngest children (p.190).

Children rec. Abington (*VR* 83-84): 1. *Jairus Fullerton Jr.*, b. 18 April 1816; m. (1) Catherine Ann Gurney, (2) Ellen C. Heard. 2. *Lydia Dunham Fullerton*, b. 21 Aug. 1818. 3. *Josiah Fullerton*, b. Dec. 1819. 4. *Samuel Newell Fullerton*, b. 8 Feb. 1822. 5. *Cyrus Fullerton*, b. 16 Dec. 1823. 6. *Caroline Fullerton*, b. 4 Sept. 1826. 7. *Spencer Fullerton*, b. 27 March 1829. 8. *Edward Fullerton*, b. 5 Nov. 1831. 9. *John Newton Fullerton*, b. 5 Sept. 1833. 10. *Lysander Fullerton*, b. 17 Dec. 1835.

iv [CHILD] FULLERTON, d. 7 May 1791, Abington (*VR* 2:281).

Sources cited: Abington VR. Mass. Vital Records 1841-1910. CENSUS: Abington, Plymouth Co. 1790 (M637-4), 1810 (M252-21), 1840 (M704-194), 1850 (M432-332).

805. RUTH FULLERTON[5] (*John Fullerton*[4], *Ruth*[3] *Samson, Caleb*[2]*, Henry*[1]), probable daughter of John Fullerton [166] and his wife Molly Noyes, was born at Abington about 1766 and died there 22 May 1848 aged 82 years (*VR* 2:314; Mass. VR 41:75). She was a descendant also of *Mayflower* passengers John Alden and Myles Standish.

She married at Abington, 1 January 1785 (*VR* 2:79, as *Fulington*; pension says 4 Jan.), **CALEB LOVELL**, who was born at Plympton 21 October 1759 (pension rec.), son of Obadiah and Ruth (Beal) Lovell, and died at Abington 19 or 20 March 1833 aged 73 of consumption (pension rec.; *VR* 2:314).

For details of Caleb Lovell's extensive service in the Revolutionary War, see *MSSR* 9: 998 and 1003-04. He served mostly around Boston and Hull, and at one time under His Excellency John Hancock. Caleb applied for a pension 29 August 1832. When Ruth applied for a widow's pension 28 July 1838, aged 71, she gave the dates of their marriage and of Caleb's death (White, 2127, citing file #W15044). She was listed as a pensioner on the 1840 census (p.146).

Children of Caleb and Ruth (Fullerton) Lovell, rec. Abington (*VR* 1:136-37); one ch. of Caleb d. 24 May 1794 (*VR* 2:314):

i CLARISSA LOVELL[6], b. 5 Oct. 1785; m. at Abington, 21 June 1807 (*VR* 2:134), LEMUEL JENKINS, b. Abington 17 Feb. 1783, d. there 4 April 1823, son of Isaiah and Huldah (Gurney) Jenkins (*VR* 1:124, 2:306).

Jenkins children rec. Abington (*VR* 1:124-25): 1. *Clarissa Jenkins*[7], b. 14 March 1810. 2. *Rebeckah Jenkins*, b. 18 Oct. 1812. 3. *Matilda Jenkins*, b. 12 March

1815. 4. *Harriet Jenkins,* b. 9 Jan. 1818. 5. *Lemuel Jenkins,* b. 8 July 1820; d. 25 Aug. 1823, "son of widow Jenkins" (*VR* 2:306).

ii RACHEL LOVELL, b. 19 Dec. 1787; m. at Abington, 20 April 1807 (*VR* 2:133), WILLIAM WALES JR., called Lieut. William in records.

    Wales children rec. Abington (*VR* 1:238-39): 1. *Rachel Wales[7],* b. 3 April 1808. 2. *Mary Noyes Wales,* b. 27 June 1810; m. Elijah Shaw. 3. *Ruth Fullarton Wales,* b. 15 Aug. 1812. 4. *William Wales,* b. 23 Dec. 1814. 5. *Austin Wales,* b. 27 May 1817. 6. *Theron Wales,* b. 10 Sept. 1818. 7. *George W. Wales,* b. 4 July 1822. 8. *Henry Newton Wales,* b. 25 Feb. 1825; d. 1832 ae 7.

iii BETSEY LOVELL, b. 3 April 1790; m. at Abington, 27 Sept. 1808 (*VR* 2:108), REUBEN HOLBROOK, b. there 29 April 1786 (*VR* 1:111), son of William and Olive (___) Holbrook. In 1850 Betsey was in Abington with Ruth ae 23, Dexter ae 25 (a boot crimper), William ae 18 and Quincy ae 28 (both shoemakers), next to her brother Jacob (p.225).

    Holbrook children rec. Abington (*VR* 1:110-12): 1. *Albert Holbrook[7],* b. 30 July 1807 [*sic – prob.* 1809]. 2. *Betsey Holbrook,* b. 7 Jan. 1812. ? 3. *Osbert Holbrook,* b. ca 1816, next to Betsey 1850; m. Catherine R. ___. 4. *Turner Holbrook,* b. 17 March 1819; m. Tirzah K. Cook. 5. *Quincy Holbrook,* b. 9 Feb. 1823. ? 6. *Dexter Holbrook,* b. late 1824, with mother 1850. 7. *Ruth Lovell Holbrook,* b. 11 April 1826. 8. *William Holbrook,* b. 16 June 1832.

iv RUTH LOVELL, b. 19 May 1792; m. at Abington, 7 Nov. 1824 (*VR* 2:134), HORATIO WHITING of Hanover, b. there 2 Nov. 1791 (*VR* 56).

v MATILDA LOVELL, b. 24 Nov. 1795; m. at Abington, 1 May 1816 (*VR* 2:134), LUCAS DUNHAM, b. Plymouth 2 Feb. 1790, son of George and Phebe (Lucas) Dunham (*VR* 391, 266). In 1850 he was a farmer at Plymouth with Matilda ae 53, Matilda E. ae 22, and Elbridge G. ae 21, a shoemaker (p.178).

    Dunham children at home 1850: 1. *Matilda E. Dunham[7],* b. ca 1828. 2. *Elbridge G. Dunham,* b. ca 1829.

vi CALEB LOVELL, b. 31 Nov. [*sic*] 1798; d. Abington 22 March 1807 ae 8 (*VR* 2:314).

vii JACOB LOVELL, b. 13 Aug. 1802; m. at Abington, 11 Oct. 1826 (*VR* 2:134), RUTH BEAL. In 1850 he was a shoemaker at Abington, ae 47, with Ruth ae 48, and all children except Sarah (p.225).

    Children rec. Abington (*VR* 1:137; census): 1. *Julia A. Lovell[7],* b. 14 June 1827. 2. *Harriet Lovell,* b. 20 Dec. 1828. 3. *Mary Lovell,* b. 12 March 1830. 4. *Henry Lovell,* b. 25 March 1831. 5. *Emily Lovell,* b. 25 Oct. 1833. 6. *Aaron Lovell,* b. 24 July 1836. 7. *Massena/Marcena Lovell,* b. 29 March 1838. 8. *Martin Van Lovell,* b. 14 Aug. 1840. 9. *Sarah Beal Lovell,* b. 31 Aug. 1842; not with family 1850. 10. *Walter Sscott Lovell,* b. 17 July 1844.

Sources cited: *Abington VR. Plymouth VR. Mass. Soldiers & Sailors.* White, *Abstracts of Rev. War Pension Files.* CENSUS: Plymouth Co., Abington 1790 (M637-4), 1820 (M33-50), 1840 (M704-194), & 1850 (M432-332), and Plymouth 1850 (M432-333).

806. WILLIAM FULLERTON[5] (*John Fullerton*[4], *Ruth*[3] *Samson, Caleb*[2], *Henry*[1]), probable son of John Fullerton [166] and his wife Molly Noyes, was born at Abington about 1773. He died at Brockton 30 June 1837 in his 65th year (*VR* 329). He was a descendant also of *Mayflower* passengers John Alden and Myles Standish.

He married at Abington (*VR* 2:79), Bridgewater (*VR* 2:143) or Brockton, 24 November 1796 (*VR* 208), **POLLY PORTER**, born at North Bridgewater 25 February 1778, daughter of James and Mary (Whitman) Porter (*VR* 265). The Abington record calls them William Fullarton and Mary Porter; in the Bridgewater and Brockton records they are William Fullerton and Polly Porter. Mary, widow of William (mistakenly called widow of *James* in one record), died at Brockton 9 October 1847 of consumption, aged 69y 8m 13d (*VR* 330). William and Mary are buried in the Leach Cemetery, "near Crescent St." [G.R. 3], Brockton.

Their first child was recorded at Abington, the next seven at Bridgewater. The marriage records of Harvey in 1827 and Calista in 1829 call them "of N. Bridgewater." The name is spelled variously in records as Fullarton, Fullerton, and Fullington, sometimes with one *l* and sometimes with two.

Children of William and Mary (Porter) Fullerton, first rec. Abington (*VR* 1:122), second - eighth rec. Bridgewater (*VR* 1:122):

i   HARVEY FULLERTON[6] [*Fulliton*], b. 5 Aug. 1798 Abington (*VR* 1:84); d.y.

ii   MEHITABLE FULLERTON, b. 1 Sept. 1800.

iii HARVEY FULLERTON, b. 27 Feb. 1803; m. at Abington 6 June 1827 (*VR* 1:80), MARY GURNEY of Abington. In 1850 Hervey was a shoemaker in East Bridgewater, with Mary and the five youngest children (p.252).

      Children rec. Abington (*VR* 1:83-84): 1. *James Harvey Fullerton*[7], b. 27 April 1828 or 29. 2. *Amanda Fullerton*, b. 24 Feb. 1830. 3. *Mary Elisabeth Fullerton*, b. 24 Dec. 1832. 4. *Almira Jane Fullerton*, b. 28 Jan. 1835. 5. *William Henry Fullerton*, b. 11 Jan. 1838. 6. *Calista Ann Fullerton*, b. 7 Jan. 1841. 7. *Noah Augustin Fullerton*, b. 5 April 1844. 8. [*Infant*] *Fullerton*, d. Abington 22 Sept. 1846 ae 2m (*VR* 2:282).

iv   ALMIRA FULLERTON, b. 7 Aug. 1805.

v   CELISTA FULLERTON, b. 21 Sept. 1807; m. at Brockton, 16 Aug. 1829 (*VR* 207), HARRISON T. MITCHELL.

vi   WILLIAM FULLERTON, b. 12 June 1810.

vii JOHN FULLERTON, b. 25 April 1813.

viii   JAMES PORTER FULLERTON, b. 25 Aug. 1815; d. Brockton 18 Oct. 1845, ae 30y 1m 2d [*sic*] (*VR* 330).

ix   MARCUS FULLERTON, b. 9 June 1818 (year rec. *Brockton VR* 57, from gs.); m. after int. at Brockton 1 Nov. 1840 (*VR* 208), SALLY ANN REYNOLDS. In 1850 Marcus was a bootmaker in North Bridgewater, with Sally Ann ae 32, and three children (p.306).

Children at home 1850; first and last rec. Brockton (*VR* 57): 1. *George H. Fullerton*[7], b. 5 Aug. 1843 at Stoughton. 2. *Ella Fullerton*, b. ca 1836. 3. *Emma Isabel Fullerton*, b. 30 Dec. 1848.

x   MARY PORTER FULLERTON, b. 11 Sept. 1821.

Sources cited: *Abington VR. Bridgewater VR. Brockton VR.* CENSUS: 1850 North Bridgewater, Plymouth Co. (M432-332).

807.   ANNA FULLERTON[5] (*John Fullerton*[4], *Ruth*[3] *Samson, Caleb*[2], *Henry*[1]), probable daughter of John Fullerton [166] and his wife Molly Noyes, was born at Abington about 1777, and died at Ashfield 20 September 1847 aged 70y 4m, of inflammation of lungs (*VR* 243). She was a descendant also of *Mayflower* passengers John Alden and Myles Standish.

She married at Abington, 20 October 1795 (*VR* 2:79), as Anna Fullington, **ZACHARIAH GURNEY**, who was born at Abington 22 August 1767, son of Joseph Jr. and Sarah (Shaw) Gurney (*VR* 1:99, 2:90). He died at Ashfield 30 March 1863, "widower aged 95, shoemaker, born Abington, son of Joseph Gurney" (Mass. VR 165:274).

In 1800 Zachary Gurney was in Abington with a household consisting of one man 26-45, one woman 16-26, and two girls under 10 (p.40). By 1810 they had moved to Ashfield; Zachariah and his wife were 26-45, the two daughters were 10-16, and a boy under 10 had been added to the family (p.268). In the 1830 census both Zachariah and Anna were 60-70 and their household included a man and a woman 20-30 and a little boy under 5 (p.15), probably son Oren and his family.

In 1850 Zachariah Gurney aged 83 was living in the household of his son Orrin at Ashfield (p.187).

Children of Zachariah and Anna (Fullerton) Gurney, first two rec. Abington (*VR* 92, 93), third Ashfield:

i   ELVIRA GURNEY[6], b. Abington 8 April 1795; d. Cummington 12 May 1853 ae 54 yrs (*VR* 214-15); m. LUTHER PACKARD, b. Abington 29 Dec. 1789, son of Luther and Abigail (Thomas) Packard (*VR* 1:158, 2:150). In

1850 Luther was a farmer at Cummington with Elvira, Ezra ae 18, a farmer, Maryett ae 26, Austin ae 3, and Eliza ae 21 (p.193).

    Packard children at home 1850: 1. *Ezra Packard*, b. ca 1822; poss. m. Eliza ___. 2. ?*Maryette Packard*, b. ca 1824.

ii   DEBORAH GURNEY, b. Abington 28 June 1797.

iii   OREN GURNEY, b. Ashfield 25 Jan. 1806 (*VR* 52); m. at Ashfield after int. 1 Aug. 1829 (*VR* 164), EMILY ELDREDGE. In 1850 he was a farmer at Ashfield with Emily, Edwin, Lucy M., and Orrin W., and his father lived with them (p.187).

    Children rec. Ashfield (*VR* 52): 1. *Lemuel Eldredge Gurney*, b. 25 Feb. 1830; d. Ashfield 14 July 1845 (*VR* 243). 2. *Henry Thomas Gurney*, b. 8 March 1832. 3. *Edwin Gurney*, b. 12 March 1835. 4. *Lucy Melvina Gurney*, b. 8 Sept. 1838. 5. *Orpha Gurney*, b. 9 March 1841; d. Ashfield 25 March 1841 ae 16d (*VR* 243). 6. *Orrin Willis Gurney*, b. 20 July 1842.

Sources cited: *Abington VR. Ashfield VR.* Mass. Vital Records 1841-1910. CENSUS: Abington, Plymouth Co. 1800 (M32-16); Ashfield, Franklin Co., 1810 (M252-19), 1830 (M19-64), & 1850 (M432-316); 1850 Cummington, Hampshire Co. (M432-320).

808.   JAMES JOYCE[5] (*Alithea Fullerton*[4], *Ruth*[3] *Samson, Caleb*[2], *Henry*[1]), son of Ebenezer Joyce and his wife Alithea Fullerton [167], was born at Marshfield 16 May 1757 (*VR* 72). He died at Swan's Island, Maine, 23 June 1833, aged 75 (Deer Isle TR 1:101). He was a descendant also of *Mayflower* passengers John Alden and Myles Standish.

He married, about 1784, **MARY (STAPLES) BABBIDGE**, who was born about 1760 and died at Swan's Island 26 February 1836 aged 75, daughter of Samuel and Mary (Cane) Staples of Deer Island, Maine, and widow of Courtney Babbidge Sr. who died at Deer Isle 13 June 1781 (Deer Isle TR 1:101).

By a deed dated 26 February 1779 in Plymouth County, James Joyce of Baggaduce, Lincoln County [Maine], sold to Thomas Joyce of Marshfield his rights to two ninth parts of the estate of his father Ebenezer Joyce of Marshfield, deceased, reserving the improvement of one-half to his grandmother Joyce, according to the will of his grandfather John Joyce, and also reserving his mother's dower (Plymouth LR 59:231). A distribution of the estate of Ebenezer Joyce on 7 April 1781 included two shares to eldest son James (Plymouth PR 28:80).

James settled at Majabagaduce, now Brooksville, about 1780, but on 1 October 1782 he sold his land there to Kenicum Limburner for £50 Halifax currency, and moved to Deer Isle (*Swan's Island History,* 89). In 1790 James Joice [*sic*] was living on Deer Isle with two boys under 16, and five females (p.27). In the

1800 census, James Joice of Deer Isle is indicated as from Marshfield, between 26 and 45, with three males and six females (*NEHGR* 105:207).

In 1806 he moved to Swan's Island, into the "Big House" that had accommodations for 13 families, and later to the east side of the Island, where he built a log house, and then another, the house where he spent his last years with his son William (*Swan's Island History*, 89).

Children of James and Mary (Staples) (Babbidge) Joyce, rec. Deer Isle, Me., to James and Molly (*VR* 8; other information from *Maine Families 1790*, 1:163-64):

   i   ALETHEA JOYCE[6], b. 23 Dec. 1783; m. at Deer Isle, 17 Feb. 1803, JEREMIAH WEED, b. 1780, d. after 1860, son of Benjamin and Hannah (Eaton) Weed (*Maine Fam. 1790*, 1:164).

        Weed children rec. Deer Isle (*VR* 11, 12, 15, 39, 40, 44, 47, 48; see also *Deer Isle History*, 131): 1. *Joan Todd Weed*, b. 16 July 1803; m. (as *Joanna*) Capt. Joseph H. Gray. 2. *Mariah Weed*, b. 4 Jan. 1805; m. Benjamin H. Eaton. 3. *Obed Weed*, b. 24 Oct. 1806. 4. *Jeremiah Weed*, b. 26 Sept. 1808. 5. *William Weed*, b. 2 July [18–]. 6. *James Joice Weed*, b. 25 July 1811. 7. *Olive Joyce Weed*, b. 24 May 1813; m. Samuel Eaton. 8. *Eleanor Stevens Weed*, b. 14 Oct. 1815; m. Nelson Haskell. 9. *Ebenezer Joice Weed*, b. 29 May 1817; m. Elsey Eaton. 10. *Mary Weed*, b. 27 May 1819; prob. m. Capt. Jonathan Gray. 11. *Randolph Weed*, b. 24 Dec. 1820. 12. *Elizabeth Weed*, b. 19 May 1823; m. William Eaton. 13. *Lucy D. Weed*, b. 19 May 182–; m. Benjamin Thompson. (One of the sons d. y.)

   ii   MERCY JOYCE, b. 18 March 1786; d. West Trenton or Ellsworth 1865 ae 80y [*sic*]; m. COURTNEY BABBIDGE, b. ca 1781, d. 1865 ae 75 yrs, son of Stephen and Hannah (Staples) Babbidge (*Swan's Isl. History*, 96). He went to Deer Island before the War of 1812, but after a short time removed to Harrington and later to West Trenton (*ibid.*).

        Babbidge children (*ibid.*, 97-98), order uncertain, first three b. Deer Isle: 1. *Ruth Babbidge*[7], m. Eben Jordan. 2. *Alfred Babbidge*, m. Hannah Hamblen. 3. *Joseph S. Babbidge*, b. 1806; m. Mary C. Hamblin. 4. *Abbie Babbidge*, b. Swan's Island; m. John Smith. 5. *Mercy Babbidge*, m. Levi B. Crockett. 6. *John Babbidge*, m. Isabella Strout. 7. *Courtney Babbidge Jr.*; m. Lucy Leighton. 8. *William Babbidge*, m. Susan York. 9. *Sarah Babbidge*, m. Thomas Hayes. 10. *Mary Babbidge*, m. Nathan McRay. 11. *Samuel Babbidge*, m. Sarah ____.

   iii   RUTH JOYCE, b. 19 Aug. 1788; m. at Swan's Island ca 1816, JOHN STOCKBRIDGE, b. Deer Isle 1796, son of Benjamin and Elizabeth (Dresser) Stockbridge. In 1850 John was a farmer on Swan's Island, ae 54, with Ruth ae 63, sons Samuel and Seth (both sailors), William (a farmer), and dau. (?Marcy; name blotted) ae 19; the family of presumed son Benjamin ae 33 was next door (p.172).

Stockbridge children (1850 census; prob. incomplete): 1. *Benjamin Stockbridge⁷*, b. ca 1817. 2. *Samuel Stockbridge*, b. ca 1824. 3. *Seth Stockbridge*, b. ca 1826. 4. *William Stockbridge*, b. ca 1829. 5. *Mary [?] Stockbridge*, b. ca 1831.

iv OLIVE JOYCE, b. 27 or 28 Jan. 1791; d. 1883; m. LEVI TORREY, b. ca 1789, d. 1863 ae 74 yrs, son of Jonathan Torrey (*Swan's Island History*, 95).

    Torrey children (*ibid.*, 95-96), order uncertain: 1. *Joseph R. Torrey⁷*, b. ca 1815; m. Roxalana Richardson. 2. *Levi Torrey Jr.*, b. ca 1816; m. Joanna Staples. 3. *Louisa Torrey*, m. John Perkins. 4. *Olive Torrey*, m. [her cousin] Isaiah B. Joyce. 5. *Emily Torrey*, d.y. 6. *Charles Torrey*, m. Ann Baker. 7. *Martha Torrey*, m. (1) Freeman Torrey, (2) Seth Stockbridge. 8. *Ezra Torrey*, m. Susan Reed. 9. *Amaziah Torrey*, m. Mary A. Nealey. 10. *Miranda Torrey*, m. George Colter.

v JAMES JOYCE, b. 19 Sept. 1793; d. Swan's Island 1873 ae 79y; m. JANE STINSON, b. Deer Isle ca 1800, dau. of John and Isabel (Dyer) Stinson. In 1850 James Joice was a farmer on Swan's Island, ae 57, with Jane ae 50, and James, Elizabeth, Abigail, Margaret, Oliver, Nancy, Sarah, and Levi (p.172).

    Children (*Swan's Island History*, 90-91; census): 1. *Mary Joyce⁷*, b. ca 1818; m. Levi Babbidge. 2. *Isabel S. Joyce* (Elizabeth on census), b. ca 1820; m. Jacob S. Reed. 3. *Asa Joyce*, b. ca 1822; m. (1) Isabel Staples, (2) Eliza Baker. 4. *Jane Joyce*, m. William A. Friend. 5. *James Joyce Jr.*, b. ca 1828, a ship carpenter 1850; m. Harriet Gott. 6. *Abigail Joyce*, b. ca 1830; m. Isaac H. Marks. 7. *Margaret Joyce*, b. ca 1832; m. William Pickering. 8. *Oliver L. Joyce*, b. ca 1834; m. Amanda Staples. 9. *Nancy E. Joyce*, b. ca 1838; m. Rodney Gott. 10. *Sarah R. Joyce*, b. ca 1841; m. James H. Hutchingson. 11. *Levi B. Joyce*, b. ca 1845; m. Matilda Staples.

vi ABIGAIL A. JOYCE, b. 27 Nov. 1795; m. SAMUEL WHITMORE, who d. ca 1862, son of Joseph and Abigail (Babbidge) Whitmore. In 1850 Samuel Whitemore was a trader at Deer Isle, ae 56, with Abigail ae 55, and children Seth, Samuel, Mary, Joseph, and William; the household included Caroline Stinson ae 19, Daniel Cole ae 21, and Warren Tr---- ae 19 (p.202).

    Whitmore children (*Deer Isle VR* 30, 39, 58, 60, 68; 1850 census): 1. *Seth Whitmore⁷*, b. 18 March 1825/7 [*sic* – prob. 1826]; a trader 1850. 2. *Susanna Whitmore*, b. 9 Oct. 1828. 3. *Lemuel Whitmore*, b. Aug. 18—. 4. *Samuel Whitmore*, b. 20 March 1831; a cooper 1850. 5. *Mary J. Whitmore*, b. 13 March 1832. 6. *James Joice Whitmore*, b. 4 Dec. 1834. 7. *Joseph Whitmore*, b. 11 May 1835 [*sic*]. 8. *William Whitmore*, b. 14 Jan. 1839.

vii EBENEZER JOYCE, b. 14 March 1797; d. Swan's Island 1875 ae 77y; m. CATHERINE STINSON, b. ca 1803, d. 1886, dau. John and Isabel (Dyer) Stinson. In 1850 Ebenezer Joice was a ship carpenter on Swan's Island, ae 51, with Catherine ae 47, and children Ebenezer S., Lucy, Roselinda, John, Reuben B., Catherine A., Maletta, and William S. (p.172). He was a representative to the State Legislature in 1859 (*Swan's Island History*, 93).

Children (*ibid.*; 1850 census), order uncertain: 1. *Sophrona Joyce*[7], m. Simeon Staples. 2. *Isaiah B. Joyce*, b. ca 1821; m. [his cousin] Olive Torrey. 3. *Roderick M. Joyce*, m. Catherine Stinson. 4. *Ebenezer S. Joyce*[7], b. ca 1826; m. Sarah Y. Stinson. 5. *Lucy Joyce*, b. ca 1830; m. Seth Staples. 6. *Roselinda Joyce*, b. ca 1832; m. Stephen Babbidge. 7. *Augustua Joyce*, m. Elias Harrington. 8. *John Joyce*, b. ca 1834. 9. *Reuben B. Joyce*, b. ca 1837; m. (1) Mary A. Lunt, (2) Abbie Young. 10. *Catherine A. Joyce*, b. ca 1839 (not in *History*). 11. *William S. Joyce*, b. ca 1844; m. Deborah Bridges. 12. *Melita Joyce*, b. ca 1847; m. Cyrus Gahan.

viii   WILLIAM JOYCE, b. 24 March 1802; d. Deer Isle 16 Feb. 1862 (*VR* 139); m. on Swan's Island ca 1820, MARY STAPLES, b. ca 1804, dau. Moses; m. (2) after 1850, BETSEY (RAFNELLE) STAPLES. In 1850 William Joice was a farmer on Swan's Island, with Mary ae 46, and eight children; son William's family was next door (p.173). He returned to Deer Isle in 1848.

Children (*Swan's Island History*, 92; 1850 census): 1. *John B. Joyce*[7], b. 1821; d. 1840. 2. *Seth Joyce*, b. ca 1823; a farmer 1850. 3. *William A. Joyce*, b. ca 1826; a fisherman 1850; m. Mary S. ___. 4. *Lemuel Joyce*, b. ca 1829. 5. *Elizabeth Joyce*, b. ca 1831; m. William Wood. 6. *Moses S. Joyce*, b. ca 1834. 7. *Hannah Joyce*, b. ca 1837; m. William Hatch. 8. *Alfred T. Joyce*, b. ca 1839. 9. *John Joyce* (again), b. ca 1840. 10. *Mary E. Joyce*, b. 1844. 11. *Justin A. Joyce*, b. 1846 (not on census).

Sources cited: *Deer Isle VR* (1997). Plymouth County Deeds. Hosmer, *An Historical Sketch of the Town of Deer Isle, Maine* (1886). Small, *History of Swan's Island, Maine* (1898). Ruth Bunker Rohrbaugh, "James Joyce," *Maine Families in 1790*, Vol. 1 (1988). CENSUS: 1790 Deer Isle, Hancock Co., Me. (M637-2); "1800 Census of Deer Isle," *NEHGR* 105 [1951]; 1850 Deer Island and Swan's Island, Hancock, Me. (M432-254). **See also:** *MF 20*: pt 1:141. Ms. from Mrs. Grace Bischof, researcher of Swan's Island Families, with Historian General (Plymouth).

809.   RUTH JOYCE[5] (*Alithea Fullerton*[4], *Ruth*[3] *Samson*, *Caleb*[2], *Henry*[1]), daughter of Ebenezer Joyce and his wife Alithea Fullerton [167], was born at Marshfield 9 November 1759 (*VR* 72), and died at Minot, Maine, 18 May 1845 (g.s.). She was a descendant also of *Mayflower* passengers John Alden and Myles Standish.

She married at Marshfield, 4 November 1779 (*VR* 174), **JOSHUA CROOKER** of Pembroke, born there 26 April 1755, son of Isaac and Desire (Bates) Crooker (*VR* 69, 260). He died at West Minot, Maine, 3 May 1820 (g.s.).

A distribution of the estate of Ruth's father, Ebenezer Joyce, on 7 April 1781 included eldest son James, Hannah Joyce, Ruth wife of Joshua Crooker, Asa Joyce, John Joyce, Abiah Joyce, Stephen Joyce, and Alathea Joyce (Plymouth PR 28:80).

Joshua served as a private in the Revolutionary War (*MSSR* 4:142). With Capt. Freedom Chamberlain's company, Col. Bailey's regiment, he marched on the alarm of 19 April 1775, serving 14 days, and then enlisted and served for 3 months, 6 days; in the fall of 1775 he was at Roxbury Camp, to receive a bounty coat or its cash value; in the fall of 1777 he marched to Rhode Island, serving just over a month with Capt. John Turner's company, Col. Theophilus Cotton's regiment.

On 11 January 1785 Joshua Crooker of Pembroke and his wife Ruth sold their one-ninth part of the estate which fell to them as heirs of their deceased father Ebenezer Joyce, late of Marshfield, in a deed they acknowledged on 7 March 1786 (Plymouth LR 65:205). In August 1786 Thomas and Joshua Crooker of Pembroke divided land there which had been willed to them by their father Isaac Crooker; and Joshua Crooker of Pembroke sold some of his Pembroke land, wife Ruth releasing her dower; Joshua acknowledged both deeds in Plymouth County on 25 August 1787 (*ibid.*, 67:123, 124; 70:106, 142). On 10 November 1789 Joshua Crooker of Bakerstown [now Poland and Minot, Maine] sold the land in Pembroke he had received in the division with his brother Thomas, acknowledged in Plymouth the next day (*ibid.*, 75:105). In 1790 Joshua was living at Bakerstown Plantation, Maine, with two boys under 16 and four females (p.9). No appropriate probate records were found in either Lincoln or Oxford County.

Pension was issued 10 February 1819 to Joshua Crooker of Minot, Cumberland County, Maine. The papers include a record of his marriage. Neighbor Nabby Gardner attested the couple had lived in Pembroke in her father's house until they moved to Minot (White, 721; file #S23875). Pension was issued 12 September 1843 to Ruth Crooker, widow of Joshua. She was aged 78, of Minot, on 2 October 1838 when she declared that Joshua died 3 May 1820, that in 1818 they had lived in Minot for 30 years; and that he had enlisted from Pembroke (*ibid.*).

Children of Joshua and Ruth (Joyce) Crooker, first three rec. Pembroke (*VR* 68-69), last five at Bakersfield Plantation, which became Poland, Me., part later set off as Minot (*NEHGR* 88:59):

   i   CHARLES CROOKER[6], b. 23 Oct. 1780; m. at Minot, Me., 27 Nov. 1800, ELIZABETH PACKARD, b. 29 May 1781 Hebron, Me., dau. of Daniel and Elizabeth (Connelly) Packard.

        Children, b. Woodstock, Me.: 1. *Charles B. Crooker*[7], b. 1 May 1801. 2. *Stephen Crooker*, b. 20 Jan. 1802; d. inf. 3. *Daniel Crooker*, b. 2 Jan. 1804. 4. *Sophronia Crooker*, b. 23 July 1806. 5. *Irene Crooker*, b. 4 April 1809. 6. *John Crooker*, b. 1 Feb. 1812. 6. *Joshua Crooker*, b. 6 March 1816. 7. *Joseph Crooker*, b. 15 Feb. 1819. 8. ? *Attice Crooker*, b. ca 1821.

   ii JOHN CROOKER, b. 20 July 1782; d. unm. at West Minot, Me., 12 May 1806.

iii   ISAAC CROOKER, b. 12 Oct. 1785; d. 3 April 1829; m. at Minot, Me.,
      8 Nov. 1812, IRENA COY, b. Poland, Me., 31 May 1792 (*NEHGR* 88:50),
      d. 8 June 1853, dau. of John and Molly (___) Coy.
          Children: 1. *Mary A. Crooker*[7], b. 18 Feb. 1813. 2. *Henry M. Crooker*, b.
      8 April 1815. 3. *Cyrus C. Crooker*, b. 15 Oct. 1817. 4. *George Crooker*, b. 22 April
      1821. 5. *Joshua Crooker / Allen Jay Crooker*, b. 16 Jan. 1823, name changed 2 May
      1849. 6. *Mary J. Crooker*, b. 8 Feb. 1826; d.y. 7. *John T. Crooker*, b. 19 April 1828.

iv   JOSHUA CROOKER, b. 28 March 1788; m. at Minot, Me., 5 July 1813,
      ALMIRA BEARSE, b. 29 Aug. 1795 at Dover-Foxcroft, Me., dau. Job and
      Betty (Turner) Bearse.
          Child: 1. *Harriet Crooker*[7], b. Hebron, Me.

v   WILLIAM CROOKER, b. 10 June 1791; m. at Minot, Me., 6 Nov. 1819,
      LUCY BEARSE. In 1850 he was a farmer at Minot with Lucy ae 54, and
      three apparent sons (p.47).
          Children at home 1850: 1. *Bearce Crooker*[7], b. ca 1821. 2. *George Crooker*
      (?twin), b. ca 1821. 3. *William A. Crooker*, b. ca 1829.

vi   COMFORT CROOKER, b. 18 April 1794; m. at Minot, Me., 4 March 1822,
      JUDITH BUCKMAN. In 1850 he was a farmer in Minot with Judith ae 50,
      four apparent sons and one daughter, and Susan Bearce ae 70, b. Mass., next
      to his brother William (p.47).
          Children at home 1850: 1. *Joel Crooker*[7], b. ca 1824; working in cotton factory
      1850. 2. *Calvin B. Crooker*, b. ca 1827; a farmer 1850. 3. *Orion Crooker*, b. ca 1830;
      a farmer 1850. 4. *Emeline Crooker*, b. ca 1837. 5. *Isaac N. Crooker*, b. ca 1836.

vii   RUTH CROOKER, b. 4 Sept. 1796; m. at Minot, Me., 4 March 1821, JOHN
      WHITTEMORE. In 1850 John ae 57, b. Me., was a farmer at Hebron, Me.,
      with Ruth and three apparent children (p.35).
          Whitemore children at home 1850: 1. *Joshua Whitemore*[7], b. ca 1826. 2. *Elthea
      Whitemore*, b. ca 1827. 3. *Harriet Whitemore*, b. ca 1834.

viii ALETHIA CROOKER, b. 17 March 1800. Her name may be a transcription
      error, as there is no further record of her, and ALEXANDER CROOKER,
      male, ae 49, was in 1850 a farmer in Minot, next to William and Comfort
      Crooker, with Roanna ae 20, Isaac ae 5, and Dexter Pingree ae 20, farmer
      (p.47). If his age is correct, he was too old to be a son of either William or
      Comfort.

Sources cited: *Marshfield VR. Pembroke VR.* Minot, Maine, Town and Vital Records. Poland,
Maine, Vital Records, in *NEHGR.* 88 [1934]. *Abstracts of Revolutionary War Pensions* and File
#S23875. Gravestone photos in GSMD #66825, MSMD #10407. CENSUS: 1790 Bakerstown
Plantation, Cumberland Co., Me. (M637-2); 1850 Minot, Cumberland Co., Me. (M432-250) &
Hebron, Oxford Co., Me. (M432-263).

810. HANNAH JOYCE[5] (*Alithea Fullerton*[4], *Ruth*[3] *Samson, Caleb*[2], *Henry*[1]), daughter of Ebenezer Joyce and his wife Alithea Fullerton [167], was born probably at Marshfield, say 1762, and died at Buckfield, Maine, 2 March 1840 (pension file). She was a descendant also of *Mayflower* passengers John Alden and Myles Standish.

She was of Bridgewater when she married, first, as his third wife, after intentions 4 May 1782 at Braintree (*VR* 884) and 9 May at Bridgewater (*VR* 2:207), **ISAAC THAYER**. He was born at Braintree 23 November 1741 (*VR* 826), son of Zachariah and Lydia (Pray) Thayer, and died 22 February 1805 at Buckfield, Maine, where he is buried on his farm (*Buckfield History*, 693). He was called "Isaac Thayer resident at Castle W^m" when he married, first, at Braintree, after intentions 19 March 1763 (*VR* 872), SARAH SPEAR, with whom he had children Isaac Thayer and Sally Thayer (*VR* 851). He married second, at Braintree 6 October 1769, "both of this town" (*VR* 875), RACHEL SAWEN, with whom he had Vashti, Shadrach, Eunice, and Eliphalet Thayer (*VR* 851; *Buckfield History*, 692).

Hannah married, second, after intentions at Buckfield, Maine, 5 August 1810, **JOSIAH SMITH**, who was born about 1763 and died 15 July 1823 (pension file), probably at Buckfield.

Isaac Thayer of Braintree served extensively in the Revolutionary War, first as a private and later as a lieutenant (*MSSR* 15:534).

A distribution of the estate of Hannah's father, Ebenezer Joyce, on 7 April 1781 included eldest son James, Hannah Joyce, Ruth wife of Joshua Crooker, Asa Joyce, John Joyce, Abiah Joyce, Stephen Joyce, and Alathea Joyce (Plymouth PR #11719, 28:80). In a deed signed and acknowledged 17 August 1789 in Suffolk County, Isaac Thayer of Braintree, gentleman, and his wife Hannah sold one-ninth share of the estate of their deceased father Ebenezer Joyce late of Marshfield, reserving dower rights of their mother (Plymouth LR 75:107).

In 1790 Isaac Thayer's household at Braintree included one boy under 16 and three females (*Heads of Fam.*,195). The family moved to Maine, about 1792. In 1800 Isaac was head of a household in Hebron that consisted of one woman 45 or older, one man and one woman 26-45, two young men 16-26, one boy 10-16, and one girl under 10 (p.221). Hebron and Buckfield are adjacent towns.

Isaac Thayer, gentleman, late of Buckfield, died intestate. On 7 October 1805 Hannah Thayer, widow, gave bond as administratrix, with Job Prince and Nathaniel Harlow as sureties. Hannah's dower was set off 5 December 1805, and on 11 May 1807 she was permitted to remove her personal belongings, the estate being insolvent (Oxford Co. PR, Early File).

Joel B. Thayer applied 2 March 1852 at Paris, Oxford County, Maine, for a pension based on his father's service in the Revolution. He stated that his father, then of Braintree, married Hannah Joyce of Bridgewater on 4 May 1782; his father died 22 February 1805 and his mother married, second, Josiah Smith, who died 15 July 1823; the widow died 2 March 1840 at Buckfield, leaving children: Joel B., John and Ebenezer Thayer, and Lydia Crooker, all living in 1852. The application was rejected on grounds that Hannah was not a widow of the date of the act, and she died before 16 August 1842 (White, 4:3187, 3457; *Rejected Pensions*).

A photograph of the Lieut. Isaac Thayer House, "oldest building in town [Buckfield, 1915]" appears in *Buckfield History* (p.693).

Children of Isaac and Hannah (Joyce) Thayer, first two rec. Braintree (*VR* 851), rest Buckfield, Me. (*Buckfield History*, 693-94):

  i   POLLY THAYER⁶, b. 15 March 1786; d. before 1840 (parents' pension); m. NATHANIEL HARLOW, b. ca 1781 in Mass. He. m. (2) Lucy ___, and in 1850 was a farmer at Buckfield with her and Nathaniel Jr. ae 23.
      Probable **Harlow** child of Nathaniel and Polly: 1. *Nathaniel Harlow⁷*, b. ca 1827 (census).

  ii JOHN THAYER, b. 13 Feb. 1788; d. autumn 1853; m. at Paris, SUSANNA HERSEY, b. 30 March 1793, a Henry Samson descendant [#815-vii]; buried Hall burying ground on Paris Hill Rd. In 1850 he was a farmer at Buckfield with Susan ae 57, sharing a dwelling with the family of son John G. Thayer (p.104).
      Children (*Buckfield History*, 694): 1. *George Washington Thayer⁷*, b. 29 Oct. 1812; m. Esther Merrill. 2. *John G. Thayer*, b. 5 Jan. 1814; m. Mary Bearce. 3. *Isaac Thayer*, b. 1827; m. Eliza Cooper.

  iii HANNAH THAYER, d. y.

  iv EBENEZER THAYER, b. 20 or 27 Feb. 1797; d. 25 Sept. 1857 (*Buckfield History*, 693); m. MARY FAUNCE, dau. Thomas Faunce, b. ca 1801 at Buckfield. In 1850 they were in Paris, Me., next to his brother Joel (p.193).
      Children (*Buckfield History*, 693): 1. *Mary Ann Thayer⁷*, m. Nathan Chase. 2. *Hannah A. Thayer*. 3. *Sarah J. Thayer*. 4. *Maria E. J., Thayer*, b. ca 1833; m. as his second wife, William Rice (*Paris History*).

  v   JOEL BRIGGS THAYER, b. 9 April 1799; d. at Paris, Me., 14 June 1880; m. (1) at Paris, 25 Aug. 1822, MARY DUDLEY, b. 3 March 1797 in Mass., d. at Paris 30 March 1871; m. (2) LOUISA (GRIFFIN) DAVIS, widow of Rev. Caleb Davis. *History of Paris* relates that on 9 Aug. 1870 "the barn of Dea. Joel B. Thayer was struck by lightning and destroyed; the house was cleared and saved by great effort and a favorable change of wind." In 1850 Joel's household included Christiana Dunham, 8, and James Crooker, 5, both b. Maine (p.193).

Children (*Paris History*): 1. *Alvin Thayer*[7], b. 11 Oct. 1823; settled in Tipton, Iowa. 2. *Angeline Thayer*, b. 2 Dec. 1828; m. Eldridge Forbes.

vi LYDIA THAYER, b. ca 1802; living 1852; m. CALVIN CROOKER, JR., prob. son of Calvin and Dorcas (Caswell) Crooker who m. at Minot in 1797 (*VR* 31). In 1850 Calvin Crooker ae 46, wheelwright, was in Greenwood, Me., with Lydia ae 48, John ae 14, and Eben ae 5 (p.49).

Crooker children (*Buckfield History*, 694): 1. *Almira Crooker*[7], m. Henry O. Bessey. 2. *Hannah J. Crooker*, m. James M. Pote. 3. *Cynthia Hill Crooker*, m. Augustus C. Richmond. 4. *Joel T. Crooker*, m. Mary A. Matthews. 5. *John B. Crooker*, b. ca 1836; m. Eliza Matthews, (2) Laura Merrill. 6. *Orlando Crooker*. 7. *Edwin M Crooker*, d.y. 8. *James Orlando Crooker*, b. 4 Dec. 1841; m. Adelia H. Higgins. ? 9. *Eben Crooker*, b. ca 1845; at home 1850.

Sources cited: *Braintree VR. Bridgewater VR.* . Buckfield, Me., VR, copied by Miss Beatrice Neal. Woodstock Vital Records, microfilm. Plymouth County Deeds. White, *Abstracts of Rev. War Pension Files*, citing #S23969 and #R9742. *Rejected or Suspended Applications for Revolutionary War Pensions* (Washington, D.C., 1852). Cole, *History of Buckfield* (1915). Lapham, *History of Paris* (1884). CENSUS: *Heads of Families 1790 – Mass.*; 1800 Hebron, Cumberland Co. (M32-6); 1850 Oxford Co., Me., Greenwood (M432-262), Buckfield & Paris (432-263).

811. ASA JOYCE[5] (*Alithea Fullerton*[4], *Ruth*[3] *Samson*, *Caleb*[2], *Henry*[1]), son of Ebenezer Joyce and his wife Alithea Fullerton [167], was born probably at Marshfield, 2 July 1766, his birth recorded as an adult at Duxbury (*VR* 100). He died at Plymouth 5 November 1826, aged 57 (*Burial Hill*, 155 #1235). He was a descendant also of *Mayflower* passengers John Alden and Myles Standish.

He married at Duxbury, 7 February 1791 (*VR* 270), **LUCY ANN SOUTHWORTH**. She was born at Duxbury 25 June 1772 (*VR* 100, *sub* Joyce), daughter of Jasper and Rumah (Southworth) Southworth (Davis, 248), died at Boston 24 July 1852, aged 81 (Mass. VR 68:42), and was buried in Burial Hill Cemetery, Plymouth, next to her husand.

Asa's father died when he was a child. On 16 February 1779 Allathea Joyce of Marshfield, widow, was appointed guardian to children of Ebenezer Joyce of Marshfield deceased: Asa Joyce aged 12, Stephen aged 9, Allathea Jr. aged 5, and Abia aged 10; a distribution of Ebenezer's estate on 7 April 1781 included eldest son James, Hannah Joyce, Ruth wife of Joshua Crooker, Asa Joyce, John Joyce, Abiah Joyce, Stephen Joyce, and Alathea Joyce (Plymouth PR #11917, 26:34-37; 28:80). The following year their mother married, second, Jacob Dingley of Marshfield.

By a deed signed and acknowledged 16 November 1787, Asa Joyce of Marshfield sold to Thomas Joyce, land in Marshfield and all rights to his mother's thirds (Plymouth LR 68:30).

In 1810 Asa and Lucy were between 26 and 45, living in Duxbury with a household consisting of one little boy and three little girls under 10, one boy and one girl 10-16, and a young man 16-26 (p.120).

Lucy Ann was not found in the 1850 census. The fact that she died in Boston suggests that one of her children may have been living there, but no confirming evidence has been found. No probate records were found for Asa or Lucy Joyce, or Jasper or Rumah Southworth.

Children of Asa and Lucy Anne (Southworth) Joyce, rec. Duxbury (*VR* 99-100):

i WILLIAM JOYCE[6], b. 23 Aug. 1792; supp. d. Duxbury 17 Nov. 1878 (not found in Mass. VR); m. at Duxbury, 15 Nov. 1818 (*VR* 270), JANE (HUNT) PRIOR [Samson #790-v], b. Duxbury 6 March 1784 (*VR* 96), d. there 25 Aug. 1865 ae 81y 5m 14d, married, of typhoid fever, dau. of Lot and Mary (Sampson) Hunt (Mass. VR 184:277). She m. (1) Ezra Prior with whom she had five children (see p. 474).

   The 1850 census lists William Joyce ae 56 with Jane ae 66, and Samuel H. ae 23 (p.64). In 1860 William Joyce ae 68 and Jane ae 76 were living in Duxbury in the household of [son-in-law] Jabez Keep.

   Children rec. Duxbury (*VR* 100): 1. *William Joyce Jr.*[7], b. 24 Sept. 1819; d. Duxbury 3 Dec. 1841 (*VR* 390). 2. *Mary S. Joyce*, b. 4 Dec. 1820; m. Jabez Keep. 3. *Hannah Otis Joyce*, b. 18 Nov. 1822; m. Samuel Holmes. 4. *Samuel Hunt Joyce*, b. 28 July 1824; d. 31 July 1825 ae 1y 3d (*VR* 389). 5. *Samuel Hunt Joyce*, b. 13 Jan. 1827; at home 1850.

ii JOHN JOYCE, b. 10 May 1794.

iii PETER JOYCE, b. 8 Aug. 1796; d. Worcester 2 Dec. 1859 ae 63 of consumption and dropsy, married, manufacturer, b. Duxbury of Asa and Lucy Ann (Mass. VR 131:181); m. (1) at Dudley, 28 Sept. 1823 (*VR* 189), SALLY WILLIAMS PERRY, d. Dudley 29 Dec. 1824 ae 23 (*VR* 270); m. (2) at Bellingham, 29 June 1826 (*VR* 122) after int. 10 June 1826 at Dudley (*VR* 189), SABRINA HOLBROOK. In 1850 Peter Joyce ae 52 (indexed as *Toyer*) was an "agent" in Worcester, with Edmund S. ae 23, Sally W. ae 25, and Sabra Holbrook [*sic*] ae 50 (p.237).

   Child with Sally: 1. *Sally Williams Joyce*[7], b. 31 Oct. 1824, Dudley (*VR* 76). Children with Sabrina, first three rec. Bellingham (*VR* 46): 2. *Edmund Sanford Joyce*, b. 28 Jan. 1828. 3. *Helen Minerva Joyce*, b. 17 Aug. 1830. 4. *Henry Clay Joyce*, b. 16 May 1834; d.y. 5. *Henry Clay Joyce*, b. 16 June 1836, Oxford (*VR* 61).

iv STEPHEN JOYCE, b. 7 Aug. 1798.

v   ABIGAIL JOYCE, b. 23 July 1802.

vi   [CHILD] JOYCE, "— child of Asa" who d. 1806 (*VR* 390).

vi   DEBORAH JOYCE, b. 3 July 1806.

vii   ALATHEA JOYCE, b. 24 Nov. 1808.

viii   HANNAH JOYCE, b. 2 Sept. 1812; perhaps d.y.

Sources cited: *Bellingham VR. Dudley VR. Duxbury VR.* Mass. Vital Records 1841-1910. Plymouth County Deeds. *Epitaphs from Burial Hill, Plymouth.* Davis, *Genealogical Register of Plymouth Families.* CENSUS, Duxbury, Plymouth Co., 1810 (M252-21), 1850 Duxbury, Plymouth Co. (M432-333) & Worcester, Worcester Co., 1850 (M432-342).

812.   STEPHEN JOYCE[5] (*Alithea Fullerton*[4], *Ruth*[3] *Samson, Caleb*[2], *Henry*[1]), son of Ebenezer Joyce and his wife Alithea Fullerton [167], was born probably at Marshfield about 1770 (guardianship rec. ae 9 in 1779), and died by 1800 when his wife was head of a household at Duxbury. He was a descendant also of *Mayflower* passengers John Alden and Myles Standish.

He married, about 1794, **LUCY PETERSON**, who was living at Duxbury in 1800. Record of the marriage has not been found, but her maiden name is given in the death record of daughter Weltha. She may be the Lucy Peterson born at Duxbury 13 June 1771, daughter of Jonathan and Lucy (Hunt) Peterson (*VR* 121). She probably married, second, at Duxbury, 28 April 1804, JOHN PATTIN (*VR* 270), whose name in the marriage record is given as John Pollin. John and Lucy Pattin had three children recorded at Duxbury: Catherine Pattin, b. 15 March 1805, John Pattin, b. 15 February 1807, and Lucy Pattin, b. 15 September 1808 (*VR* 116). Welthea (Joyce) Sampson, daughter of Stephen and Lucy Joyce, named a child Catherine Patten Sampson, apparently for her half-sister.

Stephen's father died when he was a child. On 16 February 1779 Allathea Joyce of Marshfield, widow, was appointed guardian to children of Ebenezer Joyce of Marshfield deceased: Asa Joyce aged 12, Stephen aged 9, Allathea Jr. aged 5, and Abia aged 10. A distribution of Ebenezer's estate on 7 April 1781 included eldest son James, Hannah Joyce, Ruth wife of Joshua Crooker, Asa Joyce, John Joyce, Abiah Joyce, Stephen Joyce, and Alathea Joyce (Plymouth PR #11917; 26:34-37, 28:80). The following year their mother married, second, Jacob Dingley of Marshfield.

By a deed signed and acknowledged on 28 May 1796 Stephen Joyce of Duxbury, mariner, sold land in Marshfield that had been set off to him and his sister Alethea Joyce in the division of their father's estate; his wife Lucy relinquished her dower (Plymouth LR 82:69).

In 1800 Lucy Joyce, 26-45, was living in Duxbury with two girls under 10 (p.98). In 1810 John Pattin was head of a household in Duxbury that consisted of one man 45 or older, one woman 26-45, one young man 16-26, two girls 10-16, and two boys and two girls under 10 (p.226) — figures suggesting that Lucy was his second wife. No probate records for this family have been found.

Children of Stephen and Lucy (Peterson) Joyce, rec. Duxbury (*VR* 100):

i   WELTHEA P. JOYCE[6], b. 5 Sept. 1795; d. Duxbury 18 Aug. 1889 ae 93y 11m 13d (Mass. VR 401:362); m. at Duxbury, 5 May 1816, as Wealtha B. Joyce, ALFRED SAMSON [#786-vi], son of Studley and Abigail (Prior) Samson, b. at Duxbury 12 Feb. 1790 (*VR* 137), d. there 16 Aug. 1875 (Mass. VR 275:301). They are buried in the Large Cemetery, Duxbury, where Capt. Alfred's g.s. says b. 1791, and hers says Weltha P., b. 1795 (*VR* 137, 143). See Family #786-vi (p. 467) for their children.

ii HANNAH JOYCE, b. 31 July 1798.

Sources cited: *Duxbury VR.* Mass. Vital Records 1841-1910. Plymouth County Deeds and Probate Records. CENSUS, Duxbury, Plymouth Co., 1800 (M32-16), 1810 (M252-21).

813. ALATHEA JOYCE[5] (*Alithea Fullerton[4], Ruth[3] Samson, Caleb[2], Henry[1]*), daughter of Ebenezer Joyce and his wife Alithea Fullerton [167], was born probably at Marshfield 23 March 1774 (b. rec. as w. Joseph Freeman, Duxbury [*VR* 78]), and died between 1850 (census) and August 1859, when her husband died, described as "widowed." She was a descendant also of *Mayflower* passengers John Alden and Myles Standish.

She married at Duxbury, — 1798 [*sic*] (*VR* 270), **JOSEPH FREEMAN**, who was born at Duxbury 13 May 1775 (*VR* 80, rec. as adult) and died there 4 August 1859, aged 85, widowed, son of Immanuel and Lucy (Sprague) Freeman (Mass. VR 130:203), a Henry Samson descendant [#206-iii-5].

Alathea's father died when she was a child. On 16 February 1779 Allathea Joyce of Marshfield, widow, was appointed guardian to children of Ebenezer Joyce of Marshfield deceased: Asa Joyce aged 12, Stephen 9, Allathea Jr. 5, and Abia, 10 (Plymouth PR 26:34-37). A distribution of Ebenezer's estate on 7 April 1781 included eldest son James, Hannah Joyce, Ruth wife of Joshua Crooker, Asa Joyce, John Joyce, Abiah Joyce, Stephen Joyce, and Alathea Joyce (*ibid.,* 23:110, 28:80); the following year their mother remarried. In a deed signed and acknowledged on 26 May 1795, Alethea Joyce of Marshfield, taylor, sold to Stephen Joyce of Duxbury, seaman, part of a meadow in Marshfield that had belonged to Ebenezer Joyce (Plymouth LR 78:57).

In 1850 Joseph Freeman, aged 75, was a shoemaker at Duxbury, with Alethea aged 76, and John aged 34, a laborer (p.85).

No probate records for Joseph, Immanuel, or Alathea Freeman were found in Plymouth County.

Children of Joseph and Alathea (Joyce) Freeman, rec. Duxbury (*VR* 79-81):

i JAMES FREEMAN[6], b. 30 May 1799; d. Pembroke 11 July 1852 ae 53, "fit" (Mass. VR 67:265); m. at Duxbury, Oct. 1819 (*VR* 255), SALLY OLDHAM, prob. dau. of John and Elizabeth (Chandler) Oldham b. Duxbury 17 June 1794 (*VR* 113). In 1850 James was ae 51, a shoemaker at Pembroke, with Sally ae 56, and George W. ae 21; Horace Oldham ae 18, shoemaker, was in their household (p.140).

    Children, all but George rec. Duxbury (*VR* 78-80): 1. *Allen T. Freeman[7]*, b. 31 Dec. 1821; d. 5 Feb. 1823 (*VR* 378). 2. *Henry A. Freeman*, b. 17 May 1823. 3. *Lemuel D. Freeman*, b. 20 Jan. 1825. 4. *Elisabeth O. Freeman*, b. 20 March 1828. ? 5. *George W. Freeman*, b. ca 1829; at home 1850. 6. *[Son] Freeman*, b. 8 Jan. 1833.

ii POLLY FREEMAN, b. 29 July 1801; prob. m. at Duxbury, 10 Dec. 1823 (*VR* 256), SAMUEL D. HOLMES. No children rec. Duxbury.

iii HENRY FREEMAN, b. 10 Oct. 1803.

iv RUTH FREEMAN, b. 25 June 1807.

v DEBORAH FREEMAN, b. 27 Nov. 1809.

vi SPRAGUE FREEMAN, b. 2 Oct. 1812; d. June 1878 (Mass. VR 302:210); m. at Duxbury, 14 Dec. 1836 (*VR* 256), SYLVINA DELANO, b. Duxbury 1 April 1812, daughter of Nathan and Huldah (Bates) Delano, d. there 17 March 1889 of pneumonia (Mass. VR 401:362). In 1850 Sprague Freeman was ae 38, a housewright at Duxbury, with Silvina ae 37, Huldah ae 7, and Nathan ae 5 (p.88), next door to the family of his sister Sarah.

    Children at home 1850: 1. *Huldah D. Freeman[7]*, b. 17 Aug. 1842, Duxbury (*VR* 79). 2. *Nathan Freeman*, b. Aug. 1844; d. 1885.

vii JOHN FREEMAN, b. 15 Sept. 1815; with parents 1850.

viii SARAH A. FREEMAN, b. 12 May 1819; m. at Duxbury, 22 Sept. 1839 (*VR* 256), MARTIN CHURCH, b. 1818 (g.s.); both buried Ashdod Cemetery, Duxbury (*VR* 50). In 1850 they lived next to her brother Sprague; Martin was ae 28, a housewright, with Sarah A. ae 27 [*sic*], and David F. ae 7 (p.88).

    Church children: 1. *David F. Church[7]*, b. 15 Oct. 1842 at Duxbury (*VR* 50). 2. *Henry M. Church*, b. 20 March 1846 (calc.); d. 24 Oct. 1846 ae 7m 4d; buried Ashdod Cemetery, Duxbury (*VR* 363).

Sources cited: *Duxbury VR.* Mass. Vital Records 1841-1910. Plymouth County Deeds. CENSUS: 1850 Plymouth Co.: Pembroke (M432-332) & Duxbury (M432-333).

814.   ANNA POOLE[5] (*Ruth Fullerton*[4], *Ruth*[3] *Samson, Caleb*[2], *Henry*[1]), daughter of Samuel Poole and his wife Ruth Fullerton [168], was born at Abington 13 September 1761, a twin to Alathea (*VR* 1:165), and died at Cummington 22 December 1837, aged 76, "widow of Deacon J. Whitmarsh" (*VR* 241). She was a descendant also of *Mayflower* passengers John Alden and Myles Standish.

She married at Bridgewater, 22 April 1784 (*VR* 2:403), **JACOB WHITMARSH JR.**, who was born there 14 July 1759 (*VR* 1:345), and died at Cummington 22 April 1823, aged 64, son of Jacob and Hannah (Shaw) Whitmarsh (*VR* 242).

Jacob's father, Jacob Whitmarsh of Bridgewater, housewright, in 1773 and 1774 bought land in Plantation #5 (which became Cummington in 1779), and on 23 October 1781, he sold land in Cummington to Jacob Whitmarsh of Cummington (Hampshire LR 3:449; 6:424; Hampden LR 17: 543, 544). An account of early Cummington families (*VR*, xxxvii) says, "Dea. Jacob Whitmarsh was head of the family in Cummington. He settled in the southwest corner of the town and was followed by his son, Jacob, and grandson, Nahum."

In 1790 Jacob Whitmarsh of Cummington was head of a household with two boys under 16 and four females (*Heads of Fam.*,109). In 1800 the household consisted of a man and a woman 26-45, one young man 16-26, one boy and three girls 10-16, and two boys and two girls under 10 (p.880). In 1810 Jacob and Anna were both over 45, and the family at home included one woman 16-26, two boys and one girl 10-16, and one boy under 10 (p.275). The 1820 census listed a man and a woman 45+, one young woman 16-26, two young men 18-26, and one boy under 10 (p.163); a younger Jacob Whitmarsh, probably son of this Jacob and Anna, was living at Plainfield.

No appropriate probate records were found for this family in Berkshire, Franklin, Hampden, or Hampshire counties. Several of the next generation moved on to Michigan and Ohio; news of them appears in letters published in introductory material in *Cummington VR.*

Children of Jacob and Anna (Poole) Whitmarsh, rec. Cummington (*VR* 87):

i   ANNA WHITMARSH[6], b. 11 Sept. 1785; d. Cummington 1 Jan. 1805 ae 20 yrs (*VR* 203); m. at Cummington, 2 Dec. 1804 (*VR* 129, poss. an error in date), WILLIAM KNAPP, b. there, son of Jonathan Knapp, d. there 15 July

1853 ae 71 (*VR* 204). He m. (2) MARTHA ___, with whom he several
more children.

Knapp child: 1. *William W. Knapp[7]*, b. 20 Dec. 1804; m. Maria H. Austin
(*Whitmarsh Gen.,* 31).

ii ALETHEA WHITMARSH, b. 17 Jan. 1787; m. at Cummington, 8 Feb. 1810
(*VR* 109), GORHAM COTTRELL, b. Worthington 25 April 1780, son of
Asa and Sindah [Lucinda] (?Clapp) Cottrell (*VR* 26). They settled ca 1836 in
Gorham, Ohio, which was named for him but later renamed Fayette. In
1850 he was a farmer ae 70 in Gorham, with Althea ae 63, and children
Gershom and Alethea; Ann Latham ae 9, b. Ohio, and George Ten Eyck,
laborer, shared the household (p.345).

Cottrell children, b. Mass., prob. Worthington (*Whitmarsh Gen.,* 31):
1. *Erastus Cottrell[7]*, b. 27 Aug. 1811; m. Emily Rogers. 2. *Ann Cottrell,* b. 21 Feb.
1813; m. Chester Latham. 3. *Joseph Cottrell,* b. 4 April 1815; m. Hannah Maria
Lloyd. 4. *Sardis Cottrell,* b. 30 Oct. 1817; m. Anna Willett; living next to parents
1850. 5. *Lucy Cottrell,* b. 10 March 1820; m. (1) James A. Rodgers, (2) George R.
Joy. 6. *Jane Cottrell,* b. 22 March 1824; m. Philetus W. Morris. 7. *Gorham Cottrell,*
b. 11 Oct. 1826; at home 1850. 8. *Alethea Cotrell,* b. 28 Feb. 1829; at home 1850.

iii JACOB WHITMARSH, b. 1 Jan. 1789; d. Cummington 9 Feb. 1872, ae 83
(*VR* 242); m. at Cummington, 29 Dec. 1814 (*VR* 169), OLIVE
PACKARD, b. there 9 Oct. 1793, d. there 25 July 1870 ae 76y 10m 9d of
apoplexy, dau. of Adam and Abigail (Porter) Packard (*VR* 242; Mass. VR
230:53). In 1850 Jacob was a farmer ae 61 at Plainfield, with Olive ae 56,
Fordyce ae 24, Rachel ae 19, and Nahum ae 15 (p.199).

Children (*Plainfield History,* 186-87; *Whitmarsh Gen.,* 37): 1. *Polly Packard
Whitmarsh[7]*, b. 19 Nov. 1815; m. (1) Robert A. Latham, (2) William Warner.
2. *Florintha Whitmarsh,* b. 15 April 1817; m. (1) Verren Dawes, (2) Isaac Bates, (3)
Lewis Ford. 3. *Mary Ann Whitmarsh,* b. 14 Jan. 1819; m. Newell Dyer. 4. *Jacob
Sebert Whitmarsh,* b. 9 June 1823; m. (1) Polly Bartlett, (2) Maria S. Nash. 5. *Fordyce
Whitmarsh,* b. 29 April 1826; m. (1) Eliza Allen, (2) Marion C. Dyer. 6. *Rachel
Whitmarsh,* b. 21 May 1831; m. Levi N. Campbell. 7. *Nahum Whitmarsh,* b. 16 Oct.
1834; m. Mary Lucas.

iv POLLY WHITMARSH, b. 14 Dec. 1790; d. 10 April 1825; m. 8 Feb. 1810,
JOHN SHAW, d. 27 Oct. 27 Oct. 1826; res. Worthington.

Shaw children (*Whitmarsh Gen.,* 32): 1. *Silena Shaw[7]*, b. 12 Jan. 1811; m.
Norton Warner. 2. *Lyanda Shaw,* b. 7 March 1813; m. Alonzo Mitchell.
3. *Nathan Shaw,* b. 18 April 1820; m. Ann B. Ford.

v CLARISSA WHITMARSH, b. 21 Oct. 1792; m. at Cummington, 23 Oct.
1817 (*VR* 116), CYRUS FORD, b. there 16 May 1790, son of Hezekiah
and Huldah (___) Ford and twin to Darius Ford (*VR* 26). They moved to

Ohio in 1837, where Cyrus was involved in an unsuccessful "venture to grow and sell mulberry trees, silk worms, and silk for the satinette factories" (*Cummington VR*, xviii). Letters he wrote from 1837 to 1852 to his brother Lewis in Cummington "depict the hard times in both Cummington and Ohio, the shortage of money, the longing for home of the women and children" (*ibid.*), and mention visits to relatives and friends in Michigan and Ohio. In 1850 Cyrus Ford ae 60 was a farmer in East Cleveland, Ohio, with Clarissa ae 58, and sons Horace, Henry, Francis, and Lewis (p.304).

   Ford children rec. Cummington (*VR* 27, 90; spouses from *Whitmarsh Gen.*, 32-33): 1. *Horace Ford*[7], b. 22 Oct. 1823; m. (1) Sarah A. Dawes, (2) Mary C. Hovey, (3) Eliza Talbot. 2. *Horatio C. Ford*, b. 24 July 1825; m. Martha Cordelia Cozad. 3. *Henry Ford*, b. 24 Nov. 1826; m. Martha Slaght. 4. *Francis Ford*, b. 1 May 1828; m. Mercy Fuller; an engineer 1850. 5. *Lewis W. Ford*, b. 12 Dec. 1830; m. Ann Fenn; a student 1850. 6. *George Ford*, b. 1 May 1832; d. Cummington 15 June 1832.

vi   NAHUM WHITMARSH, b. 20 Oct. 1794; d. 7 Feb. 1857; called Lieut. Nahum when he m. at Cummington, 13 Nov. 1828 (*VR* 169), MARY ANN WARNER. They removed to Palmyra, Mich., where Nahum was a farmer ae 55 in 1850, with Mary A. ae 45, and three children (p.194).

   Children (1850 census; *Whitmarsh Gen.*, 37): 1. *Charles Carroll Whitmarsh*[7], b. 13 March 1830 Mass. 2. *Clarissa Warner Whitmarsh*, b. 28 Sept. 1832 Mass.; m. ___ Benedict. 3. *Lewis Whitmarsh*, b. 6 Dec. 1834; d. ae 6m. 4. *Lewis W. Whitmarsh*, b. 10 July 1838 Mich.

vii   ALVAH WHITMARSH, b. 15 Aug. 1796; d. 9 Sept. 1862; m. (1) 14 Dec. 1820, LYDIA CLARK, d. 23 Dec. 1828; of Springfield when m. (2) 1 Jan. 1830 after int. Southampton 12 Dec. 1829 (*VR*, Corbin), Lydia's sister, NAOMI MATILDA CLARK. Rem. from Cummington to Princeton, Ill., 1841 (*Whitmarsh Gen.*, 37).

   Children, with second wife (*ibid.*,37-38): 1. *Thomas Cranmer Whitmarsh*[7], b. 13 Sept. 1822. 2. *Mary Ann Whitmarsh*, b. 15 June 1825; m. George W. Sisler. 3. *Lewis Clark Whitmarsh*, b. 5 March 1827. 4. *Lydia Clark Whitmarsh*, b. 7 Dec. 1828; m. Lucius Warner. 5. *Samuel Pool Whitmarsh*, b. 8 July 1831. 6. *Alvah Mason Whitmarsh*, b. 15 June 1835; m. Mary Steele. 7. *Jerusha Bartlett Whitmarsh*, b. 3 July 1840; m. Atherton Clark. 8. *Horace Edson Whitmarsh*, b. 21 April 1843.

viii   HANNAH WHITMARSH, b. 29 Sept. 1798; m. at Cummington, 1 Jan. 1828 (*VR* 107), FREEMAN COFFIN of Worthington, b. ca 1786. They were in Gorham, Ohio, by 1836 and Freeman ae 64 was a farmer there in 1850, with Hannah ae 51 and three children (p.345).

   Coffin children at home 1850, all b. Mass. (b. dates and spouses, *Whitmarsh Gen.*, 33): 1. *George W. Coffin*[7], b. 5 Oct. 1829; m. Emily Hill. 2. *Rosamond Coffin*, b. 4 June 1831; m. ___ Fuller. 3. *Ellen W. Coffin*, b. 10 July 1833.

ix   HORACE WHITMARSH, b. 5 Jan. 1801; d. 10 April 1896; of Springfield
      when he m. (1) at Cummington, 9 or 19 Aug. 1831 (*VR* 169) or 16 Sept.
      1831 (*Whitmarsh Gen.*, 38), CLARISSA M. WARNER, d. 23 Jan. 1839; m. (2)
      22 March 1842, LOUISA LEWIS, d. 8 Feb. 1893. They removed to
      Palmyra, Mich., and res. also Quincy, Mich., Hiawatha, Kans., and Bluff
      Point, N.Y. (*ibid.*).
           Children (*ibid.*):   1. *Ellen Augusta Whitmarsh⁷*, b. 30 Oct. 1832; m. Almon
      Whitman. 2. *Horace P. Whitmarsh*, b. 18 May 1834. 3. *Laura Whitmarsh*, b. 12 Oct.
      1836; m. James Miller. 4. *Clarissa Whitmarsh*, b. 5 Jan. 1839; m. W. H. Colvin.
      5. *Mary Louise Whitmarsh*, b. 22 Oct. 1853. 6. *Alice E. Whitmarsh*, b. 24 July 1856.

x   ERASTUS WHITMARSH, b. 6 Oct. 1803; d. 15 July 1805 ae 1y 9m 9d.

Sources cited: *Bridgewater VR. Cummington VR.* Southampton VR, Corbin. Hampshire County
Deeds. Hampden County Deeds. Dyer, *History of Plainfield* (1891). Bates, *Genealogy of the Descendants
of John Whitmarsh of Weymouth, Mass.* (1916). CENSUS: *Heads of Families 1790 – Mass.*; Cummington,
Hampshire Co., 1800 (M32-15), 1810 (M252-19), 1820 (M33-50); 1850 Plainfield, Hampshire Co.
(M432-320), E. Cleveland, Cuyahoga Co., Ohio (M432-672), Gorham, Fulton Co., Ohio (M432-
681), Palmyra, Lenawee Co., Mich. (M432-355).

815.   ALATHEA POOLE⁵ (*Ruth Fullerton⁴, Ruth³ Samson, Caleb², Henry¹*),
daughter of Samuel Poole and his wife Ruth Fullerton [168], was born at Abington
13 September 1761, a twin to Anna (*VR* 1:165), and died at Sumner, Maine, 7 May
1845, aged 80 (cem rec.). She was a descendant also of *Mayflower* passengers John
Alden and Myles Standish.

She was "of Minot, Maine," 11 October 1781 when she married at Bridgewater, after intentions 10 April 1781, **JAMES HEARSEY JR.**, who was born at
Abington 12 December 1758, son of James and Betty (Noyes) Hearsey (*VR*
1:106). He died at Sumner, Maine, 27 May 1846. James and Alethea are buried in
the Hearsey Cemetery, Sumner, Maine (g.s.).

James was a sergeant in the Revolutionary War. He lived in Abington, then
moved to Minot, Maine, and about 1801 to Sumner.

A James Hassa was living in Bakerstown Plantation [now Poland, Me.], in
1790 with three boys under 16 and two females. In 1800 James Hersy was in
Cumberland County, Maine, his household consisting of a man and a woman 26-
45, three little girls under 10, one boy and one girl 10-16, and two young men 16-
26 (p.213).

In an application for pension dated 14 August 1832, James Hearsey, aged 74,
then residing in Sumner, Maine, claimed that he had enlisted from Abington in the

spring of 1775 and several times thereafter; that he was born in Abington in 1758; and that he had lived in Oxford County for about 31 years.

No appropriate probate records for James or Alathea were found in Oxford County.

Children of James and Alathea (Poole) Hearsey, first ten rec. Poland, Maine (*NEHGR* 88:49), all except first Alethea rec. also East Sumner, Maine (1:48):

    i   SIMEON HEARSEY[6], b. Bridgewater 8 July 1782; m. LOIS ___, b. Maine ca 1783; res. Sumner, Me., 1850, a farmer; no children at home (p.153).

    ii   JAMES HEARSEY, b. at New Gloucester, Me., 11 Nov. 1783; living 1850 at Sumner, ae 66, a farmer with real estate worth $2700; m. ABIGAIL _____, b. ca 1796 in Maine. In 1850 their household included Sylvina B. Keen ae 32, Cynthia Keen ae 11, and Zephira Keen ae 7, all b. Maine (p.152). Next door was Harriett D. Hearsey ae 30, with children Eliza ae 6 and James ae 4. (White, 1589, citing Rev. War Pension #S31121, says a son "Joseph Jr." was a JP for Oxford Co., Me., in 1832; this is prob. an error for James Jr.)

   iii SAMUEL HEARSEY, b. Poland, Me., 14 May 1786; m. POLLY B. ___, b. Maine ca 1894; res. Sumner, Me., 1850, a farmer, with Polly and two children; Daniel Fletcher ae 19 was also in the household (p.156).
          Children at home 1850: 1. *Henry B. Hearsey*[7], b. ca 1834; a farmer. 2. *Eunice M. Hearsey*, b. ca 1836.

   iv ALETHEA HEARSEY, b. Poland, Me., 27 Dec. 1787; d. 1 Aug. 1788.

    v ALETHEA HEARSEY, b. Poland, Me., 14 May 1789; m. 1813 JOHN BRADBURY (*Hersey Fam.*, 28).

   vi ANNA HEARSEY, b. Poland, Me., 3 July 1791; m. MESCHACH KEEN who d. 4 March 1852, suicide (*Hersey Fam.*, 28).

  vii SUSANNA HEARSEY, b. Poland, Me., 30 March 1793; m. in 1812 her cousin JOHN THAYER, b. 13 Feb. 1788, son of Isaac and Hannah (Joyce) Thayer, a Henry Samson descendant [#810-ii], *q.v.*, p. 508.

 viii RUTH HEARSEY, b. 17 Poland, Me., Jan. 1795; m. BENJAMIN HAMMOND, b. ca 1789 Maine. In 1850 he was a farmer at Lincoln, Me., with Ruth ae 55, and three sons (p.357).
          Hammond children at home 1850 (prob. incomplete): 1. *Augustus F. Hammond*[7], b. ca 1816; m. Hannah ___. 2. *Peter Hammond*, b. ca 1821. 3. *Edwin Hammond*, b. ca 1837.

   ix OLIVE HEARSEY, b. Poland, Me., 15 Dec. 1796; m. STEPHEN COBB, b. Me. ca 1794. In 1850 he was a farmer in Sumner, Me., ae 56, with Olive ae 52, and two children (p.149).

Cobb children at home 1850: 1. *Rosetta J. Cobb*[7], b. ca 1828. 2. *Lewis A. Cobb*, b. ca 1834.

x MERIA HEARSEY, b. Poland, Me., 20 Nov. 1798; m. EZRA COBB.

xi IRA HEARSEY, b. Sumner, Me., 25 Jan. 1802.

xii SOPHRONIA HEARSEY, b. Sumner, Me., 3 Sept. 1803; m. HIRAM HEALD, b. Me. ca 1798. In 1850 they were living next to the family of her sister Olive; Hiram was a farmer ae 52, and the household included nine children and Rebeckah Heald ae 83 (p.149).

Heald children at home 1850: 1. *Marsella Heald*[7], b. ca 1825. 2. *Albert Heald*, b. ca 1831. 3. *Abel Heald*, b. ca 1833. 4. *Stephen Heald*, b. ca 1835. 5. *Emergene Heald*, b. ca 1837. 6. *James Heald*, b. ca 1839. 7. *Alethea Heald*, b. ca 1841. 8. *Franklin Heald*, b. ca 1843. 9. *Oscar Heald*, b. ca 1847.

Sources cited: *Abington VR. Bridgewater VR.* Poland, Maine, Vital Records, *NEHGR* 88 [1934]. East Sumner, Maine, Town Records and Sumner Cemetery Records, letter from Miss Beatrice Neal, Center Minot Town Clerk, to Robert M. Sherman. Rev. War Pension File #S31121. Stephen E. Hersey, *The Hersey Family* (1994). CENSUS: 1800 Cumberland Co., Me. (M32-6); 1850 Oxford Co., Me., Buckfield & Sumner (M432-263), Lincoln, Penobscot Co. (M432-266).

816.   SAMUEL POOL[5] (*Ruth Fullerton*[4], *Ruth*[3] *Samson, Caleb*[2], *Henry*[1]), son of Samuel Pool and his wife Ruth Fullerton [168], was born at Abington 3 August 1764 (*VR* 1:170) and died at Minot, Maine, 24 February 1850 aged 85y 6m (*VR* 295). He was a descendant also of *Mayflower* passengers John Alden and Myles Standish.

He married, first, at Bridgewater 2 March 1786(*VR*2:301), **ABIGAIL PORTER**, who was born 18 December 1763 at Bridgewater, daughter of Samuel Jr. and Hannah (Green) Porter (*VR* 1:264). "Abigal, wife of Samuel Pool, Deceast December 10, 179[7]" at Poland, Maine (VR, *NEHGR* 88:248).

He married, second, at Minot 3 January 1799 (*VR* 31) by Rev. Jonathan Scott (*MD* 10:85), **MARY HERSEY**, who died at Minot 9 February 1839, aged 75, "wife of Dea. Samuel Pool" (*VR* 293). Both were "of Poland" at the time of marriage.

Dea. Samuel Pool published intentions at Minot 17 November 1839 to marry Miss FIDELIA MILLET (*VR* 73), but no marriage record has been found.

Samuel served in the Revolutionary War. In 1790 he was living in Bakerstown Plantation [later Poland and Minot, Maine] with one boy under 16, and two females (p.9). In 1800 Samuel Pool was in Cumberland County, himself and wife 26-45, with a household consisting of one boy and two girls under 10, and one boy and one girl 10-16 (p.211).

The town of Minot was incorporated in 1802 from Poland. In 1810 Samuel Pool was listed in Minot with a household consisting of a man and a woman 45 or older, one young woman between 16 and 26, one boy and one girl between 10 and 16, and one little boy under 10; Samuel Pool Jr. was nearby (p.361). In 1820 two Samuels were listed fifteen pages apart, neither labeled "Jr." Figures for one, 45 or older, are indistinct, but it appears that he had one young man between 16 and 26 and one woman between 26 and 45 in the household (p.295). The other Samuel was probably his son, between 26 and 45 with one boy and two girls under ten. Deborah Hersey [his paternal aunt] was next door.

The *Edward Poole of Weymouth* genealogy appears to have confused this Samuel with another man of the same name. No record has been found of the children attributed by that source to his second marriage (Benjamin, George, Thomas, Henry, Olive, and Susan, all "d." except Susan, "living 1890"). These children are not recorded at Minot, and are not consistent with census figures.

No appropriate probate records were found in Lincoln or Oxford counties.

Children of Samuel and Abigail (Porter) Poole, rec. together at Poland, Me. (*NEHGR* 88:51):

i NABBY POOL[6], b. 11 Dec. 1786; d. evidently before 1818; m. at Minot, Me., 16 Feb. 1806 (*VR* 34), JOHN CHANDLER JR. He m. (2) at Minot, after int. 17 Jan. 1818 (*VR* 26, 43), Polly Bates.

ii SAMUEL PORTER POOL, b. 23 April 1789; m. at Minot, 1 Dec. 1808 (*VR* 37), BETSEY PERKINS.

Children, rec. Minot, Me. (*VR* 250). 1. *Oliver Pool*, b. 13 June 1809; d. Minot 6 Sept. 1812 (*VR* 250) 2. *Sidney P. Pool*, b. 18 Sept. 1811. 3. *Oliver Pool*, b. 23 Aug. 1813; d. Minot 27 Aug. 1815 (*VR* 293). 4. *Sally W. Pool*, b. 18 Sept. 1815. 5. *Eliza Jane Pool*, b. 29 Oct. 1818. 6. *Ann S. Pool*, b. 29 Oct. 1820. 7. *Naham A. Pool*, b. 28 Jan. 1824. 8. *Alvah P. Pool*, b. 14 Jan. 1826.

iii POLLY POOL, b. 12 Oct. 1792; d. evidently 1850-1860; m. at Minot, 23 Feb. 1815 (*VR* 41), JONAH BUKER of Bowdoin. In 1830 Jonah Buker at Foxcroft, Me., ae 30-40, had two boys and one girl 10-15, one girl 5-10, and two girls under 5 (p.396). Jonah Buker ae 55, b. Me., in 1850 was a farmer at Alexander, Ohio, with wife Mary ae 57, b. Me.; the household included Mariam Merril ae 25, b. Me., Hannah Buker ae 23, and three young children (p.62). In 1860 Jonah was living at Rockford, Ill., with the family of Horace Buker ae 42, a silversmith b. Me., (p.175), and in 1870 at Rockford with the family of S. P. Buker ae 54, farmer b. Me. (p.11).

Probable **Buker** children (census), list incomplete: 1. *S. P. [Samuel Pool?] Buker*[7], b. ca 1816; m. Abby ____. 2. *Horace Buker*, b. ca 1818; m. Helen M. ____; a silversmith. 3. *? Mariam Buker*, b. ca 1825; m. ____ Merril. 4. *Hannah Buker*, b. ca 1827; at home 1850.

iv   DAVID POOL, b. 22 March 1795; m. at Minot, 28 Nov. 1816 (*VR* 42), SARAH WASHBURN.
>   Child rec. Minot (*VR* 193): 1. *James Dunham Pool*, b. 15 July 1817.

v   HANNAH POOL, b. 6 Oct. 1797; m. at Minot, 29 April 1819 (*VR* 43), ALDEN CROOKER, b. Poland 2 Aug. 1796, son of Isaac and Sarah (___) Crooker (*Minot VR* 137).

Sources cited: *Bridgewater VR. Minot, Me. VR.* Poland, Maine, Vital Records, *NEHGR* 88 (1934). Minot, Maine, Church Records and Town Records, letter from Miss Beatrice Neal, Town Clerk, to Robert M. Sherman. "Marriage Records of Rev. Jonathan Scott," *MD* Vol. 10 (1908). *History of Edward Poole of Weymouth* (1893). CENSUS: Cumberland Co., Me., 1790, Bakerstown Plantation (M637-2); Poland 1800 (M32-6); Minot 1810 (M252-11), 1820 (M33-33):295, 310; 1830 Foxcroft, Penobscot Co., Me. (M19-396); 1850 Alexander, Athens Co., Ohio (M432-660); Rockford, Winnebago Co., Ill., 1860 (M653-240) & 1870 (M593-294).

817.   OLIVE POOLE[5] (*Ruth Fullerton*[4], *Ruth*[3] *Samson, Caleb*[2]*, Henry*[1]), daughter of Samuel Poole and his wife Ruth Fullerton [168], was born at Abington 8 January 1768 (*VR* 1:169), and died in Boston 27 March 1850 aged 83y 2m, "relict of Rev. William [Reed]" (Mass. VR 48:56). She was a descendant also of *Mayflower* passengers John Alden and Myles Standish.

She married at Bridgewater, 20 May 1784 (*VR* 2:319), **WILLIAM REED** of Easton. He was born at Abington 8 June 1755, son of William and Silence (Nash) Reed (*VR* 1:193), and died at Easton 16 November 1809, aged 54, "having been settled in the ministry [there] 25 years and about 7 months" (VR 163).

William was a private in the Revolution, serving in the fortifications at Roxbury during the seige of Boston (*Poole Gen.*, 82). He graduated from Harvard in 1782. He was a minister, first in Taunton and in Easton from 1784 until his death.

History of Easton includes a long and interesting account of Rev. William Reed and Olive, the story of their unusual courtship (p.265), and a picture of her taken from a daguerrotype, facing p. 266.

Inventory was requested in January 1810 of the estate of William Reed late of Easton (Bristol PR 45:315, 558). Accounts filed by Calvin Brett and Olive Read, administrators, include a receipt from the Congregational Parish for the salary due William Read; setting aside the dower of the widow Olive; an agreement January 1813 by the heirs of William Reed late of Easton, signed by William Reed, David Reed, and Jacob and Mehitable Deane (*ibid.*, 46:486; 48:58; file of William Reed).

Children of William and Olive (Poole) Reed, rec. together at Easton (VR 163):

i   MEHITABLE REED[6], b. 20 June 1785; m. at Abington in 1808 (*VR* 2:177), JACOB DEANE. In 1850 he was a farmer ae 69 in Mansfield, with Mehitable R. ae 64, Nancy Deane ae 71, and three other people (p.55).
    Deane child (*Poole Gen.*, 89): 1. *William Reed Deane[7]*.

ii WILLIAM REED, b. 12 Dec. 1787; Brown Class of 1810, Harvard Divinity School 1831. He m. (1) in 1812 (*Abington VR* 2:181) BETSEY DRAKE, d. Milton 9 Aug. 1821, dau. of Bethuel Drake of Easton (*Easton History*, 711); m. (2) in Nov. 1822 (*Abington VR* 2:181), ABIGAIL (___) HOWE, widow of Calvin Howe of Boston. He was a teacher at Plymouth, then at Milton Academy, and after 1831 he preached but never took charge of a parish; in mid-life he settled on his father's homestead in Easton (*ibid.*).
    Children (*ibid.*, 710): 1. *William Gurney Reed[7]*, b. Plymouth 25 Sept. 1813. 2. *Lieuphemia Eustatia Reed*, b. Easton 13 Sept. 1815. 3. *Charles Henry Reed*, b. Milton 5 Feb. 1818.

iii DAVID REED, Rev., b. 6 Feb. 1790; d. 7 or 8 June 1870 at 65 Bainbridge St., Boston (Mass. VR 231:89); m. 2 May 1836, MARY ANN WILLIAMS, dau. of Capt. Howell Williams of Brooklyn, Conn. (*Easton History*, 710). After years of preaching, he established the *Christian Register*, as an "organ of the Liberal Faith" (*ibid.*). In 1850 he was ae 60, a publisher, in a boarding house in Ward 9, Boston, with Mary A. ae 45, William H. ae 13, and Fidelia ae 22; among the many other boarders were [his brother] Lucius Reed ae 45 and two of his children (p.285).
    Children at home 1850: 1. *Fidelia Reed[7]*, b. ca 1828; d. before 1886. 2. *William H. Reed*, b. ca 1837. 3. [*Child*] *Reed*, d. before 1886 (*Easton History*, 710).

iv OLIVE REED, b. 13 April 1792; d. at Easton 22 Aug. 1793 ae 1y 4m (her d. and funeral are described in *Easton History*, 266).

v   JASON REED, b. 14 Oct. 1795; d. Milton 13 July 1873 of "disability," widowed, a lawyer (Mass. VR 257:313); Harvard Class of 1816; m. at Abington, 19 May 1824 (*VR* 2:174), NANCY E. COATES, b. ca 1800. In 1850 he was a counselor at law in Milton with Nancy E. ae 50 and Elizabeth ae 23 (p.230).
    Child at home 1850: 1. *Elizabeth L. Reed[7]*, b. ca 1827.

vi DANIEL REED, b. 22 March 1797; d. Easton 2 Oct. 1878 of heart disease, "mechanic," widowed (Mass. VR 301:82). He m. (1) at Easton (VR 289) or Abington, 17 Sept. 1821 (*VR* 2:171), SALLY WILD, d. Easton 14 July 1826 ae 26y 26d (*VR* 336); m. (2) at Abington, 10 Feb. 1828 (*VR* 2:171), PERSIS E. HAMMOND, d. Easton 31 March 1831 ae 23y (VR 336); m. (3) at Abington, 15 May 1831 (*VR* 2:172) BETSEY T. HAMMOND, d. Abington 11 Oct. 1843 (*VR* 2:337).

Children, rec. together at Easton (VR 336): With Sally: 1. *Fidelia Reed*, b. 13 Aug. 1822. 2. *Sally Wild Reed*, b. 31 July 1825. With Persis: 3. *Persis Hammond Reed*, b. 26 June 1829. With Betsey: 4. *Charlotte Augusta Reed*, b. Boston 21 Feb. 1833; d. 2 March 1835. 5. *Almira Hammond Reed*, b. Boston 9 Feb. 1835. 6. *Melissa Cobb Reed*, b. Boston 6 Feb. 1835. 7. *Olive Janette Reed*, b. 20 March 1839. 8. *Thomas Hammond Reed*, b. 25 March 1841.

vii   SETH REED, b. 22 Aug. 1799; d. ca 1887; res. 141 N. Fremont St., Baltimore, Md. (*Poole Fam.*, 89); m. at Abington, 22 July 1827 (*VR* 2:179), LUCY HOLDEN, b. Mass. ca 1804. He was in the wholesale commission business; had a dau. who was a missionary in Indian Territory (*Poole Fam.*, 89). In 1860 Seth Read [*sic*] was a seaman with property worth $10,000, in Baltimore, Catonsville P.O., with Lucy, Wallace, Charlotte, and Mary L.; in 1870 they were in Baltimore Ward 20 (p.526).

Children (census): 1. *Wallace W. Reed*, b. ca 1838. ? 2. *Seth Reed*, b. ca 1843 (*Poole Fam.*). 3. *Charlotte Reed*, b. ca 1846. 4. *Mary L. Reed*, b. ca 1849

viii LYMAN REED, b. 28 Dec. 1801; d. Boston, 19 Woodbine St., 16 Feb. 1876 ae 74y 1m 19d of heart disease, widowed, a merchant (Mass. VR 285:45); m. at Abington, 22 Oct. 1832 (*VR* 2:179), MARIA ANN HARRIS.

ix   LUCIUS REED, b. 27 Oct. 1805; m. at Abington, 19 Aug. 1831 (*VR* 2:176), ABBY SUMNER HARRIS, d. 6 Nov. 1839 (*Ab. VR* 2:336). In 1850 he was a clerk, living in a boarding house in Boston with the family of his brother David (p.285), with two apparent sons: 1. *William Reed*, b. ca 1832. 2. *Lucius Reed*, b. ca 1835.

Sources cited: *Abington VR* (entries taken from record kept by Mrs. Jane Bates, a niece of Rev. William Reed; some events prob. took place in Easton although rec. Abington). *Bridgewater VR.* Easton Vital Records. Mass. Vital Records 1841-1910. Bristol County Probate Records. Chaffin, *History of Easton* (1886). *The History of Edward Poole of Weymouth* (1893). CENSUS: 1850 Boston, Ward 9, Suffolk Co. (M432-337), Mansfield, Bristol Co. (M432-307); Baltimore, Md., 1860 (M653-467) & 1870 (M593-580).

818.   JOHN POOLE[5] (*Ruth Fullerton*[4], *Ruth*[3] *Samson, Caleb*[2], *Henry*[1]), son of Samuel Poole and his wife Ruth Fullerton [168], was born at East Bridgewater (d. rec.) 11 May 1770 and died at Easton 1 May 1865 aged 94y 11m 19d of influenza and old age (Mass. VR 183:80). He was a descendant also of *Mayflower* passengers John Alden and Myles Standish.

He was of Easton when he married at Abington, 29 December 1794 (*VR* 2:158), **MARY BROWN**. She was born at Abington 22 April 1776 (*VR* 1:40) and died at Easton 20 August 1865 (Mass. VR 183:80), aged 89y 4m, daughter of Samuel and Deborah (Torrey) Brown. The will of Samuel Brown of Abington, dated 2 July, presented 27 July 1787, names his wife Deborah and among others his youngest daughter Mary Brown (Plymouyh PR #3080, 30:193).

In 1850 John Pool was a farmer at Easton with wife Mary and daughter Mary; Charles Berry aged 12 was also in the household, and sons Harrison, Horace M., and Nahum lived nearby (pp.2-4).

The will of John Pool of Easton, dated 5 April 1862, proved 2 June 1865, names his wife Mary; three sons John, Horace M., and Harrison; daughters Mary, unmarried, Clarissa wife of Almon Gurney, Harriet M. wife of Jesse Packard; Lydia B. widow of his deceased son Nahum, and her son Edwin R. Poole (Bristol PR 183:609; 189:29).

Children of John and Mary (Brown) Pool, births rec. Easton by John Pool, Town Clerk (VR 197):

    i   JOHN POOL[6], b. 12 Jan. 1796; d. Easton 12 Sept. 1865, a farmer, ae 69y 8m of dropsy of heart (Mass. VR 183:80); m. (1) at Brockton, 16 Jan. 1822 (*VR* 268), ZIBEA/ZIBIE PACKARD, b. Brockton 22 July 1797 (*VR* 117), d. 1842 (*Poole Fam.*, 38), dau. of Cyrus and Keziah (Kingman) Packard; m. (2) at Foxboro, 15 April 1845 (*VR* 169), LEVARNA (PACKARD) SMITH, b. Foxboro Dec. 1803, dau. of Jedediah and Mehitable (___) Packard and widow of Ithiel Smith (*VR* 80). John Pool was a manufacturer of nautical and surveyors' instruments. In 1850 he was at Easton with Levarna and seven children; the family of son John was next door (pp.1-2).

           Children (1850 census): 1. *Julia A. Pool*, b. ca 1824; m. 1853 Joseph Russell (Mass. VR 69:101). 2. *John Murray Pool*, b. ca 1825; m. 1849 Rachael H. Gilmore (Mass. VR 37:75). 3. *Charles Babbitt Pool*, b. ca 1827. 4. *Augusta Pool*, b. ca 1829. 5. *Emory B. Pool*, b. ca 1831; a shoemaker 1850. 6. *Elizabeth Pool*, b. ca 1833. 7. *Anthony B. Pool*, b. ca 1835. 8. *Emeline B. Pool*, b. ca 1838.

    ii   NAHUM POOL, b. 9 Jan. 1798; d. Easton 30 Dec. 1853, farmer, married, of consumption (Mass. VR 75:60); m. at Easton, 4 Dec. 1822 (VR 290), LIDEA HARVEY, b. ca 1800. In 1850 he was a "Math. Inst." at Easton with Lydia B. ae 50, son Edward R. ae 21 (named in grandfather's will as Edwin R.), and John R. Hunt ae 15 (p.4).

           Child: 1. *Edwin/Edward R. Pool*, b. ca 1829; at home, a shoemaker in 1850.

    iii   MARY POOL, b. 31 Jan. 1800; unm. 1862; with parents 1850.

    iv   HORACE MINOT POOL, b. 9 July 1803; d. Easton 1 Nov. 1878 (Mass. VR 301:82); m. at Easton, 30 Sept. 1832 (VR 304), ABBY ANN AVERY, b. Norwich, Conn., 16 Feb. 1811 (calc.), d. Easton 22 Dec. 1863, dau. Oliver and Louisa Avery (Mass. VR 165:77). In 1850 he was a "Math. Inst.," at Easton with Abby and two children ae 16, apparently twins (pp.2-3).

Children (*Poole Fam.*, 62); at home 1850: 1. *Ann M. Pool*, b. ca 1834. 2. *Horace F. Pool*, b. ca 1834; occupation 1850 "Math Inst."

v   CLARISSA POOLE, b. 16 Feb. 1808; d. Whitman 5 April 1889 ae 81y 1m 20d, chronic bronchitis (Mass. VR 401:399); m. ALMON GURNEY, b. Bridgewater 17 Sept. 1806 (*VR* 126), d. E. Bridgewater 13 May 1873, son of Seth and Rebecca (Packard) Gurney (Mass. VR 257:358). In 1850 he was a farmer in E. Bridgewater with Clarisa and six children (p.253).

      Gurney children (census): 1. *Lucius Gurney*[7], b. ca 1831. 2. *Harriet M. Gurney*, b. ca 1835. 3. *Edward P. Gurney*, b. ca 1839. 4. *Caroline Gurney* (twin?), b. ca 1839. 5. *Almon A. Gurney*, b. ca 1841. 6. *Nahum B. Gurney*, b. ca 1848.

vi   HARRIET MARIA POOL, b. 19 Oct. 1812; d. Bridgewater 5 Dec. 1897 of old age and gastritis, widow (Mass. VR 473:603); bur. Halifax; m. at Bridgewater, 11 Dec. 1838 (*VR* 2:277), as his second wife, JESSE PACKARD, b. Bridgewater 6 July 1810, son of Jacob and Hannah (Kingman) Packard (*VR* 1:243), d. prob. Halifax 1884 (Mass. VR 356:303). Jesse m. (1) at Bridgewater in 1833 (*VR* 2:277) Lucinda T. Hayward, who was the mother of his dau. Lucinda. In 1850 he was a shoemaker at North Bridgewater with Harriet M., four Packard children including Lucinda ae 14, plus Augustus Poole ae 21, shoemaker, and Patrick Mahan ae 31, laborer b. Ireland (p.299).

      Packard children of Jesse and Harriet, rec. Bridgewater (*VR* 1:242): 1. *Harrison Davis Packard*[7], b. 16 July 1840;; m. (1) Lucy M. Thompson, (2) Lucy W. Morton. 2. *Horace F. Packard*, b. 31 May 1842; m. Frances M. Holmes. 3. *Harriet Frances Packard*, b. 5 April 1847; m. William S. Daby.

vii HARRISON POOLE, b. 8 March 1816; d. 6 Aug. 1869 of chronic inflammation of liver and dropsy, a mathematical instrument maker (Mass. VR 220:85); m. at Easton, 25 Dec. 1844, MARY JANE REED ae 19 (Mass. VR 12:44). In 1844 he was a mechanic; in 1850 he was a "Math. Inst." at Easton with Mary J. ae 23 [*sic*] and two children (p.3), next to his parents.

      Children at home 1850: 1. *Mary F. Pool*, b. 3 Nov. 1845 (Mass. VR 16:66). 2. *Everett E. Pool*, b. 3 Dec. 1847 (Mass. VR 28:53).

Sources cited: *Abington VR. Bridgewater VR. Brockton VR.* Easton VR. Mass. Vital Records 1841-1910. Bristol County and Plymouth County Probate Records. *Edward Poole of Weymouth* (1893). CENSUS: 1850 Easton, Bristol Co. (M432-307), Bridgewater, Plymouth Co. (M432-332)

819.   DEBORAH POOLE[5] (*Ruth Fullerton*[4], *Ruth*[3] *Samson, Caleb*[2], *Henry*[1]), daughter of Samuel Poole and his wife Ruth Fullerton [168], was baptized at Abington 15 June 1772 (*VR* 1:166), and died at Minot, Maine, 18 December 1857 aged 85y 7m (*NEHGR* 103:151). She was a descendant also of *Mayflower* passengers John Alden and Myles Standish.

She was of Bridgewater when she married at Abington, 7 February 1793 (*VR* 2:159), **THOMAS HEARSEY**. He was born at Abington 26 March 1771 (*VR* 1:107) and died there 24 January 1816 (*VR* 2:295) of consumption, aged 45, son of Joseph and Mary (___) Hearsey.

In 1800 Thomas Hearsey was in Abington with a household consisting of himself and his wife (26-45), and three boys and one girl under 10 (p.37). In 1820 Deborah Hersey was listed in the census at Minot, Maine, next to her nephew Samuel P. Poole (p.310). In 1850 Deborah Hersey, aged 78, was living with the family of her son Cyrus in Auburn, Me. (pp.12-13).

No Plymouth County probate record was found for Thomas.

Children of Thomas and Deborah (Poole) Hearsey, b. Abington (*VR* 1: 104-06):

i   SILVENUS HEARSEY[6], b. 10 Aug. 1793; d. Rockport, Ill., 29 Dec. 1876; m. 7 Oct. 1821, RHODA WEST, b. New Bedford 1 Sept. 1801, d. 2 Aug. 1862 or 1863, dau. of Stephen and Rhoda (McFarland) West (*Hersey Family*, 49).
      Children, first two b. New Bedford, others Foxcroft, Me. (*ibid.*): 1. *William Shaw Hersey[7]*, b. 12 Aug. 1822. 2. *Almy Ann Hersey*, b. 29 May 1826; m. John Thayer. 3. *Nehemiah West Hersey*, b. 18 March 1827. 4. *Susan S. Hersey*, b. 4 April 1829; m. Reuben Lucas. 5. *Cyrus Warren Hersey*, b. 25 June 1834; m. Abbie Ferry. 6. *Moses Howe Hersey*, b. 22 Aug. 1836. 7. *Charlotte Hersey*, b. 23 Feb. 1838; d. 1866. 8. *Charles Estes Hersey*, b. 30 Nov. 1841; drowned Sebec, Me., 18 May 1862 or 1864.

ii   CHARLOTTE HEARSEY, b. 18 Sept. 1795; d. 4 Nov. 1864; m. at Easton, 20 Aug. 1815 (*VR* 287), IRA DEAN of Mansfield, b. 23 Jan. 1794 Mass., d. Floyd Co., Iowa, 18 March 1878 (*Hersey Fam.*, 27). They were in Piscataquis Co., Me., by 1819, in Dover-Foxcroft 1830. In 1850 he was a farmer at Franklin, DeKalb Co., Ill., with Charlotte ae 54, and four children (p.312); his home was twice destroyed by tornadoes in 1853 and 1860 (*DeKalb Co. History*, 463). They moved on to Rock Grove, Iowa, where they died and are buried in Evergreen Cemetery, Floyd.
      Dean children, all b. Maine, last four at home 1850: 1. *Sally Ann Dean[7]*, b. 15 Jan. 1819. 2. *Edwin Dean*, b. 16 Jan. 1821. 3. *Charlotte Dean*. 4. *Angeline Dean*. 5. *Charles Dean*, b. ca 1825. 6. *William Dean*, b. ca 1828. 7. *Thomas Dean*, b. 9 Nov. 1829. 8. *Ira Dean Jr.*, b. ca 1832. 9. *Julia A. Dean*, b. ca 1834. 10. *Louisa Dean*, b. ca 1836. 11. *Daniel Dean*, b. ca 1837.

iii LORING HEARSEY, b. 21 Feb. 1798; m. 1825 MARTHA PERKINS, b. ca 1799 Mass., d. 22 March 1874 (*Hersey Fam.*, 27). He was a farmer at. Auburn, Me., 1850 (p.1), no children in the household.

iv   WARREN HEARSEY, b. 30 June 1800; d. Abington 18 Feb. 1803 ae 3y (*VR* 2:295).

v CYRUS HEARSEY, b. 17 Oct. 1802; d. Auburn, Me., 26 Oct. 1899; m. 4 Dec. 1845, PHILA SHAW, b. Minot, Me., 5 Nov. 1816, d. Auburn 4 Jan. 1904, dau. of Edward and Rhoda (Prince) Shaw (*Hersey Family*, 49). In 1850 he was a farmer at Auburn, Me., with Phila and his mother in his household, and children Edward ae 3 and Sarah A. ae 1 (pp.12-13).

Children, b. Auburn, Me. (*Hersey Fam.*, 49): 1. *Edward Shaw Hersey[7]*, b. 6 March 1847. 2. *Arvilda Sarah Hersey*, b. 29 Jan. 1849. 3. *Izetta Deborah Hersey*, b. 24 April 1851; m. Luke Woodward. 4. *Charles Byron Hersey*, b. 24 March 1853; d. 24 June 1853. 5. *Rose Caroline Hersey*, b. 23 July 1856; m. A. Carroll Fuller.

vi THOMAS HEARSEY, b. 19 March 1805; d. Boston 28 Jan. 1894; m. at Turner, Me., 20 March 1832, ABIGAIL PERRY, b. Harrison, Me., 25 May 1805, d. S. Turner, Me., 4 Feb. 1884, dau. of Levi and Nancy (Dwyer) Perry (*Hersey Fam.*, 49). In 1850 he was a farmer at Auburn, Me. (p.12).

Children, b. Minot, Me. (*Hersey Fam.*, 49); at home 1850: 1. *Thomas Welcome Hersey[7]*, b. 27 Feb. 1833 (*VR* 250); m. Olive Tirrell. 2. *Levi Perry Hersey*, b. 1 June 1838.

vii MARY HEARSEY, b. 10 July 1807; d. 16 July 1861; m. 15 Nov. 1825, BARTLETT ROBBINS, b. ca 1799 Mass. In 1850 he was a farmer at Abington with Mary ae 42, and five children (p.183).

Robbins children at home 1850: 1. *Mary B. Robbins[7]*, b. ca 1827. 2. *Thomas H. Robbins*, b. ca 1835; a shoemaker ae 15 in 1850. 3. *Loring Robbins*, b. ca 1842. 4. *William H. Robbins*, b. ca 1845. 5. *Martha A. Robbins*, b. ca 1848.

viii APOLLOS HEARSEY, b. 14 March 1810; d. Auburn, Me., 22 Jan. 1900; m. 2 Oct. 1837, SOPHRONIA PERRY, b. Minot, Me., 24 Nov. 1814, d. 4 May 1896, dau. of Thomas and Hulda (Tirrell) Perry (*Hersey Family*, 49). He was a farmer at Minot in 1850 with Zophrona and the three oldest children (p.37).

Children, b. Auburn, Me. (*Hersey Family*, 49): 1. *Benjamin F. Hersey[7]*, b. 8 Aug. 1838. 2. *William Henry Hersey*, b. 1 Aug. 1843; d. in Civil War service. 3. *Susan Ellen Hersey*, b. 29 July 1848; m. James Weston. 4. *Thomas Edgar Hersey*, b. 13 Feb. 1851. 5. *Martha Rosette Hersey*, b. 7 Jan. 1853; m. Cyrus Packard. 6. *Louise Adelaide Hersey*, b. 29 April 1856; m. Josiah F. Dunbar.

ix WELCOME HEARSEY, b. 27 March 1812; d. Abington (as "Whitcom") 27 Oct. 1813 ae 1y 7m (*VR* 2:295).

x WELCOME HEARSEY, b. 23 Nov. 1814; d. Auburn, Me., 10 July 1901; m. at Auburn, 18 March 1841, m. MARY CURTIS, b. Lewiston, Me., 7 April 1820, d. 1 Jan. 1896, dau. of John and Phebe (Jepson) Curtis (*Hersey Fam.*, 49). In 1850 he was a farmer in Auburn with Mary and four children (p.12).

Children, first three b. Minot, Me., rest prob. Auburn (*Hersey Family*, 50): 1. *Olive Curtis Hersey[7]*, b. 23 Oct. 1841. 2. *Stephen Wallace Hersey*, b. 13 June 1844. 3. *Henry Atwood Hersey*, b. 20 July 1846. 4. *Stillman Percival Hersey*, b. 28 Sept.

1848. 5. *Mary Abbie Hersey*, b. 12 Dec. 1851; m. William Briggs Knight. 6. *Elizabeth Evelyn Hersey*, b. 30 Aug. 1854. 7. *Isabelle Augusta Hersey*, b. 24 July 1857; m. Ammi D. Randall. 8. *John Gilbert Hersey*, b. 11 May 1860. 9. *Alice Edna Hersey*, b. 3 Feb. 1864; d. 14 Sept. 1868.

Sources cited: *Abington VR. Bridgewater VR. Minot [Me.] VR. NEHGR* 103 [1949]. *The Hersey Family* (1994). CENSUS: Abington, Plymouth Co., 1800 (M32-16), 1850 (M432-332); Cumberland Co., Me.: Minot 1820 (M33-33), Auburn., 1850 (M432-250).

820.   RUTH POOLE[5] (*Ruth Fullerton*[4], *Ruth*[3] *Samson, Caleb*[2], *Henry*[1]), daughter of Samuel Poole and his wife Ruth Fullerton [168], was baptized at Abington in July 1774 (*VR* 1:169), and died after 1800 when her presence was indicated in the census. In 1797 she was living at Hebron, Maine. She was a descendant also of *Mayflower* passengers John Alden and Myles Standish.

She was of Bridgewater when she married at Abington, 16 September 1796 (*VR* 2:159), **ELIPHAZ CURTIS**. He was born at Bridgewater 16 January 1771 (*VR* 1:87), son of Ashley and Susanna (Fuller) Curtis, and died after 1800. He was a descendant of *Mayflower* passengers Samuel Fuller and Francis Cooke.

In 1800 Eliph[z] Curtis was living at Buckfield, Maine, aged 26-45, with an apparent wife the same age, and two boys, one 10-16, the other under 10 (p.238). He has not been located in any later census.

Child of Eliphaz and Ruth (Poole) Curtis:

i   ALVAH CURTIS[6], b. Hebron, Maine, 16 Nov. 1797; evidently living 1800.

Sources cited: *Abington VR.*   Cole, *History of Buckfield* (1915). CENSUS: 1800 Buckfield, Cumberland Co., Me. (M32-6).

821.   OLIVER POOLE[5] (*Ruth Fullerton*[4], *Ruth*[3] *Samson, Caleb*[2], *Henry*[1]), Samuel Poole and his wife Ruth Fullerton [168], was born about 1775, and died at Albany, N.Y., in 1842 (*Poole Family*, 22). He was a descendant also of *Mayflower* passengers John Alden and Myles Standish.

He married at Easton, 26 November 1801 (VR 223), both of Easton, **HANNAH KEITH**. She was probably the daughter Hannah born at Easton 22 March 1780 to Lieut. David and Sarah (Randell) Keith (VR 133). This couple's next child was Calvin Keith, born in 1782, who died in October 1805, and it is noteworthy that Oliver and Hannah Pool named their second child, born in September 1805, Calvin Keith Pool. Record of Hannah's death has not been found.

Oliver Poole served in the War of 1812 as a captain, from Easton (*Poole Family*, 22). The family evidently removed from Massachusetts to New York State between 1818 when son Augustus was born, and 1820 when they were listed in the census at Lyme, Jefferson County, N.Y. Oliver Poole in 1820 was head of a household consisting of himself and wife 26-45, two young men 16-25, one of whom was 16-18, one boy and one girl 10-16, and three little boys under 10; four family members were engaged in manufacturing (p.443).

Children of Oliver and Hannah (Keith) Pool, first rec. Easton (*VR* 240), all in *Poole Family* (p.37):

i THACHER POOL[6], b. Easton 13 Oct. 1802; d. after 1840 when he was living in Ward 5, Albany, N.Y., himself and wife between 40 and 50, with two boys and one girl 5-10 and two girls 10-15 (p.395). He is listed in Albany City Directories from 1827 as a carpenter, wood/furniture/carriage tradesman. *Poole Family* says he m. CATHERINE ANN ___, who d. at Albany 13 Dec. 1844, and that he d. at Oswego, N.Y.

    Child (*Poole Family*, 37): 1. *Calvin Keith Pool*, b. 1837; d. 27 Nov. 1857.

ii CALVIN KEITH POOL, b. 20 Sept. 1805 in Mass.; d. 4 Sept. 1874 (g.s.); m. JANE S. WILLIAMS (*Poole Family*, 37), b. N.Y. 18 Nov. 1815, d. 6 May 1892[?9] (g.s.), both buried St. John's Episcopal Cemetery, Cape Vincent, N.Y. In 1840 he was living at Lyme, N.Y. In 1850 Calvin K. Pool, 44, a cabinetmaker b. Mass., was living at Cape Vincent, N.Y., with wife Jane S., ae 34, b. N.Y., and four children (p.396).

    Children, b. N.Y. (census; *Poole Family*, 37): 1. *Judah Williams Pool*, b. ca 1838; unm. 1883. 2. *Oliver Perry Pool*, d. ae 7; not with family 1850. 3. *Morris Merrill Pool*, b. 23 Nov. 1842; d. 14 Jan. 1864 in Civil War service, Co. M, 10th N.Y. (g.s.); unm. 4. *Mary Elizabeth Pool*, b. ca 1845; unm. 1883. 5. *Emma Louisa Pool*, d. infancy; prob. the "female Pool" who d. at Cape Vincent 7 June 1849 ae 3 of scarlet fever. 6. *Charles Augustus Pool*, b. 1849. 7. *George Calvin Pool*, b. after 1850; unm. 1883. 8. *Russell Herbert Pool*, b. after 1850; unm. 1883.

iii OLIVER POOL, b. ca 1812; d. 3 March 1837 ae 25 yrs; buried Market Street Cemetery, Cape Vincent Village, N.Y. (g.s.)

iv AUGUSTUS POOL, b. 30 March 1818, Easton; d. ca 1882 (*Poole Fam.*, 37); m. MAY or MARY ___, (2) FRANCES RATHBUN COOPER (*ibid.*). In 1850 Augustus Poole ae 33, physician, was living in Ward 1, Oswego, N.Y., with May ae 30, b. N.Y., and two children; the household included Betsey George ae 35, b. Mass., her dau. Hannah ae 12, and David Williams, 28, a painter b. N.Y. (p.135). Augustus Pool was a homeopathic physician.

    Children, first two at home 1850, rest from *Poole Family*, order uncertain:: 1. *Calvin Pool*, b. ca 1835. 2. *Mary / Mary Adelaide Pool*, b. ca March 1850; m.

Clarence Parsons. 3. *Josephine Augusta Pool*, m. William J. Robertson. 4. *Charles Henry Pool*. 6. *William H. Pool*, b. 18 March 1870. 5. *Kittie Keith Pool*.

v   [SON] POOL, b. between 1810 and 1820.

Sources cited: Easton VR. Gravestone inscriptions from Cape Vincent Cemeteries, on line. *History of Oswego County 1789-1877* (1878). Albany City Directories, 1827, 1828-9, 1830-31. *Edward Poole of Weymouth* ... (1893). CENSUS: 1820 Lyme, Jefferson Co., N.Y. (M33-72); 1840 Albany, Albany Co., N.Y. (M704-264); 1850 Census, Cape Vincent, Jefferson Co., N.Y. (M432-514); Oswego, Oswego Co., N.Y. (432-576).

822.   WILLIAM POOLE[5] (*Ruth Fullerton*[4], *Ruth*[3] *Samson, Caleb*[2], *Henry*[1]), son of Samuel Poole and his wife Ruth Fullerton [168], was born at Easton 5 May 1777 and baptized at Abington 7 July 1777 (*VR* 1:170). He died at Beaumont, Pennsylvania, 6 January 1852 (*Poole Family*, 23). He was a descendant also of *Mayflower* passengers John Alden and Myles Standish.

He was of Bridgewater when he married at Abington, 3 September 1795 (*VR* 2:160) or East Bridgewater (*VR* 277), **SARAH PACKARD** of either Abington or Bridgewater. She was born 26 December 1776 at Sheffield (son John's d. rec.) and died at Abington 10 or 23 September 1846 aged 70, of consumption, as "Sally Packard Pool, wife of William" (*VR* 2:329), daughter of Daniel Packard. (See *Poole Family*, 22, for information about her family.)

In 1800 William Pool was in Bridgewater with a household consisting of a man and a woman 16-26, and two boys and one girl under 10 (p.64).

William served in the War of 1812 as a private in the Abington Artillery Company, stationed with the garrison at the Fort at the Gurnet in Plymouth Harbor. *Poole Family* (p.22), describes him as "a farmer, physician, merchant and lumber manufacturer ... [he] removed to Beaumont, Pa., where he resided many years. He was a man of wealth, highly respected ... In personal appearance he was large, height about 6 feet, and weight about 200 pounds, with smoothly shaven face, brown hair and blue eyes. [Sarah] was slender, with pale complexion, brown hair and blue eyes." In 1850 he was living with the family of his son Amos Pool at Monroe, Pa.

Children of William and Sarah (Packard) Pool, first four rec. Bridgewater (*VR* 262-263), others except Ann and Amos at Abington (*VR* 1:167-70); Willard and John are rec. as of William and *Eunice*, but this is evidently a confusion with another couple, James and Eunice (Lazell) Poole, who were having children recorded at Abington in the same time period; all in *Poole Family* (p.23):

i   WILLIAM POOL[6], b. 2 March 1796; d. Lancaster, Pa.; m. 27 June 1817 after
    int. at Easton 6 Feb. 1817 (VR 288), MARY W. TISDALE, dau. of Rev.
    William Tisdale of Taunton (*Poole Family*, 34).
        Children (*ibid.*): 1. *Mary A. Pool*, b. 18 Feb. 1817; m. (1) Henry Keely, (2)
    John W. Wein, 3) Charles B. Moyer. 2. *Harriet Pool*, b. 19 July 1818; m. Isaac
    Grow. 3. *William Pool*, b. 29 April 1820. 4. *Sarah Pool*, b. 4 April 1822; m.
    William Bingaman. 5. *Elizabeth Bates Pool*, b. 21 Jan. 1824; m. Frederick R.
    Holbert. 6. *Willard Augustus Pool*, b. 12 Nov. 1825. 7. *Annie Poole*, b. 6 March
    1827; m. William Holbert. 8. *Tacy F. Pool*, b. 29 Nov. 1829; m. Harlow James.
    9. *Warren Pool*, b. 21 July 1831; d. 5 Aug. 1831 Manayunk, Pa. 10. *Maria Pool*, b.
    10 Oct. 1833; d. 27 Jan. 1834 Manayunk, Pa. 11. *Lucy Ann Pool*, b. 25 Nov. 1834;
    m. (1) Albert Schafnear, (2) Henry Oakes. (See *Poole Family* for further
    information.)

ii DANIEL POOL, b. 10 June 1797; d. 5 March 1864, Mt. Carmel, Ill.; m.
    ANNA REBECCA GARDNER, b. 7 Jan. 1807 Philadelphia, Pa., d. 28 May
    1885, Smithboro, N.Y., dau. of Valentine and Mary Magdalene (Hinckle)
    Gardner. Daniel was an inventor, and *Poole Family* devotes pp. 31-34 to his
    biography. In 1850 Daniel Pool ae 52, b. Mass., "machinist," lived in Mount
    Carmel, Wabash Co., Ill., with Anna R. ae 43 and children J. F. Henry ae 19
    (a lathe sawyer), C. Louis ae 16 (a sawyer), E. Caroline ae 13, and Mary E., ae
    4, all b. Pa.; Jacob Gould ae 20, teamster, b. Pa., was also with them (p.381).
        Children (*Poole Fam.*, 34): 1. *Edward Valentine Pool*, b. 3 April 1826.
    2. *Theodore W. Pool*, b. 15 July 1828; d. 29 June 1847, Philadelphia. 3. *Francis Henry*
    Pool, b. 12 April 1831. 4. *Charles Lewis Pool*, b. 10 Feb. 1834. 5. *Emily Caroline*
    Pool, b. 11 July 1836 Dauphin, Pa.; m. James Henry Clark. 6. *Mary Eliza Pool*, b.
    21 July 1845 Philadelphia; d. 3 Jan. 1855 on board steamer *Jacob Strader* on Ohio
    River. (See *Poole Family* for further information.)

iii SALLY POOL, b. 14 May 1799; d. 1886 (*Poole Fam.*; rec. not found); m. (1) at
    Easton, 6 Feb. 1817 (VR 288) JOSEPH ELLIS of Dedham; m. (2) ____
    HAMMOND (*Poole Fam.*, 88; rec. not found). Sally Ellis was admitted to the
    Orthodox Church at Dedham from the Easton Church 2 Sept. 1821
    (*Dedham VR* 618).
        Ellis children (*Poole Fam.*, 89): 1. *Sarah Elizabeth Ellis*[7]. 2. *Francis C. Ellis*.
    3. *Hosea Ballou Ellis*. 4. *Maria Ellis*; m. ____ Crane. 5. *Almira Ellis*, m. ____
    Sherman. 6. *Susan Ellis*. 7. *Josephine Ellis*; m. ____ Abbott.

iv BELINDA POOL, b. 9 Feb. 1801; m. at Abington, 20 July 1819 (*VR* 2:156),
    GEORGE M. ARNOLD, b. ca 1799 Abington, d. Cohasset 3 June 1875 ae
    76, son of Thomas H. and Polly (____) Arnold (Mass. VR 275:243). In 1850
    he was a shoemaker in Scituate, with Belindy ae 49, and six children (p.54).

Arnold children at home 1850: 1. *Andrew Arnold*, b. ca 1830. 2. *Nathaniel T. Arnold,* b. ca 1832. 3. *Edward H. Arnold,* b. ca 1834. 4. *Ann M. Arnold,* b. ca 1836. 5. *Susan F. Arnold,* b. ca 1839. 6. *George T. Arnold,* b. ca 1840.

v   SAMUEL POOL, b. 15 July 1803 at Abington; m. at Abington, 30 May 1830 (*VR* 2:159), MARIA BAKER, b. ca 1805 Mass. In 1850 Samuel Pool ae 46 was a shoemaker in Dedham, with Maria ae 45, five children, and Hannah Abington ae 36, b. Ireland (p.252).

    Children at home 1850 (four in *Poole Family,* 38): 1. *Andrew J. Pool,* b. ca 1831; m. (1) ____; a mariner ae 33, b. Hanson, when m. (2) Hanover, 1 Nov. 1864, Ellen A. Bates (Mass. VR 172:258). 2. *Anna Maria Pool,* b. ca 1832; m. Edmund S. Hunt. 3. *James H. Pool,* b. April 1835. 4. *Mary F. Pool,* b. ca 1839; not in *Poole Family.* 5. *Ethan A. Pool,* b. ca 1844.

vi   WILLARD POOL, b. 15 Oct. 1805 at Abington; m. at Hanson, 16 April 1829 (*VR* 75), BETSEY B. WHITE, b. Pembroke 3 Feb. 1810, dau. of Caleb and Betsey (___) White (*VR* 217; *VR* 438, from gs., incorrectly says d. 1839). In 1850 Willard was ae 45, a tack nailer at Pembroke, with Betsey B. ae 40, and three children; Betsey White ae 73 lived with them (p.144). Willard and Betsey were still there in 1860 with only Peregrine at home (p.125). *Poole Family* says res. Pembroke 1893; d. recs. not in Mass. VR.

    Children (census; *Poole Family,* 35; only one rec. Pembroke but all prob. b. there): 1. *Andrew E. Pool,* b. 1 Sept. 1830. 2. *Sarah Ann White Pool,* b. 2 Feb. 1833; m. Hanson, 31 Dec. 1850, James Bonney (Mass. VR 46:210). 3. *Peregrine White Pool,* b. 4 July 1842 Pembroke (*VR* 166).

vii   ANN POOL, b. 29 Feb. 1808; m. at Dorchester, 6 Jan. 1831 (*VR* 180), LORING W. REED of Milton, b. ca 1803 in Mass., d. Boston 1890 (Mass. VR 411:86). In 1850 he was a paper hanger ae 47 at Roxbury, with Ann P. ae 43, and five children; the household included several other people, prob. boarders (p.118).

    Reed children, all at home 1850 (see also *Poole Family,* 88): 1. *Anna F. Reed,* b. ca 1831. 2. *Charles L. Reed,* b. ca 1832. 3. *Sarah Reed,* b. ca 1834; m. John M. Way. 4. *Thomas Reed,* b. ca 1836. 5. *William Reed,* b. ca 1842.

viii   HANNAH POOL, b. 12 May 1810 at Abington; d. Woonsocket, R.I., 9 March 1846 (*Poole Family,* 88); m. CHARLES KENNEY.

    Kenney children (*ibid.*): 1. *Frank Kenney*, d. ae ca 25. 2. *Daniel Kenney.* 3. *Augustus Kenney,* b. ca 1845; res. Rockland, unm.

ix   JOHN POOL, b. 30 Aug. 1812 at Abington, later called John Gardner Poole; d. Randolph 25 March 1882 of heart disease (Mass. VR 338:273); m. (1) after int. at Brockton 29 Sept. 1832 (*VR* 269), VESTA C. LORING, b. 1814, d. 3 June 1851; m. (2) at Randolph, 13 July 1863 (Mass. VR 163:200), ELIZABETH A. DYER, who d. 1 Oct. 1880; m. (3) at Randolph, 25 Sept.

1881, MARY C. (MANSFIELD) (___) LUNT, ae 49, b. Salem, dau. of John and Lucy (Borden) Mansfield, 3rd m. for both (Mass. VR 316:319). In 1850 John G. Pool ae 37 was a bootmaker at Quincy with Vesta C. ae 36, three children, and George S. Page ae 28, bootmaker; all b. Mass. (p.276). From at least 1863 until his death he was postmaster at Randolph.

Children, with Vesta (*Poole Family*, 35-36; three oldest at home 1850): 1. *John Franklin Pool*, b. 19 March 1834; a bootmaker 1850. 2. *James Loring Pool*, b. 3 March 1836. 3. *Vesta Jane Pool*, b. 27 Feb. [1838]; m. Samuel Burrill. 4. *Sarah Packard Pool*, b. 12 Jan. 1840 at N. Bridgewater; d. 19 Oct. 1840 at Quincy.

x   LEONARD POOL, b. 22 March 1816 at Abington; d. ca 1885 (*Poole Family*, 36); m. 24 Sept. 1837, LUCINDA HAYDEN, b. ca 1817 in Mass. In 1850 he was a bootmaker in Randolph, ae 34, with Lucinda, and one dau.; Samuel Burrell ae 18 and Esther Kennedy ae 19 were in the household (p.222). He spent over 30 years in California and Idaho in the Gold Rush (*Poole Family*, 36, *q.v.* for more detail).

Children (*ibid.*): 1. *Maria Louise Pool*, b. 11 June 1838; at home 1850. 2. *Mary White Pool*, b. 18 Feb. 1843; d. 5 Dec. 1847.

xi   AMOS TURNER POOL, b. 30 Sept. 1818, rep. at Hanover; m. (1) 24 June 1840, MELISSA BLOOMFIELD KNOX, b. 28 Aug. 1815 Herrick Centre, Pa., d. 28 Nov. 1871 Kingston, Pa., dau. of Oliver and Mary Urania (Kent) Knox (*Poole Family*, 36); m. (2) 27 March 1873, Mrs. SARAH ANN (WINTERS) RINKER, b. 27 March 1833 Hamilton Twp., Monroe Co., Pa. (*ibid.*). In 1850 Amos Pool was a miller in Monroe, Wyoming Co., Pa., with Melissa ae 25, five children, and his father, ae 73 (p.102).

Children, first seven b. Beaumont, Pa. (*Poole Family*, 36; census): 1. *Julia Ann Pool*, b. 15 Aug. 1842; m. (1) Freeman McCarty, div., (2) Henry Noah Gridley. 2. *Louisa Maria Pool*, b. 18 March 1844; m. (1) Albert Canfield, (2) Phineas A. Watt. 3. *William Penn Pool*, b. 14 June 1846. 4. *George Wallace Pool*, b. 14 June 1848. 5. *Francis Henry Pool*, b. 7 Dec. 1849. 6. *Loring Reed Pool*, b. 1 Feb. 1852; d. 1865. 7. *Melissa Almira Pool*, b. 2 Feb. 1854; m. Melmont Little Luke. 8. *Cora May Pool*, b. 30 Jan. 1874 at Forty Fort, Pa.; m. John Martin.

Sources cited: *Abington VR. Bridgewater VR. Dorchester VR* [BRC 36]. *East Bridgewater VR.* Easton VR. *Edward Poole of Weymouth* (1893). CENSUS: 1800 Bridgewater, Plymouth Co. (M32-16); 1850, Norfolk Co.: Dedham (M432-330), Quincy (M432-331), Roxbury (M432-330), & Randolph (M432-329), Plymouth Co.: Pembroke & Scituate (M432-332), Mount Caramel, Wabash Co., Ill. (432-130), Monroe, Wyoming Co., Pa. (M432-838).; 1860 Pembroke, Plymouth Co. (M653-519).

823.   DEBORAH VINING[5] (*Deborah Fullerton*[4], *Ruth*[3] *Samson, Caleb*[2], *Henry*[1]), daughter of Elisha Vining and his wife Deborah Fullerton [169], was born at Abington 7 August 1766 (*VR* 1:236). She died there 11 March 1852 aged 85y 9m, of old age (Mass. VR 67:238). She was a descendant also of *Mayflower* passengers John Alden and Myles Standish.

The Abington record of a marriage of Deborah Vining to Snow House of Hanover in 1795 does not seem to relate to this Deborah. She was called "Deborah Vining" in 1802 when her daughter was born, and Laura's death record also says "dau. of Deborah Vining." Deborah's death record confirms her parents' names and single status. Census figures for Elisha Vining's household support their presence there.

In 1850 Deborah Vining, aged 84, was living at Abington in the household of Emerson Orcutt, aged 70, a shoemaker, and Mehitable Orcutt, 74 (p.195).

Child, rec. Abington (*VR* 1:237):

i   LAURA VINING[6], b. 28 Aug. 1802, "dau. Deborah"; d. Abington 8 April 1826 ae 24 (*VR* 2:253); m. at Abington, 18 July 1820 (*VR* 2:33), STEPHEN BLANCHARD, b. Abington 30 March 1799, son of Adam B. Jr. and Rebecca (Pain) Blanchard (*VR* 1:35), d. there 28 Oct. 1844 of consumption (Mass. VR 15:76). He m. (2) int. at Abington 20 Aug. 1826 (*VR* 2:33), Charlottie Thayer of Weymouth. In 1850 all three children were at Randolph with their families; Lewis and Elisha Blanchard and Betsey's husband all bootmakers (p.196).

 Blanchard children, first two rec. Abington (*VR* 1:33-34): 1. *Lewis Austin Blanchard*, b. 1 Dec. 1820; m. Lydia ___. 2. *Betsey Ann Blanchard*, b. 4 Aug. 1822; m. George Belcher. 3. *Elisha Vining Blanchard*, b. 3 July 1825; m. Emaline ___.

Sources cited: *Abington VR.* Mass. Vital Records 1841-1910. CENSUS: 1850 Abington, Plymouth Co. (M432-332), Randolph, Norfolk Co. (M432-329).

---

824.   JERUSHA BARTLETT ROBINSON[5] (*Jerusha Bartlett[4], Jerusha[3] Samson, Caleb[2], Henry[1]*), daughter of James Robinson and his wife Jerusha Bartlett [170], was born at Bridgewater 19 July 1753 (*VR* 1:281), and died at Duxbury between 14 November 1797 when her last child was born, and 25 January 1799 when her husband remarried. She was a descendant also of *Mayflower* passengers John Alden and Myles Standish.

She married at Duxbury, 14 March 1774 (*VR* 326), **WAIT WADSWORTH JR.** He was born at Duxbury 7 October 1754, son of Wait and Abigail (Bradford) Wadsworth (*VR* 183, 326), and died there 11 March 1840 aged 85 (*VR* 433). He was a descendant of *Mayflower* passengers William Bradford, William Brewster, and Thomas Rogers. He married, second, at Duxbury 25 January 1799 (*VR* 326), PRISCILLA WESTON, who was living 17 May 1841.

The will of James Robinson of Cummington, housewright, dated 16 July 1790, proved 1 September 1793, names among others his daughter Jerusha Bartlett Robinson (Hampshire PR Box 123 #25).

Wait Jr. was a captain in the Revolutionary War. In 1790 he was living at Duxbury with three boys under 16 and five females (*Heads of Fam.*, 169). In 1800 Wait Wadsworth was living at Duxbury, head of a household consisting of himself, 45 or over, a woman 26-45 (presumably Priscilla), one young man 16-26, two girls 10-16, and two boys and one girl under 10.

On 13 April 1840 Zenas Faunce of Duxbury was appointed administrator of the estate of Wait Wadsworth late of Duxbury, yeoman, deceased, and a petition to sell the entire estate was presented the third Monday in May 1840 (Plymouth PR 10A:342). An account allowed 17 May 1841 included cash paid to Priscilla Wadsworth for relinquishing her thirds (*ibid.*, 83:205). No Plymouth County probate record was found for Jerusha.

Children of Wait and Jerusha Bartlett (Robinson) Wadsworth, b. Duxbury (*VR* 181-84):

i ROBERT WADSWORTH[6], b. 3 July 1774; d. Duxbury 23 Sept. 1850 ae 78 [*sic*], mariner, b. Plymouth, son of Wait Wadsworth (Mass. VR 49:151) m. at Duxbury, 15 Aug. 1799 (*VR* 326), WELTHEA DELANO, b. 10 Jan. 1778 (*Duxbury VR* 66, as "wife of Robert Wadsworth"); d. 23 Oct. 1848 ae 74y 9m 28d at Plymouth, rec. Duxbury (*VR* 433).

Children rec. Duxbury (*VR* 181, 183, 184): 1. *George Wadsworth*[7], b. 17 Aug. 1802. 2. *Wait Wadsworth*, b. 2 Aug. 1805. 3. *Thomas C. Wadsworth*, b. 7 May 1809. 4. *Welthea Wadsworth*, b. 19 May 1813; d. 23 Oct. 1848 at Duxbury (*VR* 433). 5. *James Wadsworth*, b. 13 Dec. 1815.

ii MATILDA WADSWORTH, b. 23 July 1776; m. at Duxbury, 27 March 1798 (*VR* 234), THOMAS CHANDLER, d. Jan. 1825, "lost at sea on a voyage to N. Carolina" (g.s., *Duxbury VR* 361).

iii SYLVIA WADSWORTH, b. 28 July 1781; d. at Duxbury 20 July 1825, ae 43y 11m 22d (*VR* 388); m. at Duxbury, 10 Oct. 1802 (*VR* 326), ZIBA HUNT, son of Lot and Mary (Sampson) Hunt, a Henry Samson descendant. (See **Family #790-iv** for their children.) She m. (2) NATHANIEL HOLMES, b. Kingston 19 Sept. 1775, d. Duxbury 20 Sept. 1821, son of Nathaniel and Mary (Rickard) Holmes (*Delano 2004*, 159).

iv LUCINDA WADSWORTH, b. 6 Sept. 1785.

v JERUSHA WADSWORTH, b. 25 May 1789 (also on g.s.) ; d. Duxbury 26 April 1881 ae 91y 11m 1d, of old age (Mass. VR 329:305); m. at Duxbury, 29 Oct. 1812 (*VR* 325), ZENAS FAUNCE, b. 29 June 1784 (g.s.), d. Duxbury

21 March 1875 of consumption, ae 69y 9m, blacksmith, b. Kingston, son of
Elezar and Susannah (___) Faunce (Mass. VR 85:199).

    Faunce children rec. Duxbury (*VR* 74): 1. *Zenas Faunce Jr.*[7], b. 26 Oct. 1813;
m. Christiana Prior. 2. *[Son] Faunce*, b. and d. 18 Oct. 1816 ae 6 hrs (*VR* 376).
3. *George Faunce*, b. 14 July 1818. 4. *Jerusha Faunce*, b. 17 Aug. 1822; m. Thomas
Dingley Hathaway. 5. and 6. *[Twin daughters] Faunce*, b. 19 Sept. 1825; d. Sept.
1825 (*VR* 376).

vi   JAMES WADSWORTH, b. 14 Feb. 1792.

vii WAITY WADSWORTH, b. 14 Nov. 1797; d. at Duxbury in 1884 (Mass. VR
356:300); m. at Duxbury, 21 June 1821 (*VR* 326), NATHAN SAMPSON,
b. Duxbury 7 April 1799, d. there 2 March 1872 of angina pectoris (Mass.
VR 248:383), son of Ichabod and Deborah (Jones) Sampson, a desc. of
Abraham Sampson (*Giles Mem.*, 426). In 1850 he was a shipwright ae 51 at
Duxbury with Waty ae 50 and Henry L. ae 22 (p.62).

    Sampson child rec. Duxbury (*VR* 139; *Giles Mem.*): 1. *Henry Lewis Sampson*[7],
b. 10 April 1828; at home 1850.

Sources cited: *Bridgewater VR. Duxbury VR.* Mass. Vital Records 1841-1910 . Plymouth County
Probate Records. *Giles Memorial* (1864). CENSUS: *Heads of Families 1790 – Mass.*; Duxbury,
Plymouth Co., 1800 (M16–95), 1850 (M432-333).

825. MARGARET ROBINSON[5] *(Jerusha Bartlett*[4]*, Jerusha*[3] *Samson, Caleb*[2]*,
Henry*[1]*)*, daughter of James Robinson and his wife Jerusha Bartlett [170], was born
at Bridgewater 21 October 1754 (*VR* 1:281). She died at Hamilton, N.Y., in 1839
(*Robinson Gen.*, 2:80). She was a descendant also of *Mayflower* passengers John Alden
and Myles Standish.

    She married at Cummington, 5 April 1786 (*VR* 115), **ELIJAH FAY** of Plain-
field. He was born at Southboro 31 May 1746, son of Edward and Sarah (Joslin)
Fay (*Fay Gen.*, 235, not in *VR*), and died 28 July 1823 at Earlville, N.Y. (*Pioneer
Settlers of Madison Co.*, 88). Elijah and Margaret are buried in Earlville Cemetery,
Madison County, N.Y. (*ibid.*).

    The will of James Robinson of Cummington, housewright, dated 16 July 1790,
proved 1 September 1793, names among others his daughter Margaret Fay
(Hampshire PR Box 123 #25).

    Elijah served in the Revolutionary War as a private in Capt. Moses Harring-
ton's company, Col. Dike's regiment, from 1 December 1776 to 1 March 1777,
credited to Southborough. He enlisted again 21 August 1777 in Capt. Seth
Newton's (Cavalry) company, Col. Whitney's regiment and was discharged six days

later after having marched on an alarm at Bennington, with rations allowed on the march from Southborough to Hadley (*MSSR* 5:574).

In 1790 he was living at Plainfield with one boy under 16 and three females (*Heads of Fam.*, 121). In 1800 Elijah Fay of Plainfield had a household consisting of one boy and two girls under 10, one girl 10-16, one man 26-45, and one woman 45 or older (p.307). He is probably the E. Fay at Hamilton, N.Y., in 1810, head of a household consisting of a man and a woman 45 or older, two young women 16-26, and two boys 10-16 (p.200).

In his will dated 20 November 1822, proved 11 August 1823, Elijah Fay of Hamilton left to beloved wife Margaret half of his real estate, and to his only son James R. Fay the other half. Heirs of oldest daughter Margaret Pool were to have a feather bed after his wife's decease; second daughter Sarah Nash and youngest daughter Susannah Green each received a feather bed and $50. Son James was named executor (Madison Co. Surrogate's Records, DX:133).

Children of Elijah and Margaret (Robinson) Fay, b. Plainfield (VR 1:475):

i ELIJAH FAY[6], b. 3 Nov. 1786; d.y. (*Fay Gen.*, 235).

ii MARGARET FAY, b. 11 Dec. 1788; d. by 1822; m. _____ POOL. She left children who are mentioned but not named in her father's will.

iii SARAH / SALLY FAY, b. 12 Dec. 1789; m. THOMAS NASH, b. 24 March 1788 in Mass., d. 1842 ae 53, son of Elijah and Hannah (Thayer) Nash who settled in Hamilton, N.Y., 1800 (*Pioneer Settlers of Madison Co.*, 175). In 1850 Sarah was living in the home of her son C. R. Nash at Hamilton, N.Y. (p.80).
　　Nash children included: 1. *Elijah Fay Nash*[7], b. Hamilton 1814 (*Pioneer Settlers of Madison Co.*, 175). 2. *C. R.* [prob. *Clark Robinson*] *Nash*, b. ca 1821; m. Prudence _____, b. ca 1828; a merchant at Hamilton, N.Y., 1850.

iv SUSAN / SUSANNAH FAY, b. 1791; m. WILLIAM GREEN, b. ca 1785 N.Y. In 1850 he was a farmer at Genoa, Cayuga Co., N.Y., with Susan ae 56 b. Mass., and Barr ae 21; also in the household were Adaline Wise ae 17, Miranda A. Pierce ae 3, Thomas Clegg ae 17 (b. England), Charles Curtis ae 14, and Harvey Wise ae 24 (p.83).
　　Green children (said to be six in all): 1. *Barr Green*[7], b. ca 1829; at home 1850. 2. *James Fay Green*, res. Moravia, N.Y. (*Robinson Gen.*, 2:80).

v ELIJAH FAY, b. 27 Nov. 1793; not in father's will 1822.

vi JOANNA FAY, b. 17 March 1795; not in father's will 1822.

vii JAMES ROBINSON FAY, b. 8 March 1797; d. Earlville 23 Nov. 1858; bur. Earlville Cem.; res. family homestead in Hamilton; m. at Hamilton, 16 Sept. 1818, MARILLA NASH (*Hillsdale History*, 114), b. Plainfield 2 April 1801, daughter of Elijah Nash. James was executor of his father's will 1823. In 1850 he was a farmer at Hamilton, but the census entry is garbled; his age is given as 25, with Marina ae 50, both b. Mass.; the household included children Zenas F., Clara N., Cordelia D., Henry L., and Gaines L., and son William L. ae 25 was next door with wife Marrilia ae 24, their entry perhaps the reason for the confusion (p.89). James' probate records name widow Marilla Fay, and children James L. Fay, Henry L. Fay, Calphurnia Lord, William L. Fay, Cleora Bligh of Bay City, Mich., Cleopatra Whittemore of Detroit, Mich., Cordelia Giffard of Peoria, Ill., and Zenus L. Fay; and Charles L. Remming of Eaton, great-grandson of Gain L. Fay (Madison Co. Surrogate's Recs. G:43).

Children (PR; *Robinson Gen.*, 2:81; *Fay Gen.*, 235): 1. *Calphurnia Fay*[7], b. 1820; m. George Lord, res. Bay City, Mich. 2. *James LeRoy Fay*, b. 1822; m. Marcia Pearl. 3. *William LeFountain Fay*, b. ca 1824; m. Arvilla Cushman. 4. *Zenas LaFleur Fay*, b. ca 1826; m. Sarah Cushman. 5. *Margaret Cleopatra Fay*, b. 1828; m. Joseph B./P. Whittemore of Detroit. 6. *Delphia Nash Fay*, b. 1830; d.y.; not at home 1850. 7. *Cloria Marilla Fay*, b. ca 1832; m. Theodore Bligh. 8. *Cordelia Daniels Fay*, b. ca 1834; m. William Gilbert or Giffard. 9. *Henry LaMotte Fay*, b. ca 1836. 10. *Gain LaFitte Fay*, b. ca 1839; m. Maria Peck.

Sources cited: *Cummington VR.* Plainfield VR, on Holbrook microfiche. Madison County, N.Y., Surrogate's Records. *History of Hillsdale* (1883). Bracy, ed., *Names and Sketches of Pioneer Settlers of Madison County* (1984). *John Fay of Marlboro ...* (1898). *Robinson Genealogy*, Vol. 2 (1933). CENSUS: 1800 Plainfield, Hampshire Co. (M32-15); Hamilton, Madison Co., N.Y., 1810 (M252-28), 1850 (M432-527).

826.   WATSON ROBINSON[5] (*Jerusha Bartlett*[4], *Jerusha*[3] *Samson, Caleb*[2], *Henry*[1]), son of James Robinson and his wife Jerusha Bartlett [170], was born at Plymouth 16 October 1757 (*Robinson Gen.*, 2:79; not in VRs). He died in Wayne County, N.Y., probably between 1810 and 1820. He was a descendant also of *Mayflower* passengers John Alden and Myles Standish.

He was of Cummington when he published marriage intentions there 25 June 1784 (*VR* 150), with **ANNA WEBSTER** of Goshen. She was born at Chesterfield 15 April 1768, daughter of Robert and Molly (Burt) Webster (*Chesterfield Families*, 397). She is said to have died, and Watson married, second, a wife whose name has not been learned (*Robinson Gen.*).

Family recollections of Watson's niece, Lucretia Bradish (*Robinson Gen.*, 2:73-74), describe him as "a daring little fellow and, in the water, like a duck," whose father would toss him into deeper water and let him paddle. He served on a ship as a cabin boy, and when the Revolution began he enlisted at age 18.

He served extensively from Bridgewater for several enlistments from April 1776 until 1781, including at Valley Forge in January 1778. He was a private and then a sergeant; a descriptive list in 1777 gives his age as 20, and another in 1781 as aged 26, 5 ft. 5 in. tall with light complexion and dark hair (*MSSR* 13:469). In April 1790 bounty land was awarded to Watson Robertson [*sic*] who had served as a sergeant in the Massachusetts Line (White, 2914), but there is no record of a pension.

The will of James Robinson of Cummington, housewright, dated 16 July 1790, proved 1 September 1793, names among others his son Watson Robinson (Hampshire PR Box 123 #25). Goshen was Watson's wife's home, and in 1790 he was living there with two boys under 16 and three females (*Heads of Fam.*, 110). That same year, however, he was among more than eighty individuals warned out of town to prevent them from gaining legal settlement there (*Goshen History*, 23-24). On 4 April 1791 Constable Justin Parsons reported that he had "warned as directed, and said inhabitants reside in said town no longer" (*ibid.*, 24).

Watson Robinson has not been found in the 1800 census, but by 1810 he was living at Palmyra, N.Y., head of a household consisting of one man and one woman 45 or older, one man and one woman 16-26, one boy and one girl 10-16, and one boy and two girls under 10 (p.210).

In 1820 sons Timothy and James were living in Palmyra next to each other, both 26-45 (p.338). Watson is not listed, and no land or probate records were found for him in Ontario County.

Children of Watson and probably Anna (Webster) Robinson (*Robinson Gen.*, 2:81-82):

i   JAMES ROBINSON[6]; b. say 1785; d. prob. 1835 (g.s., Palmyra Village Cem.); living Palmyra 1820 with no ch.

ii   TIMOTHY ROBINSON, b. say 1787; living Palmyra 1820 with one woman 26-45 and three little boys under 10; went to Ohio (*Robinson Gen.*, 2:81).

iii WILLIAM DAMOND ROBINSON; went to Plymouth, Mich. (*ibid.*).

iv   MARY ANN ROBINSON; m. ___ FORMAN; res. St. John's, Clinton Co., Mich. (*ibid.*).

Child of Watson and ___ (___) Robinson:

v   JERUSHA ROBINSON.

Sources cited: *Cummington VR.* Hampshire County Probate Records. Baker, *Chesterfield Families* (1962). Barrus, *History of Goshen* (1881). *Robinson Genealogy*, Vol. 2 (1933). CENSUS: Palmyra, Ontario Co., N.Y., 1810 (M252-33), 1820 (M33-62).

827. MARY ROBINSON[5] (*Jerusha Bartlett*[4], *Jerusha*[3] *Samson, Caleb*[2], *Henry*[1]), daughter of James Robinson and his wife Jerusha Bartlett [170], was born at Plymouth 20 December 1758 (*Robinson Gen.*, 2:79) and died at Palmyra, N.Y., in 1811 (*ibid.*, 82). She was a descendant also of *Mayflower* passengers John Alden and Myles Standish.

She married before 1790, **MATTHEW ORR** of Bridgewater, and they settled in Nine Partners, Dutchess County, N.Y., where he died (*Hillsdale History*, 98, 114). The will of James Robinson of Cummington, housewright, dated 16 July 1790, proved 1 September 1793, names among others his daughter Mary Orr (Hampshire PR Box 123 #25).

There has been some confusion over the given name of Mary's husband. Mitchell in *History of Bridgewater* says she married *David* Orr and went to the Nine Partners (p.287). *History of Little Nine Partners* (p.372), says, "Robert Orr, the first of the name, resided in what is now 'Milan' in the NorthEast Precinct, in 1769, and David about the same time, and Hugh in 1774. David deceased 1803 leaving sons David, Matthew, Watson, and William. A daughter married Benjamin Toms, who has descendants bearing his name, but none of the name Orr are in the town." The *Robinson Genealogy* says Mary married *Matthew* Orr. Hugh Orr was recording children in Bridgewater in the 1750s (*VR* 1:236-237), including a Robert born 1745, but the names David and Matthew do not appear.

In 1790 Matthew Orr was in Hillsdale, Columbia County, N.Y., with one boy under 16 and two females (p.63). The only Matthew Orr in the 1800 census of N.Y. was in Franklin, Delaware County, aged 26-45 (p.1310).

Hillsdale History (1883) says, "After the death of her husband, [Mary] removed to Palmyra, N.Y., where she died."

Attempts to locate children and grandchildren in census records, using as clues the recollections of Lucretia Bradish (*Robinson Genealogy*), have proved frustrating. More work is needed to sort out this family.

Children of Matthew and Mary (Robinson) Orr (*Robinson Gen.*, 2:82; *Hillsdale History*, 98); order uncertain:

 i MARGARET ORR[6]; m. JOHN STAFFORD of Rhode Island, and settled in Farmington, N.Y. (*Robinson Gen.*, 83):
     Stafford children (*ibid.*): 1. prob. *Samantha Stafford*[7], b. ca 1806; m. David Payne (see 1850 census, Farmington, N.Y.). 2. *Anna Stafford.* 3. *Jeanette Stafford.* 4. *Watson Orr Stafford.* 5. *Corbett Stafford.* 6. *Robert Stafford.* 7. *John Stafford.* 8. *James Stafford;* m. Polly Potter.

 ii ANNA ORR; m. FITCH AVERILL.

 iii JENNET ORR (not mentioned in *Hillsdale History*).

iv   WATSON ORR, b. prob. ca 1780; m. LOVINA WHEELER, dau. of John and Harmie (Knowlton) Wheeler (*Wheeler Fam.,* 669). He res. Schoharie Co., N.Y., and represented that county in the State Legislature in 1834. In 1840 he was in Summit, Schoharie Co., N.Y., ae 60-70 with one woman 70-80, one woman 50-60, one man and one woman 20-30, and two young men 15-20; David J. Orr ae 20-30, was next door (p.149). In 1850 Watson Orr ae 70, b. Mass., was in Jackson, Guersey Co., Ohio, 1850, with Lovina ae 60, b. N.Y., next to Parker Orr, 27, b. NY. (p.335).

　　　　Children included prob.: 1. *David J. Orr⁷,* b. 1810-1820. 2. *Parker Orr,* b. ca 1823 N.Y.; m. Sarah _____.

v   CORBETT ORR, b. ca 1782; "commanded a sloop on the Hudson River." Corbert Orr ae 78 and Elizabeth Orr ae 21 were living in 1850 in the household of Philander Smith ae 56 and wife Maria ae 41, in Davenport, Delaware Co., N.Y. (p.137).

　　　　Possible child: 1. *Elizabeth Orr⁷,* b. ca 1829.

vi   ROBERT ORR (not mentioned in. *Hillsdale Hist.*); m. and res. Farmington, N.Y. (*Robinson Gen.,* 2:82); not located in census.

vii   JOHN ORR; went to Ohio and/or Michigan (*ibid.*).

viii   JAMES ORR, b. prob. ca 1789; perhaps the James Orr ae 61, b. N.Y., who in 1850 was a farmer at Orwell, Ashtabula Co., Ohio, with wife SALLY _____ ae 53 and four children (p.470).

　　　　Children at home 1850, first two b. N.Y., last two in Ohio: 1. *Rebecca Orr⁷,* b. ca 1828. 2. *Madison Orr,* b. ca 1834. 3. *Jerome Orr,* b. ca 1837. 4. *Emma Orr,* b. ca 1840.

ix   MARIA ORR (not mentioned in *Hillsdale Hist.*).

Sources cited: Mitchell, *History of Bridgewater* (1840). Collin, *History of Hillsdale* (1883). *Robinson Genealogy,* Volume 2 (1933). *Genealogical and Encyclopedic History of the Wheeler Family in America* (1914). Huntting, *History of the Little Nine Partners* (1897). CENSUS: 1790 Hillsdale, Columbia Co., N.Y. (M637-6); 1810 Franklin, Delaware Co., N.Y. (M32-22); 1840 Jackson Co., Ind. (M704-83) & Summit, Schoharie Co., N.Y. (M704-338); 1850: Davenport, Delaware Co., N.Y. (M432-494), Hamilton, Jackson Co., Ind. (M432-152); Orwell, Ashtabula Co., Ohio (M432-659), & Jackson, Guernsey Co., Ohio (M432-684) .

828.   ELIZABETH ROBINSON⁵ (*Jerusha Bartlett⁴, Jerusha³ Samson, Caleb², Henry¹*), daughter of James Robinson and his wife Jerusha Bartlett [170], was born at Plymouth in October 1760 (not in VR), and died in Niagara County, N.Y., in 1811 ("MacIntyre Clan," 164). She was a descendant also of *Mayflower* passengers John Alden and Myles Standish.

She married after intentions at Cummington 27 September 1782 (*VR* 134), **ALEXANDER McINTYRE**. The will of James Robinson of Cummington, housewright, dated 16 July 1790, proved 1 September 1793, names among others his daughter Elizabeth McIntyre (Hampshire PR Box 123 #25). Nothing to identify Alexander was found in Hampshire County probate or land records, or in Hampden County deeds.

In 1790 Alexander McIntire was in Hillsdale, Columbia County, N.Y., with two boys under 16 and three females (p.64). In 1800 both he and his brother-in-law Gain Robinson were in Palmyra, N.Y. (then in Ontario Co.; incorrectly indexed as Northampton on line, p.352). Alexander's family consisted of one man and one woman 26-45, one girl 10-16, and one boy and two girls under 10. "The first settlement [in Chautauqua Co.] was made at Mayville, in 1804, by Dr. Alexander McIntyre" (French, *Gazeteer of NY,* 211).

Children of Alexander and Elizabeth (Robinson) McIntyre ("MacIntyre Clan," 165); order uncertain (census suggests two boys and two girls b. 1783-90, one boy and two girls b. 1790-1800):

i   THOMAS McINTYRE[6], "a preacher … had several children" (*ibid.,* 164).

ii ALEXANDER McINTYRE, b. ca 1792; d. Palmyra, N.Y., 22 July 1859 ae 67 (g.s., Palmyra Village Cem.); m. ANN BECKWITH, b. ca 1800 Conn, d. 20 Aug. 1855 ae 58 (g.s.). He lived from boyhood with his uncle, Dr. Gain Robinson, in Palmyra, N.Y. ("MacIntyre Clan," 165). In 1850 he was a physician and surgeon in Palmyra, ae 56, b. Mass., with Ann ae 50, Elizabeth Lampson ae 27, Dewitt C. McIntyre ae 23, physician, Samuel B. McIntyre ae 21, student, James Touhey ae 19, laborer b. Ireland, Catherine Johnson ae 19, b. N.Y., and William Lampson ae 28, clerk b. N.H. (p.3). (See also *Robinson Gen.,* 2:84.)

Children, b. N.Y. ("MacIntyre Clan," 165): 1. *Ann Elizabeth McIntyre[7],* b. ca 1823; m. William Lampson of Keene, N.H. 2. *[Son] McIntyre,* d. inf. 3. *DeWitt Clinton McIntyre,* b. ca 1827. 3. *Samuel Beckwith McIntyre,* b. 1 Nov. 1828; m. Anna Eliza Pomeroy.

iii ABNER McINTYRE; had several children ("MacIntyre Clan," 165). He may be the Abner McIntire in Elbridge, N.Y., in 1830, a man 40-50, with one woman 30-40, two men 20-30, two young women 15-20, one girl 10-15, and one boy under 5 (p.93).

iv LUCRETIA McINTYRE, d. ae 18 yrs.

v   MARTHA McINTYRE, d.y.

vi ELIZABETH McINTYRE; m. _____ THRASHER. (George, Benjamin, and Samuel Threasher were heads of families in Palmyra, N.Y. in 1820.)

vii ESTHER McINTYRE, b. 22 Aug. 1800; d. Grant Twp., Neb., 26 Dec. 1873 of pleurisy at home of dau. Sophia; m. (1) ca 1820, JOHN WOODMAN, b. Madison, N.Y., 18 March 1797, d. 1 March 1835, son of Sylvester and Meribah (Brownell) Woodman; m. (2) at Palmyra, N.Y., 1839, JEREMIAH HURLBURT, b. ca 1794 Conn. [18 Feb. 1791 Wyoming Valley, Pa.], d. Brighton, Wisc., 15 Aug. 1850, son of John and Hannah (Millet) Hurlburt; m. (3) at Dover, Wisc., 31 Dec. 1852, REUBEN NORTH, b. 1801 England (*Woodmans of RI*, #E-296), from whom divorced. In 1850 Jeremiah Hurlburt was a farmer in Brighton, Wisc., with Esther ae 52, Lucy B. Woodman ae 16, Delos B. Hurlburt ae 9, and Philo Blanden ae 20, laborer, all b. N.Y. (p.203).

Woodman children (*Woodmans of RI*, #E-296): 1. *Sophia Ann Woodman[7]*, b. 22 Feb. 1821; m. Nehemiah E. Burgess. 2. *William B. Woodman*, b. ca 1823. 3. *Susannah Ide Woodman*, b. ca 1824; m. ___ Brown. 4. *Alexander McIntyre Woodman*, b. ca 1826; d.y. 5. *Thomas Jefferson Woodman*, b. ca 1829; m. (1) Rebecca ___, (2) Mrs. Lidda Granger. 6. *Harriet Ludentia Woodman*, b. 10 July 1832; m. Amos F. W. Fuller. 7. *Lucy B. Woodman*, b. ca 1834.

Hurlburt child: 1. *Deloss Bradley Hurlburt[7]*, b. 10 Sept. 1840.

Sources cited: *Cummington VR.* Hampshire County Probate Records. *History of Hillsdale* (1883). Robert Harry McIntire, "The MacIntyre, McIntyre and McIntire Clan: of Scotland, Canada, and New England," typescript, 1949, HeritageQuest Online. *Robinson Genealogy*, Vol. 2 (1933). Helen D. Woodman, *The Woodmans of Rhode Island* (1989). Louise Havens, LouiseH@cox.net. CENSUS: 1790, Hillsdale, Columbia Co., N.Y. (M637-6); Palmyra [in Ontario Co.], N.Y., 1800 (M32-28); Palmyra [in Wayne Co.], N.Y., 1850 (M432-612).

829. JANE ROBINSON[5] (*Jerusha Bartlett[4], Jerusha[3] Samson, Caleb[2], Henry[1]*), daughter of James Robinson and his wife Jerusha Bartlett [170], was born on Clark's Island in Plymouth Harbor 6 August 1763 (*Hillsdale Cem.*), and died at Hillsdale, N.Y., 7 April 1836 (*Hillsdale History*, 115). She was a descendant also of *Mayflower* passengers John Alden and Myles Standish.

She married at Bridgewater, 8 November 1779 (*VR* 2:327), **WILLIAM JOHNSON**. He was born at Bridgewater 17 January 1753 "New Style," son of Benjamin and Ruth (Holman) Johnson (*VR* 1:178), and died at Hillsdale, N.Y., in April 1818 (*Hillsdale History*, 71). William and Jane are buried in Hillsdale Rural Cemetery, Old Town Road, Hillsdale.

The will of James Robinson of Cummington, housewright, dated 16 July 1790, proved 1 September 1793, names among others his daughter Jane Johnson (Hampshire PR Box 123 #25).

William Johnson of Bridgewater served a private in the Revolutionary War in Capt. Elisha Mitchell's company, Col. Simon Cary's regiment, for seven days in 1776 on an alarm (*MSSR* 8:879).

After the birth of daughter Ruth, the family went to Cummington, where William's household in 1790 included five females (*VR* 248).

Children of William and Jane (Robinson) Johnson:

i   RUTH HOLMAN JOHNSON[6], b. Bridgewater 16 Sept. 1780 (*VR* 1:178); d. Hillsdale, N.Y., 2 Dec. 1868; m. ca 1799, JOHN COLLIN of Hillsdale. Ruth was memorialized in *Hillsdale History* (p.14-15) by her son John Francis Collin, the author and compiler.

    Collin children (*Hillsdale History*, 71): 1. *James Collin*[7], b. 16 Jan. 1800. 2. *John Francis Collin*, b. 30 April 1802. 3. *Sarah Amanda Collin*, b. 21 April 1804. 4. *Jane Miranda Collin*, b. 14 Feb. 1807. 5. *Hannah Collin*, b. 19 Dec. 1809. 6. *Ruth Maria Collin*, b. 1 March 1813; d. May 1838. 7. *Henry Augustus Collin*, b. 6 Jan. 1817. 8. *William Quincy Collin*, b. 23 Nov. 1819; d. 30 July 1822. 9. *Clynthia A. Collin*, b. 10 Dec. 1822; d. 5 Aug. 1828.

ii   SOPHIA JOHNSON, b. Cummington 7 Jan. 1784; d. Hawley 25 Nov. 1831 (*Hawley History*, 75); m. ca 1804, ELIAS FORD, b. Plainfield 25 Nov. 1780 (*ibid.*, 58), son of Andrew and Maria (Beal) Ford. He m. (2) at Cummington, Sept. 1833 (*VR* 71), Anna Carr.

    Ford children (*Hawley History*, 58): 1. *Sophia Ford*[7], b. 18 May 1805; m. Noah Ford. 2. *Elias Ford*, b. 20 July 1807. 3. *Maria Ford*, b. 14 Jan. 1810; m. Isaac Atkins. 4. *Mary/Polly Ford*, b. 12 May 1812; m. Shubael Bradford. 5. *William C. Ford*, b. 30 Nov. 1816. 6. *Sarah C. Ford*, m. Daniel W. Temple. 7. *Jane M. Ford*, b. 25 May 1823. 8. *Clynthia T. Ford*, b. 14 Aug. 1831; m. William B. Martin.

iii MELINDA JOHNSON, b. Cummington 7 Dec. 1785; d. 9 March 1792.

iv   CLYNTHIA JOHNSON, b. Cummington 7 April, bp. 13 July 1788 (*VR* 38); d. before 1883; m. 9 Feb. 1809, REV. HARRY TRUESDELL, son of Thomas and Hannah (Collin) Truesdell.

    Truesdell children (*Hillsdale History*, 72): 1. *Arnold Fletcher Truesdell*[7], b. 6 Jan. 1810. 2. *Sarah Madaline Truesdell*, b. 12 May 1812. 3. *John Quincy Truesdell*, b. 22 Feb. 1825.

v   QUINCY JOHNSON, b. Cummington 5 April 1791; d. before 1883; of Hillsdale, N.Y., when he m. (1) after int. at Otis 19 April 1812 (*VR* 96), ABIGAIL COOK; m. (2) EVELINE (JOHNSON) FOSTER, dau. Lemuel Johnson and widow of Capt. Isaac Foster. In 1850 Quincy Johnson was living at Hillsdale, N.Y., a farmer ae 59, with Abbigel, 64, b. Mass., Leonard, 33, James L., 28, and Malinda, 26, "insane" (p.328). He held high offices in the town of Hillsdale and was a Trustee of the Hillsdale Rural Cemetery Association (*Hillsdale Cem.*).

Children (*Hillsdale History*, 72, 73): 1. *Wesley Johnson*[7], b. 24 Feb. 1813; bp. Otis 12 June 1814 as *Alva Wesley* (*VR* 36); d. 1 July 1844. He helped establish the colony of Liberia and was physician to the family of the governor there. 2. *Marvin Johnson*, b. 16 Dec. 1814; d. 20 Sept. 1841. 3. *William Leonard Johnson*, b. 5 Sept. 1816. 4. *Jane Johnson*, b. 24 April 1818; d. 24 Nov. 1830. 5. *John Quincy Johnson*, b. 28 Aug. 1820. 6. *Melinda Johnson*, b. 31 Dec. 1823. 7. *James Leroy Johnson*, b. 17 April 1822; d. 1869.

vi MELINDA JOHNSON, b. 29 Sept. 1801; res. Evanston, Ill.; m. (1) 10 Sept. 1820, ARNOLD TRUESDELL, son of Thomas and Hannah (Collin) Truesdell, who d. Wilmington, Ohio, 28 March 1835; m. (2) in 1836, Rev. LEONIDAS L. HAMLINE, b. Burlington, Conn., 10 May 1797, d. Mt. Pleasant, Iowa, 23 March 1865. Educated as a lawyer, he became a Methodist minister and a Bishop of M.E. Church (*20ᵗʰ Century Biog. Dict.*, 5:192). In 1870 Melinda was living in the household of her stepson Dr. Leon Hamline ae 41 at Evanston (p.107). *Hillsdale History* (p.73), says she had a son by her second marriage, but only the stepson has been found.

Sources cited: *Bridgewater VR. Cummington VR. East Bridgewater VR. Mass. Soldiers & Sailors.* Cemetery inscriptions, Rickard Collection, Columbia County Historical Society, Kinderhook, N.Y. John Francis Collin, *History of Hillsdale* (1883), *q.v.* for further information. *Robinson Genealogy*, Vol. 2 (1933). *20ᵗʰ Century Biographical Dictionary of Notable Americans* (1904). CENSUS: 1790 Cummington, Hampshire Co., in *Cummington VR*; 1850 Hillsdale, Columbia Co., N.Y. (M432-492); 1870 Evanston, Cook Co., Ill. (M593-212).

830. ESTHER ROBINSON[5] (*Jerusha Bartlett*[4], *Jerusha*[3] *Samson*, *Caleb*[2], *Henry*[1]), daughter of James Robinson and his wife Jerusha Bartlett [170], was born at Bridgewater 30 January 1767 (*Robinson Gen.*, not in *VR*), and died at Hawley 21 December 1858 aged 92, named only as "widow [of] Mrs. Amos King" (Mass. VR 120:196). She was a descendant also of *Mayflower* passengers John Alden and Myles Standish.

She married at Cummington, 29 June 1786 (*VR* 128), **AMOS KING**. He was born at Brimfield 12 March 1758, son of Thomas and Abigail (Warriner) King and a twin to his sister Abigail, and died at Hawley 13 July 1839 aged 81 (*Hawley History*, 248). The will of James Robinson of Cummington, housewright, dated 16 July 1790, proved 1 September 1793, names among others his daughter Esther King (Hampshire PR Box 123 #25).

Amos served as a private in the Revolutionary War (*MSSR* 9:242). In 1790 he was living at Plantation No. 7 [later Hawley] with one boy under 16 and two females. In 1800 his household in Hawley consisted of one man 45 or older, one woman 26-45, one boy and one girl 10-16, and four little girls under 10 (p.807).

In his will dated 22 August 1838, presented 15 October 1839, Amos King of Hawley, husbandman, named his wife Esther as executrix; son Warriner; daughters Jerusha, Esther, Lydia Molton, Minerva, Roena, Abigail (single), and Sementha; and Lydia Molton's two daughters Loizamariah Griggs and Samentha Griggs (Franklin PR #2750).

In 1850 Esther was living in the household of her son Warriner in Hawley (p.264).

Children of Amos and Esther (Robinson) King, rec. Hawley (*Hawley Hist.*, 248-49):

i   WARRINER KING[6], b. 28 May 1787; d. Hawley 27 Feb. 1877; m. ELIZABETH CROWELL, b. 21 Sept. 1788, d. 16 Dec. 1853 (*Hawley History*, 248). In 1850 he was a farmer in Hawley with Elizabeth ae 62, and his mother Esther ae 83 in his household (p.264).

ii   JERUSHA KING, b. 25 Nov. 1788; d. 29 May 1882; m. at Hawley, 21 Sept. 1806 (*Hawley Marriages* 70), EZRA KING, b. 1 Aug. 1784, d. 6 Dec. 1841, son of Thomas and Mercy (Vincent) King (*Hawley History*, 249).
     King children (*ibid.*): 1. *Hiram King*[7], b. 21 Aug. 1806. 2. *Mercy King*, b. 7 June 1808; m. George Rice. 3. *Joanna King*, b. 15 Jan. 1810. 4. *Chloe R. King*, b. 26 Jan. 1812; m. (1) Elisha Ford, (2) Merritt Jones. 5. *Esther King*, b. 14 March 1814; m. James Ferry. 6. *Olive B. King*, b. 4 March 1816; m. Edward Coope. 7. *Ezra King*, b. 20 Dec. 1817. 8. *John Warriner King*, b. 15 Nov. 1819. 9. *Sylvia L. King*, b. 26 Oct. 1821; d. 1837. 10. *Abigail King*, b. 20 Feb. 1823; m. Abner Longley. 11. *Mahaleth King*, b. 8 Oct. 1824; m. Nelson Joy. 12. *Jerusha King*, m. Henry Joy.

iii ESTHER KING, b. 5 Dec. 1790; m. (1) at Hawley, 28 March 1811 (*Hawley Marriages* 70), ZIBA FENTON, (2) in 1837, LEMUEL LOMBARD.

iv   LYDIA MOULTON KING, b. 2 Oct. 1792; d. 24 Feb. 1852; m. at Hawley, 13 June 1816 (*Hawley Marriages* 70), CHESTER F. GRIGGS, d. 24 Feb. 1853. He was a farmer in Hawley in 1850 ae 55 with Lydia ae 57 and Charles ae 14 [?] (p.265).
     Griggs children (grandfather's will): 1. *Loisamariah Griggs*[7]. 2. *Samentha Griggs*.

v   MINERVA KING, b. 27 Sept. 1794; m. at Hawley, 1 Oct. 1818 (*Hawley Marriages* 70) WILLARD NASH; settled Madison Co., N.Y. (*Hillsdale History*, 114). In 1850 he was a farmer in Hamilton, N.Y., ae 54, with Minerva ae 55, and five children (p.92).
     Nash children at home 1850, all b. N.Y.: 1. *Kirkland Nash*[7], b. ca 1830. 2. *James R. Nash*, b. ca 1832. 3. *Dipha Nash*, b. ca 1834. 4. *Esther S. Nash*, b. ca 1837. 5. *Charlotte S. Nash*, b. ca 1841.

vi   ABIGAIL KING, b. 24 April 1796; d. 29 July 1800.

vii   ROANA KING, b. 22 April 1798; m. at Hawley, 1 Sept. 1818 (*Hawley Marriages* 70), DENNIS BANGS, b. ca 1796 Mass. In 1850 he was a farmer in Sangerfield, N.Y., ae 56, with Roana ae 52 and three children (p.42).

   Bangs children at home 1850, all b. N.Y.: 1. *Gain R. Bangs⁷*, b. ca 1831; a farmer. 2. *Marilla J. Bangs*, b. ca 1843. 3. *Julia E. Bangs*, b. ca 1839.

viii   ABIGAIL KING 2ⁿᵈ, b. 25 July 1800; m. (1) at Hawley, 20 Nov. 1838 (*Hawley Marriages*, 71), JEREMIAH TAYLOR, (2) after 1850, SUMNER BARTON. In 1850 Abigail Taylor was head of a household in Hawley that included two children (p.264); Sumner Barton was a farmer ae 49 living in Plainfield with wife Temperance and two children (p.200).

   Taylor children (1850 census): 1. *Abigail M. Taylor⁷*, b. ca 1839. 2. *Amos Taylor*, b. ca 1842.

ixi   AMOS KING, b. 9 Aug. 1802; d.y.

x   JOANNA KING, b. 10 Aug. 1804; d. 19 Sept. 1806.

xi   SAMANTHA KING, b. 1 Jan. 1807; m. at Hawley, 2 Oct. 1826 (*Hawley Marriages* 71), THERON SKEELS, b. Madison Co., N.Y., ca 1804. In 1850 Theron "Keels" was a farmer in Bedford, Cuyahoga Co., Ohio, ae 46, with Semantha ae 44, b. Ohio [*sic*] and five children. The 1860 census of Bedford is almost illegible; indexed as "Skorb," and the two children at home seem to be Frederick A. Skorb ae 4 and Harvey Bacus ae 8, but county of birthplace is given: Theron's as Madison Co., N.Y., Samantha's as Franklin Co., Mass., and that of the two boys as Bedford Co., Ohio (p.229). In 1880 Theron Skeels Sen. ae 76 was a farmer in Bedford, with wife Samantha ae 73, both b. N.Y. [*sic*], in the household of their son Theron N. Skeels ae 45 (p.9).

   Skeels children (census), b. Ohio; list prob. incomplete: 1. *Amos Skeels⁷*, b. ca 1832, a farmer at home 1850. 2. *Theron N. Skeels*, b. ca 1835 (listed as Theresa, female, 1850); m. Augusta ___. 3. *Ruth Skeels*, b. ca 1835; at home 1850. 4. *Rufus Skeels*, b. ca 1837; at home 1850. 5. *Frederick Skeels*, b. ca 1845; at home 1860.

Sources cited: *Brimfield VR. Cummington VR.* Johnson, *History of Hawley* (1953), includes VR. Collin, *History of Hillsdale* (1883). Mass. Vital Records 1841-1910. CENSUS: Hawley, Franklin Co., 1800 (M32-15), 1850 Hawley, Franklin Co. (M432-317), Plainfield, Hampshire Co. (M432-320), Madison Co., N.Y. (M432-527), Sangerfield, Oneida Co., N.Y. (M432-562); 1880 Bedford, Cuyahoga Co., Ohio (T9-1009).

831.   GAIN ROBINSON⁵ (*Jerusha Bartlett⁴, Jerusha³ Samson, Caleb², Henry¹*), son of James Robinson and his wife Jerusha Bartlett [170], was born at Plymouth 24 January 1769 (*Robinson Gen.*, 2:89). He died at Palmyra, N.Y., 21 June 1831 (g.s., Palmyra Village Cemetery), aged 62y 4m 28d, from an "aneurism of the heart"

(*Robinson Gen.*, 2:90). He was a descendant also of *Mayflower* passengers John Alden and Myles Standish.

Dr. Gain Robinson married at Cummington, 15 December 1796 (*VR* 150), **CHLOE BRADISH**, who was born at Hardwick 29 April 1775, daughter of John Jr. and Hannah (Warner) Bradish (*Hardwick History*, 341), and died 16 October 1866 aged 91 years (g.s.). Gain and Chloe are buried in Palmyra Village Cemetery, Vienna Street, Palmyra, N.Y.

Gain's sister Bethiah Robinson married Chloe's brother Charles Bradish [Family #834]. The will of John Bradish of Palmyra, dated 19 November 1812, proved 13 June 1825, names wife Hannah and daughter Chloe Robinson (Ontario Co. Wills A:73): "… unto my daughter Chloe Robinson in grain or neat stock twenty dollars to be paid her within eighteen months after my decease by my son Charles Bradish."

The will of James Robinson of Cummington, housewright, dated 16 July 1790, proved 1 September 1793, names among others his son Gain Robinson, who was to be executor (Hampshire PR Box 123 #25).

Gain Robinson, physician, and Clark Robinson, housewright, both of Cummington, sold land there 7 March 1796 (Hampshire LR 16:558). In 1800 Gain Robinson's household in Palmyra, Ontario County, N.Y., consisted of a man 26-45, two women 16-26, a boy 10-16, and one boy and two girls under 10 (p.352). In 1810 the family consisted of a man and two women 26-45, one boy and one girl 10-16, and five boys and one girl under 10 (p.208). His brother-in-law Alexander McIntyre was listed on the same census page.

The town of Macedon was set off from Palmyra on 29 January 1823, and Gain Robinson was the first physician in that town. In *Hillsdale History* (p.112, which has his birth and death dates wrong), it is written of him, "He was a man with talents of the first order, of fine appearance, of easy and gentlemanly address, interesting in conversation, and distinguished as a physician."

Although she is buried at Palmyra, Chloe may have died in Buffalo, N.Y., as in 1850 she was living there with the family of her daughter Chloe Niles.

Children of Gain and Chloe (Bradish) Robinson, b. Palmyra, N.Y. (*Hillsdale History*, 112-13; birth dates from *Robinson Gen.* 2:90):

> i AMANDA ROBINSON[6], b. 11 Sept. 1797; d. Aug. 1874, Brooklyn, N.Y.; m. PHILIP GRANDEN, b. ca 1802 N.Y. In 1850 Phillip Gorandin [*sic*] ae 48, occ. U.S. Customs, was living in Ward 3, Brooklyn, N.Y., with Amanda ae 52 b. Mass. [*sic*], Cullen ae 24, [his wife] Eliza ae 26, Hellen ae 19, Martin ae 17, in a household headed by Susan B. Thorne ae 50, b. N.Y. (p.270).

Granden children: 1. *William Gain Granden[7]*, grad. West Point Military Academy. 2. *Maria Grandin*, m. Barberic Throckmorton. 3. *Robert Grandin*, a lawyer; lived in the South. 4. *Cullen Granden*, b. ca 1826; m. Eliza Shirley; a clerk 1850. 5. *Helen Grandin*, b. ca 1831; m. William Rawlins. 6. *Martin Van Buren Grandin*, b. ca 1833 (twin); at home 1850. 7. *Andrew Jackson Grandin*, b. ca 1833 (twin); d. inf. *Robinson Gen.* adds twin daughters d. in infancy.

ii WILLIAM CULLEN ROBINSON, b. 16 Sept. 1799; d. in Illinois, unm.

iii CAIUS CASSIUS ROBINSON, b. 8 July 1801; d. 1837, N.Y.C.; grad. Fairfield, N.Y., Medical College; res. Palmyra, N.Y.; m. at Cummington, 10 Oct. 1825 (*VR* 150), ELIZA WARNER, dau. of Stephen Warner of Cummington. She probably m. (2) Henry B. Pomeroy, b. ca 1810 Mass., who in 1850 was a wool grower in Palmyra, Mich., ae 40, with Eliza ae 40 [*sic*], b. Mass., and Lucius G. Robinson ae 22, student, b. N.Y., in his household (p.199).

Child: 1. *Lucius Gain Robinson[7]*, b. ca 1828, Palmyra, N.Y.

iv ABIGAIL BLACKMAN ROBINSON, b. 13 Nov. 1803; d. Tecumseh, Mich.; m. ALEXANDER R. TIFFANY, b. ca 1799 Canada, d. Palmyra, Mich., 14 Jan. 1868 (*Mem. of Lenawee Co.*, 596). They went from Palmyra, N.Y., to Michigan in 1832 (*ibid.*). In 1850 he was a lawyer in Adrian, Mich., with Abigail ae 46 and four children (p.398).

Tiffany children at home 1850, first two b. N.Y., last two Mich., marriages from *Robinson Gen.*, 2:91): 1. *Alexander R. Tiffany[7]*, b. ca 1826. 2. *Frances M. Tiffany*, b. ca 1832; m. George Curtis. 3. *George S. Tiffany*, b. ca 1844. 4. *Margaret S. Tiffany*, b. ca 1845; m. George Archibald.

v CLARK ROBINSON, b. 24 Dec. 1805; m. DELIA STRONG, b. ca 1812 Conn. In 1850 he was a Justice in Buffalo, N.Y., with Delia ae 38, and Christian Metz ae 42 lived in their household (p.493).

Child: 1. *Mary S. Robinson[7]*, d. at ae 17 (*Robinson Gen.*, 2:91).

vi ERASMUS DARWIN ROBINSON, b. 24 Jan. 1808; d. 1890, Howard City, Mich. (*Robinson Gen.*, 2:92); m. CALISTA PECK, b. ca 1807 in N.Y.; res. 1883 White Pigeon, Mich. In 1850 Erasmus D. Robinson was a "forwarder," in Ward 2, Buffalo, N.Y., with Celestia D. ae 43, Gain ae 20, Harriet N. ae 16 (all b. N.Y.), and Ednah Randall ae 65, b. Conn. Also in the household were his brother Rollin Robinson ae 40 and Celestia ae 35 (p.166).

Children (*Robinson Gen.*, 2:92): 1. *Harriet Newell Robinson[7]*, d. before 1883; m. Hon. John Newbury of Detroit. 2. *Gain Robinson*, d. 1862; m. Catherine Washburn (line continued in *Robinson Gen.*). 3. *Cullen Robinson*, d. y., Palmyra, N.Y.

vii [CHARLES] ROLLIN ROBINSON, b. 3 June 1810; m. CALISTA
     CORBETT, b. ca 1815 N.Y. In 1850 they were living with his brother
     Erasmus in Buffalo, and his occupation was "forwarding and comissioner"
     (p.166). Later res. Palmyra, Mich.
        Child: 1. *Margaret Robinson[7]*, d. before 1883; not with parents 1850.
viii CHLOE ROBINSON, b. 1 May 1813; d. 1881, Chicago, Ill.; m. HIRAM
     NILES, b. 18 April 1805 Groton, Conn. (VR, Barbour), son of Silas
     Northrup and Bridget (?Avery) Niles. In 1850 H. Niles ae 41 was a merchant
     in Buffalo, N.Y., with Cloa ae 34, and five daughters; [his mother-in-law]
     Cloa Robinson ae 75, b. Mass. was also in the household (p.451).
        Niles children, all b. N.Y.: 1. *Frederick Montaban Niles[7]*, d.y. 2. *Julia Niles*, b.
     ca 1835; m. William Brewster. 3. *Delia Niles*, b. ca 1837; unm. 4. *Mary Helen
     Niles*, b. ca 1841; m. Edward Brewster. 5. *Margaret Niles*, b. ca 1844; d. in 17th yr.
     6. *Frances Niles*, b. ca 1849; d. inf.
ix   HELEN ELIZABETH ROBINSON, b. 27 April 1816; m. GEORGE
     ELTWEED POMEROY; res. Toledo, Ohio (*Robinson Gen.*, 2:94; not men-
     tioned in *Hillsdale History*).
x   MARGARET SOPHIA ROBINSON, b. 11 June 1819; m. at First Presby-
     terian Church, Albany, N.Y., 28 Nov. 1840 (*Early Settlers NY*, 1:680), JOHN
     E. GAVIT, b. N.Y.C., 29 Oct. 1817, d. Aug. 1874 Stockbridge, Mass. He
     had a distinguished career in bank note engraving and was known also for
     his interests in microscopy and natural science (*Am. Biog. Lib.*, 157). In 1870
     his household consisted of himself ae 52, "Pres. National Bank Note Co.",
     Margaret ae 51, children William, Nellie, Clark, Julia, Chloe B., and Pauline;
     Charles F. Adams ae 26, banker, and wife Greta ae 24 and baby Karl, and a
     cook, a waitress, and a domestic servant (p.737).
        Gavit children: 1. *John Gavit[7]*, b. 4 Aug. 1841; d. inf. 2. *Joseph Gavit*, b.
     22 Dec. 1842. 3. *Margaret Gavit*, b. 22 March 1845; prob. m. Charles F. Adams.
     4. *William Edmonds Gavit*, b. 10 Feb. 1848. 5. *Helen Elizabeth Gavit*, b. 26 Nov.
     1849. 6. *Clark Gavit*, b. 27 June 1851. 7. *Julia Niles Gavit*, b. 22 Feb. 1854.
     8. *Chloe Gavit*, b. 29 April 1865. 9. *Pauline Gavit*, b. 3 Feb. 1859.

Sources cited: *Cummington VR.* Groton, Conn., VR, per Barbour Collection. Paige, *History of
Hardwick* (1883). Gravestone inscriptions from Wayne County Cemeteries, on line. Hampshire
County Deeds. Ontario County Wills, cited in H. M. Wiles, "Wayne County, N.Y., Abstracts of
Wills," NYGBS [Wayne Co. was set off from Ontario Co. 1823]. Collins, *A History of Hillsdale,
Columbia County, New York* (1883). *Early Settlers of N.Y. American Biographical Library.* CENSUS:
Palmyra, Ontario Co., N.Y. 1800 (M32-28), 1810 (M252-33); 1850 Brooklyn, King's Co., N.Y.,
(M432-517), Buffalo, Erie Co., N.Y. (M432-501 & 502), & Palmyra, Lenawee Co., Mich. (M432-
355); 1870 Stockbridge, Berkshire Co. (M593-602).

832. CLARK ROBINSON[5] (*Jerusha Bartlett*[4], *Jerusha*[3] *Samson*, *Caleb*[2], *Henry*[1]), son of James Robinson and his wife Jerusha Bartlett [170], was born at Plymouth 12 December 1771 (*Robinson Gen.*, 2:79). He died at Cummington (*VR* 224), as Major Clark Robison, 14 or 15 August 1805, aged 34. He was a descendant also of *Mayflower* passengers John Alden and Myles Standish. The will of James Robinson of Cummington, housewright, dated 16 July 1790, proved 1 September 1793, names among others his son Clark Robinson (Hampshire PR Box 123 #25). Clark was named after the place of his birth, Clark's Island in Plymouth Harbour (*Robinson Gen.*, 2:89).

He and **RHODA WARNER**, both of Cummington, were married there 19 October 1797 (*VR* 150). Rhoda, daughter of Joseph and Mary (Whipple) Warner, was born at Cummington 10 January 1774 and died there 19 June 1853, aged 79, of consumption (*VR*, 224; Mass. VRs 76:7). Clark and Rhoda Robinson are buried buried in the Bryant Cemetery, Cummington, with his parents and the family of their son James (Corbin Coll.).

The will of Joseph Warner of Cummington, gentleman, dated 29 March 1813, presented 11 August 1818, names his daughter Rhoda Robinson (Hampshire PR Box 154, No. 12).

Clark Robinson of Cummington on 2 March 1793 bought land in Cummington from Stephen Warner (Hampshire LR 9:349). On 2 April 1794 and 7 March 1796 Gain Robinson, physician, and Clark Robinson, yeoman and housewright, both of Cummington, sold land there (*ibid.*, 10:468; 16:558). In 1800 Clark Robinson's household at Cummington consisted of himself and presumably his wife 26-45, two women 45 or older, one boy 10-16, and one boy and one girl under 10 (p.304).

On 24 September 1805 Rhoda Robinson, widow, administratrix of the estate of Major Clark Robinson late of Cummington deceased, was ordered to advertise, and on 28 January 1806 she posted bond as guardian to Lidia, James, Zarina, and Lucius Clark (Hampshire PR Box 123 No. 20).

Children of Clark and Rhoda (Warner) Robinson, rec. Cummington (*VR* 64-65):

i LYDIA ROBINSON[6], b. 21 Oct. 1798, bp. 8 June 1800; m. at Cummington, 29 Sept. 1818 (*VR* 115) HENRY/ HARVEY FENTON, b. Brimfield 1789 (*VR* 56). The m. rec. calls him Henry but it was Harvey Fenton ae 61 who was a farmer at Brimfield in 1850 with Lydia ae 51, Lucius ae 28; Pliny F. Spaulding ae 28 and wife Laura A. ae 26 shared the household which also included Ellen Lonergan ae 17 b. Ireland, and Mary Cobb ae 19 (p.257).

 Fenton children rec. Brimfield to Harvey and Lydia (*VR* 56-57): 1. *Czarina Warner Fenton*[7], b. 21 Oct. 1820. 2. *Lucius Fenton*[7], b. ca 1822, bp. 4 Nov. 1831.

       3. *Laura Ann Fenton*, b. 29 Aug. 1823; m. Pliny F. Spaulding. 4. *Adeline L. Fenton*, b. 1827; d. 24 Oct. 1849 (*VR* 285).

ii   JAMES ROBINSON, b. 22 July 1800; d. at Cummington 15 or 16 Feb. 1846, ae 45, of typhus fever (g.s.; *VR* 223); m. after int. at Cummington 12 Nov. 1827 (*VR* 150), ADALINE RANDALL, b. ca 1803, d. Cummington 15 Jan. 1873 (*VR* 223). They are buried in the Bryant Cemetery (Corbin Coll.).

       Children rec. Cummington (*VR* 64-65, 223): 1. *Lucius C. Robinson⁷*, d. 2 Jan. 1829. 2. *Lucius Clark Robinson*, b. 6 Oct. 1830. 3. *Czarina Aurelia Robinson*, b. 27 Dec. 1831. 4. *Emily Ann Robinson*, b. 12 Dec. 1833. 5. *Mary Warner Robinson*, b. 18 Feb. 1840.

iii   CZARINA ROBINSON, b. 6 June 1802; m. at Cummington, 21 Nov. 1827 (*VR* 107), AUSTIN COBB, prob. Amos Austin Cobb, son of Amos and Rachel (___) Cobb, b. Cummington 26 Jan. 1802 (*VR* 17). In 1850 Austin was a farmer in Cummington ae 48, with Czarina and four children (p.189).

       Cobb children rec. Cummington (*VR* 17-18):   1. *Ellen Louisa Cobb⁷*, b. 6 Dec. 1829; not at home 1850. 2. *Henry Austin Cobb*, b. 25 Aug. 1831. 3. *Charles Cobb*, b. 14 June 1833; not at home 1850. 4. *Marshall Norton Cobb*, b. 21 Aug. 1836. 5. *Josephine Robinson Cobb*, b. 3 June 1839. 6. *Dewey Austin Cobb*, b. 22 Dec. 1841.

iv   LUCIUS CLARK ROBINSON, b. 20 April 1805; d. 30 June 1806, ae 14m 10d (*VR* 224); bur. with parents.

Sources cited: *Cummington VR.* Mass.Vital Records 1841-1910. Hampshire County Deeds and Probate Records at Northampton. Cummington Cemetery Records, Corbin Collection, NEHGS. *Robinson Genealogy*, Vol. 2 (1933). CENSUS: Cummington, Hampshire Co., 1800 (M32-15), 1850 (M432-320).

833. ELEANOR ROBINSON⁵ (*Jerusha Bartlett⁴, Jerusha³ Samson, Caleb², Henry¹*), daughter of James Robinson and his wife Jerusha Bartlett [170], was born at Plymouth 24 December 1774 (*Robinson Gen.*, 79; not in *VR*). At the time of her birth the family lived on Clark's Island, Plymouth. She died at Enfield, 1 January 1842, "Mrs. ____ Woods, wife of Dea. Aaron Woods," aged 66 [*sic*], of inflammation of the lungs (Mass. VR 1:161). She was a descendant also of *Mayflower* passengers John Alden and Myles Standish.

    She married, first, at Cummington, 3 April 1795 (*VR* 108) as his second wife, **JACOB CONVERSE JR.** of Windsor. He was born at Thompson, Conn., about 1766, baptized there 11 May 1776 (*Brown Univ. Cat.*, 76), son of Lt. Jacob and Anna (White) Converse, and died at Palmer 23 May 1808 aged 42 (*VR* 207). He is buried in Palmer Old Center Cemetery (G.R. #2).

Eleanor married, second, at Palmer, 5 June 1812 (*VR* 113), as his second wife, **JAIRUS HOWARD** of Greenwich. He was born about 1764 in Greenwich and was buried at Enfield 23 June 1828, aged 64 (Quabbin Park Cem. Rec., 96). He married, first, ALICE CUTLER, with whom he had a son Daniel Howard, who married Eleanor's oldest daughter, Miriam Keith Converse.

Eleanor married, third, before 1840, Deacon **AARON WOODS** of Enfield. He was born in the 1760s and died at Enfield in 1844 (Mass. VR 14:160).

Jacob Converse was a medical student in the Brown University Class of 1790 (*Brown Univ. Cat.*, 76), but evidently did not practice medicine, "but was Professor of the dead languages at Providence and later Palmer" (*Converse Family*, 1:107).

The will of James Robinson of Cummington, housewright, dated 16 July 1790, proved 1 September 1793, names among others his daughter Eleanor Robinson (Hampshire PR Box 123 #25).

Jacob Converse Jr. of Palmer, in his will dated 25 March 1808, proved 4 October 1808, named his wife Eleanor and five children: Maxcy Manning oldest, Lorenzo second son, Miriam Keith Converse eldest daughter; Anne Converse second daughter, Becca Converse third daughter; executors were to be his wife Eleanor Converse and Alpheus Converse (Hampshire PR Box 35 # 5).

Jacob's father, Jacob Converse of Palmer, gentleman, made his will 29 September 1808, after Jacob Jr.'s death, and it was proved 8 February 1810 (Hampshire PR Box 35 #4½). He named his wife Anna, only son Chester Converse (executor), and grandchildren (children of Jacob Jr., deceased): Maxcy Manning, Lorenzo, Miriam Keith, Anna, Becca, and Ellinor Converse.

In 1810 Eleanor Converse widow was head of a household in Palmer, consisting of one man and one woman 26-45, three boys and one girl 10-16, and one boy and three girls under 10 (p.163). In 1820 figures for the household of Jarius [*sic*] Howard in Enfield (p.167) suggest that the family of his son Daniel, who married her daughter Miriam, lived with their parents. In 1840 the household of Aaron Woods in Enfield consisted of one man 70-80, one woman 60-70, two women 40-50, and one young man and one young woman 15-20 (p.304).

Enfield is one of the "drowned towns" taken for the Quabbin Reservoir. The 1905 *Converse Family* includes much reliable and interesting information on this family.

Children of Jacob and Eleanor (Robinson) Converse (*Converse Family*, 1:62, 106, 232-44), b. at Palmer but not rec. there:

i   MIRIAM KEITH CONVERSE[6], b. 29 Jan. 1797; d. Enfield 24 Aug. 1833 (*Converse Family*, 1:232-34); m. ca 1815, DANIEL HOWARD, b. ca 1793 Enfield, d. Byron, Ill., 1846, son of Jairus and Alice (Cutler) Howard (*ibid.*).

Howard children (*ibid.*): 1. *Jacob Converse Howard[7]*, b. Enfield 30 Nov. 1816; m. Martha Fagan. 2. *Daniel Howard,* b. 1818; d. 29 Sept. 1820 ae 1y 10m. 3. *Alice C. Howard,* b. ca Jan. 1821; d. 23 June 1822 ae 1y 5m. 4. *Marion Josephine Howard,* b. 8 July 1823; m. William Sumner Jr. 5. *Frances Miriam Howard,* b. 1833; d. 3 Nov. 1867, bur. Enfield.

ii   MAXCY MANNING CONVERSE, b. 10 Dec. 1799; d. Elmira, N.Y., 1864, while rescuing children from a fire that destroyed the Presbyterian Church there; m. at Brimfield, 8 Nov. 1821 (*VR* 179), ANNE GUTHRIE, b. Providence, R.I., 1800, dau. of Dr. Amos R. and Anna (___) Guthrie. He was named for two presidents of Brown University; res. Warren and Westfield before moving to Elmira, where he taught music. In 1850 he was a "lumberman" in Elmira, ae 50, with Ann ae 48, Frank ae 15, and Charlotte ae 13; Hannah Reilley b. Ireland and Georgiana Gibson ae 1 b. N.Y. were also in the household (p.226). The next household was that of Lyman Gibson, ae 48, lumberman, and Georgiana ae 24 b. Mass., and included Henrietta Converse ae 22, b. Mass. See *Converse Family,* 1:235-42, for a long account of this family with photographs.

Children (*Converse Family*): 1. *Mozart Manning Converse[7]*, b. 15 Feb. 1822; m. Julia Robinson. 2. *Georgiana Converse,* b. 16 March 1827; m. (1) Lyman Gibson, (2) Ariel Standish Thurston. 3. *Henrietta Converse,* b. ca 1828; m. James T. Jackson of Detroit, Mich. 4. *Charles Crozat Converse,* b. 7 Oct. 1832 Warren; m. Lida Lewis. 5. *Frank Buchanan Converse,* b. ca 1835; m. Harriet Maxwell. 6. *Charlotte A. Converse,* b. 21 June 1839 Westfield; m. Robert Lowry of Fort Wayne, Ind.

iii   LORENZO CONVERSE, b. 6 Oct. 1800; d. New Braintree 27 July 1853 of epilepsy (Mass. VR 77:147); m. at Rutland, 17 March 1841 (*VR* 75), ELIZA REID, b. there 17 Jan. 1812, d. Oakham 6 June 1881, dau. of Abel and Hannah (Gleason) Reid.

Children, rec. New Braintree (*VR* 18): 1. *Eleanor Robinson Converse[7]*, b. 1 Jan. 1842; m. Rev. Charles Sylvester Brooks. 2. *Josiah Clark Converse,* b. 12 Aug. 1843; m. Ruth A. Whitney. 3. *Elisa Jane Converse,* b. 22 Aug. 1845.

iv   ANNA CONVERSE, b. ca 1803; d. Brimfield 6 May 1849 ae 46 of "protracted and painful sickness" (*VR* 285), consumption (Mass. VR 40:39); m. 5 May 1826, HEZEKIAH FERRY, b. Palmer 18 Sept. 1795, son of Hezekiah and Hannah (___) Ferry, d. Brimfield 4 Oct. 1882 ae 87y 16d, paralysis, widowed (Mass. VR 337:346). He m. (2) at Brimfield, 7 March 1852, Martha L. Hitchcock (Mass. VR 60:243).

Ferry children, bp. Brimfield 10 Sept. 1835 (*VR* 57), b. dates from *Converse Fam.*: 1. *Ann Frances Ferry[7]*, b. 11 Dec. 1826; m. Jonathan C. Dix. 2. *Lorenzo Converse Ferry,* b. 25 Aug. 1831; m. Lydia Ornelia Alexander.

v REBECCA CONVERSE, b. 18 April 1805; d. evidently before 1838; m. 15 May 1825, JOHN CROSBY, b. Enfield 16 July 1801, d. there 19 March 1870 of typhoid pneumonia, married, son of Joshua and Lydia (___) Crosby (Mass. VR 230:56). He m. (2) before 1838, Harriet ___. In 1850 he was a farmer at Enfield ae 49, with Harriet ae 38, Rebecca C. ae 21, Lydia A. ae 19, Mary D. ae 12, and Sophronia G. ae 4 (p.337).

Crosby children of John and Rebecca, rec. Enfield (Corbin Ms): 1. *Rebecca Converse Crosby[7]*, b. 17 Oct. 1828; m. Charles Edson Davis. 2. *Lydia Augusta Crosby*, b. 1 June 1830.

vi ELEANOR CONVERSE, b. prob. ca 1807; d. Brimfield 4 Aug. 1853 ae 45 of consumption (Mass. VR 75:201); m. at Brimfield, 24 Nov. 1831 (*VR* 204), SOLOMON HOMER, b. there 1 Oct. 1804 (*VR* 77), d. there 2 Jan. 1879 of consumption, widowed (Mass. VR 310:324), son of Solomon and Abigail (___) Hoar (*VR* 75). The name Hoar was changed to Homer (see *Brimfield VR*).

Homer children, bp. and bur. Brimfield (*VR* 75, 297-8), b. dates from *Converse Family*: 1. *[Child] Homer[7]*, stillborn 27 July 1832. 2. *Charlotte Jane Homer*, b. 8 Oct. 1833; bp. Jan. 1834; d. 1836. 3. *Henry DeWitt Homer*, b. 4 April 1842; d. 29 June 1842. 4. *Abbie Georgietta Homer*, b. 5 Nov. 1843; m. Lyman B. Kellogg.

Sources cited: *Brimfield VR. Cummington VR.* Enfield VR, Corbin Collection, NEHGS. *Palmer VR.* Mass. Vital Records 1841-1910. *Historical Catalogue of Brown University 1764-1904* (Providence, 1905). "Quabbin Park Cemetery Records," L. Lovell (1940), typescript NEHGS. Collin, *A History of Hillsdale* (1883). *Robinson Genealogy*, Vol. 2 (1933). Charles Allen, *Some of the Ancestors and Descendants of Samuel Converse, Jr., of Thompson parish, Killingly, Conn.* ... (1905). CENSUS: Hampshire Co., 1810 Palmer (M252-19), Enfield 1820 (M33-50) & 1850 (M432-321).

834. BETHIAH ROBINSON[5] (*Jerusha Bartlett[4], Jerusha[3] Samson, Caleb[2], Henry[1]*), daughter of James Robinson and his wife Jerusha Bartlett [170], was born at East Bridgewater 30 December 1779 (*Robinson Gen.*, 2:95; not in *VR*), and died at Palmyra, N.Y., 26 July 1850 aged 70 years (g.s.). She was a descendant also of *Mayflower* passengers John Alden and Myles Standish.

Bethiah married at Palmyra, N.Y., 18 September 1804, **CHARLES BRADISH** (*Robinson Gen.*, 2:95). He was born at Hardwick 20 April 1778 (*Hardwick History*, 341), son of Col. John and Hannah (Warner) Bradish, and died 12 July 1857 aged 79 years (g.s.). Charles and Bethiah are buried in Palmyra Village Cemetery.

The will of James Robinson of Cummington, housewright, dated 16 July 1790, proved 1 September 1793, names among others his daughter Bethiah Robinson

(Hampshire PR Box 123 #25). Bethiah moved to Palmyra, N.Y., in 1799 with her brother Gain Robinson (*Robinson Gen.,* 2:95).

Charles Bradish's parents removed from Hardwick to Cummington soon after his birth (*Hardwick History,* 341), and later settled in Palmyra, N.Y. The will of John Bradish of Palmyra, dated 19 November 1812, proved 13 June 1825, names his wife Hannah and among others his son Charles (Wayne Co. Wills, A:73):

> ... Unto my son Charles Bradish each and every part of my real estate by him deeded to me except such parts of improvement of the same and for the time before mentioned as I have bequeathed unto my wife his mother, also one half of all my other estate [after debts and mother's legacy] ... also one half of all my wearing apparel and the whole of my silver watch this being in competition with my fire arms given to my son Calvin on condition he my son Charles pay unto my daughter Chloe Robinson in grain or neat stock twenty dollars ... and one dollar to my son Luther and one dollar to my daughter Rowena at my decease and thirty dollars in the whole to the natural born children of my daughter Rowena Comstock ... Sons Calvin and Charles to be executors ...

Charles's sister Chloe Bradish married Bethiah's brother Dr. Gain Robinson [Family #831]. Another sister, Sarah, named in their father's will as Sarah Robinson, was the wife of Bartlett Robinson (son of Robert Robinson, and *not* a sibling of Bethiah and Gain Robinson), who also moved from Bridgewater to Macedon, N.Y. and died there.

In 1820 Charles Bradish was at Palmyra, head of a household consisting of himself and Bethia 26-45, one man 45 or older, two boys and two girls 10-16, and three little boys under 10. On 29 January 1823, the town of Macedon was set off from Palmyra, and in 1830 the family was listed in Macedon, Wayne County (set off from Ontario), Charles and Bethia 50-60, with two men 20-30, two young men and one young woman 15-20, and one boy and one girl 10-15 (p.101). In 1850 Charles, 72, a farmer with real estate worth $9,000, b. Mass., was living in Macedon with Bethiah R., 70, Bartlett R., 38, laborer b. N.Y., and Lucretia E., 36, b. N.Y. Charles H. Bradish and his family were living next door (p.73).

Children of Charles and Bethia (Robinson) Bradish (*Robinson Gen.,* 2:95-98, unless otherwise cited):

i   ALEXANDER HAMILTON BRADISH[6], b. 15 Sept. 1805; d. 7 Aug. 1807.

ii WILLIAM FESSENDEN BRADISH, b. 1 March 1807; d. Medina, N.Y., 11 June 1875; m. (1) 2 April 1834, REBECCA HILLMAN WARREN, b. ca 1807 N.Y., d. 10 Oct. 1862; m. (2) Mrs. PERSIS (___) DE FORREST, d. 1892. In 1850 William was a laborer, ae 43, b. N.Y., at Macedon, N.Y.;

Anna Carpenter ae 70 was a member of their household (p.74). The family has not been found in 1860.

Children (1850 census; cem. recs.), all b. N.Y.: 1. *Amy J./Emma Jane Bradish[7]*, b. 22 March 1835; m. John Schuyler Johnson. 2. *Chloe Elizabeth Bradish,* b. 29 March 1837; d. 17 Aug. 1842 ae 5y 5m; bur. with grandparents. 3. *Clark Robinson Bradish,* b. 16 Oct. 1838; m. Maria Corser; in 1900 census, Medina, Mich. 4. *James Warren Bradish,* b. 22 May 1844; killed 27 April 1867 in destruction of steamer *Sultana* on the Mississippi River.

iii CHARLES HAMILTON BRADISH, b. Palmyra, N.Y., 8 May 1809; d. 5 April 1898; m. 2 Jan. 1849, AMY ANN ALDRICH, b. 17 Nov. 1817 in N.Y., d. 2 May 1899, dau. of Mowry Aldrich (*Robinson Gen.,* 2:98). He was issued a patent for 80 acres in Michigan 2 March 1837 at the Bronson Land Office (Michigan LR). In 1850 he was a farmer in Macedon, N.Y., ae 41, next door to his parents; his household included John Brayn ae 45, laborer, and Joanna Croyer ae 15, b. Ireland (p.73). In 1860 they were in Madison (P.O. Adrian), Mich. (p.22).

Children (census; *Robinson Gen.,* 2:98): 1. *Zim Rhoda / Ziruroda Bradish[7]*, b. 21 Dec. 1849, N.Y. 2. *Alexander Hamilton Bradish,* b. 12 Aug. 1854, Madison, Mich.; d. 16 Sept. 1866.

iv SETH WILLISTON BRADISH, b. Palmyra, N.Y., 13 Sept. 1810; d. 19 Oct. 1837, Palmyra, Mich. Seth W. Bradish was issued a patent for 80 acres in Michigan 2 March 1837 at the Bronson Land Office, described as 1 E ½ SW Michigan-Toledo Strip No 8 S 1 E 9 (Michigan LR).

v BARTLETT ROBINSON BRADISH, b. 22 July 1812; d. Adrian, Mich., 9 Oct. 1863; m. 1850 – 1860, CORA PHILLIPS, b. ca 1830 N.Y. On 5 March 1839 Bartlett R. Bradish was issued a patent for 80 acres in Michigan, described as 1 W ½ SW Michigan-Toledo Strip No 8 S 1 E 9 (Michigan LR). In 1850 he was with his parents; in 1860 he was a painter in Ward 3, Adrian, Mich., with Cora, Sarah Tuck ae 13, and Elizabeth Phillips ae 25, dressmaker, all b. N.Y., but no Bradish children.

vi LUCRETIA ELIZABETH BRADISH, b. 18 Oct. 1814; d. 6 May 1904, unm.; bur. with parents. In 1860 she was a teacher of music in Palmyra, N.Y., in the household of Morgan Robinson ae 52 (p.25). She was the author of the "Historical Notes" about the family in *Robinson Gen.,* 2:73-78.

vii PHILANDER PACKARD BRADISH, b. 4 Oct. 1816; d. 1911 at Batavia, N.Y.; m. 6 Jan. 1848, MARIA T. BRADLEY of Lyons, N.Y., b. ca 1822, d. 1 Nov. 1915, Batavia. In 1850 he was a merchant at Lyons, N.Y. (p.413); in 1860 he was a farmer at Batavia, N.Y.; his household included Jacob Acsted ae 20, laborer b. Germany, and Mary McGwin ae 21, servant, b. Ireland, and three Bradish sons (p.272).

Children, first three at home 1850:   1. *John Holley Bradish*[7], b. 18 Dec. 1848. 2. *Edmund Foster Bradish*, b. 31 Jan. 1852.   3. *William Hamilton Bradish*, b. 7 April 1856; m. Henrietta Louise Richert.   4. *Francis Bradish*, b. 7 Dec. 1857; d. 1858.

Sources cited: Paige, *History of Hardwick* (1883).   Wayne County Cemetery Records, on line. Wayne County, N.Y., Surrogate's Records. *Robinson Genealogy*, Vol. 2 (1933).   Collin, *History of Hillsdale, N.Y.* (1883). Michigan Land Records, on line. CENSUS: Wayne Co., N.Y., Macedon 1830 (M19-117), 1850 (M432-612), & Lyons 1850 (M432-613); 1860 Palmyra (M653-877); Batavia, Genesee Co., N.Y. (M653-757) & Adrian, Lenawee Co., Mich. (M653-551).

Additions and Corrections
to *Mayflower Families*, Volume 20, Part Two

Italics are used to emphasize new or corrected material.

(Page 29)

190. THOMAS DAMON[5] (*Elizabeth Oldham[4], Mercy Sprout[3], Elizabeth[2] Samson, Henry[1]*). Thomas's first wife, Alice, was probably **ALICE *PEIRCE***, daughter of Abraham Peirce and his first wife Abigail Peterson.

In his will dated 30 March 1784, Abraham Peirce of Pembroke, yeoman, advanced in age, named his beloved wife Luriana, and made bequests: to sons Abraham and Christopher, land; to son Daniel the residue; to son Joseph, 5s; to son Lemuel, £2 5s; to granddaughter Abigail Simmons, £2 5s; *to the children of daughter Alice Damon, deceased, 5s*; to daughter Hannah Simmons 5s. John Turner Esq. was to be sole executor, but he refused, and John Turner Jr. was appointed in his place. (Plymouth PR 29:335)

(Page 60)

206. SARAH OLDHAM[5] (*Elizabeth Oldham[4], Mercy Sprout[3], Elizabeth[2] Samson, Henry[1]*), and husband **SAMUEL SPRAGUE**.

Their eldest son, Uriah Sprague (husband of Lydia Samson #781), was born probably 11 Jan. 1747/8, and therefore should be listed as the *third* child, not the first. See discussion above, page 455.

Their daughter :

iii LUCY / LUCIA SPRAGUE[6] m. *at Marshfield 19 Jan. 1769* (*V*R 163), MANUEL / EDMOND FREEMAN. They evidently had a *son Joseph* whose birth was recorded (as an adult) as "Joseph, h[usband of] Alathea" at Duxbury, as 13 May 1775 (*V*R 80). This date must be in error, as it is too close to the previous child, Lucia, b. 21 Nov. 1774, and the next recorded child, Arnold, was b. 15 March 1777. Joseph's parents are listed on his death record as Immanuel and Lucy (Sprague) Freeman (Mass. VR 130:203). He married Alathea Joyce[5] [Samson #813]. See Part 3: 512.

(Pages 252-53)

326. MERCY/MARCY HOLMES[5] (*Josiah Holmes[4], John Holmes[3], Hannah[2] Samson, Henry[1]*) and husband **OBEDIAH DAMON**.

Change the birthdate of their son Nathaniel Damon's last child to:

8. *Nabby Daman*, b. *12 April 1804*.

(Page 344)

 # 393. JOHN NORCUTT[5]. His wife **SUSANNA WINSLOW** was almost certainly the daughter of James and Rhoda (Chase) Winslow, born at Tisbury 23 August 1758 (*VR* 94). James Winslow died in 1805; the division of his real estate in 1825 lists among his heirs Susan Oncutt [*sic*] (Dukes PR 27:281). Judith Haddock Swan (who searched long, hard, and unsuccessfully for a suitable Susan Oncutt) points out a network of family relationships here among Henry Samson descendants: John Norcutt's aunt Elizabeth Norcutt [#85] married Micah Bryant; among their children were Benjamin Bryant [#389], Micah Bryant [#390], Jerusha Bryant [#391], and Amasa Bryant {#392], all of whom were thus first cousins of John Norcutt [#393]. Susanna (Winslow) Norcutt's grandmother, Susannah (Conant) Winslow, married in 1744, for her second husband, Jesse Bryant, brother of Micah. In an article that went to press just before the Norcutt information appeared in Volume 20 Part 2, Mrs. Swan published "The Case for the Parentage of James Winslow of Martha's Vineyard," in *Mayflower Descendant*, 55 (Winter 2006): 1: 1.

(Pages 347-48)

 # 395. WILLIAM NORCUTT[5] *John Norcutt[4], Elizabeth Bonney[3], Dorcas[2] Samson, Henry[1]*), born ca 1760, married, first, _____, whose name has not been learned. He married, second, at Berkley, 10 June 1810, **ESTHER BRIGGS**, born there 12 Dec. 1785, d. there 8 Dec. 1881 (Mass. VR 328:82), daughter of Hathaway and Hannah (Briggs) Briggs. (*Delete Esther as the wife of William Norcutt[6], son of Zenas Norcutt #396, on page 350.*)

A typescript at the Dallas Public Library, consulted by Michael Norcutt [see CMN in Bibliography,] titled "Index to Massachusetts Revolutionary War Pensions" (abstracted by Lloyd Bockstruck) includes "William Norcut, matross, Berkley, $50, by his widow Esther." This entry does not appear in White's *Abstracts of Revolutionary War Pension Files*, and the original source has not been located.

In 1852 Alanson Norcutt petitioned Congress in behalf of Esther, widow of William Norcutt who had served in both the Revolutionary War and the War of 1812 (*Journal of the House of Representatives of the United States ... 6 December 1852, Serial Set Vol. No. 672, 32nd Congress, 2nd Session*).

Esther has not been found on the 1850 census, but her name at death was "Easter Norcutt."

Probable children of William Norcutt and his first wife:

    i   SALLY NORCUT[6], b. ca 1799; of Northfield when she m. at Greenwich, Oct. 1816, SOLOMON MILLER of Greenwich (VR 115). In 1850 he was a farmer (ae 51? - figure unclear) at Winfield, Herkimer Co., N.Y., with Sarah (ae 51?), Lovina ae 19, and Olive ae 12 (p.144).

Miller children (deaths rec. *Hardwick VR* 310; others from census): 1. *[Child] Miller*[7], b. 1819; d. 30 Aug. 1820 ae 10m. 2. *Catharine Miller*, b. ca March 1821; d. 2 Sept. 1823 ae 2y 6m. 3. *Alanson Miller*, b. ca 1823; m. Amanda ___; res. next to parents 1850. 4. *[Child] Miller*, d. 14 June 1828 ae –m. 5. *Lovina Miller*, b. ca 1831 Mass. 6. *Olive Miller*, b. ca 1838 N.Y.

ii   ALANSON NORCUTT, b. ca 1804; of Greenwich when he m. at Dana, 11 Dec. 1828 (VR 39), ELIZA HAVEN of Dana, b. ca 1806. In 1850 he was a farmer ae 46 at Hardwick, with Eliza ae 44 and seven children (p.352). Record of his death has not been found, but in 1860 Eliza was head of the household in Hardwick, with Julia J. ae 22, Frances ae 16, and Emily E. ae 13; both Eliza and Julia were "palm leaf weavers" (p.93).

Children: 1. *Alanson H. Norcutt*[7], b. ca 1831. 2. *Eliza M. Norcutt*, b. ca 1833. 3. *Catherine C. Norcutt*, b. ca 1835. 4. *Josephine / Julia Norcutt*, b. ca 1838; d. rec. both Hardwick and Dana (Mass. VR 258: 304 & 324), 17 or 18 March 1873, unm., of typhoid or of liver complaint; the Dana rec. says father b. Petersham, mother Dana, but Hardwick rec. has father's birthplace blank. 5. *Hortense F. Norcut*, b. ca 1841. 6. *Ansel Sheridan Norcut*, b. 1842; d. Hardwick 9 Feb. 1843 ae 2m, whooping cough (*VR* 312). 7. *Frances Ophelia Norcut*, b. 25 Feb. 1844, Hardwick (*VR* 79). 8. *Emely J. E. Norcut*, b. 2 Dec. 1846, Hardwick (*VR* 79).

Sources cited: *Dana VR. Greenwich VR. Hardwick VR.* Mass. Vital Records 1841-1910. *Journals of the House of Representatives of the United States,* index on line. Lloyd Bockstruck, "Index to Massachusetts Revolutionary War Pensions" (n.d., Dallas Public Library). CENSUS: Winfield, Herkimer Co., N.Y., 1850 (M432-512), Hardwick, Worcester Co., 1850 (M432-344) & 1860 (M653-533).

(Page 348)

 # 396. ZENAS NORCUTT[5] is surely the Zenas Orcutt listed on the 1790 census in Middleborough, with one man, two boys under 16, and three females (M637-4,p.173). These figures suggest another possible daughter born before 1790, unless the birthdates given for the known daughters are incorrect.

(Page 350)

 # 396-iv: WILLIAM NORCUTT[6], b. 1790 (son of Zenas). Delete his marriage to Esther Briggs (see above for her corrected marriage).

Following page 350, *add* the following:

 # 396A. ELIZABETH NORCUTT[5] (*John Norcutt*[4], *Elizabeth Bonney*[3], *Dorcas*[2] *Samson, Henry*[1]), probable daughter of John Norcutt [86] and his wife Mary Hayford, was born probably at Middleboro about 1768. Record of her death has not been found. An Elizabeth Pratt who died at Middleborough 4 June 1859 aged 90y 4m 5d, not further identified (Mass. VR 130:220) appears in the 1850 census in Middleborough as the wife of Job Pratt.

Elizabeth Norrecut [*sic*] married at Middleborough, 4 March 1786 (VR 2:149), **EBENEZER PRATT**, both of Middleborough. He was probably the man of that name born at Middleborough 16 May 1766, son of Ebenezer and Abial (Alger) Pratt (VR 1:198).

Both the 1790 and 1800 censuses list the family in Middleborough with figures that check with the list below. In 1810 (indexed as "Ernest" Pratt), Ebenez[r] Pratt was head of a household consisting of a man and a woman 26-45, and three boys and one girl under 10, figures that suggest two more sons born after 1803 (p.202).

Children, rec. Middleborough (*VR* 1:265, 266, 280, 319):

I   SELENDAH PRATT[6], b. 16 May 1787.

ii   THOMAS PRATT, b. 18 Aug. 1789.

iii   EBENEZER PRATT, b. 25 Aug. 1791.

iii   BETSEY PRATT, b. 4 May 1794.

iv   SAMUEL PRATT, b. 22 Aug. 1796.

v   JAMES PRATT, b. 6 Aug. 1798.

vi   DANIEL PRATT, b. 7 Jan. 1801.

vii   WYBRIA PRATT, b. 4 April 1803.

? viii   ANDREW PRATT, b. 1813 (Middleboro Births online index; parents' names given; not in published *VR*).

Sources cited: *Middleborough VR.* CENSUS: Middleboro 1790 (M637-4), 1800 (M32-16), 1810 (M252-21).

(Page 354)

 # 399 - i HANNAH PHILLIPS, dau. of William and Hannah (Prior) Phillips. *Delete her marriage.* The Hannah married Prince Hatch was daughter of Jeremiah and Hannah (Glover) Phillips, b. 28 July 1759. Jeremiah Hatch sold land to his daughter Hannah Hatch of Marshfield and to Prince Hatch of Marshfield. See MF 22 [Bradford], 407-08).

(Page 440)

409 - v KETURAH / CATHARINE SAMSON's husband EBENEZER BENNETT was the son of Edward and Elisabeth (Akin) Bennett, born at Dartmouth 16 Feb. 1779. He was the brother of Amy Bennett who married Stephen Tobey[5] [# 453]. More information may be found in Dorman Bridgeman Eaton Kent, "Bennett Family" (Calais, Vt.), manuscript at Vermont Historical Society.

(Page 475)

 # 480. RHODA HILLMAN, m. MALACHI MERRY.
Malachi Merry and his second wife, Jedidah, are buried in Countyline Cemetery on Townline Road on the borders of Schenectady and Montgomery Counties, N.Y. The cemetery is overgrown and uncared for in 2006. Inscriptions were listed in Clarence Foote, *Memorial Census of Duanesburg*, reprinted as *The Cemeteries of Duanesburg and Princetown, New York* (Schenectady County Historical Society, 2002). (Kathleen Heise, a descendant of this family, provided this information.)

(Page 487)

The line "Children of Joseph and Love (Samson) Mayhew ..." should read "Children of Joseph and Love (*Hillman*) Mayhew ..."

(Page 539)

(Bibliography): CMN: Michael Norcutt is the *son* (not nephew) of Charles Norcutt.

BIBLIOGRAPHY

Every source used for each family is included in the list of "Sources cited" at the end of the relevant account, often with the title abbreviated but usually including the date of publication. Further details may be found in the following list. Sources used in Part Two of the Fifth Generation but not in this volume are *not* included here, but will be found in the Bibliography for that volume.

Please note that in the following list most titles are arranged under headings that indicate *Subject*, usually a *Family Surname* or *a Geographical Location*. Places not otherwise designated are in Massachusetts.

Abington

Vital Records of the Town of Abington, Massachusetts, to the Year 1850, 2 vols. (1912).

Albany , N.Y.

Albany Cemetery Records: Jane Devlin, transc, Albany Cemetery Records, State Street Burials, Betty Frank, transc., on line at *www.freepagesgenealogyrootsweb.com/ ~clifflamere*.

Rev. J. McClusky, *The History of the First Presbyterian Church of Albany* (Albany, 1877).

Records of the Reformed Dutch Church of Albany, New York 1683-1809: Marriages, Baptisms, Members, Etc., Excerpted from Year Books of the Holland Society of New York (Baltimore: GPC, Inc., 1978).

Alden Kindred

Web site of the Alden Kindred: <www.alden.org>. Please note caveats there concerning proof of lineage.

Ashfield

Vital Records of the Town of Ashfield, Massachusetts, to the Year 1850 (1942).

Barbour Collection *see* Connecticut

Barnard, Vt.

William M. Newton, *History of Barnard with family genealogies 1761-1927* ..., 2 vols. (Montpelier, Vt., 1928).

Bath, Maine

Parker McCobb Reed, *History of Bath and environs, Sagadahoc County, Maine: 1607–1894* (Portland: Lakeside Press, Printers, 1894).

Bellingham

Vital Records of Bellingham, Massachusetts to the Year 1850 (Boston, 1904).

Bennett Family

Dorman Bridgeman Eaton Kent, "Bennett Family" (Calais, Vt.), manuscript at Vermont Historical Society.

Benson Family

Richard H. Benson, *The Benson Family of Colonial Massachusetts* (Boston, 2003).

Bethel, Maine

William B. Lapham, *The History of the Town of Bethel, Maine* (1891; reprint Somersworth, N.H.: New England History Press with Bethel Historical Society, 1981).

Bible and Family Records: are described in each relevant "Sources cited" paragraph.

Biographical Dictionaries

> *The Twentieth Century Biographical Dictionary of Notable Americans* (Boston: The Biographical Society, 1904).

> *Biographical Directory of the American Congress, 1774-1971, The Continental Congress ... and the Congress of the United States* ... (Washington, D.C.: U. S. Government Printing Office, 1971).

Boothbay, Maine

> Alfred Weston Bennett, *Boothbay, Maine, Marriage Intentions, 1766 to 1904* (Metcalfe, Ont.: A. W. Bennett, 2001), prepared for the Boothbay Region Historical Society.

> Francis Byron Greene, *History of Boothbay, Southport, and Boothbay Harbor, Maine 1623-1905* (1906; reprint Camden, Me.: Picton Press, 1999).

> George Wharton Rice, *The Shipping Days of Old Boothbay* (1938; reprint Camden, Me.: Picton, 1984).

> "Rev. John Murray's Book of Records, Boothbay & Surrounding Towns" (typescript, Maine DAR 1947).

Boston

> *John Haven Dexter's Memoranda of the Town of Boston in the 18th & 19th Centuries,* transcribed, compiled & annotated by Robert J. Dunkle and Ann Smith Lainhart (Boston, 1997).

> *Boston Vital Records: Reports of the Record Commissioners of the City of Boston* [BRC], Vols. 9 and 24, births, marriages and deaths 1630-1699 and births 1700-1800; Vols. 28 and 30, marriages 1700-1751 and 1751-1809 (Boston, 1883, 1894, 1898, 1903).

> Ogden Codman, comp., *Index of Obituaries in Boston Newspapers 1704-1800*, 3 vols. (Boston, 1968).

> *Boston Churches CD:* Robert J. Dunkle and Ann S. Lainhart, transcribers, *The Records of the Churches of Boston and The First Church, Second Parish, and Third Parish of Roxbury Including Baptisms, Marriages, Deaths, Admissions, and Dismissals* (Boston, 2001).

> *Records of the Church in Brattle Square, Boston 1699–1872* (Boston: The Benevolent Fraternity of Churches, 1902).

> Robert J. Dunkle and Ann Smith Lainhart, *Hollis Street Church Boston Records of Admissions, Baptisms, Marriages and Deaths 1732–1887, from copy by Ogden Codman (1918)* (Boston, 1998).

> Thomas B. Wyman, compiler, Robert J. Dunkle, transcriber, and Ann S. Lainhart, editor, *The New North Church, Boston, 1714-1799* (Boston, 1995).

> *The Records of Trinity Church, Boston 1728–1830,* Vol. 2 Publications of the Colonial Society of Massachusetts, 56 (1982).

> *Boston Transcript:* Genealogical column of newspaper *Boston Evening Transcript,* Boston 1906-1941, on microfilm at Boston Public Library, clippings file at NEHGS; microcards at Godfrey Memorial Library, Middletown, Conn.

Bosworth Family

> Mary B. Clarke, *A History of the Descendants of Edward Bosworth who Arrived in America in 1634,* 6 vols. (San Francisco, 1926-1940).

> *See also* Swanton

Braintree

Samuel A. Bates, *Records of the Town of Braintree 1640-1793* (Randolph, Mass.: Daniel H. Huxford, Printer, 1886), Births, Marriages, and Deaths, pages 728-889.

Waldo C. Sprague, "Genealogies of the Families of Braintree, Massachusetts, 1640-1850. Including the Modern Towns of Randolph and Holbrook and the City of Quincy," manuscript on cards at NEHGS, also on CD (Boston, 2001).

Brewer, Maine

Brewer, Maine, History , includes VR.

Brewster Family

Emma C. B. Jones, *The Brewster Genealogy 1566 – 1907 : Record of the Descendants of William Brewster of the Mayflower*, 2 vols. (New York, 1908).

Bridgewater

Nahum Mitchell, *History of the Early Settlements of Bridgewater* (Boston, 1840; reprinted Bridgewater, 1897, Baltimore, 1970).

Vital Records of Bridgewater, Massachusetts to the Year 1850, 2 vols. (Boston, 1916).

Brimfield

Vital Records of Brimfield, Massachusetts to the Year 1850 (Boston, 1931).

Bristol County

Bristol County Deeds and Probate Records, original records at Taunton; microfilmed. Early probate files are not numbered.

Bristol, Maine

Vital Records of Old Bristol and Nobleboro in the County of Lincoln, Maine including the present towns of Bremen, Damariscotta, South Bristol and the Plantation of Monhegan to the Year 1892, Christine Houston Dodge, ed., 2 vols. (Portland: Maine Historical Society, 1947, 1951).

Brockton

Vital Records of Brockton, Massachusetts to the Year 1850 (Boston, 1911).

Brookfield

Vital Records of Brookfield, Massachusetts to the End of the Year 1849 (Worcester, 1909)

Brown University

Historical Catalogue of Brown University 1764-1904 (Providence: The University, 1905)

Brunswick, Maine

George Augustus Wheeler and Henry Warren Wheeler, *History of Brunswick, Topsham and Harpswell, Maine* (Boston, 1878).

Buckfield, Maine

Alfred Cole, *A History of Buckfield, Oxford County, Maine, From the Earliest Explorations to the Close of the Year 1900* (Buckfield, Me., 1915; repr. Bridgton, Me.: Coburn Press, 1977).

Buckfield, Maine, Vital Records, copied by Miss Beatrice Neal. (Buckfield VR 1752–1891 now available from Picton Press on CD.)

Buckland

Fannie Shaw Kendrick, *The History of Buckland [Mass.], 1779-1935, with genealogies by Lucy Cutler Kellogg* (Rutland, Vt.: Tuttle Publishing Co., 1937).

Vital Records of Buckland, Colrain, and Montague, Massachusetts to the End of the Year 1849 (Salem, 1934).

Cambridge

Thomas W. Baldwin, *Vital Records of Cambridge, Massachusetts to the Year 1850*, 2 vols. (Boston, 1914, 1915)

Cape Cod

Leonard H. Smith, Jr. *Cape Cod Library of Local History and Genealogy* (Baltimore, 1992).

Cape Vincent, N.Y.

Gravestone inscriptions from Cape Vincent Cemeteries, on line courtesy of A. E. Rogers, Ellen and John Bartlett, *www.rootsweb.com/ nyjeffer/ capevin.htm.*

Carver

Vital Records of Carver, Massachusetts to the Year 1850 (Boston, 1911).

CENSUS (Federal)

Federal, 1790 – 1900, indicated by year, place, census number and reel number of microfilm, e.g. "1790 Plymouth, Plymouth Co. (M632-21)" and with page number in parentheses in text. Various sources have been used, including the printed series, *Heads of Families in 1790* for the various states, and on line images on both Ancestry.com® and HeritageQuest®. *Caveat.* The original census pages often bear more than one number, and Ancestry and HeritageQuest sometimes use different page numbers — however, reel numbers are always the same.

Charlestown VR

Roger Joslyn, *Vital Records of Charlestown, Massachusetts to the year 1850*, 2 vols. (Boston, 1984).

Charlotte, Maine

"Charlotte, Maine, Vital Records" contributed by Mrs. Myrtie Fisher Seaverns of Melrose, Mass., *NEHGR* 101 (1947), 102 (1948), 103 (1949).

Chase Family

John Carroll Chase and George Walter Chamberlain, *Seven Generations of the Descendants of Thomas and Aquila Chase* (Derry, N.H., 1928).

Gladys Marie Chase, *William Chase of Yarmouth, Massachusetts* (St. Petersburg, Fla., 1984).

Chatham

Sheila M. Dann Westgate and Anna Lowell Tomlinson, *Vital Records, Town of Chatham, Massachusetts, 1696-1850* (Chatham, 1991).

William C. Smith, *History of Chatham* (1909).

Chautauqua County, N.Y.

Andrew W. Young, *History of Chautauqua County, N.Y.* (Buffalo, N.Y., 1895).

Chelsea

Thomas W. Baldwin, *Vital Records of Chelsea, Massachusetts to the Year 1850* (Boston, 1916)

Mellen Chamberlain, *A Documentary of Chelsea : Including the Boston Precincts of Winnisimmet, Rumney Marsh, and Pullen Point, 1624 – 1824*, 2 vols. (Boston: Mass. Historical Society, 1908).

Chenango County, N.Y.

Nelson B. Tiffany, *Revolutionary War Veterans [of] Chenango County – New York* (1998).

Cheney Family

Charles Henry Pope, *The Cheney Genealogy* (Boston:, 1897).

Chesterfield

Ruth A. Baker, *History and Genealogy of the Families of Chesterfield, Massachusetts* (Northampton, 1962).

Chesterfield VR, in Corbin Collection, NEHGS SG/COR/5/22A.

Churchill Family

Gardner Asaph Churchill and Nathaniel Wiley Churchill, *The Churchill Family in America* (pub. by the family of Gardner A. Churchill, 1904).

Clark Family

John Clark, *Records of the descendants of Hugh Clark of Watertown, Mass., 1640 – 1866* (Boston: J. Clark, 1866).

Cobb Family

Philip L. Cobb, *A History of the Cobb Family* (Cleveland, 1907).

Cohasset

George Lyman Davenport and Elizabeth Osgood Davenport, *The Genealogies of the Families of Cohasset, Massachusetts* (Cohasset, 1909).

Thomas W. Baldwin, *Vital Records of Cohasset, Massachusetts to the Year 1850* (Boston, 1916).

Colcord Family

Meredith B. Colket, Jr., "The Descendants of Edward Colcord of New Hampshire," *TAG* 18 (1941-42).

Doane B. Colcord, *Descendants of Edward Colcord of New Hampshire — 1630 to 1909* (Coudersport, Pa.: Mahlon J. Colcord, 1908).

Colrain

Vital Records of Colrain, Massachusetts to the end of the year 1849 (Salem, 1934).

Columbia, Conn.

Columbia Cemetery Inscriptions, NEHGR 60 (1906).

Columbia Vital Records, from Barbour Collection.

Columbia County, N.Y.

Cemetery inscriptions, Rickard Collection, Columbia County Historical Society, Kinderhook, N.Y.

Columbian Centinel

Index of Deaths in Massachusetts Centinel and Columbian Centinel 1784-1849, compiled by the American Antiquarian Society, 12 vols. (1952).

Concord

Concord, Massachusetts, Births, Marriages, and Deaths, 1635-1850 (Boston: Beacon Press for the Town, ca 1895; repr. Bowie, Md., 1992).

CONNECTICUT (see also names of individual towns)

Barbour Index

An index to the vital records of most Connecticut towns to ca 1850, consisting of index slips and bound typescript volumes at Connecticut State Library and on film elsewhere. A new edition published by GPC in 46 soft-cover volumes does not match the pagination of the old typescript volumes, but both refer to original sources and the alphabetical arrangement is the same in both.

Early Conn. Marriages

Bailey, Frederick W., *Early Connecticut Marriages as Found in Ancient Church Records of the Colony of Connecticut Prior to 1800* (7 vols., New Haven, 1896-1906; reprint with additions, 7 vols. in 1, Baltimore, Md., 1968).

Record of Service of Connecticut Men in the I. War of the Revolution, II. War of 1812, III. Mexican War, compiled by authority of the General Assembly, under direction of the Adjutants-General (Hartford: Case, Lockwood & Brainard Co., 1889).

Hale Collection of Connecticut Cemetery Inscriptions, Conn. State Library and microfilm.

Converse Family

Charles Allen, *Some of the Ancestors and Descendants of Samuel Converse, Jr., of Thompson parish, Killingly, Conn.* ... (1905).

Conway

Vital Records of Conway, Massachusetts to the Year 1850 (Boston, 1943).

Copeland Family

Warren Turner Copeland, *The Copeland Family: A Copeland Genealogy* (Rutland, Vt.: Tuttle, 1937).

Corbin Collection

Manuscript collection at NEHGS, microfilmed; some on CD-ROM.

Coventry, Conn.

Susan W. Dimock, *Births, Marriages, Baptisms and Deaths from the Records from the Town and Churches of Coventry, Conn., 1711 – 1844* (New York: Taylor and Baker Co., 1897).

Cumberland County, Maine

Judith Holbrook Kelley, *Marriage Returns of Cumberland County, Maine prior to 1892* (Rockport: Picton Press, 1998).

Cummington

Helen H. Foster and William W. Streeter, *Only One Cummington* (1974).

William W. Streeter and Daphne H. Morris, *The Vital Records of Cummington, Massachusetts 1762 – 1900* (Bloomfield, Conn., c1979).

Cutler Family

Nahum S. Cutler, *Cutler Memorial and Genealogical History* (1889).

Cuyahoga County, Ohio

E. H. Sherman and G. E. Metler, "Cuyahoga County Cemeteries, Strongsville Township" (1929), at Western Reserve Historical Society Library, Cleveland.

Damon Family

Richard A. Damon, Jr., *The Damon Family of of Wayland, Mass.* (Camden, Me.: Penobscot Press, 1997).

Samuel Chenery Damon, *Damon Memorial : or notices of Three Damon Families* (Philadelphia for A. F. Damon and the Author, 1882).

Dana

Thomas W. Baldwin, *Vital Records of Dana, Massachusetts to the Year 1850 (Boston, 1925).*

Danby, Vt.

Williams, *The History and Map of Danby, Vermont* (1869).

Margaret Jenks, *Danby and Mount Tabor Cemetery Inscriptions* (1988, rev. 1993).

DAR Patriot Index

Patriot Index, National Society of the Daughters of the American Revolution (Washington DC, 1966); supplements: 1 (1969); 2 (1983); 3 (1976); ***Centennial Edition*** (Washington, 1996).

Dartmouth

Vital Records of Dartmouth, Massachusetts to the Year 1850, 3 vols. (Boston, 1929, 1930)

Dedham VR

Robert Brand Hanson, ed., *Vital Records of Dedham, Mass., 1635-1845,* revised and expanded edition (Camden, Me.: Picton Press, 1997), includes notes from Jason Haven Diary and church records.

Deerfield

Thomas W. Baldwin, *Vital Records of Deerfield, Massachusetts to the Year 1850* (Boston, 1920).

George Sheldon, *A History of Deerfield, Massachusetts* 2 vols. (1895-96).

Deer Isle, Maine

Vital Records of Deer Isle, Maine, Prior to 1867, transcribed by Benjamin Lake Noyes (Camden, Me.: Picton Press, 1997).

George L. Hosmer, *An Historical Sketch of the Town of Deer Isle, Maine* (1886, repr. Deer Isle - Stonington Historical Society, 1983).

Delano Family

Joel A. Delano and Mortimer D. de Lannoy, *The Genealogy, History and Alliances of the American House of Delano, 1621 to 1899* (New York, 1899).

Muriel Curtis Cushing, *Philip Delano of the "Fortune" 1621 and His Descendants for Four Generations* (Plymouth, Mass., 1991), and ... *His Descendants in the Fifth and Sixth Generations,* Part One ((Plymouth, 2004).

Sanford R. Delano, "Alpheus Delano," *Maine Families in 1790,* Vol. 5 (1996).

Delaware County, N.Y.

History of Delaware County, N.Y. with Illustrations, Biographical Sketches, and Portraits of Some Pioneers and Prominent Residents (New York: W.W. Munsell & Co., 1880).

Dennysville, Maine

Dennysville Vital Records, Births and Deaths 1790-1892 (FHL microfilm #010,828).

Dewey Family

Adelbert M. Dewey, *Life of George Dewey, rear admiral, U.S.N.; and Dewey Family History ...,* Louis Marinus Dewey *et al* comp. (Westfield, Mass.: privately published, 1898).

Dighton

"Vital Records of Dighton, Massachusetts," transcribed by Louis Hatherly Carr, 9 volumes, bound typescript (1984), copy at NEHGS.

Dorchester

Dorchester Births, Marriages, and Deaths to the End of 1825, [21st] Report of the Boston Record Commissioners (Boston: Rockwell and Churchill, 1890).

Vital Records of the town of Dorchester from 1826 to 1849, Document no. 54, Registry Department of the city of Boston (Boston: Municipal Printing Office, 1905).

Douglas

Vital Records of Douglas, Massachusetts to the End of the Year 1849 (Worcester, Mass., 1906).

W. E. Emerson, *History of Douglas* (1879).

Drake Family

Louis Stoughton Drake, *The Drake Family in England and America 1360-1896 and The Descendants of Thomas Drake of Weymouth, Mass. 1635-1691* (Boston, 1896).

Dutchess County, N.Y.

Isaac Huntting, *History of Little Nine Partners, of North East precinct, and Pine Plains, New York, Dutchess County* (Amenia, N.Y.: Charles Walsh & Co., printers, 1897).

Dudley

Vital Records of Dudley, Massachusetts to the End of the Year 1849 (Worcester, Mass., 1908).

Durham, Maine

Everett S. Stackpole, *History of Durham, Maine, with Genealogical Notes* (Lewiston, Me.: Press of Lewiston Journal, 1899).

Duxbury

Justin Winsor, *History of the Town of Duxbury, Mass. with Genealogical Registers* (Boston, 1849; reprint Boston, 1970).

George Etheridge, *Copy of the Old Records of the Town of Duxbury, Mass. from 1642 to 1770* (Plymouth, 1893).

Vital Records of Duxbury, Massachusetts to the Year 1850 (Boston, 1911)

East Bridgewater

Vital Records of East Bridgewater, Massachusetts to the Year 1850 (Boston, 1917).

Easton

Easton Vital Records Book 1, town clerk's office, FHL microfilm #1,059,951, and on line transcription courtesy of John A. Maltby.

William L. Chaffin, *History of the Town of Easton, Massachusetts* (Cambridge: John Wilson & son, University Press, 1886).

Eddy Family

Ruth Story Devereux Eddy, *The Eddy Family in America* (Boston, 1930; repr. Ann Arbor, Mich., 1978).

Falmouth

Oliver B. Brown, *Vital Records of Falmouth, Massachusetts, to the year 1850* (Warwick, R.I.: R.I. Society of Mayflower Descendants, 1976).

Falmouth, Maine

"Records of Falmouth (now Portland) Maine," *NEHGR* 16 (1862) – 17 (1863).

Baptisms & Admissions, Records from the records of the First Church in Falmouth, now Portland, Maine, Marquis F. King, comp. (Portland: Maine Historical Society, 1898).

Farmington, Maine

Dorothy Wirth, "36 Cemeteries of Franklin County, Maine" (typescript, NEHGS A4724).

Francis Gould Butler, *A History of Farmington, Maine 1776 – 1885* (1885; repr. 1983).

Fay Family

Orlin P. Fay, *Fay Genealogy: John Fay of Marlboro and his Descendants* (Cleveland, Ohio: Press of J. S. Savage, 1898).

Fiske Family

Frederick Clifton Pierce, *Fisk and Fiske Family ...* (Chicago, 1896).

Ford Family

Elizabeth C. Stewart, *The Descendants of Andrew Ford of Weymouth, Massachusetts* (Montpelier, Vt.: Capitol City Press, 1968).

Foxboro

Mr. and Mrs. Clifford W. Lane, *This was Foxborough!* (Foxborough, 1966).

Vital Records of Foxborough, Massachusetts to the Year 1850 (Boston, 1911).

Framingham

J. H. Temple, *History of Framingham, Massachusetts, early known as Danforth's Farms, 1640–1880, with a Genealogical Register* (Framingham: the Town, 1887).

Vital Records of Framingham to the Year 1850 (Boston, 1911).

Franklin

Orestes T. Doe, ed., *The Record of Births, Marriages, and Deaths in the Town of Franklin, from 1778 to 1872* (Franklin, Mass., 1898)

Fullerton family

See Mrs. John E. Barclay, "The Early Sampsons, With special reference to Ruth (Sampson) wife of John Fullerton of Marshfield," *The American Genealogist*, 28 (1952), 1-11.

Geauga Co., Ohio

Pioneer and General History of Geauga County, Ohio (Historical Society of Geauga Co., 1880)

Claridon Township Cemetery Files, Geauga Co. Genealogical Society., Chardon Library, 110 E. Park St., Chardon, Ohio 44024.

Georgetown, Maine

Vital Records of Georgetown, Maine, to the Year 1892, Mary Pelham Hill, ed., 2 vols. (Portland: Maine Historical Society, 1939, 1941).

Giles Memorial

John A. Vinton, *The Giles Mem.orial Genealogical Memoirs of the Families Bearing the Names of Giles, Gould, Holmes (and others)* (Boston, 1864).

Goshen

Hiram Barrus, *History of the Town of Goshen, Hampshire County, Massachusetts from its First Settlement in 1761 to 1881 with Family Sketches* (Boston, 1881).

Goshen, N.Y.

The Early Records of the First Presbyterian Church at Goshen, New York: from 1767 to 1885 (Goshen: printed by the Democrat Printing Co., ca 1934).

Grafton

Vital Records of Grafton, Massachusetts to the End of the Year 1849 (Worcester, 1906).

Graves of Revolutionary War Patriots

Patricia Law Hatcher, *Abstract of Graves of Revolutionary Patriots,* 4 vols. (Dallas: Pioneer Heritage Press, 1987-1988).

Green Family

Richard Henry Greene, *Greene (Green) Family of Plymouth Colony* (N.Y.: privately printed, 1909).

Greenwich

Greenwich Vital Records, typescript, on *Early Vital Records of Worcester County Massachusetts to about 1850* (CD ROM, Wheat Ridge, Colorado: Search & ReSearch, 2000).

Guilford, Conn.

Alvan Talcott, comp., Jacqueline Ricker, ed., *Families of Ancient Guilford, Connecticut* (Baltimore: GPC, 1984).

Hadley

Lucius M. Boltwood, *Genealogies of Hadley Families Embracing the Early Settlers of Hatfield, South Hadley, Amherst, and Granby* (1862; reprint Baltimore, Md.: GPC, 1979).

Halifax

George Ernest Bowman, *Vital Records of the Town of Halifax, Massachusetts to the End of the Year 1849* (Boston, 1905)

Hanover

John S. Barry, *A Historical Sketch of the Town of Hanover Mass. with Family Genealogies* (1853).

L. Vernon Briggs, *History and Records of the First Congregational Church, Hanover, Massachusetts 1727-1865,* Vol. 1 (Boston, 1895).

Jedediah Dwelley et al., *A Copy of the Records of Births, Marriages and Deaths and of Intentions of Marriage of the Town of Hanover, Mass., 1727-1857* (Rockland, 1898)

Jedediah Dwelley and John F. Simmons, *History of the Town of Hanover Mass. with Family Genealogies* (1910).

Hanson

Vital Records of Hanson, Massachusetts to the Year 1850 (Boston, 1911)

Hardwick

Lucius R. Paige, *History of Hardwick, Massachusetts ...* (1882).

Thomas W. Baldwin, *Vital Records of Hardwick, Massachusetts to the Year 1850* (Boston:, 1917).

Harlow Family

The Genealogy Committee of the Harlow Family Association, Alicia Crane Williams, ed., *Harlow Family, Descendants of Sgt. William Harlow (1624/5–1691) of Plymouth, Massachusetts* (Baltimore: Gateway Press, Inc., 1997).

Harpswell, Maine

George Augustus Wheeler and Henry Warren Wheeler, *History of Brunswick, Topsham and Harpswell, Maine* (Boston, 1878).

Harrison, Maine

Moulton, Sampson, & Fernald, *Centennial History of Harrison* [Maine] (1909).

Harvard Grads

John L. Sibley, *Biographical Sketches of Graduates of Harvard University in Cambridge, Mass.* (Cambridge, vol. 1, 1873).

Haskell Family

Ira J. Haskell, *Chronicles of the Haskell Family* (Lynn, Mass., 1943).

Haskell, Haynor and Allied Families (N.Y.: American Historical Society, 1926).

Hawley

Louise Hale Johnson, *History of the Town of Hawley ....* (Mystic, Conn.: Charter Oak House, 1953), updates William Giles Atkins' 1887 *History of Hawley* and includes Hawley Vital Records.

Hersey Family

Stephen E. Hersey, *The Hersey Family [:] Tracing the Descendants of William Hersey of Hingham, Massachusetts 1635–1994* (n.p., October 1994).

Hill Family (Maine)

William Berry Lapham, *John Hill of Dover in 1649* (Augusta, Me.: Maine Farmer Job Print, 1889).

Hillsdale, N.Y.

John Francis Collin, *History of Hillsdale* (1883).

Hingham

History of the Town of Hingham, Mass., 3 vols. (1893; reprint Somersworth, N.H., 1982).

Hinsdale

Vital Records of Hinsdale, Massachusetts to the Year 1850 (Boston, 1902).

Hiram, Maine

William Teg, *History of Hiram, Maine, Sesquicentennial Edition* (Cornish, Me.; Carbrook Press, 1964).

Holden

Samuel Chenery Damon, *History of Holden, Mass. 1667–1841* (Worcester: Wallace and Ripley, printers, 1841).

David Foster Estes, *History of Holden, Mass. 1684–1894* (Worcester: Press of C. F. Lawrence & Co., 1894).

Holliston

Vital Records of Holliston, Massachusetts to the Year 1850 (Boston, 1908).

Hopkinton

Vital Records of Hopkinton, Massachusetts to the Year 1850 (Boston, 1911).

Horsford Family

Ye Horseforde Booke: Horseford-Hosford families in the United States of America (1936).

Howe Family

Daniel Wait Howe, *Howe Genealogies … John Howe of Sudbury and Marlborough, Massachusetts* (Boston: NEHGS, 1929).

Hubbardston

Vital Records of Hubbardston, Massachusetts to the End of the Year 1849 (Worcester, Mass., 1907).

Hull

Thomas W. Baldwin, *Vital Records of Hull, Massachusetts to the Year 1850* (Boston, 1911).

Huron County, Ohio

Frank E. Weeks, *Wakeman Twp, Huron Co., Ohio* (n.d.).

"Cemetery Records of Huron County, Ohio," typescript at Western Reserve Historical Society Library, Cleveland.

IGI

International Genealogical Index of the Church of Jesus Christ of Latter-day Saints. Good for clues but information must be verified in other sources.

Illinois

Helen Maxwell Williams, comp., *Belvidere Cemeteries 1836-1900* (Rockford, Ill.: Kishwaukee Genealogical Soc., 1988).

Charles Bent, *History of Whiteside County, Illinois* (1877).

Industry, Maine

William Allen, *A History of the Town of Industry, Franklin County, Maine, from the Earliest settlement in 1787 down to the present times ...* (Skowhegan, Me.: Smith & Emery, printers, 1869).

Islesborough, Maine

John Pendleton Farrow, *History of Islesborough, Maine* (Bangor, 1893; repr. Islesboro Historical Society, 1965, 1982, with index Camden, Me.: Picton Press, 1991).

Marlene Hinkley Groves, comp., *Vital Records of Islesboro, Maine* (Rockport, Me.: Picton Press, 2000), Maine Genealogical Society Special Publication No. 34.

Jefferson, Maine

"Rev. John Murray's Book of Records ..." (1947 Maine DAR).

Jefferson, Me., VR, *NEHGR* 73 (1919) and at Maine State Archives (now available in CD format from Picton Press).

Alberto A. Bennett, *Centennial Celebration of the Town of Jefferson* (Lewiston, Me.: Journal Printing Co., 1908).

Jefferson County, N.Y.

Gravestone inscriptions from Cape Vincent Cemeteries, on line courtesy of A. E. Rogers, Ellen and John Bartlett, *www.rootsweb.com/ nyjeffer/ capevin.htm*.

Jericho, Vt.

Chauncey H. Hayden, Luther C. Stevens, La Fayette Wilbur, Rev. S. H. Barnum, *History of Jericho, Vermont* (Burlington, Vt.: Free Press Printing Co., 1916).

Jordan Family

Tristram Frost Jordan, *The Jordan Memorial. Family Records of the Rev. Robert Jordan and his Descendants in America* (1882; repr. Somersworth, N.H.: New England History Press, 1982).

Kendall Family

Christine R. and Donald V. Brown, *The Kendalls of the Kennebec* (Knoxville, Tenn., 1977).

Kennebec County, Maine

Robert Charles Anderson and Roger D. Joslyn, "Part of Kennebec County, Maine, in 1800," *NEHGR* 145 (1991).

Illustrated History of Kennebec County, Maine, ed. by Henry D. Kingsbury and Simeon L. Deyo, 2 vols. (New York: H. W. Blake & Co., 1892).

Maine Cemetery Inscriptions of Kennebec County, Maine Old Cemetery Association Special Publication No. 2, 6 vols. (Camden, Me.: Picton Press, 2000), available also in CD format.

Kingfield, Maine

Riverside Cemetery, Kingfield, Maine, [inscriptions] copied August 25, 1986 by George and Janet Thompson, on line at rootsweb.com

Kingston

Vital Records of Kingston, Massachusetts to the Year 1850 (Boston, 1911).

Lancaster

Henry S. Nourse, ed., *The Birth, Marriage and Death Register, Church Records and Epitaphs of Lancaster, Massachusetts, 1643-1850* (Lancaster, 1890).

Lawry Family

A. E. Sutton, *The Lawry Family of Friendship, Maine 1754–1982* (Camden, Me.: Penobscot Press, 1992).

Lee

Vital Records of Lee, Massachusetts to the Year 1850 (Boston, 1903).

Leeds, Maine

Leeds (Maine) Vital Records, "Births & Deaths 1785-1891," at Maine State Archives; filmed.

Mabel R. Whiting, "Part of Book I, Leeds Monthly Meeting of Friends …" (typescript, n.d., Patience Stanley Chapter, DAR, Winthrop, Me).

J. C. Stinchfield, *History of the Town of Leeds, Androscoggin County, Maine, from its Settlement June 10, 1780* (Lewiston, Me.: Journal Press, 1901).

Leicester

Vital Records of Leicester, Massachusetts to the End of the Year 1849 (Worcester, Mass., 1903).

Lewiston, Maine

Douglas I. Hodgkin, *Records of Lewiston, Maine,* 2 vols. (Rockport, Me.: Picton Press, 2001, 2002).

Lincoln County, Maine

"Record of Marriages by Nathaniel Thwing, Justice of the Peace, Lincoln County, Mass. (now Maine)," *NEHGR* 37 (1883).

William D. Patterson, ed. *The Probate Records of Lincoln County, Maine, 1760 to 1800* (1895).

Lincoln County Deeds and Probate Records at Wiscasset, Me.

Elizabeth Freeman Reed, "Miscellaneous Records of Lincoln County, Maine," typescript, Pemaquid Chapter, DAR, copy at Maine Historical Society.

Litchfield, Maine

History of Litchfield and an account of its centennial celebration 1895 (Augusta, Me.: Kennebec Journal Print, 1897).

Lo-Lathrop Family

Rev. E. B. Huntington, *A Genealogical Memoir of the Lo-Lathrop Family, embracing the Descendants, as far as known, of the Rev. John Lothrop of Scituate and Barnstable, Massachusetts* (Ridgefield, Conn., 1884).

LR

Deeds, or land records, from county or town repositories (towns in Connecticut, Rhode Island, and Vermont, counties in all other states).

Lynn

Vital Records of Lynn, Massachusetts to the End of the Year 1849, 2 vols. (Salem, 1905, 1906).

Madison County, N.Y.

William H. Tuttle, ed. by Isabel Bracy, *Names and Sketches of the Pioneer Settlers of Madison County New York* (Interlaken, N.Y.: Heart of the Lakes Publishing, 1984).

MAINE (see also specific counties and towns)

"Cemetery Inscriptions of Central Maine," by Mabel G. Hall (typescript NEHGS, ME 60 40, 1939).

George Thomas Little, *Genealogy and History of the State of Maine* (N.Y.: Historical Publishing Co., 1909).

William Willis, *A History of the Law, the Courts, and the Lawyers of Maine: from its First Colonization to the Early Part of the Present Century* (Portland, Me.: Bailey & Noyes, 1863).

James Alfred Spalding, *Maine Physicians of 1820, A Record of the Members of the Massachusetts Medical Society Practicing in the District of Maine at the Date of the Separation* (1928).

Joseph W. Porter, editor, *The Bangor [ME] Historical Magazine later the Maine Historical Magazine 1885-1894* (reprint, Camden, Me.: Picton Press, 1993).

Maine Genealogist and Biographer, A Quarterly Journal, William Berry Lapham, ed. (Augusta:, Me. Maine Genealogical and Biographical Society, 1 [1875-76]).

MeHGR : S. M. Watson, *Maine Historical and Genealogical Recorder,* 9 vols. (Portland, Me., 1884-1898; reprinted in 3 vols.; Baltimore, Md., 1973).

Sprague's Journal of Maine History, John Francis Sprague, ed. (1913-1926), now on CD, *Maine Genealogical Society Special Publication No. 35* (Picton Press, 2000).

Maine Families in 1790, Ruth Gray and Joseph Crook Anderson II, editors

Volume 1 (1988)	Volume 4 (1994)	Volume 7 (2001)
Volume 2 (1990)	Volume 5 (1996)	Volume 8 (2003)
Volume 3 (1992)	Volume 6 (1998)	Volume 9 (2006)

The Maine Seine, published by The Maine Genealogical Society 1978-1990; succeeded by *The Maine Genealogist,* whose editor in 2005 is Joseph C. Anderson II.

Maine Newspapers

David C. & Elizabeth Keene Young, *Vital Records from Maine Newspapers, 1785 - 1820* (1993).

David C. Young and Benjamin Lewis Keene, *Death Notices (1833-1852) and Items from the Maine Farmer (1833-1924)* (1997).

Vital Records from the Eastport Sentinel 1818-1900, Kenneth L. Willey, ed. (1996; repr. Maine Gen. Society SP #24, Picton Press, 2003).

Malden

Deloraine P. Corey, *Births, Marriages, and Deaths in the Town of Malden, Massachusetts, 1649-1850* (Cambridge, 1903).

Mansfield, Conn.

Susan W. Dimock, *Births, Baptisms, Marriages and Deaths from the Records of the Town and Churches in Mansfield, Connecticut, 1703-1850* (New York: Baker and Taylor Co., 1898). Not part of the Barbour Collection.

Marsh Family

D. W. Marsh, *Genealogy of the Marsh Family* (1886).

Marshfield

Baptisms from First Church, Marshfield, *Mayflower Descendant,* 31 (1933) and 32 (1934).

Barbara L. Merrick, "The Second Church of Christ at Marshfield, Massachusetts, Baptisms by the Rev. Atherton Wales, 1739–1788," *Mayflower Quarterly,* 46 (1980) – 47 (1981).

Betty Magoun Bates, "The Second Church of Christ at Marshfield, Massachusetts, The Rev. Elijah Leonard's Record of Deaths, 1789-1834," *Mayflower Quarterly,* 49 (1983) and 50 (1984).

Lysander S. Richards, *History of Marshfield,* 2 vols. (Plymouth: Memorial Press, 1901, 1905)

Robert M. Sherman and Ruth Wilder Sherman, *Vital Records of Marshfield, Massachusetts to the Year 1850* (Ann Arbor, Michigan, 1970)

Marston Family

Nathan W. Marston, *The Marston Genealogy* (South Lubec, Me., 1888; repr. 1985).

Martha's Vineyard

Charles E. Banks, *History of Martha's Vineyard, with Genealogy,* 3 vols. (Boston, 1911-25; reprint Edgartown , Mass., 1966).

Dorothy Cottle Poole, *A New Vineyard* (Edgartown: Dukes County Historical Society, 1976).

Massachusetts

List of Persons whose names have been changed in Massachusetts 1780 – 1883 (Boston: Wright & Potter Printing Co., 1885).

MSSR *Massachusetts Soldiers and Sailors of the Revolutionary War, a Compilation from the Archives, 17 volumes (Boston 1896-1908).*

Mass. VR

Massachusetts Vital Records 1841-1910 (copies provided to State by town clerks), at Mass. Archives, Columbia Point, Boston; on microfilm at NEHGS; on line at newenglandancestors.org.

Mayflower Descendant (MD)

The Mayflower Descendant: a quarterly magazine of Pilgrim history and genealogy, published by the Massachusetts Society of Mayflower Descendants, Boston Vols. 1 [1899] – 34 [1937]; vols. 35 [1985] – ongoing. Scott Andrew Bartley is editor in 2005.

Mayflower Families (MF) [The "Silver Books"]

Mayflower Families Through Five Generations; Descendants of the Pilgrims who landed at Plymouth, Mass. December 1620. Series published by the General Society of Mayflower Descendants, Plymouth, Mass. See p. ii for full listing. The following were used in this volume:

MF3: ***George Soule*** by Anne Borden Harding, *et al.* (1980). See *MFIP Soule* for corrections and additions.

MF6: ***Stephen Hopkins*** by John D. Austin (2001).

MF12: ***Francis Cooke*** by Ralph Van Wood, Jr. (1996).

MF14: ***Myles Standish*** by Russell L. Warner and Robert S. Wakefield (1997).

MF15: ***James Chilton*** by Robert M. Sherman and Verlo Delano Vincent, rev. by Robert S. Wakefield. ***Richard More*** by Robert M. Sherman, Robert S. Wakefield and Lydia Dow Finlay (1997).

MF16: ***John Alden,*** by Esther Littleford Woodworth-Barnes; Alicia Crane Williams, ed., 3 parts to date (1999, 2001, 2004), more forthcoming.

MF18: ***Richard Warren*** by Robert S. Wakefield, 3 parts (2004, 1999, 2001).

MF19: ***Thomas Rogers*** by Alice Westgate, rev. [of Vol. 2] by Ann T. Reeves (2000).

MF20: ***Henry Samson*** Part 1 [Generations 1-4] by Robert M. Sherman, Ruth W. Sherman, and Robert S. Wakefield (2000); Part 2 by Jane Fletcher Fiske, Robert M. Sherman, and Ruth W. Sherman [Fifth Gen., pt.1] (2005).

MF22: ***William Bradford*** by Ann S. Lainhart and Robert S. Wakefield (2004).

MFIP — Mayflower Families in Progress. [Soft-cover] series published by the General Society of Mayflower Descendants, Plymouth, Mass.

George Soule, four generations, by Robert S. Wakefield (1995), revision of first four generations of *MF 3.*

George Soule, *fifth and sixth generation descendants,* by Louise Walsh Throop, Parts 1 (2000), 2 (2002), and 3 (2003).

Mayflower Quarterly [*MQ*]

The Mayflower Quarterly, published four times a year since 1935 by The General Society of Mayflower Descendants. Alice Teale is editor in 2006.

McIntyre Family

Robert Harry McIntire, "The MacIntyre, McIntyre and McIntire Clan: of Scotland, Canada, and New England," typescript, 1949, HeritageQuest Online.

Medfield

Vital Records of Medfield, Massachusetts to the Year 1850 (Boston, 1903).

Medway

Vital Records of Medway, Massachusetts to the Year 1850 (Boston, 1905).

Mendon

Thomas W. Baldwin, *Vital Records of Mendon, Massachusetts to the Year 1850* (Boston, 1920).

Michigan Land Records , database on line, Ancestry.com.

Middleborough

Alfred Wood, *Records of Deaths, Middleboro, Massachusetts* (Boston, 1947).

Thomas Weston, *History of Middleborough* ... (Boston & New York: Houghton Mifflin & Co., Riverside Press, Cambridge, 1906).

Middleborough, Massachusetts Vital Records, Barbara L. Merrick and Alicia C. Williams, eds., 2 vols. (Plymouth: The Massachusetts Society of Mayflower Descendants, 1986).

Milford

Thomas W. Baldwin, *Vital Records of Milford, Massachusetts to the Year 1850* (Boston, 1917).

Adin Ballou, *History of Milford to 1881* (1882)

Milton

A. K. Telle, *History of Milton, Massachusetts, 1640-1887* (Boston, 1887).

Milton Records. Births, Marriages and Deaths 1662–1843, alphabetically and chronologically arranged (Boston: Alfred Mudge & Son, Printers, 1900).

Minot, Maine

Joseph C. Anderson II, *Vital Records of Minot, Maine* (Rockport, Me.: Picton Press, 2005).

Montville, Maine

Montville, Maine, Town Records, microfilm, NEHGS (now available in CD format from Picton Press).

Name Changes *see* Massachusetts.

Nantucket

Vital Records of Nantucket, Massachusetts to the Year 1850, 5 vols. (Boston, 1925–1928)

Alexander Starbuck, *History of Nantucket: county, island, and town, including genealogies of the first settlers* (Boston: C. E. Goodspeed, 1924).

NEHGR

New England Historical and Genealogical Register, quarterly journal of the New England Historic Genealogical Society, volumes 1 (1847) - ongoing. The editors in 2006 are Henry B. Hoff and Helen S. Ullmann.

New Bedford

Daniel Ricketson, *The History of New Bedford, Bristol County, Massachusetts* (New Bedford, 1858).

New Bedford Mercury Obits: "Deaths Reported in *New Bedford Mercury* 1807-1845," typescript (1970) at New Bedford Public Library.

Vital Records of New Bedford, Massachusetts to the Year 1850, 3 vols. (Boston, 1941).

New Braintree

Vital Records of New Braintree, Massachusetts to the Year 1850 (Boston, 1904).

Newcomb Family

Bethuel Merrit Newcomb, *Andrew Newcomb 1618-1686 and his Descendants*. A revised edition of *Genealogical Memoir of the Newcomb Family* published in 1874 by John Bearse Newcomb (New Haven, Conn., 1923).

New England

Cutter, *New England Families Genealogical and Memorial:* Third Series (1915).

NEW HAMPSHIRE (see also names of individual towns)

New Hampshire Genealogical Record, quarterly journal of the New Hampshire Society of Genealogists, published at Exeter, N.H. The editor in 2005 is Melinde Lutz Sanborn.

Newspapers (see also under Maine):

David C. Young and Robert L. Taylor, *Death Notices from Freewill Baptist Publications 1811-1851* (Bowie, Md.: Heritage Books, Inc., 1985).

New Haven, Conn.

D. L. Jacobus, *Families of Ancient New Haven*, Vol. 2 (Rome, N.Y., 1924).

New Windsor, N.Y.

"Marriages at New Windsor Presbyterian Church," on line courtesy of Glenn Marshall, Historian of the Town of New Windsor.

NEW YORK STATE (see also names of specific towns and counties)

New York in the Revolution as Colony and State (Albany, 1898).

Janet Wethy Foley, ed., *Early Settlers of New York State* (serially 1934-1942; repr. in 2 vols. Baltimore, 1993).

Fred Q. Bowman, *10,000 Vital Records of Eastern New York 1777-1834* (Baltimore: GPC, 1987).

Fred Q. Bowman, *10,000 Vital Records of Western New York 1809-1850* (Baltimore: GPC, 1985).

William Richard Cutter, *Genealogical and Family History of Western New York* (N.Y.: Lewis Historical Publishing Co., 1912).

Nobleboro, Maine

Vital Records of Old Bristol and Nobleboro in the County of Lincoln, Maine including the present towns of Bremen, Damariscotta, South Bristol and the Plantation of Monhegan to the Year 1892, Christine Houston Dodge, ed., 2 vols. (Portland: Maine Historical Society, 1947, 1951).

Norcutt Family

CMN: research of Charles M. Norcutt (GSMD #70,097) and his son Michael Norcutt.

Northborough

Gilman B. Howe, *Vital Records of Northborough, Massachusetts to the End of the Year 1850* (Worcester, Mass., 1901).

Northbridge

Thomas W. Baldwin, *Vital Records of Northbridge, Massachusetts to the Year 1850* (Boston, 1916).

North Brookfield

Josiah H. Temple, *History of North Brookfield: Records 1686-1783 with a Genealogical Register* (Boston, 1887).

Northfield

J. H. Temple and George Sheldon, *A History of the Town of Northfield, Massachusetts ... with family genealogies* (Albany, N.Y.: J. Munsell, 1875).

North Haven, Maine

Elizabeth M. Mosher, *Vital Records of North Haven, Maine* (Rockport, Me.: Picton Press, 2002).

North Yarmouth, Maine

Ruth Wilder Sherman, *Vital Records of North Yarmouth Maine to the Year 1850* (Society of Mayflower Descendants in the State of Rhode Island, 1980, 2nd ed. Camden, Me., 1993).

Norway, Maine

William Berry Lapham, *Centennial History of Norway, Oxford County, Maine 1786-1886* (1886).

Charles F. Whitman, *A History of Norway from the Earliest Settlements to the Close of the Year 1922* (Norway, Me., 1924).

Norwell

Wilford Jacob Litchfield, "Records of the Second Church of Scituate, Now the First Unitarian Church of Norwell, Mass.," *NEHGR* 58 (1904), 59 (1905), and 60 (1906).

Norwich, Conn.

Vital Records of Norwich 1659 – 1848, 2 vols. (Hartford: Society of Colonial Wars in the State of Connecticut, 1913).

Nova Scotia

W. A. Calnek, *History of the County of Annapolis* (1897; repr. Belleville, Ont.: Mika Studio, 1972).

Arthur Wentworth Hamilton Eaton, *The History of Kings County* (1910; Belleville, Ont.: Mika Studio, 1972).

Marriage Bonds of Nova Scotia, 1763-1849, Nova Scotia Archives & Records Management, on line.

Muriel M. Davidson, "Early Records of Liverpool, N.S. from Extracts: The Diary of Simeon Perkins" (ms., Brampton, Ont., 1994).

"Vital Records of Liverpool, N.S.," in *NEHGR* 126 [1972] and 127 [1973].

Allan Everett Marble, *Deaths, Burials, and Probate of Nova Scotians, 1749 – 1799, From Primary Sources*, 2 vols., Genealogical Association of Nova Scotia (Halifax, 1990).

Allan Everett Marble, *Deaths, Burials, and Probate of Nova Scotians, 1800 – 1850, From Primary Sources*, 4 vols., Genealogical Association of Nova Scotia, Publication No. 25 (Halifax, 1999).

Lorna Woodman Evans, *Township Books, Kings County, Nova Scotia : Aylesford, Cornwallis, Horton* (Kentville, N.S.: Kings Historical Society, 1996). Also, Cornwallis Township Book, microfilm of original at NEHGS.

Nova Scotia Poll tax rolls, 1791-1793, RG1 vol. 444, NSARM microfilm no. 13580.

Oakham

H. B. Wright and E. D. Harvey, *The Settlement and Story of Oakham, Massachusetts* (1947; repr. Salem: Higginson Book Co., 1998).

Orange

Orange Vital Records, transcription on *Western Massachusetts Vital Records to about 1850* (CD, Wheat Ridge, Colorado: Search and ReSearch, 2000).

Cemetery inscriptions, Jones Cemetery, Orange, copied 4 Aug. 1928 by Mrs. Grace F. Weymouth, database on line at newenglandancestors.org.

Orange County, N.Y.

Orange County Surrogate's Records (probates).

Otsego County, N.Y.

Otsego County Cemeteries, on line through www.rootsweb.com

Paris, Maine

William Berry Lapham, *History of the Town of Paris, Maine* (Paris, Me., 1884; reprint Somersworth, N.H.: New England History Press, 1983).

Parsons Family

Henry Parsons, *Parsons Family, Descendants of Cornet Joseph Parsons, Springfield, 1636 – Northampton, 1655*, 2 vols. (N.Y.: Frank Allaben Genealogical Co., 1912, 1920).

Gerald James Parsons for the Parsons Family of America, *The Parsons Family, Volume One* (Baltimore: Gateway Press, 2002). H. Parsons, *Parsons Family* (1912).

Pawlet, Vt.

Hiel Hollister, *Pawlet for One Hundred Years* (Albany, 1867; repr. 1976, Bowie, Md.: Heritage Books, 1999).

Pembroke

Elroy M. Avery, "Baptisms in the Second Church of Christ in Pembroke, Mass., from 1748 to 1803," *NEHGR*, 49 [1895] and 50 [1896].

Barbara L. Merrick, "The Original Church Records of Gad Hitchcock, D.D., 1748 to 1803: Deaths," *NEHGR*, 136 [1982].

Vital Records of Pembroke, Massachusetts to the Year 1850 (Boston, 1911).

Pembroke Friends Records, "Births, Deaths, Marriages," on FHL microfilm #0,001,335.

Pendleton Family

Everett Hall Pendleton, *Brian Pendleton and His Descendants 1599–1910* (1910).

Pension Records

Virgil D. White, *Genealogical Abstracts of Revolutionary War Pension Files*, 4 vols. (Waynesboro, Tenn., 1990-1992).

Peru

Vital Records of Peru, Massachusetts to the Year 1850 (Boston, 1902).

"Tombstone Inscriptions of Peru," Manuscript, Berkshire Athenaeum, Pittsfield.

Petersham

Vital Records of Petersham, Massachusetts to the End of the Year 1849 (Worcester, Mass., 1904).

Phillips, Maine

Phillips, Maine, Vital Records 1813-1891, on FHL microfilm #0011744 (now available on CD from Picton Press).

Phillipston

Vital Records of Phillipston, Massachusetts to the End of the Year 1849 (Worcester, Mass., 1906).

Phippsburg, Maine

Vital Records of Phippsburg Maine (1935) (CD of originals now available from Picton Press).

Pierce Family

Ebenezer W. Peirce, *The Peirce Family of the Old Colony or the Lineal Descendants of Abraham Peirce* (Boston, 1870).

Pineo Family

"Pineo Family History," FHL microfilm #564390-564393. This multi-volume manuscript was donated to the Family History Library by Mrs. Floyd Nielsen, 531 North Laurel St., Ashland, Oregon 97520 and filmed by the Genealogical Society of Utah in February 1968. The original manuscript cannot now be found and may have been destroyed after it was filmed. It consisted of many notebooks, evidently kept over a period of considerable time. Some of the volumes, although they bear no date, begin with a notation, "this book belongs to Rev. Addison P. Foster, Beacon St., Room 85, Boston, Mass." Included are transcriptions of some documents, newspaper clippings, and names and addresses of family members with whom the compiler was in contact. As a source, it has proven reliable when checked against available evidence.

Plainfield

Plainfield Vital Records, microfiche, Holbrook Research Institute.

Elmer I. Shepard, "Cummington & Plainfield Marriages," NEHGS Mss C 2487

Plainfield Cemetery Records, Corbin Collection, NEHGS.

Charles N. Dyer, *History of the Town of Plainfield, Hampshire County, Mass., From its Settlement to 1891 ...* (Northampton, Mass.: Press of Gazette Printing Co., 1891).

Plymouth

William T. Davis, *Ancient Landmarks of Plymouth, Part II: Genealogical Register of Plymouth Families.* (Boston: Damrell & Upham, 1899).

Bradford Kingman, *Epitaphs from Burial Hill, Plymouth, Massachusetts, from 1657 to 1892, with biographical and historical notes* (Brookline, Mass. 1892; reprint Baltimore, Md., 1977).

Barbara J. Bradford Robinson and Howard E. Robinson, *Burial Hill in the 1990s – A six-year cemetery mapping project with descriptions, conditions, and some photographs* (Portland, Ore., 1999).

Plymouth Church Records, 1620-1859, 2 vols. (New York, 1920-23; reprint Baltimore, Md., 1975).

Plymouth County Court Records 1686- 1859, David T. Konig, ed., 16 vols. (Wilmington, Del., 1978). The book has no index but there is a widely available CD (Boston, 2003) that is fully searchable but does not show page numbers from the book. We have sometimes used references to court term and docket number for the Court of Common Pleas; General Sessions cases are cited by date and/or by page number in the printed volumes.

Vital Records of Plymouth, Massachusetts to the year 1850, Lee D. van Antwerp, comp., Ruth Wilder Sherman, ed. (Camden, Me.: Picton Press, 1993).

Plympton

Vital Records of Plympton, Massachusetts to the Year 1850 (Boston, 1923).

Poland, Maine

Vital Records, *NEHGR* 88 (1934) – 89 (1935; cemetery inscriptions, 98 (1945) – 99 (1946).

Pomeroy Family

A. A. Pomeroy, *History and Genealogy of the Pomeroy Family* (1912).

Poole Family

Murray Edward Poole, *The History of Edward Poole of Weymouth, Mass. (1635) and His Descendants* (Ithaca, N.H.: Press of the Ithaca Democrat, 1893).

Portland, Maine

Vital Records of Portland, Maine, Volume 1, Angela M. Foster transcriber (Rockport, Me.: Picton Press, 2004).

"Records of Intentions of Marriage from Falmouth (now Portland), Maine," *NEHGR* 17 (1863).

Burial Records 1717-1962 of the Eastern Cemetery, Portland, Maine, comp. by William B. Jordan, Jr. (Bowie, Md.: Heritage Books, Inc., 1987).

Geo. F. Bacon, *Portland: Its Representative Business Men and its Points of Interest* (Newark, N.J.: Glenwood Pub. Co., 1891).

Pownalboro, Maine (Name changed to **Wiscasset** in 1802)

"A Return and true Representation of the East side of the Town of Pownalborough ... taken in pursuance of an order of the General Court June 19, 1766," *Documentary History of Maine*, Volume 13.

PR

Probate records (wills, administrations, and guardianships), kept in *Districts* in Vermont and Connecticut, in *Towns* in Rhode Island, and in *Counties* in other states. In New York they are called Surrogate's Records.

Putnam Family

Eben Putnam, *A History of the Putnam Family* (Salem, 1891).

Reading

Thomas W. Baldwin, *Vital Records of Reading, Massachusetts to the Year 1850* (Boston, 1912).

Revolutionary War *see* Pension Records

RHODE ISLAND

RIHCTP: Rhode Island Historic Cemeteries Transcription Project Data Base, John Sterling *et al*, at Rhode Island Historical Society, index on line.

Jay Mack Holbrook, *Rhode Island 1782 Census* (Oxford, Mass.: Holbrook Research Institute, 1979).

VRRI: James Newell Arnold, *Vital Record of Rhode Island 1636-1850*, 21 vols. (Providence, R.I., 1891-1912).

Robinson Family

Robinson Genealogy, Volume 2: *Descendants of Moses and Gain Robinson* (1933).

Rogers Family

Elizabeth S. Daniel and Jeanne E. Sawtelle, for the Thomas Rogers Society, *Thomas Rogers, Pilgrim, and Some of His Descendants* (Baltimore: Gateway Press, 1980).

Royalsborough, Maine, *see* Durham, Maine

Royalton, Vt.

Evelyn M. Wood Lovejoy, *The History of Royalton, Vermont, with family genealogies, 1769-1911* (Royalton, Vt.: The Town and the Royalton Woman's Club, 1911).

Sabin Family

Gordon Alan Morris and Philip Sabin Hibbard I, *William Sabin and his Descendants 1609 – 2000*, 2 vols. (Yarmouth, N.S.: Shirley Isabel Bradshaw, 2000).

St. George, Maine

Vital Records of St. George, Maine, transcribed by Marlene A. Groves (Maine Gen. Society Special Pub. No. 43, Picton Press, 2003).

Sampson Family

Robert M. Sherman and Ruth Wilder Sherman, *MF 20: The Henry Samson Family*, Part One, Generations 1 – 4 (Plymouth, 2000).

Jane Fletcher Fiske, Robert M. Sherman, and Ruth Wilder Sherman, *MF 20: The Henry Samson Family*, Part Two, Fifth Generations Descendants of Henry Samson's daughters and son James (Plymouth, 2005).

John Adams Vinton, *The Giles Memorial. Genealogical Memoirs of the Families Bearing the Names of Giles, Gould, Holmes, Jennison, Leonard, Lindall, Curwen, Marshall, Robinson, Sampson, and Webb* ... (Boston, 1864).

Sandisfield

Elizur Yale Smith, *Vital Records of Sandisfield, Massachusetts to the Year 1850 : Sandisfield Revolutionary Soldiers* (Rutland, Vt., 1936).

Scituate

Vital Records of Scituate, Massachusetts to the Year 1850, 2 vols. (Boston, 1909; reprint in 1 vol., 1976).

Wilford Jacob Litchfield, "Records of the Second Church of Scituate, Now the First Unitarian Church of Norwell, Mass.," *NEHGR* 58 (1904), 59 (1905), and 60 (1906).

Samuel Deane, *History of Scituate, Mass., from its settlement to 1831* (Boston, 1831; reprint No. Scituate 1899; reprint Scituate 1975).

Scovil Family

Jennie M. Scoville Holley and Homer Worthington Brainard, *Arthur Scovell and His Descendants in America, 1660 – 1900* (Rutland, Vt.: Tuttle Pub. Co., 1941).

Sebec, Maine

Town Records, card file index to Vital Records at Maine State Archives (TR now available in CD format from Picton Press).

Sebec Village Cemetery Records, courtesy of Betty Ellis.

Sherborn

Thomas W. Baldwin, *Vital Records of Sherborn, Massachusetts to the Year 1850* (Boston, 1911).

Sherburne, N.Y.

Joel Hatch, *Reminiscences, anecdotes and statistics of the Early Settlers and the 'Olden Time' in the Town of Sherburne* ... (Utica, N.Y., 1862).

Sherman Family

John H. Sherman, *Sherman Directory* (Baltimore: Gateway Publishing Co., 1991)

Shipbuilding on North River

L. Vernon Briggs, *History of Shipbuilding on the North River, Plymouth County, Massachusetts* (Boston, 1899).

Shurtleff Family

Benjamin Shurtleff, *The Descendants of William Shurtleff* (1912).

Soule Family

G.T. Ridlon Sr., *History, Biography and Genealogy of the Families Named Soule, Sowle and Soulis,* Volume 1 (Lewiston, Me.: Journal Press, 1926).

Louise Walsh Throop, *George Soule of the Mayflower,* MFIP (GSMD, 2000, 2002, 2003, 2004).

Southeastern Mass.

J. H. Beers & Co., *Representative Men and Old Families of Southeastern Massachusetts* (Chicago, 1912).

Cemeteries of Southeastern Massachusetts — a compilation of records by Charles M. Thatcher in the late 1880s (Middleborough Public Library, 1995).

Southampton

Southampton Vital Records, Corbin Collection.

Spencer

James Draper, History of Spencer, Mass. (1860; 2nd ed., Worcester, n.d.).

Vital Records of Spencer, Massachusetts to the End of the Year 1849 (Worcester, Mass., 1909).

Sprague Family

Waldo Vincent Sprague, *Sprague Families in America* (1913)

Springfield

Clifford L. Stott, comp., *Vital Records of Springfield, Massachusetts to 1850,* 4 vols. (Boston, 2003).

Sterling

Frances Pratt Tapley, *Vital Records of Sterling, Massachusetts* (Sterling Historical Commission, 1976).

Stetson Family

John Stetson Barry, *A Genealogical and Biographical Sketch of the Name and Family of Stetson from the year 1634, to the year 1847* (Boston: William A. Hall & Co., 1847).

Stone Family

J. Gardner Bartlett, *Gregory Stone Genealogy: Ancestry and Descendants of Gregory Stone of Cambridge, Mass., 1320-1917* (Boston: Stone Family Association, 1918).

Stowell Family

W. H. H. Stowell, *The Stowell Genealogy: A Record of the Descendants of Samuel Stowell of Hingham, Massachusetts* (Rutland, Vt.: Tuttle, 1922).

Sumner Family

William Appleton, *Records of the Descendants of William Sumner of Dorchester, Mass.* (Boston: D. Clapp, 1879).

Susquehanna County, Pa.

Emily C. Blackman, *History of Susquehanna County, Pennsylvania* (Philadelphia, 1873; repr. Baltimore: GPC, 1980).

Sutton

Vital Records of Sutton, Massachusetts to the End of the Year 1849 (Worcester, 1907).

William A. Benedict, *History of the town of Sutton, Massachusetts, from 1704 to 1876; including Grafton until 1735; Millbury until 1813; and parts of Northbridge, Upton and Auburn* (Worcester, Pub. for the Town by Sanford and Co., 1878).

Swan's Island, Maine

H. W. Small, *History of Swan's Island, Maine* (1898; repr. Camden, Me., Picton Press, 2001).

Swanton Family

Louise May Swanton, *The Swanton Genealogy : Descendants of Patrick Swanton of Boston, Massachusetts from 1716 to 1976* (Baltimore: Gateway, 1976).

Swanzey, N.H.

Benjamin Read, *The History of Swanzey, New Hampshire, from 1734 to 1890* (Salem: The Salem Press Publishing and Printing Co., 1892).

W. F. Oakman, "Swanzey Cemetery Records," typescript (1941), New Hampshire Historical Society.

Sylvester Family

Albert H. Silvester, "Richard Silvester of Weymouth and some of his descendants," *NEHGR* 85 (1931) and 86 (1932).

Taft Family

Pat Allen, "Descendants of Matthew Taft," on line at rootsweb.com.

TAG

The American Genealogist, an independent quarterly journal started by Donald Lines Jacobus in 1922 as *The New Haven Review;* published at Demorest, Georgia, since 1991. The editors in 2006 are David L. Greene, Robert Charles Anderson, and Joseph C. Anderson II.

Taunton

Samuel Hopkins Emery, *History of Taunton, Massachusetts*, 2 vols. (Syracuse, N.Y., 1893; facsimile reprint Heritage Books, 1992).

Vital Records of Taunton, Massachusetts to the Year 1850, 3 vols. (Boston, 1928).

Temple, Maine

Vital Records, 1803–1896, on FHL microfilm #012,263 (1773–1892 available in CD format, Picton Press).

Thayer Family

Bezaleel Thayer, *Memorial of the Thayer Name, from the Massachusetts Colony of Weymouth and Braintree, Embracing Genealogical and Biographical Sketches of Richard and Thomas Thayer, and Their Descendants, from 1636 to 1874* (Oswego, N.Y.: R. J. Oliphant, 1874).

Ruth Thayer Ravenscroft, "Martin Clinton Thayer," 6 vols., typescript (1943-48), NEHGS Mss 790.

Dr. F.C. Thayer, comp., *Some Data relative to the Descendants of Stephen Thayer, M.D. of Waterville, Maine* (Waterville, 1906).

Waldo Chamberlain Sprague (1903-1960), "Thomas Thayer," Ms., part of "Family Genealogies" in his "Braintree Families" Collection (Wollaston, Mass., 1952), NEHGS, SG SPR 17 (not paginated). Mr. Sprague consulted an exhaustive variety of material, and his references, including book and page of original deeds and probates, make this a tremendously valuable resource.

Thayer Cemetery Records on line at www.thayer.com.

Thomas Family

John Marshall Raymond, *Thomas Families of Plymouth County, Massachusetts* (Itasca, Ill.: Thomas Family Pub., 1980).

Thomson Family

H. J. Amy, *Descendants of David & Amyes (Colle) Thomson* … (1962).

Thorndike, Maine

Elizabeth M. Mosher, transcriber, *Vital Records of Thorndike, Maine, Prior to 1892* (Rockport, Me.: Picton Press, 1993, repr. 1998, 2003).

Topsham, Maine

George Augustus Wheeler and Henry Warren Wheeler, *History of Brunswick, Topsham and Harpswell, Maine* (Boston, 1878).

Mary Pelham Hill, *Vital Records of Topsham, Maine, to the year 1892* (Concord, N.H.: Rumford Press, 1929-1930).

Torrey Family

D. Torrey, *A contribution toward a genealogy of all Torreys in America : being genealogical notes showing the paternal line of descent from William Torrey, of Combe St. Nicholas, Somerset County, England, A.D. 1557, to Abner Torrey, of Weymouth, Massachusetts with all descendants of Abner Torrey* (Detroit: John F. Eby, 1895).

Tyler Family

Willard I. T. Brigham, *The Tyler Genealogy: Descendants of Job Tyler of Andover, Mass., 1619-1700* 2 vols. (Plainfield, N.J. and Tylerville, Conn., 1912).

Upton

Vital Records of Upton, Massachusetts to the End of the Year 1849 (Worcester, Mass., 1904).

Upton Family

John A. Vinton, *Upton Memorial* (Boston, 1874).

Uxbridge

Thomas W. Baldwin, *Vital Records of Uxbridge, Massachusetts to the Year 1850* (Boston, 1916).

VERMONT (see also names of specific towns)

Vermont Vital Records to 1870 [card index], at Vermont State Archives and on microfilm

Abby Maria Hemenway, *The Historical Gazetteer of Vermont*, 5 vols. (Burlington, Vt., 1868-1923).

Marsha H. Rising, *Vermont Newspaper Abstracts, 1783 – 1816* (Boston: NEHGS, 2001).

Alden M. Rollins, *Vermont Religious Certificates* (Rockport, Me.: Picton Press, 2003).

Alden M. Rollins, *Vermont Warnings Out*, 2 vols. (Camden, Me.: Picton Press, 1995, 1997).

Vose Family

Ellen F. Vose, *Robert Vose and His Descendants* (Boston, 1932).

Waitsfield, Vt.

Matt Bushnell Jones, *History of the Town of Waitsfield, Vermont 1782 – 1908 with Family Genealogies* (Boston: George E. Littlefield, 1909).

Waitsfield Vital Records, on microfilm.

Waldoboro, Maine

Waldoboro, Maine, Vital Records: 1773 to 1923: Marriages, Intentions, Births and Deaths compiled from the original by Mrs. Warren Colwell; compiled from her records by Mrs. Esther Gross, Waldoboro, Me: compiled from the records of Esther Gross by Georgiana Lilly and Grace Blake Maxwell for Mary Kelton Dummer Chapter of D.A.R., Hallowell, Maine, 1949-50 (Salem, Higginson Books, 1998).

Waldoboro Cemetery Inscriptions, copied by Georgiana Lilly, recopied by Virginia T. Merrill (Solon, Me., ?1989).

Samuel L. Miller, *History of the Town of Waldoboro, Maine* (Wiscasset, Me., 1910).

Jasper J. Stahl, *History of Old Broad Bay and Waldoboro, Maine* (Portland: Bond, Wheelwright, 1956).

Warren, Maine

Cyrus Eaton, *Annals of the Town of Warren: with the Early History of St. George's, Broad Bay, and the neighboring settlements on the Waldo Patent* (Hallowell: Masters, Smith, 1851).

Warwick

Warwick Vital Records, microfiche by Holbrook Research Institute; also FHL microfilm #1,888,692.

Jonathan Blake, *History of the Town of Warwick, Massachusetts* (Boston, 1873).

Washington, D.C.

Washington, D.C., obits on line: <www.congressionalcemetery.org>.

Washington County, Maine

Leonard F. Tibbetts and Darryl B. Lamson, *Early Pleasant River Families of Washington County, Maine* (Camden, Me.: Picton Press, 1997).

Wayne County, N.Y.

Wayne County Cemeteries, *www.rootsweb/nywayne/cemeteries....*

West Bridgewater

Vital Records of West Bridgewater, Massachusetts to the Year 1850 (Boston, 1911).

Western Mass.

Early Vital Records of Western Massachusetts to about 1850 (CD ROM, Wheat Ridge, Colorado: Search & ReSearch, 2000).

Weston Family

Thomas Weston, Jr., "The Descendants of Edmund Weston of Duxbury, Mass., for Five Generations," *NEHGR* 41 [1887].

Samuel N. Weston, "Genealogy of the Weston Families of Duxbury" (typescript at Duxbury Public Library, from will of Samuel N. Weston 1916). It has proven reliable when checked against other available sources, and the author's reminiscences and knowledge of the families and places concerned add a valuable dimension.

Weyman Ms

Wesley Weyman (1877-1931), "Descendants of Capt. Myles Standish, male and female lines also material on the Bennett, Ramsdell, and Wyman families," 8 cartons, NEHGS Ms. SG STA 4 [273]. Consists of 4" x 6" sheets tightly packed into numbered bundles with generations treated successively, some lines carried to 11th generation. Some sheets include name and address of his contact on that family. The form of the material makes it difficult and time-consuming to use, but the compiler was obviously very careful and there is much there beyond the generations covered in this volume.

Weymouth

Vital Records of Weymouth, Massachusetts to the Year 1850, 2 vols. (Boston, 1910).

George Walter Chamberlain, *Genealogies of the Early Families of Weymouth*, originally published as Vols. 3 and 4 of *History of Weymouth* (1923), 2 vols. in one (Baltimore: GPC, 1984).

Wheeler Family

The Genealogical and Encyclopedic History of the Wheeler Family in America, compiled under direction of Albert Gallatin Wheeler Jr. (Boston: American College of Genealogy, 1914).

White Family

Thomas J. Lothrop, Nicholas White Family 1643 – 1900 (Taunton, 1902).

Whitmarsh Family

Newton Whitmarsh Bates, Genealogy of the Descendants of John Whitmarsh of Weymouth, Mass. (Ashtabula, Ohio, 1916).

Whittemore Family

Bradford Adams Whittemore and Edgar Whittemore, "The Whittemore Family in America," NEHGR 108 (1954).

Wight Family

Danforth Phipps Wright, The Wight Family Memoir of Thomas Wight of Dedham, Mass., with genealogical notices of his descendants, From 1637 to 1840 (1848).

Williamstown

Vital Records of Williamstown, Massachusetts to the Year 1850 (Boston, 1907).

Winslow Family

David Parsons Holton and Mrs. Frances K. Holton, Winslow Memorial: Family Record of Winslows and their descendants in America, etc. (1888).

Wiscasset, Maine (name changed from Pownalborough in 1802)

Wiscasset, Maine, Town Records, including VR (FHL microfilm #0,012,309).

Wood Family

Norris Philip Wood, Descendants and Ancestors of Consider Wood and his wife Mary Adams … (1998).

John Sumner Wood, Sr., Wood Family Index - a given name Index (Germantown, Md., 1966).

Woodman Family

Helen D. Woodman, The Woodmans of Rhode Island: Descendants of John Woodman of Little Compton, R.I. (St. Petersburg, Fla.: Genealogical Publishing Service, 1989).

Worcester

Franklin P. Rice, Worcester Births, Marriages, and Deaths (Worcester, Mass., 1894).

Worcester County

Probate Records and Deeds, formerly at Court House, Worcester, many now moved to Massachusetts Archives; microfilmed.

Early Vital Records of Worcester County, Massachusetts to about 1850 (CD ROM, Wheat Ridge, Colorado: Search & ReSearch, 2000).

Worcester County, Massachusetts, Warnings, 1737-1788 (Worcester, 1899; reprint Camden, Me.: Picton Press, 1992).

Wrentham

Vital Records of Wrentham, Massachusetts to the Year 1850, 2 vols. (Boston, 1910).

Wyoming County, N.Y.

History of Wyoming County, New York (New York: F. W. Beers & Co., 1880).

Yates County, N.Y.

Yates County Genealogical & Historical Society, Inc., The Oliver House Museum, Penn Yan, N.Y.

INDEX

All names in the text appear in the index (with the exception noted below for John Alden and Myles Standish). Married women are indexed under both their married name[s] with maiden name in parentheses, and separately under maiden name, if known. Unknown maiden names are indicated thus: (—). Some surnames and many given names have been standardized, with variants listed and cross-references inserted where relevant. A list of commonly used nicknames for women appears on page viii of the Introduction.

Note: John Alden and Myles Standish have not been included in the index for pages 257-557, as *all* Samson/Sampsons treated in that part of the book [#671 – 834]are descendants also of both Alden and Standish.

BROCKAWAY
Bridget (Norris) 200
BRONSON
Amanda 236
Elizabeth (—) 121
Smisson 121
Susan 121
BROOKS
— Capt. 335
Asa 38
Charles Sylvester 554
Eleanor Robinson
(Converse) 554
Jennie 256
Mary (—) 38
Matthew 38
Nabby Jones 38
BROUWER
Femetjie 304
BROWN
— 305, 543
— Col. 185
Adriana 257
Amos 257
Anne (Nelson) (Rawson)
122
Benjamin 257, 362
Cata (Holbrook) 148
Charles 257, 452
Cornelia (Little) 257
Daniel 193
Deborah (Torrey) 523
Eliza Ann (Bartlett) 275
Elizabeth 257
Elizabeth French 227
George 148
Hannah P. 227
Henry S. 99
Isaac 328
Jeremiah 257
Joanna 451
John 43, 122, 193, 257
John T. 452
Lydia (Bosworth) 257
Maria 452
Mary 274, 523, 524
Mary Ann 66, 171
Nancy 257

BROWN *cont'd*
Oliver 196
Peggy (Shepherd) 95
Phebe 258
Rhoda 257
Rhoda (Winsor) 257
Russell 296
Sally 153
Samuel 523
Sarah 61, 213, 223, 225,
227
Sarah (Freeman) 257
Sarah Anne (Bliss) 328
Sarah Prince 287
Squire 305
Stephen Palmer 275
Susanna Ide (Woodman)
543
Wealthy (Strong) 296
Zilpha (McCurdy) 452
BROWNELL
Benjamin C. 400
Lydia (—) 400
Meribah 542
BRUCE
Abigail 241-243, 246,
248, 249, 252
Caroline Moore 244
Charles 241-245
Charles Otis 245
Delia Augusta 238
Eliza 238
Eliza W. 244
Eliza Wilder 244
Elizabeth 244, 253-255
Elizabeth (Farnsworth)
238
Elizabeth Eager 238
Emma S. 240
George 239, 241-245
George Henry 244
George W. 239, 240
Hannah 241-243
Hannah (Lovett) 239,
241-245
Harriet Fay 238
Harriet (Fay) 238
Henry 239, 240, 242

BRUCE *cont'd*
James S. 239, 242, 244
James Savage 240
James W. 240
Jane (Savage) 239, 240
Joseph 238
Joseph Edward 238
Julia Lambert (Whitney)
245
Lucy (Nickerson) 240
Martha 243
Martha/ Patty 243
Mary E. 245
Phineas 239-241
Sarah 238, 239
Sarah (Whipple) 238
Sarah Whipple 238
Simon 238
Stephen 240, 242-244
Susan (Wilder) 244
Susan Wilder 244
William 241-244
William A. 240, 242
William Charles 244
William Simon 238
BRYANT
Agatha 372
Esther 484
Sarah 307
BUCK
Eleanor 224
BUCKINGHAM
Rebecca 291, 292
Rebecca (Clark) 291
William 291
BUCKLEY
Nellie 467
BUCKMAN
Judith 506
BUCKNAM
Abigail (Samson) 3
Jeremiah 2
John 3
Mary (Pote) 2
BUDD
Abram 207
BUFFUM / BUFFAM
Allen 145

ELLS
___ (Robinson) 315
Elisha 315
George 315
John 315
Mary 305
Phebe 315
Phebe (Pineo) 315
Sarah 315
Sophia 315
Watson 315
ELSMORE / ELMORE / ELSIMORE
Bridget 311
Charles B. 311
Edward 311
Edward O. 311
Eliza J. 311
George F. 311
Gilbert 311
Hiram 311
Leonice 311
Lydia (—) 311
Moses 311
Ruby W. (Pineo) 311
EMERSON
Lois 130, 131
EMERY
David J. 136
Mary B. (Thayer) 136
EMMONS
Maria 188
ESTES
Elizabeth 255
EVANS
Richard 55
EVARTS
Mary V. 62
Philo 62
Venera (Carr) 62
EVERSON
Jane Barnes 438
Josiah 29
Patience 274
EWELL
— Capt. 368
EWEN
Albert 222

EWEN *cont'd*
Esther 222
Henry 222
Richard 221, 222
Susan (Stephens) 221, 222
FAIRBANKS
— 109
Amos 165
Charles 132
Joseph 442
Martha Keith (Sampson) 442
Nancy 122
Ruth (Adams) 165
Susan Sophia (Tyler) 109
FAIRFIELD
Hannah 256
Mary 255
FALES
Oliver 267
FARLEY
Esther (Nelson) 208
Joseph 368
Thomas 208
William I. 267
FARMER
Alzada (Sampson) 443
Ella A. 441
Moses 443
N. S. 256
FARNHAM / FARNAM / FARNUM / VARNUM
Abigail (Plummer) 331-333
Abigail (Taylor) 333
Albion 336
Alexander 341
Alexander R. 341
Ambrose C. 336
Andrew 331
Ansel 330, 332, 334-336
Betsey (Plummer) 335
Beufield 333
Bezaleel 324, 328
Chapin/Chafin 330, 332-336
Charles 341

FARNHAM *cont'd*
David 333, 341
Dorcas 330, 331, 334
Dorcas (Barnes) 330, 331
Dorcas (Holbrook?) 331, 334
Dorcas (Sargent) 341
Eben F. 341
Eben Francis 341
Ebenezer 330, 332, 339-341
Edward Watts 341
Eleanor 338
Eleanor (Samson) 330, 332, 334, 335, 337, 340
Eliza A. 331
Elizabeth 162, 333
Elizabeth (Plummer) 336
Ephraim 341
Eunice 341
Eunice (Taylor) 341
Frederic F. 336
George 331, 332
George M. 336
Hannah 330
Hannah (Smalley) 333
Hannah Barnes 332
Hanson 334
Harriet 339, 340
Isaac 331
Israel 331
Israel Harvey 331
James 333, 338
Jemima (Gamage) 336
John 330-334, 336, 340
John Albert 341
Jonathan 330, 332, 334, 335
Joseph 330-337, 340, 341
Joseph C. 341
Joshua 166
Laura 341
Levi 341
Lucinda 336
Lucy 341
Lydia (Watts) 341

FARNHAM *cont'd*
  Lydia M. 341
  Marcia 341
  Margaret (Thayer) 166
  Maria (Mann) 336
  Marriah 341
  Martha 334, 337, 341
  Mary 333, 334, 337, 341
  Mary (—) 331
  Mary (Herrin) 339, 340
  Mary Augusta 341
  Mary J. 336
  Mary J. (Farnham) 331,
    336
  Meriam 324, 328
  Micah 333
  Nancy 331, 333
  Nancy (Farnham) 331,
    333, 336
  Nancy Jane 331
  Olive 166-168
  Joseph 331
  Joshua 166
  Margaret (Thayer) 166
  Mary J. 331
  Meriam 324, 328
  Nancy 336
  Olive 166-168
  Phebe 324, 325, 329
  Phebe (Kirtland) 324,
    328
  Rachel 342
  Royal 147
  Sarah 130, 132, 137, 138,
    333, 341
  Sarah Barnes 331
  Simon H. 336
  William G. 336
FARNSWORTH
  Abigail (Pineo) 308
  Elizabeth 238
  Elizabeth W. (Pineo) 310
  Joseph W. 310
  Lewis 83, 84
  Peter 308
  Robert 368
  William 368
Farnum *see* Farnham

FARR
  Areal J. 253
  Elijah 433
  Emeline 253
  Lorin 433
  Lydia 433
  Lyman M. 253
  Maria 433
  Mary J. 253
  Matilda (Patterson) 253
  Nelson H. 252, 253
  Ruth (Sampson) 433
  Samuel 253
  Wealthy C. (Hazeltine)
    252, 253
FARRAR
  Granville 153
  Lydia (Staples) 153
FARRINGTON
  Abigail (—) 456
  David 456
FAUNCE
  Christiana (Prior) 536
  Eleanor (Bradford) 285,
    287
  Elizabeth (Sylvester) 287
  Elizabeth A. (Morton)
    287
  George 536
  Jerusha 536
  Jerusha (Wadsworth)
    535
  John 22, 27
  Lemuel B. 287
  Lydia Vaughan (Wood)
    287
  Mary 508
  Mary Olive (Harlow)
    287
  Solomon 287
  Thaddeus 287
  Thomas 508
  William 287
  Zenas 535, 536
FAY
  Calphurnia 538
  Clevia Marilla 538
  Cordelia Daniels 538

FAY *cont'd*
  Delphia Nash 538
  Edward 536
  Elijah 536, 537
  Gain La Fitte 538
  Harriet 238
  Henry La Motte 538
  James 537
  James Le Roy 538
  James R. 537
  James Robinson 537
  Joanna 537
  Marcia (Pearl) 538
  Margaret 537
  Margaret (Robinson) 536
  Margaret Cleopatra 538
  Marilla (Nash) 537
  Sarah 537
  Sarah (Joslin) 536
  Susan/Susannah 537
  William Le Fountain 538
  Zenas La Fleur 538
FELKER
  Jane (Veazie) 8
  Michael 8
FELLOWS
  — 89
  Melinda Fiske (Parsons)
    89
FENDERSON
  Bridget (Elsmore) 311
  D. A. 311
FENN
  Ann 516
FENNER
  Amelia (Pineo) 302
  Gurdon 302
FENNO
  Elizabeth 310
  Elizabeth (Torrey) 460
  George Washington 310
  Jerusha (Robinson) 310
  Joseph 310
  Joseph William 310
  Mary (—) 310
  Mary A. (Pineo) 310
  Mary Ann 310
  Oliver 460

FULLER *cont'd*
Edward 113
Elizabeth (Weston) 401
Elmiria (Thayer) 172
Emeline 181, 402
Ezra 401
Hannah (Cooper) 276
Harriet Ludentia
(Woodman) 543
James 401
John 276
Jonathan Clarke 290
Mary 401
Mary (Little) 293
Mary Little (Dewey) 293
Mehitable 199, 200
Mercy 516
Molly 401
Nancy Adelia (Holbrook)
290
Nathan F. 8
Rosamond (Coffin) 517
Rose Caroline (Hersey)
527
Samuel 401, 528
Susanna 401, 411, 528
FULLERTON
Abigail (Keene) 497
Alathea 512
Alethea 501, 504, 507,
509, 511, 512
Almira 499
Almira Jane 499
Amanda 499
Anna 500
Arabella (Brewster) 496
Asa 495, 496
Betsey Jane 496
Betty 406
Calista 499
Calista Ann 499
Caroline 497
Cyrus 497
Daniel Morton 496
Deborah 534
Edward 497
Ella 500
Emma Isabel 500

FULLERTON *cont'd*
George H. 500
Hannah Reed 496
Hannah (Reed) 496
Harvey 499
Henry Williams 496
Jacob 496
Jairus 496, 497
James Harvey 499
James Porter 500
James Reed 496
John 261, 495-497, 499,
500
John Newton 497
Josiah 497
Lucretia Persons 496
Lydia Dunham 497
Lysander 497
Marcus 500
Martha T. (Packard) 496
Mary 496
Mary (Gurney) 499
Mary (Hunt) 496
Mary (Porter) 499
Mary (Torrey) 496
Mary Elizabeth 499
Mehitable 499
Mercy 62, 480, 482, 484,
486, 489, 491, 492
Molly (Noyes) 495-497,
499, 500
Myra 496
Nahum 496
Noah 496
Noah Augustin 499
Oliver 496
Rachel (Ford) 496
Ruth 497, 514, 517, 519,
521, 523, 525, 528, 530
Sally Ann (—) 500
Sally Ann (Reynolds)
500
Samuel Newell 497
Sarah (Noyes) 495
Silence Dailey 496
Silence (Dayley) 496
Spencer 497
Timothy Reed 496

FULLERTON *cont'd*
William 499
William Henry 499
FULSOM
Peter 481
Ruby (Soule) (Dudley)
481
GAHAN
Cyrus 504
Melita (Joyce) 504
Galaspy *see* Gillespie
GALE
Daniel 280
Harriet (Sampson) 280
GALLAGHER
Araminta Abigail (Taft)
127
P. O. 127
GALLUP
Josiah 236
Lucy A. 236
Mary A. 236
Violatra (Pomeroy) 236
GAMAGE
Jemima 336
GAMMON
Anna 228
GAMMOND
E. H. 211
Sarah Jane (Cutler) 211
GARDINER
Ephia (Linnekin)
(Whitney) 340
Obediah 340
GARDNER
Amos 434
Andrew 20
Anna Rebecca 531
Betsey (—) 434
David 434
Deborah 1
Hannah (Sampson) 431,
434
Helena 476
John 431, 434
Mary Magdalene
(Hinckle) 531
Nabby 505

HUBBARD *cont'd*
  Lusannah (Wadsworth)
    (Osgood) 34
  Martha (Bradley) 192
  Nelson O. 213
  Phineas 213
  Thomas 213
HUDSON
  Silence 397
Hughs *see* Hewes
HUMES
  Diana (Thayer) 155, 158
  Miranda (Thayer) 155,
    158
  Moses 158
  Nahum 158
HUNT
  Abigail W. 411
  Abigail (Sampson)
    (Hanks) 473
  Abigail (Soule) 474, 485
  Adeline (Cone) 296
  Allan Melville 474
  Andrew W. 58
  Anna Maria (Pool) 532
  Anne 396
  Asa 362, 363, 474, 485
  Asenith 404, 494
  Betty (Oldham) 361
  Beulah 473
  Bwys 362
  Caroline (—) 474
  Caroline (Wadsworth)
    474
  Cassius 58
  Charlotte 171
  Deborah 360
  Deborah (Churchill) 467,
    474
  Deborah (Freeman) 474
  Deborah (Sampson)
    (Churchill) 474
  Deborah (Soule) 473
  Deborah Cushman
    (Delano) 392
  Diana (Chandler) 474
  Edmund S. 532
  Edward Gray 474

HUNT *cont'd*
  Edwin 58
  Eldred 294, 296
  Elizabeth B. 411
  Ellis W. 411
  Emma (Prior) 474
  Esther 363
  Esther (Wright) 361
  Hane 510
  Hannah 474
  Hannah (Gray) 474
  Hannah C. (Sampson)
    474
  Hannah Cushing 474
  Hannah Gray 457, 474
  Henry 473, 474
  Henry A. 58
  Hiram 474
  Huldah (Benton) 294,
    296
  Jane 363, 473, 474
  Joanna 76
  John 361, 362, 364, 367,
    370, 373, 473
  John O. 296
  Jonathan 496
  Judah 361
  Lois 292
  Lot 473, 475, 485, 510,
    535
  Louisa (Little) 295, 296
  Louisa A. 296
  Lucia W. (Prior) 474
  Lucy 484, 511
  Lydia S. (Samson) 58
  Marcia 411
  Maria 363
  Martha 411
  Mary 376, 473, 474, 496
  Mary (Sampson) 472,
    473, 485, 510, 535
  Mary (Simmons) 361,
    362, 373
  Mary J. (Kirkland) 296
  Mary Lewis 474
  Mary S. 58
  Melzar 392
  Mercy 363, 372

HUNT *cont'd*
  Nancy 294
  Nathaniel 363
  Nathaniel K. 411
  Orren 296
  Peter Bucklin 215
  Rebecca 363
  Ruth (Nelson) 215
  Sally 363
  Samuel 363, 411, 467,
    473, 474
  Sarah 411, 473
  Sarah (—) 496
  Sarah Simmons
    (Robbins) (Woodcock)
    363
  Sarah Smith (Kent) 411
  Susan T. 411
  Susanna (Fuller) 411
  Sylvia (Wadsworth) 474,
    535
  Thomas 411
  Wadsworth 58
  Ziba 473, 474, 535
  Zilpha S. 411
HUNTING
  Sarah 214
HUNTINGTON
  Henry 222
  Margaret 43
  Roxana 222
  Unice 222
HUNTLEY
  —— 315
  Daniel 305
  David Rufus 305
  Esther 305
  Margaret (Pineo) 315
  Rebecca Ann 305
  Ruby (Pineo) 305
  Sarah Jane 305
  William 315
HUNTOON
  Martha J. 201
HURLBURT
  Delos Bradley 543
  Esther (McIntyre)
    (Woodman) 542

KING *cont'd*
Warriner 546
KINGMAN
Abigail 390
Abigail (Hall) 390
David 390
Hannah 525
Keziah 524
KINGSLAND
Richard 134
Sarah M. (Thayer) 134
KINGSLEY
Darius 293
Elizabeth (Scoville) 293
KINNEY
Henry 93
Sarah J. (Fisk) 93
KINSMAN
Mary 317
Mehitable (Rand) 317
Robert 317
KIRKLAND
Mary J. 296
KIRKPATRICK
Jesse Jackson 231
Phebe Elvira (Thayer)
231
KIRTLAND
Phebe 324, 328
KITCHEL
Albert 197
KNAPP
Anna (Whitmarsh) 514
Jonathan 514
Maria H. (Austin) 515
Martha (—) 515
Mary Ann 136
William 514
William W. 515
KNEELAND
Elizabeth (Samson) 22
John 22
KNIGHT
Daniel 30
Fanny 142
Hannah 308
Lydia 30
Mary (Winslow) 30

KNIGHT *cont'd*
Mary Abbie (Hersey)
527
Phebe (Burnham) 143
Susan R. 309
Thomas 142
William Briggs 527
KNOWLES
Anne (Pineo) 316
Baldwin 316
Lydia 7
Nathan 316
Rebecca 316
KNOWLTON
Cynthia 206
Harmie 541
Harriet B. 206
KNOX
— Gen. 363
Mary Urania (Kent) 533
Melissa Bloomfield 533
Oliver 533
KRIEGER
John George 43
LABYN
Caroline (Thayer) 188
LAMB
C. M. 326
Charlotte 255
Hannah 308
James 309
Louisa Maria
(Hutchinson) 326
LAMBERT
Hannah 438
LAMPSON
Ann Elizabeth
(McIntyre) 542
Elizabeth 542
Jane 172
William 542
LANCASTER
Susan (Damon) 205
LANDERS
Lucy 212
LANDMAN
Polly 491

LANG
Charles 342
David 342
Eleanor 342
Harriet 342
John 342
Mary 342
Rachel (Farnham) 342
Sarah 342
LAPHAM
Elizabeth 153, 154
Joshua 52
Lemuel 52, 53
Lydia (Magoun) 52, 53
Margaret V. 153
Mary (Wood) 52
Melzar 52, 53
Robert 52, 53
Sarah (Alden) 52
LARRABEE
Abby F. 406
Charles W. 406
Lucy (Weston) 405, 406
Mary W. 406
Nathaniel 6
Nehemiah 405, 406
Sophia S. 406
LASELL
Betsey 325
LATHAM
Ann (Cottrell) 515
Charles 66
Chester 515
LATHROP / LOTHROP
Darius 292
Elizabeth 32, 292, 293
John Backus 292
Jonathan 292
Lydia (McCall) 292
Mary (Little) 292, 293
Mira 292, 293
Sophia 292, 293
Theoda (Woodworth)
292
Thomas 37, 391, 464,
482
LAUGHLEN
Jennie 444

TAFT *cont'd*
Susan (Benedict) 127
Susanna 135
Thaddeus 134
Willard 248, 249
William Schenck 127
TAGGART
Daniel 82
Lovina (Fisk) 81, 82
TALBOT
Eliza 516
TARBELL
Joannah 188
Sarah 188
TASKER
Hannah (Carr)
(Batchelor) 446
John 446
TAY
Charlotte E. (Tirrell)
(Turner) 418
Joseph N. 418
Lucy H. 418
Rufus L. 418
Rufus T. 418
TAYLOR
—— 109
Abigail 333, 392
Abigail M. 547
Abigail (King) 547
Amos 547
Betsey 381
Eben 392
Elizabeth (Adams) 315
Eunice 341
Frances (Tyler) 109
Jemima 278
Jeremiah 547
John 41
John B. 85
Lemuel 98
Love 212
Luana (Barnard) 85
Lucinda (——) 234
Lucinda Wright (Smith)
85
Lucy 277, 280
Marcy (——) 41

TAYLOR *cont'd*
Mary 85
Mary (Cutler) 212
Mary E. 228
Mercy 41
Quintus 234
Roseltha 116
Samuel 98, 212
Seth 85
Sophronia (Delano) 392
TEFFT
Elizabeth (Dye) 439
John 439
Rhoda 439
TEMPLE
Daniel W. 544
Sarah C. (Ford) 544
TEN EYCK
George 515
TENNEY
Achsah 89
TERRILL / TYRRELL
Hannah 82
Isaac 82
Mary (——) 82
THACHER
Hannah B. 17, 18
Thair *see* Thayer
THAXTER
Delia (Pineo) 310
Robert 310
THAYER / THAIR
Aaron 171, 172, 179
Aaron Chance/ Cheney
178, 179
Aaron Everett 181
Abigail 127, 185, 186,
188-190, 199, 206
Abigail (Belcher) 195,
198
Abigail (Jones) 185-187,
189, 191, 192, 195
Abigail (Tilden) 179
Adaline 178
Adeline (Kelly) 177
Alanson 188
Albert 141, 155, 178
Albert C. 140, 141

THAYER *cont'd*
Alberton Delos 188
Alexander 157
Alfred 172
Alfred B. 172
Alice (Hood) 157
Alice Jane (Tomlinson)
231
Alinda 178
Allen 188
Alma 180
Almira 135, 140, 141,
155, 156, 178, 180
Almira (Taft) 134
Almira M. 232
Almy 180
Almy Ann (Hersey) 526
Alonzo 135
Alva/Alvah Barnes 142
Alvin 143
Alvira Caroline 181
Alzada 155, 156
Amanda 178
Amanda M. 180
Ambrose K. 179, 182
Amory 133, 135, 176
Amos 130, 191-193
Amos Leonard 195
Amy (Mathewson) 156
Andrew 194
Andrew Jackson 136
Angeline 509
Angenette 136
Anjeline L. 135, 136
Ann 171
Ann (Smith) 199
Ann E. (Putnam) 140,
141
Ann Elizabeth 181
Ann Louisa 143
Ann Maria (Sutton) 157
Ann Maria 186
Anna 171, 185, 186
Anna (Barnes) 143
Anna (Twitchell) 170
Anna F. 136
Anne (Barnes) 142
Antoinette (——) 136